Haynes

Land Rover Discovery
Service and Repair Manual

Steve Rendle, Mark Coombs and RM Jex

Models covered *(3016 - 5AH7 - 416)*

Land Rover Discovery models (including Commercial) with V8 petrol and four-cylinder TDi diesel engines

3.5 litre (3528 cc) and 3.9 litre (3947 cc) petrol engines

2.5 litre (2495 cc) diesel engines

Does not cover 2.0 litre MPi petrol engine, or revised range introduced December 1998

T0385041

ABCDE
FG
2

A book in the **Haynes Service and Repair Manual Series**

ISBN **978 1 78521 330 4**

British Library Cataloguing in Publication Data
A catalogue record for this book is available from the British Library.

Printed in Malaysia

J H Haynes & Co. Ltd.
Sparkford, Yeovil, Somerset BA22 7JJ, England

Haynes North America, Inc
859 Lawrence Drive, Newbury Park, California 91320, USA

Printed using NORBRITE BOOK 48.8gsm (CODE: 40N6533) from NORPAC; procurement system certified under Sustainable Forestry Initiative standard. Paper produced is certified to the SFI Certified Fiber Sourcing Standard (CERT - 0094271)

Contents

LIVING WITH YOUR LAND ROVER DISCOVERY

Contents

The Discovery was introduced to the UK market in late 1989, in three-door body style, with both petrol and diesel engines. The 200 TDi Diesel engine is unique to the Discovery, and has not been used in any other Land Rover vehicles.

In Autumn 1990, a five-door version became available, and in June 1993, a Commercial ('Van') model was introduced, based on the three-door version with the rear side windows deleted.

For 1994 model year, the 3.5 litre V8 engine was replaced by a larger 3.9 litre unit.

In the Spring of 1994, the Discovery range was facelifted, and at the same time, the 300 TDi diesel engine was introduced. Based on the previous 200 TDi engine, a number of improvements were made, including an Electronic Diesel Control (EDC) system for certain markets. The most notable feature of the EDC system is that a 'drive-by-wire' accelerator control system is used, with no mechanical link (accelerator cable) between the accelerator pedal and the fuel injection pump.

The V8 petrol engine is the famous all-alloy 'Rover V8' engine, with chain-driven camshaft, overhead valves and hydraulic tappets. Early models had twin SU carburettors, which were superseded by Lucas fuel injection after 1990.

The diesel engines fitted to the Discovery are of pushrod overhead-valve design, and the cylinder block-mounted camshaft is driven from the crankshaft via a toothed belt. The engines use direct fuel injection.

Models are available with a five-speed manual, or four-speed automatic, transmission. The drive from the transmission is picked up by a transfer gearbox, which provides permanent four-wheel-drive to the front and rear axles, via propeller shafts.

A wide range of standard and optional equipment is available within the Discovery range to suit most tastes, including central locking, electric windows, electric sunroof, anti-lock braking system, and air bags.

Due to the rugged construction of the vehicle, the number of items requiring regular maintenance (mainly the need for regular lubrication checks) is higher than that found on many smaller vehicles, but the Discovery is a straightforward vehicle to maintain, and most of the items requiring frequent attention are easily accessible.

Land Rover Discovery 3-door (1989 model)

HAYNES

Land Rover Discovery 5-door (1997 model)

Your Discovery manual

The aim of this manual is to help you get the best value from your vehicle. It can do so in several ways. It can help you decide what work must be done (even should you choose to get it done by a garage). It will also provide information on routine maintenance and servicing, and give a logical course of action and diagnosis when random faults occur. However, it is hoped that you will use the manual by tackling the work yourself. On simpler jobs it may even be quicker than booking the vehicle into a garage and going there twice, to leave and collect it. Perhaps most important, a lot of money can be saved by avoiding the costs a garage must charge to cover its labour and overheads.

The manual has drawings and descriptions to show the function of the various components so that their layout can be understood. Tasks are described and photographed in a clear step-by-step sequence. The illustrations are numbered by the Section number and paragraph number to which they relate - if there is more than one illustration per paragraph, the sequence is denoted alphabetically.

References to the 'left' or 'right' of the vehicle are in the sense of a person in the driver's seat, facing forwards.

Acknowledgements

Thanks are due to Draper Tools Limited, who provided some of the workshop tools, and to all those people at Sparkford who helped in the production of this manual.

Working on your car can be dangerous. This page shows just some of the potential risks and hazards, with the aim of creating a safety-conscious attitude.

General hazards

Scalding

• Don't remove the radiator or expansion tank cap while the engine is hot.
• Engine oil, automatic transmission fluid or power steering fluid may also be dangerously hot if the engine has recently been running.

Burning

• Beware of burns from the exhaust system and from any part of the engine. Brake discs and drums can also be extremely hot immediately after use.

Crushing

• When working under or near a raised vehicle, always supplement the jack with axle stands, or use drive-on ramps. ***Never venture under a car which is only supported by a jack.***

TWIT 1

• Take care if loosening or tightening high-torque nuts when the vehicle is on stands. Initial loosening and final tightening should be done with the wheels on the ground.

Fire

• Fuel is highly flammable; fuel vapour is explosive.
• Don't let fuel spill onto a hot engine.
• Do not smoke or allow naked lights (including pilot lights) anywhere near a vehicle being worked on. Also beware of creating sparks (electrically or by use of tools).
• Fuel vapour is heavier than air, so don't work on the fuel system with the vehicle over an inspection pit.
• Another cause of fire is an electrical overload or short-circuit. Take care when repairing or modifying the vehicle wiring.
• Keep a fire extinguisher handy, of a type suitable for use on fuel and electrical fires.

Electric shock

• Ignition HT voltage can be dangerous, especially to people with heart problems or a pacemaker. Don't work on or near the ignition system with the engine running or the ignition switched on.

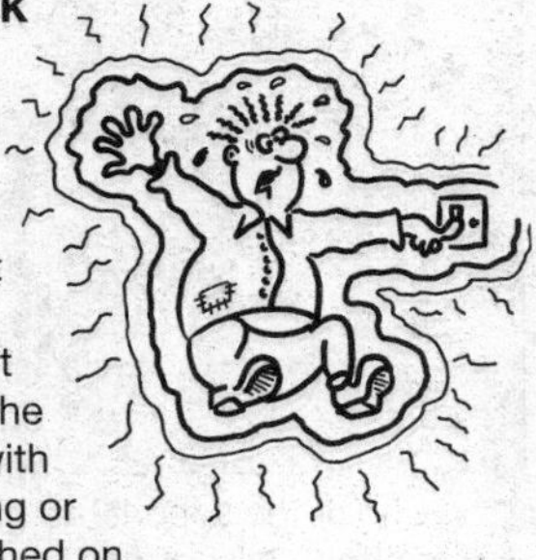

• Mains voltage is also dangerous. Make sure that any mains-operated equipment is correctly earthed. Mains power points should be protected by a residual current device (RCD) circuit breaker.

Fume or gas intoxication

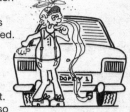

• Exhaust fumes are poisonous; they often contain carbon monoxide, which is rapidly fatal if inhaled. Never run the engine in a confined space such as a garage with the doors shut.

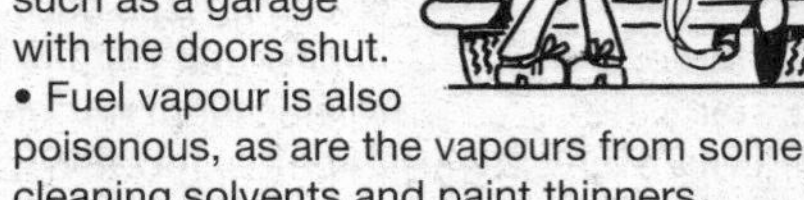

• Fuel vapour is also poisonous, as are the vapours from some cleaning solvents and paint thinners.

Poisonous or irritant substances

• Avoid skin contact with battery acid and with any fuel, fluid or lubricant, especially antifreeze, brake hydraulic fluid and Diesel fuel. Don't syphon them by mouth. If such a substance is swallowed or gets into the eyes, seek medical advice.
• Prolonged contact with used engine oil can cause skin cancer. Wear gloves or use a barrier cream if necessary. Change out of oil-soaked clothes and do not keep oily rags in your pocket.
• Air conditioning refrigerant forms a poisonous gas if exposed to a naked flame (including a cigarette). It can also cause skin burns on contact.

Asbestos

• Asbestos dust can cause cancer if inhaled or swallowed. Asbestos may be found in gaskets and in brake and clutch linings. When dealing with such components it is safest to assume that they contain asbestos.

Special hazards

Hydrofluoric acid

• This extremely corrosive acid is formed when certain types of synthetic rubber, found in some O-rings, oil seals, fuel hoses etc, are exposed to temperatures above $400^{\circ}C$. The rubber changes into a charred or sticky substance containing the acid. *Once formed, the acid remains dangerous for years. If it gets onto the skin, it may be necessary to amputate the limb concerned.*
• When dealing with a vehicle which has suffered a fire, or with components salvaged from such a vehicle, wear protective gloves and discard them after use.

The battery

• Batteries contain sulphuric acid, which attacks clothing, eyes and skin. Take care when topping-up or carrying the battery.
• The hydrogen gas given off by the battery is highly explosive. Never cause a spark or allow a naked light nearby. Be careful when connecting and disconnecting battery chargers or jump leads.

Air bags

• Air bags can cause injury if they go off accidentally. Take care when removing the steering wheel and/or facia. Special storage instructions may apply.

Diesel injection equipment

• Diesel injection pumps supply fuel at very high pressure. Take care when working on the fuel injectors and fuel pipes.

⚠ ***Warning: Never expose the hands, face or any other part of the body to injector spray; the fuel can penetrate the skin with potentially fatal results.***

Remember...

DO

• Do use eye protection when using power tools, and when working under the vehicle.

• Do wear gloves or use barrier cream to protect your hands when necessary.

• Do get someone to check periodically that all is well when working alone on the vehicle.

• Do keep loose clothing and long hair well out of the way of moving mechanical parts.

• Do remove rings, wristwatch etc, before working on the vehicle – especially the electrical system.

• Do ensure that any lifting or jacking equipment has a safe working load rating adequate for the job.

DON'T

• Don't attempt to lift a heavy component which may be beyond your capability – get assistance.

• Don't rush to finish a job, or take unverified short cuts.

• Don't use ill-fitting tools which may slip and cause injury.

• Don't leave tools or parts lying around where someone can trip over them. Mop up oil and fuel spills at once.

• Don't allow children or pets to play in or near a vehicle being worked on.

The following pages are intended to help in dealing with common roadside emergencies and breakdowns. You will find more detailed fault finding information at the back of the manual, and repair information in the main chapters.

If your car won't start and the starter motor doesn't turn

- ☐ If it's a model with automatic transmission, make sure the selector is in 'P' or 'N'.
- ☐ Open the bonnet and make sure that the battery terminals are clean and tight.
- ☐ Switch on the headlights and try to start the engine. If the headlights go very dim when you're trying to start, the battery is probably flat. Get out of trouble by jump starting (see next page) using a friend's car.

If your car won't start even though the starter motor turns as normal

- ☐ Is there fuel in the tank?
- ☐ Is there moisture on electrical components under the bonnet? Switch off the ignition, then wipe off any obvious dampness with a dry cloth. Spray a water-repellent aerosol product (WD-40 or equivalent) on ignition and fuel system electrical connectors like those shown in the photos. On petrol models, pay special attention to the ignition coil wiring connector and HT leads. Diesel engines are not generally as susceptible to damp problems, but all accessible wiring and connectors should still be checked.

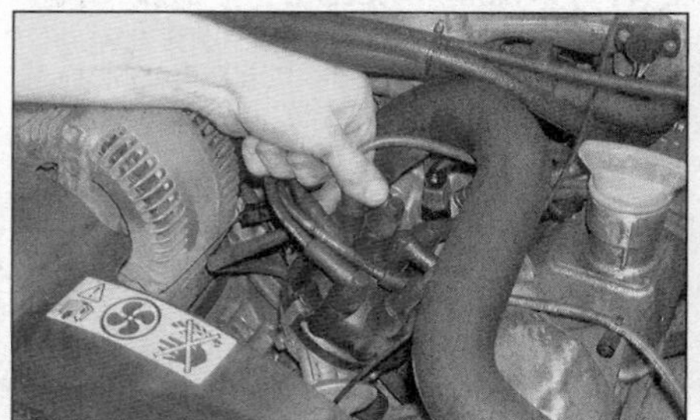

A On petrol models, check that the HT leads are securely connected to the distributor, and that the cap is clean and properly fitted.

B On petrol models, check that the HT lead and wiring connections are securely connected to the ignition coil.

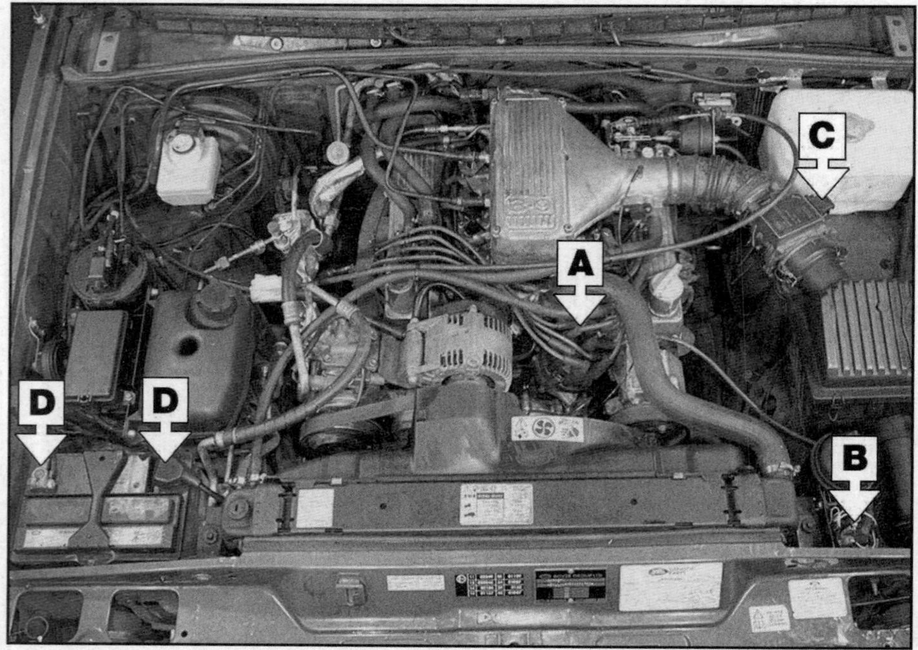
C
A
D
D
B

Check that electrical connections are secure (with the ignition switched off) and spray them with a water-dispersant spray like WD-40 if you suspect a problem due to damp.

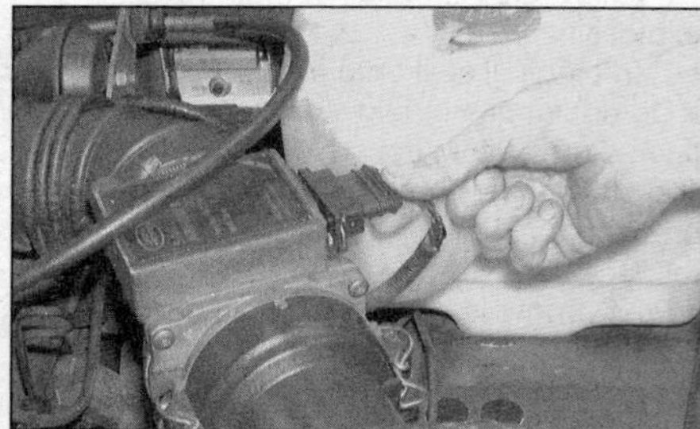

C Check all fuel system wiring and connectors for security.

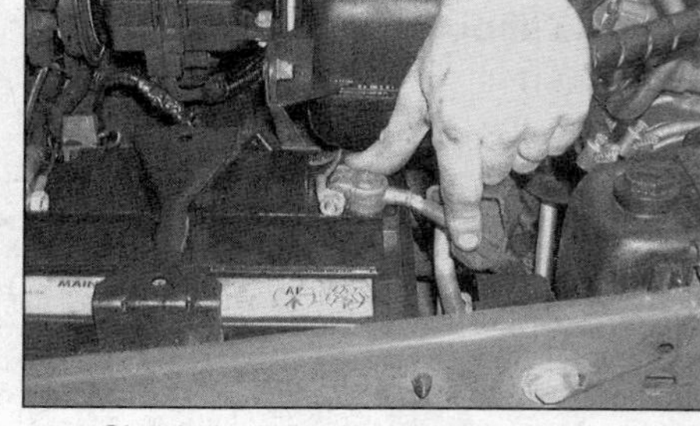

D Check the security and condition of the battery terminals.

Jump starting

HAYNES HiNT *Jump starting will get you out of trouble, but you must correct whatever made the battery go flat in the first place. There are three possibilities:*

***1** The battery has been drained by repeated attempts to start, or by leaving the lights on.*

***2** The charging system is not working properly (alternator drivebelt slack or broken, alternator wiring fault or alternator itself faulty).*

***3** The battery itself is at fault (electrolyte low, or battery worn out).*

When jump-starting a car using a booster battery, observe the following precautions:

- ✔ Before connecting the booster battery, make sure that the ignition is switched off.
- ✔ Ensure that all electrical equipment (lights, heater, wipers, etc) is switched off.
- ✔ Take note of any special precautions printed on the battery case.
- ✔ Make sure that the booster battery is the same voltage as the discharged one in the vehicle.
- ✔ If the battery is being jump-started from the battery in another vehicle, the two vehicles MUST NOT TOUCH each other.
- ✔ Make sure that the transmission is in neutral (or PARK, in the case of automatic transmission).

1 Connect one end of the red jump lead to the positive (+) terminal of the flat battery

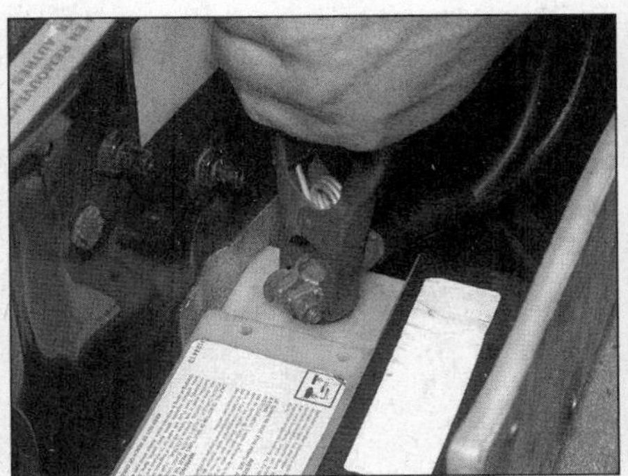

2 Connect the other end of the red lead to the positive (+) terminal of the booster battery.

3 Connect one end of the black jump lead to the negative (-) terminal of the booster battery

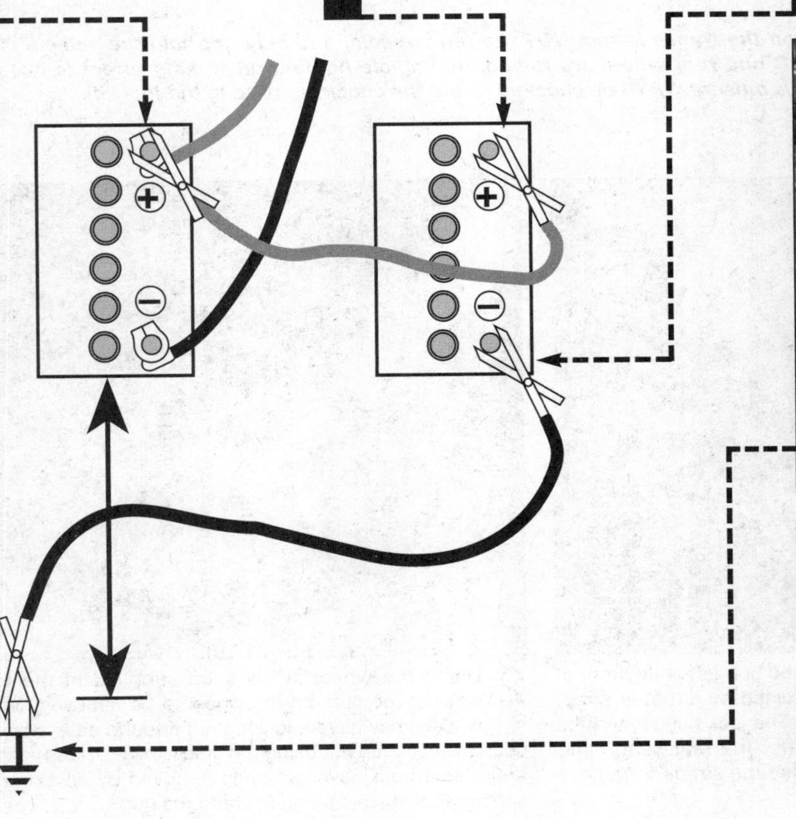

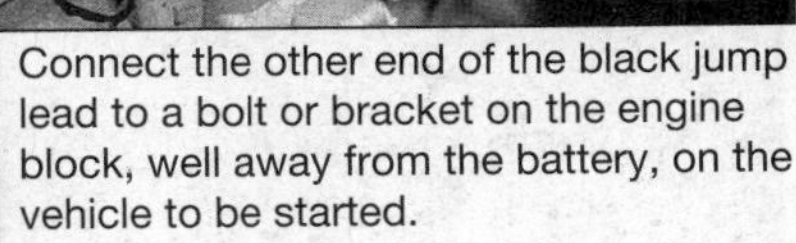

4 Connect the other end of the black jump lead to a bolt or bracket on the engine block, well away from the battery, on the vehicle to be started.

5 Make sure that the jump leads will not come into contact with the fan, drive-belts or other moving parts of the engine.

6 Start the engine using the booster battery and run it at idle speed. Switch on the lights, rear window demister and heater blower motor, then disconnect the jump leads in the reverse order of connection. Turn off the lights etc.

Wheel changing

Warning: Do not change a wheel in a situation where you risk being hit by another vehicle. On busy roads, try to stop in a lay-by or a gateway. Be wary of passing traffic while changing the wheel - it is easy to become distracted by the job in hand.

Preparation

- ☐ When a puncture occurs, stop as soon as it is safe to do so.
- ☐ Park on firm level ground, if possible, and well out of the way of other traffic.
- ☐ Use hazard warning lights if necessary.
- ☐ If you have one, use a warning triangle to alert other drivers of your presence.
- ☐ Apply the handbrake and engage first or reverse gear (or Park on models with automatic transmission).
- ☐ Select 'Low' range in the transfer gearbox, and engage the differential lock.
- ☐ Chock the wheel opposite the one being removed – a chock is supplied in the vehicle tool kit.
- ☐ If the ground is soft, use a flat piece of wood to spread the load under the jack.
- ☐ If the vehicle is coupled to a trailer, disconnect the trailer from the vehicle before commencing jacking. This is to prevent the trailer pulling the vehicle off the jack and causing personal injury.

Changing the wheel

Warning: The handbrake acts on the transmission, NOT the rear wheels, and may not hold the vehicle stationary when jacking. If one front wheel AND one rear wheel are raised, no vehicle holding or braking effect is possible using the handbrake. Therefore, the wheels must ALWAYS be chocked (using the chock supplied in the tool kit).

1 The jack and the wheel chock are under the bonnet, at the front of the engine compartment. The jack is retained by a rubber strap, and the chock is secured by a wing nut. The jack handle and the wheel nut wrench are located in a bag under the rear seats, and secured by straps. Raise the seats and release the straps to remove the bag.

2 Using the wheel nut wrench supplied in the tool kit, initially slacken the nuts on the wheel to be removed. Models with alloy wheels may have a locking nut fitted to each wheel, including the spare. Unlock the nut using the small key provided - later models have an indented nut cover which is removed by an extractor tool, and a special socket which then fits onto the nut.

3 Assemble the two-piece jack operating lever, ensuring that the locking clip engages fully with the corresponding slot. Check that the release valve at the bottom of the jack body is closed (turned fully clockwise).

4 The jack head must now be located under the correct part of the front or rear axle, adjacent to the wheel to be changed - refer to *Jacking and vehicle support* at the end of this manual for more information. Engage the operating lever with the jack, then pump the lever up and down to raise the vehicle.

5 Once the wheel is clear of the ground, remove the wheel nuts, and lift off the wheel.

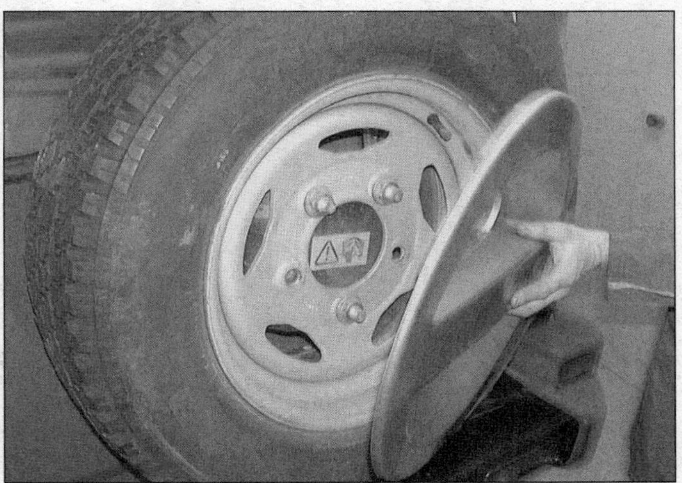

6 Again using the wheel nut wrench, remove the nuts securing the plastic spare wheel cover, then unscrew the three nuts securing the spare wheel to the carrier, and lift off the wheel. Take care not to mix up the spare wheel cover nuts and spare wheel nuts.

7 Locate the spare wheel on the studs, then refit the original wheel nuts, and tighten firmly using the wrench. **Do not** use the spare wheel cover nuts to secure the wheel. Lower the vehicle to the ground, and withdraw the jack. Tighten the wheel nuts using the wrench, with hand pressure only.

Finally...

- ☐ Remove the wheel chock.
- ☐ Stow the jack, chock and tools in their correct locations.
- ☐ Fit the removed wheel to the spare wheel carrier, and where applicable, refit the cover (it may not be possible to fit the cover to certain alloy wheels).
- ☐ Check the tyre pressure on the tyre just fitted. If it is low, or if you don't have a pressure gauge with you, drive slowly to the next garage and inflate the tyre to the correct pressure.
- ☐ On completion, disengage the differential lock and select the 'High' range in the transfer gearbox.
- ☐ Have the punctured wheel repaired as soon as possible, or another puncture will leave you stranded.

Identifying leaks

Puddles on the garage floor or drive, or obvious wetness under the bonnet or underneath the car, suggest a leak that needs investigating. It can sometimes be difficult to decide where the leak is coming from, especially if the engine bay is very dirty already. Leaking oil or fluid can also be blown rearwards by the passage of air under the car, giving a false impression of where the problem lies.

Warning: Most automotive oils and fluids are poisonous. Wash them off skin, and change out of contaminated clothing, without delay.

HAYNES
HiNT

The smell of a fluid leaking from the car may provide a clue to what's leaking. Some fluids are distinctively coloured. It may help to clean the car carefully and to park it over some clean paper overnight as an aid to locating the source of the leak. Remember that some leaks may only occur while the engine is running.

Sump oil

Engine oil may leak from the drain plug...

Oil from filter

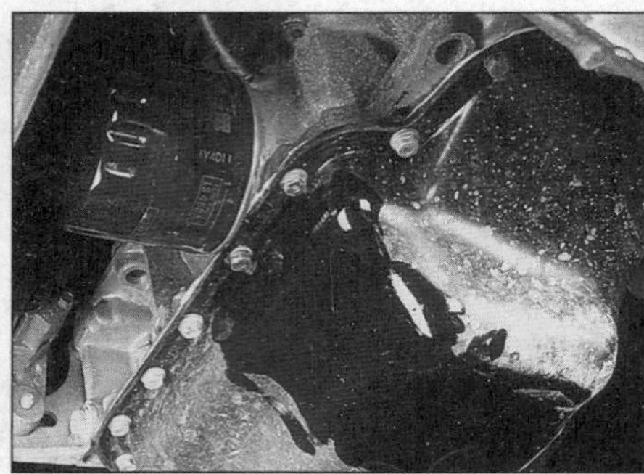

...or from the base of the oil filter.

Gearbox oil

Gearbox oil can leak from the seals at the inboard ends of the driveshafts.

Antifreeze

Leaking antifreeze often leaves a crystalline deposit like this.

Brake fluid

A leak occurring at a wheel is almost certainly brake fluid.

Power steering fluid

Power steering fluid may leak from the pipe connectors on the steering rack.

Towing

When all else fails, you may find yourself having to get a tow home – or of course you may be helping somebody else. Long-distance recovery should only be done by a garage or breakdown service. For shorter distances, DIY towing using another car is easy enough, but observe the following points:

☐ Land Rover Discovery models must not be towed with either the front or the rear wheels raised (suspended tow). The car should ideally be transported on a trailer, with all four wheels off the ground - this approach should particularly be used if a transmission problem is suspected.

☐ Use a proper tow-rope – they are not expensive. The vehicle being towed must display an ON TOW sign in its rear window.

☐ Always turn the ignition key to the 'on' position when the vehicle is being towed, so that the steering lock is released, and that the direction indicator and brake lights will work.

☐ A single towing eye is provided below the front bumper, and two are provided at the rear. Two lashing rings are also provided at the front of the car - these must **not** be used for towing.

☐ Before being towed, release the handbrake and select neutral. Also select neutral on the transfer gearbox, and ensure that the differential lock is in the unlocked position, or the transmission may be damaged - if in doubt, seek professional assistance.

☐ Note that greater-than-usual pedal pressure will be required to operate the brakes, since the vacuum servo unit is only operational with the engine running. Similarly, greater-than-usual steering effort will also be required.

☐ The driver of the car being towed must keep the tow-rope taut at all times to avoid snatching.

☐ Make sure that both drivers know the route before setting off.

☐ Only drive at moderate speeds and keep the distance towed to a minimum. Drive smoothly and allow plenty of time for slowing down at junctions.

Introduction

There are some very simple checks which need only take a few minutes to carry out, but which could save you a lot of inconvenience and expense.

These Weekly checks require no great skill or special tools, and the small amount of time they take to perform could prove to be very well spent, for example;

☐ Keeping an eye on tyre condition and pressures, will not only help to stop them wearing out prematurely, but could also save your life.

☐ Many breakdowns are caused by electrical problems. Battery-related faults are particularly common, and a quick check on a regular basis will often prevent the majority of these.

☐ If your car develops a brake fluid leak, the first time you might know about it is when your brakes don't work properly. Checking the level regularly will give advance warning of this kind of problem.

☐ If the oil or coolant levels run low, the cost of repairing any engine damage will be far greater than fixing the leak, for example.

Underbonnet check points

3.9 litre petrol (3.5 litre similar)

A *Engine oil level dipstick*
B *Engine oil filler cap*
C *Coolant expansion tank*
D *Brake fluid reservoir*
E *Power steering fluid reservoir*
F *Screen washer fluid reservoir*
G *Battery*

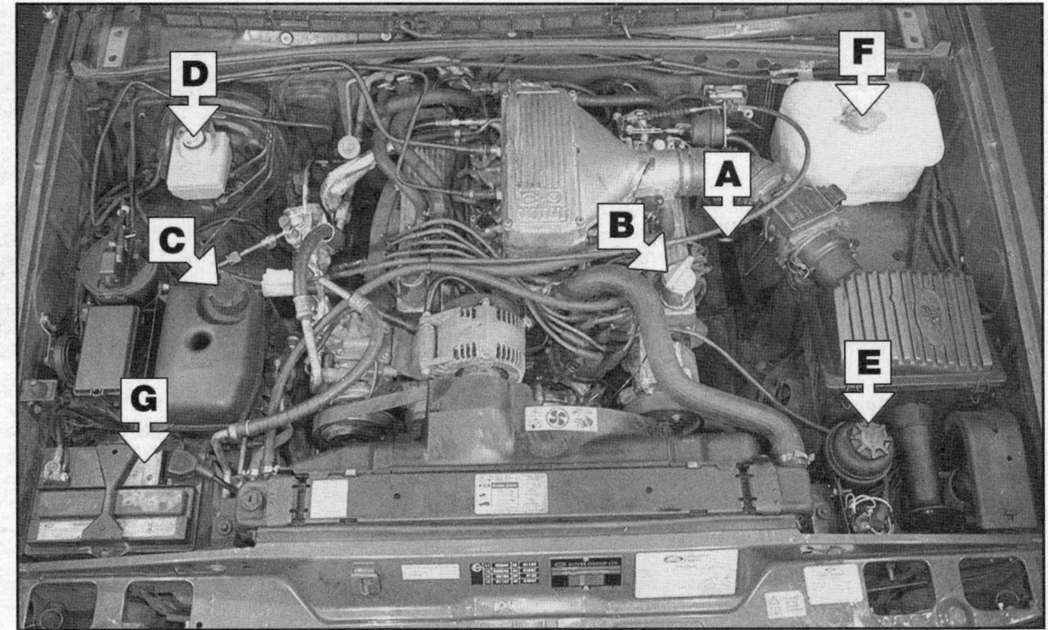
D
F
A
B
C
E
G

300 TDi diesel (200 TDi similar)

A *Engine oil level dipstick*
B *Engine oil filler cap*
C *Coolant expansion tank*
D *Brake fluid reservoir*
E *Power steering fluid reservoir*
F *Screen washer fluid reservoir*
G *Battery*

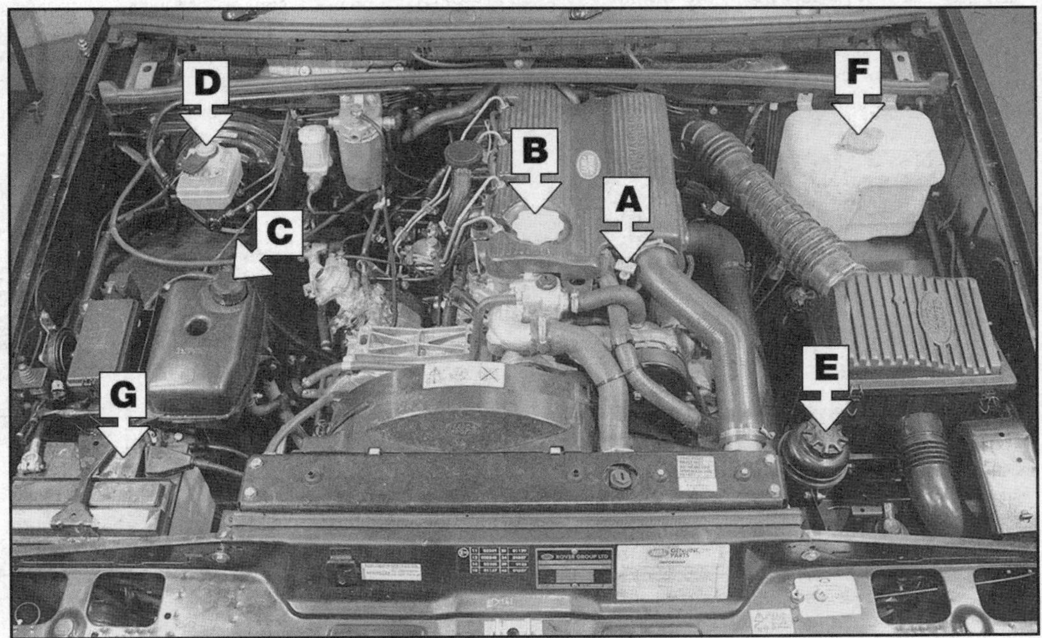
D
F
B
A
C
E
G

Engine oil level

Before you start

✔ Make sure that your car is on level ground.
✔ Check the oil level before the car is driven, or at least 5 minutes after the engine has been switched off.

HAYNES
HiNT

If the oil is checked immediately after driving the vehicle, some of the oil will remain in the upper engine components, resulting in an inaccurate reading on the dipstick!

The correct oil

Modern engines place great demands on their oil. It is very important that the correct oil for your car is used (See "Lubricants and fluids").

Car Care

● If you have to add oil frequently, you should check whether you have any oil leaks. Place some clean paper under the car overnight, and check for stains in the morning. If there are no leaks, the engine may be burning oil, or the oil may only be leaking when the engine is running.

● Always maintain the level between the upper and lower dipstick marks. If the level is too low severe engine damage may occur. Oil seal failure may result if the engine is significantly overfilled by adding too much oil.

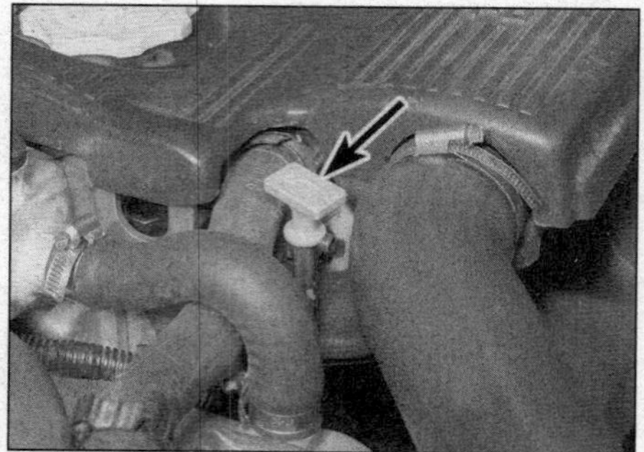

1 On some engines, the dipstick is brightly coloured for easy identification (see *Underbonnet check points* on page 0•11 for exact location). Withdraw the dipstick.

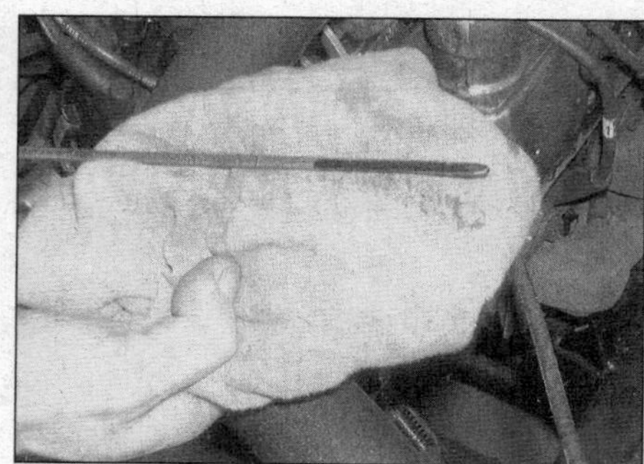

2 Using a clean rag or paper towel remove all oil from the dipstick. Insert the clean dipstick into the tube as far as it will go, then withdraw it again.

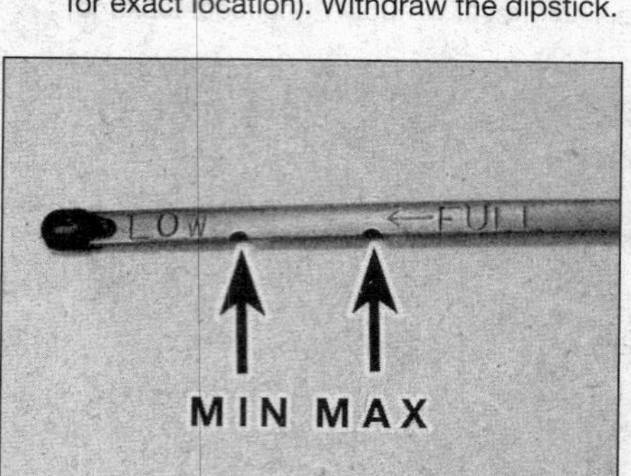
LOW
FULL
MIN MAX

3 Note the oil level on the end of the dipstick, which should be between the upper (MAX, HIGH, or FULL) mark and lower (MIN, LOW or ADD OIL) mark.

4 Oil is added through the filler cap. Unscrew the cap and top-up the level; a funnel may help to reduce spillage. Add the oil slowly, allowing time for the oil to reach the sump, and checking the level on the dipstick often. Don't overfill (see *Car care*).

Coolant level

Warning: DO NOT attempt to remove the expansion tank pressure cap when the engine is hot, as there is a very great risk of scalding. Do not leave open containers of coolant about, as it is poisonous.

Car Care

● With a sealed-type cooling system, adding coolant should not be necessary on a regular basis. If frequent topping-up is required, it is likely there is a leak. Check the radiator, all hoses and joint faces for signs of staining or wetness, and rectify as necessary.

● It is important that antifreeze is used in the cooling system all year round, not just during the winter months. Don't top-up with water alone, as the antifreeze will become too diluted.

1 The coolant reservoir is located on the right-hand inner wing, behind the battery. To check the coolant level, **wait until the engine is cold**. Slowly unscrew the expansion tank cap, to release any pressure present in the cooling system, and remove it.

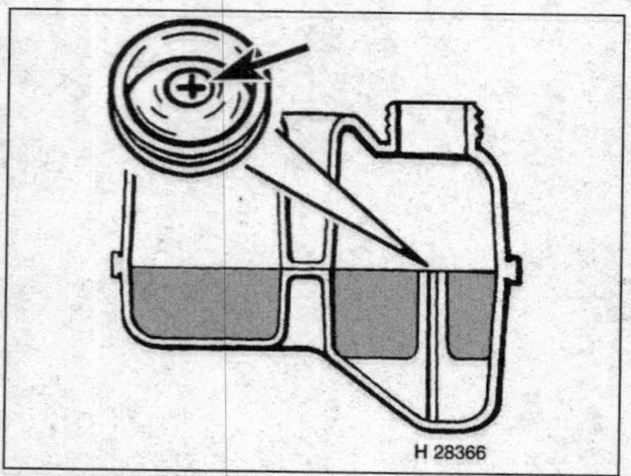
H 28366

2 The coolant level should be up to the top of the level indicator visible inside the tank.

3 Add a suitable mixture of water and antifreeze to the expansion tank until the coolant is at the correct level (see Chapter 1A or 1B for antifreeze mixtures). Refit the cap and tighten it securely.

Brake fluid level

Warning:

- ***Brake fluid can harm your eyes and damage painted surfaces, so use extreme caution when handling and pouring it.***
- ***Do not use fluid that has been standing open for some time, as it absorbs moisture from the air, which can cause a dangerous loss of braking effectiveness.***

HAYNES
HiNT

The fluid level in the reservoir will drop slightly as the brake pads wear down, but the fluid level must never be allowed to drop below the MIN mark.

Before you start

- Make sure that your car is on level ground.

Safety First!

- If the reservoir requires repeated topping-up this is an indication of a fluid leak somewhere in the system, which should be investigated immediately.
- If a leak is suspected, the car should not be driven until the braking system has been checked. Never take any risks where brakes are concerned.

1 The MAX and MIN marks are indicated on the reservoir. The fluid level must be kept between the marks at all times. If topping-up is necessary, disconnect the wiring plug from the filler cap.

2 Wipe clean the area around the filler cap to prevent dirt entering the hydraulic system. Unscrew the reservoir cap and carefully lift it out of position, taking care not to damage the level sender float. Place the cap on a clean piece of absorbent rag. Inspect the reservoir, if the fluid is dirty, the hydraulic system should be drained and refilled (see Chapter 1A or 1B).

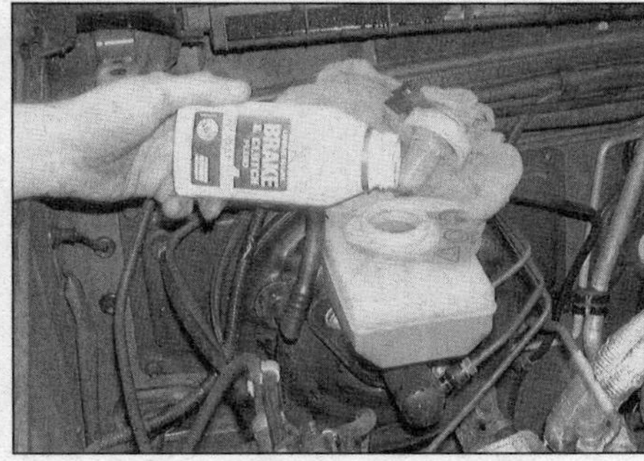

3 Carefully add fluid, taking care not to spill it onto the surrounding components. Use only the specified fluid; mixing different types can cause damage to the system. After topping-up to the correct level, securely refit the cap and wipe off any spilt fluid. Refit the wiring plug.

Power steering fluid level

Before you start:

✔ Park the vehicle on level ground.
✔ Set the steering wheel straight-ahead.
✔ The engine must be cold (wait at least 2 hours after switching off).

HAYNES
HiNT

For the check to be accurate, the steering wheel must not be turned after switching the engine off.

Safety First!

- The need for frequent topping-up indicates a leak, which should be investigated immediately.

1 The power steering fluid reservoir is located in the front left-hand corner of the engine compartment, mounted onto the side of the radiator. Unscrew the filler cap from the top of the reservoir, and wipe all fluid from the cap dipstick with a clean rag. Refit the filler cap fully, then remove it again.

2 Note the fluid level on the dipstick. When the engine is cold, the fluid level should be between the upper and lower marks on the dipstick. If the level is checked when the engine is at normal operating temperature, the fluid level should be up to the upper mark on the dipstick.

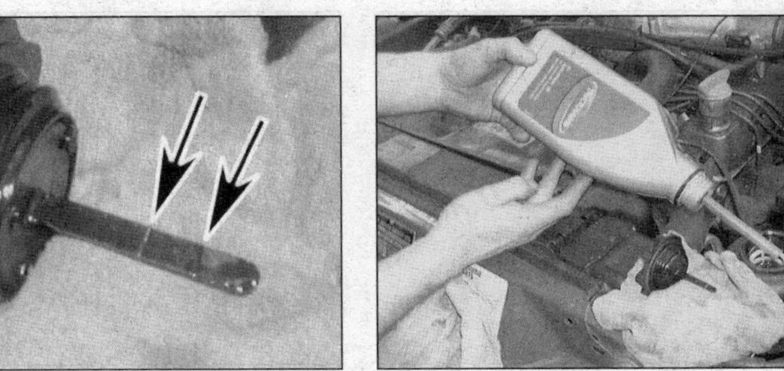

3 If necessary, top-up with the specified type of fluid, then refit the filler cap securely.

Tyre condition and pressure

It is very important that tyres are in good condition, and at the correct pressure - having a tyre failure at any speed is highly dangerous. Tyre wear is influenced by driving style - harsh braking and acceleration, or fast cornering, will all produce more rapid tyre wear. As a general rule, the front tyres wear out faster than the rears. Interchanging the tyres from front to rear ("rotating" the tyres) may result in more even wear. However, if this is completely effective, you may have the expense of replacing all four tyres at once!

Remove any nails or stones embedded in the tread before they penetrate the tyre to cause deflation. If removal of a nail does reveal that the tyre has been punctured, refit the nail so that its point of penetration is marked. Then immediately change the wheel, and have the tyre repaired by a tyre dealer.

Regularly check the tyres for damage in the form of cuts or bulges, especially in the sidewalls. Periodically remove the wheels, and clean any dirt or mud from the inside and outside surfaces. Examine the wheel rims for signs of rusting, corrosion or other damage. Light alloy wheels are easily damaged by "kerbing" whilst parking; steel wheels may also become dented or buckled. A new wheel is very often the only way to overcome severe damage.

New tyres should be balanced when they are fitted, but it may become necessary to re-balance them as they wear, or if the balance weights fitted to the wheel rim should fall off. Unbalanced tyres will wear more quickly, as will the steering and suspension components. Wheel imbalance is normally signified by vibration, particularly at a certain speed (typically around 50 mph). If this vibration is felt only through the steering, then it is likely that just the front wheels need balancing. If, however, the vibration is felt through the whole car, the rear wheels could be out of balance. Wheel balancing should be carried out by a tyre dealer or garage.

A
B

1 *Tread Depth - visual check*
The original tyres have tread wear safety bands (B), which will appear when the tread depth reaches approximately 1.6 mm. The band positions are indicated by a triangular mark on the tyre sidewall (A).

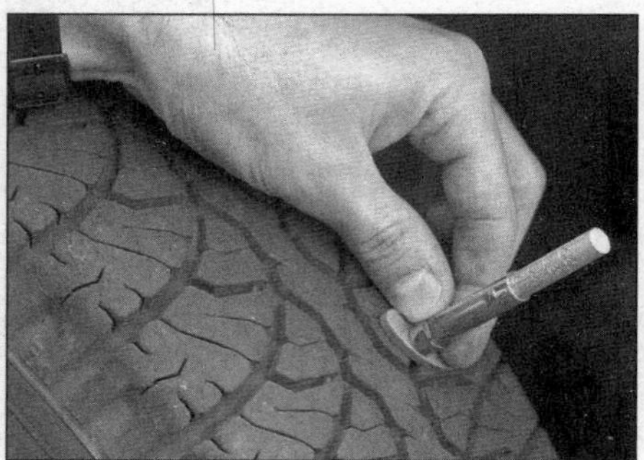

2 *Tread Depth - manual check*
Alternatively, tread wear can be monitored with a simple, inexpensive device known as a tread depth indicator gauge.

3 *Tyre Pressure Check*
Check the tyre pressures regularly with the tyres cold. Do not adjust the tyre pressures immediately after the vehicle has been used, or an inaccurate setting will result. Tyre pressures are shown on page 0•18.

Tyre tread wear patterns

Shoulder Wear

Underinflation (wear on both sides)
Under-inflation will cause overheating of the tyre, because the tyre will flex too much, and the tread will not sit correctly on the road surface. This will cause a loss of grip and excessive wear, not to mention the danger of sudden tyre failure due to heat build-up.
Check and adjust pressures
Incorrect wheel camber (wear on one side)
Repair or renew suspension parts
Hard cornering
Reduce speed!

Centre Wear

Overinflation
Over-inflation will cause rapid wear of the centre part of the tyre tread, coupled with reduced grip, harsher ride, and the danger of shock damage occurring in the tyre casing.
Check and adjust pressures

If you sometimes have to inflate your car's tyres to the higher pressures specified for maximum load or sustained high speed, don't forget to reduce the pressures to normal afterwards.

Uneven Wear

Front tyres may wear unevenly as a result of wheel misalignment. Most tyre dealers and garages can check and adjust the wheel alignment (or "tracking") for a modest charge.
Incorrect camber or castor
Repair or renew suspension parts
Malfunctioning suspension
Repair or renew suspension parts
Unbalanced wheel
Balance tyres
Incorrect toe setting
Adjust front wheel alignment
Note: *The feathered edge of the tread which typifies toe wear is best checked by feel.*

Battery

Caution: Before carrying out any work on the vehicle battery, read the precautions given in 'Safety first' at the start of this manual.

✔ Make sure that the battery tray is in good condition, and that the clamp is tight. Corrosion on the tray, retaining clamp and the battery itself can be removed with a solution of water and baking soda. Thoroughly rinse all cleaned areas with water. Any metal parts damaged by corrosion should be covered with a zinc-based primer, then painted.

✔ Periodically (approximately every three months), check the charge condition of the battery as described in Chapter 5A.

✔ If the battery is flat, and you need to jump start your vehicle, see *Roadside Repairs*.

1 The battery is located at the front of the engine compartment on the right-hand side - where necessary, unclip and remove the cover for access. The exterior of the battery should be inspected periodically for damage such as a cracked case or cover.

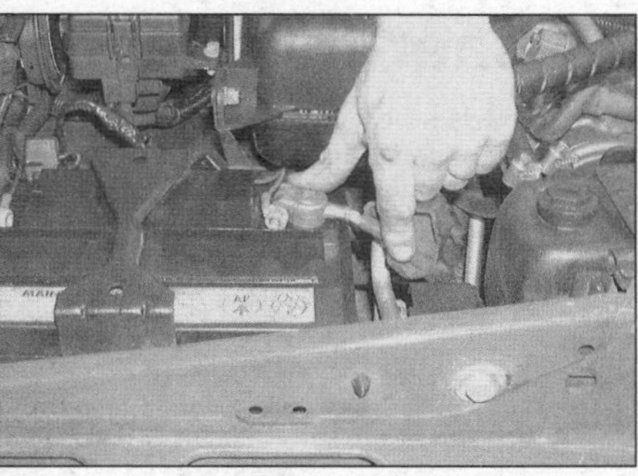

2 Check the tightness of battery clamps to ensure good electrical connections. You should not be able to move them. Also check each cable for cracks and frayed conductors.

HAYNES HINT

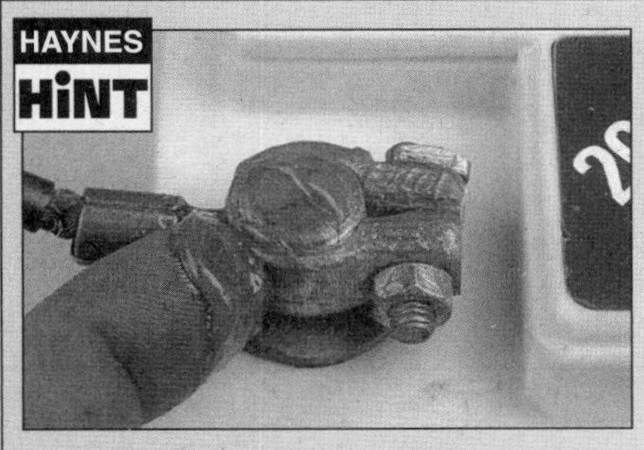

Battery corrosion can be kept to a minimum by applying a layer of petroleum jelly to the clamps and terminals after they are reconnected.

Freedo
Batter

3 If corrosion (white, fluffy deposits) is evident, remove the cables from the battery terminals, clean them with a small wire brush, then refit them. Automotive stores sell a tool for cleaning the battery post . . .

4 . . . as well as the battery cable clamps

Bulbs and fuses

✔ Check all external lights and the horn. Refer to the appropriate Sections of Chapter 13 for details if any of the circuits are found to be inoperative.

✔ Visually check all accessible wiring connectors, harnesses and retaining clips for security, and for signs of chafing or damage.

HAYNES
HINT

If you need to check your brake lights and indicators unaided, back up to a wall or garage door and operate the lights. The reflected light should show if they are working properly.

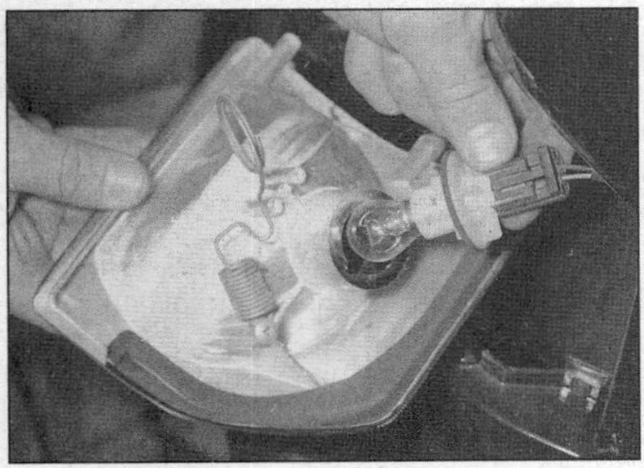

1 If a single indicator light, stop-light or headlight has failed, it is likely that a bulb has blown and will need to be replaced. Refer to Chapter 13 for details. If both stop-lights have failed, it is possible that the switch is faulty (see Chapter 10).

2 If more than one indicator light or headlight has failed, it is likely that either a fuse has blown or that there is a fault in the circuit (see Chapter 13). The main fuses are located in the fusebox situated behind a facia panel on the driver's side, although other fuses may be found in a fusebox under the bonnet.

3 To replace a blown fuse, make sure the ignition is switched off, then simply pull it out - use the plastic tweezers provided, where applicable. Fit a new fuse of the same rating (see Chapter 13). If the fuse blows again, it is important that you find out why - a complete checking procedure is given in Chapter 13.

Washer fluid level

- On models so equipped, the screenwasher fluid is also used to clean the headlights and the tailgate rear window.
- Screenwash additives not only keep the winscreen clean during foul weather, they also prevent the washer system freezing in cold weather - which is when you are likely to need it most. Don't top up using plain water as the screenwash will become too diluted, and will freeze during cold weather. ***On no account use coolant antifreeze in the washer system - this could discolour or damage paintwork.***

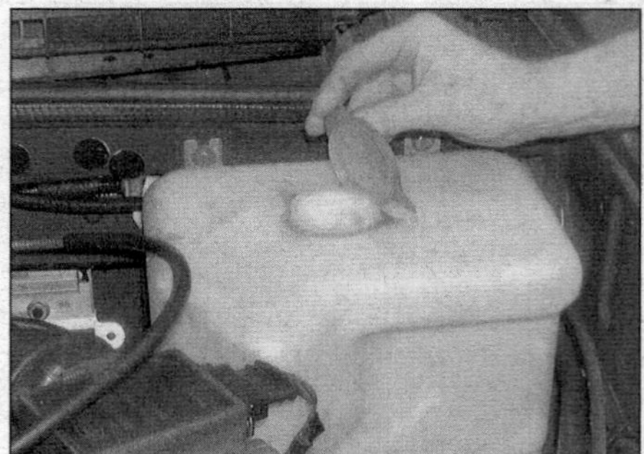

1 The washer fluid reservoir is located at the left-hand rear corner of the engine compartment. The washer level should be maintained just below the reservoir filler neck (the precise level is not critical).

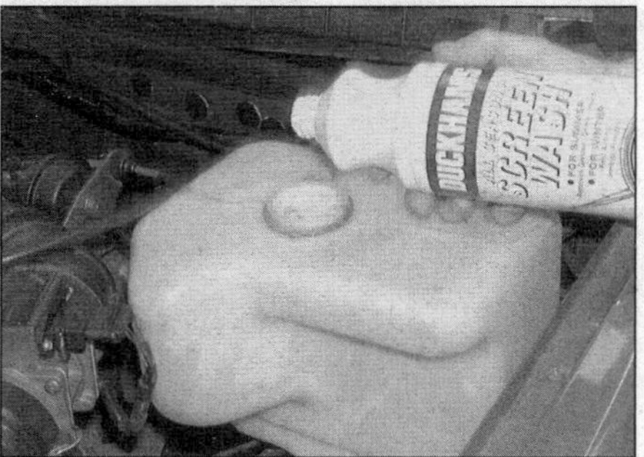
DUCKHAMS
SCREEN
WASH

2 If topping-up is required, release the cap. When topping-up the reservoir, a screenwash additive should be added in the quantities recommended on the bottle.

Wiper blades

Note: *Fitting details for wiper blades vary according to model, and according to whether genuine Land Rover wiper blades have been fitted. Use the procedures and illustrations shown as a guide for your vehicle.*

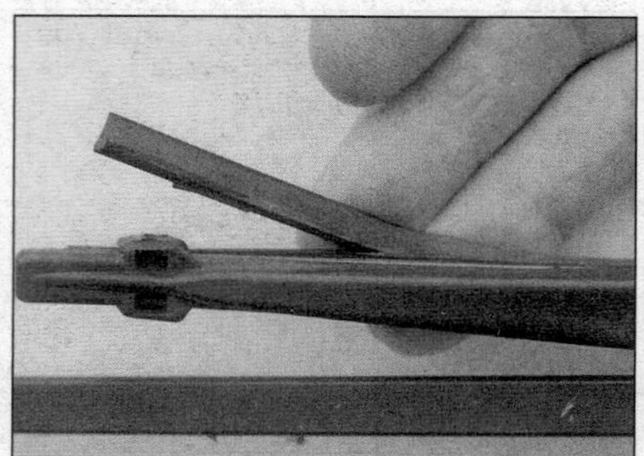

1 Check the condition of the wiper blades; if they are cracked or show any signs of deterioration, or if the glass swept area is smeared, renew them. Wiper blades should be renewed annually.

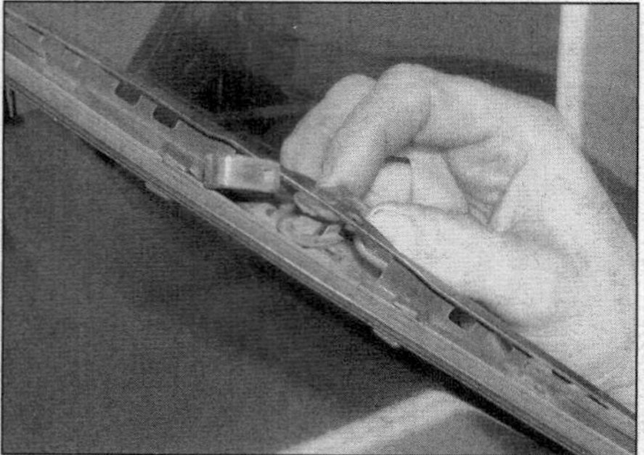

2 To remove a wiper blade, pull the arm fully away from the glass until it locks. Swivel the blade through 90°, press the locking tab with your fingers, and slide the blade out of the arm's hooked end.

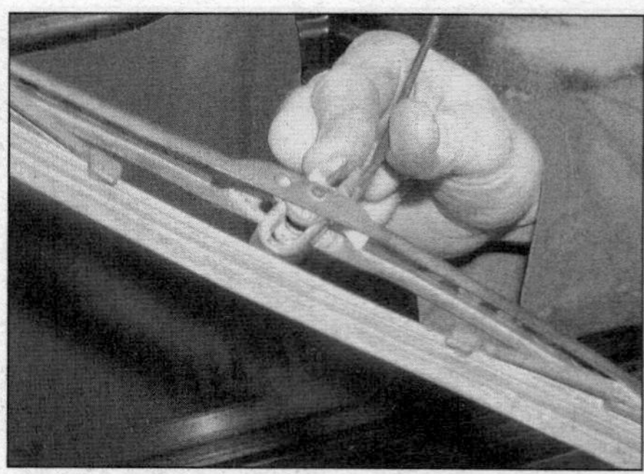

3 Don't forget to check the tailgate wiper blade as well - these are removed in the same way as the windscreen wiper blades.

Lubricants and fluids

Engine:	
Petrol	Multigrade engine oil, viscosity SAE 5W/30 to 10W/40, to ACEA A2:96, API SH or better
Diesel	Multigrade engine oil, viscosity SAE 5W/30 to 15W/40, to ACEA B2:96, API CE or better
Cooling system	Ethylene glycol-based antifreeze
Manual transmission	Dexron IID type automatic transmission fluid (ATF)
Automatic transmission	Dexron IID type automatic transmission fluid (ATF)
Transfer gearbox	Hypoid gear oil, viscosity SAE 80EP or SAE 90EP to API GL4, MIL-L-2105, or better
Front and rear axles, swivel pin housings*	Hypoid gear oil, viscosity SAE 80EP or SAE 90EP to API GL4, MIL-L-2105, or better
Propeller shaft joints	Multi-purpose lithium-based grease to NLGI-2
Brake and clutch fluid reservoirs	Hydraulic fluid to FMVSS 116 DOT 4
Power steering fluid reservoir	Dexron IID type automatic transmission fluid (ATF)

***Note:** *From approximately 1998 onwards, Land Rover (and their dealers) drain the oil and fill the swivel pin housing with a special grease, which then requires no further maintenance - consult a dealer for more information. This grease is available from Land Rover dealers, under part number FTC3435.*

Choosing your engine oil

Engines need oil, not only to lubricate moving parts and minimise wear, but also to maximise power output and to improve fuel economy.

HOW ENGINE OIL WORKS

• *Beating friction*

Without oil, the moving surfaces inside your engine will rub together, heat up and melt, quickly causing the engine to seize. Engine oil creates a film which separates these moving parts, preventing wear and heat build-up.

• *Cooling hot-spots*

Temperatures inside the engine can exceed 1000° C. The engine oil circulates and acts as a coolant, transferring heat from the hot-spots to the sump.

• *Cleaning the engine internally*

Good quality engine oils clean the inside of your engine, collecting and dispersing combustion deposits and controlling them until they are trapped by the oil filter or flushed out at oil change.

OIL CARE - FOLLOW THE CODE

To handle and dispose of used engine oil safely, always:

OIL CARE
FOLLOW THE CODE
OIL BANK LINE
0800 66 33 66
www.oilbankline.org.uk

- ***Avoid skin contact with used engine oil. Repeated or prolonged contact can be harmful.***
- ***Dispose of used oil and empty packs in a responsible manner in an authorised disposal site. Call 0800 663366 to find the one nearest to you. Never tip oil down drains or onto the ground.***

Tyre pressures (cold)

Note: *Pressures apply only to original equipment tyres, and may vary if any other make of tyre is fitted; check with the tyre manufacturer or supplier for correct pressures if necessary.*

Normal use	**Front**	**Rear**
205 R 16 tyres	1.9 bars (28 psi)	2.6 bars (38 psi)
235/70 R 16 tyres	1.8 bars (26 psi)	2.3 bars (33 psi)
Off-road use*		
All tyres	1.2 bars (17 psi)	1.8 bars (26 psi)

**Vehicle speed must not exceed 25 mph (40 km/h) whilst off-road pressures are being used.*

Advanced driving

INSTITUTE ADVANCED MOTORISTS
I
A M

Many people see the words 'advanced driving' and believe that it won't interest them or that it is a style of driving beyond their own abilities. Nothing could be further from the truth. Advanced driving is straightforward safe, sensible driving - the sort of driving we should all do every time we get behind the wheel.

An average of 10 people are killed every day on UK roads and 870 more are injured, some seriously. Lives are ruined daily, usually because somebody did something stupid. Something like 95% of all accidents are due to human error, mostly driver failure. Sometimes we make genuine mistakes - everyone does. Sometimes we have lapses of concentration. Sometimes we deliberately take risks.

For many people, the process of 'learning to drive' doesn't go much further than learning how to pass the driving test because of a common belief that good drivers are made by 'experience'.

Learning to drive by 'experience' teaches three driving skills:

- ☐ Quick reactions. (Whoops, that was close!)
- ☐ Good handling skills. (Horn, swerve, brake, horn).
- ☐ Reliance on vehicle technology. (Great stuff this ABS, stop in no distance even in the wet...)

Drivers whose skills are 'experience based' generally have a lot of near misses and the odd accident. The results can be seen every day in our courts and our hospital casualty departments.

Advanced drivers have learnt to control the risks by controlling the position and speed of their vehicle. They avoid accidents and near misses, even if the drivers around them make mistakes.

The key skills of advanced driving are **concentration,** effective all-round **observation, anticipation** and **planning.** When **good vehicle handling** is added to these skills, all driving situations can be approached and negotiated in a safe, methodical way, leaving nothing to chance.

Concentration means applying your mind to safe driving, completely excluding anything that's not relevant. Driving is usually the most dangerous activity that most of us undertake in our daily routines. It deserves our full attention.

Observation means not just looking, but seeing and seeking out the information found in the driving environment.

Anticipation means asking yourself what is happening, what you can reasonably expect to happen and what could happen unexpectedly. (One of the commonest words used in compiling accident reports is 'suddenly'.)

Planning is the link between seeing something and taking the appropriate action. For many drivers, planning is the missing link.

If you want to become a safer and more skilful driver and you want to enjoy your driving more, contact the Institute of Advanced Motorists at www.iam.org.uk, phone 0208 996 9600, or write to IAM House, 510 Chiswick High Road, London W4 5RG for an information pack.

Chapter 1 Part A:
Routine maintenance & servicing - petrol models

Contents

Degrees of difficulty

Easy, suitable for novice with little experience 	**Fairly easy,** suitable for beginner with some experience 	**Fairly difficult,** suitable for competent DIY mechanic 	**Difficult,** suitable for experienced DIY mechanic 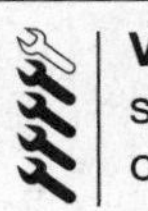	**Very difficult,** suitable for expert DIY or professional

Lubricants and fluids

Refer to end of *Weekly checks* on page 0•17

Capacities

Engine oil:	
Sump capacity (drain and refill, including oil filter):	
3.5 litre engine	5.7 litres
3.9 litre engine	6.7 litres
Cooling system:	
Manual transmission models	11.3 litres
Automatic transmission models	11.7 litres
Manual transmission	2.7 litres
Automatic transmission	9.8 litres
Transfer gearbox:	
Up to suffix D	2.3 litres
From suffix E	2.8 litres
Front axle	1.7 litres
Rear axle	1.7 litres
Steering box and power steering reservoir:	
Right-hand-drive models	3.4 litres
Left-hand-drive models	2.9 litres
Swivel pin housing oil (each)	0.35 litre
Fuel tank:	
Models built up to March 1993	81.8 litres
Models built from April 1993	89.0 litres
Washer fluid reservoir	7.0 litres

Cooling system

Antifreeze mixture:	
Minimum strength	25% antifreeze, 75% water
Maximum strength	60% antifreeze, 40% water
Protection to -36°C	50% antifreeze, 50% water

Fuel system

Idle speed:	
Carburettor engines	700 ± 50 rpm
Fuel injection engines (non-adjustable)	665 to 735 rpm
Mixture/CO level:	
Carburettor engines	1.0 to 2.0 %
Fuel injection engines (non-adjustable)	0.5 to 1.0 %

Ignition system

Ignition timing (UK market):		
Carburettor models	6 ± 1° BTDC at 750 ± 50 rpm	
3.5 litre fuel injection models:		
Low-compression engine	6 ± 1° BTDC at idle	
High-compression engine	TDC (0° BTDC) ± 1° at idle	
3.9 litre fuel injection models:		
Low-compression engine, non-catalyst	2 ± 1° BTDC at idle	
High-compression engine:		
Non-catalyst	4 ± 1° BTDC at idle	
With catalyst	5 ± 1° BTDC at idle	
Ignition timing (Australian market):		
3.5 litre fuel injection models	3 ± 2° BTDC at idle	
3.9 litre fuel injection models	2 ± 1° BTDC at idle	
Firing order	1-8-4-3-6-5-7-2	
Location of No 1 cylinder	Pulley end left (left as seen from driver's seat - odd numbers on left bank, evens on right)	
Spark plugs:	**Type**	**Electrode gap**
3.5 litre models	Bosch WR 7 D+	0.8 mm
3.9 litre models	Bosch WR 9 D+	0.8 mm

Brakes

Minimum front brake disc pad thickness	3.0 mm
Minimum rear brake disc pad thickness	3.0 mm

Tyre pressures

Refer to end of *Weekly checks* on page 0•18

Alternator drivebelt

Tension figures - 1994 to 1995 model year:	
New belt	470 to 500 N (106 to 113 lbf)
Used belt	400 to 420 N (90 to 95 lbf)

Torque wrench settings

	Nm	lbf ft
Distributor clamp nut	20	15
Engine sump drain plug:		
3.5 litre engine	30	22
3.9 litre engine	40	30
Fuel filter pipe unions	30	22
Propeller shaft and rubber coupling securing bolts	47	35
Roadwheel nuts	129	95
Spark plugs	20	15
Transfer gearbox oil drain plug	30	22
Transfer gearbox oil filler/level plug	30	22

Maintenance schedule

The maintenance intervals in this manual are provided with the assumption that you, not the dealer, will be carrying out the work. These are the minimum intervals recommended for vehicles driven daily. If you wish to keep your vehicle in peak condition at all times, you may wish to perform some of these procedures more often. We encourage frequent maintenance, since it enhances the efficiency, performance and resale value of your vehicle.

When the vehicle is new, it should be serviced by a dealer service department, in order to preserve the factory warranty.

Every 250 miles (400 km) or weekly

- ☐ Refer to *Weekly checks*

Every 6000 miles (10 000 km) or 6 months, whichever comes first

- ☐ Renew the engine oil and filter (Section 3)
- ☐ Check the battery electrolyte level, where possible (Section 4)

Continued overleaf . . .

Every 12 000 miles (20 000 km) or 12 months, whichever comes first

In addition to all the items listed above, carry out the following:

- ☐ Check the clutch fluid level (Section 5)
- ☐ Check the automatic transmission fluid level (Section 6)
- ☐ Renew the spark plugs (Section 7)
- ☐ Check the condition of the ignition system components (Section 8)
- ☐ Renew the air cleaner element (Section 9)
- ☐ Check the condition of the crankcase breather system hoses (Section 10)
- ☐ Top-up the carburettor piston dampers, where applicable (Section 11)
- ☐ Check and if necessary adjust the idle speed and mixture settings (Section 12)
- ☐ Check and lubricate the accelerator mechanism (Section 13)
- ☐ Check the cooling and heater system hoses for security and leaks (Section 14)
- ☐ Check the brake vacuum servo hose for security (Section 15)
- ☐ Check the condition of the auxiliary drivebelt(s), and adjust if necessary (Section 16)
- ☐ Check and if necessary adjust the steering gear backlash (Section 17)
- ☐ Check the security of the jack and tools (Section 18)
- ☐ Renew the manual transmission fluid (Section 19)
- ☐ Check the transfer gearbox oil level (Section 20)
- ☐ Check the front and rear axle oil levels (Section 21)
- ☐ Check the swivel pin housing oil level (Section 22)
- ☐ Lubricate the propeller shaft universal joints and sliding joints (Section 23)
- ☐ Lubricate the handbrake linkage (Section 24)
- ☐ Check all underbody brake, fuel and clutch pipes and hoses for leaks and condition (Section 25)
- ☐ Check the exhaust system for security and condition (Section 26)
- ☐ Check the steering and suspension components, including all hydraulic pipes and hoses, for leaks and condition (Section 27)
- ☐ Check the tightness of the propeller shaft coupling bolts (Section 28)
- ☐ Check the front and rear axle breathers for obstructions (Section 29)
- ☐ Drain the flywheel housing, where applicable (Section 30)
- ☐ Check the security of the fuel tank (Section 31)
- ☐ Check the security of the towing bracket (Section 32)
- ☐ Check the handbrake adjustment (Section 33)
- ☐ Carry out a road test (Section 34)
- ☐ Check and if necessary adjust the headlight and auxiliary light adjustment (Section 35)
- ☐ Check the operation of the sunroofs, and clear sunroof drain tubes (Section 36)
- ☐ Check the front wheel alignment (Section 37)

Every 12 000 miles (20 000 km) or 12 months, whichever comes first (continued)

- ☐ Check the condition of the brake pads and discs (Section 38)
- ☐ Check the condition of the spare wheel (Section 39)
- ☐ Check and lubricate all door, bonnet and tailgate locks (Section 40)
- ☐ Check the condition and operation of all seat belts (Section 41)

Every 24 000 miles (40 000 km) or 2 years, whichever comes first

In addition to all the items listed above, carry out the following:

- ☐ Check the ignition timing and adjust if necessary (Section 42)
- ☐ Renew the transfer gearbox oil (Section 43)
- ☐ Renew the front and rear axle oil (Section 44)
- ☐ Renew the swivel pin housing oil (Section 45)
- ☐ Renew the automatic transmission fluid and oil screen (Section 46)
- ☐ Clean the plenum chamber ventilation duct (Section 47)

Every 2 years, regardless of mileage

- ☐ Renew the brake fluid (Section 48)
- ☐ Renew the coolant (Section 49)

Every 36 000 miles (60 000 km) or 3 years, whichever comes first

In addition to all the items listed above, carry out the following:

- ☐ Check all shock absorbers for condition and operation (Section 50)
- ☐ Renew all braking system hydraulic fluid seals, the vacuum servo filter, and all flexible brake fluid hoses (Section 51)

Every 48 000 miles (80 000 km) or 4 years, whichever comes first

- ☐ Check the fuel evaporative emission control system for leaks (Section 52)
- ☐ Renew the fuel filter on fuel injected engines (Section 53)

Every 96 000 miles (154 000 km)

- ☐ Renew the emission control components, where applicable (Section 54)

Every 10 years

- ☐ Renew the airbag module, where applicable (Section 55)

Underbonnet view of a fuel injection model

1. *Battery*
2. *Fusebox*
3. *Coolant expansion tank*
4. *Charcoal canister (catalyst models)*
5. *Brake fluid reservoir*
6. *Automatic transmission fluid dipstick*
7. *Plenum chamber*
8. *Accelerator cable*
9. *Washer fluid reservoir*
10. *Air cleaner casing*
11. *Engine oil level dipstick*
12. *Engine oil filler cap*
13. *Wheel chock and jack*
14. *Ignition coil*
15. *Power steering fluid reservoir*
16. *Radiator top hose*
17. *Distributor cap*
18. *Auxiliary drivebelt*
19. *Radiator filler cap*
20. *Engine breather filter*

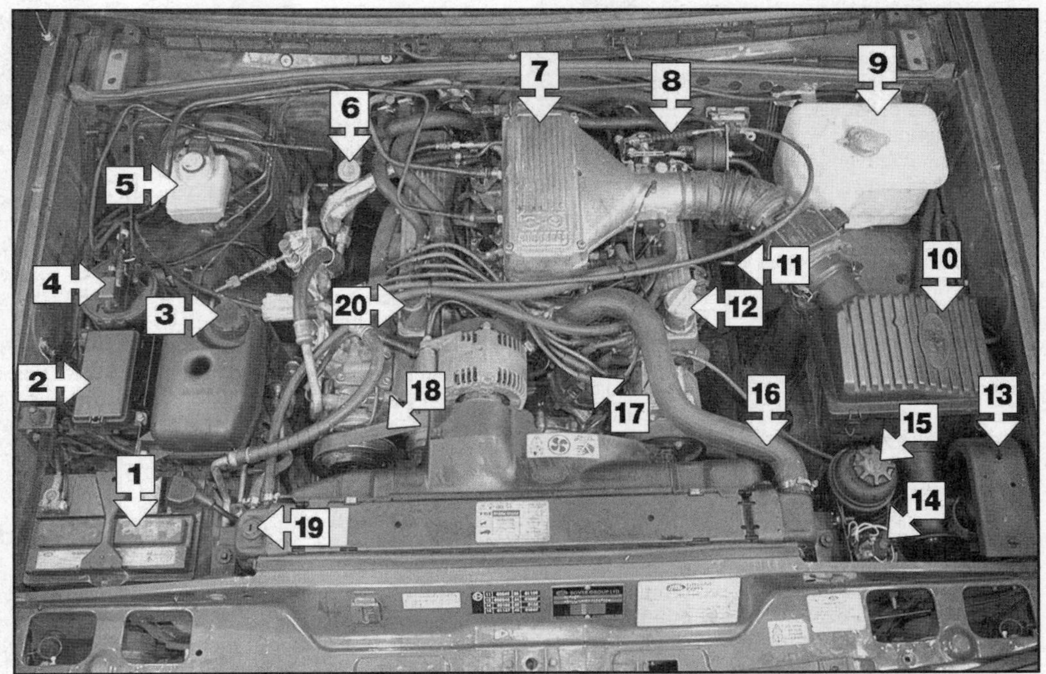
1
2
3
4
5
6
7
8
9
10
11
12
13
14
15
16
17
18
19
20

Front underbody view

1. *Panhard rod*
2. *Steering box*
3. *Oil filter*
4. *Drag link*
5. *Swivel pin housing*
6. *Track rod*
7. *Anti-roll bar*
8. *Radius arm*
9. *Exhaust (catalytic converters)*
10. *Engine oil drain plug*
11. *Steering damper*
12. *Front axle drain plug*

Note: *For centre and rear underbody views, see Chapter 1B*

1
2
3
4
5
5
6
7
8
8
9
9
10
11
12

1 Introduction

This Chapter is designed to help the home mechanic maintain his/her vehicle for safety, economy, long life and peak performance.

The Chapter contains a master maintenance schedule, followed by Sections dealing specifically with each task in the schedule. Visual checks, adjustments, component renewal and other helpful items are included. Refer to the accompanying illustrations of the engine compartment and the underside of the vehicle for the locations of the various components.

Servicing your vehicle in accordance with the mileage/time maintenance schedule and the following Sections will provide a planned maintenance programme, which should result in a long and reliable service life. This is a comprehensive plan, so maintaining some items but not others at the specified service intervals will not produce the same results.

As you service your vehicle, you will discover that many of the procedures can - and should - be grouped together, because of the particular procedure being performed, or because of the proximity of two otherwise unrelated components to one another. For example, if the vehicle is raised for any reason, the exhaust can be inspected at the same time as the suspension and steering components.

The first step in this maintenance programme is to prepare yourself before the actual work begins. Read through all the Sections relevant to the work to be carried out, then make a list and gather all the parts and tools required. If a problem is encountered, seek advice from a parts specialist, or a dealer service department.

2 Regular maintenance

1 If, from the time the vehicle is new, the routine maintenance schedule is followed closely, and frequent checks are made of fluid levels and high-wear items, as suggested throughout this manual, the engine will be kept in relatively good running condition, and the need for additional work will be minimised.

2 It is possible that there will be times when the engine is running poorly due to lack of regular maintenance. This is even more likely if a used vehicle, which has not received regular and frequent maintenance checks, is purchased. In such cases, additional work may need to be carried out, outside of the regular maintenance intervals.

3 If engine wear is suspected, a compression test (refer to the relevant Part of Chapter 2) will provide valuable information regarding the overall performance of the main internal components. Such a test can be used as a basis to decide on the extent of the work to be carried out. If, for example, a compression test indicates serious internal engine wear, conventional maintenance as described in this Chapter will not greatly improve the performance of the engine, and may prove a waste of time and money, unless extensive overhaul work is carried out first.

4 The following series of operations are those most often required to improve the performance of a generally poor-running engine:

Primary operations

a) Clean, inspect and test the battery (See Weekly checks and Section 4, where applicable).
b) Check all the engine-related fluids (See Weekly checks).
c) Check the condition and tension of the auxiliary drivebelt (Section 16).
d) Renew the spark plugs (Section 7).
e) Inspect the distributor cap and rotor arm (Section 8).
f) Check the condition of the air filter, and renew if necessary (Section 9).
g) Check the fuel filter (Section 53).
h) Check the condition of all hoses, and check for fluid leaks (Sections 10 and 14).
i) Check the exhaust gas emissions (Section 12).

5 If the above operations do not prove fully effective, carry out the following secondary operations:

Secondary operations

All items listed under *Primary operations*, plus the following:

a) Check the charging system (see Chapter 5A).
b) Check the ignition system (see Chapter 5B).
c) Check the fuel system (see relevant part of Chapter 4).
d) Renew the distributor cap and rotor arm (see Chapter 5B).
e) Renew the ignition HT leads (see Chapter 5B)

Every 6000 miles or 6 months, whichever comes first

3 Engine oil and filter renewal

Frequent oil and filter changes are the most important preventative maintenance procedures that can be undertaken by the DIY owner. As engine oil ages, it becomes diluted and contaminated, which leads to premature engine wear.

1 Before starting this procedure, gather together all the necessary tools and materials. Also make sure that you have plenty of clean rags and newspapers handy, to mop up any spills. Ideally, the engine oil should be warm, as it will drain better and more built-up sludge will be removed with it. Take care, however, not to touch the exhaust or any other hot parts of the engine when working under the vehicle. To avoid any possibility of scalding, and to protect yourself from possible skin irritants and other harmful contaminants in used engine oils, it is advisable to wear rubber gloves when carrying out this work.

2 Access to the underside of the vehicle will be greatly improved if it can be raised on a lift, driven onto ramps, or jacked up and supported on axle stands (see *Jacking and vehicle support*). Whichever method is chosen, make sure that the vehicle remains as level as possible, to enable the oil to drain fully.

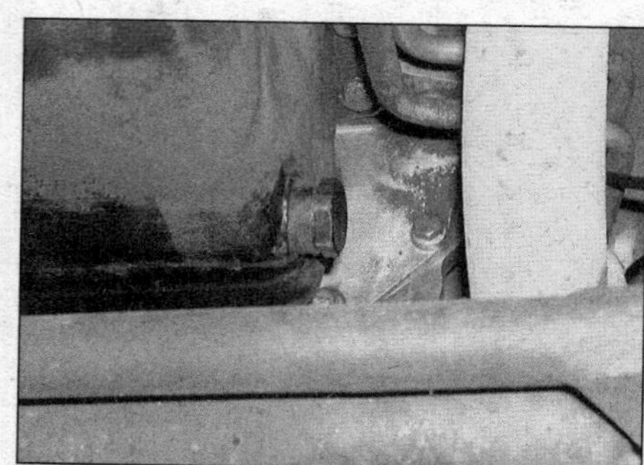

3.4 Sump drain plug location

3 Remove the oil filler cap from the top of the engine, then position a suitable container beneath the sump.

4 Taking care to avoid the hot exhaust, clean the drain plug (located at the bottom left-hand side of the sump) and the area around it **(see illustration)**. Slacken the plug using a suitable socket or spanner, and remove it.

If possible, try to keep the plug pressed into the sump while unscrewing it by hand the last couple of turns. As the plug releases from the threads, move it away sharply, so that the stream of oil issuing from the sump runs into the container, not up your sleeve.

5 Allow some time for the old oil to drain, noting that it may be necessary to reposition the container as the oil flow slows to a trickle.

6 After all the oil has drained, wipe off the drain plug with a clean rag, and check the condition of the copper sealing washer.

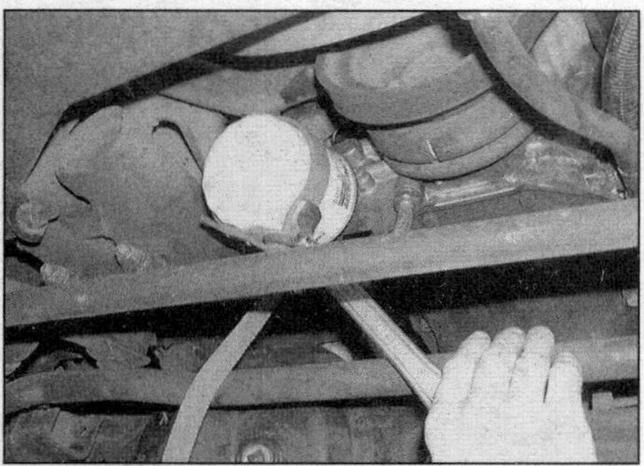
3.8 Slackening the oil filter using a strap wrench

GENUINE
PARTS
ERR3340
3.12 Fitting the new oil filter

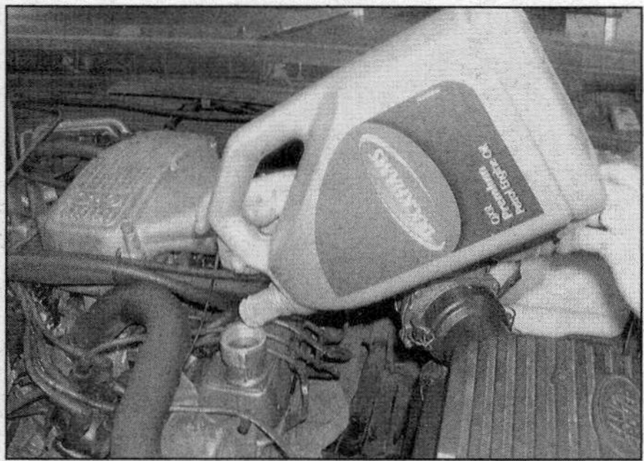
3.14 Filling the engine with oil

Renew the washer if necessary. Clean the area around the drain plug opening, then refit and tighten the plug to the specified torque setting.

7 Move the container into position under the oil filter, screwed onto the adapter on the front of the engine.

Caution: On this engine, when the oil filter is removed, there is a danger that the oil pump will drain down too far to self-prime when the fresh oil is added to the sump. The likelihood of this happening during a routine oil change is remote, but work quickly, and always fill the new filter with fresh oil before fitting, as stated in paragraph 11.

8 Using an oil filter removal tool if necessary, slacken the filter initially **(see illustration)**. Loosely wrap some rags around the oil filter, then unscrew it, and immediately position it with its open end uppermost to prevent further spillage of oil. Remove the oil filter from the engine compartment, and empty the oil into the container.

9 Use a clean rag to remove all oil, dirt and sludge from the filter sealing area on the engine. Check the old filter to make sure that the rubber sealing ring hasn't stuck to the engine. If it has, carefully remove it.

10 Apply a light coating of clean oil to the sealing ring on the new filter.

11 It is advisable to pre-fill the new oil filter with fresh oil, to avoid oil pressure problems when the engine is re-started. Holding the filter at the approximate fitted angle, pour as much clean oil into the filter as possible.

12 Screw the filter into position on the engine **(see illustration)**. Tighten the filter firmly by hand only - do not use any tools. Wipe clean the exterior of the oil filter.

13 Remove the old oil and all tools from under the vehicle, then (if applicable) lower the vehicle to the ground.

14 Fill the engine with the specified quantity and grade of oil **(see illustration)**. Pour the oil in slowly, otherwise it may overflow. Take particular care not to overfill the engine, particularly if the oil filter was pre-filled with oil (paragraph 11). Check that the oil level is up to the correct level on the dipstick (see *Weekly checks*), then refit and tighten the oil filler cap.

15 Start the engine without racing it, and let it idle. The oil warning light should go out after a short delay. If the light stays on, this means that the oil pump has not primed itself - switch off the engine and refer to Chapter 2A, Section 13.

16 Run the engine for a few minutes, and check that there are no leaks around the oil filter seal and the sump drain plug.

17 Switch off the engine, and wait a few minutes for the oil to settle in the sump once more. With the new oil circulated and the filter now completely full, recheck the level on the dipstick, and add more oil if necessary.

18 Dispose of the used engine oil safely with reference to *General repair procedures* in the Reference Section of this manual.

4 Battery electrolyte level check

Warning: The electrolyte inside a battery is diluted acid - it is a good idea to wear suitable rubber gloves. When topping-up, don't overfill the cells so that the electrolyte overflows. In the event of any spillage, rinse the electrolyte off without delay. Refit the cell covers and rinse the battery with copious quantities of clean water. Don't attempt to siphon out any excess electrolyte.

1 The battery is located in the front right-hand corner of the engine compartment. Where applicable, unclip and remove the cover from the top of the battery.

2 Some models covered by this manual will be fitted with a maintenance-free battery as standard equipment, or may have had one fitted as a replacement. If the battery in your vehicle is marked 'Freedom', 'Maintenance-Free' or similar, electrolyte level checking may not be possible (the battery is often completely sealed, preventing any topping-up).

3 Batteries which do require their electrolyte level to be checked can be recognised by the presence of removable covers over the six battery cells - the battery casing is also sometimes translucent, so that the electrolyte level can be more easily checked.

4 Remove the cell caps or covers (these either unscrew, or are prised/pulled out), and look down inside the battery to see the level webs or the separators between the cells **(see illustration)**. The electrolyte should cover the battery plates (maximum 3 mm above the plates), and should be up to the level of the indicator webs or separators. If markings are provided on the battery casing, these can be used instead.

5 If necessary, top up a little at a time with distilled (de-ionised) water until the level in all six cells is correct - don't fill the cells up to the brim **(see illustration)**. Wipe up any spillage, then refit the cell covers.

6 Further information on the battery, charging and jump starting can be found at the start of this manual and in Chapter 5A.

4.4 Removing the battery cell covers

4.5 Topping-up the battery electrolyte level

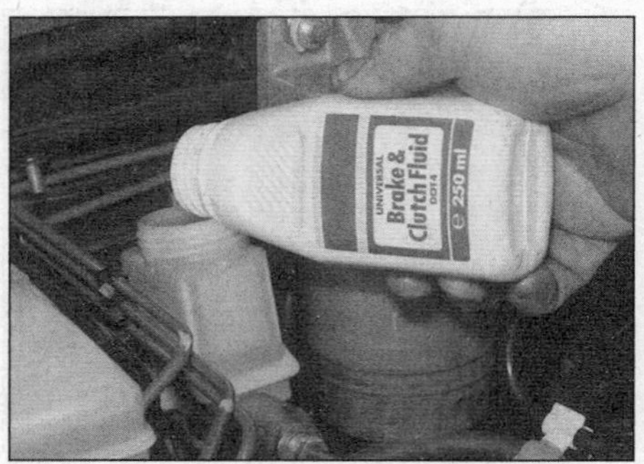
Brake & Clutch Fluid
250 ml

5.3 Topping-up the clutch fluid level

6.5a Removing the transmission fluid dipstick

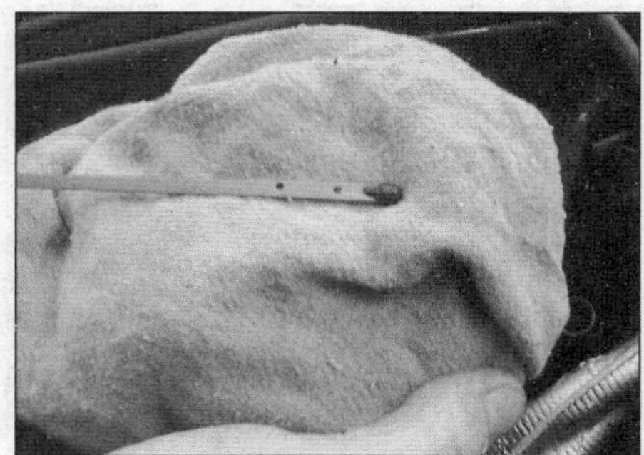

6.5b Wipe the dipstick, then re-insert it and check the level

Every 12 000 miles or 12 months, whichever comes first

5 Clutch fluid level check

Warning: Hydraulic fluid is poisonous; wash off immediately and thoroughly in the case of skin contact, and seek immediate medical advice if any fluid is swallowed or gets into the eyes. Hydraulic fluid is also an effective paint stripper, and will attack plastics; if any is spilt, it should be washed off immediately, using copious quantities of clean water. Finally, it is hygroscopic (it absorbs moisture from the air). While this is not as important in the clutch system as it is in the braking system, old fluid may be too contaminated for further use. When topping-up or renewing the fluid, always use the recommended type, and ensure that it comes from a freshly-opened, sealed container.

1 The clutch fluid reservoir is attached to the master cylinder, which is located on the right-hand side of the engine compartment on right-hand-drive models, or on the left-hand side of the engine compartment on left-hand-drive models.

2 On models with level marks on the side of the reservoir, the fluid level should be maintained between the MAX and MIN marks. On models with no level markings, the fluid level should be up to the lower edge of the filler neck on the reservoir.

3 If topping-up is required, wipe round the reservoir and filler cap before unscrewing the cap - it is important not to introduce dirt into the system. Using the fluid recommended at the end of *Weekly checks*, top up to the required level **(see illustration)**.

4 On completion, refit the filler cap, tightening it securely, and wipe up or wash away any fluid spillage.

5 There should be no significant drop in fluid level during normal operation of the clutch. Any significant loss of fluid is likely to be due to a leak in the hydraulic system, and should be investigated and corrected.

6 Automatic transmission fluid level check

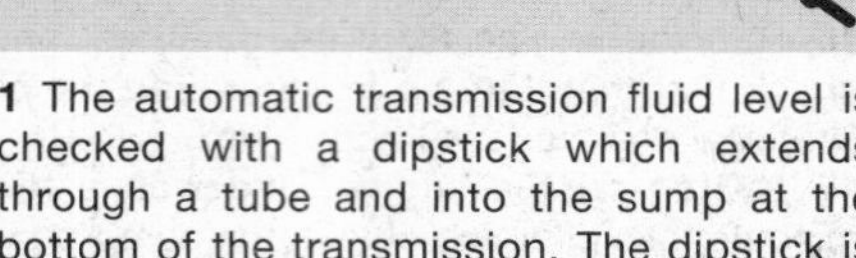

1 The automatic transmission fluid level is checked with a dipstick which extends through a tube and into the sump at the bottom of the transmission. The dipstick is located on the right-hand side of the engine (right as seen from the driver's seat).

2 The fluid level should be checked with the transmission cold, as follows.

3 Check that the vehicle is parked on level ground.

4 With the handbrake fully applied, and the engine running at normal idle speed, select position P with the transmission selector lever.

5 Withdraw the dipstick from the tube, and wipe it clean **(see illustrations)**.

6 Re-insert the dipstick to its full depth, and remove it for a second time to take a reading.

7 The fluid level should be maintained between the two level marks on the dipstick.

8 If necessary, top-up the fluid level, using the correct type of fluid (see end of *Weekly checks*) through the dipstick tube **(see illustration)**. **Do not** overfill the transmission. Note that 0.25 litre of fluid will raise the level from the 'low' to the 'high' mark on the dipstick.

9 Ensure that the dipstick is inserted correctly after checking the level.

6.8 Topping-up the transmission fluid

10 Any significant loss of fluid should be investigated and corrected.

7 Spark plug renewal

Note: *There is very little clearance between the body of the spark plug and the cylinder head. The best tool is the box spanner and tommy-bar usually supplied in the vehicle tool kit, as this is thin enough to fit.*

1 The correct functioning of the spark plugs is vital for the correct running and efficiency of the engine. It is essential that the plugs fitted are appropriate for the engine (the suitable type is specified at the beginning of this Chapter). If this type is used and the engine is in good condition, the spark plugs should not need attention between scheduled replacement intervals. Spark plug cleaning is rarely necessary, and should not be attempted unless specialised equipment is available, as damage can easily be caused to the firing ends.

2 Before removing the spark plugs, allow the engine time to cool.

3 If the marks on the original-equipment spark plug (HT) leads cannot be seen, mark the leads 1 to 8, according to which number cylinder the lead serves (number 1 cylinder is at the front of the left-hand bank). Pull the leads from the plugs by gripping the end fitting, not the lead, otherwise the lead connection may be fractured. Don't detach the HT leads from their clips on the valve covers more than necessary.

4 It is advisable to remove the dirt from the spark plug recesses using a clean brush, vacuum cleaner or compressed air before removing the plugs, to prevent dirt dropping into the cylinders.

5 Unscrew the plugs using either the tool supplied in the vehicle tool kit (mentioned in the note above), a spark plug spanner, suitable box spanner, or a deep socket and extension bar **(see illustrations)**. Keep the tool aligned with the spark plug if it is forcibly moved to one side, the ceramic insulator may be broken off. As each plug is removed, examine it as follows.

7.5a Pull off the HT leads . . .

7.5b . . . then using a suitable plug socket, unscrew . . .

7.5c . . . and remove the spark plugs

6 Examination of the spark plugs will give a good indication of the condition of the engine. If the insulator nose of the spark plug is clean and white, with no deposits, this is indicative of a weak mixture or too hot a plug (a hot plug transfers heat away from the electrode slowly, a cold plug transfers heat away quickly).

7 If the tip and insulator nose are covered with hard black-looking deposits, then this is indicative that the mixture is too rich. Should the plug be black and oily, then it is likely that the engine is fairly worn, as well as the mixture being too rich.

8 If the insulator nose is covered with light tan to greyish-brown deposits, then the mixture is correct and it is likely that the engine is in good condition.

9 The spark plug electrode gap is of considerable importance as, if it is too large or too small, the size of the spark and its efficiency will be seriously impaired. The gap should be set to the value specified at the start of this Chapter. **Note:** *Spark plugs with multiple earth electrodes are becoming an increasingly common fitment, especially to vehicles equipped with catalytic converters. Unless there is clear information to the contrary, no attempt should be made to adjust the plug gap on a spark plug with more than one earth electrode.*

HAYNES HiNT

It is very often difficult to insert spark plugs into their holes without cross-threading them. To avoid this possibility, fit a short length of 5/16 inch internal diameter rubber hose over the end of the spark plug. The flexible hose acts as a universal joint to help align the plug with the plug hole. Should the plug begin to cross-thread, the hose will slip on the spark plug, preventing thread damage to the alloy cylinder head

10 To set the gap, measure it with a feeler blade and then bend open, or closed, the outer plug electrode until the correct gap is achieved. The centre electrode should never be bent, as this may crack the insulator and cause plug failure, if nothing worse. If using feeler blades, the gap is correct when the appropriate-size blade is a firm sliding fit.

11 Special spark plug electrode gap adjusting tools are available from most motor accessory shops, or from some spark plug manufacturers.

12 Before fitting the spark plugs, check that the threaded connector sleeves are tight, and that the plug exterior surfaces and threads are clean. It's often difficult to screw in new spark plugs without cross-threading them - this can be avoided using a piece of rubber hose **(see Haynes Hint)**.

13 Remove the rubber hose (if used), and tighten the plug to the specified torque using the spark plug socket and a torque wrench **(see illustration)**. If a torque wrench is not available, tighten the plug by hand until it just seats, then tighten it by no more than a quarter of a turn further with the plug socket and handle. Refit the remaining spark plugs in the same manner.

7.13 Tighten the plugs using a torque wrench, if available

8 Ignition system components check

HT leads

1 The spark plug and ignition coil HT leads should be checked on a regular basis, as they are vital to the correct running of the engine. The HT leads should also be checked whenever new spark plugs are installed in the engine (Section 7).

2 Before removing them, check that the HT leads are numbered for position **(see Haynes Hint)**. Pull the HT leads from the plugs by gripping the end fitting, not the lead, otherwise the lead connection may be fractured.

3 Check inside the end fitting for signs of corrosion, which will look like a white crusty powder **(see illustration)**.

4 Push the end fitting back onto the spark plug, ensuring that it is a tight fit on the plug. If it isn't, remove the lead again and use pliers to carefully crimp the metal connector inside the end fitting until it fits securely on the end of the spark plug.

HAYNES HiNT

Ensure that the leads are numbered before removing them, to avoid confusion when refitting. Number 1 plug lead is at front of the left-hand bank of the engine (left as seen from the driver's seat). Wrap numbered labels around the leads if no other markings are found

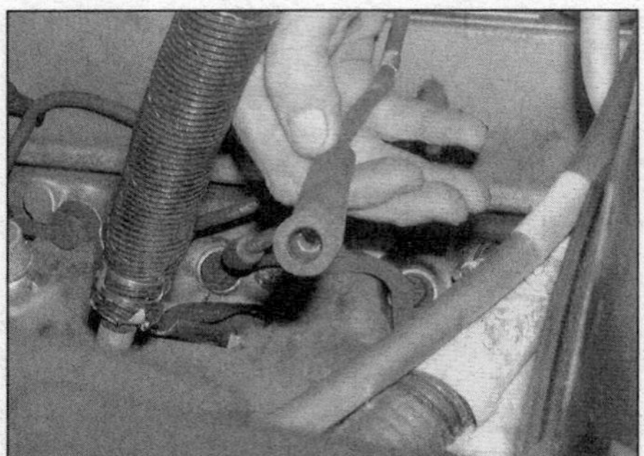

8.3 Check the HT lead end fittings at the plugs

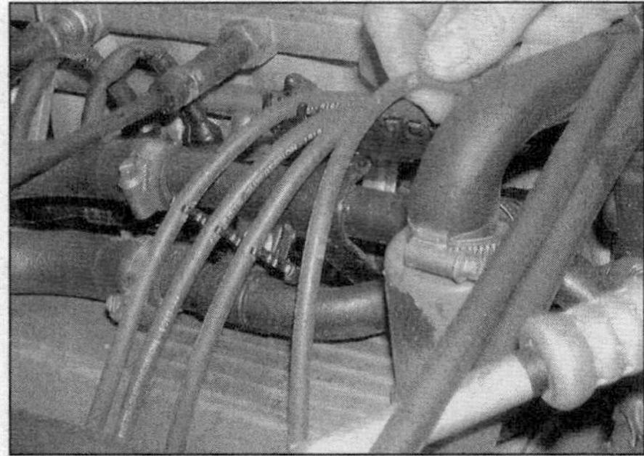

8.5a Unclip the HT leads from the clips around the engine . . .

8.5b . . . then wipe them clean

5 Unclip each lead then, using a clean rag, wipe the entire length of the lead to remove any built-up dirt and grease **(see illustrations)**. Once the lead is clean, check for burns, cracks and other damage. Do not bend the lead excessively or pull the lead lengthways - the conductor inside might break.

6 Disconnect the other end of the lead from the distributor cap - again, pull only on the end fitting. Check for corrosion and a tight fit in the same manner as the spark plug end. Refit the lead securely on completion.

7 Check the remaining HT leads one at a time, in the same way. Don't forget to include the HT which links the centre terminal on the distributor cap to the ignition coil (the 'king' lead) **(see illustration)**. It is most important that the leads are routed so they cross over each other as little as possible - this reduces the chance of the leads arcing, which would cause a misfire.

8 If new HT leads are required, purchase a set for your specific vehicle and engine.

9 Even with the ignition system in first class condition, some engines may still occasionally experience poor starting attributable to damp ignition components. To disperse moisture, a water-repelling aerosol spray can be very effective.

Distributor cap and rotor arm

10 It is preferable to remove the distributor cap with the HT leads attached, even though this makes handling the cap more awkward. If the HT leads are to be removed, make sure their locations on the cap are marked.

11 Release the clip either side, and lift the cap off the top of the distributor **(see illustrations)**.

12 Wipe the cap clean and carefully inspect it inside and out for signs of cracks, carbon tracks (tracking) and worn, burned or loose contacts **(see illustration)**.

13 Check that the cap's carbon brush is unworn, free to move against spring pressure and making good contact with the rotor arm. Similarly inspect the rotor arm. Renew these components if any defects are found.

14 It is common practice to renew the cap and rotor arm whenever new HT leads are fitted. The rotor arm is simply pulled off the distributor shaft, and the notch in the shaft ensures it can only fit in one position **(see illustration)**.

HAYNES
HiNT

When fitting a new cap, remove the HT leads from the old cap one at a time (if not already removed) and fit them to the new cap in the exact same location - do not simultaneously remove all the leads from the old cap, or firing-order confusion may occur.

Distributor - lubrication

15 Remove the distributor cap and rotor arm as described above, and apply 3 drops of engine oil down through the spindle on which the rotor arm sits **(see illustration)**.

16 On completion, refit the rotor arm and distributor cap.

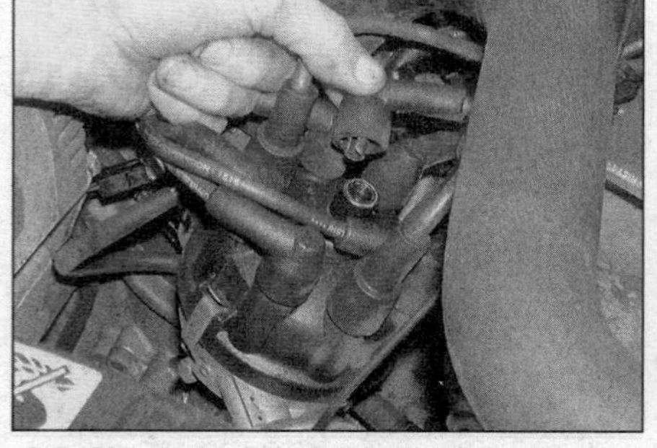

8.7 Check the king lead at the distributor cap and at the coil

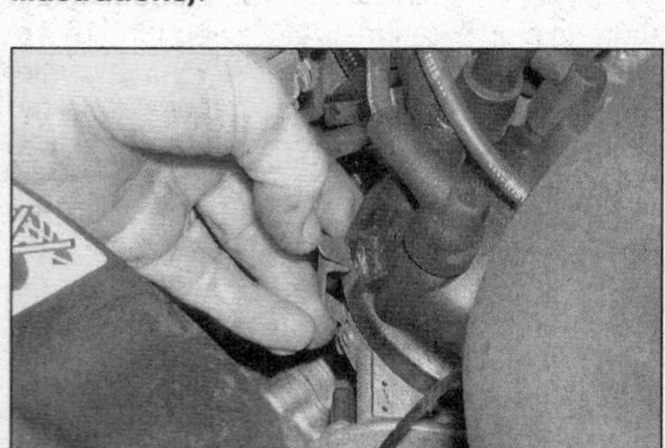

8.11a Release the clip at either side . . .

8.11b . . . and remove the distributor cap

8.12 Inspect the inside of the distributor cap

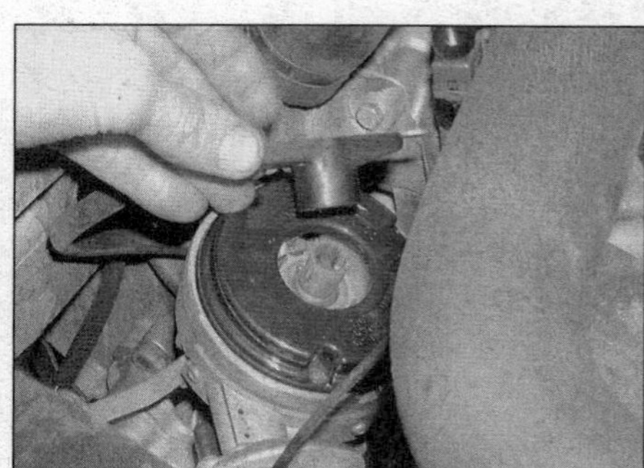

8.14 The rotor arm pulls off the spindle

8.15 Lubricate the distributor through the spindle

9 Air cleaner element renewal

Carburettor models

1 Slacken the hose clips on either end of the air cleaner, and pull the elbows from the carburettors and air cleaner assembly. Check the condition of the rubber seals fitted on the elbows, and renew if the rubber is cracked or perished.

2 Using two open-ended spanners, disconnect the one-way valve hose from the flame trap.

3 Remove the air cleaner assembly from the retaining posts by lifting it and pulling it forwards. As the assembly is withdrawn, disconnect the crankcase breather hose from its base. Note that a new breather filter should be fitted whenever the air filters are changed - see Section 10.

4 Release the clips on each end of the air cleaner canister in turn, and withdraw the end cover and air filter element from both ends.

5 Remove the wing nut and retaining plate from the inner end of each assembly, and remove the elements **(see illustration)**.

6 Fit a new element to each assembly, and refit the retaining plate and wing nut. Check that the sealing washers on the end cover and retaining plate are in good condition, otherwise they must be renewed. Wipe clean the element housing, and check that the dump valve in the base of the housing is clear by squeezing it open **(see illustration)**.

7 Refit each assembly into the end of the housing, and secure it with the spring clips. Refit the air cleaner into position, making sure that the breather hoses are reconnected. Reconnect the flame trap to the one-way valve, then refit the elbows and secure the hose clips.

Fuel injection models

Canister-type air filter (early models)

8 Release the three over-centre wire clips securing the housing end cover and air inlet spout, and remove the cover.

9 Unscrew the nut and remove the air filter element retaining plate **(see illustrations)**.

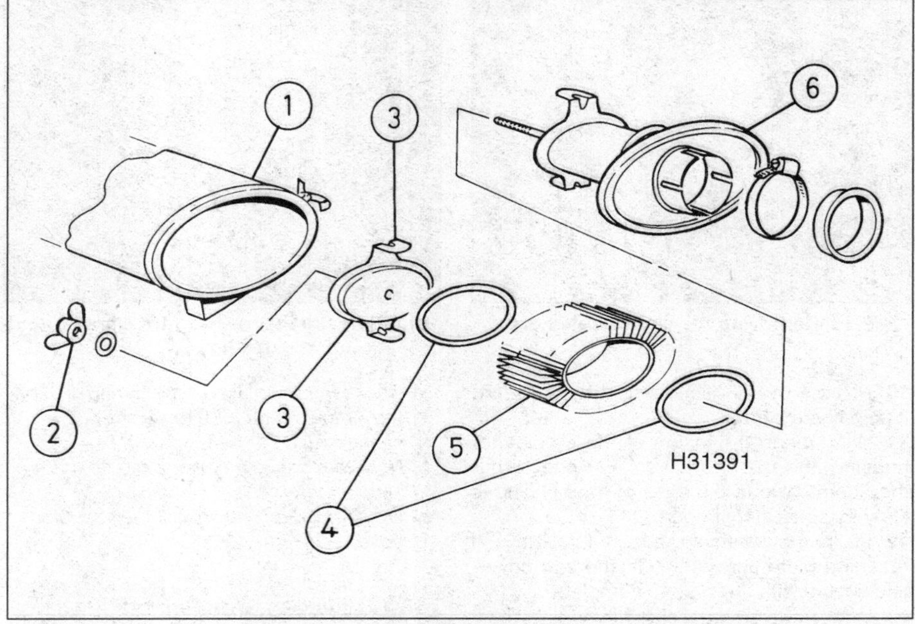
1
2
3
3
4
5
6
H31391

9.5 Air cleaner details - carburettor models

1 Clip
2 Wing nut
3 Retaining plate
4 Rubber seals
5 Filter element
6 End cover

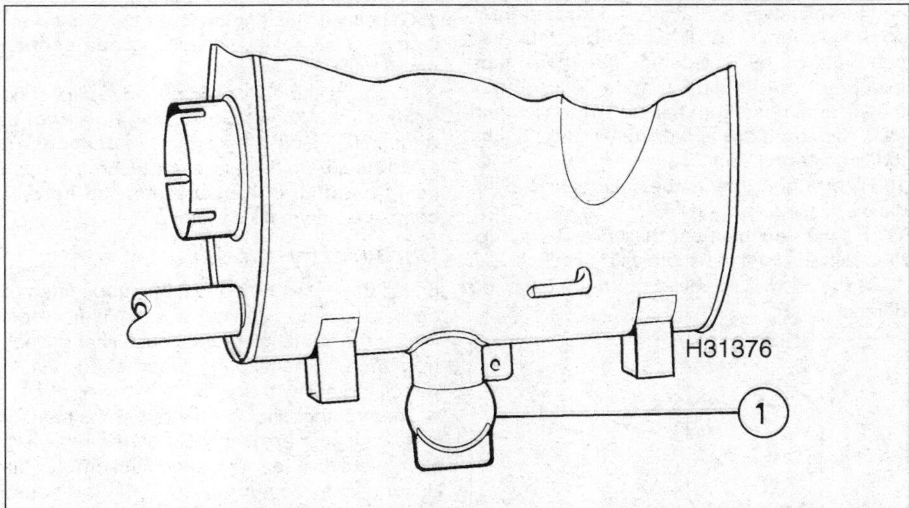
H31376
1

9.6 Air cleaner dump valve (1) - carburettor models

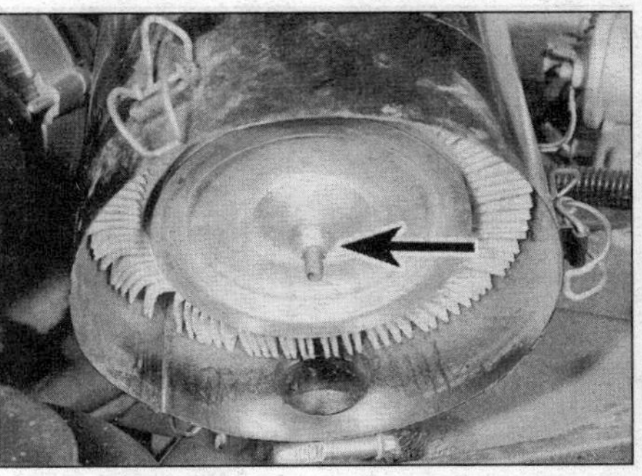

9.9a Undo the retaining nut (arrowed) . . .

9.9b . . . and remove the filter element retaining plate

9.10 Removing the air filter element

9.13 Release the over-centre clips around the lid . . .

9.14 . . . then lift up the lid and remove the filter element

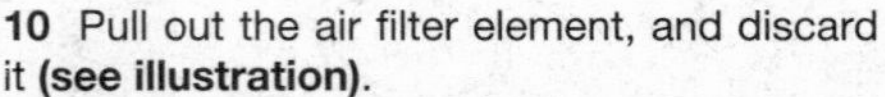

10 Pull out the air filter element, and discard it **(see illustration)**.

11 Wipe clean the inside of the air cleaner housing and the end cover, and check that the dump valve in the base of the housing is clear by squeezing it open.

12 Fit the new element, and secure with the retaining plate and nut. Refit the end cover, and secure with the clips to complete.

Square-type air filter (later models)

13 Release the four over-centre wire clips securing the lid to the air cleaner assembly **(see illustration)**.

14 Lift up the lid, and lift out the element, noting which way up it fits **(see illustration)**.

15 If wished, the lid can be removed completely, by releasing the two clips securing it to the airflow meter. Disconnect the vacuum hose from the side of the lid, and ease the lid off the airflow meter stub, noting the large O-ring seal.

16 Thoroughly clean the inside of the air cleaner casing and the lid.

17 Fit the new element the correct way up, then refit the lid and secure with the clips.

18 If the lid was removed, note the following points:

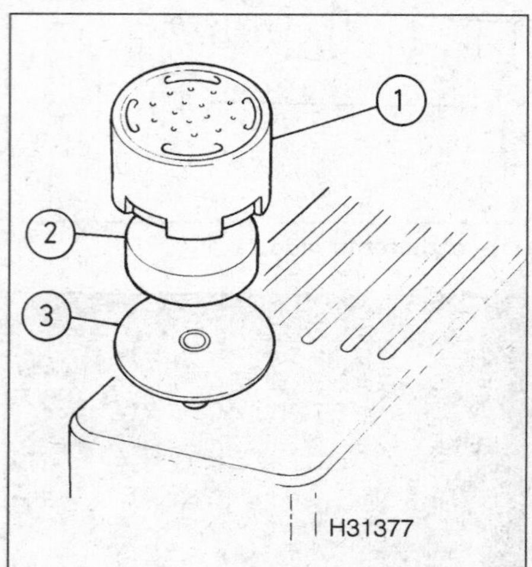
1
2
3
H31377

10.6 Crankcase ventilation air inlet filter details

1 *Filter cover*
2 *Foam filter*
3 *Mounting plate*

a) Check the condition of the O-ring seal on the airflow meter stub, and renew if necessary.
b) Note that the lid fits over a pip on the airflow meter stub.
c) On completion, reconnect the vacuum hose to the lid.

10 Crankcase breather system check

General

1 Check all the engine breather hoses for signs of cracking, leaks, and general deterioration.

2 It is advisable to loosen the hose clips, and remove each hose to check for a build-up of deposits, which may cause restrictions or even blockage. If necessary, clean the hose using paraffin, but ensure that the hose is completely dry before refitting.

Carburettor models

3 Pull the hoses from the flame traps fitted to each carburettor, and remove the flame traps. Check the condition of the gauze filter in each trap then, if necessary, wash each unit in petrol and allow to dry.

4 The breather filter connected to the base of the air cleaner assembly should be renewed. Remove the air cleaner assembly as described in Section 9, then pull the hoses from the filter and fit the new unit.

Fuel injection models

Early models (up to 1994)

5 The crankcase ventilation air inlet filter is located under a round plastic cover, at the rear of the left-hand rocker cover.

6 To renew the filter, prise up the plastic filter cover and separate the foam filter from the filter body **(see illustration)**. The filter should be discarded, and a new one fitted. If a new filter is not available, the old one could be cleaned in petrol and allowed to dry before refitting, though this is not recommended.

7 Reassemble the filter, and press it fully back down into the rocker cover to complete.

All models

8 The main crankcase filter is fitted to the front of the right-hand rocker cover, and is connected via a hose to the plenum chamber.

9 To check the rest of the system, first loosen the hose clip and disconnect the hose from the top of the filter body **(see illustration)**. Clean the end of the hose, then try to blow through it to check for blockages. If the hose appears to be blocked, disconnect the other end from the plenum chamber (and release any cable-ties), then remove the hose completely and clean using petrol or degreasant.

10 Unscrew the filter body from the rocker cover, and recover the sealing O-ring. If the O-ring is in poor condition, a new one must be fitted **(see illustrations)**.

11 Wash the filter thoroughly in petrol or degreasant, then allow it to dry. Check the

10.9 Disconnect the hose from the crankcase filter

10.10a Unscrew the filter from the rocker cover . . .

10.10b . . . and check the condition of the O-ring

condition of the wire mesh inside the filter - if the mesh is in poor condition, or is still blocked, fit a new filter.

12 Refit the filter body to the rocker cover, using a new O-ring if necessary, and screw it firmly into place. Reconnect the hose, ensuring the hose clip(s) are tight.

11 Carburettor piston damper oil level top-up

Note: *This procedure should be carried out at the specified interval, and also prior to any form of emissions testing. If symptoms of poor idle quality become apparent, low piston damper oil level could be the cause.*

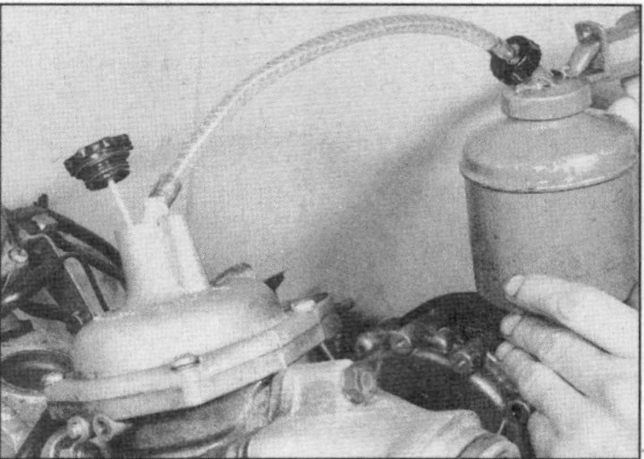

11.2 Topping-up the carburettor piston damper

1 Unscrew the piston damper from the top of each carburettor.

2 Using clean engine oil, top-up the oil level to the top of the hollow piston rod visible in the top of the carburettor **(see illustration)**.

3 Slowly insert the piston dampers back into place, and screw firmly into place.

12 Idle speed and mixture check and adjustment

Note: *Strictly speaking, this check need only be carried out if the engine is not running well, if fuel consumption is excessive, or if the exhaust gas emissions are thought to be too high. Adjusting the carburettor accurately is an involved procedure for the DIY mechanic, requiring several items of specialist equipment - if not done accurately, it would be better left to a suitably-equipped garage. With the right equipment, the check itself is a simple task, and should not therefore be an expensive one to entrust to a garage.*

Carburettor models

1 Before starting the procedure, it will be necessary to obtain a carburettor balancer and an exhaust gas analyser. The ambient air temperature should be between 15°C and 26°C, and an accurate tachometer should be used. The engine must be at normal temperature at least 5 minutes after the thermostat has opened, and the adjustment should be preceded by running the engine at 2500 rpm for one minute. Only run the engine at this speed every two minutes, to prevent the engine overheating. Make sure that the piston dampers are topped-up before starting the procedure (see Section 11).

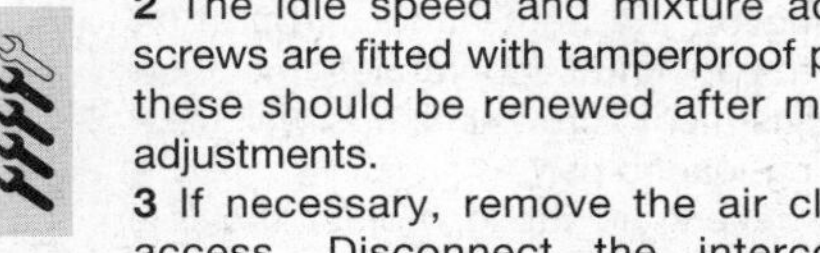

2 The idle speed and mixture adjustment screws are fitted with tamperproof plugs, and these should be renewed after making the adjustments.

3 If necessary, remove the air cleaner for access. Disconnect the interconnecting throttle link between the two carburettors, then unscrew the idle adjusting screws on each carburettor until clear of the throttle levers **(see illustration)**. Now turn each adjusting screw until it just touches the throttle lever.

4 Start the engine and allow it to idle. Turn each adjusting screw clockwise by equal amounts until the idle speed is between 700 and 800 rpm **(see illustration)**.

5 Connect the carburettor balancer to each carburettor in turn in accordance with the equipment manufacturer's instructions, and if necessary adjust the idle screws to give the same reading on each carburettor. The idle speed must also be maintained.

6 With the carburettor balance set, reconnect the throttle interconnecting link.

7 Working on one carburettor at a time, remove the carburettor suction chamber, piston and spring, and adjust the jet flush with the bridge (see Chapter 4A). This provides a datum position for adjusting the mixture. Refit

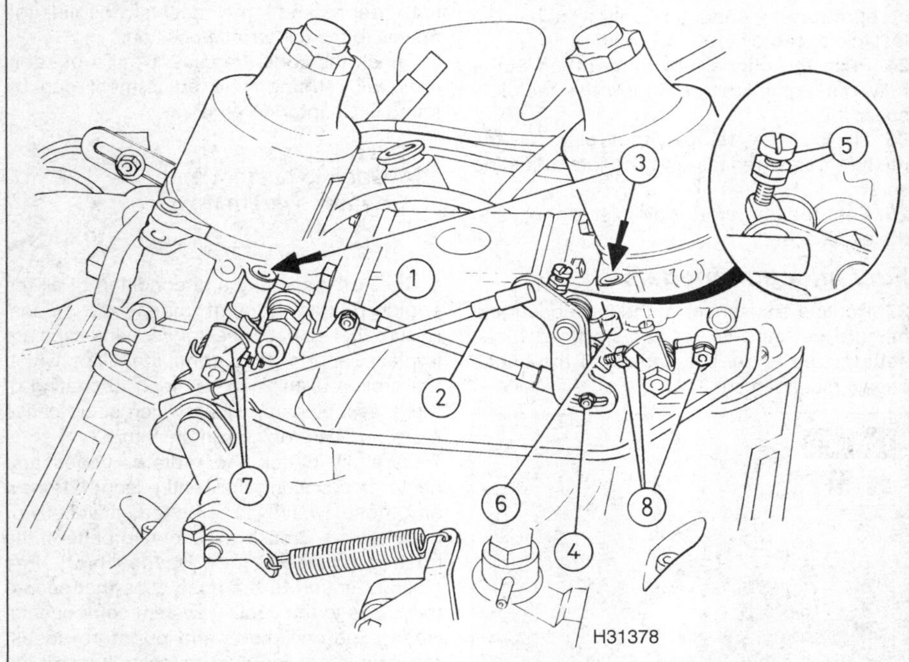
1
2
3
4
5
6
7
8
H31378

12.3 Carburettor adjustment details (seen from rear of engine)

1 *Inboard interconnecting link*
2 *Outboard interconnecting link*
3 *Idle speed screws*
4 *Interconnecting link ball nut*
5 *Lost motion screw and locknut*
6 *Right-hand throttle lever*
7 *Left-hand fast idle cam and screw*
8 *Right-hand fast idle cam and screw, and link rod screw*

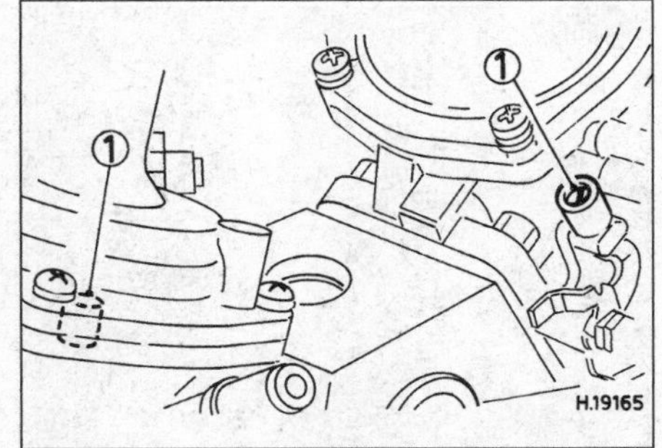
1
1
H.19165

12.4 Idle speed screws (1)

the suction chambers to the carburettors and make sure that the dampers are topped-up with engine oil to the top of the hollow piston rod.

8 Turn each mixture adjustment screw 3 1/2 turns clockwise **(see illustration)**.

9 Insert the exhaust gas analyser probe into the end of the exhaust pipe as far as possible, then start the engine and allow it to stabilise for approximately 2 minutes.

10 With the engine idling, check the CO reading, and if necessary adjust each mixture adjustment screw by equal amounts to achieve the specified CO readin. If the reading is not satisfactory after two minutes, run the engine at 2000 to 2500 rpm for a minute before proceeding.

11 Loosen the nut at the left-hand carburettor securing the interconnecting link ball to the throttle cam lever.

12 Disconnect the interconnecting link between the carburettors at the left-hand carburettor.

13 Working on the right-hand carburettor, unscrew the locknut and loosen the lost-motion adjustment screw until it is well clear of the spring-loaded pad.

14 With the engine idling, adjust the idle screw so that the specified idle speed is maintained, then re-check the CO reading and adjust if necessary.

15 Re-connect the interconnecting link to the left-hand carburettor.

16 While holding the right-hand throttle lever against the idle screw stop, adjust the lost-motion screw until contact is made with the spring-loaded pad, then tighten the locknut.

17 Check the idle speed and balance, and adjust the lost-motion screw if necessary to maintain balance.

18 Ensure that the roller is firmly seated in the lower corner of the cam lever, then tighten the nut securing the interconnecting link ball to the cam lever.

19 Switch off the engine and carry out the fast idle adjustment as follows.

20 First pull out the choke control until the scribed line on the left-hand fast idle cam is aligned with the centre of the fast idle screw. Check that the scribed line on the right-hand fast idle cam is also aligned with the fast idle screw. If not, loosen the fast idle cam link rod screw at the right-hand carburettor and move the cam until the scribed line is aligned with the centre of the screw. Tighten the cam rod screw.

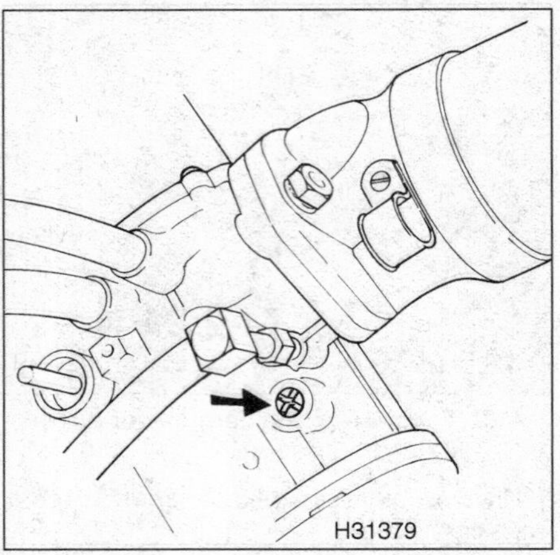
H31379

12.8 Mixture screw (arrowed)

13.3 Lubricating the throttle linkage

21 Turn each fast idle screw clockwise until just clear of the cam.

22 With the engine idling, turn the fast idle screw of the leading (left-hand) carburettor clockwise until a slight change in engine speed is noted. Working on the right-hand carburettor, turn the fast idle screw down until a further slight change of engine speed is noted.

23 Adjust the fast idle screws of both carburettors by equal amounts to achieve a fast idle speed of 1100 to 1150 rpm.

24 Push the choke fully home, then pull it fully out again and re-check the fast idle speed.

25 Fit the new tamperproof caps to the mixture screw recess and the idle adjusting screw.

26 Refit the carburettor air inlet elbows and the air cleaner.

Fuel injection models

27 Routine adjustment of the idle speed and mixture settings is not required, as these settings are under the control of the Lucas engine management ECU.

28 Experienced home mechanics equipped with an accurate tachometer and a carefully-calibrated exhaust gas analyser may be able to check the exhaust gas CO content and the engine idle speed. If these are found to be out of specification, then the vehicle must be taken to a suitably-equipped Land Rover dealer for assessment - incorrect test results indicate a fault within the fuel injection system. Apart from the base idle speed adjustment described in Chapter 4B, any adjustments which may be required must be performed by a Land Rover dealer.

HAYNES HiNT

A leak in the cooling system will usually show up as white or rust-coloured deposits on the area adjoining the leak

13 Accelerator mechanism checking and lubrication

1 Check the operation of the accelerator pedal. Make sure that the pedal pivots freely, and if necessary, lightly lubricate the pivot bushes using a little light oil.

2 Check the condition of the accelerator cable. Make sure that the cable is routed correctly, free from kinks, and clear of surrounding components. Check the cable for signs of chafing and fraying, particularly at the injection pump end, and renew the cable if necessary.

3 Lubricate the accelerator (and cruise control/kickdown cable, where fitted) linkages and pivots using a little light oil **(see illustration)**.

4 Check that when the accelerator pedal is fully depressed, the accelerator linkage moves to the full-throttle position.

5 Check the cable freeplay. Details of cable removal, refitting, and adjustment can be found in Chapter 4A or 4B.

14 Cooling system and heater system hose check

1 Check the security and condition of all the engine-related coolant pipes and hoses. Ensure that all cable-ties or securing clips are in place, and in good condition. Clips which are broken or missing can lead to chafing of the hoses, pipes or wiring which could cause more serious problems in the future.

2 Carefully check the radiator hoses and heater hoses along their entire length. Renew any hose which is cracked, swollen or deteriorated. Cracks will show up better if the hose is squeezed **(see Haynes hint)**. Pay close attention to the hose clips that secure the hoses to the cooling system components. Hose clips can pinch and puncture hoses, resulting in cooling system leaks. If wire-type hose clips are used, it may be a good idea to replace them with screw-type clips.

3 Inspect all the cooling system components (hoses, joint face, etc.) for leaks. Where any problems of this nature are found on system components, renew the component or gasket with reference to Chapter 3.

15 Brake vacuum servo hose check

1 Working from the servo unit, examine the vacuum hose for signs of damage or deterioration; at the same time, also check the servo unit check valve rubber grommet. If necessary, renew the hose/grommet, referring to the information given in Chapter 10.

16 Auxiliary drivebelt checking and renewal

1 Correct tensioning of each drivebelt will ensure that it has a long life. Beware, however, of overtightening, as this can cause excessive wear in the ancillary components.

2 To improve access, remove the viscous cooling fan and coupling as described in Chapter 3.

3 The belt should be inspected along its entire length, and if it is found to be worn, frayed or cracked, it should be renewed as a precaution against breakage in service. It is advisable to carry a spare drivebelt of the correct type in the vehicle at all times.

Up to 1995 model year (four drivebelts)

Power steering pump drivebelt checking and adjustment

4 The belt tension should be checked at the mid-point of the belt run between the pulleys **(see illustration)**. Under normal finger pressure, the belt should deflect by 4 to 6 mm.

5 If adjustment is required, first slacken the alternator mounting and adjuster bolts as described later in this Section.

6 Loosen the pump front and rear mounting bolts, and the clamp bolt on the adjustment slide.

7 Pivot the pump as necessary to achieve the correct tension, but do not lever against the pump casing itself, as this could lead to fluid leakage.

8 When the correct tension is achieved, tighten the adjuster clamp bolt and the pump mounting bolts.

9 Re-check the tension, and adjust if necessary. Do not be tempted to run the belt too tight, as this will damage the pump bearings.

10 If a new drivebelt has been fitted, start the engine and run it for five minutes at a fast idle, then re-check the tension and adjust if necessary.

11 Where applicable, refit the viscous fan and coupling as described in Chapter 3.

Power steering pump drivebelt removal and refitting

12 To remove the belt, first remove the alternator and water pump drivebelts as described later in this Section. Loosen the pump mounting and adjuster bolts, and pivot the pump sufficiently to slip the belt from the pulleys.

13 Refit the pump drivebelt and tension it as described previously, then refit and tension the alternator and water pump belts removed for access, as described later in this Section.

Alternator drivebelt checking and adjustment - up to 1994 model year

14 Prior to checking the alternator belt tension, check and if necessary adjust the power steering pump drivebelt tension as described previously.

15 The alternator belt tension should be checked at the mid-point of the belt run between the pulleys **(see illustration)**. Under normal finger pressure, the belt should deflect by 4 to 6 mm.

16 If adjustment is required, slacken the alternator lower mounting bolt, and the alternator adjuster link mounting bolt below the distributor cap.

17 Slacken the clamp bolt securing the alternator to the adjuster link.

18 Pivot the alternator as necessary to achieve the correct belt tension, taking care not to lever directly against the alternator body, or near the distributor cap.

19 When the correct tension is achieved, tighten the adjuster link clamp bolt and the remaining two bolts.

20 Re-check the tension, and adjust if necessary. Do not be tempted to run the belt too tight, as this will damage the alternator bearings.

21 If a new drivebelt has been fitted, start the engine and run it for five minutes at a fast idle, then re-check the tension and adjust if necessary.

22 Where applicable, refit the viscous fan and coupling as described in Chapter 3.

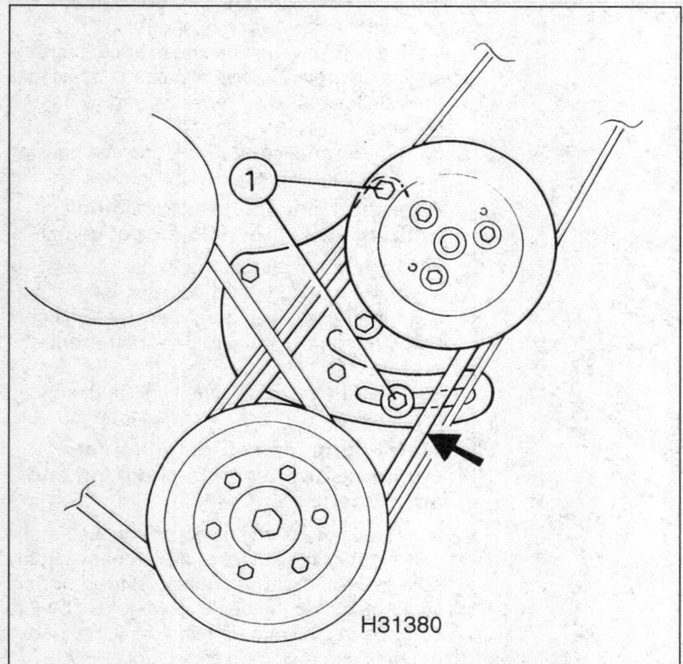
1
H31380

16.4 Power steering pump drivebelt checking (1994 model shown)

Arrow indicates tension checking point
1 Pump mounting bolts

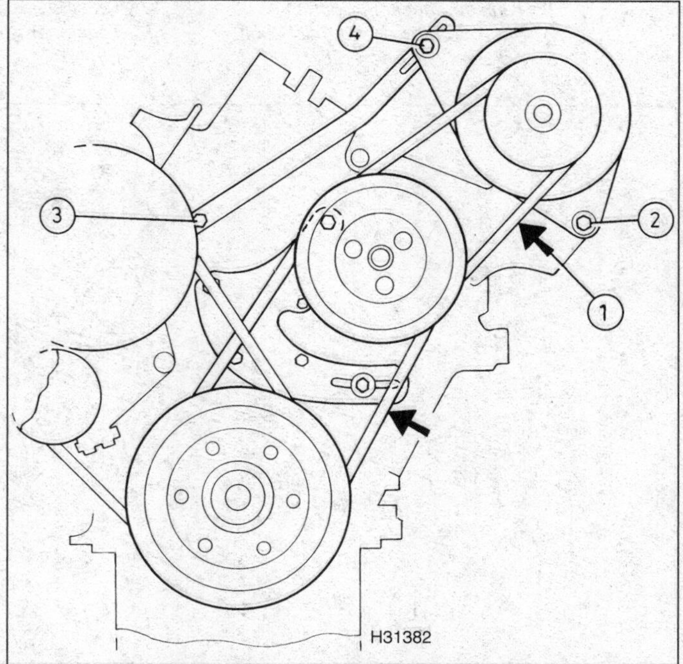
4
3
2
1
H31382

16.15 Alternator drivebelt details - up to 1994 model year

1 Tension checking point
2 Alternator lower mounting bolt
3 Adjusting link lower mounting bolt
4 Adjusting link clamp bolt

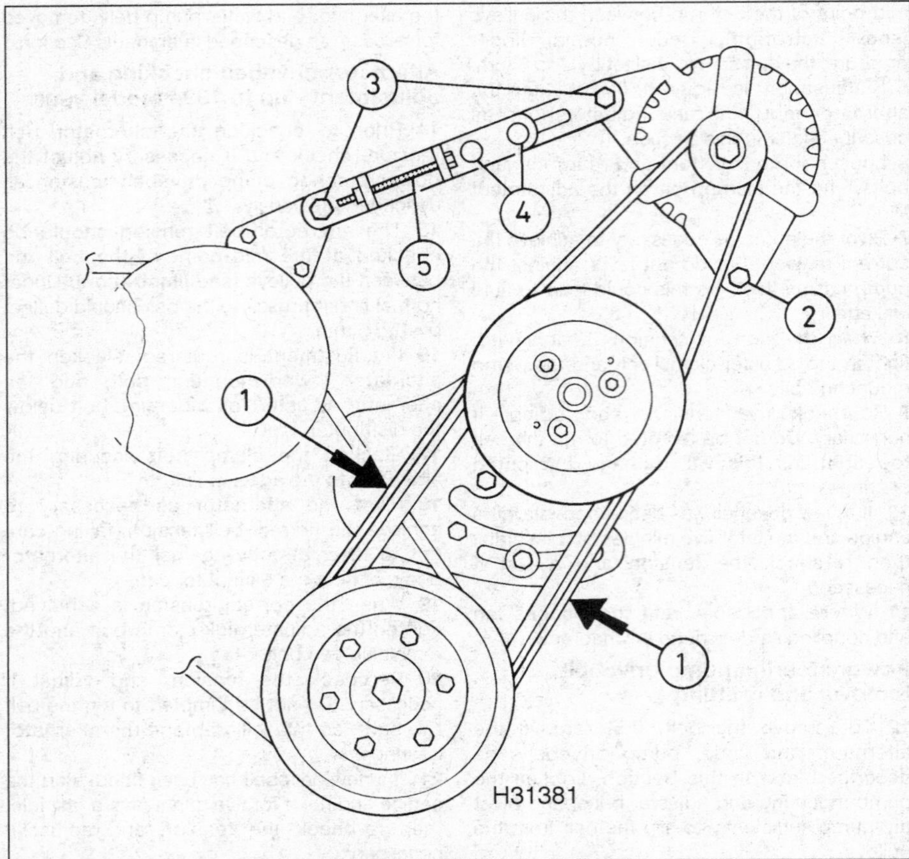
3
4
5
2
1
1
H31381

16.26a Alternator drivebelt details - 1994 to 1995 model year

1 Tension checking points
2 Alternator lower mounting bolt
3 Adjuster link end bolts
4 Tensioner assembly bolts
5 Tensioner bolt

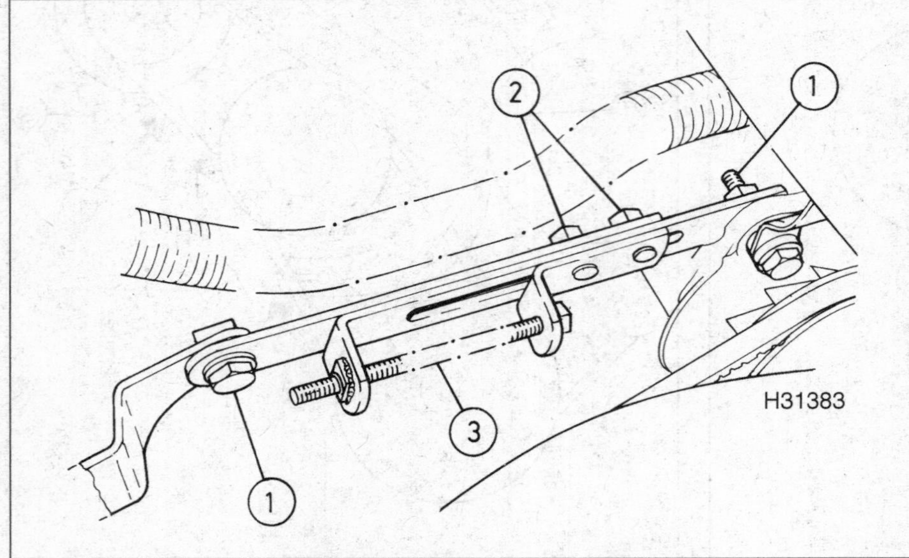
2
1
3
1
H31383

16.26b Alternator tensioner details - 1994 to 1995 model year

1 Adjuster link end bolts *2 Tensioner assembly bolts* *3 Tensioner bolt*

Alternator drivebelt removal and refitting - up to 1994 model year

23 To remove the belt, simply loosen the alternator mounting and adjuster link bolts as described previously, and pivot the alternator sufficiently to slip the belt from the pulleys.

24 Refit the belt and tension it as described previously.

Alternator drivebelt checking and adjustment - 1994 to 1995 model year

25 Measure the length of the belt run between the centres of the pulleys. As a rough guide, under normal finger pressure, the belt should deflect by 0.5 mm for every 25.0 mm of belt run between pulley centres. Otherwise, Land Rover only publish tension figures for use with a special belt tension gauges - if one is available, the tension figures are given in the Specifications.

26 If adjustment is required, slacken the alternator lower mounting bolt, the bolt at either end of the adjuster link, and the two bolts securing the tensioner assembly to the adjuster link **(see illustrations)**.

27 Slacken the power steering pump mounting and adjuster bolts as described previously.

28 Turn the alternator tensioner bolt as necessary to achieve the correct belt tension.

29 Tension the power steering pump belt as described previously in this Section.

30 When the correct tension is achieved in both belts, securely tighten all mounting, adjuster and adjuster link bolts.

31 Re-check the tension of both belts, and adjust if necessary. Do not be tempted to run the belts too tight, as this will damage the alternator and/or pump bearings.

32 If a new drivebelt has been fitted, start the engine and run it for five minutes at a fast idle, then re-check the tension and adjust if necessary.

33 Where applicable, refit the viscous fan and coupling as described in Chapter 3.

Alternator drivebelt removal and refitting - 1994 to 1995 model year

34 To remove the belt, simply loosen the alternator mounting and adjuster link bolts as described previously, and turn the tensioner bolt sufficiently to slip the belt from the pulleys.

35 Refit the belt and tension it as described previously.

Water pump and air conditioning compressor drivebelts checking and adjustment

36 The belt tension should be checked at the mid-point of the longest belt run between the pulleys. As a rough guide, under normal finger pressure, the belt should deflect by 4 to 6 mm, or by 0.5 mm for every 25.0 mm of belt run between pulley centres.

37 If adjustment is required, loosen the clamp bolt on the jockey wheel midway between the main pulleys **(see illustrations)**. Turn the jockey wheel as necessary to achieve the correct tension, then tighten the clamp bolt securely.

38 If a new drivebelt has been fitted, start the engine and run it for five minutes at a fast idle, then re-check the tension and adjust if necessary.

39 Where applicable, refit the viscous fan and coupling as described in Chapter 3.

Water pump and air conditioning compressor drivebelts removal and refitting

40 To remove the water pump belt, simply loosen the jockey wheel clamp bolt as described previously, and turn the wheel sufficiently to slip the belt from the pulleys.

41 The procedure for removing the air conditioning belt is identical to that for the water pump belt described above, but the water pump belt must be removed first.

42 Refit each belt as applicable and tension it as described previously.

1995 model year onwards (one drivebelt)

Checking and adjustment

43 An automatic drivebelt tensioner is fitted, and no checking of the tension is necessary, however the belt should be inspected for wear or damage at the recommended intervals.

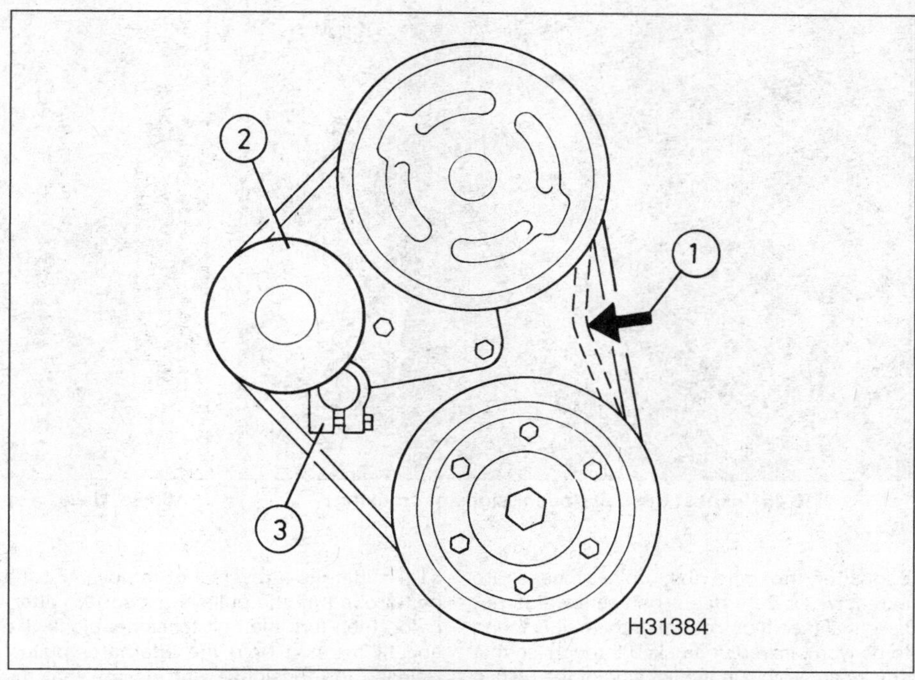
2
1
3
H31384

16.37a Water pump drivebelt details - up to 1995 model year

1 Tension checking point *2 Jockey wheel* *3 Clamp bolt*

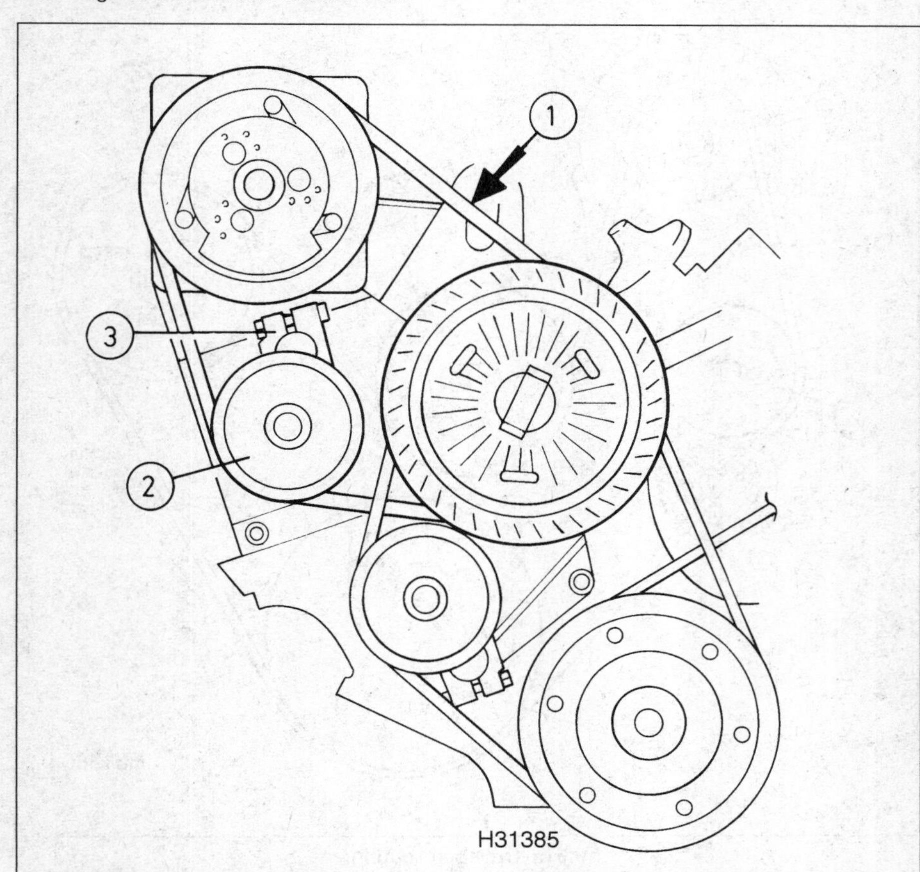
1
3
2
H31385

16.37b Air conditioning compressor drivebelt details - up to 1995 model year

1 Tension checking point *2 Jockey wheel* *3 Clamp bolt*

44 To improve access, remove the cooling fan upper cowl by releasing the two over-centre clips **(see illustrations)**.

45 The belt should be inspected along its entire length. Note that it is not unusual for a ribbed belt to exhibit small cracks in the

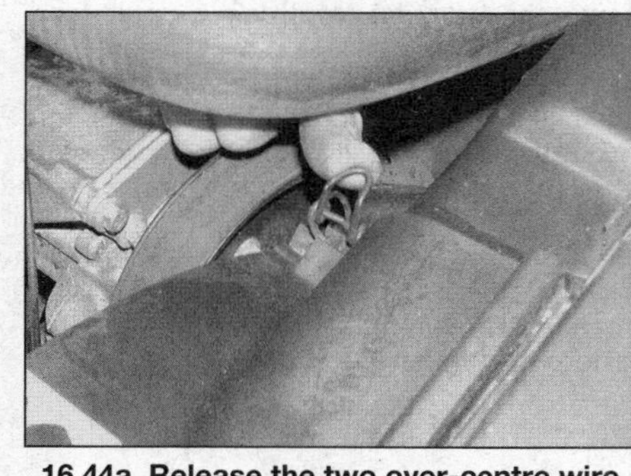

16.44a Release the two over-centre wire clips . . .

16.44b . . . and lift out the cooling fan upper cowl

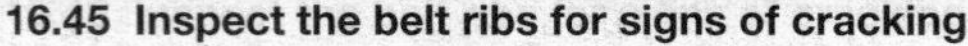

16.45 Inspect the belt ribs for signs of cracking

16.48a Using a spanner on the tensioner bolt, release the belt tension . . .

edges of the belt ribs; unless these are extensive or very deep, belt renewal is not essential **(see illustration)**. If the belt is found to be worn, frayed or cracked through (so that cracks are visible in the flat side of the belt), it should be renewed as a precaution against breakage in service.

46 Refit the upper cooling fan cowl on completion.

Removal and refitting

47 Remove the upper cooling fan cowl by releasing the two over-centre clips.

48 Using a suitable ring spanner on the belt tensioner pulley retaining bolt, turn the tensioner clockwise and relieve the tension in the belt. Slide the belt from the alternator pulley, then release the tensioner **(see illustrations)**.

49 If the original belt is to be refitted, mark the running direction to ensure correct refitting.

50 Remove the belt from the remaining pulleys, then if the fan was not removed, manipulate the belt over the viscous fan blades, and remove it.

51 Refitting is a reversal of removal. Fit the belt around all the pulleys except the alternator, then turn the belt tensioner clockwise and fit the belt onto the alternator pulley. Release the tensioner, and ensure that the belt is correctly seated on the pulleys **(see illustrations)**.

52 On completion, refit the upper cooling fan cowl.

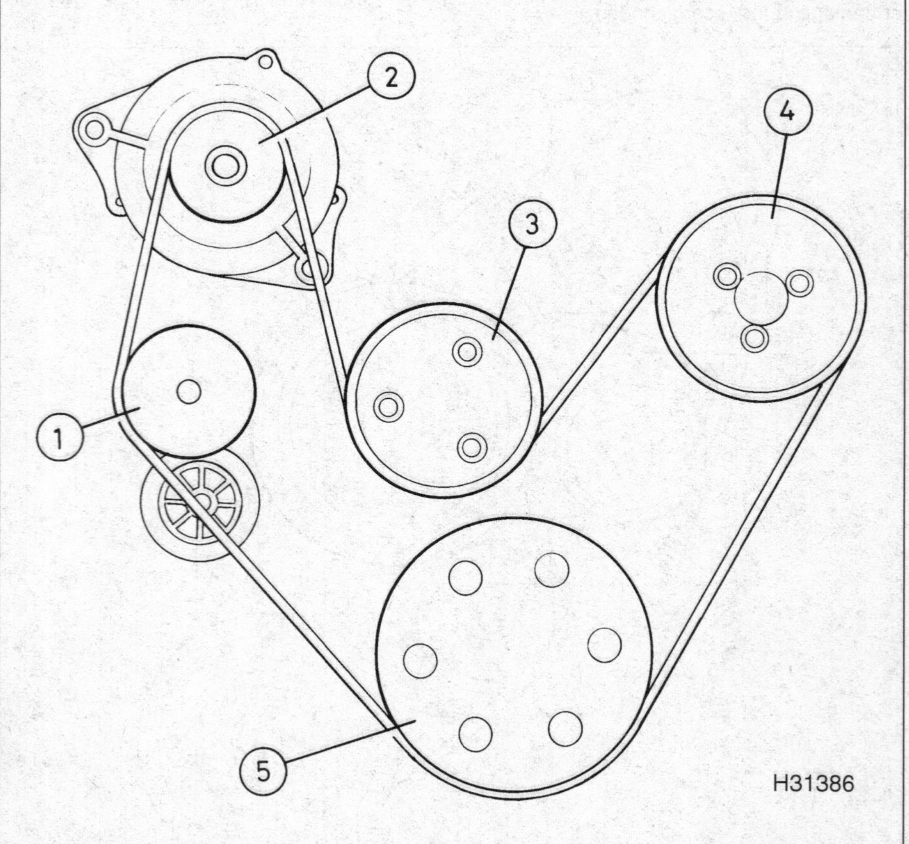

1
2
3
4
5
H31386

16.51a Drivebelt routing - models without air conditioning

1 Tensioner
2 Alternator
3 Water pump
4 Power steering pump
5 Crankshaft pulley

16.48b . . . and slip the drivebelt off the alternator pulley

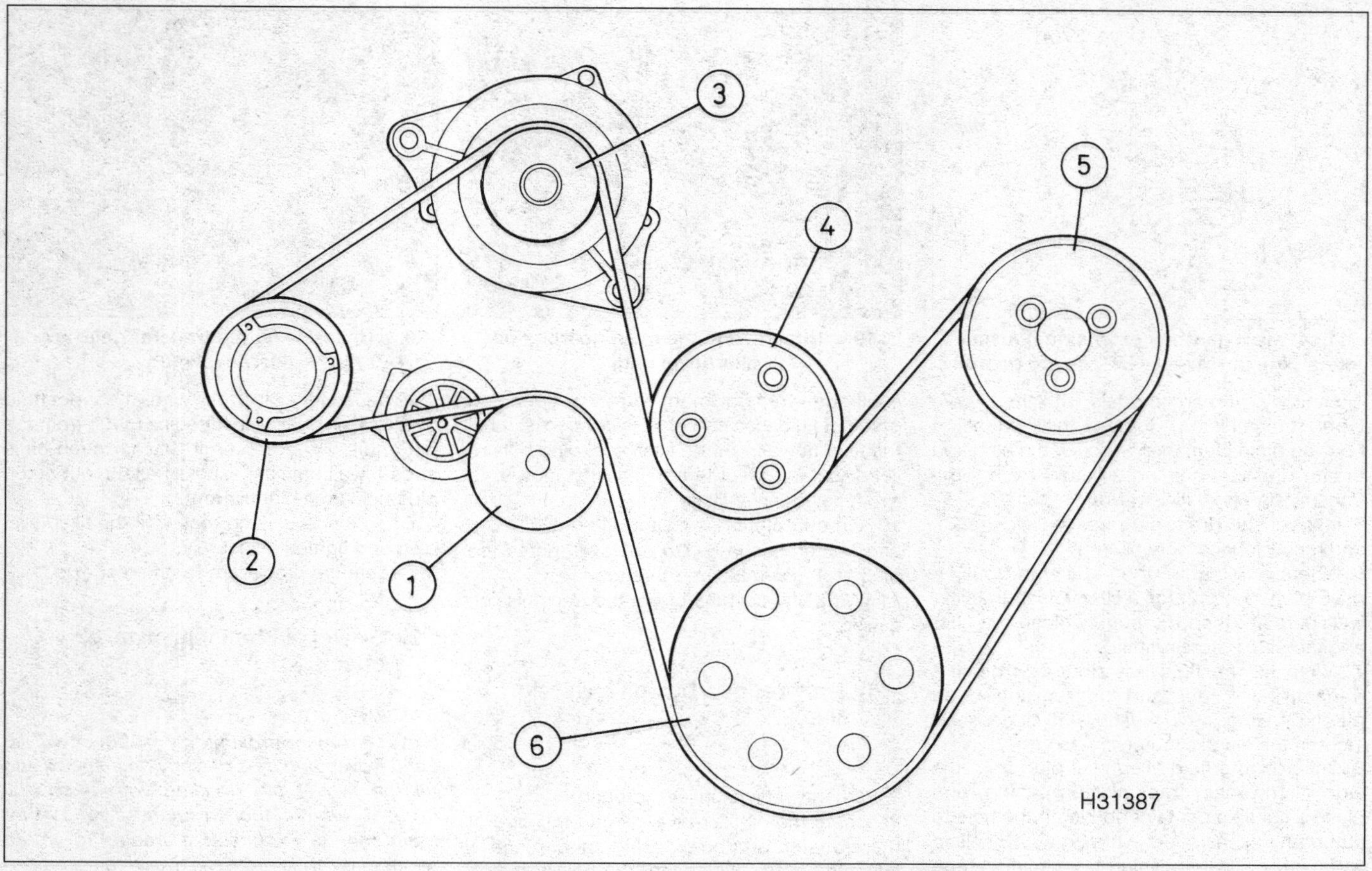

16.51b Drivebelt routing - models with air conditioning

1 Tensioner
2 Air conditioning compressor
3 Alternator
4 Water pump
5 Power steering pump
6 Crankshaft pulley

17 Steering gear backlash check

If at any time it is noted that the steering action has become stiff or sloppy, the vehicle should be taken to a Land Rover dealer for the steering components to be checked. Adjustments to the steering components and power steering box are possible, but specialist knowledge and equipment are needed. Therefore, this task must be entrusted to a Land Rover dealer.

18 Jack and tools security check

1 Lift the bonnet, and check that the vehicle jack and the wheel chock are securely stowed in their bay at the front of the engine compartment. Check the condition of the strap securing the jack, and check that the wing nut or turn-clip securing the wheel chock is tight **(see illustration)**.

2 Similarly, check the security of the jack handle and the wheel nut wrench, which are located in a bag under the rear seats. Tilt the rear seat cushions forwards for access.

3 If the car has alloy wheels, one of the roadwheel nuts on each wheel may be of locking type. If so, check that the removal key or removal tools are present. Standard-equipment locking wheel nuts may have an indented cover fitted over the nut.

18.1 Checking the jack retaining strap

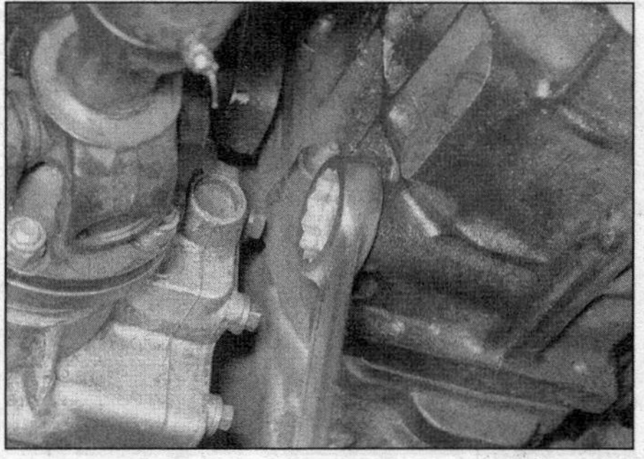

19.3 Unscrewing the main gearbox drain plug

19 Manual transmission fluid renewal

1 Park the vehicle on level ground.

2 Working under the vehicle, locate the main transmission casing drain plug, and place a suitable container beneath the plugs to catch the escaping fluid.

3 Unscrew the drain plug, and allow the fluid to drain. Allow at least ten minutes for all the fluid to drain **(see illustration)**.

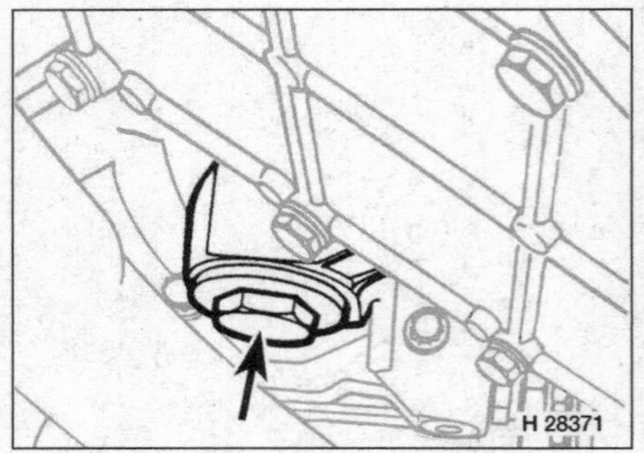
H 28371

19.4 Main gearbox extension housing drain plug (arrowed) - LT 77-type gearbox

4 Similarly, on early models with the LT 77-type transmission, locate the extension housing drain plug, then unscrew the plug and drain the remaining fluid from the transmission **(see illustration)**.

5 Inspect the drain plug sealing washer(s), and renew if necessary.

6 Where applicable, the extension housing drain plug incorporates a filter. Clean the filter with paraffin, then thoroughly clean the filter and the plug before refitting.

7 When all the fluid has drained from the transmission, refit and tighten the drain plug(s), using new washers if necessary. Tighten the plugs securely.

8 Unscrew the fluid filler/level plug from the side of the main transmission casing, and place a suitable container beneath the hole to catch any excess fluid which may be spilled when the transmission is filled **(see illustration)**.

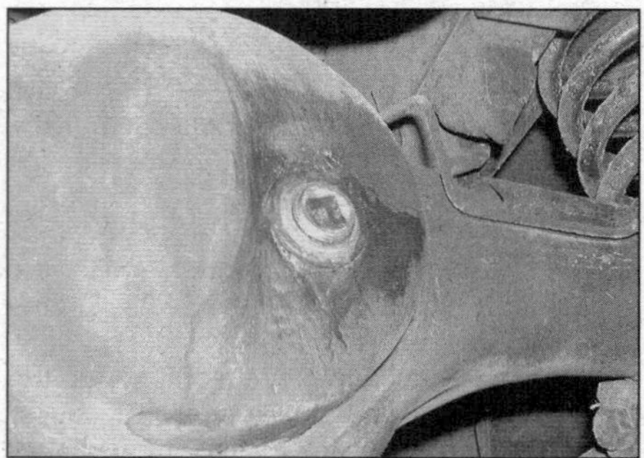

21.2 Axle oil filler/level plug

21.4 Topping-up the axle oil level

19.8 Unscrewing the main gearbox oil filler/level plug

9 Fill the transmission with the specified grade of fluid (see end of *Weekly checks*), until the fluid flows from the filler/level plug hole. It is advisable to fill the transmission slowly, to avoid a sudden spillage.

10 On completion, refit the filler/level plug, and tighten securely. **Do not** overtighten the plug, as it has a tapered thread.

11 Wipe any split fluid from the transmission casing.

20 Transfer gearbox oil level check

1 Park the vehicle on level ground.

2 Locate the oil filler/level plug in the side of the transfer gearbox casing, and place a suitable container beneath the hole to catch any escaping oil.

3 Unscrew the filler/level plug, and check the oil level. The level should be up to the lower edge of the filler/level plug hole **(see illustration)**.

4 If necessary, add oil of the specified type (see end of *Weekly checks*) until the oil overflows from the filler/level hole.

5 Clean and refit the filler/level plug, and tighten to the specified torque. **Do not** over-tighten the plug, as it has tapered threads.

6 Wipe any split oil from the gearbox casing.

21 Axle oil level check

Note: *A 13 mm square-section wrench will be required to undo the axle filler/level plug. These wrenches can be obtained from most motor factors or your Land Rover dealer. It may be possible to use the square fitting of a half-inch-drive socket handle as a substitute.*

1 Ensure that the vehicle is standing on level ground, and that the handbrake is applied.

2 Working underneath the vehicle, unscrew the front axle oil filler/level plug, which is located in the differential housing **(see illustration)**.

3 The oil level should be up to the lower edge of the filler/level plug hole.

20.3 Unscrewing the transfer gearbox oil filler/level plug

4 If necessary, top-up with the specified grade of oil, until oil just begins to run from the plug hole. Do not overfill - if too much oil is added, wait until the excess has run out of the plug hole **(see illustration)**.

5 Once the level is correct, refit the filler/level plug and tighten it securely.

6 Repeat the procedure for the rear axle.

22 Swivel pin housing oil level check

Note: *From approximately 1998 onwards, Land Rover (and their dealers) drain the oil and fill the swivel pin housing with a special grease, which then requires no further maintenance - consult a dealer for more information. This grease is available from Land Rover dealers, under part number FTC3435.*

1 Ensure that the vehicle is standing on level ground, and that the handbrake is applied.

2 Working underneath the vehicle, unscrew the left-hand swivel pin housing level plug. The level plug has a square-section head, and is situated approximately halfway up the housing **(see illustration)**.

3 The oil level should be up to the lower edge of the level plug hole.

4 If topping-up is necessary, unscrew the filler plug from the top of the swivel pin housing; the filler plug also has a square-section head. Top-up the housing via the filler plug hole using the specified grade of oil, until oil just begins to run from the level plug hole. Do not overfill - if too much oil is added, wait

2
1

22.2 Swivel pin housing level plug (1) and filler plug (2)

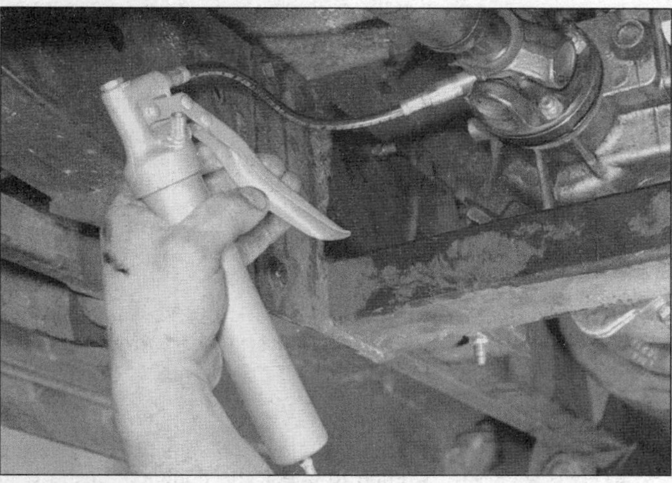

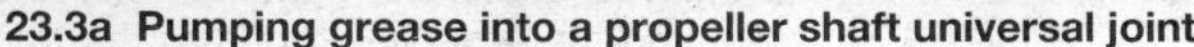

23.3a Pumping grease into a propeller shaft universal joint

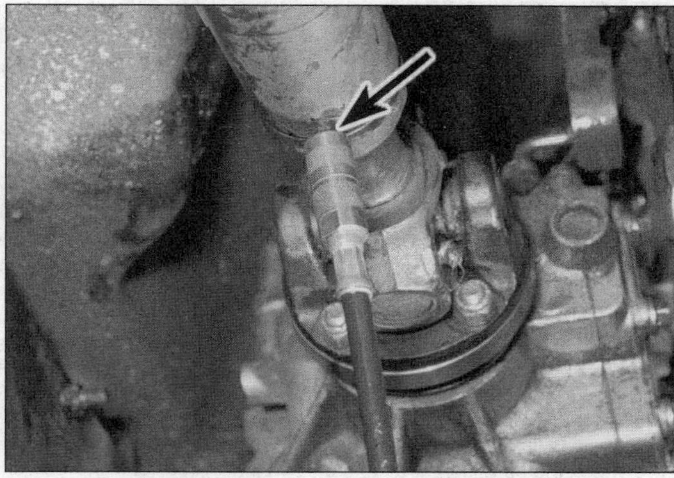

23.3b Greasing a propeller shaft sliding joint (grease nipple arrowed)

until the excess has run out of the level plug hole.

5 Once the level is correct, refit both the filler and level plugs, and tighten them securely.

6 Repeat the above procedure on the right-hand swivel pin housing.

23 Propeller shaft joint lubrication

Note: *A low-pressure grease gun will be required for this operation.*

1 Working under the vehicle, locate the grease nipples on the front and rear propeller shafts universal joint spiders, and the shaft sliding joints.

2 Thoroughly clean the around each nipple. This is essential - if the area is not clean, the grease will either not go in, or will take in dirt with it.

3 Fill a suitable grease gun with the recommended type of grease (see end of *Weekly checks*), then apply the grease gun to each of the nipples in turn, and pump grease into the joints **(see illustrations)**. Apply grease until it emerges from the end of the nipple, then wipe away the excess.

24 Handbrake linkage lubrication

Early models (with rod-actuated brake assembly)

1 To improve access, firmly apply the handbrake, then jack up the front of the vehicle and support it on axle stands.

2 Thoroughly degrease the handbrake rod linkage assembly, which is mounted onto the side of the transfer box. Apply fresh high-melting point grease to all the linkage pivot points and to the exposed end of the handbrake cable, then lower the vehicle to the ground.

Later models (with cable-actuated brake assembly)

3 On these models, no lubrication is necessary.

25 Underbody component, pipe, hose and wiring check

1 Visually inspect the engine joint faces, gaskets and seals for any signs of water or oil leaks. Pay particular attention to the areas around the rocker covers, cylinder heads, oil filter and sump joint faces. Bear in mind that over a period of time some very slight seepage from these areas is to be expected - what you are really looking for is any indication of a serious leak. Should a leak be found, renew the offending gasket or oil seal by referring to the appropriate Chapter(s) in this manual.

2 Similarly, check the transmission components for oil leaks, and investigate and rectify and problems found.

3 Check the security and condition of all the engine-related pipes and hoses. Ensure that all cable-ties or securing clips are in place and in good condition. Clips which are broken or missing can lead to chafing of the hoses, pipes or wiring, which could cause more serious problems in the future.

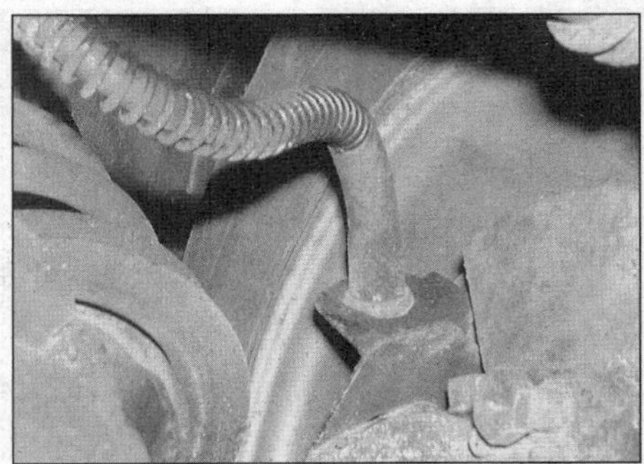

25.6 Check all brake pipes and hoses

4 Carefully check the condition of all coolant, fuel and brake hoses. Renew any hose which is cracked, swollen or deteriorated. Cracks will show up better if the hose is squeezed gently. Pay close attention to the hose clips that secure the hoses to the system components. Hose clips can pinch and puncture hoses, resulting in leaks. If wire-type hose clips are used, it may be a good idea to replace them with screw-type clips.

5 With the vehicle raised, inspect the fuel tank and filler neck for punctures, cracks and other damage. The connection between the filler neck and tank is especially critical. Sometimes, a rubber filler neck or connecting hose will leak due to loose retaining clamps or deteriorated rubber.

6 Similarly, inspect all brake hoses and metal pipes **(see illustration)**. If any damage or deterioration is discovered, do not drive the vehicle until the necessary repair work has been carried out. Renew any damaged sections of hose or pipe.

7 Carefully check all rubber hoses and metal fuel lines leading away from the petrol tank. Check for loose connections, deteriorated hoses, crimped lines and other damage. Pay particular attention to the vent pipes and hoses, which often loop up around the filler neck and can become blocked or crimped. Follow the lines to the front of the vehicle carefully inspecting them all the way. Renew damaged sections as necessary.

8 From within the engine compartment, check the security of all fuel hose attachments and pipe unions, and inspect the fuel hoses and vacuum hoses for kinks, chafing and deterioration.

9 Check the condition of the oil cooler hoses and pipes.

10 Check the condition of the power steering

26.3 Exhaust mounting rubber

fluid hoses and pipes and, where applicable, check the condition of the automatic transmission fluid hoses and pipes.

11 Check the condition of all exposed wiring harnesses, paying particular attention to the ABS wheel sensor wiring harnesses, where applicable.

26 Exhaust system check

1 With the engine cold (at least an hour after the vehicle has been driven), check the complete exhaust system from the engine to the end of the tailpipes. Ideally the inspection should be carried out with the vehicle raised (see *Jacking and vehicle support*).

2 Check the exhaust pipes and connections for evidence of leaks, severe corrosion and damage. Make sure that all brackets and mountings are in good condition and tight. Leakage at any of the joints or in other parts of the system will usually show up as a black sooty stain in the vicinity of the leak.

3 Rattles and other noises can often be traced to the exhaust system, especially the brackets and mountings **(see illustration)**. Try to move the pipes and silencers. If the components can come into contact with the body or suspension parts, secure the system with new mountings; if possible, separate the joints, and twist the pipes as necessary to provide additional clearance.

4 Run the engine at idle speed, then temporarily place a cloth rag over the rear end of

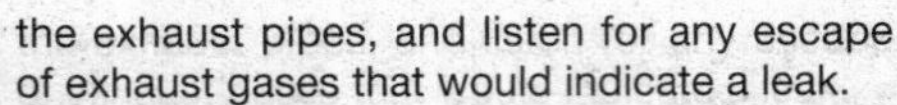

the exhaust pipes, and listen for any escape of exhaust gases that would indicate a leak.

5 On completion, where applicable, lower the vehicle to the ground.

27 Steering and suspension component check

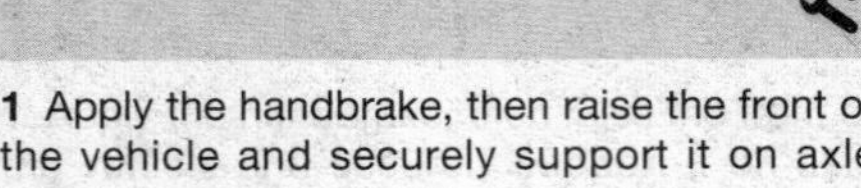

1 Apply the handbrake, then raise the front of the vehicle and securely support it on axle stands.

2 Visually inspect the balljoint dust covers for splits, chafing or deterioration. Any damage will cause loss of lubricant, together with dirt and water entry, resulting in rapid deterioration of the balljoints.

3 Check the power steering fluid hoses for chafing or deterioration, and the pipe and hose unions for fluid leaks. Also check for signs of fluid leakage under pressure from the steering box, which would indicate failed fluid seals within the steering box assembly.

4 Grasp the roadwheel at the 12 o'clock and 6 o'clock positions, and try to rock it. Very slight freeplay may be felt, but if the movement is appreciable, further investigation is necessary to determine the source. Continue rocking the wheel while an assistant depresses the footbrake. If the movement is now eliminated or significantly reduced, it is likely that the hub bearings are at fault. If the freeplay is still evident with the footbrake depressed, then there is wear in the suspension joints or mountings.

5 Now grasp the wheel at the 9 o'clock and 3 o'clock positions, and try to rock it as before. Any movement felt now may again be caused by wear in the hub bearings or the steering track rod and drag link balljoints. If a balljoint is worn, the visual movement will be obvious.

6 Using a large screwdriver or flat bar, check for wear in the suspension mounting bushes by levering between the relevant suspension component and its attachment point. Some movement is to be expected as the mountings are made of rubber, but excessive wear should be obvious. Also check the condition of any visible rubber bushes, looking for splits, cracks or contamination of the rubber.

7 With the vehicle standing on its wheels, have an assistant turn the steering wheel back and forth. There should be very little, if any, lost movement between the steering wheel and roadwheels. If this is not the case, closely observe the joints and mountings previously described, but in addition, check the steering column universal joints for wear. The steering box backlash is adjustable, but adjustment should be entrusted to a Land Rover dealer (see Section 17).

28 Propeller shaft securing bolt check

1 Working under the vehicle, use a torque wrench to check the tightness of the bolts securing the propeller shafts to the transfer gearbox and axle drive flanges.

2 Also check the bolts securing the rear propeller shaft rubber coupling, where applicable.

29 Axle breather check

1 Ensure that the vehicle is standing on level ground, and that the handbrake is applied. To access the rear axle breather, jack up the rear of the car and support on axle stands under the chassis. The front axle breather is routed into the engine compartment, at the base of the left-hand inner wing.

2 Check that both the front and rear axle breather tubes are securely retained by all the relevant retaining clips, and show no signs of damage or deterioration **(see illustrations)**.

3 If renewal is necessary, unscrew the union bolt securing the breather hose to the top of the axle, and recover the sealing washers from the hose union. Free the hose from its retaining clips, and remove it from the vehicle.

4 Position a new sealing washer on each side of the hose union, and refit the union bolt. Ensure that the hose is correctly routed and retained by all the necessary clips, then securely tighten the union bolt.

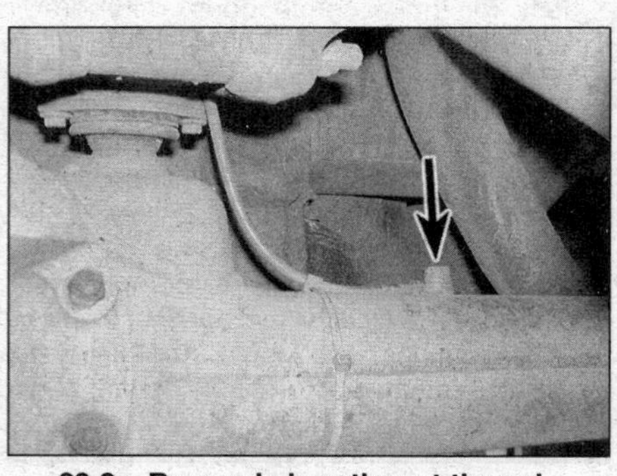

29.2a Rear axle breather at the axle end . . .

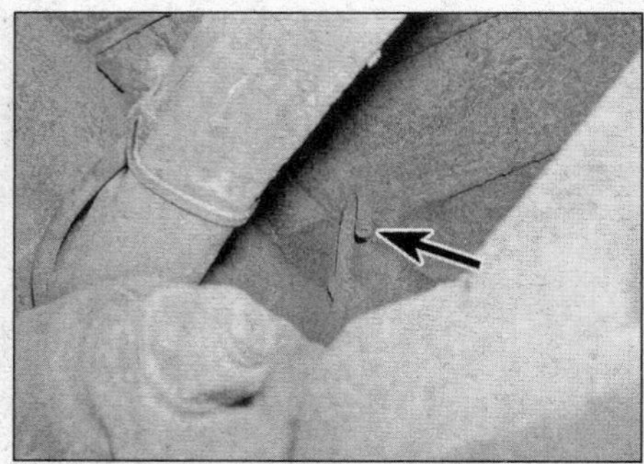

29.2b . . . and showing the hose end (arrowed)

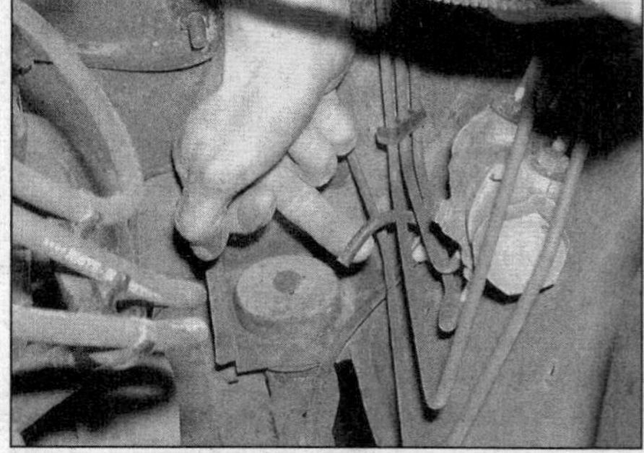

29.2c Front axle breather is routed into the engine compartment

30 Flywheel housing draining

1 In production, the flywheel housing plug is not normally fitted. The plug can be fitted to the oil drain hole in the housing, to seal the housing if the vehicle is likely to be used off-road in very muddy conditions, or under severe wading conditions. A suitable plug can be obtained from a Land Rover dealer **(see illustration)**.

2 If the vehicle is regularly used in adverse conditions, the plug should be fitted permanently, but if the vehicle is normally used on the road, the plug should be removed.

3 If the plug is permanently fitted, it should be removed at the recommended intervals to allow any accumulated oil to drain from the housing.

4 Clean the plug before refitting.

31 Fuel tank security check

1 Working under the vehicle, check the fuel tank for any signs of damage or corrosion.

2 If there is any sign of significant damage or corrosion, remove the fuel tank (see the relevant part of Chapter 4) and take it to a professional for repair. **Do not** under any circumstances attempt to weld or solder a fuel tank.

32 Towing bracket check

1 Where applicable, check the security of the towbar bracket mountings. Also check that all wiring is intact, and that the trailer electrical systems function correctly.

33 Handbrake adjustment

1 The handbrake mechanism is mounted onto the rear of the transfer box assembly. Place the transmission in gear (manual) or P (automatic), then release the handbrake lever and chock the front wheels.

2 Jack up the rear of the vehicle, and support it on axle stands so the wheels are clear of the ground.

Early models (with rod-actuated brake)

3 From underneath the vehicle, slacken the cable locknut, then loosen the adjuster nut to obtain plenty of freeplay in the cable.

4 Using a suitable spanner, rotate the adjuster on the rear of the handbrake assembly clockwise until both shoes are fully expanded against the drum.

30.1 Flywheel housing drain plug location (arrowed)

5 With the shoes in full contact with the drum, remove all but a slight amount of freeplay from the handbrake cable, using the adjuster nut. Hold the adjuster nut in this position, and securely tighten the cable locknut.

6 Rotate the handbrake drum adjuster in an anti-clockwise direction, until the drum is free to rotate easily.

7 Applying normal, moderate pressure, pull the handbrake lever to the fully-applied position whilst counting the number of clicks emitted from the handbrake ratchet mechanism. The handbrake should be fully-applied on the second or third click of the ratchet mechanism. If necessary, adjust by rotating the drum adjuster in the relevant direction.

8 When adjustment is correct, release the handbrake lever, and check that the drum is free to rotate easily.

9 Apply a smear of high-melting point grease to all the linkage pivot points and to the exposed end of the handbrake cable, then lower the vehicle to the ground.

Later models (with cable-actuated brake)

10 Release the handbrake lever gaiter from the console, and remove the switch panel cover plate. Undo the retaining screws, then withdraw the switch panel and disconnect its wiring connectors. Access can then be gained to the handbrake cable knurled adjuster nut **(see illustration)**.

11 Slacken the cable knurled cable adjuster ring to obtain some freeplay in the cable.

12 From underneath the vehicle, using a suitable spanner, rotate the adjuster on the rear of the handbrake assembly clockwise until both shoes are fully expanded against the drum.

13 With the shoes in full contact with the drum, rotate the handbrake adjuster in an anti-clockwise direction until the handbrake drum is free to rotate easily.

14 Applying normal, moderate pressure, pull the handbrake lever to the fully-applied position, counting the number of clicks emitted from the handbrake ratchet mechanism. The handbrake should be fully-applied on the third click of the ratchet mechanism. If necessary, adjust the cable setting using the adjuster nut.

15 When adjustment is correct, release the handbrake lever, and check that the drum is free to rotate easily. If all is well, lower the vehicle to the ground.

16 Reconnect the wiring connectors to the centre console switch panel, and refit the panel to the console. Securely tighten the panel retaining screws, and clip the cover plate and handbrake lever gaiter back into position.

34 Road test

Instruments and electrical equipment

1 Check the operation of all instruments and electrical equipment.

2 Make sure that all instruments read correctly, and switch on all electrical equipment in turn to check that it functions properly.

Steering and suspension

3 Check for any abnormalities in the steering, suspension, handling or road 'feel'.

4 Drive the vehicle, and check that there are no unusual vibrations or noises.

5 Check that the steering feels positive, with no excessive sloppiness, or roughness, and check for any suspension noises when cornering and driving over bumps.

Drivetrain

6 Check the performance of the engine, clutch (where applicable), transmission and propeller shafts.

7 Listen for any unusual noises from the engine, clutch and transmission.

8 Make sure that the engine runs smoothly when idling, and that there is no hesitation when accelerating.

9 Where applicable, check that the clutch action is smooth and progressive, that the drive is taken up smoothly, and that the pedal travel is not excessive. Also listen for any noises when the clutch pedal is depressed.

33.10 On later models, access to the handbrake cable adjuster nut (arrowed) can be gained once the switch panel has been removed from the centre console

10 Check that all gears can be engaged smoothly without noise, and that the gear lever action is not abnormally vague or 'notchy'. This check applies to both the manual/automatic transmission and the transfer gearbox.

Braking system

11 Make sure that the vehicle does not pull to one side when braking, and that the wheels do not lock prematurely when braking hard.
12 Check that there is no vibration through the steering when braking.
13 Check that the handbrake operates correctly without excessive movement of the lever, and that it holds the vehicle stationary on a slope.
14 Test the operation of the brake servo unit as follows. With the engine switched off, depress the footbrake four or five times to exhaust the vacuum, then start the engine, keeping the pedal depressed. As the engine starts, there should be a noticeable 'give' in the brake pedal as vacuum builds up. Allow the engine to run for at least two minutes, and then switch it off. If the brake pedal is now depressed, it should be possible to detect a hiss from the servo as the pedal is depressed. After about four or five applications, no further hissing should be heard, and the pedal should feel considerably harder.

35 Headlight and auxiliary light adjustment check

1 Check the operation of all the electrical equipment, ie lights, direction indicators, horn, etc. Refer to the appropriate Sections of Chapter 13 for details if any of the circuits are found to be inoperative.
2 Note that stop-light switch adjustment is described in Chapter 10.
3 Visually check all accessible wiring connectors, harnesses and retaining clips for security, and for signs of chafing or damage. Rectify any faults found.
4 Accurate adjustment of the headlight beam is only possible using optical beam-setting equipment, and this work should therefore be carried out by a Land Rover dealer or service station with the necessary facilities.
5 Basic adjustments can be carried out in an emergency, and further details are given in Chapter 13.
6 On models with an electrically-operated headlight levelling system, check the operation of both headlight motors. Refer to the appropriate Sections of Chapter 13 if any of the circuits are found to be inoperative.

36 Sunroof maintenance

1 Check the operation of each sunroof (on cars so equipped). If the action is at all stiff, clean and lubricate the sunroof guide rails and slides with a little multi-purpose grease.
2 With the sunroof open, check that the sunroof drain tubes at the corners of the sunroof aperture are clear. Carefully pour a little water into the drain channel, and have an assistant watch for the water emerging under the car. Beware of probing the drain tubes with wire, as this may damage the tubes. If available, an air line should be used to clear any blockages.

37 Front wheel alignment check

Check the front wheel alignment as described in Chapter 11.

38 Brake pad and disc check

1 Jack up the vehicle, support securely on axle stands, then remove the roadwheels (see *Jacking and vehicle support*).
2 For a quick check, the thickness of friction material remaining on each pad can be measured through the slot in the caliper body **(see illustration)**. If any pad is worn to the specified minimum thickness or less, all four pads must be renewed (see Chapter 10).
3 For a comprehensive check, the brake pads should be removed and cleaned. This will allow the operation of the caliper to be checked, and the condition of the brake disc itself to be fully examined on both sides (see Chapter 10).

39 Spare wheel check

Refer to *Weekly checks* and Section 18.

40 Hinge and lock check and lubrication

1 Lubricate the hinges of the bonnet, doors and tailgate with a light general-purpose oil. Similarly, lubricate all latches, locks and lock strikers **(see illustration)**. At the same time, check the security and operation of all the locks, adjusting them if necessary (see Chapter 12).
2 Lightly lubricate the bonnet release mechanism and cable with a suitable grease.

41 Seat belt check

1 Carefully examine the seat belt webbing for cuts, or any signs of serious fraying or deterioration. If the seat belt is of the retractable type, pull the belt all the way out, and examine the full extent of the webbing.
2 Fasten and unfasten the belt, ensuring that the locking mechanism holds securely, and releases properly when intended. If the belt is of the retractable type, check also that the retracting mechanism operates correctly when the belt is released.
3 Check the security of all seat belt mountings and attachments which are accessible, without removing any trim or other components, from inside the vehicle.
4 Renew any worn components as described in Chapter 12.

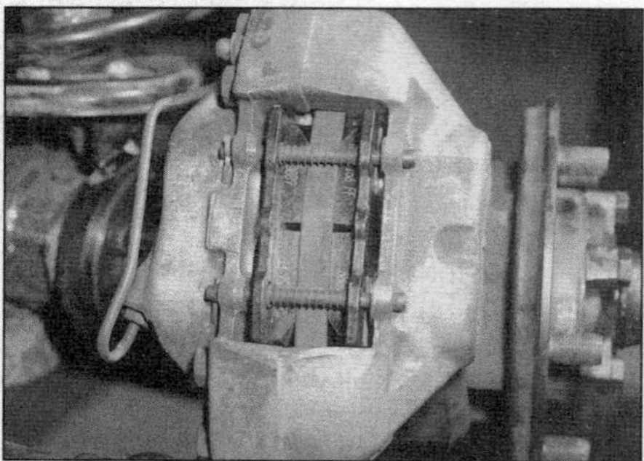

38.2 Brake pad friction material thickness can be checked with the caliper in position

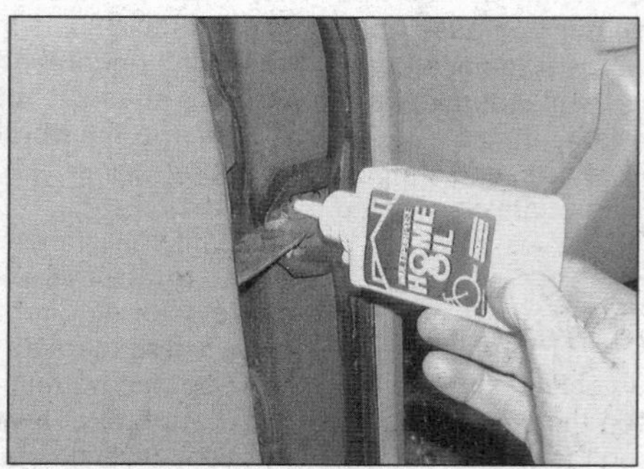

40.1 Lubricating a front door check strap pivot

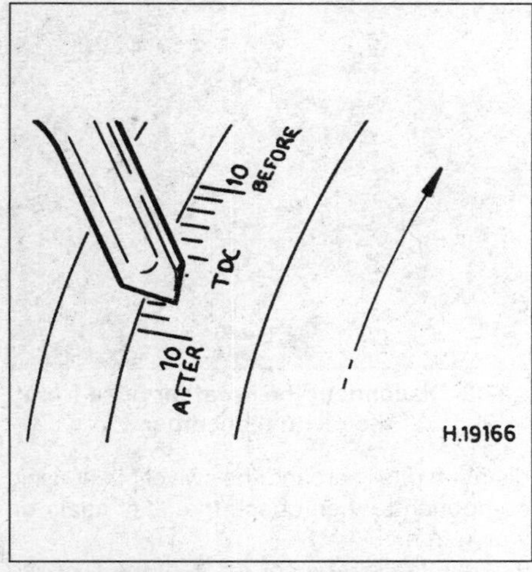
10
BEFORE
TDC
10
AFTER
H.19166

42.5 Ignition timing pointer and scale

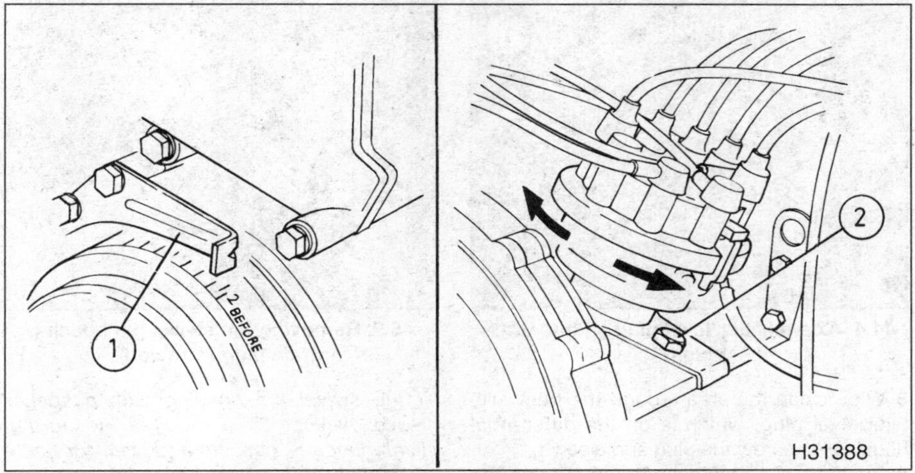
1
2
BEFORE
2
H31388

42.6 Ignition timing pointer (1) and distributor clamp bolt (2)

Every 24 000 miles or 2 years, whichever comes first

42 Ignition timing check and adjustment

1 Correct ignition timing is vital for the proper running of the engine. If the ignition is over-advanced, pre-ignition (pinking), and possible piston damage, will result; if the ignition is retarded, there will be loss of power, overheating and high fuel consumption.

2 The engine must be at normal operating temperature. Disconnect the distributor vacuum hose - the idle speed should not rise above 800 rpm when this is done.

3 Connect a timing light (strobe) into the ignition system in accordance with the equipment manufacturer's instructions - usually to the No 1 HT lead. Some lights also require a connection to be made to the battery or to a mains power supply.

4 Depending on the brightness of the timing light and the ambient light level, it may be necessary to highlight the specified timing mark (on the scale on the pulley) and the pointer with quick-drying white paint. Typist's correcting fluid is ideal.

5 Start the engine and allow it to idle. Point the timing light at the timing marks and pointer. The timing marks will appear stationary, and if the timing is correct, the specified mark on the scale will be aligned with the pointer **(see illustration)**. Take care not to let the light or its leads come into contact with moving parts of the engine.

6 If the timing is incorrect, stop the engine, slacken the distributor clamp bolt and move the distributor in the required direction (clockwise to retard, anti-clockwise to advance) to correct the timing **(see illustration)**. Access to the clamp bolt is not easy, and is best achieved from under the power steering pump, using a long extension handle. Tighten the clamp bolt and recheck the timing.

7 Note that if the engine idle speed is too high, it will be impossible to set the timing correctly since the centrifugal advance mechanism in the distributor will have started to operate. Connect a tachometer to the engine if in doubt.

8 With the ignition timing set, check the operation of the centrifugal advance mechanism by slowly increasing the engine speed. As the engine speed is increased, the timing scale will appear to drift relative to the pointer in the advanced (BTDC) direction. Accurate checking is difficult without special equipment, but any jerkiness or sticking in the advancement should be regarded with suspicion.

9 The vacuum advance system can be checked in a similar way, once the distributor vacuum hose is reconnected.

10 On completion, disconnect the timing light, and make sure (if not already done) that the distributor vacuum hose is reconnected.

43 Transfer gearbox oil renewal

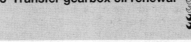

1 Park the vehicle on level ground.

2 Locate the filler/level plug in the side of the transfer gearbox casing, the unscrew the plug (see Section 20).

3 Place a suitable container beneath the drain plug in the bottom of the gearbox casing, then unscrew the drain plug and allow the oil to drain **(see illustration)**. Recover the sealing washer.

4 When the oil has finished draining, refit and tighten the drain plug, using a new sealing washer if necessary.

5 Refill the gearbox with oil of the specified type (see end of *Weekly checks*) through the filler/level hole, until the oil level reaches the lower edge of the hole (place a container beneath the hole to catch any escaping oil).

6 Clean and refit the filler/level plug, and tighten to the specified torque. **Do not** overtighten the plug, as it has tapered threads.

7 Wipe any split oil from the gearbox casing.

44 Axle oil renewal

Note: *A 13 mm square-section wrench will be required to undo the axle filler/level plug. These wrenches can be obtained from most motor factors or your Land Rover dealer. It may be possible to use the square fitting of a half-inch-drive socket handle as a substitute.*

1 This operation is much quicker and more efficient if the car is first taken on a journey of sufficient length to warm the axle oil up to normal operating temperature.

2 Park the car on level ground, switch off the ignition and apply the handbrake firmly.

43.3 Unscrewing the transfer gearbox oil drain plug

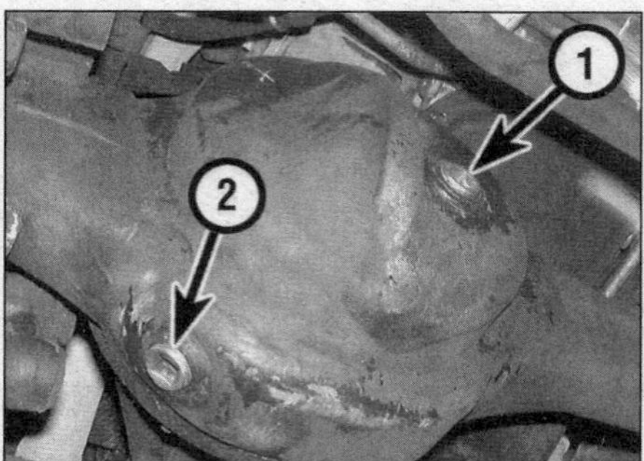
1
2

44.4 Axle oil filler/level plug (1) and drain plug (2)

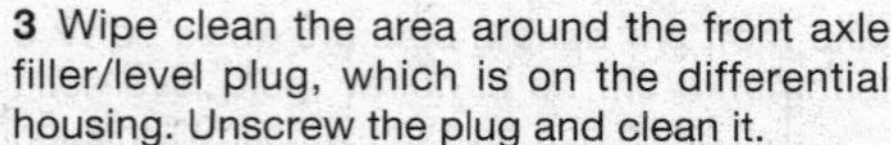

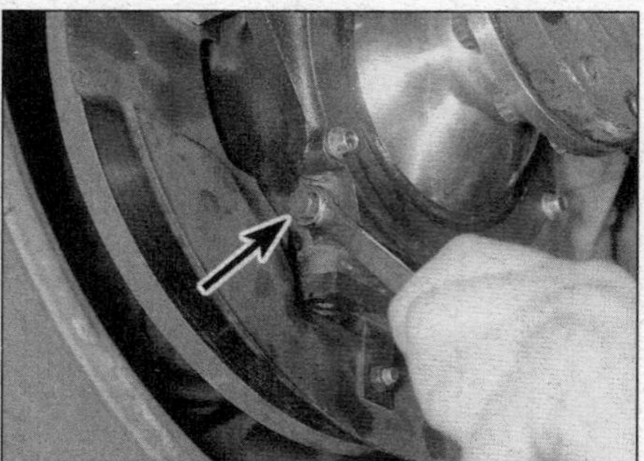

45.5 Removing the swivel pin housing drain plug (arrowed)

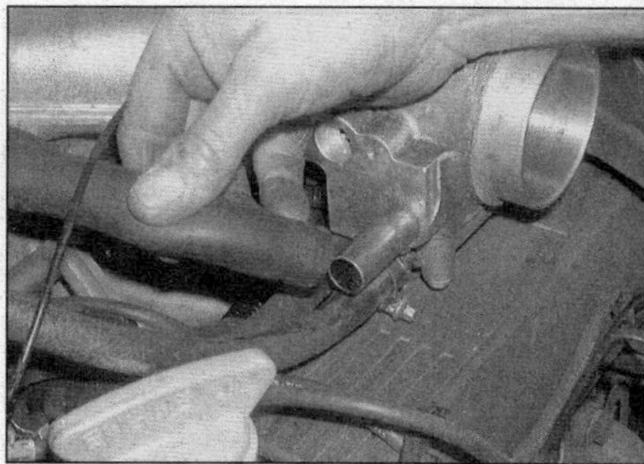

47.2 Disconnect the breather hose from the plenum chamber

3 Wipe clean the area around the front axle filler/level plug, which is on the differential housing. Unscrew the plug and clean it.

4 Position a suitable container under the drain plug situated on the base of the differential housing **(see illustration)**.

5 Unscrew the drain plug, and allow the oil to drain completely into the container. If the oil is hot, take precautions against scalding. Examine the sealing washer for signs of damage, renewing it if necessary, and clean both the filler/level and the drain plugs.

6 When the oil has finished draining, clean the drain plug threads and those of the differential casing, then refit the drain plug and washer, tightening it securely.

7 Refilling the axle is an extremely awkward operation. Above all, allow plenty of time for the oil level to settle properly before checking it. Note that the car must be parked on flat level ground when checking the oil level.

8 Refill the axle with the exact amount of the specified type of oil, then check the oil level as described in Section 21. If the correct amount was poured into the housing, and a large amount flows out on checking the level, refit the filler/level plug, and take the car on a short journey so that the new oil is distributed fully around the axle components, then check the level again on your return.

9 When the level is correct, refit the filler/level plug, tightening it securely, and wash off any spilt oil.

10 Repeat the procedure for the rear axle.

45 Swivel pin housing oil renewal

Note: *From approximately 1998 onwards, Land Rover (and their dealers) drain the oil and fill the swivel pin housing with a special grease, which then requires no further maintenance - consult a dealer for more information. This grease is available from Land Rover dealers, under part number FTC3435.*

1 This operation is much quicker and more efficient if the car is first taken on a journey of sufficient length to warm the swivel pin housing oil up to normal operating temperature.

2 Park the car on level ground, switch off the ignition and apply the handbrake firmly.

3 Working underneath the vehicle, unscrew the left-hand swivel pin housing level plug and filler. Both plugs can be identified by their square-section heads (see Section 22).

4 Position a suitable container under the drain plug situated on the base of the swivel pin housing.

5 Unscrew the drain plug, and allow the oil to drain completely into the container **(see illustration)**. If the oil is hot, take precautions against scalding. Examine the sealing washer for signs of damage, renewing it if necessary, and clean the threads of all removed plugs.

6 When the oil has finished draining, clean the drain plug threads and those of the housing, then refit the drain plug and washer, tightening it securely.

7 Refilling the housing is an extremely awkward operation. Above all, allow plenty of time for the oil level to settle properly before checking it. Note that the car must be parked on flat level ground when checking the oil level.

8 Refill the housing with the exact amount of the specified type of oil, then check the oil level as described in Section 22. If the correct amount was poured into the housing, and a large amount flows out on checking the level, refit the filler and level plugs, and take the car on a short journey so that the new oil is distributed fully around the swivel pin housing components, then check the level again on your return.

9 When the level is correct, refit the filler and level plugs, tightening them securely, and wash off any spilt oil.

10 Repeat the above operation on the right-hand swivel pin housing.

46 Automatic transmission fluid and oil screen renewal

This is an involved operation, and is best entrusted to a Land Rover dealer.

47 Plenum chamber ventilation duct cleaning

1 Loosen the hose clamp and remove the large air inlet hose from the plenum chamber.

2 Disconnect the crankcase breather hose from the front of the plenum chamber **(see illustration)**, and also disconnect the T-piece further down the same hose.

3 To prevent any debris being drawn into the inlet manifold, stuff a clean piece of rag down into the plenum chamber main air inlet, making sure that it can easily be retrieved.

4 Using an air line or a soft piece of wire, clean the crankcase breather duct at the front of the plenum chamber. Using the breather hose, blow through the duct to ensure that it is clear.

5 Similarly, check and clean the T-piece removed previously.

6 Remove the rag from the plenum chamber, then refit all disconnected hoses to complete.

Every 2 years, regardless of mileage

48 Brake fluid renewal

The procedure is similar to that for the bleeding of the hydraulic system as described in Chapter 10, except that the brake fluid reservoir should be emptied by siphoning, using a (clean) old battery hydrometer or similar before starting, and allowance should be made for the old fluid to be expelled from the circuit when bleeding each section of the circuit.

49 Coolant renewal

Warning: Wait until the engine is cold before starting this procedure. Do not allow antifreeze to come in contact with your skin, or with the painted surfaces of the vehicle. Rinse off spills immediately with plenty of water. Never leave antifreeze lying around in an open container, or in a puddle in the driveway or garage floor. Children and pets are attracted by its sweet smell, but antifreeze is fatal if ingested. Refer to the 'Antifreeze mixture' sub-Section before proceeding.

Cooling system draining

1 To drain the cooling system, first cover the expansion tank cap with a wad of rag, and slowly turn the cap anti-clockwise to relieve the pressure in the cooling system (a hissing sound will normally be heard). Wait until any pressure remaining in the system is released, then continue to turn the cap until it can be removed.

2 To assist draining, unscrew and remove the radiator filler plug fitted to the top right-hand side of the radiator, and recover the O-ring.

3 Position a suitable container beneath the radiator bottom hose connection, then slacken the hose clip and ease the hose from the radiator stub **(see illustration)**. If the hose joint has not been disturbed for some time, it will be necessary to manipulate the hose to break the joint. Allow the coolant to drain into the container.

4 To fully drain the system, also slacken and remove the square-headed coolant drain plug fitted to each side of the cylinder block, below the exhaust manifold, and allow any residual coolant to drain from the block **(see illustration)**.

TOOL TiP

In the absence of a proper tool, the left-hand block drain plug can be removed using a short 3/8-inch extension bar as a 'socket', with a 10 mm open-ended spanner fitted to the square end fitting. Lack of access prevents this method on the right-hand side, but a 10 mm spanner alone can be used.

5 When the flow of coolant has stopped, wipe clean the threads of the drain plugs and block. Apply a smear of suitable sealant to the drain plug threads, then refit the drain plugs to the block, and tighten securely.

6 If the coolant has been drained for a reason other than renewal, then provided it is clean and less than two years old, it can be re-used.

Cooling system flushing

7 If coolant renewal has been neglected, or if the antifreeze mixture has become diluted, then in time, the cooling system may gradually lose efficiency, as the coolant passages become restricted due to rust, scale deposits, and other sediment. The cooling system efficiency can be restored by flushing the system clean.

8 The radiator should be flushed independently of the engine, to avoid unnecessary contamination.

9 To flush the radiator, disconnect the top hose at the radiator, refit the radiator filler plug, then insert a garden hose into the radiator top inlet. Direct a flow of clean water through the radiator, and continue flushing until clean water emerges from the radiator bottom outlet (the bottom radiator hose should have been disconnected to drain the system).

10 If after a reasonable period, the water still does not run clear, the radiator can be flushed with a good proprietary cleaning agent. It is important that the cleaning agent manufacturer's instructions are followed carefully. If the contamination is particularly bad, insert the hose in the radiator bottom outlet, and flush the radiator in reverse ('reverse-flushing').

11 Remove the thermostat as described in Chapter 3, then temporarily refit the thermostat cover.

12 With the radiator top and bottom hoses disconnected from the radiator, insert a hose into the radiator bottom hose. Direct a clean flow of water through the engine, and continue flushing until clean water emerges from the radiator top hose.

13 On completion of flushing, refit the thermostat with reference to Chapter 3, and reconnect the hoses.

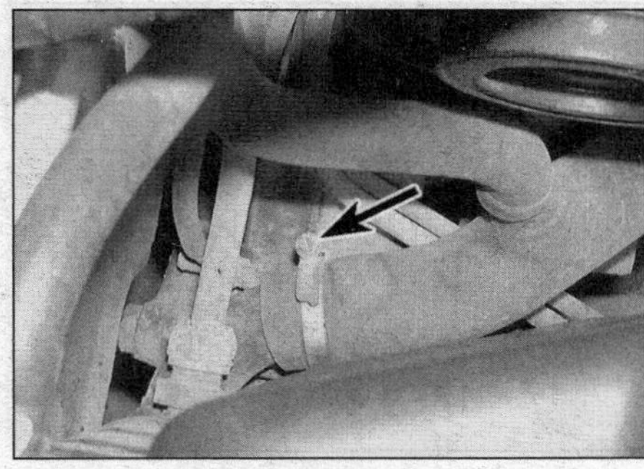

49.3 Radiator bottom hose connection (arrowed)

Antifreeze mixture

14 Always use an ethylene-glycol based antifreeze which is suitable for use in mixed-metal cooling systems. The quantity of antifreeze and levels of protection are indicated in the Specifications.

15 Before adding antifreeze, the cooling system should be completely drained, preferably flushed, and all hoses and clips checked for condition and security.

16 After filling with antifreeze, a label should be attached to the radiator or expansion tank, stating the type and concentration of antifreeze used, and the date installed. Any subsequent topping-up should be made with the same type and concentration of antifreeze.

Cooling system filling

17 Before attempting to fill the cooling system, make sure that all hoses and clips are in good condition, and that the clips are tight. Note that an antifreeze mixture must be used all year round, to prevent corrosion of the alloy engine components.

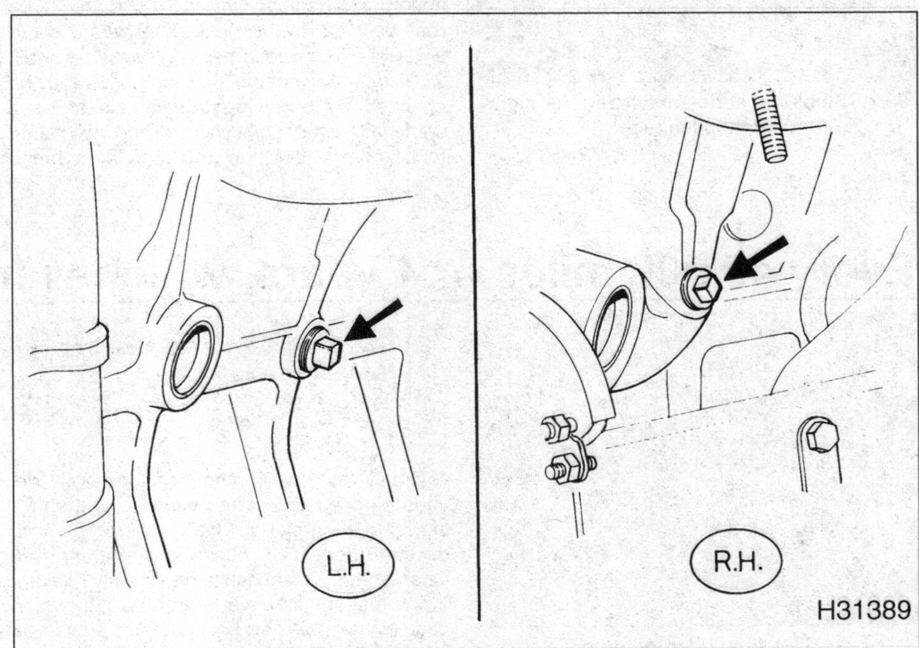
L.H.
R.H.
H31389

49.4 Engine block drain plugs (arrowed)

49.18 Removing the radiator filler cap

18 Remove the expansion tank cap, and (if not already done) unscrew the filler cap from the top of the radiator **(see illustration)**. In both cases, check the cap sealing ring (where fitted), and renew it if it shows signs of damage or deterioration.

19 Fill the system slowly to prevent airlocks from forming. Pour the coolant mixture into the expansion tank until coolant free of air bubbles emerges from the radiator filler. Refit the radiator filler cap, tightening it securely, and add more coolant until the level in the expansion tank is correct. Refit and tighten the expansion tank cap.

20 Start the engine and run it until it reaches normal operating temperature, then stop the engine and allow it to cool for several hours (preferably overnight).

21 Check for leaks, particularly around disturbed components.

22 Check the coolant level in the expansion tank, and top-up if necessary. Note that the system must be cold before an accurate level is indicated in the expansion tank.

Airlocks

23 If, after draining and refilling the system, symptoms of overheating are found which did not occur previously, then the fault is almost certainly due to trapped air at some point in the system, causing an airlock and restricting the flow of coolant; usually, the air is trapped because the system was refilled too quickly.

24 If an airlock is suspected, first try gently squeezing all visible coolant hoses. A coolant hose which is full of air feels quite different to one full of coolant, when squeezed. After refilling the system, most airlocks will clear once the system has cooled, and been topped-up.

25 While the engine is running at operating temperature, switch on the heater and heater fan, and check for heat output. Provided there is sufficient coolant in the system, lack of heat output could be due to an airlock in the system.

26 Airlocks can have more serious effects than simply reducing heater output - a severe airlock could reduce coolant flow around the engine. Check that the radiator top hose is hot when the engine is at operating temperature - a top hose which stays cold could be the result of an airlock (or a non-opening thermostat).

27 If the problem persists, stop the engine and allow it to cool down **completely**, before unscrewing the expansion tank filler cap or partially disconnecting hoses to bleed out the trapped air. In the worst case, the system will have to be at least partially drained (this time, the coolant can be saved for re-use) and flushed to clear the problem.

Every 36 000 miles or 3 years, whichever comes first

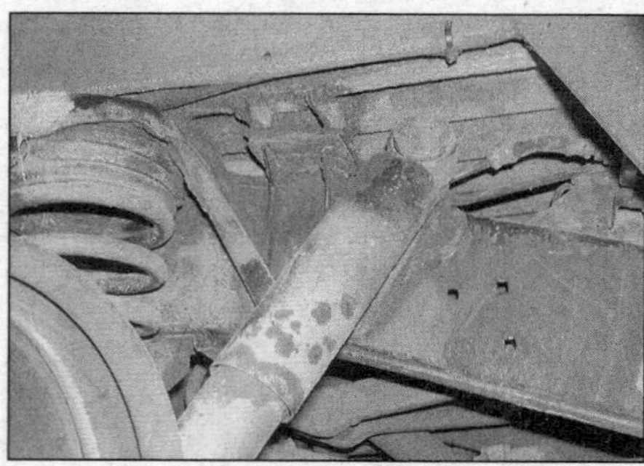

50.1 Check the shock absorbers for signs of fluid leakage

50 Shock absorber check

1 Check for any signs of fluid leakage around the shock absorber body, or from the rubber gaiter around the piston rod **(see illustration)**. Should any fluid be noticed, the shock absorber is defective internally and should be renewed. **Note:** *Shock absorbers should always be renewed in pairs on the same axle.*

2 The efficiency of the shock absorber may be checked by bouncing the vehicle at each corner. Generally speaking, the body will return to its normal position and stop after being depressed. If it rises and returns on a rebound, the shock absorber is probably suspect. Examine also the shock absorber upper and lower mountings for any signs of wear.

51 Braking system seal, vacuum servo filter and hose renewal

Land Rover recommend that all the braking system and rubber hoses are renewed, and the hydraulic system filled with fresh fluid. At the same time, the vacuum servo unit filter should also be renewed. Refer to the relevant Sections of Chapter 10 for renewal information.

Every 48 000 miles or 4 years, whichever comes first

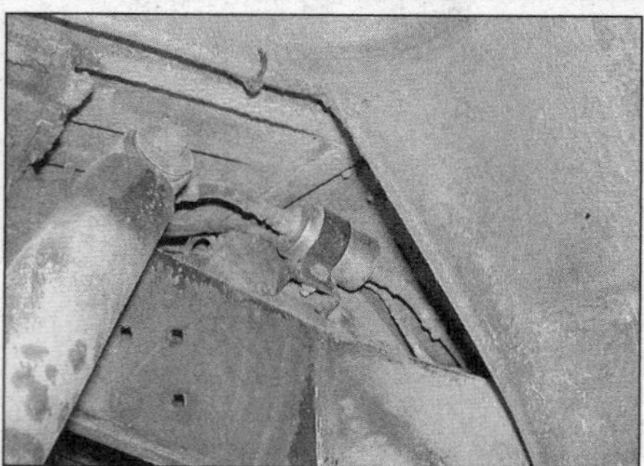

53.3 Fuel filter location

52 Evaporative emission control system check

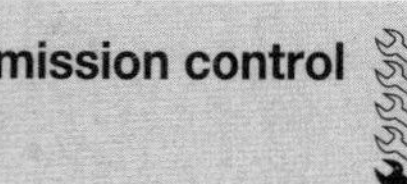

Check all the engine vacuum and fuel vapour hoses associated with the system for signs of cracking, leaks, and general deterioration. For more information, see Chapter 4D. This check is particularly relevant if any fuel smells have been noted, in which case all fuel pipes and connections should be closely inspected.

53 Fuel filter renewal

Warning: Ensure that this operation is carried out in a well-ventilated area.

1 Depressurise the fuel system as described in Chapter 4B.

2 Disconnect the battery negative terminal.

3 The fuel filter is accessed through the right-hand rear wheel arch **(see illustration)**. Loosen the right-hand rear wheel nuts, then jack up the rear of the vehicle and support it on stands (see *Jacking and vehicle support*). Remove the right-hand rear roadwheel.

4 Using pipe clamps, clamp the inlet and outlet hoses at the fuel filter. If only one clamp is available, clamp the inlet hose **(see illustration)**.

5 Slacken the fuel pipe unions and disconnect the inlet and outlet pipes **(see illustration)**. Plug the pipe ends after removal to prevent dirt ingress.

6 Unscrew the filter clamp bolt and remove the filter from the clamp. Note the fitted position of the direction-of-flow arrow on the filter body, and ensure that the new filter is fitted with the arrow pointing the same way **(see illustration)**.

7 Refitting is the reversal of removal, noting the following points:

a) *Tighten the fuel pipe unions to the specified torque, then remove the hose clamps.*

b) *Before lowering the vehicle, reconnect the battery and switch on the ignition without starting the engine. This will pressurise the fuel system (the fuel pump should briefly run). With the system pressurised, check carefully around the disturbed connections for signs of leakage.*

c) *On completion, refit the rear wheel and lower the vehicle to the ground. Tighten the wheel nuts to the specified torque.*

d) *If, after renewing the filter, any petrol smell is noted, trace and rectify the cause without delay.*

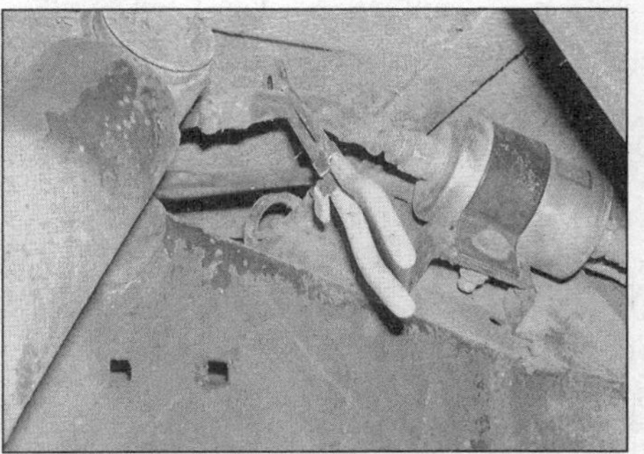

53.4 Clamp the fuel inlet hose before disconnecting

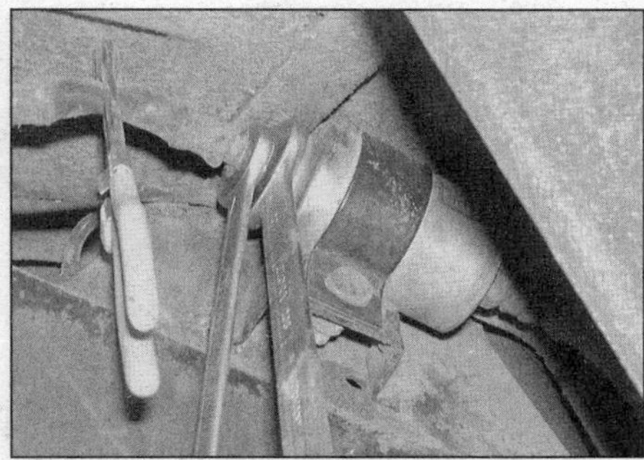

53.5 Slacken the fuel unions as shown

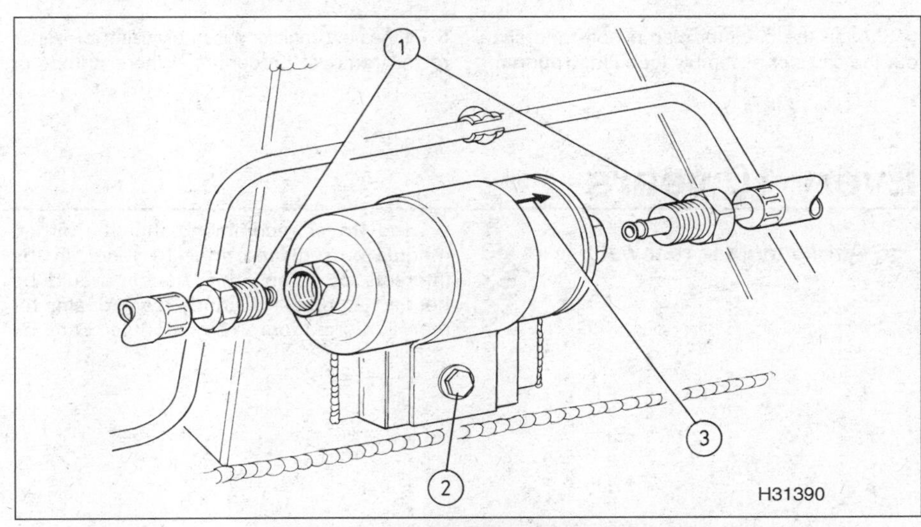
1
2
3
H31390

53.6 Fuel filter removal details

1 Fuel unions *2 Filter clamp bolt* *3 Fuel direction-of-flow arrow*

Every 96 000 miles

54 Emission control component renewal

1 Land Rover recommend that the charcoal canister, exhaust gas oxygen sensors, and catalytic converters be renewed at this mileage. For more information, refer to Chapter 4D - the sensors and converters need only be renewed if they are no longer effective, and this can only be established using emissions testing equipment.

Charcoal canister renewal

2 Disconnect the battery negative lead.

3 Disconnect the wiring multi-plug from the purge valve on top of the canister **(see illustration)**.

4 Noting their locations, loosen the hose clips and disconnect the purge valve (upper) and fuel tank (lower) hoses from the top of the canister. It may be necessary to cut the clips to remove them - make sure suitable replacement clips are available **(see illustrations)**.

54.3 Disconnect the wiring plug from the purge valve

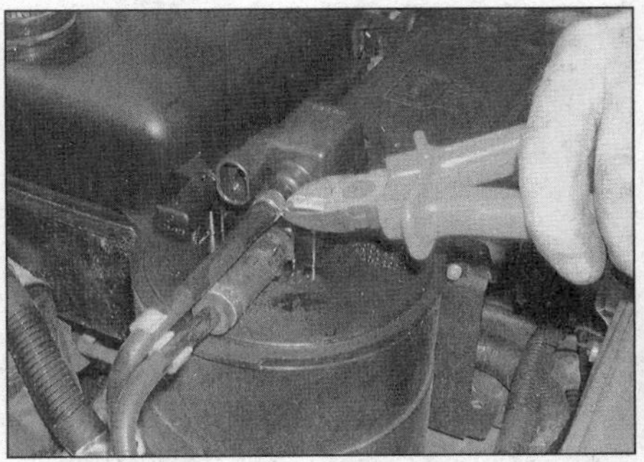

54.4a The crimped clip on the upper hose had to be cut . . .

54.4b . . . before the hose could be disconnected

54.4c Disconnecting the fuel tank hose from the charcoal canister

54.5a Loosen the canister clamp bolt . . .

54.5b . . . then withdraw the canister from the engine compartment

5 Loosen the canister clamp bolt, and slide out the canister assembly **(see illustrations)**.

6 Fit the new canister assembly using a reversal of the removal procedure. Where crimp- or spring-type clips were used, replace these with screw-type fuel pipe clips when reassembling.

Every 10 years

55 Airbag module renewal

Land Rover recommend that the airbag module be replaced after 10 years. In the interests of safety, this advice should be heeded - consult a Land Rover dealer for more information. The module can be removed and refitted as described in Chapter 13, but on completion, its operation should be checked by a Land Rover dealer.

Chapter 1 Part B:
Routine maintenance & servicing - diesel models

Contents

Degrees of difficulty

Easy, suitable for novice with little experience 

Fairly easy, suitable for beginner with some experience 

Fairly difficult, suitable for competent DIY mechanic 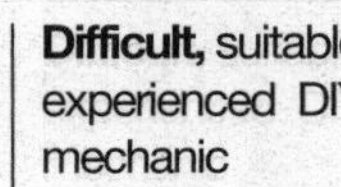

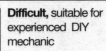

Difficult, suitable for experienced DIY mechanic 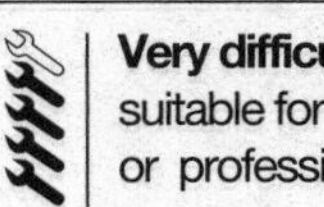

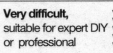

Very difficult, suitable for expert DIY or professional

Servicing specifications - diesel models

Lubricants and fluids

Refer to end of *Weekly checks* on page 0•17

Capacities

Engine oil:	
Sump capacity (drain and refill, including oil filter):	
200 TDi engine	6.9 litres
300 TDi engine	6.7 litres
Cooling system:	
Manual transmission models	11.5 litres
Automatic transmission models	11.7 litres
Manual transmission	2.7 litres
Automatic transmission	9.8 litres
Transfer gearbox:	
Up to suffix D	2.3 litres
From suffix E	2.8 litres
Front axle	1.7 litres
Rear axle	1.7 litres
Steering box and power steering reservoir:	
Right-hand-drive models	3.4 litres
Left-hand-drive models	2.9 litres
Swivel pin housing oil (each)	0.35 litre
Fuel tank:	
Models built up to March 1993	81.8 litres
Models built from April 1993	89.0 litres
Washer fluid reservoir	7.0 litres

Engine

Valve clearances (inlet and exhaust)	0.20 mm

Cooling system

Antifreeze mixture:	
Minimum strength	25% antifreeze, 75% water
Maximum strength	60% antifreeze, 40% water
Protection to -36°C	50% antifreeze, 50% water

Fuel system

Glow plugs	Bosch 0 250 202 040
Turbocharger maximum boost pressure	0.8 to 1.0 bar

Brakes

Minimum front brake disc pad thickness	3.0 mm
Minimum rear brake disc pad thickness	3.0 mm

Tyre pressures

Refer to end of *Weekly checks* on page 0•18

Torque wrench settings

	Nm	lbf ft
Engine sump drain plug:		
200 TDi engine	45	33
300 TDi engine	35	26
Propeller shaft and rubber coupling securing bolts	47	35
Roadwheel nuts	129	95
Transfer gearbox oil drain plug	30	22
Transfer gearbox oil filler/level plug	30	22

The maintenance intervals in this manual are provided with the assumption that you, not the dealer, will be carrying out the work. These are the minimum intervals recommended for vehicles driven daily. If you wish to keep your vehicle in peak condition at all times, you may wish to perform some of these procedures more often. We encourage frequent maintenance, since it enhances the efficiency, performance and resale value of your vehicle.

When the vehicle is new, it should be serviced by a dealer service department, in order to preserve the factory warranty.

Every 250 miles (400 km) or weekly

- ☐ Refer to *Weekly checks*

Every 6000 miles (10 000 km) or 6 months, whichever comes first

- ☐ Renew the engine oil and filter (Section 3)
- ☐ Check and if necessary adjust the valve clearances* (Section 4)
- ☐ Check the battery electrolyte level, where possible (Section 5)
- ☐ Check and if necessary adjust the engine idle speed* (Section 6)

**Check at first 6000 miles (10 000 km), then at 12 000 miles (20 000 km) intervals*

Every 12 000 miles (20 000 km) or 12 months, whichever comes first

In addition to all the items listed above, carry out the following:

- ☐ Check the clutch fluid level (Section 7)
- ☐ Check the automatic transmission fluid level (Section 8)
- ☐ Renew the fuel filter element (Section 9)
- ☐ Renew the air cleaner element (Section 10)
- ☐ Clean the engine breather filter (Section 11)
- ☐ Check the cooling and heater system hoses for security and leaks (Section 12)
- ☐ Check the brake vacuum servo hose for security (Section 13)
- ☐ Check the condition and security of the glow plug wiring (Section 14)
- ☐ Check the condition of the crankcase breather system hoses (Section 15)
- ☐ Check the condition of the air cleaner dump valve - 200 TDi engine models (Section 16)
- ☐ Check the condition of the auxiliary drivebelt(s), and adjust if necessary (Section 17)
- ☐ Check the operation of the accelerator mechanism, and lubricate the moving components (Section 18)
- ☐ Check and if necessary adjust the steering gear backlash (Section 19)
- ☐ Check the security of the jack and tools (Section 20)
- ☐ Renew the manual transmission fluid (Section 21)
- ☐ Check the transfer gearbox oil level (Section 22)
- ☐ Check the front and rear axle oil levels (Section 23)
- ☐ Check the swivel pin housing oil level (Section 24)
- ☐ Lubricate the propeller shaft universal joints and sliding joints (Section 25)
- ☐ Lubricate the handbrake linkage (Section 26)
- ☐ Check all underbody pipes and hoses for leaks and condition (Section 27)

Every 12 000 miles (20 000 km) or 12 months, whichever comes first (continued)

- ☐ Check the exhaust system for security and condition (Section 28)
- ☐ Check the steering and suspension components, including all hydraulic pipes and hoses, for leaks and condition (Section 29)
- ☐ Check the tightness of the propeller shaft coupling bolts (Section 30)
- ☐ Check the front and rear axle breathers for obstructions (Section 31)
- ☐ Clean the fuel sedimenter (Section 32)
- ☐ Drain the flywheel housing and timing belt housing, where applicable (Section 33)
- ☐ Check the security of the fuel tank (Section 34)
- ☐ Check the security of the towing bracket (Section 35)
- ☐ Check the handbrake adjustment (Section 36)
- ☐ Carry out a road test (Section 37)
- ☐ Check and if necessary adjust the headlight and auxiliary light adjustment (Section 38)
- ☐ Check the operation of the sunroof(s), and clear sunroof drain tubes (Section 39)
- ☐ Check the front wheel alignment (Section 40)
- ☐ Check the condition of the brake pads and discs (Section 41)
- ☐ Check the condition of the spare wheel (Section 42)
- ☐ Check and lubricate all door, bonnet and tailgate locks (Section 43)
- ☐ Check the condition and operation of all seat belts (Section 44)

Every 24 000 miles (40 000 km) or 2 years, whichever comes first

In addition to all the items listed above, carry out the following:

- ☐ Renew the transfer gearbox oil (Section 45)
- ☐ Renew the front and rear axle oil (Section 46)
- ☐ Renew the swivel pin housing oil (Section 47)
- ☐ Check the turbocharger boost pressure (Section 48)
- ☐ Renew the automatic transmission fluid and oil screen (Section 49)

Every 2 years, regardless of mileage

- ☐ Renew the brake fluid (Section 50)
- ☐ Renew the coolant (Section 51)

Continued overleaf . . .

Every 36 000 miles (60 000 km) or 3 years, whichever comes first

In addition to all the items listed above, carry out the following:

- ☐ Check all shock absorbers for condition and operation (Section 52)
- ☐ Renew all braking system hydraulic fluid seals, the vacuum servo filter, and all flexible brake fluid hoses (Section 53)
- ☐ Renew the timing belt (Section 54)

Note: *The normal interval for timing belt renewal is 72 000 miles (100 000 km), it is strongly recommended that the interval is halved to 36 000 miles (60 000 km) or 3 years, particularly on vehicles which are subjected to intensive use, ie. mainly short journeys, stop-start driving, off-road driving or towing. Land Rover recommend this shorter interval in any case for vehicles used in dusty conditions or high ambient temperatures. The actual belt renewal interval is therefore very much up to the individual owner, but bear in mind that severe engine damage will result if the belt breaks.*

Every 48 000 miles (80 000 km) or 4 years, whichever comes first

- ☐ Clean the intercooler element (Section 55)

Every 96 000 miles (154 000 km)

- ☐ Check and renew the catalytic converter, if applicable (Section 56)

Every 10 years

- ☐ Renew the airbag module, where applicable (Section 57)

Maintenance - component location

Underbonnet view of a 300 TDi engine model

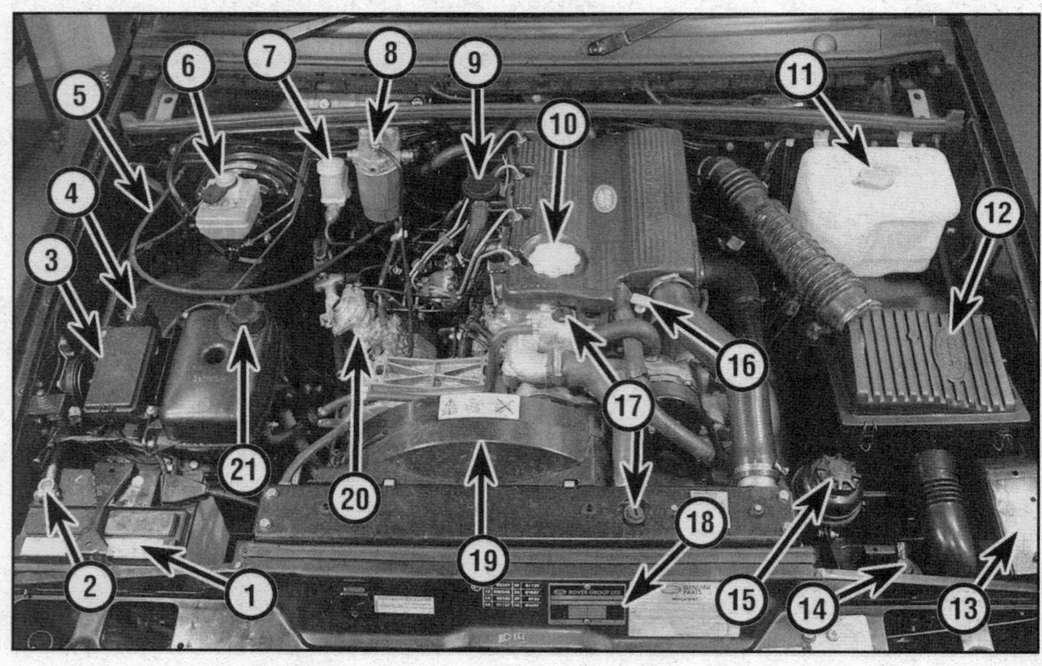
1
2
3
4
5
6
7
8
9
10
11
12
13
14
15
16
17
18
19
20
21

1. *Battery*
2. *Battery negative lead*
3. *Fusebox*
4. *Preheating system relay/timer unit*
5. *Accelerator cable*
6. *Brake fluid reservoir*
7. *Clutch fluid reservoir*
8. *Fuel filter assembly*
9. *Engine breather filter*
10. *Engine oil filler cap*
11. *Washer fluid reservoir*
12. *Air cleaner casing*
13. *Wheel chock*
14. *Jack*
15. *Power steering fluid reservoir*
16. *Engine oil level dipstick*
17. *Cooling system bleed screw*
18. *VIN plate*
19. *Cooling fan cowl*
20. *Fuel injection pump*
21. *Coolant expansion tank cap*

Front underbody view

1 *Crankshaft pulley*
2 *Exhaust*
3 *Sump*
4 *Gearbox bellhousing*
5 *Drag link*
6 *Track rod*
7 *Panhard rod*
8 *Anti-roll bar*
9 *Steering damper*
10 *Steering box*
11 *Swivel pin housing*
12 *Radius arm*

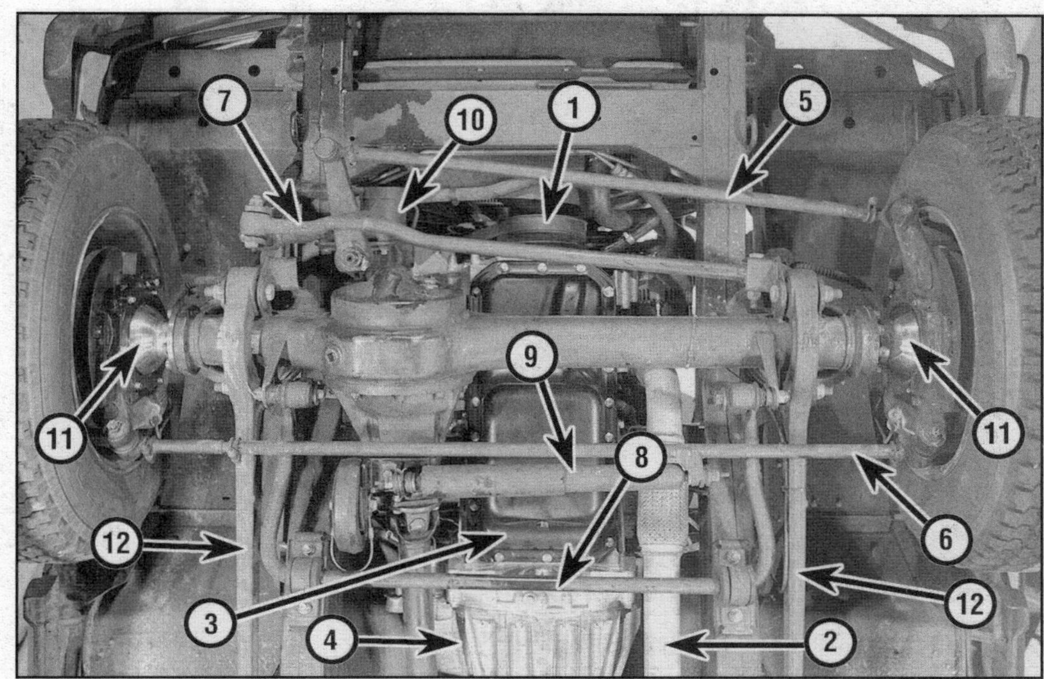
7
10
1
5
9
11
11
8
6
12
12
3
4
2

Centre underbody view

1 *Crankshaft pulley*
2 *Sump drain plug*
3 *Exhaust*
4 *Handbrake drum*
5 *Transfer gearbox*
6 *Front propeller shaft*
7 *Main gearbox bellhousing*

2
3
1
7
6
5
4

Rear underbody view

3
4
7
6
6
5
8
1
2
5

1 *Fuel sedimenter*
2 *Exhaust*
3 *Fuel tank*
4 *Anti-roll bar*
5 *Lower link*
6 *Shock absorber*
7 *Differential unit*
8 *Upper links*

Maintenance procedures

1 Introduction

This Chapter is designed to help the home mechanic maintain his/her vehicle for safety, economy, long life and peak performance.

The Chapter contains a master maintenance schedule, followed by Sections dealing specifically with each task in the schedule. Visual checks, adjustments, component renewal and other helpful items are included. Refer to the accompanying illustrations of the engine compartment and the underside of the vehicle for the locations of the various components.

Servicing your vehicle in accordance with the mileage/time maintenance schedule and the following Sections will provide a planned maintenance programme, which should result in a long and reliable service life. This is a comprehensive plan, so maintaining some items but not others at the specified service intervals will not produce the same results.

As you service your vehicle, you will discover that many of the procedures can - and should - be grouped together, because of the particular procedure being performed, or because of the proximity of two otherwise unrelated components to one another. For example, if the vehicle is raised for any reason, the exhaust can be inspected at the same time as the suspension and steering components.

The first step in this maintenance programme is to prepare yourself before the actual work begins. Read through all the Sections relevant to the work to be carried out, then make a list and gather all the parts and tools required. If a problem is encountered, seek advice from a parts specialist, or a dealer service department.

2 Regular maintenance

1 If, from the time the vehicle is new, the routine maintenance schedule is followed closely, and frequent checks are made of fluid levels and high-wear items, as suggested throughout this manual, the engine will be kept in relatively good running condition, and the need for additional work will be minimised.

2 It is possible that there will be times when the engine is running poorly due to lack of regular maintenance. This is even more likely if a used vehicle, which has not received regular and frequent maintenance checks, is purchased. In such cases, additional work may need to be carried out, outside of the regular maintenance intervals.

3 If engine wear is suspected, a compression test (refer to the relevant Part of Chapter 2) will provide valuable information regarding the overall performance of the main internal components. Such a test can be used as a basis to decide on the extent of the work to be carried out. If, for example, a compression test indicates serious internal engine wear, conventional maintenance as described in this Chapter will not greatly improve the performance of the engine, and may prove a waste of time and money, unless extensive overhaul work is carried out first.

4 The following series of operations are those most often required to improve the performance of a generally poor-running engine:

Primary operations

a) Clean, inspect and test the battery (See Weekly checks, Section 5 and Chapter 5A).
b) Check all the engine-related fluids (See Weekly checks).
c) Drain the water from the fuel filter (Section 9).
d) Check the condition and tension of the auxiliary drivebelt(s) (Section 17).
e) Check the condition of the air filter, and renew if necessary (Section 10).
f) Check the condition of all hoses, and check for fluid leaks (Sections 12 and 15).
g) Check the engine idle speed setting (Chapter 4C).

5 If the above operations do not prove fully effective, carry out the following secondary operations:

Secondary operations

All items listed under *Primary operations*, plus the following:

a) Check the charging system (see Chapter 5A).
b) Check the preheating system (see Chapter 5C).
c) Renew the fuel filter (Section 9) and check the fuel system (see Chapter 4C).

3.4 Slackening the sump drain plug

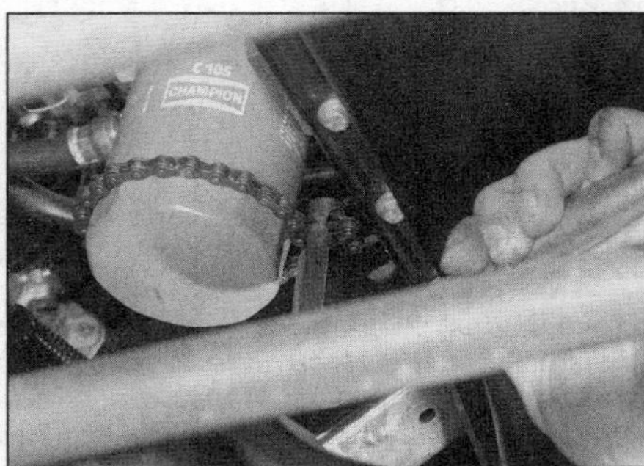
CHAMPION
3.8 Slackening the oil filter using a chain wrench

4.3 Measuring a valve clearance

Every 6000 miles or 6 months, whichever comes first

3 Engine oil and filter renewal

HAYNES
HiNT

Frequent oil and filter changes are the most important preventative maintenance procedures that can be undertaken by the DIY owner. As engine oil ages, it becomes diluted and contaminated, which leads to premature engine wear.

1 Before starting this procedure, gather together all the necessary tools and materials. Also make sure that you have plenty of clean rags and newspapers handy, to mop up any spills. Ideally, the engine oil should be warm, as it will drain better and more built-up sludge will be removed with it. Take care, however, not to touch the exhaust or any other hot parts of the engine when working under the vehicle. To avoid any possibility of scalding, and to protect yourself from possible skin irritants and other harmful contaminants in used engine oils, it is advisable to wear rubber gloves when carrying out this work.

2 Access to the underside of the vehicle will be greatly improved if it can be raised on a lift, driven onto ramps, or jacked up and supported on axle stands (see *Jacking and vehicle support*). Whichever method is chosen, make sure that the vehicle remains as level as possible, to enable the oil to drain fully.

3 Remove the oil filler cap from the valve cover, then position a suitable container beneath the sump.

4 Clean the drain plug (located at the bottom left-hand side of the sump) and the area around it, then slacken it using a suitable socket or spanner **(see illustration)**. If possible, try to keep the plug pressed into the sump while unscrewing it by hand the last couple of turns. As the plug releases from the threads, move it away sharply, so that the stream of oil issuing from the sump runs into the container, not up your sleeve.

5 Allow some time for the old oil to drain, noting that it may be necessary to reposition the container as the oil flow slows to a trickle.

6 After all the oil has drained, wipe off the drain plug with a clean rag, and check the condition of the copper sealing washer. Renew the washer if necessary. Clean the area around the drain plug opening, then refit and tighten the plug to the specified torque setting.

7 Move the container into position under the oil filter, screwed onto the adapter on the right-hand side of the cylinder block.

8 Using an oil filter removal tool if necessary, slacken the filter initially **(see illustration)**. Loosely wrap some rags around the oil filter, then unscrew it, and immediately position it with its open end uppermost to prevent further spillage of oil. Remove the oil filter from the engine compartment, and empty the oil into the container.

9 Use a clean rag to remove all oil, dirt and sludge from the filter sealing area on the engine. Check the old filter to make sure that the rubber sealing ring hasn't stuck to the engine. If it has, carefully remove it.

10 Apply a light coating of clean oil to the sealing ring on the new filter, then screw it into position on the engine. Tighten the filter firmly by hand only - do not use any tools. Wipe clean the exterior of the oil filter.

11 Remove the old oil and all tools from under the vehicle, then (if applicable) lower the vehicle to the ground.

12 Fill the engine with the specified quantity and grade of oil. Pour the oil in slowly, otherwise it may overflow from the top of the valve cover. Check that the oil level is up to the correct level on the dipstick (see *Weekly checks*), then refit and tighten the oil filler cap.

13 Run the engine for a few minutes, and check that there are no leaks around the oil filter seal and the sump drain plug.

14 Switch off the engine, and wait a few minutes for the oil to settle in the sump once more. With the new oil circulated and the filter now completely full, recheck the level on the dipstick, and add more oil if necessary.

15 Dispose of the used engine oil safely with reference to *General repair procedures* in the Reference Section of this manual.

4 Valve clearances checking and adjustment

Warning: If the crankshaft is rotated with excessive valve clearances, it is possible for the pushrods to become dislodged, and fracture the tappet slides. To prevent the possibility of damage, turn the adjusters to eliminate all clearance from any loose rocker arms before turning the crankshaft to check the valve clearances.

1 Remove the valve cover, as described in Chapter 2B.

2 Using a spanner or socket on the crankshaft pulley bolt (the bolt is most easily reached from underneath the vehicle), turn the crankshaft until No 8 valve is fully open (valve spring fully compressed). The valves are numbered from the front of the engine. Turning the engine will be much easier if the glow plugs are removed first - see Chapter 5C.

3 Using a feeler blade of the specified thickness (refer to the Specifications at the start of this Chapter), check the clearance between the top of No 1 valve stem, and the valve stem contact face of the rocker arm**(see illustration)**.

4 If the clearance is not as specified, slacken the adjuster locknut, and turn the tappet adjuster screw as required to give the specified clearance **(see illustration)**. Turn the adjuster

4.4 Adjusting a valve clearance

screw clockwise to reduce the clearance, and anti-clockwise to increase the clearance.

5 When the clearance is correct, tighten the adjuster locknut. Hold the adjuster screw stationary as the locknut is tightened.

6 With the locknut tightened, re-check the clearance, and re-adjust if necessary.

7 Turn the crankshaft, and continue to check the remaining valve clearances in the following order.

Valve fully open	Valve clearance to be checked
No 6	*No 3*
No 4	*No 5*
No 7	*No 2*
No 1	*No 8*
No 3	*No 6*
No 5	*No 4*
No 2	*No 7*

8 When all the valve clearances have been checked, refit the valve cover as described in Chapter 2B.

5 Battery electrolyte level check

Warning: The electrolyte inside a battery is diluted acid - it is a good idea to wear suitable rubber gloves. When topping-up, don't overfill the cells so that the electrolyte overflows. In the event of any spillage, rinse the electrolyte off without delay. Refit the cell covers and rinse the battery with copious quantities of clean water. Don't attempt to siphon out any excess electrolyte.

1 The battery is located in the front right-hand corner of the engine compartment. Where applicable, unclip and remove the cover from the top of the battery.

2 Some models covered by this manual will be fitted with a maintenance-free battery as standard equipment, or may have had one fitted as a replacement. If the battery in your vehicle is marked 'Freedom', 'Maintenance-Free' or similar, electrolyte level checking may not be possible (the battery is often completely sealed, preventing any topping-up).

3 Batteries which do require their electrolyte level to be checked can be recognised by the presence of removable covers over the six battery cells - the battery casing is also sometimes translucent, so that the electrolyte level can be more easily checked.

4 Remove the cell caps or covers (these either unscrew, or are prised/pulled out), and look down inside the battery to see the level webs or the separators between the cells. The electrolyte should cover the battery plates (maximum 3 mm above the plates), and should be up to the level of the indicator webs or separators. If markings are provided on the battery casing, these can be used instead.

5 If necessary, top up a little at a time with distilled (de-ionised) water until the level in all six cells is correct - don't fill the cells up to the brim. Wipe up any spillage, then refit the cell covers.

6 Further information on the battery, charging and jump starting can be found at the start of this manual and in Chapter 5A.

6 Idle speed checking and adjustment

Refer to Chapter 4C.

Every 12 000 miles or 12 months, whichever comes first

7 Clutch fluid level check

Warning: Hydraulic fluid is poisonous; wash off immediately and thoroughly in the case of skin contact, and seek immediate medical advice if any fluid is swallowed or gets into the eyes. Hydraulic fluid is also an effective paint stripper, and will attack plastics; if any is spilt, it should be washed off immediately, using copious quantities of clean water. Finally, it is hygroscopic (it absorbs moisture from the air). While this is not as important in the clutch system as it is in the braking system, old fluid may be too contaminated for further use. When topping-up or renewing the fluid, always use the recommended type, and ensure that it comes from a freshly-opened, sealed container.

1 The clutch fluid reservoir is attached to the master cylinder, which is located on the right-hand side of the engine compartment on right-hand-drive models, or on the left-hand side of the engine compartment on left-hand-drive models.

2 On models with level marks on the side of the reservoir, the fluid level should be maintained between the MAX and MIN marks. On models with no level markings, the fluid level should be up to the lower edge of the filler neck on the reservoir.

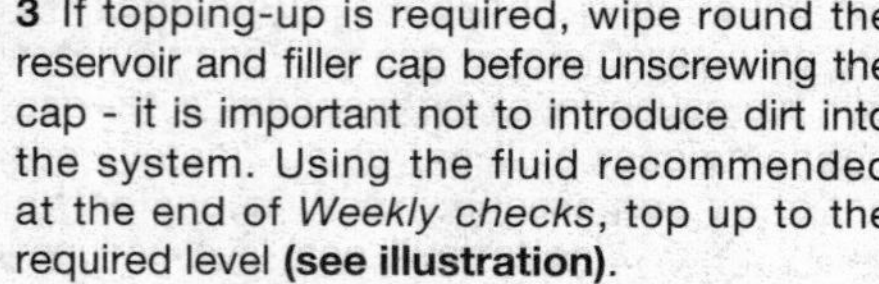

3 If topping-up is required, wipe round the reservoir and filler cap before unscrewing the cap - it is important not to introduce dirt into the system. Using the fluid recommended at the end of *Weekly checks*, top up to the required level **(see illustration)**.

4 On completion, refit the filler cap, tightening it securely, and wipe up or wash away any fluid spillage.

5 There should be no significant drop in fluid level during normal operation of the clutch. Any significant loss of fluid is likely to be due to a leak in the hydraulic system, and should be investigated and corrected.

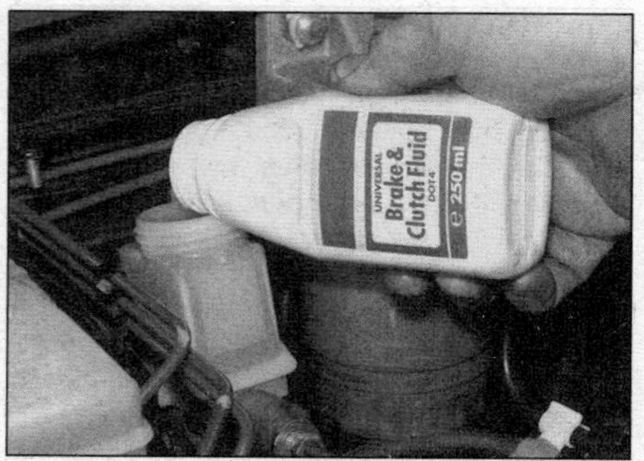
Brake & Clutch Fluid

7.3 Topping-up the clutch fluid level

8 Automatic transmission fluid level check

1 The automatic transmission fluid level is checked with a dipstick which extends through a tube and into the sump at the bottom of the transmission. The dipstick is located on the right-hand side of the engine.

2 The fluid level should be checked with the transmission cold, as follows.

3 Check that the vehicle is parked on level ground.

4 With the handbrake fully applied, and the engine running at normal idle speed, select position P with the transmission selector lever.

5 Withdraw the dipstick from the tube, and wipe it clean.

6 Re-insert the dipstick to its full depth, and remove it for a second time to take a reading.

7 The fluid level should be maintained between the two level marks on the dipstick.

8 If necessary, top-up the fluid level, using the correct type of fluid (see end of *Weekly checks*) through the dipstick tube. **Do not** overfill the transmission. Note that 0.25 litre of fluid will raise the level from the 'low' to the 'high' mark on the dipstick.

9 Ensure that the dipstick is inserted correctly after checking the level.

10 Any significant loss of fluid should be investigated and corrected.

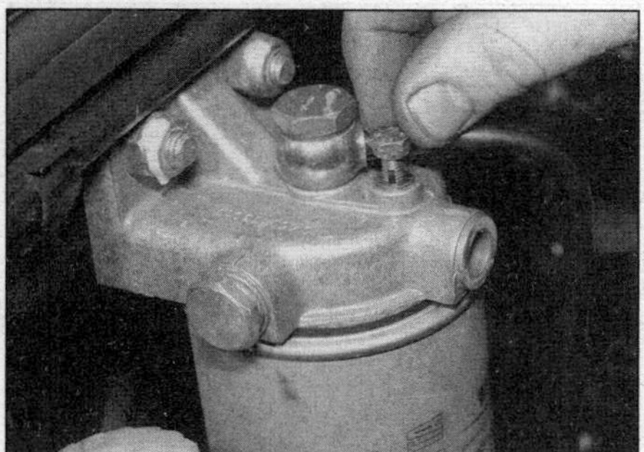
9.2a Loosen the bleed screw . . .

9.2b . . . and unscrew the drain tap (arrowed) to drain the water

9.4 Removing the fuel filter element

9 Fuel filter renewal

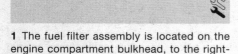

1 The fuel filter assembly is located on the engine compartment bulkhead, to the right-hand side of the engine.

2 Before the filter is renewed, any water present should be drained from the filter bowl as follows:

*a) Loosen the bleed screw on the top of the filter head **(see illustration)**.*

*b) Hold a small container beneath the drain tap at the bottom of the filter, then unscrew the tap by half a turn **(see illustration)**.*

c) Drain off water and sediment until clean fuel flows from the tap.

d) Immediately close the tap when fuel flows from it - failure to do so may result in the fuel system requiring bleeding.

3 Clean the area around the filter head, and place a container beneath the filter.

4 Unscrew the filter, and catch the fuel which is released **(see illustration)**. A strap wrench can be used to grip the base of the filter if necessary.

5 Lubricate the seals of the new filter with a little fuel.

6 Screw the new filter into position, and tighten the filter firmly by hand only.

7 Make sure that the drain tap at the base of the filter is closed.

8 Prime the fuel system by operating the priming lever on the fuel lift pump until fuel free from air bubbles emerges from the bleed screw on the filter head, then tighten the bleed screw.

9 Start the engine and check for leaks around the filter.

10 Air cleaner element renewal

200 TDi engine

1 Working in the engine compartment, slacken the clip at the front of the air cleaner casing, and pull the air outlet ducting from the casing **(see illustration)**.

2 Release the two clips securing the air cleaner body to the mounting bracket, and lift the air cleaner away from the engine compartment, easing the air inlet spout from the inlet on the front body panel.

3 Unscrew the nut securing the air cleaner lid to the body, then withdraw the lid **(see illustration)**.

4 Unscrew the now-exposed wing nut securing the air cleaner element, and recover the sealing washer.

5 Pull the element from the casing, and discard it.

6 Thoroughly clean the inside of the air cleaner casing and the lid.

7 Squeeze open the air cleaner dump valve, which is located at the bottom of the casing. Check that the valve is flexible, and is in good condition.

8 If it needs cleaning, pull the dump valve from the air cleaner casing. Fit a new valve if necessary.

9 Fit the new element to the casing, ensuring that the sealing rubber is towards the air cleaner outlet.

10 Refit the wing nut to the casing, ensuring that the sealing washer is in place, and tighten to secure the element.

11 Refit the air cleaner lid, and tighten the securing nut.

12 Refit the air cleaner to the mounting bracket, ensuring that the air inlet spout engages with the inlet on the front body panel.

13 Push the air outlet ducting into position on the front of the casing, ensuring that the locating lug on the casing engages with the corresponding cut-out in the air outlet ducting elbow. Tighten the clip.

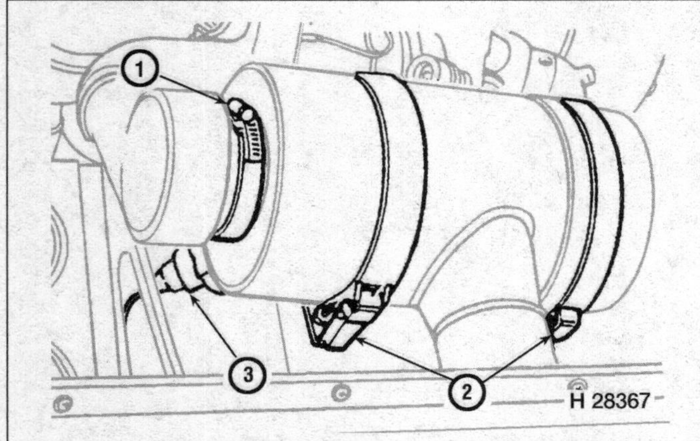
1
2
3
H 28367
10.1 Air cleaner location - 200 TDi engine

1 Air outlet ducting clip
2 Air cleaner mounting clips
3 Dump valve

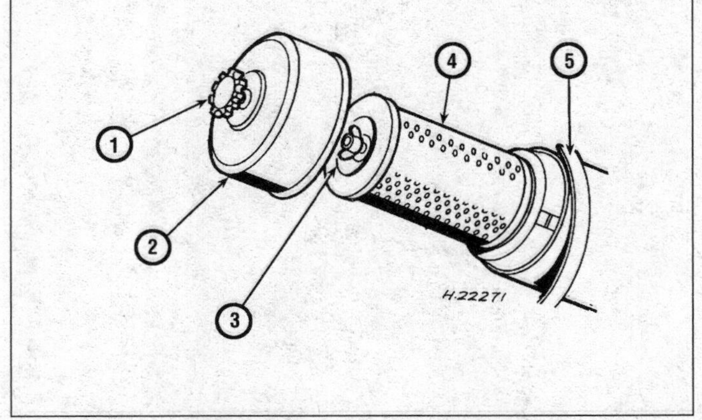
1
2
3
4
5
H.22271
10.3 Air cleaner element components - 200 TDi engine

1 Nut
2 Lid
3 Wing nut
4 Element
5 Mounting clip

10.15 Releasing an air cleaner lid securing clip - 300 TDi engine

14 Secure the air cleaner in position with the two clips.

300 TDi engine

15 Working under the bonnet, release the four clips securing the lid to the air cleaner assembly **(see illustration)**.

16 Lift off the lid, taking care not to strain the air outlet hose, and lift out the element **(see illustration)**.

17 Thoroughly clean the inside of the air cleaner casing and the lid.

18 Fit the new element, then refit the lid and secure with the clips.

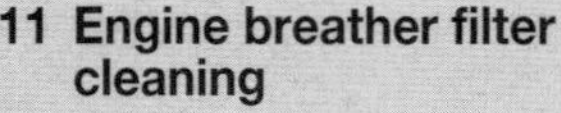

11 Engine breather filter cleaning

Note: *A new gasket will be required when refitting the filter.*

1 The filter is located at the rear right-hand corner of the valve cover **(see illustration)**.

2 Loosen the clips securing the hoses to the top and bottom of the filter, noting their locations to ensure correct refitting.

3 Unscrew the two bolts securing the filter to the valve cover, then carefully pull the filter away from the valve cover, and recover the gasket.

10.16 Lifting out the air cleaner element - 300 TDi engine

4 Fill a suitable container with clean paraffin, then immerse the filter in the paraffin to dissolve any oily deposits which may have formed inside.

5 Once satisfied that the filter is clean, remove it from the paraffin, and dry thoroughly. **Note:** *It is **vital** that the filter is absolutely dry before it is refitted to the engine.*

6 Refit the filter to the valve cover, using a new gasket, and tighten the securing bolts.

7 Reconnect the two hoses to the filter, ensuring that the clips are securely tightened to produce a gas-tight seal.

12 Cooling system and heater system hose check

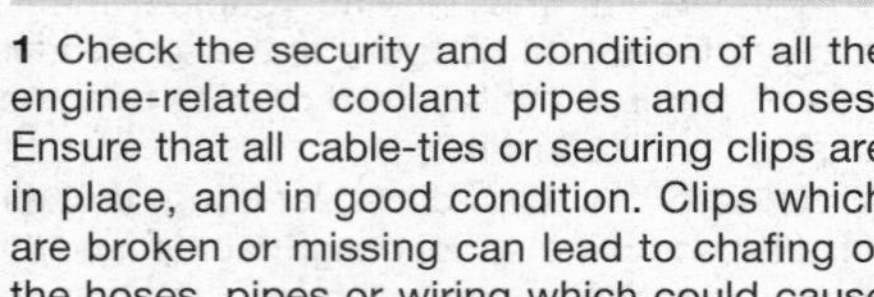

1 Check the security and condition of all the engine-related coolant pipes and hoses. Ensure that all cable-ties or securing clips are in place, and in good condition. Clips which are broken or missing can lead to chafing of the hoses, pipes or wiring which could cause more serious problems in the future.

2 Carefully check the radiator hoses and heater hoses along their entire length. Renew any hose which is cracked, swollen or deteriorated. Cracks will show up better if the hose is squeezed. Pay close attention to the hose clips that secure the hoses to the cooling system components. Hose clips can pinch and puncture hoses, resulting in cooling system leaks. If wire-type hose clips are used, it may be a good idea to replace them with screw-type clips.

HAYNES
HiNT

A leak in the cooling system will usually show up as white or rust-coloured deposits on the area adjoining the leak.

3 Inspect all the cooling system components (hoses, joint faces etc.) for leaks. Where any problems of this nature are found on system components, renew the component or gasket with reference to Chapter 3.

13 Brake vacuum servo hose check

1 Working from the vacuum pump back to the servo unit, examine the vacuum hose for signs of damage or deterioration; at the same time, also check the servo unit check valve rubber grommet. If necessary, renew the hose/grommet, referring to the information given in Chapter 10.

14 Glow plug wiring check

1 Where applicable, to improve access, remove the oil filler cap, and unclip the plastic cover from the valve cover.

2 Check all the glow plug wiring for signs of fraying, chafing and general deterioration **(see illustration)**.

3 Check that the nuts securing the wiring to the glow plugs are secure. Also check the security of the wiring connector at the

11.1 Engine breather filter (arrowed) - 300 TDi engine

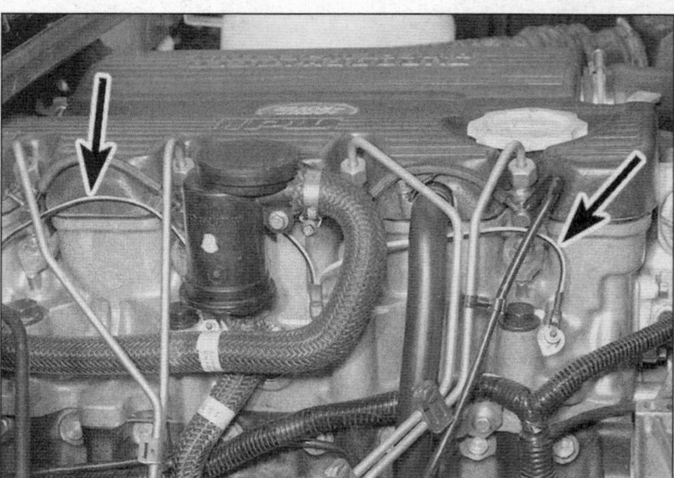

14.2 Check the condition of the glow plug wiring (arrowed)

preheating system relay/timer unit, located on the rear of the fusebox at the right-hand side of the engine compartment (see Chapter 5C).

15 Crankcase breather hose check

1 Check all the engine breather hoses for signs of cracking, leaks, and general deterioration.

2 It is advisable to loosen the hose clips, and remove each hose to check for a build-up of deposits, which may cause restrictions or even blockage. If necessary, clean the hose using paraffin, but ensure that the hose is completely dry before refitting.

16 Air cleaner dump valve check (200 TDi engine models)

Refer to Section 10.

17 Auxiliary drivebelt checking and renewal

200 TDi engine

Cooling fan/coolant pump/power steering pump drivebelt checking and adjustment

1 Correct tensioning of the drivebelt will ensure that it has a long life. Beware, however, of overtightening, as this can cause excessive wear in the ancillary components.

2 To improve access, remove the viscous cooling fan and coupling as described in Chapter 3.

3 The belt should be inspected along its entire length, and if it is found to be worn, frayed or cracked, it should be renewed as a precaution against breakage in service. It is advisable to carry a spare drivebelt of the correct type in the vehicle at all times.

4 The belt tension should be checked at the mid-point of the belt run between the coolant pump and the power steering pump **(see illustration)**.

5 Measure the length of the belt run between the centres of the coolant pump and power steering pump pulleys. Under normal finger pressure, the belt should deflect by 0.5 mm for every 25.0 mm of belt run between pulley centres.

6 If adjustment is required, slacken the front and rear alternator mounting bolts, and the alternator adjuster link mounting bolt at the power steering pump plate.

7 Slacken the bolt securing the alternator to the adjuster link.

8 Slacken the three power steering pump mounting plate bolts, then turn the power steering pump as necessary to achieve the correct belt tension. **Do not** lever against the power steering pump body to move it.

9 When the correct tension is achieved, tighten the power steering pump mounting plate bolts, then re-check the tension and repeat the adjustment procedure if necessary.

10 On completion, adjust the alternator drivebelt tension as described later in this Section.

11 If a new drivebelt has been fitted, start the engine and run it for five minutes at a fast idle, then re-check the tension of both drivebelts and adjust if necessary.

12 Where applicable, refit the viscous fan and coupling as described in Chapter 3.

Cooling fan/coolant pump/power steering pump drivebelt removal and refitting

13 To remove the belt, simply loosen the alternator mounting bolts, the alternator adjuster link bolts, and the power steering pump mounting plate bolts, as described previously, and slacken the belt sufficiently to slip it from the pulleys.

14 Refit the belt and tension it as described previously.

Alternator drivebelt checking and adjustment

15 Proceed as described in paragraphs 1 to 3 inclusive.

16 The belt tension should be checked at the mid-point of the belt run.

17 Measure the length of the belt run between the centres of the power steering pump and alternator pulleys. Under normal finger pressure, the belt should deflect by 0.5 mm for every 25.0 mm of belt run between pulley centres.

18 If adjustment is required, slacken the front and rear alternator mounting bolts, and the alternator adjuster link bolts.

19 Pivot the alternator as necessary to achieve the correct belt tension. **Do not** lever against the alternator body to move it.

20 When the correct tension is achieved, tighten the alternator mounting bolts and the adjuster link bolts, then re-check the tension and repeat the adjustment procedure if necessary.

21 If a new drivebelt has been fitted, start the engine and run it for five minutes at a fast idle, then re-check the tension of both drivebelts and adjust if necessary.

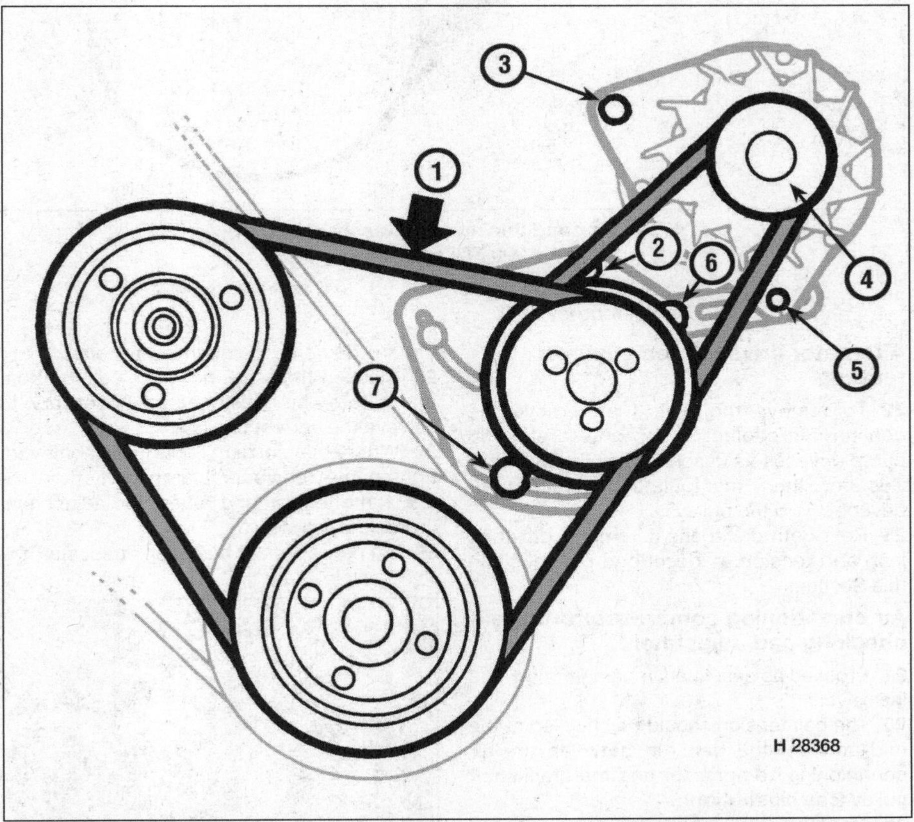
3
1
2
6
4
5
7
H 28368

17.4 Cooling fan/coolant pump/power steering pump drivebelt and alternator drivebelt - 200 TDi engine

1 *Belt tension checking point*
2 *Power steering pump mounting bolts*
3 *Alternator mounting bolt*
4 *Alternator pulley*
5 *Alternator-to-adjuster link bolt*
6 *Adjuster link mounting bolt*
7 *Power steering pump pulley*

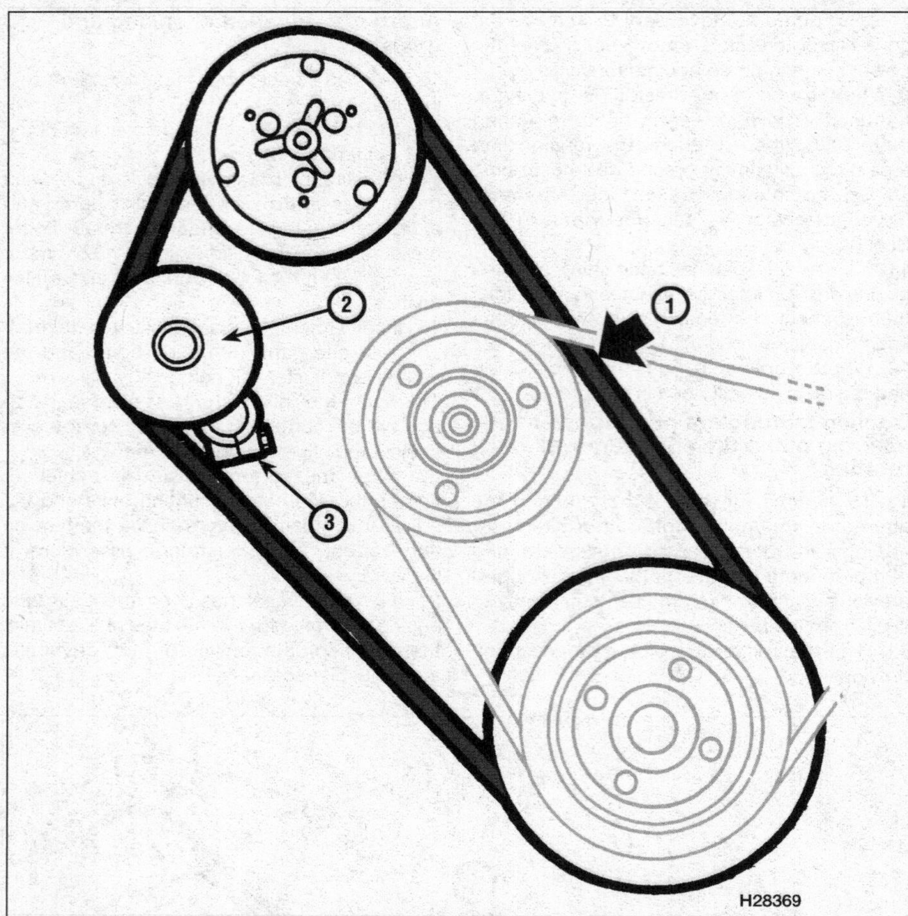
1
2
3
H28369

17.25 Air conditioning compressor drivebelt - 200 TDi engine

1 Belt tension checking point
2 Tensioner pulley
3 Tensioner clamp bolt

Alternator drivebelt removal and refitting

22 To remove the belt, first remove the cooling fan/coolant pump/power steering pump drivebelt as described previously in this Section, then manipulate the alternator drivebelt from the pulleys.

23 Refit both drivebelts (alternator drivebelt last) and tension as described previously in this Section.

Air conditioning compressor drivebelt checking and adjustment

24 Proceed as described in paragraphs 1 to 3 inclusive.

25 The belt tension should be checked at the mid-point of the belt run between the air conditioning compressor and the crankshaft pulley **(see illustration)**.

26 Measure the length of the belt run between the centres of the air conditioning compressor and crankshaft pulleys. Under normal finger pressure, the belt should deflect by 0.5 mm for every 25.0 mm of belt run between pulley centres.

27 If adjustment is required, firstly ensure that the compressor mounting bolts are tight.

28 Slacken the tensioner pulley clamp bolt, and rotate the tensioner as necessary to achieve the correct tension.

29 When the correct tension is achieved, tighten the tensioner clamp bolt, then re-check the tension and repeat the adjustment procedure if necessary.

30 If a new drivebelt has been fitted, start the engine and run it for five minutes at a fast idle, then re-check the tension of both drivebelts and adjust if necessary.

17.40 Levering the belt tensioner to relieve the tension in the drivebelt (viewed with engine removed for clarity) - 300 TDi engine

Air conditioning compressor drivebelt removal and refitting

31 To remove the belt, first remove the cooling fan/coolant pump/power steering pump drivebelt as described previously in this Section.

32 Slacken the air conditioning compressor drivebelt tensioner pulley bolt. Rotate the tensioner as necessary to allow the belt to be slipped from the pulleys.

33 Refit both drivebelts (air conditioning compressor drivebelt last), and tension as described previously in this Section.

300 TDi engine

Cooling fan/coolant pump/power steering pump/alternator drivebelt checking and adjustment

34 Proceed as described in paragraphs 1 to 3 inclusive.

35 An automatic drivebelt tensioner is fitted, and no checking of the tension is necessary, however the belt should be inspected for wear or damage at the recommended intervals.

36 To improve access, remove the cooling fan upper cowl.

37 The belt should be inspected along its entire length, and if it is found to be worn, frayed or cracked, it should be renewed as a precaution against breakage in service. It is advisable to carry a spare drivebelt of the correct type in the vehicle at all times.

38 Refit the upper cooling fan cowl on completion.

Cooling fan/coolant pump/power steering pump/alternator drivebelt removal and refitting

39 Remove the upper cooling fan cowl.

40 Using a suitable ring spanner, lever the belt tensioner pulley retaining bolt to move the tensioner and relieve the tension in the belt **(see illustration)**.

41 Slide the belt from the pulleys, and manipulate it over the viscous fan blades.

42 If the original belt is to be refitted, mark the running direction to ensure correct refitting.

43 Refitting is a reversal of removal, but ensure that the belt is correctly seated on the pulleys.

44 On completion, refit the upper cooling fan cowl.

Air conditioning compressor drivebelt checking and adjustment

45 Proceed as described in paragraphs 1 to 3 inclusive.

46 Correct tensioning of the drivebelt will ensure that it has a long life. Beware, however, of overtightening, as this can cause excessive wear in the ancillary components.

47 To improve access, remove the air conditioning compressor shield.

48 Loosen the three bolts securing the belt tensioner to the timing belt cover **(see illustration)**.
49 Fit a suitable square-drive extension to a torque wrench, and engage the extension with the square hole in the centre of the tensioner.
50 Apply and hold a torque of 35 Nm (26 lbf ft), then tighten the tensioner securing bolts.
51 Rotate the engine through two full turns.
52 Again, apply and hold a torque of 35 Nm (26 lbf ft) to the tensioner pulley, then fully loosen and tighten the tensioner securing bolts. Tighten the bolts securely.
53 Refit the air conditioning compressor shield.

Air conditioning compressor drivebelt removal and refitting

54 Remove the cooling fan/coolant pump/ power steering pump/alternator drivebelt, as described previously in this Section.
55 Remove the air conditioning compressor shield.
56 Loosen the three belt tensioner securing bolts, then move the tensioner sufficiently to allow the belt to be removed.
57 If the original belt is to be refitted, mark the running direction to ensure correct refitting.
58 Refit and tension the belt as described previously in this Section.

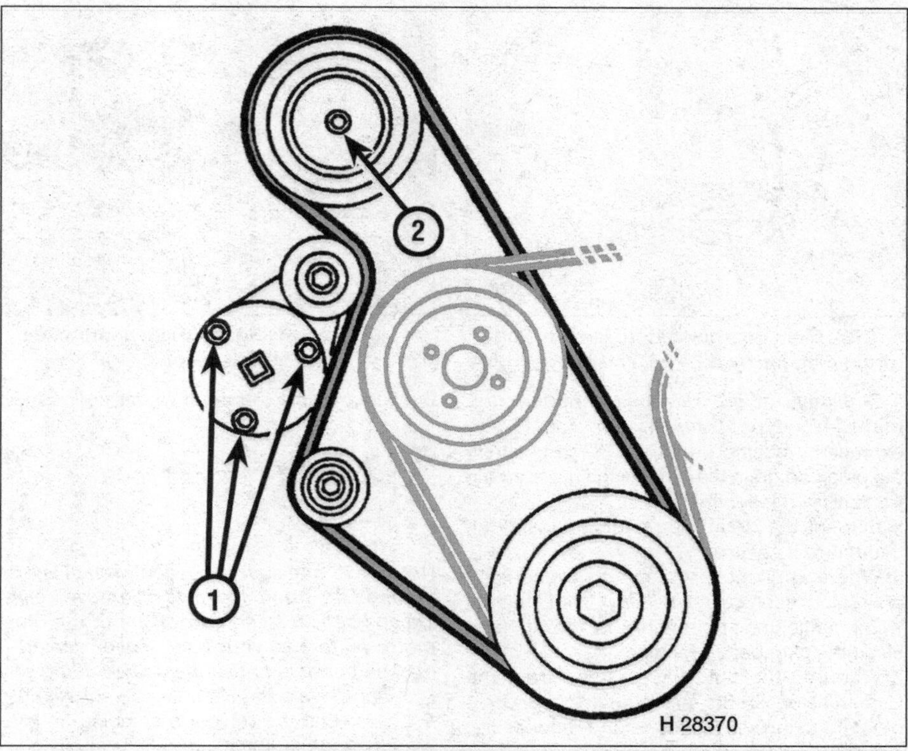
2
1
H 28370

17.48 Air conditioning compressor drivebelt - 300 TDi engine

1 Tensioner securing bolts *2 Air conditioning compressor pulley*

18 Accelerator mechanism checking and lubrication

Note: *On models with Electronic Diesel Control (EDC - see Chapter 4C), no throttle cable is fitted, and no adjustment of the throttle pedal position sensor is possible. If an EDC system is fitted, the operation of the accelerator pedal should be checked, but any suspected problems with the operation of the throttle should be referred to a Land Rover dealer or a suitably-equipped specialist.*

1 Check the operation of the accelerator pedal. Make sure that the pedal pivots freely, and if necessary, lightly lubricate the pivot bushes using a little multi-purpose grease.
2 On models with an accelerator cable (all except models with EDC - see Chapter 4C), check the condition of the accelerator cable. Make sure that the cable is routed correctly, free from kinks, and clear of surrounding components. Check the cable for signs of chafing and fraying, particularly at the injection pump end, and renew the cable if necessary.
3 Lubricate the accelerator (and cruise control, where fitted) linkages and pivots using a little multi-purpose grease.
4 Check that when the accelerator pedal is fully depressed, the accelerator lever on the injection pump moves to the full-throttle position.
5 Check the cable freeplay. Details of cable removal, refitting, and adjustment can be found in Chapter 4C.

19 Steering gear backlash check

If at any time it is noted that the steering action has become stiff or sloppy, the vehicle should be taken to a Land Rover dealer for the steering components to be checked. Adjustments to the steering components and power steering box are possible, but specialist knowledge and equipment are needed. Therefore, this task must be entrusted to a Land Rover dealer.

20 Jack and tools security check

1 Lift the bonnet, and check that the vehicle jack and the wheel chock are securely stowed in their bay at the front of the engine compartment. Check the condition of the rubber strap securing the jack, and check that the wing nut securing the wheel chock is tight.
2 Similarly, check the security of the jack handle and the wheel nut wrench, which are located in a bag under the rear seats. Tilt the rear seat cushions forwards for access.
3 If the car has alloy wheels, one of the roadwheel nuts on each wheel may be of locking type. If so, check that the removal key or removal tools are present. Standard-equipment locking wheel nuts may have an indented cover fitted over the nut.

21 Manual transmission fluid renewal

1 Park the vehicle on level ground.
2 Working under the vehicle, locate the main transmission casing drain plug, and place a suitable container beneath the plugs to catch the escaping fluid.
3 Unscrew the drain plug, and allow the fluid to drain. Allow at least ten minutes for all the fluid to drain **(see illustration)**.

21.3 Unscrewing the main gearbox drain plug

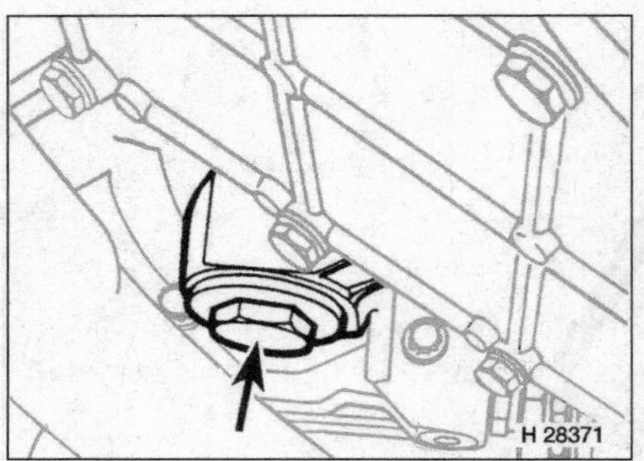
H 28371

21.4 Main gearbox extension housing drain plug (arrowed) - LT 77-type gearbox

4 Similarly, on 200 TDi engine models with the LT 77-type transmission, locate the extension housing drain plug, then unscrew the plug and drain the remaining fluid from the transmission **(see illustration)**.

5 Inspect the drain plug sealing washer(s), and renew if necessary.

6 Where applicable, the extension housing drain plug incorporates a filter. Clean the filter with paraffin, then thoroughly dry the filter and clean the plug before refitting.

7 When all the fluid has drained from the transmission, refit and tighten the drain plug(s), using new washers if necessary. Tighten the plugs securely.

8 Unscrew the fluid filler/level plug from the side of the main transmission casing, and place a suitable container beneath the hole to catch any excess fluid which may be spilled when the transmission is filled **(see illustration)**.

9 Fill the transmission with the specified grade of fluid (see end of *Weekly checks*), until the fluid flows from the filler/level plug hole. It is advisable to fill the transmission slowly, to avoid a sudden spillage.

10 On completion, refit the filler/level plug, and tighten securely. **Do not** overtighten the plug, as it has a tapered thread.

11 Wipe any split fluid from the transmission casing.

22 Transfer gearbox oil level check

1 Park the vehicle on level ground.

2 Locate the oil filler/level plug in the side of the transfer gearbox casing, and place a suitable container beneath the hole to catch any escaping oil.

3 Unscrew the filler/level plug, and check the oil level. The level should be up to the lower edge of the filler/level plug hole **(see illustration)**.

4 If necessary, add oil of the specified type (see end of *Weekly checks*) until the oil overflows from the filler/level hole.

5 Clean and refit the filler/level plug, and tighten to the specified torque. **Do not** over-tighten the plug, as it has tapered threads.

21.8 Unscrewing the main gearbox oil filler/level plug

6 Wipe any split oil from the gearbox casing.

23 Axle oil level check

Note: *A 13 mm square-section wrench will be required to undo the axle filler/level plug. These wrenches can be obtained from most motor factors or your Land Rover dealer. It may be possible to use the square fitting of a half-inch-drive socket handle as a substitute.*

1 Ensure that the vehicle is standing on level ground, and that the handbrake is applied.

2 Working underneath the vehicle, unscrew the front axle oil filler/level plug, which is located in the differential housing.

3 The oil level should be up to the lower edge of the filler/level plug hole.

4 If necessary, top-up with the specified grade of oil, until oil just begins to run from the plug hole. Do not overfill - if too much oil is added, wait until the excess has run out of the plug hole **(see illustration)**.

5 Once the level is correct, refit the filler/level plug and tighten it securely.

6 Repeat the procedure for the rear axle.

24 Swivel pin housing oil level check

Note: *From approximately 1998 onwards, Land Rover (and their dealers) drain the oil and fill the swivel pin housing with a special grease,*

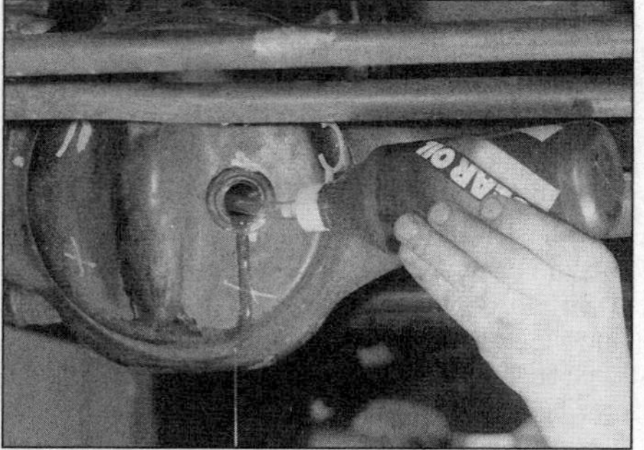

23.4 Topping-up the axle oil level

22.3 Unscrewing the transfer gearbox oil filler/level plug

which then requires no further maintenance. This grease is available from Land Rover dealers, under part number FTC3435.

1 Ensure that the vehicle is standing on level ground, and that the handbrake is applied.

2 Working underneath the vehicle, unscrew the left-hand swivel pin housing level plug. The level plug has a square-section head, and is situated approximately halfway up the housing **(see illustration)**.

3 The oil level should be up to the lower edge of the level plug hole.

4 If topping-up is necessary, unscrew the filler plug from the top of the swivel pin housing; the filler plug also has a square-section head. Top-up the housing via the filler plug hole using the specified grade of oil, until oil just begins to run from the level plug hole. Do not overfill - if too much oil is added, wait until the excess has run out of the level plug hole.

5 Once the level is correct, refit both the filler and level plugs, and tighten them securely.

6 Repeat the above procedure on the right-hand swivel pin housing.

25 Propeller shaft joint lubrication

Note: *A low-pressure grease gun will be required for this operation.*

1 Working under the vehicle, locate the grease nipples on the front and rear propeller shafts universal joint spiders, and the shaft sliding joints.

2 Thoroughly clean the around each nipple.

2
1

24.2 Swivel pin housing level plug (1) and filler plug (2)

3 Fill a suitable grease gun with the recommended type of grease (see end of *Weekly checks*), then apply the grease gun to each of the nipples in turn, and pump grease into the joints **(see illustrations)**. Apply grease until it emerges from the end of the nipple, then wipe away the excess.

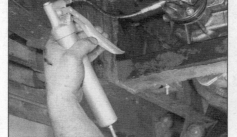

26 Handbrake linkage lubrication

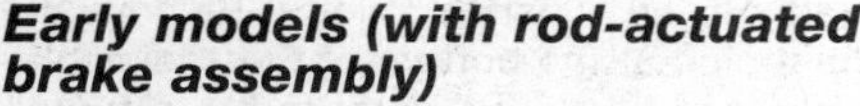

Early models (with rod-actuated brake assembly)

1 To improve access, firmly apply the handbrake, then jack up the front of the vehicle and support it on axle stands.
2 Thoroughly degrease the handbrake rod linkage assembly, which is mounted onto the side of the transfer box. Apply fresh high-melting point grease to all the linkage pivot points and to the exposed end of the handbrake cable, then lower the vehicle to the ground.

Later models (with cable-actuated brake assembly)

3 On these models, no lubrication is necessary.

27 Underbody component, pipe, hose and wiring check

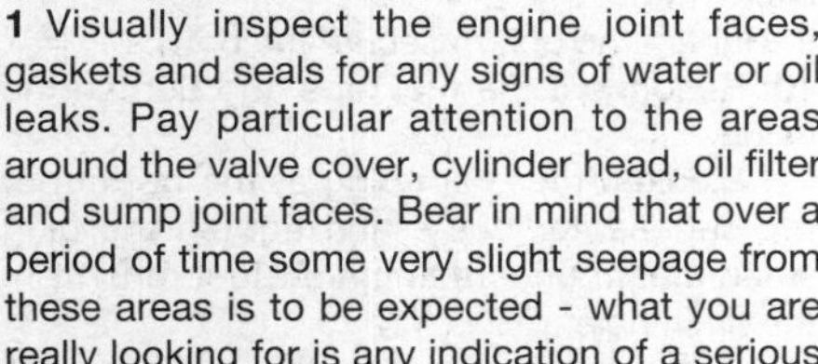

1 Visually inspect the engine joint faces, gaskets and seals for any signs of water or oil leaks. Pay particular attention to the areas around the valve cover, cylinder head, oil filter and sump joint faces. Bear in mind that over a period of time some very slight seepage from these areas is to be expected - what you are really looking for is any indication of a serious leak. Should a leak be found, renew the offending gasket or oil seal by referring to the appropriate Chapter(s) in this manual.
2 Similarly, check the transmission components for oil leaks, and investigate and rectify and problems found.
3 Check the security and condition of all the engine-related pipes and hoses. Ensure that all cable-ties or securing clips are in place and in good condition. Clips which are broken or missing can lead to chafing of the hoses, pipes or wiring, which could cause more serious problems in the future.
4 Carefully check the condition of all coolant, fuel and brake hoses. Renew any hose which is cracked, swollen or deteriorated. Cracks will show up better if the hose is squeezed gently. Pay close attention to the hose clips that secure the hoses to the system components. Hose clips can pinch and puncture hoses, resulting in leaks. If wire-type hose clips are used, it may be a good idea to replace them with screw-type clips.
5 With the vehicle raised, inspect the fuel tank and filler neck for punctures, cracks and other damage. The connection between the filler neck and tank is especially critical. Sometimes, a rubber filler neck or connecting hose will leak due to loose retaining clamps or deteriorated rubber.
6 Similarly, inspect all brake hoses and metal pipes. If any damage or deterioration is discovered, do not drive the vehicle until the necessary repair work has been carried out. Renew any damaged sections of hose or pipe.
7 Carefully check all rubber hoses and metal fuel lines leading away from the fuel tank. Check for loose connections, deteriorated hoses, crimped lines and other damage. Pay particular attention to the vent pipes and hoses, which often loop up around the filler neck and can become blocked or crimped. Follow the lines to the front of the vehicle carefully inspecting them all the way. Renew damaged sections as necessary.
8 From within the engine compartment, check the security of all fuel hose attachments and pipe unions, and inspect the fuel hoses and vacuum hoses for kinks, chafing and deterioration.
9 Check the condition of the oil cooler hoses and pipes.
10 Check the condition of the power steering fluid hoses and pipes and, where applicable, check the condition of the automatic transmission fluid hoses and pipes.
11 Check the condition of all exposed wiring harnesses, paying particular attention to the ABS wheel sensor wiring harnesses, where applicable.

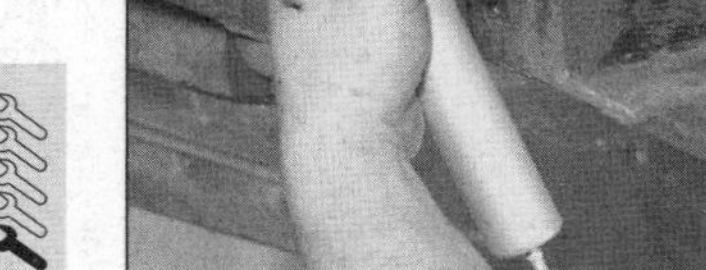

25.3a Pumping grease into a propeller shaft universal joint

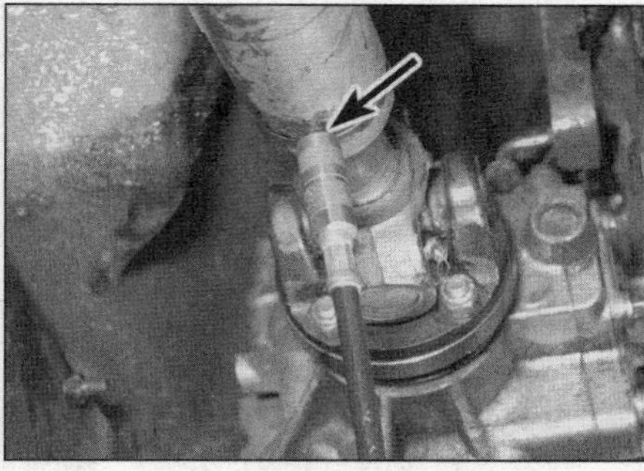

25.3b Greasing a propeller shaft sliding joint (grease nipple arrowed)

28 Exhaust system check

1 With the engine cold (at least an hour after the vehicle has been driven), check the complete exhaust system from the engine to the end of the tailpipe. Ideally the inspection should be carried out with the vehicle raised (see *Jacking and vehicle support*).
2 Check the exhaust pipes and connections for evidence of leaks, severe corrosion and damage. Make sure that all brackets and mountings are in good condition and tight. Leakage at any of the joints or in other parts of the system will usually show up as a black sooty stain in the vicinity of the leak.
3 Rattles and other noises can often be traced to the exhaust system, especially the brackets and mountings **(see illustration)**. Try to move the pipes and silencers. If the components can come into contact with the body or suspension parts, secure the system with new mountings; if possible, separate the joints, and twist the pipes as necessary to provide additional clearance.
4 Run the engine at idle speed, then temporarily place a cloth rag over the rear end of the exhaust pipe, and listen for any escape of exhaust gases that would indicate a leak.
5 On completion, where applicable, lower the vehicle to the ground.

29 Steering and suspension component check

1 Apply the handbrake, then raise the front of the vehicle and securely support it on axle stands.
2 Visually inspect the balljoint dust covers for splits, chafing or deterioration. Any damage will cause loss of lubricant, together with dirt and water entry, resulting in rapid deterioration of the balljoints.
3 Check the power steering fluid hoses for chafing or deterioration, and the pipe and hose unions for fluid leaks. Also check for signs of fluid leakage under pressure from the steering box, which would indicate failed fluid seals within the steering box assembly.

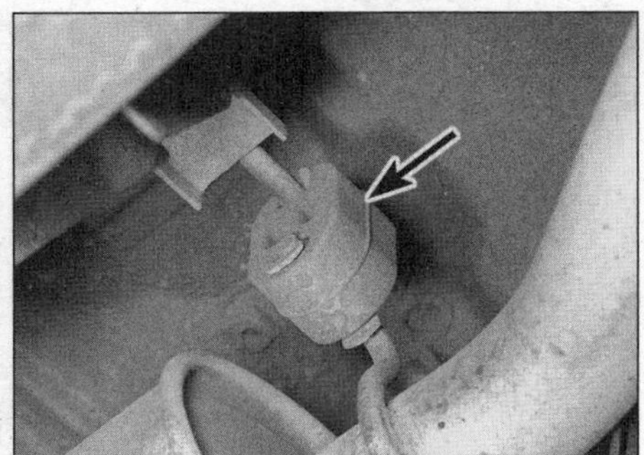

28.3 Rear exhaust mounting rubber (arrowed)

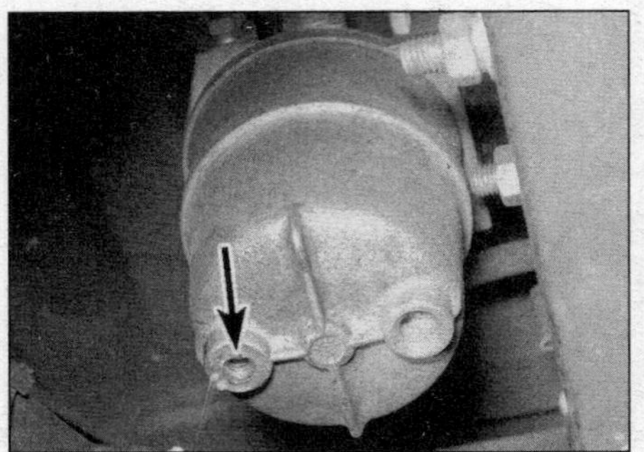
32.3 Allow any water to drain from the fuel sedimenter drain hole (arrowed)

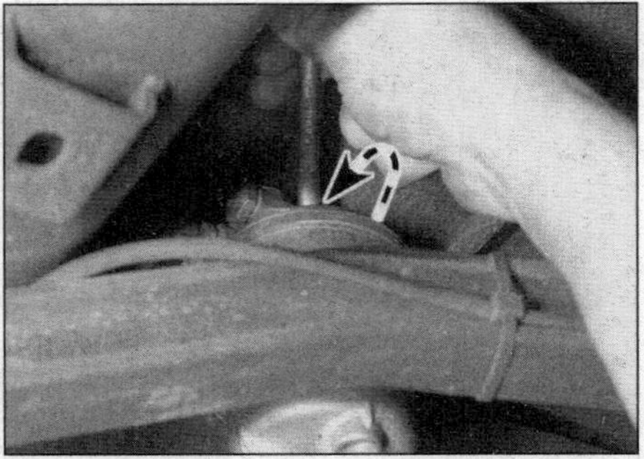
32.5 Unscrewing the fuel sedimenter securing bolt

4 Grasp the roadwheel at the 12 o'clock and 6 o'clock positions, and try to rock it. Very slight freeplay may be felt, but if the movement is appreciable, further investigation is necessary to determine the source. Continue rocking the wheel while an assistant depresses the footbrake. If the movement is now eliminated or significantly reduced, it is likely that the hub bearings are at fault. If the freeplay is still evident with the footbrake depressed, then there is wear in the suspension joints or mountings.

5 Now grasp the wheel at the 9 o'clock and 3 o'clock positions, and try to rock it as before. Any movement felt now may again be caused by wear in the hub bearings or the steering track rod and drag link balljoints. If a balljoint is worn, the visual movement will be obvious.

6 Using a large screwdriver or flat bar, check for wear in the suspension mounting bushes by levering between the relevant suspension component and its attachment point. Some movement is to be expected as the mountings are made of rubber, but excessive wear should be obvious. Also check the condition of any visible rubber bushes, looking for splits, cracks or contamination of the rubber.

7 With the vehicle standing on its wheels, have an assistant turn the steering wheel back and forth. There should be very little, if any, lost movement between the steering wheel and roadwheels. If this is not the case, closely observe the joints and mountings previously described, but in addition, check the steering column universal joints for wear. The steering box backlash is adjustable, but adjustment should be entrusted to a Land Rover dealer (see Section 19).

30 Propeller shaft securing bolt check

1 Working under the vehicle, use a torque wrench to check the tightness of the bolts securing the propeller shafts to the transfer gearbox and axle drive flanges.

2 Also check the bolts securing the rear propeller shaft rubber coupling, where applicable.

31 Axle breather check

1 Ensure that the vehicle is standing on level ground, and that the handbrake is applied.

2 Check that both the front and rear axle breather tubes are securely retained by all the relevant retaining clips, and show no signs of damage or deterioration.

3 If renewal is necessary, unscrew the union bolt securing the breather hose to the top of the axle, and recover the sealing washers from the hose union. Free the hose from its retaining clips, and remove it from the vehicle.

4 Position a new sealing washer on each side of the hose union, and refit the union bolt. Ensure that the hose is correctly routed and retained by all the necessary clips, then securely tighten the union bolt.

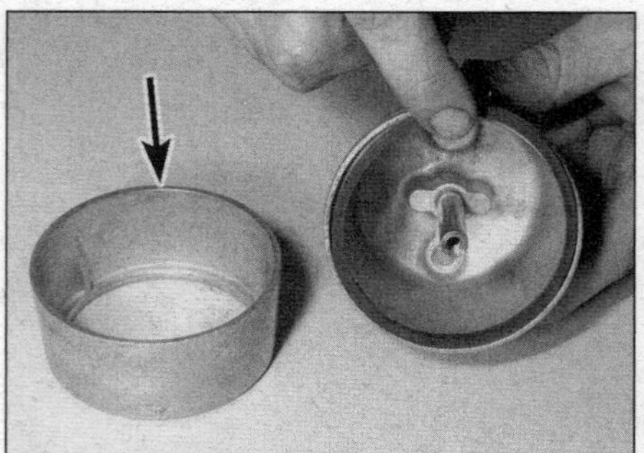
32.7 Fit a new seal to the top of the sedimenter bowl. Sleeve arrowed

32.8 Fitting the plastic collar to the sedimenter head. Seals arrowed

32 Fuel sedimenter cleaning

1 The fuel sedimenter is designed to increase the life of the fuel filter, by removing the larger droplets of water and dirt from the fuel before it reaches the filter.

2 The sedimenter is located under the vehicle, on the inboard right-hand side of the chassis, forward of the rear axle.

3 Before cleaning the sedimenter element, drain off the water as follows. Remove the drain plug at the bottom of the sedimenter body, and allow the water to run out **(see illustration)**. When clean, uncontaminated fuel runs from the drain hole, refit and tighten the drain plug.

4 Disconnect the fuel inlet pipe from the sedimenter, and lift the pipe above the level of the fuel tank. Alternatively, plug the end of the pipe to prevent fuel draining from the tank.

5 Support the sedimenter bowl, then unscrew the bolt at the top of the sedimenter head, until the bowl can be removed **(see illustration)**.

6 Remove the sedimenter sleeve from the bowl, and recover the plastic collar, then clean the components in clean paraffin.

7 Fit new seals to the sedimenter head, and fit a new seal to the top of the bowl, then fit the sleeve to the bowl **(see illustration)**.

8 Fit the plastic collar to the sedimenter head, then fit the bowl/sleeve assembly **(see illustration)**.

9 Tighten the bolt to secure the bowl.

10 Reconnect the fuel pipe and tighten the union.

11 Slacken the drain plug at the bottom of the sedimenter body, and tighten the plug when clean, uncontaminated fuel runs from the drain hole.

12 Prime the fuel system as described in Chapter 4C.

13 Start the engine, and check for fuel leaks around the sedimenter.

33 Flywheel housing and timing belt housing draining

Flywheel housing

1 In production, the flywheel housing plug is not normally fitted. The plug can be fitted to the oil drain hole in the housing, to seal the housing if the vehicle is likely to be used off-road in very muddy conditions, or under severe wading conditions. A suitable plug can be obtained from a Land Rover dealer **(see illustration)**.

2 If the vehicle is regularly used in adverse conditions, the plug should be fitted permanently, but if the vehicle is normally used on the road, the plug should be removed.

3 If the plug is permanently fitted, it should be removed at the recommended intervals to allow any accumulated oil to drain from the housing.

4 Clean the plug before refitting.

Timing belt housing

5 Refer to paragraphs 1 to 4, but note that the plug should be treated as an inspection plug - there should be no oil in the timing belt housing **(see illustration)**. If oil is present, investigate the cause immediately, as the timing belt will deteriorate if contaminated with oil.

34 Fuel tank security check

1 Working under the vehicle, check the fuel tank for any signs of damage or corrosion.

2 If there is any sign of significant damage or corrosion, remove the fuel tank (see the relevant part of Chapter 4) and take it to a professional for repair. **Do not** under any circumstances attempt to weld or solder a fuel tank.

35 Towing bracket check

1 Where applicable, check the security of the towbar bracket mountings. Also check that all wiring is intact, and that the trailer electrical systems function correctly.

36 Handbrake adjustment

1 The handbrake mechanism is mounted onto the rear of the transfer box assembly. Place the transmission in gear (manual) or P (automatic), then release the handbrake lever and chock the front wheels.

2 Jack up the rear of the vehicle, and support it on axle stands so the wheels are clear of the ground.

Early models (with rod-actuated brake)

3 From underneath the vehicle, slacken the cable locknut, then loosen the adjuster nut to obtain plenty of freeplay in the cable.

4 Using a suitable spanner, rotate the adjuster on the rear of the handbrake assembly clockwise until both shoes are fully expanded against the drum.

5 With the shoes in full contact with the drum, remove all but a slight amount of freeplay from the handbrake cable, using the adjuster nut. Hold the adjuster nut in this position, and securely tighten the cable locknut.

6 Rotate the handbrake drum adjuster in an anti-clockwise direction, until the drum is free to rotate easily.

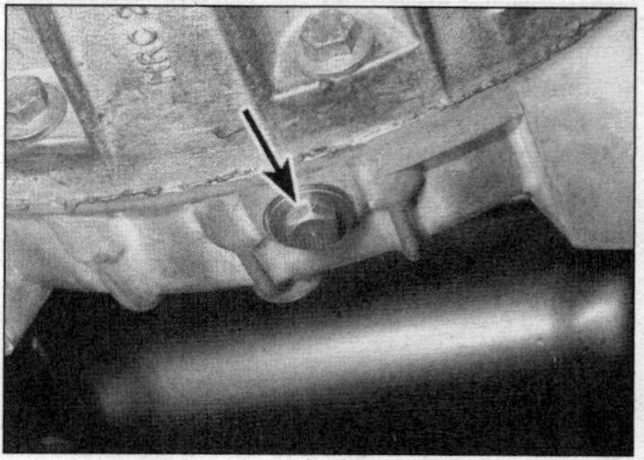

33.1 Flywheel housing drain plug location (arrowed)

33.5 Timing belt housing inspection hole location (arrowed)

7 Applying normal, moderate pressure, pull the handbrake lever to the fully-applied position whilst counting the number of clicks emitted from the handbrake ratchet mechanism. The handbrake should be fully-applied on the second or third click of the ratchet mechanism. If necessary, adjust by rotating the drum adjuster in the relevant direction.

8 When adjustment is correct, release the handbrake lever, and check that the drum is free to rotate easily.

9 Apply a smear of high-melting point grease to all the linkage pivot points and to the exposed end of the handbrake cable, then lower the vehicle to the ground.

Later models (with cable-actuated brake)

10 Release the handbrake lever gaiter from the console, and remove the switch panel cover plate. Undo the retaining screws, then withdraw the switch panel and disconnect its wiring connectors. Access can then be gained to the handbrake cable knurled adjuster nut **(see illustration)**.

11 Slacken the cable knurled cable adjuster ring to obtain some freeplay in the cable.

12 From underneath the vehicle, using a suitable spanner, rotate the adjuster on the rear of the handbrake assembly clockwise until both shoes are fully expanded against the drum.

13 With the shoes in full contact with the drum, rotate the handbrake adjuster in an anti-clockwise direction until the handbrake drum is free to rotate easily.

14 Applying normal, moderate pressure, pull the handbrake lever to the fully-applied position, counting the number of clicks emitted from the handbrake ratchet mechanism. The handbrake should be fully-applied on the third click of the ratchet mechanism. If necessary, adjust the cable setting using the adjuster nut.

15 When adjustment is correct, release the handbrake lever, and check that the drum is free to rotate easily. If all is well, lower the vehicle to the ground.

16 Reconnect the wiring connectors to the centre console switch panel, and refit the panel to the console. Securely tighten the panel retaining screws, and clip the cover plate and handbrake lever gaiter back into position.

37 Road test

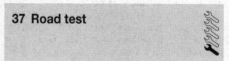

Instruments and electrical equipment

1 Check the operation of all instruments and electrical equipment.

2 Make sure that all instruments read correctly, and switch on all electrical equipment in turn to check that it functions properly.

Steering and suspension

3 Check for any abnormalities in the steering, suspension, handling or road 'feel'.

4 Drive the vehicle, and check that there are no unusual vibrations or noises.

5 Check that the steering feels positive, with no excessive sloppiness, or roughness, and check for any suspension noises when cornering and driving over bumps.

Drivetrain

6 Check the performance of the engine, clutch (where applicable), transmission and propeller shafts.

36.10 On later models, access to the handbrake cable adjuster nut (arrowed) can be gained once the switch panel has been removed from the centre console

7 Listen for any unusual noises from the engine, clutch and transmission.

8 Make sure that the engine runs smoothly when idling, and that there is no hesitation when accelerating.

9 If applicable, check that the clutch action is smooth and progressive, that the drive is taken up smoothly, and that the pedal travel is not excessive. Also listen for any noises when the clutch pedal is depressed.

10 Check that all gears can be engaged smoothly without noise, and that the gear lever action is not abnormally vague or 'notchy'. This check applies to both the manual/automatic transmission and the transfer gearbox.

Braking system

11 Make sure that the vehicle does not pull to one side when braking, and that the wheels do not lock prematurely when braking hard.

12 Check that there is no vibration through the steering when braking.

13 Check that the handbrake operates correctly without excessive movement of the lever, and that it holds the vehicle stationary on a slope.

14 Test the operation of the brake servo unit as follows. With the engine switched off, depress the footbrake four or five times to exhaust the vacuum, then start the engine, keeping the pedal depressed. As the engine starts, there should be a noticeable 'give' in the brake pedal as vacuum builds up. Allow the engine to run for at least two minutes, and then switch it off. If the brake pedal is now depressed, it should be possible to detect a hiss from the servo as the pedal is depressed. After about four or five applications, no further hissing should be heard, and the pedal should feel considerably harder.

38 Headlight and auxiliary light adjustment check

1 Check the operation of all the electrical equipment, ie lights, direction indicators, horn, etc. Refer to the appropriate Sections of Chapter 13 for details if any of the circuits are found to be inoperative.

2 Note that stop-light switch adjustment is described in Chapter 10.

3 Visually check all accessible wiring connectors, harnesses and retaining clips for security, and for signs of chafing or damage. Rectify any faults found.

4 Accurate adjustment of the headlight beam is only possible using optical beam-setting equipment, and this work should therefore be carried out by a Land Rover dealer or service station with the necessary facilities.

5 Basic adjustments can be carried out in an emergency, and further details are given in Chapter 13.

6 On models with an electrically-operated headlight levelling system, check the operation of both headlight motors. Refer to the appropriate Sections of Chapter 13 if any of the circuits are found to be inoperative.

39 Sunroof maintenance

1 Check the operation of each sunroof (on cars so equipped). If the action is at all stiff, clean and lubricate the sunroof guide rails and slides with a little multi-purpose grease.

2 With the sunroof open, check that the sun-roof drain tubes at the corners of the sunroof aperture are clear. Carefully pour a little water into the drain channel, and have an assistant watch for the water emerging under the car. Beware of probing the drain tubes with wire, as this may damage the tubes. If available, an air line should be used to clear any blockages.

40 Front wheel alignment check

Check the front wheel alignment as described in Chapter 11.

41 Brake pad and disc check

1 Jack up the vehicle, support securely on axle stands, then remove the roadwheels (see *Jacking and vehicle support*).

2 For a quick check, the thickness of friction material remaining on each pad can be measured through the slot in the caliper body **(see illustration)**. If any pad is worn to the specified minimum thickness or less, all four pads must be renewed (see Chapter 10).

3 For a comprehensive check, the brake pads should be removed and cleaned. This will allow the operation of the caliper to be checked, and the condition of the brake disc itself to be fully examined on both sides (see Chapter 10).

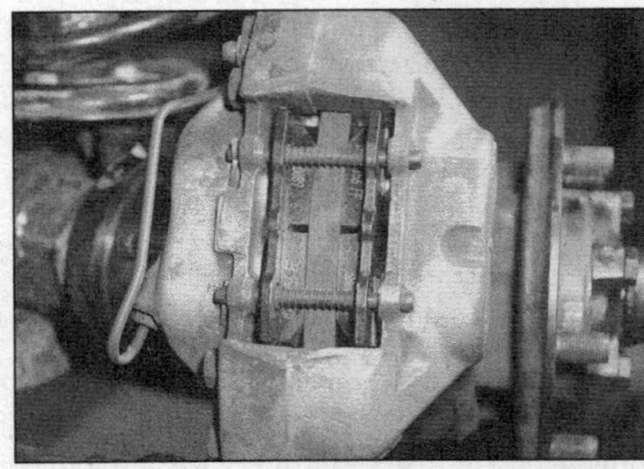

41.2 Brake pad friction material thickness can be checked with the caliper in position

42 Spare wheel check

Refer to *Weekly checks* and Section 20.

43 Hinge and lock check and lubrication

1 Lubricate the hinges of the bonnet, doors and tailgate with a light general-purpose oil. Similarly, lubricate all latches, locks and lock strikers. At the same time, check the security and operation of all the locks, adjusting them if necessary (see Chapter 12).

2 Lightly lubricate the bonnet release mechanism and cable with a suitable grease.

44 Seat belt check

1 Carefully examine the seat belt webbing for cuts, or any signs of serious fraying or deterioration. If the seat belt is of the retractable type, pull the belt all the way out, and examine the full extent of the webbing.

2 Fasten and unfasten the belt, ensuring that the locking mechanism holds securely, and releases properly when intended. If the belt is of the retractable type, check also that the retracting mechanism operates correctly when the belt is released.

3 Check the security of all seat belt mountings and attachments which are accessible, without removing any trim or other components, from inside the vehicle.

4 Renew any worn components as described in Chapter 12.

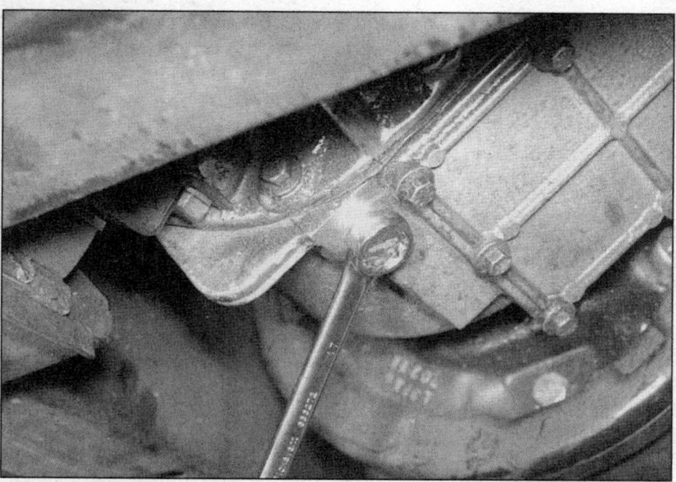
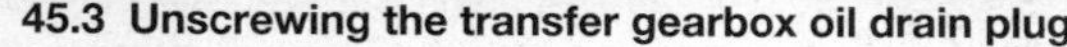

45.3 Unscrewing the transfer gearbox oil drain plug

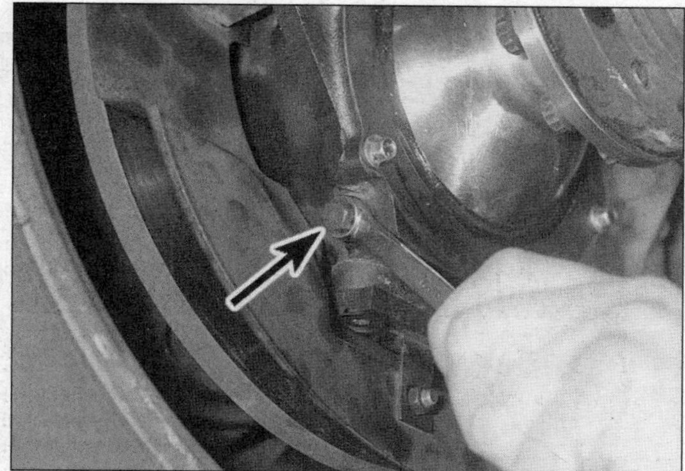

47.5 Removing the swivel pin housing drain plug (arrowed)

Every 24 000 miles or 2 years, whichever comes first

45 Transfer gearbox oil renewal

1 Park the vehicle on level ground.
2 Locate the filler/level plug in the side of the transfer gearbox casing, the unscrew the plug (see Section 22).
3 Place a suitable container beneath the drain plug in the bottom of the gearbox casing, then unscrew the drain plug and allow the oil to drain **(see illustration)**. Recover the sealing washer.
4 When the oil has finished draining, refit and tighten the drain plug, using a new sealing washer if necessary.
5 Refill the gearbox with oil of the specified type (see end of *Weekly checks*) through the filler/level hole, until the oil level reaches the lower edge of the hole (place a container beneath the hole to catch any escaping oil).
6 Clean and refit the filler/level plug, and tighten to the specified torque. **Do not** overtighten the plug, as it has tapered threads.
7 Wipe any split oil from the gearbox casing.

46 Axle oil renewal

Note: *A 13 mm square-section wrench will be required to undo the axle filler/level plug. These wrenches can be obtained from most motor factors or your Land Rover dealer. It may be possible to use the square fitting of a half-inch-drive socket handle as a substitute.*
1 This operation is much quicker and more efficient if the car is first taken on a journey of sufficient length to warm the axle oil up to normal operating temperature.
2 Park the car on level ground, switch off the 'ignition' and apply the handbrake firmly.
3 Wipe clean the area around the front axle filler/level plug, which is on the differential housing. Unscrew the plug and clean it.
4 Position a suitable container under the drain plug situated on the base of the differential housing.
5 Unscrew the drain plug, and allow the oil to drain completely into the container. If the oil is hot, take precautions against scalding. Examine the sealing washer for signs of damage, renewing it if necessary, and clean both the filler/level and the drain plugs.
6 When the oil has finished draining, clean the drain plug threads and those of the differential casing, then refit the drain plug and washer, tightening it securely.
7 Refilling the axle is an extremely awkward operation. Above all, allow plenty of time for the oil level to settle properly before checking it. Note that the car must be parked on flat level ground when checking the oil level.
8 Refill the axle with the exact amount of the specified type of oil, then check the oil level as described in Section 23. If the correct amount was poured into the housing, and a large amount flows out on checking the level, refit the filler/level plug, and take the car on a short journey so that the new oil is distributed fully around the axle components, then check the level again on your return.
9 When the level is correct, refit the filler/level plug, tightening it securely, and wash off any spilt oil.
10 Repeat the procedure for the rear axle.

47 Swivel pin housing oil renewal

Note: *From approximately 1998 onwards, Land Rover (and their dealers) drain the oil and fill the swivel pin housing with a special grease, which then requires no further maintenance. This grease is available from Land Rover dealers, under part number FTC3435.*
1 This operation is much quicker and more efficient if the car is first taken on a journey of sufficient length to warm the swivel pin housing oil up to normal operating temperature.
2 Park the car on level ground, switch off the 'ignition' and apply the handbrake firmly.
3 Working underneath the vehicle, unscrew the left-hand swivel pin housing level plug and filler. Both plugs can be identified by their square-section heads (see Section 24).
4 Position a suitable container under the drain plug situated on the base of the swivel pin housing.
5 Unscrew the drain plug, and allow the oil to drain completely into the container **(see illustration)**. If the oil is hot, take precautions against scalding. Examine the sealing washer for signs of damage, renewing it if necessary, and clean the threads of all removed plugs.
6 When the oil has finished draining, clean the drain plug threads and those of the housing, then refit the drain plug and washer, tightening it securely.
7 Refilling the housing is an extremely awkward operation. Above all, allow plenty of time for the oil level to settle properly before checking it. Note that the car must be parked on flat level ground when checking the oil level.
8 Refill the housing with the exact amount of the specified type of oil, then check the oil level as described in Section 24. If the correct amount was poured into the housing, and a large amount flows out on checking the level, refit the filler and level plugs, and take the car on a short journey so that the new oil is distributed fully around the swivel pin housing components, then check the level again on your return.

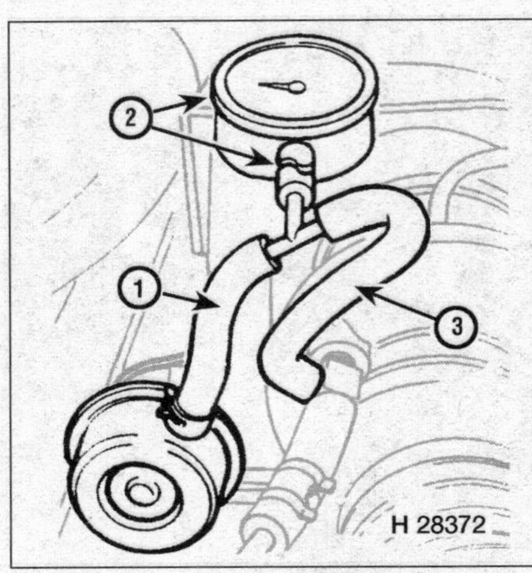
2
1
3
H 28372

48.2 Turbocharger boost pressure checking

1 *Wastegate actuator hose*
2 *T-piece and pressure gauge*
3 *Hose to turbocharger*

9 When the level is correct, refit the filler and level plugs, tightening them securely, and wash off any spilt oil.
10 Repeat the above operation on the right-hand swivel pin housing.

48 Turbocharger boost pressure check

Note: *A pressure gauge capable of registering pressure in excess of 1 bar will be required for this check.*
1 Working in the engine compartment, disconnect the hose connecting the wastegate actuator to the turbocharger, at the turbocharger.
2 Connect the hose to a T-piece, and use a short length of hose to connect the T-piece to the turbocharger **(see illustration)**.
3 Obtain a length of hose long enough to run from the T-piece in the engine compartment to the passenger compartment, to enable a pressure gauge to be read by the driver or passenger whilst the vehicle is being driven. Note that the hose must be long enough to enable it to be routed so that it is not trapped when the bonnet is closed.
4 Connect the hose between the T-piece and the pressure gauge. Carefully lower the bonnet, taking care not to trap the hose. Do not fully close the bonnet (as this will trap the hose), but ensure that the safety catch is engaged, so that there is no risk of the bonnet opening when the vehicle is driven. As a safety precaution, it is advisable to secure the bonnet using a length of string or a cable-tie around the lock and striker.
5 Start the engine, and drive the vehicle normally until the engine reaches normal operating temperature.
6 When the engine is warm, drive the vehicle normally, up a suitable shallow hill, in such a manner that full throttle can be maintained, with the engine speed held steady between 2500 and 3000 rpm.
7 Under these conditions, the maximum boost pressure should be as specified at the start of this Chapter.
8 If the reading is not as specified, it is likely that there is a fault with the turbocharger wastegate. In this case, have the problem investigated by a Land Rover dealer.

49 Automatic transmission fluid and oil screen renewal

This is an involved operation, and is best entrusted to a Land Rover dealer.

Every 2 years, regardless of mileage

50 Brake fluid renewal

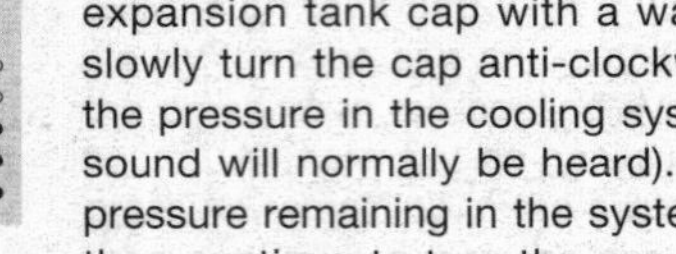

1 The procedure is similar to that for the bleeding of the hydraulic system as described in Chapter 10, except that the brake fluid reservoir should be emptied by siphoning, using a (clean) old battery hydrometer or similar before starting, and allowance should be made for the old fluid to be expelled from the circuit when bleeding each section of the circuit.

51 Coolant renewal

Warning: Wait until the engine is cold before starting this procedure. Do not allow antifreeze to come in contact with your skin, or with the painted surfaces of the vehicle. Rinse off spills immediately with plenty of water. Never leave antifreeze lying around in an open container, or in a puddle in the driveway or garage floor. Children and pets are attracted by its sweet smell, but antifreeze is fatal if ingested. Refer to the 'Antifreeze mixture' sub-Section before proceeding.

Cooling system draining

1 To drain the cooling system, first cover the expansion tank cap with a wad of rag, and slowly turn the cap anti-clockwise to relieve the pressure in the cooling system (a hissing sound will normally be heard). Wait until any pressure remaining in the system is released, then continue to turn the cap until it can be removed.
2 Position a suitable container beneath the radiator bottom hose connection, then slacken the hose clip and ease the hose from the radiator stub. If the hose joint has not been disturbed for some time, it will be necessary to manipulate the hose to break the joint. Allow the coolant to drain into the container.
3 To fully drain the system, also slacken and remove the coolant drain plug from the left-hand side of the cylinder block, and allow any residual coolant to drain from the block. When the flow of coolant has stopped, wipe clean the threads of the drain plug and block. Where the plug was fitted with a sealing washer, fit a new sealing washer; where no washer was fitted, apply a smear of suitable sealant to the drain plug threads. Refit the drain plug to the block, and tighten it securely.
4 If the coolant has been drained for a reason other than renewal, then provided it is clean and less than two years old, it can be re-used.

Cooling system flushing

5 If coolant renewal has been neglected, or if the antifreeze mixture has become diluted, then in time, the cooling system may gradually lose efficiency, as the coolant passages become restricted due to rust, scale deposits, and other sediment. The cooling system efficiency can be restored by flushing the system clean.
6 The radiator should be flushed independently of the engine, to avoid unnecessary contamination.
7 To flush the radiator, disconnect the top hose at the radiator, then insert a garden hose into the radiator top inlet. Direct a flow of clean water through the radiator, and continue flushing until clean water emerges from the radiator bottom outlet (the bottom radiator hose should have been disconnected to drain the system). If after a reasonable period, the water still does not run clear, the radiator can be flushed with a good proprietary cleaning agent. It is important that the cleaning agent manufacturer's instructions are followed carefully. If the contamination is particularly bad, insert the hose in the radiator bottom outlet, and flush the radiator in reverse ('reverse-flushing').
8 Remove the thermostat as described in Chapter 3, then temporarily refit the thermostat cover.
9 With the radiator top and bottom hoses disconnected from the radiator, insert a hose into the radiator bottom hose. Direct a clean flow of water through the engine, and continue flushing until clean water emerges from the radiator top hose.
10 On completion of flushing, refit the thermostat with reference to Chapter 3, and reconnect the hoses.

Antifreeze mixture

11 Always use an ethylene-glycol based antifreeze which is suitable for use in mixed-metal cooling systems. The quantity of antifreeze and levels of protection are indicated in the Specifications.

12 Before adding antifreeze, the cooling system should be completely drained, preferably flushed, and all hoses and clips checked for condition and security.

13 After filling with antifreeze, a label should be attached to the radiator or expansion tank, stating the type and concentration of antifreeze used, and the date installed. Any subsequent topping-up should be made with the same type and concentration of antifreeze.

Cooling system filling

14 Before attempting to fill the cooling system, make sure that all hoses and clips are in good condition, and that the clips are tight. Note that an antifreeze mixture must be used all year round, to prevent corrosion of the alloy engine components.

15 Remove the expansion tank cap. On 200 TDi engines, unscrew the filler cap from the top of the radiator; on 300 TDi engines, unscrew the filler cap from the top of the thermostat housing **(see illustration)**. Recover the cap sealing ring (where fitted), and renew it if it shows signs of damage or deterioration.

16 Fill the system by slowly pouring the coolant into the radiator/thermostat housing (as applicable) to prevent airlocks from forming.

17 If the coolant is being renewed, begin by pouring in a couple of litres of water, followed by the correct quantity of antifreeze, then top-up with more water.

18 When coolant free of air bubbles emerges from the filler, refit the filler cap and tighten it securely.

19 Top-up the expansion tank level up to the indicator (see *Weekly checks*), then refit the expansion tank cap.

20 Start the engine and run it until it reaches normal operating temperature, then stop the engine and allow it to cool for several hours (preferably overnight).

21 Check for leaks, particularly around disturbed components.

22 Check the coolant level in the expansion tank, and top-up if necessary. Note that the system must be cold before an accurate level is indicated in the expansion tank.

Airlocks

23 If, after draining and refilling the system, symptoms of overheating are found which did not occur previously, then the fault is almost certainly due to trapped air at some point in the system, causing an airlock and restricting the flow of coolant; usually, the air is trapped because the system was refilled too quickly.

24 If an airlock is suspected, first try gently squeezing all visible coolant hoses. A coolant hose which is full of air feels quite different to one full of coolant, when squeezed. After refilling the system, most airlocks will clear once the system has cooled, and been topped-up.

25 While the engine is running at operating temperature, switch on the heater and heater fan, and check for heat output. Provided there is sufficient coolant in the system, lack of heat output could be due to an airlock in the system.

51.15 On 300 TDi engines, the filler cap (arrowed) is situated on the top of the thermostat housing

26 Airlocks can have more serious effects than simply reducing heater output - a severe airlock could reduce coolant flow around the engine. Check that the radiator top hose is hot when the engine is at operating temperature - a top hose which stays cold could be the result of an airlock (or a non-opening thermostat).

27 If the problem persists, stop the engine and allow it to cool down **completely**, before unscrewing the expansion tank filler cap or partially disconnecting hoses to bleed out the trapped air. In the worst case, the system will have to be at least partially drained (this time, the coolant can be saved for re-use) and flushed to clear the problem.

Every 36 000 miles or 3 years, whichever comes first

52 Shock absorber check

1 Check for any signs of fluid leakage around the shock absorber body, or from the rubber gaiter around the piston rod. Should any fluid be noticed, the shock absorber is defective internally and should be renewed. **Note:** *Shock absorbers should always be renewed in pairs on the same axle.*

2 The efficiency of the shock absorber may be checked by bouncing the vehicle at each corner. Generally speaking, the body will return to its normal position and stop after being depressed. If it rises and returns on a rebound, the shock absorber is probably suspect. Examine also the shock absorber upper and lower mountings for any signs of wear.

53 Braking system seal, vacuum servo filter and hose renewal

Land Rover recommend that all the braking system and rubber hoses are renewed, and the hydraulic system filled with fresh fluid. At the same time, the vacuum servo unit filter should also be renewed. Refer to the relevant Sections of Chapter 10 for renewal information.

54 Timing belt renewal

The timing belt renewal procedure is described in Chapter 2B.

Every 48 000 miles or 4 years, whichever comes first

55 Intercooler element cleaning

1 Remove the intercooler as described in Chapter 4C.

2 Check the element for damage and deterioration, and renew if necessary.

3 If the original element is to be refitted, flush the element with ICI Genklene or a suitable alternative, following the instructions supplied with the cleaner.

4 Dry the element thoroughly, then refit as described in Chapter 4C.

Every 96 000 miles

56 Catalytic converter check and renewal

The catalytic converter is integral with the exhaust front section. For more information, refer to Chapter 4D - the converter need only be renewed if it is no longer effective.

Every 10 years

57 Airbag module renewal

Land Rover recommend that the airbag module be replaced after 10 years. In the interests of safety, this advice should be heeded - consult a Land Rover dealer for more information. The module can be removed and refitted as described in Chapter 13, but on completion, its operation should be checked by a Land Rover dealer.

Chapter 2 Part A:
Petrol engine in-car repair procedures

Contents

Degrees of difficulty

Easy, suitable for novice with little experience 	**Fairly easy,** suitable for beginner with some experience 	**Fairly difficult,** suitable for competent DIY mechanic 	**Difficult,** suitable for experienced DIY mechanic 	**Very difficult,** suitable for expert DIY or professional

Specifications

General

Engine type	V8, 4-stroke, water-cooled, ohv
Cubic capacity:	
3.5 litre engine	3528 cc
3.9 litre engine	3947 cc
Bore:	
3.5 litre engine	88.90 mm
3.9 litre engine	94.00 mm
Stroke	71.12 mm
Compression ratio:	
Low-compression engines	8.13 : 1
High-compression engines	9.35 : 1
Power output (DIN):	
3.5 litre carburettor engines	144.5 bhp at 5000 rpm
3.5 litre fuel injection engines	152 bhp at 4750 rpm
3.9 litre low-compression engines	165 bhp at 4550 rpm
3.9 litre high-compression engines	174 bhp at 4750 rpm
Firing order	1 - 8 - 4 - 3 - 6 - 5 - 7 - 2
Cylinder numbering (front to rear):	
Left-hand bank	1 - 3 - 5 - 7
Right-hand bank	2 - 4 - 6 - 8
Compression pressure at cranking speed, engine warm:	
Low-compression engines	150 psi minimum
High-compression engines	170 psi minimum

Flywheel

Minimum thickness (after machining)	39.9 mm

Lubrication system

Oil pump type	Gear
Oil pump drive	From bottom end of distributor driveshaft, off camshaft gear
Clearance between pump gears and front cover	0.05 mm
Oil pressure at 2400 rpm, engine warm	30 to 40 psi

Torque wrench settings	Nm	lbf ft
Alternator mounting bracket	34	25
Alternator mounting/adjuster bolts	24	18
Big-end bearing bolts	51	38
Clutch cover bolts	27	20
Crankshaft pulley bolt	280	207
Cylinder head bolts (up to 1995 model year with only 14 bolts):		
Inner and centre rows (nos 1 to 10)	92	68
Outer row (nos 11 to 14)	58	43
Cylinder head bolts (1995 model year onwards with 10 bolts):		
Stage 1	20	15
Stage 2	Angle-tighten a further 180 ± 5°	
Distributor clamp nut	20	15
Distributor drivegear retaining bolt	58	43
Driveplate to adaptor plate**	41	30
Driveplate-to-starter ring gear bolts (automatic transmission models)	25	18
Engine mounting nuts	20	15
Engine sump drain plug:		
3.5 litre engine	30	22
3.9 litre engine	40	30
Engine-to-transmission bellhousing bolts	40	30
Exhaust manifold bolts	20	15
Flywheel/adaptor plate to crankshaft**	80	59
Inlet manifold bolts	51	38
Main bearing cap bolts*:		
Nos 1 to 4	72	53
No 5 (rear cap)***	90	66
Oil cooler pipes:		
Oil filter housing unions	45	33
Radiator unions	30	22
Oil pressure relief valve plug	61	45
Oil pump cover bolts	13	10
Rocker cover bolts	9	7
Rocker shaft pedestal bolts	38	28
Spark plugs	20	15
Starter motor bolts	44	32
Sump bolts:		
Up to 1995 model year:		
Front bolts	10	7
Rear bolts	18	13
1995 model year onwards	18	13
Timing chain cover bolts	27	20
Timing chain sprocket to camshaft	58	43
Viscous fan bolt	12	9

**Use new fasteners.*
***Use locking fluid.*
****Use lubricant EXP 16A.*

1 General description

Using this Chapter

Chapter 2 is divided into three Parts; A, B and C. Repair operations that can be carried out with the engine in the vehicle are described in Parts A (petrol engines) and B (diesel engines). Part C covers the removal of the engine/transmission as a unit, and describes the engine dismantling and overhaul procedures.

In Parts A and B, the assumption is made that the engine is installed in the vehicle, with all ancillaries connected. If the engine has been removed for overhaul, the preliminary dismantling information which precedes each operation may be ignored.

Engine description

The engine is an overhead valve V8, based on a Buick design. The cylinder block and cylinder heads are aluminium alloy castings, and the two banks of four cylinders are set at 90° to each other, forming a vee **(see illustration)**. The cylinder liners are of cast iron, and are integral with the block so they can be rebored within certain tolerances. The valve guides and seats are also of iron and can be renewed.

The camshaft is mounted centrally at the base of the cylinder banks, and is driven by a chain from the crankshaft. The valves are operated by pushrods and self-adjusting hydraulic tappets, meaning that routine valve clearance adjustment is not required.

The crankshaft runs in five main bearings; crankshaft endfloat is controlled by a thrust bearing on the centre main bearing.

Engine coolant is circulated by a pump, driven by the crankshaft via an auxiliary drivebelt. A viscous-type fan is fitted to the water pump pulley. For details of the cooling system, refer to Chapter 3.

Lubrication is by a gear-driven oil pump at the front of the engine, which delivers oil under pressure to all the main, big-end and camshaft bearings, the valve gear, distributor driveshaft and cylinder bores **(see illustration)**. A full-flow cartridge type of disposable oil filter is fitted at the front of the engine.

Note: *Because the engine is of aluminium construction, it is vital when refitting engine components that the specified torque settings are strictly observed. It is also of equal* *importance that bolt lengths are noted, so that different-length bolts are refitted in the same location from which they were removed.*

Repairs possible with the engine installed in the vehicle

The following operations can be performed without removing the engine:

a) Cylinder heads - removal and refitting.*
b) Rocker gear, pushrods and hydraulic tappets - removal and refitting.
c) Camshaft - removal and refitting.
d) Timing chain and sprockets - removal and refitting.
e) Coolant pump - removal and refitting (see Chapter 3).
f) Crankshaft oil seals - renewal.
g) Crankshaft pulley - removal and refitting.
h) Engine mountings - inspection and renewal.
i) Sump - removal and refitting.
j) Oil pump - removal and refitting.

**Cylinder head dismantling procedures are detailed in Chapter 2C.*

Note: *It is possible to remove the pistons and connecting rods (after removing the cylinder head and sump) without removing the engine. However, this is not recommended. Work of this nature is more easily and thoroughly completed with the engine on the bench, as described in Chapter 2C.*

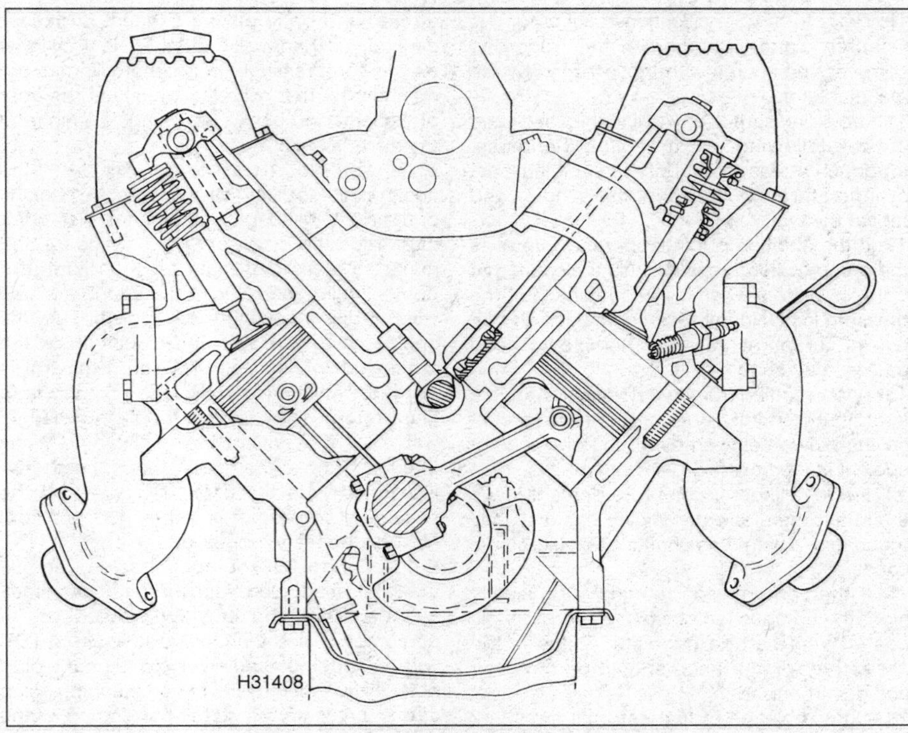
H31408

1.3 Sectional view of the engine from the front

2 Compression test - description and interpretation

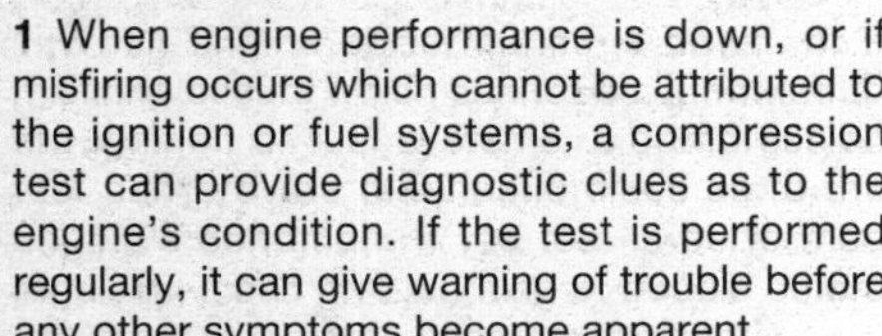

1 When engine performance is down, or if misfiring occurs which cannot be attributed to the ignition or fuel systems, a compression test can provide diagnostic clues as to the engine's condition. If the test is performed regularly, it can give warning of trouble before any other symptoms become apparent.

2 The engine must be fully warmed-up to normal operating temperature, the battery must be fully charged, and all the spark plugs must be removed (refer to Chapter 1A). The aid of an assistant will also be required.

3 Disable the ignition system by disconnecting the ignition HT coil lead from the distributor cap and earthing it on the cylinder block. Use a jumper lead or similar wire to make a good connection.

4 Where applicable, to prevent possible damage to the catalytic converter, depressurise and disable the fuel injection system by removing the fuel pump fuse or relay (see Chapter 4B).

5 Fit a compression tester to the No 1 cylinder spark plug hole - the type of tester which screws into the plug thread is preferable.

6 Have an assistant hold the accelerator pedal in the full-throttle position, then crank the engine on the starter motor; after one or two revolutions, the compression pressure should build up to a maximum figure, and then stabilise. Record the highest reading obtained.

7 Repeat the test on the remaining cylinders, recording the pressure in each. Keep the accelerator pedal fully depressed.

8 All cylinders should produce very similar pressures; a difference of more than 2 bars between any two cylinders indicates a fault (the manufacturer quotes a maximum difference between the highest and lowest of all four readings).

9 Note that the compression should build up quickly in a healthy engine; low compression on the first stroke, followed by gradually-increasing pressure on successive strokes, indicates worn piston rings. A low compression reading on the first stroke, which does not build up during successive strokes, indicates leaking valves or a blown head gasket (a cracked head could also be the cause). Deposits on the undersides of the valve heads can also cause low compression.

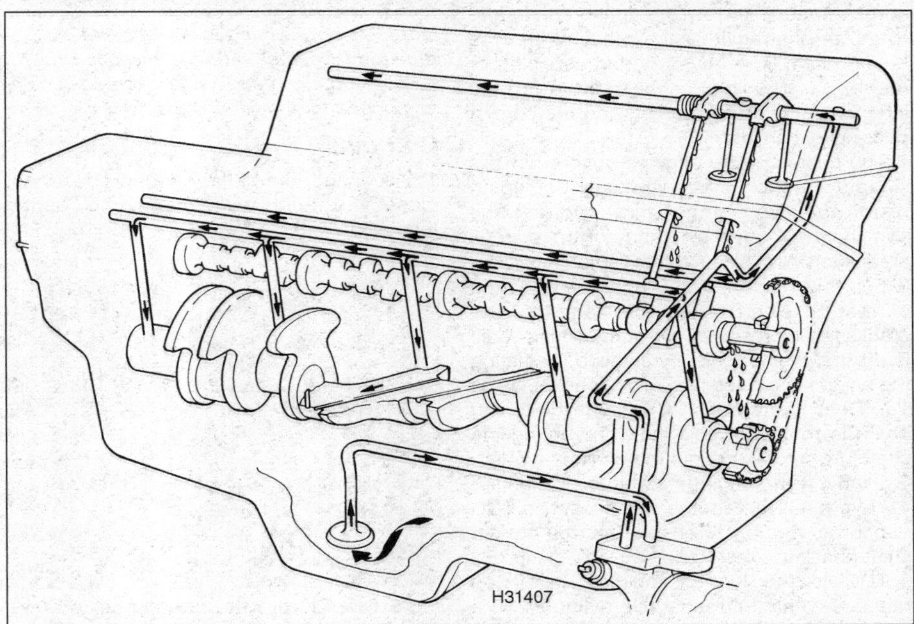
H31407

1.7 Lubrication system

10 Refer to the Specifications section of this Chapter, and compare the recorded compression figures with those stated by the manufacturer.
11 If the pressure in any cylinder is low, carry out the following test to isolate the cause. Introduce a teaspoonful of clean oil into that cylinder through its spark plug hole, and repeat the test.
12 If the addition of oil temporarily improves the compression pressure, this indicates that bore or piston wear is responsible for the pressure loss. No improvement suggests that leaking or burnt valves, or a blown head gasket, may be to blame.
13 A low reading from two adjacent cylinders is almost certainly due to the head gasket having blown between them; the presence of coolant in the engine oil will confirm this.
14 If one cylinder is about 20 percent lower than the others and the engine has a slightly rough idle, a worn camshaft lobe could be the cause.
15 If the compression reading is unusually high, the combustion chambers are probably coated with carbon deposits. If this is the case, the cylinder head should be removed and decarbonised.
16 On completion of the test, refit the spark plugs and restore the ignition and fuel systems.

3 Top dead centre (TDC) for No 1 piston - locating

Note: *This sub-Section has been written with the assumption that the distributor, HT leads and timing chain are correctly fitted.*
1 The crankshaft pulley and camshaft sprocket are linked by the timing chain, and rotate in phase with each other. When the timing chain is removed during servicing or repair, it is possible for the shafts to rotate independently of each other, and the correct phasing is then lost.
2 The design of the engines covered in this Chapter is such that potentially damaging piston-to-valve contact may occur if the camshaft is rotated when any of the pistons are stationary at, or near, the top of its stroke.
3 For this reason, it is important that the correct phasing between the camshaft and crankshaft is preserved whilst the timing chain is off the engine. This is achieved by setting the engine in a reference condition (known as Top Dead Centre or TDC) before the timing chain is removed, and then preventing the shafts from rotating until the chain is refitted. Similarly, if the engine has been dismantled for overhaul, the engine can be set to TDC during reassembly to ensure that the correct shaft phasing is restored.
4 TDC is the highest position a piston reaches within its respective cylinder - in a four-stroke engine, each piston reaches TDC twice per cycle; once on the compression stroke, and once on the exhaust stroke. In general, TDC normally refers to No 1 cylinder on the compression stroke (the cylinders are numbered 1 to 8, with No 1 being at the front of the left-hand bank - left being as seen from the driver's seat).
5 To set No 1 piston at TDC on the compression or firing stroke, note the position of the No 1 cylinder HT lead on the distributor cap (trace the lead from No 1 cylinder), and make an alignment mark on the distributor body. Unclip and remove the distributor cap without disconnecting the HT leads. Turn the engine using a socket and extension on the crankshaft pulley bolt until the rotor arm is aligned with the No 1 HT lead position **(see illustration)**. The crankshaft pulley is marked with a scale for ignition timing, and a pointer is fitted just above the pulley. When the pointer is aligned with the 0 or TDC mark on the scale, the crankshaft is in the TDC position, No 1 piston on compression.
6 To confirm TDC on compression, remove the No 1 spark plug. Turning the engine back a little from the position described in paragraph 5, and then forwards again to TDC with a finger placed over No 1 spark plug hole. If No 1 piston is rising on a compression stroke, pressure will be felt building up as the engine is turned forwards to TDC.
7 Once No 1 cylinder has been positioned at TDC on the compression stroke, TDC for any of the other cylinders can then be located by rotating the crankshaft clockwise 180° at a time and following the firing order (see Specifications).

4 Timing cover, chain and gears - removal, inspection and refitting

Note: *A new timing cover gasket will be required, together with some sealant for the sump mating face and thread-locking compound for the timing cover bolts.*

Removal

1 Disconnect the battery negative lead, and place the lead away from the battery terminals.

3.5 Distributor rotor arm in position for No 1 cylinder firing (1995 model shown - earlier distributors may differ)

2 Referring to Chapter 3, remove the radiator fan cowl and the viscous fan assembly. Although not strictly necessary, access will be further improved if the radiator is also removed.
3 Remove the auxiliary drivebelts (or single drivebelt on later models) as described in Chapter 1A.
4 Drain the cooling system as described in Chapter 1A, then disconnect the hoses from the water pump.
5 Drain the engine oil as described in Chapter 1A, then remove the oil filter. Where applicable, also disconnect the oil cooler pipe unions from the oil filter housing (see Section 14).
6 Using the information in Section 3, set the engine to TDC on No 1 cylinder.
7 Lift off the distributor cap and leads, and place it to one side. Also disconnect the distributor vacuum pipe and wiring plug.
8 Unbolt and remove the power steering pump mounting bracket from the water pump. Loosen the steering pump mounting and adjuster bolts, and pivot the pump body away from the timing cover. Tighten the adjuster bolt to hold the pump in this position.
9 Disconnect the wiring from the oil pressure switch.
10 On models with multiple auxiliary drivebelts, unbolt the alternator adjuster link from the water pump. Detach any wiring from the adjuster link. Also unbolt the alternator support strut from the timing cover, and move it to one side.
11 The crankshaft pulley must now be removed. As the engine has been set to TDC, try to turn the pulley as little as possible as the bolt is loosened.
12 Apply the handbrake, then jack up the front of the vehicle and support on axle stands. Remove the engine undertray, and then remove the bolts securing the transmission bellhousing lower cover, for access to the flywheel teeth.
13 Have an assistant jam the flywheel teeth so that the crankshaft cannot turn, then slacken and remove the crankshaft pulley bolt. Particularly on models where a starter dog is incorporated into the bolt head, a deep socket will be needed. The bolt is extremely tight - be sure to use only good-quality, close-fitting tools, and be prepared for the bolt to loosen suddenly under high pressure. Remove the bolt and recover the special washer.
14 Check that the engine is still at TDC, then slide off the crankshaft pulley. This should come off easily by hand, but a puller may be required.
15 Make an alignment mark between the distributor body and the timing cover, so that the distributor can be accurately refitted. Loosen the distributor clamp bolt, and withdraw the distributor from the engine.
16 Remove the two sump bolts nearest the front, which screw through the base of the timing cover. Also loosen the four sump bolts next nearest the front **(see illustration)**.

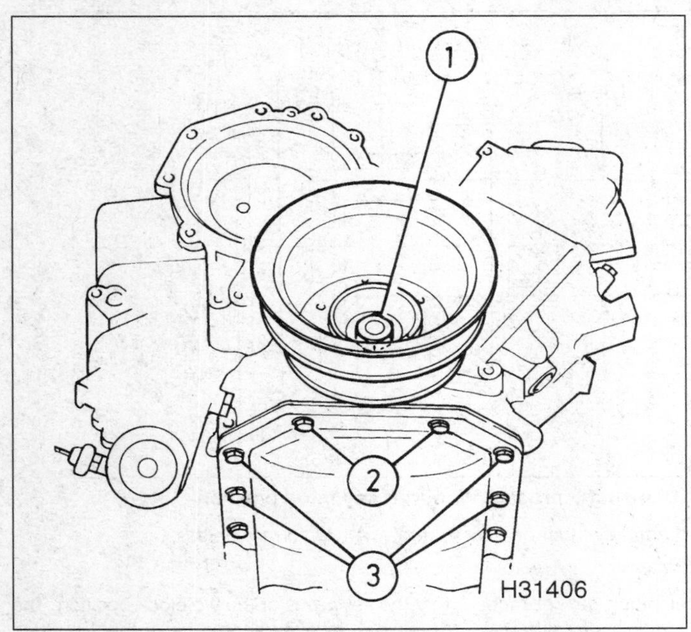
1
2
3
H31406

4.16 Timing cover removal details

1 Crankshaft pulley bolt
2 Remove these two bolts
3 Loosen these four bolts

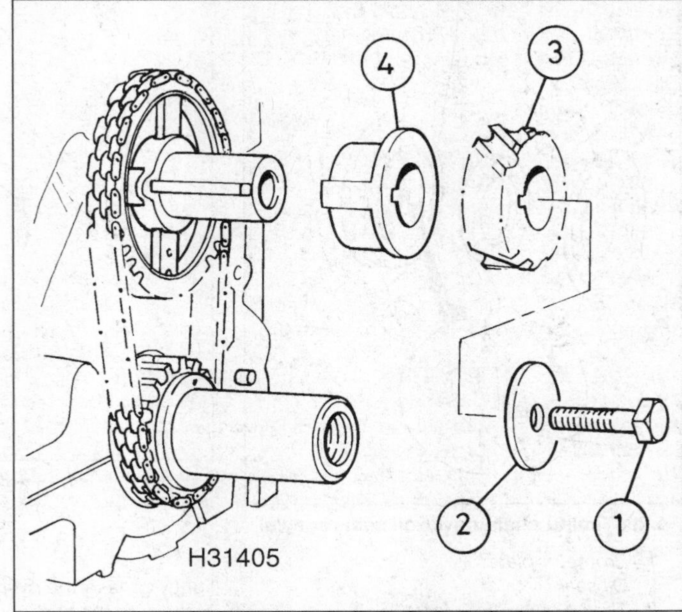
4
3
2
1
H31405

4.18 Distributor drivegear details

1 Drivegear retaining bolt
2 Washer
3 Drivegear
4 Spacer

17 Loosen and remove the nine timing cover retaining bolts, noting their locations, as they are of different lengths. Separate the cover from the front of the engine, taking great care not to damage the sump gasket, and recover the two dowels. The cover is removed complete with the water and oil pumps.

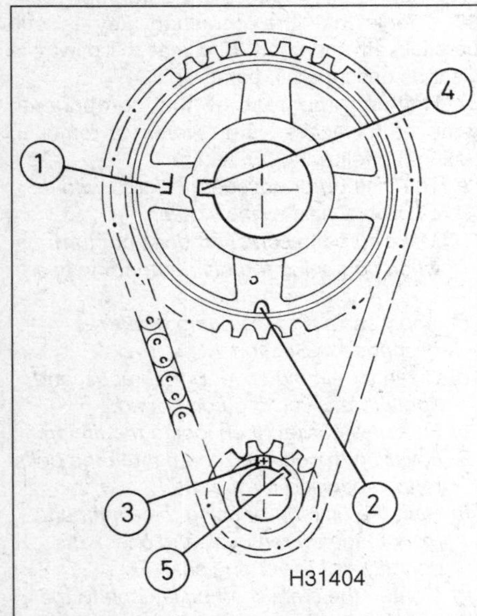
4
1
F
3
2
5
H31404

4.19 Timing chain and related components set to TDC

1 F mark on camshaft sprocket
2 Notch in camshaft sprocket spoke
3 Punch mark in crankshaft sprocket
4 Camshaft sprocket keyway (at 9 o'clock)
5 Crankshaft sprocket keyway (at 1 o'clock)

Recover the gasket, if possible - a new gasket will of course be needed when refitting.

18 Making sure the camshaft does not turn, loosen and remove the distributor drivegear retaining bolt and washer. Take off the distributor drivegear and spacer, noting which way round the gear fits **(see illustration)**.

19 As a final check that the engine is set to TDC, note that the punched dot mark in the crankshaft sprocket hub and the notch in one of the camshaft sprocket spokes should be adjacent to each other, and aligned vertically - check this with a straight-edge. It is also worth noting the respective positions of the sprocket keyways, particularly if a new timing chain is being fitted **(see illustration)**.

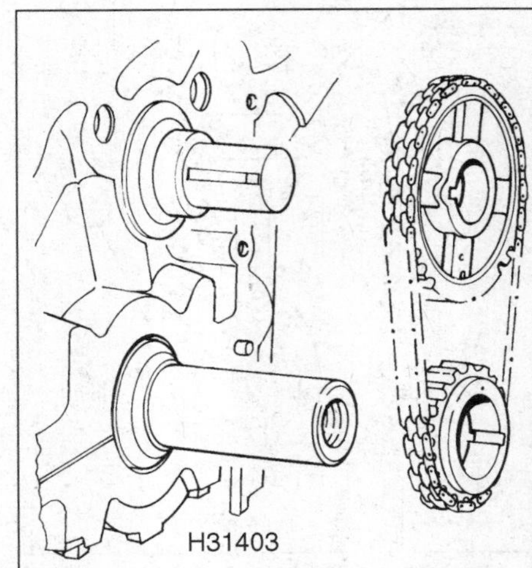
H31403

4.20 Removing the timing chain and sprockets

20 Carefully slide off the crankshaft and camshaft sprockets, together with the timing chain **(see illustration)**. Recover the Woodruff keys from the shafts if they are loose.

Inspection

21 Examine the teeth on the camshaft and crankshaft sprockets. If they are worn, or have taken on a hooked appearance, they should be renewed. Note that a new chain should not be fitted onto old sprockets.

22 Inspect the camshaft sprocket for signs of cracking.

23 Inspect the chain for wear, and the links for slackness. Remove the chain from the sprockets, and squeeze it together into a straight line. Pick the chain up at one end, and try to hold it horizontal, to check the side play - if the chain droops too much, the link pins are worn **(see illustration)**.

24 Temporarily refit the chain to the engine - there should be no undue slackness or sag between the sprockets. As a guide, if the chain can be lifted clear of the sprocket teeth at the top or bottom of its run, it has stretched

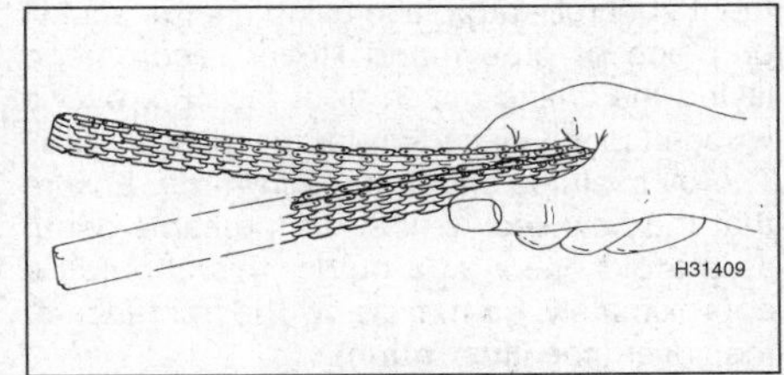
H31409

4.23 Checking timing chain for wear

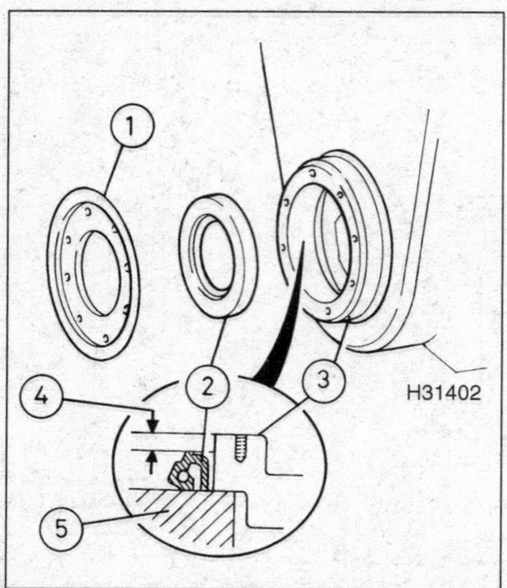
1
2
3
4
5
H31402

4.29 Timing chain cover oil seal renewal

1 Protector plate
2 Oil seal
3 Timing cover front face
4 Oil seal fitted depth (1.5 mm)
5 Wooden block placed under timing cover (Land Rover method)

too far, and must be renewed. There is no chain tensioner, and a slack chain could jump off the sprockets, with potentially disastrous results. Renew the chain if necessary, but note that a new chain should not be fitted onto old sprockets.

25 Check the condition of the front cover oil seal. Although it can be renewed without removing the timing cover, it would be worth fitting a new one as a matter of course, since the job is far easier with the cover removed.

26 Unscrew the eight screws securing the protector plate from the front of the seal, then remove the plate and note the seal's fitted depth in the cover.

27 Drive the seal squarely from its location, taking care not to damage the seal seating, and noting which way round it is fitted. Alternatively, drill two small holes on opposite sides of the front face of the seal and screw in two self-tapping screws, leaving enough of each screw sticking out so that it can be gripped with a pair of pliers. The seal can then be worked out of the front cover.

28 After extracting the old seal, clean the housing and remove any burrs on the front edge.

29 When fitting the new seal, lubricate it and tap it squarely into place using a large socket or piece of pipe (Land Rover recommend laying the timing cover, front face up, over a wooden block placed under the oil seal bore). The oil seal lips should face inwards. Ensure that the new seal is fitted to the same depth as the old one - as a guide, this should be approximately 1.5 mm below the front face of the cover **(see illustration)**.

30 Thoroughly clean the mating faces of the timing cover and the cylinder block, then lightly grease the cylinder block gasket face. Make sure the two cover dowels are refitted to their locations.

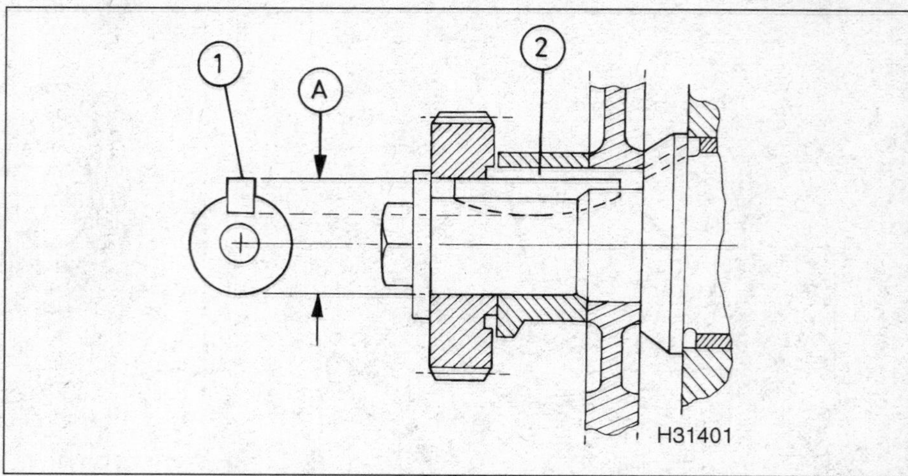
1
A
2
H31401

4.31 Camshaft sprocket Woodruff key fitted position

1 Woodruff key must be fully seated
2 Oilway
A 30.15 mm or less

Refitting

31 It is essential that the Woodruff key for the camshaft sprocket is correctly fitted. The oil feed for the timing chain is made through a channel in the distributor drivegear spacer. If the key is not fitted so that its top edge is absolutely parallel with the top of the shaft, or if it is loose in its groove and can move under centrifugal force, it will block the oil supply to the timing chain and gears, with serious results. The Woodruff key must also be fully seated in its groove in the shaft, so that the overall height of shaft and key does not exceed 30.15 mm **(see illustration)**.

32 If the camshaft has been disturbed, check that the keyway is at the 9 o'clock position. The crankshaft keyway should be at the 1 o'clock position **(see illustration)**.

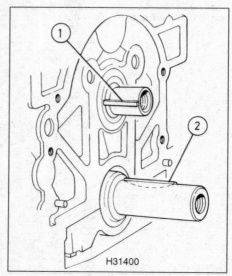

4.32 Camshaft (1) and crankshaft (2) Woodruff key positions, prior to fitting timing chain

33 Fit the chain to the sprockets with the timing marks and keyways aligned as noted on removal. The F or FRONT marking on the camshaft sprocket must be visible when fitted.

34 Offer up the sprockets and chain to both the camshaft and crankshaft simultaneously, ensuring that the timing marks stay in line.

35 Fit the sprockets over the keys on both shafts and push them home. Check that the alignment is still correct - see paragraph 19.

36 Check that the camshaft key is still parallel with the shaft, and that the oilway is clear as described in paragraph 31.

37 Refitting the rest of the components removed for access is a reversal of removal, noting the following points:

a) The distributor drivegear is fitted with its oil groove next to the spacer.
b) Make sure the camshaft does not turn when tightening the distributor drivegear bolt..
c) Apply sealant to the sump gasket as described in Section 12.
d) Clean the timing cover bolt threads, and apply thread-locking compound.
e) Fit a new gasket, then locate the timing cover on the dowels, and tighten the bolts to the specified torque.
f) Refit the distributor using the alignment mark made on removal, and check the condition of the O-ring seal.
g) Tighten the crankshaft pulley bolt to the specified torque, preventing crankshaft rotation as on removal.
h) When all remaining components have been refitted and the engine is refilled with oil and coolant, start the engine and check for oil leaks around the timing cover.
i) Check and if necessary adjust the ignition timing as described in Chapter 1A.

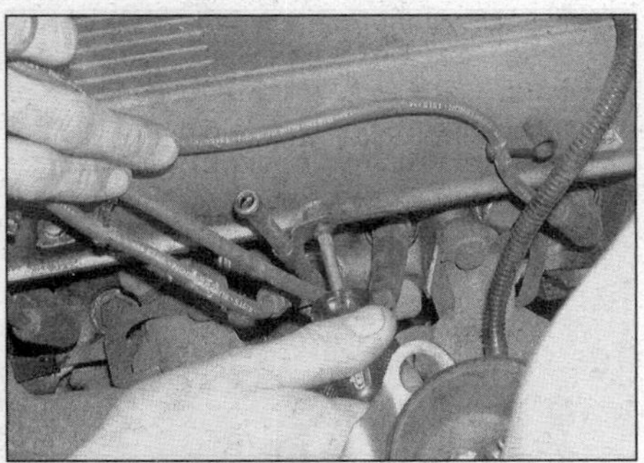

5.3 Remove the bolt securing the top of the dipstick tube

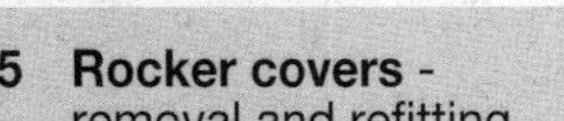

5 Rocker covers - removal and refitting

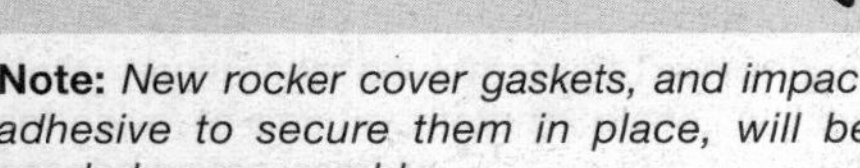

Note: *New rocker cover gaskets, and impact adhesive to secure them in place, will be needed on reassembly.*

Left-hand cover

Removal

1 On carburettor engines, remove the air cleaner as described in Chapter 1A.

2 On fuel injection engines, refer to Chapter 4B and remove the plenum chamber.

3 Pull out the engine oil dipstick, and place it to one side. Unbolt the dipstick tube clamp from the rocker cover **(see illustration)**, then slide the clamp over the top of the tube. If the cylinder heads are to be removed, pull the tube upwards and remove it.

5.7a Unscrew the four bolts . . .

5.8 Loosen the hose clip, and pull off the breather hose

5.4 Unclip the HT leads from the rocker cover

4 Make sure that the HT leads are marked for position, then pull the leads from the spark plugs. Unclip the leads from the clips on top of the rocker cover and engine lifting bracket, noting how they are routed **(see illustration)**.

5 Where applicable, remove the alternator heat shield securing nut from the rocker cover.

6 Release any wiring or cables attached to the rocker cover from the cable-ties or clamps, and place to one side as far as possible. Pull off the breather hose from the rear of the cover **(see illustrations)**.

7 Loosen and remove the four rocker cover bolts, and lift off the cover **(see illustrations)**. If it is stuck, try to rock it free - if the cover has to be prised off, do not use force, or the sealing surfaces between the cover and cylinder head will be damaged. Recover the gasket, and note that the outer two bolts are longer than the inner ones.

5.7b . . . then lift off the rocker cover and gasket

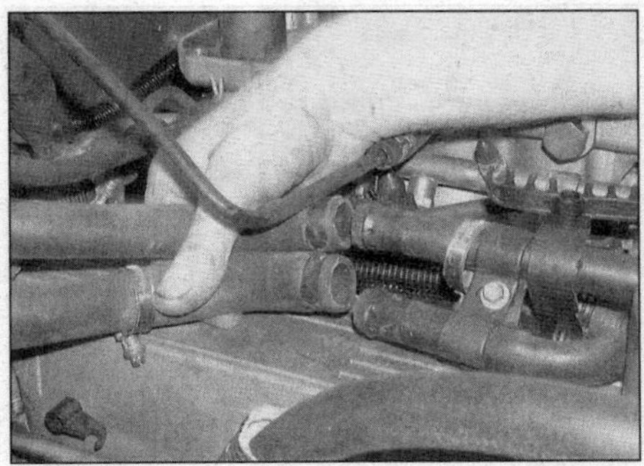

5.12 Disconnecting the heater hoses from the rigid pipes

5.6a Release the wiring harness from the rocker cover . . .

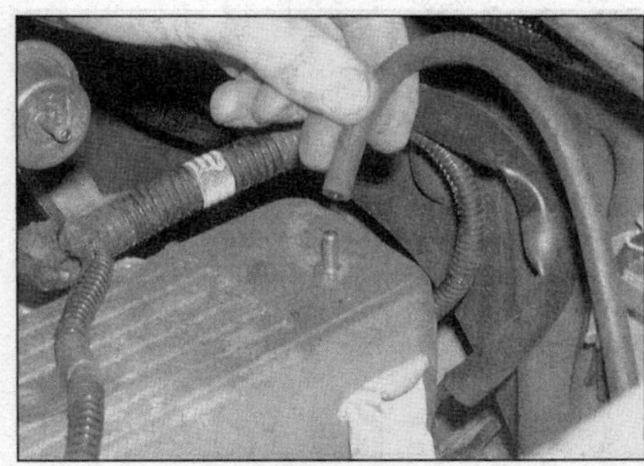

5.6b . . . and pull off the breather hose at the rear

Right-hand cover

Removal

8 Disconnect the hose from the crankcase breather filter **(see illustration)**.

9 On carburettor engines, remove the air cleaner as described in Chapter 1A.

10 Partially drain the cooling system, using the information in Chapter 1A.

11 Make sure that the HT leads are marked for position, then pull the leads from the spark plugs. Unclip the leads from the clips on top of the rocker cover and heater pipes, noting how they are routed.

12 Loosen the hose clips and detach the heater hoses from the rigid pipes **(see illustration)**.

13 Remove the bolt clamping the two rigid heater pipes together, then detach the heater hose from the inlet manifold **(see illustrations)**.

5.13a Remove the heater pipe clamp bolt . . .

5.13b . . . then disconnect the heater hose from the inlet manifold

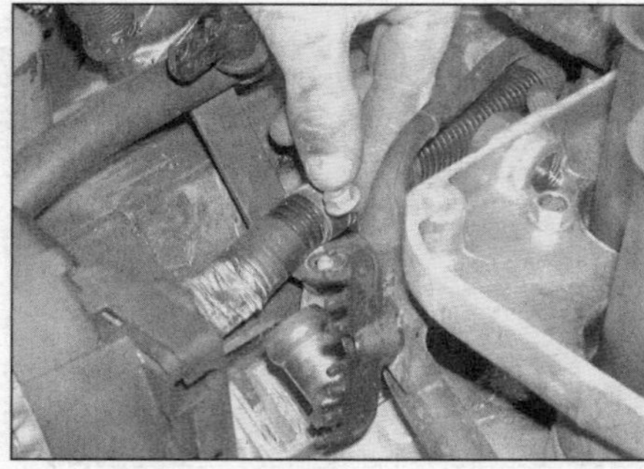

5.14 Remove the nut securing the heater pipe bracket

5.15 Unclip and disconnect the fuel injection supply and return hoses

5.17 Removing the right-hand rocker cover

14 Remove the nut and detach the heater hose bracket from the inlet manifold **(see illustration)**. One heater pipe can now be removed completely - move the pipe which was not removed to one side as far as possible.

15 On fuel injection engines, depressurise the fuel system as described in Chapter 4B, then unclip and disconnect the fuel supply and return hoses **(see illustration)**.

16 Release any wiring or cables attached to the rocker cover from the cable-ties or clamps, and place to one side as far as possible.

17 Loosen and remove the four rocker cover bolts, and lift off the cover, manoeuvring it out past the coolant pipes **(see illustration)**. If the cover is stuck, try to rock it free - if the cover has to be prised off, do not use force, or the sealing surfaces between the cover and cylinder head will be damaged. Recover the gasket, and note that the outer two bolts are longer than the inner ones.

Refitting - both covers

18 Refitting is a reversal of removal, noting the following points:

a) Always fit a new gasket. Clean all traces of the old gasket from the cover and cylinder head mating surfaces, then apply a suitable impact adhesive (Bostik 1775) to the rocker cover mating face and to the rocker cover side of the new gasket. When the adhesive is touch-dry, accurately fit the gasket, starting at one end, and press firmly into place. Wait 30 minutes before fitting the rocker cover to the engine.

b) The shorter rocker cover bolts are fitted to the inside of the cover. Tighten the bolts to the specified torque.

c) Check that the lip of the gasket is visible all round the edge of the cover, to ensure a good seal.

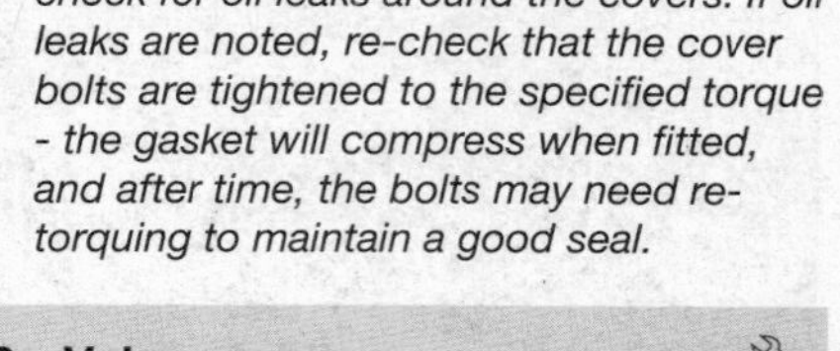

d) Refit all components removed for access. On completion, start the engine and check for oil leaks around the covers. If oil leaks are noted, re-check that the cover bolts are tightened to the specified torque - the gasket will compress when fitted, and after time, the bolts may need re-torquing to maintain a good seal.

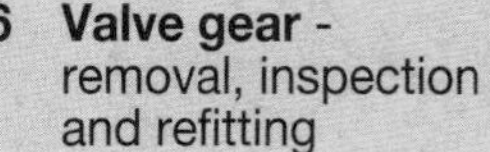

6 Valve gear - removal, inspection and refitting

Removal

1 Remove the rocker covers as described in Section 5.

2 If the hydraulic tappets are to be removed, refer to Chapter 4A or 4B as applicable, and remove the inlet manifold.

3 It is most important that the original fitted position of all components is maintained - this applies particularly to the pushrods and hydraulic tappets. Take care to identify all removed components for position, as described in the following paragraphs.

4 Undo the four rocker shaft assembly retaining bolts in stages so that the assembly rises evenly on the pressure of the valve springs **(see illustration)**.

5 Lift out the assembly complete with bolts, and place it to one side **(see illustration)**.

6 To avoid confusion when refitting, mark the rocker shafts for position (ie left and right). The shafts should be marked with a notch at one end - this is at the front on the right-hand shaft, and at the rear on the left-hand shaft.

7 Make up two pieces of card with 8 numbered holes punched in it, with an arrow to indicate the front of the engine - also mark the cards left and right. Remove the pushrods slowly, and place them in order through the holes in the card **(see illustration)**.

HAYNES
HiNT

If the pushrods are removed slowly, the hydraulic tappets will usually lift up as the pushrod is pulled upwards, and the tappets can then be removed more easily.

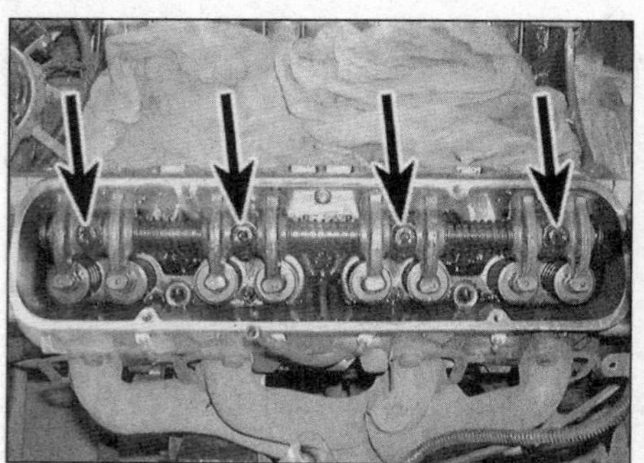

6.4a Rocker shaft retaining bolts (arrowed)

6.4b Loosen the rocker shaft bolts evenly

6.5 Lifting out the rocker shaft assembly

L/H
1 2 3 4 5 6 7 8

6.7 Take out the pushrods, and store them in a clearly-marked piece of card

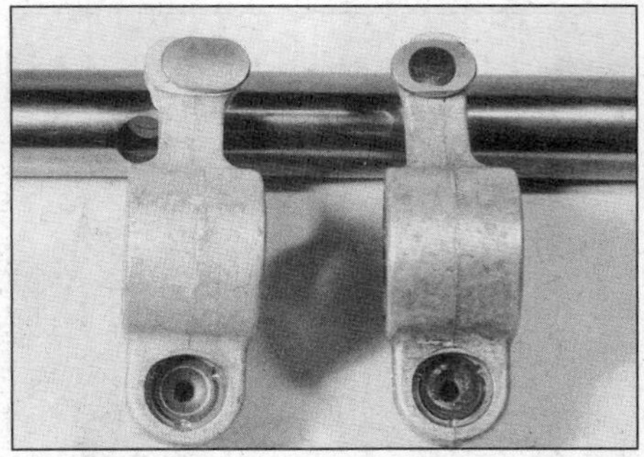

6.12 New rocker (left) compared with old one (right). Note damage to cup

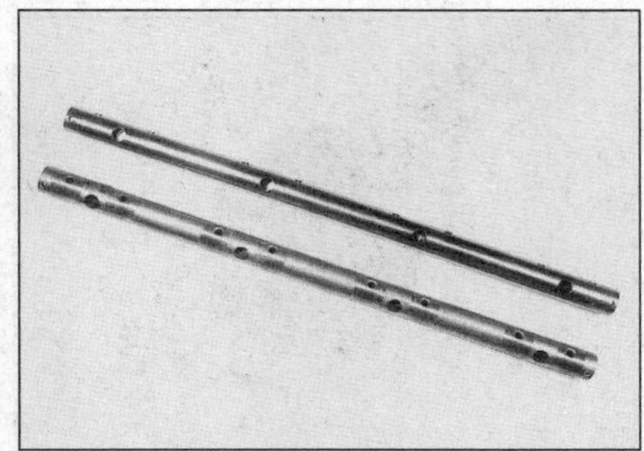

6.13 Worn (bottom) and new (top) rocker shafts being compared

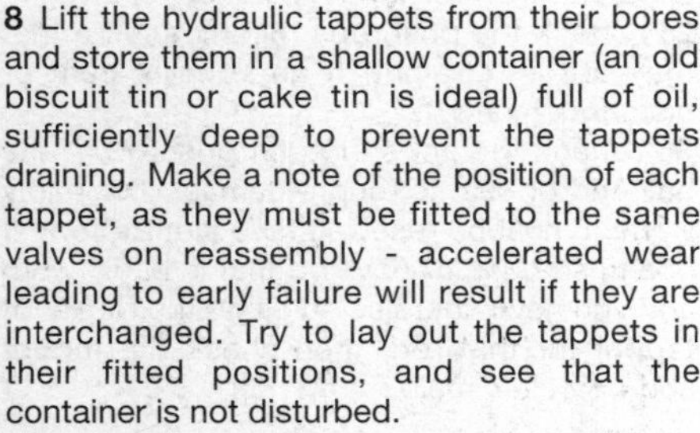

8 Lift the hydraulic tappets from their bores and store them in a shallow container (an old biscuit tin or cake tin is ideal) full of oil, sufficiently deep to prevent the tappets draining. Make a note of the position of each tappet, as they must be fitted to the same valves on reassembly - accelerated wear leading to early failure will result if they are interchanged. Try to lay out the tappets in their fitted positions, and see that the container is not disturbed.

9 If a tappet is difficult to remove, and the engine is being completely stripped, leave it until the camshaft has been withdrawn, and then push it downwards to remove it (the tappet will then have to be removed from the crankcase once the sump has been removed). Otherwise, try using a magnetic probe tool to pull out the tappet.

Inspection

Rocker shafts

10 With the rocker shaft assemblies removed, the first job is to inspect the rockers and shafts for wear, in order to determine whether the assemblies need to be stripped and overhauled.

11 Take one assembly at a time, and do not mix up left and right-hand assemblies. The shafts are handed, and can only fit one way.

12 First examine the rockers. The rockers themselves are alloy, but they have hardened inserts at each end. The pads bear on the ends of the valve stems, and the cups fit over the upper ends of the pushrods. With high mileage or hard wear, the hardened cup inserts tend to crack up and wear badly. If bad wear is evident in a cup, then the pushrod will be badly worn as well. Similarly the pads will wear, and if this is noticeable the rockers need renewing **(see illustration)**.

13 Check the amount of lateral movement of the rockers on the shafts. If play is evident, then look further. Slide the rockers along the shaft against their springs, and examine the rocker shaft itself. If this is done from above only, the wear pattern on the rocker shaft may be missed, as the wear occurs on the *underside* of the shaft - the rockers cut into the shaft under pressure from the valves and pushrods below. With high-mileage engines, those which have been used for hard work, or where there has been a lack of oil being fed to the top of the engine, the amount of wear can be quite severe **(see illustration)**.

14 Remove the pedestal bolts, and slide the pedestals along the shaft. Check for wear in the pedestal/shaft contact areas.

15 To overhaul the rocker shaft assembly, proceed as follows. Remove the split pin from one end of the rocker shaft, and slide off the components, carefully retaining them in the correct order of sequence for reassembly.

16 If new rocker arms are being fitted, ensure that the protective coating material used in storage is removed from the oil holes, and the new rocker given a smearing of clean oil before fitting to the shaft. **Note:** *The rocker arms are handed each side of the pedestals, and must be fitted correctly so that the metal pads locate over the valve stems. The valve ends of the rocker arms should slope away from the pedestals* ***(see illustrations)***.

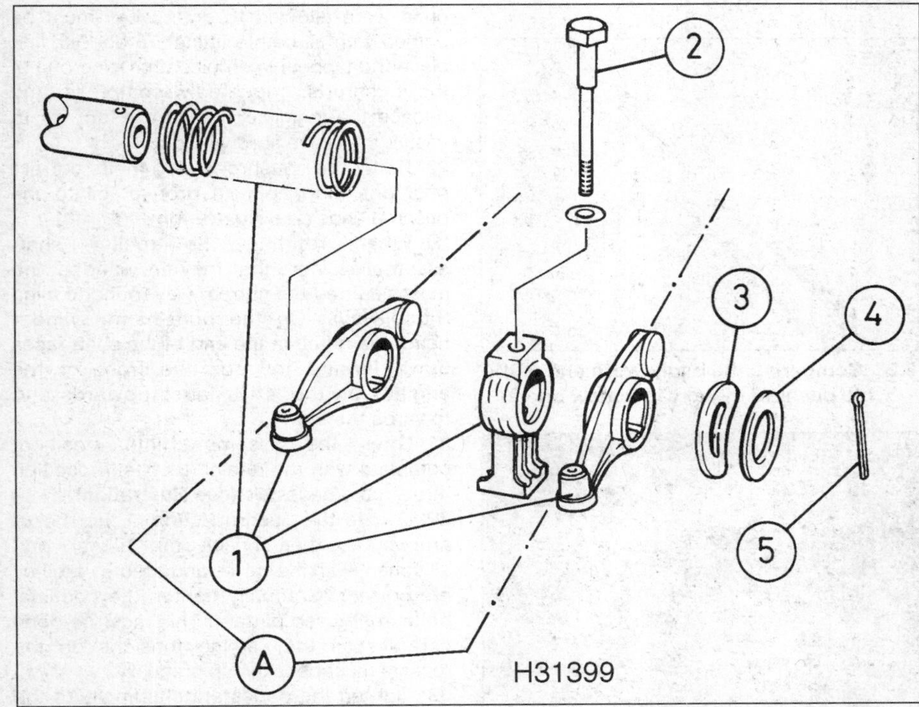
1
2
3
4
5
A
H31399

6.16a Dotted lines (A) indicating slope of rocker arms away from the pedestals

1 Pedestal, rocker arms and spring
2 Bolt
3 Wave washer
4 Plain washer
5 Split pin

6.16b Two rockers with pedestal between - note relationship of pushrod bearing faces away from pedestal

6.17 Refit split pin, plain washer and wave washer - notch in shaft uppermost

17 The rocker shafts are notched at one end, to ensure that the oil feed holes are positioned correctly facing upwards. The notches must be located uppermost **(see illustration)**. On the right-hand bank (viewed from the driver's seat) the notch must be facing towards the front of the engine, and on the left-hand bank it must be facing towards the rear of the engine. Always use new split pins.

18 Refit the baffle plate (where applicable) and pedestal bolts to the shaft. Note that the plate fits at the opposite end of the shaft to the notch.

19 The rocker shaft assembly is now ready for refitting. Carry out the same inspection and overhaul procedure for the other assembly.

Tappets and pushrods

20 If a hydraulic tappet has to be removed downwards (see paragraph 9) then there is a good chance that the lower end has become belled or rimmed. Inspect and renew if wear is bad.

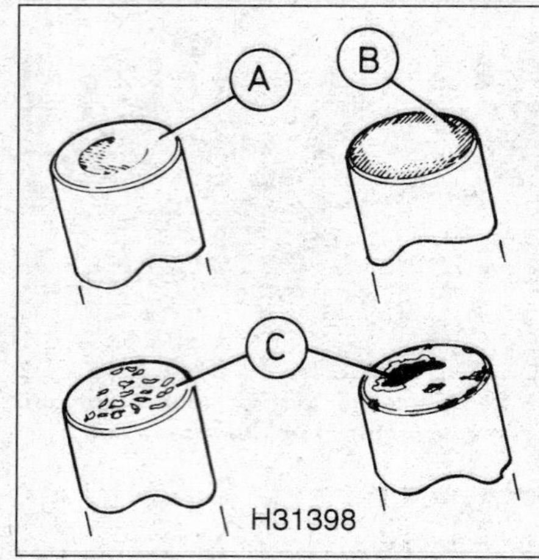
A
B
C
H31398

6.23 Tappet wear patterns

A Correct rotating wear pattern
B Wear pattern for non-rotating tappet
C Typical examples of excessive wear

21 If there is a prominent wear pattern just above the lower end of the body, this should only merit renewal of the tappet if it is badly grooved or scored. This condition is caused by the side thrust of the cam against the body whilst the tappet moves vertically in its guide.

22 Inspect the tappet inner and outer surfaces for blow holes and scoring. Renew the tappet if the body is roughly grooved or scored, or has a blow hole extending through the wall.

23 Inspect the tappet/camshaft lobe contact area. Fit a new tappet if the surface is badly worn or damaged. The tappet must rotate as it moves up and down, and should produce an even circular wear pattern. If the tappet has not been rotating, the wear pattern will be square with a dip in the centre **(see illustration)**. Non-rotating tappets must be renewed. Check the wear on the camshaft lobe if there is a non-rotating tappet. When renewing a tappet, check that it moves freely in the guide in the cylinder block.

24 Check the pushrod contact end of the tappet for roughness or damage **(see illustration)**. If either sorts of wear are apparent, then the tappet must be renewed.

25 Check the pushrods. Firstly ensure that they are all straight. If any one is bent or distorted, renew it.

26 Check the ends of each pushrod. If the ball end or seat is rough, damaged or badly worn, it must be renewed **(see illustration)**. If one pushrod is discovered that is badly worn and you have not rejected either the rocker or tappet for that rod, then check the tappet and/or rocker again.

6.24 Check the pushrod seat in the top of the tappet

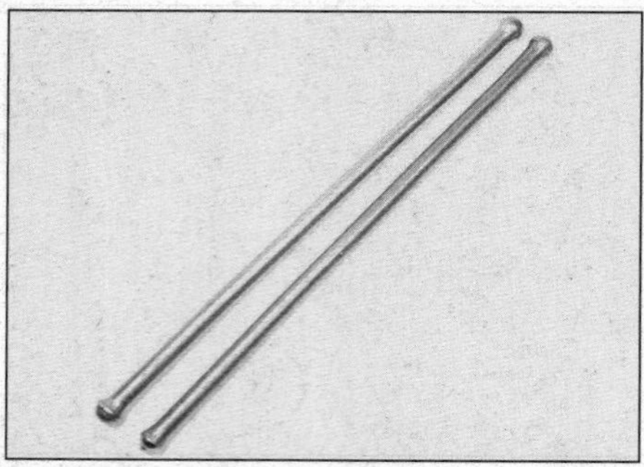

6.26 Comparing the badly-worn end of the old pushrod (right) with a new one

6.29 Oil the ends of the pushrods before fitting the rocker gear

6.31 Offer the rocker gear into position, aligning the pushrods and rockers

Refitting

27 Refit the tappets the right way up in the positions from which they were removed. New tappets must be fitted to the positions where tappets have been discarded for reasons of wear, etc. Check the tappet oilways before refitting.

28 If new tappets are being fitted, or if the old ones were allowed to drain, they must be primed with oil before fitting. To do this, first place the tappets in an oil bath. Using one of the pushrods, repeatedly compress and release the inner section of the tappets to ensure they have filled with oil.

29 Refit the pushrods to their correct positions, and apply a drop of oil to the pushrod ends **(see illustration)**.

30 When refitting the rocker shaft assemblies, note that they are handed and must be fitted the correct way round to align the oilways. On the right-hand cylinder head, the notch in the end of the shaft faces upwards and towards the front of the engine. On the left it faces upwards and towards the rear.

31 Offer the assembly into position, complete with the retaining bolts in position through the pedestals **(see illustration)**.

32 Locate the pushrod ends in the rocker arm cups, then check the rocker pad alignment with the valves and ensure that they are correct. Gradually tighten the pedestal bolts in an even pattern. This must be done carefully as the varying tensions on the rockers must be taken up gradually.

33 Tighten the pedestal bolts finally to the specified torque **(see illustration)**.

34 Rotate the crankshaft to ensure that all the valves, rockers and tappets function correctly.

6.33 Tighten the pedestal bolts to the specified torque

35 Refit the inlet manifold as described in Chapter 4A or 4B.

36 Refit the rocker covers as described in Section 5.

7 Camshaft - removal, inspection and refitting

Removal

1 Remove the radiator as described in Chapter 3.

2 Remove the timing cover and timing chain as described in Section 4.

3 Using the information in Section 6, remove the rocker gear, pushrods and hydraulic tappets.

4 If any of the hydraulic tappets cannot be removed, action must be taken to lift the tappets clear of the camshaft as far as possible before attempting to remove the camshaft. Insert the tappet next to the one which is stuck, and lift up the stuck tappet as far as possible in its bore. Wrap a stout rubber band tightly around the tops of the two tappets, so that they are lifted clear of the camshaft **(see illustration)**.

5 Withdraw the camshaft slowly from the engine, taking care not to twist it, otherwise it will hang up on the lobes, which may cause damage to the camshaft and bearing surfaces. It may be necessary to turn the shaft as it is removed, but at no time should any force be used. Take care not to drop the shaft as it emerges from the engine - insert a screwdriver into the threaded end of the shaft to help support it **(see illustration)**.

Inspection

6 Thoroughly clean the camshaft and dry off, handling with care.

7 Examine all the bearing surfaces for obvious defects, wear, score marks, etc.

8 Similarly inspect the cam lobes for excessive wear.

9 Ensure that the key or keyway is not damaged or burred, and that the key is a tight fit in its keyway - this is most important (see Section 4, paragraph 31).

10 If in doubt about the camshaft's condition, seek professional advice and/or replace with a new component.

11 If a new camshaft is fitted, it may be advisable to replace all the hydraulic tappets as a set - re-using worn tappets on a new shaft will only lead to premature wear. Seek the advice of a Land Rover dealer or engine rebuilding specialist.

12 The camshaft bearings in the cylinder block are not renewable. If they are badly worn or damaged, a new block will be required.

Refitting

13 Refitting is a reversal of removal, noting the following points:

a) *Ensure that the camshaft is absolutely clean when refitting. Lubricate the cam lobes and bearings with clean engine oil as the shaft is inserted.*

b) *As with removal, insert the shaft slowly and carefully, to avoid damaging the surfaces - keep it aligned perpendicular to the front of the engine at all times.*

c) *Refit all the remaining components as described in Sections 4 and 6, then refit the radiator as described in Chapter 3.*

d) *If a new camshaft and tappets have been fitted, the engine should be run-in for the first few hundred miles, and the oil changed soon after.*

8 Cylinder heads - removal and refitting

Note: *This procedure assumes that both cylinder heads are to be removed. New head gaskets must be used. On models with 14 head bolts, Loctite 572 thread sealant will also be needed.*

Removal

1 Remove the valve gear and pushrods as described in Section 6.

2 To improve access, remove the cooling fan as described in Chapter 3. Although not essential, the job will be made easier if the radiator is also removed.

3 Refer to Chapter 4A or 4B as applicable, and remove the inlet manifold.

4 On early models with multiple auxiliary drivebelts, remove the alternator as described in Chapter 5A. Where applicable, unbolt the air conditioning compressor, and move it to one side, without straining or disconnecting any pipework. Refer to Chapter 11 and unbolt the power steering pump, moving it aside without disconnecting the fluid hoses.

5 On later models with a single drivebelt, unbolt the power steering pump as described in Chapter 11, and lay it to one side with the fluid hoses attached. Remove the mounting bolt from the drivebelt tensioner, and slide the tensioner off, disengaging its locating peg. Remove the four bolts securing the alternator mounting bracket, then slide the bracket

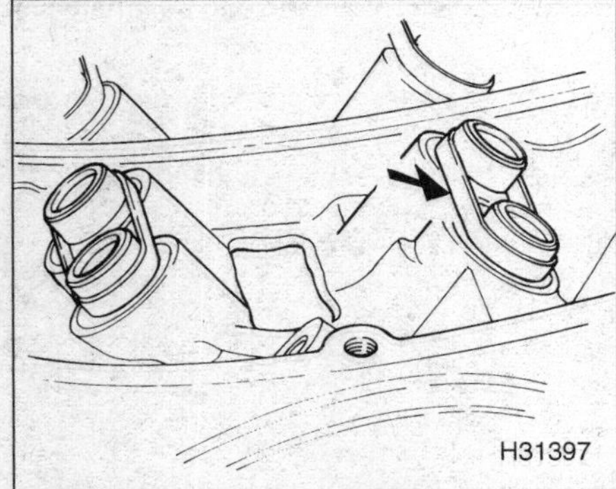
H31397

7.4 Rubber band (arrowed) used to retain hydraulic tappets in position for camshaft removal

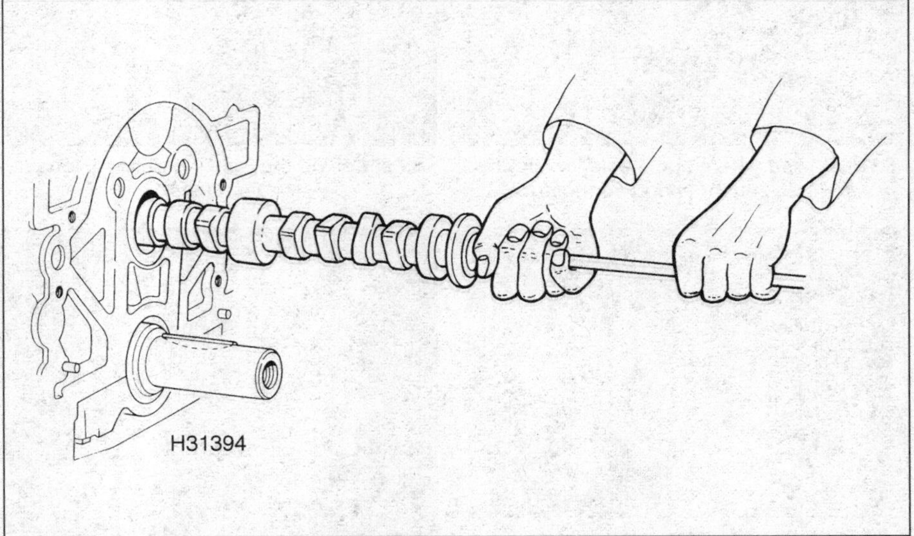
H31394

7.5 Removing the camshaft - note use of screwdriver to support the shaft

8.5a Remove the drivebelt tensioner mounting bolt . . .

8.5b . . . and slide off the tensioner, noting the mounting peg (arrowed)

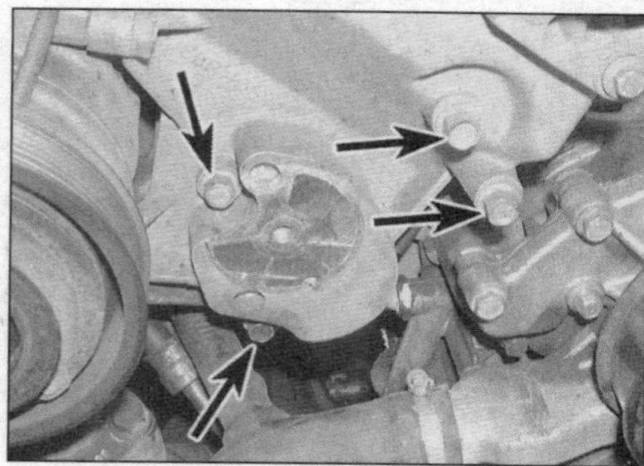
8.5c Alternator mounting bracket bolts (arrowed)

forwards slightly, to clear the right-hand cylinder head, but without straining the alternator wiring or air conditioning hoses (where applicable) **(see illustrations)**.

6 Unbolt and remove the exhaust manifolds as described in Chapter 4D. **Note:** *On later models with only 10 head bolts, the exhaust manifolds can be left on, and the exhaust separated at the manifold-to-downpipe connections (three nuts each side, accessed from below). If this method is used, the locktabs used to secure the manifold bolts will have to be bent to gain access to the outer row of head bolts.*

8.7a Remove the nut and stud from behind the left-hand head . . .

7 Remove the nut and stud, and disconnect the earth leads (and automatic transmission kickdown cable, where applicable) from the rear of the left-hand cylinder head. On models with a catalytic converter, unclip the lambda sensor wiring connector from the rear of the head - the connector halves do not have to be separated **(see illustrations)**.

8 At the rear of the right-hand head, remove the two bolts securing the engine lifting eye, and move it to the rear **(see illustrations)**.

9 Make sure that all wiring, hoses and cables have been detached from the heads, and moved clear to permit removal.

10 Models up to 1995 have, in addition to the ten main head bolts, a row of four small bolts on the spark plug side of each head. Models after this date have had the four additional bolts deleted.

11 Using the reverse of the relevant tightening sequence **(see illustration 8.32 or 8.34)**, loosen each bolt a quarter-turn at a time until all the bolts are completely loose **(see illustrations)**.

12 Make a careful note of where each bolt fits, since there are three different sizes - two different lengths of main head bolts, and also the four smaller additional bolts (on models so equipped) **(see illustration)**. Label the bolts as they are removed, or store them in their fitted order.

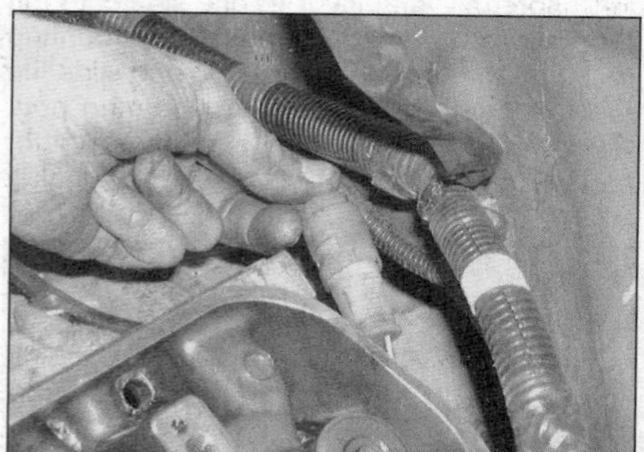
8.7b . . . and where applicable, unclip the lambda sensor wiring connector

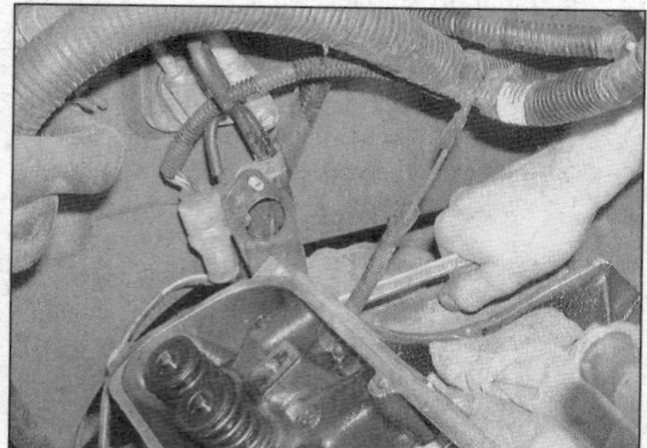
8.8a Behind the right-hand head, loosen the two bolts . . .

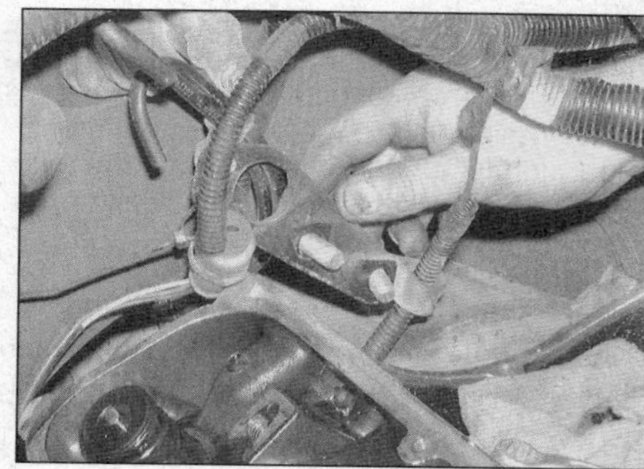
8.8b . . . and remove the engine lifting eye

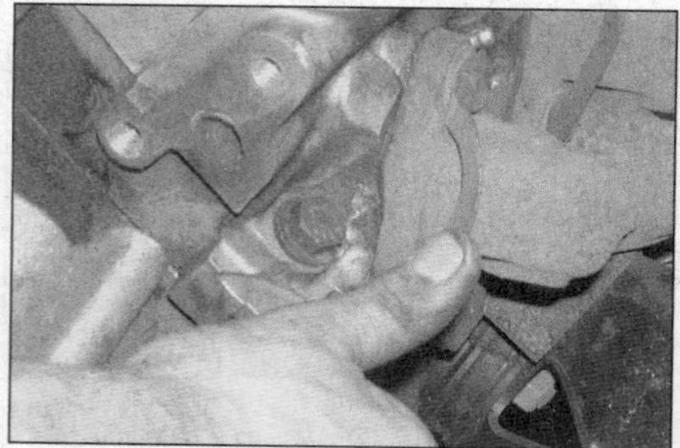
8.11a If the exhaust manifolds were not removed, bend the locktabs for access to the bolts

8.11b Loosening the cylinder head bolts

8.12 Removing one of the long head bolts - later model with 10 bolts per head

8.13 Lifting off the cylinder head

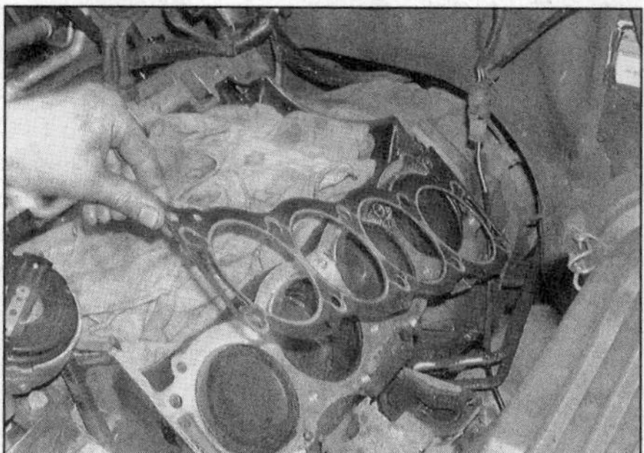

8.15 Recover the old cylinder head gasket

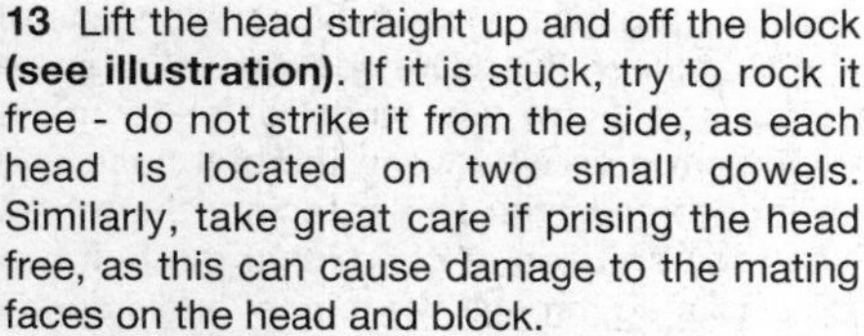

13 Lift the head straight up and off the block **(see illustration)**. If it is stuck, try to rock it free - do not strike it from the side, as each head is located on two small dowels. Similarly, take great care if prising the head free, as this can cause damage to the mating faces on the head and block.

14 Repeat the operation for the other cylinder head if that is also to be removed. It would be worth identifying the heads as being left and right, if there is any danger that they might become mixed up during overhaul.

15 Remove the gasket from the top of the block **(see illustration)**. Do not discard the gasket yet.

16 If the cylinder head is to be dismantled for overhaul, refer to Chapter 2C.

Preparation for refitting

17 The mating faces of the cylinder heads and cylinder block/crankcase must be perfectly clean before refitting the head.

18 Remove the locating dowels, noting their locations. Use a hard plastic or wood scraper to remove all traces of gasket and carbon; also clean the piston crowns.

19 Take particular care during the cleaning operations, as aluminium alloy is easily damaged. Also, make sure that the carbon is not allowed to enter the oil and water passages - this is particularly important for the lubrication system, as carbon could block the oil supply to the engine's components. Using adhesive tape and paper, seal the water, oil and bolt holes in the cylinder block/crankcase.

20 Check the mating surfaces of the cylinder block/crankcase and the cylinder heads for nicks, deep scratches and other damage. If slight, they may be removed carefully with a file, but if excessive, machining may be the only alternative to renewal.

21 If warpage of a cylinder head gasket surface is suspected, use a straight-edge to check it for distortion. Refer to Part C of this Chapter if necessary.

22 Check the condition of the cylinder head bolts, and particularly their threads, whenever they are removed. Clean off all traces of thread sealant, then wash the bolts in suitable solvent, and wipe them dry.

23 Check each bolt for any sign of visible wear or damage, renewing any bolt if necessary. Measure the length of each bolt, to check for stretching (although this is not a conclusive test, if all bolts have stretched by the same amount). Land Rover do not actually specify that the bolts must be renewed - however, it is strongly recommended that the bolts should be renewed as a complete set, particularly if this is not the first time the heads have been removed.

24 Clean out the cylinder head bolt drillings using a suitable tap. If a tap is not available, make a home-made substitute **(see Tool Tip)**. Clean out the bolt holes in the block using a pipe cleaner, or a rag and screwdriver. Make sure that all oil or coolant is removed, otherwise there is a possibility of the block being cracked by hydraulic pressure when the bolts are tightened.

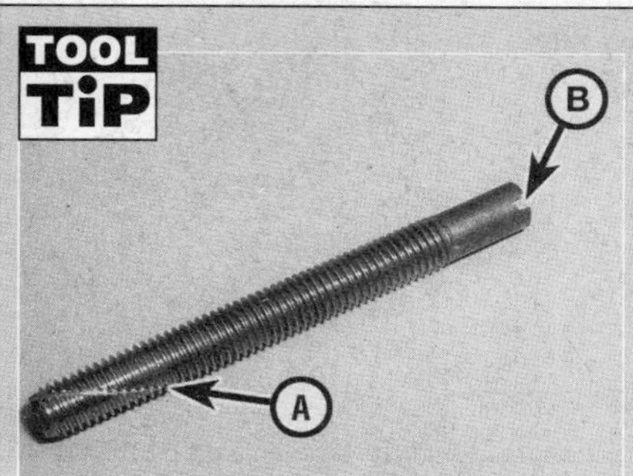
TOOL
TiP
B
A

If a tap is not available, make a home-made substitute by cutting a slot (A) down the threads of one of the old cylinder head bolts. After use, the bolt head can be cut off, and the shank can then be used as an alignment dowel to assist cylinder head refitting. Cut a screwdriver slot (B) in the top of the bolt, to allow it to be unscrewed

Refitting

25 When refitting the cylinder heads, it may be found easier to work on one head at a time. Once one head has been refitted, repeat the following procedure on the remaining head.

26 Refit the two locating dowels to their locations.

27 Fit a new gasket to the cylinder block, and engage it on the two small dowels **(see illustrations)**. Note that the gasket is marked TOP to show which way up it should fit. Do not use any sealant.

28 Identify each head for position, as noted on removal. Lift up the cylinder head and lower it into position on the two dowels, to ensure that it is aligned correctly **(see illustration)**. Take care not to trap any wiring, etc, between the head and the block.

29 On models with 14 head bolts per cylinder head, apply thread sealant to each bolt in turn and refit it to its appropriate position. Land Rover recommend Loctite 572 thread lubricant and sealant for this purpose.

8.27a Lay the new gasket into position . . .

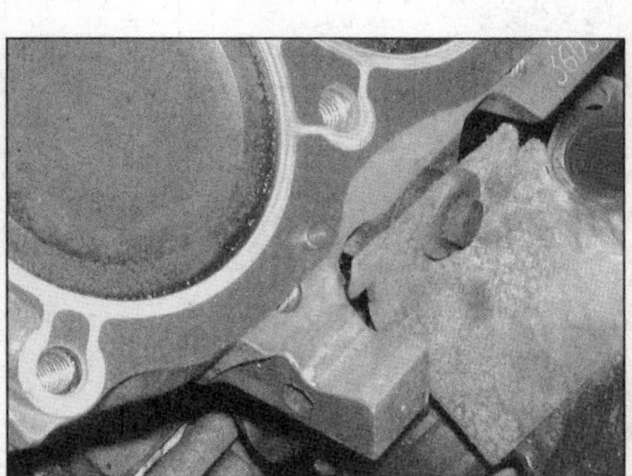

8.27b . . . and locate it over the dowels

8.28 Lift the head into position, and locate it over the dowels

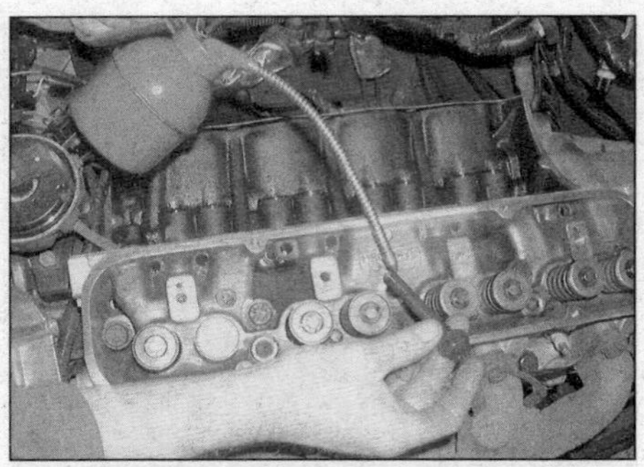

8.30 Lightly oil the threads of the head bolts (later models only)

30 On later models with just 10 bolts per head, lightly oil each bolt, and insert it into position **(see illustration)**.

31 Of the 10 main head bolts, there are 3 long bolts, and 7 medium length bolts. The long bolts fit in the three central holes in the centre of the cylinder head (1, 3 and 5 in the tightening sequence). On models with 14 head bolts, the four shortest bolts fit on the outermost (spark plug) side of the head.

Models with 14 head bolts

32 Tighten the cylinder head bolts gradually, in the sequence shown, to the specified torque **(see illustration)**. Note that the four outermost bolts (the last four in the sequence) are tightened to a lesser torque than the ten main bolts.

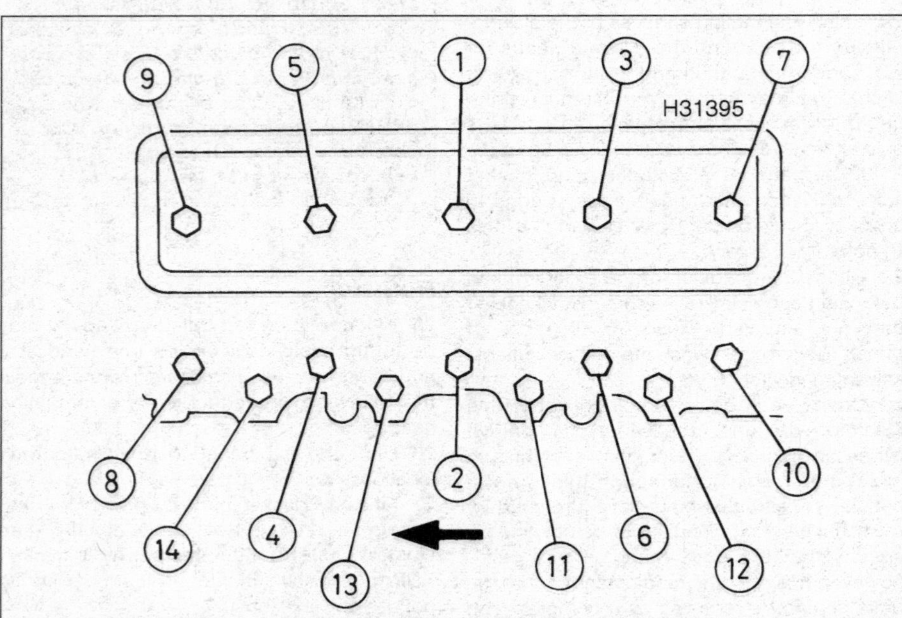
9
5
1
3
7
H31395
8
2
10
14
4
6
13
11
12

8.32 Cylinder head bolt tightening sequence - models with 14 head bolts

33 Once all the bolts have been tightened, go around again with the torque wrench, and re-check that all are correctly tightened.

Models with 10 head bolts

34 Working in the sequence shown, first gradually tighten all the bolts to the Stage 1 setting **(see illustration)**.

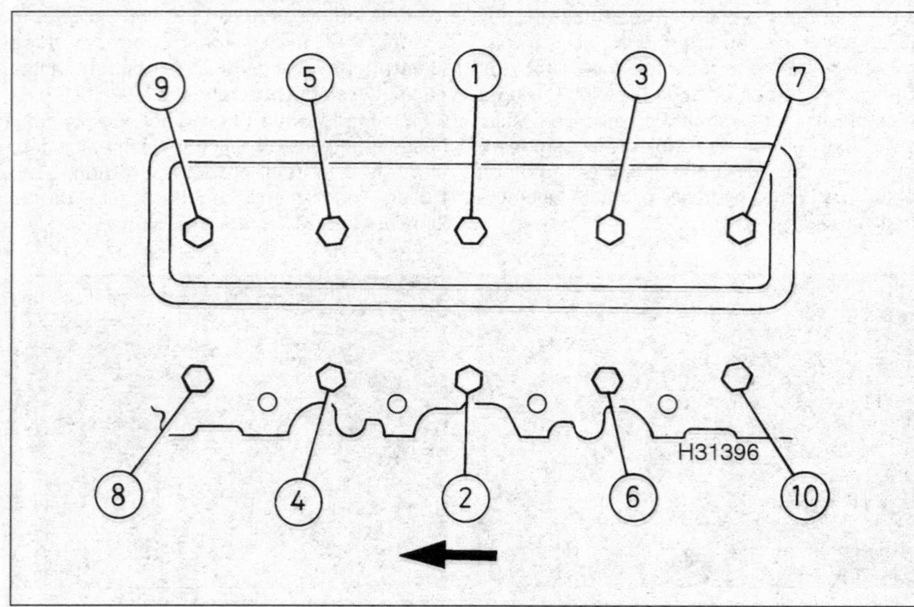
9
5
1
3
7
H31396
8
4
2
6
10

8.34 Cylinder head bolt tightening sequence - models with 10 head bolts

35 The bolts should now be angle-tightened further, in the same sequence, through the specified Stage 2 angle, using a socket and extension bar.

36 It is recommended that an angle-measuring gauge is used during this stage of the tightening, to ensure accuracy. If a gauge is not available, use white paint to make alignment marks between the bolt head and cylinder head prior to tightening; the marks can then be used to check that the bolt has been rotated through the correct angle during tightening **(see illustration)**.

37 If the cylinder heads are being refitted with the engine in the vehicle, tightening through 180° is not possible, at least not in one movement. We found in the workshop that a more practical solution was to tighten all bolts through 90°, and then to go around again, tightening all bolts a further 90°, making 180° in total.

All models

38 Refit all components removed for access, using a reverse of the removal procedure.

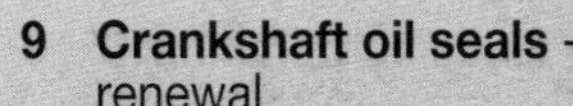

9 Crankshaft oil seals - renewal

Crankshaft front oil seal (in timing cover)

1 This seal can be renewed in one of two ways. If the timing cover gasket is also leaking, refer to Section 4 and remove the timing cover - the oil seal (which fits in the timing cover) can then more easily be replaced, and a new gasket fitted.

2 If the front oil seal is to be replaced on its own, proceed as follows.

8.36 Use an angle gauge for Stage 2 tightening

3 Referring to Chapter 3, remove the radiator fan cowl and the viscous fan assembly. Although not strictly necessary, access will be further improved if the radiator is also removed.

4 Remove the auxiliary drivebelts as required (or single drivebelt on later models) as described in Chapter 1A.

5 Apply the handbrake, then jack up the front of the vehicle and support on axle stands. Remove the engine undertray, and then remove the bolts securing the transmission bellhousing lower cover, for access to the flywheel teeth.

6 Have an assistant jam the flywheel teeth so that the crankshaft cannot turn, then slacken and remove the crankshaft pulley bolt. Particularly on models where a starter dog is incorporated into the bolt head, a deep socket will be needed. The bolt is extremely tight - be sure to use only good-quality, close-fitting tools, and be prepared for the bolt to loosen suddenly under high pressure. Remove the bolt and recover the special washer.

7 Slide off the crankshaft pulley. This should come off easily by hand, but a puller may be required.

8 Unscrew the eight screws securing the protector plate from the front of the seal **(see illustration)**, then remove the plate and note the seal's fitted depth in the cover.

9 Drill two small holes on opposite sides of the front face of the seal, and screw in two self-tapping screws, leaving enough of each screw sticking out so that it can be gripped with a pair of pliers. The seal can then be worked out of the front cover.

10 After extracting the old seal, clean the housing and remove any burrs on the front edge.

11 Offer the new seal into position, lips facing inwards, and lubricate it with engine oil **(see illustration)**.

12 Tap the seal squarely into place using a large socket or piece of pipe - whatever method is chosen, take care not to damage the new seal or its seat during fitting **(see illustration)**.

13 Ensure that the new seal is fitted to the same depth as the old one - as a guide, this should be approximately 1.5 mm below the front face of the cover **(see illustration)**.

14 Refitting is a reversal of removal, noting the following points:

a) Tighten the crankshaft pulley bolt to the specified torque, preventing crankshaft rotation as on removal.

b) When all remaining components have been refitted and the engine is refilled with oil, start the engine and check for oil leaks.

Timing cover gasket

15 Refer to Section 4.

Crankshaft rear oil seal

Note: *Besides the main oil seal, new bearing cap side seals and sealant must be obtained.*

9.8 Undo the screws and remove the protector plate

9.12 Drive the seal into position using a suitable piece of tube

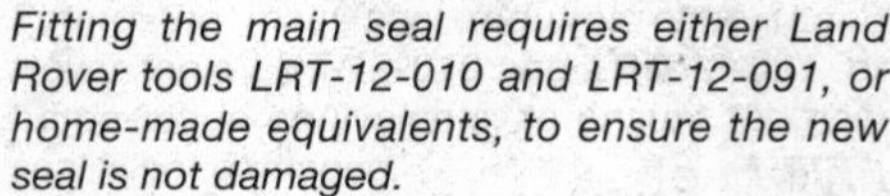

Fitting the main seal requires either Land Rover tools LRT-12-010 and LRT-12-091, or home-made equivalents, to ensure the new seal is not damaged.

16 Remove the flywheel or driveplate as described in Section 10, and the sump as described in Section 12.

17 Remove the bolts securing the rear main bearing cap, then screw two of the sump retaining bolts into the holes at the front of the cap. Using pliers or a pair of large screwdrivers on the bolt heads, carefully pull or prise the cap from its location, taking care not to damage any sealing surfaces.

18 Recover the side seals from the bearing cap, then remove the crankshaft oil seal, noting its fitted depth.

19 Thoroughly clean the bearing cap and the oil seal area of the engine block, removing all traces of oil and sealant. Also check for burrs or sharp edges which may damage the new seals on fitting.

20 Apply a coating of suitable sealant (Land Rover recommend Hylomar SQ32M, available from dealers) to the areas shown, and fit the new side seals to the bearing cap **(see illustrations)**.

21 Lubricate the bearing shell and side seals with clean engine oil, then carefully fit the bearing cap into position.

22 Ensure that the cap is seated squarely,

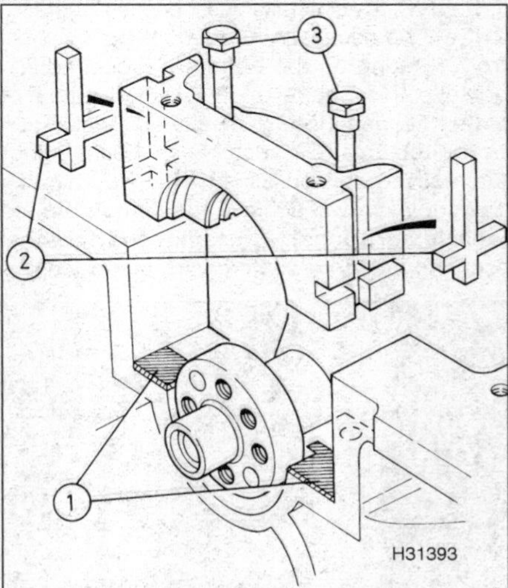
3
2
1
H31393

9.20a Crankshaft rear main bearing cap fitting details

1 Apply sealant here
2 Side seals
3 Main bearing cap bolts

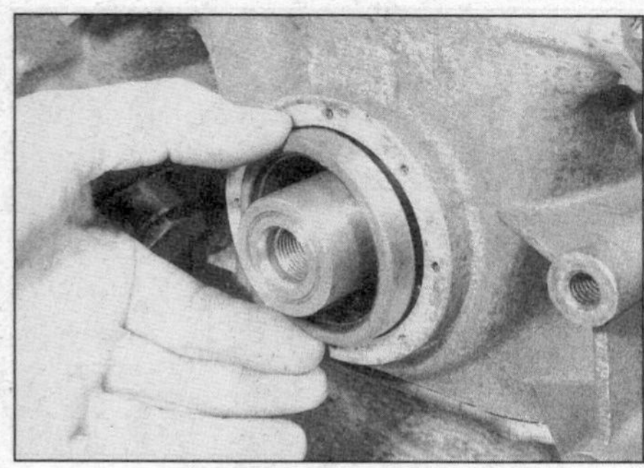

9.11 Offer up the new seal

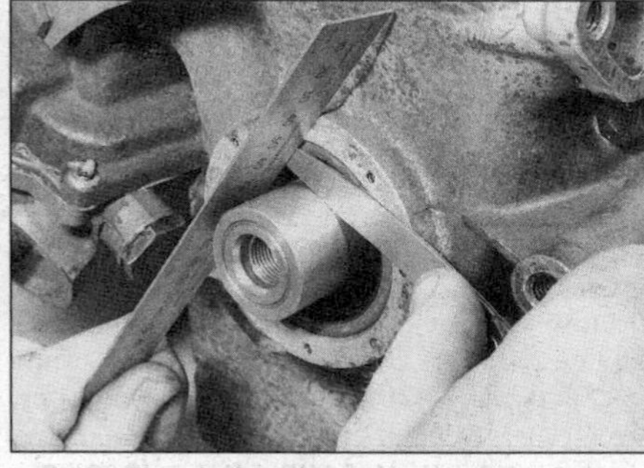

9.13 Check the fitted depth of the new seal

9.20b Fitting new side seals

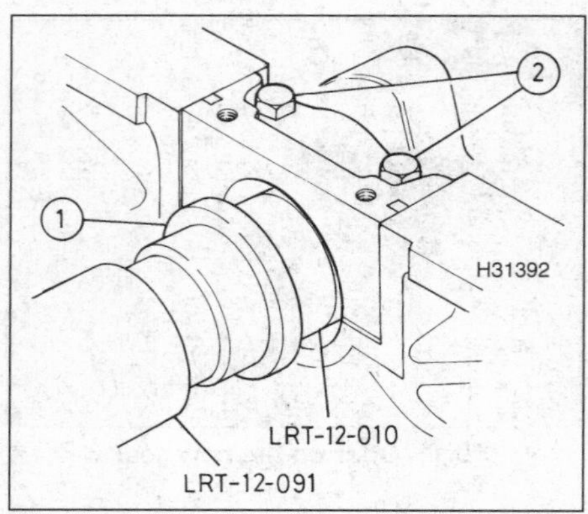
2
1
H31392
LRT-12-010
LRT-12-091

9.23 Land Rover special tools used to fit the crankshaft oil seal

1 *Oil seal*
2 *Main bearing cap bolts*

and is pressed fully home (note that the side seals should protrude by 1.5 mm from the face - do not trim them flat). Lubricate and insert the cap retaining bolts, but do not tighten them more than hand-tight at this stage. Clean the oil seal recess in the bearing cap and block - any oil will prevent the new seal from staying in position.

23 When fitting the new crankshaft oil seal, do not handle the inner lips, and ensure that the outside of the seal remains dry. To fit the seal successfully, Land Rover dealers use two special tools (LRT-12-010 and LRT-12-091) **(see illustration)**. These tools are basically two pieces of tube, one exactly the same diameter as the inside diameter of the oil seal, and one slightly larger, which fits over the first tube, and bears fully on the seal face. If these tools cannot be purchased or borrowed, make up your own from suitable pipe - if these tools are not used, there is a danger that the lips of the new seal will be damaged or folded back on fitting, rendering it useless.

24 Lightly oil the inside of the new seal, the outer surface of the crankshaft flange, and the surfaces of any tools used to fit it **(see illustration)**. The outer surface of the seal must not be lubricated, or it will not stay in position when clamped down by the bearing cap.

25 Fit the seal over the first tube, and butt the tube accurately up against the end of the crankshaft. Use the second tube to fit the seal

9.24 Lightly lubricate the crankshaft outer flange

(lips facing inwards) over the end of the crankshaft, taking care that the seal lips do not get caught up or folded as this is done.

26 Using the larger tube, gradually slide the seal fully and squarely into the recess formed by the cap and block, until it abuts the machined step in the recess.

27 Once the seal is fully home, tighten the main bearing cap bolts to the specified torque.

28 Refit the sump as described in Section 12, and the flywheel or driveplate as described in Section 10. On completion, start the engine and check for signs of oil leakage.

10 Flywheel/driveplate - removal, inspection and refitting

Flywheel (manual transmission models)

Note: *New flywheel securing bolts and thread-locking fluid must be used on refitting. Two medium-length 3/8-inch UNC bolts will be required to lift the flywheel from the crankshaft.*

Removal

1 Remove the clutch as described in Chapter 6.

2 It will be necessary to prevent the flywheel from rotating as the bolts are loosened. To achieve this, make up a notched piece of plate to engage the flywheel teeth, which can be bolted to the transmission bellhousing. Alternatively, it is possible to make up a metal wedge which will achieve the same purpose **(see illustrations)**. Note that the flywheel securing bolts are coated with thread-locking compound, and considerable effort may be required to unscrew them.

3 Before removing the flywheel, it is worth marking a line across the end of the crankshaft, to indicate the flywheel's fitted position. While this is not essential, since the flywheel will only fit one way, it will help when offering the (heavy) flywheel into place initially.

4 Support the flywheel, then remove the six securing bolts **(see illustration)**.

5 Carefully lift the flywheel from the crankshaft.

Warning: The flywheel is heavy - take care not to drop it.

Inspection

6 If the clutch friction disc contact surface of the flywheel is scored, or on close inspection, shows signs of small hairline cracks (caused by overheating), it may be possible to have the flywheel surface-ground, provided the overall thickness of the flywheel is not reduced below the minimum limit (see *Specifications*). Consult a Land Rover dealer or a specialist engine repairer, and if grinding is not possible, renew the flywheel complete.

7 If the teeth on the flywheel starter ring are badly worn, or if some are missing, then it will be necessary to remove the ring and fit a new one.

8 To renew the ring gear, firstly drill a 10 mm hole in the side of the ring gear between the roots of any two gear teeth, and the inner diameter of the ring gear. The hole should be just deep enough to weaken the gear - *take great care not to allow the drill to touch the flywheel*.

9 Clamp the flywheel securely in a vice, and cover it with a large cloth to reduce the possibility of personal injury.

Warning: Wear eye protection during the following procedure.

10 Place a cold chisel between the gear teeth above the drilled hole, then split the gear with the chisel. Take great care not to damage the flywheel during this operation, and wear eye protection at all times. Once the ring has been split, it will spread apart, and can be lifted from the flywheel.

11 The new ring gear must be heated to between 170 and 175°C, and unless facilities

10.2a Typical home-made tool for locking the flywheel

10.2b It is also possible to use a metal wedge to prevent flywheel rotation

10.4 The flywheel is secured by six bolts

10.15 Tighten the flywheel bolts to the specified torque - note the metal wedge (arrowed)

10.21b . . . torque converter adaptor plate . . .

for heating by oven or flame are available, leave the fitting to a Land Rover dealer or engineering works. The new ring gear must not be overheated during this work, or the temper of the metal will be affected.

12 The ring should be tapped gently down onto its register, and left to cool naturally - the contraction of the metal on cooling will ensure that it is a secure and permanent fit.

Refitting

13 Commence refitting by thoroughly cleaning the mating faces of the flywheel and the crankshaft. Also apply a little thread-locking fluid to the new flywheel bolt threads.

14 Turn the flywheel so that the marks made on removal are aligned. Lift the flywheel onto the end of the crankshaft, and support it carefully while the new flywheel bolts are aligned and fitted - the bolts are offset, so the flywheel will only fit one way. Initially tighten the bolts so that the flywheel is just lightly gripped.

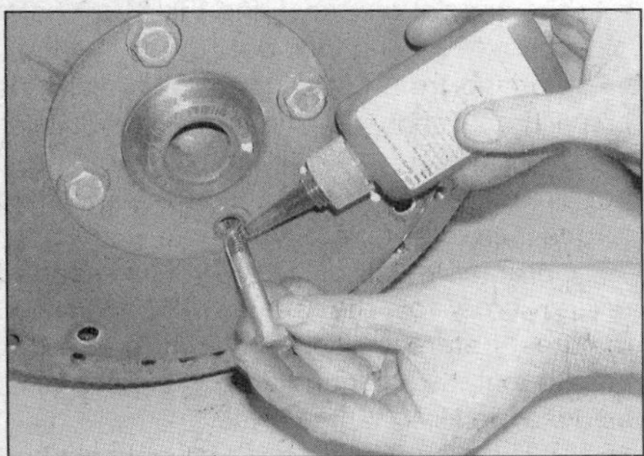

10.26a Apply a little thread-locking fluid to the new bolts . . .

10.18 Home-made tool for preventing driveplate rotation

10.21c . . . driveplate boss . . .

15 Take up any play in the flywheel by turning it against the direction of rotation, then tighten the bolts to the specified torque, preventing the crankshaft from turning as during removal **(see illustration)**.

16 Refit the clutch as described in Chapter 6.

Driveplate (automatic transmission models)

Removal

17 Remove the engine as described in Part C of this Chapter.

18 It will be necessary to prevent the driveplate from rotating as the bolts are loosened. To achieve this, make up a notched piece of plate to engage the teeth, which can be bolted to the transmission bellhousing **(see illustration)**. Note that the driveplate securing bolts are coated with thread-locking compound, and considerable effort may be required to unscrew them.

10.26b . . . then insert and tighten them to the specified torque

10.21a With the bolts removed, take off the outer shim plate . . .

10.21d . . . and the driveplate itself

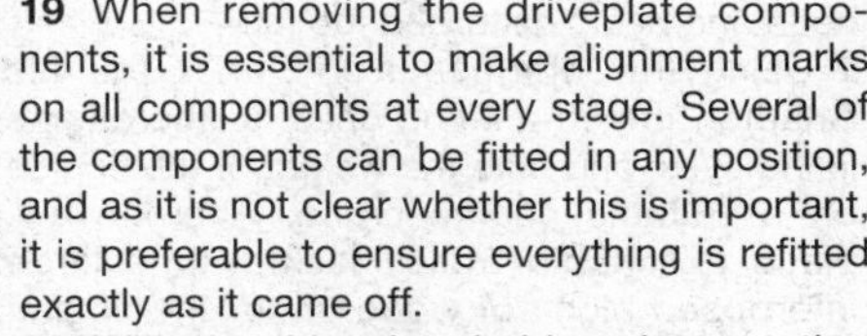

19 When removing the driveplate components, it is essential to make alignment marks on all components at every stage. Several of the components can be fitted in any position, and as it is not clear whether this is important, it is preferable to ensure everything is refitted exactly as it came off.

20 With the driveplate held against rotation and supported by an assistant, loosen and remove the four retaining bolts.

21 Taking precautions that every component is marked for alignment as it is removed, take off the outer shim plate and the torque converter adaptor plate. Supporting the driveplate, slide off the boss, then take out the driveplate **(see illustrations)**.

Inspection

22 Refer to paragraphs 6 to 12, noting that the driveplate itself is not subject to wear in the same way as a flywheel.

Refitting

23 Commence refitting by thoroughly cleaning the mating faces of the driveplate and the crankshaft.

24 Offer up the driveplate so that the marks made on removal are aligned, and fit it over the end of the crankshaft.

25 Fit the boss, torque converter adaptor plate and shim plate, using the marks made on removal to align all components correctly.

26 Apply a little thread-locking fluid to the new driveplate bolt threads. Fit the bolts into position, and tighten them to the specified torque, holding the driveplate against rotation as on removal **(see illustrations)**.

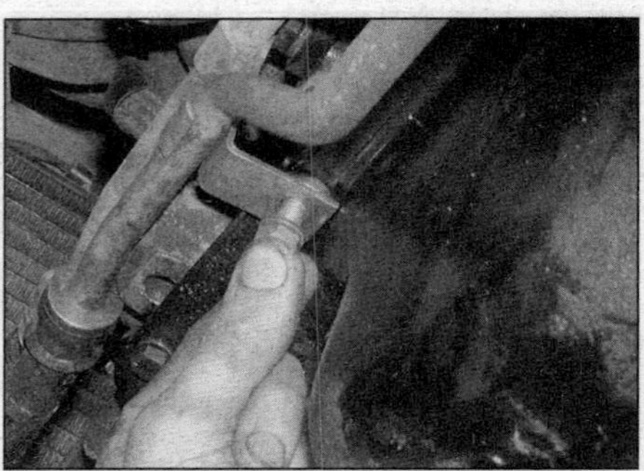

12.4 Removing the sump bolt which also secures the transmission fluid pipes

12.6 Lowering the sump out from under the car

11 Engine mounting rubbers - removal and refitting

Removal

1 Referring to the engine removal procedure in Part C of this Chapter, disconnect any wiring, hoses or other components which will prevent the engine from being lifted the few inches necessary to clear the engine mountings. On models with air conditioning, the compressor must be unbolted and moved to one side, as the rigid refrigerant pipes will not stand being disturbed too far.

2 Using the information in Part C of this Chapter, attach a lifting chain to the engine lifting eyes, and take the weight of the engine on a suitable engine crane. Alternatively, place a suitable trolley jack with a large interposed block of wood under the engine sump, to just take the weight of the engine. Ensure that the engine is safely supported before proceeding.

3 Working from the relevant side of the engine compartment and from below, unscrew the nuts securing the engine mountings to the brackets on either side of the cylinder block.

4 Taking care that no wiring or hoses are strained unduly, lift the engine clear of the mountings, so that the rubbers can be unbolted from the engine.

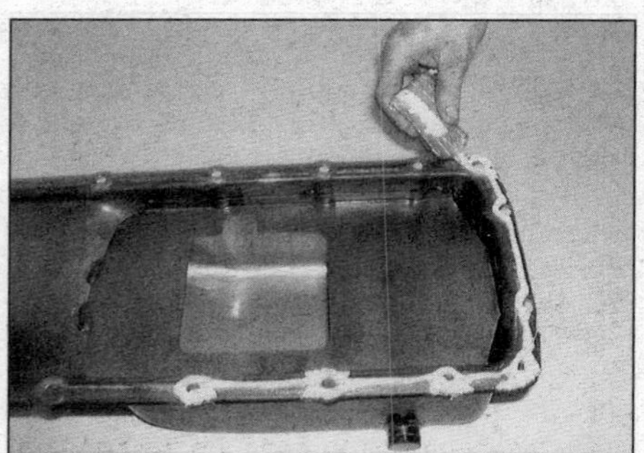

12.11 Applying a bead of sealant to the sump - note that the sealant runs to the inside of the two rear bolt holes

Refitting

5 Bolt the new rubbers into position on the engine, then lower the engine back onto the mountings.

6 Tighten the engine mounting nuts to the specified torque.

7 On completion, reconnect and refit any wiring, hoses or other components removed to allow the engine to be lifted.

12 Sump - removal and refitting

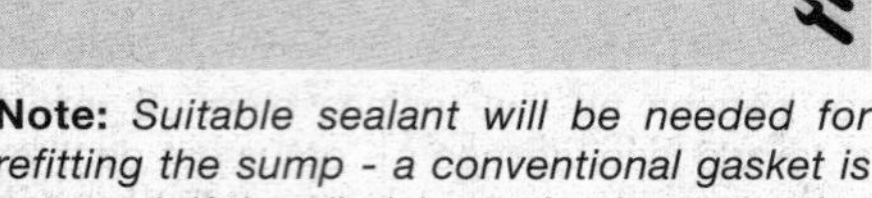

Note: *Suitable sealant will be needed for refitting the sump - a conventional gasket is not used. If the oil pick-up pipe is removed, a new gasket must be used when refitting.*

Removal

1 Drain the engine oil as described in Chapter 1A. When jacking up the vehicle, place the stands under the chassis, NOT under the axle - in order for the sump to clear the axle, the axle must be hanging free.

2 To allow clearance for the sump to be removed, the steering damper and track rod must first be removed, as described in Chapter 11. Note that the track rod need only be detached at one end - the rod can then be swung to one side.

3 Where necessary, remove the bolt securing the dipstick tube to the rocker cover.

4 Working from the centre outwards, progressively loosen the sump retaining bolts by a quarter-turn at a time until they have all been removed. Note that, on automatic transmission models, one of the sump bolts secures the transmission fluid cooler pipes - this bolt is longer than the others, and has a spacer fitted above it **(see illustration)**.

5 If the sump has stuck to the bottom of the engine, try running a sharp knife around the joint between the sump and engine, to cut through the bead of sealant used. If this is not successful, remove the oil drain plug. Insert a large screwdriver (with a piece of card wrapped around it to protect the threads) into the drain plug hole, and carefully use it as a lever to break the sump joint. This method is preferable to prising between the sump face and base of the block, as the mating surfaces could be damaged, and the sump would no longer seal. Take care during removal that the base of the sump does not get damaged through contact with the front axle.

6 Withdraw the sump past the front axle and the oil pick-up pipe inside the sump, and lower it to the ground **(see illustration)**.

7 While the sump is removed, examine the condition of the oil pick-up pipe and strainer. If there is any evidence that the strainer is blocked, remove the two bolts and withdraw the oil pick-up pipe and strainer for cleaning.

8 If the sump has been badly dented or otherwise damaged, there's little point in refitting it. Try to source one in better condition from a vehicle breakers, or fit a new one.

Refitting

9 Clean the sump out thoroughly, and remove all traces of sealant from the sump and crankcase mating surfaces. Degrease the mating surfaces before proceeding.

10 If removed, refit the oil pick-up pipe, using a new gasket.

11 Apply a 2 mm bead of suitable RTV silicone rubber sealant (Land Rover recommend a Hylosil product, available from dealers) to the sump mating surface. Run the bead of sealant around all the holes apart from the rear two - the bead should just run inside the edges of these **(see illustration)**. **Do not** apply excess sealant, which may enter the engine when the sump is refitted.

12 Apply a smear of sealant also at the joint between the timing cover and the crankcase - a coating 13 to 19 mm wide will suffice.

13 Insert one of the sump bolts through one of the bolt holes at the corner of the sump, to act as a guide, then offer the sump up into position. Once in position, try to disturb the sump as little as possible, so that the sealant will spread evenly and not enter the sump. Quickly insert all the bolts, and tighten initially by hand. On automatic transmission models, refit the special bolt securing the fluid cooler pipes, not forgetting the spacer.

14 Working from the central bolts outwards in a diagonal sequence, tighten all the bolts to the specified torque. Refit the oil drain plug, if not already done, and tighten to the specified torque (see Chapter 1A).

15 On completion, allow the recommended drying time for the sealant (typically 30 minutes) before refilling the sump - use this time to refit the steering damper and track rod as described in Chapter 11.

16 Refill the sump with fresh oil as described in Chapter 1A, then start the engine and check for oil leaks.

13.3 Disconnect the oil pressure switch wiring

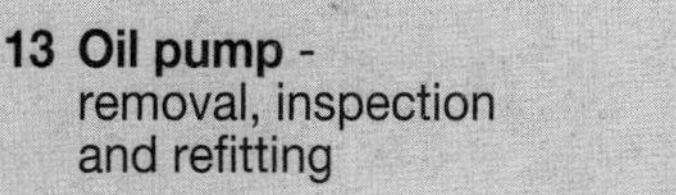

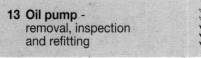

13 Oil pump - removal, inspection and refitting

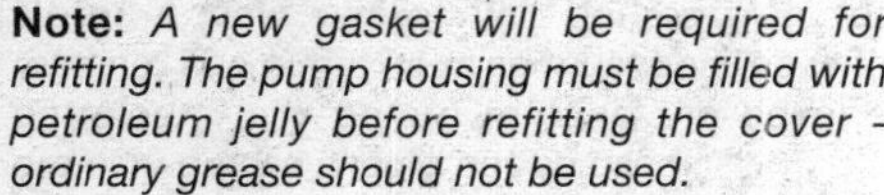

Note: *A new gasket will be required for refitting. The pump housing must be filled with petroleum jelly before refitting the cover - ordinary grease should not be used.*

Removal

1 The engine oil does not have to be drained for this operation, but anticipate a small amount of spillage as the pump is removed, by placing a drain tray below the pump.

2 Unscrew and remove the oil filter, referring to Chapter 1A if necessary. If the same filter is to be re-used, do not allow the oil to drain.

3 Disconnect the electrical connector from the oil pressure switch **(see illustration)**.

4 On models with an oil cooler, the coolant unions to the cooler must be disconnected. Anticipate some oil spillage, and have ready suitable plugs or tape to cover the pipe ends. Unscrew the unions, and move the pipes to one side **(see illustration)**.

5 Unscrew and remove the six bolts securing the pump cover, taking care not to damage the oil pressure switch **(see illustration)**. Remove the cover, taking care that the pump gears do not fall out as the cover is removed.

6 Noting the fitted position of the oil pump driven gear, slide out the driven gear and the oil pump driveshaft **(see illustration)**.

7 Remove and discard the old cover gasket, and thoroughly clean the pump mating surfaces.

13.4 Disconnecting the oil cooler pipes

Inspection

8 If the vehicle has covered a high mileage and the engine is being overhauled, renew all the working parts contained in the oil pump as a matter of course.

9 First clean all the components as they are dismantled.

10 Visually check the gears for obvious scoring or chipping of the teeth. Renew if they are in poor condition.

11 Dismantle the pressure relief valve, and inspect it for excessive wear and/or scoring **(see illustration)**. Pay special attention to the pressure relief valve spring. Note whether it shows signs of wear on its sides, or whether it is on the point of collapse.

12 Thoroughly clean the gauze filter housed within the relief valve bore.

13 Test the valve in its bore in the cover; it should have no more clearance than to make it an easy sliding fit. If any side movement is obviously apparent, then the valve and/or the cover will have to be renewed.

14 Wash the stripped casting in clean paraffin or petrol, and dry with a clean rag. Smear all parts with clean engine oil before reassembly.

15 With the gears refitted in the pump housing, check the pump gear endfloat. Lay a straight-edge across the two gear wheels and, with a feeler gauge, measure the clearance between the straight-edge and the surface of the front cover **(see illustration)**. The clearance should be within the specified limits. If the measurement is less than the minimum specified, inspect the front cover recess for signs of wear.

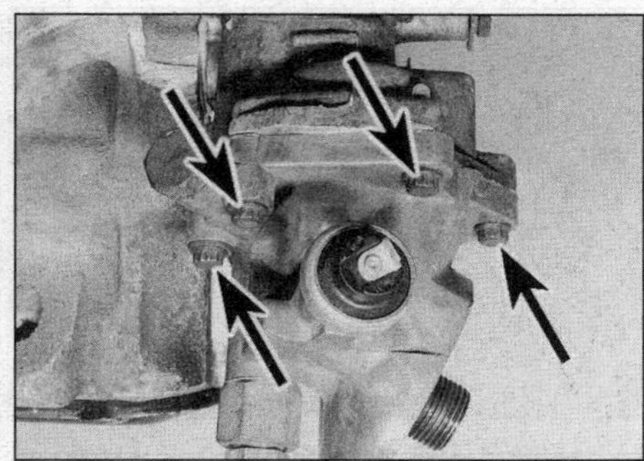

13.5 The oil pump cover is retained by six bolts (four arrowed)

13.6 Sliding out the pump gears

16 Lubricate the relief valve and fit it into its bore, then insert the relief valve spring. Fit the washer to the plug and screw it home, tightening it to the specified torque.

17 The pump housing must now be packed with petroleum jelly. This is essential, otherwise the oil pump will not prime itself with oil when the engine is started **(see illustration)**. Ordinary grease must not be used as a substitute, since it will not dissolve fully in the engine oil, and may block the hydraulic tappets or oil pick-up strainer.

18 Locate the pump gears into their correct positions, ensuring that the petroleum jelly is filling every visible cavity.

Refitting

19 Fit a new gasket on the pump cover, then offer up the pump cover to the body and locate it in position. Refit the six securing bolts hand-tight to start with.

13.11 Inspect the pressure relief valve assembly

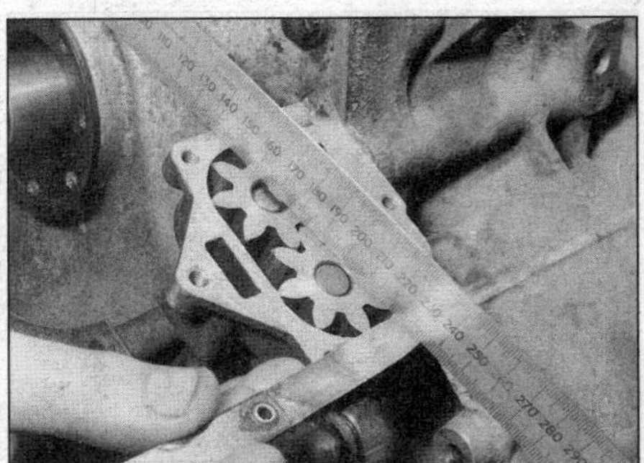

13.15 Checking the pump gear endfloat

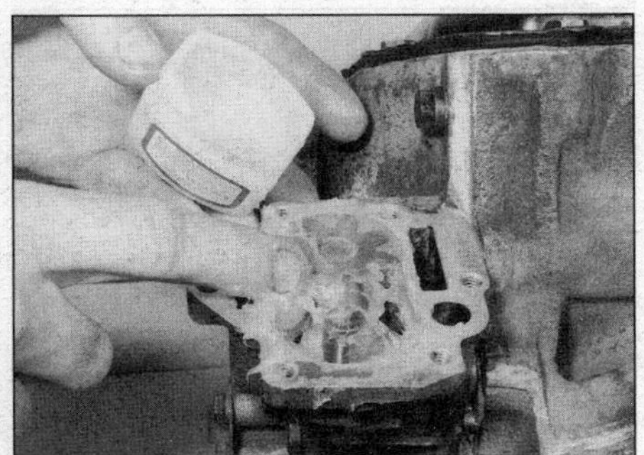

13.17 Packing the pump housing with petroleum jelly

14.2a Unscrew the clamp nut and bolt . . .

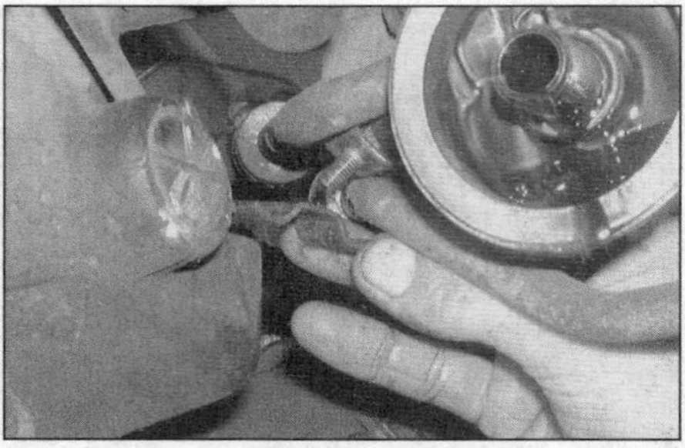

14.2b . . . and separate the clamp joining the two oil cooler pipes

14.3a Loosen the union nuts . . .

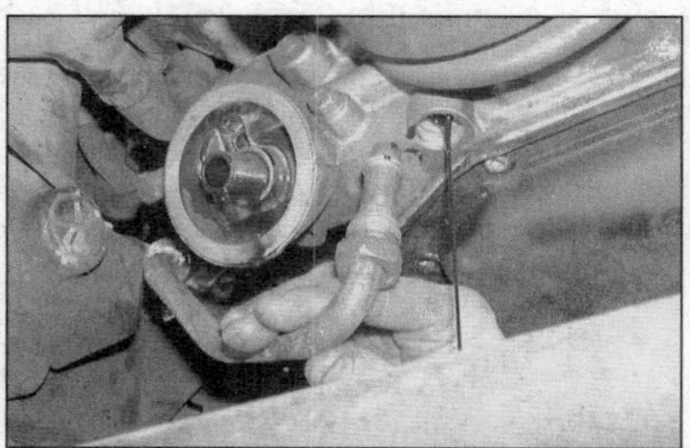

14.3b . . . and disconnect the pipes from the base . . .

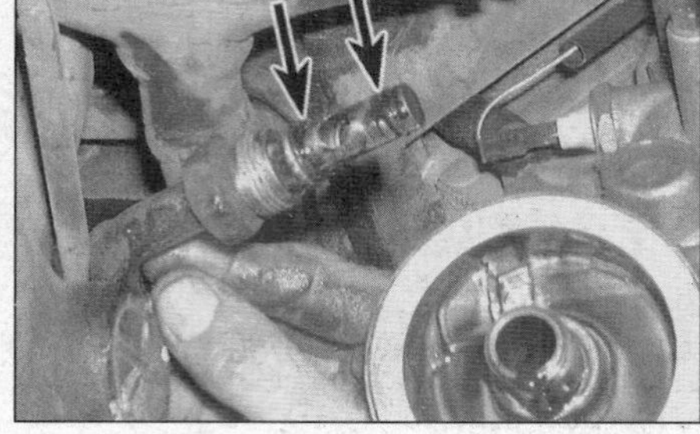

14.3c . . . and from the side of the oil filter housing - note O-rings (arrowed)

14.4 Disconnecting the upper oil cooler pipe

20 Finally tighten all the securing bolts evenly, working in alternate sequence to the final torque figure given in the Specifications.

21 Reconnect the wiring to the oil pressure warning light switch.

22 On models with an oil cooler, reconnect the pipes, tightening the union nuts to the specified torque.

23 Refit the oil filter, ensuring that it is pre-filled with oil, as described in Chapter 1A.

24 Check the oil level in the sump and top up as necessary.

25 Start the engine without racing it, and let it idle. The oil pressure warning light should go out after a short delay - failure to do so indicates that either the pump is worn, incorrectly assembled, or was not sufficiently packed with petroleum jelly on reassembly. Another reason could be that the oil pump pick-up strainer is blocked - remove the sump and clean the strainer as described in Section 12.

26 Once the warning light has gone out, leave the engine running for a few minutes, and check carefully for leaks from the oil pump cover.

14 Oil cooler pipes - removal and refitting

Removal

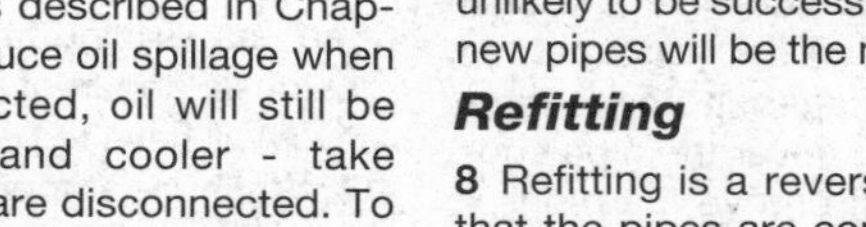

1 Drain the engine oil as described in Chapter 1A. While this will reduce oil spillage when the pipes are disconnected, oil will still be present in the pipes and cooler - take precautions when these are disconnected. To improve access, also remove the oil filter.

2 At the engine end of the pipes, unscrew the bolt from the clamp which secures the two pipes together, and recover the clamp, washer and nut **(see illustrations)**.

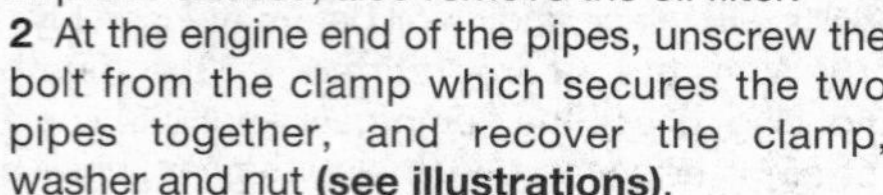

3 Loosen the union nuts, and withdraw the pipe ends from the oil filter housing. Recover the O-rings, which often remain inside the housing **(see illustrations)**.

4 Loosen the union nuts at the cooler fittings, and withdraw the pipes **(see illustration)**. Anticipate some oil spillage as this is done, and recover the O-rings.

5 Where applicable, unscrew the bolt from the upper clamp which secures the two pipes together, and recover the clamp, washer and nut.

6 Withdraw the pipes individually, noting how each one is routed.

7 If oil is leaking from the crimped joint where the flexible hose joins the rigid pipe, repair is unlikely to be successful - in the long run, fitting new pipes will be the most effective solution.

Refitting

8 Refitting is a reversal of removal, ensuring that the pipes are correctly routed, and using new O-rings. Tighten the union nuts to the specified torque.

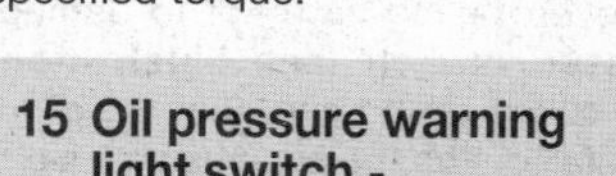

15 Oil pressure warning light switch - removal and refitting

Removal

Note: *A new sealing ring may be required on refitting.*

1 The oil pressure warning light switch is located in the oil filter housing at the front of the cylinder block.

2 Disconnect the battery negative lead, then release the wiring connector from the switch **(see illustration 13.3)**.

3 Carefully unscrew the switch, and withdraw it from the cylinder block **(see illustrations)**. Be prepared for some oil spillage.

4 Recover the sealing ring, where applicable.

Refitting

5 Refitting is a reversal of removal, but clean the threads of the switch before screwing it into the cylinder block, and if applicable, use a new sealing ring.

15.3a Unscrew the switch . . .

15.3b . . . then remove it from the oil filter housing

Chapter 2 Part B:
Diesel engine in-car repair procedures

Contents

Degrees of difficulty

Easy, suitable for novice with little experience 

Fairly easy, suitable for beginner with some experience 

Fairly difficult, suitable for competent DIY mechanic

Difficult, suitable for experienced DIY mechanic 

Very difficult, suitable for expert DIY or professional

Specifications

General

Engine type	Four-cylinder, in-line, water-cooled. Single belt-driven camshaft, operating valves via pushrods and rocker gear	
Manufacturer's engine codes:*		
200 TDi engine	12L00001	
300 TDi engine:		
Manual transmission and EDC (Electronic Diesel Control)	17L00001	
Manual transmission and DETOX system (not UK)	18L00001	
Automatic transmission and EDC (Electronic Diesel Control)	19L00001	
Automatic transmission and DETOX system (not UK)	20L00001	
Manual transmission and EGR (Exhaust Gas Recirculation)	21L00001	
Automatic transmission and EGR (Exhaust Gas Recirculation)	22L00001	
Bore	90.47 mm	
Stroke	97.00 mm	
Capacity	2495 cc	
Firing order	1-3-4-2 (No 1 at timing belt end)	
Direction of crankshaft rotation	Clockwise (viewed from timing belt end of engine)	
Compression ratio	19.5:1 ± 0.5:1	
Maximum power (DIN)	111 bhp at 4000 rpm	
Maximum torque (DIN)	265 Nm (196 lbf ft) at 1800 rpm	
Compression pressure difference between cylinders (typical)	70 psi max.	

**For details of engine code location, see 'Vehicle identification numbers'.*

Timing belt

Tension (using gauge-type torque wrench - see text):	**Nm**	**lbf ft**
200 TDi engine	18 to 20	13 to 15
300 TDi engine:		
New belt	14 to 16	10 to 12
Used belt	11 to 13	8 to 10

Rocker arms

Rocker arm freeplay on rocker shaft	0.1010 to 0.1270 mm

Lubrication system

Normal oil pressure (engine at normal operating temperature and operating speeds)	25.0 to 55.0 psi
Oil pump type:	
200 TDi engine	Double gear-type, driven by camshaft via skew gear and driveshaft
300 TDi engine	Rotor type, driven directly from front of crankshaft
Oil pump clearances (200 TDi engine):	
Maximum gear-to-housing clearance (endfloat)	0.026 to 0.135 mm
Maximum gear lobe-to-housing clearance	0.025 to 0.075 mm
Maximum gear backlash	0.100 to 0.200 mm

Flywheel

Maximum permissible lateral run-out of flywheel	0.050 to 0.070 mm
Minimum permissible thickness of flywheel after refinishing	36.960 mm

Torque wrench settings

	Nm	lbf ft
Air conditioning compressor bracket-to-timing belt housing bolts	45	33
Air conditioning compressor/alternator drivebelt idler pulley bolt	45	33
Air conditioning compressor/alternator drivebelt tensioner bolt	25	18
Alternator mounting bracket bolts (models with air conditioning)	45	33
Auxiliaries mounting bracket-to-cylinder block nuts and bolts	25	18
Auxiliary drivebelt tensioner securing nut	45	33
Big-end cap nuts**	59	44
Camshaft oil jet	7	5
Camshaft sprocket bolt (200 TDi engine)	45	33
Camshaft sprocket hub-to-camshaft bolt (300 TDi engine)	80	59
Camshaft sprocket-to-camshaft hub bolts (300 TDi engine)	25	18
Camshaft thrust plate bolts	9	7
Coolant pipe stub-to-cylinder head	22	16
Coolant pump securing bolts (200 TDi engine)	26	19
Coolant temperature sensor/blanking plug	14	10
Crankcase breather cover bolts (300 TDi engine)	25	18
Crankshaft damper bolt (200 TDi engine)	340	251
Crankshaft pulley bolt (300 TDi engine):		
Stage 1	80	59
Stage 2	Angle-tighten a further 90°	
Crankshaft rear oil seal housing bolts (300 TDi engine)	25	18
Cylinder block coolant drain plug	25	18
Cylinder block ladder frame bolts (200 TDi engine)	25	18
Cylinder block oil gallery rear plug	37	27
Cylinder block oil jets	17	13
Cylinder head bolts:		
200 TDi engine (all bolts):		
Stage 1	40	30
Stage 2	Angle-tighten a further 60°	
Stage 3	Angle-tighten a further 60°	
300 TDi engine:		
Stage 1 (all bolts)	Tighten until bolt heads just contact cylinder head	
Stage 2 (all bolts)	40	30
Stage 3 (all bolts)	Angle-tighten a further 60°	
Stage 4 (all bolts)	Angle-tighten a further 60°	
Stage 5 **(M12 x 140 mm bolts only)**	Angle tighten a further 20°	
Dipstick tube bolt	25	18
Driveplate access panel (automatic transmission models)	9	7
Driveplate-to-starter ring gear bolts (automatic transmission models)	25	18
Driveplate-to-torque converter bolts (automatic transmission models)*	39	29
Engine lifting bracket bolts	25	18
Engine mounting bracket-to-chassis nuts	45	33
Engine mounting bracket-to-cylinder block bolts	85	63
Engine mounting bracket-to-flywheel housing bolts	45	33
Engine mounting rubber-to-bracket nuts	85	63
Engine-to-transmission bolts:		
Automatic transmission	45	33
Manual transmission	40	30
Exhaust manifold bracket-to-cylinder block bolts	25	18
Exhaust manifold nuts:		
200 TDi engine	25	18
300 TDi engine	45	33

Torque wrench settings (continued)

	Nm	lbf ft
Flywheel housing drain plug	12	9
Flywheel housing-to-bellhousing bolts:		
Automatic transmission	45	33
Manual transmission	40	30
Flywheel housing-to-cylinder block bolts	45	33
Flywheel/driveplate securing bolts**	146	108
Fuel injection pump rear mounting bracket-to-cylinder block bolts	25	18
Fuel injection pump sprocket-to-hub bolts	25	18
Inlet manifold nuts and bolts	25	18
Main bearing cap bolts**	133	98
Oil baffle-to-crankcase breather cover bolts (300 TDi engine)	4	3
Oil cooler pipe-to-oil filter adapter unions	45	33
Oil drain/return pipes-to-cylinder block	25	18
Oil filter adapter bolts	45	33
Oil pick-up pipe-to-bracket bolt (200 TDi engine)	25	18
Oil pick-up pipe-to-oil pump nut (200 TDi engine)	45	33
Oil pick-up/strainer pipe-to-bearing cap bolts (300 TDi engine)*	9	7
Oil pick-up/strainer pipe-to-timing belt housing bolts (300 TDi engine)	25	18
Oil pressure relief valve plug	30	22
Oil pressure warning light switch	17	13
Oil pump cover-to-oil pump bolts (200 TDi engine)	25	18
Oil pump driveshaft bush-to-cylinder block screw (200 TDi engine)	25	18
Oil pump-to-cylinder block bolts (200 TDi engine)	25	18
Oil separator-to-valve cover bolt	9	7
Oil thermostat housing-to-oil filter adapter bolts	9	7
Power steering pump bracket-to-auxiliary mounting bracket bolts	25	18
Rocker shaft pedestal bolts:		
200 TDi engine	30	22
300 TDi engine:		
Stage 1	5	4
Stage 2	Angle-tighten a further 50°	
Sump drain plug:		
200 TDi engine	45	33
300 TDi engine	35	26
Sump securing bolts	25	18
Tappet adjuster nut:		
200 TDi engine	25	18
300 TDi engine	16	12
Tappet guide locating screws	14	10
Thermostat cover-to-thermostat housing bolts:		
200 TDi engine	9	7
300 TDi engine	25	18
Thermostat housing-to-cylinder head bolts	25	18
Timing belt cover bolts	25	18
Timing belt housing-to-cylinder block bolts	25	18
Timing belt idler pulley nut	45	33
Timing belt tensioner bolt	45	33
Turbocharger oil drain adapter to cylinder block	42	31
Turbocharger oil feed adapter to cylinder block	25	18
Valve cover securing bolts:		
200 TDi engine	4	3
300 TDi engine	10	7
Wiring harness bracket bolts	25	18

**Use thread-locking fluid.*
***New fasteners must be used on refitting.*

1 General information

How to use this Chapter

This Part of Chapter 2 describes the repair procedures which can reasonably be carried out on the engine while it remains in the vehicle. If the engine has been removed from the vehicle and is being dismantled as described in Chapter 2C, any preliminary dismantling procedures can be ignored.

Note that while it may be possible physically to overhaul items such as the piston/connecting rod assemblies while the engine is in the vehicle, such tasks are not usually carried out as separate operations, and usually require the execution of several additional procedures (not to mention the cleaning of components and of oilways); for this reason, all such tasks are classed as major overhaul procedures, and are described in Chapter 2C.

Chapter 2C describes the removal of the engine/transmission from the vehicle, and the full overhaul procedures which can then be carried out.

Engine description

The engine is of four-cylinder in-line, overhead valve type, and is mounted longitudinally at the front of the vehicle. The engine uses direct diesel injection, and the combustion chambers are incorporated in the pistons.

The crankshaft runs in five shell-type bearings, and the centre bearing incorporates thrustwashers to control crankshaft endfloat.

The connecting rods are attached to the crankshaft by horizontally-split shell-type big-end bearings. The pistons are attached to the connecting rods by gudgeon pins, which are a push-fit in the connecting rod small-end bores. The gudgeon pins are retained by circlips. The aluminium-alloy pistons are fitted with three piston rings - two compression rings and an oil control ring.

The camshaft is driven from the crankshaft by a toothed composite-rubber belt, which also drives the fuel injection pump.

The camshaft runs in four bearings pressed into the cylinder block. Each cylinder has two valves (one inlet and one exhaust), operated from the camshaft via pushrods and rocker arms. To minimise camshaft wear, tappet rollers act on the camshaft lobes, The rollers act on tappet slides, which in turn operate the pushrods. The rocker arms pivot on a shaft bolted to the cylinder head, and incorporate adjuster pins to enable valve clearance adjustment.

The inlet and exhaust valves are each closed by a single valve spring, and operate in guides pressed into the cylinder head.

On 200 TDi engines, a gear-type oil pump is located in the sump, and is driven from the camshaft via a skew gear and driveshaft.

On 300 TDi engines, a rotor type oil pump is fitted, and the pump is driven directly from the front of the crankshaft.

The fuel lift pump and the brake vacuum pump are driven via pushrods acting on lobes on the camshaft.

The coolant pump is located in a housing at the front of the engine, and is driven by the auxiliary drivebelt.

Repair operations possible with the engine in the vehicle

The following operations can be carried out without having to remove the engine from the vehicle:

a) Removal and refitting of the valve operating (rocker) gear.
b) Removal and refitting of the cylinder head.
c) Removal and refitting of the timing belt and sprockets.
d) Removal and refitting of the sump.
e) Removal and refitting of the big-end bearings, connecting rods, and pistons.*
f) Removal and refitting of the oil pump.
g) Renewal of the engine mountings.
h) Removal and refitting of the flywheel/driveplate.

** Although the operation marked with an asterisk can be carried out with the engine in the vehicle (after removal of the sump), it is preferable for the engine to be removed, in the interests of cleanliness and improved access. For this reason, the procedure is described in Chapter 2C.*

2 Compression and leakdown tests - description and interpretation

Compression test

Note: *A compression tester specifically designed for diesel engines must be used for this test.*

1 When engine performance is down, or if misfiring occurs which cannot be attributed to the fuel system, a compression test can provide diagnostic clues as to the engine's condition. If the test is performed regularly, it can give warning of trouble before any other symptoms become apparent.

2 A compression tester specifically designed for diesel engines must be used, because of the higher pressures involved. The tester is connected to an adapter which screws into the glow plug or injector hole. It is unlikely to be worthwhile buying such a tester for occasional use, but it may be possible to borrow or hire one - if not, have the test performed by a garage.

3 Unless specific instructions to the contrary are supplied with the tester, observe the following points:

a) The battery must be in a good state of charge, the air filter must be clean, and the engine should be at normal operating temperature.
b) All the injectors or glow plugs should be removed before starting the test. If removing the injectors, also remove the copper washers (which must be renewed when the injectors are refitted - see Chapter 4C), otherwise they may be blown out.
c) It is advisable to disconnect the stop solenoid on the fuel injection pump, to reduce the amount of fuel discharged as the engine is cranked.

4 There is no need to hold the accelerator pedal down during the test, because the diesel engine air inlet is not throttled.

5 The actual compression pressures measured are not so important as the balance between cylinders. Land Rover do not specify compression pressures, but a typical value for the maximum difference between cylinders is given in the Specifications.

6 The cause of poor compression is less easy to establish on a diesel engine than on a petrol one. The effect of introducing oil into the cylinders ('wet' testing) is not conclusive, because there is a risk that the oil will sit in the recess on the piston crown instead of passing to the rings. However, the following can be used as a rough guide to diagnosis.

7 All cylinders should produce very similar pressures; any difference greater than that specified indicates the existence of a fault. Note that the compression should build up quickly in a healthy engine; low compression on the first stroke, followed by gradually-increasing pressure on successive strokes, indicates worn piston rings. A low compression reading on the first stroke, which does not build up during successive strokes, indicates leaking valves or a blown head gasket (a cracked head could also be the cause). Deposits on the undersides of the valve heads can also cause low compression.

8 A low reading from two adjacent cylinders is almost certainly due to the head gasket having blown between them; the presence of coolant in the engine oil will confirm this.

9 If the compression reading is unusually high, the cylinder head surfaces, valves and pistons are probably coated with carbon deposits. If this is the case, the cylinder head should be removed and decarbonised (see Chapter 2C).

Leakdown test

10 A leakdown test measures the rate at which compressed air fed into the cylinder is lost. It is an alternative to a compression test, and in many ways it is better, since the escaping air provides easy identification of where pressure loss is occurring (piston rings, valves or head gasket).

11 The equipment needed for leakdown testing is unlikely to be available to the home mechanic. If poor compression is suspected, have the test performed by a suitably-equipped garage.

3 Top dead centre (TDC) for No 1 piston - locating

Note: *Suitable tools will be required to lock the flywheel and the fuel injection pump spindle in position during this operation. The Land Rover special tool available to lock the flywheel is LRT-12-044 for models with a conventional fuel injection system, or LRT-12-085 for models with EDC (see Chapter 4C). Special flywheel locking tool LRT-12-044 can be improvised by obtaining a spare flywheel housing blanking plug, and accur-ately drilling a hole though its centre to accept a 3/16 in twist drill. To lock the fuel injection pump sprocket, special tool LRT-12-045 will be required - this tool can be improvised using a short length (approximately 50.0 mm) of 3/8 in (9.5 mm) diameter round bar.*

1 On models with a manual transmission, unscrew the blanking plug from the timing hole in the base of the flywheel housing.

2 On models with automatic transmission, unscrew the larger bolt from the cover plate located on the engine backplate, to the rear of the sump. Pivot the cover plate away from the bolt hole.

3 Screw the appropriate flywheel locking tool (see note at the beginning of this Section) into the timing hole on models with manual transmission, or into the larger cover plate bolt hole on models with automatic transmission. Do not engage the locking tool centre pin at this stage **(see illustrations)**.

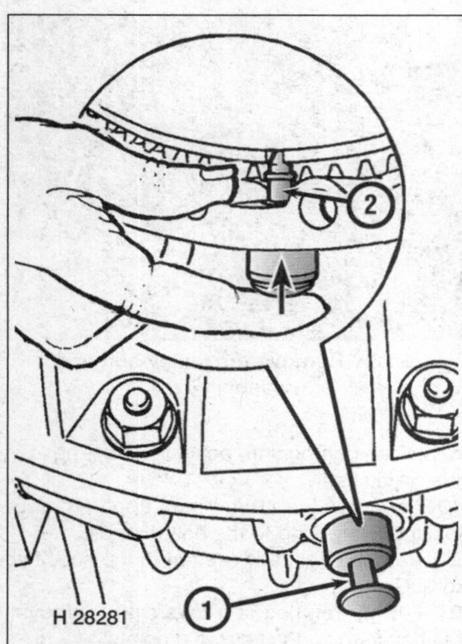
2
1
H 28281

3.3a Special tool LRT-12-044 in position on manual transmission model
1 *Special tool LRT-12-044*
2 *Tool centre pin*

4 On models with air conditioning, remove the air conditioning compressor drivebelt as described in Chapter 1B, Section 17. If desired, unscrew the securing bolts, and move the compressor to one side, clear of the working area - **do not** disconnect the refrigerant lines (refer to the precautions in Chapter 3).

5 Remove the three securing screws, and withdraw the injection pump hub cover plate from the timing belt cover **(see illustration)**. Note that on models with air conditioning, the air conditioning drivebelt tensioner pulley is secured to the cover plate. Recover the gasket.

6 Insert the pump timing pin (Tool No LRT-12-045), or an improvised equivalent, through the U-shaped slot in the pump hub then, using a suitable tool on the crankshaft pulley/damper bolt, turn the crankshaft until the timing pin can be slid through the pump hub into the pump body **(see illustration)**. The tool should slide easily into position.

3.7 Improvised flywheel locking tool centre pin engaged with flywheel (viewed with transmission removed)

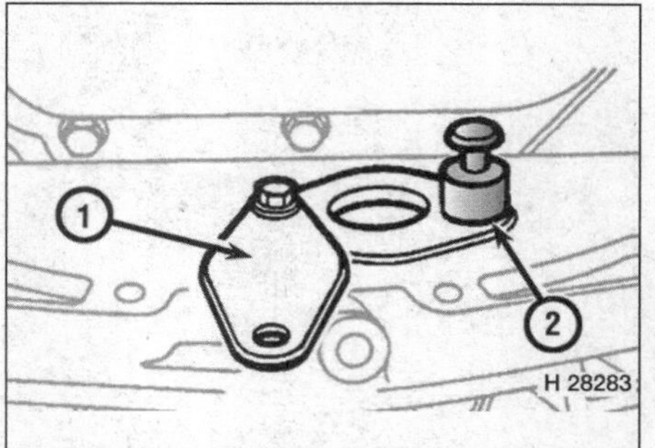
1
2
H 28283

3.3b Special tool LRT-12-044 in position on automatic transmission model
1 *Cover plate*
2 *Special tool LRT-12-044*

3.5 Remove the injection pump hub cover plate and gasket - viewed with engine removed

7 The flywheel locking tool centre pin should now slide easily into engagement with the timing slot in the flywheel (if the tool does not slide easily into position, this indicates that the injection pump timing is incorrect - see Chapter 4C) **(see illustration)**.

8 The engine is now locked with No 1 piston at top dead centre.

4 Valve cover - removal and refitting

Removal

Note: *A new valve cover gasket may be required on refitting (the manufacturers recommend that the gasket is re-used a maximum of five times). New securing bolt sealing washers may be required, and on 200 TDi engines, new semi-circular seals and suitable liquid sealant may be required.*

1 Where applicable, unscrew the oil filler cap, then unclip the plastic cover from the top of the valve cover **(see illustration)**.

2 Loosen the hose clip(s), and disconnect the breather hose(s) from the valve cover, and from the breather filter on the side of the valve cover, where applicable.

3 Unscrew the three securing bolts, and recover the sealing washers if they are loose, then lift the valve cover from the cylinder head.

4 Recover the gasket.

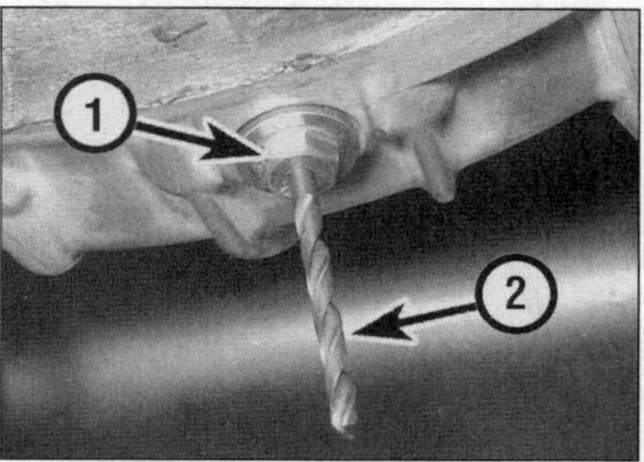
1
2

3.3c Improvised flywheel locking tool in position on manual transmission model
1 *Blanking plug*
2 *3/16 in twist drill*

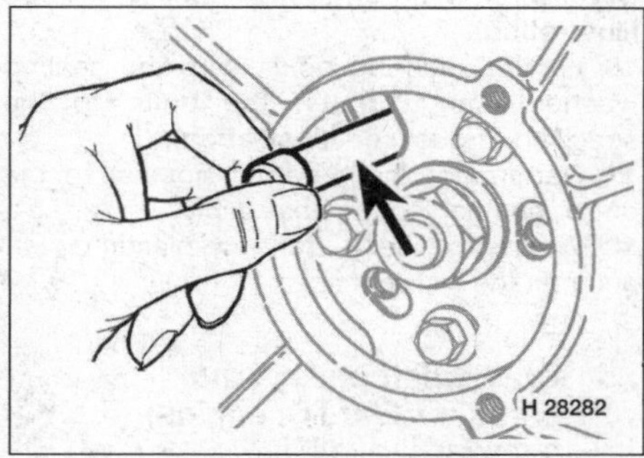
H 28282

3.6 Injection pump timing pin (arrowed) in position

Refitting

5 Commence refitting by thoroughly cleaning the gasket faces of the cover and the cylinder head.

6 On 200 TDi engines, check the condition of the semi-circular seals at each end of the cylinder head, and renew if necessary. To renew the seals, prise them from the cut-outs in the cylinder head, then thoroughly clean the cut-outs, and fit the new seals using suitable liquid sealant.

7 Check the condition of the sealing washers on the securing bolts, and renew if necessary.

8 Check the condition of the valve cover gasket, and renew if necessary. Note that the manufacturers recommend that the gasket is only re-used a maximum of five times, regardless of apparent condition.

4.1 Removing the plastic cover from the valve cover - 300 TDi engine

4.9 Fitting the gasket to the valve cover - 300 TDi engine

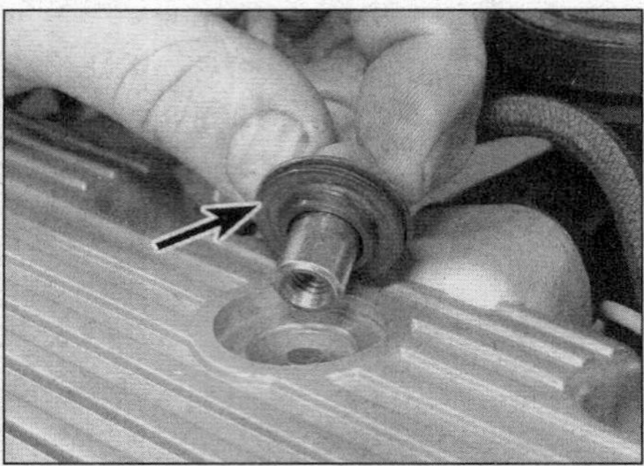

4.10 Ensure that the sealing washers (arrowed) are in place on the valve cover bolts

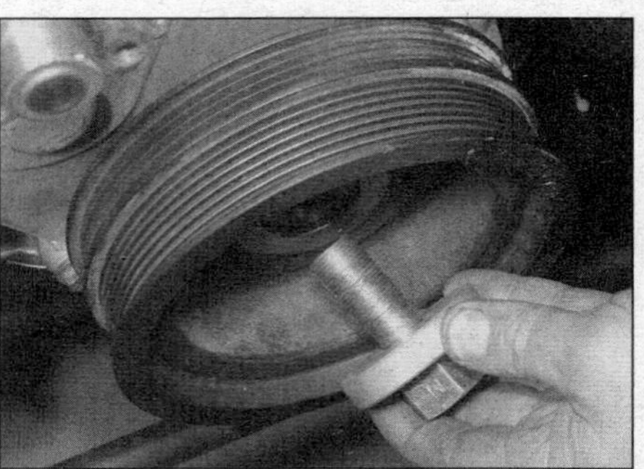

5.28a Remove the pulley bolt and washer . . .

9 Fit the gasket to the cover, then place the cover in position on the cylinder head **(see illustration)**.

10 Fit the securing bolts (with the sealing washers), and tighten the bolts to the specified torque **(see illustration)**.

11 Reconnect the breather hose(s) to the cover, and tighten the hose clip(s).

12 Where applicable, refit the plastic cover, and refit the oil filler cap.

5 Crankshaft pulley (and damper - 200 TDi engine) - removal and refitting

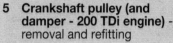

200 TDi engine

Warning: The crankshaft damper securing bolt is tightened to a very high torque, and both the damper and bolt are coated with thread-locking compound. Ensure that adequate, good-quality tools are used to hold the damper, and to loosen and tighten the bolt. Check the condition of the tools before use, to avoid the possibility of failure and resulting personal injury. Suitable thread-locking compound will be required to coat the threads of the bolt and the damper on refitting.

Removal

1 Disconnect the battery negative lead.

2 On models with air conditioning, proceed as follows:

a) Remove the air conditioning compressor drivebelt, as described in Chapter 1B, Section 17.

b) Disconnect the wiring from the temperature sensor located in the thermostat housing.

*c) Remove the four bolts securing the air conditioning compressor to the engine, and move the compressor to one side, clear of the working area. Take care not to strain the refrigerant hoses - **do not** under any circumstances disconnect the hoses.*

3 Drain the cooling system as described in Chapter 1B.

4 Remove the viscous cooling fan and coupling as described in Chapter 3.

5 Loosen the securing clip, and disconnect the intercooler-to-inlet manifold air trunking at the manifold.

6 Loosen the securing clips and remove the radiator top hose.

7 Unscrew the two nuts securing the cooling fan cowl to the top of the radiator, and withdraw the cowl.

8 Remove the alternator and power steering pump drivebelts as described in Chapter 1B, Section 17.

9 Unscrew the four securing bolts, and remove the crankshaft pulley from the crankshaft damper.

10 To remove the damper, proceed as follows.

11 A suitable tool will now be required to hold the damper stationary as the damper bolt is loosened - note that the bolt is very tight! This is most easily achieved by bolting a suitable metal bar to the damper, using bolts screwed into at least two of the pulley bolt holes. Alternatively, carry out the following:

a) Apply the handbrake.

b) Engage the differential lock.

c) Engage the 'Low' range in the transfer gearbox.

d) On manual transmission models, engage first gear in the main transmission.

e) On automatic transmission models, move the selector lever to position P.

f) Remove the 'ignition' key.

12 Hold the damper stationary, and loosen the damper bolt using a suitable socket and extension bar.

13 Where applicable, unbolt the tool used to hold the damper stationary, then remove the damper bolt and recover the washer.

14 Withdraw the damper from the crankshaft, using a suitable puller to free it if necessary.

Refitting

15 Clean all traces of thread-locking compound from the damper and the securing bolt.

16 Smear the crankshaft contact surfaces of the damper spigot with thread-locking compound.

17 Fit the damper to the crankshaft, then fit the washer and bolt.

18 Using the tool to hold the damper stationary, as during removal, tighten the bolt to pull the damper into position on the nose of the crankshaft.

19 Unscrew the bolt, then apply thread-locking compound to the bolt threads.

20 Refit the bolt, and tighten to the specified torque.

21 Further refitting is a reversal of removal, bearing in mind the following points:

a) Tighten the crankshaft pulley bolts securely.

b) Refit and tension the power steering pump and alternator drivebelts as described in Chapter 1B, Section 17.

c) Refit the viscous cooling fan and coupling as described in Chapter 3.

d) On models with air conditioning, refit the air conditioning compressor drivebelt as described in Chapter 1B, Section 17.

e) On completion, refill the cooling system as described in Chapter 1B.

300 TDi engine

Note: *Suitable thread-locking compound will be required to coat the threads of the damper bolt on refitting.*

Removal

22 Disconnect the battery negative lead.

23 Drain the cooling system as described in Chapter 1B.

24 Disconnect the radiator top hose.

25 Loosen the securing clips, and remove the air trunking connecting the intercooler to the inlet manifold.

26 Remove the viscous fan unit and cowl, as described in Chapter 3.

27 Remove the auxiliary drivebelt, as described in Chapter 1B.

28 Proceed as described in paragraphs 11 to 14 inclusive, substituting the word pulley for damper **(see illustrations)**.

Refitting

29 Refitting is a reversal of removal, bearing in mind the following points:

a) Lightly grease the pulley spigot before fitting.

b) Apply suitable thread-locking compound to the bolt threads, and tighten the bolt to the specified torque, holding the pulley stationary as during removal.

5.28b . . . and withdraw the pulley - 300 TDi engine

c) Refit and tension the auxiliary drivebelt as described in Chapter 1B.
d) Refit the viscous fan, coupling and fan cowl assembly, as described in Chapter 3.
e) On completion, refill the cooling system as described in Chapter 1B.

6 Timing belt cover - removal and refitting

200 TDi engine

Note: *A new timing belt cover gasket and a new coolant pump gasket must be used on refitting, and it is advisable to fit a new crankshaft dust seal to the cover.*

Removal

1 Remove the crankshaft pulley and damper, as described in Section 5.
2 Loosen the hose clip, and disconnect the hoses from the coolant pump.
3 If necessary, hold the coolant pump pulley stationary by wrapping the drivebelt tightly round the pulley, then unscrew the three securing bolts, and withdraw the pulley.
4 Unscrew the securing bolts, and withdraw the coolant pump. Recover the gasket.
5 Loosen the hose clips, and withdraw the air trunking connecting the air cleaner to the turbocharger. Where applicable, disconnect the breather hose from the air trunking.
6 Disconnect the wiring from the alternator, then unscrew the through-bolt and nut, and remove the alternator from its mounting bracket.
7 Unscrew the through-bolt and nut, and remove the power steering pump from the mounting bracket. There is no need to disconnect the fluid hoses - just move the pump to one side clear of the working area, taking care not to strain the hoses.
8 Unscrew the securing bolts, and remove the alternator/power steering pump mounting bracket.
9 Unscrew the nine securing bolts, and remove the timing belt cover. Note the locations of the bolts, as they are of different lengths. Recover the gasket.

Refitting

10 Commence refitting by cleaning all traces of old gasket from the mating faces of the timing belt cover and housing.
11 It is advisable to fit a new crankshaft dust seal to the cover, as follows:
a) Prise the old seal from the aperture in the cover using a suitable screwdriver.
b) Clean the seal seat in the cover.
c) Press a new seal into position using a suitable socket or tube. Take care not to damage the seal lips.
12 Refit the cover to the housing, using a new gasket, then refit the securing bolts in their correct locations as noted before removal **(see illustration)**. Tighten the bolts to the specified torque.
13 Refit the alternator/power steering pump mounting bracket, and tighten the securing bolts.
14 Refit the power steering pump and alternator to the bracket, and reconnect the alternator wiring.
15 Refit the air trunking, and tighten the securing clips.
16 Clean all traces of old gasket from the mating faces of the coolant pump and housing, then refit the coolant pump using a new gasket. Tighten the securing bolts to the specified torque.
17 Refit the coolant pump pulley, and tighten the securing bolts. Hold the pulley using the drivebelt, as during removal.
18 Reconnect the hoses to the coolant pump.
19 Refit the crankshaft damper and pulley as described in Section 5.

300 TDi engine

Note: *New gaskets must be used on refitting, and it is advisable to fit a new crankshaft dust seal to the cover.*

Removal

20 Remove the crankshaft pulley as described in Section 5.
21 Unscrew and withdraw the fourteen bolts securing the timing belt cover to the housing. Note the locations of the bolts, as they are of different lengths. Note also that the top two bolts secure the thermostat coolant hose clips.
22 Unbolt the viscous fan pulley if desired.
23 Withdraw the cover, and recover the gasket. Where applicable, also recover the small gasket located around the cover centre securing bolt boss. **Note:** *If quantities of black dust are found inside the cover when it is removed, this is an indication of premature timing belt wear, and the belt should be carefully inspected for wear (especially on the edges of the belt) without delay.*

Refitting

24 Commence refitting by cleaning all traces of old gasket from the mating faces of the timing belt cover and housing.

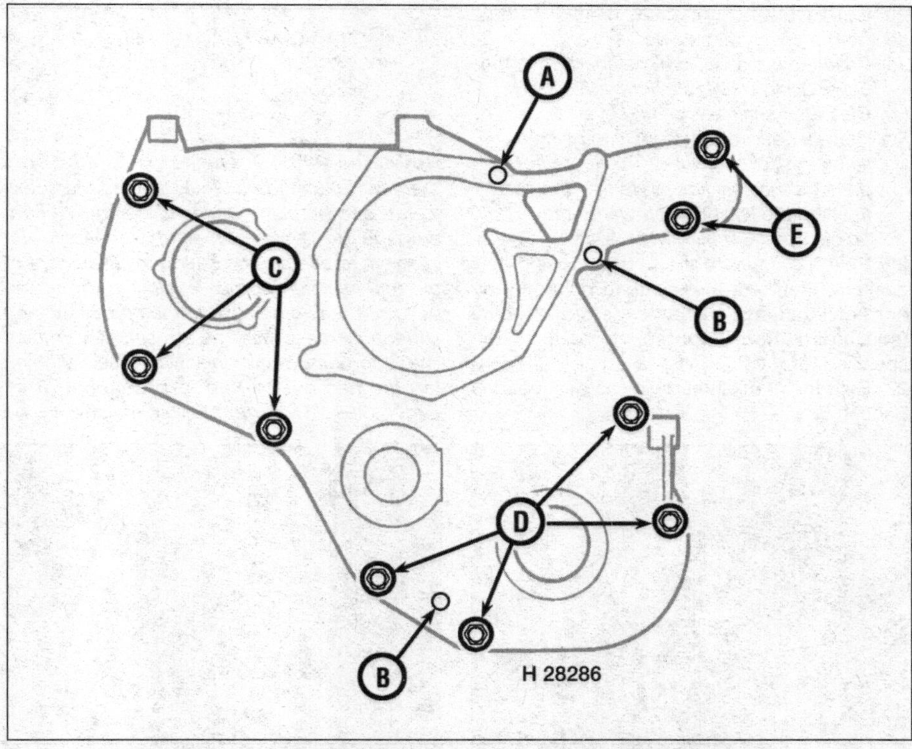
A
C
E
B
D
B
H 28286

6.12 Timing belt cover securing bolt locations - 200 TDi engine

A Stud hole
B Dowel hole
C 25 mm long bolt
D 80 mm long bolt
E 90 mm long bolt

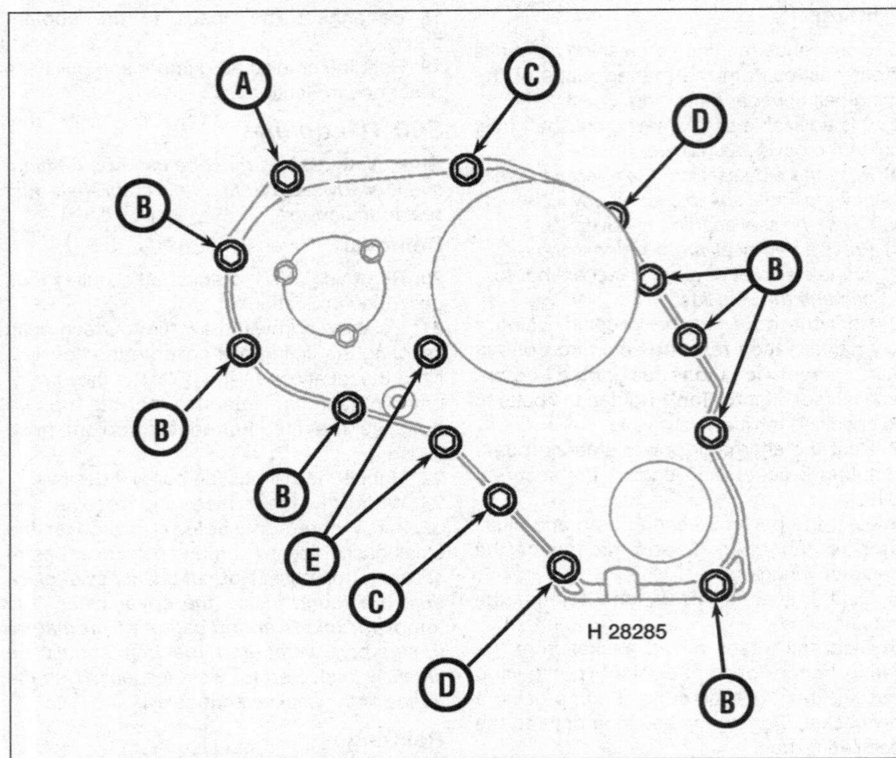
A
B
C
D
E
H 28285

6.26 Timing belt cover securing bolt locations - 300 TDi engine

A 25 mm long bolt
B 35 mm long bolt
C 50 mm long bolt
D 100 mm long bolt
E 110 mm long bolt

25 It is advisable to fit a new crankshaft dust seal to the cover, as follows:

a) Prise the old seal from the aperture in the cover using a suitable screwdriver.

b) Clean the seal seat in the cover.

c) Press a new seal into position using a suitable socket or tube. Take care not to damage the seal lips. Note that the seal fits with the lips facing towards the outside of the timing belt cover.

26 Refit the cover to the housing, using new gaskets, then refit the securing bolts in their correct locations as noted before removal **(see illustration)**. Tighten the bolts to the specified torque.

27 Refit the crankshaft pulley as described in Section 5.

7 Timing belt - inspection, removal and refitting

Note: *The 300 TDi engine can suffer from premature timing belt wear, leading ultimately to the belt breaking in service, and resultant damage to pushrods and rockers. The problem appears to be due to misalignment of the fuel injection pump, leading to the timing belt not running parallel on the sprockets, and suffering excess wear as a result. A modified injection pump mounting, with a self-aligning ferrule, has been fitted in production from early 1999. This modified part should be available from Land Rover dealers, who may also be able to advise on its fitment - regrettably, no further details were available at time of writing.*

Inspection

1 Remove the timing belt cover as described in Section 6.

2 Temporarily refit the crankshaft damper /pulley bolt to the end of the crankshaft.

3 Ensure that the transmission is in neutral, then using a suitable spanner or socket on the crankshaft damper/pulley bolt, rotate the crankshaft so that the full length of the timing belt can be progressively checked. Examine the belt carefully for any signs of uneven wear, splitting or oil contamination, and renew it if there is the slightest doubt about its condition. If the belt exhibits signs of wear on its edges, this is also a sign that it has been weakened, and a new one should be fitted.

4 On completion, refit the timing belt cover as described in Section 6.

Removal

Note: *If the original belt is to be refitted, it must be refitted so that it rotates in the original running direction - mark the running direction before removal. When removed from the engine, timing belts must be stored on edge, on a clean surface.* ***Do not*** *bend the belt through acute angles (radius less than 50 mm), as damage and premature failure may result. A gauge- or pointer-type torque wrench will be required to tension the belt during refitting - a 'break' or 'click' type torque wrench is not suitable.*

5 Remove the timing belt cover as described in Section 6.

6 If the camshaft sprocket (sprocket hub on 300 TDi engines) is to be removed for any reason, the sprocket/hub securing bolt should be loosened at this stage, before the timing belt is removed (see Section 8).

7 Temporarily refit the crankshaft damper/ pulley bolt to the end of the crankshaft, then turn the crankshaft (using a suitable spanner or socket on the damper/pulley bolt) to bring No 1 piston to TDC and lock it in place, as described in Section 3. Ignore the references to removal of the air conditioning compressor and the injection pump hub cover plate.

8 Check that the timing marks are aligned as follows:

a) The timing mark on the camshaft sprocket should be aligned with the web on the timing belt housing ***(see illustration).***

b) The Woodruff key in the end of the crankshaft should be aligned with the arrow on the timing belt housing ***(see illustration).***

9 Slacken the belt tensioner pulley bolt.

10 Slide the timing belt from the sprockets **(see illustration)**. If the original belt is to be refitted, mark the running direction of the belt to ensure correct refitting.

7.8a Camshaft sprocket timing mark aligned with web on timing belt housing - 300 TDi engine

7.8b Crankshaft Woodruff key aligned with arrow on timing belt housing - 300 TDi engine

7.10 Slacken the belt tensioner pulley bolt (arrowed) and slide off the timing belt - 300 TDi engine shown

Warning: Do not turn the camshaft once the timing belt has been removed.

If the belt cannot easily be slid from the sprockets, unscrew the securing nut, and remove the belt idler pulley.

Refitting

Note: *During refitting, the timing belt tensioning procedure is effectively carried out twice. This double-tensioning procedure* ***must*** *be carried out as described, to avoid the possibility of belt failure and resultant engine damage.*

11 Slacken the three bolts securing the injection pump sprocket to the pump hub **(see illustration)**.

12 Carefully fit the belt over the sprockets, ensuring that the direction of rotation marks are correctly orientated if the original belt is being refitted. Take care not to move the sprockets, and make sure that the timing marks are still aligned as described in paragraph 8.

13 Where applicable, refit the idler pulley, and tighten the securing nut.

14 If necessary, adjust the position of the belt, so that it sits correctly on the sprockets, with the timing marks still aligned.

15 Tighten the belt tensioner pulley bolt finger-tight.

16 Engage a half-inch square-drive extension bar with the hole in the tensioner pulley mounting plate.

17 Using a gauge-type torque wrench held vertically, turn the extension bar to tension the belt to the specified torque. Tighten the tensioner pulley bolt, taking care to maintain the correct torque **(see illustration)**.

18 Tighten the injection pump sprocket-to-hub securing bolts to the specified torque.

19 Remove the pump timing pin from the injection pump sprocket, and withdraw the flywheel locking tool centre pin from the slot in the flywheel.

20 Turn the crankshaft clockwise through two complete turns, until the timing marks are aligned again, as described in paragraph 8.

7.11 Unscrew the three bolts (arrowed) securing the injection pump sprocket to the pump hub - 300 TDi engine shown

21 Slacken the tensioner pulley bolt, and repeat the tensioning procedure described in paragraph 17.

22 Turn the crankshaft through two complete revolutions clockwise, then re-engage the fly wheel locking tool with the slot in the flywheel, and check that the pump timing pin can still be inserted easily. If the pump timing pin cannot be easily inserted into position, proceed as follows, otherwise proceed to paragraph 30.

23 Withdraw the flywheel locking tool centre pin from the slot in the flywheel, then turn the crankshaft as necessary, until the timing pin can be inserted easily into the injection pump.

24 Loosen the pump locking screw, and remove the keeper plate (located at the front of the pump, behind the timing belt housing). Tighten the locking screw to lock the pump spindle in position.

25 Loosen the three pump sprocket-to-hub bolts.

26 Turn the crankshaft the small amount to TDC, and engage the flywheel locking tool centre pin with the timing slot in the flywheel.

27 Re-check to ensure that the pump timing pin is an easy sliding fit in the pump.

28 Tighten the pump sprocket-to-hub bolts to the specified torque.

29 Loosen the pump locking screw, then refit the keeper plate, and tighten the locking screw.

30 Remove the timing pin from the pump, and withdraw the flywheel locking tool centre pin from the slot in the flywheel.

7.17 Tensioning the timing belt - 300 TDi engine

31 If necessary, tighten the camshaft sprocket to the specified torque.

32 Refit the timing belt cover as described in Section 6.

8 Timing belt sprockets and tensioner - removal and refitting

Camshaft sprocket - 200 TDi engine

Note: *New retaining plate O-rings must be used on refitting.*

Removal

1 Remove the timing belt as described in Section 7.

Warning: Do not turn the crankshaft or the camshaft once the timing belt has been removed.

2 Unscrew the sprocket securing bolt (the bolt should have been loosened before the timing belt was removed). Recover the washer, the small O-ring, the retaining plate, and the larger O-ring.

3 Withdraw the sprocket from the end of the camshaft.

Refitting

4 Refitting is a reversal of removal, bearing in mind the following points:

a) Use new O-rings when refitting the sprocket retaining plate. Note that the larger O-ring fits between the retaining plate and the sprocket. The smaller O-ring fits between the retaining plate and the washer.

b) Do not fully tighten the sprocket securing bolt until the timing belt has been refitted.

c) Refit the timing belt as described in Section 7, but before refitting the timing belt cover, tighten the sprocket securing bolt to the specified torque.

Camshaft sprocket and hub - 300 TDi engine

Note: *The sprocket is bolted to a hub (with three bolts and a retaining plate) on 300 TDi engines, and the hub is in turn bolted to the end of the camshaft. If the sprocket is to be removed, leaving the hub on the camshaft, the sprocket retaining plate* ***must*** *be locked in position on the sprocket by fitting and tightening two M8 bolts in the holes provided. If this is not done, it is possible for the valve timing to be altered when the sprocket is refitted (the bolt holes are elongated), which may adversely affect the performance of the engine.*

Removal

5 Remove the timing belt as described in Section 7.

Warning: Do not turn the crankshaft or the camshaft once the timing belt has been removed.

6 If the sprocket/hub assembly is to be removed as a complete unit, proceed as

8.7 Removing the camshaft sprocket/hub assembly - 300 TDi engine

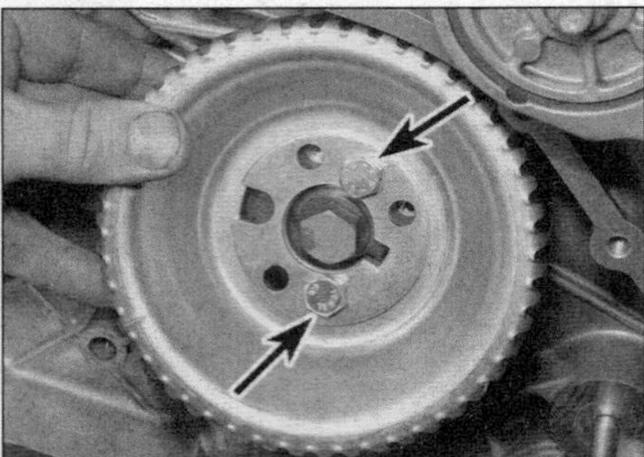
8.9 Removing the camshaft sprocket from the hub. Note M8 bolts (arrowed) locking retaining plate to hub - 300 TDi engine

8.12 Withdraw the crankshaft sprocket . . .

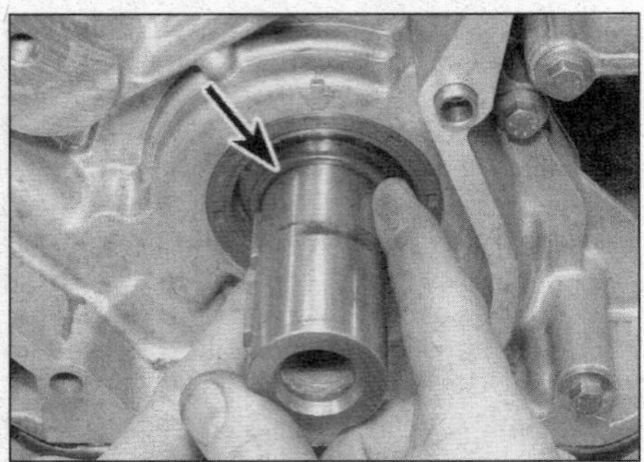
8.13 . . . and recover the O-ring (arrowed) from the crankshaft - 300 TDi engine

follows. If the sprocket is to be removed leaving the hub in place on the camshaft, proceed to paragraph 8.

7 If the sprocket/hub assembly is to be removed as a complete unit (such as for camshaft renewal), unscrew the hub securing bolt (the bolt should have been loosened before the timing belt was removed), then recover the washer and withdraw the assembly from the end of the camshaft **(see illustration)**. If the sprocket is to be removed from the hub, ensure that the retaining plate is locked in position first, as described in the note at the beginning of this sub-Section.

8 If the sprocket is to be removed leaving the hub in place on the camshaft, refer to the note at the beginning of this sub-Section, and fit two M8 bolts to lock the retaining plate in position on the sprocket.

9 Counterhold the camshaft using a suitable socket on the hub securing bolt, then unscrew the three bolts securing the sprocket to the hub, and withdraw the sprocket from the hub **(see illustration)**.

Refitting

10 Refitting is a reversal of removal, bearing in mind the following points:

a) *Where applicable, do not fully tighten the sprocket hub securing bolt until the timing belt has been refitted.*
b) *Refit the timing belt as described in Section 7, but before refitting the timing belt cover, where applicable, tighten the sprocket hub securing bolt to the specified torque, and/or remove the two bolts used to lock the retaining plate to the sprocket.*

Crankshaft sprocket

Note: *On 300 TDi engines, a new O-ring should be used when refitting the sprocket.*

Removal

11 Remove the timing belt as described in Section 7.

12 Withdraw the sprocket from the end of the crankshaft **(see illustration)**. If the sprocket is tight, a suitable puller should be used. If a puller is used, do not allow the puller to bear on the end of the crankshaft - temporarily refit the pulley/damper bolt, and allow the puller to bear on the bolt head.

13 Recover the Woodruff key if it is loose, and on 300 TDi engines, recover the O-ring which fits behind the sprocket **(see illustration)**.

Refitting

14 Refitting is a reversal of removal, bearing in mind the following points:

a) *Ensure that the Woodruff key is securely fitted to the end of the crankshaft.*
b) *On 300 TDi engines, refit the sprocket using a new O-ring.*
c) *If the sprocket is a tight fit on the crankshaft, carefully tap it into position using a soft-faced mallet. On 300 TDi engines, ensure that the O-ring is properly seated.*
d) *Refit the timing belt as described in Section 7.*

Fuel injection pump sprocket

Removal

15 Remove the timing belt as described in Section 7.

16 Slacken the three bolts securing the injection pump sprocket to the pump hub.

17 Loosen the pump locking screw, and remove the keeper plate (located at the front of the pump, behind the timing belt housing). Tighten the locking screw to lock the pump spindle in position.

18 Ensure that the flywheel locking tool is engaged with the slot in the flywheel - no attempt must be made to turn the crankshaft or the fuel injection pump once the pump spindle has been locked.

19 Remove the injection pump timing pin from the pump.

20 Remove the sprocket securing bolts, then recover the retaining plate, and withdraw the sprocket from the pump hub **(see illustrations)**.

8.20a Remove the three securing bolts . . .

8.20b . . . recover the retaining plate . . .

8.20c . . . and withdraw the sprocket

Refitting

21 Fit the sprocket to the pump hub, then fit the retaining plate, and the securing bolts. Do not fully tighten the securing bolts at this stage.
22 Fit the injection pump timing pin, and engage the pin with the pump hub.
23 Loosen the pump locking screw, then refit the keeper plate, and tighten the locking screw.
24 Refit the timing belt as described in Section 7.

Idler pulley

25 Remove the timing belt as described in Section 7.
26 Unscrew the securing nut, recover the washer, and withdraw the idler pulley **(see illustration)**.
27 Refitting is a reversal of removal, but refit the timing belt as described in Section 7.

Timing belt tensioner

Removal

28 Remove the idler pulley as described previously in this Section.
29 Unscrew the securing bolt, recover the washer, and withdraw the tensioner. On 300 TDi engines, recover the spacer washer from the idler pulley stud **(see illustrations)**.
30 Check the tensioner for signs of wear, or of roughness when the wheel is spun. If the tensioner is known to have completed a high mileage, or if there is any doubt as to its condition, renew it.

Refitting

31 Refitting is a reversal of removal, bearing in mind the following points:

a) On 200 TDi engines, make sure that the hole in the tensioner plate locates over the lug on the timing belt housing.

b) On 300 TDi engines, make sure that the spacer washer is in place on the idler pulley stud, and make sure that the tensioner plate locates over the stud.

32 Refit the idler pulley, and refit the timing belt as described in Section 7.

9 Valve operating (rocker) gear - removal, inspection and refitting

Note: *In order to remove the cam follower components, the cylinder head must be removed. Removal of the cam follower components is described in Section 11.*

200 TDi engine

Removal

1 Remove the valve cover as described in Section 4.
2 Progressively unscrew the five rocker shaft securing bolts, but do not remove the bolts from the shaft - if the bolts are removed, the rocker assembly will fall apart when removed from the cylinder head.

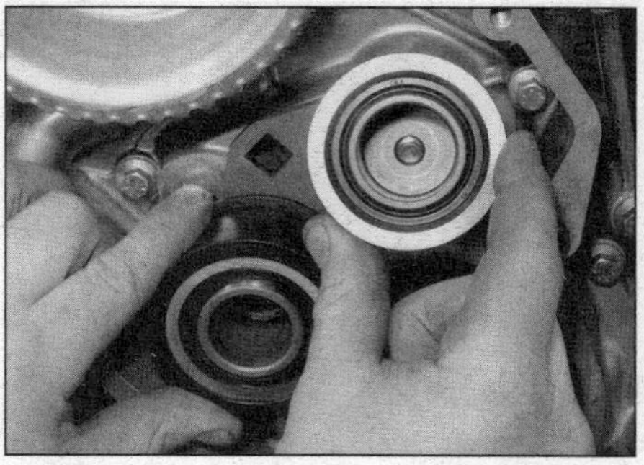

8.26 Removing the timing belt idler pulley - 300 TDi engine

8.29a Unscrew the securing bolt and recover the washer . . .

8.29b . . . withdraw the tensioner . . .

8.29c . . . and recover the spacer washer - 300 TDi engine

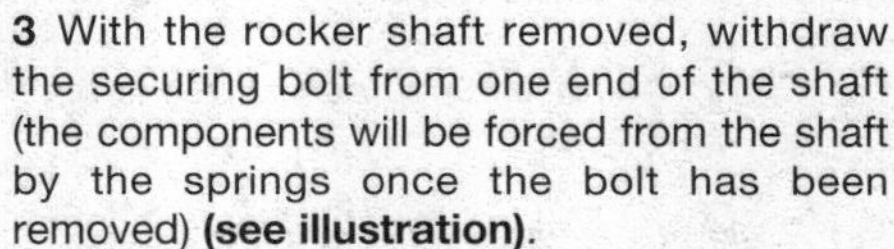

3 With the rocker shaft removed, withdraw the securing bolt from one end of the shaft (the components will be forced from the shaft by the springs once the bolt has been removed) **(see illustration)**.
4 Withdraw the spacers, bearing cap, rocker arm, and spring from the shaft. Lay all the components out in order of removal. Take care not to mix the components up, as they must be refitted to the rocker shaft in their original positions.
5 Working progressively along the shaft,

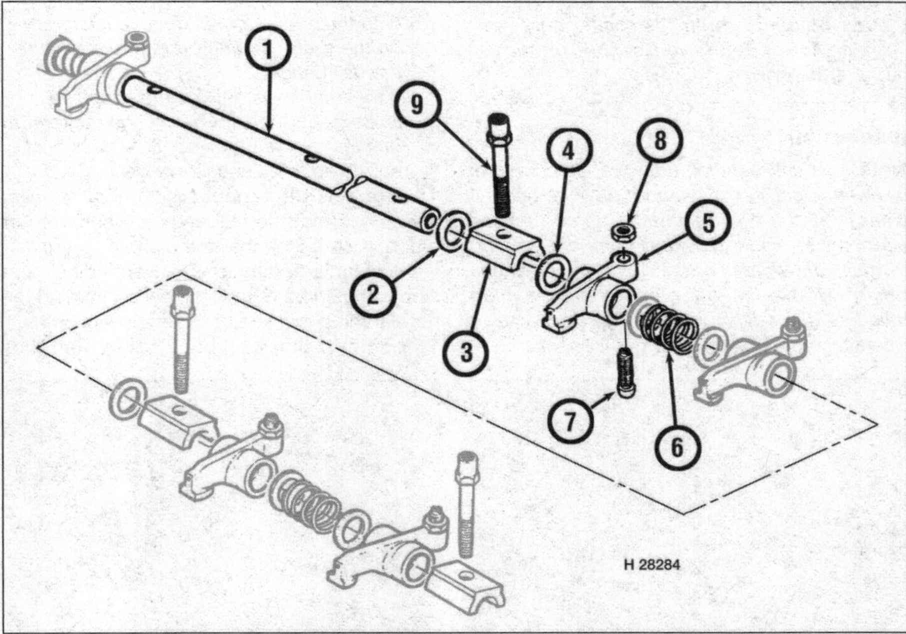
1
9
4
8
5
2
3
7
6
H 28284

9.3 Valve operating gear components - 200 TDi engine

1 Rocker shaft
2 Spacer
3 Bearing cap
4 Spacer
5 Rocker arm
6 Spring
7 Tappet adjustment screw
8 Tappet locknut
9 Rocker shaft securing bolt

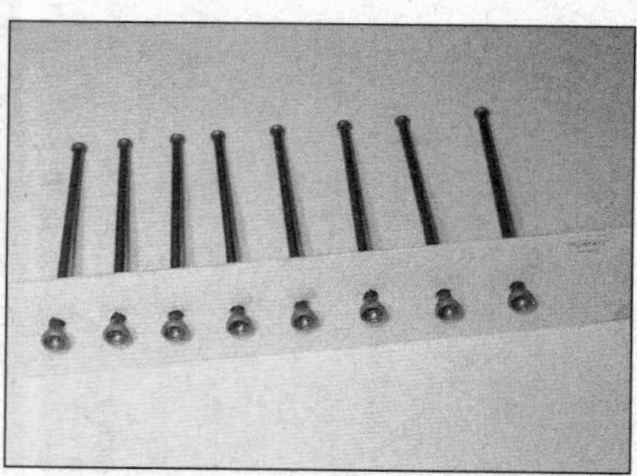
9.7 Store the pushrods in order by pushing them through holes in piece of card

withdraw the remaining rocker shaft securing bolts, and slide the remaining components from the shaft, keeping them in order.

6 Make suitable holes to accommodate the pushrods in a piece of card, then number the holes from 1 to 8 (No 1 at the timing belt end of the engine).

7 Working from the timing belt end of the cylinder head, lift the pushrods from their bores in the cylinder head, and insert them through the holes in the card, in order of removal **(see illustration)**.

8 Where applicable, remove the valve stem caps from the tops of the valve stems. Keep them in order so that they can be refitted to their original locations.

To keep the rocker shaft components in order, slide them onto a 'dummy shaft' in order of removal. The dummy shaft can be made from a suitable length of thin bar or rod, which must be longer than the rocker shaft in order to accommodate the uncompressed springs.

Inspection

Note: *It is unlikely that individual components will wear significantly, without obvious general wear in all the components. It can be a false economy to renew individual components, and if significant wear is evident, or if the engine is being overhauled after completing a high mileage, it is advisable to renew all the valve operating and cam follower components.*

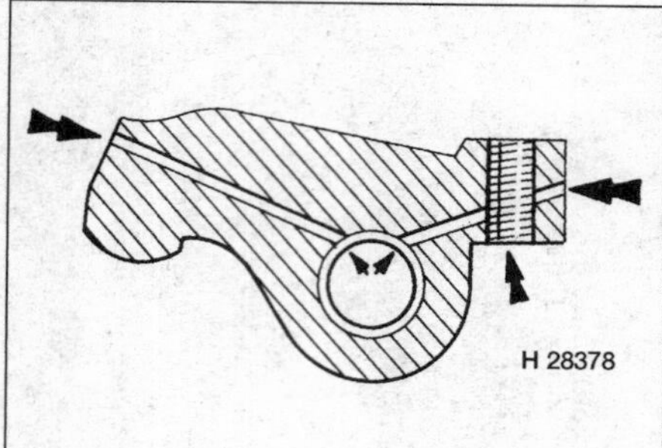
H 28378
9.11 Check that the oil holes (arrowed) in the rocker arms are clear - 200 TDi engine

9 Clean all the components thoroughly, one by one, keeping them in order.

10 Examine the rocker shaft for wear. Check the bearing surfaces, and check that the oilways are clear. If there is any sign of wear, scoring or pitting on the bearing surfaces, the shaft must be renewed.

11 Inspect the rocker arm pads (the areas which contact the valve stems) for wear. If excessive wear is evident, the rocker arms must be renewed - it is not permissible to grind the pads to compensate for wear. Check that the oil holes in the rocker arms are free from obstructions **(see illustration)**.

12 Check the freeplay of the rocker arms on the shaft. This is most easily accomplished as follows:

a) Clamp the rocker shaft horizontally in a soft-jawed vice.
b) Slide the rocker arm onto the shaft.
c) Position a suitable dial test indicator to read from the cylindrical section of the rocker arm.
d) Grip the rocker arm and move it laterally on the shaft, reading off the freeplay on the dial gauge.
e) If the freeplay is outside the specified limits (see 'Specifications'), the rocker arm bushes can be renewed, but this is best entrusted to a Land Rover dealer.

13 Examine the tappet adjustment screws, and check that the ball-ends are not worn or pitted. Also check that the oil holes are clear. If any wear is evident, the relevant adjustment screw should be renewed (bearing in mind the note at the beginning of this sub-Section).

14 Examine the pushrods. Ensure that they are all straight, and if any one is bent or distorted, renew it. Check the ends of each pushrod. If either end is rough, damaged or badly worn, the pushrod must be renewed. If it is discovered that one pushrod is worn, examine the corresponding rocker arm and tappet slide also (see Section 10).

15 Examine the rocker shaft springs for damage and deterioration. It is advisable to renew all the springs as a matter of course.

16 Check the condition of the valve stem caps where applicable, and renew them if there is any sign of significant wear. Note that if no valve stem caps are fitted, it is permissible to fit caps (the caps must be fitted to all the valves as a set, and are available from Land Rover dealers) to compensate for wear in the valve stems and/or the rocker arm pads.

Refitting

17 Commence refitting by ensuring that all components are clean. Check all oilways for obstructions.

18 Lightly lubricate the tops of the tappet slides with clean engine oil of the correct grade, then refit the pushrods in their original locations. Make sure that the ball-end of each pushrod locates correctly in the tappet slide **(see illustration)**.

19 Where applicable, refit the valve stem caps to the tops of the valves, in their original locations **(see illustration)**.

20 Lubricate the rocker shaft, then slide one of the end bearing caps onto the shaft, and refit one of the rocker shaft securing bolts to retain the bearing cap.

21 Slide the spacers, rocker arms, springs and bearing caps onto the shaft, keeping them in their original order. Refit the relevant rocker shaft securing bolt as each bearing cap is fitted, to retain the components on the shaft.

22 With the rocker shaft reassembled, lubricate the rocker arm contact faces of the pushrods and valve stems.

23 Refit the rocker shaft assembly to the cylinder head. If necessary, loosen the locknuts, and back off the tappet adjuster screws to aid refitting. Ensure that the ball ends of the tappet adjuster screws locate correctly in the pushrod cups.

24 Progressively tighten the securing bolts to the specified torque.

25 Adjust the valve clearances as described in Chapter 1B.

Warning: If the crankshaft is rotated with excessive valve clearances, it is possible for the pushrods to become dislodged, and fracture the tappet slides. To prevent the possibility of damage, turn the adjusters to eliminate all clearance from any loose rocker arms before turning the crankshaft to check the valve clearances.

26 On completion, refit the valve cover as described in Section 4.

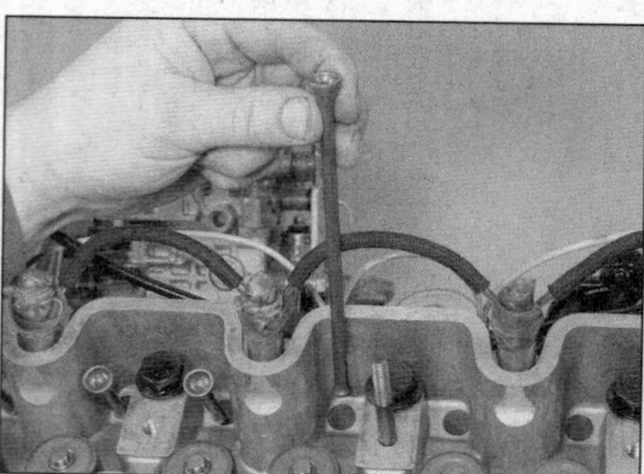
9.18 Fitting a pushrod

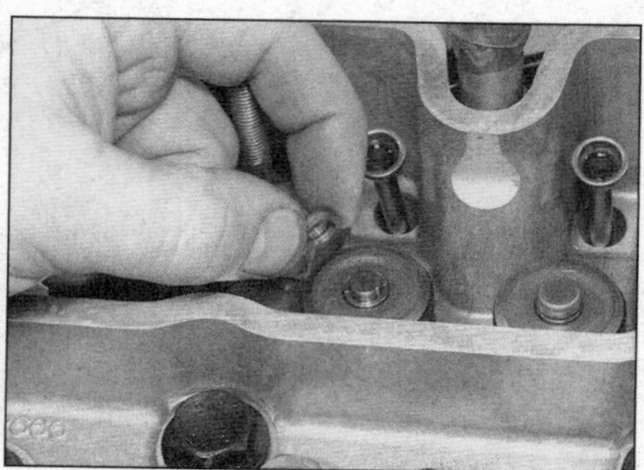
9.19 Fitting a valve stem cap

300 TDi engine

Removal

27 Remove the valve cover as described in Section 4.

28 Progressively unscrew the three nuts and two bolts securing the rocker shaft to the cylinder head, then lift the assembly from the cylinder head studs **(see illustrations)**. Hold the end pedestals as the assembly is removed, to prevent the components from falling off the rocker shaft. Take care not to dislodge the valve stem caps from the tops of the valves as the rocker gear is removed.

29 With the rocker shaft removed, withdraw the pedestals, spacers, rocker arms and springs from the shaft. Lay all the components out in order of removal. Take care not to mix the components up, as they must be refitted to the rocker shaft in their original positions.

To keep the rocker shaft components in order, slide them onto a 'dummy shaft' in order of removal. The dummy shaft can be made from a suitable length of thin bar or rod, which must be longer than the rocker shaft in order to accommodate the uncompressed springs.

30 Remove the pushrods, as described in paragraphs 6 and 7.

31 Remove the caps from the tops of the valve stems. Again, keep them in order so that they can be refitted to their original locations.

9.28a Removing a rocker shaft securing bolt - 300 TDi engine

9.28b Removing the rocker shaft - 300 TDi engine

Inspection

32 Proceed as described in paragraphs 9 to 16.

Refitting

33 Commence refitting by ensuring that all components are clean. Check all oilways for obstructions.

34 Lightly lubricate the tops of the tappet slides with clean engine oil of the correct grade, then refit the pushrods in their original locations. Make sure that the ball-end of each pushrod locates correctly in the tappet slide.

35 Refit the valve stem caps to the tops of the valves, in their original locations.

36 Lubricate the rocker shaft, then slide the components onto the shaft, keeping them in their original order **(see illustrations)**.

37 With the rocker shaft reassembled, lubricate the rocker arm contact faces of the pushrods and the valve stems.

38 Refit the rocker shaft assembly to the cylinder head, ensuring that the three locating studs pass through the shaft and the pedestals. If necessary, loosen the locknuts, and back off the tappet adjuster screws to aid refitting. Ensure that the ball ends of the tappet adjuster screws locate correctly in the pushrod cups.

39 Refit the securing nuts and bolts, and tighten progressively to the specified torque in the two stages given in the Specifications **(see illustrations)**.

40 Proceed as described in paragraphs 25 and 26.

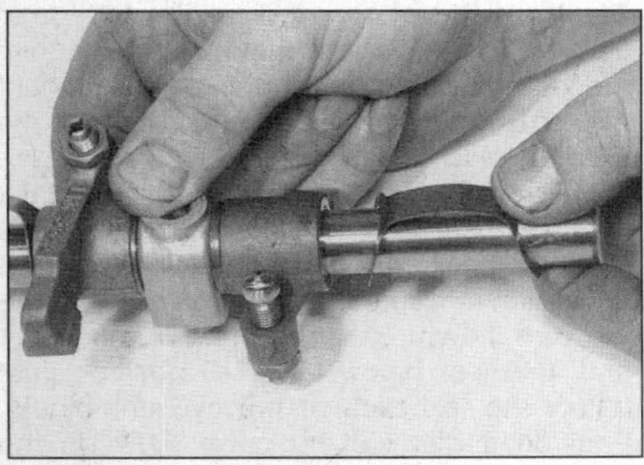

9.36a Refit the spring . . .

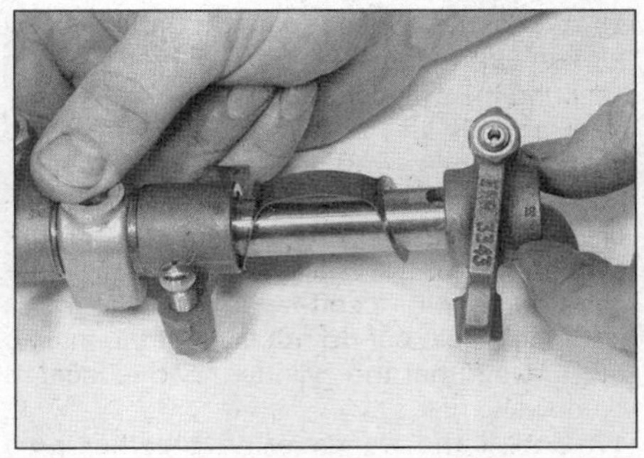

9.36b . . . rocker arm . . .

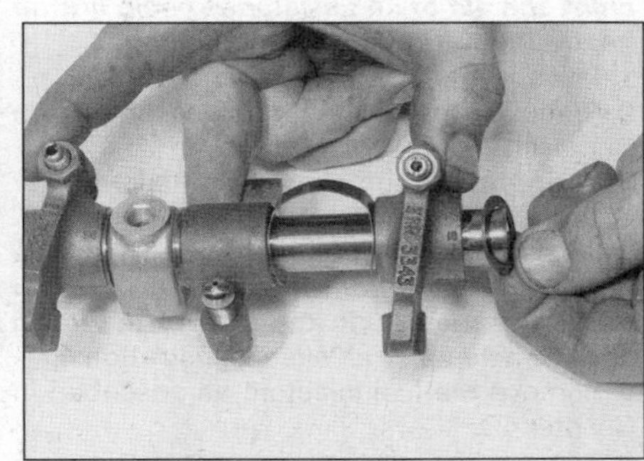

9.36c . . . washer . . .

9.36d . . . and end pedestal to the end of the rocker shaft - 300 TDi engine

9.39a Refit the rocker shaft securing nuts and bolts . . .

9.39b . . . and tighten to the specified torque, then through the specified angle - 300 TDi engine

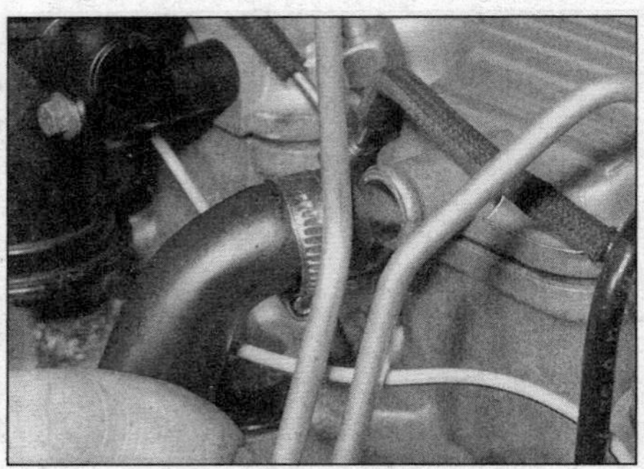

10.4a Disconnect the breather hoses from the valve cover . . .

10.4b . . . and the breather - 300 TDi engine

10 Cylinder head - removal, inspection and refitting

Removal

Note: *The cylinder head bolts may be re-used a maximum of five times. Unless the history of the cylinder head bolts is certain (make marks to indicate the number of times they have been used), it is advisable to use new bolts when refitting the cylinder head. A new cylinder head gasket must be used on refitting.*

Warning: Access to lift the cylinder head is awkward, due to the width of the engine compartment. Although the cylinder head is not unusually heavy, it is advisable to enlist the aid of an assistant to help lift the head - do not attempt the job alone.

1 Disconnect the battery negative lead.

2 Remove the bonnet as described in Chapter 12.

3 Drain the cooling system as described in Chapter 1B.

4 Loosen the hose clips, and disconnect the breather hose(s) from the valve cover, and from the breather on the side of the valve cover, where applicable **(see illustrations)**.

5 Remove the fuel injectors as described in Chapter 4C.

6 Remove the glow plugs as described in Chapter 5C.

7 Disconnect the coolant hoses from the thermostat housing and cover **(see illustration)**.

10.7 Disconnecting the coolant hose from the thermostat housing - 300 TDi engine

8 Disconnect the wiring from the temperature gauge sender, located in the thermostat housing.

9 Remove the inlet manifold, exhaust manifold and turbocharger, as described in the relevant part of Chapter 4.

10 Disconnect the coolant hose connecting the coolant pipe (mounted on the manifold studs) to the water pump, then move the coolant pipe clear of the working area.

11 Disconnect the coolant hose from the rear of the cylinder head.

12 Unbolt the wiring harness bracket from the cylinder head.

13 Remove the valve operating gear as described in Section 9.

14 Where applicable, lift the valve stem caps from the tops of the valves. Keep the caps in order, so that they can be refitted in their original positions.

15 Working in a spiral pattern, progressively loosen and remove the eighteen bolts securing the cylinder head.

16 Carefully lift the cylinder head from the cylinder block, and move it forwards for access to the bolt securing the transmission breather pipe bracket to the rear of the cylinder head. If necessary, tap the cylinder head gently with a soft-faced mallet to free it from the block, but **do not** lever at the mating faces. Note that the cylinder head is located on dowels.

17 Unbolt the transmission breather pipe bracket from the cylinder head then, with the aid of an assistant, lift the cylinder head from the vehicle.

18 Recover the cylinder head gasket, and discard it.

Inspection

19 The mating faces of the cylinder head and block must be perfectly clean before refitting the head. Use a scraper to remove all traces of gasket and carbon, and also clean the tops of the pistons. Take particular care with the aluminium cylinder head, as the soft metal is damaged easily. Also, make sure that debris is not allowed to enter the oil and water channels - this is particularly important for the oil circuit, as carbon could block the oil supply to the camshaft or crankshaft bearings. Using adhesive tape and paper, seal the water, oil and bolt holes in the cylinder block. Clean the piston crowns in the same way.

HAYNES
HiNT

To prevent carbon entering the gap between the pistons and bores, smear a little grease in the gap. After cleaning the piston, rotate the crankshaft so that the piston moves down the bore, then wipe out the grease and carbon with a cloth rag.

20 Check the block and head for nicks, deep scratches and other damage. If slight, they may be removed carefully with a file. More serious damage may be repaired by machining, but this is a specialist job.

21 If warpage of the cylinder head is suspected, use a straight-edge to check it for distortion. Refer to Part C of this Chapter if necessary.

22 Clean out the bolt holes in the block using a pipe cleaner, or a rag and screwdriver. Make sure that all oil is removed, otherwise there is a possibility of the block being cracked by hydraulic pressure when the bolts are tightened.

23 Examine the bolt threads and the threads in the cylinder block for damage. If necessary, use the correct-size tap to chase out the threads in the block, and use a die to clean the threads on the bolts.

Gasket selection

24 When the pistons are at the top dead centre (TDC) position, they protrude above the top face of the cylinder block. The amount of protrusion determines the thickness of the cylinder head gasket required. The protrusion of all the pistons above the cylinder block must be measured, and the thickness of the gasket to be used is determined by the largest protrusion measured.

25 Turn the crankshaft to bring piston Nos 1 and 4 to just below the TDC position (just below the top face of the cylinder block). Position a dial test indicator (DTI) on the cylinder block, and zero it on the block face. Transfer the probe to the crown of No 1 piston (as close as possible to the centre, avoiding the combustion chamber), then slowly turn the crankshaft back and forth past TDC, noting the highest reading produced on the indicator. Record this reading.

26 Repeat this measurement procedure on No 4 piston, then turn the crankshaft half a turn (180°) and repeat the procedure on Nos 2 and 3 pistons **(see illustration)**. Ensure that all measurements are taken along the longitudinal centreline of the crankshaft (this will eliminate errors due to piston slant).

27 If a dial test indicator is not available, piston protrusion may be measured using a straight-edge and feeler blades or vernier calipers. However, these methods are inevitably less accurate, and cannot therefore be recommended **(see illustration)**.

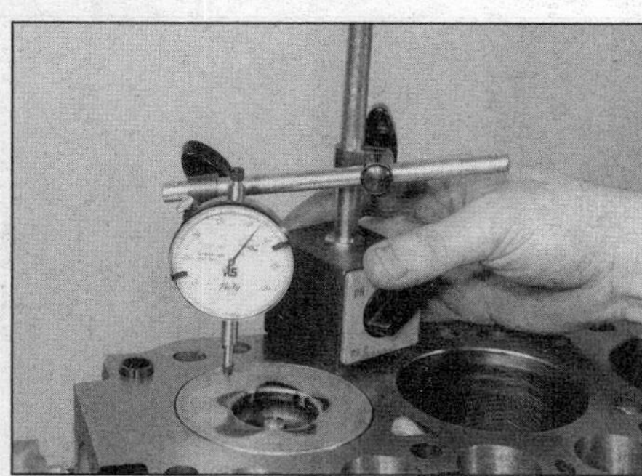

10.26 Measuring piston protrusion using a dial gauge

Ensure that measurements are taken along the longitudinal centreline of the crankshaft (this will eliminate errors due to piston slant)

28 Ascertain the greatest piston protrusion measurement, and use this to determine the correct cylinder head gasket from the table. The gasket identification holes are located at the rear right-hand (fuel injection pump) side of the gasket **(see illustration)**.

Piston protrusion	Gasket identification
0.5000 to 0.6000 mm	1 hole
0.6100 to 0.7000 mm	2 holes
0.7100 to 0.8000 mm	3 holes

Refitting

29 Ensure that the cylinder head locating dowels are fitted to the cylinder block, then fit the correct gasket the right way round on the cylinder block, with the identification mark(s) at the rear right-hand (fuel injection pump) side of the gasket. The TOP mark should be uppermost on the fuel injection pump side of the engine **(see illustration)**.

30 Lower the cylinder head onto the block, to enable the transmission breather pipe to be refitted. Refit the bolt securing the breather pipe bracket, then position the head over the two positioning dowels in the cylinder block.

31 Refer to the note at the beginning of this Section, and fit new cylinder head bolts if there is any doubt about the number of times the original bolts have been used.

32 Lightly lubricate the cylinder head bolt threads, then loosely fit the bolts. Note that there are three different sizes of bolt, and the bolts should be fitted to the locations shown **(see illustrations)**.

33 Tighten the bolts in the order shown in illustration 10.32a, and in the stages given in the Specifications - ie, tighten all bolts in sequence to the Stage 1 torque, then tighten all bolts in sequence to the Stage 2 torque, and so on **(see illustration)**.

34 Where applicable, refit the valve stem caps to the tops of the valves in their original locations, as noted before removal.

35 Refit the valve operating gear as described in Section 9.

36 Refit the wiring harness bracket, and tighten the securing bolt.

10.27 Measuring piston protrusion using a straight-edge and feeler blades

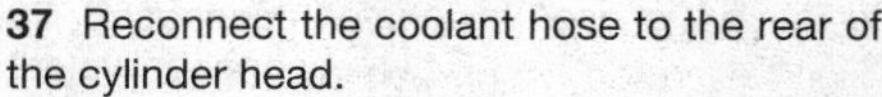

37 Reconnect the coolant hose to the rear of the cylinder head.

38 Reconnect the coolant hose connecting the manifold-mounted coolant pipe to the water pump.

39 Refit the exhaust manifold, turbocharger and inlet manifold, as described in the relevant part of Chapter 4.

40 Reconnect the temperature gauge sender wiring, and reconnect the coolant hoses to the thermostat housing and cover.

41 Refit the glow plugs as described in Chapter 5C.

42 Refit the fuel injectors as described in Chapter 4C.

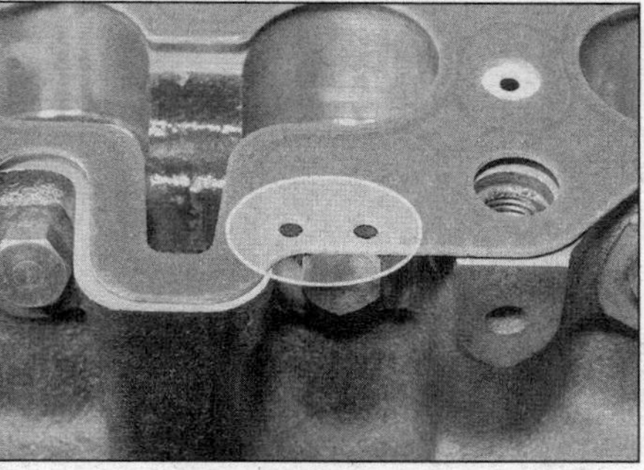

10.28 Cylinder head gasket identification holes

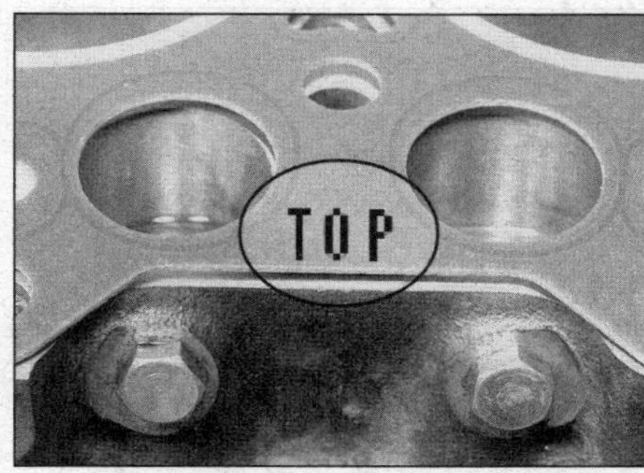
TOP

10.29 Cylinder head gasket TOP mark

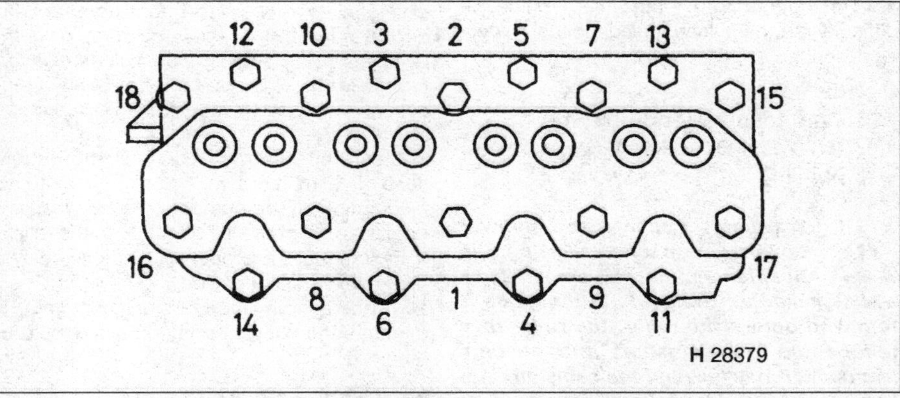
12
10
3
2
5
7
13
18
15
16
17
8
1
9
14
6
4
11
H 28379

10.32a Cylinder head bolt locations and tightening sequence

M10 x 117 mm bolts at locations 3, 5, 12 and 13
M12 x 140 mm bolts at locations 1, 2, 7, 8, 9, 10, 15, 16, 17 and 18
M12 x 100 mm bolts at locations 4, 6, 11 and 14

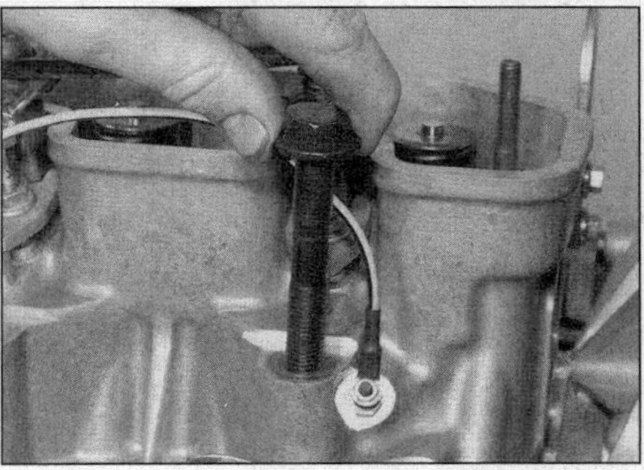

10.32b Refit the cylinder head bolts . . .

10.33 . . . and tighten to the specified torque, then through the specified angle

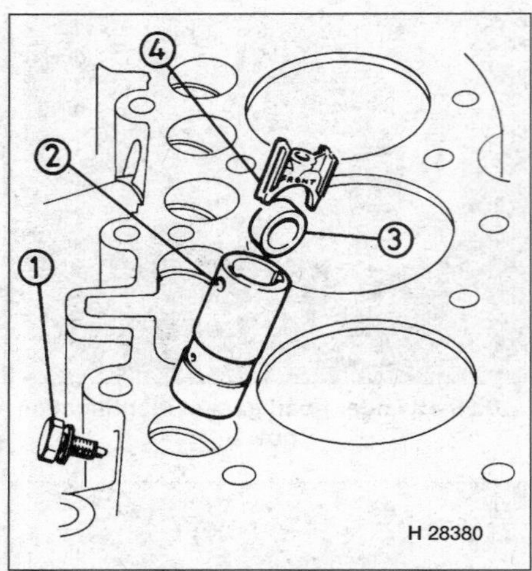
4
2
3
1
H 28380

11.2a Cam follower components

1 Guide locating screw
2 Guide
3 Roller
4 Tappet slide

43 Reconnect the breather hoses to the valve cover and the breather filter, if not already done.
44 Refill the cooling system as described in Chapter 1B.
45 Refit the bonnet as described in Chapter 12.
46 Reconnect the battery negative lead.
47 On completion, start the engine. If difficulty is experienced, bleed the fuel system as described in Chapter 4C.

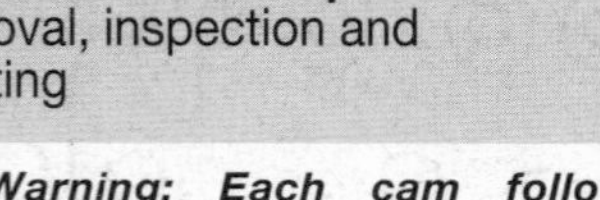

11 Cam follower components - removal, inspection and refitting

Warning: Each cam follower consists of a solid roller, held in position against the camshaft by a slide inside a fixed guide. If the guide is removed before the roller, the roller may fall behind the camshaft and become jammed, or may fall past the camshaft into the crankcase. The following procedure must therefore be followed exactly when removing the cam followers.

Removal

Note: *New guide locating screws must be used on refitting.*
1 Remove the cylinder head as described in Section 10.
2 Starting at the front of the engine, loosen the first cam follower guide locating screw (accessed from the camshaft side of the cylinder block), until the end of the screw rests just below the hole in the inner bore of the guide **(see illustrations)**.
3 Using a suitable length of wire with a hooked end, lift out the tappet slide. Note that the FRONT or F mark on the slide should face the timing belt end of the engine **(see illustration)**.
4 Using the same piece of wire, lift out the roller **(see illustration)**. Mark the roller on the side facing the timing belt end of the engine, so that it can be refitted in its original position.
5 Remove the guide locating screw, and lift out the guide **(see illustration)**. On 200 TDi engines, recover the washer from under the screw head.
6 Repeat the procedure on the remaining components, and number the components from 1 to 8, so that they can be refitted in their original locations.

11.2b Cam follower guide locating screws (arrowed)

Inspection

Note: *It is unlikely that individual components will wear significantly, without obvious general wear in all the components. It can be a false economy to renew individual components, and if significant wear is evident, or if the engine is being overhauled after completing a high mileage, it is advisable to renew all the cam follower and valve operating components as a set.*
7 Clean all the components thoroughly, keeping them in order.
8 Examine all the components for wear and damage. Pay particular attention to the rollers.
9 Ensure that the tappet slides move freely in their relevant guides.
10 If there is any sign of significant wear or damage, the relevant components should be renewed.

Refitting

11 Insert the first guide into its original location in the cylinder block, and align the locating screw holes in the block and the guide.

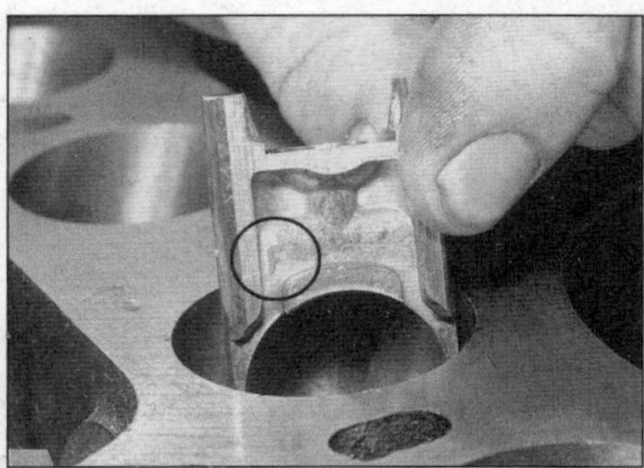

11.3 Lifting out a tappet slide. Note F mark faces timing belt end of engine

12 Fit a new guide locating screw, but do not allow the end of the screw to protrude into the inner bore of the guide at this stage.
13 Fit the relevant roller, making sure that the mark made before removal faces the timing belt end of the engine. New rollers can be fitted either way round.
14 Before fitting the tappet slide, check that the oilways are clear.
15 Fit the tappet slide with the FRONT or F mark facing the timing belt end of the engine.
16 Tighten the tappet guide locating screw to the specified torque.
17 Repeat the procedure for the remaining components, ensuring that all components are refitted in their original locations.
18 Refit the cylinder head as described in Section 10.

12 Sump - removal and refitting

Removal

Note: *Suitable sealant will be required on refitting.*
1 Drain the engine oil as described in Chapter 1B. When jacking up the vehicle, place the stands under the chassis, NOT under the axle - in order for the sump to clear the axle, the axle must be hanging free.
2 To allow clearance for the sump to be removed, the steering damper and track rod must first be removed, as described in Chapter 11. Note that the track rod need only

11.4 Lifting out a roller

11.5 Lifting out a tappet guide

be detached at one end - the rod can then be swung to one side.

3 Where necessary, remove the bolt securing the dipstick tube to the rocker cover.

4 Support the sump, then remove the bolts (on 200 TDi engines, note the locations of the bolts, as bolts of different lengths are used).

5 If the sump has stuck to the bottom of the engine, try running a sharp knife around the joint between the sump and engine, to cut through the bead of sealant used. If this is not successful, remove the oil drain plug. Insert a large screwdriver (with a piece of card wrapped around it to protect the threads) into the drain plug hole, and carefully use it as a lever to break the sump joint. This method is preferable to prising between the sump face and base of the block, as the mating surfaces could be damaged, and the sump would no longer seal. Take care during removal that the base of the sump does not get damaged through contact with the front axle.

6 Withdraw the sump past the front axle and the oil pick-up pipe inside the sump, and lower it to the ground.

7 While the sump is removed, examine the condition of the oil pick-up pipe and strainer. If there is any evidence that the strainer is blocked, remove the two bolts and withdraw the oil pick-up pipe and strainer for cleaning.

8 If the sump has been badly dented or otherwise damaged, there's little point in refitting it. Try to source one in better condition from a vehicle breakers, or fit a new one.

Refitting

9 Clean the sump out thoroughly, and remove all traces of sealant from the sump and crankcase mating surfaces. Degrease the mating surfaces before proceeding.

10 Examine the sump mating face for damage or distortion. Check the condition of the drain plug threads.

11 Apply a 2.0 mm wide bead of RTV sealant to the mating face of the sump flange, ensuring that the sealant is applied inboard of the bolt holes. **Do not** apply excess sealant, which may enter the engine when the sump is refitted. Also apply sealant to the groove between the timing belt housing and the cylinder block.

12 Lift the sump into position, then loosely fit the securing bolts sufficiently to locate the sump securely on the engine. On 200 TDi engines, ensure that the bolts are refitted to their correct locations, as noted before removal - the three longest bolts fit at the front of the sump.

13 Progressively tighten the securing bolts to the specified torque.

14 Ensure that the sump drain plug has been refitted and tightened, using a new sealing ring, then lower the vehicle to the ground.

15 On completion, allow the recommended drying time for the sealant (typically 30 minutes) before refilling the sump - use this time to refit the steering damper and track rod as described in Chapter 11.

16 Refill the sump with fresh oil as described in Chapter 1B, then start the engine and check for oil leaks.

13 Oil pump and skew gear (200 TDi engine) - removal, inspection and refitting

Oil pump

Removal

1 Remove the sump as described in Section 12.

2 Loosen the two bolts securing the oil pump to the cylinder block **(see illustration)**. Note that access to the right-hand bolt may require the use of a socket with a universal joint adapter.

3 Remove the bolts and recover the washers, then lower the oil pump from the engine.

4 Recover the gasket.

5 Where possible, withdraw the oil pump driveshaft.

Inspection

6 With the pump removed from the engine, thoroughly clean the external surfaces.

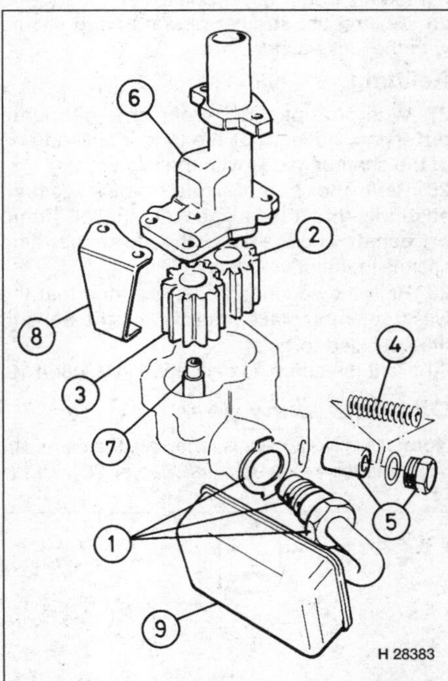
6
2
8
4
3
7
5
1
9
H 28383

13.8 Oil pump components - 200 TDi engine

1 *Lockwasher, O-ring and union nut*
2 *Driven gear*
3 *Idler gear*
4 *Pressure relief valve spring*
5 *Pressure relief valve plunger and plug*
6 *Pump cover*
7 *Idler gear spindle*
8 *Oil strainer support bracket*
9 *Oil strainer*

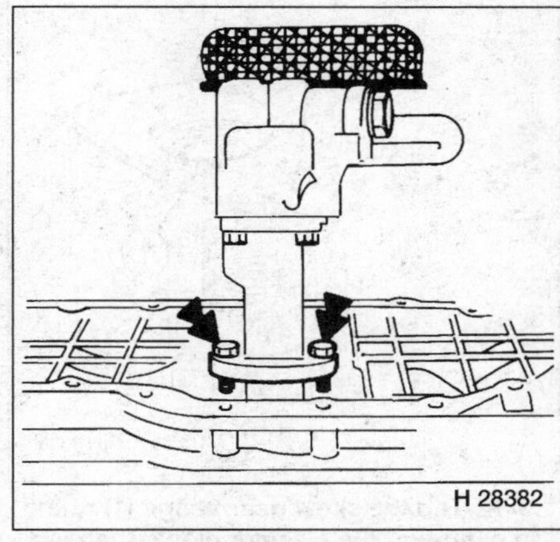
H 28382

13.2 Oil pump securing bolts (arrowed) - 200 TDi engine

7 Unscrew the bolt securing the oil strainer to the support bracket, and recover the washers.

8 Using a suitable screwdriver, bend back the lockwasher, then unscrew the nut securing the strainer pipe to the pump body. Withdraw the strainer, and recover the O-ring if it is loose **(see illustration)**.

9 Unscrew the four securing bolts and washers, and lift off the pump cover. Note that two of the bolts also secure the oil strainer support bracket.

10 Lift out the gears, noting their locations so that they can be refitted in their original positions.

11 Unscrew the oil pressure relief valve plug, and recover the sealing washer. Lift out the relief valve spring and plunger.

12 Examine the gears for wear, scoring and pitting, and if there is any evidence of wear or damage, renew the gears. Note that both gears must be renewed as a pair.

13 If the gears appear to be serviceable, check the endfloat as follows. Thoroughly clean the pump body, and refit the gears. Place a straight-edge across the pump body, then using a feeler blade, measure the clearance between the end face of the pump body and the gears **(see illustration)**.

14 Also check the clearance between the gear lobes and the pump body, again using a feeler blade.

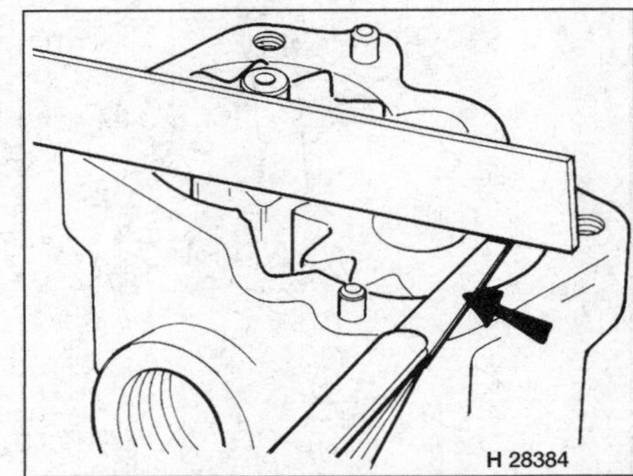
H 28384

13.13 Checking the oil pump gear endfloat using a feeler blade (arrowed) - 200 TDi engine

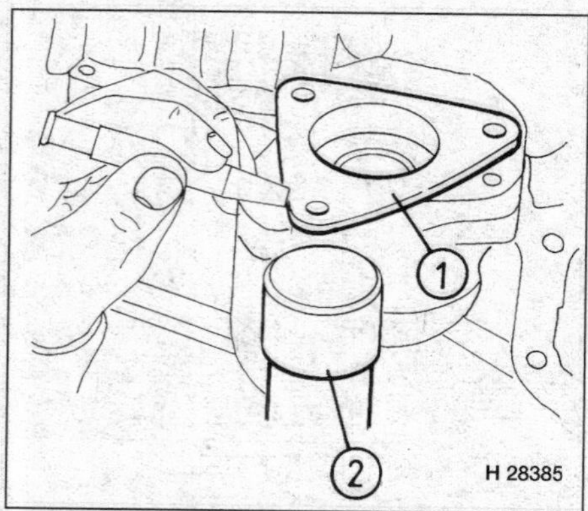
1
2
H 28385

13.34 Tap the skew gear flange (1) round to overhang the cylinder block, then tap upwards using a suitable tool (2) - 200 TDi engine

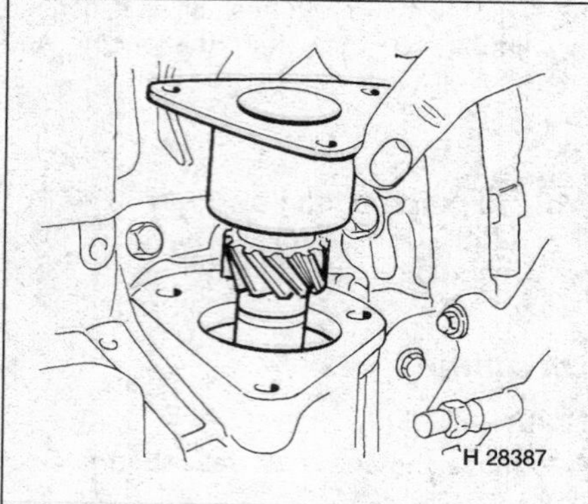
H 28387

13.35 Withdrawing the skew gear assembly from the cylinder block - 200 TDi engine

15 If either of the measurements is outside the specified limits (see *Specifications*), the pump should be renewed.

16 Examine the relief valve plunger for wear or scoring, and check the condition of the spring. Renew the components if there is any sign of wear or damage.

17 Examine the condition of the idler gear spindle in the pump body. This is unlikely to show wear, but if necessary, the spindle can be renewed as follows. Drive or press the spindle from the pump body, and drive or press the new spindle into position up to the locating shoulder on the spindle.

18 Check the pump cover for signs of wear or scoring, and renew if necessary.

19 Reassemble the pump as follows.

20 Fit the idler gear to the spindle.

21 Fit the driven gear to the pump body, with the plain section of the bore uppermost (facing the pump cover).

22 Fit the pump cover, then refit the securing bolts, ensuring that the oil strainer support bracket is in place on the bolts. Do not fully tighten the bolts at this stage.

23 Hold the pump body so that the pressure relief valve bore is vertical, then fit the relief valve plunger, solid end first. Fit the spring, then fit the plug using a new sealing washer. Tighten the plug to the specified torque.

24 Fill the pump with oil through the strainer pipe orifice in the pump body, then slide the lockwasher over the end of the oil strainer pipe. Fit a new O-ring to the end of the pipe, and engage the pipe with the pump body. Loosely tighten the securing nut.

25 Refit and tighten the bolt securing the strainer assembly to the support bracket, then tighten the pump cover bolts.

26 Tighten the strainer pipe nut, and secure with the lockwasher.

Refitting

27 Where applicable, refit the oil pump driveshaft, noting that the longer splined end of the shaft engages with the oil pump.

28 Refit the pump using a new gasket, ensuring that the splines on the oil pump driveshaft engage with the corresponding splines in the driven gear.

29 Refit the securing bolts, ensuring that the washers are in place, and tighten the bolts to the specified torque.

30 Refit the sump as described in Section 12.

Oil pump skew gear

Note: *If the skew gear is renewed, the camshaft must also be renewed (see Chapter 2C). This is necessary to preserve the meshing of the skew gear teeth with the teeth on the camshaft. New skew gear shaft O-rings will be required on refitting.*

Removal

31 The skew gear drives the oil pump driveshaft, which also drives the brake vacuum pump.

32 Remove the brake vacuum pump as described in Chapter 10.

33 Make alignment marks between the skew gear flange and the cylinder block, so that the skew gear assembly can be refitted in its original position. Similarly, make alignment marks between the inner face of the skew gear shaft, and the skew gear flange. This is necessary because the skew gear teeth must mesh with the same teeth on the camshaft when the skew gear is refitted.

34 Using a suitable punch or similar tool, tap the skew gear flange round so that the edges overhang the cylinder block **(see illustration)**.

35 Carefully tap the skew gear flange upwards until the assembly can be lifted from the cylinder block **(see illustration)**.

36 Remove the O-rings from the inside diameter of the skew gear shaft, and from the outside diameter of the skew gear flange, and discard them.

37 Using a pair of long-nosed pliers, or a suitable length of wire, withdraw the oil pump driveshaft from the cylinder block **(see illustration)**.

38 If desired, the skew gear guide can be removed from the cylinder block as follows:

a) *Remove the oil filter adapter assembly for access to the guide retaining screw.*
b) *Working at the side of the cylinder block, using a suitable Allen key, unscrew the guide retaining screw* ***(see illustration)****.*
c) *Using a suitable length of hooked wire, lift the guide from the cylinder block.*

Inspection

39 Thoroughly clean the skew gear and oil pump driveshaft components

40 Check that the oil pump driveshaft is straight, and check the condition of the splines on the ends of the shaft. If the shaft is bent, or the splines are worn or damaged, the shaft should be renewed. Note that if the splines at the oil pump end of the shaft are damaged or worn, then the condition of the corresponding splines on the oil pump should be checked (remove the oil pump as described previously in this Section).

41 Check the condition of the skew gear teeth, and if there is any sign of wear or damage, renew the assembly (note that in this case, the camshaft must also be renewed - see note at the beginning of this sub-Section).

42 If the condition of the skew gear is satisfactory, turn the gear in the flange to check the condition of the bearing. If the gear does not turn smoothly, or if there is excessive play in the bearing, the bearing should be renewed. To renew the bearing, proceed as follows **(see illustration)**:

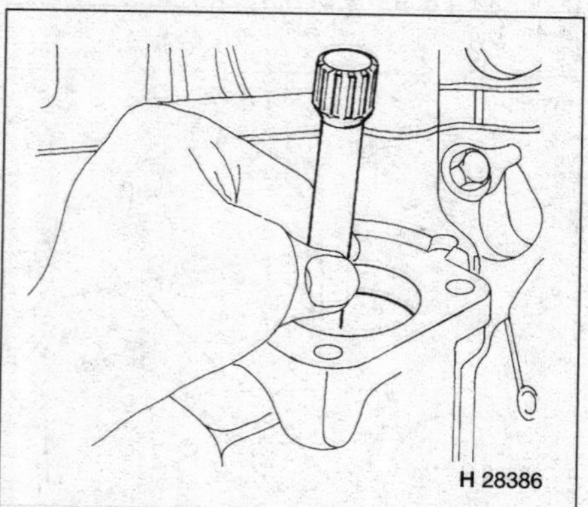
H 28386

13.37 Withdrawing the oil pump driveshaft from the cylinder block - 200 TDi engine

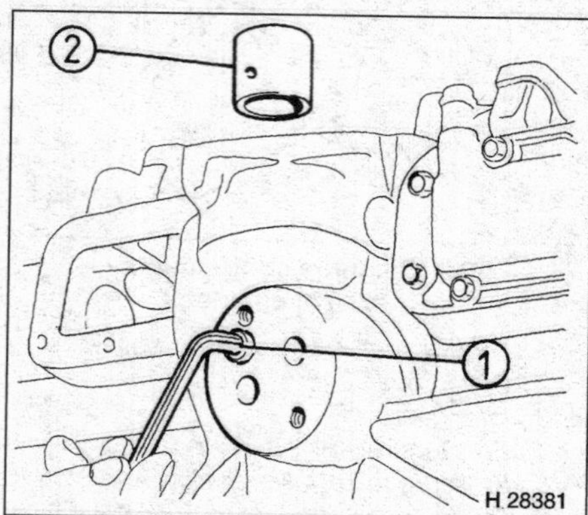
2
1
H 28381

13.38 Unscrew the retaining screw (1) to remove the skew gear guide (2) - 200 TDi engine

a) Using a suitable pair of circlip pliers, remove the retaining circlip from the skew gear shaft.
b) Similarly, remove the bearing retaining circlip from the groove in the skew gear flange.
c) Support the skew gear flange, then press the bearing and the skew gear from the flange.
d) Support the bearing, then press the skew gear from the bearing.
e) Using a tube or socket of suitable diameter on the bearing outer race, press the bearing into the flange up to the shoulder.
f) Refit the bearing retaining circlip.
g) Support the bearing inner race using a socket or tube of suitable diameter, then press the skew gear into the bearing.
h) Refit the retaining circlip to the skew gear shaft.

43 Examine the internal surfaces of the skew gear guide for wear or damage, and renew if necessary.

Refitting

44 Where applicable, fit the skew gear guide to the cylinder block, ensuring that the retaining screw hole in the guide aligns with the corresponding hole in the cylinder block. Refit and tighten the guide retaining screw, ensuring that the screw locates correctly in the hole in the guide. Refit the oil filter adapter, using a new gasket.

45 Fit the oil pump driveshaft, noting that the longer splined end of the shaft engages with the oil pump.

14.3 Removing the oil pump cover plate - 300 TDi engine

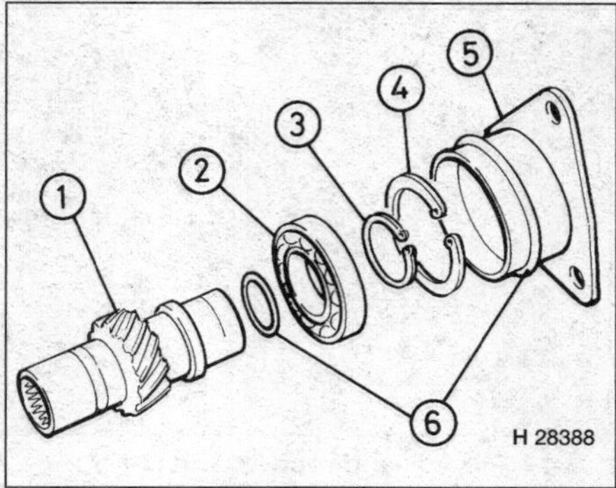
1
2
3
4
5
6
H 28388

13.42 Oil pump skew gear components - 200 TDi engine

1 Skew gear
2 Bearing
3 Skew gear shaft circlip
4 Bearing retaining circlip
5 Housing
6 O-rings

46 Fit new O-rings to the inside diameter of the skew gear shaft, and to the outside diameter of the flange.

47 Refit the skew gear assembly to the cylinder block, ensuring that the marks made on the inner face of the skew gear shaft and the skew gear flange, and on the skew gear flange and the cylinder block, are aligned. Manipulate the flange and the skew gear as necessary until all the marks are aligned, noting that the skew gear will move as it is engaged with the camshaft.

48 Refit the brake vacuum pump as described in Chapter 10.

14 Oil pump and strainer (300 TDi engine) - removal, inspection and refitting

Oil pump

Removal

1 The rotor-type oil pump is driven from the front of the crankshaft, and the rotors are located in the timing belt housing.

2 Remove the timing belt housing as described in Section 16.

3 Working at the rear of the timing belt housing, unscrew the securing screws, and remove the oil pump cover plate **(see illustration)**.

4 Mark the face of the outer oil pump rotor so that it can be refitted the same way round, then lift out the oil pump rotors **(see illustrations)**.

Inspection

5 At the time of writing, no information was available regarding wear limits for the oil pump rotors. It is recommended that if there is any sign of obvious wear, the rotors are renewed. Always renew the rotors as a pair.

6 Unscrew the oil pressure relief valve plug, using a suitable large-bladed screwdriver, and lift out the spring and plunger **(see illustration)**. Note the orientation of the plunger, to ensure correct refitting.

7 Examine the relief valve plunger for wear or scoring, and check the condition of the spring. Renew the component if there is any sign of wear or damage.

8 Refit the relief valve plunger and spring, ensuring that the plunger is orientated as noted before removal.

9 Coat the threads of the relief valve plug with suitable thread-locking compound, then refit the plug and tighten securely.

Refitting

10 Ensure that the rotors are clean, then lubricate them with clean engine oil, and refit them to the housing. Ensure that the mark made on the outer rotor is visible, indicating that the rotor is orientated correctly.

11 Ensure that the mating faces of the pump cover and the housing are clean, then refit the cover and tighten the screws securely.

Strainer

Note: *A new pick-up pipe O-ring must be used on refitting. The pick-up pipe and support bracket bolts must be coated with thread-locking fluid when refitting.*

Removal

12 Remove the sump as described in Section 12.

13 Unscrew the two bolts securing the strainer support bracket to the main bearing cap.

14 Unscrew the bolt securing the oil pick-up pipe to the timing belt housing, then withdraw

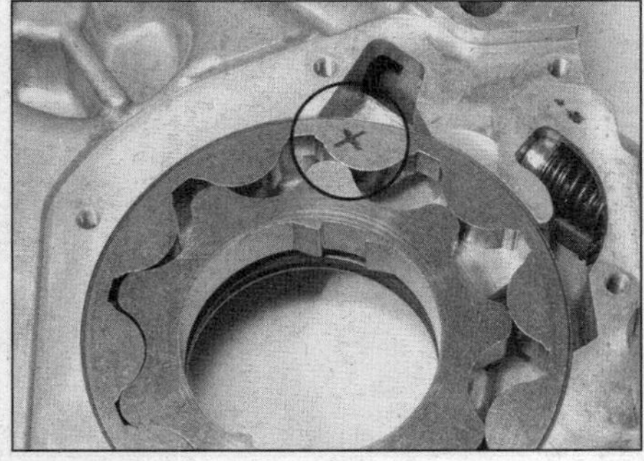

14.4a Mark the face of the outer oil pump rotor . . .

14.4b . . . then lift the rotors from the housing - 300 TDi engine

14.6 Oil pressure relief valve plug (arrowed) - 300 TDi engine

14.14a Withdraw the oil strainer . . .

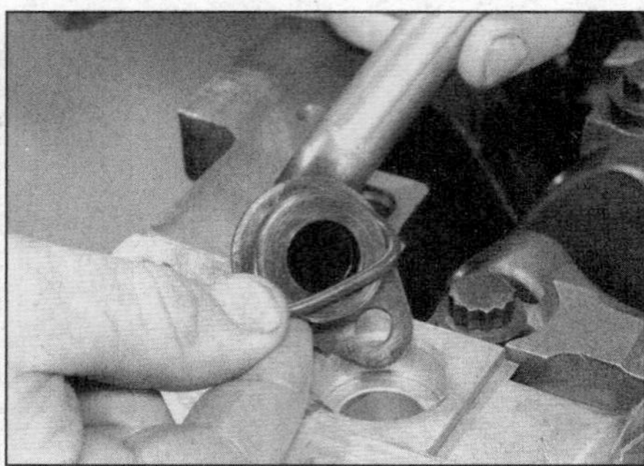

14.14b . . . and recover the O-ring - 300 TDi engine

14.16 Coat the threads of the strainer support bracket bolts with thread-locking compound - 300 TDi engine

the strainer. Recover the O-ring from the pick-up pipe **(see illustrations)**.

Inspection

15 Check the strainer gauze and the pick-up pipe for obstructions, and clean the assembly thoroughly before refitting.

Refitting

16 Refitting is a reversal of removal, bearing in mind the following points:

a) *Use a new pick-up pipe O-ring.*
b) *Coat the threads of the pick-up pipe and strainer support bracket bolts with suitable thread-locking compound* ***(see illustration)****, and tighten all fixings to the specified torque.*
c) *Refit the sump as described in Section 12.*

15 Oil seals - renewal

Crankshaft front (timing belt cover) dust seal

1 The procedure is described with the timing belt cover removal and refitting procedure in Section 6.

Crankshaft front (timing belt housing) oil seal

2 Remove the crankshaft sprocket, as described in Section 8.

3 Prise out the old oil seal using a small screwdriver, taking care not to damage the surface of the crankshaft.

HAYNES HiNT

An oil seal can be removed by drilling two small holes diagonally opposite each other, and inserting self-tapping screws in them. A pair of grips can then be used to pull out the oil seal, by pulling on each side in turn.

4 Wipe clean the oil seal seating, then dip the new seal in fresh engine oil, and locate it over the crankshaft with its closed side facing outwards. Make sure that the oil seal lip is not damaged as it is located over the crankshaft.

5 Using a tube of suitable diameter, drive the oil seal squarely into the housing until the outer edge of the seal is approximately 0.5 mm below the face of the housing.

6 Refit the crankshaft sprocket as described in Section 8.

Crankshaft rear oil seal

200 TDi engine

7 Remove the flywheel/driveplate as described in Section 17.

8 Proceed as described in paragraphs 3 to 5, bearing in mind the following points:

a) *Wind a length of tape around the crankshaft nose, to prevent damage to the oil seal lips as the seal is fitted over the crankshaft.*
b) *Take care to ensure that the seal enters its housing squarely, and make sure that the seal lip does not fold over.*
c) *Press the seal into position until it rests against the shoulder in the housing.*

9 Refit the flywheel/driveplate as described in Section 17.

300 TDi engine

Note: *The oil seal is retained in a housing, and the seal and housing must be renewed as an assembly. A new assembly is supplied fitted with a former/seal guide.* ***Do not*** *remove the former/seal guide before fitting the assembly to the engine. If a new assembly is received without a former/seal guide fitted, return it to the supplier. Used formers/seal guides must be discarded. Three M8 studs (or bolts with the heads cut off) will be required when fitting the new seal.*

10 Remove the flywheel/driveplate as described in Section 17.

11 Unscrew the five securing bolts, and remove the seal/housing assembly from the cylinder block. Recover the gasket, and the housing rubber seal if it is loose.

12 Thoroughly clean the gasket faces of the cylinder block and the new seal/housing assembly.

13 Screw three M8 studs (or bolts with the heads cut off, and slots cut in the top to enable removal) into the cylinder block bolt holes, then fit a new seal housing gasket over the studs **(see illustration)**.

14 Fit a new rubber seal to the rear of the new oil seal housing **(see illustration)**.

15 Fit the new assembly, with the former/seal guide in place, over the studs and the crankshaft flange. The former/seal guide will be ejected as the assembly is fitted **(see illustration)**.

15.13 M8 stud locations (arrowed) for fitting of crankshaft rear oil seal housing - 300 TDi engine

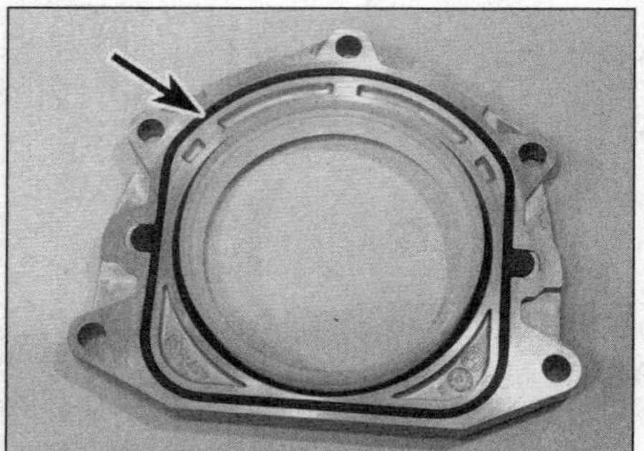

15.14 Fit a new rubber seal (arrowed) to the housing - 300 TDi engine

15.15 Fitting the new crankshaft rear oil seal/housing assembly

16 Loosely fit the two bolts to the holes not occupied by the studs.
17 Unscrew one of the studs, and loosely refit the bolt in its place. Repeat the procedure for the two remaining studs.
18 Progressively tighten the seal/housing securing bolts to the specified torque.
19 Refit the flywheel/driveplate as described in Section 17.

Camshaft front oil seal

20 Remove the camshaft sprocket as described in Section 8.
21 Proceed as described in paragraphs 3 to 5.
22 Refit the camshaft sprocket as described in Section 8.

16 Timing belt housing gasket - renewal

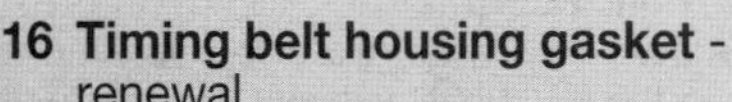

200 TDi engine

1 Remove the fuel injection pump as described in Chapter 4C.
2 Remove the timing belt sprockets, and the timing belt tensioner, as described in Section 8.
3 Unscrew the three bolts securing the sump and the ladder frame to the timing belt housing **(see illustration)**.
4 Unscrew the five bolts securing the timing belt housing to the cylinder block, noting their locations, as different lengths of bolt are used.
5 Withdraw the timing belt housing from the front of the engine. Recover the main gasket, the coolant aperture gasket, and the gasket washer which fits around the timing belt tensioner pulley bolt hole **(see illustration)**.
6 Thoroughly clean all traces of old gasket from the mating faces of the cylinder block and the timing belt housing.

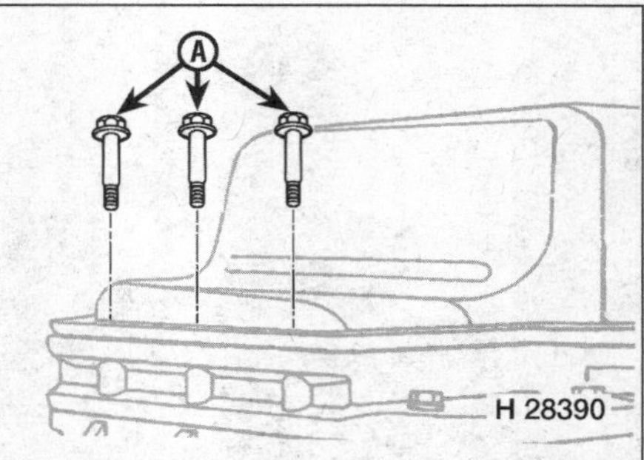
A
H 28390

16.3 Unscrew the three bolts (A) securing the sump and ladder frame to the cylinder block - 200 TDi engine

7 Note that whilst the timing belt housing is removed, it is advisable to renew the camshaft oil seal and the crankshaft front oil seal, as described in Section 15.
8 Fit a new main gasket to the cylinder block, using a little grease to hold it in position.
9 Similarly, fit new gaskets to the coolant aperture and the timing belt tensioner bolt hole in the cylinder block.
10 Carefully offer the timing belt housing to the cylinder block, taking care not to damage the oil seals as they are passed over the crankshaft and camshaft. Ensure that the housing fits over the locating stud.
11 Refit the five securing bolts to their original locations, as noted before removal, and progressively tighten the bolts to the specified torque **(see illustration)**.
12 Refit the three bolts securing the sump and the ladder frame to the timing belt housing, and tighten to the specified torque.
13 Refit the timing belt tensioner, and the timing belt sprockets, as described in Section 8.

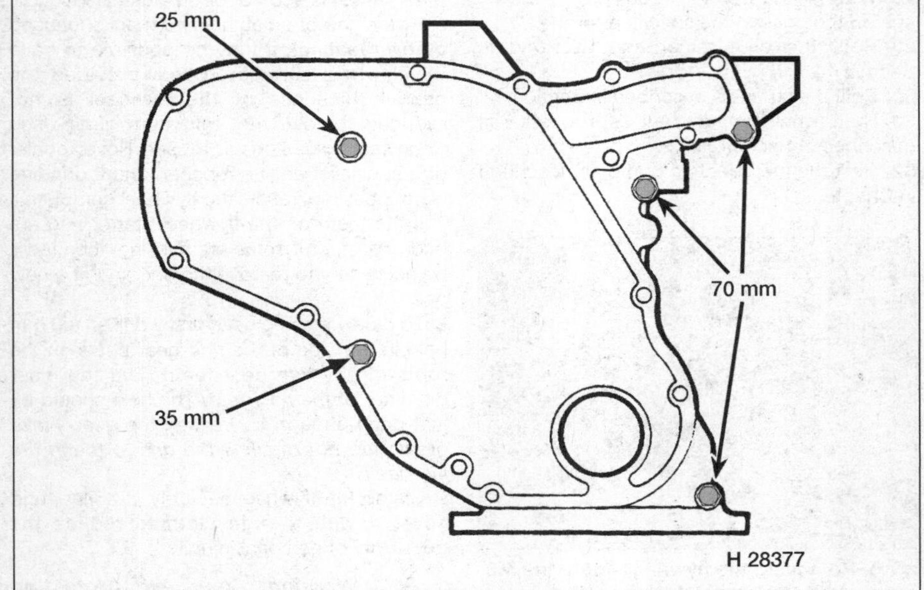
25 mm
70 mm
35 mm
H 28377

16.11 Timing belt housing securing bolt locations - 200 TDi engine

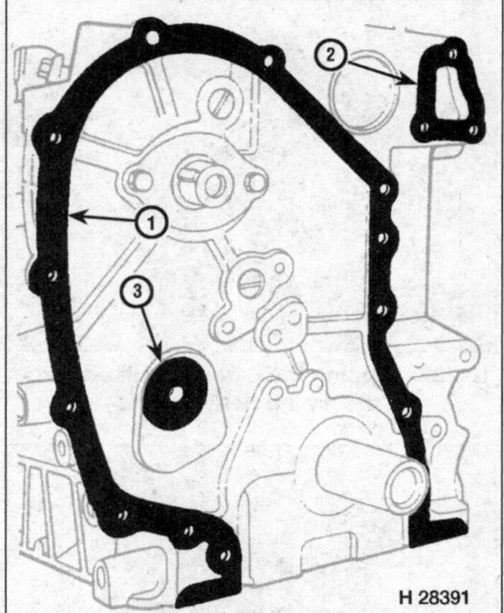
2
1
3
H 28391

16.5 Timing belt housing main gasket (1), coolant aperture gasket (2) and washer gasket (3) - 200 TDi engine

14 Refit the fuel injection pump as described in Chapter 4C.

300 TDi engine

Note: *Six M8 studs (or bolts with the heads cut off) will be required when refitting the housing.*
15 Remove the fuel injection pump as described in Chapter 4C.
16 Remove the timing belt sprockets as described in Section 8.
17 Remove the sump as described in Section 12.
18 Remove the oil strainer as described in Section 14.
19 Unscrew the ten timing belt housing securing bolts, noting their locations, as several different lengths of bolt are used.
20 Withdraw the timing belt housing from the front of the engine, and recover the gasket **(see illustration)**. Note that the housing locates on two dowels.
21 Thoroughly clean the gasket faces of the cylinder block and the timing belt housing.
22 Note that whilst the timing belt housing is removed, it is advisable to renew the

16.20 Withdrawing the timing belt housing (engine shown inverted) - 300 TDi engine

16.22a Tapping the camshaft oil seal from the timing belt housing

16.22b Fitting a new camshaft oil seal to the timing belt housing using a socket

16.23 Fitting the timing belt housing gasket. M8 guide stud locations arrowed (engine shown inverted) - 300 TDi engine

16.25 Using a screwdriver to align the oil pump rotor with the flats on the crankshaft (engine shown inverted) - 300 TDi engine

camshaft oil seal and the crankshaft front oil seal. The seals can be tapped from the housing using a suitable punch, and the new seals can be fitted by tapping into position using a suitable socket or tube **(see illustrations)**.

23 Fit six M8 studs (or bolts with the heads cut off, and slots cut in the top to enable removal) to the bolt holes in the cylinder block, then locate the new gasket over the studs **(see illustration)**.

24 Align the flats on the oil pump driven rotor with the corresponding flats on the crankshaft.

25 Carefully offer the timing belt housing to the cylinder block, taking care not to damage the oil seals as they are passed over the crank-shaft and camshaft. Locate the housing on the studs, and the two dowels. If necessary, alter the position of the oil pump rotor using a small screwdriver, to enable it to engage with the crankshaft as the housing is fitted **(see illustration)**.

26 Refit bolts of the correct length to the holes not occupied by the studs, but do not fully tighten them at this stage.

27 Remove one of the studs, and fit the correct length of bolt to the relevant hole. Repeat the procedure for the remaining studs.

28 With all the bolts refitted, progressively tighten the bolts to the specified torque.

29 Refit the oil strainer as described in Section 14.

30 Refit the sump as described in Section 12.

31 Refit the timing belt sprockets as described in Section 8.

32 Refit the fuel injection pump as described in Chapter 4C.

17.3 Using a length of bar to counterhold the flywheel as the bolts are unscrewed. M8 bolt locations arrowed - 300 TDi engine

17.5 Removing the flywheel - note the M8 bolts being used as 'handles'

17 Flywheel/driveplate - removal, inspection and refitting

Flywheel (manual transmission models)

Note: *New flywheel securing bolts must be used on refitting. Two M8 bolts will be required to lift the flywheel from the crankshaft.*

Removal

1 Remove the clutch as described in Chapter 6.

2 Fit two long M8 bolts to two of the clutch cover bolt holes in the flywheel, diametrically opposite each other.

3 Using a suitable length of bar positioned between the two bolts, prevent the crankshaft from turning as the flywheel securing bolts are unscrewed **(see illustration)**. It will be necessary to reposition the M8 bolts and the bar, using different clutch cover bolt holes, in order to reach all of the flywheel securing bolts. Note that the flywheel securing bolts are coated with thread-locking compound, and considerable effort may be required to unscrew them.

4 Remove all the flywheel securing bolts, and where applicable withdraw the reinforcing plate from the centre of the flywheel.

5 Carefully lift the flywheel from the crankshaft, using the two bolts as 'handles' **(see illustration).** Note that the flywheel locates on a dowel in the end of the crankshaft.

Warning: The flywheel is heavy - take care not to drop it.

Inspection

6 If the clutch friction disc contact surface of the flywheel is scored, or on close inspection, shows signs of small hairline cracks (caused by overheating), it may be possible to have the flywheel surface-ground, provided the overall thickness of the flywheel is not reduced below the minimum limit (see *Specifications*). Consult a Land Rover dealer or a specialist engine repairer, and if grinding is not possible, renew the flywheel complete.

7 If the teeth on the flywheel starter ring are badly worn, or if some are missing, then it will be necessary to remove the ring and fit a new one.

8 To renew the ring gear, firstly drill an 8.0 mm hole in the side of the ring gear between the roots of any two gear teeth, and the inner diameter of the ring gear. The hole should be just deep enough to weaken the gear - *take great care not to allow the drill to touch the flywheel*.

9 Clamp the flywheel securely in a vice, and cover it with a large cloth to reduce the possibility of personal injury.

Warning: Wear eye protection during the following procedure.

10 Place a cold chisel between the gear teeth above the drilled hole, then split the gear with the chisel. Take great care not to damage the flywheel during this operation, and wear eye protection at all times. Once the ring has been split, it will spread apart, and can be lifted from the flywheel **(see illustration)**.

11 The new ring gear must be heated to between 225 and 250°C, and unless facilities for heating by oven or flame are available, leave the fitting to a Land Rover dealer or engineering works. The new ring gear must not be overheated during this work, or the temper of the metal will be affected.

12 The ring should be tapped gently down onto its register, and left to cool naturally - the contraction of the metal on cooling will ensure that it is a secure and permanent fit.

Refitting

13 Commence refitting by thoroughly cleaning the mating faces of the flywheel and the crankshaft.

14 If the two M8 'handle' bolts have been removed, refit them to the flywheel.

15 Align the dowel hole in the flywheel with the crankshaft dowel, then lift the flywheel onto the end of the crankshaft.

16 Where applicable, refit the reinforcing plate, then fit new flywheel securing bolts, and tighten them to the specified torque, preventing the crankshaft from turning as during removal.

17 With all the flywheel bolts tightened, and the two M8 bolts removed, check the flywheel run-out as follows:

a) Mount a dial test indicator securely on the end face of the flywheel housing.

b) Position the probe to read from the flywheel face at a radius of 114.0 mm from the centre of the crankshaft.

c) Turn the crankshaft through one complete revolution, and check that the run-out does not exceed the specified limit.

18 If the run-out is excessive, remove the flywheel again, and check for damage or dirt between the mating faces of the crankshaft and the flywheel, and the locating dowel. Refit the flywheel, and check the run-out again as described previously. If the problem persists, have the flywheel checked by a suitable engine repair specialist.

19 Refit the clutch as described in Chapter 6.

18.3 Spigot bush location (arrowed) in end of crankshaft

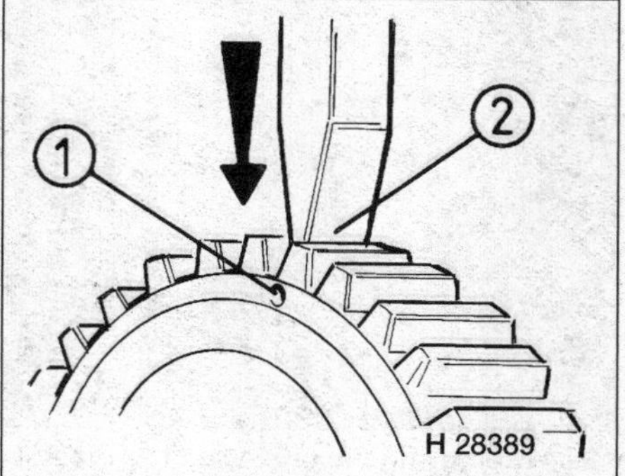
1
2
H 28389

17.10 Removing the ring gear from the flywheel

1 *Drill an 8.0 mm hole*
2 *Split the gear using a cold chisel*

Driveplate (automatic transmission models)

20 At the time of writing, no information was available regarding the removal and refitting of the driveplate.

21 Once the transmission has been separated from the engine, the procedure should prove similar to that described previously for the flywheel, noting the following points. Consult a Land Rover dealer for further details.

a) On 200 TDi engine models, a separate torque converter plate and driveplate are fitted. Mark the relationship of the two plates before the components are removed.

b) Note the locations of any spacers and shims, and ensure that they are refitted to their original locations.

c) On 200 TDi engines, selective shims are used to set the position of the torque converter in relation to the driveplate. Consult a Land Rover dealer for details of how to select the appropriate shim.

d) Use new driveplate securing bolts on refitting.

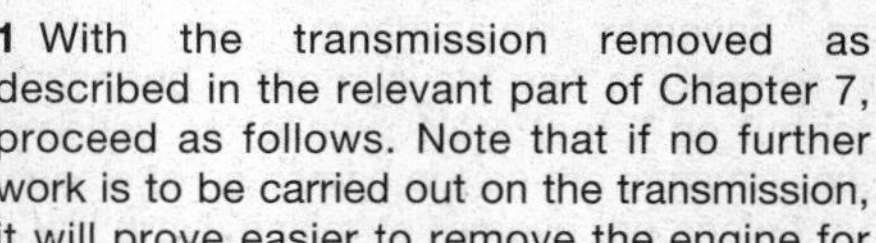

18 Crankshaft spigot bush - renewal

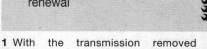

1 With the transmission removed as described in the relevant part of Chapter 7, proceed as follows. Note that if no further work is to be carried out on the transmission, it will prove easier to remove the engine for access, as described in Chapter 2C.

2 Where applicable, remove the clutch as described in Chapter 6.

3 Using a suitable tap, thread the bore of the bush, located in the end of the crankshaft **(see illustration)**.

4 Screw a suitable bolt into the bush, then use the bolt to pull the bush from the end of the crankshaft using a suitable pair of pliers or grips.

5 Alternatively, the bush can be removed as follows.

a) Obtain a short length of metal rod, with a diameter which provides a firm sliding fit in the bore of the bush.

b) Pack the bore of the bush with grease.

c) Insert the metal rod into the bush, and cover the rod and bush with a cloth or rag (to prevent the possibility of injury due to grease splashes or the ejection of the bush).

d) Give the rod a sharp tap with a hammer - the grease should force the bush from the crankshaft.

6 Thoroughly clean the bush location in the end of the crankshaft, and make sure that the new bush is absolutely clean.

7 Tap the bush into position in the end of the crankshaft using a suitable drift. Take care not to produce any burrs on the edge of the bush. The bush should be fitted flush with the end of the crankshaft.

8 Where applicable, refit the clutch as described in Chapter 6, then refit the engine as described in Chapter 2C.

19 Engine mountings - removal and refitting

Removal

1 Place a suitable trolley jack with a large interposed block of wood under the engine sump, to just take the weight of the engine. Ensure that the engine is safely supported before proceeding.

2 Working from the relevant side of the engine compartment, unscrew the two upper bolts securing the engine mounting bracket to the cylinder block.

3 Working underneath the vehicle, unscrew the two lower bolts securing the engine mounting bracket to the cylinder block, and the two bolts securing the mounting bracket to the flywheel housing **(see illustration)**.

4 Again working underneath the vehicle, unscrew the nut securing the engine mounting to the bracket on the chassis.

5 Working from the engine compartment, lift the complete engine mounting assembly from

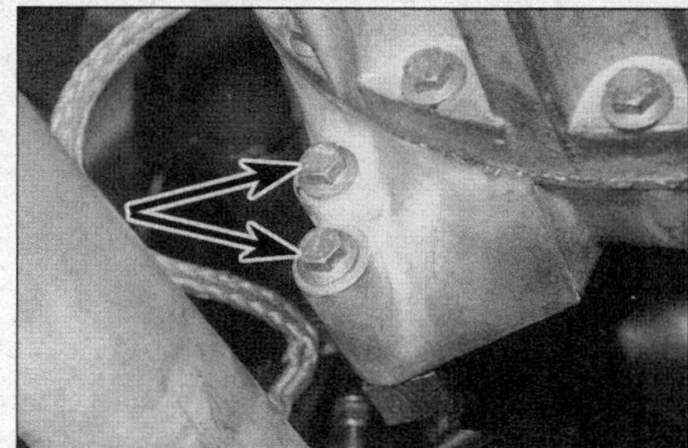

19.3 Left-hand engine mounting bracket-to-flywheel housing bolts (arrowed) - 300 TDi engine

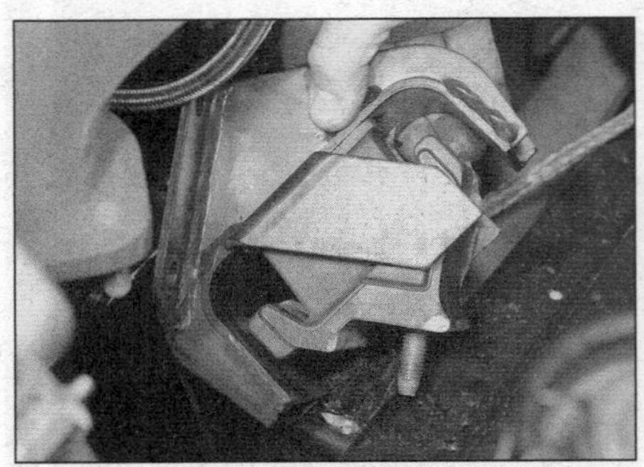
19.5 Lifting the left-hand engine mounting from the engine compartment - 300 TDi engine

20.4 Removing the engine oil thermostat cover

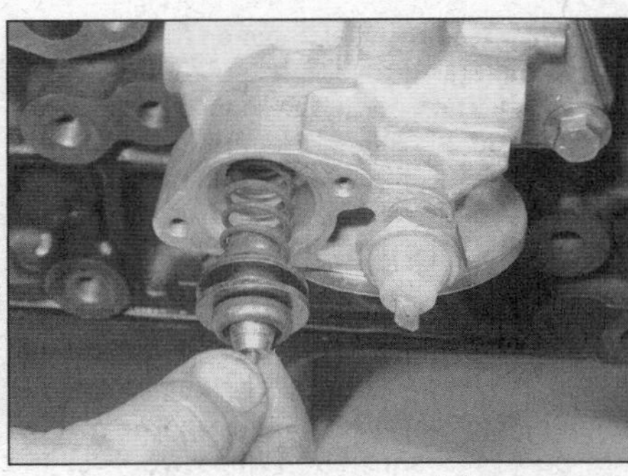
20.5 Removing the engine oil thermostat

the vehicle, taking care not to damage surrounding components in the engine compartment **(see illustration)**.

6 If desired, the mounting rubber can be renewed by unscrewing the nut securing it to the engine mounting bracket.

Refitting

7 Refitting is a reversal of removal, but tighten all fixings to the specified torque.

20 Engine oil cooler and thermostat - removal and refitting

Oil cooler

1 The oil cooler is integral with the radiator. Refer to Chapter 3 for removal and refitting details.

Thermostat

Note: *A new thermostat cover O-ring must be used on refitting.*

Removal

2 The oil cooler thermostat is located in the oil filter adapter on the right-hand side of the cylinder block.

3 Place a suitable container beneath the oil filter adapter, then disconnect the oil cooler hose union from the thermostat cover. Be prepared for oil spillage, and cover the open end of the hose to prevent further spillage and dirt ingress.

4 Unscrew the two securing bolts, and remove the thermostat cover **(see illustration)**.

5 Lift out the thermostat assembly **(see illustration)**.

Refitting

6 Refitting is a reversal of removal, but use a new O-ring when refitting the thermostat cover, and on completion, check the oil level.

21 Oil pressure warning light switch - removal and refitting

Removal

Note: *A new sealing ring may be required on refitting.*

1 The oil pressure warning light switch is located in the oil filter adapter at the right-hand side of the cylinder block **(see illustration)**.

21.1 Oil pressure warning light switch (arrowed) - 300 TDi engine

2 Disconnect the battery negative lead, then release the wiring connector from the switch.

3 Carefully unscrew the switch, and withdraw it from the cylinder block. Be prepared for some oil spillage.

4 Recover the sealing ring, where applicable.

Refitting

5 Refitting is a reversal of removal, but clean the threads of the switch before screwing it into the cylinder block, and where applicable, use a new sealing ring. Check the oil level.

Chapter 2 Part C:
Engine removal and overhaul procedures

Contents

Degrees of difficulty

Easy, suitable for novice with little experience 	**Fairly easy,** suitable for beginner with some experience 	**Fairly difficult,** suitable for competent DIY mechanic 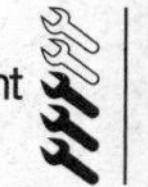	**Difficult,** suitable for experienced DIY mechanic 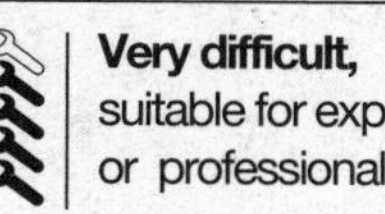	**Very difficult,** suitable for expert DIY or professional 

Specifications

Petrol engines

Camshaft

Material	Cast-iron
Location	Central, in vee of cylinder block
Drive	Inverted tooth chain (54 links)
Bearings:	
Number	5
Type	Steel-backed, babbit-lined

Cylinder heads

Material	Aluminium alloy
Type	Two separate heads, in-line valves, separate inlet manifold
Valve seat material	Piston ring iron
Valve seat angle	46° ± 1/4°
Oversize inserts available	+ 0.25 and 0.50 mm
Inlet valve seat diameter	37.03 mm
Exhaust valve seat diameter	31.50 mm)
Maximum permissible distortion of sealing face (typical value)	0.0100 mm

Valves

Overall length	116.59 to 117.35 mm
Angle of face	45° to 45.5°
Valve lift	9.49 mm
Valve clearance	Not adjustable (hydraulic self-adjusting tappets)
Valve head diameter:	
Inlet	39.75 to 40.00 mm
Exhaust	34.226 to 34.480 mm
Valve stem diameter:	
Inlet	8.664 to 8.679 mm
Exhaust	8.651 to 8.666 mm
Stem-to-guide clearance:	
Inlet	0.025 to 0.066 mm
Exhaust	0.038 to 0.078 mm
Valve spring length (nominal, fitted)	40.4 mm at 29.5 kgf
Maximum permissible valve stem play in guide (typical value)	0.1500 mm

Petrol engines (continued)

Cylinder block

Material	Aluminium alloy
Cylinder liner type	Dry, cast integrally with block
Liner material	Cast-iron
Maximum cylinder bore ovality (typical value)	0.1270 mm
Maximum cylinder bore taper (typical value)	0.2540 mm

Crankshaft and bearings

Material	Iron, spheroidal graphite
Number of main bearings	5
Main bearing journal diameter (standard)	58.409 to 58.422 mm
Main bearing clearance	0.010 to 0.048 mm
Undersizes available	0.254 and 0.508 mm
Big-end bearing journal diameter (standard)	50.800 to 50.812 mm
Big-end bearing clearance	0.015 to 0.055 mm
Undersizes available	As for main bearings
Journal ovality	0.04 mm maximum
Crankshaft endthrust	Taken on centre (No 3) main bearing shell flanges
Crankshaft endfloat	0.10 to 0.20 mm

Pistons

Type	Aluminium alloy, with flat or concave crown
Clearance in bore (measured at bottom of skirt)	0.008 to 0.041 mm
Piston grades:	
Standard (Grade Z)	Nominal size to + 0.0075 mm
Grade A	+ 0.0075 to 0.0150 mm
Grade B	+ 0.0150 to 0.0225 mm
Grade C	+ 0.0225 to 0.0300 mm
Grade D	+ 0.0300 to 0.0375 mm
Grade letter location	Piston crown and cylinder block face
Oversize pistons available after rebore (ungraded)	+ 0.25 and 0.50 mm

Piston rings

Number of compression rings	2
Number of oil rings	1
Number one compression ring	Chrome or molybdenum barrel-faced
Number two compression ring	Stepped or tapered, marked TOP or T
Compression ring end gap in bore	0.40 to 0.65 mm
Compression ring clearance in groove	0.05 to 0.10 mm
Oil control ring type	Expander ring with top and bottom rails
Oil control ring gap in bore	0.38 to 1.40 mm

Connecting rods

Type	Horizontally-split big-end, solid small-end
Length between centres	143.71 to 143.81 mm
Endfloat on crankpin	0.15 to 0.36 mm

Gudgeon pins

Length	72.67 to 72.79 mm
Diameter	22.215 to 22.220 mm
Fit in connecting rod	Press fit
Fit in piston	Sliding fit
Clearance in piston	0.002 to 0.007 mm

Torque wrench settings

Refer to Chapter 2A Specifications.

Diesel engines

Camshaft

Endfloat	0.1 to 0.2 mm

Cylinder head

Material	Aluminium alloy
Maximum permissible distortion of sealing face (typical value)	0.0100 mm
Valve seat angle:	
Inlet	30°
Exhaust	45°

Diesel engines (continued)

Cylinder head (continued)

Valve recess in cylinder head:	
200 TDi engine (inlet and exhaust)	0.9000 to 1.1000 mm
300 TDi engine:	
Inlet	0.8100 to 1.0900 mm
Exhaust	0.8600 to 1.1400 mm

Valves

Valve clearance (inlet and exhaust)	0.20 mm
Valve stem diameter:	
Inlet	7.9600 to 7.9750 mm
Exhaust	7.9400 to 7.9600 mm
Valve head diameter:	
200 TDi engine:	
Inlet	39.3500 to 39.6500 mm
Exhaust	36.3500 to 36.6500 mm
300 TDi engine:	
Inlet	38.7500 to 39.0500 mm
Exhaust	36.3500 to 36.6500 mm
Maximum permissible valve stem play in guide	0.1500 mm

Cylinder block

Material	Cast-iron
Maximum cylinder bore ovality	0.1270 mm
Maximum cylinder bore taper	0.2540 mm
Cylinder bore wear limit	0.1770 mm
Cylinder rebore oversizes	0.5000 mm and 1.0100 mm

Crankshaft and bearings

Number of main bearings	5
Main bearing journal diameter:	
Production standard	63.4750 to 63.4870 mm
Regrind (0.25 mm undersize)	63.2330 to 63.2460 mm
Main bearing running clearance	0.0792 to 0.0307 mm
Main bearing journal wear limit	0.1140 mm
Big-end bearing journal diameter:	
Production standard	58.7250 to 58.7440 mm
Regrind (0.25 mm undersize)	58.4710 to 58.4900 mm
Big-end bearing running clearance	0.0250 to 0.0750 mm
Big-end bearing journal wear limit	0.0880 mm
Maximum bearing journal ovality	0.0400 mm
Maximum bearing journal taper	0.0250 mm
Maximum run-out of centre main bearing journal (front and rear main bearings supported in V-blocks)	0.0760 mm
Crankshaft endfloat	0.0500 to 0.1500 mm
Thrustwasher oversizes	0.0625 mm, 0.1250 mm, 0.2500 mm
Maximum variation in thickness between thrustwashers	0.0800 mm
Connecting rod side play	0.1500 to 0.3560 mm

Pistons

Piston-to-bore clearance*	0.0250 to 0.0500 mm
Maximum piston protrusion	0.8000 mm

***Note:** *New standard service pistons are supplied 0.0250 mm oversize to allow for production tolerance on new engines. Pistons are also available in 0.5000 and 1.0100 mm oversizes.*

Piston rings

Number of rings (per piston)	2 compression, 1 oil control
Ring end gap:	
Top compression	0.4000 to 0.6000 mm
Middle compression	0.3000 to 0.5000 mm
Oil control	0.3000 to 0.6000 mm
Clearance in piston groove:	
Top compression	0.1670 to 0.2320 mm
Middle compression	0.0500 to 0.0800 mm
Oil control	0.0500 to 0.0800 mm

Connecting rods

Maximum distortion	0.1270 mm

Diesel engines (continued)

Gudgeon pins

Diameter	30.1564 to 30.1625 mm
Clearance in connecting rod:	
200 TDi engine	0.0036 to 0.0196 mm
300 TDi engine	0.0025 to 0.0163 mm

Torque wrench settings

Refer to Chapter 2B Specifications.

1 General information

This part of Chapter 2 includes details of engine removal and refitting, and general overhaul procedures for the cylinder head(s), cylinder block/crankcase and internal engine components.

The information ranges from advice concerning preparation for an overhaul and the purchase of replacement parts, to detailed step-by-step procedures covering removal, inspection, renovation and refitting of internal engine components.

The following Sections have been compiled based on the assumption that the engine has been removed from the vehicle. For information concerning in-car engine repair, as well as information on the removal and refitting of the external components necessary to facilitate overhaul, refer to Chapter 2A or 2B, and to Section 6 of this Part.

2 Engine overhaul - general information

It is not always easy to determine if an engine should be completely overhauled, as a number of factors must be considered.

High mileage is not necessarily an indication that an overhaul is needed, while low mileage does not preclude the need for an overhaul. Frequency of servicing is probably the most important consideration. An engine which has had regular and frequent oil and filter changes, as well as other required maintenance, will most likely give many thousands of miles of reliable service. Conversely, a neglected engine may require an overhaul very early in its life.

Excessive oil consumption is an indication that piston rings, valve seals and/or valve guides are in need of attention. Make sure that oil leaks are not responsible before deciding that the rings and/or guides are worn. Perform a cylinder compression check or a leakdown test to determine the extent of the work required.

Check the oil pressure with a gauge fitted in place of the oil pressure sender, and compare it with the Specifications (Chapter 2A or 2B). If it is extremely low, the main and big-end bearings and/or the oil pump are probably worn out.

Loss of power, rough running, knocking or metallic engine noises, excessive valve gear noise and high fuel consumption may also point to the need for an overhaul, especially if they are all present at the same time. If a complete tune-up does not remedy the situation, major mechanical work is the only solution.

An engine overhaul involves restoring the internal parts to the specifications of a new engine. During an overhaul, the pistons and rings are replaced and the cylinder bores are reconditioned. New main bearings, connecting rod bearings and camshaft bearings are generally fitted, and if necessary, the crankshaft may be reground to restore the journals. The valves are also serviced as well, since they are usually in less-than-perfect condition at this point. While the engine is being overhauled, other components, such as the starter and alternator, can be overhauled as well. The end result should be a like-new engine that will give many trouble-free miles. **Note:** *Critical cooling system components such as the hoses, drivebelts, thermostat and water pump MUST be renewed when an engine is overhauled. The radiator should be checked carefully, to ensure that it is not clogged or leaking. Also it is a good idea to renew the oil pump whenever the engine is overhauled.*

Before beginning the engine overhaul, read through the entire procedure, to familiarise yourself with the scope and requirements of the job. Overhauling an engine is not difficult if you follow all of the instructions carefully, have the necessary tools and equipment, and pay close attention to all specifications; however, it can be time-consuming. Plan on the vehicle being tied up for a minimum of two weeks, especially if parts must be taken to an engineering works for repair or reconditioning. Check on the availability of parts, and make sure that any necessary special tools and equipment are obtained in advance. Most work can be done with typical hand tools, although a number of precision measuring tools are required for inspecting parts to determine if they must be renewed. Often, the engineering works will handle the inspection of parts, and offer advice concerning reconditioning and renewal. **Note:** *Always wait until the engine has been completely disassembled, and all components (especially the engine block) have been inspected, before deciding what service and repair operations must be performed by an engineering works. Since the condition of the block will be the major factor to consider when determining whether to overhaul the original engine or buy a reconditioned unit, do not purchase parts or have overhaul work done on other components until the block has been thoroughly inspected. As a general rule, time is the primary cost of an overhaul, so it does not pay to fit worn or substandard parts.*

As a final note, to ensure maximum life and minimum trouble from a reconditioned engine, everything must be assembled with care in a spotlessly-clean environment.

3 Engine removal - methods and precautions

If you have decided that an engine must be removed for overhaul or major repair work, several preliminary steps should be taken.

Locating a suitable place to work is extremely important. Adequate work space, along with storage space for the vehicle, will be needed. If a garage is not available, at the very least a flat, level, clean work surface is required.

Cleaning the engine compartment and engine before beginning the removal procedure will help keep tools clean and organised.

An engine hoist or A-frame will also be necessary. Make sure the equipment is rated in excess of the weight of the engine. Bear in mind that the petrol or diesel Discovery engine weighs considerably more than a typical unit found in an ordinary vehicle. Safety is of primary importance, considering the potential hazards involved in lifting the engine out of the vehicle.

If the engine is being removed by a novice, an assistant should be available. Advice and aid from someone more experienced would also be helpful. There are many instances when one person cannot simultaneously perform all of the operations required when lifting the engine out of the vehicle.

Plan the operation ahead of time. Arrange for, or obtain, all of the tools and equipment you will need, prior to beginning the job. Some of the equipment necessary to perform engine removal and installation safely and with relative ease are (in addition to an engine hoist) a heavy-duty floor jack, complete sets

4.9a Loosen the union nuts . . .

of spanners and sockets as described at the rear of this manual, wooden blocks, and plenty of rags and cleaning solvent for mopping up spilled oil, coolant and fuel. If the hoist must be hired, make sure that you arrange for it in advance, and perform all of the operations possible without it beforehand. This will save you money and time.

Plan for the vehicle to be out of use for quite a while. An engineering works will be required to perform some of the work which the do-it-yourselfer cannot accomplish without special equipment. These places often have a busy schedule, so it would be a good idea to consult them before removing the engine, in order to accurately estimate the amount of time required to rebuild or repair components that may need work.

Always be extremely careful when removing and refitting the engine. Serious injury can result from careless actions. Plan ahead, take your time, and you will find that a job of this nature, although major, can be accomplished successfully.

The sequence of operations listed is not critical; the position of the person undertaking the work, or the tool in his hand, will determine to a certain extent the order in which the work is tackled. Obviously the engine cannot be removed until everything is disconnected from it, and the following sequence should ensure that nothing is forgotten.

Assemble a collection of containers for the small parts, nuts and bolts, etc, that are removed and keep them in convenient groups.

The engine is most easily removed by separating it from the transmission, and lifting the engine upwards from the engine compartment.

4 Petrol engine - removal and refitting

Removal

1 Ensure that the vehicle is parked on level ground, and apply the handbrake.

2 On fuel injection models, depressurise the fuel system as described in Chapter 4B.

3 Disconnect the battery negative lead.

4 Drain the engine oil and cooling system with reference to Chapter 1A.

5 Remove the bonnet as described in Chapter 12.

6 Remove the viscous fan unit and cowl, as described in Chapter 3.

7 Loosen the hose clips, and disconnect the top hose and the expansion tank hose from the top of the radiator. Disconnect the top hose from the thermostat housing, and the bottom hose from the coolant pump, and remove both hoses.

8 Unscrew the union nuts, and disconnect the engine oil cooler pipes from the right-hand side of the cooler. Be prepared for oil spillage, and cover the open ends of the pipes, to prevent further spillage and dirt ingress.

9 On models with automatic transmission, similarly disconnect the transmission fluid cooler pipes from the fluid cooler **(see illustrations)**. Release the clamps securing the pipes to the engine.

10 Unscrew the nut and bolt securing the right-hand radiator mounting bracket to the front body panel, and remove the bracket.

11 Similarly, unbolt the left-hand radiator mounting bracket, noting that the power steering fluid reservoir is mounted on the bracket. Move the bracket/reservoir clear of the engine, leaving the fluid hoses connected.

12 Carefully lift the complete radiator assembly from the engine compartment **(see illustration)**.

13 On carburettor models, refer to Chapter 4A and disconnect the accelerator and choke cables from the left-hand carburettor. Disconnect the fuel return pipe from the right-hand carburettor, and tuck it out of the way.

4.9b . . . and disconnect the fluid pipes from the radiator

14 On fuel injection models with manual transmission, disconnect the accelerator cable from the bracket **(see illustration)**. On automatic transmission models, unbolt the cable bracket from the plenum chamber, and lay it to one side, without disturbing the kickdown cable - see Chapter 4B.

15 Again on fuel injection models, disconnect the fuel feed union from the fuel rail. Unclip and disconnect the fuel return hose and vacuum pipe from the fuel pressure regulator. In all cases, seal the open pipe ends with tape, to prevent fuel loss and dirt entry.

16 Disconnect the two heater hoses from the rigid pipes on top of the right-hand rocker cover **(see illustration)**. Loosen and remove the bolt securing the pipe bracket to the rocker cover, then disconnect the shorter rigid pipe from the short section of hose feeding into the inlet manifold.

17 On carburettor models, remove the air cleaner assembly as described in Chapter 4A.

18 On fuel injection models, also remove the airflow sensor, plenum chamber and ram housing as described in Chapter 4B.

19 Remove the alternator as described in Chapter 5A.

20 On models with air conditioning, unscrew and remove the coolant expansion tank mounting nuts, and remove the tank from its mounting bracket. Unbolt the compressor and, **without** disconnecting any of the pipes, move it aside and tie it to the expansion tank bracket **(see illustrations)**. Make sure when

4.12 Lifting out the radiator

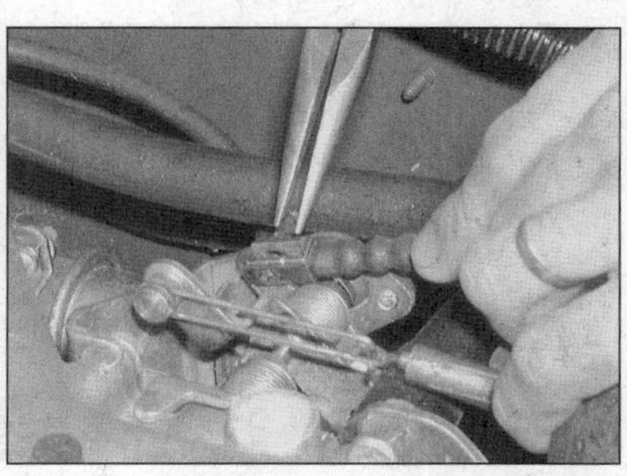

4.14 Disconnecting the accelerator cable

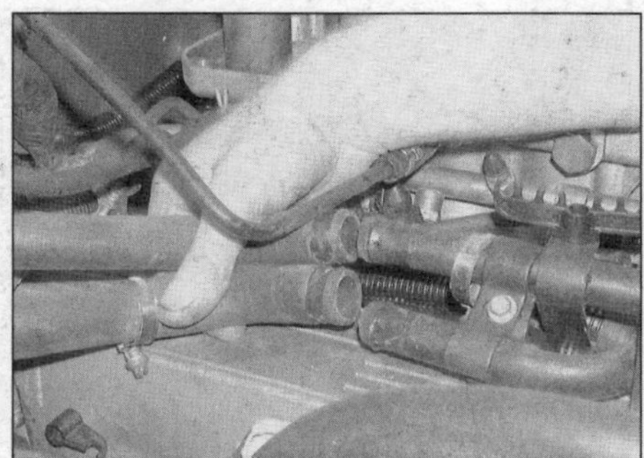

4.16 Disconnect the two heater hoses from the rigid pipes

4.20a Unbolt and lift out the expansion tank . . .

4.20b . . . then remove the air conditioning compressor bolts (arrowed) and move the unit aside

4.23a Disconnecting the oil pressure switch wiring

this is done that the engine oil cooler pipes do not get trapped, as these will be coming out with the engine. Take care also that the large flexible hose from the compressor does not get damaged as the engine is removed.

21 Referring to Chapter 11, unbolt and remove the power steering pump from the left-hand cylinder head, and move it aside. There is no need to disconnect the fluid pipes.

22 Unclip and remove the distributor cap, complete with leads. Making sure they are marked for position, disconnect the HT leads from the plugs and coil, and remove the cap and leads as an assembly.

23 Disconnect the wiring from the following, as applicable:

a) *Coolant temperature sensor on the thermostat housing.*
b) *Fuel temperature sensor on the fuel rail.*
c) *Oil pressure switch above the oil filter **(see illustration)** and oil level sensor on the side of the sump (where fitted).*
d) *Release the lambda sensor wiring plugs from the rear of the cylinder heads (the plug halves do not have to be separated).*
e) *Fuel injectors (label each plug for position).*
f) *Ignition module at the distributor or ignition coil **(see illustration)**.*
g) *Distributor pick-up wiring plug.*
h) *Earth strap from rear of left-hand cylinder head, and earth strap at the left-hand front of the block **(see illustration)**.*
i) *Release all wiring from the retaining clips at the rear of the engine.*

24 Release the transmission breather pipes from the retaining clip on the rear lifting eye. Remove the bottom bolt from the rear lifting eye, and detach the starter motor wiring.

25 Particularly on later models with fuel injection, the wiring harness must now be detached from the engine itself and the engine compartment earth points. The degree to which this is required will depend on the year of the vehicle, and on the equipment fitted.

26 Trace the loom to the earth points at the front left- and right-hand inner wings. One of the earth points is found inside the engine compartment fusebox, and the end fitting is released by removing the retaining screw; another earth point on the same side has the wiring secured by a single nut. The loom also has an earth connection at one of the ignition coil mounting bolts **(see illustrations)**.

27 Once the earth points have been disconnected, feed the wiring back to the engine, releasing it from any cable-ties or mounting clips. It may be necessary to disconnect or remove more of the heater pipework to feed the wiring underneath **(see illustration)**. Move the loom as far to the rear of the engine compartment as possible, so that it is completely clear of the engine.

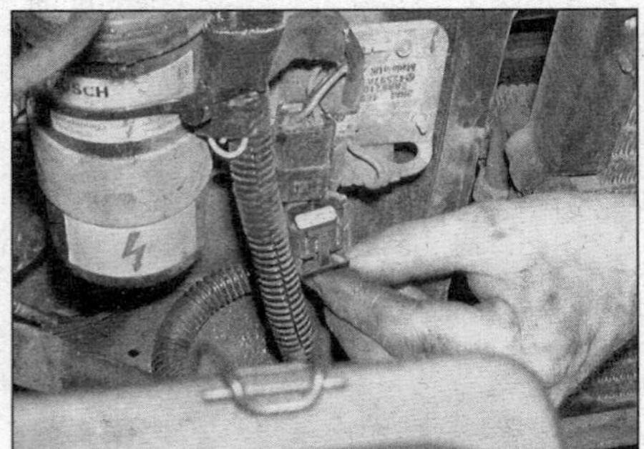

4.23b Unplug the wiring harness from the ignition module

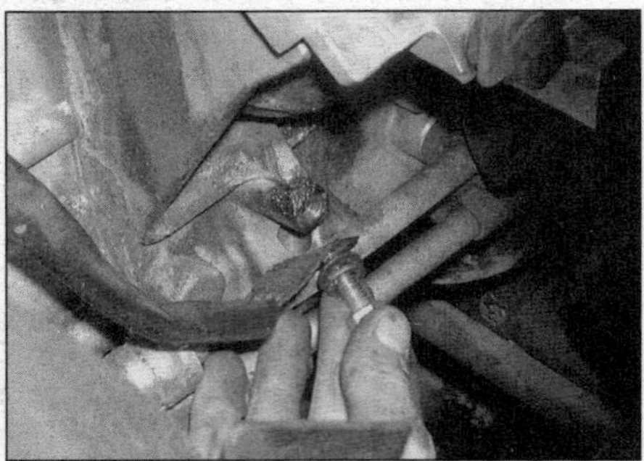

4.23c Disconnecting the front earth strap

4.26a Removing the screw from the harness earth terminal in the fusebox

4.26b Harness earth point (arrowed) below the fusebox

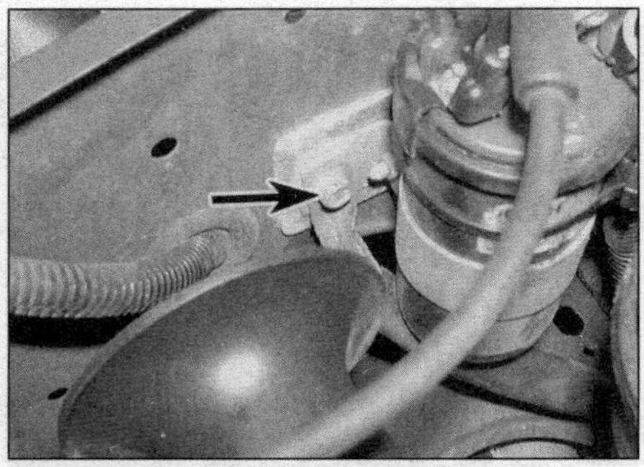

4.26c Earth strap (arrowed) secured by one of the ignition coil mounting bolts

4.27 Feeding the wiring loom under the heater pipework

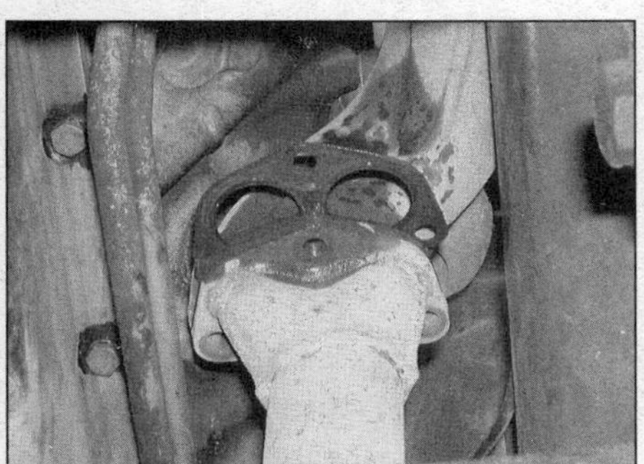

4.30 Exhaust system separated at manifold-to-downpipe connection

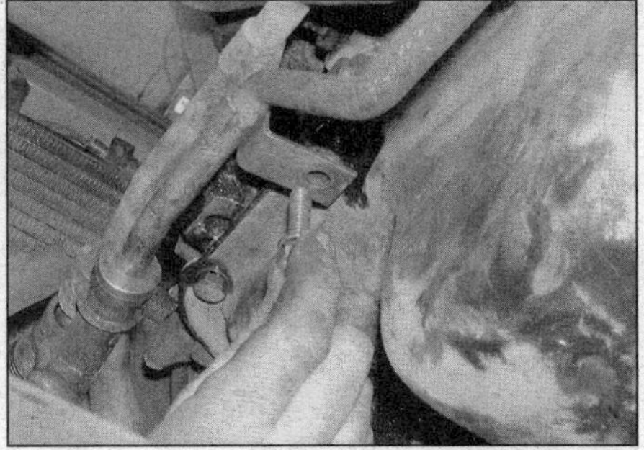

4.32a Removing the transmission fluid pipe clamp bolt

28 Jack up the front of the vehicle, and support it securely on axle stands. This operation is simply to gain access to the underside of the engine - once the engine has been separated from the transmission, it will be lifted out from above.

29 Disconnect the starter motor wiring, including the chassis earth strap.

30 Remove the heatshield from the right-hand exhaust downpipe (two bolts), then unscrew the exhaust manifold-to-downpipe nuts, and separate the exhaust pipes **(see illustration)**.

31 Loosen all the engine-to-bellhousing bolts accessible from below. Those bolts which cannot be accessed when the vehicle is lowered should be removed now.

32 On models with automatic transmission, proceed as follows:

a) *Unscrew and remove the bolt which secures the fluid pipe clamp to the engine sump, and ensure the pipes are free of the engine* ***(see illustration).***

b) *Working under the vehicle, unscrew the securing bolts, and remove the driveplate front access plate from the transmission bellhousing. Note that two of the bolts are different to the rest - these are tapered, to help align the plate when it is refitted* ***(see illustration).***

c) *Remove the three retaining bolts, and take off the round cover plate from the base of the transmission* ***(see illustration).***

d) *Working through the bellhousing aperture, make alignment marks between the torque converter and the driveplate* ***(see illustration).***

e) *Unscrew the four torque converter-to-driveplate securing bolts, rotating the crankshaft as necessary to gain access to each bolt in turn.*

33 Position a hydraulic jack and a large block of wood under the bellhousing, and raise it to support the transmission when the engine is separated from it. Ensure that the jack is completely secure, and that the transmission is steady on top of the jack, as some force may be needed to separate the engine. Arrange the jack so that the jack handle can be operated with the vehicle on its wheels.

34 Lower the front of the vehicle back onto its wheels.

35 Check that there is nothing still connected to the engine which would prevent it from being lifted out, or which would be damaged when the engine is removed. On models with air conditioning, it would be worth placing a large piece of card or board behind the condenser, to prevent it being damaged as the engine is removed.

36 Fit lifting chains to the engine lifting eyes. To lift the engine safely, chains should be fitted to the left- and right-hand side of the engine, and one to the rear. If necessary, make up your own lifting eyes, and bolt them securely to the engine - the mounting points for the alternator or air conditioning compressor could be used, for example **(see illustrations)**.

37 Take the weight of the engine using a suitable engine crane or hoist, then loosen and remove the remaining engine-to-bellhousing bolts - there are eight in total.

38 With the engine supported, unscrew and remove the engine mounting nuts on either side of the engine. Lift the engine so that it is clear of the mounting brackets **(see illustrations)**.

4.32b Driveplate front access plate - two special bolts arrowed

4.32c Round cover plate on the base of the transmission

4.32d Alignment marks and one of the torque converter bolts (arrowed)

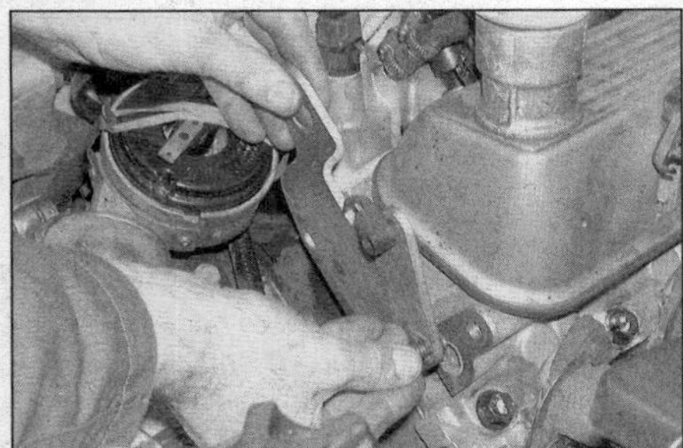

4.36a Refit the power steering pump mounting bracket/lifting eye, using shorter bolts

4.36b Home-made lifting eye attached to the drivebelt tensioner mounting bolt with an extra nut

4.38a Remove the nut from below the engine mounting . . .

4.38b . . . and raise the engine so that the mounting bolt clears the bracket

4.40 Where necessary, unbolt the left-hand engine mounting completely

39 Raise the hydraulic jack under the bellhousing, so that the weight of the transmission is still supported.

40 On models with air conditioning, unbolt and remove the engine left-hand mounting completely (left as seen from the driver's seat) **(see illustration)**. This will allow the engine to swing over and clear the air conditioning pipes at the rear of the engine compartment, next to the rear lifting eye.

41 Carefully ease the engine forwards to disengage it from the transmission, noting that it is located on dowels. It may be necessary to raise or lower the engine as this is done, to achieve the optimum alignment, but (on manual transmission models) do not allow the weight of the engine to be taken by the input shaft, as damage may occur. As the engine is removed, check carefully that no wires, pipes, etc, become snagged.

42 Once the engine is clear of the transmission, lift it carefully out of the engine bay with the help of an assistant **(see illustration)**. Either lower it to the floor or move it onto an engine stand. If the engine must be rested on the floor (this may result in damage to the sump), place blocks under the front of the sump as additional support.

HAYNES
HiNT

On models with a manual transmission, fasten a suitable hose clip around the transmission input shaft to prevent the release bearing from being inadvertently pushed forwards on the shaft whilst the engine is removed from the vehicle.

4.42 Lifting out the engine

43 On models with automatic transmission, if the transmission is to be left in position in the vehicle, and the engine is to be removed for some time, bolt a suitable bar across the transmission bellhousing (using the engine-to-transmission bolts) to retain the torque converter in position in the bellhousing.

Refitting

44 On models with manual transmission, ensure that the clutch friction disc has been centralised as described in Chapter 6.

45 On models with automatic transmission, unbolt the torque converter retaining tool from the bellhousing.

46 Where applicable, remove the hose clip from the transmission input shaft.

47 On manual transmission models, apply a little high-melting-point grease to the splines of the transmission input shaft. Do not apply too much grease, as it may contaminate the clutch.

48 Attach the hoist and lifting tackle to the engine, as during the removal procedure, and lift the engine into position over the engine bay.

49 Lower the engine into position, taking care not to damage the surrounding components.

50 Manipulate the engine and transmission as necessary to enable the two assemblies to be mated together. Alter the position of the jack supporting the transmission, and the hoist supporting the engine, until the two assemblies are correctly aligned. On manual transmission models, ensure that the weight of the engine is not allowed to hang on the input shaft, and ensure that the input shaft engages with the splines of the clutch friction disc.

51 Fit as many engine-to-bellhousing bolts as possible, and tighten by hand to help align the engine - do not tighten them fully until all the bolts are fitted. Engage the engine fully on the bellhousing dowels.

52 Refit the engine mounting (where removed), then lower the engine slowly, until it is resting fully on the engine mounts. Refit the engine mounting nuts, and tighten by hand - do not tighten the mountings fully until all the engine-to-bellhousing bolts are tightened.

53 Remove the engine lifting crane, and unbolt any home-made lifting eyes used. Jack up the front of the vehicle, and support it securely on axle stands.

54 Refit all the engine-to-bellhousing bolts, and tighten to the specified torque.

55 On models with automatic transmission, proceed as follows:

a) Clean the threads of the torque converter-to-driveplate bolts, then coat them with thread-locking compound.

b) Turn the crankshaft as necessary to align the marks made on the driveplate and torque converter before removal.

c) Refit the first accessible torque converter-to-driveplate bolt, ensuring that the marks are still aligned.

d) Refit the remaining torque converter-to-driveplate bolts, turning the crankshaft as necessary to gain access to each bolt location in turn.

e) Tighten the torque converter-to-driveplate bolts to the specified torque (Chapter 7B).

f) Clean the round cover plate and transmission mating faces, then refit the plate and secure with the three bolts.

g) Clean the driveplate front access plate and bellhousing mating faces, then refit the plate. Fit all the bolts finger-tight, then tighten the two tapered bolts fully (to align the plate), followed by the remaining bolts.

h) Refit and tighten the bolt securing the transmission fluid pipes to the base of the engine sump.

56 Reconnect the starter motor wiring, including the chassis earth strap.

57 Reconnect the exhaust pipes to the manifolds, using the information in Chapter 4D, and refit the heatshield to the right-hand pipe.

58 Lower the vehicle back onto its wheels.

59 Tighten the remaining engine-to-bellhousing bolts, and the engine mounting nuts.

60 The remainder of refitting is a reversal of removal, noting the following points:

a) Tighten all bolts to the specified torque, and use new seals and gaskets, as applicable.

b) Make sure that all wiring is securely re-connected, and the wiring harness is retained as before removal - use new clips and cable-ties as necessary.

c) When reconnecting fuel pipes and hoses, check the condition of the hose ends, and use new hose clips where necessary. Make sure that all hoses and pipes are routed as before removal, ie clear of any hot or moving parts.

d) On completion, if the engine has been rebuilt, refer to Section 20 when restarting for the first time.

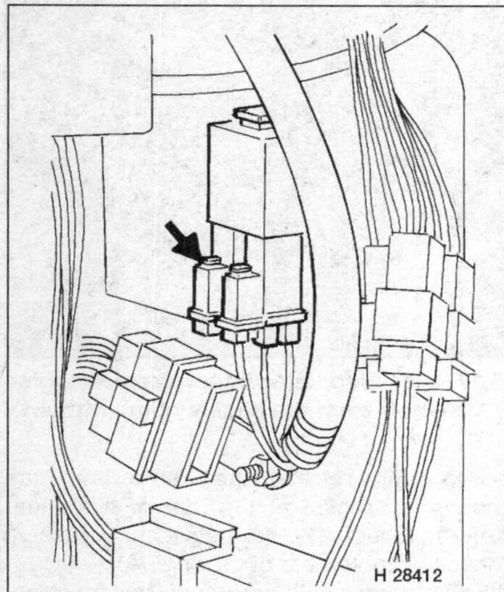
H 28412

5.7 Air conditioning relay wiring plug (arrowed) - 300 TDi engine model

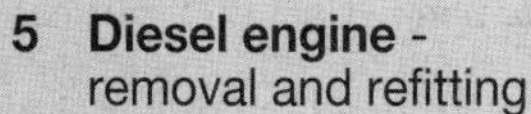

5 Diesel engine - removal and refitting

Note: *An engine hoist and suitable lifting tackle will be required for this operation. Suitable jointing compound will be required to coat the mating faces of the flywheel housing and the transmission bellhousing on refitting. New power steering and oil cooler pipe O-rings should be used on refitting.*

Removal

1 Ensure that the vehicle is parked on level ground, and apply the handbrake.

2 Disconnect the battery negative lead.

3 Drain the engine oil with reference to Chapter 1B.

4 Drain the cooling system as described in Chapter 1B.

5 Remove the bonnet as described in Chapter 12.

6 On 300 TDi engines, remove the oil filler cap, then unclip the plastic cover from the valve cover.

7 On models fitted with air conditioning, release the securing clips and remove the right-hand footwell trim panel, then disconnect the wiring from the air conditioning relay **(see illustration)**.

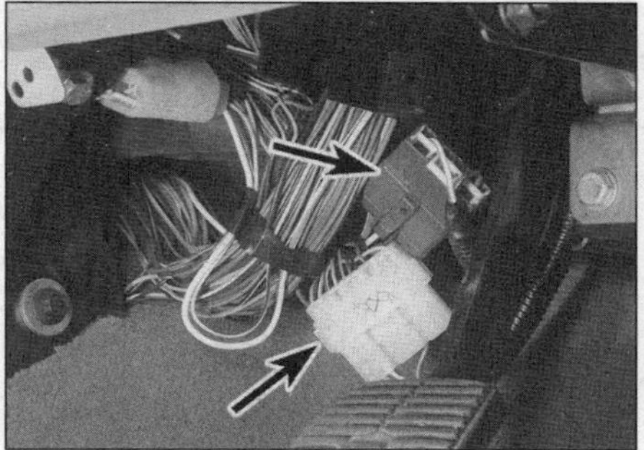

5.8a Engine wiring harness plugs (arrowed) - 300 TDi engine model

5.10 Disconnecting the expansion tank hose from the radiator

8 On 300 TDi engine models, working in the right-hand footwell, release the securing clips and remove the lower facia trim panel, then disconnect the two engine wiring harness plugs. Prise the wiring harness grommet from the engine compartment bulkhead, then feed the wiring harness through into the engine compartment **(see illustrations)**.

9 Remove the viscous fan unit and cowl, as described in Chapter 3.

10 Loosen the hose clips, and disconnect the top hose and the expansion tank hose from the top of the radiator **(see illustration)**.

11 Unscrew the union nuts, and disconnect the engine oil cooler pipes from the right-hand side of the radiator. Be prepared for oil spillage, and cover the open ends of the oil cooler and pipes, to prevent further oil spillage and dirt ingress. Recover the O-ring seals from the unions **(see illustrations)**.

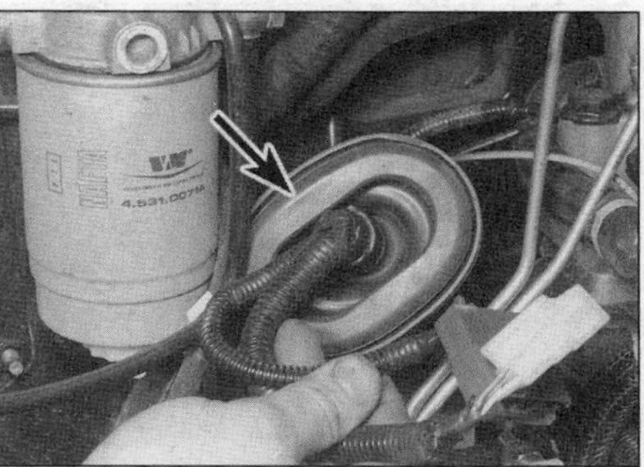

5.8b Prise the wiring grommet (arrowed) from the bulkhead - 300 TDi engine model

5.11a Disconnect the oil cooler pipes (arrowed) . . .

12 Similarly, disconnect the oil pipes from the oil filter adapter on the cylinder block, and remove the pipes.

13 On models with automatic transmission, similarly disconnect the transmission fluid cooler pipes from the fluid cooler.

14 Loosen the hose clips, and remove the intercooler air trunking from the engine compartment **(see illustrations)**.

15 Unscrew the nut and bolt securing the right-hand radiator mounting bracket to the front body panel, and remove the bracket.

16 Similarly, unbolt the left-hand radiator mounting bracket, noting that the power steering fluid reservoir is mounted on the bracket. Move the bracket/reservoir clear of the engine, leaving the fluid hoses connected **(see illustrations)**.

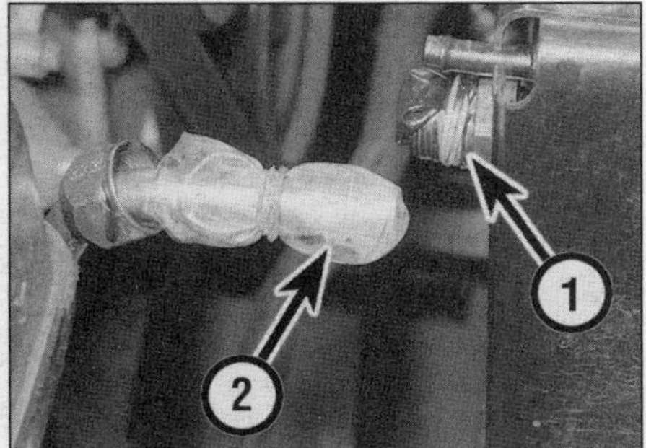
1
2

5.11b . . . and cover the open ends of the oil cooler (1) and the pipes (2)

5.14a Remove the upper . . .

5.14b . . . and lower intercooler air trunking

5.16a Unscrew the securing nut and bolt . . .

5.16b . . . and move the left-hand radiator mounting bracket/power steering reservoir clear of the engine

5.17 Lift the radiator/intercooler/oil cooler assembly from the engine compartment

17 Carefully lift the complete radiator/intercooler/oil cooler assembly from the engine compartment **(see illustration)**.

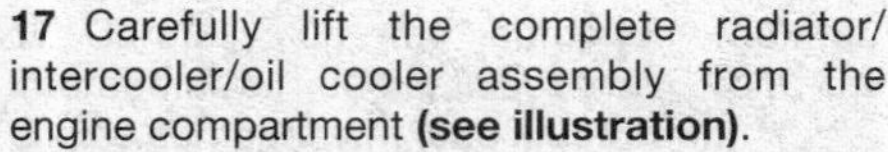

18 On models with air conditioning, have the system discharged by a Land Rover dealer, or a suitably-qualified specialist. Once the system has been discharged, unscrew the union bolts, and disconnect the refrigerant pipes from the air conditioning compressor.

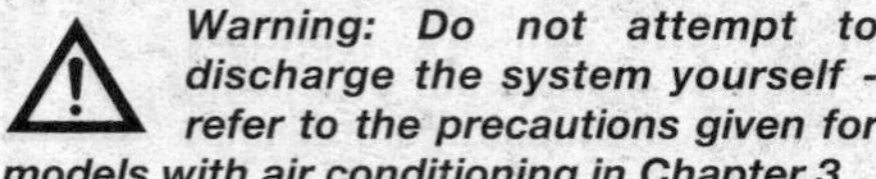

Warning: Do not attempt to discharge the system yourself - refer to the precautions given for models with air conditioning in Chapter 3.

19 Where applicable, loosen the securing clip, and disconnect the engine breather hose from the air trunking which connects the air cleaner to the to the turbocharger. Loosen the securing clips, and remove the air trunking **(see illustration)**.

20 Disconnect the coolant hoses from the rear of the cylinder head, and the rear of the manifold-mounted coolant pipe **(see illustration)**.

21 Place a suitable container beneath the power steering pump to catch escaping fluid, then unscrew the union nut and disconnect the high-pressure fluid hose from the pump. Plug or clamp the open ends of the hose and the pump, to prevent dirt ingress and further fluid loss. Similarly, loosen the hose clip, and disconnect the fluid return hose from the pump.

22 Disconnect the coolant bypass hose from the thermostat housing then, where applicable, release the hose from the clips on the engine **(see illustrations)**.

23 Where applicable, disconnect the accelerator cable from the fuel injection pump, and release the cable from the mounting bracket at the rear of the pump (refer to Chapter 4C for details if necessary). Move the cable clear of the engine.

24 On models with automatic transmission, disconnect the kickdown cable from the fuel injection pump and the mounting bracket, and move the cable clear of the engine (refer to Chapter 7B for details if necessary).

25 Unscrew the banjo bolt and nut, and disconnect the fuel supply and return pipes from the fuel injection pump (note that it will be necessary to counterhold the union on the pump when disconnecting the return pipe) **(see illustration)**. Be prepared for fuel spillage. Recover the sealing washers from the banjo unions.

HAYNES
HiNT

Cover the open ends of the pipes, and plug the openings in the injection pump, to keep dirt out (the banjo bolt can be refitted to the pump and covered).

26 Similarly, disconnect the fuel hoses from the fuel lift pump (on the right-hand side of the engine). Again, be prepared for fuel spillage, and cover or plug the open ends of the hoses and the pump.

27 Release the securing clip, and disconnect the vacuum hose from the brake vacuum pump.

28 Disconnect the exhaust front section from the manifold, with reference to Chapter 4D.

29 Loosen the hose clips, and disconnect the

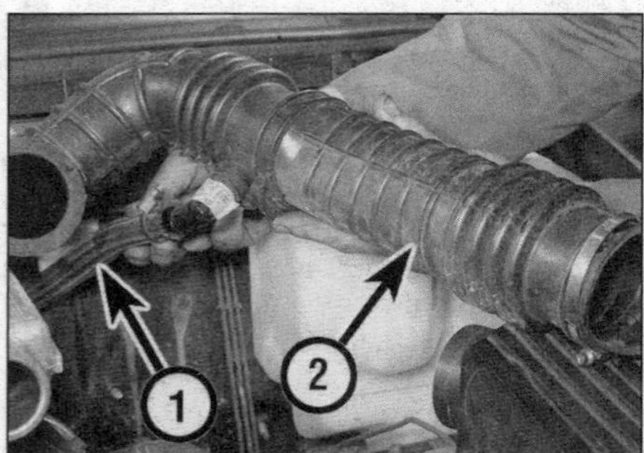
1
2
5.19 Disconnect the engine breather hose (1) and remove the air trunking (2)

1
2
5.20 Disconnect the coolant hoses from the rear of the cylinder head (1) and the coolant pipe (2)

5.22a Disconnect the coolant bypass hose . . .

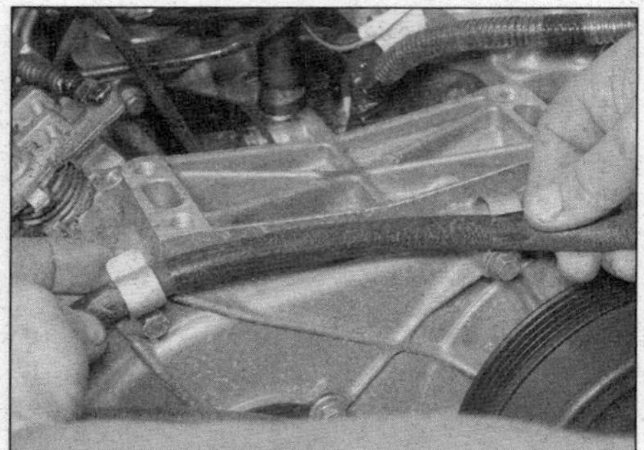
5.22b . . . and release the hose from the clips

5.25 Disconnecting the fuel return hose (arrowed) from the fuel injection pump

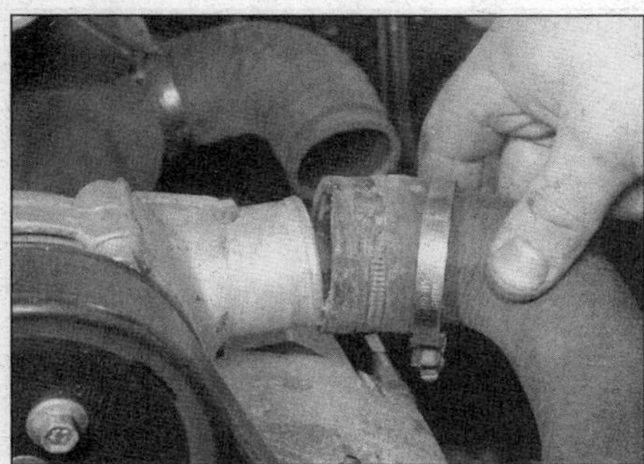

5.29a Disconnect the coolant hoses from the coolant pump . . .

coolant hoses from the coolant pump and the front of manifold-mounted coolant pipe **(see illustrations)**.

Cover the alternator with a plastic bag, to prevent escaping coolant from entering the alternator during the engine removal procedure.

30 On 200 TDi engines, unscrew the bolt securing the starter motor earth strap to the cylinder block. On 300 TDi engines, unscrew the bolt and disconnect the earth strap from the starter motor **(see illustration)**.

31 On 200 TDi engines, disconnect the engine wiring harness connections as follows:

a) Working at the rear of the engine compartment, separate the two halves of the engine wiring harness connector at the bulkhead.

5.29b . . . and the front of the coolant pipe (arrowed)

b) Remove the cable-ties securing the engine wiring harness to the lighting wiring harness.

c) Release the engine wiring harness from the clips on the bulkhead.

d) Disconnect the wiring from the brake fluid level sensor on the top of the brake fluid reservoir.

e) Pull the rubber boot from the wiring terminal at the bulkhead, and disconnect the wiring from the terminal.

f) Check that all relevant engine wiring harness connections have been disconnected, then release the harness from any remaining clips in the engine compartment, and lay the harness on the engine (the harness is removed complete with the engine). Note the routing of the wiring harness, to ensure correct refitting.

32 On 300 TDi engines, disconnect the engine wiring harness connections as follows:

5.30 Unscrew the earth strap bolt (arrowed) - 300 TDi engine

a) Unclip the cover from the fusebox at the right-hand side of the engine compartment, then unclip the circuit breaker cover plate **(see illustration)**.

b) Remove the securing screw, and disconnect the left-hand wire from the fusebox connector plate **(see illustration)**.

c) Disconnect the battery positive lead. Unscrew the bolt from the lead clamp, and separate the secondary leads from the clamp **(see illustration)**.

d) Unscrew the securing nut, and disconnect the earth wires from the body panel under the fusebox **(see illustration)**.

e) Disconnect the wiring plug from the preheating system relay/timer unit at the rear of the fusebox **(see illustration)**.

f) Unscrew the two nuts securing the wiring harness clamps to the right-hand body panel **(see illustration)**, *then release the*

5.32a Unclip the circuit breaker cover plate . . .

5.32b . . . then disconnect the left-hand wire from the connector plate

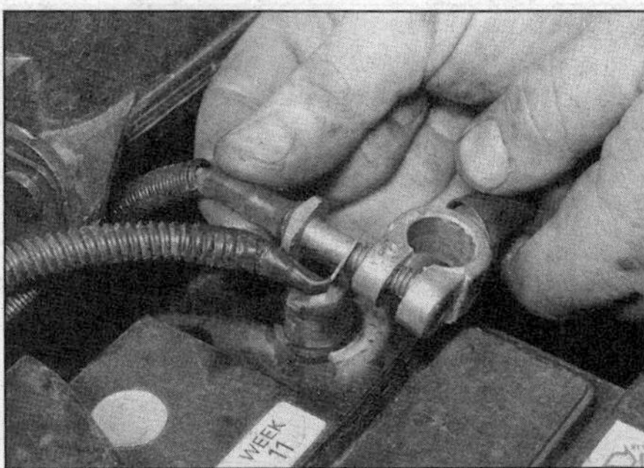

5.32c Separate the secondary leads from the battery positive lead clamp

5.32d Unscrew the nut (arrowed) and disconnect the earth leads from the body panel

5.32e Disconnect the wiring plug from the preheating system relay/timer unit

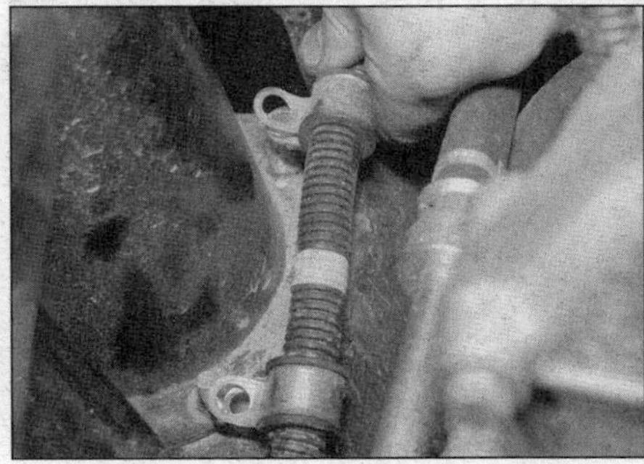

5.32f Release the wiring harness clamps from the body panel

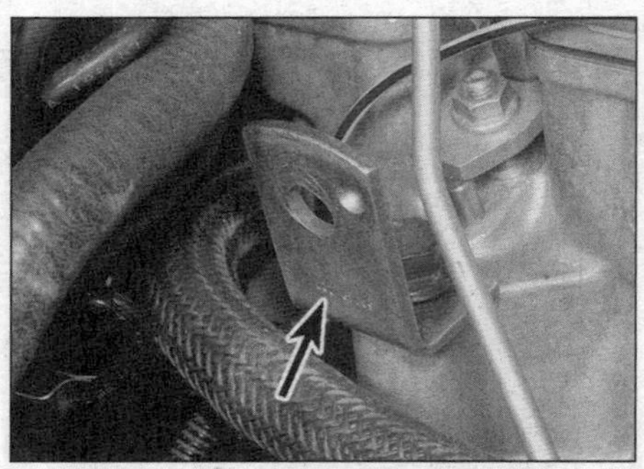
5.38 Engine lifting bracket (arrowed) in position on rear cylinder head bolt

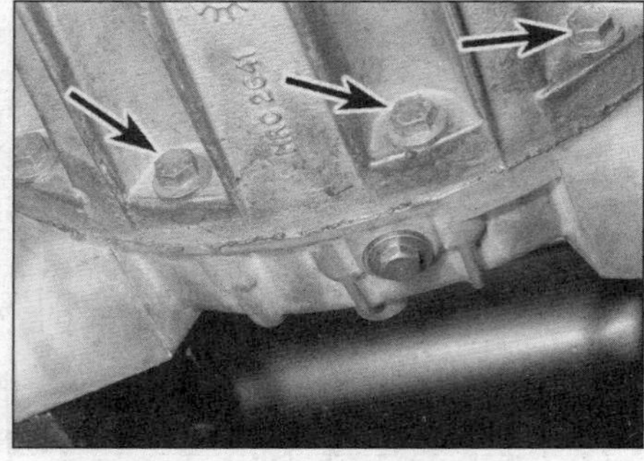
5.41 Three of the flywheel housing-to-bellhousing bolts (arrowed)

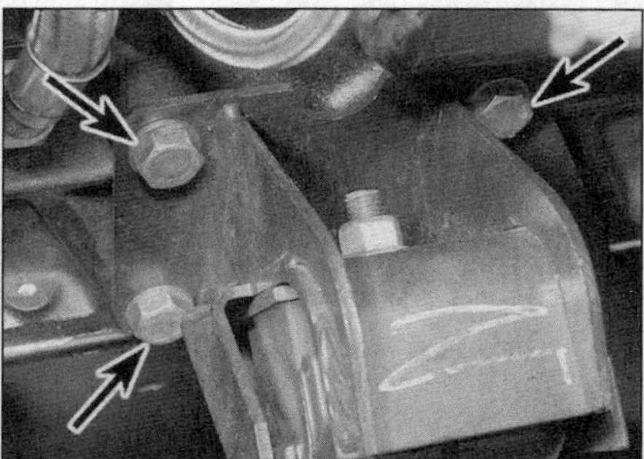
5.42 Engine left-hand mounting bracket-to-cylinder block bolts (arrowed)

wiring harness from any remaining clips in the engine compartment, and lay the harness on the engine (the harness is removed complete with the engine). Note the routing of the wiring harness, to ensure correct refitting.

33 On models with Electronic Diesel Control (EDC), disconnect all relevant wiring from the system components in the engine compartment (refer to Chapter 4C for further details) to enable the wiring harness to be removed complete with the engine.

34 On models with automatic transmission, where applicable, unbolt the transmission fluid cooler pipe bracket from the cylinder block, and move the pipes to one side, clear of the engine.

35 Place a trolley jack under the transmission, with an interposed block of wood to spread the load. Raise the jack to support the transmission.

36 On models with automatic transmission, proceed as follows:

a) *Working under the vehicle, unscrew the securing bolts, and remove the driveplate access panel from the transmission bellhousing. Recover the gasket.*
b) *Working through the bellhousing aperture, make alignment marks between the torque converter and the driveplate.*
c) *Unscrew the four torque converter-to-driveplate securing bolts, rotating the crankshaft as necessary to gain access to each bolt in turn.*

37 Make up an engine rear lifting bracket from a suitable piece of steel bar - the bracket should be constructed so that it can be secured by the right-hand rear cylinder head bolt. Ensure that the bracket is strong enough to carry the weight of the engine.

38 Carefully unscrew the right-hand rear cylinder head securing bolt, then fit the lifting bracket, and refit and tighten the cylinder head bolt to secure the bracket **(see illustration)**.

39 Connect a suitable hoist and lifting tackle to the front and rear engine lifting brackets on the cylinder head.

40 Raise the hoist sufficiently to just take the weight of the engine.

41 Working underneath the vehicle, unscrew, but do not remove, all accessible flywheel housing-to-bellhousing bolts and nuts **(see illustration)**.

42 Working at each side of the engine in turn, unscrew the four bolts (on each side) securing the front engine mounting brackets to the cylinder block **(see illustration)**.

43 Similarly, remove the two bolts on each side, securing the front engine mountings to the flywheel housing.

44 Unscrew the nuts, and recover the washers securing the front engine mountings to the chassis, then withdraw both engine mounting assemblies from the vehicle **(see illustration)**.

45 Lower the engine and transmission, using the hoist and jack, for access to the three upper flywheel housing-to-bellhousing nuts.

46 Unscrew and remove the upper flywheel housing-to-bellhousing nuts. Access is difficult, and is easiest from underneath the vehicle, using a suitable socket and extension bar **(see illustrations)**.

HAYNES
HiNT

Have an assistant guide the socket onto the flywheel housing-to-bellhousing nuts from above.

47 Working in the engine compartment, unscrew and remove the bolt securing the transmission breather pipe bracket to the rear of the cylinder head, then move the pipe to one side, clear of the engine.

48 Working under the vehicle, remove the remaining flywheel housing-to-bellhousing bolts and nuts. Leave the starter motor in position.

49 Carefully raise the hoist, and lift the engine from the transmission. On manual transmission models, it will be necessary to pull the engine forwards to disengage the transmission input shaft from the clutch - take care not to allow the weight of the engine or transmission to hang on the input shaft. If necessary, alter the position of the jack supporting the transmission, and the hoist supporting the engine, until the engine is free. Note that there is sealant between the mating faces of the flywheel housing and the bellhousing.

50 Make a final check to ensure that all hoses, pipes and wires have been disconnected from the engine to allow removal.

51 With the aid of an assistant, carefully raise

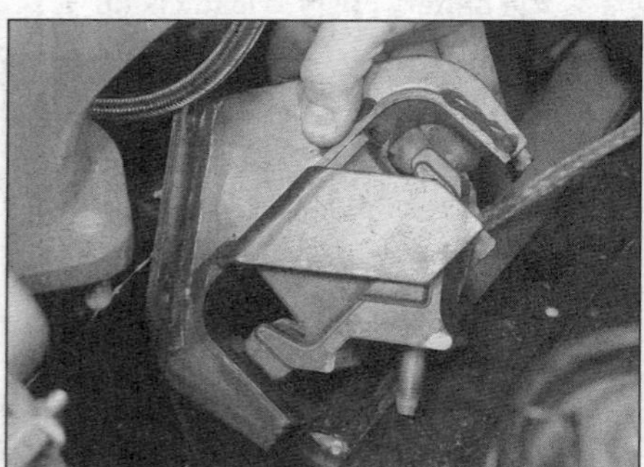
5.44 Removing the engine left-hand mounting

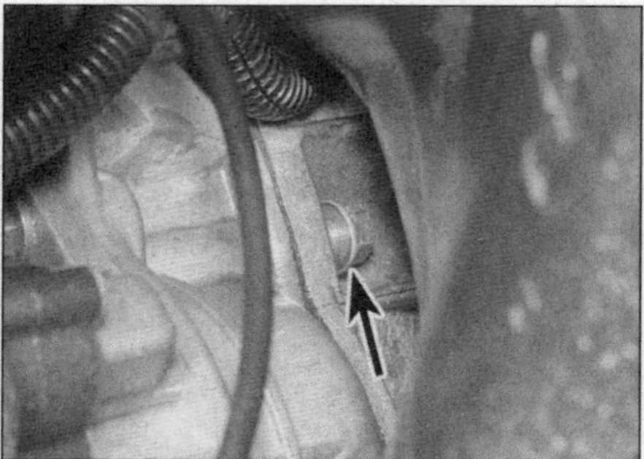
5.46a Left-hand . . .

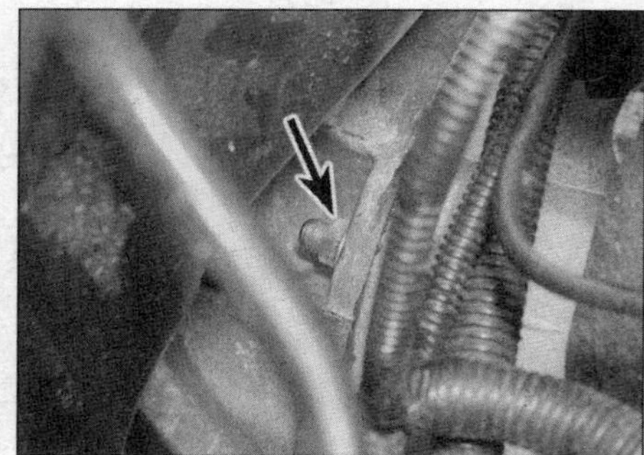
5.46b . . . and right-hand upper flywheel housing-to-bellhousing nuts (arrowed) - there is one more nut at the very top

the hoist to lift the engine from the vehicle, taking care not to damage surrounding components in the engine compartment **(see illustration)**.

On models with a manual transmission, fasten a suitable hose clip around the transmission input shaft to prevent the release bearing from being inadvertently pushed forwards on the shaft whilst the engine is removed from the vehicle.

52 On models with automatic transmission, if the transmission is to be left in position in the vehicle, and the engine is to be removed for some time, bolt a suitable bar across the transmission bellhousing (using the engine-to-transmission bolts) to retain the torque converter in position in the bellhousing.

Refitting

53 Check that the rear engine lifting bracket is in position on the right-hand rear cylinder head bolt.

54 On models with a manual transmission, ensure that the clutch friction disc has been centralised as described in Chapter 6.

55 On models with automatic transmission, unbolt the torque converter retaining tool from the bellhousing.

56 Where applicable, remove the hose clip from the transmission input shaft.

57 Apply jointing compound to the cylinder block mating faces of the transmission bellhousing.

58 On manual transmission models, apply a little high-melting-point grease to the splines of the transmission input shaft. Do not apply too much grease, as it may contaminate the clutch.

59 Attach the hoist and lifting tackle to the engine, as during the removal procedure, and lift the engine into position over the vehicle engine compartment.

60 Lower the engine into position, taking care not to damage the surrounding components.

61 Manipulate the engine and transmission as necessary to enable the two assemblies to be mated together. Alter the position of the jack supporting the transmission, and the hoist supporting the engine, until the two assemblies are correctly aligned. On manual transmission models, ensure that the weight of the engine or transmission is not allowed to hang on the input shaft, and ensure that the input shaft engages with the splines of the clutch friction disc.

62 Fit the flywheel housing-to-bellhousing bolts and nuts, and tighten them to the specified torque. If necessary, lower the engine/transmission assembly to gain access to the top nuts, as during removal.

63 Wipe any excess jointing compound from the area around the flywheel housing-to-bellhousing mating faces.

5.51 Lifting the engine from the vehicle

64 Refit and tighten the bolt securing the transmission breather pipe bracket to the rear of the cylinder head.

65 If necessary, raise the engine slightly, then place the front engine mountings in position. Refit and tighten the bolts securing the engine mountings to the cylinder block and the flywheel housing.

66 Carefully withdraw the jack and the block of wood used to support the transmission.

67 Lower the engine, ensuring that the engine mounting studs engage with the corresponding holes in the chassis brackets, then refit the engine mounting washers and nuts, and tighten the nuts to the specified torque.

68 Disconnect the hoist and lifting tackle from the cylinder head.

69 On models with automatic transmission, proceed as follows.

a) Coat the threads of the torque converter-to-driveplate bolts with thread-locking compound.

b) Turn the crankshaft as necessary to align the marks made on the driveplate and torque converter before removal.

c) Refit the first accessible torque converter-to-driveplate bolt, ensuring that the marks are still aligned.

d) Refit the remaining torque converter-to-driveplate bolts, turning the crankshaft as necessary to gain access to each bolt location in turn.

e) Tighten the torque converter-to-driveplate bolts to the specified torque (Chapter 7B).

f) Clean all traces of old gasket from the driveplate access panel and bellhousing mating faces, then refit the access panel using a new gasket. Tighten the securing bolts to the specified torque.

70 Unscrew the right-hand rear cylinder head bolt, and remove the engine lifting bracket. Refit the cylinder head bolt, and tighten to the specified torque in the stages given in the Specifications.

71 On models with automatic transmission, where applicable, refit the bolt securing the fluid cooler pipe bracket to the cylinder block.

72 Reconnect all relevant engine harness wiring, and clip the harness into position, ensuring that it is routed as noted before removal (refer to paragraphs 31 to 33).

73 Refit the bolt securing the starter motor earth strap.

74 Reconnect the coolant hoses to the coolant pump and the front of the manifold-mounted coolant pipe.

75 Reconnect the exhaust front section to the manifold as described in Chapter 4D.

76 Reconnect the vacuum hose to the brake vacuum pump.

77 Reconnect the fuel hoses to the fuel lift pump, and tighten the banjo unions.

78 Similarly, reconnect the fuel supply and return pipes to the fuel injection pump.

79 On models with automatic transmission, reconnect and adjust the kickdown cable as described in Chapter 7B.

80 Where applicable, reconnect and adjust the accelerator cable as described in Chapter 4C.

81 Reconnect the coolant bypass hose to the thermostat housing, and clip the hose into position on the timing belt cover.

82 Reconnect the fluid hoses to the power steering pump, using new O-ring seals.

83 Reconnect the coolant hoses to the rear of the cylinder head and to the manifold-mounted coolant pipe.

84 Refit the air trunking connecting the air cleaner to the turbocharger and, where applicable, reconnect the engine breather hose to the air trunking.

85 On models with air conditioning, reconnect the refrigerant pipes to the air conditioning compressor.

86 Refit the radiator/intercooler/oil cooler assembly, and secure with the mounting brackets, ensuring that the power steering fluid reservoir hoses are correctly routed.

87 Refit the intercooler air trunking, and tighten the securing clips.

88 On models with automatic transmission, reconnect the transmission fluid cooler pipes to the fluid cooler.

89 Reconnect the oil cooler pipes to the oil filter adapter and the oil cooler, using new O-ring seals.

90 Reconnect the top hose and the expansion tank hose to the radiator.

91 Refit the viscous fan unit and cowl as described in Chapter 3.

92 On 300 TDi engine models, feed the engine wiring harness through the bulkhead, and push the bulkhead grommet into position.

93 Where applicable, working in the footwell, reconnect the engine wring harness plugs, and on models with air conditioning, reconnect the wiring to the air conditioning relay. Refit the lower facia trim panel.

94 Where applicable, clip the plastic cover into position on the valve cover, then refit the oil filler cap.

95 Refit the bonnet as described in Chapter 12.

96 Check the power steering fluid level, and top-up as necessary as described in Chapter 1B.

97 On models with automatic transmission, check and if necessary top-up the transmission fluid level as described in Chapter 1B.

6.3a Removing the oil filter adapter

6.3b Remove the bolts securing the injection pump bracket . . .

6.3c . . . then remove the crankcase breather housing - 300 TDi engine

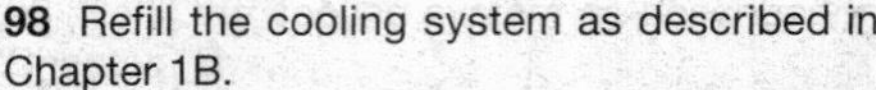

98 Refill the cooling system as described in Chapter 1B.

99 Refill the engine with oil as described in Chapter 1B.

100 Before starting the engine, the turbocharger **must** be primed with oil as follows. Failure to carry out this procedure may result in serious (and expensive) damage to the turbocharger.

a) Unscrew the oil feed pipe banjo bolt from the top of the turbocharger housing. Recover the two sealing washers, and move the feed pipe away from the oil hole in the housing.

b) Fill the housing with clean engine oil of the correct type and grade, from a freshly-opened sealed container.

c) Reconnect the oil feed pipe, and refit the banjo bolt, ensuring that one sealing washer is positioned on each side of the pipe. Tighten the banjo bolt to the specified torque.

101 On models with air conditioning, have the system re-charged with refrigerant by a Land Rover dealer, or a suitably-equipped specialist.

102 Reconnect the battery negative lead.

6 Engine overhaul - dismantling sequence

It is far easier to dismantle and work on the engine if it is mounted on a portable engine stand. These stands can often be hired from a tool hire shop. Depending on the type of stand used, the flywheel/driveplate may have to be removed from the engine, to allow the engine stand bolts to be tightened into the end of the cylinder block.

If a stand is not available, it is possible to dismantle the engine while supported on blocks on a sturdy workbench, or on the floor. Be extra-careful not to tip or drop the engine when working without a stand.

Before starting the overhaul procedure, the external engine ancillary components must be removed (this is the case even if a reconditioned engine is to be fitted, in which case, the components from the old engine must be transferred to the reconditioned unit). These components include the following (check with the supplier of a reconditioned unit to see which components are included):

6.3d To remove the auxiliary mounting bracket on 300 TDi engines, unscrew the nut . . .

6.3e . . . and remove the auxiliary drivebelt tensioner . . .

a) Wiring looms (note all connections and routing).

b) Spark plugs or glow plugs.

c) Fuel injectors.

d) Diesel injection pump.

e) Coolant pump.

f) Alternator.

g) Starter motor.

h) Power steering pump.

i) Manifolds and turbocharger (diesel models).

j) Thermostat and housing.

k) Clutch.

l) Oil pressure switch.

m) Temperature gauge sender.

*n) Oil filter adapter **(see illustration)**.*

*o) Crankcase breather and oil separator components **(see illustrations)**.*

p) Dipstick and tube.

*q) Auxiliary component mounting bracket(s) **(see illustrations)**.*

6.3f . . . for access to the bracket securing nut (arrowed)

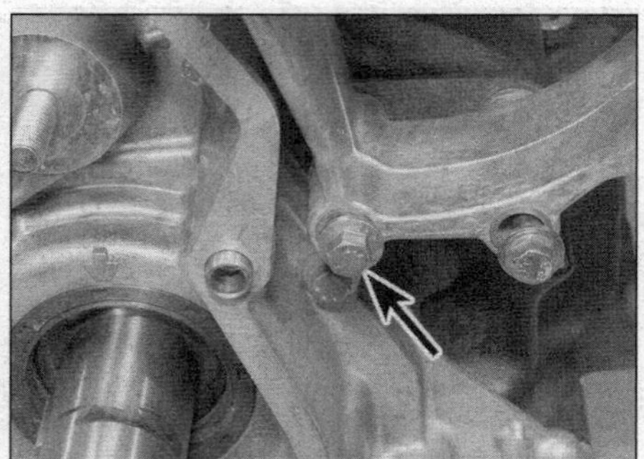

6.3g Remove the securing bolt (arrowed) . . .

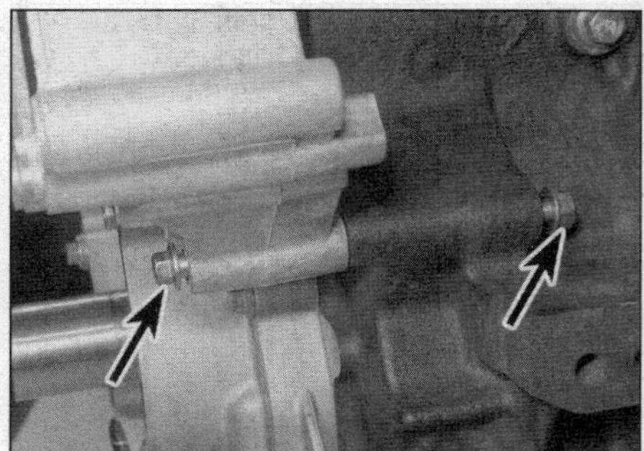

6.3h . . . and the through-bolt and nut (arrowed) . . .

6.3i . . . then withdraw the bracket . . .

6.3j . . . and recover the gasket

7.5 Measuring the camshaft endfloat - engine shown inverted

7 Camshaft (diesel engines) - removal, inspection and refitting

Note 1: *On 200 TDi engines, if the camshaft is renewed, the oil pump/brake vacuum pump drive skew gear must also be renewed (see Chapter 2B, Section 13). This is necessary to preserve the meshing of the skew gear teeth with the teeth on the camshaft.*

Note 2: *On petrol engines, camshaft removal is covered in part A of this Chapter.*

Removal

1 With the engine removed, if not already done, remove the cylinder head, cam follower components, and the fuel lift pump (see Chapters 2B and 4C). On 200 TDi engines, remove the oil pump driveshaft, as described in part B of this Chapter. On 300 TDi engines, remove the brake vacuum pump (Chapter 10).

2 Remove the timing belt housing, as described in part B of this Chapter (Section 16).

3 Before removing the camshaft, check the camshaft endfloat as follows.

4 Mount a dial gauge on the end of the cylinder block, and position the probe to read from the end of the camshaft.

5 Push the camshaft fully into the cylinder block, and zero the dial gauge **(see illustration)**.

6 Pull the camshaft fully towards the front of the engine, and note the reading on the dial gauge.

7 If the reading is outside the specified limits (see *Specifications*), fit a new thrust plate on reassembly.

8 Unscrew the two securing bolts, and remove the camshaft thrust plate, noting which way round it is fitted **(see illustration)**.

9 Carefully withdraw the camshaft from the front of the cylinder block, taking care not to allow the end of the camshaft to drop onto the bearings in the cylinder block as it is removed **(see illustration)**.

Inspection

10 Examine the camshaft bearing surfaces and cam lobes for wear ridges, pitting or scoring. Renew the camshaft if evident.

11 Examine the camshaft bearing surfaces in the cylinder block **(see illustration)**. Deep scoring or other damage means that the bearings must be renewed. To determine the extent of wear, the internal diameter of the bearings can be measured using a suitable internal micrometer. Renewal of the bearings is a specialist job, and should be entrusted to a suitably-equipped specialist with access to line-boring equipment.

Refitting

12 Carefully offer the camshaft into position in the cylinder block, taking care not to damage the bearings or the cam lobes.

13 Refit the camshaft thrust plate, ensuring that it is positioned as noted before removal, and tighten the securing bolts to the specified torque.

14 Refit the timing belt housing, as described in part B of this Chapter.

15 Refit the cam follower components, the cylinder head, and the fuel lift pump (Chapters 2B and 4C). On 200 TDi engines, refit the oil pump driveshaft, as described in part B of this Chapter. On 300 TDi engines, refit the brake vacuum pump as described in Chapter 10.

8 Cylinder head - dismantling

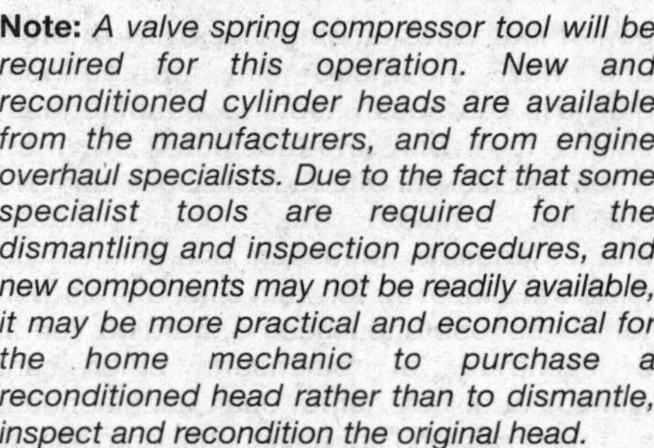

Note: *A valve spring compressor tool will be required for this operation. New and reconditioned cylinder heads are available from the manufacturers, and from engine overhaul specialists. Due to the fact that some specialist tools are required for the dismantling and inspection procedures, and new components may not be readily available, it may be more practical and economical for the home mechanic to purchase a reconditioned head rather than to dismantle, inspect and recondition the original head.*

1 With the cylinder head removed as described in Chapter 2A or 2B, clean away all external dirt, and if desired, remove any ancillaries such as engine lifting brackets, thermostat housing, etc, which are still attached to the cylinder head.

Petrol engines

2 Before starting to remove the valves from the cylinder head, take a piece of cardboard and pierce 8 numbered holes in it. If both cylinder heads are being done together, then make two such cards and mark one LEFT and the other RIGHT. Alternatively, bag each valve

7.8 Remove the thrust plate . . .

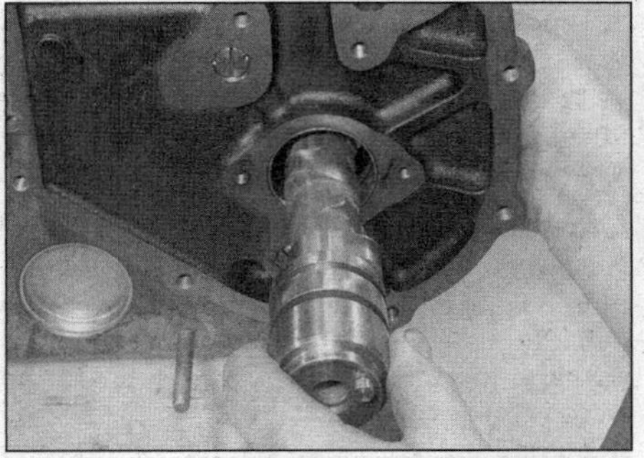
7.9 . . . and withdraw the camshaft - engine shown inverted

7.11 Examine the camshaft bearings in the cylinder block (arrowed) - engine shown inverted

8.4 Clamp the compressor tool and remove the collet halves

and its components once removed, and label the bag No 1 LEFT, and so on. Small food or freezer bags are ideal for this, especially the self-closing type.

3 The procedure for each cylinder head is the same. Start at the front of the head and arrange a valve spring compressor tool over the first valve.

4 Clamp the tool and remove the two split collets, then release the tool **(see illustration)**.

If the spring cap sticks to the valve stem, support the compressor tool, and give the end a light tap with a soft-faced mallet to help free the spring cap.

5 Remove the upper cup, valve spring and valve from the cylinder head **(see illustrations)**.

6 Place the valve in the No 1 hole in the card and the spring(s), collets and upper cup in a suitably-marked container, or put all components in a clearly-marked bag.

7 Remove the rest of the valves in turn in each cylinder head, making sure that they are put into the correct holes in the card for their particular head.

Diesel engines

8 If not already done, remove the caps from the tops of the valve stems, keeping them in order so that they can be refitted in their original positions.

9 To remove a valve, fit a valve spring compressor tool. Ensure that the arms of the compressor tool are securely positioned on the head of the valve and the spring cap. As the valves are recessed into the cylinder head, a suitable extension piece may be required for the spring compressor **(see illustration)**.

10 Compress the valve spring to relieve the pressure of the spring cap acting on the collets.

If the spring cap sticks to the valve stem, support the compressor tool, and give the end a light tap with a soft-faced mallet to help free the spring cap.

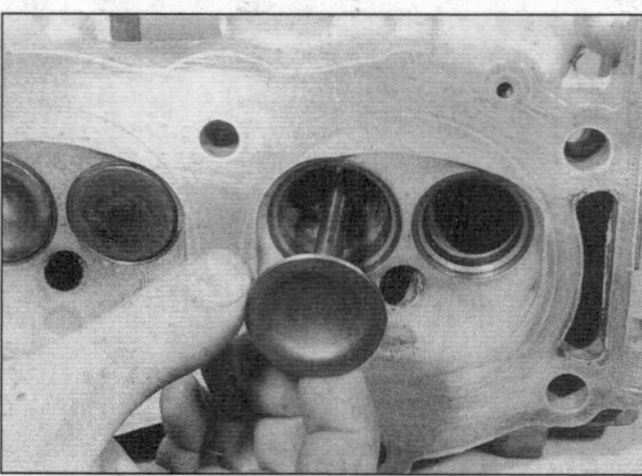

8.5a Remove the upper cup and valve spring . . .

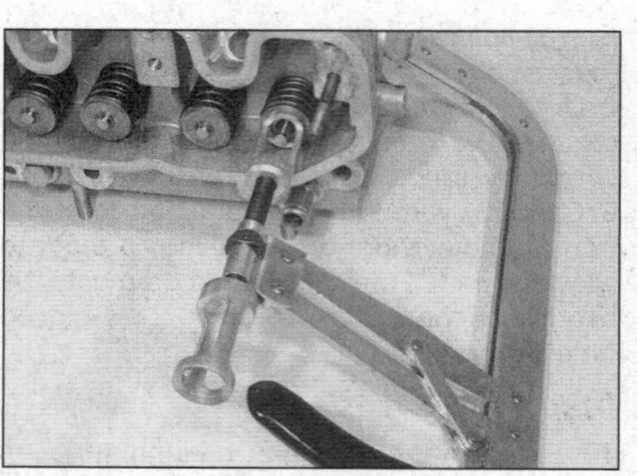

8.9 Valve spring compressor tool in position on No 8 valve

11 Extract the two split collets, then slowly release the compressor tool.

12 Remove the spring cap, spring, valve stem oil seal (using long-nosed pliers if necessary), and the spring seat, then withdraw the valve from the cylinder head.

13 Repeat the procedure for the remaining valves, keeping all components in strict order so that they can be refitted in their original positions, unless all the components are to be kept and used again. If the components are to be renewed. If the components are to be kept and used again, place each valve assembly in a labelled polythene bag or a similar small container. Note that as with cylinder numbering, the valves are normally numbered from the timing belt end of the engine **(see illustration)**.

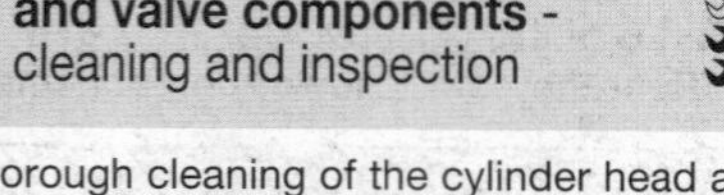

9 Cylinder head and valve components - cleaning and inspection

1 Thorough cleaning of the cylinder head and valve components, followed by a detailed inspection, will enable a decision to be made on whether further work is necessary before reassembling the components.

Cleaning

2 Scrape away all traces of old gasket material and sealing compound from the cylinder head surfaces. Take care not to damage the cylinder head surfaces, as the head is made of light alloy.

3 Scrape away the carbon from the combustion chamber mating faces of the cylinder head, then wash the cylinder head thoroughly with paraffin or a suitable solvent.

4 Scrape off any heavy carbon deposits that may have formed on the valves, then use a power-operated wire brush to remove deposits from the valve heads and stems.

Inspection

Note: *Be sure to perform all the following inspection procedures before concluding that the services of a machine shop or engine overhaul specialist are required. Make a list of all items that require attention.*

Cylinder head(s)

5 Inspect the head(s) very carefully for cracks, evidence of coolant leakage, and other damage. If cracks are found, a new cylinder head should be obtained.

6 Use a straight-edge and feeler blade to check that the cylinder head surface is not distorted **(see illustration)**. If the specified

8.5b . . . followed by the valve

8

8.13 Place the valve components in a labelled polythene bag

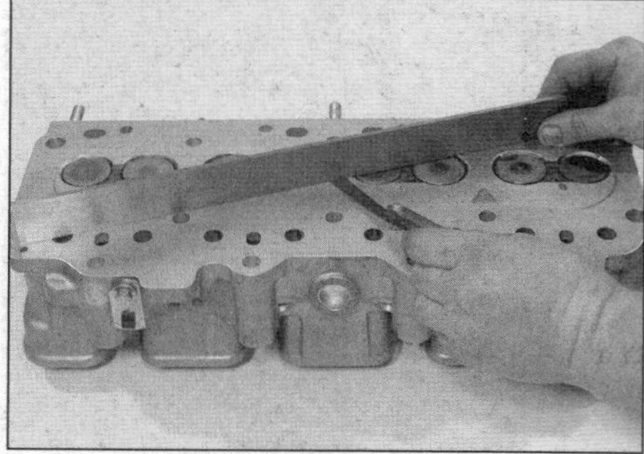

9.6 Checking the cylinder head surface for distortion

distortion limit is exceeded, it may be possible to have the cylinder head resurfaced - consult a Land Rover dealer for further information.

7 Examine the valve seats in the cylinder head. If the seats are severely pitted, cracked or burned, then they will need to be recut by an engine overhaul specialist. If only slight pitting is evident, this can be removed by grinding the valve heads and seats together with coarse, then fine, grinding paste, as described later in this Section.

8 If the valve guides are worn, indicated by a side-to-side motion of the valve, the guides can be renewed. This work is best carried out by an engine overhaul specialist. To measure the valve stem play in the guide, insert the valve into the relevant guide, with the valve head positioned approximately 8.0 mm from the seat. A dial gauge positioned against the edge of the valve head may be used to determine whether the amount of side play of the valve exceeds the specified maximum. If new valve guides have been fitted, repeat the measuring procedure, and if the valve stem play still exceeds the maximum limit, renew the valve.

9 Check the condition of the rocker shaft bearing surfaces in the cylinder head for signs of wear or damage. If evident, the cylinder head must be renewed, as no repair is possible.

Valves - petrol engines

Note: *A micrometer will be required for this operation.*

10 Examine the head of each valve for pitting, burning, cracks and general wear, and check the valve stem for scoring and wear ridges. Rotate the valve, and check for any obvious indication that it is bent. Look for pitting and excessive wear on the end of each valve stem. If the valve appears satisfactory at this stage, measure the valve stem diameter at several points using a micrometer **(see illustration)**. Any significant difference in the readings obtained indicates wear of the valve stem. Should any of these conditions be apparent, the valve(s) must be renewed.

11 Fit each valve in turn into the guide from which it was removed, unless the valves are new ones.

12 Check the height of the valve stems above the valve spring seat surface. This distance **must not** exceed 47.63 mm. If necessary, grind the end of the valve stem to reduce the height. However, if this is going to entail too much grinding, new valves or even valve seats may be required.

13 The valves they should be ground (lapped) onto their respective seats to ensure a smooth gas-tight seal.

14 Valve grinding is carried out as follows. Place the cylinder head upside down on a bench, with a block of wood at each end to give clearance for the valve stems.

15 Smear a trace of coarse carborundum paste on the seat face in the cylinder head, and press a suction grinding tool onto the relevant valve head.

16 With a semi-rotary action, grind the valve head to its seat, lifting the valve occasionally to redistribute the grinding paste **(see illustration)**.

A light spring placed under the valve head will greatly ease the grinding-in operation.

17 When a dull, matt, even surface is produced on the faces of both the valve seat and the valve, wipe off the paste, and repeat the process with fine carborundum paste. When a smooth unbroken ring of light grey matt finish is produced on both the valve and seat faces, the grinding operation is complete.

18 Carefully clean away every trace of grinding paste, taking great care to leave none in the ports or in the valve guides. Clean the valves and valve seats with a paraffin-soaked rag, then with a clean rag, and finally, if an air line is available, blow the valves, valve guides and cylinder head ports clean.

Warning: Wear eye protection when using compressed air

19 Repeat the valve inspection and grinding-in operations described in paragraphs 10 to 16 on the other cylinder head.

Valves - diesel engines

20 Examine the head of each valve for pitting, burning, cracks and general wear, and check the valve stem for scoring and wear ridges. Rotate the valve, and check for any obvious indication that it is bent. Look for pitting and excessive wear on the end of each valve stem. If the valve appears satisfactory at this stage, measure the valve stem diameter at several points using a micrometer **(see illustration 9.10)**. Any significant difference in the readings obtained indicates wear of the valve stem. Should any of these conditions be apparent, the valve(s) must be renewed.

21 The valves they should be ground (lapped) onto their respective seats to ensure a smooth gas-tight seal.

22 Valve grinding is carried out as follows. Place the cylinder head upside down on a bench, with a block of wood at each end to give clearance for the valve stems.

23 Smear a trace of coarse carborundum paste on the seat face in the cylinder head, and press a suction grinding tool onto the relevant valve head.

24 With a semi-rotary action, grind the valve head to its seat, lifting the valve occasionally to redistribute the grinding paste **(see illustration 9.16)**.

A light spring placed under the valve head will greatly ease the grinding-in operation.

9.10 Measuring a valve stem diameter

25 When a dull, matt, even surface is produced on the faces of both the valve seat and the valve, wipe off the paste, and repeat the process with fine carborundum paste. When a smooth unbroken ring of light grey matt finish is produced on both the valve and seat faces, the grinding operation is complete.

26 Carefully clean away every trace of grinding paste, taking great care to leave none in the ports or in the valve guides. Clean the valves and valve seats with a paraffin-soaked rag, then with a clean rag, and finally, if an air line is available, blow the valves, valve guides and cylinder head ports clean.

27 After carrying out the valve grinding operation, the valve recess from the face of the cylinder head must be measured as follows.

28 With the cylinder head supported upside-down, as during the valve grinding operation, insert the valve into its relevant guide, and push the valve onto its seat.

29 Place a straight-edge across the surface of the cylinder head, so that the straight-edge passes across the centre of the valve.

30 Using a feeler blade, measure the recess of the valve below the surface of the cylinder head. The recess should be within the specified limits, if not, new valves or even valve seats may be required. Repeat the measurement for all the valves.

Valve springs

31 Check that all the valve springs are intact. If any one is broken, all should be renewed.

32 Stand each spring on a flat surface, and check it for squareness. If possible, check the

9.16 Grinding-in a valve

10.2 Fitting a spring seat

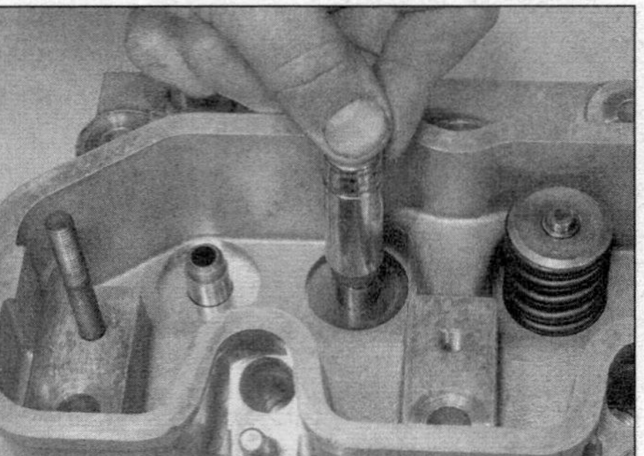
10.3 Fitting a valve stem oil seal using a socket

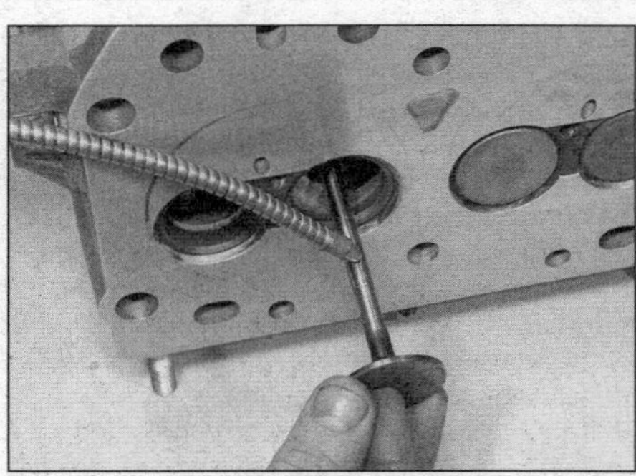
10.4 Fitting a valve

free height of the springs against a new spring. If a spring is found to be too short, or damaged in any way, renew all the springs as a set. Springs suffer from fatigue, and it is a good idea to renew them, even if they look serviceable.

Valve stem oil seals

33 All valve stem oil seals should be renewed as a matter of course.

Valve stem caps

34 Certain engines may be fitted with valve stem caps, which are designed to reduce wear between the rocker arms and the valve stems. Where fitted, the caps should be renewed as a matter of course. Note that, on diesel engines, if no valve stem caps are fitted, it is permissible to fit caps (the caps must be fitted to all the valves as a set, and are available from Land Rover dealers) to compensate for wear in the valve stems and/or the rocker arm pads.

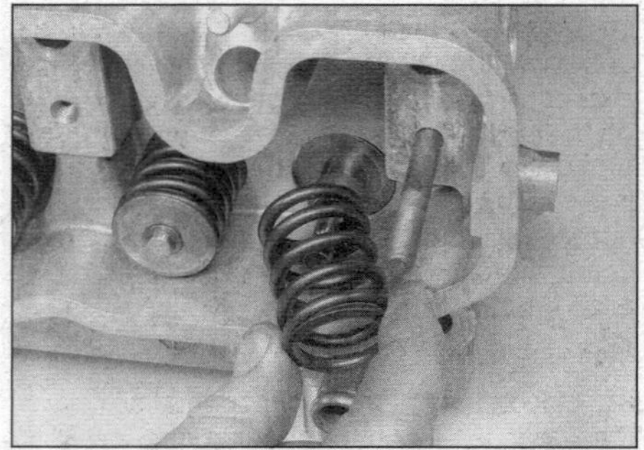
10.5a Fitting a valve spring . . .

10 Cylinder head - reassembly

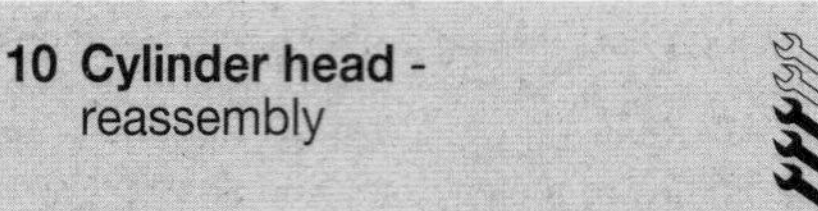

Note: *A valve spring compressor will be required for this operation. New valve stem oil seals and (where applicable) new valve stem caps, should be fitted on reassembly.*

1 With all the components cleaned, starting at one end of the cylinder head, fit the valve components as follows. If the original components are being refitted, all components must be refitted in their original positions.

2 On diesel engines, fit the spring seat to its location in the cylinder head **(see illustration)**.

3 Lubricate the valve stem oil seal with clean engine oil, then fit the oil seal by pushing it into position on the spring seat using a suitable socket **(see illustration)**. Ensure that the seal engages correctly over the valve guide. On petrol engines, seals are fitted to the inlet valves only.

4 Insert the appropriate valve into its guide (if new valves are being fitted, insert each valve into the location to which it has been ground), ensuring that the valve stem is well-lubricated with clean engine oil **(see illustration)**. Take care not to damage the valve stem oil seal as the valve is fitted.

5 Fit the valve spring (either way up) and the spring cap **(see illustrations)**.

6 Fit the spring compressor tool, and compress the valve spring until the spring cap passes beyond the collet groove in the valve stem.

7 Apply a little grease to the collet groove, then fit the split collets into the groove, with the narrow ends nearest the spring **(see illustration)**. The grease should hold them in the groove.

8 Slowly release the compressor tool, ensuring that the collets are not dislodged from the groove. When the compressor is fully released, give the top of the valve assembly a tap with a soft-faced mallet to settle the components **(see illustration)**.

9 Where applicable, fit a new valve stem cap.

10 Repeat the procedure for the remaining valves, ensuring that if the original components are being used, they are all refitted in their original positions.

11 On petrol engines, repeat the procedures to reassemble the remaining cylinder head.

12 Where applicable, refit any brackets, etc, which were removed before dismantling the cylinder head.

11 Piston/connecting rod assembly - removal

Petrol engines

1 Before proceeding, the following components must be removed as described in Chapter 2A:

a) Cylinder heads.
b) Sump.

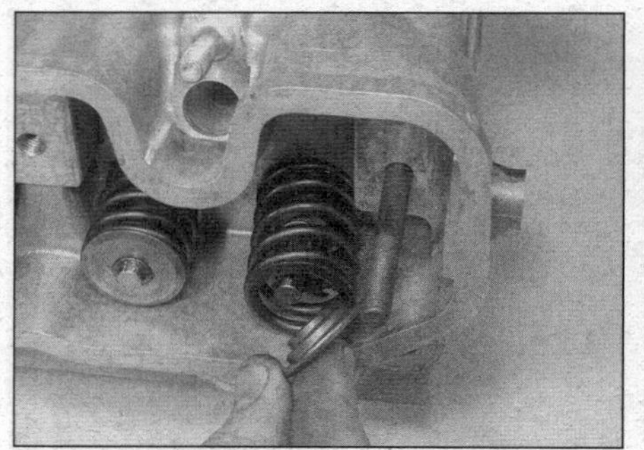
10.5b . . . and a spring cap

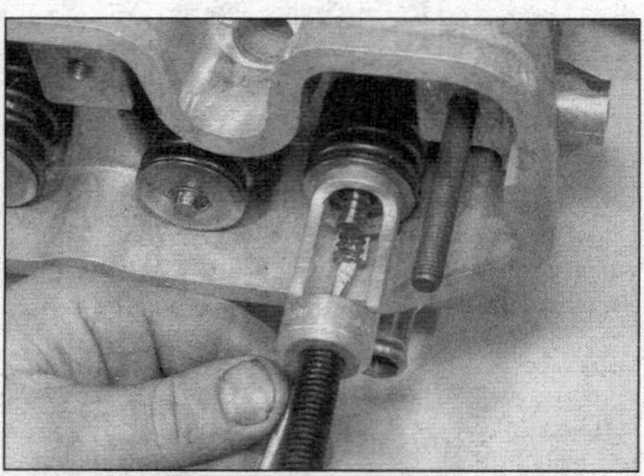
10.7 Fitting a split collet

10.8 Valve components assembled with collets correctly seated

11.2 Removing the oil pick-up pipe and strainer

11.7 Take off the No 1 cylinder connecting rod cap

11.11 Withdrawing the piston and connecting rod assembly - note tubing fitted to bolt threads

2 Unscrew the two bolts securing the oil pick-up pipe and strainer, and remove the assembly, recovering the gasket **(see illustration)**.

3 Note that the cylinders are numbered from front to rear, even numbers on the right-hand bank and odd numbers on the left-hand bank. The big-end caps for the odd numbered assemblies are on the front of the shared crankshaft journals, and the even numbered assemblies fit on the rear of the journals.

4 The big-end caps and con-rods are not marked, so great care must be taken and each connecting rod and cap must be scribed with its appropriate number as it is removed. So that no confusion can arise, make up two boxes big enough to each take four piston and connecting rod assemblies. Mark one box 2-4-6-8 and the other one 1-3-5-7. Place each assembly in order in its correct box as it is removed.

5 If the operation is being carried out with the engine in the vehicle, since it is easy to withdraw the pistons through the tops of both banks of cylinders with the engine upright, the assemblies can be removed from front to rear, starting at No 1 and working through to No 8.

6 With the engine on the workbench it is easier to work down one side, removing the odd or even numbered assemblies first, and then to turn the cylinder block over onto the other side and repeat the operation for the other cylinder bank.

7 Rotate the crankshaft so that the connecting rod cap nuts for No 1 cylinder are easily accessible. Undo and remove the nuts and withdraw the cap **(see illustration)**.

8 Mark the cap with the appropriate cylinder number.

9 Cut two short lengths of plastic tubing and fit them over the connecting rod bolts so that when the assembly is withdrawn, the bolt threads do not damage the journals or cylinder walls.

10 Push the connecting rod and piston assembly up the bore; if necessary, tap the end of the connecting rod bolts with the wooden handle of a hammer.

11 Withdraw the piston and connecting rod through the top of the bore, and remove the protective tubing from the bolts **(see illustration)**. Note that if there is a pronounced wear ridge at the top of the bore, there is a risk of damaging the piston as the rings foul the ridge. However, it is reasonable to assume that a rebore and new pistons will be required in any case if the ridge is so pronounced.

12 Scribe the connecting rod with the cylinder number and then refit the connecting rod cap and nuts to the assembly. Note that the rib on the bearing cap faces in the same direction as the boss on the connecting rod.

13 Place the assembly in the appropriate box in its correct place.

14 Rotate the crankshaft to reach the next pair of connecting rod cap nuts, and repeat the operations already described for all the other piston and connecting rod assemblies.

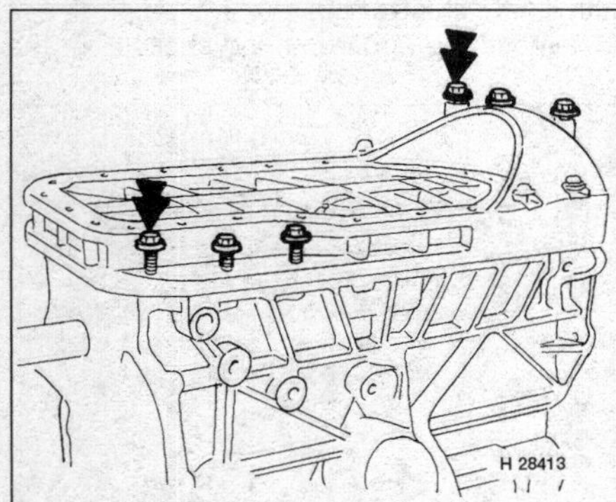
H 28413
11.16 Unscrew the securing bolts (arrowed) and remove the ladder frame - 200 TDi engine

200 TDi engine

15 Before proceeding, the following components must be removed as described in Chapter 2B:

a) *Cylinder head.*
b) *Sump.*
c) *Oil pump.*

16 Unscrew and remove the ten bolts securing the ladder frame to the lower face of the cylinder block **(see illustration)**.

17 Gently tap the ladder frame with a soft-faced mallet to break the seal, then withdraw the ladder frame from the cylinder block.

18 Rotate the crankshaft so that No 1 big-end cap (nearest the timing belt end of the engine) is at the lowest point of its travel. If the big-end cap and connecting rod are not already numbered, mark them with a centre-punch. Mark both cap and rod to identify the cylinder they operate in, noting that No 1 is nearest the timing belt end of the engine (normally, the connecting rods and caps are already numbered, the numbers being read from the camshaft side of the engine).

19 Before removing the big-end cap, use a feeler blade to check the amount of side play between the connecting rod/cap and the crankshaft webs (the limit is given in the *Specifications*).

20 Unscrew and remove the big-end bearing cap nuts. Withdraw the cap, complete with bearing shell, from the connecting rod **(see illustration)**. Strike the cap with a wooden or copper mallet if it is stuck.

HAYNES
HiNT
Tape the bearing shell to the cap if it is to be re-used.

21 If only the bearing shells are being attended to, push the connecting rod up and off the crankpin, and remove the upper bearing shell. Tape the bearing shell to the rod if it is to be re-used.

22 If desired, push the connecting rod up, and remove the piston and rod assembly from the bore. Note that if there is a pronounced wear ridge at the top of the bore, there is a risk of damaging the piston as the rings foul the ridge. However, it is reasonable to assume that a rebore and new pistons will be required in any case if the ridge is so pronounced.

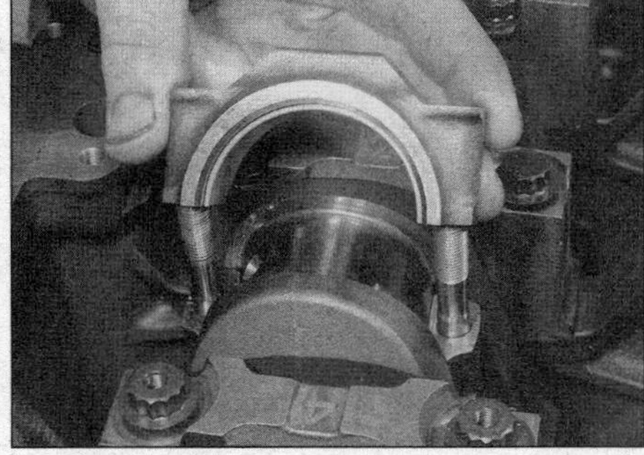
11.20 Removing a big-end bearing cap

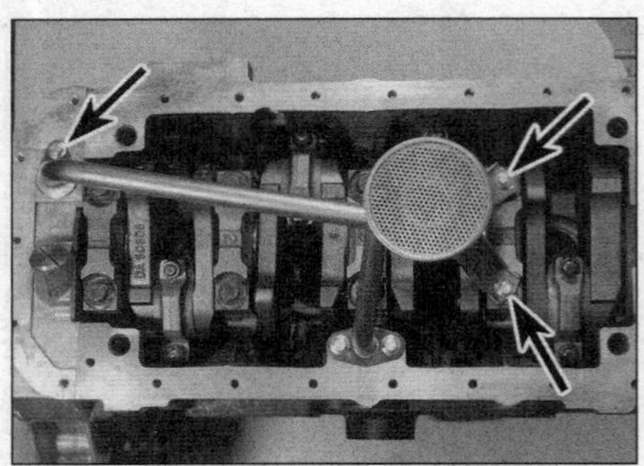
11.26 Oil strainer securing bolts (arrowed) - 300 TDi engine

11.27 Removing the oil return pipe - 300 TDi engine

12.3 Checking the crankshaft endfloat at the centre bearing

12.5 Removing the centre main bearing cap with its flanged bearing shell

23 Repeat the procedure for the remaining piston/connecting rod assemblies. Ensure that the caps and rods are marked before removal, as described previously, and keep all components in order.

300 TDi engine

24 Before proceeding, the following components must be removed as described in Chapter 2B:

a) *Cylinder head.*
b) *Sump.*

25 Unscrew the two bolts securing the oil strainer support bracket to the main bearing cap.

26 Unscrew the bolt securing the oil pick-up pipe to the timing belt housing, then withdraw the strainer **(see illustration)**. Recover the O-ring from the pick-up pipe.

27 Unscrew the two bolts securing the oil return pipe to the cylinder block **(see illustration)**. Recover the gasket.

28 Proceed as described in paragraphs 18 to 23 inclusive.

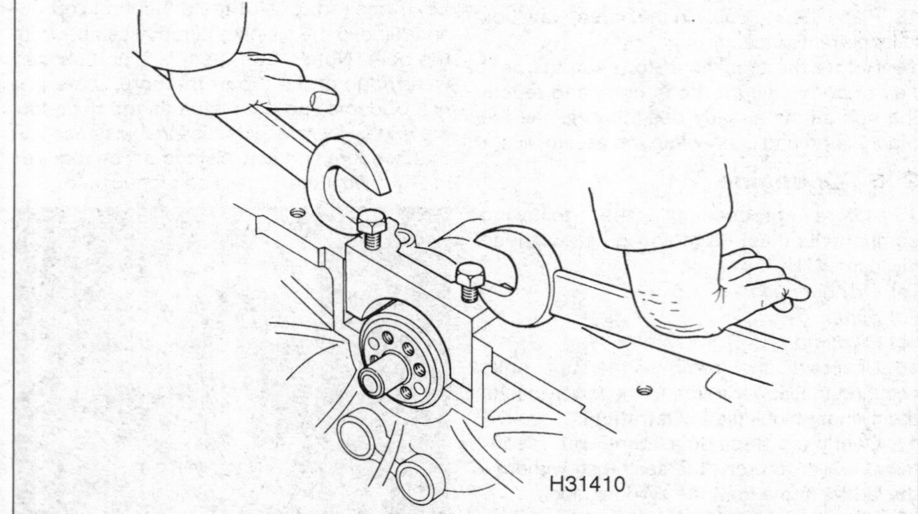
H31410
12.6 Using a pair of large spanners to prise up the rear main bearing cap

12 Crankshaft - removal

Petrol engines

1 Before proceeding, the following components must be removed:

a) *Timing chain and cover (Chapter 2A).*
b) *Flywheel (Chapter 2A).*
c) *Piston/connecting rod assemblies (Section 11).*

2 Before the crankshaft is removed, check the endfloat using a dial gauge in contact with the end of the crankshaft. Push the crankshaft fully one way, and then zero the gauge. Push the crankshaft fully the other way, and check the endfloat. If the result is out of specification, this will be due to wear in the flanges on the centre (No 3) bearing shell (diesel engines have thrustwashers in the same location). Endfloat is corrected by fitting flanged shells (or thrustwashers) of the correct size.

3 If a dial gauge is not available, feeler blades can be used. First push the crankshaft fully towards the flywheel end of the engine, then slip the feeler blade between the web of No 2 crankpin and the thrustwasher of No 3 main bearing (located in the crankcase) **(see illustration).**

4 Undo the main bearing cap retaining bolts.

5 Remove the first four bearing caps and bolts, together with the lower bearing shells **(see illustration)**. Note that the first four caps are numbered from the front 1-2-3-4. The rear one, which is larger and easily identified, is not marked. The caps also have arrows on them which point to the front of the engine.

6 The rear cap will have to be eased out, as it also forms part of the rear oil seal construction. Remove the bolts securing the rear main bearing cap, then screw two of the sump retaining bolts into the holes at the front of the cap. Using pliers or a pair of large spanners on the bolt heads, carefully pull or prise the cap from its location, taking care not to damage any sealing surfaces **(see illustration).**

7 Hold the crankshaft at both ends, and lift it out carefully; the rear oil seal will come out with it **(see illustration).**

8 Remove the upper bearing shells from the

12.7 Lifting out the crankshaft

12.11 Removing the flywheel housing - 300 TDi engine

12.13 Checking the crankshaft endfloat using a dial gauge

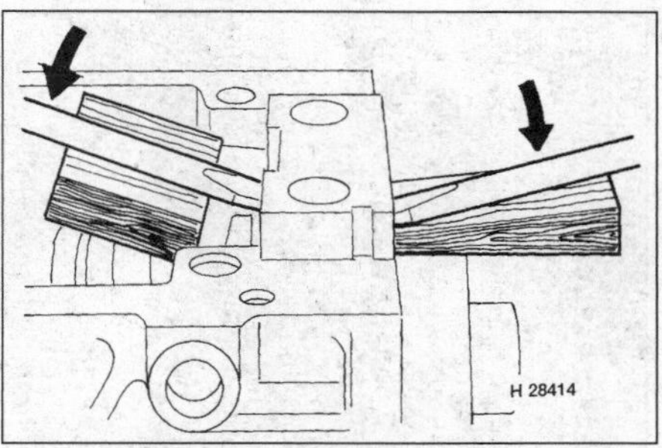
H 28414
12.16 Using two screwdrivers to lever No 5 main bearing cap from its location. Note location of blocks of wood

bearing seats. Note that the centre bearing (No 3) has a flanged shell, as this bearing takes the endthrust of the crankshaft. Identify the shells if they are to be re-used.

9 Remove the lower bearing shells from the bearing caps only if they are to be renewed.

Diesel engines

10 Before proceeding, the following components must be removed:

a) Timing belt housing (Chapter 2B, Section 16).
b) Flywheel (Chapter 2B).
c) Piston/connecting rod assemblies (Section 11).

11 Working at the rear of the cylinder block, unscrew the securing bolts, and remove the flywheel housing **(see illustration)**. Note the locations of any brackets secured by the external housing bolts. Where applicable, recover the gasket.

12 On 300 TDi engines, unscrew the securing bolts, and remove the crankshaft rear oil seal housing from the rear of the cylinder block. Discard the housing, and recover the gasket (and the sealing ring, if it is loose).

13 Before the crankshaft is removed, check the endfloat as described in paragraphs 2 and 3 **(see illustration)**. The result can be compared with the specified amount, and will give an indication as to whether new thrustwashers are required.

14 Check the main bearing caps for identification marks, and if none are present, number them so that the numbers can be read from the timing belt end of the engine, using a centre-punch, as was done for the connecting rods and caps. Again note that No 1 cylinder is at the timing belt end of the engine.

15 Unscrew and remove the main bearing cap securing bolts.

16 Withdraw the caps, complete with bearing shells. Tap the caps with a wooden or copper mallet if they are stuck (the caps locate on dowels). Note that the sides of No 5 bearing cap are sealed to the cylinder block using plastic seals on each side, which may cause difficulty in removing the cap. If necessary, the cap can be levered from its location using a suitable bar inserted in the hole in the inside face of the cap - place a suitable piece of wood on the crankshaft web, and lever against the wood **(see illustration)**.

17 Carefully lift the crankshaft from the crankcase.

18 Remove the thrustwashers at each side of No 3 main bearing, then remove the bearing shell upper halves from the crankcase **(see illustration)**. Place each shell with its respective bearing cap.

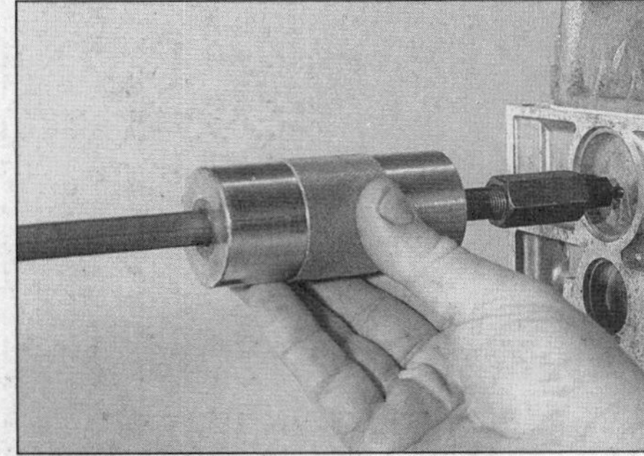
13.1 Using a slide hammer to remove a core plug

13 Cylinder block/crankcase - cleaning and inspection

Cleaning

1 For complete cleaning, the core plugs should be removed. Drill a small hole in them, then insert a self-tapping screw and pull out the plugs using a pair of grips or a slide-hammer **(see illustration)**. Also remove all external components, brackets and senders (if not already done), noting their locations.

2 On diesel engines, remove the securing bolts, and withdraw the piston oil spray jets from the bottom of the cylinder block **(see illustration)**. Where applicable, recover the sealing washers.

3 Remove all oil gallery plugs, and where applicable, recover the sealing washers. Note that the plugs may be fitted using sealant.

4 Scrape all traces of gasket and sealant from the cylinder block, taking care not to damage the head and sump (or ladder frame on 200 TDi engines) mating faces.

5 Where applicable, also remove all traces of sealant from the mating faces of the cylinder block and the flywheel housing.

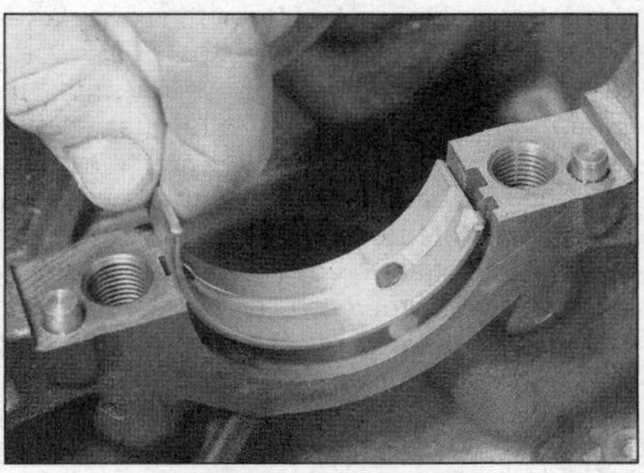
12.18 Removing a main bearing shell upper half from the crankcase (engine inverted)

6 If the block is extremely dirty, it should be steam-cleaned.

7 After the block has been steam-cleaned, clean all oil holes and oil galleries one more time. Flush all internal passages with warm water until the water runs clear, then dry the block thoroughly and wipe all machined surfaces with a light rust-preventative oil. If you have access to compressed air, use it to speed up the drying process, and to blow out all the oil holes and galleries.

Warning: Wear eye protection when using compressed air.

8 If the block is not very dirty, you can do an adequate cleaning job with hot soapy water and a stiff brush. Take plenty of time, and do a thorough job. Regardless of the cleaning method used, be sure to clean all oil holes and galleries very thoroughly, dry the block

13.2 Removing a piston oil spray jet - 300 TDi engine

13.9 Using a tap to clean a cylinder block bolt thread

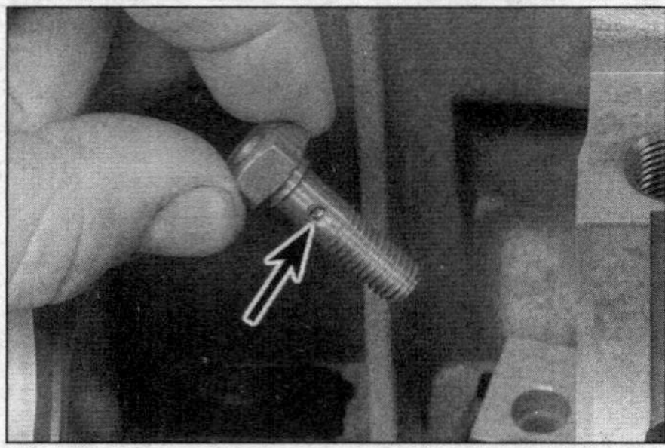

13.12 Check the oil holes (arrowed) in the piston oil jet securing bolts for blockage - 300 TDi engine

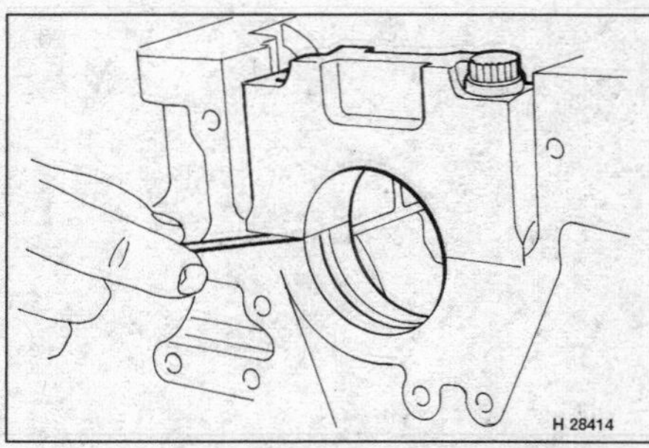
H 28414

13.26 Checking the clearance between the mating face of a main bearing cap and the cylinder block

completely, and coat all machined surfaces with light oil.

9 The threaded holes in the block must be clean, to ensure accurate torque wrench readings during reassembly. Run the proper-size tap into each of the holes to remove rust, corrosion, thread sealant or sludge, and to restore damaged threads **(see illustration)**. If possible, use compressed air to clear the holes of debris produced by this operation, noting the warning given in paragraph 7. Now is a good time to clean the threads on the head bolts and the main bearing cap bolts as well.

10 After coating the mating surfaces of the new core plugs with suitable sealant, refit them in the cylinder block. Make sure that they are driven in straight and seated properly, or leakage could result. Special tools are available for this purpose, but a large socket, with an outside diameter that will just slip into the core plug, will work just as well.

11 Refit the oil gallery plugs, using new sealing washers or sealant where applicable.

12 On diesel engines, check the oil holes in the piston oil spray jet securing bolts, and the oil holes in the jets themselves for blockage **(see illustration)**. Clean if necessary, then refit the jets and tighten the securing bolts. Ensure that the locating pegs on the jets engage with the corresponding holes in the cylinder block. Where applicable, ensure that the larger-diameter sealing washer fits under the bolt head.

13 If the engine is not going to be reassembled right away, cover it with a large plastic bag, to keep it clean and prevent it rusting.

14 On 200 TDi engines, thoroughly clean both the cylinder block and sump mating faces of the ladder frame, and remove all traces of old sealant.

Inspection

15 Visually check the block for cracks, rust and corrosion. Look for stripped threads in the threaded holes. If there has been any history of internal water leakage, it may be worthwhile having an engine overhaul specialist check the block with special equipment. If defects are found, have the block repaired, if possible, or renewed.

16 Check the cylinder bores for scuffing and scoring. Normally, bore wear will be evident in the form of a wear ridge at the top of the bore. This ridge marks the limit of piston travel.

17 Measure the diameter of each cylinder at the top (just under the ridge area), centre and bottom of the cylinder bore, parallel to the crankshaft axis.

18 Next measure each cylinder's diameter at the same three locations across the crankshaft axis. If the measurements taken indicate excessive cylinder bore taper or ovality (see *Specifications*), then remedial action must be considered.

19 Repeat this procedure for the remaining cylinders.

20 If the cylinder walls are badly scuffed or scored, or if they are excessively out-of-round or tapered, have the cylinder block rebored. New pistons (oversize in the case of a rebore) will also be required.

21 If the cylinders are in reasonably good condition, then it may only be necessary to renew the piston rings.

22 If this is the case, the bores should be honed, in order to allow the new rings to bed-in correctly and provide the best possible seal. The conventional type of hone has spring-loaded stones, and is used with a power drill. You will also need some paraffin or honing oil and rags.

23 The hone should be moved up and down the cylinder to produce a crosshatch pattern, and plenty of honing oil should be used. Ideally, the crosshatch lines should intersect at approximately a 60° angle. Do not take off more material than is necessary to produce the required finish.

24 If new pistons are being fitted, the piston manufacturers may specify a finish with a different angle, so their instructions should be followed. Do not withdraw the hone from the cylinder while it is still being turned - stop it first. After honing a cylinder, wipe out all traces of the honing oil.

25 If equipment of this type is not available, or if you are not sure whether you are competent to undertake the task yourself, an engine overhaul specialist will carry out the work at a moderate cost.

26 Refit the main bearing caps, without the bearing shells, and tighten the old bolts to the specified torque. Loosen and remove the bolt on one side of each bearing cap, and check, using a feeler blade, that no clearance exists between the mating faces of the bearing cap and the cylinder block **(see illustration)**. If a clearance exists, this indicates one of the following problems:

a) One of the bearing cap bolts is bent.
b) The bearing cap is distorted.
c) The block and/or the bearing cap has been filed or machined in a misguided attempt to compensate for bearing wear.

27 Main bearing caps are not available separately from the cylinder block, and if a clearance exists between the cap and the block, the block must be renewed.

28 Where applicable, refit all external components and senders in their correct locations, as noted before removal.

29 On 200 TDi engines, check that the ladder frame is not distorted, and is free from burrs and damage to the mating faces, which may cause oil or gas leaks. Renew the ladder frame if it is damaged.

14 Piston/connecting rod assembly - inspection

1 Before the inspection process can begin, the piston/connecting rod assemblies must be cleaned, and the original piston rings removed from the pistons.

2 Carefully expand the old rings over the top of the pistons. The use of two or three old feeler blades will be helpful in preventing the rings dropping into empty grooves **(see illustration)**. Note that the oil control ring has two sections.

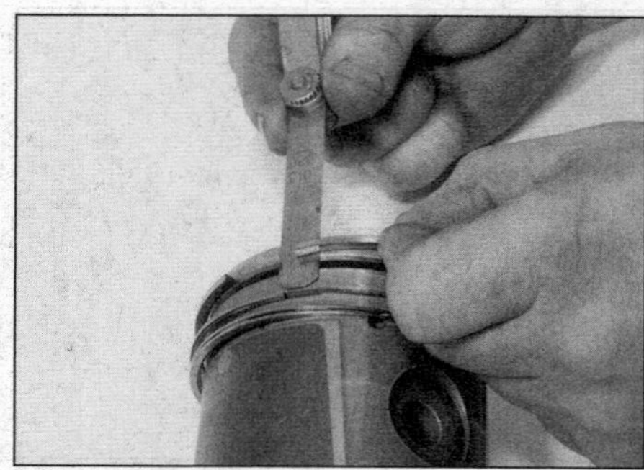

14.2 Using a feeler blade to aid removal of a piston ring

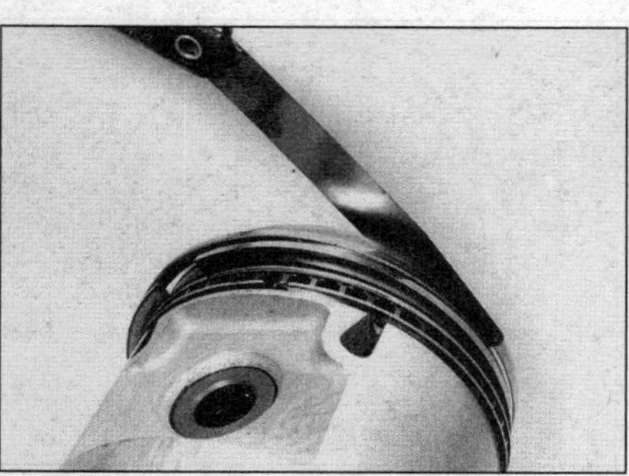
14.10 Checking the piston ring-to-groove clearance

14.13a Prise out the circlip . . .

14.13b . . . and push out the gudgeon pin

3 Scrape away all traces of carbon from the top of the piston. A hand-held wire brush or a piece of fine emery cloth can be used once the majority of the deposits have been scraped away.

4 Remove the carbon from the ring grooves in the piston by cleaning them using an old ring. Break the ring in half to do this. Be very careful to remove only the carbon deposits; do not remove any metal, nor nick or scratch the sides of the ring grooves. Protect your fingers - piston rings are sharp.

5 Once the deposits have been removed, clean the piston/connecting rod assembly with paraffin or a suitable solvent, and dry thoroughly. Make sure that the oil return holes in the back sides of the ring grooves are clear.

6 If the pistons and cylinder bores are not damaged or worn excessively, and if the cylinder block does not need to be rebored, the original pistons can be re-used. Normal piston wear appears as even vertical wear on the piston thrust surfaces, and slight looseness of the top ring in its groove. New piston rings, however, should always be used when the engine is reassembled.

7 Carefully inspect each piston for cracks around the skirt, at the gudgeon pin bosses, and at the piston ring lands (between the piston ring grooves).

8 Look for scoring and scuffing on the sides of the skirt, holes in the piston crown, and burned areas at the edge of the crown. If the skirt is scored or scuffed, the engine may have been suffering from overheating and/or abnormal combustion, which caused excessively-high operating temperatures. The cooling and lubricating systems should be checked thoroughly. Scorch marks on the sides of the pistons show that blow-by has occurred. A hole in the piston crown, or burned areas at the edge of the piston crown indicates that abnormal combustion (pre-ignition, knocking, or detonation) has been occurring. If any of the above problems exist, the causes must be investigated and corrected, or the damage will occur again. The causes may include incorrect injection pump or ignition timing, or a fuel system fault.

9 Corrosion of the piston, in the form of small pits, indicates that coolant is leaking into the combustion chamber and/or the crankcase. Again, the cause must be corrected, or the problem may persist in the rebuilt engine.

10 If new rings are being fitted to old pistons, measure the piston ring-to-groove clearance by placing a new piston ring in each ring groove and measuring the clearance with a feeler blade **(see illustration)**. Check the clearance at three or four places around each groove. If the measured clearance is outside the specified limits, new pistons will be required. If the new ring is excessively tight, the most likely cause is dirt remaining in the groove.

11 Check the piston-to-bore clearance by measuring the cylinder bore (see Section 12) and the piston diameter. Measure the piston across the skirt, at a 90° angle to the gudgeon pin, approximately halfway down the skirt. Subtract the piston diameter from the bore diameter to obtain the clearance. If this is greater than the figures given in the Specifications, the block will have to be rebored, and new pistons and rings fitted.

12 Check the fit of the gudgeon pin by twisting the piston and connecting rod in opposite directions. Any noticeable play indicates excessive wear, which must be corrected.

13 On diesel engines, separate a piston from its connecting rod, prise out the circlips and push out the gudgeon pin **(see illustrations)**. Hand pressure is sufficient to remove the pin. Identify the piston and rod to ensure correct reassembly.

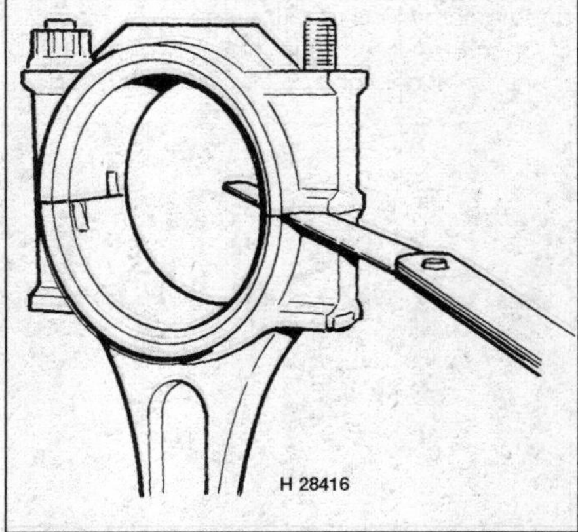
H 28416
14.16 Checking for a clearance between a big-end bearing cap and connecting rod

14 The gudgeon pins on petrol engines cannot be removed without access to a hydraulic press.

15 The connecting rods themselves should not need renewal, unless seizure or some other major mechanical failure has occurred. Check the alignment of the connecting rods visually, and if the rods are not straight, take them to an engine overhaul specialist for a more detailed check.

16 Fit the appropriate bearing cap to each of the connecting rods, then refit the securing nuts, and tighten them to the specified torque. Loosen and remove the nut on one side of the bearing cap, and check, using a feeler blade, that no clearance exists between the mating faces of the bearing cap and the connecting rod **(see illustration)**. If clearance is evident, this suggests that the connecting rod is distorted, or the mating faces of the big-end caps and connecting rods have been machined or filed, in a mistaken attempt to take up bearing wear. If there is any clearance, then the connecting rod and the bearing cap must be renewed.

17 Where applicable, reassemble the pistons and rods. Make sure that the pistons are fitted the right way round:

*a) On diesel engines, the arrow on the piston crown should point towards the timing belt end of the engine, and the bearing shell locating cut-outs in the connecting rod and bearing cap should be positioned on the camshaft side of the cylinder block **(see illustrations)**. Oil the gudgeon pins before fitting them. When*

14.17a The arrow on the piston crown should point towards the timing belt end of the engine . . .

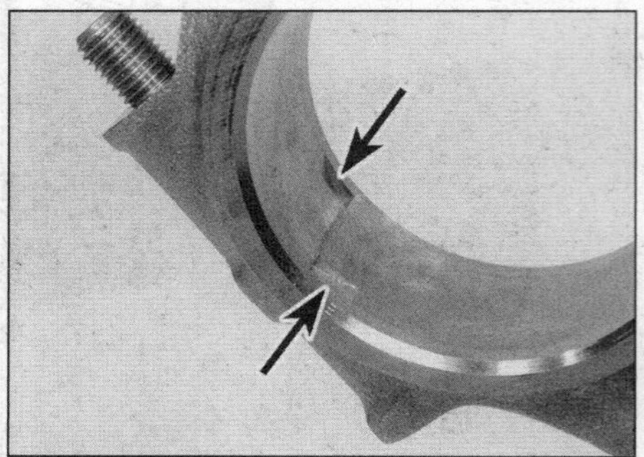

14.17b . . . and the bearing shell locating cut-outs (arrowed) should be on the camshaft side of the cylinder block

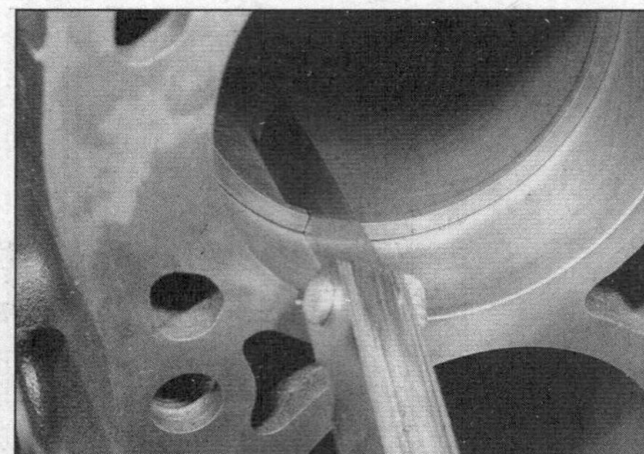

14.18 Measuring a piston ring end gap

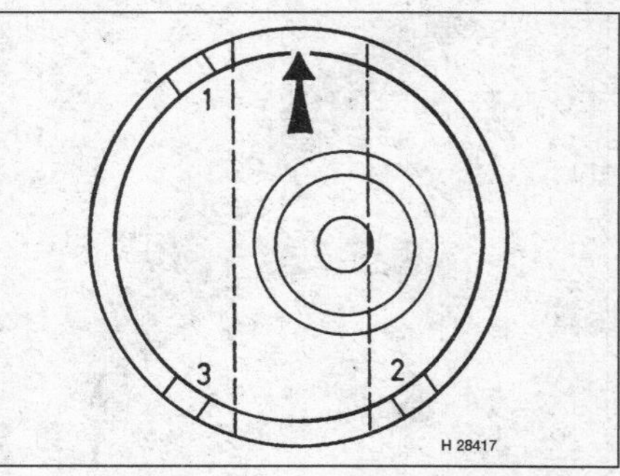
1
2
3
H 28417

14.25 Piston ring end gap positions (viewed from top of piston)

1 Top compression ring gap
2 Lower compression ring gap
3 Oil control ring gap

assembled, the piston should pivot freely on the rod.

b) On petrol engines, the domed boss on the connecting rod must face forwards for the right-hand bank of cylinders (2-4-6-8) and rearwards for the left bank (1-3-5-7). When the assemblies are refitted, the domed bosses should face each other on the crankshaft journals.

18 Before refitting the rings to the pistons, check their end gaps by inserting each of them in their cylinder bores. Use the piston to make sure that they are square. Check that the gaps are within the specified limits **(see illustration)**. Land Rover rings are supplied pre-gapped; no attempt should be made to adjust the gaps by filing.

19 Once the ring end gaps have been checked, the rings can be fitted to the pistons.

20 Fit the piston rings using the same technique as for removal. Fit the bottom (oil control) ring first, and work up. **Note:** *Always follow the instructions supplied with the new piston ring sets - different manufacturers may specify different procedures. Do not mix up the top and middle rings, as they have different cross-sections.*

Petrol engines

21 When fitting the oil control ring, first insert the expander so that the ends do not overlap but just abut each other. Fit the rails, one at a time, making sure that they locate snugly within the piston groove.

22 Where applicable, ensure that the TOP marking on the face of the piston ring faces the piston crown.

23 Fit the compression rings so that the gap in each ring is diametrically opposite, and the oil control ring so that its gap appears on the same side between gudgeon pin and the piston thrust face but staggered. Locate the rail ring gaps approximately 25 mm either side of the expander join.

Diesel engines

24 When fitting the oil control ring, first insert the expander, then fit the ring.

25 Where applicable, ensure that the TOP marking on the face of the piston ring faces the piston crown. Position the oil control ring gap to the manifold side of the piston (the left-hand side, when viewed with the arrow on the piston crown pointing forwards). Arrange the gaps of the middle and upper rings 90° either side of the oil control ring gap, but make sure that no gap is positioned on the thrust side of the piston **(see illustration)**.

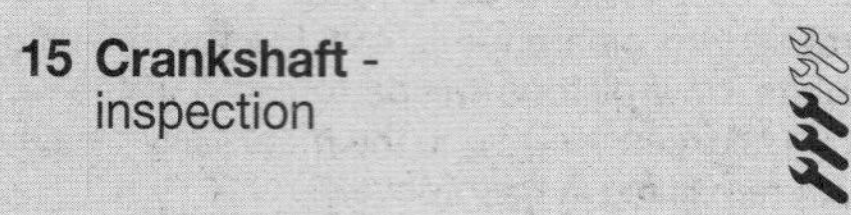

15 Crankshaft - inspection

Note: *A micrometer will be required for this operation.*

1 Clean the crankshaft using paraffin or a suitable solvent, and dry it, preferably with compressed air if available. Be sure to clean the oil holes with a pipe cleaner or similar probe, to ensure that they are not obstructed.

Warning: Wear eye protection when using compressed air.

2 Check the main and big-end bearing journals for uneven wear, scoring, pitting and cracking.

3 Big-end bearing wear is accompanied by distinct metallic knocking when the engine is running, particularly noticeable when the engine is pulling from low revs, and some loss of oil pressure.

4 Main bearing wear is accompanied by severe engine vibration and rumble - getting progressively worse as engine revs increase - and again by loss of oil pressure.

5 Check the bearing journal for roughness by running a finger lightly over the bearing surface.

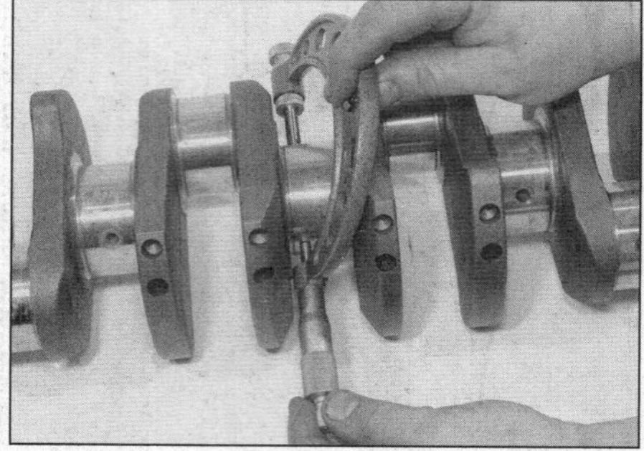

15.7 Measuring a crankshaft main bearing journal

Any roughness (which will be accompanied by obvious bearing wear) indicates the that the crankshaft requires regrinding.

6 If the crankshaft has been reground, check for burrs around the crankshaft oil holes (the holes are usually chamfered, so burrs should not be a problem, unless regrinding has been carried out carelessly). Remove any burrs with a fine file or scraper, and thoroughly clean the oil holes as described previously.

7 Using a micrometer, measure the diameter of the main and big-end bearing journals, and compare the results with the Specifications **(see illustration)**. By measuring the diameter at a number of points around each journal's circumference, you will be able to determine whether or not the journal is out-of-round. Take the measurement at each end of the journal, near the webs, to determine if the journal is tapered. If the crankshaft journals are damaged, tapered, out-of-round or worn beyond the limits given in the Specifications, the crankshaft will have to be reground, and undersize bearings fitted.

8 Check the oil seal contact surfaces at each end of the crankshaft for wear and damage. If the seal has worn an excessive groove in the surface of the crankshaft, consult an engine overhaul specialist, who will be able to advise whether a repair is possible or whether a new crankshaft is necessary.

16 Main and big-end bearings - inspection

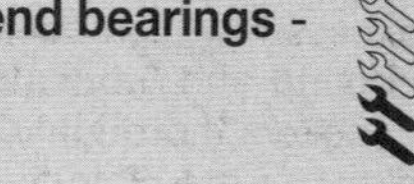

1 Even though the main and big-end bearings should be renewed during engine overhaul, the old bearings should be retained for close examination, as they may reveal valuable information about the condition of the engine. The bearing shells carry identification marks to denote their size, in the form of a code marked on the back of the shell. If the shells are to be renewed, without carrying out any crankshaft regrinding, the old shells should be taken along when obtaining new shells, to ensure that the correct shells are obtained.

2 Bearing failure occurs because of lack of lubrication, the presence of dirt or other foreign particles, overloading the engine, or corrosion **(see illustration)**. If a bearing fails, the cause must be found and eliminated before the engine is reassembled, to prevent the failure from happening again.

3 To examine the bearing shells, remove them from the cylinder block, the main bearing caps, the connecting rods and the big-end bearing caps, and lay them out on a clean surface, in the same order as they were fitted to the engine. This will enable any bearing problems to be matched with the corresponding crankshaft journal.

4 Dirt and other foreign particles can enter the engine in a variety of ways. Contamination may be left in the engine during assembly, or it may pass through filters or the crankcase ventilation system. Normal engine wear produces small particles of metal, which can eventually cause problems. If particles find their way into the lubrication system, it is likely that they will eventually be carried to the bearings. Whatever the source, these foreign particles often end up embedded in the soft bearing material, and are easily recognised. Large particles will not embed in the bearing, and will score or gouge the bearing and journal. To prevent possible contamination, clean all parts thoroughly, and keep everything spotlessly-clean during engine assembly. Once the engine has been installed in the vehicle, ensure that regular engine oil and filter changes are carried out at the recommended intervals.

5 Lack of lubrication (or lubrication breakdown) has a number of interrelated causes. Excessive heat (which thins the oil), overloading (which squeezes the oil from the bearing face) and oil leakage (from excessive bearing clearances, worn oil pump or high engine speeds) all contribute to lubrication breakdown. Blocked oil passages, which may be the result of misaligned oil holes in a bearing shell, will also starve a bearing of oil, and destroy it. When lack of lubrication is the cause of bearing failure, the bearing material is wiped or extruded from the steel backing of the bearing. Temperatures may increase to the point where the steel backing turns blue from overheating.

6 Driving habits can have a definite effect on bearing life. Full-throttle, low-speed operation (labouring the engine) puts very high loads on bearings, which tends to squeeze out the oil film. These loads cause the bearings to flex, which produces fine cracks in the bearing face (fatigue failure). Eventually the bearing material will loosen in pieces, and tear away from the steel backing. Regular short journeys can lead to corrosion of bearings, because insufficient engine heat is produced to drive off the condensed water and corrosive gases which form inside the engine. These products collect in the engine oil, forming acid and sludge. As the oil is carried to the bearings, the acid attacks and corrodes the bearing material.

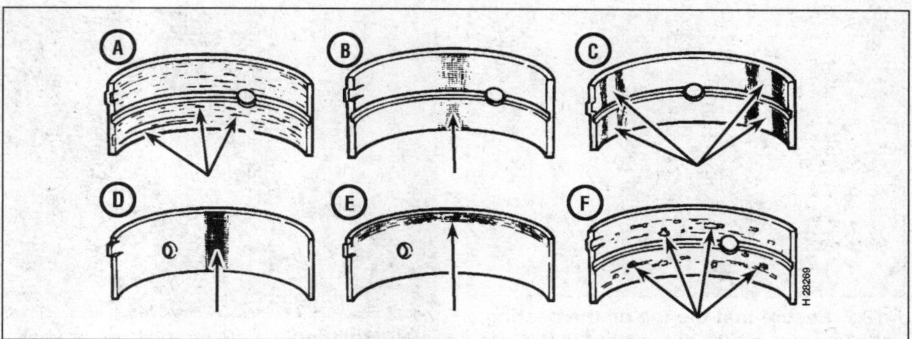
A
B
C
D
E
F
H 28269

16.2 Typical bearing failures

A Scratched by dirt; dirt embedded into bearing material
B Lack of oil; overlay wiped out
C Improper seating; bright (polished) sections
D Tapered journal; overlay gone from entire surface
E Radius ride
F Fatigue failure; craters or pockets

7 Incorrect bearing installation during engine assembly will also lead to bearing failure. Tight-fitting bearings leave insufficient bearing lubrication clearance, and will result in oil starvation. Dirt or foreign particles trapped behind a bearing shell results in high spots on the bearing, which can lead to failure.

8 If new bearings are to be fitted, the bearing running clearances should be measured before the engine is finally reassembled, to ensure that the correct bearing shells have been obtained (see Sections 18 and 19). If the crankshaft has been reground, the engineering works which carried out the work will advise on the correct-size bearing shells to suit the work carried out. If there is any doubt as to which bearing shells should be used, seek advice from a Land Rover dealer.

17 Engine overhaul - reassembly sequence

Before reassembly begins, ensure that all new parts have been obtained, and that the tools are available. Read through the entire procedure, to familiarise yourself with the work involved, and to ensure that all items necessary for reassembly are at hand. In addition to all normal tools and materials, some thread-locking compound will be needed. Note also that certain nuts and bolts must be renewed when reassembling the engine.

To save time and avoid problems, reassembly can be carried out in the following order:

Petrol engines

a) Crankshaft.
b) Pistons/connecting rod assemblies.
c) Sump.
d) Flywheel/driveplate.
e) Camshaft.
f) Timing cover and chain.
g) Cylinder heads.
h) Engine external components (use appropriate new gaskets and seals where necessary).

Diesel engines

a) Crankshaft.
b) Pistons/connecting rod assemblies.
c) Ladder frame (200 TDi engine only).
d) Flywheel housing and flywheel/driveplate.
e) Oil pump.
f) Timing belt housing.
g) Camshaft.
h) Timing belt.
i) Sump.
j) Cylinder head(s).
k) Engine external components (use appropriate new gaskets and seals where necessary).

18 Crankshaft - refitting and main bearing running clearance check

Note: *Suitable seals will be required when refitting No 5 main bearing cap - see text. A new gasket or suitable sealant will be required when refitting the flywheel housing - see text. New main bearing cap bolts, and new crankshaft oil seals, must also be used on refitting.*

Main bearing running clearance check

Note: *Suitable measuring equipment will be required for this check - see text.*

1 Clean the backs of the bearing shells, and the bearing recesses in both the cylinder block and main bearing caps. If new shells are being fitted, ensure that all traces of the protective grease are cleaned off using paraffin.

2 Press the bearing shells without oil holes into the caps, ensuring that the tag on the shell engages in the cut-out in the cap **(see illustration)**. Note that No 5 bearing shells are wider than the remaining bearing shells.

3 Press the bearing shells with the oil holes/grooves into the recesses in the

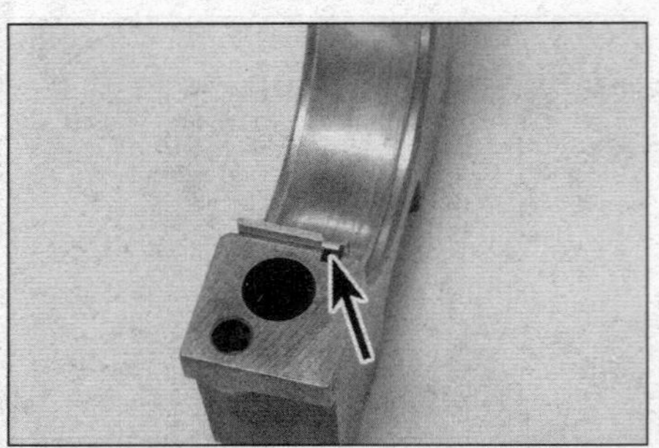
18.2 Ensure that the tag on the bearing shell engages with the cut-out in the cap (arrowed)

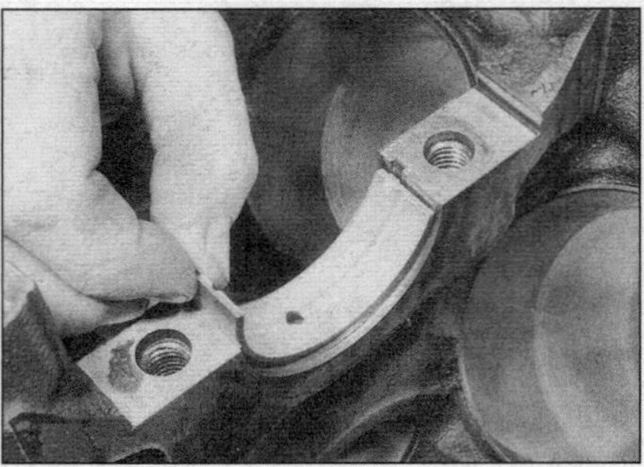
18.5 Refitting a main bearing upper shell - note oil groove

18.6 Plastigauge in place on crankshaft main bearing journal

cylinder block. Note that if the original main bearing shells are being re-used, these must be refitted to their original locations in the block and caps.

4 Before the crankshaft can be permanently installed, the main bearing running clearance should be checked; this can be done in either of two ways:

a) *One method is to fit the main bearing caps to the cylinder block, with the bearing shells in place. With the original cap retaining bolts tightened to the specified torque, measure the internal diameter of each assembled pair of bearing shells using a vernier dial indicator or internal micrometer. If the diameter of each corresponding crankshaft journal is measured, and then subtracted from the bearing internal diameter, the result will be the main bearing running clearance.*

b) *The second (and more accurate) method is to use an American product known as Plastigauge. This consists of a fine thread of perfectly-round plastic, which is compressed between the bearing cap and the journal. When the cap is removed, the deformation of the plastic thread is measured with a special card gauge supplied with the kit. The running clearance is determined from this gauge. Plastigauge is sometimes difficult to obtain in the UK, but enquiries at one of the larger specialist chains of quality motor factors should produce the name of a stockist in your area. The procedure for using Plastigauge is as follows.*

5 With the upper main bearing shells in place (the upper shells have oil grooves), carefully lay the crankshaft in position **(see illustration)**. Do not use any lubricant; the crankshaft journals and bearing shells must be perfectly clean and dry.

6 Cut several pieces of the appropriate-size Plastigauge (they should be slightly shorter than the width of the main bearings), and place one piece on each crankshaft journal axis **(see illustration)**.

7 With the bearing shells in position in the caps (the shells have no oil grooves), fit the caps to their numbered or previously-noted locations. Take care not to disturb the Plastigauge.

8 Starting with the centre main bearing and working outward, tighten the original main bearing cap bolts progressively to their specified torque setting. Don't rotate the crankshaft at any time during this operation.

9 Remove the bolts and carefully lift off the main bearing caps, keeping them in order. Don't disturb the Plastigauge or rotate the crankshaft. If any of the bearing caps are difficult to remove, tap them from side-to-side with a soft-faced mallet.

10 Compare the width of the crushed Plastigauge on each journal to the scale printed on the Plastigauge envelope, to obtain the main bearing running clearance **(see illustration)**.

11 If the clearance is not as specified, the bearing shells may be the wrong size (or excessively-worn, if the original shells are being re-used). Before deciding that different-size shells are needed, make sure that no dirt or oil was trapped between the bearing shells and the caps or block when the clearance was measured.

12 If the Plastigauge was wider at one end than at the other, the journal may be tapered.

13 Carefully scrape away all traces of the Plastigauge material from the crankshaft and bearing shells, using a fingernail or something similar which is unlikely to score the shells.

Final refitting - petrol engines

14 Carefully lift the crankshaft out of the cylinder block once more.

15 Liberally lubricate each bearing shell in the cylinder block, and lower the crankshaft into position **(see illustration)**.

16 Lubricate the bearing shells, then fit Nos 1 to 4 bearing caps in their numbered or previously-noted locations. Fit the new main bearing cap bolts, but tighten them only hand-tight at this stage. Check the crankshaft endfloat as described in Section 12.

17 Thoroughly clean the No 5 bearing cap and the oil seal area of the engine block, removing all traces of oil and sealant. Also check for burrs or sharp edges which may damage the new seals on fitting.

18 When refitting the No 5 (rear) bearing cap, refer to the crankshaft rear oil seal renewal procedure (Chapter 2A, Section 9).

19 Progressively tighten the bearing cap bolts to the specified torque, working outwards from the centre (No 3) bearing cap **(see illustration)**. Note that the No 5 bearing cap bolts are tightened to a greater torque than those for Nos 1 to 4, and requires a special lubricant (see *Specifications*).

18.10 Measuring the width of the deformed Plastigauge using the card gauge

18.15 Lubricate the main bearing shells generously

18.19 Tightening the main bearing cap bolts

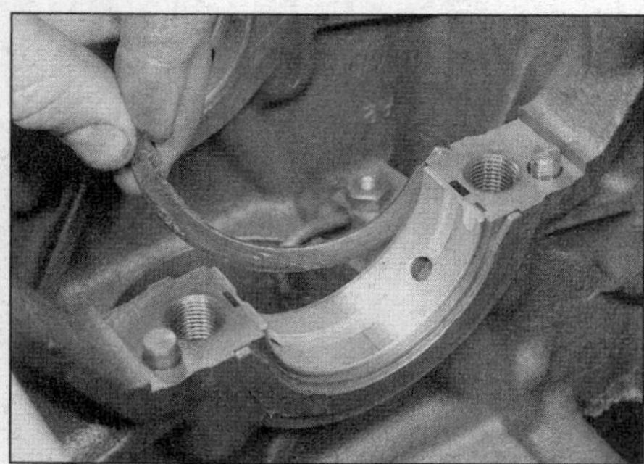
18.22 Fitting the thrustwashers to No 3 main bearing location

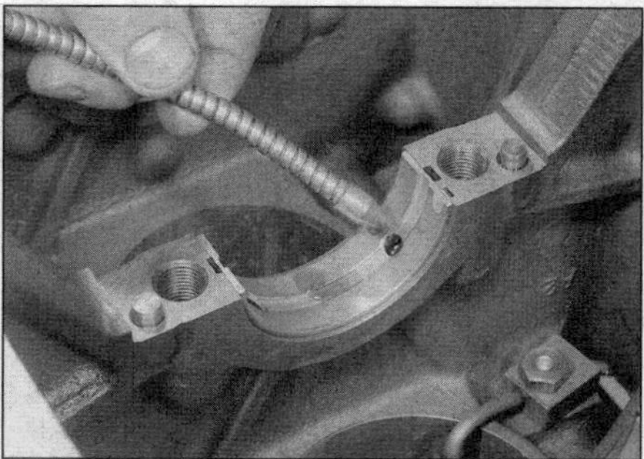
18.23 Lubricate the bearing shells

18.26 Fit the seals to No 5 main bearing cap

20 Check that the crankshaft is free to turn. Some stiffness is normal if new components have been fitted, but there must be no jamming or tight spots.

Final refitting - diesel engines

21 Carefully lift the crankshaft out of the cylinder block once more.
22 Use a little grease to stick the thrustwashers to each side of No 3 main bearing location in the crankcase. Ensure that the oilway grooves on each thrustwasher face outwards from the bearing location, towards the crankshaft webs **(see illustration)**.
23 Liberally lubricate each bearing shell in the cylinder block **(see illustration)**, and lower the crankshaft into position.
24 Lubricate the bearing shells, then fit Nos 1 to 4 bearing caps in their numbered or previously-noted locations. Ensure that the caps locate correctly over the dowels. Check the crankshaft endfloat as described in Section 12.
25 To prevent the possibility of the No 5 main bearing cap oil seals becoming trapped between the bearing cap and the crankcase, chamfer the lower inner edge of each seal to between 0.40 and 0.80 mm wide.
26 Smear the seals with clean engine oil, then locate the seals in the bearing cap. Do not trim the seals **(see illustration)**.
27 To prevent damage to the No 5 main bearing cap oil seals, make up two seal guide tools as shown. Ensure that the tools are fitted parallel to the edge of the cylinder block, and use two of the sump bolts to secure them **(see illustration)**. Alternatively, two old feeler blades can be used to protect the seals as the bearing cap is fitted.
28 If feeler blades are to be used to protect the seals, lay the feeler blades in position between the cylinder block and the bearing cap.

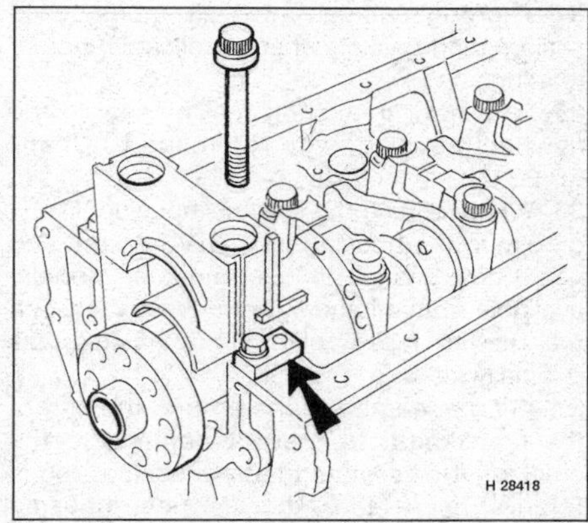
H 28418
18.27 No 5 main bearing cap seal guide tool (arrowed) in position on cylinder block

Carefully fit the bearing cap, complete with the bearing shell **(see illustration)**. If feeler blades have been used, withdraw the feeler blades as the bearing cap is pushed into position. If guide tools have been used, remove the tools once the bearing cap is in position.
29 Fit new main bearing cap bolts, noting that the bolts with the threaded holes for the oil pick-up pipe should be fitted to No 4 bearing cap, and progressively tighten the bolts to the specified torque, working outwards from the centre (No 3) bearing cap **(see illustrations)**.
30 Trim the No 5 main bearing cap seals to approximately 0.80 mm above the face of the cylinder block. Also trim the seals flush with end face of the cylinder block **(see illustrations)**.

18.28 Feeler blades (arrowed) in position to protect No 5 main bearing cap seals

18.29a Fit the main bearing cap bolts with the threaded holes to No 4 bearing cap

18.29b Tighten the main bearing cap bolts to the specified torque

18.30a Using a 0.80 mm feeler blade and knife to trim the No 5 main bearing cap seals

18.30b Trimming No 5 main bearing cap seal (arrowed) flush with the end face of the cylinder block

31 Check that the crankshaft is free to turn. Some stiffness is normal if new components have been fitted, but there must be no jamming or tight spots.

32 Refit the flywheel housing as follows, according to engine type.

Early 200 TDi engines

33 On early models, the mating faces of the cylinder block and flywheel housing are sealed, using a bead of RTV sealant in an annular groove around the oil seal housing. No gasket was fitted in production, but note that a gasket may have been fitted if the housing has been removed previously during service.

34 Thoroughly clean away all traces of old sealant (and gasket, where applicable) before refitting.

35 Fit a new crankshaft rear oil seal to the flywheel housing, with reference to Chapter 2B.

36 When refitting the flywheel housing, fill the groove in the housing with RTV sealant, and use a new gasket (as used on later models, available from a Land Rover dealers) between the mating faces, even if no gasket was originally fitted.

37 Wind a length of tape around the end of the crankshaft, to prevent damage to the crankshaft oil seal as the flywheel housing is fitted. Ensure that the flywheel housing engages with the dowels in the cylinder block.

38 Refit the securing bolts, ensuring that any brackets are in position as noted before removal, and tighten the bolts to the specified torque.

39 Remove the tape from the end of the crankshaft.

40 Proceed to paragraph 54.

Later 200 TDi engines

41 On later models, the mating faces of the cylinder block and flywheel housing are sealed using a gasket.

42 Thoroughly clean away all traces of old gasket before refitting.

43 Fit a new crankshaft rear oil seal to the flywheel housing, with reference to Chapter 2B.

44 Wind a length of tape around the end of the crankshaft, to prevent damage to the crankshaft oil seal as the flywheel housing is fitted, then refit the flywheel housing using a new gasket. Ensure that the flywheel housing engages with the dowels in the cylinder block.

18.50 Apply a bead of RTV sealant to the flywheel housing mating face of the cylinder block - 300 TDi engine

45 Refit the flywheel housing securing bolts, ensuring that any brackets are in position as noted before removal, and tighten the bolts to the specified torque.

46 Remove the tape from the end of the crankshaft.

47 Proceed to paragraph 54.

300 TDi engines

48 On 300 TDi engines, the mating faces of the cylinder block and flywheel housing are sealed using RTV sealant around the periphery of the cylinder block mating face.

49 Thoroughly clean away all traces of old sealant from the cylinder block and flywheel housing before refitting. Also clean the crankshaft rear oil seal housing mating face of the cylinder block.

50 Apply a bead of suitable RTV sealant to the periphery of the cylinder block mating face, then fit the flywheel housing **(see illustration)**. Ensure that the flywheel housing engages with the dowels in the cylinder block.

51 Refit the securing bolts, ensuring that any brackets are in position as noted before removal, and tighten the bolts to the specified torque. Note that the longer, shouldered bolts fit at the top.

52 Clean away any surplus sealant.

53 Fit a new crankshaft rear oil seal assembly as described in Chapter 2B.

All models

54 On completion, refit the piston/connecting rod assemblies as described in Section 19. Refit the flywheel and timing belt housing as described in Chapter 2B.

19 Piston/connecting rod assembly - refitting and big-end bearing running clearance check

Note: *A piston ring compressor tool will be required for this operation. A new oil pick-up pipe gasket will be needed on petrol engines. On diesel engines, new big-end bolts and nuts must be used on refitting. Suitable sealant will be required when refitting the sump, and the ladder frame on 200 TDi engines. On 300 TDi engines, a new oil pick-up pipe O-ring and a new oil return pipe gasket must be used on refitting.*

1 On diesel engines, remove the big-end bolts from the connecting rods (carefully tap them out using a hammer if necessary), and fit new bolts **(see illustration)**. Where applicable, ensure that the eccentrics on the bolt heads locate correctly in the connecting rod recesses.

2 Clean the backs of the big-end bearing shells and the recesses in the connecting rods and big-end caps. If new shells are being fitted, ensure that all traces of the protective grease are cleaned off using paraffin. Wipe the shells and connecting rods dry with a lint-free cloth.

3 Press the big-end bearing shells into the connecting rods and caps, in their correct locations if the original shells are to be re-used. Make sure that the locating tabs on the shells are engaged with the cut-outs in the connecting rods and bearing caps **(see illustrations)**.

Big-end bearing running clearance check

Note: *Suitable measuring equipment will be required for this check - see text.*

4 Lubricate No 1 piston and piston rings, and check that the piston ring end gaps are positioned as described in Section 14.

5 Wrap a layer of tape around the connecting rod bolts, or fit plastic sleeves over the bolt threads, to prevent damage to the crankshaft bearing surfaces as the rods are fitted.

19.1 Tapping a big-end bolt from a connecting rod

19.3a Fitting a new bearing shell to the connecting rod big-end

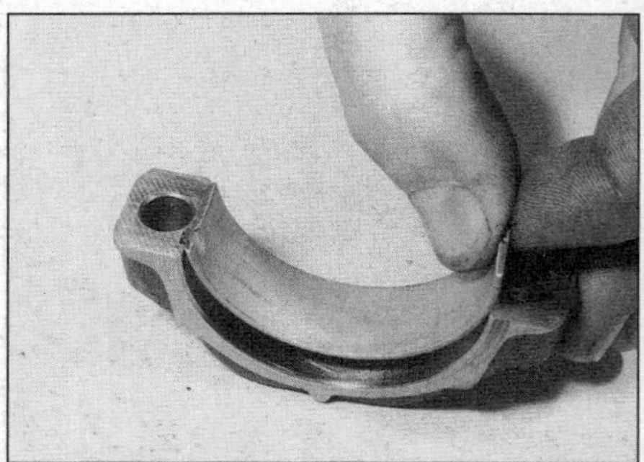

19.3b Engage the tab in the cut-out when fitting the big-end cap shells

19.9a Insert the piston and connecting rod into the cylinder with a piston ring compressor fitted . . .

19.9b . . . then drive the piston into the cylinder

6 Fit a ring compressor to No 1 piston, then insert the piston and connecting rod into No 1 cylinder.

7 On petrol engines, the domed boss on the connecting rod must face forwards for the right-hand bank of cylinders (2-4-6-8) and rearwards for the left bank (1-3-5-7). When the assemblies are refitted, the domed bosses should face each other on the crankshaft journals.

8 On diesel engines, the arrow on the piston crown should point towards the timing belt end of the engine, and the combustion chamber in the piston crown should be on the camshaft side of the engine. Note also that the bearing shell locating cut-outs in the connecting rod and bearing cap should be positioned on the camshaft side of the engine.

9 With No 1 crankpin at its lowest point, drive the piston carefully into the cylinder with the wooden handle of a hammer, at the same time guiding the connecting rod onto the crankpin **(see illustrations)**.

10 To measure the big-end bearing running clearance, refer to the information contained in Section 18; the same general procedures apply.

11 If the Plastigauge method is being used, ensure that the crankpin journal and the big-end bearing shells are clean and dry, then engage the connecting rod with the crankpin. Place the Plastigauge strip on the crankpin, fit the bearing cap in its previously-noted position (see Section 11), then tighten the nuts to the specified torque. Do not rotate the crankshaft during this operation. Remove the cap and check the running clearance by measuring the Plastigauge as previously described.

12 Repeat the above procedures on the remaining piston/connecting rod assemblies **(see Tool Tip)**.

Final refitting

13 Having checked the running clearance of all the crankpin journals and taken any corrective action necessary, clean off all traces of Plastigauge from the bearing shells and crankpin.

14 Liberally lubricate the crankpin journals and big-end bearing shells. Refit the bearing caps once more, ensuring correct positioning as previously described. On petrol engines, the rib on the edge of the cap faces in the same direction as the domed boss on the connecting rod, so that when the two connecting rods and caps are refitted to each of the four journals, the ribs face each other **(see illustrations)**.

15 Tighten the big-end bearing cap nuts to the specified torque, and turn the crankshaft each time to make sure that it is free before moving on to the next assembly **(see illustration)**.

16 Proceed as follows according to engine type.

Petrol engines

17 Check the oil strainer gauze and the pick-up pipe for obstructions, and clean the assembly thoroughly before refitting.

TOOL
TiP

To turn the crankshaft, refit two of the flywheel securing bolts to the end of the crankshaft, and use a screwdriver to lever the crankshaft round

18 Refit the oil pick-up pipe, using a new gasket. Coat the threads of the securing bolts with suitable thread-locking compound, and tighten the bolts securely.

19 Refit the sump and the cylinder heads, as described in Chapter 2A.

200 TDi engine

Note: *Since the sealant used to seal the ladder frame to the cylinder block and the sump to the ladder frame cures within fifteen minutes, it is important that the ladder frame, oil pump and sump are fitted together without undue delay.*

20 Check that the cylinder block and sump mating faces of the ladder frame are clean.

21 Apply Hylogrip Primer to the mating faces of the cylinder block and the ladder frame. This will clean the surfaces, and speed up curing of the sealant.

22 Apply RTV sealant to the joint between the cylinder block and the flywheel housing at the ladder frame mating face.

23 Apply Hylogrip 2000 to the cylinder block mating face of the ladder frame, then loosely fit the ladder frame to the cylinder block.

24 Fit the bolts securing the ladder frame to the cylinder block, and the four bolts securing the ladder frame to the flywheel housing, then tighten the bolts to the specified torque.

25 Refit the oil pump, the sump and the cylinder head, as described in Chapter 2B.

19.14a Lubricate the crankshaft journal as the connecting rod is drawn onto it

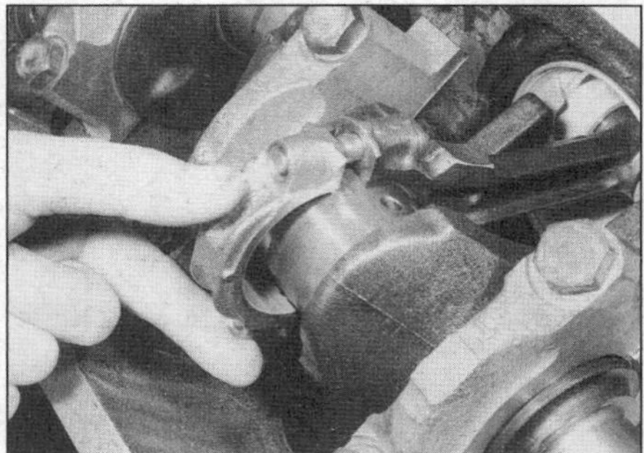

19.14b Refitting a petrol engine big-end cap - note rib on cap

19.15 Tightening the big-end bearing cap nuts

300 TDi engine

26 Check the oil strainer gauze and the pick-up pipe for obstructions, and clean the assembly thoroughly before refitting.
27 Refit the oil return pipe, using a new gasket. Coat the threads of the securing bolts with suitable thread-locking compound, and tighten the bolts to the specified torque.
28 Refit the oil strainer using a new pick-up pipe O-ring. Coat the threads of the securing bolts with suitable thread-locking compound, and tighten the bolts to the specified torque.
29 Refit the sump and the cylinder head, as described in Chapter 2B.

20 Engine - initial start-up after overhaul

1 With the engine refitted to the vehicle, double-check the engine oil and coolant levels, and check that the battery is well charged. Make a final check that everything has been reconnected. Make sure that there are no tools or rags left in the engine compartment.

Petrol models

2 Remove the spark plugs, referring to Chapter 1A for details.
3 The engine must be immobilised such that it can be turned over using the starter motor, without starting. Disconnect the HT lead from the ignition coil. On fuel injection models, also disable the fuel pump by removing the fuel pump fuse (refer to the information on depressurising the system in Chapter 4B).
Caution: On vehicles with a catalytic converter, it is potentially damaging to immobilise the engine by disabling the ignition system without first disabling the fuel system, as unburnt fuel could be supplied to the catalyst. When the engine is later started, the unburnt fuel in the converter may ignite and irreparably damage the converter.
4 Turn the engine using the starter motor until the oil pressure warning light goes out. If the light fails to extinguish after several seconds of cranking, check the engine oil level and that the oil filter is secure. Assuming these are correct, check the security of the oil pressure switch wiring - do not progress any further until you are satisfied that oil is being pumped around the engine at sufficient pressure.
5 Refit the spark plugs and ignition coil wiring, and refit the fuel pump fuse, where applicable.

Diesel models

6 Prime the fuel system as described in Chapter 4C.
7 Before starting the engine, the turbocharger **must** be primed with oil as follows. Failure to carry out this procedure may result in serious (and expensive) damage to the turbocharger.
- a) *Unscrew the oil feed pipe banjo bolt from the top of the turbocharger housing. Recover the two sealing washers, and move the feed pipe away from the oil hole in the housing.*
- b) *Fill the housing with clean engine oil of the correct type and grade, from a freshly-opened sealed container.*
- c) *Reconnect the oil feed pipe, and refit the banjo bolt, ensuring that one sealing washer is positioned on each side of the pipe. Tighten the banjo bolt to the specified torque.*

8 Prime the remainder of the lubrication circuit by disconnecting the stop solenoid in the injection pump and cranking the engine on the starter motor in several ten-second bursts, pausing for half a minute or so between each burst. Reconnect the solenoid when satisfied that oil pressure has been established (ensure that the oil pressure warning light on the facia extinguishes when the engine is cranked).
9 Fully depress the accelerator pedal, then turn the ignition key to position M and wait for the preheating warning light to go out.

All models

10 Start the engine, but be aware that as fuel system components have been disturbed, the cranking time may be a little longer than usual.
11 Once started, keep the engine running at fast tickover. Check that the oil pressure light stays out, then check that there are no leaks of oil, fuel or coolant. Check the power steering pipe/hose unions for leakage. On models with automatic transmission, check the transmission fluid cooler pipe unions for leakage. Do not be alarmed if there are some odd smells and smoke from parts getting hot and burning off oil deposits.
12 On petrol models, the hydraulic tappets may initially run noisily, but the engine should quieten down after a few seconds' running.
13 Assuming all is well, keep the engine idling until hot water is felt circulating through the top hose.
14 Check the ignition timing or fuel injection pump timing, as applicable, as described in Chapter 5B or 4C.
15 Check the engine idle speed as described in the relevant part of Chapter 4, then switch off the engine and allow it to cool.
16 Once the engine has cooled, recheck the oil and coolant levels, and top-up as necessary.
17 There is no need to re-tighten the cylinder head bolts once the engine has been run following reassembly.
18 If new pistons, rings or crankshaft bearings have been fitted, the engine must be treated as new, and run-in for the first 600 miles (1000 km). *Do not* operate the engine at full-throttle, or allow it to labour at low engine speeds in any gear. It is recommended that the engine oil and filter are changed at the end of this period.

Chapter 3
Cooling, heating and ventilation systems

Contents

Degrees of difficulty

Easy, suitable for novice with little experience 	**Fairly easy,** suitable for beginner with some experience 	**Fairly difficult,** suitable for competent DIY mechanic	**Difficult,** suitable for experienced DIY mechanic	**Very difficult,** suitable for expert DIY or professional 

Specifications

General

Expansion tank cap opening pressure	1.0 bars
Antifreeze type	See end of *Weekly checks*
Cooling system capacity	See Chapter 1A or 1B Specifications

Thermostat

Opening temperatures:	
3.5 litre petrol and 200 TDi engines	82°C
3.9 litre petrol and 300 TDi engines	88°C

Torque wrench settings

Torque wrench settings	Nm	lbf ft
Coolant pump nut and bolts (diesel)	26	19
Coolant pump housing bolts (petrol)*	28	21
Cooling fan mounting bolts	35	26
Radiator oil/fluid cooler unions	30	22
Thermostat housing bolts	28	21

**Long bolts must be coated with thread-locking fluid - see text*

1 General information and precautions

General information

The cooling system is of pressurised type, comprising a belt-driven coolant pump, an aluminium crossflow radiator, the cooling fan, and a thermostat. The radiator incorporates an oil cooler on diesel engines; on petrol engines, a coolant supply is taken to a heat exchanger on the oil filter mounting.

The system functions as follows. Cold coolant from the radiator passes through the hose to the coolant pump, where it is pumped around the cylinder block and head passages. After cooling the cylinder bores, combustion surfaces and valve seats, the coolant reaches the underside of the thermostat, which is initially closed. The coolant passes through the heater, and is returned via the cylinder block to the coolant pump.

When the engine is cold, the coolant circulates only through the cylinder block, cylinder head(s), expansion tank and heater. When the coolant reaches a predetermined temperature, the thermostat opens, and the coolant passes through to the radiator. As the coolant circulates through the radiator, it is cooled by the inrush of air when the car is in forward motion. Once it has passed through the radiator, the coolant is cooled and the cycle is repeated.

The cooling fan is driven via a viscous coupling. The viscous coupling varies the fan speed, according to engine temperature. At low temperatures, the coupling provides very little resistance between the fan and pump pulley, so only a slight amount of drive is transmitted to the cooling fan. As the temperature of the coupling increases, so does its internal resistance, therefore increasing drive to the cooling fan.

Refer to Section 11 for information on the air conditioning system.

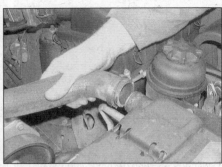

2.3 Disconnecting the radiator top hose (petrol model)

Precautions

Warning: Do not attempt to remove the expansion tank filler cap, nor disturb any part of the cooling system, while the engine is hot, as there is a high risk of scalding. If the expansion tank filler cap must be removed before the engine and radiator have fully cooled (even though this is not recommended) the pressure in the cooling system must first be relieved. Cover the cap with a thick layer of cloth, to avoid scalding, and slowly unscrew the filler cap until a hissing sound can be heard. When the hissing has stopped, indicating that the pressure has reduced, slowly unscrew the filler cap until it can be removed; if more hissing sounds are heard, wait until they have stopped before unscrewing the cap completely. At all times, keep well away from the filler cap opening.

3.4a Disconnecting the top hose (diesel model)

Warning: Do not allow antifreeze to come into contact with skin or painted surfaces of the vehicle. Rinse off spills immediately with plenty of water. Never leave antifreeze lying around in an open container or in a puddle in the driveway or on the garage floor. Children and pets are attracted by its sweet smell, but antifreeze can be fatal if ingested.

Warning: Refer to Section 11 for precautions to be observed when working on models with air conditioning.

2 Cooling system hoses - disconnection and renewal

Note: *Refer to the warnings given in Section 1 of this Chapter before proceeding.*

1 If the checks described in Chapter 1A or 1B reveal a faulty hose, it must be renewed as follows.

2 First drain the cooling system (see the relevant part of Chapter 1). If the coolant is not due for renewal, it may be re-used if it is collected in a clean container.

3 To disconnect a hose, use a screwdriver to slacken the clips, then move them along the hose, clear of the relevant inlet/outlet union. Carefully work the hose free **(see illustration)**. The hoses can be removed with relative ease when new - on an older vehicle, they may have stuck.

4 If a hose proves stubborn, try to release it by rotating it on its unions before attempting to work it off. Gently prise the end of the hose with a blunt instrument (such as a flat-bladed screwdriver), but do not apply too much force, and take care not to damage the pipe stubs or hoses. Note in particular that the radiator hose unions are fragile; do not use excessive force when attempting to remove the hoses.

If all else fails, cut the hose with a sharp knife, then slit it so that it can be peeled off in two pieces. While expensive, this is preferable to buying a new radiator. Check first, however, that a new hose is readily available.

5 Before fitting a hose, make sure the pipe unions are clean. On an older engine, there is often a build-up of crusty white deposits, which should be cleaned off to provide a better seal.

6 When fitting a hose, first slide the clips onto the hose, then work the hose into position. If clamp-type clips were originally fitted, it is a good idea to replace them with screw-type clips when refitting the hose. If the hose is stiff, use a little washing-up liquid as a lubricant, or soften the hose by soaking it in hot water.

7 Work the hose into position, checking that it is correctly routed, then slide each clip along the hose until it passes over the flared end of the relevant inlet/outlet union, before tightening the clips securely.

8 Refill the cooling system with reference to the relevant part of Chapter 1.

9 Check thoroughly for leaks as soon as possible after disturbing any part of the cooling system.

3 Radiator - removal, inspection and refitting

If leakage is the reason for wanting to remove the radiator, bear in mind that minor leaks can be often be cured using a radiator sealant with the radiator in situ.

Removal

1 Disconnect the battery negative lead.

2 Drain the cooling system as described in the relevant part of Chapter 1.

3 Remove the cooling fan and cowl as described in Section 5.

4 Slacken the retaining clips, and detach the expansion tank hose, and the top and bottom hoses from the radiator **(see illustrations)**.

5 Slacken the union nuts and disconnect the engine oil cooler pipes from the radiator **(see illustration)**. Be prepared for some oil or coolant spillage as the pipes are disconnected; plug or cap the pipe and cooler

3.4b Disconnecting the expansion tank hose - petrol model. . .

3.4c . . . disconnecting the expansion tank hose - diesel model

3.5 . . . then slacken the union nut and disconnect the oil cooler pipe (arrowed) from the radiator

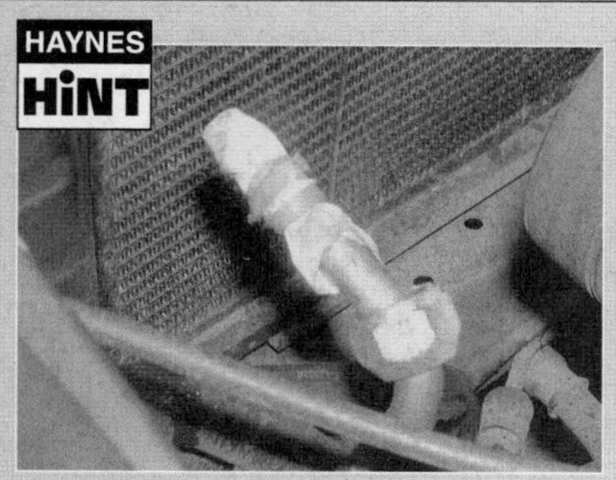
HAYNES
HiNT

Cut the finger from an old pair of rubber gloves, and secure it to the cooler pipe with a strong elastic band, to prevent loss of oil/fluid

unions, to minimise fluid loss and to prevent dirt entering the lubrication system **(see Haynes Hint)**.

6 On models with automatic transmission, slacken the union nuts and disconnect the fluid pipes from the radiator **(see illustration)**. Be prepared for fluid spillage, and be sure to plug or cap over the open unions, to prevent dirt from entering the transmission.

7 On diesel engines, slacken the retaining clips, and disconnect both hoses from the intercooler **(see illustration)**.

8 Unscrew the mounting bracket retaining nuts and bolts, then free both mounting brackets from the radiator, and recover the upper mounting rubbers. Support the left-hand mounting bracket so that the fluid does not spill from the power steering reservoir **(see illustrations)**.

3.6 Disconnect the transmission fluid cooler pipes from the radiator

3.7 Slacken the retaining clips, and disconnect the hoses from the intercooler

9 Lift the radiator assembly out from the engine compartment, and recover its lower mounting rubbers **(see illustrations)**. On vehicles with air conditioning, in order to remove the radiator, it may first be necessary to undo the air conditioning compressor mounting bolts and reposition the compressor slightly to gain the necessary clearance required - **DO NOT** *disconnect any of the refrigerant lines.*

10 Examine the mounting rubbers for signs of damage or deterioration, and renew if necessary.

Refitting

11 Fit the lower mounting rubbers, then manoeuvre the radiator assembly into position, making sure that its lower mounting pegs are correctly engaged.

12 Install the upper mounting rubbers and mounting brackets, and securely tighten their retaining nuts and bolts.

13 Reconnect the cooling system and intercooler hoses (as applicable), and securely tighten their retaining clips.

14 Reconnect the oil cooler pipes, and securely tighten their union nuts. Where applicable, similarly reconnect the automatic transmission fluid cooler pipes.

15 Refit the cooling fan and cowl as described in Section 5, then refill the cooling system as described in the relevant part of Chapter 1.

4 Thermostat - removal, testing and refitting

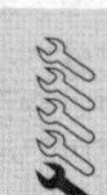

1 As the thermostat ages, it will become slower to react to changes in water temperature. Ultimately, the unit may stick in the open or closed position, and this causes problems. A thermostat which is stuck open will result in a very slow warm-up; a thermostat which is stuck shut will lead to rapid overheating.

2 Before assuming the thermostat is to blame for a cooling system problem, check the coolant level. If the system is draining due to a leak, or has not been properly filled, there may be an airlock in the system (see *Coolant renewal* in the relevant part of Chapter 1).

3 If the engine seems to be taking a long time to warm up (based on heater output or temperature gauge operation), the thermostat is probably stuck open.

3.8a Undo the radiator mounting bracket nuts and bolts . . .

3.8b . . . move the power steering fluid reservoir and left-hand bracket clear . . .

3.8c . . . and remove the right-hand mounting bracket

3.9a Lifting the radiator assembly out of position - diesel model . . .

3.9b . . . and petrol model

4.13 Removing the radiator top hose from the thermostat housing

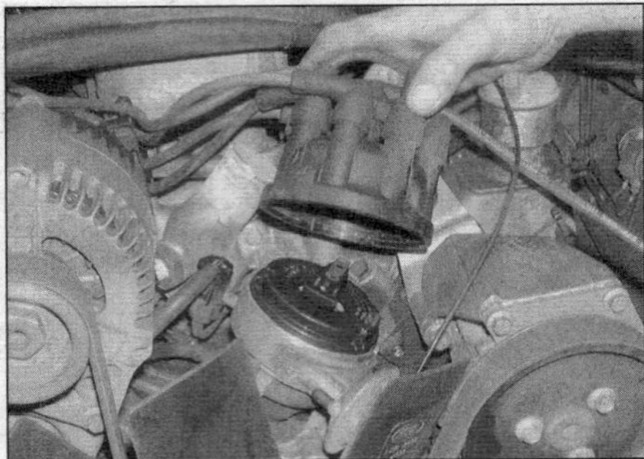
4.14 Take off the distributor cap

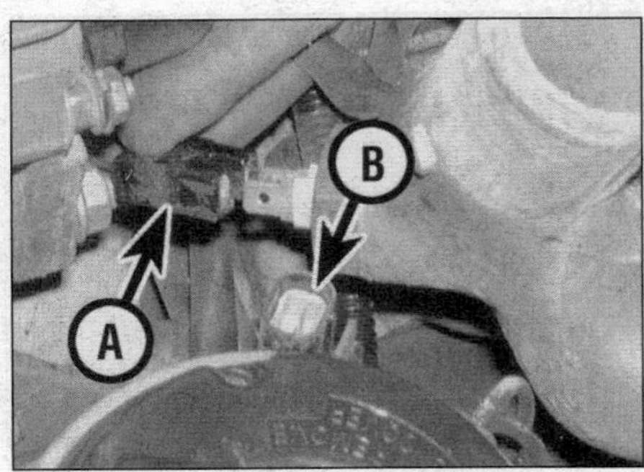
B
A
4.15 Disconnect the temperature switch (A) and distributor wiring plug (B)

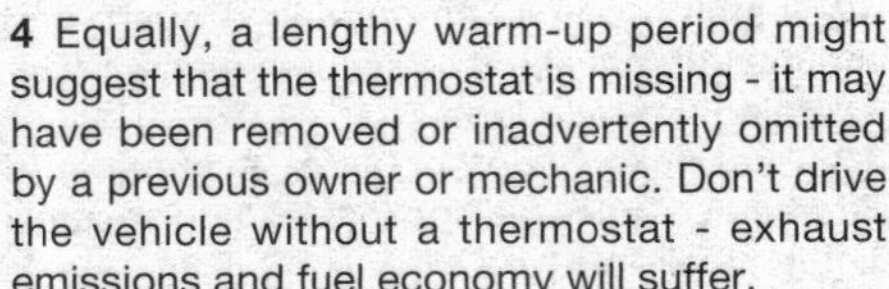

4 Equally, a lengthy warm-up period might suggest that the thermostat is missing - it may have been removed or inadvertently omitted by a previous owner or mechanic. Don't drive the vehicle without a thermostat - exhaust emissions and fuel economy will suffer.

5 If the engine runs hot, use your hand to check the temperature of the radiator top hose. If the hose isn't hot, but the engine is, the thermostat is probably stuck closed, preventing the coolant inside the engine from escaping to the radiator - renew the thermostat. Again, this problem may also be due to an airlock (see *Coolant renewal* in the relevant part of Chapter 1).

6 If the radiator top hose is hot, it means that the coolant is flowing and the thermostat is open. Consult the *Fault finding* section at the end of this manual to assist in tracing possible cooling system faults.

7 To gain a rough idea of whether the thermostat is working properly when the engine is warming up, without dismantling the system, proceed as follows.

4.16a Slacken the housing cover bolts . . .

8 With the engine completely cold, start the engine and let it idle, while checking the temperature of the radiator top hose. Periodically check the temperature indicated on the coolant temperature gauge - if overheating is indicated, switch the engine off immediately.

9 The top hose should feel cold for some time as the engine warms up, and should then get warm quite quickly as the thermostat opens.

10 The above is not a precise or definitive test of thermostat operation, but if the system does not perform as described, remove and test the thermostat as described below.

Removal

Note: *A new thermostat housing gasket and sealing ring will be required on refitting - also see paragraph 27.*

11 Disconnect the battery negative lead.

12 Drain the cooling system as described in the relevant part of Chapter 1, and proceed as described under the relevant sub-heading.

Petrol engines

13 Slacken the retaining clip, and disconnect the top hose from the thermostat housing **(see illustration)**.

14 Remove the distributor cap as described in Chapter 1A, Section 8 **(see illustration)**.

15 On models with air conditioning, disconnect the wiring from the temperature switch screwed into the front of the thermostat cover. To improve access, also disconnect the wiring plug on the distributor body **(see illustration)**.

16 Slacken and remove the retaining bolts, recover the washers, and remove the thermostat housing cover from the engine **(see illustrations)**.

17 Withdraw the thermostat from its housing, noting its fitted position, and recover its sealing ring **(see illustrations)**.

200 TDi diesel engine

18 Slacken the retaining clip, and disconnect the coolant hose from the thermostat housing.

19 Slacken and remove the retaining bolts, and remove the thermostat housing cover from the engine. Recover the housing gasket, and discard it.

20 Withdraw the thermostat from its housing.

300 TDi diesel engine

21 Slacken the retaining clip, and disconnect the coolant hose(s) from the thermostat housing.

22 Disconnect the wiring connectors from the switches which are screwed into the underside of the thermostat cover (where fitted).

23 Slacken and remove the retaining bolts, and remove the thermostat housing cover from the engine **(see illustration)**.

24 Withdraw the thermostat from its housing, and recover its sealing ring.

Testing

25 To test it fully, suspend the (closed) thermostat on a length of string in a container of cold water, with a thermometer beside it;

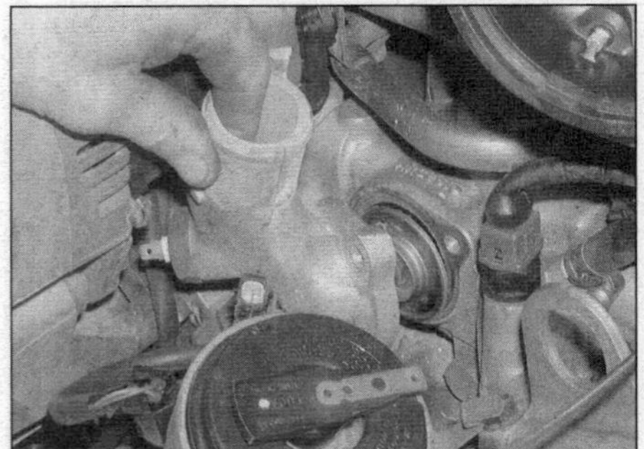
4.16b . . . then withdraw the cover for access to the thermostat

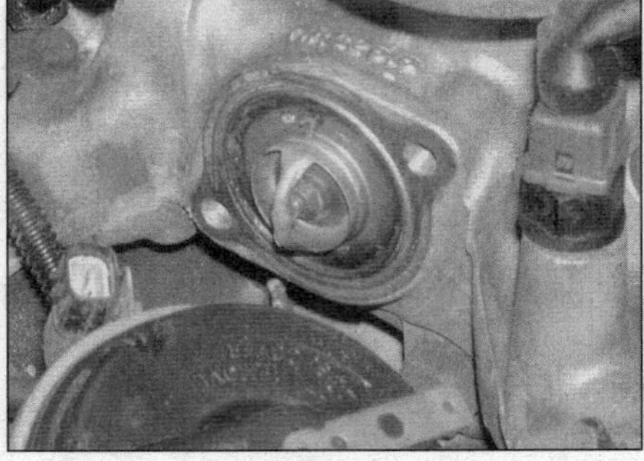
4.17a Note the correct fitted position of the thermostat . . .

4.17b . . . then remove it from the housing

4.23 On 300 TDi engines, remove the housing cover then withdraw the thermostat and recover its sealing ring (arrowed)

ensure that neither touches the side of the container.

26 Heat the water, and check the temperature at which the thermostat begins to open; compare this value with that specified. This value is also stamped on the thermostat body. It's difficult to check the fully-open temperature, because this occurs very near the boiling point of water at normal atmospheric pressure. If the temperature at which the thermostat began to open was as specified, then it is most likely that the thermostat's OK. Remove the thermostat and allow it to cool down; check that it closes fully.

27 If the thermostat does not open and close as described, or if it sticks in either position, it must be renewed. Frankly, if there is any question about the operation of the thermostat, renew it - they are not expensive.

Refitting

28 Refitting is the reverse of the relevant removal procedure, using a new gasket/sealing ring (as applicable), and making sure that the thermostat is correctly seated in its housing **(see illustration)**. Tighten the housing retaining bolts to the specified torque. On petrol engines, the jiggle pin/vent hole must be positioned uppermost. On completion, refill the cooling system as described in the relevant part of Chapter 1.

5 Cooling fan and viscous coupling - removal and refitting

Note: *A special slim open-ended spanner will be required to remove the fan and viscous coupling assembly. On the project vehicles seen, petrol engines had a 36 mm nut, and diesel engines a 32 mm nut.*

Removal

1 Disconnect the battery negative lead.

2 Where applicable, release the two wire clips and lift out the upper section of the fan cowl - this is not essential for removing the fan, but it will improve access **(see illustrations)**.

3 Hold the coolant pump pulley against rotation, by wedging a long screwdriver across two of the pulley bolts. Using the special open-ended spanner, unscrew the viscous coupling from the coolant pump/camshaft **(see illustration)**. **Note:** *On diesel engines, the viscous coupling has a* ***left-hand thread*** *- ie it unscrews* ***clockwise.***

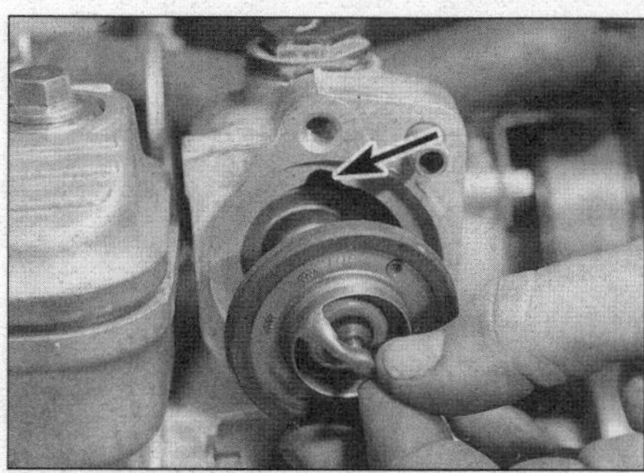

4.28 On 300 TDi engines, ensure that the thermostat is correctly engaged with the housing cut-out (arrowed) so its TOP marking is uppermost

4 On 200 TDi engines, remove the fan and coupling assembly, then undo the two upper retaining nuts, and manoeuvre the fan cowl out from the engine compartment.

5 On all other engines, lift out the fan and coupling assembly. If necessary, undo the retaining nuts, release the remaining clips, and remove the remainder of the cowl **(see illustrations)**.

6 On all models, if necessary, slacken and remove the retaining bolts, and separate the cooling fan from the coupling, noting which way around the fan is fitted.

Refitting

7 Where necessary, refit the fan to the viscous coupling and tighten its retaining bolts to the specified torque. Make sure that

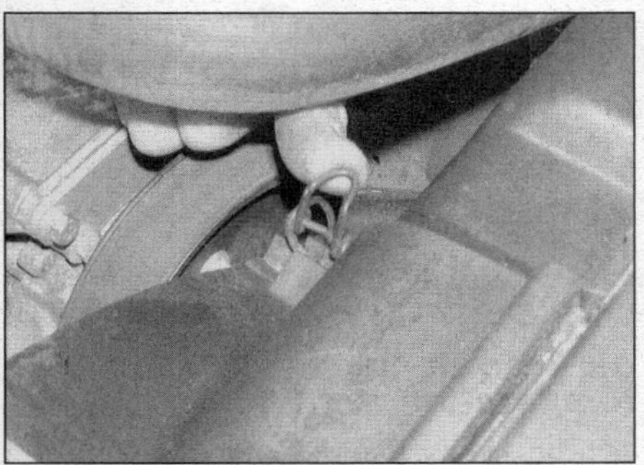

5.2a Release the two clips . . .

5.2b . . . and lift out the fan cowl access panel

5.3 Hold the pulley against rotation, and use a special cranked spanner to loosen the viscous fan nut

5.5a Removing the fan and viscous coupling

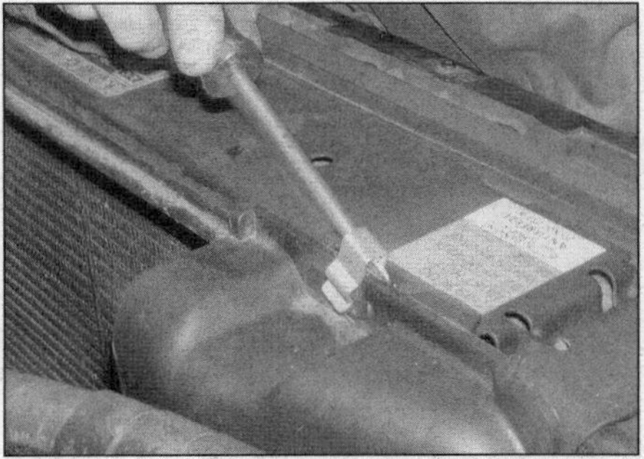

5.5b If necessary, release the clips . . .

5.5c . . . and remove the main cowl from the radiator

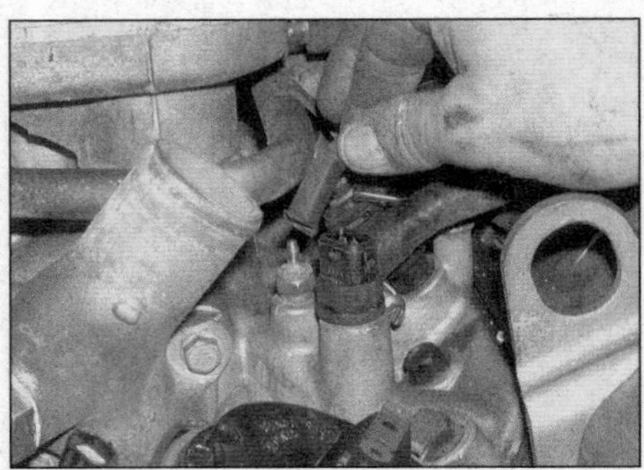
6.9a Disconnect the wiring plug . . .

6.9b . . . then unscrew the sender from its location (later petrol model shown) . . .

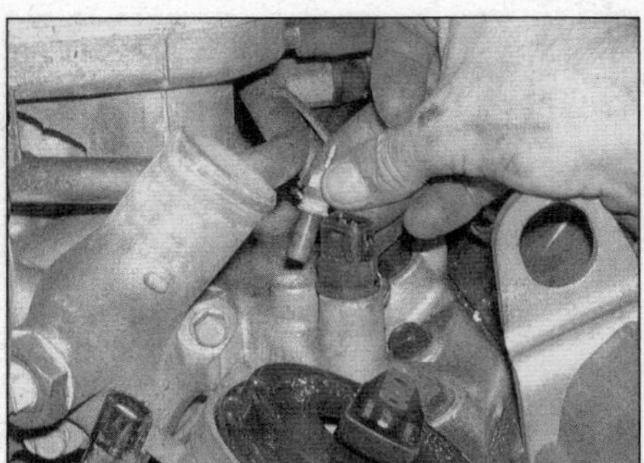
6.9c . . . and withdraw it

the fan is fitted the correct way round; the fan should be marked FRONT on one side, this side should face the radiator when the fan is installed. **Note:** *If the fan is fitted the wrong way round, the efficiency of the cooling system will be significantly reduced.*

8 Further refitting is a reversal of removal. Bear in mind that, on diesel engines, the coupling is screwed on anti-clockwise.

6 Cooling system electrical switches - testing, removal and refitting

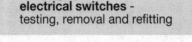

Coolant temperature gauge sender

Testing

1 The coolant temperature gauge, mounted in the instrument panel, is fed with a stabilised voltage supply from the instrument panel feed (via the 'ignition' switch and a fuse), and its earth is controlled by the sender.

2 The sender is screwed into the thermostat housing on diesel models, while petrol models have the sender screwed into the inlet manifold, behind the distributor (the smaller of the two plugs visible on fuel injection models). The sender contains a thermistor, which consists of an electronic component whose electrical resistance decreases at a predetermined rate as its temperature rises. When the coolant is cold, the sender resistance is high, current flow through the gauge is reduced, and the gauge needle points towards the cold end of the scale. If the sender is faulty, it must be renewed.

3 If the gauge develops a fault, first check the other instruments; if they do not work at all, check the instrument panel electrical feed. If the readings are erratic, there may be a fault in the voltage resistor, which will necessitate renewal of the printed circuit (see Chapter 13, Section 10). If the fault lies in the temperature gauge alone, check it as follows.

4 If the gauge needle remains at the cold end of the scale, disconnect the sender wire, and earth it to the cylinder head. If the needle then deflects when the 'ignition' is switched on, the sender unit is proved faulty, and should be renewed. If the needle still does not move, remove the instrument panel (Chapter 13) and check the continuity of the wiring between the sender unit and the gauge, and the feed to the gauge unit. If continuity is shown, and the fault still exists, then the gauge is faulty, and the gauge unit should be renewed.

5 If the gauge needle remains at the hot end of the scale, disconnect the sender wire. If the needle then returns to the cold end of the scale when the 'ignition' is switched on, the sender unit is proved faulty and should be renewed. If the needle still does not move, check the remainder of the circuit as described previously.

Removal

6 Either partially drain the cooling system to just below the level of the sender (see the relevant part of Chapter 1), or have ready a suitable plug which can be used to plug the sender aperture whilst it is removed. If a plug is used, take great care not to damage the sender unit threads, and do not use anything which will allow foreign matter to enter the cooling system.

7 On petrol models, remove the distributor cap as described in Chapter 1A, Section 8. Also disconnect the top hose from the thermostat housing, taking precautions against spillage if the cooling system has only been partially drained.

8 Disconnect the battery negative lead.

9 Disconnect the wiring from the sender, then unscrew the unit; recover the sealing washer (where fitted). On later petrol models, a 12 mm cranked spanner will be needed - if this is not available, it may be necessary to remove the injection system temperature sender for access **(see illustrations)**.

Refitting

10 If the sender unit was fitted with a sealing washer, fit a new washer. Where no washer was fitted, ensure that the sender threads are clean, and apply a smear of suitable sealant to them.

11 Refit the sender, tightening it securely, and reconnect the wiring.

12 Top-up the cooling system as described in the relevant part of Chapter 1.

13 On completion, start the engine and check the operation of the temperature gauge. Also check for coolant leaks.

Air conditioning system fan temperature switch

14 The switch screwed into the thermostat housing controls the fans for the air conditioning system, and can be removed as follows. *Do not attempt to remove the pressure switches which are fitted to the air conditioning refrigerant lines; these cannot be removed without first discharging the air conditioning system (see Section 11).*

15 To improve access, remove the upper section of the fan cowl and, on petrol models, the distributor cap (Chapter 1A, Section 8).

16 Disconnect the wiring plug from the switch.

17 To unscrew the switch from the housing, a large spanner is required. On the (petrol) project car, this proved to be a 1 1/8 in size, and access was still not easy **(see illustrations)**. If the required spanner is not available, the best option is to remove the thermostat housing as

6.17a Using a large spanner, loosen . . .

6.17b . . . then unscrew and remove the air conditioning fan temperature switch

7.3 Slacken the coolant pump pulley bolts, using a screwdriver to prevent rotation

7.5 Remove the pulley, noting its fitted orientation

7.6 Slacken the hose clip, then disconnect the bottom hose from the pump

described in Section 4, grip the switch in a vice, and (effectively) unscrew the housing from the switch.

18 On refitting, coat the threads of the switch with a smear of suitable sealant, and tighten securely. If the thermostat housing had to be removed, refit it as described in Section 4, using a new gasket/sealing ring.

Fuel injection system temperature switch

19 Refer to Chapter 4B, Section 6.

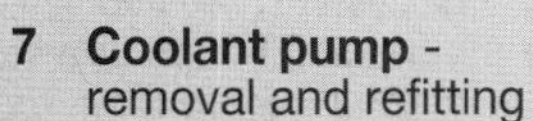

7 Coolant pump - removal and refitting

Removal

1 Drain the cooling system as described in Chapter 1A or 1B, and proceed as described under the relevant sub-heading.

Petrol engines

2 Remove the cooling fan and viscous coupling as described in Section 5.

3 Slacken, but do not remove, the bolts securing the pulley to the coolant pump. Hold the pulley against rotation using a large screwdriver between the pulley hub and one of the bolts **(see illustration)**.

4 Remove the coolant (water) pump drivebelt as described in Chapter 1A, Section 16.

5 Unscrew the retaining bolts and remove the drive pulley, noting which way around it is fitted **(see illustration)**.

6 Slacken the retaining clip, and disconnect the coolant hose from the pump **(see illustration)**.

7 Evenly and progressively slacken and remove the pump retaining bolts **(see illustration)**. Note each bolt's correct fitted location, as they are of different lengths and sizes. It was found that, on inspection, the location of the three long (11 mm fitting) bolts was obvious, and confusion is unlikely in practice.

8 Remove the pump assembly from the engine, and recover the gasket **(see illustration)**.

200 TDi diesel engine

9 Remove the cooling fan and viscous coupling as described in Section 5.

10 Slacken the bolts securing the pulley to the coolant pump.

11 Remove the coolant pump drivebelt as described in Chapter 1B, Section 17.

12 Unscrew the retaining bolts and remove the drive pulley, noting which way around it is fitted.

13 Slacken the retaining clip, and disconnect the coolant hose from the top of the pump.

14 Evenly and progressively slacken and remove the pump retaining nut and bolts. Note each bolt's correct fitted location, as they are of different lengths.

15 Remove the pump assembly from the engine, and recover the gasket.

300 TDi diesel engine

16 To improve access, slacken the retaining clips, and remove the radiator top hose and the intercooler top hose.

17 Slacken the bolts securing the pulleys to the coolant pump and power steering pump.

18 Remove the auxiliary drivebelt as described in Chapter 1, Section 17.

19 To improve access, undo the auxiliary drivebelt tensioner retaining nut, then slide the tensioner assembly off its retaining stud. Alternatively, the tensioner can be left in position, but this will mean the tensioner arm will have to be lifted to access the lower retaining bolts.

20 Unscrew the retaining bolts, and remove both the coolant pump and power steering pump drive pulleys, noting which way around each one is fitted.

21 Evenly and progressively slacken and remove the pump retaining nut and bolts. Note each bolt's correct fitted location, as they are of different lengths **(see illustration)**.

22 Remove the pump assembly from the engine, and recover the gasket **(see illustration)**.

7.7 Slacken and remove the pump retaining bolts

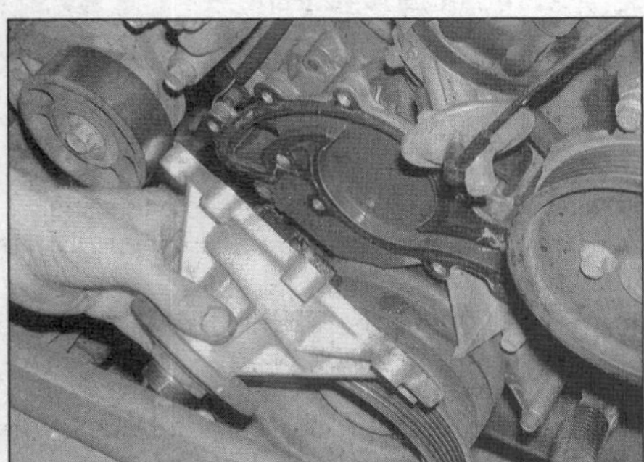
7.8 Removing the coolant pump

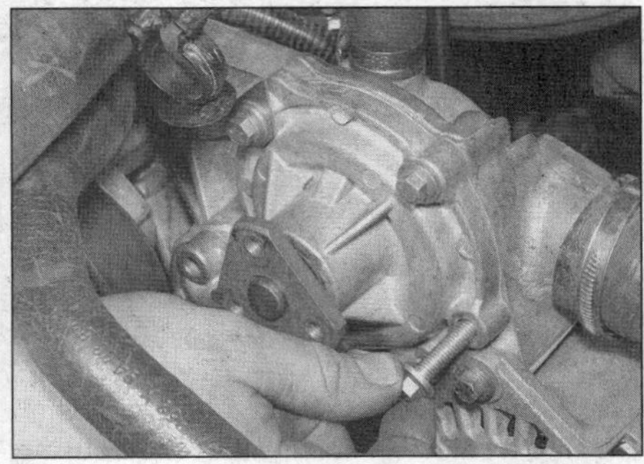
7.21 On 300 TDi engines, unscrew the retaining bolts . . .

7.22 . . . and remove the coolant pump from the front of the engine

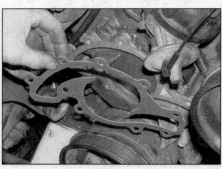

7.24 Use a little grease or sealant to stick the new gasket in position

Refitting

Petrol engines

23 Ensure that the pump and cylinder block mating surfaces are clean and dry.

24 Apply a smear of grease or sealant to the new pump gasket, and position it on the pump housing **(see illustration)**.

25 Clean the threads of the long coolant pump retaining bolts (which pass through the housing and screw into the cylinder block) and apply a smear of suitable sealant to each one's threads. Land Rover recommend Loctite 572 thread lubricant-sealant, available from dealers.

26 Install the coolant pump and refit the retaining bolts, making sure that each one is installed in its correct position **(see illustrations)**. Tighten all by hand, then go around in a diagonal sequence, and evenly and progressively tighten them to the specified torque setting.

27 Reconnect the hose to the pump, and securely tighten its retaining clip.

28 Refit the drive pulley, making sure that it is the correct way around, then refit the drivebelt as described in Chapter 1A, Section 16. Once the belt is correctly tensioned, securely tighten the pulley retaining bolts.

29 Refit the cooling fan and coupling as described in Section 5, then refill the cooling system as described in Chapter 1A.

200 TDi diesel engine

30 Ensure that the pump and cylinder block mating surfaces are clean and dry.

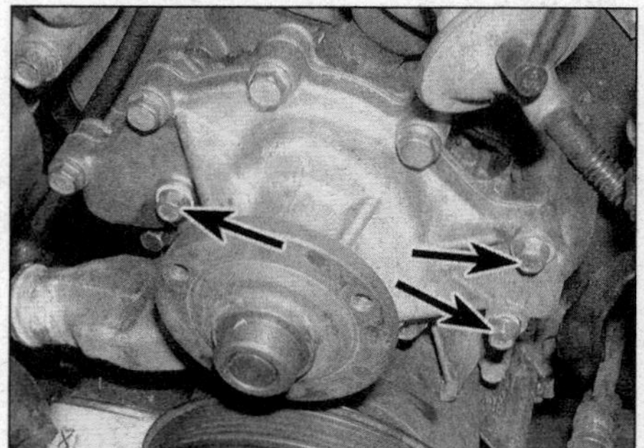

7.26b Locations (arrowed) of the three long bolts

7.26a Fit the coolant pump bolts - one of the long ones shown

31 Apply a smear of silicone grease to the new pump gasket, and position it on the pump housing.

32 Clean the threads of the long coolant pump retaining bolts (which pass through the housing and screw into the cylinder block) and apply a smear of suitable sealant to each one's threads.

33 Install the coolant pump and refit the retaining bolts, making sure that each one is installed in its correct position. Also refit the retaining nut. Tighten all by hand, then go around in a diagonal sequence, and evenly and progressively tighten them to the specified torque setting.

34 Reconnect the hose to the top of the pump, and securely tighten its retaining clip.

35 Refit the drive pulley, making sure that it is the correct way around, then refit the drivebelt as described in Chapter 1B, Section 17. Once the belt is correctly tensioned, securely tighten the pulley retaining bolts.

36 Refit the cooling fan and coupling as described in Section 5, then refill the cooling system as described in Chapter 1B.

300 TDi diesel engine

37 Ensure that the pump and cylinder block mating surfaces are clean and dry, then fit a new gasket to the housing **(see illustration)**.

38 Install the coolant pump and refit the retaining bolts, making sure that each one is installed in its correct position. Tighten all the bolts by hand, then go around in a diagonal sequence, and evenly and progressively tighten each one to the specified torque.

7.37 On refitting, ensure that the housing mating surfaces are clean and dry, and fit a new gasket

39 Refit the drive pulleys to the coolant and power steering pumps, making sure that both are fitted the correct way around.

40 Slide the tensioner assembly onto its stud. Make sure that the tensioner locating pins are correctly engaged with the mounting bracket, then refit the retaining nut and tighten it securely.

41 Refit the auxiliary drivebelt as described in Chapter 1B, Section 17, then securely tighten all the pulley retaining bolts.

42 Refit the intercooler and coolant hoses, and securely tighten their retaining clips.

43 Refill the cooling system as described in Chapter 1B.

8 Heating and ventilation system - general information

1 The heating/ventilation system consists of a four-speed blower motor, face-level vents in the centre and at each end of the facia, and air ducts to the front footwells.

2 The control unit is located in the facia, and the controls operate flap valves to deflect and mix the air flowing through the various parts of the heating/ventilation system. The flap valves are contained in the air distribution housing, which acts as a central distribution unit, passing air to the various ducts and vents.

3 Cold air enters the system through the grille at the rear of the engine compartment.

4 The airflow, which can be boosted by the blower, then flows through the various ducts, according to the settings of the controls. Stale air is expelled through ducts at the rear of the vehicle. If warm air is required, the cold air is passed through the heater matrix, which is heated by the engine coolant.

5 A recirculation lever enables the outside air supply to be closed off, while the air inside the vehicle is recirculated. This can be useful to prevent unpleasant odours entering from outside the vehicle, but should only be used briefly, as the recirculated air inside the vehicle will soon become stale.

9 Heater/ventilation components - removal and refitting

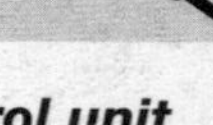

Heater/ventilation control unit

Early models (pre-March 1994)

1 Disconnect the battery negative terminal.

2 Remove the facia panel assembly as described in Chapter 12.

3 Mark the wiring connectors for identification purposes, then disconnect the wiring from the heater/ventilation control unit switches.

4 Undo the retaining screw, and remove the switches from the control unit.

5 Release the retaining clip, and disconnect the cable from the temperature control lever.

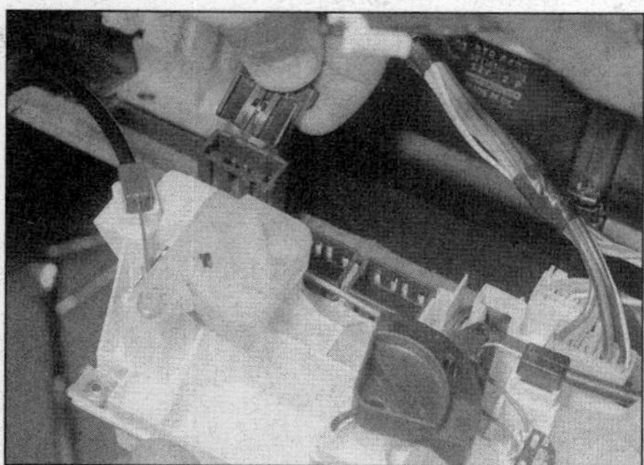

9.9 On later (March 1994 onwards) models, disconnect the wiring connectors . . .

6 Undo the retaining bolts, and lower the control unit assembly out of position. On models with air conditioning, as the unit is removed, disconnect the temperature control potentiometer wiring connector, and free its arm from the control lever. If necessary, the potentiometer can then be removed.

7 Refitting is the reverse of removal, making sure that all wiring is correctly routed and securely reconnected.

Later models (March 1994 onwards)

8 Remove the facia centre vent panel as described in Chapter 12.

9 Disconnect the wiring connectors from the rear of the control unit **(see illustration)**.

10 Noting each cable's correct fitted location, release each heater outer cable retaining clip, and release them from the rear of the unit **(see illustration)**. Remove the control unit from the facia.

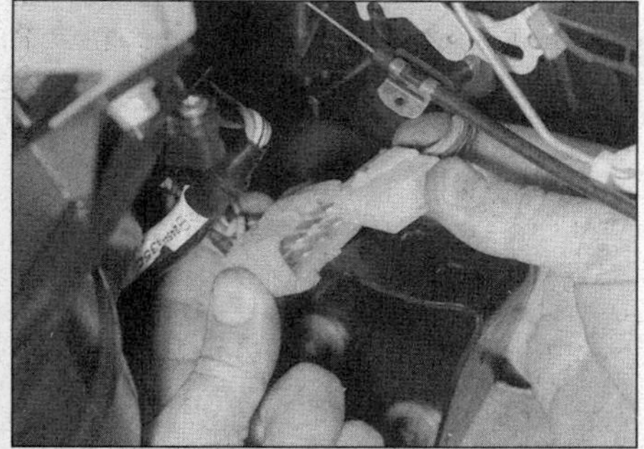

9.25 Disconnect the wiring connectors . . .

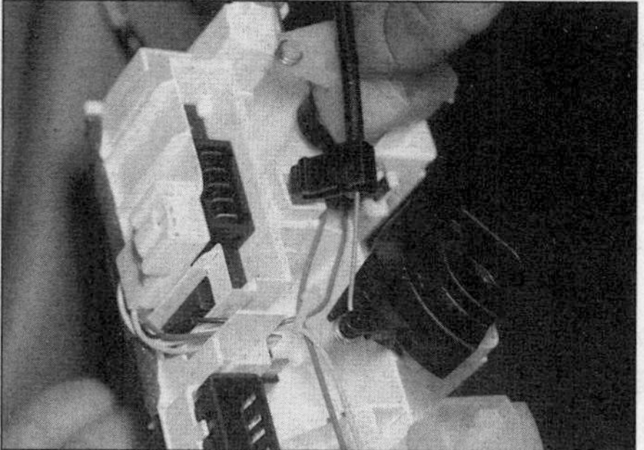

9.10 . . . then release the retaining clips and detach the control cables from the rear of the heater control unit

11 On refitting, reconnect each cable to its original location on the control unit. Temporarily refit the control knobs to the unit, and check the operation of each cable before proceeding further. The remainder of refitting is a direct reversal of the removal procedure.

Air distribution housing assembly

Early models (pre-March 1994)

12 Drain the cooling system as described in the relevant part of Chapter 1.

13 Working in the engine compartment, slacken the retaining clips and disconnect the coolant hoses from the heater matrix unions.

14 Remove the facia panel assembly as described in Chapter 12.

15 Free the rear passenger heater ducts and facia vent ducts from the air distribution housing.

16 Trace the wiring back from the heater blower motor, and disconnect it at the wiring connector.

17 Noting their correct fitted locations, disconnect the wiring connectors from the heater control switches.

18 Disconnect the wiring connectors from the air recirculation solenoid which is mounted onto the blower motor cover. Also disconnect the vacuum supply hose from the solenoid.

19 On models with air conditioning, disconnect the wiring connector from the temperature control potentiometer.

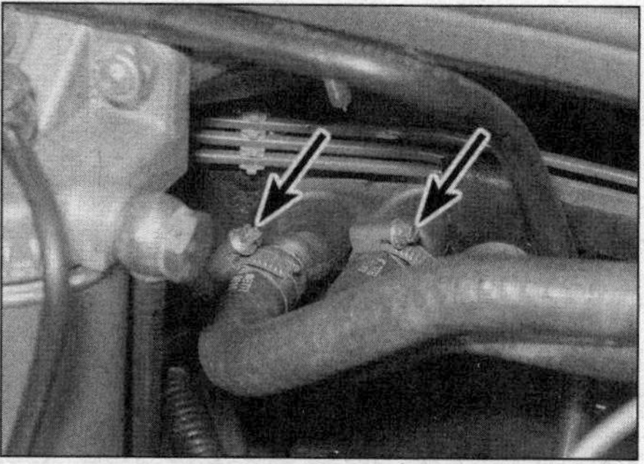

9.23 Slacken the retaining clips, and disconnect the coolant hoses from the heater matrix unions (arrowed)

20 Slacken and remove the four retaining bolts, then manoeuvre the air distribution housing assembly out of position. **Note:** *Keep the matrix unions uppermost as the matrix is removed, to reduce coolant spillage.*

21 Refitting is the reverse of removal.

HAYNES
HiNT

Mop up any spilt coolant immediately, and wipe the affected area with a damp cloth to prevent staining.

Later models (March 1994 onwards) without air conditioning

22 Drain the cooling system as described in the relevant part of Chapter 1.

23 Working in the engine compartment, slacken the retaining clips and disconnect the coolant hoses from the heater matrix unions **(see illustration)**.

24 Remove the facia panel assembly as described in Chapter 12.

25 Disconnect the wiring connectors from the blower motor housing components **(see illustration)**.

26 Slacken and remove the retaining nuts and bolt, then disengage the blower motor housing from the air distribution housing, and remove it from the vehicle **(see illustrations)**.

27 Disconnect the rear passenger footwell ducts and the rubber drain hoses from the base of the housing **(see illustrations)**.

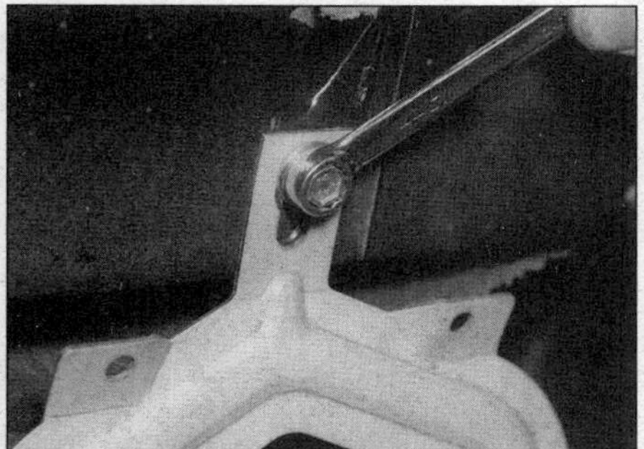

9.26a . . . then undo the retaining nuts and bolt . . .

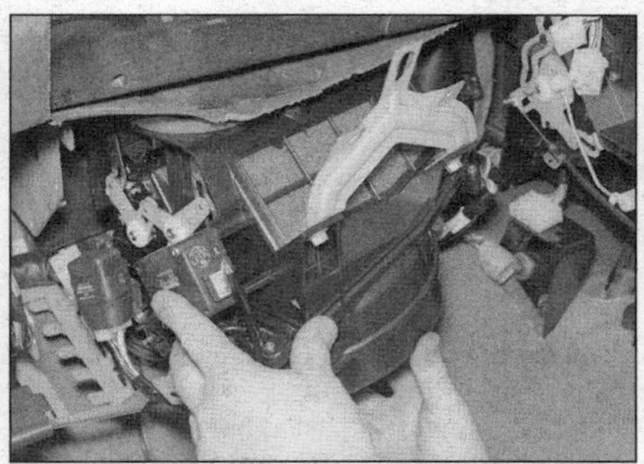

9.26b . . . and manoeuvre the blower motor housing out of position

9.27a Disconnect the rear passenger ducts . . .

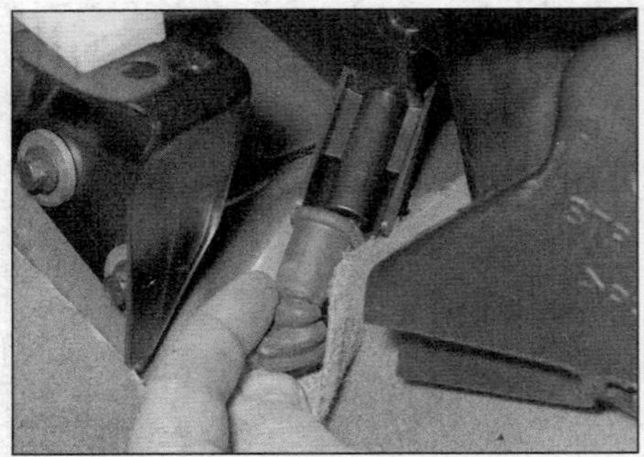

9.27b . . . and the drain hoses . . .

9.29 . . . then undo the air distribution housing retaining bolts

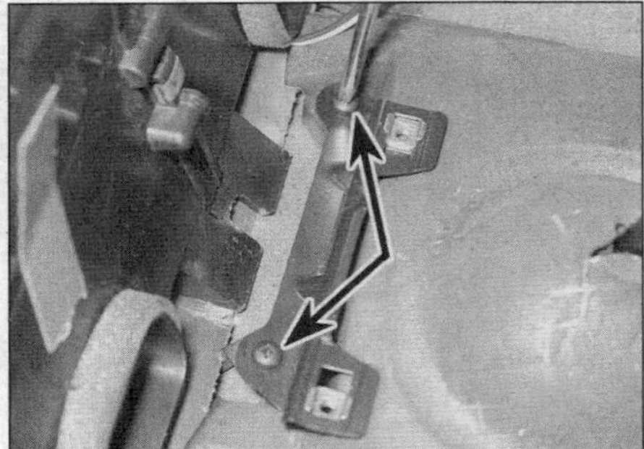

9.30a Undo the two retaining screws (arrowed) . . .

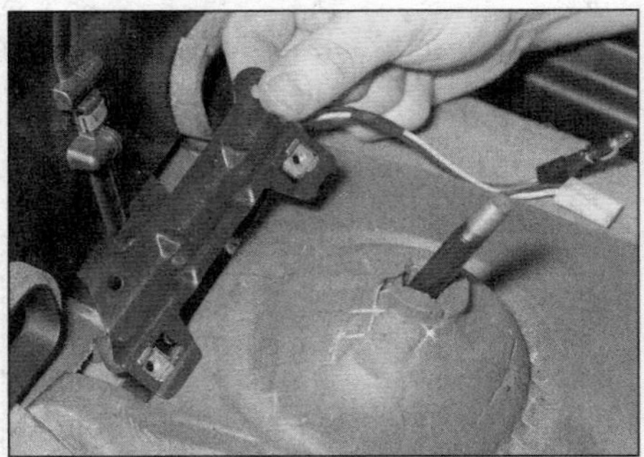

9.30b . . . and remove the centre console bracket . . .

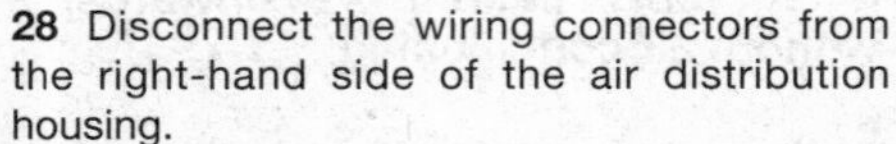

9.31 . . . then withdraw the air distribution housing from the vehicle

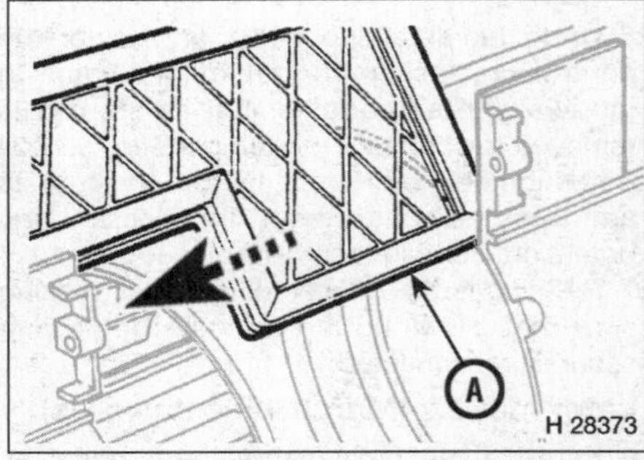
A
H 28373

9.38 On early (pre-March 1994) models, position the inlet flap (A) as shown when separating the air distribution housing casing halves

28 Disconnect the wiring connectors from the right-hand side of the air distribution housing.

29 Slacken and remove the bolts securing the air distribution housing to the bulkhead **(see illustration)**.

30 Manoeuvre the housing assembly out of position, noting that it may be necessary to undo the retaining screws and remove the centre console bracket to allow the housing to be removed **(see illustrations)**.

31 Ease the assembly away from the bulkhead, and remove it from the vehicle **(see illustration)**. **Note:** *Keep the matrix unions uppermost as the matrix is removed, to reduce coolant spillage.* Mop up any spilt coolant immediately, and wipe the affected area with a damp cloth to prevent staining. Recover the mounting rubber from the air distribution housing locating peg.

32 Refitting is a reverse of the removal procedure, making sure that the air distribution housing and blower motor housing are correctly joined.

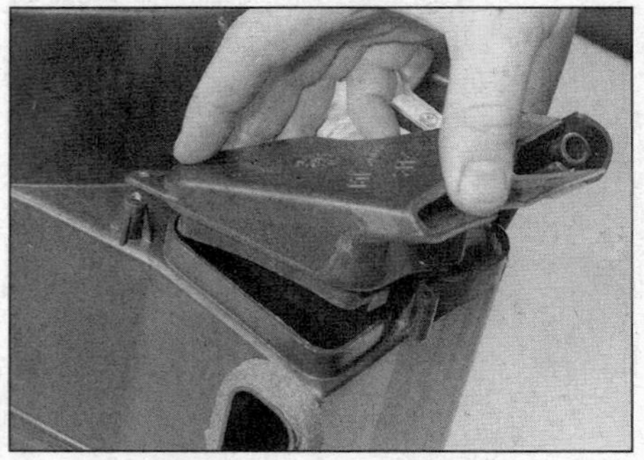

9.44 Removing the right-hand front duct from the housing

Later models (March 1994 onwards) with air conditioning

33 On models with air conditioning, it is not possible to remove the air distribution housing without opening the refrigerant circuit (See Section 11). Therefore, this task must be entrusted to a Land Rover dealer.

Heater matrix

Early models (pre-March 1994)

34 Remove the air distribution housing as described above.

35 Release the retaining clips, and detach the left-hand duct outlet union from the housing.

36 Carefully release its retaining clip, then disconnect the left-hand vent control rod from the housing.

37 Release the retaining clips and circlips securing the two halves of the air distribution housing together.

38 Position the inlet flap correctly, then carefully slide its lower edge through the gap between the blower motor housing and outer case, whilst at the same time separating each half of the housing **(see illustration)**.

39 Make a note of the correct fitted location of all the distribution housing flaps, to use as a guide on refitting, then separate the air distribution housing casing halves.

40 Remove the pad from around the heater matrix coolant hose unions, then remove the matrix access panel.

41 Carefully withdraw the heater matrix from the housing, complete with its sponge packing.

42 Refitting is the reverse of the removal procedure. Prior to installing the air distribution housing, check that each housing ventilation flap is correctly clipped into position, and opens and closes easily and smoothly.

Later models (March 1994 onwards) without air conditioning

43 Remove the air distribution housing as described above.

44 Undo the two retaining screws, and remove the right-hand front duct outlet from the housing **(see illustration)**.

45 Undo the retaining screw, and remove the heater matrix pipe retaining clip from the right-hand side of the air distribution housing.

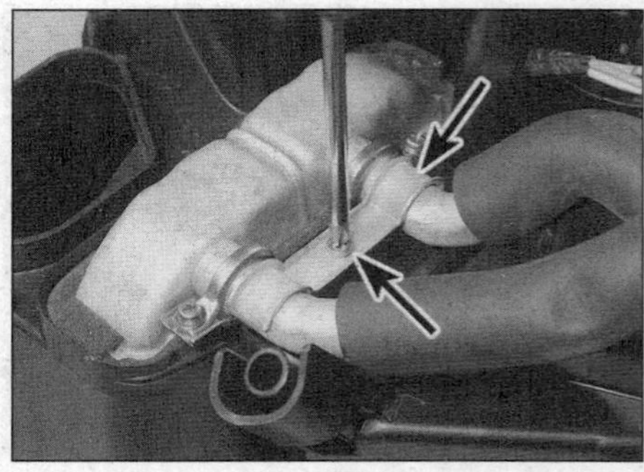

9.45a Undo the retaining screw, and remove the pipe retaining clip (arrowed) . . .

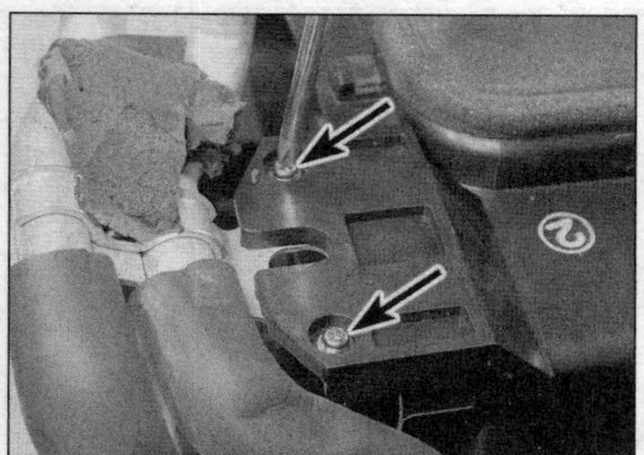
9.45b . . . then undo the two screws (arrowed) securing the pipes to the front of the distribution housing

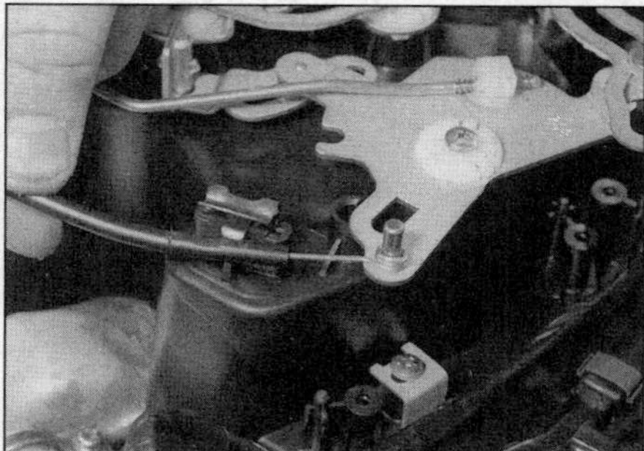
9.46a To allow the matrix to be removed, disconnect the cable . . .

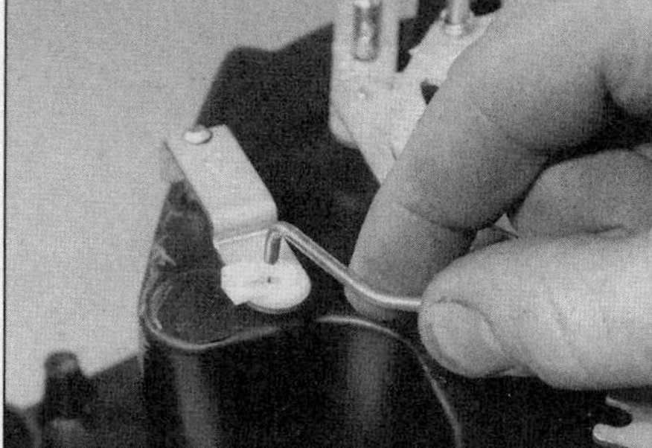
9.46b . . . and free the relevant housing link rod

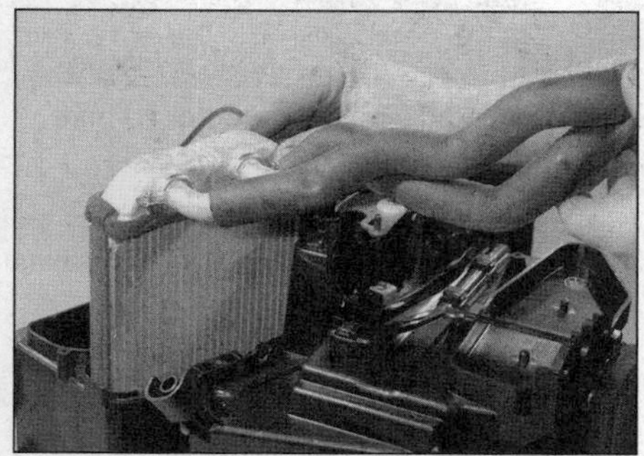
9.46c Slide the matrix and pipe assembly out of the housing . . .

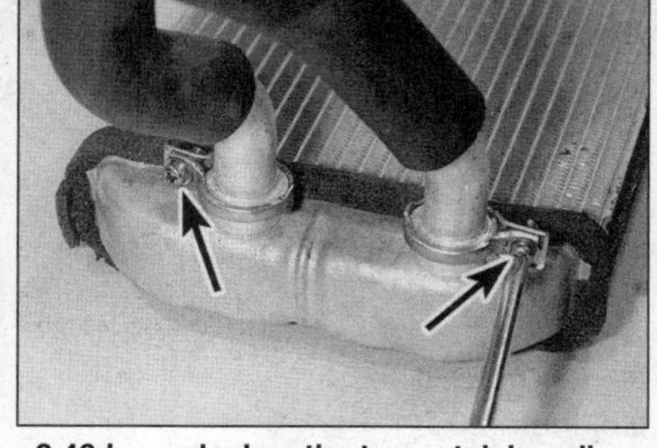
9.46d . . . slacken the two retaining clips (arrowed) . . .

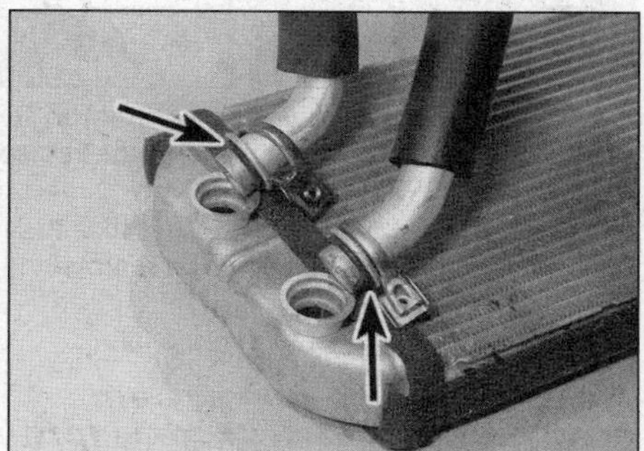
9.46e . . . then detach the pipes and recover the O-ring seals (arrowed)

Undo the two screws, and free the pipes from the front of the housing **(see illustrations)**.

46 Slide the heater matrix assembly, complete with hoses, out from the air distribution housing, noting that it may be necessary to detach the housing link rod and free the cable retaining clip to allow this. With the matrix removed, slacken the retaining clips and detach the pipes from the matrix. Recover the O-rings from the pipe unions, and discard them **(see illustrations)**.

47 Refitting is the reverse of removal, using new O-rings on the pipe unions.

Later models (March 1994 onwards) with air conditioning

48 On models with air conditioning, it is not possible to remove the heater matrix without opening the refrigerant circuit (see Section 11). Therefore, this task must be entrusted to a Land Rover dealer.

Heater blower motor

Early models (pre-March 1994)

49 Separate the air distribution housing casing as described above in paragraphs 34 to 39.

50 Release the wiring grommet, then undo the retaining screws securing the left-hand motor end cover in position.

51 Carefully detach the vacuum diaphragm unit from the inlet flap, then ease the cover away from the distribution housing. Free the blower motor resistor from its retaining clips, and remove the cover.

52 Release the blower motor retaining clips, and withdraw the motor assembly, complete with resistor, from the left-hand casing half.

53 Refitting is a reverse of the removal procedure. Prior to installing the air distribution housing, check that each housing ventilation flap is correctly clipped into position, and opens and closes easily and smoothly.

Later models (March 1994 onwards)

54 Open up the glovebox, release its hinge springs, then slacken and remove the hinge retaining screws and remove the glovebox from the facia.

55 Release the clips and remove the undercover panel from the passenger side of the facia, to gain access to the blower motor.

56 Disconnect the motor wiring connector, then undo the three retaining screws, and lower the motor assembly out from the housing **(see illustration)**.

57 If necessary, release the retaining clip, lift off the fan, then undo the retaining screws and separate the motor and casing.

58 Refitting is the reverse of removal, making sure that an airtight seal is made between the blower motor housing and the air distribution housing.

Heater blower motor resistor

Early models (pre-March 1994)

59 Remove the air distribution housing as described above.

60 Release the wiring grommet, then undo the retaining screws securing the left-hand motor end cover in position.

61 Carefully detach the vacuum diaphragm unit from the inlet flap, then ease the cover away from the distribution housing. Free the blower motor resistor from its retaining clips, and remove the cover.

62 Make identification marks on the wiring connectors, disconnect them from the resistor, and remove the resistor.

63 Refitting is the reverse of removal, making sure that the wiring connectors are correctly reconnected.

Later models (March 1994 onwards)

64 Disconnect the battery negative terminal.

65 Open up the glovebox, and release its hinge springs. This will allow the lid to be fully opened, so that access can be gained to the blower motor resistor, which is mounted on the side of the blower motor housing.

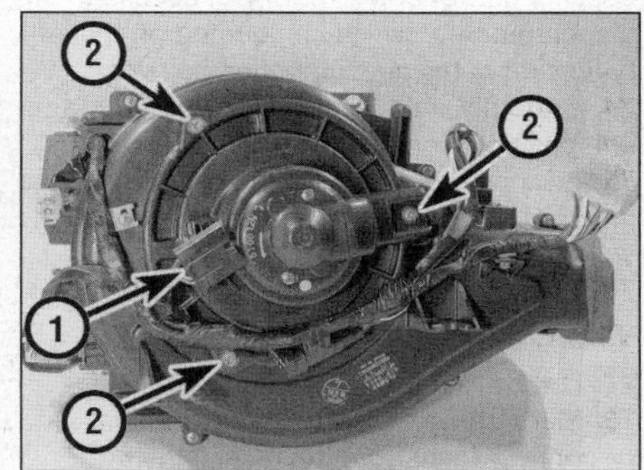
2
2
1
2
9.56 Blower motor wiring connector (1) and retaining screws (2) - shown with housing removed for clarity

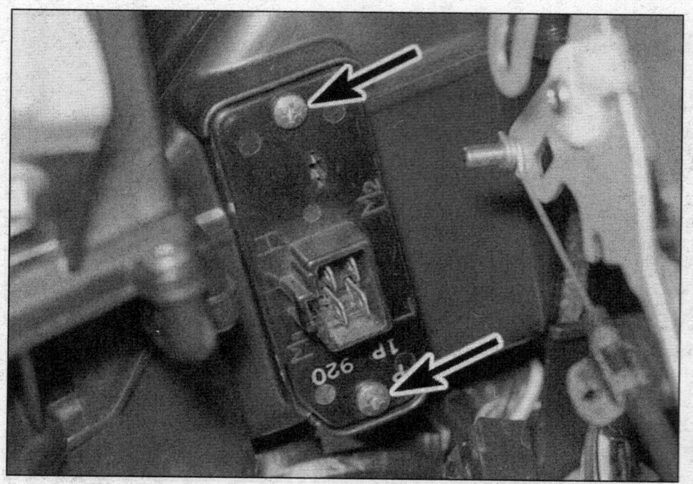

9.66 **Disconnect the wiring connector, then undo the retaining screws (arrowed) and remove the resistor from the housing**

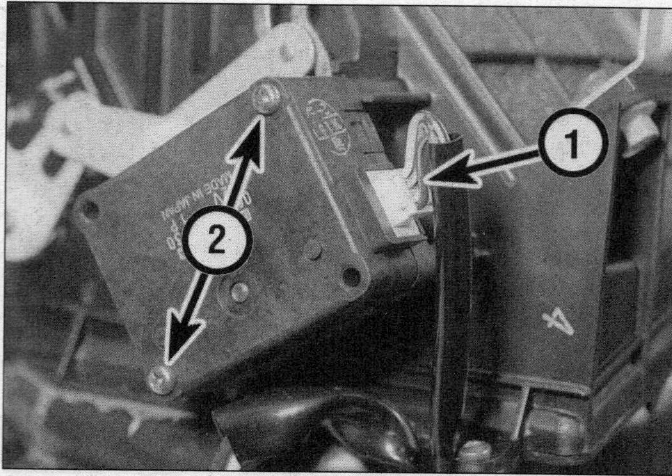
1
2

9.83 **Air recirculation flap solenoid wiring connector (1) and retaining screws (2)**

66 Disconnect the wiring connector, then undo the two retaining screws and remove the resistor unit **(see illustration)**.

67 Refitting is the reverse of removal.

Air recirculation flap system components - early models (pre-March 1994)

Switch

68 Refer to Chapter 13.

Solenoid valve

69 Remove the facia panel assembly as described in Chapter 12 to gain access to the solenoid, which is mounted on the left-hand side of the air distribution housing.

70 Mark the wiring connectors for identification, and disconnect them from the solenoid.

71 Disconnect the vacuum hoses from the solenoid, then undo the retaining screw and remove the solenoid.

72 Refitting is reverse of removal, making sure that the wiring connectors are correctly reconnected.

Vacuum diaphragm unit

73 Remove the facia panel assembly as described in Chapter 12 to gain access to the diaphragm unit, which is mounted on the left-hand side of the air distribution housing.

74 Carefully detach the vacuum diaphragm unit pushrod from the inlet flap.

75 Disconnect the vacuum hose, then undo the retaining screws and remove the unit from the vehicle.

76 Refitting is the reverse of removal.

Vacuum reservoir

77 Disconnect the battery negative lead.

78 Mark the hoses for identification, and disconnect them from the reservoir.

79 Undo the retaining nuts and washers, and remove the reservoir from the engine compartment.

Air recirculation flap system components - later models (March 1994 onwards)

Switch

80 Refer to Chapter 13.

Solenoid unit

81 Disconnect the battery negative terminal.

82 Open up the glovebox, and release its hinge springs. This will allow the lid to be fully opened, so that access can be gained to the solenoid unit, which is mounted on the side of the blower motor housing.

83 Disconnect the wiring connector and undo the two solenoid retaining screws **(see illustration)**.

84 Pivot the retaining clip away from the solenoid link rod, then free the rod from the housing and remove the solenoid unit.

85 Refitting is the reverse of removal.

10 Heater/ventilation vents - removal and refitting

Removal

Early models (pre-March 1994)

1 Remove the facia panel assembly as described in Chapter 12.

2 To remove a side vent, release the retaining clips and disconnect the duct, then push the duct out from behind the facia.

3 To remove a centre vent, undo the retaining nuts and free the duct housing from the rear of the facia. The centre vents can then be pushed out of position.

Later models (March 1994 onwards)

4 The centre vents are an integral part of the facia centre panel, and are not available separately. Refer to Chapter 12 for centre panel removal and refitting details.

5 To remove a side vent, first remove the facia panel assembly as described in Chapter 12. The vent can then be pushed out from behind the facia.

Refitting

6 Refitting is the reverse of the relevant removal procedure.

11 Air conditioning system - general information and precautions

General information

1 An air conditioning system is available on certain models. It enables the temperature of incoming air to be lowered, and also dehumidifies the air, which makes for rapid demisting and increased comfort.

2 The cooling side of the system works in the same way as a domestic refrigerator **(see illustration opposite)**. Refrigerant gas is drawn into a belt-driven compressor, and passes into a condenser mounted in front of the radiator, where it loses heat and becomes liquid. The liquid passes through an expansion valve to an evaporator, where it changes from liquid under high pressure to gas under low pressure. This change is accompanied by a drop in temperature, which cools the evaporator. The refrigerant returns to the compressor and the cycle begins again.

3 Air blown through the evaporator passes to the air distribution unit, where it is mixed with hot air blown through the heater matrix, to achieve the desired temperature in the passenger compartment.

4 The heating side of the system works in the same way as on models without air conditioning (see Section 8).

5 The operation of the system is controlled electronically by the coolant temperature switches (see Section 6), which are screwed into the thermostat housing, and pressure switches which are screwed into the compressor high-pressure line. Any problems with the system should be referred to a Land Rover dealer.

Precautions

6 When an air conditioning system is fitted, it is necessary to observe special precautions whenever dealing with any part of the system, and its associated components. If for any reason the system must be disconnected, entrust this task to your Land Rover dealer or a refrigeration engineer.

Warning: The refrigeration circuit contains a liquid refrigerant (Freon), and it is therefore dangerous to disconnect any part of the system without specialised knowledge and equipment.

7 The refrigerant is potentially dangerous, and should only be handled by qualified persons. If it is splashed onto the skin, it can cause frostbite. It is not itself poisonous, but in the presence of a naked flame (including a cigarette) it forms a poisonous gas. Uncontrolled discharging of the refrigerant is dangerous, and potentially damaging to the environment.

8 Do not operate the air conditioning system if it is known to be short of refrigerant, as this may damage the compressor.

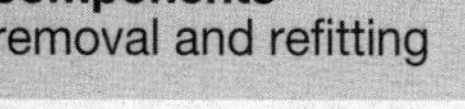

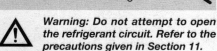

12 Air conditioning system components - removal and refitting

Warning: Do not attempt to open the refrigerant circuit. Refer to the precautions given in Section 11.

1 The only operation which can be carried out easily without discharging the refrigerant is renewal of the compressor drivebelt, which is covered in *Auxiliary drivebelt checking and renewal* in the relevant part of Chapter 1. All other operations must be referred to a Land Rover dealer or an air conditioning specialist.

2 If necessary, the compressor can be unbolted and moved aside, *without disconnecting its flexible hoses*, after removing the drivebelt.

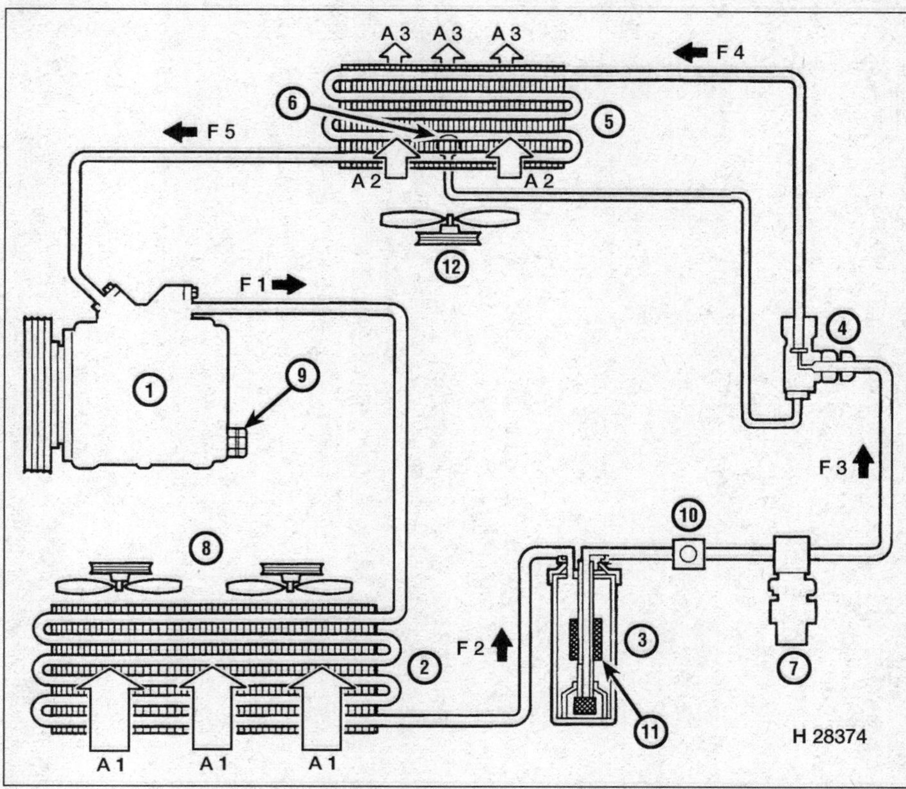
A 3
A 3
A 3
F 4
F 5
A 2
A 2
F 1
F 3
F 2
A 1
A 1
A 1
1
2
3
4
5
6
7
8
9
10
11
12
H 28374

11.2 Schematic layout of the air conditioning system components

1 *Compressor*
2 *Condenser*
3 *Receiver/drier*
4 *Thermostatic expansion valve*
5 *Evaporator*
6 *Capillary tube*
7 *Dual pressure switch*
8 *Cooling fans*
9 *Compressor high-pressure relief valve*
10 *Refrigerant sight glass*
11 *Drying agent*
12 *Blower motor*

A1 Air flow through condenser
A2 Air flow through fan and evaporator
A3 Cooled air supply to vehicle interior
F1 High-pressure high-temperature refrigerant vapour
F2 High-pressure slightly subcooled refrigerant
F3 High-pressure slightly subcooled refrigerant liquid with moisture, vapour and foreign matter removed
F4 Low-pressure low-temperature mixed liquid and vapour
F5 Low-pressure slightly superheated refrigerant vapour

Chapter 4 Part A:
Fuel system - carburettor models

Contents

Degrees of difficulty

Easy, suitable for novice with little experience 

Fairly easy, suitable for beginner with some experience 

Fairly difficult, suitable for competent DIY mechanic

Difficult, suitable for experienced DIY mechanic

Very difficult, suitable for expert DIY or professional

Specifications

General

System type	Twin SU carburettors, manual choke operation. Electric fuel pump, mounted in tank
Minimum octane rating (all models)	95 RON unleaded

Carburettors

Type	2 x SU HIF44
Jet size	2.5 mm
Needle	BGV
Idle speed	700 ± 50 rpm
Fast idle speed	1100 ± 50 rpm
CO content (at idle)	1.0 to 2.0 %

Torque wrench settings	**Nm**	**lbf ft**
Fuel pump/sender unit locking ring	50	37
Inlet manifold bolts	50	37
Inlet manifold gasket clamp bolts	20	15

1 General information and precautions

Early Discovery models are fitted with twin SU carburettors, with manual choke operation for cold starting.

The fuel system comprises a fuel tank with a submerged low-pressure electric fuel pump, a fuel filter, fuel supply and return lines, and the twin carburettors.

The fuel pump delivers a constant supply of fuel through a cartridge filter to the carburettors. A spill pipe returns excess fuel from the carburettors back to the fuel tank.

Inlet air is drawn into the engine through the air cleaner, which contains two renewable paper filter elements.

For information on the exhaust and emission control systems, refer to part D of this Chapter.

SU HIF carburettor - description

The SU HIF (Horizontal Integral Float chamber) carburettor is the last significant development of the SU design which has been around since the 1960s. Each carburettor is of the variable-choke, constant-depression type, incorporating a sliding piston which automatically controls the mixture of air and fuel supplied to the engine with respect to the throttle valve position and engine speed.

The carburettor functions as follows. When the engine is started and is allowed to idle, the throttle valve passes a small amount of air. Because the piston is in a low position, it offers a large restriction, and the resultant pressure reduction draws fuel from the jet, and atomisation occurs to provide a combustible mixture. Since the inside section of the tapered needle is across the mouth of the jet, a relatively small amount of fuel is passed.

When the throttle valve is opened, the amount of air passing through the carburettor is increased, which causes a greater depression beneath the sliding piston. An internal passageway connects this depression with the suction chamber above the piston, which now rises. The piston offers less of a restriction and the depression is reduced, with the result that a point is reached where the forces of depression, gravity, and spring tension balance out. The tapered needle has now been raised, and more fuel passes from the jet.

If the throttle is opened suddenly, the natural tendency of the air valve piston to rise - causing a weak mixture when it is least required (ie during acceleration) - is prevented by a hydraulic damper which delays the piston in its upward travel. The air intake is thus restricted and a proportionately larger quantity of fuel to air is drawn through.

Incorporated in the jet adjusting (mixture) screw mechanism is a bi-metal strip which alters the position of the jet to compensate for varying fuel densities resulting from varying fuel temperatures.

For cold starting, the carburettor incorporates a disc valve which allows additional fuel to flow into the mixture stream. The disc valve itself incorporates several orifices which are progressively uncovered as the disc is moved when the choke control is pulled. The throttle butterfly is also opened a small amount. Also included is a temperature-controlled valve which weakens the mixture under light load and idling conditions when the engine is hot.

The overall effect of this type of carburettor is that it will remain in tune during the lengthy service intervals and also under varying operating conditions and temperature changes. The design of the unit and its related systems ensures a fine degree of mixture control over the complete throttle range, coupled with enhanced engine fuel economy.

Precautions

Warning: Many of the procedures in this Chapter require the removal of fuel lines and connections, which may result in some fuel spillage. Before carrying out any operation on the fuel system, refer to the precautions given in Safety first! at the beginning of this manual, and follow them implicitly. Petrol is a highly-dangerous and volatile liquid, and the precautions necessary when handling it cannot be overstressed.

Do not smoke, or allow any naked flames or uncovered light bulbs near the work area. Note that gas-powered domestic appliances with pilot flames, such as heaters boilers and tumble-dryers, also present a fire hazard - bear this in mind if you are working in an area where such appliances are present. Always keep a suitable fire extinguisher close to the work area, and familiarise yourself with its operation before starting work. Wear eye protection when working on fuel systems, and wash off any fuel spilt on bare skin immediately with soap and water. Note that fuel vapour is just as dangerous as liquid fuel - possibly more so; a vessel (such as the fuel tank) that has been emptied of liquid fuel will still contain vapour, and can be potentially explosive.

Although a low-pressure electric fuel pump is used, some residual fuel pressure may still remain in the fuel system, long after the engine has been switched off. This pressure must be relieved in a controlled manner before disconnecting any part of the fuel system - refer to Section 6 for details.

When working with fuel system components, pay particular attention to cleanliness - dirt entering the fuel system may cause blockages, which will lead to poor running.

In the interests of personal safety, many of the procedures in this Chapter suggest that the negative lead be removed from the battery terminal. This eliminates the possibility of accidental short-circuits being caused as the vehicle is being worked upon, which would be particularly dangerous if the fuel system is open.

2 Air cleaner - removal and refitting

1 The air cleaner is an oval metal cylinder. A paper disposable air filter is fitted into each end and alloy elbows feed the air to the twin carburettors. The air cleaner is located on mounting pegs attached to the rear of the inlet manifold, and the air intake protrudes forward between the carburettors.

Removal

2 Slacken the hose clips on either end of the air cleaner and pull the elbows from the carburettors and air cleaner assembly.

3 Using two open-ended spanners, disconnect the one-way valve hose from the flame trap.

4 Remove the air cleaner assembly from the retaining posts by lifting it and pulling it forwards. As the assembly is withdrawn, disconnect the crankcase breather hose from its base.

Refitting

5 Refit the air cleaner into position, making sure that the breather hoses are reconnected. Reconnect the flame trap to the one-way valve, then refit the elbows and secure the hose clips.

3 Accelerator cable - removal, refitting and adjustment

Removal

Note: *New split-pins should be used to secure the cable end clevis pins on refitting.*

1 Remove the air cleaner as described in Section 2.

2 Remove the split pin and clevis pin, and disconnect the cable end from the operating linkage.

3 Slide back the rubber cover, and loosen the locknut and adjuster nut so that the adjuster can be removed from the bracket.

4 Where applicable, release the accelerator cable from the bracket on the engine compartment bulkhead, noting the cable routing.

5 Working inside the vehicle, release the securing clips, and withdraw the driver's side lower facia panel. This will allow access to the accelerator pedal assembly.

6 Remove the split-pin, and withdraw the clevis pin securing the end of the cable to the accelerator pedal.

7 Release the cable grommet from the bulkhead, then withdraw the cable through the bulkhead into the engine compartment.

Refitting

8 Refitting is a reversal of removal, bearing in mind the following points:

a) Ensure that the cable is routed as noted before removal.

b) Use new split-pins to secure the cable end clevis pins.

c) On completion, check the cable adjustment, as described in the following paragraphs.

Adjustment

9 Ensure the throttle lever is in the fully-closed position, by pressing the lever fully against its stop.

10 Loosen the locknut, then turn the adjuster nut to give a small amount of freeplay in the inner cable, so that the throttle lever is free to return to the closed (idle) position, but without undue slack. If there is any reluctance to return to idle, lubricate the throttle linkages with a few drops of light oil.

11 With the aid of an assistant, check that the accelerator lever moves to the full-throttle position when the accelerator pedal is fully depressed.

12 With the handbrake applied and the transmission in neutral, start the engine. Press and release the accelerator pedal several times, and ensure the engine returns to idle promptly. On completion, check and if necessary adjust the idle speed as described in Chapter 1A.

4 Accelerator pedal - removal and refitting

Removal

1 Working inside the vehicle, release the securing clips, and withdraw the driver's side lower facia panel. This will allow access to the accelerator pedal assembly.

2 Remove the split-pin, and withdraw the clevis pin securing the end of the cable to the accelerator pedal.

3 Using a suitable pair of circlip pliers, remove the circlip from one end of the pedal pivot pin.

4 Withdraw the pivot pin from the pedal bracket, and recover the bushes, noting their locations. Withdraw the pedal and return spring, noting the orientation of the spring.

Refitting

5 Refitting is a reversal of removal, bearing in mind the following points:

a) Ensure that the pedal return spring and the pivot bushes are located as noted during removal. Lubricate the pivot pin with a little light oil or grease.

b) On completion, check the accelerator cable adjustment, as described in Section 3.

5 Choke cable - removal and refitting

Removal

1 The choke cable is attached to the trunnion at the front of the left-hand carburettor (left and right are as seen from the driver's seat). Undo the screw to release it. If the cable is to be refitted, note how far the inner cable protrudes from the trunnion.

2 Disconnect the outer cable from the cable clamp by the carburettor and the clip on the air cleaner housing. Again, note the fitted position of the outer cable if it is to be refitted.

3 Working inside the vehicle, release the securing clips, and withdraw the driver's side lower facia panel. Disconnect the choke warning light switch cables from the choke control assembly.

4 Pull out the outer cable retaining clip, then release the bulkhead grommet and withdraw the choke control knob and cable complete.

Refitting

5 Refitting is a reversal of removal, bearing in mind the following points:

a) If the old cable is being refitted, position the inner and outer cables as noted on removal.

b) On completion, check the cable adjustment, as described below.

Adjustment

6 Before starting the adjustment, make sure that the fast idle adjustment procedure has been carried out, as described in Chapter 1A, Section 12.

7 Pull out the choke control to the full choke position.

8 At the left-hand carburettor, check to see whether the choke lever has been pulled against its stop. Now push the choke control fully home, and ensure the choke lever has returned to the off position. If not, proceed as follows.

9 There are two ways to adjust the choke cable - neither way is uniquely right, and some trial-and-error may be required.

10 To adjust the outer cable, loosen the cable clamp and move the cable as necessary. If the choke is not operating enough, pull the cable out of the clamp slightly, and tighten the clamp. If the choke is not returning, push the cable through the clamp before retightening it. Push the choke control fully in, then pull it fully out again, and re-check the adjustment.

11 Adjusting the inner cable is similar to the outer cable - on an older car, it is likely that the inner cable will have stretched, causing the choke not to operate sufficiently. Holding the choke lever in the full-choke position, loosen the inner cable screw and pull the cable through taut, tightening the screw when in the right position. Push the choke control fully in, then pull it fully out again, and re-check the adjustment.

6 Fuel system - depressurisation

Note 1: *Observe the precautions in Section 1 before working on any component in the fuel system.*

Note 2: *The fuel pressure on carburettor models is lower than that found in those with fuel injection, but there is still a risk of uncontrolled fuel spray if the procedures below are not followed.*

***Warning:** The following procedure will merely relieve the pressure in the fuel system - remember that fuel will still be present in the system components, and take precautions accordingly before disconnecting any of them.*

1 The fuel system referred to in this Section is defined as the tank-mounted fuel pump, the fuel filter, and the metal pipes and flexible hoses of the fuel lines between these components. All these contain fuel, which will be under pressure while the engine is running and/or while the ignition is switched on. The pressure will remain for some time after the ignition has been switched off, and must be relieved before any of these components are disturbed for servicing work. Ideally, the engine should be allowed to cool completely before work commences.

2 Identify and remove the fuel pump fuse from the fusebox (see Chapter 13).

3 With the fuel pump disabled, crank the engine for about ten seconds. The engine may fire and run for a while, but let it continue running until it stops. This will lower the line fuel pressure, and reduce the risk of fuel spraying out when a fuel line is disturbed.

4 Switch off the ignition, disconnect the battery negative terminal, then refit the fuel pump fuse.

5 Place a suitable container beneath the relevant connection/union to be disconnected, and have a large rag ready to soak up any escaping fuel not being caught by the container.

6 Slowly loosen the connection to avoid a sudden release of pressure, and position the rag around the connection to catch any fuel spray which may be expelled. Once the pressure has been released, disconnect the fuel line. Insert plugs to minimise fuel loss and prevent the entry of dirt into the fuel system.

7 Carburettors - removal and refitting

Removal

1 Depressurise the fuel system as described in Section 6.

2 Remove the air cleaner as described in Section 2.

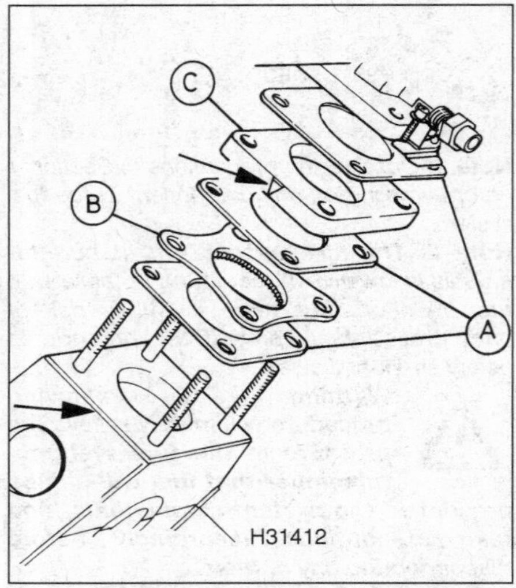
C
B
A
H31412
7.9 Correct fitted order of the carburettor gaskets (A), liner (B) and insulator (C)
Arrows indicate insulator alignment markings

3 Disconnect the rocker cover breather pipes from the carburettors, as applicable.

4 Disconnect the main fuel and choke fuel supply pipes which run between the carburettors.

5 To remove the left-hand carburettor (left as seen from the driver's seat), disconnect the following:
- *a) Accelerator cable (Section 3).*
- *b) Choke cable (Section 5).*
- *c) Fuel supply pipe at the front of the carburettor.*
- *d) Throttle linkage between the carburettors.*
- *e) Vacuum pipe to the distributor.*

6 To remove the right-hand carburettor, disconnect the following:
- *a) Fuel return pipe from the union in front of the carburettor.*
- *b) Throttle linkage between the carburettors.*
- *c) Brake vacuum servo hose from inlet manifold (for convenience).*

7 Undo the four retaining nuts and spring washers for each carburettor, and lift it away.

8 The gaskets and insulator can then be removed if necessary. Note that there is a liner fitted inside the insulator on some models.

Refitting

9 Refitting of the carburettors is the reverse of the removal procedure, but the following points should be noted:
- *a) Clean the mating faces of the carburettors and the inlet manifold.*
- *b) Fit the inner gasket, followed by the liner (where applicable), taking care to ensure that the lugs locate properly in the insulator recesses and do not stand proud.* ***Note:*** *The liner can only be fitted one way round, that is with the teeth engaged in the slots.*
- *c) Fit the next gasket and the insulator, making sure that the arrow is uppermost and pointing towards the centre of the manifold. Fit the final gasket, then the carburettor can be mounted in place* ***(see illustration)****.*
- *d) Refit the retaining nuts and spring washers, and tighten evenly.*

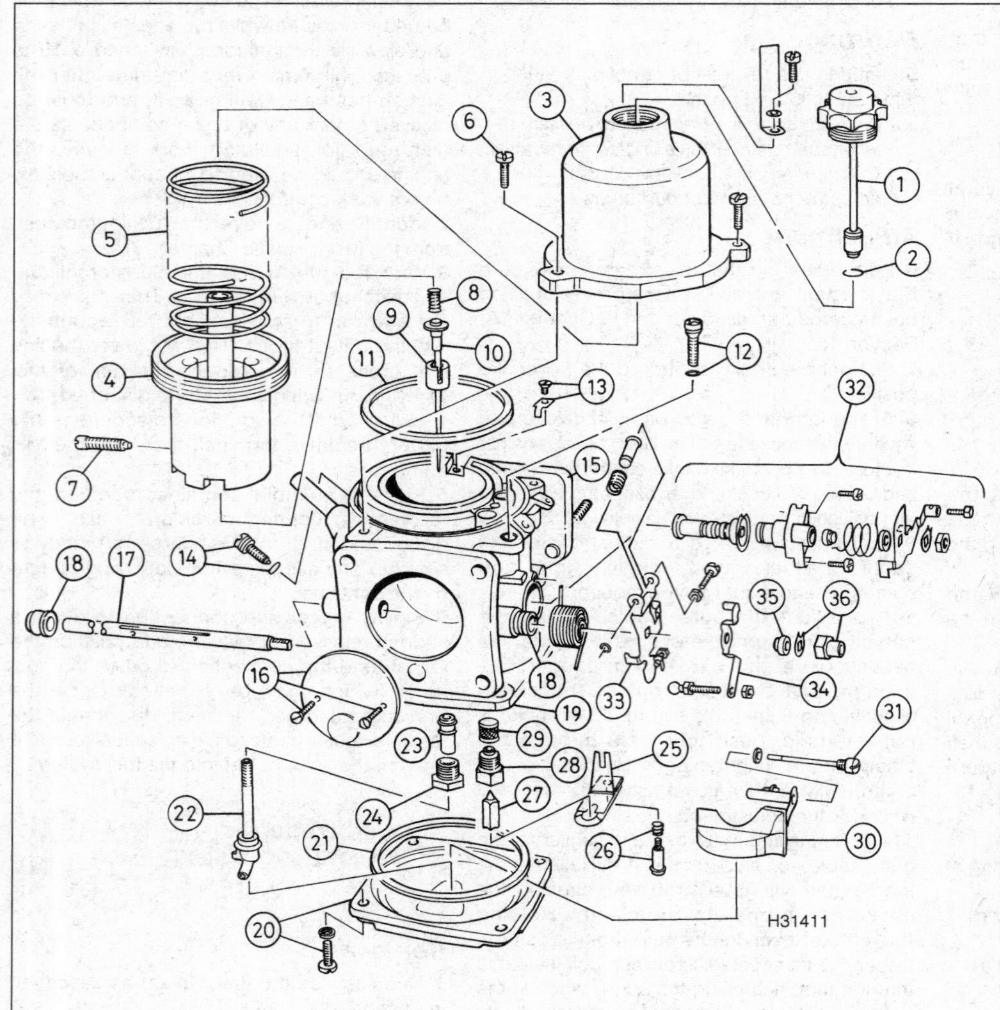
H31411

1 Piston damper
2 Spring clip
3 Suction chamber
4 Piston
5 Piston spring
6 Suction chamber retaining screws
7 Needle retaining screw
8 Needle bias spring
9 Needle guide
10 Needle
11 Suction chamber sealing ring
12 Throttle adjusting screw and seal
13 Piston key and retaining screw
14 Mixture adjusting screw and seal
15 Carburettor body
16 Throttle butterfly and retaining screws
17 Throttle spindle
18 Throttle spindle seals
19 Float chamber
20 Float chamber cover and retaining screws
21 Seal
22 Jet assembly
23 Jet bearing
24 Jet bearing nut
25 Bi-metal jet lever
26 Jet retaining screw and spring
27 Float needle
28 Float needle seat
29 Float needle seat filter
30 Float
31 Float pivot spindle
32 Cold start and cam lever assembly
33 Throttle adjusting lever and lost motion assembly
34 Throttle actuating lever
35 Bush washer
36 Throttle lever assembly retaining nut and lock washer

8.4 Exploded view of the SU HIF carburettor

10 The remainder of the fitting procedure is a direct reversal of the removal sequence. On completion, adjust the carburettors as described in Chapter 1A, Section 12.

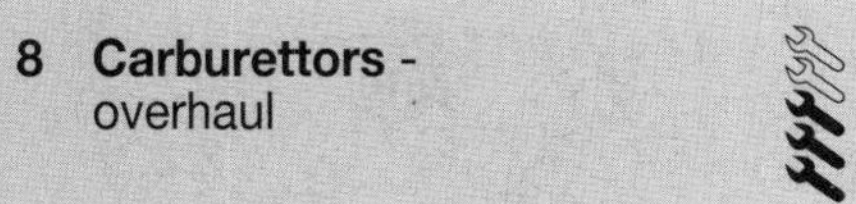

8 Carburettors - overhaul

Note: *The following procedure is for the right-hand carburettor. The left-hand carburettor procedure is similar.*

Dismantling

1 Remove the carburettor from the engine as described in Section 7, and clean it with fuel or paraffin.
2 Remove the nuts and spring washers, and remove the air inlet adaptor and the gasket.
3 Unscrew the piston damper and drain the oil into a suitable container.
4 Mark the suction chamber and piston body in relation to each other with a pencil. Remove the screws and withdraw the suction chamber, together with the piston and spring **(see illustration opposite)**.
5 Extract the circlip from the top of the piston rod, and remove the piston and spring.
6 Unscrew the metering needle guide locking screw and remove the needle, guide and spring assembly from the piston. If difficulty is experienced, carefully grip the needle in a soft-jawed vice close to the piston, and give the piston a sharp pull. Take care not to bend the needle.
7 Invert the carburettor, then loosen the screws and remove the float chamber cover plate and sealing ring from the bottom of the carburettor.
8 Unscrew the jet adjusting lever mounting screw, and remove the spring.
9 Remove the jet, together with the bi-metal lever, and separate the lever from the jet.
10 Hold the float, then unscrew and remove the pivot spindle and remove the washer. Withdraw the float.
11 Remove the needle valve from its seat.
12 Unscrew and remove the needle valve seat, and remove the filter.
13 Unscrew the jet bearing nut, then invert the carburettor and extract the jet bearing. If necessary, tap the carburettor to release the bearing.
14 Loosen the screw and remove the piston guide key. Remove the suction chamber sealing ring.
15 Unscrew and remove the mixture adjusting screw and seal, using thin-nosed pliers to withdraw the screw.
16 Bend back the tabs and remove the cam lever nut and lockwasher. Remove the cam lever and spring.
17 Remove the end seal cover and seal.
18 Remove the screws and withdraw the cold start valve body and seal, together with the valve spindle **(see illustration)**. Remove the gasket.

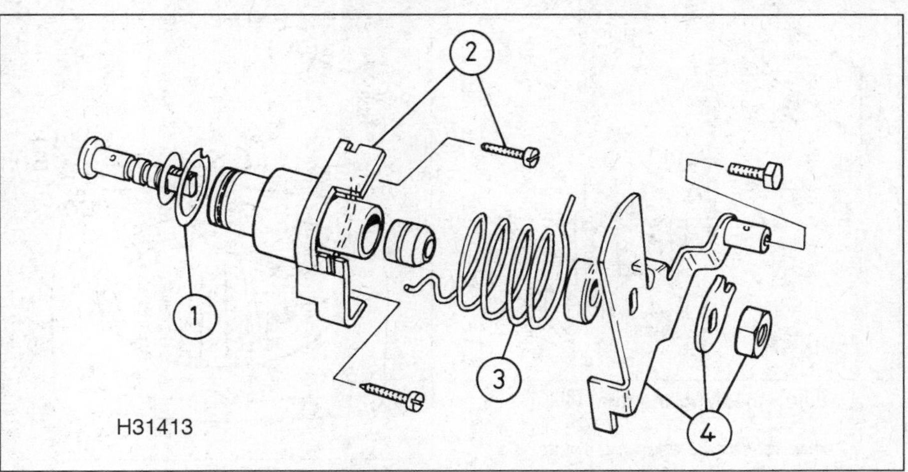
1
2
3
4
H31413

8.18 Cold start valve components

1 *Washer with half-moon cut-out*
2 *Body and screws*
3 *Return spring*
4 *Cam lever, lock washer and nut*

19 Note the positions of the throttle levers and the return spring, then bend back the tab and remove the throttle lever nut. Withdraw the lockwasher, bush washer and the throttle actuating lever.
20 Release the throttle return spring, and remove the throttle adjusting lever from the throttle butterfly spindle. Remove the return spring.
21 With the butterfly shut, mark the butterfly in relation to the carburettor flange. Unscrew the remaining screws and withdraw the butterfly from the spindle.
22 Remove the throttle butterfly spindle from the carburettor body, together with the two seals.

Inspection

23 Wash all components in fuel or paraffin, and examine them for wear and damage.
24 In particular, check the throttle spindle and bearing for excessive play, the float needle and seating for wear, the float for punctures, the carburettor body for cracks, the metering needle for wear and scoring, and the bi-metal jet for cracks.
25 Check all springs and renew all seals.
26 Clean the inside of the suction chamber and the piston, then locate the piston in the chamber without the spring. Hold the assembly horizontal and spin the piston - it should spin freely in all positions. If there is any tendency to stick, check for any foreign matter or for distortion, and renew the components as necessary.

Reassembly

27 Commence reassembly by inserting the throttle spindle into the carburettor body, then insert the butterfly into the spindle in its correct position as noted on removal. Insert the screws but before tightening them, close the throttle firmly to ensure that the butterfly is centred correctly. After tightening the screws, carefully splay the inner ends to lock them.
28 Locate the new seals on both ends of the throttle spindle, making sure that they are the correct way round.
29 Locate a new O-ring to the cold start valve body, and assemble the valve spindle to the valve body. Fit the new gasket to the valve, noting that the half-moon cut-out in the washer is positioned for the top retaining screw.
30 Refit the cold start assembly to the carburettor body, and fit and tighten the screws.
31 Fit the end seal and cover, followed by the spring.
32 Refit the cam lever and tension the spring, then fit a new lockwasher and secure with the nut. Bend over the locktab to secure. Check that the spring is located correctly and re-position the coils if necessary.
33 Refit the throttle lever return spring so that the longest leg rests against the throttle adjusting screw housing.
34 Refit the throttle adjusting lever and lost motion assembly, and tension the return spring.
35 Fit the throttle actuating lever, then refit the bush washer and lockwasher. Refit the special nut and bend over the locktabs to lock.
36 Refit the jet bearing with its long end towards the float, then refit the bearing nut.
37 Clean the filter and refit it followed by the float seat. Tighten securely.
38 Locate the needle valve in the seat, with its spring-loaded pin uppermost.
39 Locate the float in the carburettor body, then insert the pivot pin with the washer and tighten.
40 With the carburettor inverted and the needle valve closed by the weight of the float only, use a straight-edge and check that the ridge on the float is 0.5 to 1.5 mm below the level of the float chamber face. If not, adjust the position by bending the brass pad until the correct dimension is achieved **(see**

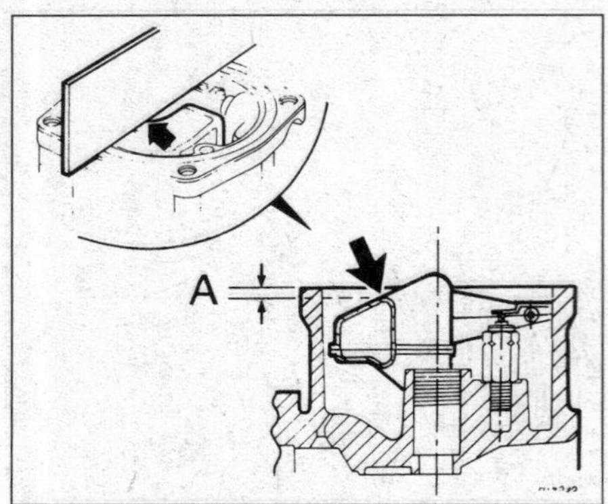
A

8.40 Checking the float level

Arrows indicate checking points
A 0.5 to 1.5 mm

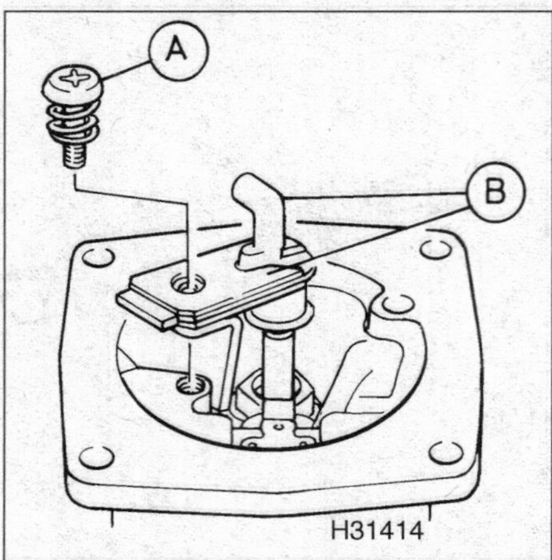
A
B
H31414

8.42 Spring-loaded screw (A) secures bi-metal jet assembly (B)

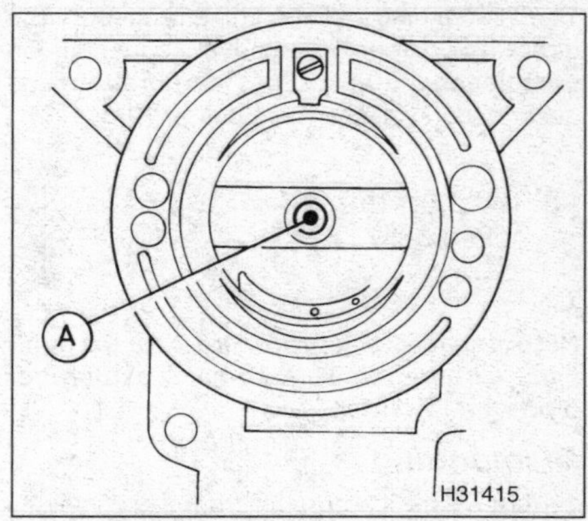
A
H31415

8.43 Adjust the jet (A) flush with the carburettor bridge - use a straight edge to check

illustration). Make sure that the float pivots correctly on the spindle.

41 Assemble the jet to the bi-metal jet lever, and make sure that the jet head moves freely in the cut-out.

42 Refit the jet and bi-metal jet lever to the carburettor, and secure with the spring-loaded jet retaining screw **(see illustration)**.

43 Refit the mixture adjusting screw and adjust until the jet is flush with the carburettor bridge, then turn the screw 3 1/2 turns clockwise **(see illustration)**.

44 Refit the float chamber cover together with a new gasket. Insert the screw and washer, and tighten securely.

45 Locate the needle, spring and guide assembly to the piston, making sure that the etched arrow head on the needle locating guide is aligned between the piston transfer holes. Insert and tighten the screw, making sure that the guide is flush with the piston and that the screw locates in the guide slot **(see illustration)**.

46 Locate the piston key on the body and tighten the screw. Splay the end of the screw to lock it.

47 Locate a new sealing ring in the groove in the carburettor body.

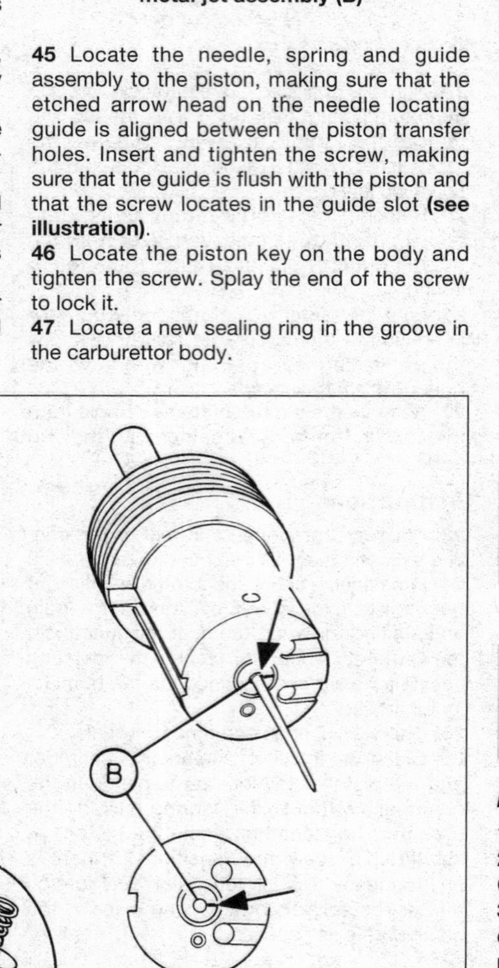
A
B
H31416

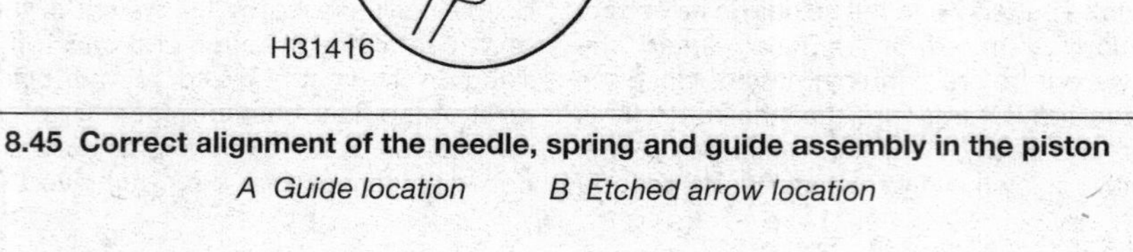

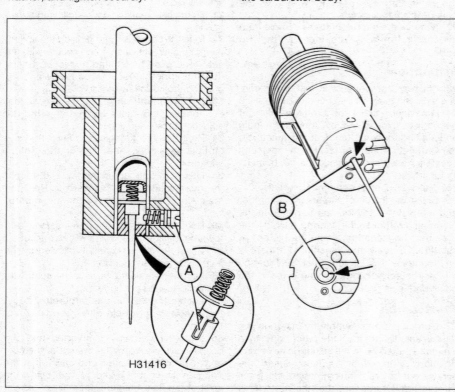

8.45 Correct alignment of the needle, spring and guide assembly in the piston

A Guide location B Etched arrow location

48 Locate the piston and needle assembly in the carburettor body, followed by the spring.

49 Hold the suction chamber over the spring in its correct position in relation to the body, then lower the chamber onto the spring and onto the body, taking care not to rotate the chamber. Failure to observe this may result in the spring being 'wound up'. Insert and tighten the screws, then check that the piston moves up and down freely.

50 With the piston held at the top of its stroke, refit the circlip.

51 Top-up the piston with the correct quantity of oil, then insert the piston damper and tighten.

52 Refit the air inlet adaptor together with a new gasket, and refit the carburettor as described in Section 7.

9 Carburettors - tuning and adjustment

Refer to Chapter 1A, Section 12.

10 Inlet manifold - removal and refitting

Removal

1 Disconnect the battery negative lead.

2 Drain the cooling system as described in Chapter 1A.

3 Remove the air cleaner assembly as described in Section 2. If the manifold is being removed as part of an engine overhaul procedure, the carburettors need not be removed separately, and can be removed with the manifold as an assembly.

4 Disconnect the following items first, if they have not already been removed:

a) Distributor advance/retard vacuum pipe. This can be disconnected from the left-hand carburettor and its retaining bracket from the inlet manifold, or from the distributor.

b) The engine breather hoses and flame traps from between the carburettors and rocker covers.
c) The bypass hoses from the front of the inlet manifold to the water pump, and the heater hoses.
d) The brake servo vacuum pipe.

5 There are twelve bolts securing the inlet manifold to the cylinder heads. These should be loosened progressively in a diagonal sequence, starting with the outermost bolts and working inwards. The bolts are of differing lengths, so take note of their exact locations as they are removed.

6 Any bolts removed from the cylinder heads or block should have their threads cleaned with a wire brush dipped in paraffin or clean petrol. If this cleaning cannot be carried out immediately, it is vital that they are stored in petrol or paraffin, as the sealant used when the bolts were originally fitted will tend to harden on exposure to the air, making its removal difficult.

7 Move aside the heater hoses and the hose from the water pump, and ease the manifold away from the cylinder head.

8 Before removing the gasket clamps, ensure that there is no coolant lying on top of the gasket. Remove the clamps and lift away the gasket, followed by the rubber gasket seals. Discard the gasket and seals - new items must be fitted on assembly.

Refitting

9 As the inlet manifold also serves to cover the pushrod cavities of the cylinder block, a single manifold gasket is fitted. Made from sheet metal, this gasket extends downwards over the inlet port face of each cylinder head, and over each of the respective pushrod cavities. Rubber seals are fitted at each end, to seal the manifold to the timing chest and rear flange. It is important that the gasket and seals are carefully fitted, or oil leaks may develop.

10 Clean all the mating surfaces of the manifold, and the cylinder heads and block.

11 Apply a blob of suitable sealant (Land Rover recommend Loctite Superflex) to the four outer notches formed between the cylinder heads and block, where the new seals will be fitted.

12 Locate the new seals to the front and rear walls of the engine. The seals must be smeared on both sides with silicone grease and their ends must locate in the notches between the cylinder head and cylinder block joints.

13 Apply gasket sealing compound to the joints between the seals and cylinder heads, and around the manifold gasket cylinder head and inlet manifold water passages.

14 Fit the new gasket with the word FRONT at the front. The open notch should be at the right-hand side front (right as seen from the driver's seat).

15 Refit the two gasket clamps, but do not tighten the bolts fully. Note that the two clamps are different, and can only fit at one end or the other.

16 Lower the inlet manifold into position. Note that the open bolt hole aligns with the open hole in the gasket.

17 If not already done, clean the threads of the manifold securing bolts, then coat the threads with locking compound (Land Rover recommend Loctite 572, available from dealers).

18 Refit the manifold bolts to their positions as noted on removal - the bolts with the slotted heads fit to the two central positions each side.

19 Tighten the bolts evenly and gradually, working on alternate sides from the centre to the ends. Do not exceed the specified torque.

20 Tighten the gasket clamps front and rear to the specified torque.

21 The remainder of refitting is a reversal of removal. On completion, start the engine and check for oil and water leaks.

11 Fuel pump and gauge sender unit - removal and refitting

Note: *Refer to the precautions given in Section 1 before proceeding.*

Removal

1 Depressurise the fuel system as described in Section 6.

2 Remove the securing screws, and withdraw the carpet retainer from the rear edge of the luggage compartment.

3 Manipulate the carpet from under the lower trim panels behind the rear seats.

4 Lift the carpet to expose the sound insulation, then fold back the sound insulation to expose the fuel level sender cover.

5 Remove the securing screws, and recover the washers, then withdraw the cover from the floor **(see illustration)**.

6 Disconnect the wiring plug from the sender unit, or separate the two halves of the wiring connector, as applicable.

7 Where applicable, remove the insulating sealant from the earth lead connection on the sender unit, then disconnect the earth lead.

8 Unscrew the union nuts, and disconnect the fuel pipes from the top of the sender unit. Note the positions of the pipes, although confusion on refitting is unlikely **(see illustration)**. Be prepared for fuel spillage, and plug the open ends of the pipes and the sender unit to reduce further fuel spillage, and to prevent dirt ingress.

9 Unscrew the locking ring - Land Rover dealers have a special tool (LST 131) for this, but a pair of slip-joint (water pump) pliers may be used as a substitute.

10 Carefully withdraw the sender unit and pump from the fuel tank. Again, be prepared for fuel spillage.

11 At the time of writing, the pump and sender unit are only available as an assembly - if either one is proved faulty, renewal of the whole assembly will be required. Consult a Land Rover dealer or automotive electrical specialist to see if repairs can be made, however.

Refitting

12 Refitting is a reversal of removal, noting the following points:

a) There is a torque specified for the pump/sender unit locking ring (see Specifications). Without the special Land Rover tool, tightening to this torque is not possible, but make sure whatever method is used that the locking ring is secure.
b) Make sure that all fuel line and electrical connections are securely made.
c) Once the fuel lines have been reconnected, before refitting the cover, carpet and insulation, switch on the ignition and check that the pump can be heard working. Run the engine, and check carefully for any signs of fuel leakage from the disturbed fuel lines.

12 Fuel tank - removal and refitting

Note: *Refer to the precautions given in Section 1 before proceeding.*

Removal

1 A drain plug is not provided on the fuel tank, and it is therefore preferable to carry out the removal operation when the tank is nearly

11.5 Withdrawing the fuel gauge sender unit cover

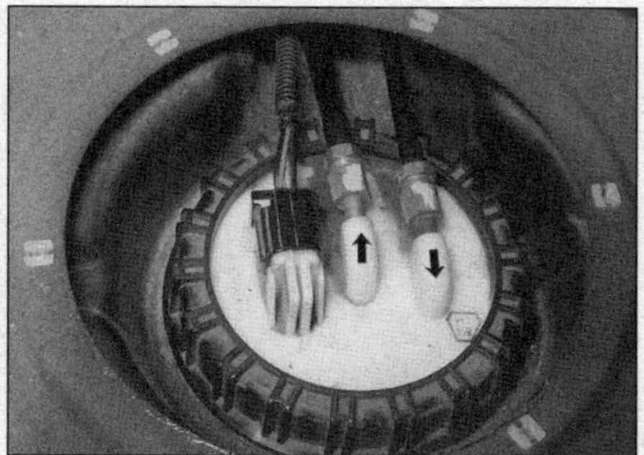

11.8 Flow direction arrows are stamped into the fuel gauge sender unit casing

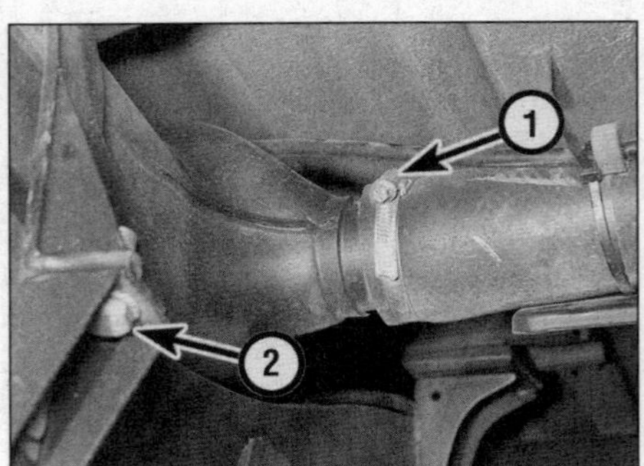
1
2
12.5 Fuel tank filler hose clamp (1) and right-hand tank strap securing bolt (2)

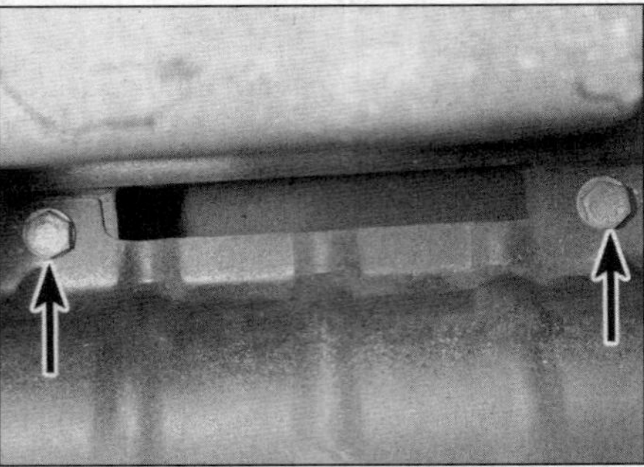
12.8 Fuel tank cradle rear securing bolts (arrowed)

empty. Before proceeding, disconnect the battery negative lead, then syphon or hand-pump the remaining fuel from the tank.

2 To improve access, apply the handbrake, jack up the vehicle, and support securely on axle stands positioned under the axles, as described in *Jacking and vehicle support*.

3 Disconnect the fuel pipes and the wiring from the fuel gauge sender unit, as described in Section 11.

4 Working under the vehicle, where applicable, mark the positions of the anti-roll bar mounting rubbers on the bar. Unscrew the bolts, withdraw the mounting brackets, then allow the anti-roll bar to swing down clear of the fuel tank.

5 Loosen the securing clips, disconnect the fuel tank filler and, where applicable, the breather hoses from the tank, noting their routing **(see illustration)**. Note that the tank may have to be lowered before the breather hose can be disconnected.

6 Remove the nut and bolt securing the right-hand side of the fuel tank strap to the bracket on the chassis.

7 On certain models, it may be necessary to unbolt the towing hitch bracket from the chassis, to allow sufficient clearance to remove the fuel tank.

8 Remove the two bolts and plate-nuts securing the rear of the fuel tank cradle to the underbody **(see illustration)**.

9 Remove the two front fuel tank cradle securing nuts and bolts, and recover the washers. Withdraw the fuel tank cradle.

10 Where applicable, manipulate the fuel tank for access to the breather hose connection, and disconnect the breather hose.

11 With the aid of an assistant, tilt the right-hand side of the tank upwards, then manipulate the tank around the chassis member, and withdraw the tank from under the vehicle.

12 If the tank is contaminated with sediment or water, remove the sender unit as described in Section 11, and swill the tank out with clean fuel. If the tank is damaged, or if leaks are apparent, it should be repaired by a specialist, or alternatively, renewed.

Refitting

13 Refitting is a reversal of removal, but note the following points:

a) *Ensure that the fuel filler and breather hoses are securely reconnected and correctly routed.*
b) *Where applicable, align the anti-roll bar mounting rubbers with the marks made on the bar before removal, and tighten the mounting bolts to the specified torque (see Chapter 11).*
c) *On completion, check very carefully for any sign of fuel leakage.*

13 Unleaded petrol - general information and usage

Note: *The information given in this Chapter is correct at the time of writing, and applies only to petrols currently available in the UK. Check with a Land Rover dealer as more up-to-date information may be available. If travelling abroad, consult one of the motoring organisations (or a similar authority) for advice on the petrols available and their suitability for your vehicle.*

1 The fuel recommended by Land Rover is given in the Specifications of this Chapter.

2 RON and MON are different testing standards; RON stands for Research Octane Number (also written as RM), while MON stands for Motor Octane Number (also written as MM).

Chapter 4 Part B:
Fuel system - petrol injection models

Contents

Degrees of difficulty

Easy, suitable for novice with little experience 	**Fairly easy,** suitable for beginner with some experience 	**Fairly difficult,** suitable for competent DIY mechanic 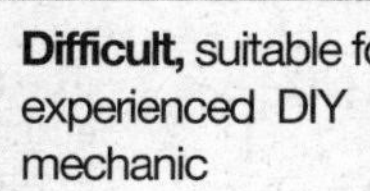	**Difficult,** suitable for experienced DIY mechanic 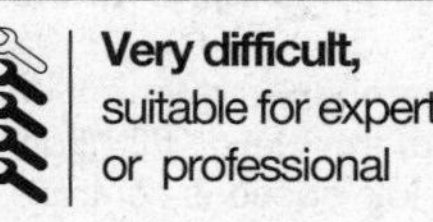	**Very difficult,** suitable for expert DIY or professional 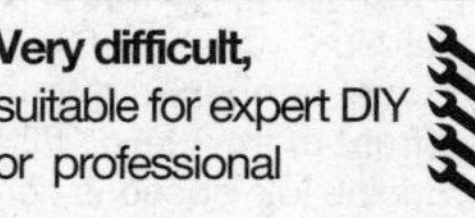

Specifications

General

System type	Lucas Hot-Wire multiport fuel injection
ECU type	Lucas 14 CUX
Idle speed (non-adjustable)	665 to 735 rpm
Base idle speed	525 ± 25 rpm
Mixture/CO level (non-adjustable)	0.5 to 1.0 %
Minimum octane rating:	
Low-compression, non-catalyst engine	91 RON unleaded
All other engines	95 RON unleaded
Fuel pump delivery pressure	2.4 to 2.6 bar

Torque wrench settings	**Nm**	**lbf ft**
By-pass air valve	20	15
Fuel union to fuel rail	22	16
Inlet manifold bolts	38	28
Inlet manifold gasket clamp bolts	18	13
Lambda sensor	20	15
Plenum chamber to ram housing	28	21
Ram housing to inlet manifold	27	20

1 General information and precautions

The fuel injection system comprises a fuel tank, an electric fuel pump, a fuel filter, fuel supply and return lines, a fuel rail, a fuel pressure regulator, eight electronic fuel injectors, and an Electronic Control Unit (ECU) together with its associated sensors, actuators and wiring.

For information on the exhaust and emission control systems, refer to part D of this Chapter.

Lucas Hot-Wire injection system - description

A Lucas Hot-wire electronic fuel injection system is fitted to all petrol Discovery models from 1991 model year. The system ensures that the correct air/fuel mixture is supplied to the engine under all engine operating conditions. This is achieved by using various sensors which send signals to the ECU, and this information is then computed and the injectors opened for the correct period. The injectors are operated on each bank separately (ie each set of four injectors is triggered together).

The ECU is located behind the kick panel in the driver's footwell, and is connected to the main harness by a 40-pin multi-plug.

The injectors are located on a common fuel rail, but electrically they are arranged in two banks of four.

A tune select resistor is located next to the ECU, which allows the system to be set up for different world markets (for example, a different value of resistor is fitted if the vehicle has a catalytic converter).

A coolant temperature thermistor is located by the front left-hand branch of the inlet manifold.

A fuel temperature thermistor is located on the front of the fuel distribution rail.

Engine idle speed is controlled by a by-pass air valve located on the rear of the air inlet plenum chamber. The by-pass air valve maintains the engine idle speed constant when differing loads are applied to the engine, such as when the air conditioning system or headlights are switched on. When the valve is energised by the ECU, extra air passes into the inlet manifold - this fools the system into supplying more fuel, raising the idle speed.

On engines fitted with catalytic converters, Lambda sensors are located just forward of the front converters to monitor the oxygen content of the exhaust gases. The sensors are heated by an internal element to improve their response time - see part D of this Chapter for more information.

The fuel pressure regulator located on the rear of the fuel rail maintains the fuel pressure at 2.5 bars above the inlet manifold pressure.

The high-pressure fuel pump is located in the top of the fuel tank.

The airflow sensor is of the hot-wire type. A proportion of air flowing through the sensor is passed through a by-pass in which two wires are located. One wire is a sensing wire, and the other is a compensating wire. An electronic module mounted on the side of the airflow sensor passes a small current through the sensing wire to produce a heating effect. The air passing over the sensing wire has a cooling effect, which changes the wire's resistance, and this signal is passed back to the module. The compensating wire is not heated, but reacts to the temperature of the air passing through the meter. The electronic module monitors the reaction of the wires in proportion to the airflow, and sends output signals to the ECU.

A throttle potentiometer is mounted on the side of the plenum chamber inlet neck, and is attached to the throttle valve shaft. This device monitors the position of the throttle, and its rate of opening.

A vehicle speed sensor is located on the side of the transfer box, adjacent to the handbrake, and it sends signals to the ECU. It is also used to operate the electronic speedometer (and cruise control, on models so equipped).

An inertia switch is located either beneath the driver's side of the facia, to the left of the steering wheel, or latterly at the rear of the engine compartment, next to the washer reservoir. In the event of a sudden impact, the switch opens and disconnects the fuel pump. The switch may be reset by pressing the top button.

Two fuel injection relays are fitted. The main relay supplies current to the fuel injection system, while the fuel pump relay energises the fuel pump - both relays are controlled by the ECU.

Should the fuel injection system develop a fault, a warning light on the instrument panel will illuminate, and the fuel injection system should then be investigated to find the fault. The system incorporates a 'limp-home' feature, enabling the vehicle to be driven carefully to a garage.

The fuel pump delivers a constant supply of fuel through a cartridge filter to the fuel rail. The return pipe from the pressure regulator returns excess fuel back to the fuel tank.

Inlet air is drawn into the engine through the air cleaner, which contains a renewable paper filter element.

For information on the exhaust and emission control systems, refer to part D of this Chapter.

Precautions

Warning: Many of the procedures in this Chapter require the removal of fuel lines and connections, which may result in some fuel spillage. Before carrying out any operation on the fuel system, refer to the precautions given in Safety first! at the beginning of this manual, and follow them implicitly. Petrol is a highly-dangerous and volatile liquid, and the precautions necessary when handling it cannot be overstressed.

Do not smoke, or allow any naked flames or uncovered light bulbs near the work area. Note that gas-powered domestic appliances with pilot flames, such as heaters boilers and tumble-dryers, also present a fire hazard - bear this in mind if you are working in an area where such appliances are present. Always keep a suitable fire extinguisher close to the work area, and familiarise yourself with its operation before starting work. Wear eye protection when working on fuel systems, and wash off any fuel spilt on bare skin immediately with soap and water. Note that fuel vapour is just as dangerous as liquid fuel - possibly more so; a vessel (such as the fuel tank) that has been emptied of liquid fuel will still contain vapour, and can be potentially explosive.

Residual fuel pressure always remains in the fuel system, long after the engine has been switched off. This pressure must be relieved in a controlled manner before disconnecting any part of the fuel system - refer to Section 5 for details.

When working with fuel system components, pay particular attention to cleanliness - dirt entering the fuel system may cause blockages, which will lead to poor running.

In the interests of personal safety, many of the procedures in this Chapter suggest that the negative lead be removed from the battery terminal. This eliminates the possibility of accidental short-circuits being caused as the vehicle is being worked upon, which would be particularly dangerous if the fuel system is open.

2 Air cleaner - removal and refitting

Canister-type air filter (early models)

1 Slacken the connecting hose retaining clip, then undo the two mounting bracket nuts and bolts, and remove the unit from the engine compartment.

2 Refitting is a reversal of removal.

Square-type air filter (later models)

3 Release the clip and disconnect the small vacuum hose from the front of the air cleaner lid **(see illustration)**.

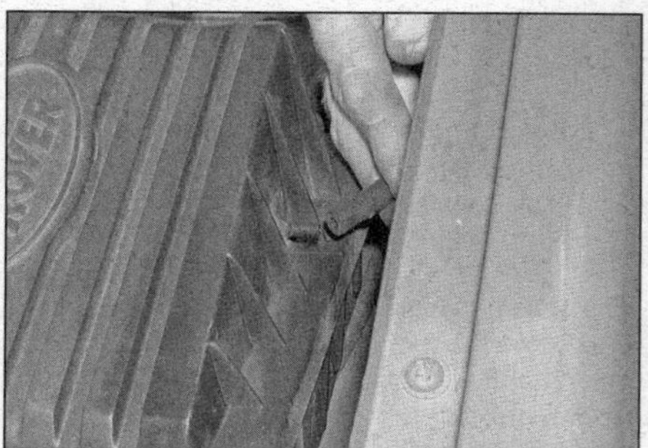

2.3 Disconnect the breather hose from the side of the air cleaner lid

2.4 Release the two clips, then move the airflow sensor rearwards to release the lid

2.6 Removing the air cleaner housing - disengage the locating pegs (arrowed)

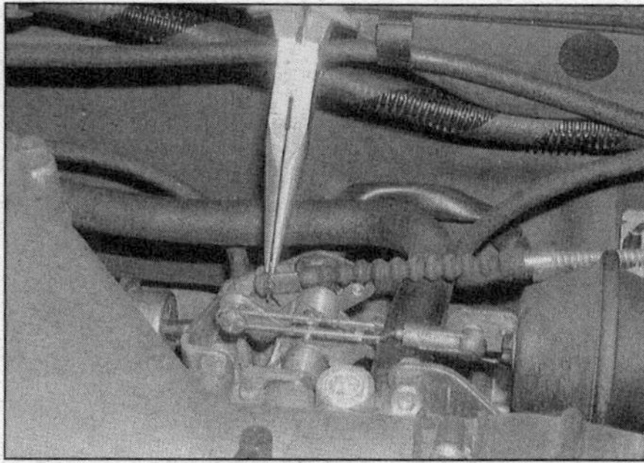

3.1a Using pliers, take out the split-pin . . .

4 Release the four over-centre clips securing the lid to the air cleaner assembly, and the two clips securing the air cleaner to the airflow sensor **(see illustration)**.

5 Lift the lid away, and lift out the filter element, noting which way up it fits.

6 Ease the air cleaner housing up to disengage the two rubber locating pegs from the inner wing. If difficulty is experienced, reach in under the wing, and push the rubber mountings up from below. As the housing is withdrawn, also disengage the front corner locating pegs **(see illustration)**.

7 Refitting is a reversal of removal. When offering the housing into position, some trial-and-error may be required before all the locating pegs engage, and the air cleaner lid can be reconnected to the airflow sensor. The rubber pegs can be pulled down through the holes in the wing if this is easier.

3 Accelerator cable - removal, refitting and adjustment

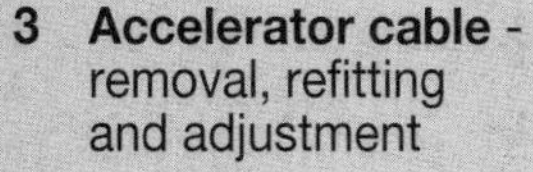

Removal

Note: *New split-pins should be used to secure the cable end clevis pins on refitting.*

1 Extract the split-pin and remove the washer and clevis pin securing the cable to the throttle linkage **(see illustrations)**.

2 Carefully prise the cable adjuster assembly out of the linkage mounting bracket, and withdraw the cable from the bracket **(see illustrations)**.

3 Work back along the cable, releasing it from its retaining clips and cable-ties in the engine compartment **(see illustration)**.

4 Working inside the vehicle, release the securing clips, and withdraw the driver's side lower facia panel. This will allow access to the accelerator pedal assembly.

5 Remove the split-pin, and withdraw the clevis pin securing the end of the cable to the accelerator pedal.

6 Release the cable grommet from the bulkhead, then withdraw the cable through the bulkhead into the engine compartment.

Refitting

7 Refitting is a reversal of removal, bearing in mind the following points:

a) *Ensure that the cable is routed as noted before removal, and secured with new cable-ties where necessary.*
b) *Use new split-pins to secure the cable end clevis pins.*
c) *On completion, check the cable adjustment, as described in the following paragraphs.*

Adjustment

8 Ensure the throttle lever is in the fully-closed position, by pressing the lever fully against its stop.

9 Turn the adjuster wheel to give a small amount (1.5 mm) of freeplay in the inner cable, so that the throttle lever is free to return to the closed (idle) position, but without undue slack. If there is any reluctance to return to idle, lubricate the throttle linkages with a few drops of light oil.

10 With the aid of an assistant, check that the accelerator lever moves to the full-throttle position when the accelerator pedal is fully depressed.

11 With the handbrake applied and the transmission in neutral, start the engine. Press and release the accelerator pedal several times, and ensure the engine returns to idle promptly.

12 The idle speed is not adjustable. Any reluctance to return to idle may be due to mechanical resistance in the throttle linkage (which should be curable by cleaning and lubricating) or in the cable (which may be due to poor routing of the cable).

13 If poor idle quality is experienced, this may indicate a problem with another

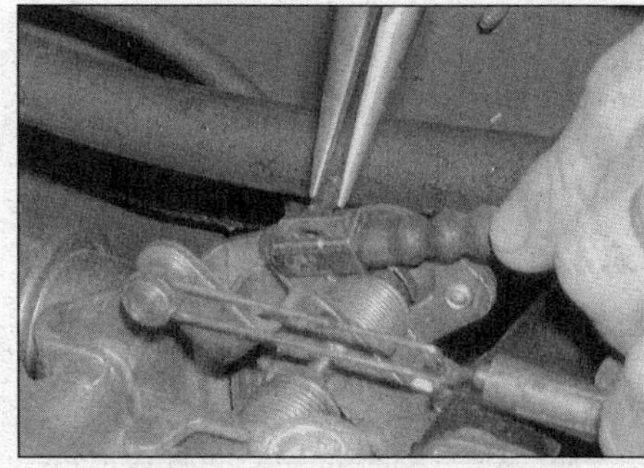

3.1b . . . then extract the clevis pin securing the cable end fitting

3.2a Prise the cable adjuster out of the mounting bracket . . .

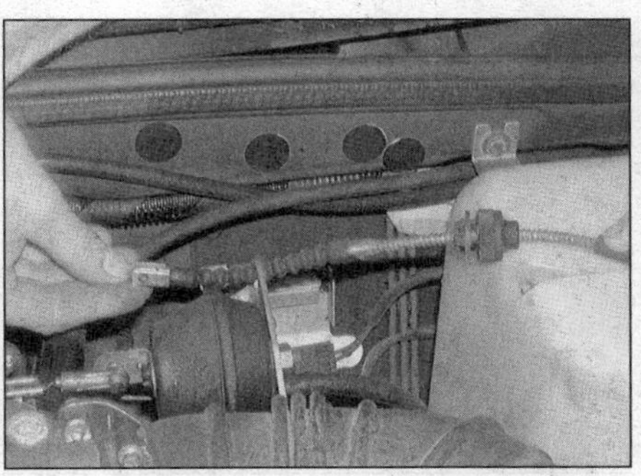

3.2b . . . then feed the cable through it

3.3 This cable-tie had to be cut to release the cable

5.2a Lift off the cover from the engine compartment fusebox . . .

5.2b . . . and remove the fuel pump fuse

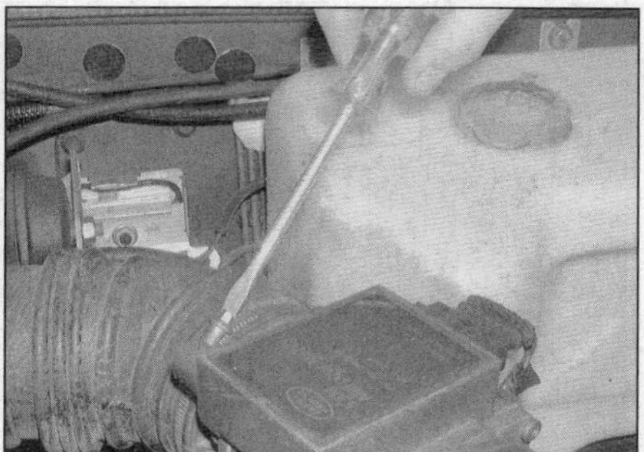

6.2a Loosen the hose clip . . .

component in the injection system - possibly an air leak or a partially-blocked injector (see Section 11). A faulty speed sensor (see Sections 1 and 6) could also give rise to idle problems, as the signal from the sensor (on whether the vehicle is moving) engages and disengages the idle air control mode.

4 Accelerator pedal - removal and refitting

Refer to part A of this Chapter. On completion, the cable should be adjusted as described in Section 3 above.

5 Fuel injection system - depressurisation

Note: *Observe the precautions in Section 1 before working on any component in the fuel system.*

Warning: The following procedure will merely relieve the pressure in the fuel system - remember that fuel will still be present in the system components, and take precautions accordingly before disconnecting any of them.

1 The fuel system referred to in this Section is defined as the tank-mounted fuel pump, the fuel filter, the fuel rail and injectors, the fuel pressure regulator, and the metal pipes and flexible hoses of the fuel lines between these components. All these contain fuel, which will be under pressure while the engine is running and/or while the ignition is switched on. The pressure will remain for some time after the ignition has been switched off, and must be relieved before any of these components are disturbed for servicing work. Ideally, the engine should be allowed to cool completely before work commences.

2 Referring to Section 6, remove the fuel pump relay. Alternatively (and more easily), identify and remove the fuel pump fuse from the fusebox **(see illustrations)**. Refer to Chapter 13 if necessary to positively identify the fuse.

3 With the fuel pump disabled, crank the engine for about ten seconds. The engine may fire and run for a while, but let it continue running until it stops. The fuel injectors should have opened enough times during cranking to considerably reduce the line fuel pressure, and reduce the risk of fuel spraying out when a fuel line is disturbed.

4 Switch off the ignition, disconnect the battery negative terminal, then refit the fuel pump fuse or relay.

5 Place a suitable container beneath the relevant connection/union to be disconnected, and have a large rag ready to soak up any escaping fuel not being caught by the container.

6 Slowly loosen the connection or union nut (as applicable) to avoid a sudden release of pressure, and position the rag around the connection to catch any fuel spray which may be expelled. Once the pressure has been released, disconnect the fuel line. Insert plugs to minimise fuel loss and prevent the entry of dirt into the fuel system.

6 Fuel injection system components - removal and refitting

Airflow sensor

1 Disconnect the battery negative lead.

2 Loosen the hose clip and disconnect the air inlet hose from the rear of the airflow sensor **(see illustrations)**.

3 Disconnect the multi-plug from the unit **(see illustration)**.

4 Release the two clips securing the airflow sensor to the air cleaner, then withdraw it from the engine compartment **(see illustrations)**.

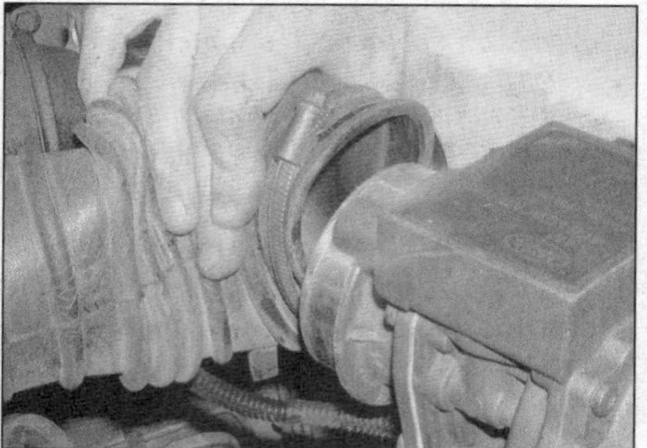

6.2b . . . and disconnect the air inlet hose

6.3 Disconnect the airflow sensor wiring plug

6.4a Release the two over-centre wire clips . . .

6.4b . . . and remove the airflow sensor

6.5 The pip in the airflow sensor engages with a notch in the air cleaner lid

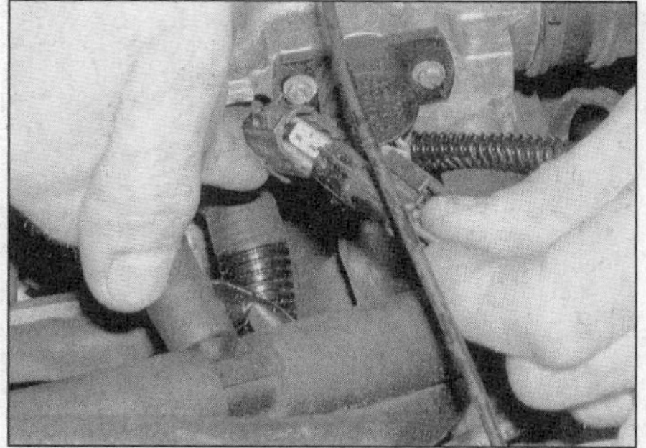

6.7 Disconnect the potentiometer wiring plug

6.8a Loosen and remove the two securing screws . . .

5 Refitting is a reversal of the removal procedure, noting the following points:

a) Make sure that the multi-plug is securely reconnected.

b) A large O-ring is fitted at each end of the airflow sensor - check that these have not been omitted, and that they are in good condition.

*c) Ensure that the pip on the airflow meter engages with the notch in the air cleaner lid **(see illustration)**.*

d) The hoses and clips must be fitted correctly, to avoid air leaks.

Throttle potentiometer

6 Disconnect the battery negative terminal.

7 Trace the wiring from the potentiometer back to its wiring multi-plug, and disconnect it **(see illustration)**.

8 Undo the two screws securing the throttle potentiometer to the side of the plenum chamber and carefully pull the switch from the throttle spindle. Remove the gasket **(see illustrations)**.

9 If the unit is to be removed for some time, note that the throttle must not be operated while the unit is removed.

10 Refitting is a reversal of removal, using a new gasket. Align the end of the potentiometer with the slot in the throttle shaft before inserting and tightening the screws.

By-pass air valve

11 Disconnect the battery negative lead.

12 Disconnect the wiring multi-plug **(see illustration)**.

13 There are two ways of removing the air valve, as follows:

*a) Disconnect the air hose from the valve, then unscrew the three Allen bolts securing the housing to the rear of the plenum chamber. Remove the housing, recover the gasket, and disconnect the air hose **(see illustration)**. The valve can then be unscrewed on the bench.*

*b) Unscrew the valve from the rear of the plenum chamber (this requires a large spanner), and remove the fibre washer **(see illustrations)**.*

14 Refitting is a reversal of the removal procedure, but use a new fibre washer (and housing gasket, where removed). Clean the threads and apply locking fluid (such as Loctite 241) before tightening the valve to the specified torque.

Vehicle speed sensor

Removal

15 The sensor is located in the transfer gearbox casing, next to the handbrake **(see illustration)**.

16 Disconnect the battery negative lead.

6.8b . . . and withdraw the potentiometer and gasket

6.12 Disconnect the wiring plug from the air valve

6.13a Removing the air valve housing

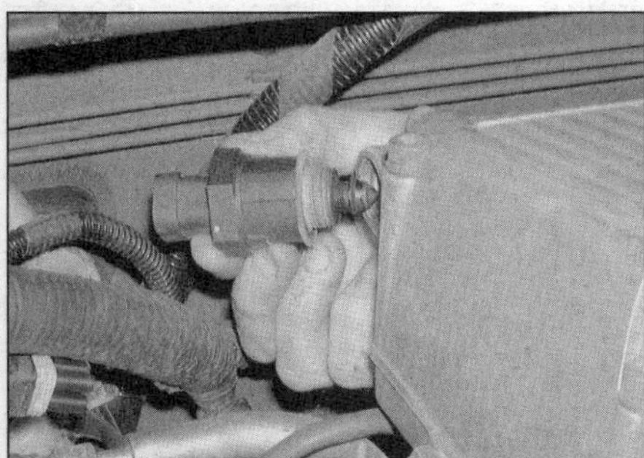

6.13b Unscrew and remove the valve from the housing . . .

6.13c . . . noting the fibre washer

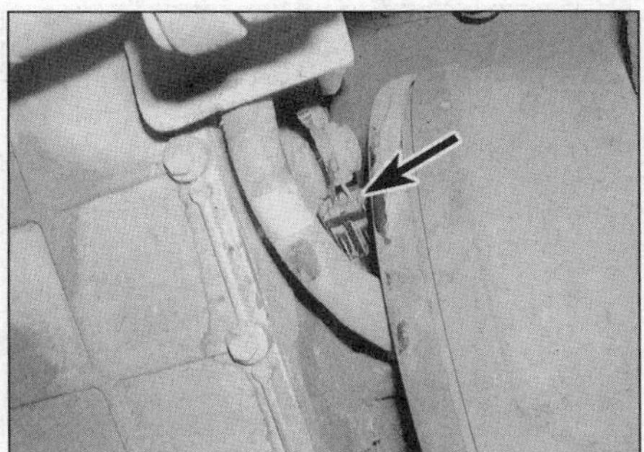

6.15 Vehicle speed sensor (arrowed)

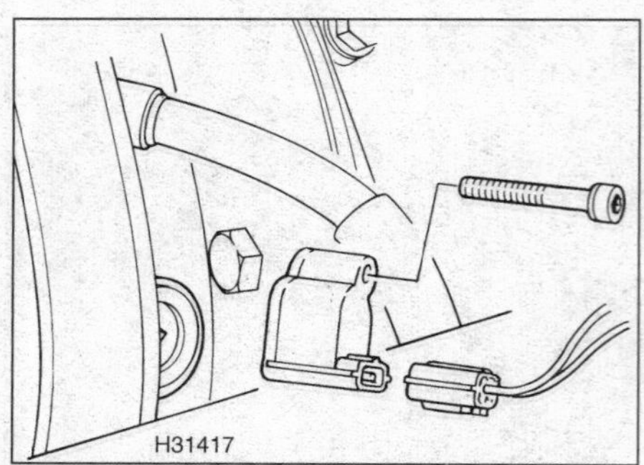
H31417

6.18 Speed sensor mounting details

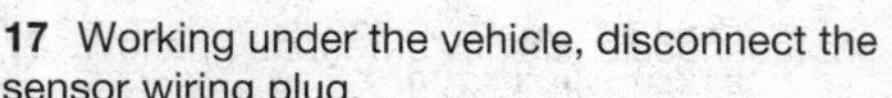

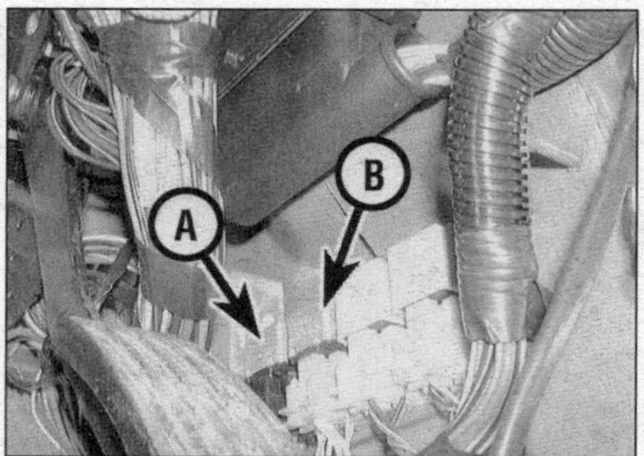
A
B

6.22 Fuel injection system relay (A) and fuel pump relay (B)

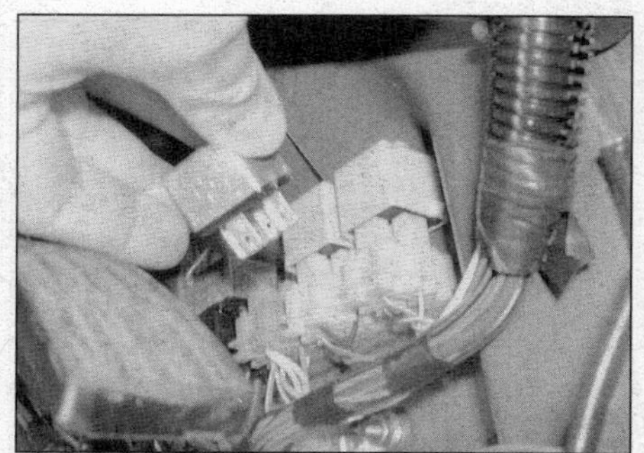

6.24 Removing the fuel pump relay

17 Working under the vehicle, disconnect the sensor wiring plug.

18 Unscrew the sensor securing bolt, and recover the washer **(see illustration)**.

19 Withdraw the sensor from the transfer gearbox.

20 Check the condition of the wiring plug and terminals on the sensor, and clean as necessary.

Refitting

21 Refitting is a reversal of removal. The sensor drive peg must engage correctly with the hole in the drivegear - turn the drive peg as necessary until it fits.

Fuel injection relays

22 The two relays are located either on a small bracket beneath the facia, to the right of the centre console, or behind the right-hand kick panel in the driver's footwell, below the main ECU. The fuel pump relay is mounted on a blue terminal block, and the main relay is mounted on a black terminal block **(see illustration)**.

23 Disconnect the battery negative lead.

24 Pull the relevant relay directly from its socket **(see illustration)**.

25 Refitting is a reversal of the removal procedure.

Electronic control unit (ECU)

26 It is essential that the ignition is switched off when the ECU multi-plug is disconnected, or the ECU could be irreparably damaged. Disconnect the battery negative lead.

27 Release the clips, and remove the driver's side lower facia panel, and the right-hand kick panel from the driver's footwell.

28 Release the multi-plug retaining clip from the front end, and pull the front edge of the multi-plug down **(see illustration)**. Unhook the rear end of the multi-plug and disconnect it completely from the ECU.

29 Remove the two nuts/screws at the side of the unit, and release the ECU from the spring clip on the opposite side **(see illustration)**.

30 Refitting is a reversal of the removal procedure. Ensure that the ECU multi-plug is fully and securely reconnected.

Fuel temperature thermistor

Note: *It is not necessary to depressurise the fuel system, as the thermistor is not in direct contact with the fuel.*

31 Disconnect the battery negative lead.

32 Disconnect the engine breather hoses as required for access to the thermistor.

33 Disconnect the multi-plug from the thermistor - prise the wire clip aside with a small screwdriver **(see illustration)**.

34 Unscrew the thermistor from the fuel rail **(see illustrations)**.

35 Refitting is a reversal of the removal procedure. Ensure that the thermistor is securely screwed into the fuel rail.

Coolant temperature sender

36 Partially drain the cooling system with reference to Chapter 1A.

37 Remove the top hose from the thermostat housing.

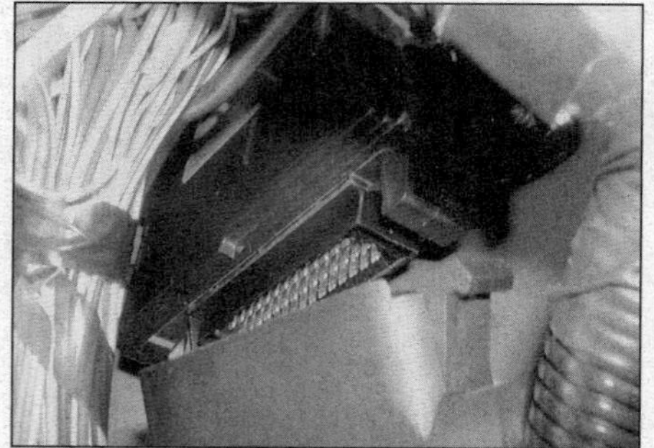

6.28 Release the front end of the ECU multi-plug

6.29 Removing the fuel injection ECU

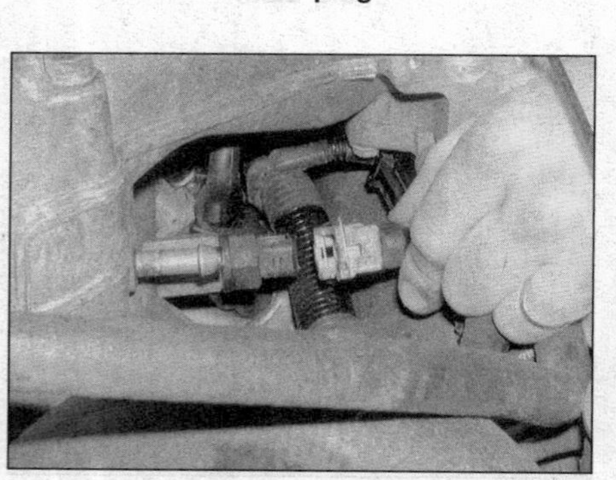

6.33 Disconnect the thermistor wiring plug

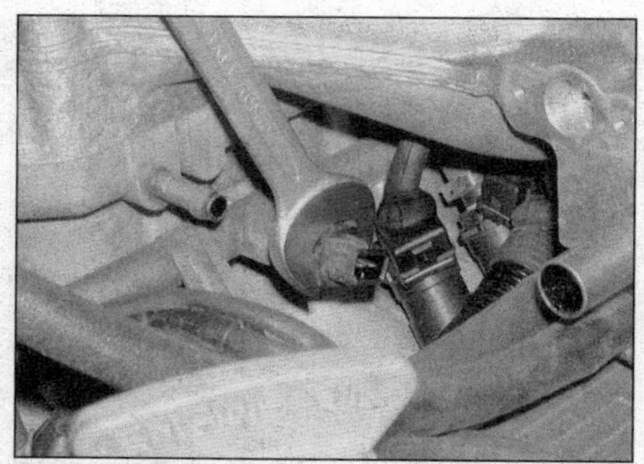

6.34a Loosen the thermistor . . .

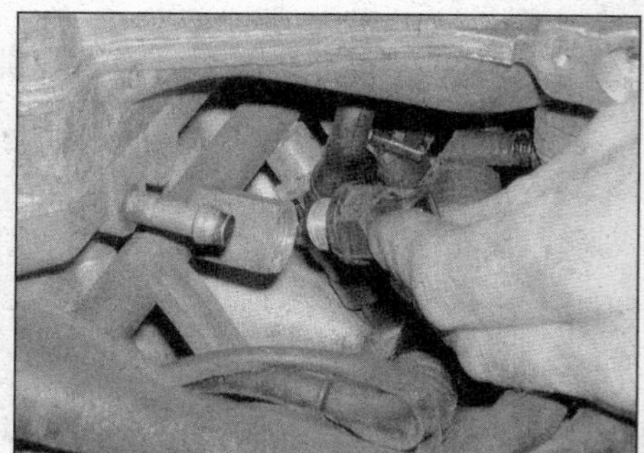

6.34b . . . and remove it from the fuel rail

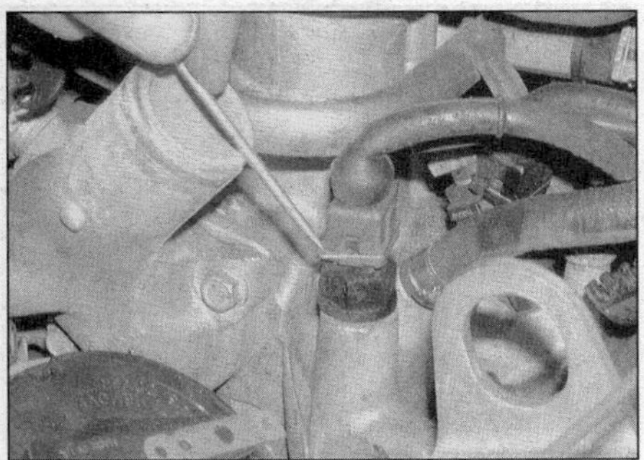
6.39a Ease out the wire clip with a small screwdriver . . .

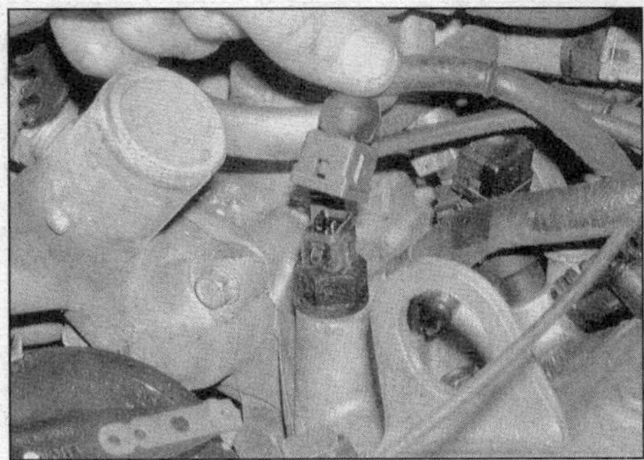
6.39b . . . then disconnect the wiring plug

6.39c Unscrew the temperature sensor . . .

38 Release the two clips securing the distributor cap, then lift off the cap complete with HT leads and place it to one side.

39 Disconnect the multi-plug, and unscrew the sender from the left-hand front branch of the inlet manifold (square wiring plug) **(see illustrations)**. Remove the copper washer.

40 Refitting is a reversal of the removal procedure, but fit a new copper washer and refill the cooling system with reference to Chapter 1A. On completion, run the engine and check for coolant leaks.

Inertia switch

41 Disconnect the battery negative lead.

42 On models up to 1995 model year, the switch is under the driver's side of the facia, to the left of the steering wheel. Release the clips and remove the driver's side lower facia panel for access.

43 From 1995 model year onwards, the inertia switch is at the rear of the engine compartment, behind the washer reservoir. Remove the reservoir as described in Chapter 13 for access.

44 Disconnect the multi-plug from the base of the switch **(see illustration)**.

45 Remove the switch retaining screws, or unclip the switch from its mounting bracket, and remove it **(see illustration)**.

46 Refitting is a reversal of removal.

Plenum chamber

47 Disconnect the battery negative lead.

48 Partially drain the cooling system with reference to Chapter 1A.

49 Loosen the clips and remove the air hose between the airflow sensor and plenum chamber.

50 Disconnect the distributor vacuum hose, and the crankcase ventilation hose **(see illustrations)**.

51 Identify their locations, then disconnect the coolant hoses from the bottom of the plenum chamber **(see illustration)**.

52 Disconnect the multi-plug from the air bypass valve. To avoid damage to the throttle potentiometer wiring, remove the potentiometer completely as described previously in this Section.

53 Disconnect the small vacuum hose from the rear of the plenum chamber below the air by-pass valve location.

54 Disconnect the hose between the air by-

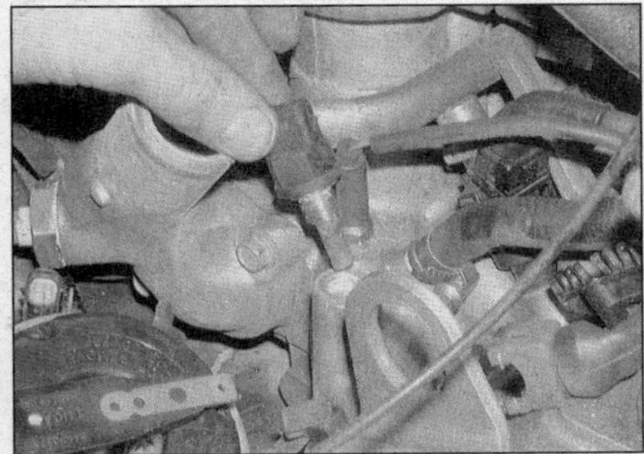
6.39d . . . and remove it from the inlet manifold

6.44 With the washer bottle removed, disconnect the wiring plug from the inertia switch

6.45 Remove the retaining screws, and take out the inertia switch

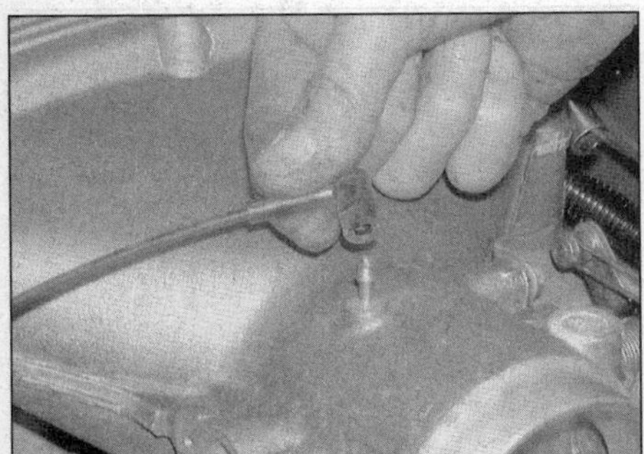
6.50a Disconnect the distributor vacuum hose . . .

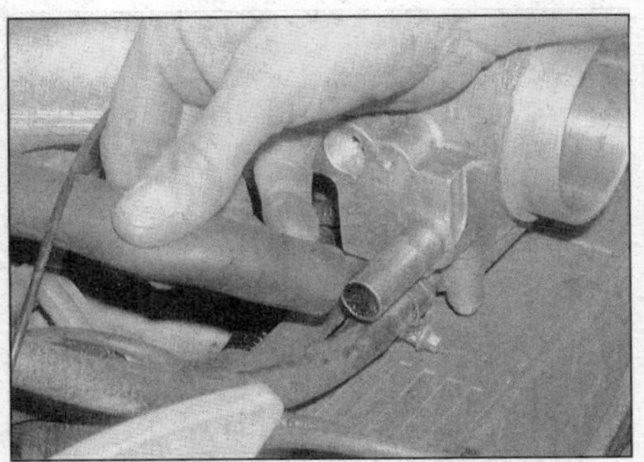
6.50b . . . and the crankcase breather hose

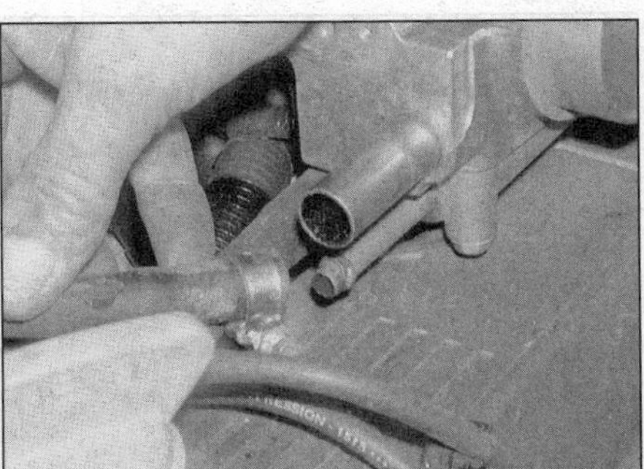
6.51 Disconnect the two coolant hoses at the base of the plenum chamber

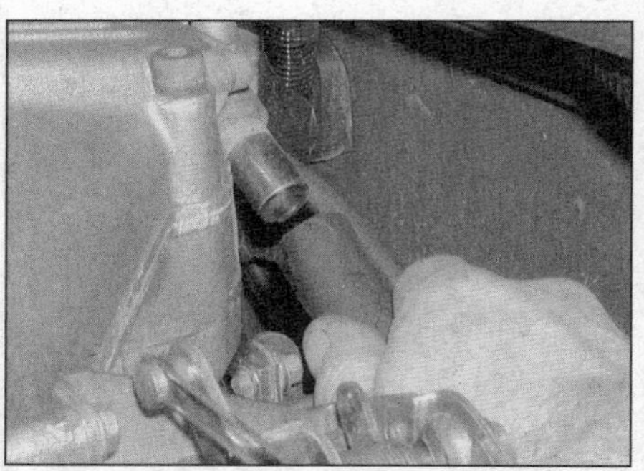

6.54 Disconnecting the air hose from the by-pass valve

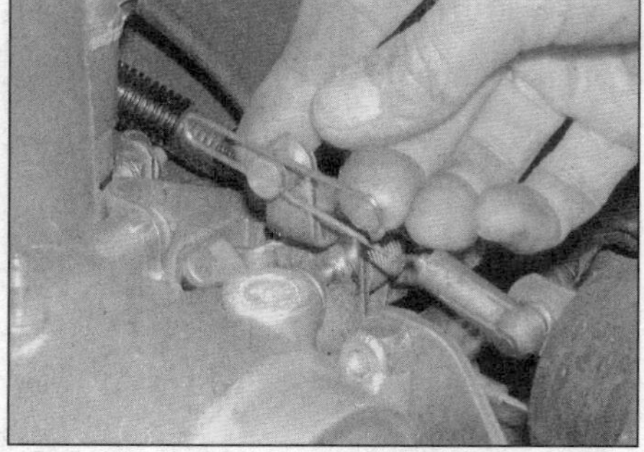

6.56a Unhook the control link . . .

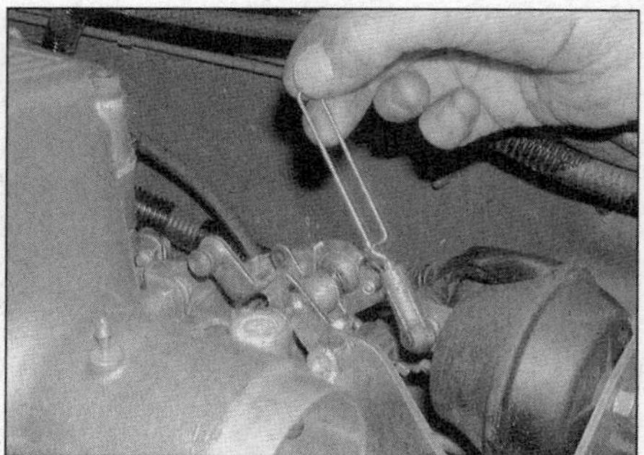

6.56b . . . and lift it clear

pass valve and plenum chamber **(see illustration)**.

55 On models without cruise control, remove the three bolts (and recover the spring washers) securing the throttle linkage assembly bracket to the plenum chamber, and lay the assembly to one side without disconnecting any cables.

56 On models with cruise control, dismantle the throttle linkage as follows:

a) *Unhook the control link for the vacuum control unit, and lift the link out of the way* ***(see illustrations)****.*

b) *Unhook the small overtravel spring at the base of the throttle linkage* ***(see illustration)****.*

c) *Hold the throttle plate open slightly for access, then loosen and remove the bolts securing the throttle linkage bracket* ***(see illustration)****.*

d) *Press down the spring leg nearest the front of the linkage, and slide the leg out of the locating slot* ***(see illustration)****.*

e) *Unhook the front throttle plate tab from the jaws in the rear throttle plate, and separate the two sections of the linkage. Move the throttle linkage assembly to one side* ***(see illustration)****.*

57 Unscrew the six socket-headed bolts and lift the plenum chamber from the ram housing **(see illustrations)**. Cover the ram housing to prevent the ingress of foreign matter.

58 With the plenum chamber removed, the coolant supply elbow gasket can be renewed if necessary. The elbow is secured by four bolts. Clean the mating surfaces thoroughly before refitting the elbow using a new gasket **(see illustrations)**.

59 Refitting is a reversal of the removal procedure, noting the following points:

a) *Clean the mating faces, and apply gasket sealant to the plenum chamber mating face.*

6.56c Unhook the overtravel spring

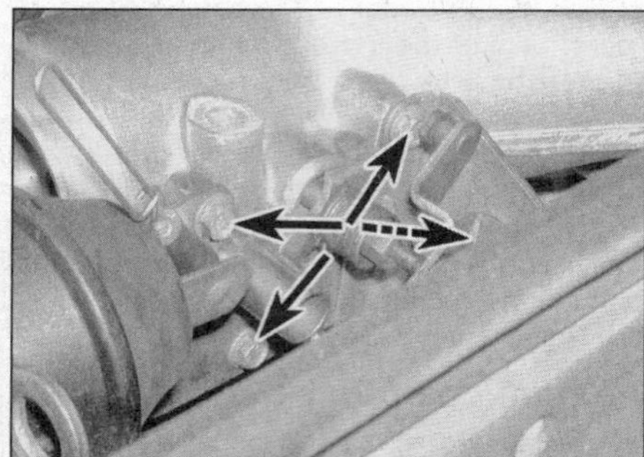

6.56d Remove the bolts (three of four arrowed) securing the throttle linkage bracket

A
B

6.56e Front spring leg slides down out of slot (A). Front throttle plate tab (B) disengages from the jaws in the rear plate

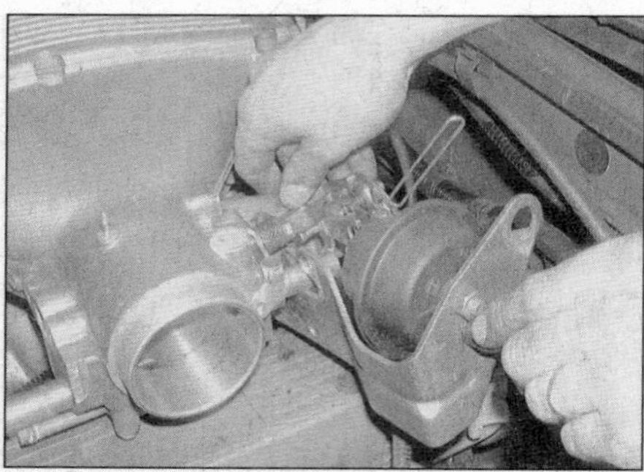

6.56f Remove the throttle linkage assembly, and place to one side

6.57a Remove the six bolts . . .

6.57b . . . and lift off the plenum chamber

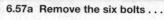

6.58a If necessary, remove the four bolts . . .

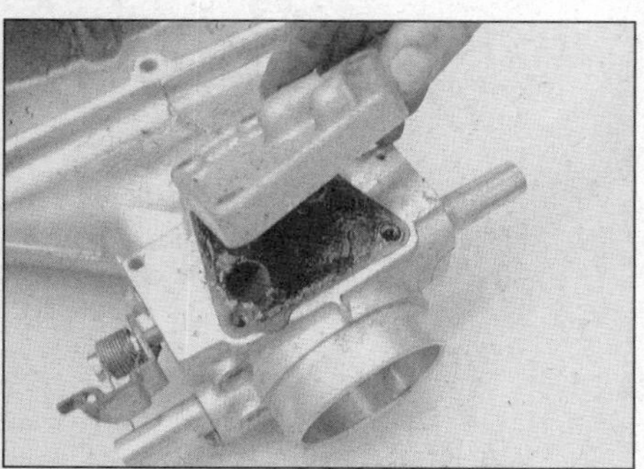
6.58b . . . and take off the coolant supply elbow

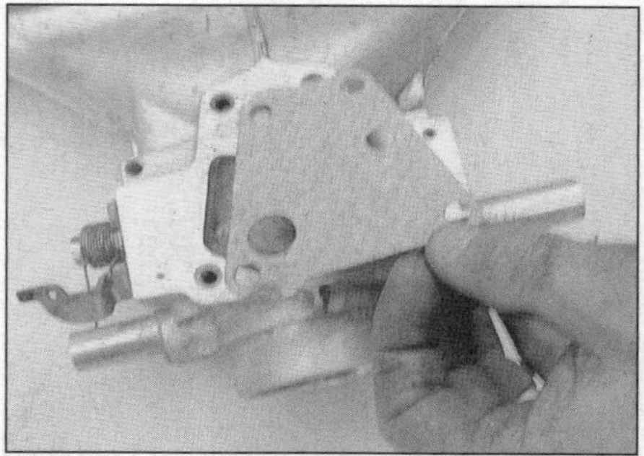
6.58c On refitting, use a new gasket

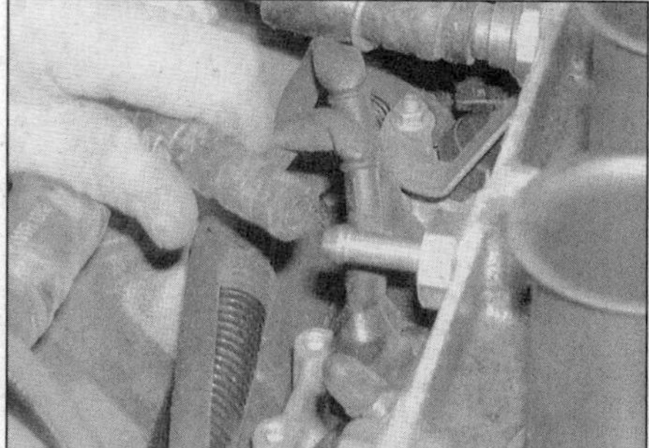
6.61a Disconnect the charcoal canister hose . . .

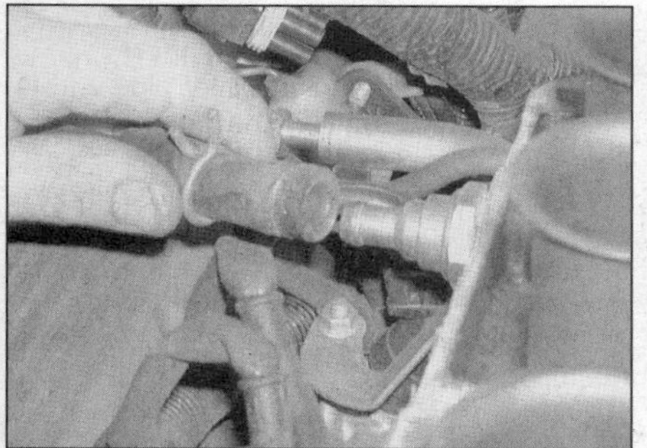
6.61b . . . the brake servo vacuum hose . . .

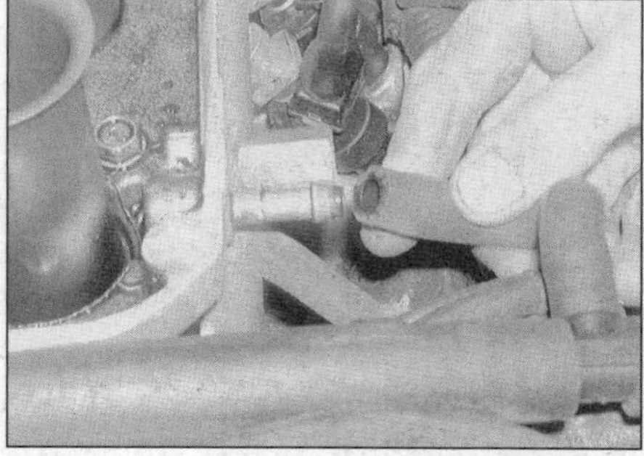
6.61c . . . and the crankcase breather hose

6.63 Removing the ram housing

b) Tighten the plenum chamber bolts evenly to the specified torque.
c) Make sure that all hoses are correctly and securely reconnected, to prevent air leaks.

Ram housing

60 Remove the plenum chamber as described previously.
61 Disconnect the hoses from the outer edges of the ram housing, noting their locations. Depending on model, these will include a small breather hose on the air cleaner side, and vacuum hoses for the brake servo and charcoal canister on the other side **(see illustrations)**.

HAYNES HiNT

If the housing is stuck, do not lever against the fuel rail, nor lever between the mating faces. Loosely fit two bolts to the ram housing, then temporarily refit the plenum chamber. Using a suitable piece of wood, lever gently between the plenum chamber and the rocker cover to release the ram housing joint

62 Unscrew and remove the six through-bolts and washers holding the ram housing to the inlet manifold.
63 Withdraw the ram housing from the inlet manifold, and cover the top of the inlet manifold to prevent the ingress of foreign matter **(see illustration and Haynes Hint)**.
64 Refitting is a reversal of the removal procedure, noting the following points:

a) Clean the mating faces, and apply gasket sealant to the inlet manifold mating face.
b) Tighten the bolts progressively to the specified torque, working diagonally outwards from the two centre bolts.
c) Make sure that all hoses are correctly and securely reconnected, to prevent air leaks.

Fuel pressure regulator

65 Depressurise the fuel system as described in Section 5.
66 Disconnect the battery negative terminal.
67 Release the fuel return hose from the clip to the inside of the right-hand rocker cover **(see illustration)**.
68 To improve access, disconnect the air hose from the by-pass air valve, then pull off the vacuum hose from the fuel pressure regulator **(see illustrations)**.
69 Undo the two nuts and bolts securing the regulator to its mounting bracket, then

6.67 Unclip the fuel return hose by pulling upwards

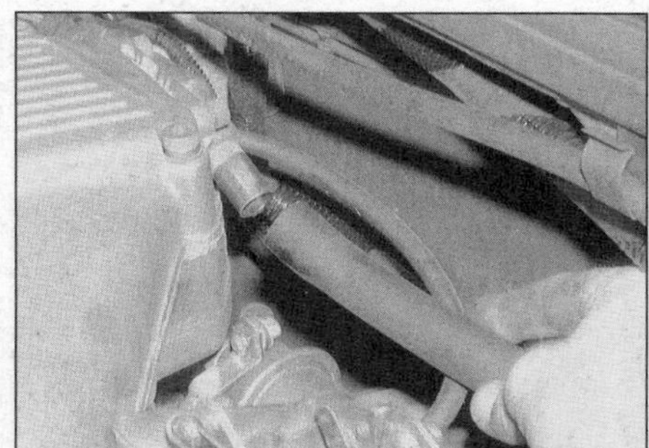
6.68a Disconnect the air by-pass valve hose for access . . .

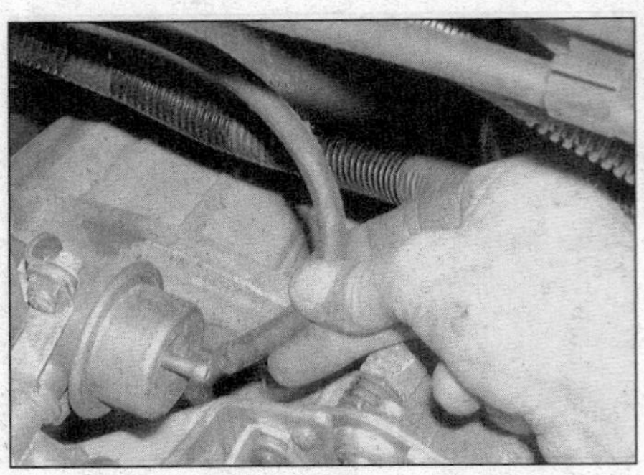

6.68b . . . then pull off the pressure regulator vacuum hose

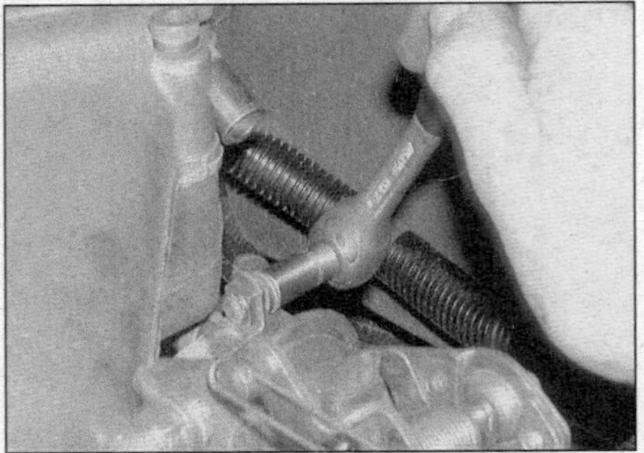

6.69a Unscrew the regulator mounting nuts and bolts . . .

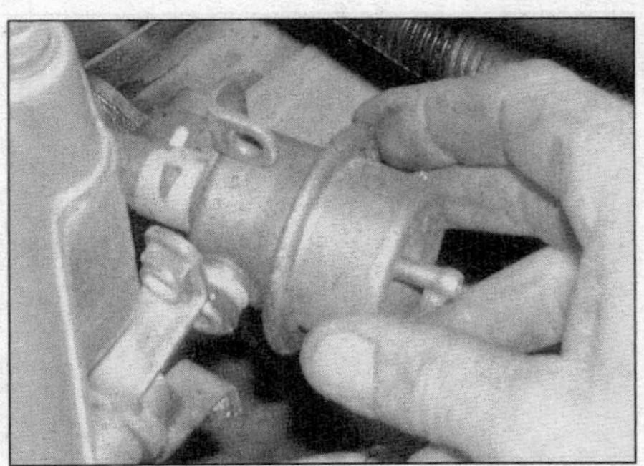

6.69b . . . then pull the regulator to the rear to release its O-ring from the fuel rail

6.70a Move the pressure regulator around the back of the plenum chamber . . .

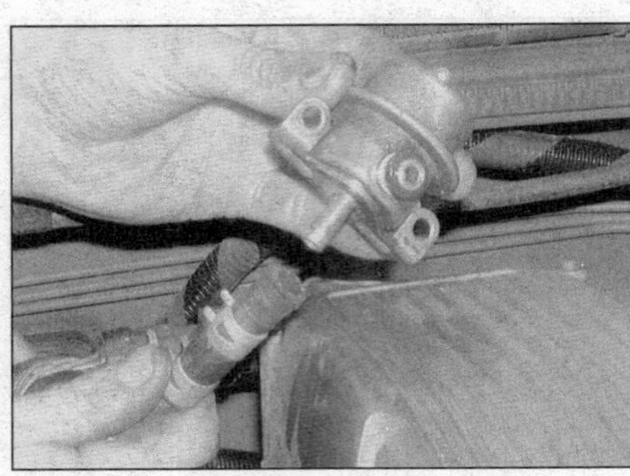

6.70b . . . then release the pipe clips and disconnect the regulator

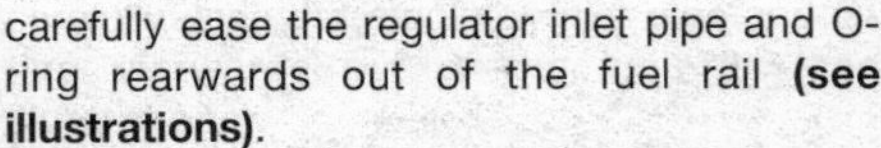

carefully ease the regulator inlet pipe and O-ring rearwards out of the fuel rail **(see illustrations)**.

70 Feed the regulator and hose behind the plenum chamber, then release the pipe clips securing the regulator to the hose, and remove the regulator **(see illustrations)**.

71 Refitting is the reversal of removal, noting the following points:

*a) Use a new O-ring, and coat it with a little silicon grease before refitting the regulator to the fuel rail **(see illustration)**.*

b) On completion, switch on the ignition to pressurise the system, and check for signs of fuel leakage.

Fuel rail and injectors

72 Depressurise the fuel system as described in Section 5.

73 Disconnect the battery negative lead.

74 Remove the plenum chamber and ram housing as described previously. Place clean cloth rags in the inlet ports to prevent ingress of dirt.

75 Unclip the fuel return hose from the right-hand rocker cover, then release the clips and disconnect the fuel return hose from the pressure regulator **(see illustrations)**.

76 Loosen the union nuts and disconnect the fuel feed hose from the fuel rail **(see illustrations)**.

77 Disconnect the multi-plug from the fuel

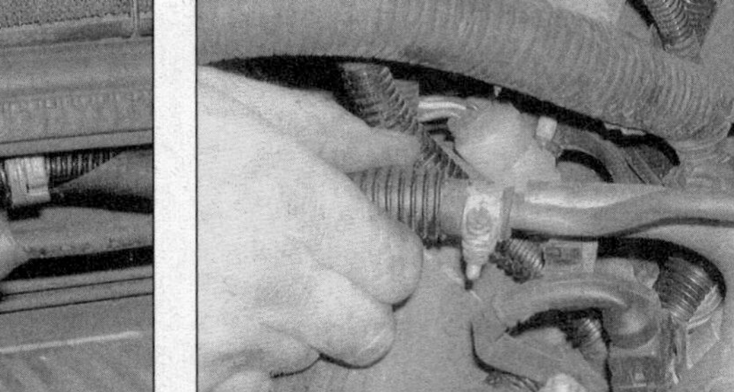

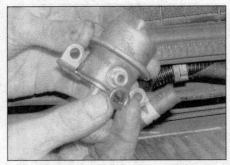

6.71 Use a new O-ring when refitting the regulator

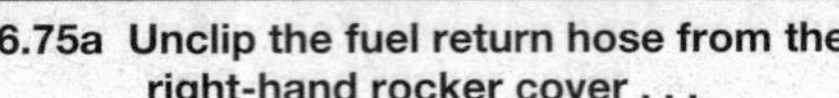

6.75a Unclip the fuel return hose from the right-hand rocker cover . . .

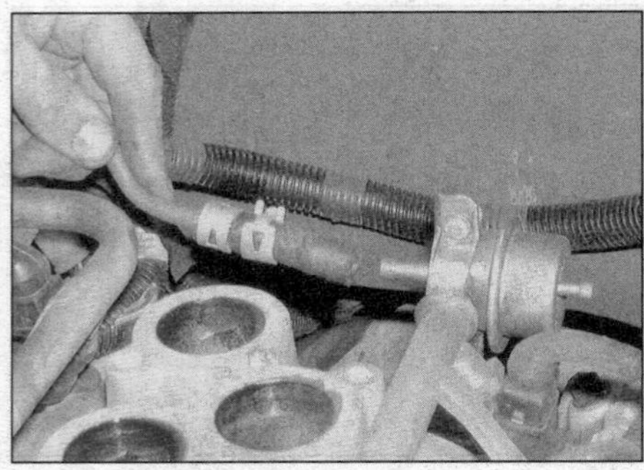

6.75b . . . then release it from the fuel pressure regulator

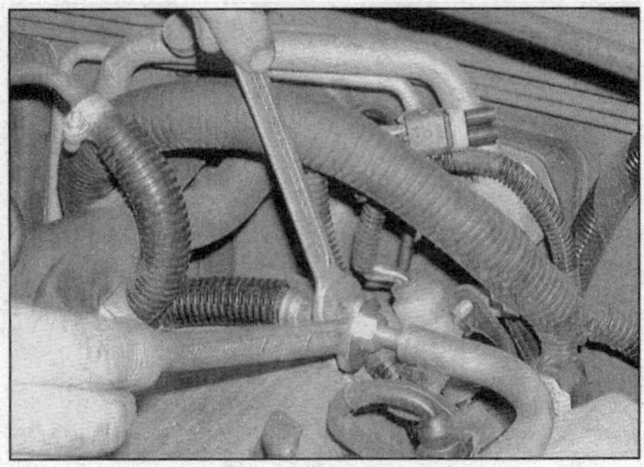

6.76a Loosen the union nuts . . .

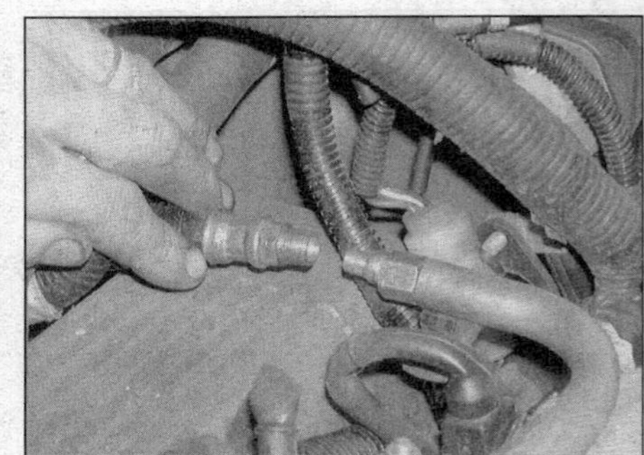

6.76b . . . and disconnect the fuel feed hose from the fuel rail

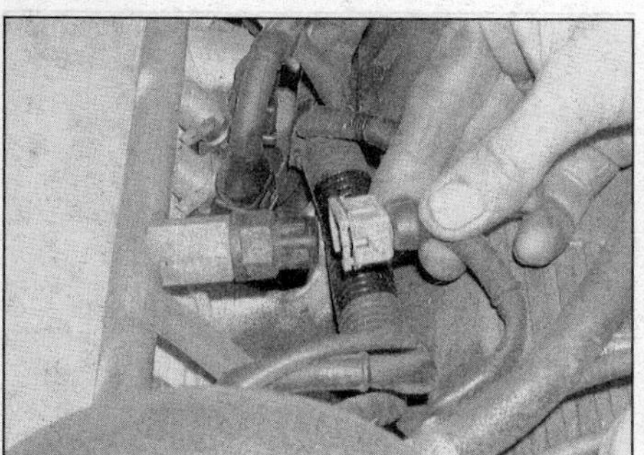
6.77 Disconnecting the wiring plug from the fuel temperature thermistor

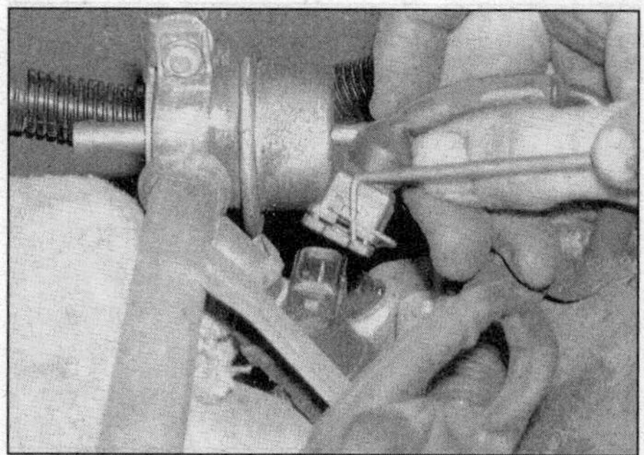
6.78 Use a suitable tool to release the clip securing the injector multi-plugs

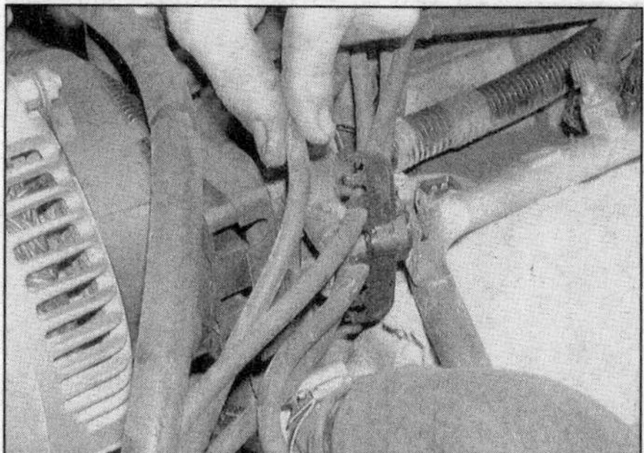
6.79 Release the HT leads from the fuel rail clip

temperature thermistor on the front of the fuel rail **(see illustration)**. Use a small screwdriver (or similar tool) to ease out the wire clip securing the plug before pulling the plug clear.

78 Disconnect the multi-plugs from the injectors, using the same method as for the fuel temperature thermistor plug **(see illustration)**. Label the plugs if necessary, to prevent any confusion on refitting.

79 Release the HT leads from the clip attached to the fuel rail **(see illustration)**.

80 Unscrew and remove the fuel rail mounting nuts **(see illustration)**.

81 Remove the heater pipe clamp bolt from the top of the rocker cover, then disconnect the heater hose leading to the inlet manifold. Move the heater pipes and wiring to one side as necessary, so that the heater pipe bracket can be lifted off the stud which is also used to locate the front right-hand fuel rail mounting **(see illustrations)**.

82 Carefully ease the fuel rail and injectors from the inlet manifold, and remove the assembly from the engine compartment **(see illustration)**.

83 Pull out the clips securing the injectors to the fuel rail, and ease the injectors from the rail **(see illustrations)**.

84 Unscrew the two nuts and bolts securing the pressure regulator to the fuel rail, and ease the regulator from the rail.

85 Prise the O-rings from the injectors, clean the grooves and fit new O-rings **(see**

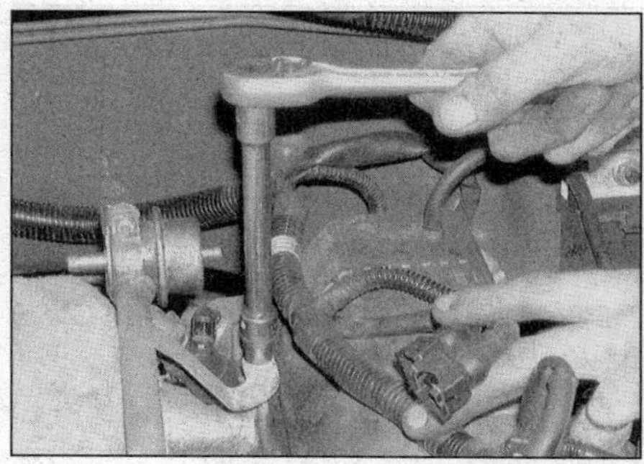
6.80 Unscrew the fuel rail mounting nuts

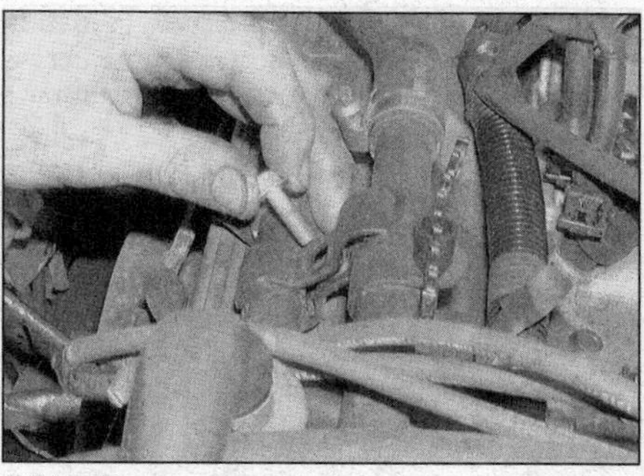
6.81a Remove the bolt and clamp from the heater pipework . . .

6.81b . . . then unscrew the hose clip and disconnect the hose from the inlet manifold . . .

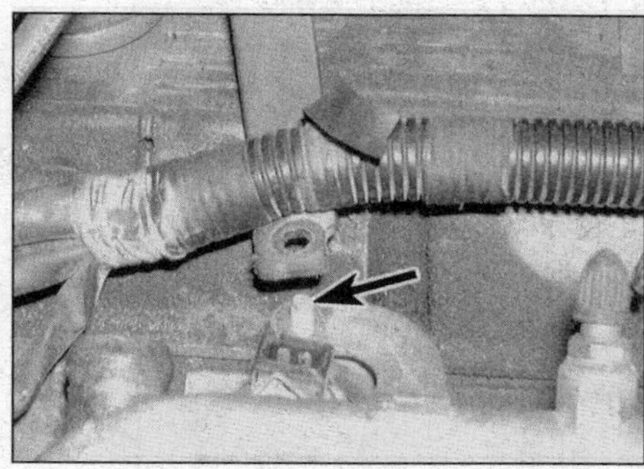
6.81c . . . to allow the heater pipe bracket to be lifted off the stud also used by the fuel rail (arrowed)

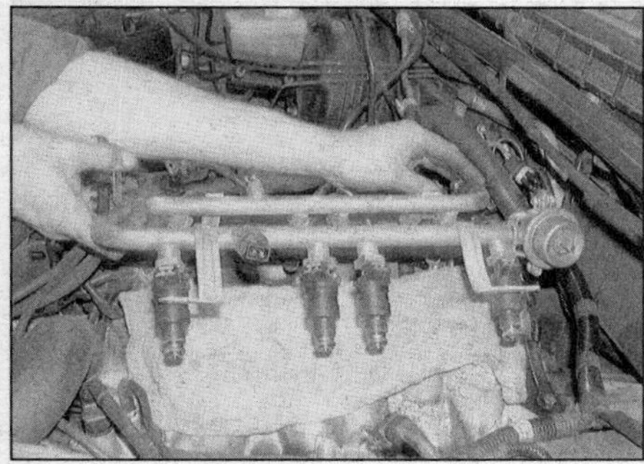
6.82 Removing the fuel rail and injectors

6.83a Prise out the injector securing clips . . .

6.83b . . . and remove the injectors from the fuel rail

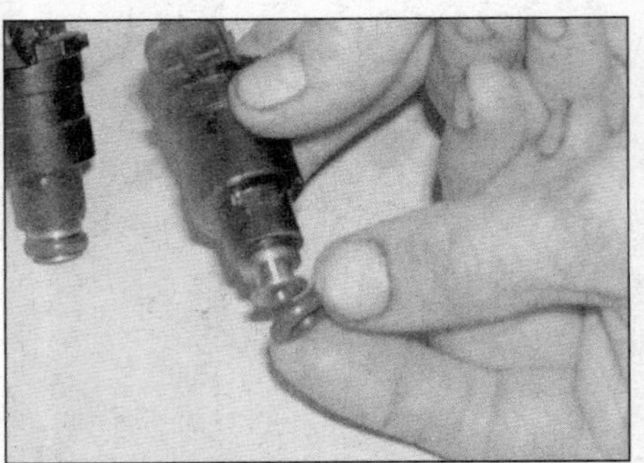
6.85 Prise out the injector O-rings, and fit new ones

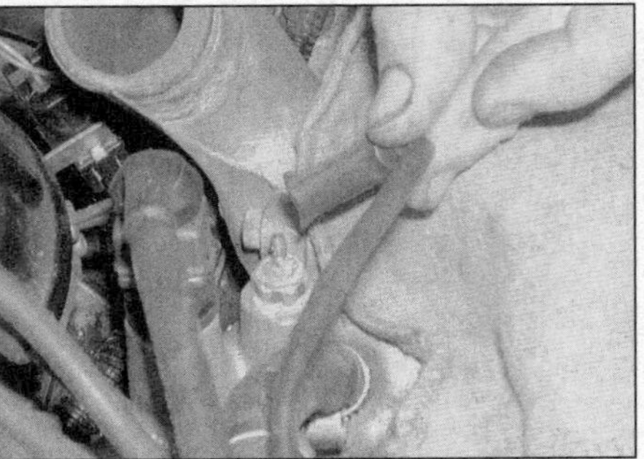
9.6 Disconnect the coolant temperature sensor wiring plugs

9.12 Unscrew the heater pipe stub from the inlet manifold

illustration). Also clean the injector locations in the fuel rail.

86 Apply a light coating of silicon grease to the O-rings then fit the injectors to the fuel rail with the multi-plug connections facing outwards. Secure with the clips.

87 Remove the O-ring from the pressure regulator, clean the location and fit a new O-ring. Apply a little silicon grease to the O-ring and press the regulator into the fuel rail. Refit and tighten the two nuts and bolts.

88 The remaining procedure is a reversal of removal. On completion switch on the ignition and check for leaks from the fuel rail.

7 Fuel pump and gauge sender unit - removal and refitting

1 Depressurise the fuel system as described in Section 5.

2 The procedure is now identical to that described in part A of this Chapter, Section 11.

8 Fuel tank - removal and refitting

1 Depressurise the fuel system as described in Section 5.

2 The procedure is now identical to that described in part A of this Chapter, Section 12.

9 Inlet manifold - removal and refitting

1 Depressurise the fuel system as described in Section 5.

2 Disconnect the radiator bottom hose and partially drain the cooling system until the level is below the thermostat housing. Refit the hose and tighten the clip. Refer to Chapter 1A if necessary.

3 Remove the plenum chamber with reference to Section 6.

4 Disconnect the wiring multi-plugs to the fuel temperature thermistor and fuel injectors. Label the injector plugs if necessary, to avoid confusion on refitting.

5 Release the injector harness from the rear of the fuel rail, and place it to one side.

6 Disconnect the two coolant temperature switches fitted to the inlet manifold, behind the distributor **(see illustration)**. Remove the top hose from the thermostat housing, and on models with air conditioning, disconnect the wiring plug from the housing.

7 To improve access, unclip and lift off the distributor cap, complete with HT leads.

8 Release the HT leads from the clip attached to the fuel rail.

9 Unclip the fuel return hose from the rocker cover, and separate the hose from the rigid pipe.

10 Taking note of the precautions given in Section 5, loosen the union, and disconnect the fuel supply hose from the fuel rail. Plug the union to prevent further loss of fuel.

11 Disconnect the hoses from the outer edges of the ram housing, noting their locations. Depending on model, these will include a small breather hose on the air cleaner side, and vacuum hoses for the brake servo and charcoal canister on the other side.

12 Unbolt the rigid heater pipes from the inlet manifold, disconnect the hose leading to the inlet manifold connection, and place the heater pipe assembly to one side. Unscrew the heater pipe stub from the inlet manifold **(see illustration)**.

13 Starting with the outermost bolts, and working in a diagonal sequence, progressively loosen the twelve bolts securing the inlet manifold to the cylinder heads. Remove the bolts, noting their positions for refitting, as they are of different lengths **(see illustration)**.

14 Any bolts removed from the cylinder heads or block should have their threads cleaned with a wire brush dipped in paraffin or clean petrol. If this cleaning cannot be carried out immediately, it is vital that they are stored in petrol or paraffin, as the sealant used when the bolts were originally fitted will tend to harden on exposure to the air, making its removal difficult.

15 Move aside the heater hoses, and ease the manifold assembly away from the engine **(see illustration)**. Take care not to damage the alternator or distributor as the assembly is lifted out.

16 Before removing the gasket clamps, ensure that there is no coolant lying on top of the gasket. Remove the clamps and lift away the gasket, followed by the rubber gasket seals **(see illustrations)**. Discard the

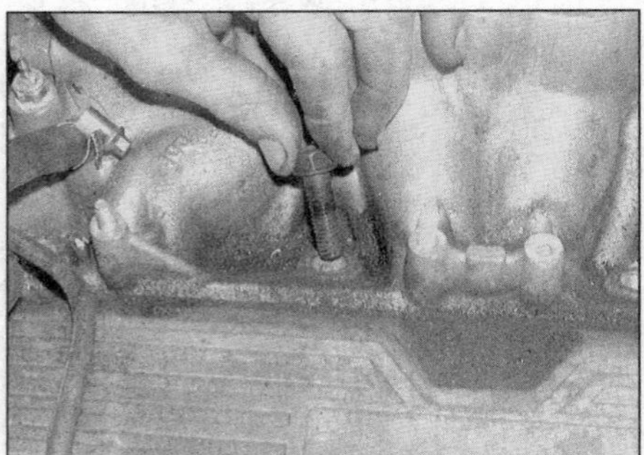
9.13 Removing an inlet manifold securing bolt

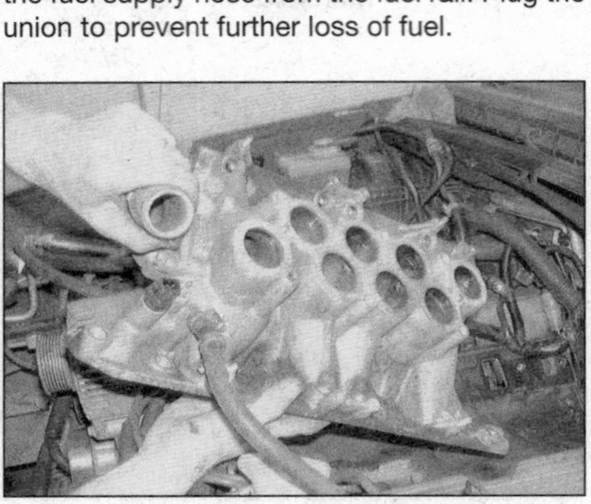
9.15 Removing the inlet manifold

9.16a Unbolt the inlet manifold gasket clamps . . .

9.16b . . . and remove the clamps and rubber seals

9.16c Removing the inlet manifold gasket

9.19 Place the rubber seals in position

gasket and seals - new items must be fitted on assembly.

Refitting

17 As the inlet manifold also serves to cover the pushrod cavities of the cylinder block, a single manifold gasket is fitted. Made from sheet metal, this gasket extends downwards over the inlet port face of each cylinder head, and over each of the respective pushrod cavities. Rubber seals are fitted at each end, to seal the manifold to the timing chest and rear flange. It is important that the gasket and seals are carefully fitted, or oil leaks may develop.

18 Clean the mating faces of the inlet manifold, and the cylinder heads and block. Also clean the threads of the manifold securing bolts.

19 Commence refitting by locating the new rubber seals in position with their ends engaged in the notches formed between the cylinder heads and cylinder block **(see illustration)**.

20 Apply a blob of suitable RTV sealant between the ends of the seals and the cylinder heads/block **(see illustration)**.

21 Locate the new manifold gasket in position, with the word FRONT to the front, and the open bolt hole to the front right-hand side (right as seen from the driver's seat). Later gaskets have no markings, however, and appear to fit either way round.

22 Refit the two gasket clamps, but do not tighten the bolts fully **(see illustration)**. Note that the two clamps are different, and can only fit at one end or the other.

23 Lower the inlet manifold into position **(see illustration)**. Note that, where applicable, the open bolt hole aligns with the open hole in the gasket.

24 Insert all the bolts to their positions as noted on removal - the two long bolts fit either side at the front of the manifold **(see illustration)**.

25 Tighten all bolts progressively in a diagonal sequence from the centre outwards to the specified torque. Tighten the gasket clamps to the specified torque **(see illustrations)**.

26 The remainder of refitting is a reversal of removal. On completion, start the engine and check for oil and water leaks.

9.20 Apply sealant to the ends of the rubber seals

9.22 Gasket clamp in position

9.23 Lowering in the inlet manifold

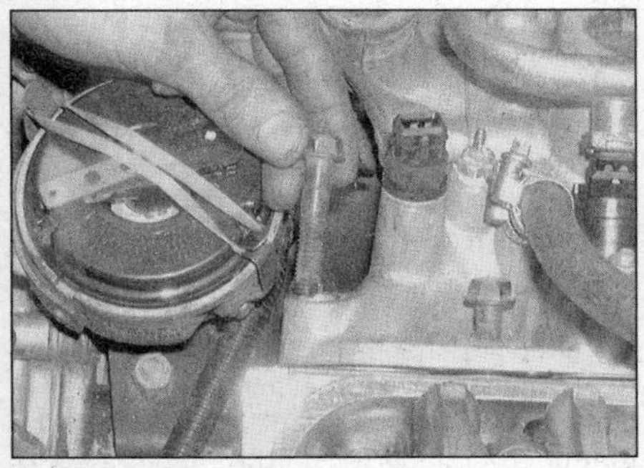
9.24 Fitting one of the longer inlet manifold bolts

9.25a Tighten the manifold bolts . . .

9.25b . . . and the gasket clamp bolts

10 Base idle speed - adjustment

1 Routine adjustment of the idle speed and mixture settings is not required, as these settings are under the control of the Lucas engine management ECU.
2 Similarly, the base idle speed is set at the factory, and unless the plenum chamber is changed, it should not require adjustment. A tamperproof plug is fitted over the adjuster screw.
3 The ECU will normally compensate for factors such as engine wear, so poor idle quality should not be blamed on the base setting being too low. Consider the possibility of an air leak into the engine, a blocked breather, or general lack of maintenance, before tampering with the base idle setting (see Section 11). A fault with the speed sensor (see Section 6) may cause poor idle quality.
4 If adjustment is to be made, run the engine to operating temperature.
5 Check the ignition timing as described in Chapter 5B.
6 To enable an accurate setting to be made, the by-pass air valve at the rear of the plenum chamber must be effectively disabled. Land Rover dealers disconnect both ends of the by-pass air hose, then fit special blanked-off sections of hose to each connection. The same effect may be achievable by fitting and tightening a hose clamp halfway along the hose.
7 Connect up an accurate tachometer to the engine, using its manufacturer's instructions. The vehicle's own tachometer will only give a rough guide for adjustment, but will suffice if necessary.
8 Start the engine, and check the base idle speed achieved against the specified value.
9 If adjustment is required, hook out the tamperproof plug from the adjuster, which is fitted to the throttle housing in front of the main throttle linkage **(see illustration)**.
10 Using a suitable Allen key inserted down the adjuster bore, turn the screw as necessary to bring the base idle speed into the specified range.

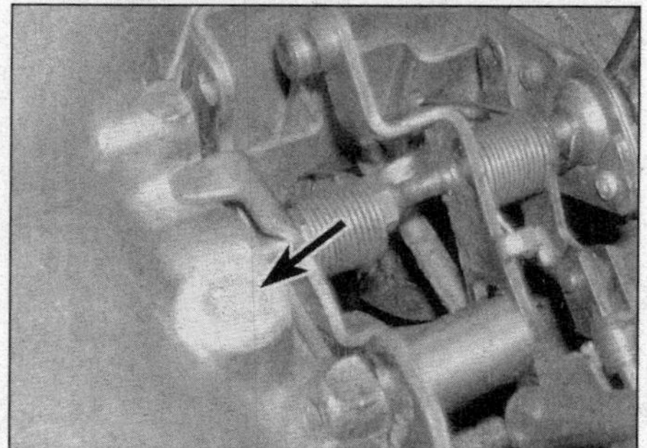

10.9 Base idle speed screw is located under tamperproof plug (arrowed)

11 Press and release the accelerator pedal a few times, then let the engine settle and re-check the adjustment. If there is any reluctance to return to idle, lubricate the throttle linkages with a few drops of light oil.

11 Fuel injection system - testing

1 If a fault appears in the fuel injection system, first ensure that all the system wiring connectors are securely connected and free of corrosion. Then ensure that the fault is not due to poor maintenance; ie, check that the air cleaner filter element is clean, the spark plugs are in good condition and correctly gapped, the cylinder compression pressures are correct, the ignition timing is correct and the engine breather hoses are clear and undamaged, referring to Chapter 1A, Chapter 2A and Chapter 5B.
2 One of the most common complaints with fuel injection systems is that of poor idle quality and frequent stalling. The reasons behind this are many and varied, but those listed below are the easiest to cure:

a) *Inlet air leaks, allowing 'unmetered' air into the engine. If the hose clips securing the various air inlet and engine breather hoses are not tight, or if the hoses themselves are damaged, air will leak into the engine, and this upsets the idle fuel/air mixture - if this is the problem, the engine will probably only run badly at idle, and no other speed.*
b) *Partially-blocked injectors, causing poor atomisation of the fuel. The fuel injected into the engine should be in the form of a fine spray, not a jet. Over time, if poor-quality petrol is used, the injectors may become partially blocked, and the fuel does not atomise. This leads not only to poor idle quality, but will adversely affect the idle mixture (emissions). Some improvement may be effected by adding a proprietary injector cleaning agent to the fuel in the tank. If this does not work, injector cleaning services may be available from local automotive specialists.*
c) *Blocked engine breathers. This really falls into the lack of maintenance category - check all the breathers as described in Chapter 1A. A blocked breather can give rise to all kinds of problems. Once the breathers are clear, consider changing the oil, and the quality of oil being used in the engine - the older the oil gets, or the lower quality it is to begin with, the more oil fumes are produced, and the more blocked the breathers will become.*
d) *Poor electrical connections and damaged wiring. This is a particularly good source of intermittent problems. Every visible wiring connection in the engine compartment should be checked, separated and cleaned. A light spray with a water-dispersant aerosol will often help restore a poor connection, but should not be used as a substitute for proper cleaning (using fine emery paper) if required. If appropriate, simpler connections may benefit from having the connector pins bent slightly, to achieve a better connection, but this should not be attempted on more complex connectors, or if there is a risk of damaging the plug. Wiring should be checked for insulation which has chafed through or been melted, or stretching (which may cause it to detach from a wiring plug, or to fracture internally). Wire also becomes brittle with age, particularly if it is exposed (as may be the case with some earth connections) - an apparently-sound connection may have fractured, and be anything but.*
e) *Ignition system problems, causing a partial misfire. Check all the ignition system components as described in Chapter 1A, paying special attention to the distributor cap, rotor arm and HT leads. Having eight cylinders may make one poor-condition or badly-fitting HT lead harder to pinpoint than on a four-cylinder engine. Pay particular attention to the routing of the leads, and arrange them so that they overlay each other as little as possible. Also check that they do not directly contact more metal surfaces than necessary, bearing in mind also that they might come into contact with the inside of the bonnet when it is closed. If any HT lead has damaged insulation, or cannot be made to connect securely, it should be renewed - if all the leads have seen long service, renew the leads as a set.*

3 If these checks fail to reveal the cause of the problem, the vehicle should be taken to a suitably-equipped Land Rover dealer for the system to be checked electronically for fault codes. A diagnostic plug (white) is located adjacent to the system ECU, into which a fault code reader can be plugged.
4 Fault codes can only be extracted from the ECU using a dedicated fault code reader. A Land Rover dealer will obviously have such a reader, but they are also available from other suppliers, including Haynes. It is unlikely to be cost-effective for the private owner to purchase a fault code reader, but a well-equipped local garage or auto electrical specialist will have one.
5 Using this equipment, faults can be pinpointed quickly and simply, even if their occurrence is intermittent. Testing all the system components individually in an attempt to locate the fault by elimination is a time-consuming operation that is unlikely to be fruitful (particularly if the fault occurs dynamically), and carries high risk of damage to the ECU's internal components.

12 Unleaded petrol - general information and usage

Note: *The information given in this Chapter is correct at the time of writing, and applies only to petrols currently available in the UK. Check with a Land Rover dealer as more up-to-date information may be available. If travelling abroad, consult one of the motoring organisations (or a similar authority) for advice on the petrols available and their suitability for your vehicle.*

1 The fuel recommended by Land Rover is given in the Specifications of this Chapter.

2 RON and MON are different testing standards; RON stands for Research Octane Number (also written as RM), while MON stands for Motor Octane Number (also written as MM).

13 Cruise control system - description and component renewal

Cruise control system - description

1 Cruise control may be fitted to later models as an option. The system incorporates the following components:

a) *Electronic control unit located behind the driver's side lower facia panel. The ECU receives information from the driver, brake pedal switch and vehicle speed sensor, and activates the throttle vacuum pump accordingly. On models with manual transmission, a further ECU in this location cuts the cruise control if the engine speed exceeds 5000 rpm.*

b) *Cruise control switches are located in the auxiliary switch panel and on the steering wheel. The steering wheel switches provide **set/accelerate** and **resume/decelerate** functions.*

c) *The clutch and brake pedal switches are mounted on the pedal bracket and, when either pedal is pressed, the ECU disengages the cruise control system and releases the throttle levers to their idle position.*

d) *The vehicle speed sensor is mounted on the side of the transfer box. Cruise control cannot be engaged at road speeds under 28 mph.*

e) *The vacuum pump fitted at the front left-hand side of the engine compartment provides the vacuum source for the actuator. A control valve in the pump allows precise control to the throttle actuator, or a quick purge of the system when the system disengages.*

f) *The actuator is located in the engine compartment and moves the throttle levers as required.*

g) *The neutral lockout relay, fitted to automatic transmission models, is located behind the driver's side right-hand footwell trim panel. Its function is to disengage the cruise control if Neutral or Park is selected in the main gearbox when the system is engaged.*

2 If the cruise control system develops a fault, first check all of the associated wiring and fuses, and the vacuum hoses.

Cruise control system components - removal, refitting and adjustment

Brake or clutch switch/vent valve

3 Disconnect the battery negative lead.

4 Release the clips and pull down the lower facia panel.

5 Disconnect the wiring and vacuum hose from the switch/vent valve.

6 Release the locking sleeve behind the switch, then release the locking tabs and remove the switch from the pedal bracket **(see illustration)**.

7 Refitting is a reversal of the removal procedure, noting the following points:

a) *The brake switch should be adjusted to provide a clearance of 1.0 mm between the switch/vent valve body and the inside shoulder of the contact button.*

b) *The clutch switch should be set to a zero clearance between the switch/vent valve body and the inside shoulder of the contact button.*

Main control switch

8 See Chapter 13, Section 4.

Steering wheel switches - models with driver's airbag

9 Disconnect the battery negative lead. Remove the airbag unit as described in Chapter 13.

10 Disconnect the cruise control switch main multi-plug in the centre, and the two horn contact wiring plugs at the base.

11 At each side of the wheel, remove the two small screws securing the switches to the wheel.

12 Unscrew the three mounting bracket bolts from the centre of the wheel, and remove the cruise control switch assembly.

13 Refitting is a reversal of the removal procedure, ensuring that the cruise control wiring harness is routed correctly. Refit the airbag unit as described in Chapter 13.

Steering wheel switches - models without driver's airbag

14 Disconnect the battery negative lead.

15 The switches must be prised from their locations in the steering wheel, and this requires significant effort with a screwdriver. The first attempt when we tried in the workshop did no more than separate the top half of the switch from the switch body - the wheel padding has to be levered aside considerably to ease out the switch complete **(see illustration)**. Take care to minimise the potential damage to the wheel padding as this is done - use stiff card behind the screwdriver shaft, for instance.

16 Once the switch has been removed,

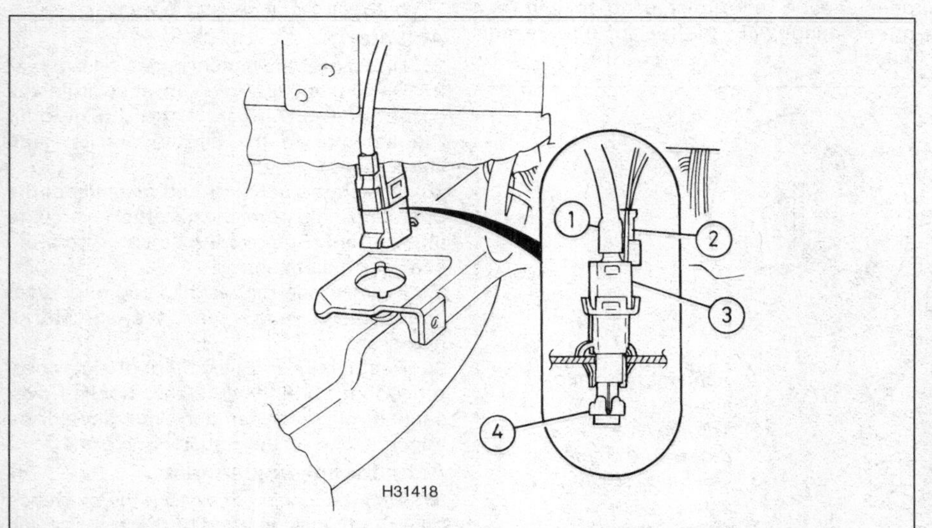
1
2
3
4
H31418

13.6 Cruise control pedal switch removal

1 Vacuum hose 2 Wiring connector 3 Wiring plug 4 Locking sleeve

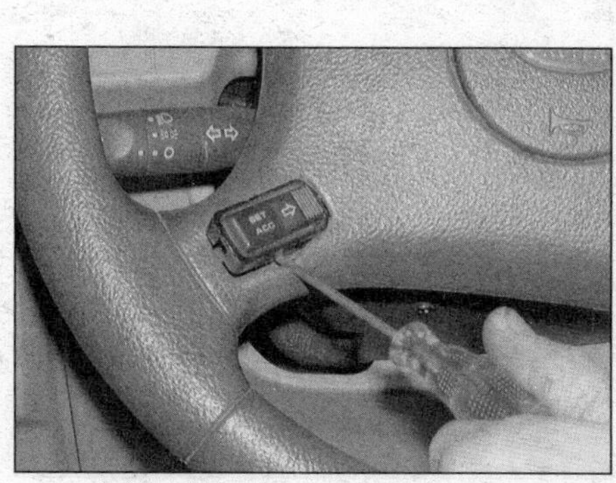

13.15 Prise out the cruise control switches from the steering wheel . . .

13.16 . . . and disconnect the wiring

13.21 Disconnect the contact unit wiring plug

13.23 Using a small screwdriver to release the contact unit retaining lugs

13.27a Disconnect the vacuum hose . . .

13.27b . . . then unscrew the actuator mounting nut

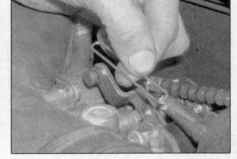

13.28 Unhook the actuator operating link from the throttle linkage

disconnect the wiring from the switch base **(see illustration)**.

17 Refitting is a reversal of removal.

Rotary contact unit

18 Disconnect the battery negative lead.

19 Set the front wheels pointing straight-ahead, then remove the steering wheel as described in Chapter 11.

20 Release the clips securing the driver's side lower trim panel, and remove the three screws securing the steering column lower shroud.

21 Disconnect the contact unit multi-plug from the steering column wiring harness **(see illustration)**, and release the harness from the ignition switch.

22 If the contact unit is to be re-used, apply adhesive tape to the upper and lower halves to prevent rotation. If this precaution is not taken, the wiring inside the unit will be damaged.

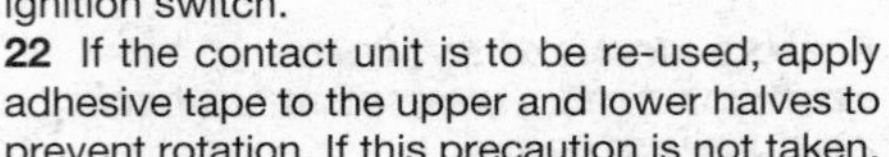

23 Pull the assembly rearwards off the steering column, then using a small screw-driver, release the upper and lower plastic lug which secures the unit to the column switches **(see illustration)**. Remove the unit from the steering column, noting how the protruding pegs engage with the steering column (two more engage with the rear of the steering wheel).

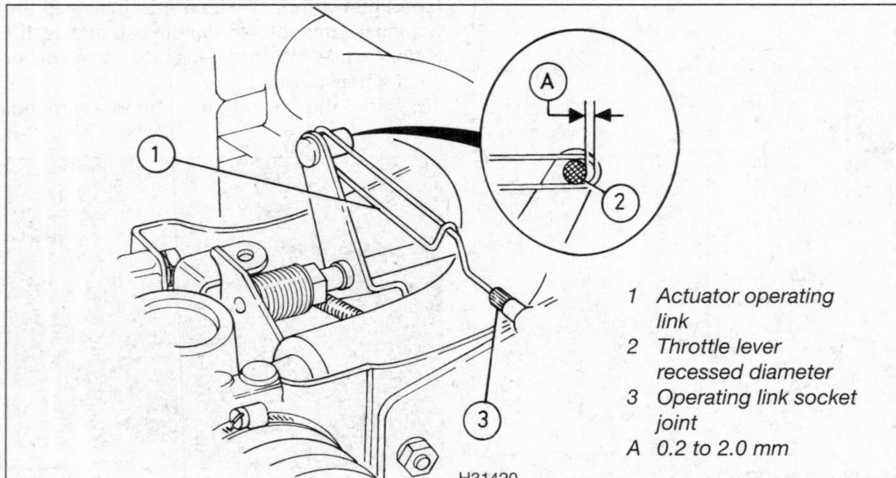
A
1
2
3
1 Actuator operating link
2 Throttle lever recessed diameter
3 Operating link socket joint
A 0.2 to 2.0 mm
H31420

13.31 Actuator link adjustment

24 While the contact unit is removed, keep it in a plastic bag, and make sure the mechanism is not rotated.

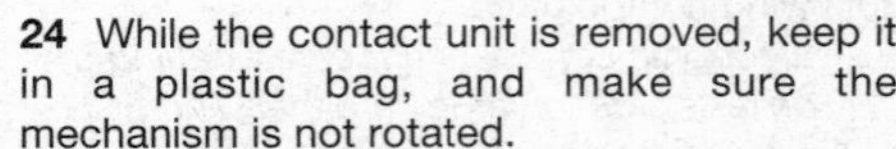

25 Refitting is a reversal of the removal procedure, noting the following points:

a) *Check that the front wheels are still in the straight-ahead position.*

b) *Make sure that the pegs on the front and rear of the unit locate in the holes on the steering column and the underside of the steering wheel.*

c) *Make sure that the wiring is not trapped between the upper and lower shroud.*

Actuator

26 Disconnect the battery negative lead.

27 Disconnect the vacuum hose from the actuator, then unscrew the nut holding the actuator to the throttle bracket **(see illustrations)**.

28 Detach the actuator and disconnect the operating link from the throttle lever **(see illustration)**. Remove the actuator from the engine compartment.

29 Examine the rubber diaphragm for wear and damage, and renew the actuator if necessary.

30 Refitting is a reversal of the removal procedure, noting that the hooked-over section of the operating link should be uppermost when the actuator is in place.

Actuator link adjustment

31 With the ignition off, check the clearance between the inside edge of the actuator link and the recessed diameter of the throttle lever. This should be between 0.2 and 2.0 mm **(see illustration)**.

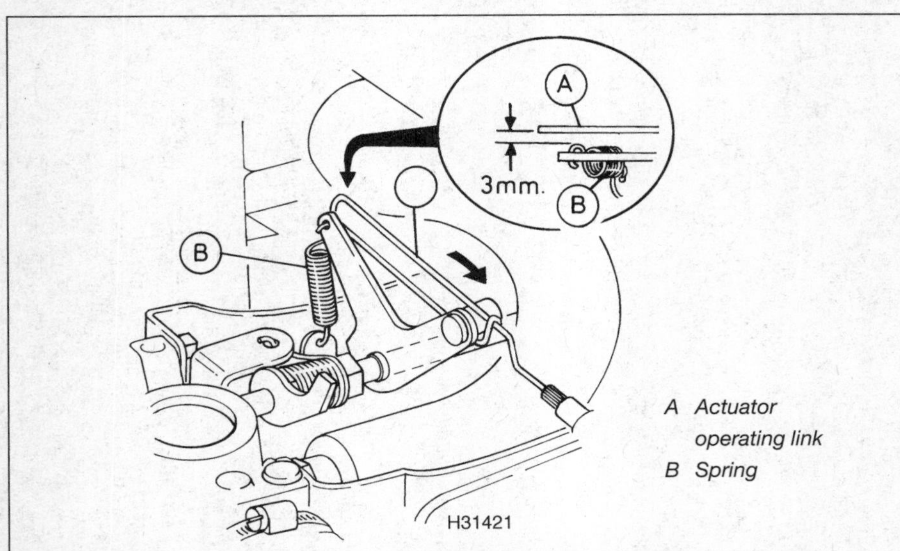
A
3mm.
B
B
A Actuator operating link
B Spring
H31421

13.33 Actuator link adjustment

32 To adjust the setting, remove the link from the actuator and rotate the socket joint on the link as required to increase or decrease the length of the link. Refit the link to the actuator and recheck the adjustment.

33 Open the throttle fully and check that a gap of 3.0 mm minimum exists between the side of the actuator link and the side of the small spring which connects the inner throttle lever to the outer throttle lever **(see illustration)**.

34 Bend the link to achieve the correct gap if it is less than 3.0 mm.

35 Check the clearance again at closed throttle and open throttle and check that the actuator link slides smoothly in the groove of the throttle lever.

Vacuum pump

36 Disconnect the battery negative lead.

37 Remove the air cleaner as described in Section 2.

38 Release the wheel chock and jack from their mountings and remove them.

39 Disconnect the vacuum pump multi-plug, then release the pump's rubber mountings and withdraw the pump **(see illustrations)**.

40 Disconnect the vacuum feed hose from the pump **(see illustration)**.

41 Refitting is a reversal of the removal procedure.

Cruise control electronic control unit (ECU)

42 The ECU is located behind the facia below the steering column. First disconnect the battery negative lead.

43 Release the clips and pull down the driver's side lower facia panel.

44 Unscrew the mounting bolt and withdraw the cruise control ECU so that the wiring multi-plug can be disconnected.

45 Refitting is a reversal of the removal procedure.

Vehicle speed sensor

46 See Section 6.

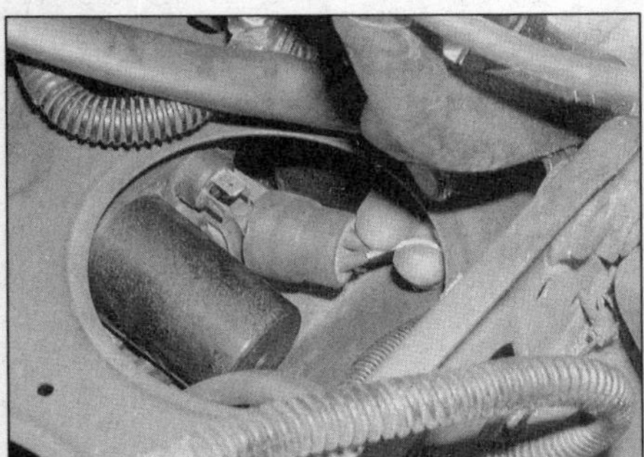

13.39a Disconnect the vacuum pump wiring plug . . .

13.39b . . . and withdraw the pump

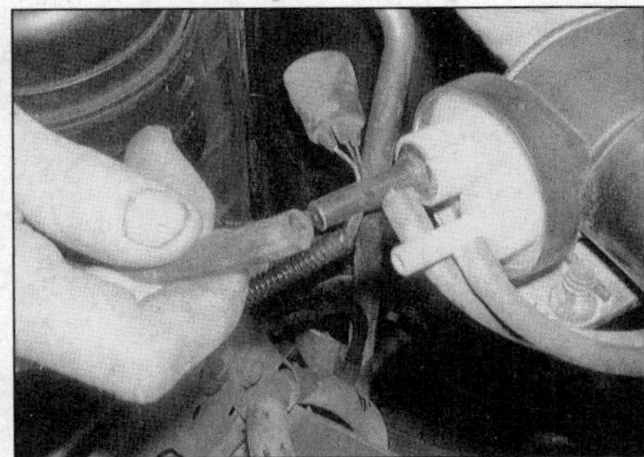

13.40 Disconnecting the vacuum feed hose

Notes

Chapter 4 Part C:
Fuel system - diesel

Contents

Degrees of difficulty

Easy, suitable for novice with little experience		**Fairly easy,** suitable for beginner with some experience		**Fairly difficult,** suitable for competent DIY mechanic		**Difficult,** suitable for experienced DIY mechanic		**Very difficult,** suitable for expert DIY or professional	

Specifications

General

System type	Rear-mounted fuel tank, distributor fuel injection pump with camshaft-driven mechanical lift pump, indirect injection. Turbocharger and intercooler
Injection pump type:	
200 TDi engine	Bosch VE4/11F
300 TDi engine	Bosch R509 (non-EDC) or R500 (EDC)
Firing order	1-3-4-2 (No 1 at timing belt end)
Direction of injection pump rotation	Clockwise (viewed from timing belt end)

Accelerator cable

Freeplay	1.5 mm

Injection timing

Note: *For reference only - see text for adjustment procedure*

200 TDi engine	1.54 mm lift at TDC
300 TDi engine:	
Engines without EDC (Electronic Diesel Control) or electronic EGR (Exhaust Gas Recirculation)	1.54 mm lift at TDC
With EDC	0.45 mm lift at TDC
With electronic EGR	1.40 mm lift at TDC

Maximum speed

No-load (all engines)	4600 + 40 - 120 rpm
Full load (cut-off begins - all engines)	4000 rpm

Idle speed

All engines	720 ± 20 rpm

Fast idle speed

Determined by idle speed - no adjustment possible

Injectors

Type	Pintle
Opening pressure:	
Initial	200 bars
Secondary:	
200 TDi engine	280 bars
300 TDi engine	300 bars

Turbocharger

Type:	
200 TDi engine	Garrett T25
300 TDi engine	Allied signal
Maximum boost pressure:	
200 TDi engine	0.78 bars
300 TDi engine	0.83 to 1.04 bars
Speed of rotation	Approximately 150 000 rpm

Torque wrench settings

	Nm	lbf ft
Air temperature sensor/blanking plug-to-inlet manifold	14	10
Boost pressure pipe-to-fuel injection pump union	10	7
Fuel hose-to-fuel filter unions:		
200 TDi engine	15	11
300 TDi engine	33	24
Fuel hose-to-fuel lift pump unions:		
200 TDi engine	12	9
300 TDi engine	33	24
Fuel injection pump front securing nuts	25	18
Fuel injection pump hub cover plate screws	25	18
Fuel injection pump rear bracket fixings	25	18
Fuel injection pump sprocket-to-hub bolts	25	18
Fuel injector clamp plate nuts	25	18
Fuel injector pipe unions	25	18
Fuel injector spill rail banjo bolt:		
200 TDi engine	2	1
300 TDi engine	10	7
Fuel leak-off pipe-to-fuel injection pump union	25	18
Fuel leak-off pipe-to-injector unions:		
Fuel lift pump securing bolts	25	18
Fuel supply hose-to-fuel injection pump union:		
200 TDi engine	12	9
300 TDi engine	25	18
Inlet manifold heat shield	6	4
Inlet manifold securing nuts and bolts	25	18
Turbocharger oil drain pipe-to-cylinder block adapter union	38	28
Turbocharger oil drain pipe-to-turbocharger union:		
200 TDi engine	45	33
300 TDi engine	25	18
Turbocharger oil feed pipe-to-cylinder block adapter union	25	18
Turbocharger oil feed pipe-to-turbocharger union	19	14
Turbocharger outlet elbow nuts (200 TDi engine)	25	18
Turbocharger-to-manifold nuts (200 TDi engine)	25	18
Turbocharger-to-manifold bolts (300 TDi engine)	45	33

1 General information and precautions

General information

The fuel system consists of a rear-mounted fuel tank, a fuel sedimenter (which removes large droplets of water and particles of contamination), a fuel filter (incorporating a secondary water separator), a fuel lift pump, a fuel injection pump, injectors and associated components **(see illustration)**. On some models, as the fuel passes through the filter, it is heated by a coolant supply flowing through the filter bowl. A turbocharger and intercooler are fitted to all engines.

For information on the exhaust and emission control systems, refer to part D of this Chapter.

Fuel is drawn from the fuel tank to the fuel injection pump by a camshaft-driven mechanical lift pump. Before reaching the fuel injection pump, the fuel passes through the fuel sedimenter and the fuel filter, where foreign matter and water are removed. Excess fuel lubricates the moving components of the pump, and is then returned to the tank.

The fuel injection pump is driven at half-crankshaft speed by the timing belt. The high pressure required to inject the fuel is achieved by a cam plate acting on a piston. The fuel passes through a central rotor with a single outlet drilling which aligns with ports leading to the injector pipes.

All 200 TDi engines, and early UK 300 TDi engines, are equipped with a conventional diesel injection system. Certain export models and later UK models may have an Electronic Diesel Control (EDC) system.

On models with a conventional fuel injection system, fuel metering is controlled by a centrifugal governor which reacts to accelerator pedal position and engine speed. The governor is linked to a metering valve which increases or decreases the amount of fuel delivered at each pumping stroke. A separate device also increases fuel delivery with increasing turbocharger boost pressure. Basic injection timing is determined when the pump is first fitted. When the engine is running, it is varied automatically to suit the prevailing engine speed, by a mechanism which turns the cam plate or ring.

On models with Electronic Diesel Control (EDC), fuel metering, injection timing and cold start control is under the control of the EDC electronic control unit. The fuel injection pump operates in fundamentally the same way as a conventional pump, but instead of using mechanical mechanisms, fuel metering is controlled by an electronically-controlled actuator, and injection timing is controlled by a solenoid. The actuator and solenoid are controlled by the EDC electronic control unit according to information provided by various sensors. The most notable feature of the EDC system is that a 'drive-by-wire' accelerator control system is used, with no mechanical link (accelerator cable) between the accelerator pedal and the fuel injection pump. Further details of the EDC system are given in Section 20.

The four fuel injectors produce a homogeneous spray of fuel into the combustion chambers. The injectors are calibrated to open and close at critical pressures to provide efficient and even combustion. Each injector needle is lubricated by fuel, which accumulates in the spring chamber and is channelled to the injection pump return hose by leak-off pipes.

Cold starting is assisted by preheater or glow plugs - one for each cylinder (see Chapter 5C for further details).

A stop solenoid cuts the fuel supply to the injection pump rotor when the engine is switched off.

Provided that the specified maintenance is carried out, the fuel injection equipment will give long and trouble-free service. The injection pump itself may well outlast the engine. The main potential cause of damage to the injection pump and injectors is dirt or water in the fuel.

Servicing of the injection pump and injectors is very limited for the home mechanic, and any dismantling or adjustment other than that described in this Chapter must be entrusted to a Land Rover dealer or fuel injection specialist.

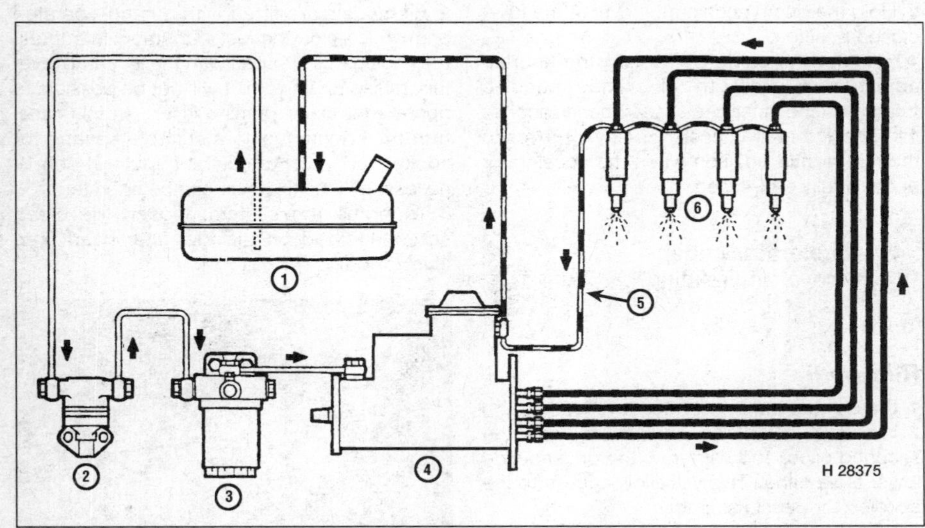
1
2
3
4
5
6
H 28375

1.1 Schematic layout of diesel fuel system

1 Fuel tank
2 Fuel lift pump
3 Fuel filter
4 Fuel injection pump
5 Fuel leak-off return line
6 Fuel injectors
Arrows show direction of fuel flow

Precautions

Warning: It is necessary to take certain precautions when working on the fuel system components, particularly the fuel injectors. Before carrying out any operations on the fuel system, refer to the precautions given in Safety first! at the beginning of this manual, and to any additional warning notes at the start of the relevant Sections.

When working on any part of the fuel system, avoid direct contact skin contact with diesel fuel - wear protective clothing and gloves when handling fuel system components. Ensure that the work area is well-ventilated, to prevent the build-up of diesel fuel vapour.

Fuel injectors operate at extremely high pressures, and the jet of fuel produced at the nozzle is capable of piercing skin, with potentially fatal results. When working with pressurised injectors, take great care to avoid exposing any part of the body to the fuel spray. It is recommended that any pressure testing of the fuel system components should be carried out by a diesel fuel systems specialist.

Under no circumstances should diesel fuel be allowed to come into contact with coolant hoses - wipe off accidental spillage immediately. Hoses that have been contaminated with fuel for an extended period should be renewed. Diesel fuel systems are particularly sensitive to contamination from dirt, air and water. Pay particular attention to cleanliness when working on any part of the fuel system, to prevent the ingress of dirt. Thoroughly clean the area around fuel unions before disconnecting them. Store dismantled components in sealed containers, to prevent contamination and the formation of condensation. Only use lint-free cloths and clean fuel for component cleansing. Avoid using compressed air when cleaning components in situ.

3.2a Remove the split-pin . . .

3.2b . . . and withdraw the accelerator clevis pin at the fuel injection pump

3.3 Unclip the cable adjuster ferrule from the bracket on the injection pump

2 Air cleaner assembly and ducting - removal and refitting

200 TDi engine

1 Removal of the air cleaner assembly is described in Chapter 1B as part of the air cleaner element renewal procedure.

2 Removal and refitting of the ducting is self-evident, but note the locations of any wiring or hose clips attached to the ducting, and ensure that they are refitted in the same locations.

300 TDi engine

Removal

3 Working in the engine compartment, loosen the securing clamp, and disconnect the air outlet hose from the air cleaner cover.

4 Unclip the air cleaner cover, and withdraw the filter element.

5 Remove the wheel chock from the corner of the engine compartment.

6 Carefully pull the air cleaner up to release the mounting rubbers from the holes in the bottom of the air cleaner casing. Note that the rubbers remain in place in the body panel.

7 Release the plastic clips securing the air inlet tube to the body side panel, then lift the air cleaner assembly from the engine compartment.

Refitting

8 Refitting is a reversal of removal, but ensure that the mounting rubbers engage securely in the air cleaner holes.

3 Accelerator cable - removal, refitting and adjustment

Note: *Does not apply to EDC-equipped models.*

Removal

Note: *New split-pins should be used to secure the cable end clevis pins on refitting.*

1 Disconnect the battery negative lead.

2 Working in the engine compartment, remove the split-pin, and withdraw the clevis pin securing the end of the accelerator cable to the accelerator lever on the fuel injection pump **(see illustrations)**.

3 Unclip the cable adjuster from the bracket on the fuel injection pump **(see illustration)**.

4 Where applicable, release the accelerator cable from the bracket on the engine compartment bulkhead, noting the cable routing.

5 Working inside the vehicle, release the securing clips, and withdraw the driver's side lower facia panel. This will allow access to the accelerator pedal assembly.

6 Remove the split-pin, and withdraw the clevis pin securing the end of the cable to the accelerator pedal.

7 Release the cable grommet from the bulkhead, then withdraw the cable through the bulkhead into the engine compartment.

Refitting

8 Refitting is a reversal of removal, bearing in mind the following points:

a) Ensure that the cable is routed as noted before removal.

b) Use new split-pins to secure the cable end clevis pins.

c) On completion, check the cable adjustment, as described in the following paragraphs.

Adjustment

9 Hold the pump accelerator lever in the fully-closed position.

10 Adjust the cable by turning the knurled adjustment wheel to give the specified freeplay in the inner cable (see *Specifications*).

11 Check that the accelerator lever moves to the full-throttle position when the accelerator pedal is fully depressed.

4 Accelerator pedal - removal and refitting

Removal

1 Disconnect the battery negative lead.

2 Working inside the vehicle, release the securing clips, and withdraw the driver's side lower facia panel. This will allow access to the accelerator pedal assembly.

3 Where applicable, remove the split-pin, and withdraw the clevis pin securing the end of the cable to the accelerator pedal.

4 Using a suitable pair of circlip pliers, remove the circlip from one end of the pedal pivot pin.

5 Withdraw the pivot pin from the pedal bracket, and recover the bushes, noting their locations. Withdraw the pedal and return spring, noting the orientation of the spring.

Refitting

6 Refitting is a reversal of removal, bearing in mind the following points:

a) Ensure that the pedal return spring and the pivot bushes are located as noted during removal.

b) On completion, check the accelerator cable adjustment, as described in Section 3, where applicable.

5 Fuel system - priming and bleeding

Note: *Refer to the precautions given in Section 1 before proceeding.*

1 After disconnecting part of the fuel supply system (or after running out of fuel), it is necessary to prime the system and bleed off any air which may have entered the system components.

2 All models are fitted with a hand-operated priming lever on the fuel lift pump. Note that if the engine has stopped with the lift pump lever fully raised on its cam, it will not be possible to operate the hand priming lever - in this case, turn the engine (using a suitable spanner or socket on the crankshaft pulley bolt if necessary) until the lever can be operated.

3 To prime the system, loosen the bleed screw, located on the fuel filter head **(see illustration)**.

5.3 Fuel filter head bleed screw (arrowed)

4 Operate the priming lever until fuel free from air bubbles emerges from the bleed screw, then retighten the screw. To operate the lever, push the lever down to release it from the catch, then pump the lever up and down.

5 Switch on the 'ignition' (to activate the stop solenoid) and continue operating the priming lever until firm resistance is felt, then pump a few more times.

6 If a large amount of air has entered the fuel injection pump, place a wad of rag around the fuel return union on the fuel injection pump (to absorb spilt fuel), then slacken the union. Operate the priming lever (with the 'ignition' switched on to activate the stop solenoid), or crank the engine on the starter motor in 10-second bursts, until fuel free from air bubbles emerges from the fuel union. Tighten the union, and mop up any split fuel.

Warning: Be prepared to stop the engine if it should fire, to avoid excessive fuel spray and spillage.

7 If air has entered the injector pipes, place wads of rag around the injector pipe unions at the injectors (to absorb spilt fuel), then slacken the unions. Crank the engine on the starter motor until fuel emerges from the unions, then stop cranking the engine and retighten the unions. Mop up spilt fuel.

Warning: Be prepared to stop the engine if it should fire, to avoid excessive fuel spray and spillage.

8 Start the engine with the accelerator pedal fully depressed. Additional cranking may be necessary to finally bleed the system before the engine starts.

6 Fuel gauge sender unit - removal and refitting

Note: *Refer to the precautions given in Section 1 before proceeding.*

Refer to part A of this Chapter, Section 11. Ignore the references to depressurising the fuel system, and to the fuel pump.

7 Fuel tank - removal and refitting

Note: *Refer to the precautions given in Section 1 before proceeding.*

Refer to part A of this Chapter, Section 12. Ignore the references to depressurising the fuel system, and to the fuel pump.

8 Fuel lift pump - removal and refitting

Note: *Refer to the precautions given in Section 1 before proceeding.*

Removal

Note: *A new gasket must be used when refitting the pump.*

1 Disconnect the battery negative lead.

2 Unscrew the union nuts, and disconnect the upper two fuel pipes connecting the fuel injectors to the fuel injection pump, from the fuel injectors. Be prepared for fuel spillage, and plug or cover the open ends of the injectors and the pipes, to prevent dirt ingress. Loosen the pipe unions at the fuel injection pump (counterhold the unions on the pump), and manipulate the pipes to allow sufficient access to remove the fuel lift pump.

3 Unscrew the unions (again, counterhold the unions on the pump), and disconnect the fuel supply and feed hoses from the fuel lift pump **(see illustration)**. Again, plug or cover the open ends of the hoses and pump.

4 Unscrew the two bolts securing the pump to the cylinder block, then withdraw the pump and the gasket(s) **(see illustrations)**. Discard the gasket(s), noting that some models may be fitted with a plastic insulating block, sandwiched between two gaskets..

5 On 200 TDi engines, if desired, the fuel lift pump housing can be unbolted from the cylinder block - note the locations of any brackets secured by the bolts. Recover the gasket.

Refitting

6 Commence refitting by cleaning all traces of old gasket from the mating faces of the pump and the cylinder block (and the insulating block, where applicable).

7 Similarly, where applicable on 200 TDi engines, clean the mating faces of the fuel pump housing, and refit the housing using a new gasket.

8 Refit the pump, and the insulating block where applicable, using new gasket(s). Ensure that the pump operating lever engages correctly with the camshaft as the pump is refitted.

9 Refit the pump securing bolts, and tighten them to the specified torque.

10 Reconnect the fuel hoses to the lift pump, and reconnect the injector pipes to the injectors. Ensure that all unions are securely tightened.

11 Start the engine. If difficulty is experienced, bleed the fuel system as described in Section 5.

9 Maximum speed - checking and adjustment

Models with conventional fuel injection system

Caution: The maximum speed adjustment screw is sealed by the manufacturers at the factory, using paint or a locking wire and a lead seal. There is no reason why it should require adjustment. Do not disturb the screw if the vehicle is still within the warranty period, otherwise the warranty will be invalidated. This adjustment requires the use of a tachometer - refer to Section 10 for alternative methods.

1 Run the engine to normal operating temperature.

2 Have an assistant fully depress the accelerator pedal, and check that the maximum engine speed is as given in the Specifications. Do not keep the engine at maximum speed for more than two or three seconds.

8.3 Disconnecting a fuel hose from the fuel lift pump

8.4a Remove the fuel lift pump . . .

8.4b . . . and recover the gasket - 300 TDi engine

2
1

9.3 Maximum speed adjustment screw (1) and locknut cover (2) - viewed from rear of pump

3 If adjustment is necessary, stop the engine then loosen the locknut, turn the maximum speed adjustment screw as necessary, and retighten the locknut. Note that the locknut may be sealed using a plastic cover **(see illustration)**.

4 Repeat the procedure in paragraph 2 to check the adjustment.

5 Stop the engine and disconnect the tachometer.

Models with Electronic Diesel Control (EDC) system

6 The maximum speed is controlled by the EDC system, as a built-in safety feature, and no adjustment is possible.

10 Idle speed - checking and adjustment

Note: *The fast idle speed is automatically set with the idle speed, and cannot be adjusted independently. Adjustment of the idle speed is permitted in service, but the manufacturers recommend that any other fuel injection pump adjustments are entrusted to authorised Bosch agents. For information purposes, details of maximum engine speed adjustment are given in Section 9.*

1 The usual type of tachometer (rev counter), which works from ignition system pulses, cannot be used on diesel engines. If it is not felt that adjusting the idle speed by ear is satisfactory, one of the following alternatives may be used:

1
2

10.4 Idle speed adjustment screw (1) and locknut (2)

a) Purchase or hire of an appropriate tachometer.

b) Delegation of the job to a Land Rover dealer or other specialist.

c) Timing light (strobe) operated by a petrol engine running at the desired speed. If the timing light is pointed at a mark on the camshaft or injection pump sprocket, the mark will appear stationary when the two engines are running at the same speed (or multiples of that speed). The sprocket will be rotating at half the crankshaft speed, but this will not affect the adjustment. (In practice, it was found impossible to use this method on the crankshaft pulley, due to the acute viewing angle.)

2 Before making adjustments, warm-up the engine to normal operating temperature. Make sure that the accelerator cable is correctly adjusted, where applicable (see Section 3).

3 With the accelerator lever resting against the idle stop, check that the engine idles at the specified speed. If necessary, adjust as follows.

4 If adjustment is necessary, loosen the idle speed adjustment screw locknut, and turn the screw as necessary to give the desired engine speed **(see illustration)**. Turn the screw clockwise to increase the engine speed, or anti-clockwise to decrease the engine speed.

5 Operate the accelerator lever to increase the engine speed for a few seconds, then re-check the idle speed.

6 When the adjustment is correct, hold the adjustment screw steady, as the locknut is tightened.

7 On completion, stop the engine and, where applicable, disconnect the tachometer.

11 Fuel injection pump - removal and refitting

Note 1: *Refer to the precautions given in Section 1 before proceeding. On 300 TDi engines, also refer to the note in Chapter 2B, Section 7.*

Note 2: *To remove the pump without disturbing the timing belt, Land Rover special tool LRT-12-045 will be required to retain the pump sprocket in position. If a suitable tool is not available, remove the timing belt as described in Chapter 2B. A new pump front gasket and a new pump hub cover plate gasket must be used on refitting.*

Conventional fuel injection system - using special tool LRT-12-045

Removal

1 Disconnect the battery negative lead.

2 Turn the crankshaft to bring No 1 piston to TDC on the compression stroke, and fit the tools to lock the crankshaft and injection pump spindle in position, as described in Chapter 2B, Section 3.

3 With the engine locked in the TDC position, proceed as follows.

4 Loosen the pump locking screw, and remove the keeper plate (located at the front of the pump, behind the timing belt housing). Tighten the locking screw to lock the pump in position **(see illustrations)**.

5 Remove the three pump sprocket-to-hub bolts, and withdraw the sprocket retaining plate. If necessary, counterhold the injection pump hub using a socket on the hub nut - **do not** rely on the pump spindle locking screw to hold the sprocket in position whilst loosening the pump sprocket-to-hub bolts.

6 Withdraw the pump timing pin.

7 Fit the sprocket retaining tool (LRT-12-045), with an 8.0 mm washer, 1.5 to 2.0 mm thick, under each bolt head, in addition to the washers supplied with the tool. Tighten the two retaining tool bolts, then re-insert the timing pin through the hole provided in the retaining tool plate **(see illustration)**.

8 Disconnect the wiring from the stop solenoid.

11.4a Unclip the wiring harness (arrowed) from the bracket on the pump . . .

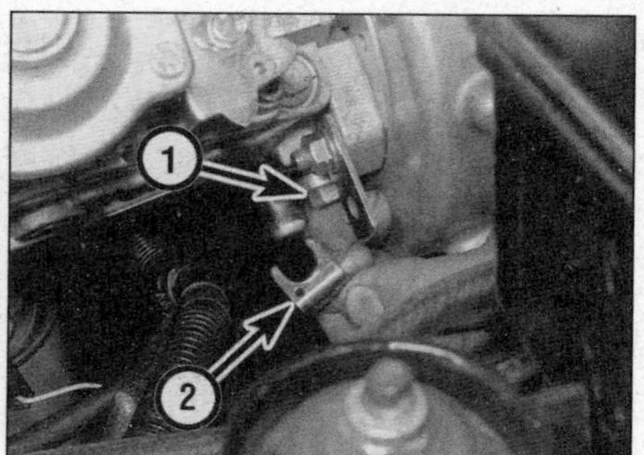
1
2

11.4b . . . then loosen the screw (1) and remove the keeper plate (2) - 300 TDi engine

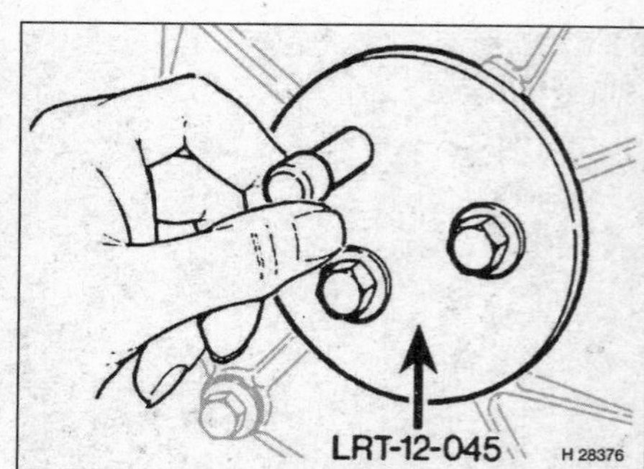
LRT-12-045
H 28376

11.7 Special tool LRT-12-045 fitted to retain fuel injection pump sprocket

11.10a Disconnecting the fuel supply pipe from the pump

11.10b Counterhold the union on the pump when unscrewing the fuel return pipe union nut

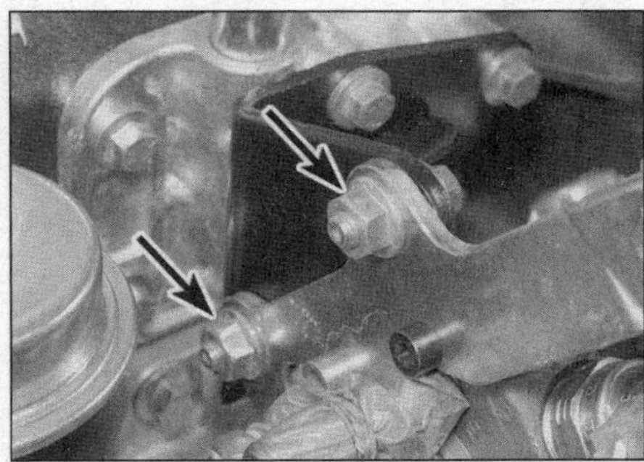

11.13 Unscrew the two nuts and bolts (arrowed) securing the pump to the rear support bracket

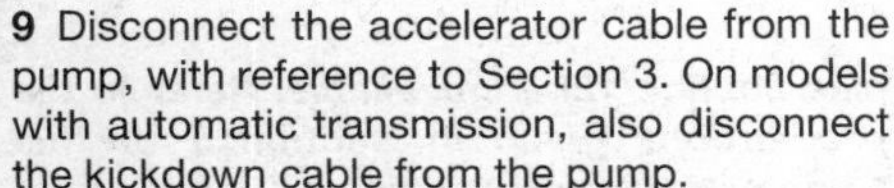

9 Disconnect the accelerator cable from the pump, with reference to Section 3. On models with automatic transmission, also disconnect the kickdown cable from the pump.

10 Unscrew the banjo bolt and the union nut, and disconnect the fuel supply and return pipes from the pump **(see illustrations)**. Be prepared for fuel spillage. Recover the sealing washers from the banjo union. Cover the open ends of the pipes, and plug the openings in the injection pump to keep dirt out (the banjo bolt can be refitted to the pump and covered).

11 Similarly, disconnect the boost pressure pipe from the pump.

12 Unscrew the union nuts, and disconnect the injector pipes from the rear of the pump, and from the injectors. Remove the pipes. Plug or cover the open ends of the pump, pipes, and injectors, to prevent dirt ingress.

13 Working at the rear of the pump, counterhold the bolts, and unscrew the two nuts securing the pump to the rear support bracket **(see illustration)**.

14 Unscrew the three nuts securing the pump to the studs at the rear of the timing belt housing, then withdraw the pump and recover the gasket. Where applicable, note the location of any brackets on the studs **(see illustrations)**.

Refitting

15 Commence refitting by thoroughly cleaning the mating faces of the pump flange and the timing belt housing.

16 Place the new gasket in position over the pump mounting studs.

11.14a Note the location of any brackets (arrowed) on the timing belt housing studs

17 If a new pump is being fitted, proceed as follows:

a) *Fit the timing pin to the pump. If necessary, rotate the pump spindle to allow the pin to locate fully.*
b) *Slacken the pump locking screw, remove the keeper plate, then tighten the screw to lock the pump.*
c) *Remove the timing pin from the pump.*

18 Place the pump in position on the mounting studs, ensuring that the gasket is correctly located, and tighten the mounting nuts to the specified torque.

19 Refit the pump rear mounting bracket to the cylinder block, but do not fully tighten the bolts at this stage.

20 Refit the nuts and bolts securing the pump to the rear mounting bracket, but again do not fully tighten at this stage.

21 Tighten the rear mounting bracket-to-cylinder block bolts, followed by the pump-to-mounting bracket bolts.

22 Refit and reconnect the injector pipes, and tighten the union nuts.

23 Reconnect the boost pressure pipe to the pump.

24 Reconnect the fuel supply and return pipes to the pump.

25 Reconnect the accelerator cable to the pump, and adjust the cable as described in Section 3. On models with automatic transmission, also reconnect and adjust the kickdown cable, with reference to Chapter 7B.

26 Reconnect the stop solenoid wiring.

27 Unscrew the securing bolts, and remove the injection pump sprocket retaining tool.

11.14b Withdrawing the fuel injection pump

28 Refit the sprocket retaining plate, then refit the pump timing pin through the pump hub into the pump body.

29 Refit and tighten the pump sprocket-to-hub bolts.

30 Loosen the pump locking screw, then refit the keeper plate, and tighten the locking screw.

31 Remove the timing pin from the pump, and withdraw the flywheel locking tool centre pin from the slot in the flywheel.

32 Turn the crankshaft through two complete revolutions, then re-engage the flywheel locking tool centre pin with the slot in the flywheel, and check that the pump timing pin can still be inserted easily.

33 If the pump timing pin cannot be easily inserted into position, proceed as follows.

34 Withdraw the flywheel locking tool centre pin from the slot in the flywheel, then turn the crankshaft as necessary, until the timing pin can be inserted easily into the injection pump.

35 Loosen the pump locking screw, and remove the keeper plate, then tighten the locking screw to lock the pump in position.

36 Loosen the three pump sprocket-to-hub bolts.

37 Turn the crankshaft back to TDC, and engage the flywheel locking tool centre pin with the timing slot in the flywheel.

38 Re-check to ensure that the pump timing pin is an easy sliding fit in the pump.

39 Tighten the pump sprocket-to-hub bolts to the specified torque.

40 Loosen the pump locking screw, then refit the keeper plate, and tighten the locking screw.

41 Remove the timing pin from the pump, and withdraw the flywheel locking tool centre pin from the slot in the flywheel.

42 Refit the blanking plug, or the cover plate bolt, as applicable, to the flywheel locking tool aperture (on models with a blanking plug, coat the threads of the plug with thread-locking compound before refitting).

43 Refit the injection pump hub cover plate, using a new gasket.

44 Where applicable, refit the air conditioning compressor, and refit the drivebelt as described in Chapter 1B.

45 Reconnect the battery negative lead.

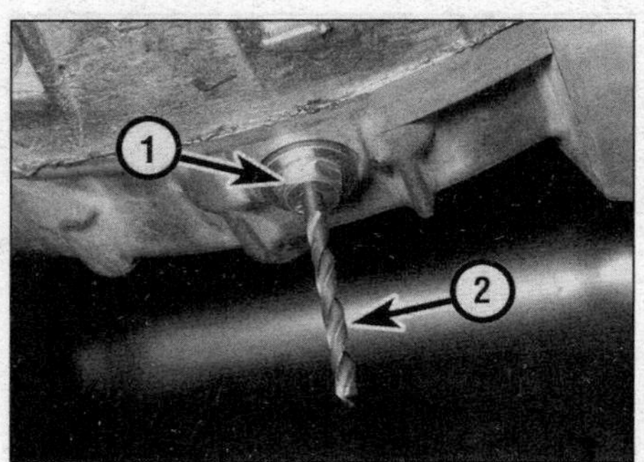
1
2

12.6a Improvised flywheel locking tool in position on manual gearbox model
1 Blanking plug 2 3/16 in twist drill

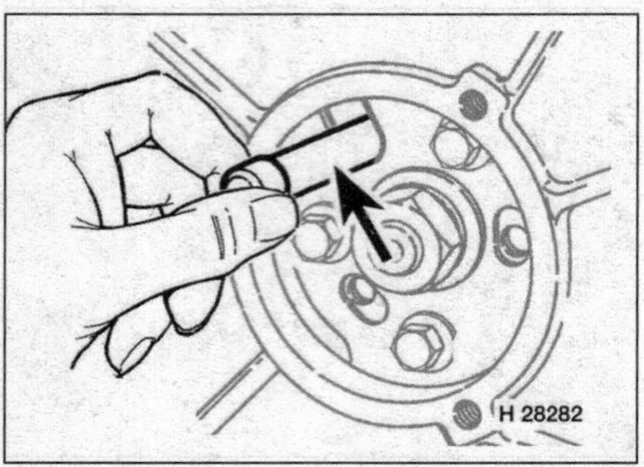
H 28282

12.6b Injection pump timing pin (arrowed) can be improvised using a length of 9.5 mm diameter bar

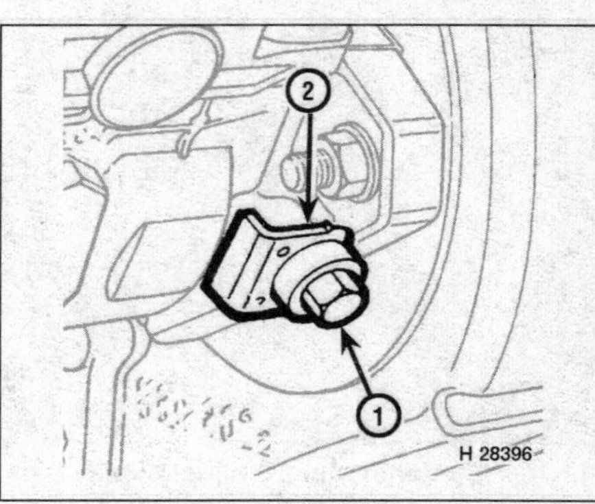
2
1
H 28396

13.5 Pump locking screw (1) and keeper plate (2)

Conventional fuel injection system - without special tool LRT-12-045

Removal

46 Remove the timing belt as described in Chapter 2B.

47 Loosen the pump locking screw, and remove the keeper plate (located at the front of the pump, behind the timing belt housing). Tighten the locking screw to lock the pump spindle in position.

48 Withdraw the pump timing pin from the pump sprocket.

49 Remove the pump sprocket-to-hub securing bolts, then withdraw the sprocket retaining plate and the sprocket.

50 Proceed as described in paragraphs 8 to 14 inclusive.

Refitting

51 Proceed as described in paragraphs 15 to 26 inclusive.

52 Refit the pump sprocket and retaining plate (noting that the U-shaped slot in the retaining plate should align with the slot in the pump hub), then refit the sprocket-to-hub bolts. Do not fully tighten the bolts at this stage.

53 Refit the pump timing pin through the sprocket into the pump body.

54 Loosen the pump locking screw, then refit the keeper plate, and tighten the locking screw.

55 Refit the timing belt as described in Chapter 2B.

Electronic Diesel Control (EDC) system

56 The removal and refitting procedure is as described previously for models with a conventional fuel injection system, bearing in mind the following points:

a) Ignore all references to the accelerator cable.

b) Disconnect all relevant wiring from the pump, noting the routing of the harnesses.

12 Injection timing - checking methods and adjustment

Checking the injection timing is not a routine operation. It is only necessary after the injection pump has been disturbed.

Dynamic timing equipment does exist, but it is unlikely to be available to the home mechanic, and there should be no need to carry out dynamic timing on the engines fitted to the Discovery. The equipment works by converting pressure pulses in an injector pipe into electrical signals. If such equipment is available, use it in accordance with its maker's instructions.

Static timing can be carried out very accurately, provided that the appropriate flywheel and injection pump spindle locking tools are available.

The Land Rover special tool available to lock the flywheel is LRT-12-044 for models with a conventional fuel injection system, or LRT-12-085 for models with EDC.

Special flywheel locking tool LRT-12-044 can be improvised by obtaining a spare flywheel housing blanking plug, and accurately drilling a hole though its centre to accept a 3/16 in twist drill.

To lock the fuel injection pump sprocket, special tool LRT-12-045 will be required - this tool can be improvised using a short length (approximately 50.0 mm) of 3/8 in (9.5 mm) diameter round bar **(see illustrations)**.

13 Injection timing - checking and adjustment

Caution: The maximum engine speed and transfer pressure settings, together with timing access plugs, are sealed by the manufacturers at the factory, using locking wire and lead seals. Do not disturb the wire if the vehicle is still within the warranty period, otherwise the warranty will be invalidated. Also do not attempt the timing procedure unless accurate locking tools (see Section 12) are available. Refer to the precautions given in Section 1 of this Chapter before proceeding.

Note: *A new injection pump hub cover plate gasket must be used on refitting.*

1 Disconnect the battery negative lead.

2 Turn the crankshaft to bring No 1 piston to TDC on the compression stroke, and fit the tools to lock the flywheel and the injection pump sprocket in position, as described in Chapter 2B, Section 3. If the flywheel and injection pump sprocket can be locked using the tools as described, the injection pump timing is correct.

3 If the flywheel locking tool centre pin cannot be engaged easily with the timing slot in the flywheel, proceed as follows.

4 Withdraw the flywheel locking tool centre pin from the slot in the flywheel, then turn the crankshaft as necessary, until the timing pin can be inserted easily into the injection pump.

5 Loosen the pump locking screw, and remove the keeper plate (located at the front of the pump, behind the timing belt housing). Tighten the locking screw to lock the pump in position **(see illustration)**.

6 Loosen the three pump sprocket-to-hub bolts.

7 Turn the crankshaft back the small amount to TDC, and engage the flywheel locking tool centre pin with the timing slot in the flywheel.

8 Re-check to ensure that the pump timing pin is an easy sliding fit in the pump.

9 Tighten the pump sprocket-to-hub bolts to the specified torque.

10 Loosen the pump locking screw, then refit the keeper plate, and tighten the locking screw.

11 Remove the timing pin from the pump, and withdraw the flywheel locking tool centre pin from the slot in the flywheel.

12 Turn the crankshaft through two complete revolutions, and check that the flywheel locking tool and the pump timing pin can still be inserted easily, both at the same time.

13 Withdraw the timing pin and the flywheel locking tool.

14 Refit the blanking plug (or the cover plate bolt, as applicable) to the flywheel locking tool aperture (on models with a blanking plug, coat

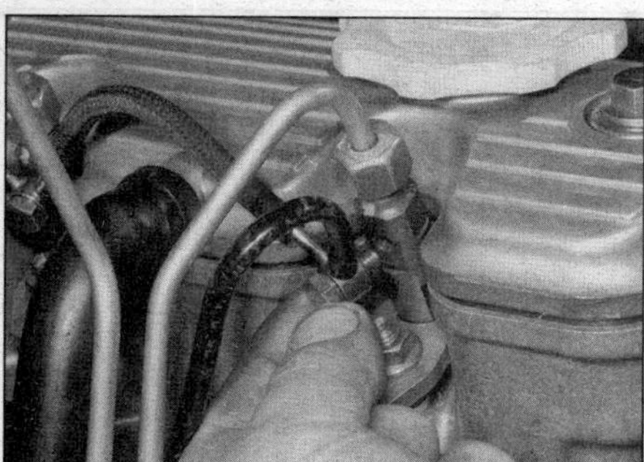

14.5 Disconnecting the leak-off pipes . . .

14.6 . . . and the injector pipe from a fuel injector

14.9 Unscrew the securing nut . . .

the threads of the plug with thread-locking compound before refitting).

15 Refit the injection pump hub cover plate, using a new gasket.

16 Where applicable, refit the air conditioning compressor, and refit the drivebelt as described in Chapter 1B.

14 Fuel injectors - testing, removal and refitting

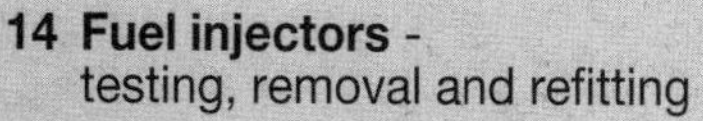

Warning: Exercise extreme caution when working on the fuel injectors. Never expose the hands or any part of the body to injector spray, as the high working pressure can cause the fuel to penetrate the skin, with possibly fatal results. You are strongly advised to have any work which involves testing the injectors under pressure carried out by a Land Rover dealer or fuel injection specialist. Refer to the precautions given in Section 1 of this Chapter before proceeding.

Testing

1 Injectors do deteriorate with prolonged use, and it is reasonable to expect them to need reconditioning or renewal after 60 000 miles (100 000 km) or so. Accurate testing, overhaul and calibration of the injectors must be left to a specialist. A defective injector which is causing knocking or smoking can be located without dismantling as follows.

2 Run the engine at a fast idle. Slacken each injector union in turn, placing rag around the union to catch spilt fuel, and being careful not to expose the skin to any spray. When the union on the defective injector is slackened, the knocking or smoking will stop.

Removal

Note: *Take great care not to allow dirt into the injectors or fuel pipes during this procedure. New sealing washers must be used when refitting the injectors.*

3 Where applicable, remove the engine oil filler cap, and unclip the plastic cover from the top of the valve cover.

4 Carefully clean around the relevant injector and injector pipe union nuts.

5 Unscrew the banjo bolt, and disconnect the leak-off pipe(s) from the injector **(see illustration)**.

6 Unscrew the union nut securing the injector pipe to the fuel injector **(see illustration)**. Cover the open ends of the injector and the pipe, using small plastic bags or fingers cut from discarded (but clean!) rubber gloves.

7 Counterhold the union on the pump, and slacken the union nut securing the relevant injector pipe to the injection pump. There is no need to disconnect the pipe from the pump.

8 If working on No 4 fuel injector on engines fitted with EDC (see Section 20), separate the two halves of the fuel injector wiring connector (the injector incorporates the EDC injection timing sensor).

9 Unscrew the nut securing the injector clamp plate to the cylinder head **(see illustration)**.

10 Withdraw the clamp plate and the injector from the cylinder head **(see illustrations)**.

11 Recover the copper washer from the cylinder head.

12 Take care not to drop the injectors, nor allow the needles at their tips to become damaged. The injectors are precision-made to fine limits, and must not be handled roughly. In particular, do not mount them in a bench vice.

Refitting

13 Fit a new copper washer to the cylinder head, with the concave side towards the injector **(see Tool Tip)**.

14 Place the injector in position, with the hole for the leak-off pipe union facing away from the cylinder head, then refit the clamp plate, locating it over the cylinder head stud.

15 Refit the clamp nut, and tighten to the specified torque.

16 Reconnect the injector pipe to the fuel injector, and tighten the union.

17 Tighten the injector pipe union at the injection pump.

18 Reconnect the leak-off pipe to the injector, and tighten the banjo bolt.

19 Where applicable, reconnect the two halves of the fuel injector wiring connector.

20 Start the engine. If difficulty is experienced, bleed the fuel system as described in Section 5.

21 On completion, where applicable, refit the plastic cover and the oil filler cap to the valve cover.

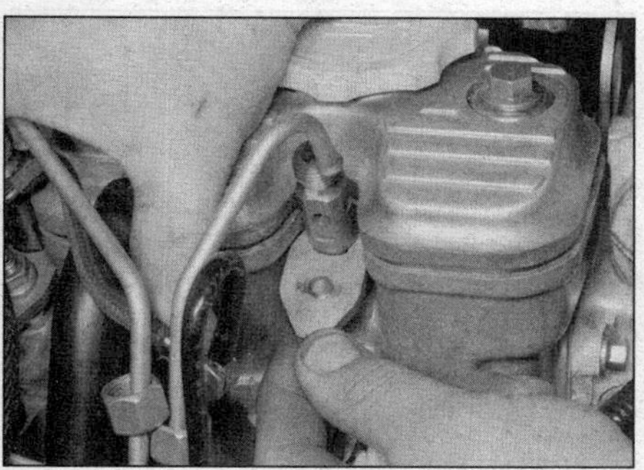

14.10a . . . then withdraw the clamp plate . . .

14.10b . . . and the injector

TOOL
TiP

The washer can be guided into position by sliding it down the shaft of a screwdriver positioned over the injector hole in the cylinder head

15 Turbocharger - description and precautions

Description

A turbocharger is fitted to all engines. It increases engine efficiency by raising the pressure in the inlet manifold above atmospheric pressure. Instead of the air simply being sucked into the cylinders, it is forced in. Additional fuel is supplied by the injection pump, in proportion to the increased amount of air.

Energy for the operation of the turbocharger comes from the exhaust gas. The gas flows through a specially-shaped housing (the turbine housing) and in so doing, spins the turbine wheel. The turbine wheel is attached to a shaft, at the end of which is another vaned wheel, known as the compressor wheel. The compressor wheel spins in its own housing, and compresses the inducted air on the way to the inlet manifold.

Between the turbocharger and the inlet manifold, the compressed air passes through an intercooler. This is an air-to-air heat exchanger, mounted at the front of the vehicle, next to the radiator, and supplied with air through the front grille. The purpose of the intercooler is to remove from the inducted air some of the heat gained in being compressed. Because cooler air is denser, removal of this heat further increases engine efficiency.

Boost pressure (the pressure in the inlet manifold) is limited by a wastegate, which diverts the exhaust gas away from the turbine wheel in response to a pressure-sensitive actuator.

The turbo shaft is pressure-lubricated by an oil feed pipe from the main oil gallery. The shaft 'floats' on a cushion of oil. A drain pipe returns the oil to the sump.

Precautions

The turbocharger operates at extremely high speeds and temperatures. Certain precautions must be observed to avoid premature failure of the turbo, or injury to the operator.

Do not operate the turbo with any parts exposed. Foreign objects falling onto the rotating vanes could cause excessive damage and (if ejected) personal injury.

Do not race the engine immediately after start-up, especially if it is cold. Give the oil a few seconds to circulate.

Always allow the engine to return to idle speed before switching it off - do not blip the throttle and switch off, as this will leave the turbo spinning without lubrication.

Allow the engine to idle for several minutes before switching off after a high-speed run.

Observe the recommended intervals for oil and filter changing, and use a reputable oil of the specified quality. Neglect of oil changing, or use of inferior oil, can cause carbon formation on the turbo shaft and subsequent failure.

16 Turbocharger - removal and refitting

200 TDi engine

Removal

Note: *A new gasket will be required when refitting the turbocharger.*

1 Disconnect the battery negative lead.

2 To improve access, remove the air cleaner assembly with reference to Section 2.

3 Disconnect the exhaust front section from the turbocharger, with reference to part D of this Chapter.

4 Loosen the securing clips, and disconnect the air trunking from the turbocharger. If desired, to improve access, remove the air trunking.

5 Place a suitable container beneath the engine to catch escaping oil, then unscrew the union nuts, and disconnect the turbocharger oil feed and return hoses from the cylinder block. Plug the open ends of the hoses and the cylinder block, to prevent dirt ingress.

6 Disconnect the turbocharger boost pressure pipe from the turbocharger.

7 Unscrew the four securing nuts, and withdraw the turbocharger from the exhaust manifold. Recover the gasket.

Refitting

8 Refitting is a reversal of removal, bearing in mind the following points:

a) Refit the turbocharger to the manifold using a new gasket, and tighten the securing nuts to the specified torque.

b) Ensure that the oil pipes are securely reconnected.

c) Reconnect the exhaust front section to the turbocharger with reference to part D of this Chapter.

9 Before starting the engine, the turbocharger **must** be primed with oil as follows. Failure to carry out this procedure may result in serious (and expensive) damage to the turbocharger:

a) Unscrew the oil feed pipe banjo bolt from the top of the turbocharger housing. Recover the two sealing washers, and move the feed pipe away from the oil hole in the housing.

b) Fill the housing with clean engine oil of the correct type and grade (see end of Weekly checks), from a freshly-opened sealed container.

c) Reconnect the oil feed pipe, and refit the banjo bolt, ensuring that one sealing washer is positioned on each side of the pipe. Tighten the banjo bolt to the specified torque.

300 TDi engine

10 On 300 TDi engines, the turbocharger is integral with the exhaust manifold. Although the turbocharger and manifold can be separated once the manifold assembly has been removed, at the time of writing, it was unclear whether the turbocharger can be renewed independently of the manifold - check with a Land Rover dealer for details.

11 Removal and refitting of the turbocharger is described as part of the exhaust manifold removal and refitting procedure in part D of this Chapter.

17 Turbocharger - examination and overhaul

1 With the turbocharger removed, inspect the housing for cracks or other visible damage.

2 Spin the turbine or the compressor wheel to verify that the shaft is intact, and to feel for excessive shake or roughness. Some play is normal, since in use the shaft is 'floating' on a film of oil. Check that the wheel vanes are undamaged.

3 The wastegate actuator is a separate unit, and can be renewed independently of the turbocharger. Testing of the wastegate actuator (boost pressure check) is described in Chapter 1B.

4 If the exhaust or inlet passages are oil-contaminated, the turbo shaft oil seals have probably failed. (On the inlet side, this will also have contaminated the intercooler, which if necessary should be flushed with a suitable solvent.)

5 Check the oil feed and return pipes for contamination or blockage, and clean if necessary.

6 No DIY repair of the turbocharger is possible. A new unit may be available on an exchange basis.

18 Intercooler - removal and refitting

200 TDi engine

Removal

1 Disconnect the battery negative lead.

2 Loosen the clips securing the two hoses to the intercooler, and carefully pull the hoses from the intercooler stubs **(see illustration)**.

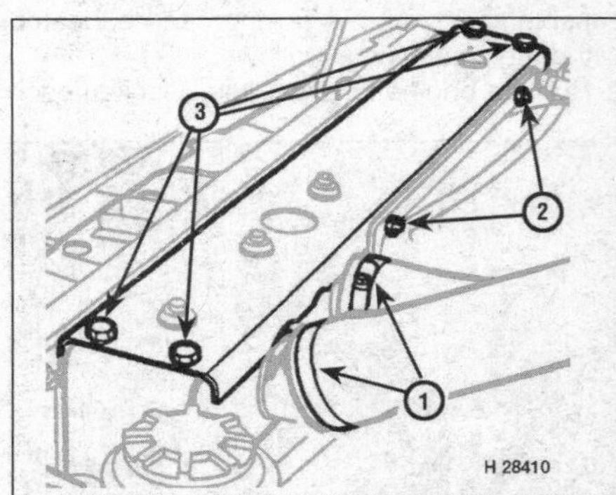
3
2
1
H 28410

18.2 Intercooler mounting details

1 Intercooler hose clips
2 Cooling fan cowl-to-radiator nuts
3 Radiator top cover bolts

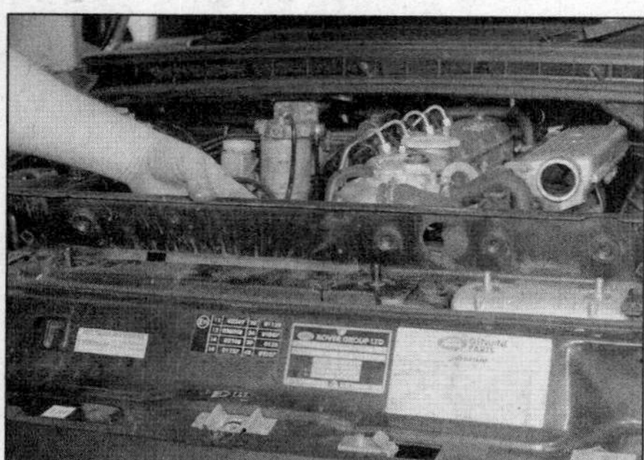
18.11 Withdrawing the radiator top cover

18.12 Remove the nut and bolt securing the power steering pump bracket

18.17 Lift the intercooler upwards and remove it from the vehicle

3 Unscrew the two nuts and washers securing the upper cooling fan cowl to the radiator.
4 Ease the fan cowl upwards to disengage the lower section from the securing clips, then move the cowl towards the rear of the vehicle, over the fan blades.
5 Remove the four bolts (two at each side) securing the radiator top cover, and withdraw the cover.
6 Lift the intercooler upwards from the support frame.

Refitting

7 Before refitting, check the condition of the intercooler locating lug grommets in the lower body panel and the radiator top cover, and renew if necessary. Also check the condition of the foam insulating pad, and ensure that it is securely attached to the intercooler.
8 Refitting is a reversal of removal, ensuring that the hose sleeves are securely reconnected.

300 TDi engine

Removal

9 Disconnect the battery negative lead.
10 Release the two clips securing the cooling fan cowl to the radiator top cover.
11 Remove the four bolts (two at each side) securing the radiator top cover, and withdraw the cover **(see illustration)**.
12 Unscrew the nut and bolt securing the power steering pump bracket to the body front panel **(see illustration)**. Recover the washer.
13 Release the power steering pump bracket from the locating lug, then position the bracket and power steering fluid reservoir assembly to one side.
14 Pull the side bracket away from the intercooler.
15 Loosen the two securing clips, and disconnect the sleeve connecting the top hose to the intercooler.
16 Similarly, disconnect the sleeve connecting the bottom hose to the intercooler.
17 Lift the intercooler upwards clear of the cooling fan shroud **(see illustration)**.

Refitting

18 Proceed as described in paragraphs 7 and 8.

19 Inlet manifold - removal and refitting

Removal

Note: *A new manifold gasket, and a new dipstick tube O-ring, may be required on refitting.*
1 Disconnect the battery negative lead.
2 Where applicable, remove the engine oil filler cap, and unclip the plastic cover from the top of the valve cover.
3 On 200 TDi engines, remove the two securing bolts, and release the dipstick tube bracket from the inlet manifold. Pull the dipstick tube from the cylinder block.
4 Where applicable, remove the securing screws, and withdraw the heat shield from the rear of the manifold.
5 On 300 TDi engines, unbolt the dipstick tube from the cylinder block, and withdraw the assembly **(see illustration)**.
6 Loosen the securing clip, and disconnect the air inlet hose from the manifold.
7 Where applicable, unbolt the EGR pipe which connects the inlet manifold to the EGR valve, and recover the gaskets.
8 Remove the two upper bolts, and the two lower nuts securing the manifold to the cylinder head, then withdraw the manifold **(see illustrations)**.

Refitting

9 Refitting is a reversal of removal, bearing in mind the following points:

a) *Check the condition of the manifold gasket, and renew if necessary (in which case, the exhaust manifold will have to be removed) - if the original gasket has deteriorated, clean all traces of old gasket from the mating faces of the cylinder head and manifold before fitting a new gasket.*
b) *Tighten the manifold securing nuts and bolts to the specified torque.*
c) *Check the condition of the lower dipstick*

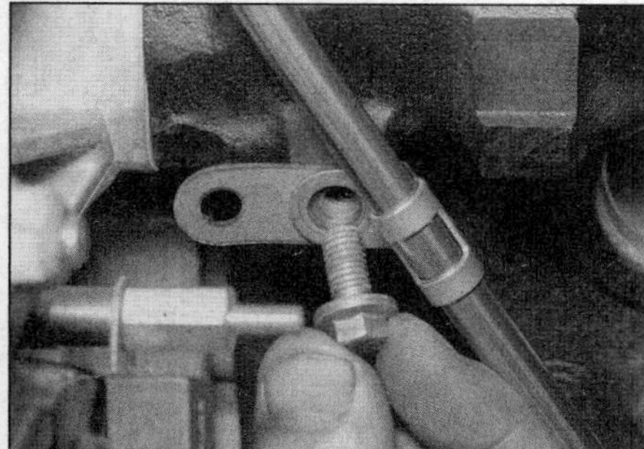
19.5 Unbolt the dipstick tube from the cylinder block - 300 TDi engine

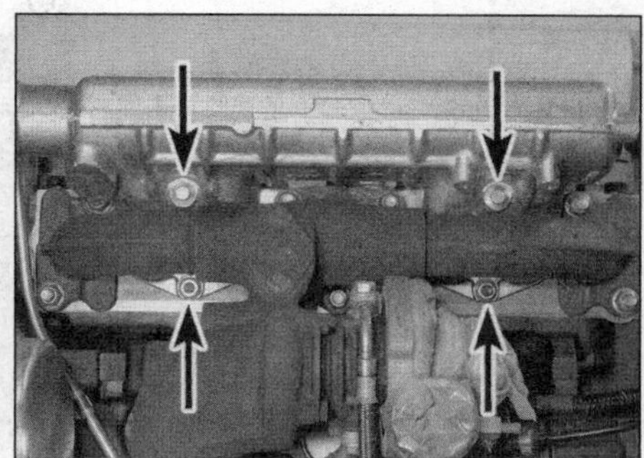
19.8a Remove the bolts and nuts (arrowed) . . .

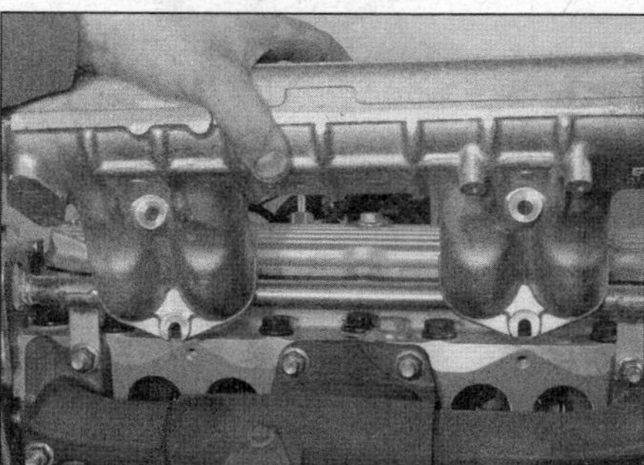
19.8b . . . and withdraw the inlet manifold - 300 TDi engine

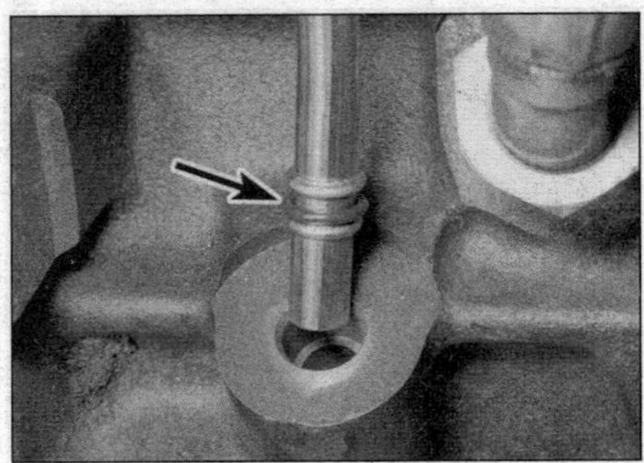

19.9 Use a new O-ring (arrowed) when refitting the dipstick tube - 300 TDi engine

tube O-ring, and renew if necessary ***(see illustration)****.*

d) Where applicable, use new gaskets when refitting the EGR pipe.

20 Electronic Diesel Control (EDC) system - general description and precautions

General description

The Electronic Diesel Control (EDC) 'drive-by-wire' system replaces certain mechanical systems used to control a conventional diesel fuel injection system with electronic controls **(see illustration)**.

The most notable feature of the EDC system is that a 'drive-by-wire' accelerator control system is used, with no mechanical link (accelerator cable) between the accelerator pedal and the fuel injection pump.

The EDC system supplies the exact amount of fuel required by the engine, according to the prevailing engine operating conditions. The engine is fitted with various sensors, which monitor the engine operating conditions, and transmit data to the EDC electronic control unit. The electronic control unit processes the data from the various sensors, and determines the optimum amount of fuel required, and the injection timing for the prevailing running conditions. Additionally, the electronic control unit activates the fuel injection pump stop solenoid, and on models fitted with EGR (see part D of this Chapter) the electronic control unit also determines the degree of exhaust gas recirculation.

The system uses the following sensors:

a) Injection timing sensor - an inductive sensor incorporated in No 4 fuel injector.

b) Airflow sensor - positioned in the air inlet trunking between the air cleaner and the turbocharger.

c) Engine speed sensor - an inductive sensor mounted on the flywheel housing, activated by slots in the flywheel.

d) Vehicle speed sensor - located in the transfer gearbox, and also acts as a speedometer sender unit.

e) Brake and clutch switches - located in the pedal box.

f) Throttle position sensor - located in the pedal box.

g) Turbocharger boost pressure sensor - located on the engine compartment bulkhead.

h) Coolant temperature sensor - located in the cylinder head.

i) Air temperature sensor.

j) Fuel temperature sensor - located in the fuel injection pump.

To control the fuelling of the engine, the system uses the following actuators:

a) Fuel delivery actuator - incorporated in the fuel injection pump.

b) Injection timing solenoid - incorporated in the fuel injection pump.

c) EGR control solenoid - mounted at the front left-hand corner of the engine compartment.

d) Engine stop solenoid, or on models from 1997 onwards, the digital diesel shut-off valve (DDS) - located in the fuel injection pump.

Safety features are built into the system to protect the engine against overspeed and overheating damage. If a component in the system fails, the electronic control unit activates a 'limp-home' mode, where a default value is

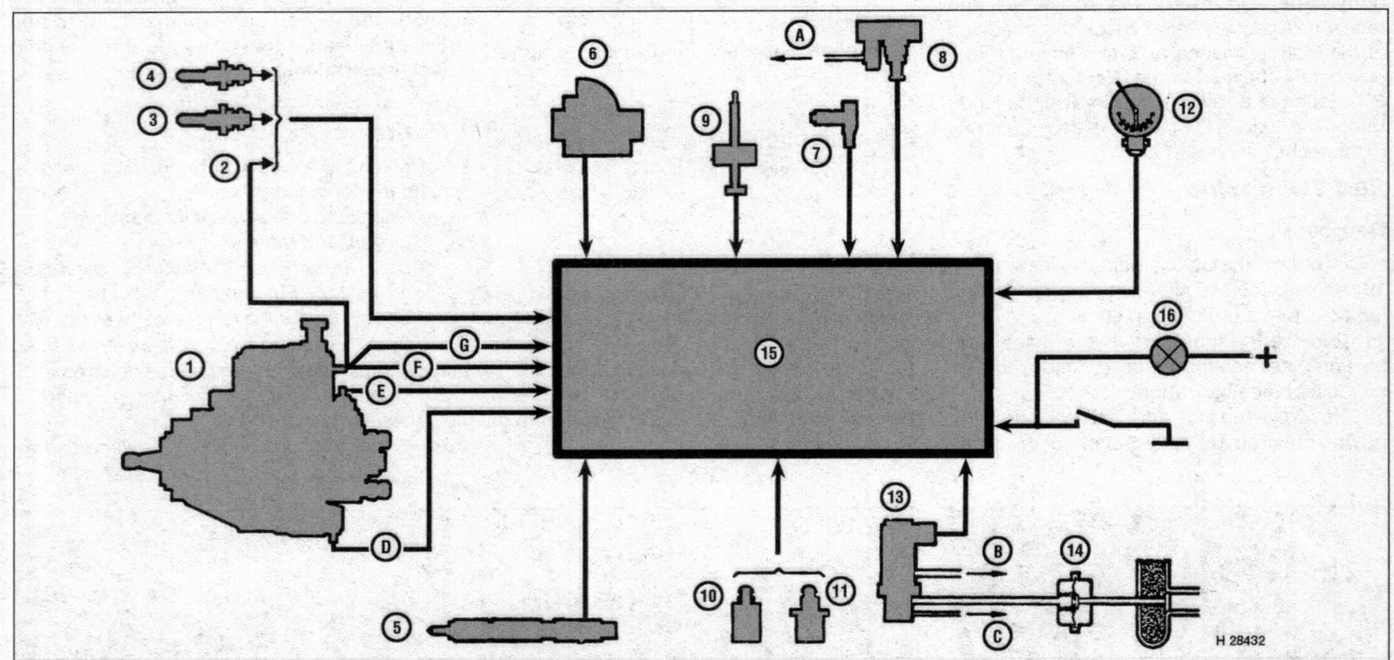

1
2
3
4
5
6
7
8
9
10
11
12
13
14
15
16
A
B
C
D
E
F
G
+
H 28432

20.1 Electronic Diesel Control system layout

1 Fuel injection pump
2 Fuel temperature sensor
3 Air temperature sensor
4 Coolant temperature sensor
5 Injection timing sensor (No 4 fuel injector)
6 Airflow sensor
7 Engine speed sensor
8 Turbocharger boost pressure sensor
9 Vehicle speed sensor
10 Clutch switch
11 Brake switch
12 Throttle position sensor
13 EGR control solenoid
14 EGR valve
15 Electronic control unit
16 Diagnostic indicator
A To turbocharger
B To air cleaner
C To brake servo vacuum hose T-piece
D Injection timing solenoid
E Engine stop solenoid
F Actuator current
G Fuel delivery actuator

substituted for the failed component - this will allow the engine to start and run, but a noticeable loss in engine performance may occur.

Precautions

Electronic control units are very sensitive components, and certain precautions must be taken, to avoid damage to the EDC control unit when working on the vehicle.

When carrying out welding operations on the vehicle using electric welding equipment, the battery and alternator should be disconnected.

Although the underbonnet-mounted modules will tolerate normal underbonnet conditions, they can be adversely affected by excess heat or moisture. If using welding equipment or pressure-washing equipment in the vicinity of an electronic module, take care not to direct heat, or jets of water or steam, at the module. If this cannot be avoided, remove the module from the vehicle, and protect its wiring plug with a plastic bag.

Before disconnecting any wiring, or removing components, always ensure that the 'ignition' is switched off.

Do not attempt to improvise fault diagnosis procedures using a test light or multi-meter, as irreparable damage could be caused to the module.

After working on any of the EDC system components, ensure that all wiring is correctly reconnected before reconnecting the battery or operating the 'ignition' switch.

21 Electronic Diesel Control (EDC) system components - removal and refitting

Injection timing sensor

1 The sensor is incorporated in No 4 fuel injector.

2 The removal and refitting procedure for the fuel injectors is given in Section 14.

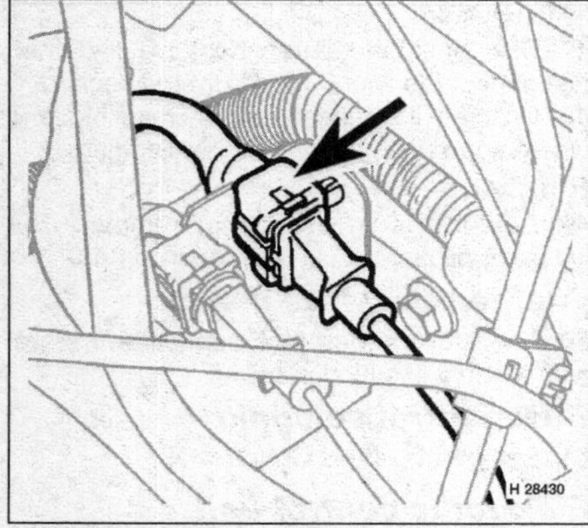
H 28430

21.13 Engine speed sensor wiring connector location (arrowed) - EDC system

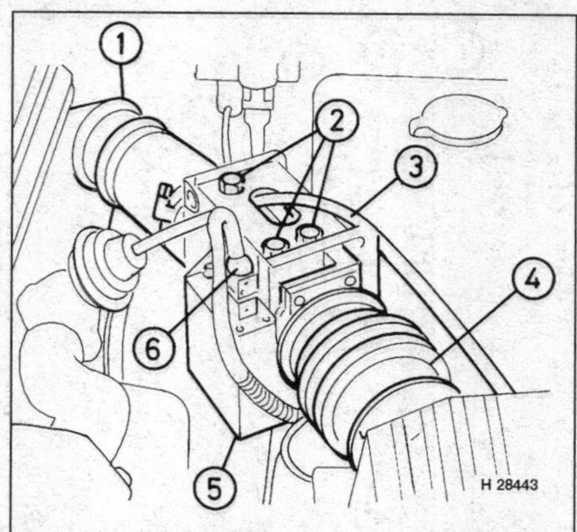
1
2
3
4
5
6
H 28443

21.3 Airflow sensor location - EDC system

1 Air outlet hose
2 Airflow sensor mounting bolts
3 EGR valve vacuum pipe
4 Air inlet hose
5 Airflow sensor
6 Wiring plug

Airflow sensor

Removal

3 The sensor is located in the air trunking between the air cleaner and the turbocharger **(see illustration)**.

4 Disconnect the battery negative lead.

5 Where applicable, disconnect the vacuum pipe from the EGR valve.

6 Disconnect the airflow sensor wiring plug.

7 Loosen the securing clips, and disconnect the air trunking from the airflow sensor.

8 Unscrew the three bolts securing the airflow sensor to the mounting bracket, and withdraw the airflow sensor.

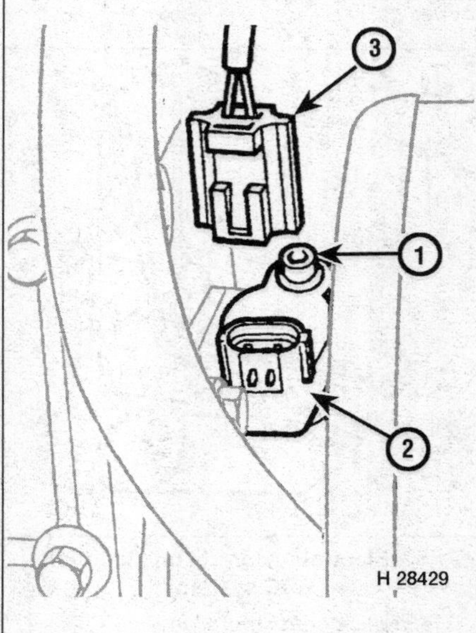
3
1
2
H 28429

21.16 Vehicle speed sensor location

1 Securing bolt 2 Sensor 3 Wiring plug

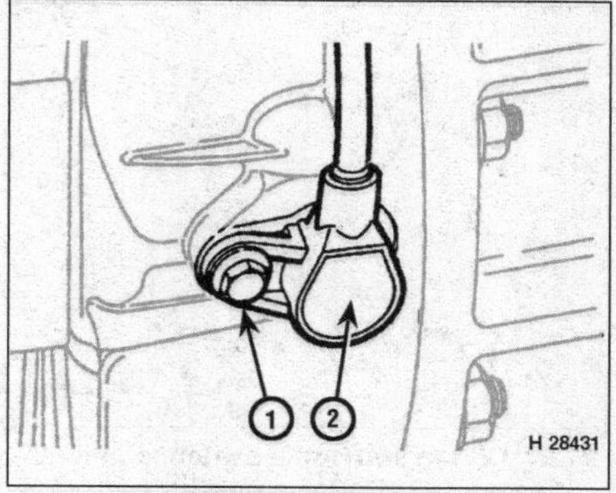
1
2
H 28431

21.10 Engine speed sensor location - EDC system

1 Securing bolt
2 Sensor

Refitting

9 Refitting is a reversal of removal, but ensure that the wiring plug is securely reconnected, and make sure that the air trunking clips are securely tightened, to prevent air leaks.

Engine speed sensor

Removal

10 The sensor is located in the gearbox bellhousing, and access is obtained from under the vehicle **(see illustration)**.

11 Disconnect the battery negative lead.

12 Jack up the vehicle, and support securely on axle stands positioned under the front and rear axles (see *Jacking and vehicle support*).

13 Unclip the sensor wiring connector from the top of the transfer gearbox, then separate the two halves of the connector **(see illustration)**.

14 Unscrew the securing bolt, and withdraw the sensor from the bellhousing.

Refitting

15 Refitting is a reversal of removal.

Vehicle speed sensor

Removal

16 The sensor is located in the transfer gearbox casing **(see illustration)**.

17 Disconnect the battery negative lead.

18 Disconnect the sensor wiring plug.

19 Unscrew the sensor securing bolt, and recover the washer.

20 Withdraw the sensor from the transfer gearbox.

Refitting

21 Refitting is a reversal of removal.

Brake and clutch pedal switches

Removal

22 The brake pedal switch is mounted in the pedal box, above the stop-light switch, and

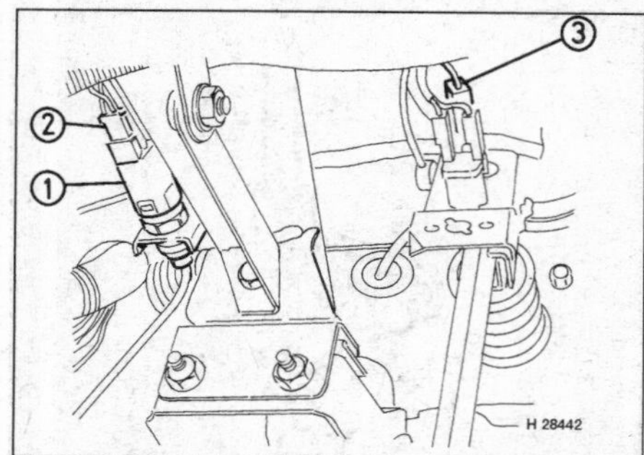
1
2
3
H 28442

21.22 Clutch and brake switch locations - EDC system

1 Clutch pedal switch
2 Clutch pedal switch wiring plug
3 Brake pedal switch wiring plug

the clutch pedal switch is mounted at the top of the clutch pedal **(see illustration)**.

23 Disconnect the battery negative lead.

24 Release the securing clips, and withdraw the driver's side lower facia panel for access to the pedals.

25 Disconnect the wiring from the switch.

26 Loosen the locknut at the rear of the switch, then unscrew the front securing nut, and withdraw the switch from the bracket.

Refitting

27 Refitting is a reversal of removal.

Throttle position sensor

Removal

Warning: Do not operate the accelerator pedal if the sensor is loosely fitted, as damage to the sensor may result.

28 The sensor is located in the pedal box **(see illustration)**.

29 Disconnect the battery negative lead.

30 Release the securing clips, and withdraw the driver's side lower facia panel for access to the pedals.

31 Working in the driver's footwell, disconnect the wiring plug from the sensor.

32 Unscrew the nut securing the accelerator pedal quadrant to the sensor, and disconnect the quadrant.

33 Unscrew the two nuts securing the sensor to the pedal box, and withdraw the sensor.

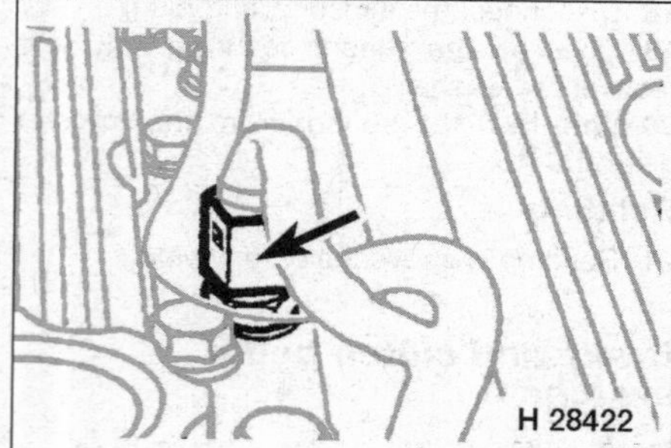
H 28422

21.41 Coolant temperature sensor location (arrowed) - EDC system

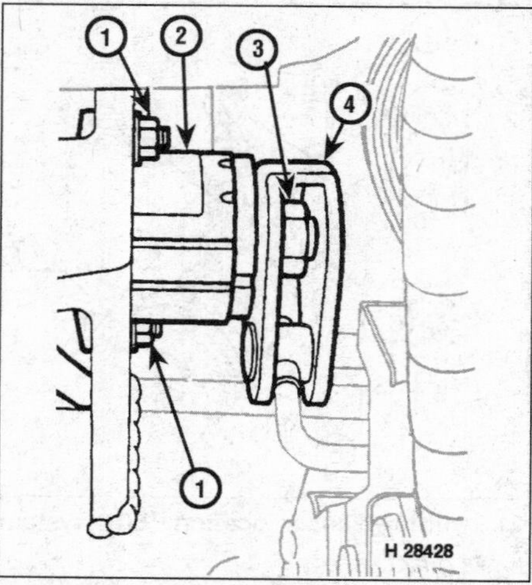
1
2
3
4
1
H 28428

21.28 Throttle position sensor location - EDC system

1 Sensor securing nuts
2 Sensor
3 Pedal quadrant-to-sensor nut
4 Pedal quadrant

Refitting

34 Refitting is a reversal of removal.

Turbocharger boost pressure sensor

Removal

Note: *New pressure pipe union copper washers will be required on refitting.*

35 The sensor is located on a bracket attached to the engine compartment bulkhead **(see illustration)**.

36 Disconnect the battery negative lead.

37 Disconnect the sensor wiring plug.

38 Unscrew the banjo bolt, and disconnect the pressure pipe from the sensor. Recover the copper washers.

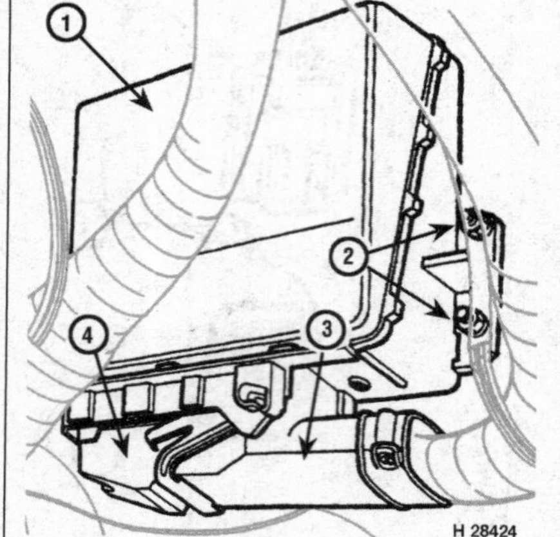
1
2
3
4
H 28424

21.52 Electronic control unit location - EDC system

1 Electronic control module
2 Securing nuts
3 Wiring plug
4 Wiring plug securing screw

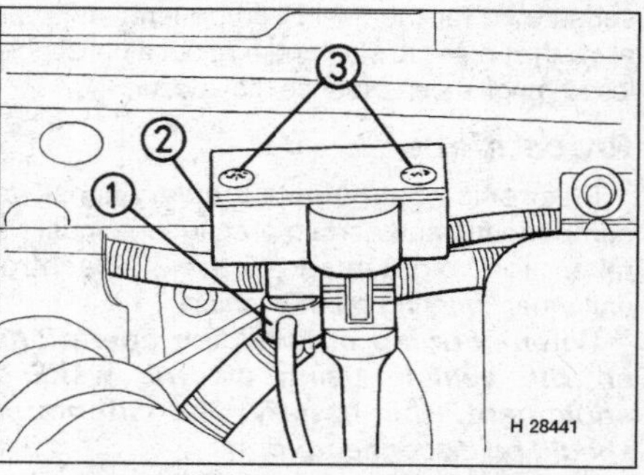
3
2
1
H 28441

21.35 Turbocharger boost pressure sensor - EDC system

1 Banjo union 2 Sensor
3 Sensor securing screws

39 Remove the two screws securing the sensor to the mounting bracket, and withdraw the sensor.

Refitting

40 Refitting is a reversal of removal, but use new copper washers when reconnecting the pressure pipe.

Coolant temperature sensor

Removal

Note: *A new copper washer must be used on refitting.*

41 The sensor is located in the top left-hand side of the cylinder head **(see illustration)**.

42 Disconnect the battery negative lead.

43 Disconnect the sensor wiring plug.

44 Unscrew the sensor from the cylinder head, and recover the copper washer. Be prepared for coolant spillage.

Refitting

45 Refitting is a reversal of removal, but use a new copper washer, and on completion, check the coolant level as described in *Weekly checks*.

Air temperature sensor

Removal

Note: *A new sealing ring may be required on refitting.*

46 The sensor is located in the rear of the inlet manifold.

47 Disconnect the battery negative lead, then disconnect the wiring plug from the sensor.

48 Unscrew the sensor from the manifold, and where applicable, recover the sealing ring.

Refitting

49 Refitting is a reversal of removal, but where applicable, use a new sealing ring.

Fuel temperature sensor

50 The fuel temperature sensor is integral with the fuel injection pump.

EGR control solenoid

51 See part D of this Chapter.

Electronic control unit

Removal

52 The unit is located behind the right-hand A-pillar trim panel **(see illustration)**.

53 Remove the A-pillar trim panel.
54 Disconnect the battery negative lead.
55 Loosen the control unit wiring plug securing screw, and disconnect the wiring plug. Move the wiring plug and the harness to one side.
56 Unscrew the securing nuts, and withdraw the control unit.

Refitting

57 Refitting is a reversal of removal.

22 Cruise control system - description and component renewal

Cruise control system - description

1 Cruise control may be fitted to later models with automatic transmission as an option. The system incorporates the following components:

a) Electronic control unit located behind the passenger's side lower facia panel. The ECU receives information from the driver, brake pedal switch and vehicle speed sensor, and activates the throttle vacuum pump accordingly.
*b) Cruise control switches are located in the auxiliary switch panel and on the steering wheel. The steering wheel switches provide **set/accelerate** and **resume/decelerate** functions.*
c) The clutch and brake pedal switches are mounted on the pedal bracket and, when either pedal is pressed, the ECU disengages the cruise control system and releases the throttle levers to their idle position.
d) The vehicle speed sensor is mounted on the side of the transfer box. Cruise control cannot be engaged at road speeds under 28 mph.
e) The vacuum pump fitted at the front left-hand side of the engine compartment provides the vacuum source for the actuator. A control valve in the pump allows precise control to the throttle actuator, or a quick purge of the system when the system disengages.
f) The actuator is located in the engine compartment and moves the throttle levers as required.
g) The neutral lockout relay is located behind the driver's side right-hand footwell trim panel. Its function is to disengage the cruise control if Neutral or Park is selected in the main gearbox when the system is engaged.

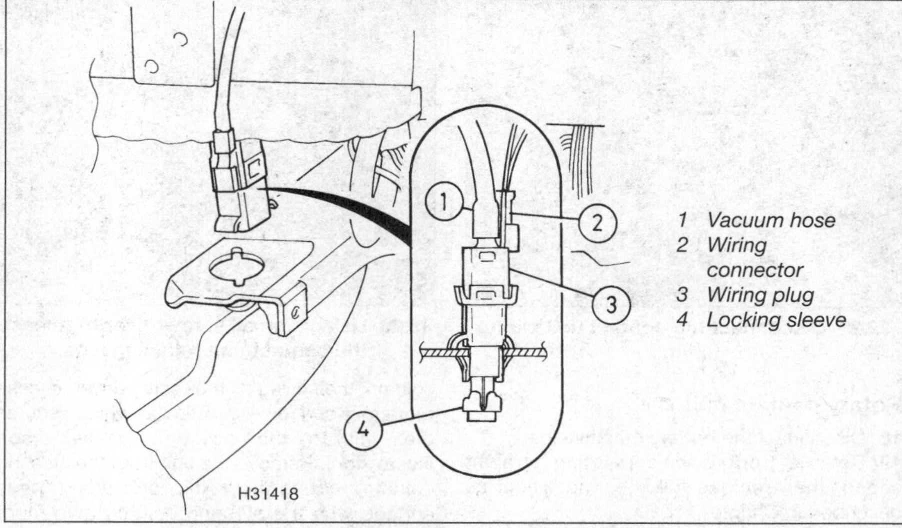
1
2
3
4
H31418
1 Vacuum hose
2 Wiring connector
3 Wiring plug
4 Locking sleeve

22.6 Cruise control pedal switch removal

2 If the cruise control system develops a fault, first check all of the associated wiring and fuses, and the vacuum hoses.

Cruise control system components - removal, refitting and adjustment

Brake or clutch switch/vent valve

3 Disconnect the battery negative lead.
4 Release the clips and pull down the lower facia panel.
5 Disconnect the wiring and vacuum hose from the switch/vent valve.
6 Release the locking sleeve behind the switch, then release the locking tabs and remove the switch from the pedal bracket **(see illustration)**.
7 Refitting is a reversal of the removal procedure, noting the following points:

a) The brake switch should be adjusted to provide a clearance of 1.0 mm between the switch/vent valve body and the inside shoulder of the contact button.
b) The clutch switch should be set to a zero clearance between the switch/vent valve body and the inside shoulder of the contact button.

Main control switch

8 See Chapter 13, Section 4.

Steering wheel switches - models with driver's airbag

9 Disconnect the battery negative lead. Remove the airbag unit as described in Chapter 13.
10 Disconnect the cruise control switch main multi-plug in the centre, and the two horn contact wiring plugs at the base.
11 At each side of the wheel, remove the two small screws securing the switches to the wheel.
12 Unscrew the three mounting bracket bolts from the centre of the wheel, and remove the cruise control switch assembly.
13 Refitting is a reversal of the removal procedure, ensuring that the cruise control wiring harness is routed correctly. Refit the airbag unit as described in Chapter 13.

Steering wheel switches - models without driver's airbag

14 Disconnect the battery negative lead.
15 The switches must be prised from their locations in the steering wheel, and this requires significant effort with a screwdriver. The first attempt when we tried in the workshop did no more than separate the top half of the switch from the switch body - the wheel padding has to be levered aside considerably to ease out the switch complete **(see illustration)**. Take care to minimise the potential damage to the wheel padding as this is done - use stiff card behind the screwdriver shaft, for instance.
16 Once the switch has been removed, disconnect the wiring from the switch base **(see illustration)**.
17 Refitting is a reversal of removal.

22.15 Prise out the cruise control switches from the steering wheel . . .

22.16 . . . and disconnect the wiring

22.21 Disconnect the contact unit wiring plug

22.23 Using a small screwdriver to release the contact unit retaining lugs

Rotary contact unit

18 Disconnect the battery negative lead.
19 Set the front wheels pointing straight ahead, then remove the steering wheel as described in Chapter 11.
20 Release the clips securing the driver's side lower trim panel, and remove the three screws securing the steering column lower shroud.
21 Disconnect the contact unit multi-plug from the steering column wiring harness **(see illustration)**, and release the harness from the ignition switch.
22 If the contact unit is to be re-used, apply adhesive tape to the upper and lower halves to prevent rotation. If this precaution is not taken, the wiring inside the unit will be damaged.
23 Pull the assembly rearwards off the steering column, then using a small screwdriver, release the upper and lower plastic lug which secures the unit to the column switches **(see illustration)**. Remove the unit from the steering column, noting how the protruding pegs engage with the steering column (two more engage with the rear of the steering wheel).
24 While the contact unit is removed, keep it in a plastic bag, and make sure the mechanism is not rotated.
25 Refitting is a reversal of the removal procedure, noting the following points:

a) Check that the front wheels are still in the straight-ahead position.
b) Make sure that the pegs on the front and rear of the unit locate in the holes on the steering column and the underside of the steering wheel.
c) Make sure that the wiring is not trapped between the upper and lower shroud.

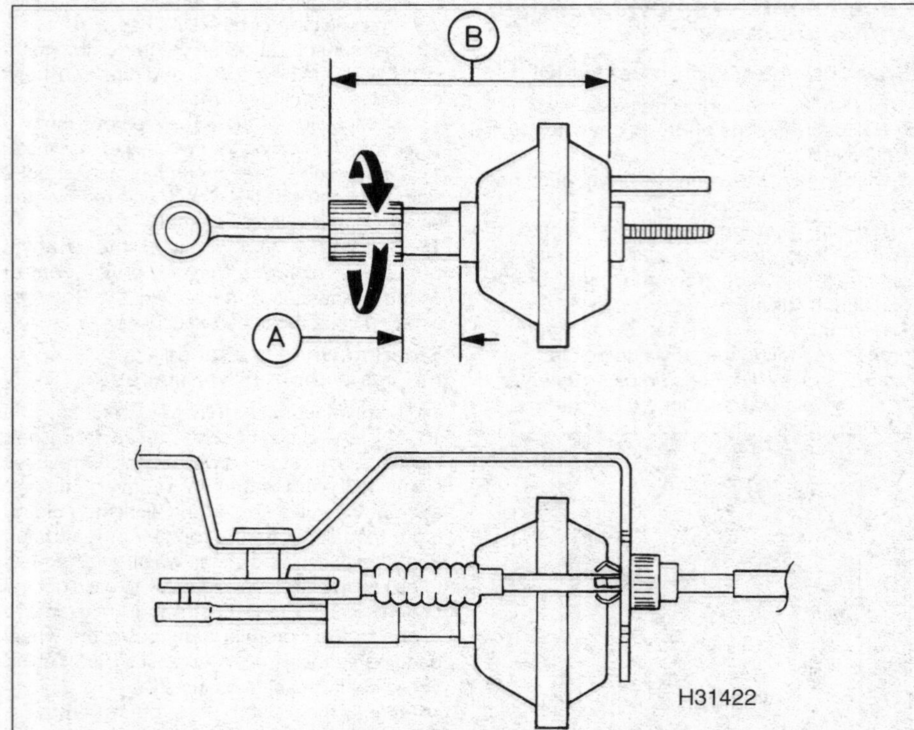
B
A
H31422

22.32 Cruise control actuator link adjustment
A 16 mm B 103 mm

Actuator

26 Disconnect the battery negative lead.
27 Remove the split pin, then withdraw the clevis pin and disconnect the cable from the actuator lever.
28 Carefully prise off the ball end fitting from the actuator lever.
29 Disconnect the vacuum hose, then unscrew the mounting nut and remove the actuator from its bracket.
30 Examine the rubber diaphragm for wear and damage, and renew the actuator if necessary.
31 Refitting is a reversal of the removal procedure, but check the link and cable adjustment as described below.

Actuator link adjustment

32 With the ignition off, check that the link setting distance (A) is correct, and that the retainer is locked in position **(see illustration)**.
33 If adjustment is required, measure the specified distance from the diaphragm collar, and mark this position. Set the link and retainer to the mark just made, and turn the retainer half a turn to secure. Check that the distance is still correct, then turn the retainer a further quarter-turn to lock it.
34 Remove any freeplay in the cable using the adjuster clip in the actuator mounting bracket. Check also that dimension (B) is correct **(see illustration 22.32)**.

Vacuum pump

35 Disconnect the battery negative lead.
36 Release the wheel chock and the jack from their locations, and remove them.
37 Release the three pump mounting rubbers from the body, then manoeuvre the pump out of its location.
38 Release the cover from the pump multi-plug, and disconnect the plug.
39 Disconnect the vacuum pipe, then withdraw the pump.
40 Refitting is a reversal of the removal procedure.

Cruise control electronic control unit (ECU)

41 The ECU is located behind the passenger's side of the facia. First disconnect the battery negative lead.
42 Release the four clips and pull down the passenger's side lower facia panel.
43 Unscrew the nut securing the ECU/relay bracket, and lower the bracket for access. Unscrew the ECU lower securing nut.
44 Open the glovebox lid, align the lid stops with the cut-outs in the facia panel, and lower the lid out of position.
45 Move the airbag harness to one side, then unscrew the ECU upper securing nut. Disconnect the ECU multi-plug, and remove the ECU from its location.
46 Refitting is a reversal of the removal procedure.

Vehicle speed sensor

47 See Section 21.

Chapter 4 Part D:
Exhaust and emission control systems

Contents

Degrees of difficulty

Easy, suitable for novice with little experience 	**Fairly easy,** suitable for beginner with some experience 	**Fairly difficult,** suitable for competent DIY mechanic 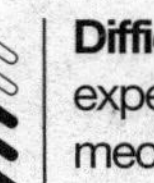	**Difficult,** suitable for experienced DIY mechanic 	**Very difficult,** suitable for expert DIY or professional

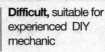

Specifications

EGR throttle position sensor

Resistance across terminals 1 and 3	1000 to 1050 ohms
Resistance across terminals 1 and 2	850 to 900 ohms

Torque wrench settings

Torque wrench settings	Nm	lbf ft
EGR delivery pipe bolts	25	18
EGR valve securing bolts	25	18
Exhaust manifold securing nuts:		
Petrol engines	20	15
200 TDi engine	25	18
300 TDi engine	45	33

1 General information

Emission control systems

All petrol-engined models can use unleaded fuel, and fuel injection models are controlled by an engine management system 'tuned' to give the best compromise between driveability, fuel consumption and exhaust emission production. In addition, a number of systems are fitted that help to minimise other harmful emissions. All models are fitted with a crankcase emission-control system that reduces the release of pollutants from the engine's lubrication system. Models from 1993 onwards have a catalytic converter that reduces exhaust gas pollutants. Models with a catalytic converter also have an evaporative loss emission control system that reduces the release of gaseous hydrocarbons from the fuel tank.

All diesel-engined models also have a crankcase emission control system. Later models are fitted with an Exhaust Gas Recirculation (EGR) system and a catalytic converter to reduce exhaust emissions.

Crankcase emission control

To reduce the emission of unburned hydrocarbons from the crankcase into the atmosphere, the engine is sealed, and the blow-by gases and oil vapour are drawn from inside the crankcase, through an oil separator, into the air cleaner, to be burned by the engine during normal combustion.

Under conditions of high manifold depression (idling, deceleration) the gases will be sucked positively out of the crankcase. Under conditions of low manifold depression (acceleration, full-throttle running) the gases are forced out of the crankcase by the (relatively) higher crankcase pressure; if the engine is worn, the raised crankcase pressure (due to increased blow-by) will cause some of the flow to return under all manifold conditions.

Exhaust emission control - petrol models

To minimise the amount of pollutants which escape into the atmosphere, later models are fitted with twin catalytic converters in the exhaust system. The fuelling system is of the closed-loop type, in which twin lambda sensors in the exhaust system provide the engine management system ECU with constant feedback, enabling the ECU to adjust the air/fuel mixture to optimise combustion.

The lambda sensor has a built-in heating element that is controlled by the ECU through the lambda sensor relay, to quickly bring the sensor's tip to its optimum operating temperature. The sensor's tip is sensitive to oxygen, and relays a voltage signal to the ECU that varies according on the amount of oxygen in the exhaust gas. If the inlet air/fuel mixture is too rich, the exhaust gases are low in oxygen, so the sensor sends a low-voltage signal, the voltage rising as the mixture weakens and the amount of oxygen rises in the exhaust gases. Peak conversion efficiency of all major pollutants occurs if the inlet air/fuel mixture is maintained at the chemically-correct ratio for the complete combustion of petrol of 14.7 parts (by weight) of air to 1 part of fuel (the stoichiometric ratio). The sensor output voltage alters in a large step at this point, the ECU using the signal change as a reference point, and correcting the inlet air/fuel mixture accordingly by altering the fuel injector pulse width. Details of the lambda sensor removal and refitting are given in Section 4.

Exhaust emission control - diesel models

An oxidation catalyst is fitted in the line with the exhaust system of all diesel-engined models. The catalytic converter consists of a canister containing a fine mesh impregnated with a catalyst material, over which the exhaust gases pass. The catalyst speeds up the oxidation of harmful carbon monoxide, unburnt hydrocarbons and soot, effectively reducing the quantity of harmful products reaching the atmosphere.

An Exhaust Gas Recirculation (EGR) system is fitted to later models. This reduces the level of nitrogen oxides produced during combustion, by introducing a proportion of the exhaust gas back into the inlet manifold, under certain engine operating conditions, via a solenoid valve. The solenoid valve is controlled by a fuel injection pump-mounted sensor on models with a conventional fuel injection system, or by the EDC electronic control unit on models with EDC.

Evaporative emission control - petrol models

To minimise the escape of unburned hydrocarbons into the atmosphere, an evaporative loss emission control system is fitted to all petrol models with a catalytic converter (1993 onwards). The fuel tank filler cap is sealed, and a charcoal canister is mounted on the right-hand inner wing to collect the petrol vapours released from the fuel contained in the fuel tank. It stores them until they can be drawn from the canister (under the control of the fuel injection system ECU) via the purge valve into the plenum chamber, where they are then burned by the engine during normal combustion.

To ensure that the engine runs correctly when it is cold and/or idling, and to protect the catalytic converter from the effects of an over-rich mixture, the purge control valve is not opened by the ECU until the engine has warmed up, and the engine is under load; the valve solenoid is then modulated on and off to allow the stored vapour to pass into the inlet tract.

Exhaust system

The exhaust system comprises the exhaust manifold(s), catalytic converter(s), two silencer units, a number of mounting brackets, and a series of connecting pipes.

2 Evaporative loss emission control system

General information

1 The evaporative loss emission control system fitted to petrol models consists of the purge valve, the activated charcoal filter canister, and a series of connecting hoses.

2 The purge valve is mounted on top of the charcoal canister, itself mounted on the right-hand inner wing (right as seen from the driver's seat) **(see illustration)**.

Component renewal

3 The charcoal canister assembly can be renewed as described in Chapter 1A, Section 54. The purge valve is only available as part of the canister assembly

3 Crankcase emission system - general information

1 The crankcase emission control system consists of a series of hoses and filters that connect the crankcase vent to the rocker cover vent (where applicable) and the air cleaner.

2 The system requires no maintenance beyond that given in the relevant part of Chapter 1. Bear in mind, however, that using low-quality engine oil (or not changing the oil regularly) will result in more oil fumes passing into the system, and a greater chance of the pipes and filters being prematurely blocked.

4 Lambda sensors - removal and refitting

Removal

1 Each lambda sensor is threaded into the exhaust pipe, ahead of the catalytic converter. Removal details are much the same for either sensor.

2 Disconnect the battery negative lead and position it away from the terminal.

3 Access to the sensors may be gained from above or below, according to preference **(see illustration)**. In either case, wait for the system to cool down completely before attempting removal.

4 Trace the wiring back from the sensor, releasing it from any securing clips. Unplug the wiring harness at the connector, located in the engine compartment, at the rear of each cylinder head **(see illustration)**.

5 Slacken and withdraw the sensor, taking care to avoid damaging the sensor probe as it is removed. **Note:** *As a flying lead remains connected to the sensor after it has been disconnected, if the correct-size spanner is not available, a slotted socket will be required to remove the sensor.*

Refitting

6 Apply a little anti-seize grease to the sensor threads only - keep the probe tip clean.

2.2 Charcoal canister - purge valve arrowed

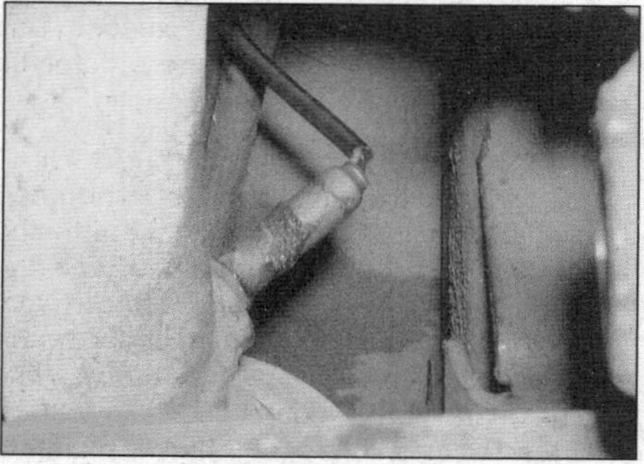

4.3 Lambda sensor (seen from below)

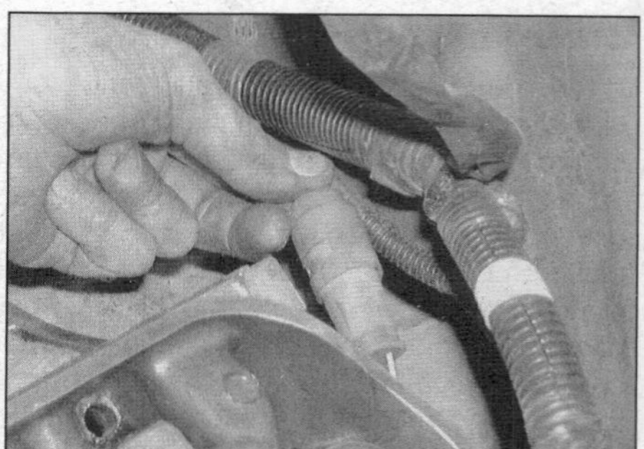

4.4 The lambda sensor wiring connectors are clipped to the rear of each cylinder head

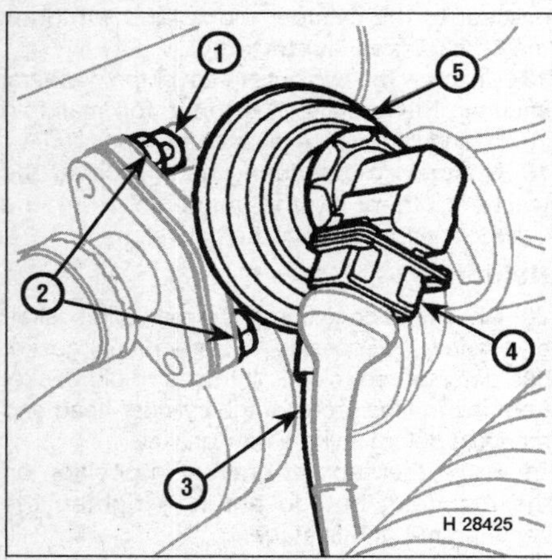
1
5
2
4
3
H 28425

5.7 EGR valve location

1 Valve securing bolts
2 EGR delivery pipe securing bolts
3 Vacuum hose
4 Wiring plug
5 Valve

7 Refit the sensor to its location, tightening it securely. Restore the harness connection. Note that the type of lambda sensor fitted depends on vehicle specification - the sensor may not be interchangeable with one obtained from another model.

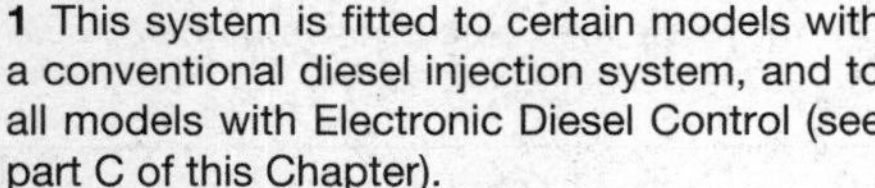

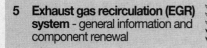

5 Exhaust gas recirculation (EGR) system - general information and component renewal

1 This system is fitted to certain models with a conventional diesel injection system, and to all models with Electronic Diesel Control (see part C of this Chapter).

2 The system is designed to recirculate small quantities of exhaust gas into the inlet tract, and therefore into the combustion process. This process reduces the level of oxides of nitrogen present in the final exhaust gas which is released into the atmosphere, and also lowers the combustion temperature.

3 The volume of exhaust gas recirculated is controlled by vacuum, via a solenoid valve. The solenoid valve is controlled by a fuel injection pump-mounted sensor on models with a conventional fuel injection system, or by the Electronic Diesel Control electronic control unit on models with EDC.

4 A vacuum-operated recirculation valve is fitted to the exhaust manifold, to regulate the quantity of exhaust gas recirculated. The valve is operated by the vacuum supplied via the solenoid valve.

5 Between idle speed and a pre-determined engine load, power is supplied to the solenoid valve, which allows the recirculation valve to open. Under full-load conditions, the exhaust gas recirculation is cut off. Additional control is provided by the engine temperature sensor, which cuts off the vacuum supply until the coolant temperature reaches 40°C, preventing

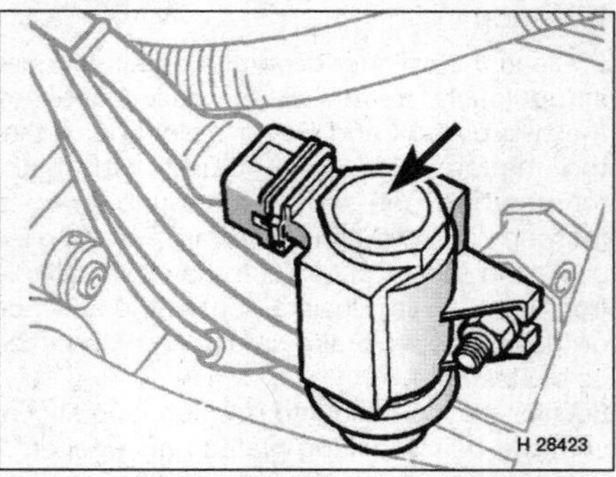
H 28423

5.12 EGR control solenoid location (arrowed) - EDC system

the recirculation valve from opening during the engine warm-up phase.

EGR valve

Removal

Note: *New EGR valve-to-manifold, and delivery pipe-to-EGR valve, gaskets must be used on refitting.*

6 Disconnect the battery negative lead then, where applicable, disconnect the wiring plug from the valve.

7 Disconnect the vacuum hose from the valve **(see illustration)**.

8 Unscrew the two bolts securing the valve to the exhaust manifold.

9 Remove the two securing bolts, and disconnect the EGR delivery pipe from the valve.

10 Withdraw the valve, and recover the gaskets.

Refitting

11 Refitting is a reversal of removal, but use new gaskets when refitting the valve and reconnecting the delivery pipe.

EGR control solenoid

Removal

12 The solenoid is located at the front left-hand corner of the engine compartment **(see illustration)**.

13 Disconnect the battery negative lead.

14 Disconnect the wiring plug from the solenoid.

15 Disconnect the three vacuum hoses from the modulator, noting their locations to ensure correct refitting.

16 Unscrew the securing nut, and withdraw the solenoid from the body panel.

Refitting

17 Refitting is a reversal of removal.

Coolant temperature sensor

18 The system uses the coolant temperature gauge sender unit. Details of removal and refitting are given in Chapter 3, Section 6.

Throttle position sensor

19 This sensor is only used on models with a conventional fuel injection system, and is located on the fuel injection pump.

Testing

20 Start the engine, and run it until normal operating temperature is reached.

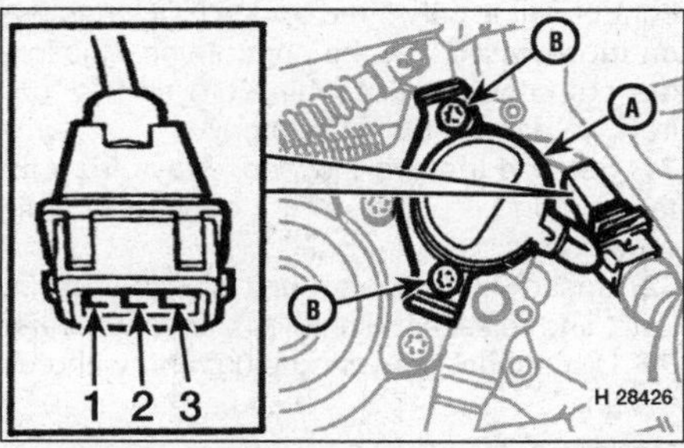
B
A
B
1 2 3
H 28426

5.22 EGR throttle position sensor location - note plug terminal numbers (inset)

A Sensor B Securing screws

21 Stop the engine, and disconnect the throttle position sensor wiring plug.

22 Connect an ohmmeter across pins 1 and 3 of the wiring plug. The reading on the ohmmeter should be as given in the Specifications **(see illustration)**.

23 Connect the ohmmeter between pins 1 and 2 of the wiring plug. Again, the reading should be as specified.

24 If the readings are not as specified, loosen the two sensor retaining screws, and rotate the sensor to achieve the correct readings. Tighten the retaining screws when the readings are correct.

25 If the correct readings cannot be obtained by rotating the sensor, then it is faulty and should be renewed.

26 Reconnect the wiring plug on completion.

Removal

27 Disconnect the battery negative lead, then disconnect the wiring plug from the sensor.

28 Unscrew the two securing screws, and withdraw the sensor.

Refitting

29 Refitting is a reversal of removal, but before tightening the securing screws, adjust the position of the sensor as described previously in this Section (*Testing*).

EGR electronic control unit

Removal

30 The unit is located in the passenger compartment, behind the right-hand side of the facia **(see illustration)**. The separate

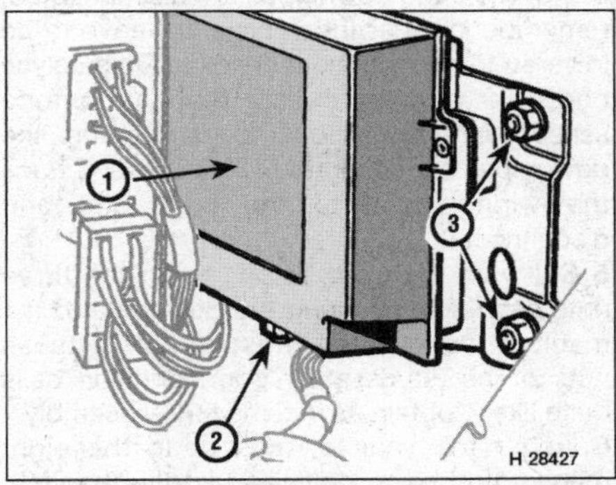
1
3
2
H 28427

5.30 EGR electronic control unit location

1 Electronic control unit
2 Wiring plug 3 Securing nuts

control unit is only fitted to non-EDC models - on those with EDC, the control unit functions are contained in the main EDC control unit (refer to part C of this Chapter).

31 Release the two glovebox stays from the facia, and pivot the glovebox fully downwards.

32 Unscrew the control unit plastic securing nuts, and release the unit from its mountings.

33 Disconnect the wiring plug, and withdraw the unit.

Refitting

34 Refitting is a reversal of removal.

6 Exhaust manifold - removal and refitting

Note: *It would be well worth obtaining new manifold bolts (or studs and nuts on diesel engines) for reassembly - the same applies to the manifold-to-downpipe fasteners. Given the corrosion which will almost certainly be evident on the old fasteners, a new set will make reassembly much easier. It may be found that some of the fasteners cannot be re-used, in any case. Take care when loosening old fasteners that the socket does not slip on rounded-off/corroded nut or bolt heads, resulting in personal injury.*

Petrol engines

Note: *The exhaust manifolds are handed. Check that any replacement parts are correct.*

Removal

1 Allow the exhaust system to cool down sufficiently if the engine has just been running.

2 Bend back the ends of the locking tabs on the eight manifold retaining bolts.

3 Make sure the handbrake is applied, then jack up the front of the vehicle and support on axle stands.

4 In order that no strain is placed on the rest of the system when the downpipes are released from the manifolds, loosen the front pipe fixings next to the transmission mounting bracket. Additionally, arrange to support the system (perhaps on a trolley jack, or an axle stand) while the downpipes are disconnected, remembering that the vehicle will have to be lowered to remove the manifolds. On catalytic converter models, ensure that the lambda sensor wiring will not be under strain when the downpipes are separated - if necessary, trace the wiring back to the multi-plug and disconnect it.

5 Still working from below, undo the three nuts each side securing the downpipe to the manifold flange **(see illustration)**. If these nuts (or their studs) are in poor condition, as is quite likely, obtain new items for reassembly.

6 Lower the vehicle, then undo the eight manifold retaining bolts and lift the manifold away. Note the fitted order of the bolts, locking plates and washers, and obtain new items as necessary for reassembly.

Refitting

7 Clean the cylinder head and manifold faces scrupulously, as no gasket is used between the two parts. Land Rover recommend that the mating faces are coated with high-temperature anti-seize compound prior to reassembly - two mentioned are Rocal Foliac J166 and Moly Paul (which may be available from Land Rover dealers), but in the absence of these, copper brake grease could be used as a substitute.

8 Offer the manifold into position, and secure with the bolts, locking plates and washers - note that the washers fit between the manifold and locking plates, not under the bolt heads. Tighten the bolts to the specified torque, but do not bend over the locking tabs at this stage.

9 Raise the front of the vehicle once more, and support on axle stands. Apply a smear of exhaust jointing compound to the manifold-to-downpipe joint face.

10 Taking care not to impose any strain on the rest of the exhaust system, offer up the downpipe to the manifold, then fit and tighten the nuts evenly and securely.

11 Lower the front of the vehicle to the ground. Start the engine, allow it to warm up and check for exhaust gas leakage.

12 Stop the engine and allow the exhaust system to cool down for several hours.

13 Check the tightness of the exhaust manifold bolts and the downpipe flange nuts. Finally bend over the ends of the locking tabs on to the manifold bolt heads.

200 TDi diesel engine

Removal

Note: *A new manifold gasket should be used on refitting (a single gasket is used for both the inlet and exhaust manifolds).*

14 Remove the inlet manifold and turbocharger as described in part C of this Chapter.

15 Where applicable, disconnect the wiring plug and the vacuum hose from the EGR valve.

16 Unscrew the nut securing the manifold support bracket to the manifold.

17 Slacken the nuts and bolts securing the two parts of the manifold support bracket together, then remove the bolts securing the bracket to the cylinder block, and withdraw the bracket **(see illustration)**.

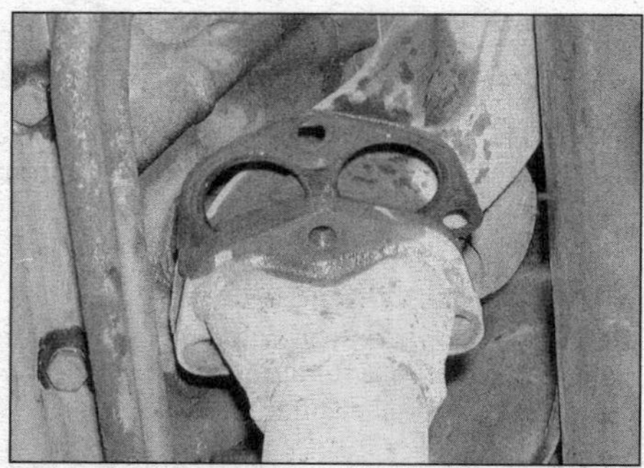

6.5 Separating the exhaust manifold-to-downpipe joint

18 Unscrew the two nuts (recover the washers) securing the coolant pipe to the top manifold studs, and lift the pipe clear of the studs.

19 Unscrew the securing nuts, recover the washers, then lift the manifold from the cylinder head. Recover the gasket.

Refitting

20 Check the condition of the manifold gasket, and renew if necessary - if the original gasket has deteriorated, clean all traces of old gasket from the mating faces of the cylinder head and manifold before fitting a new gasket.

21 Place the support bracket in position on the manifold, but do not fully tighten the securing nut at this stage.

22 Fit the gasket and the manifold, then refit the securing nuts and washers, and tighten the nuts progressively to the specified torque.

23 Refit the coolant pipe to the top manifold studs, and tighten the securing nuts. Ensure that the washers are in place.

24 Refit the bolts securing the manifold support bracket to the cylinder block, then tighten all the support bracket fixings.

25 Where applicable, reconnect the wiring plug and the vacuum pipe to the EGR valve.

26 Refit the turbocharger and inlet manifold as described in part C of this Chapter. Before the engine is started, the turbocharger **must** be primed with oil. Failure to carry out this procedure may result in serious (and expensive) damage to the turbocharger.

a) *Unscrew the oil feed pipe banjo bolt from the top of the turbocharger housing. Recover the two sealing washers, and move the feed pipe away from the oil hole in the housing.*

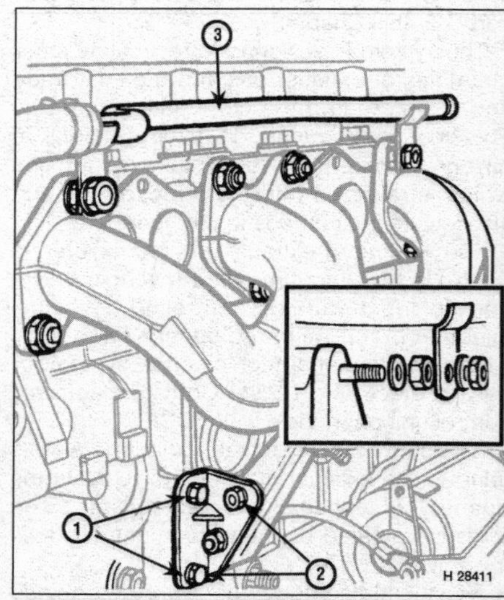
3
1
2
H 28411

6.17 Exhaust manifold mounting details - 200 TDi engine

1 *Support bracket-to-cylinder block bolts*
2 *Support bracket nuts and bolts (securing two parts of bracket together)*
3 *Coolant pipe*

6.32 Disconnecting the turbocharger oil return hose union from the cylinder block - 300 TDi engine

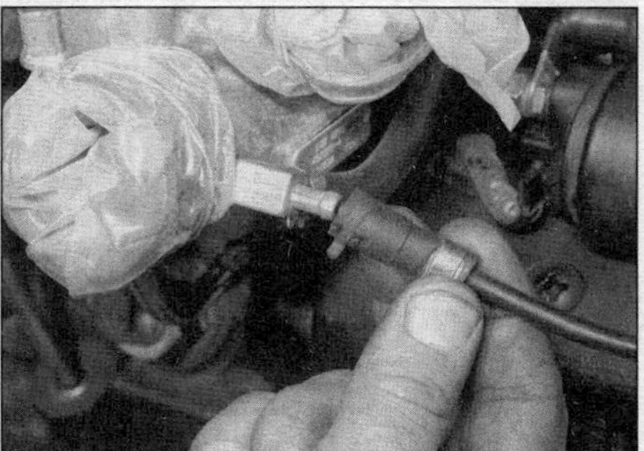

6.33 Disconnecting the boost pressure pipe from the turbocharger - 300 TDi engine

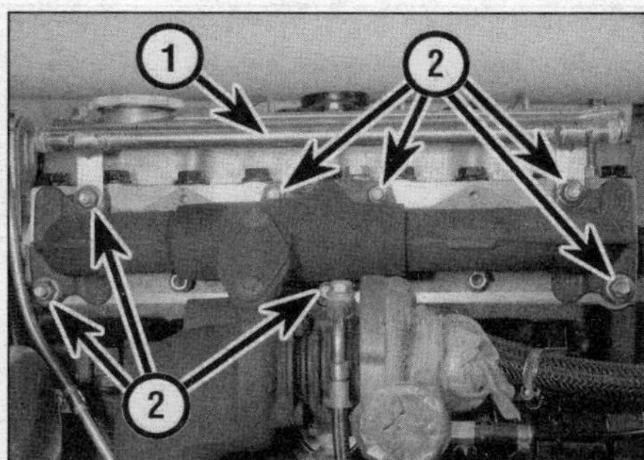
1
2
2

6.34 Coolant pipe (1) and exhaust manifold securing nuts (2) - 300 TDi engine

b) Fill the housing with clean engine oil of the correct type and grade from a freshly-opened sealed container.

c) Reconnect the oil feed pipe, and refit the banjo bolt, ensuring that one sealing washer is positioned on each side of the pipe. Tighten the banjo bolt to the specified torque.

300 TDi diesel engine

Removal

Note: *If the turbocharger is removed from the manifold, a new turbocharger-to-manifold gasket, and a new wastegate pushrod clip, will be required. On 300 TDi engines, the turbocharger is integral with the exhaust manifold. Although the turbocharger and manifold can be separated once the manifold assembly has been removed, at the time of writing, it was unclear whether the turbocharger can be renewed independently of the manifold - check with a Land Rover dealer for details. A new manifold gasket should be used on refitting (a single gasket is used for both the inlet and exhaust manifolds).*

27 Remove the inlet manifold, as described in part C of this Chapter.

28 Loosen the securing clips, and remove the air cleaner-to-turbocharger inlet trunking, and the turbocharger outlet-to-intercooler trunking. Note the breather hose connected to the inlet trunking.

29 On models with EGR, unscrew the two securing bolts and disconnect the EGR delivery pipe from the intercooler-to-inlet manifold trunking.

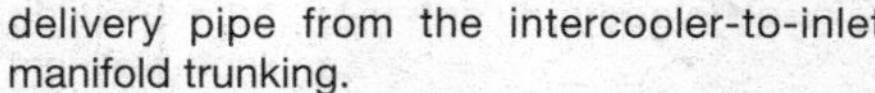

30 Where applicable, disconnect the wiring plug from the EGR valve.

31 Disconnect the exhaust front section from the turbocharger, with reference to Section 7.

32 Place a suitable container beneath the engine to catch escaping oil, then unscrew the union nuts, and disconnect the turbo-charger oil feed and return hoses from the cylinder block (counterhold the unions on the cylinder block) **(see illustration)**. Plug the open ends of the hoses and the cylinder block, to prevent dirt ingress.

33 Disconnect the turbocharger boost pressure pipe from the turbocharger **(see illustration)**.

34 Unscrew the two manifold nuts securing the coolant pipe to the top manifold studs, and lift the pipe clear of the studs **(see illustration)**.

35 Unscrew the remaining manifold securing nuts, then lift the complete manifold/ turbocharger assembly from the cylinder head. Recover the gasket.

36 It is possible that some of the manifold studs may be unscrewed from the cylinder head when the manifold securing nuts are unscrewed. In this event, the studs should be screwed back into the cylinder head once the manifolds have been removed, using two manifold nuts locked together.

37 If the turbocharger is to be removed from the manifold, refer to the note at the beginning of this sub-Section before proceeding.

38 To remove the turbocharger from the manifold, prise off the clip securing the operating lever to the wastegate pushrod, then remove the four bolts and the two clamp plates securing the turbocharger **(see illustrations)**.

39 Withdraw the turbocharger, and recover the gasket.

Refitting

40 If the turbocharger has been removed from the manifold, thoroughly clean the mating faces of the turbocharger and the manifold, then refit the turbocharger using a new gasket.

41 Reconnect the operating lever to the wastegate pushrod, using a new clip.

42 Check the condition of the manifold gasket, and renew if necessary - if the original gasket has deteriorated, clean all traces of old gasket from the mating faces of the cylinder head and manifold before fitting a new gasket.

43 Fit the gasket and the manifold, and refit the coolant pipe to the top manifold studs. Refit the securing nuts and washers, and tighten the nuts progressively to the specified torque.

44 Reconnect the turbocharger boost pressure pipe.

45 Reconnect the turbocharger oil pipes, and securely tighten the union nuts.

46 Reconnect the exhaust front section to the turbocharger, with reference to Section 7.

47 Where applicable, reconnect the EGR valve wiring plug.

48 Refit the air trunking, and reconnect the breather hose to the inlet trunking.

49 On models with EGR, reconnect the EGR delivery pipe to the intercooler-to-inlet manifold trunking, and tighten the securing bolts.

50 Refit the inlet manifold as described in Chapter 4C.

51 Before starting the engine, the turbocharger **must** be primed with oil as follows. Failure to carry out this procedure may result in serious (and expensive) damage to the turbocharger.

a) Unscrew the oil feed pipe banjo bolt from the top of the turbocharger housing. Recover the two sealing washers, and

6.38a Turbocharger wastegate pushrod securing clip (arrowed)

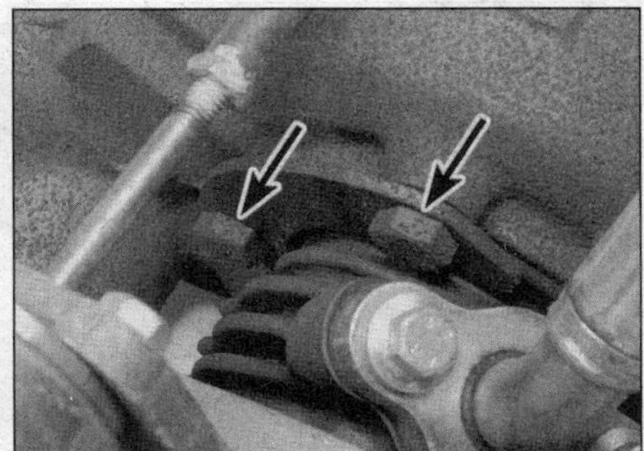

6.38b Two of the turbocharger securing bolts (arrowed)

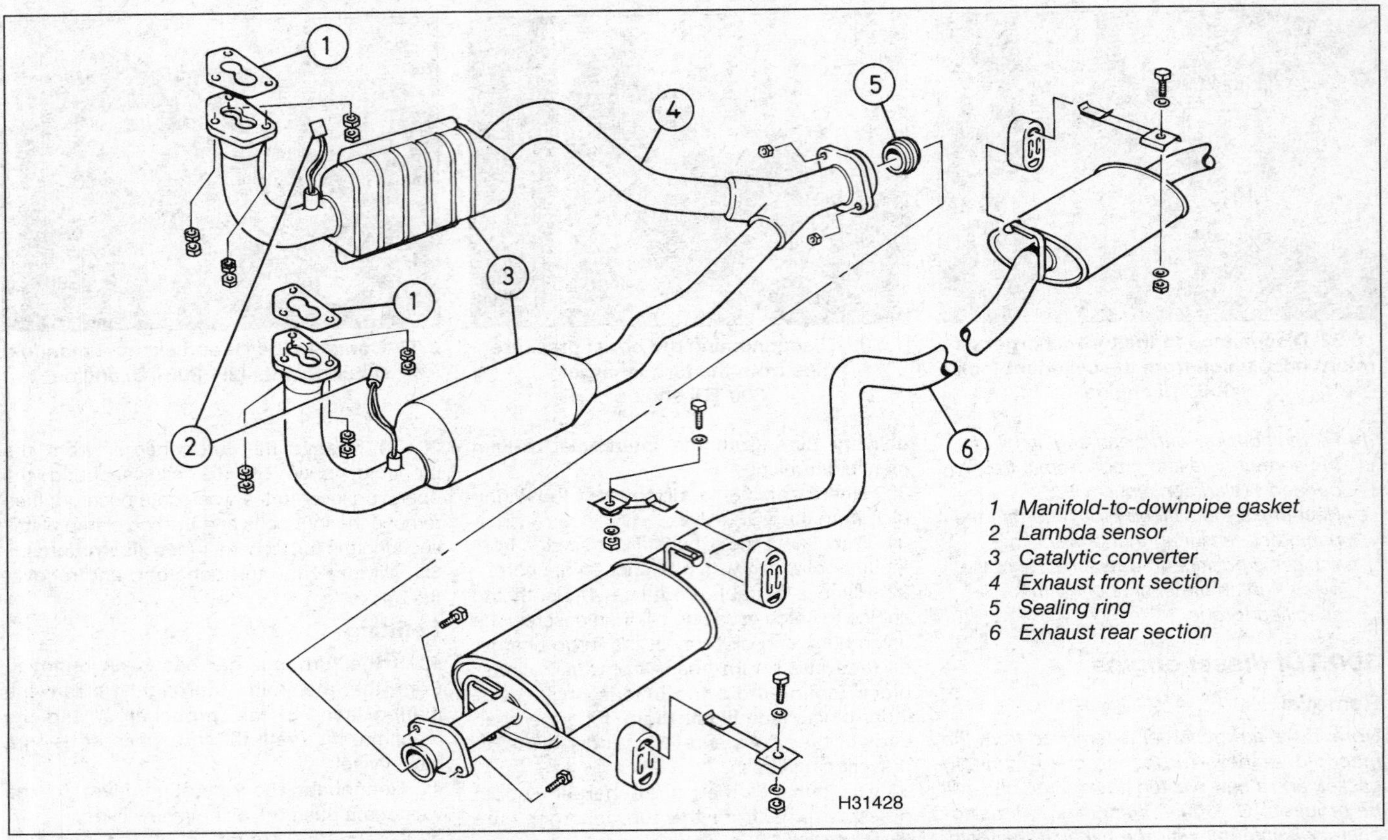

1 Manifold-to-downpipe gasket
2 Lambda sensor
3 Catalytic converter
4 Exhaust front section
5 Sealing ring
6 Exhaust rear section

H31428

7.1a Typical petrol engine exhaust system - later model with catalyst shown

move the feed pipe away from the oil hole in the housing.

b) Fill the housing with clean engine oil of the correct type and grade from a freshly-opened sealed container.

c) Reconnect the oil feed pipe, and refit the banjo bolt, ensuring that one sealing washer is positioned on each side of the pipe. Tighten the banjo bolt to the specified torque (see Chapter 4C).

7 Exhaust system - general information and component renewal

General information

1 The exhaust system consists of two or three sections, the sections varying in detail depending on model **(see illustrations)**. Each exhaust section can be renewed individually, leaving the remaining section(s) in place.

2 Where applicable, the catalytic converter(s) is/are located in the exhaust front (downpipe) section.

Component renewal - petrol models

Front section

Note: *Suitable jointing compound will be required on refitting, and a new sealing ring may be required.*

3 Jack up the front of the vehicle and support securely on axle stands (see *Jacking and vehicle support*). Arrange the axle stands so that the suspension is not compressed, to give the best clearance between the axle and the exhaust.

4 Loosen the nuts and bolts securing the front section to the centre section, in front of

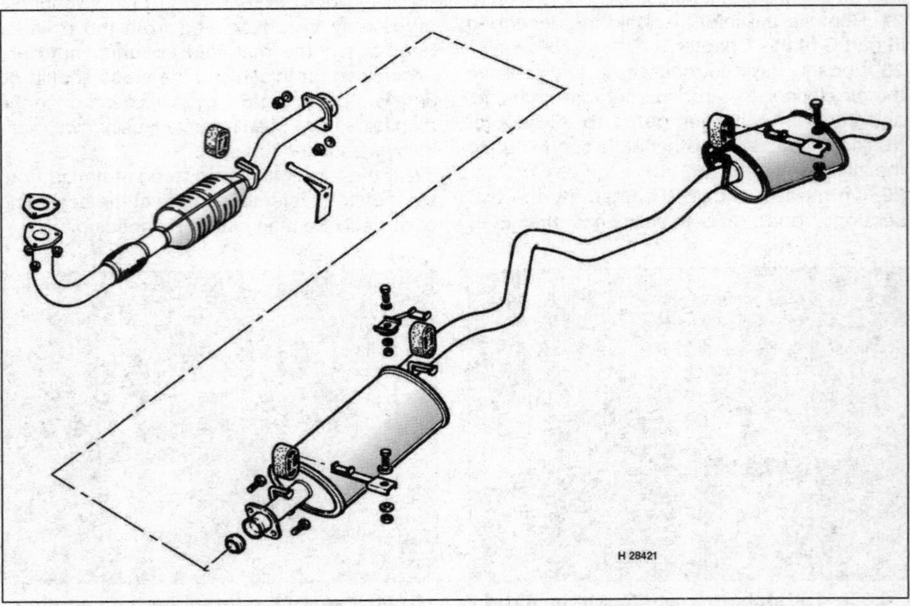
H 28421

7.1b Typical diesel engine two-piece exhaust system components

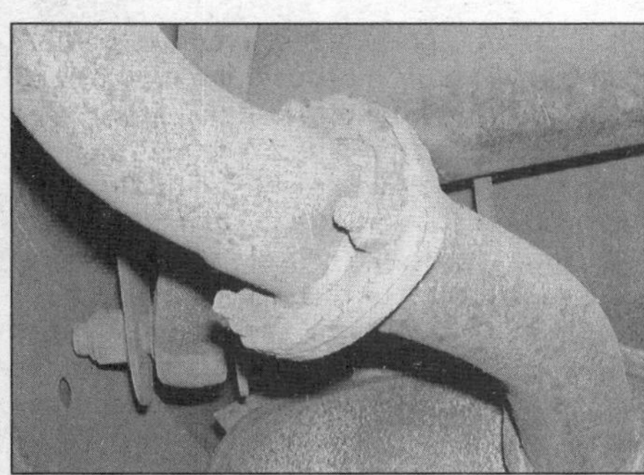

7.4 Exhaust front-to-rear section joint

the centre silencer box **(see illustration)**. Do not completely separate the joint at this stage.

5 Loosen the nuts securing the U-clamp support in front of the centre silencer, and remove the U-clamp.

6 On catalytic converter models, trace the lambda sensor wiring back to the multi-plugs (in the engine compartment, at the rear of the cylinder heads) and disconnect it.

7 Loosen the manifold-to-downpipe nuts, and separate the downpipes from the manifold flanges, supporting the front section so that it is not strained. Remove the nuts and bolts at the front silencer joint, and lower the front section out from under the vehicle. Recover the sealing ring used at the front silencer joint.

8 Refitting is a reversal of removal, bearing in mind the following points:

a) *Examine the condition of the silencer mounting rubbers, and renew if necessary.*
b) *Apply a little exhaust jointing compound to the joints, especially the manifold joints, where no gasket is used.*
c) *Examine the condition of the sealing ring, and renew if necessary. Ensure that the sealing ring is in place between the front section and the silencer.*
d) *Do not fully tighten the clamp nuts and bolts until the completion of refitting.*

Centre section - non-catalyst models

9 Jack up the front of the vehicle and support securely on axle stands (see *Jacking and vehicle support*). Arrange the axle stands so that the suspension is not compressed, to give the best clearance between the axle and the exhaust.

10 Loosen the nuts and bolts securing the front section to the centre section, in front of the centre silencer box. Do not completely separate the joint at this stage.

11 Loosen the nuts securing the U-clamp at the rear of the centre silencer, and remove the U-clamp.

12 Support the front of the centre silencer, then remove the three nuts and bolts.

13 Twist the rear section of the exhaust to separate the sleeved joint behind the rear silencer. If this approach is not successful, the sleeved joint may have corroded together - try carefully tapping the joint with a small hammer to free it.

14 To remove the centre silencer, it will have to be manipulated down or to the side, to clear the rest of the system - if necessary, loosen the U-clamp ahead of the rear silencer to give more movement.

15 Refitting is a reversal of removal, bearing in mind the following points:

a) *Examine the condition of the silencer mounting rubbers, and renew if necessary.*
b) *Apply a little exhaust jointing compound to the joints.*
c) *Examine the condition of the sealing ring, and renew if necessary. Ensure that the sealing ring is in place between the front section and the silencer.*
d) *Do not fully tighten the clamp nuts and bolts until the completion of refitting.*

Rear section - non-catalyst models

16 Jack up the rear of the vehicle and support securely on axle stands (see *Jacking and vehicle support*). Arrange the axle stands so that the suspension is not compressed, to give the best clearance between the axle and the exhaust.

17 Loosen the nuts securing the U-clamp at the rear of the centre silencer, and remove the U-clamp.

18 Loosen the U-clamp ahead of the rear silencer, but do not remove it at this stage.

19 Twist the rear section of the exhaust to separate the sleeved joint behind the rear silencer. If this approach is not successful, the sleeved joint may have corroded together - try carefully tapping the joint with a small hammer to free it.

20 Remove the U-clamp from the rear silencer, then separate the sleeved joint and manipulate the exhaust carefully from under the vehicle.

21 Refitting is a reversal of removal, bearing in mind the following points:

a) *Examine the condition of the mounting rubbers, and renew if necessary.*
b) *Apply a little exhaust jointing compound to the sleeved joint.*
c) *Do not fully tighten the clamp nuts and bolts until the completion of refitting.*

Rear section - catalyst models

22 Jack up the rear of the vehicle and support securely on axle stands (see *Jacking and vehicle support*). Arrange the axle stands so that the suspension is not compressed, to give the best clearance between the axle and the exhaust.

23 Loosen and remove the nuts and bolts securing the front section to the centre section, in front of the centre silencer box. Separate the joint so that the system can be removed.

24 Working from the front, unhook the system from the mounting rubbers (three in total). Support the system as this is done. If preferred, the mountings can be unbolted from the underside of the vehicle - if this is done, note which goes where, and also the fitted order of all components.

25 Manipulate the system from under the vehicle, and lower it to the floor. Recover the sealing ring fitted at the front joint.

26 Refitting is a reversal of removal, bearing in mind the following points:

a) *Examine the condition of the mounting rubbers, and renew if necessary.*
b) *Apply a little exhaust jointing compound to the front joint.*
c) *Examine the condition of the sealing ring, and renew if necessary. Ensure that the sealing ring is in place between the front section and the silencer.*

Heatshields

27 The heatshields fitted to the downpipes and above the centre silencer are secured by a mixture of nuts, bolts and clips. Each shield can be removed once the relevant exhaust section has been removed. Note that if the shield is being removed to gain access to a component located behind it, in some cases it may prove sufficient to remove the retaining nuts and/or bolts and simply lower the shield, avoiding the need to disturb the exhaust system.

Component renewal - diesel models

Front section (three-piece exhaust system)

Note: *Suitable jointing compound will be required on refitting, and a new sealing ring may be required.*

28 Jack up the front of the vehicle and support securely on axle stands placed under the front axle (see *Jacking and vehicle support*).

29 Working in the engine compartment, unscrew the clamp nut and bolt, and withdraw the clamp securing the exhaust front section to the turbocharger elbow.

30 Working under the vehicle, release the front exhaust silencer from the front and rear support brackets.

31 Unscrew the nuts and bolts securing the exhaust front section to the front silencer. Recover the washers, and the sealing ring, then withdraw the front section from under the vehicle.

32 Refitting is a reversal of removal, bearing in mind the following points:

a) *Examine the condition of the silencer mounting rubbers, and renew if necessary.*
b) *Apply exhaust jointing compound to the joint between the exhaust front section and the turbocharger elbow.*
c) *Examine the condition of the sealing ring, and renew if necessary. Ensure that the sealing ring is in place between the front section and the silencer.*
d) *Do not fully tighten the clamp nuts and bolts until the completion of refitting.*

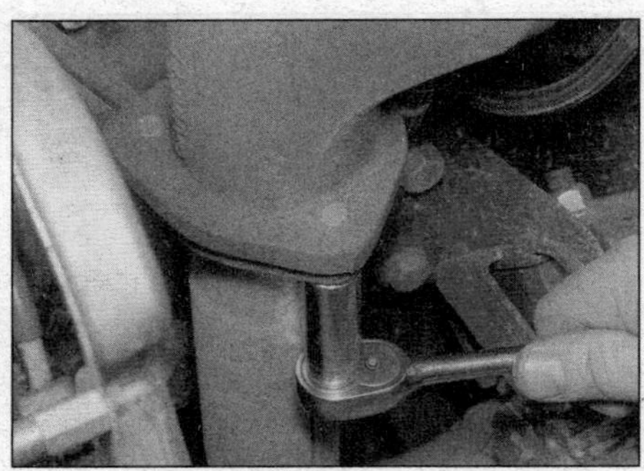
7.45a Unscrew the three securing nuts . . .

7.45b . . . and disconnect the exhaust front section from the turbocharger

Front silencer (three-piece exhaust system)

Note: *New sealing rings may be required on refitting.*

33 Jack up the front and rear of the vehicle and support securely on axle stands (see *Jacking and vehicle support*). Arrange the axle stands so that the suspension is not compressed, to give the best clearance between the axles and the exhaust.

34 Remove the exhaust rear section as described later in this Section.

35 Unscrew the nuts and bolts securing the exhaust front section to the front silencer, and recover the washers, and the sealing ring.

36 Release the silencer from the front and rear support brackets, then withdraw the silencer from under the vehicle.

37 Refitting is a reversal of removal, bearing in mind the following points:

a) *Examine the condition of the silencer mounting rubbers, and renew if necessary.*
b) *Examine the condition of the sealing rings and renew if necessary. Ensure that the sealing rings are in place between the exhaust sections.*
c) *Refit the exhaust rear section as described later in this Section.*
d) *Do not fully tighten the clamp nuts and bolts until the completion of refitting.*

Rear section (three-piece exhaust system)

Note: *New sealing rings may be required on refitting.*

38 Jack up the rear of the vehicle and support securely on axle stands (see *Jacking and vehicle support*). Arrange the axle stands so that the suspension is not compressed, to give the best clearance between the axle and the exhaust.

39 Working under the vehicle, unscrew the nuts and bolts securing the exhaust rear section to the front silencer. Recover the washers and the sealing ring.

40 Release the exhaust rear section from the rear support bracket, then manipulate the assembly from under the vehicle.

41 Refitting is a reversal of removal, bearing in mind the following points:

a) *Examine the condition of the exhaust mounting rubbers, and renew if necessary.*
b) *Examine the condition of the sealing rings, and renew if necessary. Ensure that the sealing ring is in place between the exhaust sections.*
c) *Do not fully tighten the clamp nuts and bolts until the completion of refitting.*

Front section (two-piece exhaust system)

Note: *A new exhaust-to-turbocharger gasket must be used on refitting, and a new front section-to-rear section sealing ring may be required.*

42 Jack up the vehicle, and support securely on axle stands positioned under the axles (see *Jacking and vehicle support*). Note that the axle stands must be of sufficient size to support the chassis of the vehicle with the suspension fully extended, with the wheels clear of the ground.

43 Working under the vehicle, where applicable, mark the positions of the front anti-roll bar mounting rubbers on the bar. Unscrew the bolts, withdraw the mounting brackets, then allow the anti-roll bar to swing down clear of the exhaust system.

44 Where applicable, disconnect the exhaust front section from its mounting bracket.

45 Unscrew the three securing nuts, and disconnect the exhaust front section from the turbocharger. Recover the gasket **(see illustrations)**.

46 Unscrew the nuts and bolts securing the exhaust front section to the rear section **(see illustration)**. Recover the washers and the sealing ring.

47 Place a suitable hydraulic jack under the centre of the front differential housing, then carefully jack up the front of the vehicle, and reposition the front axle stands under the chassis side-members.

48 Slowly lower the jack until the front suspension is fully extended.

49 Manipulate the exhaust front section out from under the vehicle.

50 Refitting is a reversal of removal, bearing in mind the following points:

a) *Examine the exhaust mounting rubbers, and renew if necessary.*
b) *Use a new gasket when reconnecting the exhaust to the turbocharger.*
c) *Examine the condition of the sealing ring, and renew if necessary. Ensure that the sealing ring is in place between the exhaust sections.*
d) *Align the anti-roll bar mounting rubbers with the marks made on the bar before removal, and tighten the mounting bolts to the specified torque (see Chapter 11).*
e) *Do not fully tighten the exhaust clamp nuts and bolts until the completion of refitting.*

Rear section (two-piece exhaust system)

Note: *The aid of an assistant will greatly ease this operation.*

51 Remove the exhaust front section, as described previously in this Section.

52 Unbolt the exhaust rear section brackets from the body, then carefully lower the exhaust onto the rear axle. Remove the mounting rubbers from the exhaust brackets **(see illustration)**.

53 Ensure that the axle stands are securely positioned under the front of the chassis, then withdraw the jack from under the front axle, and reposition the jack under the rear axle.

54 Jack up the rear of the vehicle, then reposition the rear axle stands under the chassis side-members, in front of the rear towing brackets.

55 Slowly lower the jack until the rear suspension is fully extended.

56 Manipulate the exhaust diagonally across the underside of the vehicle, with the front silencer positioned to the right of the vehicle.

57 Facing towards the rear of the vehicle,

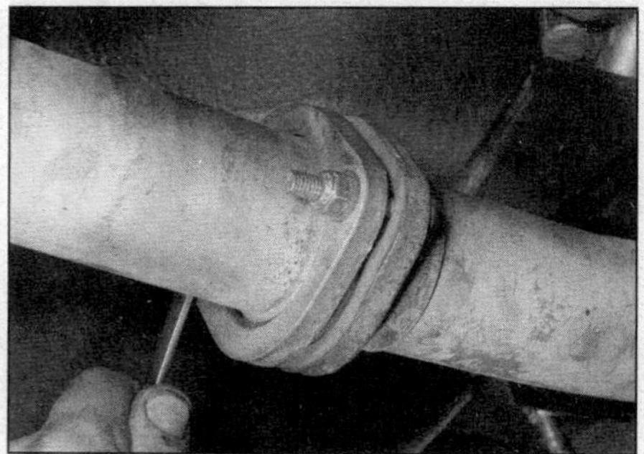
7.46 Unscrewing an exhaust clamp nut

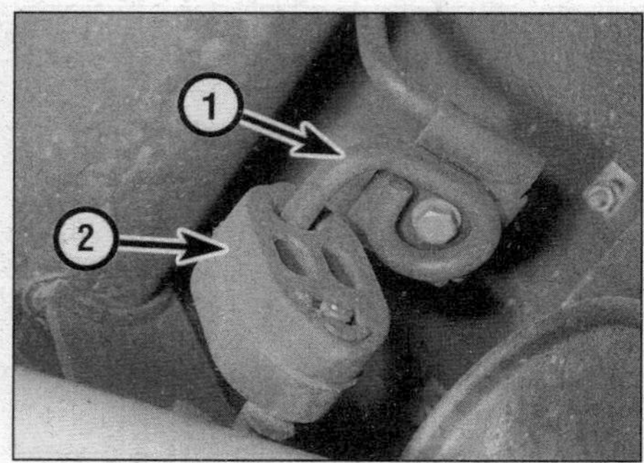
1
2
7.52 Rear exhaust mounting bracket (1) and rubber (2)

turn the exhaust assembly anti-clockwise to clear the rear axle, then manipulate the assembly out from under the vehicle.

58 Refitting is a reversal of removal, bearing in mind the following points:

- *a) Examine the condition of the exhaust mounting rubbers, and renew if necessary.*
- *b) Refit the exhaust front section as described previously in this Section.*

8 Catalytic converter - general information and precautions

The catalytic converter is a reliable and simple device which needs no maintenance in itself, but there are some facts of which an owner should be aware if the converter is to function properly for its full service life.

Petrol models

- *a) DO NOT use leaded (UK 4-star) petrol in a vehicle with a catalytic converter - the lead will coat the precious metals' reagents, reducing their converting efficiency, and will eventually destroy the converter.*
- *b) Always keep the ignition and fuel systems well-maintained in accordance with the manufacturer's schedule.*
- *c) If the engine develops a misfire, do not drive the vehicle at all (or at least as little as possible) until the fault is cured.*
- *d) DO NOT push- or tow-start the vehicle - this will soak the catalytic converter in unburned fuel, causing it to overheat when the engine does start.*
- *e) DO NOT switch off the ignition at high engine speeds, ie do not 'blip' the throttle immediately before switching off.*
- *f) In some cases a sulphurous smell (like that of rotten eggs) may be noticed from the exhaust. This is common to many catalytic converter-equipped vehicles and once the vehicle has covered a few thousand miles the problem should disappear. Low-quality fuel with a high sulphur content will exacerbate this effect.*
- *g) The catalytic converter, used on a well-maintained and well-driven vehicle, should last between 50 000 and 100 000 miles - if the converter is no longer effective it must be renewed.*

Petrol and diesel models

- *h) DO NOT use fuel or engine oil additives - these may contain substances harmful to the catalytic converter.*
- *i) DO NOT continue to use the vehicle if the engine burns oil to the extent of leaving a visible trail of blue smoke.*
- *j) Remember that the catalytic converter operates at very high temperatures. DO NOT, therefore, park the vehicle in dry undergrowth, over long grass or piles of dead leaves after a long run.*
- *k) Remember that the catalytic converter is FRAGILE - do not strike it with tools during servicing work.*

Chapter 5 Part A:
Starting and charging systems

Contents

Degrees of difficulty

Easy, suitable for novice with little experience 	**Fairly easy,** suitable for beginner with some experience 	**Fairly difficult,** suitable for competent DIY mechanic 	**Difficult,** suitable for experienced DIY mechanic 	**Very difficult,** suitable for expert DIY or professional 

Specifications

General

Electrical system type . . . . 12-volt negative earth

Battery

Type . . . . Lead-acid, low-maintenance

Alternator

Type . . . . Lucas or Magneti-Marelli
Rating . . . . 65, 80 or 100 amps
Regulated voltage . . . . 13.6 to 14.4 volts
Minimum brush length (nominal) . . . . 5 mm

Starter motor

Make and type:
- Petrol models . . . . Pre-engaged, Lucas M78R
- Diesel models . . . . Pre-engaged, Paris-Rhone or Bosch, reduction-gear type

Torque wrench settings	Nm	lbf ft
Alternator mounting bracket bolts	34	25
Alternator mountings	25	18
Starter motor mountings	45	33

1 General information and precautions

The starting and charging system is defined as the battery, alternator and starter motor, and all related wiring; because of their engine-related functions, these components are covered separately from the body electrical devices such as the lights, instruments, etc (which are covered in Chapter 13). The ignition system fitted to petrol models is covered in part B of this Chapter, with the diesel engine pre-heating system covered in part C.

The electrical system is of the 12-volt negative-earth type.

The battery is either of the low-maintenance or maintenance-free type, and is charged by the alternator, which is belt-driven from a crankshaft-mounted pulley.

The starter motor is of the pre-engaged type, incorporating an integral solenoid. On starting, the solenoid moves the drive pinion into engagement with the flywheel ring gear before the starter motor is energised. Once the engine has started, a one-way clutch prevents the motor armature being driven by the engine until the pinion disengages from the flywheel. The motor fitted to diesel models has a reduction gear mechanism, in order to achieve the high torque necessary to turn the engine against the high compression pressures encountered in a diesel engine.

Further details of the various systems are given in the relevant Sections of this Chapter. While some repair procedures are given, the usual course of action is to renew the component concerned. The owner whose interest extends beyond mere component renewal should obtain a copy of the *Automobile Electrical & Electronic Systems Manual*, available from the publishers of this manual.

Precautions

Warning: It is necessary to take extra care when working on the electrical system, to avoid damage to semi-conductor devices (diodes and transistors), and to avoid the risk of personal injury. In addition to the precautions given in* Safety first! *at the beginning of this manual, observe the following when working on the system:

Always remove rings, watches, etc before working on the electrical system. Even with the battery disconnected, capacitive discharge could occur if a component's live terminal is earthed through a metal object. This could cause a shock or nasty burn.

Do not reverse the battery connections. Components such as the alternator, pre-heating electronic control unit, or any other components having semi-conductor circuitry could be irreparably damaged.

Never disconnect the battery terminals, the alternator, any electrical wiring or any test instruments when the engine is running.

Do not allow the engine to turn the alternator when the alternator is not connected.

Never test for alternator output by 'flashing' the output lead to earth.

Always ensure that the battery negative lead is disconnected when working on the electrical system.

If the engine is being started using jump leads and a slave battery, connect the batteries ***positive-to-positive*** and ***negative-to-negative*** (see *Jump starting*). This also applies when connecting a battery charger.

Never use an ohmmeter of the type incorporating a hand-cranked generator for circuit or continuity testing.

Before using electric-arc welding equipment on the vehicle, ***disconnect the battery, alternator and components such as the electronic control units***, as applicable, to protect them from the risk of damage.

Caution: The radio/cassette unit fitted as standard equipment by Land Rover may be equipped with a built-in security code, to deter thieves. If the power source to the unit is cut, the anti-theft system will activate. Even if the power source is immediately reconnected, the radio/cassette unit will not function until the correct security code has been entered. Therefore, if you do not know the correct security code for the radio/cassette unit, do not disconnect the negative terminal of the battery, nor remove the radio/cassette unit from the vehicle. Refer to the manufacturer's handbook supplied with the vehicle for details of how to enter the security code.

2 Electrical fault finding - general information

Refer to Chapter 13.

3 Battery - testing and charging

Note: *Refer to the precautions given in Safety first! and in Section 1 of this Chapter before proceeding.*

Testing

1 If the vehicle covers a very small annual mileage, it is worthwhile checking the specific gravity of the electrolyte every three months, to determine the state of charge of the battery. Use a hydrometer to make the check, and compare the results obtained with the following table:

	Normal climates	**Tropics**
Discharged	*1.080*	*1.120*
Half-charged	*1.200*	*1.160*
Fully-charged	*1.280*	*1.230*

2 If the battery condition is suspect, where possible, first check the specific gravity of the electrolyte in each cell. A variation of 0.040 or more between cells indicates loss of electrolyte or deterioration of the internal plates.

3 An accurate test of battery condition can be made by a battery specialist, using a heavy-discharge meter. Alternatively, connect a voltmeter across the battery terminals, and (where applicable) disconnect the main feed wire to the glow plugs; operate the starter motor with the headlights, heated rear window and heater blower switched on. If the voltmeter reading remains above 9.6 volts, the battery condition is satisfactory. If the voltmeter reading drops below 9.6 volts, and the battery has already been charged, it is faulty.

Charging

Note: *The following is intended as a guide only. Always refer to the battery manufacturer's recommendations (often printed on a label attached to the battery) before charging.*

4 In normal use, the battery should not require charging from an external source, unless it is discharged accidentally (for instance by leaving the lights on). Charging can also temporarily revive a failing battery, but if frequent recharging is required (and the alternator output is correct), the battery is worn out.

5 Unless the battery manufacturer advises differently, the charging rate in amps should be no more than one-tenth of the battery capacity in amp-hours (for instance, 6.5 amps for a 65 amp-hour battery). Most domestic battery chargers have an output of 5 amps or so, and these can safely be used overnight. Rapid 'boost' charging is not recommended; if it is not carefully controlled, it can cause serious damage to the battery plates through overheating.

6 Both battery terminal leads must be disconnected before connecting the charger leads (disconnect the negative lead first). Connect the charger leads **before** switching on at the mains. When charging is complete, switch off at the mains **before** disconnecting the charger. If this procedure is followed, there is no risk of creating a spark at the battery terminals. Continue to charge the battery until no further rise in specific gravity is noted over a four-hour period, or until vigorous gassing is observed.

7 On completion of charging, check the electrolyte level (if possible) and top-up if necessary, using distilled or de-ionised water.

4 Battery - removal and refitting

Note: *Refer to the precautions given in Safety first! and in Section 1 of this Chapter before proceeding.*

Removal

1 The battery is located at the front right-hand corner of the engine compartment. First check that all electrical components are switched off, in order to avoid a spark occurring as the negative lead is disconnected. Note also that if the radio has a security coding, it will be necessary to insert this code when the battery is re-connected.

2 On models from 1996 onwards, the standard anti-theft alarm system has a battery back-up facility, meaning that the alarm will still sound even if the battery is disconnected. To avoid accidentally setting off the alarm, switch the ignition on, then off, and disconnect the battery terminals as described below **within 15 seconds**. If the alarm sounds, disarm the system with the handset, then reconnect the battery, switch on the ignition, and try again.

3 Where necessary, unclip and remove the cover fitted over the battery for access. Loosen the clamp nut and bolt, and disconnect the battery negative lead.

4 Similarly, disconnect the battery positive lead.

5 Unscrew the four nuts securing the battery clamp in position. Recover the washers **(see illustration)**.

6 Lift the clamp bracket from the studs, then lift out the battery. Take care not to drop it, as it is heavy - also try not to tilt it more than necessary.

7 Clean the battery terminal posts, clamps, tray and battery casing.

Refitting

8 Refitting is a reversal of removal, but always connect the positive terminal clamp first and the negative terminal clamp last.

5 Charging system - testing

Note: *Refer to the warnings given in Safety first! and in Section 1 of this Chapter before proceeding.*

1 If the charge warning light fails to illuminate when the ignition is switched on, first check the security of the alternator wiring connections. If satisfactory, check that the warning light bulb has not blown, and that the bulbholder is secure in its location in the instrument panel. If the light still fails to illuminate, check the continuity of the warning light feed wire from the alternator to the bulbholder. If all is satisfactory, the alternator

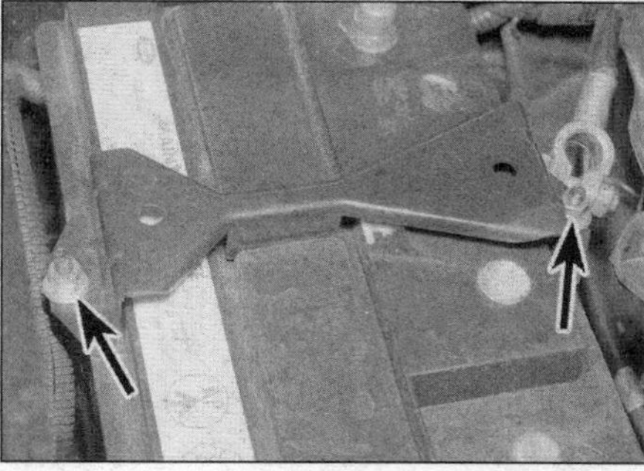

4.5 Battery clamp securing nuts (arrowed)

is at fault, and should be renewed or taken to an auto-electrician for testing and repair.

2 If the charge warning light illuminates when the engine is running, stop the engine and check that the drivebelt is correctly tensioned (Chapter 1A, Section 16 or Chapter 1B, Section 17) and that the alternator connections are secure. If all is so far satisfactory, check the alternator brushes and slip rings (see Section 7). If the fault persists, the alternator should be renewed, or taken to an auto-electrician for testing and repair.

3 If the alternator output is suspect even though the warning light functions correctly, the regulated voltage may be checked as follows.

4 Connect a voltmeter across the battery terminals, and start the engine.

5 Increase the engine speed until the voltmeter reading remains steady; as a rough guide, the reading should be between 13.6 and 14.4 volts.

6 Switch on as many electrical accessories (headlights, heated rear window, heater blower, etc) as possible, and check that the alternator maintains the regulated voltage between 13.6 and 14.4 volts. It may be necessary to increase engine speed slightly.

7 If the regulated voltage is not as stated, the fault may be due to worn brushes, weak brush springs, a faulty voltage regulator, a faulty diode, a severed phase winding, or worn or damaged slip rings. The brushes and slip rings may be checked (see Section 7), but if the fault persists, the alternator should be renewed or taken to an auto-electrician for testing and repair.

6 Alternator - removal and refitting

Note: *Refer to the precautions given in Safety first! and in Section 1 of this Chapter before proceeding.*

Removal

1 Disconnect the battery negative lead.

2 Remove the auxiliary drivebelt as described in Chapter 1A or 1B.

Petrol engines

3 Disconnect the electrical leads from the rear of the alternator, noting their locations **(see illustrations)**.

4 Remove the adjustment link bolt or upper mounting bolt, and the lower mounting bolt(s), and remove the alternator from the engine **(see illustration)**.

6.3a Disconnect the warning light wire . . .

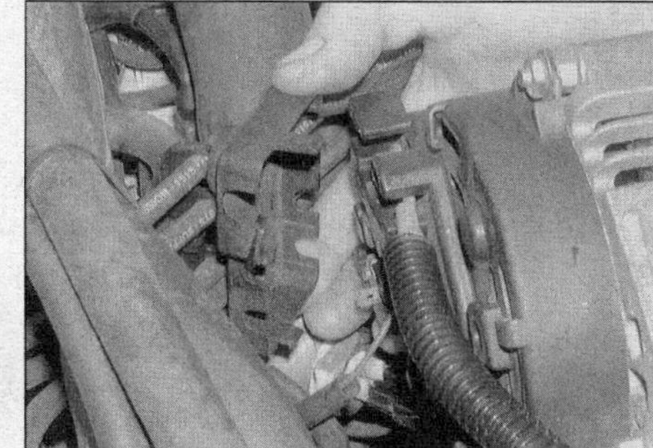

6.3b . . . then unclip the rear cover . . .

6.3c . . . and remove the nuts securing the main wiring

6.4 Loosen and remove the alternator mounting bolts, and remove the alternator

6.6 Disconnect the wiring (arrowed) from the rear of the alternator

6.7 Removing the alternator lower securing bolt - 300 TDi engine

6.10 Removing the alternator through-bolt - 300 TDi engine

Diesel engines

5 Where applicable, unscrew the three securing nuts, and withdraw the heat shield from the rear of the alternator to expose the wiring connections.

6 Disconnect the electrical leads from the rear of the alternator **(see illustration)**.

7 Remove the alternator lower securing bolt. Where applicable, recover the washers, noting their locations **(see illustration)**.

8 Working at the top of the alternator, counterhold the through-bolt, and unscrew the nut. Again recover the washers, noting their locations.

9 Where applicable, withdraw the heat shield from the rear of the through-bolt.

10 Remove the through-bolt, and withdraw the alternator from the engine **(see illustration)**.

Refitting

11 Refitting is a reversal of removal, but refit and tension the auxiliary drivebelt as described in the relevant part of Chapter 1.

7 Alternator brushes - inspection and renewal

Lucas alternator

1 For improved access, remove the alternator as described in Section 6.

2 If necessary, unscrew the suppressor securing nut from the through-bolt, then disconnect the wiring and withdraw the suppressor for access to the voltage regulator/brush box assembly **(see illustration)**.

3 Remove the three screws securing the voltage regulator/brush box assembly to the rear of the alternator.

4 Tip the outside edge of the assembly upwards, and withdraw it from its location. Disconnect the wiring plug, and withdraw the assembly from the alternator.

5 If the length of either brush is less than the minimum given in the Specifications, the complete regulator/brush box assembly must be renewed.

6 Before refitting, wipe the alternator slip rings clean with a fuel-moistened cloth. If the rings are very dirty, use fine emery paper to clean them, then wipe with the cloth.

7 Refitting is a reversal of removal, but make sure that the brushes move freely in their holders.

8 Where applicable, refit the alternator as described in Section 6.

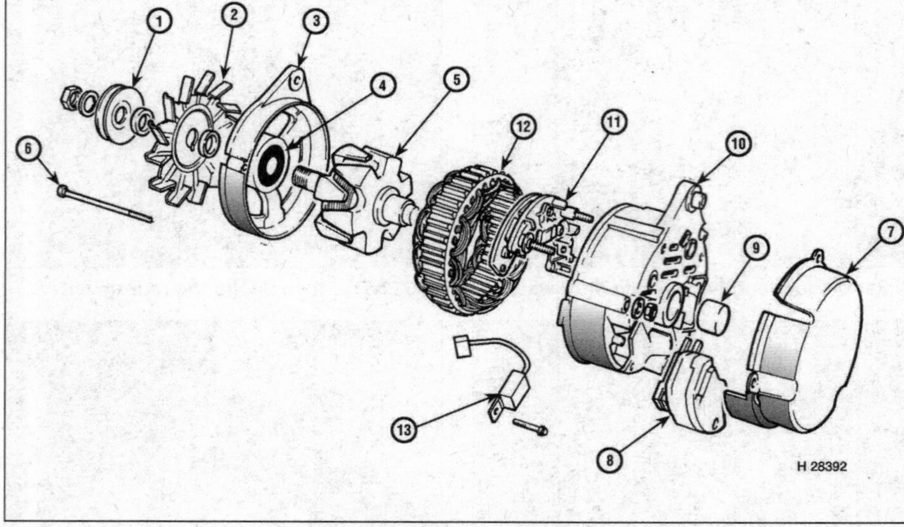
1
2
3
4
5
6
7
8
9
10
11
12
13
H 28392

7.2 Lucas A127-type alternator

1 Pulley
2 Fan
3 Drive end housing
4 Bearing
5 Rotor
6 Through-bolt
7 End cover
8 Voltage regulator/brush holder
9 Bearing
10 Slip ring end housing
11 Diode pack
12 Stator
13 Suppressor

Magneti-Marelli alternator

Note: *Check on the availability of replacement brushes before proceeding.*

9 With the alternator removed as described in Section 6, unscrew the three studs from the rear of the alternator, noting that the suppressor is secured by one of the studs **(see illustration)**.

10 Unscrew the nut and recover the washer securing the wiring terminal to the rear of the alternator, then remove the terminal **(see illustrations)**. Note that the suppressor wiring is connected to the terminal.

11 Withdraw the alternator rear cover **(see illustration)**.

12 To remove a brush, remove the screw securing the brush wiring terminal to the top of the brush plate, then withdraw the wiring, spring and brush as an assembly **(see illustration)**.

7.9 Unscrew the studs from the rear of the alternator - Marelli alternator

7.10a Unscrew the nut . . .

7.10b . . . and remove the wiring terminal - Marelli alternator

TOOL
TiP
When fitting a brush, use a small screwdriver to push the brush into position in the brush holder, as the wiring terminal is lined up with the securing screw

7.11 Withdrawing the alternator rear cover - Marelli alternator

7.12 Removing an alternator brush - Marelli alternator

13 Refitting is a reversal of removal **(see Tool Tip)**. Make sure that the brushes move freely in their holders, and make sure that the suppressor is positioned as noted before removal.

8 Starting system - testing

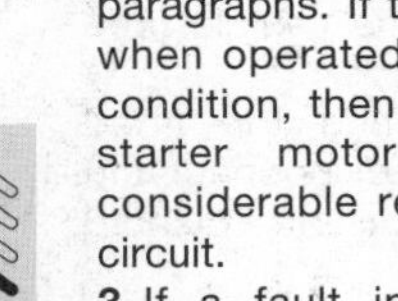

Note: *Refer to the precautions given in Safety first! and in Section 1 of this Chapter before proceeding.*

1 If the starter motor fails to operate when the ignition key is turned to the appropriate position, the possible causes are as follows:

a) The battery is faulty.
b) The electrical connections between the switch, solenoid, battery and starter motor are somewhere failing to pass the necessary current from the battery through the starter to earth.
c) The solenoid is faulty.
d) The starter motor is mechanically or electrically defective.

2 To check the battery, switch on the headlights. If they dim after a few seconds, this indicates that the battery is discharged - recharge (see Section 3) or renew the battery. If the headlights glow brightly, operate the starter switch and observe the lights. If they dim, then this indicates that current is reaching the starter motor, therefore the fault must lie in the starter motor. If the lights continue to glow brightly (and no clicking sound can be heard from the starter motor solenoid), this indicates that there is a fault in the circuit or solenoid - see the following paragraphs. If the starter motor turns slowly when operated, but the battery is in good condition, then this indicates either that the starter motor is faulty, or there is considerable resistance somewhere in the circuit.

3 If a fault in the circuit is suspected, disconnect the battery leads, the starter/solenoid wiring and the engine/transmission earth strap(s). Thoroughly clean the connections, and reconnect the leads and wiring. Use a voltmeter or test light to check that full battery voltage is available at the battery positive lead connection to the solenoid. Smear petroleum jelly around the battery terminals to prevent corrosion - corroded connections are among the most frequent causes of electrical system faults.

4 If the battery and all connections are in good condition, check the circuit by disconnecting the wire from the solenoid blade terminal. Connect a voltmeter or test light between the wire end and a good earth (such as the battery negative terminal), and check that the wire is live when the ignition switch is turned to the start position. If it is, then the circuit is sound - if not, there is a fault in the ignition/starter switch or wiring.

5 The solenoid contacts can be checked by connecting a voltmeter or test light between the battery positive feed connection on the starter side of the solenoid, and earth. When the ignition switch is turned to the start position, there should be a reading or lighted bulb, as applicable. If there is no reading or lighted bulb, the solenoid is faulty and should be renewed.

6 If the circuit and solenoid are proved sound, the fault must lie in the starter motor. Begin checking the starter motor by removing it (see Section 9), and checking the brushes (see Section 10). If the fault does not lie in the brushes, the motor windings must be faulty. In this event, the starter motor must be renewed, unless an auto-electrical specialist can be found who will overhaul the unit at a cost significantly less than that of a new or exchange starter motor.

9 Starter motor - removal and refitting

Note: *Refer to the precautions given in Safety first! and in Section 1 of this Chapter before proceeding.*

Removal

1 Disconnect the battery negative lead.

Petrol engines

Caution: On models with catalytic converters, take great care to avoid damaging the lambda sensor in the right-hand branch of the exhaust system (or its wiring) when removing the starter motor.

2 The starter motor is at the right-hand rear of the engine (right as seen from the driver's seat), and access is hindered by the right-hand exhaust downpipe. In view of this, wait until the engine (and exhaust) has cooled before starting work.

3 Apply the handbrake, then jack up the front of the vehicle and support on axle stands (see *Jacking and vehicle support).*

4 Using a suitable Allen key, loosen and remove the starter motor lower mounting bolt

9.4 Removing the lower mounting bolt

9.6 Exhaust heat shield and mounting bolts (arrowed)

9.7 Loosening the nut securing the starter motor wiring

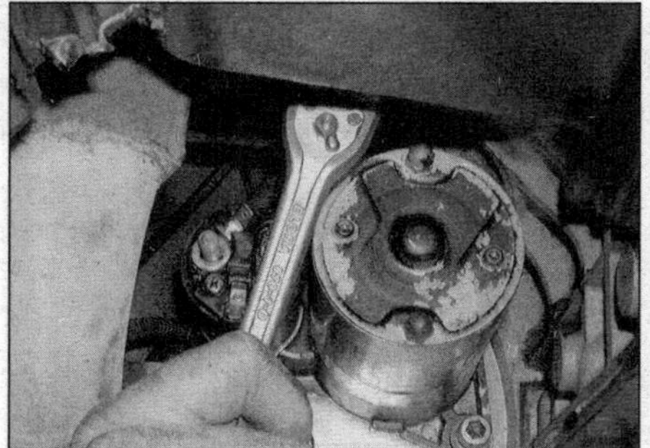
9.8a Loosen the starter motor upper mounting bolt . . .

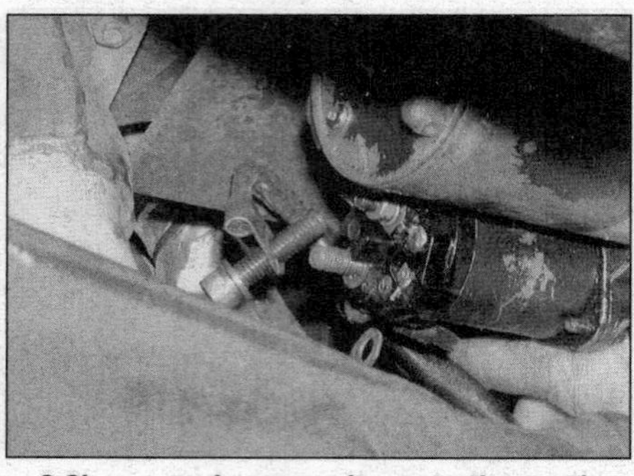
9.8b . . . and remove it - note the earth strap

9.9 Removing the starter motor

(see illustration). In the workshop, we found that access prevented using the Allen key the normal way round - with care, we used a long socket as a lever over the short end of the key. Once the heat shield is free from the mounting bolt, the lower bolt can be refitted loosely for support until the motor is finally removed.

5 The heat shield has a large spring clip which fits around the starter solenoid - manoeuvre the shield up and to one side to release the clip, taking care not to damage the lambda sensor wiring.

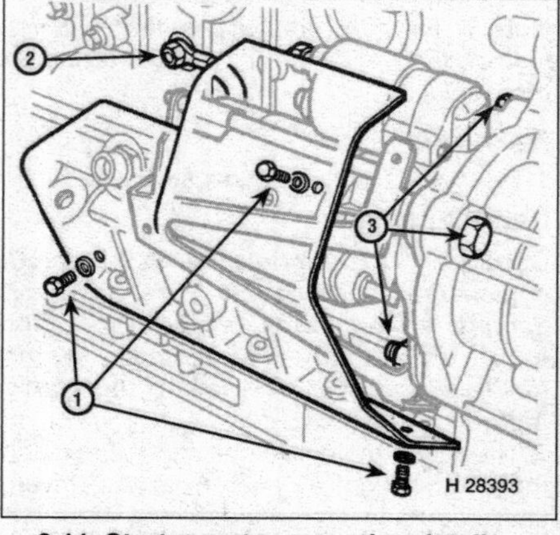
2
3
1
H 28393
9.11 Starter motor mounting details - 200 TDi engine

1 Heat shield securing bolts
2 Earth lead
3 Starter motor mounting bolts and nut

6 The exhaust heat shield must also be removed from the downpipe. The two bolts securing the shield are accessed from in front of the shield, from below the vehicle **(see illustration)**.

7 Noting their locations, and the fitted sequence of the washers, disconnect the wiring from the starter motor and solenoid **(see illustration)**.

8 Loosen and remove the starter motor upper mounting bolt, noting the earth strap located beneath the bolt **(see illustrations)**.

9 Remove the lower mounting bolt, then carefully withdraw the starter motor from the flywheel housing, and lower it to the ground **(see illustration)**.

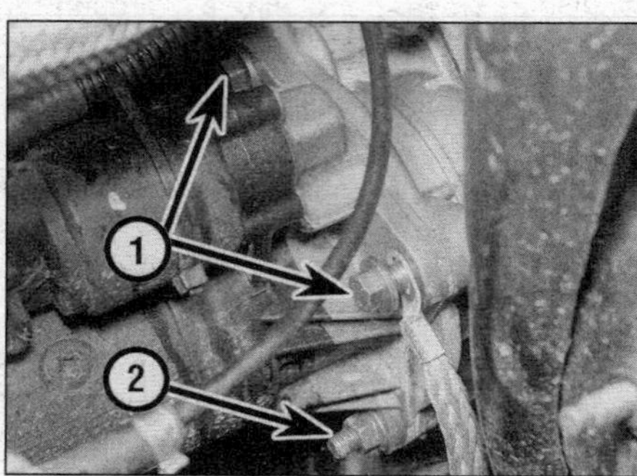
1
2
9.14 Starter motor securing bolts (1) and nut (2) - 300 TDi engine

Diesel engines

10 The starter motor is located on the left-hand side of the engine, and access is most easily obtained from above.

11 On 200 TDi engines, unscrew the three securing bolts, and remove the starter motor heat shield **(see illustration)**.

12 Disconnect the wiring from the solenoid, and where applicable release the securing clip.

13 Unbolt the earth lead from the starter motor, or the cylinder block. Note that on 300 TDi engines, the earth lead is secured by one of the starter motor mounting bolts.

14 Unscrew the securing bolt(s), and the nut, and withdraw the starter motor, complete with the heat shield bracket on 200 TDi engines **(see illustration)**.

Refitting

15 Refitting is a reversal of removal. Ensure that the wiring connections and mountings are securely tightened.

10 Starter motor - brush renewal

Starter motor brush renewal is considered to be beyond the scope of the DIY mechanic, and the task should be entrusted to a Land Rover dealer, or an automotive electrical specialist.

Chapter 5 Part B:
Ignition system - petrol engines

Contents

Degrees of difficulty

Easy, suitable for novice with little experience 	**Fairly easy,** suitable for beginner with some experience 	**Fairly difficult,** suitable for competent DIY mechanic	**Difficult,** suitable for experienced DIY mechanic	**Very difficult,** suitable for expert DIY or professional

Specifications

General

Firing order	1-8-4-3-6-5-7-2
Location of No 1 cylinder	Pulley end left (left as seen from driver's seat - odd numbers on left bank, evens on right)

Distributor

Type	Lucas 35 DLM8
Pick-up air gap	0.20 to 0.35 mm
Pick-up coil resistance	2000 to 5000 ohms

Ignition coil

Primary winding resistance (typical)	0.5 to 1.2 ohms
Secondary resistance (typical)	3000 to 4000 ohms

1 General information and precautions

All models are fitted with the Lucas Constant Energy electronic ignition system, which is a simple distributor-based non-ECU-controlled system, designed to be a direct replacement for the contact breaker systems used on earlier Land Rover models. The system is largely maintenance-free.

The ignition system comprises eight spark plugs, nine HT leads, the distributor, amplifier unit, and an electronic ignition coil, together with its associated wiring.

The electronic ignition functions in a similar manner to a conventional system, but the contact points and condenser are replaced by a magnetic sensor (pick-up) in the distributor and a control unit (amplifier). The amplifier is mounted on the side of the distributor body. As the distributor driveshaft rotates, the magnetic impulses are fed to the amplifier, which switches the primary circuit on and off.

No condenser is necessary, as the circuit is switched electronically with semi-conductor components.

The ignition advance is controlled mechanically by centrifugal weights, and by a vacuum capsule mounted on the side of the distributor.

Precautions

To prevent personal injury and damage to the ignition system, the following precautions must be observed when working on the ignition system. Also refer to the general precautions listed in Chapter 5A, Section 1.

Warning: The HT voltage generated by an electronic ignition system is extremely high and in certain circumstances, could prove fatal. Take care to avoid receiving electric shocks from the HT side of the ignition system. Do not handle HT leads, or touch the distributor or coil, when the engine is running. If tracing faults in the HT circuit, use well-insulated tools to manipulate live leads. Persons with surgically-implanted cardiac pacemaker devices should keep well clear of the ignition circuits, components and test equipment

Do not attempt to disconnect any plug lead or touch any of the HT leads when the engine is running, or being turned by the starter motor.

Ensure that the ignition is turned OFF before disconnecting any of the ignition wiring, or when connecting or disconnecting any ignition testing equipment such as a timing light.

If the HT lead is disconnected from the distributor, the lead must immediately be connected to earth and remain earthed if the engine is to be rotated by the starter motor (for example if a compression test is to be done).

If an electric arc welder is to be used on any part of the vehicle, the vehicle battery must be disconnected while welding is being done.

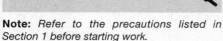

2 Ignition system - testing

Note: *Refer to the precautions listed in Section 1 before starting work.*

General

1 Most ignition system faults are likely to be due to loose or dirty connections, or to tracking (unintentional earthing) of HT voltage due to dirt, dampness or damaged insulation, rather than by the failure of any of the system's components. **Always** check all wiring thoroughly before condemning an electrical component, and work methodically to eliminate all other possibilities before deciding that a particular component is faulty.

2 The old practice of checking for a spark by holding the live end of an HT lead a short distance away from the engine is not recommended; not only is there a high risk of an electric shock, but the HT coil could be damaged. Similarly, **never** try to diagnose misfires by pulling off one HT lead at a time.

Engine will not start

3 If the engine either will not turn over at all, or only turns very slowly, check the battery and starter motor. Connect a voltmeter across the battery terminals (meter positive probe to battery positive terminal), disconnect the ignition coil HT lead from the distributor cap and earth it, then note the voltage reading obtained while turning over the engine on the starter for (no more than) ten seconds. If the reading obtained is less than approximately 9.5 volts, first check the battery, starter motor and charging systems (see Chapter 5A).

4 If the engine turns over at normal speed but will not start, check the HT circuit by connecting a timing light (following its manufacturer's instructions) and turning the engine over on the starter motor; if the light flashes, voltage is reaching the spark plugs, so these should be checked first. If the light does not flash, check the HT leads themselves, followed by the distributor cap, carbon brush and rotor arm.

5 If there is a spark, check the fuel system for faults, referring to the relevant part of Chapter 4 for further information.

6 If there is no spark, switch on the ignition and check for voltage between both coil LT terminals and earth - in both cases, almost battery voltage should be obtained. Also check for voltage between the amplifier mounting screws and earth - almost zero volts should be obtained. Compare the results with the following:

a) If the voltage at both coil terminals is low, check the ignition switch and/or wiring.

b) If the voltage at the coil negative terminal only is low, check the coil and the amplifier module.

c) If a significant voltage is obtained in the amplifier earth test, the amplifier should be removed, checked and cleaned. If there is no improvement, have the amplifier tested by a Land Rover dealer or automotive electrical specialist.

7 Next, switch off the ignition, and connect the voltmeter between the battery positive terminal and the coil negative terminal (wire to amplifier module). With the ignition off, zero volts should be obtained; switch the ignition on, and the reading should still be zero. Now crank the engine, and look for an increase in voltage. If no increase is noted, this indicates that the amplifier module is not switching. Check the pick-up coil as described in paragraph 21 onwards.

8 If there is still no spark, then the problem must lie within the amplifier unit or its wiring, or possibly in the pick-up module inside the distributor (see paragraph 15 onwards).

Engine misfires

9 An irregular misfire suggests either a loose connection or intermittent fault on the primary circuit, or an HT fault on the coil side of the rotor arm.

10 With the ignition switched off, check carefully through the system, ensuring that all connections are clean and securely fastened. If the equipment is available, check the LT circuit as described above.

11 Check that the HT coil, the distributor cap and the HT leads are clean and dry. Check the leads themselves and the spark plugs (by substitution, if necessary), then check the distributor cap, carbon brush and rotor arm.

12 Regular misfiring is almost certainly due to a fault in the distributor cap, HT leads or spark plugs. Use a timing light (paragraph 4 above) to check whether HT voltage is present at all leads.

13 If HT voltage is not present on one particular lead, the fault will be in that lead or in the distributor cap. If HT voltage is present on all leads, the fault will be in the spark plugs; check and renew them if there is any doubt about their condition.

14 If no HT voltage is present, check the HT coil; its secondary windings may be breaking down under load.

Ignition coil

15 With the ignition switched on, and without disconnecting the LT wiring, check for battery voltage at both the LT terminals on the ignition coil.

16 Switch off the ignition, then disconnect the LT wiring plugs and the HT (king) lead from the ignition coil.

17 Connect a multi-meter between terminals 1 (-) and 15 (+), and check the resistance of the primary windings.

18 Connect the multi-meter between terminals 4 (HT) and 15 (+), and check the resistance of the secondary windings.

19 Values for the primary and secondary resistances are not quoted by Land Rover, but those given in the Specifications can be used as a guide.

20 If either reading is substantially different to those quoted, or if an open-circuit or zero result is obtained, the coil is suspect. Remove the coil as described in Section 3 and take it to a Land Rover dealer or automotive electrical specialist to confirm your findings before condemning the coil.

Pick-up coil

21 The pick-up coil is located inside the distributor. The pick-up coil resistance can be checked without dismantling the distributor, as follows.

22 On early models, remove the amplifier from the distributor body, as described in Section 5. On later models, disconnect the wiring plug from the side of the distributor.

23 Connect an ohmmeter between the two pick-up terminals now visible, and compare the resistance measured with that quoted in the Specifications.

24 If the resistance is outside the specified range, dismantle the distributor as described in Section 5, and fit a new pick-up coil.

25 The pick-up air gap can be checked as described in Section 5.

3 Ignition coil - removal and refitting

Removal

1 Disconnect the battery negative lead.

2 Disconnect the HT lead from the coil, pulling on the end fitting, not the lead itself, to avoid damage to the lead **(see illustration)**.

3 Disconnect the LT wiring plugs from the ignition coil, noting the location of each, as they are very similar in appearance **(see illustration)**.

BOSCH

3.2 Disconnect the HT lead from the ignition coil . . .

3.3 . . . followed by the LT wiring

3.4a Remove the coil mounting bolts (one arrowed) . . .

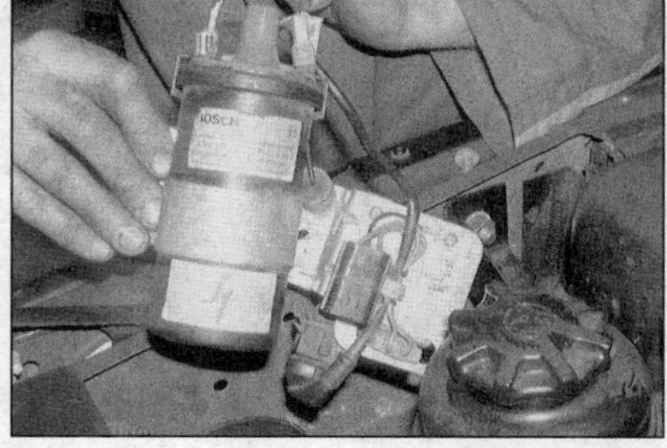
3.4b . . . and remove the coil and amplifier (later model shown)

4.3 Pull off the distributor vacuum pipe

On later models where the amplifier is located on a bracket behind the coil, do not disconnect the amplifier wiring.

4 Remove the two securing bolts, recover the washers, and remove the coil (and on later models, the amplifier) from the engine compartment **(see illustrations)**. Note that one of the bolts has an earth strap underneath it, and on later models, the other bolt secures a suppressor.

5 On later models, if the amplifier module is to be removed from the mounting bracket, unscrew the two mounting nuts, and disconnect the wiring plug and LT connectors.

Refitting

6 Refitting is a reversal of removal. Make sure that the earth strap connection is cleaned thoroughly, and apply a little petroleum jelly to the connection once this has been done.

4 Distributor - removal and refitting

Removal

1 Disconnect the battery negative lead.

2 Drain the cooling system as described in Chapter 1A, and disconnect the top hose from the thermostat housing.

3 Disconnect the vacuum pipe from the vacuum unit **(see illustration)**.

4 On early models, disconnect the low tension lead from the amplifier module on the side of the distributor body. On later models, disconnect the wiring plug from the side of the distributor **(see illustration)**.

5 Release the clip either side, and lift the cap off the top of the distributor.

6 Set the engine to TDC with No 1 piston on compression, as described in Chapter 2A, Section 3.

7 Mark the alignment of the rotor arm to the distributor body, and mark the body of the distributor to show its relationship to the timing cover **(see illustration)**.

8 Undo the clamp plate nut/bolt and remove the plate **(see illustration)**. Access is not easy, and is best achieved from under the power steering pump, using a long extension handle.

9 Withdraw the distributor from the timing cover **(see illustration)**. Note that, as this is done, the rotor arm will turn away from the alignment mark made on the distributor body. If the distributor is not disturbed from this position, when refitted, the arm will turn back to the correct position. If wished, make another mark to indicate the removed position of the rotor arm.

Refitting

10 Fit a new O-ring to the distributor shaft casing **(see illustration)**.

11 If the distributor is in the correct position for refitting, the rotor arm will be 30° anti-clockwise from the mark scribed on the body. This allows the distributor drivegear to engage correctly as the distributor is refitted. As the distributor is pushed home, so the gear will rotate and the marks will be correctly aligned.

4.4 Disconnect the wiring plug from the distributor body

4.7 Paint an alignment mark (arrowed) between the distributor body and timing cover

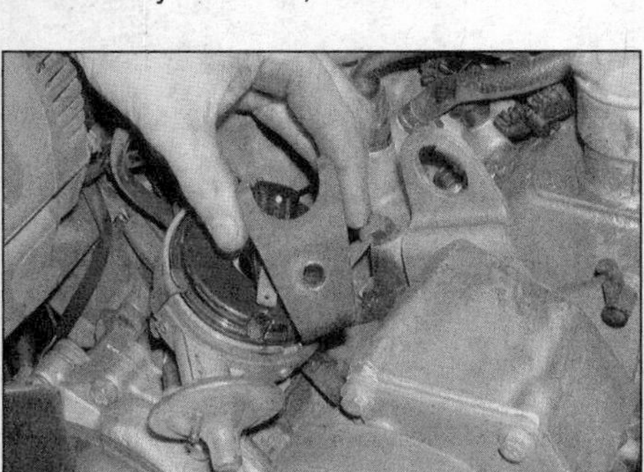
4.8 Remove the distributor clamp plate

4.9 Withdrawing the distributor

4.10 Fit a new O-ring to the distributor shaft

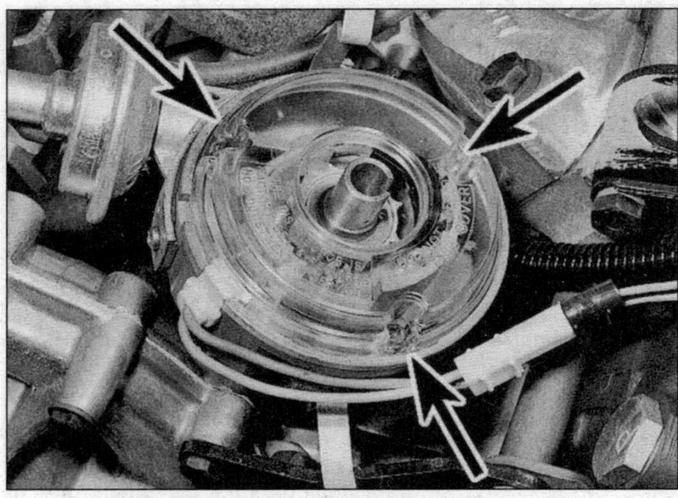

5.2 Flash shield retaining screws (arrowed)

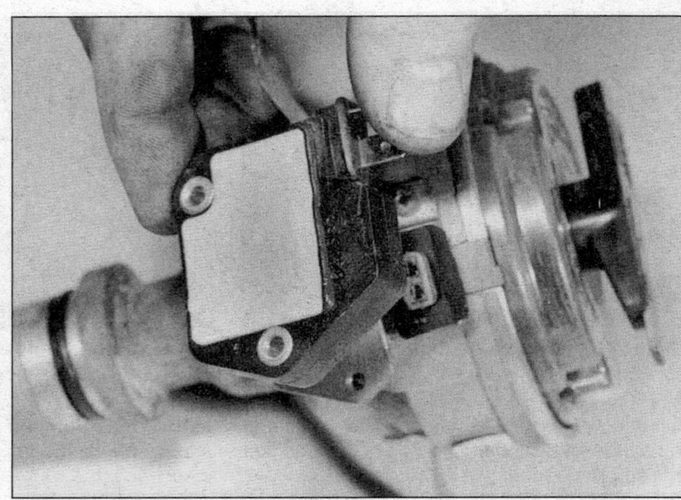

5.4a Removing the amplifier from the side of the distributor . . .

12 If a new distributor is being fitted, identify No 1 cylinder HT lead position on the distributor cap. Using this as a reference, set the rotor arm 30° anti-clockwise from this position. Note that most distributors have a notch cut in the upper rim, which indicates the alignment of the rotor arm with the No 1 cylinder segment.

13 Check that the engine is set to TDC with No 1 on compression, as described in Chapter 2A, Section 3.

14 Check as the distributor is offered up, that the oil pump driveshaft slot is correctly lined up to accept the end of the distributor driveshaft. If it is not in alignment, insert a screwdriver and set it to the correct position.

15 Refit the distributor so that the marks on the body and timing cover correctly aligned (where applicable). Make sure that the rotor arm turns to the No 1 HT lead position - if not, remove the distributor, reset the rotor arm as described in paragraphs 10 and 11, and try again.

16 Fit the clamp plate and nut/bolt, and secure the distributor in its original location.

17 Reconnect the wiring, and the vacuum pipe to the vacuum unit.

18 Refit the distributor cap, securing with the two clips.

19 On completion, reconnect the battery and check the ignition timing as described in Chapter 1A.

5 Distributor - dismantling and reassembly

Dismantling

1 Remove the distributor as described in Section 4.

2 Commence dismantling by withdrawing the rotor arm, then undo the three retaining screws and lift clear the plastic insulation cover (flash shield) **(see illustration)**.

3 Undo the two screws securing the vacuum unit and withdraw the unit, disengaging the connecting rod from the pick-up baseplate peg as it is removed.

4 On early models, unscrew the two screws and withdraw the amplifier from the side of the distributor, together with the gasket. Unscrew the two screws and remove the cast heat sink from the side of the distributor **(see illustrations)**. **Note:** *The amplifier is a sealed unit. No attempt should be made to dismantle it, as it contains beryllia, which is dangerous if handled.*

5 On all models, using a pair of circlip pliers, release the circlip securing the reluctor on the driveshaft, then withdraw the reluctor complete with the flat washer and O-ring. To assist with the removal of the reluctor, insert a small screwdriver blade under it and prise it up the shaft. Note the coupling ring located underneath the reluctor.

6 To remove the pick-up module and baseplate unit, unscrew and remove the three support pillars. Take care not to undo the two barrel nuts - these retain the pick-up module, and if disturbed, the air gap will have to be reset. Do not dismantle the distributor any further.

7 Clean and renew as necessary any items which are worn or suspect.

5.4b . . . followed by the gasket

5.4c Removing the cast heat sink from the side of the distributor

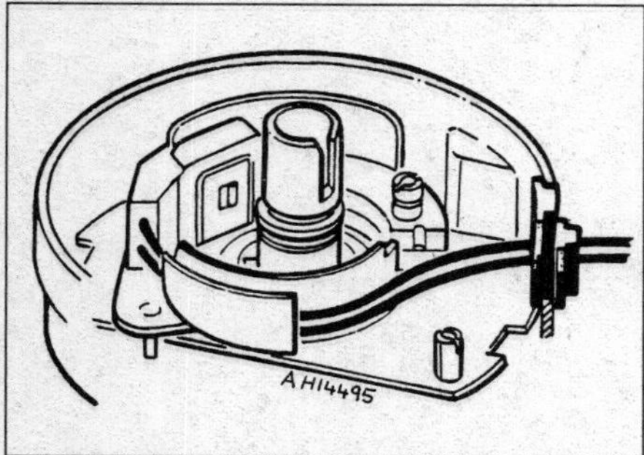
AH14495

5.8 Locate the pick-up wiring in the curved guide channel

Reassembly

8 Reassembly is a reversal of the dismantling procedure, but note the following special points:

a) When refitting the pick-up and baseplate unit, locate the pick-up leads in the curved plastic channel ***(see illustration)****.*

b) When refitting the reluctor, slide it down the shaft as far as possible, then turn the reluctor so that it engages with the coupling ring underneath the baseplate.

c) On early models. before refitting the amplifier, apply MS4 silicone grease or an equivalent heat-conducting compound to the amplifier module backplate, the seating face on the distributor body, and to both faces of the heat sink casting.

d) Apply three drops of clean engine oil to the felt pad in the top end of the rotor shaft.

e) Apply grease to the vacuum unit connecting rod seal (within the unit).

f) Apply grease to the automatic advance mechanism, the pick-up plate centre bearing, pre-tilt spring and contact area, and to the vacuum unit connecting peg and corresponding connecting rod hole.

g) Prior to refitting the insulation cover check, and if necessary adjust, the pick-up air gap as described below.

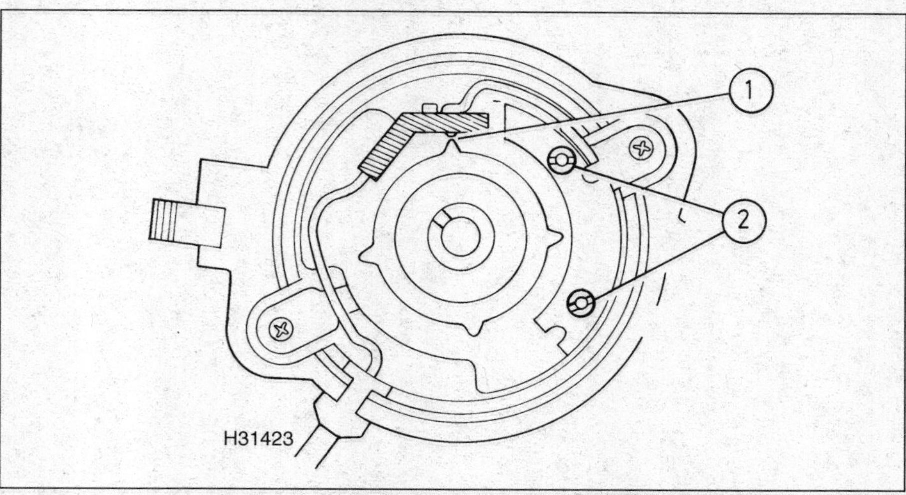
1
2
H31423

5.12 Distributor pick-up air gap adjustment
1 Air gap 2 Barrel nuts

Pick-up air gap adjustment

9 The air gap should only need checking when the distributor has been dismantled - it is not a routine operation.

10 If not already done, remove the distributor cap and rotor arm, then undo the three retaining screws and lift clear the plastic insulation cover (flash shield).

11 The air gap is checked by inserting a non-ferrous feeler gauge of the specified thickness between the pick-up limb and a reluctor tooth. An ordinary (ferrous) feeler gauge will be attracted to the pick-up magnet, making accurate adjustment very difficult.

12 Where adjustment is necessary, loosen the two barrel nuts retaining the pick-up module (these will already be loosened on a new unit) and move the module/pick-up to adjust the gap **(see illustration)**. Retighten the nuts when the gap is correct.

13 Turn the distributor shaft, and check that the air gap remains consistent as all the reluctor teeth pass the pick-up. Re-adjust if necessary.

14 On completion, refit the plastic insulation cover, rotor arm and distributor cap.

Chapter 5 Part C:
Pre-heating system - diesel models

Contents

Degrees of difficulty

Easy, suitable for novice with little experience 	**Fairly easy,** suitable for beginner with some experience 	**Fairly difficult,** suitable for competent DIY mechanic 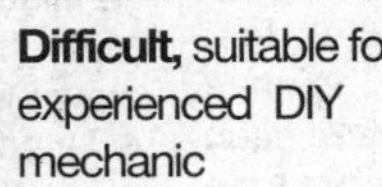	**Difficult,** suitable for experienced DIY mechanic	**Very difficult,** suitable for expert DIY or professional

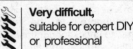

Specifications

Glow plugs		
Type	See Chapter 1B	
Torque wrench setting	**Nm**	**lbf ft**
Glow plugs	23	17

1 General information

Each cylinder has a heater plug (commonly called a glow plug) screwed into it. The plugs are electrically operated before, during, and a short time after, start-up when the engine is cold. Electrical feed to the glow plugs is controlled by the pre-heating control unit.

The glow plugs also provide a post-heating function, whereby the glow plugs remain switched on for a period after the engine has started. The length of time for which the glow plugs are switched on is dependent on underbonnet temperature, which is monitored by a temperature sensor located in the relay/timer unit. The electrical supply to the glow plugs will be interrupted by:

a) Opening of the no-load switch - a microswitch located on the fuel injection pump, which operates when the accelerator is depressed.

b) The signal from the underbonnet temperature sensor when the temperature reaches a predetermined level.

A warning light in the instrument panel tells the driver that pre-heating is taking place. When the light goes out, the engine is ready to be started. The voltage supply to the glow plugs may continue for several seconds after the light goes out. If no attempt is made to start, the timer then cuts off the supply in order to avoid draining the battery and overheating of the glow plugs.

Precautions

The heater plugs draw a very high current, and operate at very high temperatures - certain precautions must be observed when working on the system. Also refer to the general precautions listed in Chapter 5A, Section 1.

Always allow time for the glow plugs to cool before working on the system

Ensure that the battery negative lead is disconnected before working on the system, and that the ignition switch is in the off position, unless otherwise stated. Given the high current required for the system to operate, there is a high risk of damage from short-circuits, possibly even fire. If the glow plug supply cable is disconnected for testing purposes, do not let it short out against the engine or bodywork.

Take great care when trying to verify the operation of a glow plug outside of the engine. A healthy glow plug will rapidly become hot enough to glow red-hot, presenting a significant risk of personal injury and fire if carelessly handled.

2 Pre-heating system - testing

Note: *Refer to the precautions given in Safety first! and in Section 1 of this Chapter before proceeding.*

1 If the system malfunctions, testing is ultimately by substitution of known good units, but some preliminary checks may be made as follows.

2 Connect a voltmeter or 12-volt test light between the glow plug supply cable and earth (engine or vehicle metal). Make sure that the live connection is kept clear of the engine and bodywork.

3 Have an assistant switch on the 'ignition', and check that voltage is applied to the glow plugs. Note the time for which the warning light is lit, and the total time for which voltage is applied before the system cuts out. Switch off the 'ignition'.

4 At an underbonnet temperature of 20°C, typical times noted should be 5 or 6 seconds for warning light operation, followed by a further 4 to 5 seconds' supply after the light goes out (provided that the starter motor is not operated). Warning light time will increase with lower temperatures, and decrease with higher temperatures.

5 If there is no supply at all, the relay or associated wiring is at fault.

6 To locate a defective glow plug, disconnect the main supply cable and the interconnecting wire or strap from the top of the glow plugs. Be careful not to drop the nuts and washers.

7 Use a continuity tester, or a 12-volt test light connected to the battery positive terminal, to check for continuity between each glow plug terminal and earth. The resistance of a glow plug in good condition is very low (less than 1 ohm), so if the test light does not light, or the continuity tester shows a high resistance, the glow plug is certainly defective.

8 If an ammeter is available, the current draw of each glow plug can be checked. After an initial surge of around 15 to 20 amps, each plug should draw around 10 amps. Any plug which draws much more or less than this is probably defective.

9 As a final check, the glow plugs can be removed and inspected as described in Section 3.

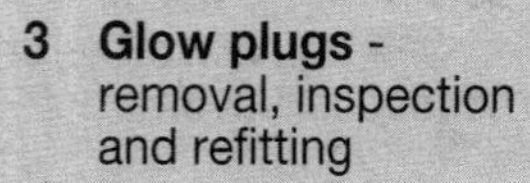

3 Glow plugs - removal, inspection and refitting

Removal

Caution: If the pre-heating system has just been energised, or if the engine has been running, the glow plugs may be very hot. Allow the system to cool before proceeding.

Note: *Refer to the precautions given in Safety first! and in Section 1 of this Chapter before proceeding. Where applicable, a new crankcase ventilation valve O-ring will be required on refitting - see text.*

1 Disconnect the battery negative lead.

2 If the No 1 cylinder (timing belt end glow plug is to be removed on 300 TDi engine models with air conditioning, proceed as follows:

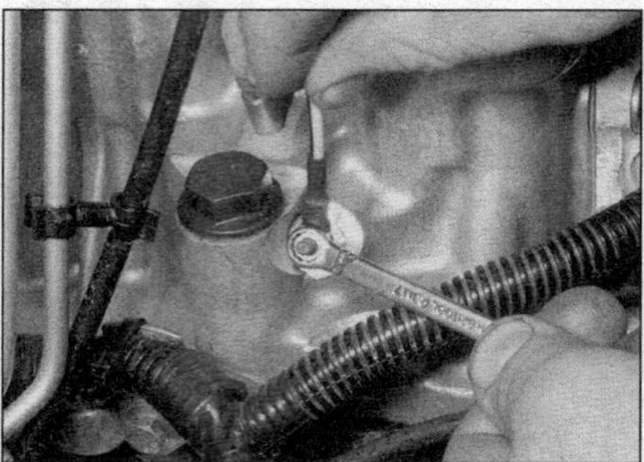

3.4 Unscrewing a glow plug wiring nut

a) Remove the air conditioning compressor drivebelt, as described in Chapter 1B, Section 17.

b) Remove the four securing bolts, and move the compressor to one side, to provide access to the glow plug. DO NOT disconnect the refrigerant lines from the compressor (see Chapter 3).

3 If the No 3 cylinder glow plug is to be removed on 300 TDi engine models, remove the securing bolt, and withdraw the crankcase ventilation system valve from the valve cover. Move the valve to one side for access to the glow plug.

4 Unscrew the nut from the relevant glow plug terminal, and recover the washer **(see illustration)**.

5 Disconnect the wiring, noting the routing if all the glow plugs are to be removed.

6 Unscrew the glow plug, and remove it from the cylinder head **(see illustration)**.

Inspection

7 Inspect the glow plugs for physical damage. Burnt or eroded glow plug tips can be caused by a bad injector spray pattern. Have the injectors checked if this sort of damage is found.

8 If the glow plugs are in good physical condition, check them electrically using a 12-volt test light or continuity tester as described in Section 2.

9 The glow plugs can be energised by applying 12 volts to them to verify that they heat up evenly and in the required time. Observe the following precautions:

4.3 Disconnecting the wiring plug from the preheating system relay/timer unit - 300 TDi engine model

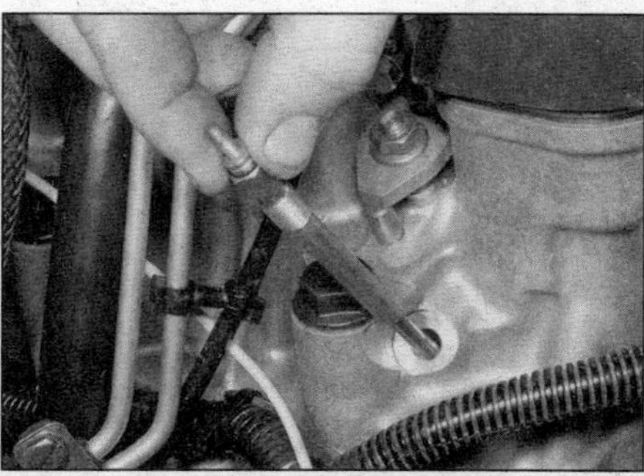

3.6 Removing a glow plug - 300 TDi engine

a) Support the glow plug by clamping it carefully in a vice or self-locking pliers. Remember, it will become red-hot.

b) Make sure that the power supply or test lead incorporates a fuse or overload trip, to protect against damage from a short-circuit.

c) After testing, allow the glow plug to cool for several minutes before attempting to handle it.

10 A glow plug in good condition will start to glow red at the tip after drawing current for 5 seconds or so. Any plug which takes much longer to start glowing, or which starts glowing in the middle instead of at the tip, is defective.

Refitting

11 Refitting is a reversal of removal, bearing in mind the following points:

a) Apply a smear of copper-based anti-seize compound to the plug threads, and tighten the glow plugs to the specified torque. Do not overtighten, as this can damage the glow plug element.

b) Ensure that the glow plug wiring is routed as noted before removal.

c) Where applicable, use a new O-ring, lubricated with clean engine oil, when refitting the crankcase ventilation valve.

d) Where applicable, refit and tension the air conditioning compressor drivebelt as described in Chapter 1B, Section 17.

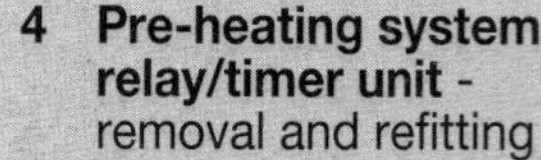

4 Pre-heating system relay/timer unit - removal and refitting

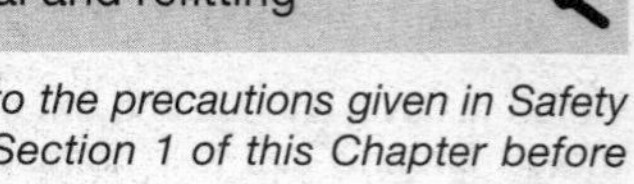

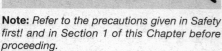

Note: *Refer to the precautions given in Safety first! and in Section 1 of this Chapter before proceeding.*

Removal

1 On 200 TDi engine models, the relay/timer unit is located on the right-hand side of the engine compartment bulkhead. On 300 TDi engine models, the unit is located on the right-hand side of the engine compartment, on a bracket attached to the rear of the fusebox.

2 Disconnect the battery negative lead.

3 Disconnect the wiring plug from the relay/timer unit **(see illustration)**.

4 Unscrew the bolt, or the nut and bolt, as applicable, and withdraw the unit.

Refitting

5 Refitting is a reversal of removal.

5 Stop solenoid - description, removal and refitting

Description

1 The stop solenoid is located on the end of the fuel injection pump. Its purpose is to cut the fuel supply when the 'ignition' is switched off. If an open-circuit occurs in the solenoid or supply wiring, it will be impossible to start the engine, as the fuel will not reach the injectors. The same applies if the solenoid plunger jams in the stop position. If the solenoid jams in the run position, the engine will not stop when the 'ignition' is switched off.

2 If the solenoid has failed and the engine will not run, a temporary repair may be made by removing the solenoid as described in the following paragraphs. Refit the solenoid body without the plunger and spring. Tape up the wire so that it cannot touch earth. The engine can now be started as usual, but it will be necessary to use the manual stop lever on the fuel injection pump (or to stall the engine in gear) to stop it.

Removal

Caution : Be careful not to allow dirt into the injection pump during this procedure. A new sealing washer or O-ring must be used on refitting.

Note: *Refer to the precautions given in Safety first! and in Section 1 of this Chapter before proceeding.*

3 Disconnect the battery negative lead.

4 Withdraw the rubber boot (where applicable), then unscrew the terminal nut and disconnect the wire from the top of the solenoid **(see illustration)**.

5 Carefully clean around the solenoid, then unscrew and withdraw the solenoid, and recover the sealing washer or O-ring (as applicable). Recover the solenoid plunger and spring if they remain in the pump. Operate the hand-priming lever on the fuel lift pump as the solenoid is removed, to flush away any dirt.

5.4 Stop solenoid location (arrowed) in the rear of the injection pump

Refitting

6 Refitting is a reversal of removal, using a new sealing washer or O-ring.

Chapter 6
Clutch

Contents

Degrees of difficulty

Easy, suitable for novice with little experience 	**Fairly easy,** suitable for beginner with some experience 	**Fairly difficult,** suitable for competent DIY mechanic 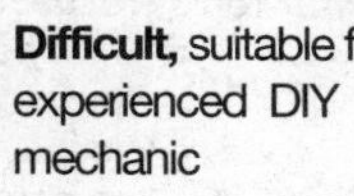	**Difficult,** suitable for experienced DIY mechanic	**Very difficult,** suitable for expert DIY or professional

Specifications

General

Clutch type	Single dry plate, diaphragm spring, hydraulically-operated
Adjustment	Automatic
Hydraulic fluid type	See end of *Weekly checks*

Clutch disc

Diameter:	
Petrol models	267 mm
Diesel models	235 mm

Torque wrench settings

	Nm	lbf ft
Clutch cover bolts	28	21
Clutch slave cylinder bolts	25	18
Hydraulic fluid pipe and hose unions	15	11

1 General information

All manual transmission models are fitted with a single dry plate clutch, which consists of five main components - friction disc, pressure plate, diaphragm spring, cover, and release bearing.

The friction disc is free to slide along the splines of the transmission input shaft, and is held in position between the flywheel and the pressure plate by the pressure exerted on the pressure plate by the diaphragm spring. Friction lining material is riveted to both sides of the friction disc, and spring cushioning between the friction linings and the hub absorbs transmission shocks, and helps to ensure a smooth take-up of power as the clutch is engaged.

The diaphragm spring is mounted on pins, and is held in place in the cover by annular fulcrum rings.

The release bearing is located on a guide sleeve at the front of the transmission, and the bearing is free to slide on the sleeve, under the action of the release arm which pivots inside the clutch bellhousing.

The release mechanism is operated by the clutch pedal, using hydraulic pressure. The pedal acts on the hydraulic master cylinder pushrod, and a slave cylinder, mounted on the transmission bellhousing, operates the clutch release lever via a pushrod.

On diesel models, a hydraulic damper is fitted between the master cylinder and the slave cylinder. The damper absorbs the small fluctuations in hydraulic pressure caused by slight variations in engine speed at low rpm.

When the clutch pedal is depressed, the release arm pushes the release bearing forwards, to bear against the centre of the diaphragm spring, thus pushing the centre of the diaphragm spring inwards. The diaphragm spring acts against the fulcrum rings in the cover, and so as the centre of the spring is pushed in, the outside of the spring is pushed out, so allowing the pressure plate to move backwards away from the friction disc.

When the clutch pedal is released, the diaphragm spring forces the pressure plate into contact with the friction linings on the friction disc, and simultaneously pushes the friction disc forwards on its splines, forcing it against the flywheel. The friction disc is now firmly sandwiched between the pressure plate and the flywheel, and drive is taken up.

The clutch is self-adjusting. As wear takes place on the friction disc over a period of time, the pressure plate automatically moves closer to the friction plate to compensate.

2 Clutch assembly - removal, inspection and refitting

Warning: Dust created by clutch wear and deposited on the clutch components may contain asbestos, which is a health hazard. DO NOT blow it out with compressed air, or inhale any of it. DO NOT use petrol (or petroleum-based solvents) to clean off the dust. Brake system cleaner or methylated spirit should be used to flush the dust into a suitable receptacle. After

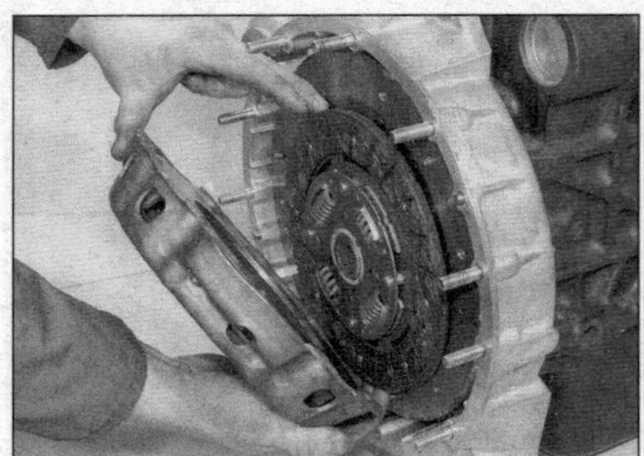

2.4 Withdrawing the clutch cover and friction disc

FWSIDE

2.11 FW SIDE mark on clutch friction disc

2.12 The pressure plate assembly locates on dowels (arrowed)

the clutch components are wiped clean with rags, dispose of the contaminated rags and cleaner in a sealed, marked container.

Removal

1 Remove the transmission, as described in Chapter 7A, or the engine, as described in Chapter 2C. Note that if no other work is to be carried out on the transmission, it is far simpler to remove the engine.

2 If the original clutch is to be refitted, make alignment marks between the clutch cover and the flywheel, so that the clutch can be refitted in its original position.

3 Progressively unscrew the bolts securing the clutch cover to the flywheel, and recover the washers. Do not disturb the three bolts located in the side of the clutch cover.

4 Withdraw the clutch cover from the flywheel. Be prepared to catch the clutch friction disc, which may drop out of the cover as it is withdrawn, and note which way round the friction disc is fitted **(see illustration)**. The greater projecting side of the hub faces the flywheel.

Inspection

5 With the clutch assembly removed, clean off all traces of dust using a dry cloth. Although most friction discs now have asbestos-free linings, some do not, and it is wise to take suitable precautions; *asbestos dust is harmful, and must not be inhaled.*

6 Examine the linings of the clutch disc for wear and loose rivets, and the disc for distortion, cracks, broken torsion springs, and worn splines. The surface of the friction linings may be highly glazed, but, as long as the friction material pattern can be clearly seen, this is satisfactory. The disc must be renewed if the lining thickness has worn down to, or just above, the level of the rivet heads.

7 If there is any sign of oil contamination, indicated by a continuous, or patchy, shiny black discolouration, the disc must be renewed. The source of the contamination must be traced and rectified before fitting new clutch components; typically, a leaking crankshaft rear oil seal or transmission input shaft oil seal - or both - will be to blame (renewal procedures are given in the relevant part of Chapter 2 and Chapter 7A respectively).

8 Check the machined faces of the flywheel and pressure plate. If either is grooved, or heavily scored, renewal is necessary. The pressure plate must also be renewed if any cracks are apparent, or if the diaphragm spring is damaged or its pressure suspect.

9 With the clutch removed, it is advisable to check the condition of the release bearing, as described in Section 3. It is considered good practice to renew the release bearing at the same time as the rest of the clutch components, given the amount of work necessary to gain access to it.

Refitting

10 It is important to ensure that no oil or grease gets onto the friction disc linings, or the pressure plate and flywheel faces. It is advisable to refit the clutch assembly with clean hands, and to wipe down the pressure plate and flywheel faces with a clean rag before assembly begins.

11 Apply a smear of molybdenum disulphide grease to the splines of the friction disc hub, then offer the disc to the flywheel, with the greater projecting side of the hub facing the flywheel (most friction discs will have a Flywheel Side or FW SIDE marking, which should face the flywheel) **(see illustration)**. Hold the friction disc against the flywheel while the cover/pressure plate assembly is offered into position.

12 Fit the clutch cover assembly, where applicable aligning the marks on the flywheel and clutch cover. Insert the securing bolts and washers, and tighten them finger-tight, so that the friction disc is gripped, but can still be moved. Note that pressure plate assembly locates on dowels **(see illustration)**.

13 The friction disc must now be centralised, so that when the engine and transmission are mated, the transmission input shaft splines will pass through the splines in the friction disc hub.

14 Ideally, a dedicated clutch aligning tool should be used, as this will eliminate much of the guesswork **(see illustrations)**. Centralisation can be carried out by inserting a round bar or a long screwdriver through the hole in the centre of the friction disc, so that the end of the bar rests in the spigot bearing in the centre of the crankshaft. Where possible, use a blunt instrument; if a screwdriver is used, wrap tape around the blade, to prevent damage to the bearing surface.

15 Moving the bar sideways or up and down as necessary, move the friction disc in whichever direction is necessary to achieve centralisation. With the bar removed, view the friction disc hub in relation to the hole in the centre of the crankshaft and the circle created by the ends of the diaphragm spring fingers. When the hub appears exactly in the centre, all is correct.

16 Tighten the cover retaining bolts gradually in a diagonal sequence, to the specified torque. Remove the alignment tool.

17 Refit the transmission or engine, as applicable, as described in Chapter 7A or Chapter 2C respectively.

2.14a Using a clutch alignment tool . . .

2.14b . . . to centre the friction disc

3.3 Sliding the clutch release bearing from the guide sleeve

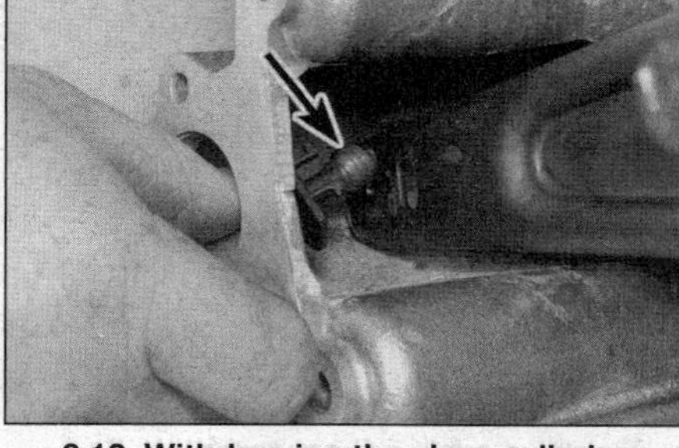

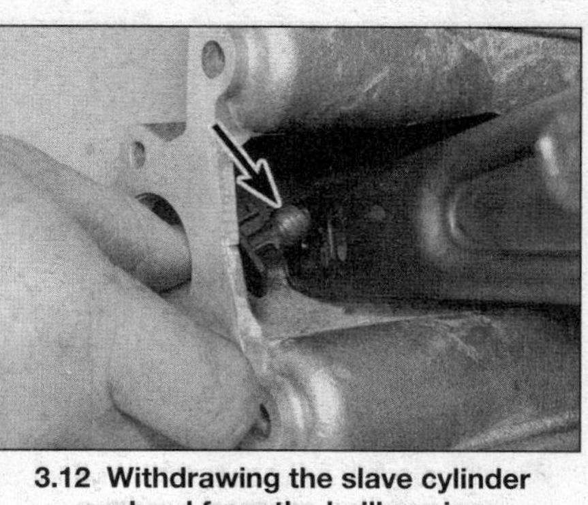

3.12 Withdrawing the slave cylinder pushrod from the bellhousing

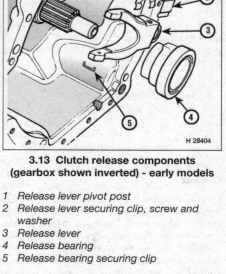

1
2
3
4
5
H 28404

3.13 Clutch release components (gearbox shown inverted) - early models

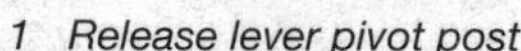

1 Release lever pivot post
2 Release lever securing clip, screw and washer
3 Release lever
4 Release bearing
5 Release bearing securing clip

3 Clutch release bearing and lever - removal, inspection and refitting

Release bearing

Removal

1 Remove the transmission, as described in Chapter 7A, or the engine, as described in Chapter 2C. Note that if no other work is to be carried out on the transmission, it is far simpler to remove the engine.

2 Where applicable, remove the clip securing the release bearing assembly to the release lever. Note that the clip is used to hold the bearing in position when mating the engine and transmission in production - the clip may fall out or become dislodged with no adverse effects.

3 Slide the bearing assembly from the guide sleeve **(see illustration)**.

4 On certain models, the bearing is attached to a separate retaining sleeve, and if the bearing is to be renewed, it must be pressed from the sleeve.

Inspection

5 Spin the release bearing, and check it for excessive roughness. Hold the outer race, and attempt to move it laterally against the inner race. If any excessive movement or roughness is evident, renew the bearing. If a new clutch has been fitted, it is wise to renew the release bearing as a matter of course.

Refitting

6 On models with a separate bearing retaining sleeve, if a new bearing is to be fitted, press the new bearing onto the retaining sleeve. Note that the domed face of the bearing must face away from the sleeve (the domed face acts on the clutch pressure plate).

7 Lightly smear the outer faces of the release bearing guide sleeve with molybdenum disulphide grease.

8 Slide the bearing assembly onto the guide sleeve, ensuring that the guide slippers on the release arm engage with the release bearing collar.

9 Where applicable, refit the clip securing the release bearing assembly to the release lever.

10 Refit the transmission or engine, as applicable, as described in Chapter 7A or Chapter 2C respectively.

Release lever

Removal

11 Remove the release bearing, as described previously in this Section, and the slave cylinder, as described in Section 4 (note that if the transmission is in position in the vehicle, there is no need to disconnect the hydraulic fluid pipe from the slave cylinder - move the slave cylinder to one side, leaving the pipe connected).

12 Unclip the slave cylinder pushrod from the end of the release lever, and withdraw the pushrod through the bellhousing **(see illustration)**.

13 Where applicable, remove the securing screw (and washer), and prise off the clip securing the release lever to the pivot post. Note that the clip locates behind the washer on the pivot post **(see illustration)**.

14 On models where there is no screw securing the release lever clip, pull the release lever out, and slide it towards the release bearing guide sleeve to release the clip from the pivot post.

15 Withdraw the release lever from the bellhousing, and (where applicable) recover the release bearing guide slippers **(see illustrations)**.

Refitting

16 Where applicable, ensure that the release bearing guide slippers are in position on the release lever.

17 Apply a little high-melting-point grease to the contact faces of the pivot post and the release lever **(see illustration)**.

18 Manipulate the release lever into position on the pivot post, and engage the securing clip. Where applicable, ensure that the

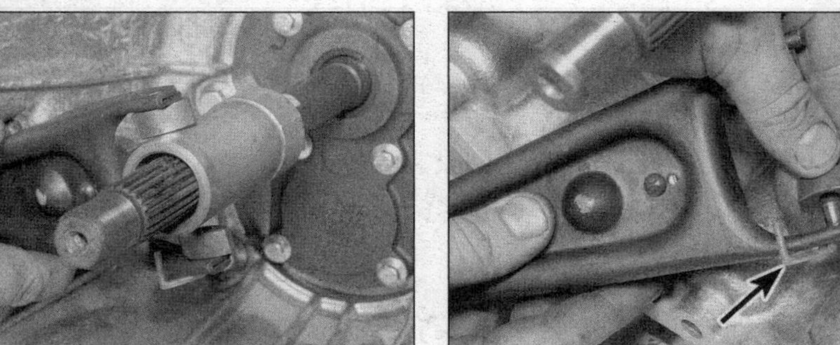

3.15a Withdraw the release lever . . .

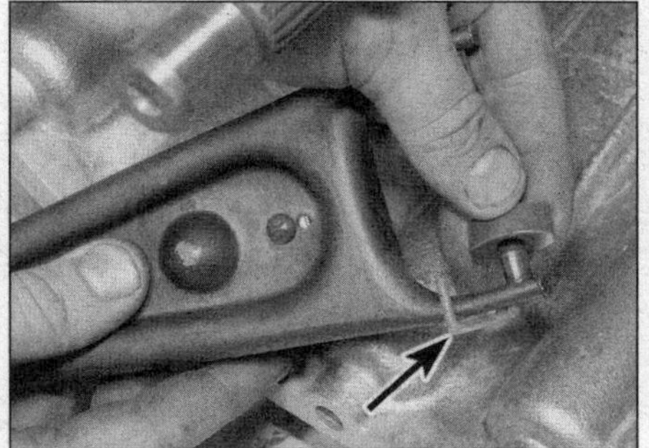

3.15b . . . and recover the release bearing guide slippers. Note release bearing securing clip (arrowed)

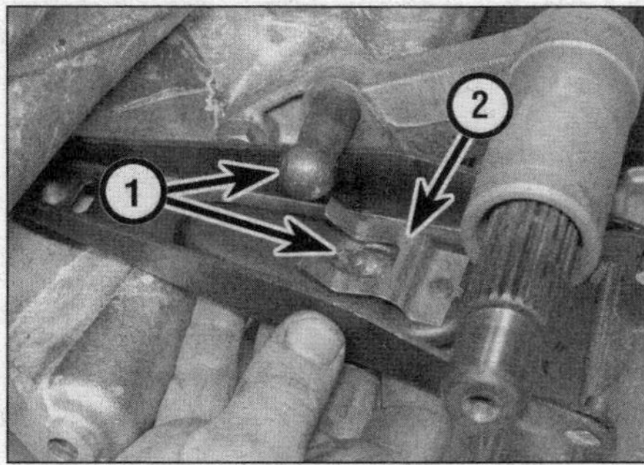

1
2

3.17 Apply high-melting-point grease to the contact faces (1). Note release lever securing clip (2)

securing clip locates behind the washer on the pivot post.

19 Where applicable, refit the securing screw and washer to the release lever securing clip.

20 Refit the slave cylinder pushrod to the end of the release arm, ensuring that the securing clip is engaged.

21 Refit the release bearing as described previously in this Section, and the slave cylinder as described in Section 4.

4 Hydraulic slave cylinder - removal, overhaul and refitting

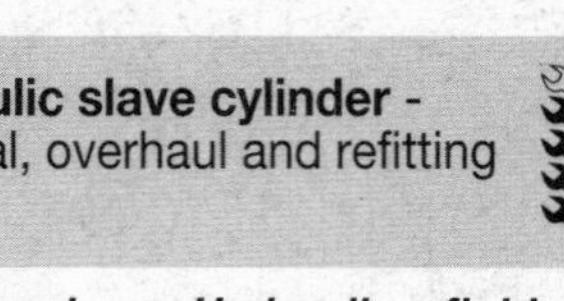

Warning: Hydraulic fluid is poisonous; wash off immediately and thoroughly in the case of skin contact, and seek immediate medical advice if any fluid is swallowed or gets into the eyes. Certain types of hydraulic fluid are inflammable, and may ignite when allowed into contact with hot components; when servicing any hydraulic system, it is safest to assume that the fluid IS inflammable, and to take precautions against the risk of fire as though it is petrol that is being handled. Finally, it is hygroscopic (it absorbs moisture from the air) - old fluid may be contaminated and unfit for further use. When topping-up or renewing the fluid, always use the recommended type, and ensure that it comes from a freshly-opened sealed container.

HAYNES
HiNT

Hydraulic fluid is an effective paint stripper, and will attack plastics; if any is spilt, it should be washed off immediately, using copious quantities of fresh water.

Removal

Note: *Suitable jointing compound will be required to coat the mating faces of the slave cylinder mounting plate on refitting.*

1 Disconnect the battery negative lead.

2 To reduce fluid spillage, drain the clutch hydraulic system. Follow the procedure described in Section 7 for bleeding the hydraulic system, but do not top-up the fluid reservoir. Pump the clutch pedal until all the hydraulic fluid has been expelled from the bleed screw.

3 Unscrew the union nuts, and remove the hydraulic fluid pipe which connects the slave cylinder to the hydraulic damper.

4 Unscrew the two securing bolts, and withdraw the slave cylinder and the mounting plate from the transmission bellhousing **(see illustration)**. Note that the bolts also secure the hydraulic damper mounting bracket - move the assembly to one side, taking care not to strain the hydraulic hose. Recover the slave cylinder pushrod if it is loose.

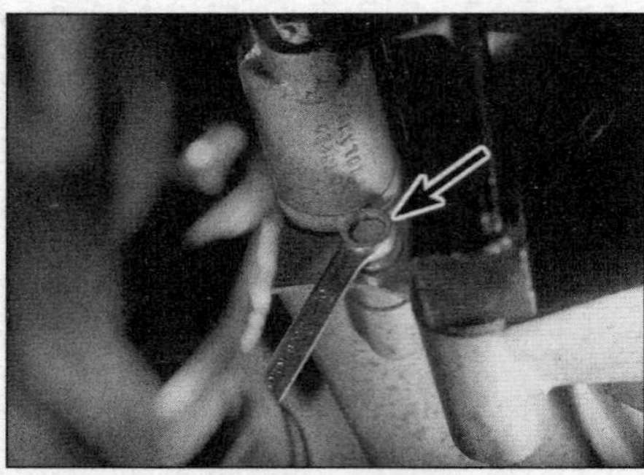

4.4 Unscrewing a clutch slave cylinder securing bolt (arrowed)

5 Both sides of the mounting plate are coated with jointing compound - if necessary, carefully separate the components, taking care not to damage the mating faces or the dust cover.

Overhaul

Note: *Before dismantling the slave cylinder, check on the availability of spares, and ensure that the appropriate overhaul kit is obtained. Suitable rubber grease will be required to pack the dust cover on refitting.*

6 With the slave cylinder removed, as described previously in this Section, thoroughly clean the exterior of the assembly, then proceed as follows.

7 If not already done, withdraw the dust cover and the pushrod from the end of the cylinder.

8 Using a suitable pair of circlip pliers, remove the piston retaining circlip from the cylinder bore **(see illustration)**.

9 Extract the piston and seal assembly from the cylinder bore. If necessary, tap the cylinder body on a clean wooden surface to dislodge the components - alternatively, apply low-pressure air (such as from a tyre foot-pump) to the fluid inlet to eject the components.

10 Prise the seal from the groove in the piston.

11 Withdraw the spring from the cylinder bore.

12 Unscrew the bleed screw from the rear of the cylinder.

13 Clean all the components thoroughly, using clean fresh hydraulic fluid, and dry them using a clean, lint-free cloth. Check that the fluid inlet port is free from obstructions.

14 Examine the cylinder bore, which must be free from corrosion, scoring and ridges. Similarly, examine the piston. If either the cylinder bore or the piston show signs of damage or wear, the complete assembly must be renewed.

15 Refit the bleed screw to the cylinder. Take care not to overtighten the screw.

16 Lubricate the new seal, the piston and the cylinder bore with clean, fresh hydraulic fluid.

17 Fit the seal to the groove in the piston, noting that the larger diameter of the seal should face towards the rear (fluid inlet end) of the cylinder.

18 Push the spring and piston assembly to the cylinder bore (using a wooden dowel if necessary), ensuring that the piston seal does not fold back. Note that the smaller diameter of the piston should seat against the spring.

19 Secure the piston assembly with the circlip.

20 Fill the dust cover with suitable rubber grease, then fit the dust cover to the groove in the end of the cylinder.

21 Where applicable, feed the pushrod through the dust cover, ensuring that the pushrod engages with the piston.

22 Refit the assembly as described in the following paragraphs.

Refitting

23 Commence refitting by cleaning all traces of sealant from the mating faces of the mounting plate, slave cylinder and bellhousing.

24 Coat both sides of the mounting plate with suitable jointing compound.

25 Fit the mounting plate to the slave cylinder. Where applicable, also fit the dust cover, ensuring that it engages with the groove in the slave cylinder.

26 Manipulate the slave cylinder into position in the bellhousing, and feed the pushrod through the slave cylinder dust cover,

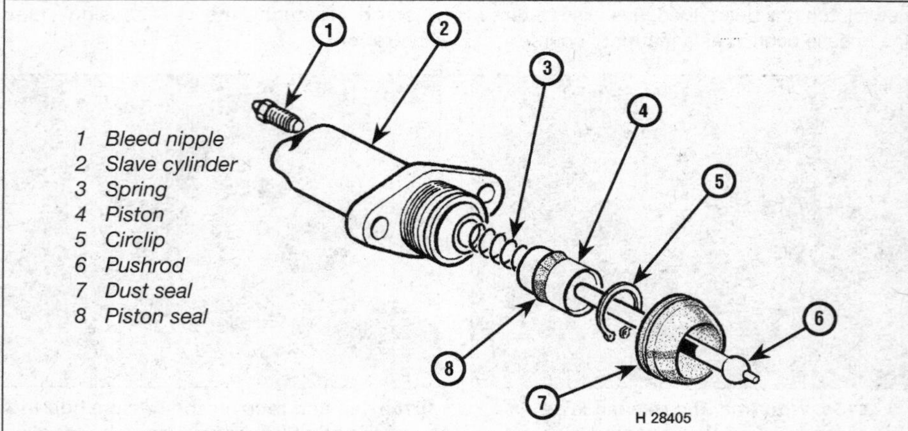
1 Bleed nipple
2 Slave cylinder
3 Spring
4 Piston
5 Circlip
6 Pushrod
7 Dust seal
8 Piston seal
1
2
3
4
5
6
7
8
H 28405

4.8 Slave cylinder components

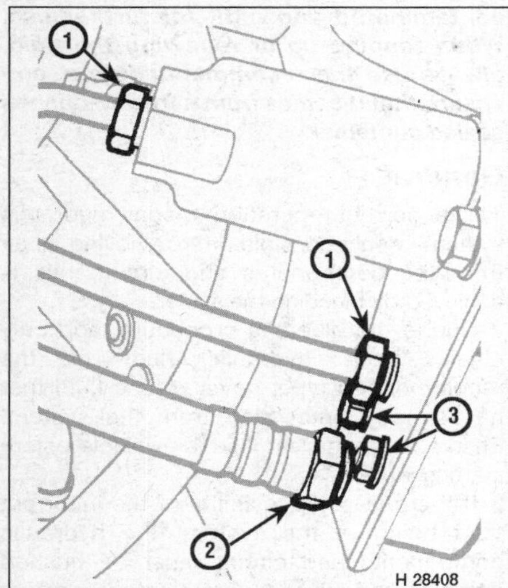
1
1
3
2
H 28408

5.3 Clutch hydraulic damper

1 Fluid pipe unions
2 Fluid hose union
3 Damper securing bolts

ensuring that the pushrod engages with the slave cylinder piston. Note that the slave cylinder should be fitted with the bleed screw uppermost.

27 Ensure that the hydraulic damper mounting bracket is in position, then refit and tighten the slave cylinder securing bolts.

28 Refit the slave cylinder-to-hydraulic damper fluid pipe, and tighten the union nuts.

29 Refill the clutch hydraulic fluid reservoir, and bleed the hydraulic system as described in Section 7.

30 Reconnect the battery negative lead.

5 Hydraulic damper (diesel models) - removal and refitting

Warning: Refer to the warning at the beginning of Section 4 before proceeding.

Removal

1 Proceed as described in Section 4, paragraphs 1 to 3.

2 Unscrew the union nut and disconnect the fluid hose from the damper.

3 Unscrew the two bolts securing the damper to the bracket, and withdraw the damper **(see illustration)**.

Refitting

4 Refitting is a reversal of removal, but on completion, refill the clutch hydraulic fluid reservoir, and bleed the hydraulic system as described in Section 7.

6 Master cylinder - removal, overhaul and refitting

Warning: Refer to the warning at the beginning of Section 4 before proceeding.

Removal

1 Disconnect the battery negative lead.

2 Drain the clutch hydraulic system. Follow the procedure described in Section 7 for bleeding the hydraulic system, but do not top-up the fluid reservoir. Pump the clutch pedal until all the hydraulic fluid has been expelled from the bleed screw.

3 Unscrew the union nut, and disconnect the fluid pipe from the master cylinder. Plug the open ends of the master cylinder and the pipe, to prevent dirt ingress.

4 Working inside the vehicle, release the securing clips and withdraw the driver's side lower facia panel for access to the clutch pedal assembly.

5 The clevis pin securing the master cylinder pushrod to the pedal must now be removed. The clevis pin may be secured by a spring clip, or by a nut and washer. Prise off the spring clip, or unscrew the securing nut (as applicable), and withdraw the clevis pin **(see illustration)**. Where applicable, recover the washer and bushes from the clevis pin, noting their locations.

6 Working in the engine compartment, unscrew the two securing bolts and recover the washers, then withdraw the master cylinder.

Overhaul

Note: *Before dismantling the master cylinder, check on the availability of spares, and ensure that the appropriate overhaul kit is obtained. Suitable rubber grease will be required to pack the dust cover on refitting.*

7 With the master cylinder removed as described previously in this Section, thoroughly clean the exterior of the assembly, then proceed as follows.

8 Pull back the dust cover from the end of the cylinder **(see illustration)**.

9 Depress the pushrod into the cylinder, then using a suitable pair of circlip pliers, extract the pushrod retaining circlip from the cylinder bore.

10 Withdraw the pushrod, complete with the dust cover, circlip and washer.

11 Remove the dust cover from the pushrod.

12 Withdraw the piston assembly and spring.

13 Prise the spring seat from the rear of the piston assembly, then remove the rear seal and the shim.

14 Prise the front seal from the piston.

15 Clean all the components thoroughly, using clean fresh hydraulic fluid, and dry them using a clean, lint-free cloth. Check that the fluid ports are free from obstructions.

16 Examine the cylinder bore, which must be free from corrosion, scoring and ridges. Similarly, examine the piston. If either the cylinder bore or the piston show signs of damage or wear, the complete assembly must be renewed.

17 Clean the fluid reservoir cap, and check

6.5 Master cylinder pushrod-to-clutch pedal clevis pin spring clip (arrowed)

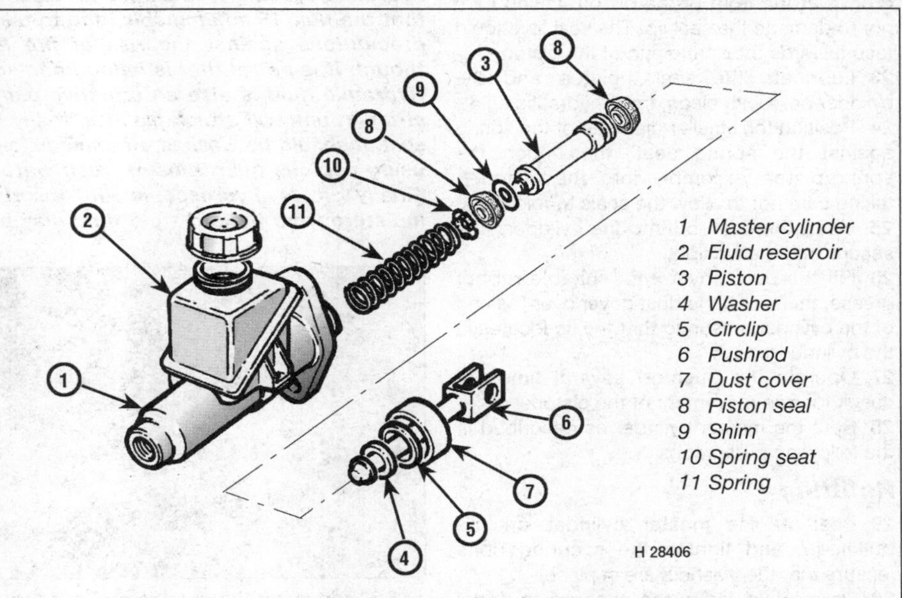
1 Master cylinder
2 Fluid reservoir
3 Piston
4 Washer
5 Circlip
6 Pushrod
7 Dust cover
8 Piston seal
9 Shim
10 Spring seat
11 Spring
H 28406

6.8 Clutch master cylinder components

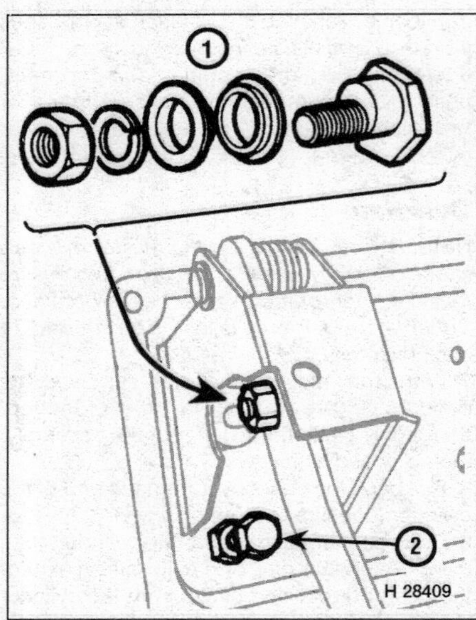
1
2
H 28409

6.31 Clutch master cylinder pushrod-to-pedal clevis pin details - early models

1 Clevis pin components
2 Pedal stop-bolt

that the vent hole in the cap is free from obstructions.
18 Fit the new dust cover to the pushrod.
19 Check that the three holes in the rear of the piston are unobstructed, then fit the new shim to the rear of the piston.
20 Fit the thinner of the two new seals to the rear of the piston, with the flat side of the seal against the shim.
21 Fit the spring seat to the end of the piston (larger diameter against the seal), ensuring that the seat locates in the piston groove.
22 Carefully fit the remaining seal to the groove at the front of the piston, taking care not to damage the seal lip. The seal lip should face towards the spring end of the piston.
23 Lubricate the seals, piston and the cylinder bore with clean, fresh hydraulic fluid.
24 Position the smaller diameter of the spring against the spring seat, then push the spring/piston assembly into the cylinder, taking care not to allow the seals to fold back.
25 Insert the pushrod into the cylinder, and secure with the circlip.
26 Fill the dust cover with suitable rubber grease, then push the dust cover over the end of the cylinder, ensuring that the lip locates in the cylinder groove.
27 Operate the pushrod several times to check for free movement of the piston.
28 Refit the master cylinder as described in the following paragraphs.

Refitting

29 Position the master cylinder on the bulkhead, and tighten the securing bolts (ensure that the washers are in place).
30 On models where the pushrod-to-pedal clevis pin is secured by a spring clip, refit the clevis pin, and secure with the spring clip. Proceed to paragraph 32.
31 On models where the pushrod-to-pedal clevis pin is secured by a nut, proceed as follows **(see illustration)**:

a) Connect the pushrod to the pedal, and refit the clevis pin. Position the bushes as noted before removal. Refit the washer and nut, but do not tighten the nut at this stage.
b) Turn the clevis pin (the pin has an eccentric shank) until the clutch pedal rests at the same height as the brake pedal, then tighten the clevis pin nut.
c) Loosen the locknut on the clutch pedal stop-bolt, and back off the stop-bolt (turn the bolt clockwise).
d) Fully depress the clutch pedal, then unscrew the stop-bolt until it just touches the pedal. Unscrew the stop-bolt one further turn, then tighten the locknut.

32 Refit the lower facia panel.
33 Reconnect the fluid pipe to the master cylinder, and tighten the union nut.
34 Refill the fluid reservoir and bleed the hydraulic system as described in Section 7.
35 Reconnect the battery negative lead.

7 Hydraulic system - bleeding

Warning: Hydraulic fluid is poisonous; wash off immediately and thoroughly in the case of skin contact, and seek immediate medical advice if any fluid is swallowed or gets into the eyes. Certain types of hydraulic fluid are inflammable, and may ignite when allowed into contact with hot components; when servicing any hydraulic system, it is safest to assume that the fluid IS inflammable, and to take precautions against the risk of fire as though it is petrol that is being handled. Hydraulic fluid is also an effective paint stripper, and will attack plastics; if any is spilt, it should be washed off immediately, using copious quantities of fresh water. Finally, it is hygroscopic (it absorbs moisture from the air) - old fluid may be contaminated and unfit for further use. When topping-up or renewing the fluid, always use the recommended type, and ensure that it comes from a freshly-opened sealed container.

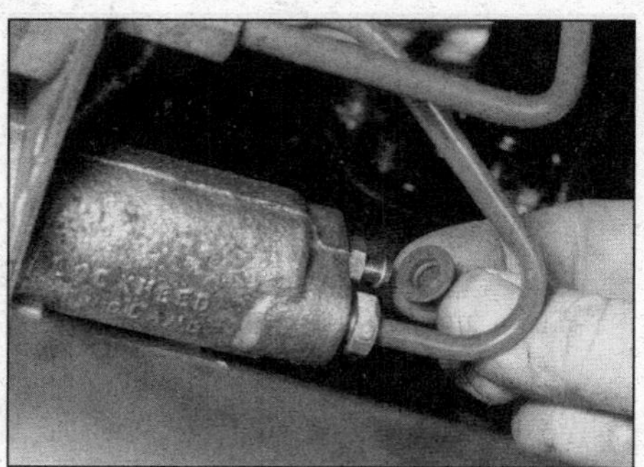

7.8 Removing the dust cover from the clutch slave cylinder bleed screw

General

1 The correct operation of any hydraulic system is only possible after removing all air from the components and circuit; this is achieved by bleeding the system.
2 During the bleeding procedure, add only clean, fresh hydraulic fluid of the recommended type; never re-use fluid that has already been bled from the system. Ensure that sufficient fluid is available before starting work.
3 If there is any possibility of the incorrect fluid being in the system, the hydraulic components and circuit must be flushed completely with uncontaminated, correct fluid, and new seals should be fitted throughout the system.
4 If hydraulic fluid has been lost from the system, or air has entered because of a leak, ensure that the fault is cured before proceeding further.

Bleeding procedure

5 Unscrew the master cylinder reservoir cap, and top the master cylinder reservoir up to the MAX level line; refit the cap loosely, and remember to maintain the fluid level at least above the MIN level line throughout the procedure, otherwise there is a risk of further air entering the system.
6 There are a number of one-man, do-it-yourself brake/clutch bleeding kits currently available from motor accessory shops. It is recommended that one of these kits is used whenever possible, as they greatly simplify the bleeding operation, and also reduce the risk of expelled air and fluid being drawn back into the system. If such a kit is not available, the basic (two-man) method must be used, which is described in detail below.
7 If a kit is to be used, prepare the vehicle as described previously, and follow the kit manufacturer's instructions, as the procedure may vary slightly according to the type being used; generally, they are as outlined below in the relevant sub-section.

Bleeding - basic (two-man) method

8 Clean the area around the bleed screw at the rear of the clutch slave cylinder (located on the transmission bellhousing). Where applicable, remove the dust cover from the bleed screw **(see illustration)**.
9 Collect a clean glass jar, a suitable length of plastic or rubber tubing which is a tight fit over the bleed screw, and a ring spanner to fit the screw. The help of an assistant will also be required.
10 Fit a suitable spanner and tube to the screw, place the other end of the tube in the jar, and pour in sufficient fluid to cover the end of the tube.

11 Ensure that the master cylinder reservoir fluid level is maintained at least above the MIN level line throughout the procedure.
12 Unscrew the bleed screw (approximately one turn).
13 Have the assistant fully depress the clutch pedal, then hold the pedal depressed. When the flow of fluid into the jar stops, tighten the bleed screw again, have the assistant release the pedal slowly, and recheck the reservoir fluid level.
14 Repeat the steps given in paragraphs 12 and 13 until the fluid emerging from the bleed screw is free from air bubbles. If the master cylinder has been drained and refilled, allow approximately five seconds between cycles for the master cylinder passages to refill.
15 When no more air bubbles appear, tighten the bleed screw securely, remove the tube and spanner, and refit the dust cap (where applicable). Do not overtighten the bleed screw.
16 On completion, recheck the fluid level in the reservoir, and top-up if necessary.
17 Discard any hydraulic fluid that has been bled from the system; it will not be fit for re-use.

Bleeding - using a one-way valve kit

18 As their name implies, these kits consist of a length of tubing with a one-way valve fitted, to prevent expelled air and fluid being drawn back into the system; some kits include a translucent container, which can be positioned so that the air bubbles can be more easily seen flowing from the end of the tube.
19 The kit is connected to the bleed screw, which is then opened. The user returns to the driver's seat, depresses the clutch pedal with a smooth, steady stroke, and slowly releases it; this is repeated until the expelled fluid is clear of air bubbles.
20 Note that these kits simplify work so much that it is easy to forget the master cylinder reservoir fluid level; ensure that this is maintained at least above the MIN level line at all times.

8 Clutch pedal - removal and refitting

General

1 In order to remove the clutch pedal, the complete pedal box assembly must be removed, complete with the brake servo and brake and clutch master cylinders. Proceed as described in the following sub-sections.

Pedal box

Warning: Refer to the warning at the beginning of Section 4 before proceeding.

Removal

2 Disconnect the battery negative lead.
3 Release the retaining clips, and withdraw the driver's side lower facia panel for access to the clutch pedal assembly.
4 Working in the engine compartment, disconnect the wiring plug(s) from the brake fluid reservoir cap.
5 Place a suitable container beneath the brake master cylinder to catch escaping fluid, then unscrew the union nuts, and disconnect the brake pipes from the master cylinder, noting their locations. Plug or cover the open ends of the pipes and master cylinder, to prevent dirt ingress and further fluid loss.
6 Similarly, unscrew the union nut, and disconnect the fluid pipe from the clutch hydraulic master cylinder.
7 Disconnect the vacuum hose from the brake vacuum servo.
8 Working inside the vehicle, disconnect the wiring plug from the brake light switch.
9 Where applicable, disconnect the accelerator cable from the accelerator pedal (see the relevant part of Chapter 4).
10 On later models, where the steering column passes through the pedal box, remove the steering column as described in Chapter 11.
11 Unscrew the fixings securing the pedal box to the bulkhead. On early models, the pedal box is secured by nuts, which are accessible from the engine compartment. On later models, the pedal box is secured by bolts - the upper bolts are accessible from the engine compartment, and the lower bolts are reached from the driver's footwell.
12 Manipulate the complete pedal box assembly into the engine compartment, and withdraw it from the vehicle.
13 Remove the clutch pedal as described in the following sub-section.

Refitting

14 Manoeuvre the pedal box into position on the bulkhead, then refit and tighten the fixings.
15 Where applicable, refit the steering column as described in Chapter 11.
16 Where applicable, reconnect the accelerator cable to the accelerator pedal.
17 Reconnect the brake light switch wiring plug.
18 Refit the lower facia panel.
19 Reconnect the hydraulic fluid pipes to the brake and clutch master cylinders, ensuring that the pipes are reconnected to their correct unions.
20 Reconnect the brake vacuum servo hose.
21 Reconnect the wiring plug(s) to the brake fluid reservoir cap.
22 Bleed the brake hydraulic system as described in Chapter 10.
23 Bleed the clutch hydraulic system as described in Section 7.
24 Reconnect the battery negative lead.

Clutch pedal

Removal

25 With the pedal box removed as described previously, proceed as follows.
26 Unscrew the nut, or prise the spring clip, as applicable, from the end of the clutch pedal-to-pushrod clevis pin **(see illustration)**.
27 Withdraw the clevis pin, and (where applicable) recover the washer and bushes, noting their locations to ensure correct refitting.
28 On early models, the pedal pivot shaft is secured by circlips, and on later models, the shaft is secured by bolts screwed into the ends of the shaft, and roll-pins.
29 Remove the circlip from the relevant end of the shaft (using circlip pliers), or unscrew the relevant bolt and extract the roll-pins, as applicable.
30 Where applicable, release the clutch assist spring from the pedal, noting its orientation.
31 Slide the pedal pivot shaft from the pedal sufficiently to enable removal or the clutch pedal. Release the return spring from the pedal as the pedal is removed - take care, as the spring tension is high.

Refitting

32 If necessary, the pedal pivot bushes can be renewed. Press the old bushes from the pedal, or remove them from the pivot shaft (as applicable), and press the new bushes into position.
33 Lightly grease the pedal pivot shaft.
34 Position the pedal in the pedal box, then reconnect the return spring, and slide the pivot shaft through the pedal.
35 Refit the circlip to the end of the pivot shaft, or refit the securing bolt and fit new roll-pins, as applicable.
36 Where applicable, reconnect the clutch assist spring to the pedal, ensuring that it is orientated as noted before removal.
37 On models where the pushrod-to-pedal clevis pin is secured by a spring clip, connect

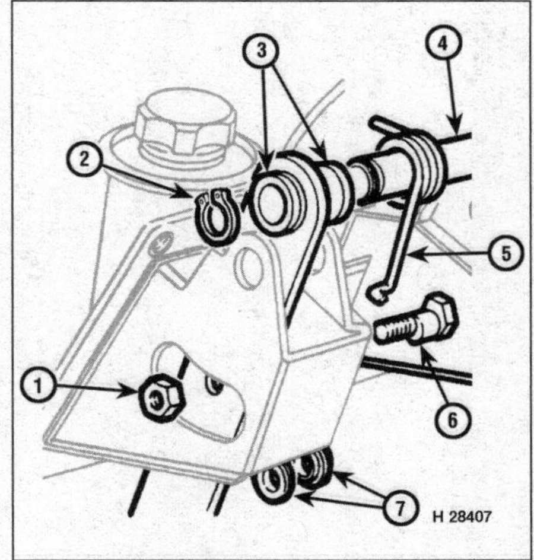
3
4
2
5
1
6
7
H 28407

8.26 Clutch pedal mounting details - early models

1 Clevis pin nut
2 Circlip
3 Pivot shaft bushes
4 Pivot shaft
5 Pedal return spring
6 Clevis pin
7 Clevis pin bushes

the pushrod to the pedal, then refit the clevis pin, and secure with the spring clip. Proceed to paragraph 39.

38 On models where the pushrod-to-pedal clevis pin is secured by a nut, proceed as follows:

a) *Connect the pushrod to the pedal, and refit the clevis pin. Position the bushes as noted before removal. Refit the washer and nut, but do not tighten the nut at this stage.*
b) *Turn the clevis pin (the pin has an eccentric shank) until the clutch pedal rests at the same height as the brake pedal, then tighten the clevis pin nut.*
c) *Loosen the locknut on the clutch pedal stop-bolt, and back off the stop-bolt (turn the bolt clockwise).*
d) *Fully depress the clutch pedal, then unscrew the stop-bolt until it just touches the pedal. Unscrew the stop-bolt one further turn, then tighten the locknut (if desired, this last operation can be carried out when the pedal box has been refitted, when the pedal will be easier to depress).*

39 Refit the pedal box as described previously.

Chapter 7 Part A:
Manual transmission

Contents

Degrees of difficulty

Easy, suitable for novice with little experience 	**Fairly easy,** suitable for beginner with some experience 	**Fairly difficult,** suitable for competent DIY mechanic	**Difficult,** suitable for experienced DIY mechanic 	**Very difficult,** suitable for expert DIY or professional

Specifications

General

Transmission type:	
Up to March 1994	LT77 type transmission; five forward speeds and reverse
March 1994 onwards	R380 type transmission; five forward speeds and reverse

Torque wrench settings

Torque wrench settings	Nm	lbf ft
Clutch slave cylinder-to-bellhousing bolts	25	18
Transfer gearbox-to-main transmission bolts	45	33
Transmission bellhousing-to-engine flywheel housing bolts and nuts	40	30

1 General information

Two different types of five-speed transmission have been available on the Discovery - models up to March 1994 had the LT77 transmission, while those after this date have the new R380 unit.

Drive from the clutch is picked up by the input shaft, which runs in parallel with the layshaft and the mainshaft. The input shaft runs on the same axis as the mainshaft, and a bearing between the two shafts allows the shafts to rotate independently. A fixed gear at the rear of the input shaft drives the layshaft. The input shaft and mainshaft gears are in constant mesh, and selection of gears is by sliding synchromesh hubs, which lock the appropriate mainshaft gear to the mainshaft. The direct-drive fourth gear is obtained by locking the input shaft to the mainshaft.

Reverse gear is obtained by sliding an idler gear into mesh with two straight-cut gears on the mainshaft (the 1st/2nd gear synchro sleeve) and the layshaft.

All the forward gear teeth are helically-cut, to reduce noise and to improve wear characteristics.

The mainshaft provides drive to the transfer gearbox, which is described in part C of this Chapter.

Gear selection is by means of a floor-mounted gearchange lever, acting directly on the gearchange rail in the transmission.

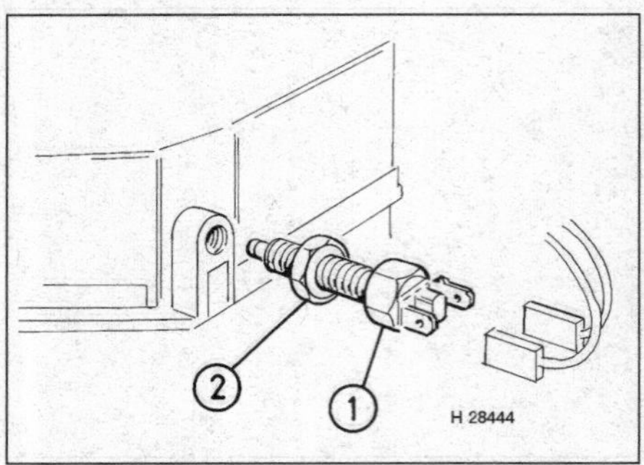
2
1
H 28444

2.1 Reversing light switch (1) and locknut (2) - LT 77 type gearbox

2 Reversing light switch - testing, removal and refitting

LT77 type transmission

Testing

1 The reversing light switch is located in the rear of the main transmission selector housing, and is accessible from under the vehicle **(see illustration)**.

2 Disconnect the battery negative lead, and disconnect the wiring from the switch.

3 Connect a continuity tester or an ohmmeter across the switch terminals. There should be no continuity (infinite resistance) between the switch terminals.

4 Engage reverse gear. There should now be continuity (close to zero resistance) between the terminals.

3.6a Remove the securing screws . . .

3.6b . . . and withdraw the selector lever insulation clamp rings

2.16 Reversing light switch location (arrowed) - R380 type gearbox

5 If the above readings are not as expected, try cleaning the switch terminals. If the readings are still not as expected, it is likely that the switch is faulty or incorrectly positioned. The switch can be tested after it is removed.

Removal

6 Disconnect the battery negative lead.

7 Disconnect the wires from the terminals on the switch.

8 Loosen the switch locknut, then unscrew the switch from the selector housing.

Refitting

9 Select reverse gear.

10 Loosely screw the switch into position in the selector housing (ensure that the locknut is fitted to the switch).

11 Connect a 12-volt supply to one of the switch terminals, and connect a test light between the remaining terminal and earth.

12 Screw the switch into the selector housing until the test light illuminates, then screw the switch into the housing a further half-turn.

13 Tighten the locknut, ensuring that the switch does not move.

14 Disconnect the test light, and reconnect the wiring to the switch.

15 Reconnect the battery negative lead.

R380 type transmission

Testing

16 The switch is located in the left-hand side of the transfer gearbox casing **(see illustration)**.

17 Testing is as described in paragraphs 1 to 5.

3.7a Prise off the C-clip . . .

3.4 Lifting the sound insulation from the top of the transmission tunnel

Removal

18 Disconnect the battery negative lead.

19 Separate the two halves of the switch wiring connector.

20 Unscrew the switch from the gearbox casing, and recover the sealing ring.

21 Examine the condition of the sealing ring, and renew if necessary.

Refitting

22 Refitting is a reversal of removal, but use a new sealing ring if necessary.

3 Manual transmission - removal and refitting

Removal

Note: *Although the following procedure is not difficult, the transmission assembly (the main transmission is removed complete with the transfer gearbox) is heavy, and awkward to handle. Read through the entire procedure before proceeding, to familiarise yourself with the steps. The help of an assistant will prove invaluable during this operation. A suitable engine lifting crane and tackle will be required, and (on diesel models) sealing compound will be required to seal the mating faces of the flywheel housing and transmission bellhousing on refitting.*

1 Disconnect the battery negative lead.

2 Jack up the vehicle, and support securely on axle stands placed under the axle tubes (see *Jacking and vehicle support*). Note that the vehicle must be raised sufficiently to give enough clearance for the transmission assembly to be removed from under the vehicle.

3 Remove the centre console as described in Chapter 12.

4 Lift the sound insulation from the top of the transmission tunnel **(see illustration)**.

5 If not already done, unscrew the securing bolt, and remove the upper section of the gear lever.

6 Remove the securing screws, and withdraw the main transmission selector lever insulation clamp rings **(see illustrations)**.

7 Prise off the C-clip, and withdraw the handbrake cable adjuster **(see illustrations)**.

3.7b . . . and withdraw the handbrake cable adjuster

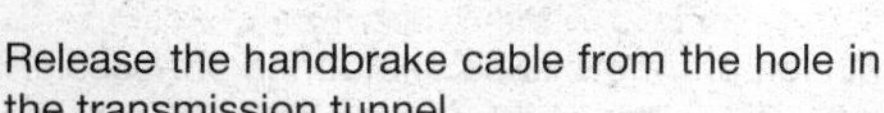

3.8a Drill out the rivets . . .

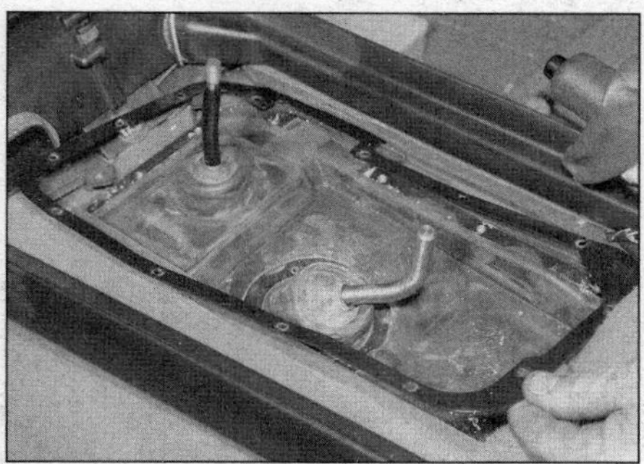

3.8b . . . remove the retaining plate . . .

Release the handbrake cable from the hole in the transmission tunnel.

8 Remove the securing screws, or drill out the rivets (as applicable), and remove the lever surround from the transmission tunnel **(see illustrations)**.

9 Move the transfer gearbox selector lever to the Low range position, to prevent the selector lever from fouling the transmission tunnel when removing the gearbox.

10 Unscrew the bolt securing the gearbox breather pipe clip to the rear of the engine.

11 Remove the viscous fan unit and cowl, as described in Chapter 3 (this is necessary to allow the engine to tilt during the transmission removal procedure).

12 If work is to be carried out on the main transmission and/or transfer gearbox, drain the oil from the main transmission and/or the transfer gearbox, with reference to the relevant part of Chapter 1 if necessary.

13 Remove the exhaust front section as described in Chapter 4D.

14 Release the exhaust centre section from its mountings, then move the exhaust system to one side. Support it by suspending it from the chassis using wire or string.

15 Unscrew the bolts securing the clutch slave cylinder to the transmission bellhousing.

16 Release the clutch slave cylinder from the bellhousing, and recover the spacer. Move the slave cylinder clear of the bellhousing, but take care not to strain the hydraulic fluid pipe.

17 Remove the propeller shafts as described in Chapter 8 (it is only strictly necessary to disconnect the propeller shafts from the transfer gearbox, but it is recommended that the shafts are removed completely, to provide additional working space).

18 Working under the vehicle, where applicable, release the securing ring, and disconnect the speedometer cable from the transfer gearbox.

19 Again working under the vehicle, disconnect all electrical wiring connectors from the main transmission and the transfer gearbox, noting their locations. Release the wiring from any clips on the main transmission/transfer gearbox casing, noting its routing.

20 The main transmission/transfer gearbox assembly must now be supported, to enable the support crossmember to be removed from underneath the vehicle. This is most easily and safely accomplished using an engine crane, as follows:

*a) Working under the vehicle, unscrew one of the top securing bolts from the power take-off cover at the rear of the transfer gearbox. Make up a lifting bracket, and bolt it to the transfer gearbox using the previously-removed bolt **(see illustration)**.*

b) Pass a lifting strap or chain around the main transmission casing. Pass the ends of the strap/chain up through the hole in the transmission tunnel.

c) Attach a second lifting strap/chain to the lifting bracket on the transfer gearbox, and again pass the end of the strap/chain up through the transmission tunnel.

d) Open one of the front doors, and secure the door in the fully-open position using a length of string.

*e) Pass the engine lifting crane in through the front door aperture, and position the lifting hook over the transmission tunnel aperture. Attach the previously-positioned lifting straps to the crane **(see illustration)**. Take care not to damage the interior trim when positioning the lifting gear.*

f) Raise the crane sufficiently to just take the weight of the transmission assembly.

21 Ensure that the transmission assembly is adequately supported before proceeding.

22 Working under the vehicle, unscrew the nuts and through-bolts securing the transmission support crossmember to the chassis **(see illustration)**.

23 Unscrew the bolts securing the mounting brackets to the transfer gearbox, then

3.8c . . . and remove the lever surround

3.20a Lifting bracket (arrowed) bolted to transfer gearbox - viewed with transmission removed

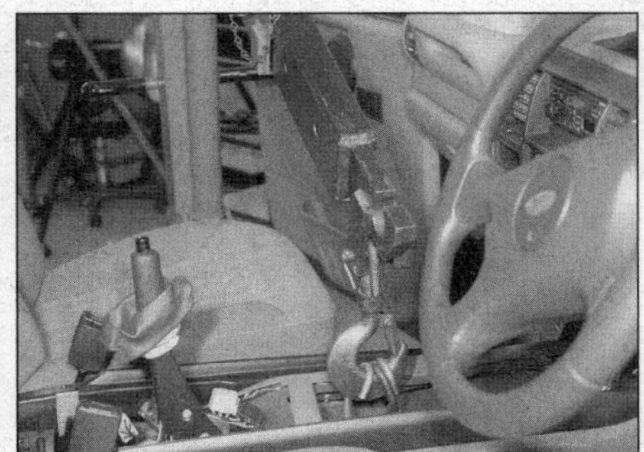

3.20b Engine crane and lifting tackle in position to support transmission assembly

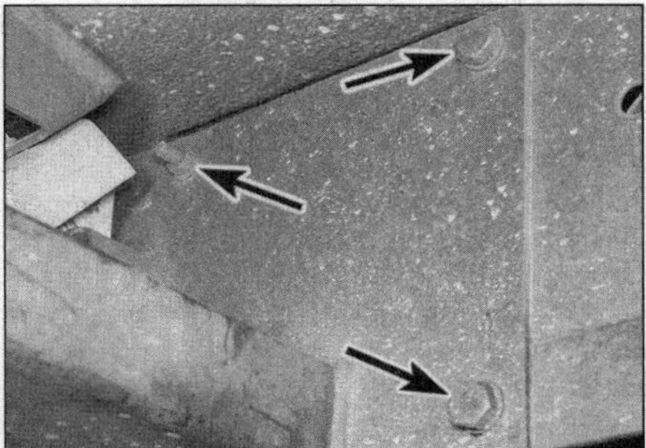

3.22 Three of the transmission support crossmember-to-chassis bolts and nuts (arrowed)

3.28 Lowering the transmission assembly from the vehicle. Note location of lifting strap (arrowed)

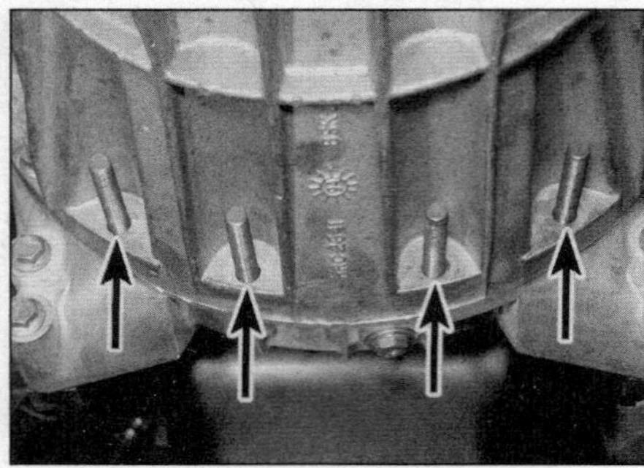
3.33 Fit four studs (arrowed) to the flywheel housing - viewed with transmission refitted

withdraw the complete crossmember/ mounting bracket assembly from under the vehicle.

24 Lower the transmission assembly slightly, using the engine crane, to gain access to the engine flywheel housing-to-transmission bellhousing nuts and bolts.

25 Unscrew and remove the upper flywheel housing-to-transmission bellhousing nuts.

26 Progressively unscrew the lower flywheel housing-to-transmission bellhousing bolts. Note that the transmission assembly may move backwards from the engine once the bolts are removed - be prepared for this, and do not allow the assembly to swing uncontrolled.

27 If necessary, carefully tap around the flywheel housing-to-bellhousing joint to break the sealant, then slide the transmission assembly back from the engine, taking care not to strain the transmission input shaft.

28 Position a trolley jack and a large block of wood under the transmission assembly (the wood should be suitably shaped to support the transmission when it is lowered), then lower the engine crane to position the transmission assembly on the trolley jack and support block **(see illustration)**.

29 Disconnect the lifting straps/chains from the transmission assembly and the engine crane, then carefully slide the transmission assembly out from under the vehicle, using the trolley jack. Take care when moving the transmission, and do not attempt to lift the assembly without suitable lifting tackle - the assembly is very heavy!

30 If desired, the transfer gearbox can be separated from the main gearbox as described in part C of this Chapter.

Refitting

31 Where applicable, refit the transfer gearbox to the main transmission, as described in part C of this Chapter. Ensure that the Low range is selected in the transfer gearbox.

32 On diesel models, thoroughly clean the mating faces of the engine flywheel housing and the transmission bellhousing, then apply sealing compound to the transmission bellhousing mating face of the engine flywheel housing.

33 Fit four M10 studs (or bolts with the heads cut off) to the lower engine-to-transmission bolt holes in the flywheel housing. The studs should be approximately 100 mm long **(see illustration)**.

34 Position the transmission assembly under the vehicle using the trolley jack and support block, then fit the lifting straps/chains to the transmission (as during removal). Pass the lifting straps/chains up through the transmission tunnel, and connect them to the engine crane.

35 Using the crane, lift the transmission assembly into position, then slide the bellhousing onto the studs previously fitted to the flywheel housing. Ensure that the wiring harness and connectors, and the breather pipes, are not trapped as the transmission is moved into position. Note that it will be necessary to tilt the rear of the engine down to align the engine and transmission (the engine can easily be tilted on its mountings if an assistant pushes the assembly from above). Push the transmission bellhousing onto the studs sufficiently to enable nuts to be fitted to the studs.

36 Manipulate the engine and transmission as necessary to align the transmission input shaft splines with the splines in the clutch friction disc hub (it may be necessary to turn the crankshaft using a spanner or socket on the pulley bolt). Once the input shaft is engaged with the clutch, progressively tighten the nuts fitted to the four studs in the flywheel housing to draw the transmission bellhousing flush against the flywheel housing.

37 Refit and tighten the engine-to-transmission upper nuts, then unscrew the nuts and studs from the lower bolt holes, and refit the four lower bolts. Tighten the bolts, then (on diesel models) wipe any surplus sealing compound from the flywheel housing/bellhousing mating face.

38 Using the crane, raise the transmission assembly sufficiently to enable the crossmember/mounting bracket assembly to be fitted, then fit the assembly and tighten all fixings.

39 The remainder of the refitting procedure is a reversal of removal, bearing in mind the following points:

a) Ensure that all wiring is routed correctly, and that all plugs are reconnected to their correct locations.

b) Refit the propeller shafts with reference to Chapter 8.

c) Refit the exhaust front section with reference to Chapter 4D.

d) Where applicable, use new pop-rivets to secure the transmission tunnel lever surround.

e) Before refitting the centre console, check the handbrake cable adjustment as described in the relevant part of Chapter 1.

f) Where applicable, on completion, refill the main transmission and transfer gearbox with oil of the correct type, as described in the relevant part of Chapter 1.

4 Manual transmission overhaul - general information

Overhauling a manual transmission is a difficult and involved job for the DIY home mechanic. In addition to dismantling and reassembling many small parts, clearances must be precisely measured and, if necessary, changed by selecting shims and spacers. Transmission internal components are also often difficult to obtain, and in many instances, extremely expensive. Because of this, if the transmission develops a fault or becomes noisy, the best course of action is to have the unit overhauled by a specialist repairer, or to obtain an exchange reconditioned unit.

Nevertheless, it is not impossible for the more experienced mechanic to overhaul a transmission, provided the special tools are available, and the job is done in a deliberate step-by-step manner so that nothing is overlooked.

The tools necessary for an overhaul include internal and external circlip pliers, bearing pullers, a slide-hammer, a set of pin punches, a dial test indicator, and possibly a hydraulic press. In addition, a large, sturdy workbench and a vice will be required.

During dismantling of the transmission, make careful notes of how each component is fitted, to make reassembly easier and more accurate.

Before dismantling the transmission, it will help if you have some idea of which area is malfunctioning. Certain problems can be closely related to specific areas in the transmission, which can make component examination and replacement easier. Refer to the *Fault finding* Section at the end of this manual for more information.

Chapter 7 Part B: Automatic transmission

Contents

Degrees of difficulty

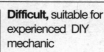

Easy, suitable for novice with little experience 	**Fairly easy,** suitable for beginner with some experience 	**Fairly difficult,** suitable for competent DIY mechanic 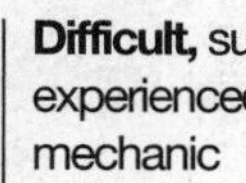	**Difficult,** suitable for experienced DIY mechanic	**Very difficult,** suitable for expert DIY or professional

Specifications

General

Type	ZF 4HP22	

Kickdown cable

Freeplay	0.25 to 1.25 mm	

Torque wrench settings	Nm	lbf ft
Dipstick tube-to-sump union nut	68	50
Engine-to-transmission bellhousing bolts	42	31
Selector lever-to-gearbox bolts	25	18
Sump drain plug	10	7
Sump securing bolts	8	6
Torque converter-to-driveplate bolts*	39	29

**Use thread-locking compound.*

1 General information

A 4-speed fully-automatic transmission is available as an option on certain models. The transmission consists of a torque converter, an epicyclic geartrain, and hydraulically-operated clutches and brakes. The transmission is a customised version of the ZF 4HP22 unit used in many other vehicles.

The torque converter provides a fluid coupling between the engine and transmission, acts as an automatic clutch, and also provides a degree of torque multiplication when accelerating.

The epicyclic geartrain provides either one of the four forward gear ratios, or reverse gear, according to which of its component parts are held stationary or allowed to turn. The components of the geartrain are held or released by brakes and clutches, which are activated by a hydraulic governor. A fluid pump within the transmission provides the necessary hydraulic pressure to operate the brakes and clutches.

First, second and third gears are reduction gears, but fourth gear is an overdrive gear for high-speed cruising. A direct-drive clutch, integral with the torque converter, operates to engage fourth gear.

Due to the complexity of the automatic transmission, any repair or overhaul work must be entrusted to a Land Rover dealer, or a suitably-qualified transmission specialist, with the necessary specialist equipment and knowledge for fault diagnosis and repair. Refer to the *Fault finding* Section at the end of this manual for further information.

2 Selector assembly - removal and refitting

Removal

1 Disconnect the battery negative lead.

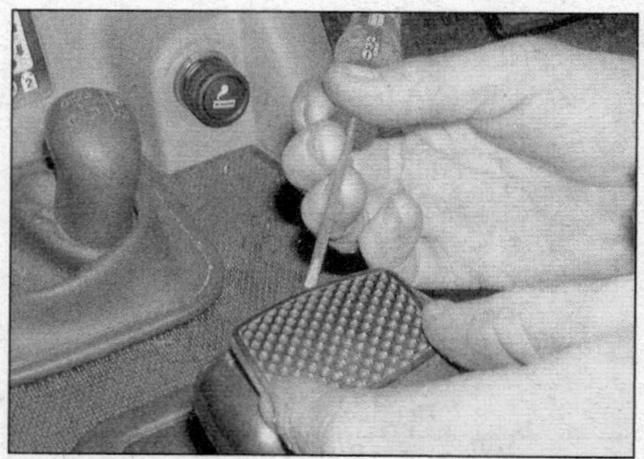

2.4 Prise up the cover from the gear knob

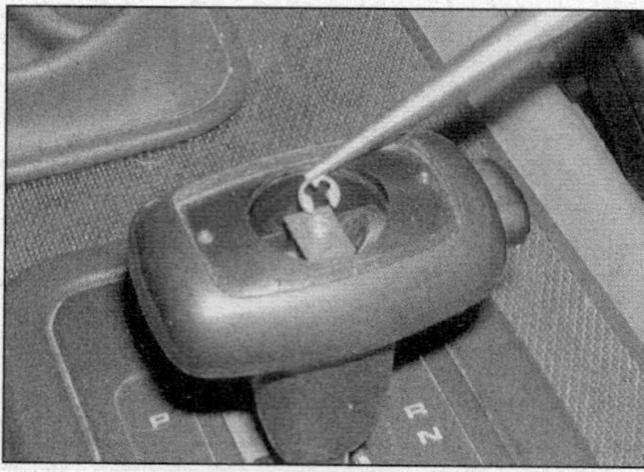

2.5a Remove the E-clip . . .

2.5b . . . and recover the spacer

2.6a Pull out the locking button . . .

2.6b . . . and recover the spring

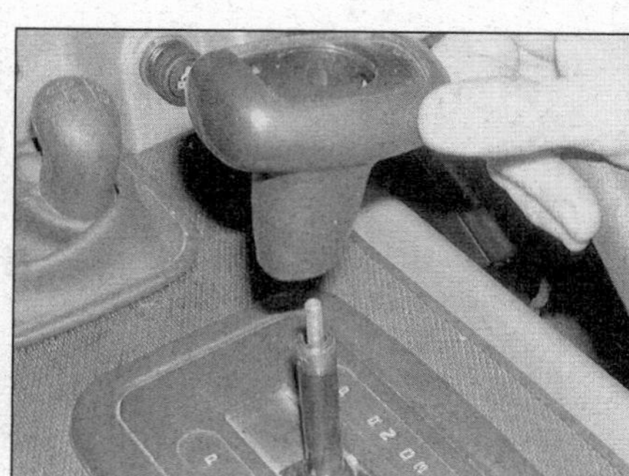

2.7a Prise out the locking clip, then unscrew the retaining nut . . .

2.7b . . . and remove the gear knob

2 Working under the vehicle, disconnect the selector cable from the lever on the side of the transmission.

3 Remove the centre console as described in Chapter 12.

4 Carefully prise the cover from the top of the gear knob **(see illustration)**.

5 Using a suitable screwdriver and pliers, prise off and remove the E-clip securing the gear lever locking button to the top of the selector lever, and recover the spacer beneath **(see illustrations)**.

6 Pull the locking button from the side of the gear lever **(see illustrations)** and (where applicable) recover the two O-rings.

7 Prise off the locking clip, then unscrew the securing nut, and withdraw the gear knob from the top of the lever **(see illustrations)**.

8 Disconnect the selector illumination panel wiring plug at the rear (the plugs at each side can remain connected), then remove the four plastic nuts, and withdraw the illumination housing **(see illustrations)**.

9 Remove the securing screws, and withdraw the selector lever assembly from the body.

Refitting

10 Refitting is a reversal of removal.

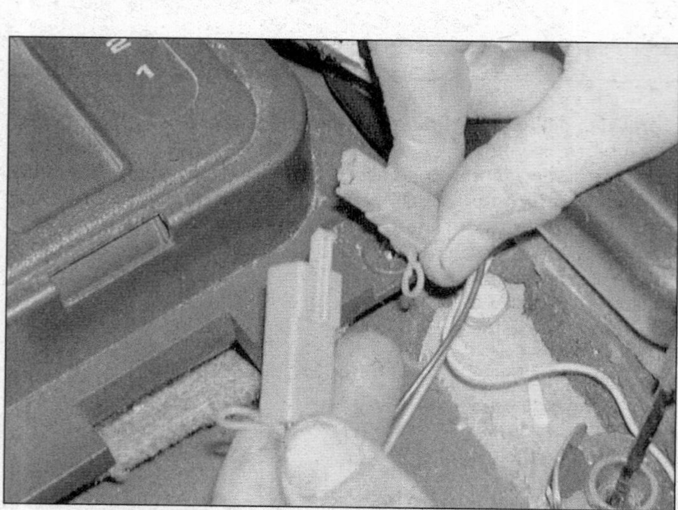

2.8a Disconnect the illumination wiring plug . . .

2.8b . . . and remove the illumination housing

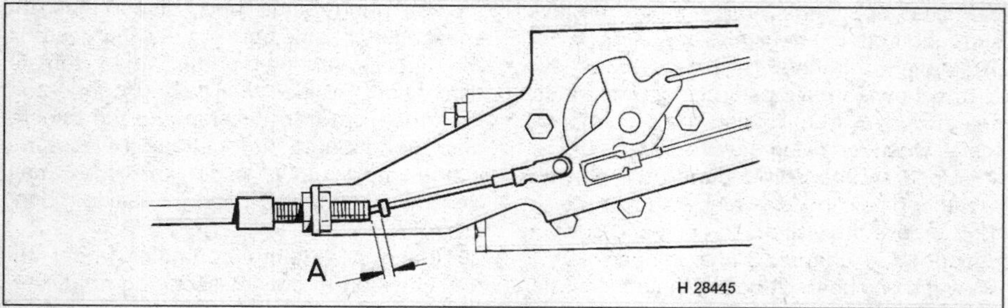
A
H 28445

3.3 Kickdown cable adjustment
A = 0.25 to 1.25 mm

3 Kickdown cable - adjustment, removal and refitting

Adjustment

1 Working under the vehicle, loosen the kickdown cable outer locknut at the cable mounting bracket on the transmission.
2 Open the bonnet, and ensure that the throttle linkage is fully closed.
3 Working at the transmission bracket, adjust the outer cable, by turning the adjuster nut as required, to achieve the desired gap (freeplay) between the end of the cable outer and the crimped collar on the inner cable **(see illustration)**.
4 When the gap is correct, tighten the locknut.
5 Again, check that the throttle linkage is fully closed, then recheck the gap and re-adjust if necessary.

Removal and refitting

6 In order to remove the kickdown cable, it is necessary to remove the transmission fluid pan. It is also necessary to use a special tool to disconnect the cable from the transmission. For these reasons, renewal of the kickdown cable should be entrusted to a Land Rover dealer.

4 Starter inhibitor/reversing light switch - description, removal and refitting

Description

1 The starter/inhibitor/reversing light switch is a dual-function switch which is screwed into the transmission casing.
2 The inhibitor function of the switch ensures that the engine can only be started with the selector lever in either the N or the P positions, therefore preventing the engine from being started with the transmission in gear. This is achieved by the switch cutting the supply to the starter motor solenoid. If at any time it is noted that the engine can be started with the selector lever in any position other than N or P, then it is likely that the inhibitor function of the switch is faulty.
3 The switch also performs the function of the reversing light switch, illuminating the reversing lights whenever the selector lever is in the R position.
4 If either function of the switch is faulty, the complete switch must be renewed as a unit.

Removal

Note: *A new O-ring will be required on refitting.*
5 Disconnect the battery negative lead.
6 Jack up the vehicle, and support securely on axle stands placed under the axle tubes (see *Jacking and vehicle support*).
7 Working under the vehicle, separate the two halves of the switch wiring connector.
8 Unscrew the clamp bolt, and remove the switch retaining plate **(see illustration)**.
9 Withdraw the switch from the transmission casing, and recover the O-ring.

Refitting

10 Commence refitting by cleaning the switch, and the switch housing in the transmission casing.
11 Lubricate a new O-ring with a little clean transmission fluid of the correct type, then fit the seal to the switch.
12 Fit the switch to the transmission casing, then refit the retaining plate and secure with the clamp bolt.
13 Reconnect the switch wiring plug.

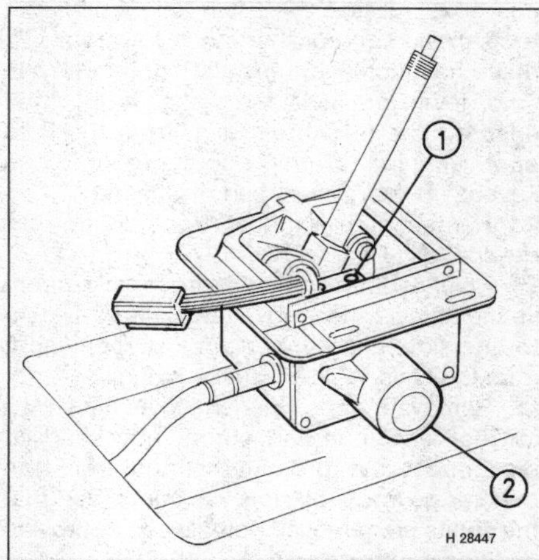
1
2
H 28447

5.3 Gear selector mechanism microswitch support bracket (1) and interlock solenoid (2)

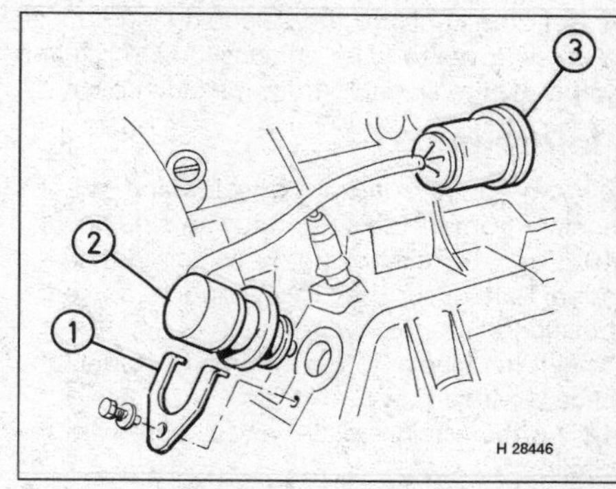
1
2
3
H 28446

4.8 Starter inhibitor/reversing light switch
1 Retaining plate 2 Switch
3 Wiring connector

14 Lower the vehicle to the ground, and reconnect the battery.

5 Gear selector interlock solenoid - removal and refitting

Removal

Note: *Suitable sealant will be required when refitting the selector housing side cover, and a new solenoid spindle C-clip will be required.*
1 Disconnect the battery negative lead.
2 Remove the selector assembly as described in Section 2.
3 Remove the screws securing the microswitch support bracket at the top of the selector assembly **(see illustration)**.
4 Remove the screws securing the side cover to the selector assembly, then withdraw the side cover, complete with the solenoid.
5 Disconnect the solenoid wiring connector.
6 Using a suitable pair of circlip pliers, remove the solenoid retaining circlip, then lift off the retainer plate **(see illustration)**.
7 Prise the C-clip from the solenoid spindle, and withdraw the sleeve.

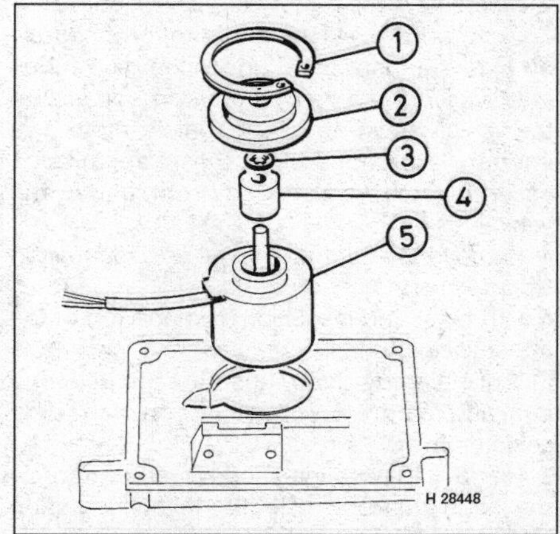
1
2
3
4
5
H 28448

5.6 Gear selector interlock components
1 Circlip
2 Retainer plate
3 C-clip
4 Sleeve
5 Solenoid

8 Refit the C-clip to the solenoid spindle; use a screwdriver to lever against the C-clip, and withdraw the solenoid from the side cover.

Refitting

9 Commence refitting by cleaning all the sealant from the selector housing side cover.
10 Push the solenoid into position in the side cover, ensuring that the wiring is correctly positioned in the cover recess.
11 Fit the sleeve to the solenoid spindle, and secure with a new C-clip.
12 Fit the retainer plate, and secure with the circlip.
13 Reconnect the solenoid wiring connector.
14 Apply suitable sealant to the mating face of the side cover, then refit the side cover and tighten the securing bolts.
15 Lightly grease all the moving parts of the gear selector mechanism.
16 Further refitting is a reversal of removal.

6 Automatic transmission - removal and refitting

Removal

Note: *Although the following procedure is not difficult, the transmission assembly (the main transmission is removed complete with the transfer gearbox) is heavy, and awkward to handle. Read through the entire procedure before proceeding, to familiarise yourself with the steps. The help of an assistant will prove invaluable during this operation. A suitable engine lifting crane and tackle will be required. Sealing compound to seal the mating faces of the flywheel housing and transmission bellhousing on refitting, and suitable thread-locking compound for the torque converter-to-driveplate bolts, may also be required.*
1 The automatic transmission is removed with the transfer gearbox as a complete unit.
2 Disconnect the battery negative lead.
3 Jack up the vehicle, and support securely on axle stands placed under the axle tubes (see *Jacking and vehicle support*). Note that the vehicle must be raised sufficiently to give enough clearance for the transmission assembly to be removed from under the vehicle.
4 Remove the centre console as described in Chapter 12.
5 Lift the sound insulation from the top of the transmission tunnel.
6 If not already done, unscrew the securing bolt, and remove the upper section of the gear selector lever.
7 Remove the securing screws, and withdraw the main gearbox selector lever insulation clamp rings.
8 Prise off the C-clip, and withdraw the hand-brake cable adjuster. Release the handbrake cable from the hole in the transmission tunnel.
9 Remove the securing screws, or drill out the rivets, as applicable, and remove the lever surround from the transmission tunnel.
10 Move the transfer gearbox selector lever to the Low range position, to prevent the selector lever from fouling the transmission tunnel when removing the gearbox.
11 Unscrew the bolt securing the gearbox breather pipe clip to the rear of the engine.
12 Remove the viscous fan unit and cowl, as described in Chapter 3 (this is necessary to allow the engine to tilt during the transmission removal procedure).
13 On left-hand-drive vehicles, disconnect the wiring from the brake fluid level sensor on the top of the fluid reservoir.
14 Release the wiring harness from the clips on the engine compartment bulkhead, and move the harness to one side, clear of the working area.
15 Disconnect the kickdown cable from the throttle linkage.
16 Drain the cooling system as described in the relevant part of Chapter 1, and disconnect the top hose from the radiator.
17 On petrol models, disconnect the large air hose from the side of the plenum chamber, and the by-pass air valve hose at the rear of the plenum chamber.
18 On diesel models, loosen the hose clips, and remove the air trunking connecting the turbocharger to the intercooler.
19 Remove the starter motor, as described in Chapter 5A.
20 Working through the starter motor aperture in the bellhousing, make alignment marks between the torque converter and the driveplate, to ensure that the alignment is maintained on refitting.
21 Again working through the starter motor aperture, unscrew and remove the four torque converter-to-driveplate bolts. It will be necessary to turn the crankshaft to gain access to each bolt in turn, and this can be done using a suitable spanner or socket on the crankshaft pulley bolt.
22 If work is to be carried out on the automatic transmission and/or the transfer gearbox, drain the fluid/oil from the transmission and/or the transfer gearbox. To drain the automatic transmission, remove the fluid level dipstick from the tube, then unscrew the fluid drain plug from the fluid pan. Draining of the transfer gearbox is covered in the relevant part of Chapter 1.
23 Remove the exhaust front section as described in Chapter 4D.
24 Release the exhaust centre section from its mountings, then move the exhaust system to one side, and support it by suspending it from the chassis using wire or string.
25 Remove the propeller shafts as described in Chapter 8 (it is only strictly necessary to disconnect the propeller shafts from the transfer gearbox, but it is recommended that the shafts are removed completely, to provide additional working space).
26 Working under the vehicle, where applicable, remove the heat shield, release the securing ring, and disconnect the speedometer cable from the transfer gearbox.
27 Again working under the vehicle, disconnect all electrical wiring connectors from the main transmission and the transfer gearbox, noting their locations. Release the wiring from any clips on the main transmission/transfer gearbox casing, noting its routing.
28 Place a suitable container under the transmission to collect escaping fluid, then unscrew the union nuts, and disconnect the transmission fluid cooler pipes from the underside of the transmission. Plug the open ends of the pipes and transmission, to prevent dirt ingress and further fluid loss.
29 Unscrew the bolt securing the fluid cooler pipe bracket to the transmission fluid pan, and move the pipes to one side.
30 Disconnect the selector cable from the lever on the side of the transmission.
31 The main transmission/transfer gearbox assembly must now be supported, to enable the support crossmember to be removed from underneath the vehicle. This is most easily and safely accomplished using an engine crane as follows.

a) Working under the vehicle, unscrew one of the top securing bolts from the power take-off cover at the rear of the transfer gearbox. Make up a lifting bracket, and bolt it to the transfer gearbox using the previously-removed bolt.
b) Pass a lifting strap or chain around the main gearbox casing. Pass the ends of the strap/chain up through the hole in the transmission tunnel.
c) Attach a second lifting strap/chain to the lifting bracket on the transfer gearbox, and again pass the end of the strap/chain up through the transmission tunnel.
d) Open one of the front doors, and secure the door in the fully-open position using a length of string.
e) Pass the engine lifting crane in through the front door aperture, and position the lifting hook over the transmission tunnel aperture. Attach the previously-positioned lifting straps to the crane. Take care not to damage the interior trim when positioning the lifting gear.
f) Raise the crane sufficiently to just take the weight of the transmission assembly.

32 Ensure that the transmission assembly is adequately supported before proceeding.
33 Working under the vehicle, unscrew the nuts and through-bolts securing the transmission support crossmember to the chassis.
34 Unscrew the bolts securing the mounting brackets to the transfer gearbox, then withdraw the complete crossmember and mounting bracket assembly from under the vehicle.
35 Lower the transmission assembly slightly, using the engine crane, to gain access to the engine flywheel housing-to-transmission bellhousing nuts and bolts.

36 Release the cable-ties and clips securing the breather pipes and wiring harness. Note the routing of the pipes and harness, to ensure correct refitting.

37 Unscrew the nut securing the transmission dipstick tube to the bellhousing.

38 Loosen the union nut securing the dipstick tube to the transmission fluid pan, and remove the dipstick tube assembly. Plug the open ends of the tube and the sump, to prevent dirt ingress.

39 Unscrew the nut securing the kickdown cable bracket to the bellhousing.

40 Working at the top of the transmission, unscrew the two bolts securing the top of the transmission bellhousing to the flywheel housing.

41 Progressively unscrew the remaining bellhousing-to-flywheel housing securing nuts and bolts. Note that the transmission assembly may move backwards from the engine once the bolts are removed - be prepared for this, and do not allow the assembly to swing uncontrolled.

42 Where necessary, carefully tap around the bellhousing-to-flywheel housing joint to break the sealant, then slide the transmission assembly back from the engine.

43 Fit a suitable strip of metal across the bellhousing, to retain the torque converter. **Do not** allow the torque converter to fall out of the transmission.

44 Position a trolley jack and a large block of wood under the transmission assembly (the wood should be suitably shaped to support the transmission when it is lowered), then lower the engine crane to position the transmission assembly on the trolley jack and support block.

45 Disconnect the lifting straps/chains from the transmission assembly and the engine crane, then carefully slide the transmission assembly out from under the vehicle, using the trolley jack. Take care when moving the transmission, and do not attempt to lift the assembly without suitable lifting tackle - the assembly is very heavy!

46 If desired, the transfer gearbox can be separated from the main gearbox as described in part C of this Chapter.

Refitting

47 If a new transmission is to be fitted, it will be necessary to transfer the following components from the existing assembly to the new unit. Take great care to prevent dirt from entering the transmission - plug all openings to prevent dirt ingress.

a) Extension shaft spacer - this is vital!
b) Transmission breather pipe union and washers.
c) Gearbox selector lever.
d) Transmission mounting assembles.
e) Fluid cooler pipe unions.

48 Where applicable, reconnect the transfer gearbox to the transmission as described in part C of this Chapter.

49 Ensure that the Low gear range is selected in the transfer gearbox.

50 On diesel models, thoroughly clean the mating faces of the engine flywheel housing and the transmission bellhousing, then apply sealing compound to the transmission bellhousing mating face of the engine flywheel housing.

51 Fit four M10 studs (or bolts with the heads cut off) to the lower engine-to-transmission bolt holes in the flywheel housing. The studs should be approximately 100 mm long.

52 Position the transmission assembly under the vehicle using the trolley jack and support block, then fit the lifting straps/chains to the transmission (as during removal). Pass the lifting straps/chains up through the transmission tunnel, and connect them to the engine crane. Remove the torque converter retaining strap from the bellhousing.

53 Using the crane, lift the transmission assembly into position, then slide the bellhousing onto the studs previously fitted to the flywheel housing. Ensure that the wiring harness and connectors, and the breather pipes, are not trapped as the transmission is moved into position. Note that it will be necessary to tilt the rear of the engine down to align the engine and transmission (the engine can easily be tilted on its mountings if an assistant pushes the assembly from above). Push the gearbox bellhousing onto the studs sufficiently to enable nuts to be fitted to the studs.

54 Progressively tighten the nuts fitted to the four studs in the flywheel housing, to draw the transmission bellhousing flush against the flywheel housing.

55 Refit and tighten the engine-to-transmission upper nuts, then unscrew the nuts and studs from the lower bolt holes, and refit the four lower bolts. Tighten the bolts, then (on diesel models) wipe any surplus sealing compound from the flywheel housing/bellhousing mating face.

56 Refit the nut securing the kickdown cable to the bracket on the bellhousing.

57 Refit the transmission fluid dipstick assembly.

58 Secure the wiring harness and breather pipes, as noted during removal, using new cable-ties where necessary.

59 Using the crane, raise the transmission assembly sufficiently to enable the crossmember/mounting bracket assembly to be fitted, then fit the assembly and tighten all fixings.

60 The remainder of the refitting procedure is a reversal of removal, bearing in mind the following points:

a) Ensure that all wiring is routed correctly, and that all plugs are reconnected to their correct locations.
b) Refit the propeller shafts with reference to Chapter 8.
c) Refit the exhaust front section with reference to Chapter 4D.
d) Apply suitable thread-locking compound to the threads of the torque converter-to-driveplate bolts.
e) If the original torque converter and driveplate components are being refitted, ensure that the marks made on the torque converter and the driveplate before removal are aligned. Tighten the bolts to the specified torque.
f) Check the kickdown cable adjustment as described in Section 3.
g) Where applicable, use new pop-rivets to secure the transmission tunnel lever surround.
h) Before refitting the centre console, check the handbrake cable adjustment as described in the relevant part of Chapter 1.
i) Where applicable, on completion, refill the main transmission and transfer gearbox with fluid and oil of the correct type, as described in the relevant part of Chapter 1.

7 Automatic transmission overhaul - general information

In the event of a fault occurring on the transmission, it is first necessary to determine whether it is of an electrical, mechanical or hydraulic nature, and to achieve this, special test equipment is required. It is therefore essential to have the work carried out by a Land Rover dealer, or a suitably-equipped specialist, if a transmission fault is suspected.

Do not remove the transmission from the vehicle for possible repair before professional fault diagnosis has been carried out, since most tests require the transmission to be in the vehicle.

Chapter 7 Part C:
Transfer gearbox

Contents

Degrees of difficulty

Easy, suitable for novice with little experience 	**Fairly easy,** suitable for beginner with some experience 	**Fairly difficult,** suitable for competent DIY mechanic 	**Difficult,** suitable for experienced DIY mechanic 	**Very difficult,** suitable for expert DIY or professional

Specifications

Overall gear ratios (final drive to axles)	**High range**	**Low range**
First	15.962:1	43.367:1
Second	9.218:1	25.040:1
Third	6.040:1	16.406:1
Fourth	4.324:1	11.747:1
Fifth	3.331:1	9.049:1
Reverse	14.827:1	40.276:1

Torque wrench settings	**Nm**	**lbf ft**
Breather pipe union nut	15	11
Transfer gearbox-to-main gearbox/transmission bolts and nuts	45	33

1 General information

The transfer gearbox is mounted in-line with the main manual gearbox/automatic transmission. The transfer gearbox is a two-speed ratio-reducing gearbox, and provides drive to the front and rear axles via the propeller shafts.

Permanent four-wheel-drive is provided, and the unit incorporates a differential assembly to allow for any difference in the rotational speed of the front and rear wheels (and a resulting difference in speed between the front and rear propeller shafts). This centre differential (the axles also incorporate differentials, to allow for the difference in rotational speed between left- and right-hand wheels on the same axle) can be locked by mechanical means, to provide increased traction in particularly slippery conditions.

Selection of the High/Low ranges and the differential lock is made using a selector lever mounted forward of the main gear lever.

2 Transfer gearbox - removal and refitting

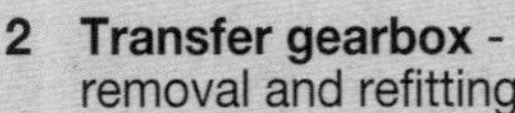

Removal

1 The transfer gearbox is most easily removed complete with the manual gearbox/ automatic transmission as an assembly. This procedure is described in part A or B of this Chapter, as applicable.

2 To separate the transfer gearbox from the manual gearbox/automatic transmission, proceed as follows.

3 Position the transmission assembly securely on a bench or a suitable stand, or rest the assembly on wooden blocks on the workshop floor.

4 Where applicable, unbolt the bracing bar connecting the transfer box to the main gearbox/transmission.

5 Unscrew the union bolt, and disconnect the breather pipe from the top of the transfer gearbox casing **(see illustration).** Recover the sealing washers.

2.5 Unscrew the breather pipe union bolt (arrowed)

6 Remove the split-pin, or the spring clip (as applicable), securing the differential lock connecting rod to the lever on the transfer gearbox, and disconnect the rod from the lever **(see illustration).** Where applicable, recover the washers.

1
2

2.6 Disconnect the differential lock connecting rod (1) from the lever (2)

7 Select the Low range by moving the transfer gear selector lever fully forwards.

8 Unscrew the transfer gear selector rod lower locknut, and withdraw the rod from the yoke **(see illustration).**

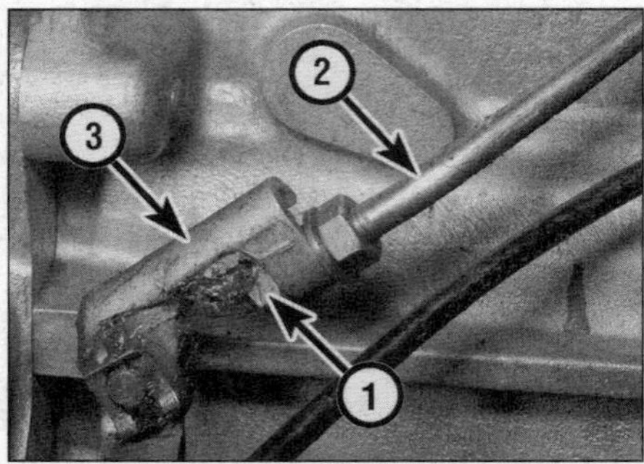
2
3
1

2.8 Unscrew the locknut (1) and withdraw the rod (2) from the yoke (3)

9 Ensure that the main gearbox/transmission and the transfer gearbox are adequately supported, then remove the transfer gearbox-to-main gearbox/transmission securing bolts, and slide the transfer gearbox rearwards from the main gearbox/transmission **(see illustration).**

2.9 Three of the transfer gearbox-to-main gearbox bolts and nuts (arrowed)

Refitting

10 Refitting is a reversal of removal, bearing in mind the following points:

a) *Thoroughly clean the mating faces of the transfer gearbox and the main gearbox/transmission.*
b) *On models with automatic transmission, before attempting to mate the main transmission and transfer gearbox together, select P in the main transmission.*
c) *Before attempting to mate the main gearbox and the transfer gearbox together, select the Low range, and engage the differential lock in the transfer gearbox.*
d) *As the two assemblies are mated together, engage the transfer gear selector rod with the yoke.*
e) *Refit the complete transmission assembly as described in Chapter 7A or B, as applicable.*

3 Transfer gearbox overhaul - general information

Overhauling a transfer gearbox is a difficult and involved job for the DIY home mechanic. In addition to dismantling and reassembling many small parts, clearances must be precisely measured and, if necessary, changed by selecting shims and spacers. Gearbox internal components are also often difficult to obtain, and in many instances, extremely expensive. Because of this, if the gearbox develops a fault or becomes noisy, the best course of action is to have the unit overhauled by a specialist repairer, or to obtain an exchange reconditioned unit.

Nevertheless, it is not impossible for the more experienced mechanic to overhaul a gearbox, provided the special tools are available, and the job is done in a deliberate step-by-step manner so that nothing is overlooked.

The tools necessary for an overhaul include internal and external circlip pliers, bearing pullers, a slide-hammer, a set of pin punches, a dial test indicator, and possibly a hydraulic press. In addition, a large, sturdy workbench and a vice will be required. Certain Land Rover special tools will be required for work on the differential assembly.

During dismantling of the gearbox, make careful notes of how each component is fitted, to make reassembly easier and more accurate.

Before dismantling the gearbox, it will help if you have some idea of which area is malfunctioning. Certain problems can be closely related to specific areas in the gearbox, which can make component examination and replacement easier. Refer to the *Fault finding* Section at the end of this manual for more information.

Chapter 8
Propeller shafts

Contents

Degrees of difficulty

Easy, suitable for novice with little experience 	**Fairly easy,** suitable for beginner with some experience 	**Fairly difficult,** suitable for competent DIY mechanic 	**Difficult,** suitable for experienced DIY mechanic 	**Very difficult,** suitable for expert DIY or professional

Specifications

General

Propeller shaft type	Tubular, splined joint
End joints	Hookes non-constant velocity joints with needle-roller bearings. Later models use flexible rubber coupling in place of universal joint at rear propeller shaft-to-differential flange joint
Shaft diameter	51.0 mm

Torque wrench settings

	Nm	lbf ft
Propeller shaft securing nuts and bolts	47	35
Rear flexible rubber coupling securing nuts and bolts	47	35

1 General information

The drive is transmitted from the transfer gearbox to the front and rear axle differentials by two tubular propeller shafts.

The front propeller shaft is fitted with non-constant velocity universal joints at each end, which run in needle-roller bearings. The universal joints cater for the varying angle between the axle and the transmission, caused by suspension movement.

On early models, the rear propeller shaft is fitted with universal joints at each end, as described previously for the front propeller shaft. On later models, the rear propeller shaft is fitted with a universal joint at the front end, and a flexible rubber coupling at the rear end.

To allow for the fore-and-aft movement between the axles and transmission, a sliding, splined joint is incorporated in each propeller shaft.

Grease nipples are fitted to the universal joints, and the universal joints and sliding joints should periodically be lubricated in accordance with the maintenance schedule given in the relevant part of Chapter 1.

2 Propeller shaft - removal and refitting

Front propeller shaft

Removal

1 Jack up the vehicle, and support securely on axle stands positioned under the axles, as described in *Jacking and vehicle support*.

2 If the original propeller shaft is to be refitted, make alignment marks between the front propeller shaft flange and the differential flange.

2.4 Making alignment marks between the rear propeller shaft flange and the transfer gearbox flange

2.10 Make alignment marks between the propeller shaft flange and the handbrake drum

3 Counterhold the bolts, and unscrew the nuts securing the front of the propeller shaft to the differential flange.

4 Again, if the original propeller shaft is to be refitted, make alignment marks between the rear propeller shaft flange and the transfer gearbox flange **(see illustration)**.

5 Unscrew the nuts securing the rear of the propeller shaft to the transfer gearbox flange.

6 Remove the bolts from the front shaft flange, then compress the propeller shaft sliding joint until the rear of the shaft can be withdrawn from the studs on the transfer gearbox flange.

7 Withdraw the propeller shaft from under the vehicle.

Refitting

8 Refitting is a reversal of removal, bearing in mind the following points:

a) *Ensure that the propeller shaft is refitted with the sliding joint towards the transfer gearbox.*
b) *If the original propeller shaft is being refitted, align the marks made on the differential flange, transfer gearbox flange, and the propeller shaft flanges before removal.*
c) *Tighten the securing nuts and bolts to the specified torque.*

Rear propeller shaft

Removal

9 Jack up the vehicle, and support securely on axle stands positioned under the axles, as described in *Jacking and vehicle support*.

10 If the original propeller shaft is to be refitted, make alignment marks between the front propeller shaft flange and the handbrake drum at the transfer gearbox **(see illustration)**.

11 Unscrew the nuts securing the front of the propeller shaft to the handbrake drum.

12 Again, if the original propeller shaft is to be refitted, make alignment marks between the rear propeller shaft flange and the rear differential flange or rubber coupling, as applicable.

13 Counterhold the bolts, and unscrew the nuts securing the rear of the propeller shaft to the rear differential flange, or the flexible rubber coupling, as applicable **(see illustration)**.

14 Withdraw the flange bolts, then compress the propeller shaft sliding joint until the front of the propeller shaft can be withdrawn from the studs on the brake drum **(see illustration)**. Note that on models with a rear flexible rubber coupling, the rear of the propeller shaft fits over a spigot on the differential flange - it is therefore necessary to pull the shaft forwards before it can be lowered.

15 Withdraw the propeller shaft from under the vehicle.

Refitting

16 Refitting is a reversal of removal, bearing in mind the following points:

a) *Ensure that the propeller shaft is refitted with the sliding joint towards the front of the vehicle (nearest the transfer gearbox).*
b) *If the original propeller shaft is being refitted, align the marks made on the handbrake drum, rear differential flange or rubber coupling, and the propeller shaft flanges before removal.*
c) *Tighten the securing nuts and bolts to the specified torque.*

2.13 Counterhold the bolts, and unscrew the nuts securing the propeller shaft to the rubber coupling

2.14 Withdraw the front of the propeller shaft from the studs on the brake drum

3 Propeller shaft - inspection and overhaul

Note: *On some later models, sealed propeller shafts are fitted, which cannot be overhauled. In the event of wear in such shafts, it is likely that the complete shaft will have to be renewed. Consult a Land Rover dealer for further information.*

Inspection

1 Wear in the universal joint needle roller bearings is characterised by vibration in the transmission, clonks on taking up the drive, and in extreme cases (lack of lubrication), unpleasant metallic noises as the bearings break up.

2 To test the universal joints for wear with the propeller shaft in place, apply the handbrake, and chock the wheels.

3 Working under the vehicle, apply leverage between the yokes using a large screwdriver or a flat metal bar. Wear is indicated by movement between the shaft yoke and the coupling flange yoke. Check all the universal joints in this way.

4 To check the splined sleeve on the front of both shafts, try to push the shafts from side to side, and look for any excessive movement between the sleeve and the shaft. A further check can be made by gripping the shaft and sleeve, and turning them in opposite directions, again looking for excessive movement. As a rough guide, if *any* movement can be seen, the splines are worn, and the shaft assembly should be renewed.

5 If a universal joint is worn, a new joint must be obtained and fitted as described later in this Section.

6 If the sliding joint is excessively worn, the complete shaft assembly must be renewed.

7 Where applicable, check the condition of the rear propeller shaft flexible rubber coupling, with reference to Section 4.

Overhaul

Dismantling

8 With the propeller shaft removed as described in Section 2, proceed as follows.

9 If working on the front propeller shaft, release the clips securing the rubber gaiter over the sliding joint, and slide the gaiter

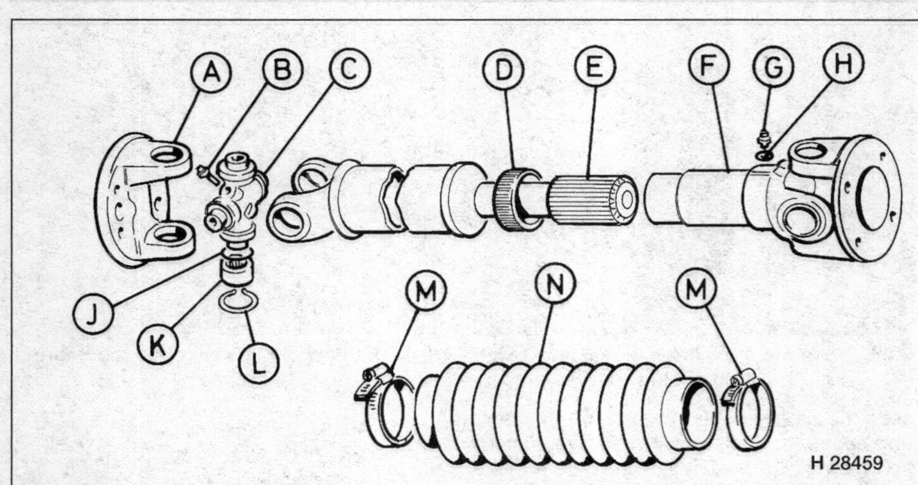
A
B
C
D
E
F
G
H
J
K
L
M
N
M
H 28459

A Yoke
B Grease nipple for universal joint
C Spider
D Dust cap
E Splined shaft
F Splined sleeve
G Grease nipple for splined joint
H Washer
J Seal
K Needle-roller bearing assembly
L Bearing retaining circlip
M Gaiter clips (front shaft only)
N Sliding joint gaiter (front shaft only)

3.9 Propeller shaft components

towards the rear of the shaft **(see illustration)**.

10 Check that alignment marks are visible on the two halves of the shaft (normally two stamped arrows) **(see illustration)**. If no marks can be found, scribe a line along the two halves of the shaft, to ensure that the two halves are reassembled in exactly the same position. This is vital, to ensure that the correct universal joint alignment and shaft balance is maintained.

11 Unscrew the dust cap, and withdraw the front section of the shaft from the splined end of the rear section.

12 Working on one of the universal joints, note the position of the grease nipple on the spider in relation to the adjacent shaft yoke, and coupling flange yoke (make alignment marks on the yokes). This is vital to ensure correct reassembly, and to ensure that the shaft balance is maintained.

13 Clean away all traces of dirt and grease from the circlips located on the ends of the joint spiders, and from the grease nipple.

14 Unscrew the grease nipple.

15 Using a suitable pair of circlip pliers, remove the four joint circlips **(see illustration)**. If a circlip proves difficult to remove, as a last resort, place a drift on the bearing cup, in the centre of the circlip, and tap the top of the bearing cup to ease the pressure on the circlip.

16 Support the end of the shaft in a vice, with the yoke in a vertical plane. Using a hammer and a suitable drift (a socket of appropriate size, for example), tap the uppermost bearing cup until the bottom bearing cup protrudes from the yoke **(see illustration)**.

17 Remove the shaft from the vice, then securely grip the protruding bearing cup in the vice jaws. Turn the shaft from side to side, at the same time lifting the shaft until the bearing cup comes free.

18 Refit the shaft to the vice, with the exposed spider uppermost. Tap the spider with the hammer and drift until the lower bearing cup protrudes, then remove the cup as described previously.

19 The coupling flange and the spider can now be removed from the shaft, and the remaining two bearing cups can be removed as described previously.

20 Where applicable, repeat the operations described in paragraphs 12 to 19 to remove the remaining joint from the shaft.

Inspection

21 With the universal joint dismantled, carefully examine the needle rollers, bearing cups and spider for wear, scoring and pitting of the surface finish. If any wear is detected, the joint must be renewed **(see illustration)**.

22 Where applicable, unscrew the sliding joint grease nipple, and thoroughly clean the nipple and its hole.

23 If working on the front propeller shaft, examine the condition of the sliding joint rubber gaiter, and renew if necessary.

24 Temporarily fit the front section of the shaft to the rear section, ensuring that the alignment marks are correctly positioned. Grip the front section of the shaft in a vice, and check for wear in the sliding joint splines, as described in paragraph 4.

Reassembly

25 If a new joint is being fitted, remove the bearing cups from the new spider. Check that

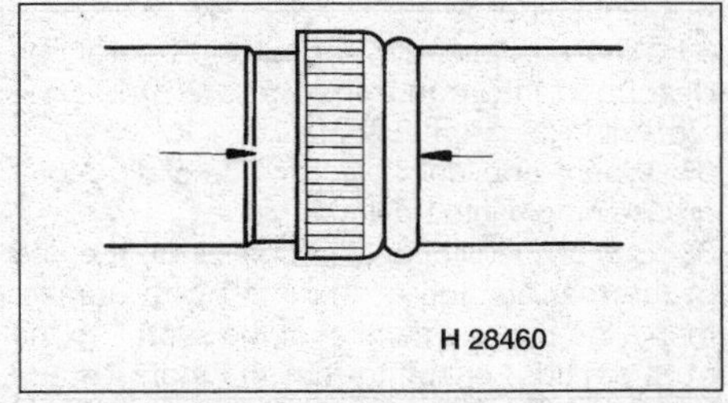
H 28460

3.10 Alignment marks on two halves of propeller shaft

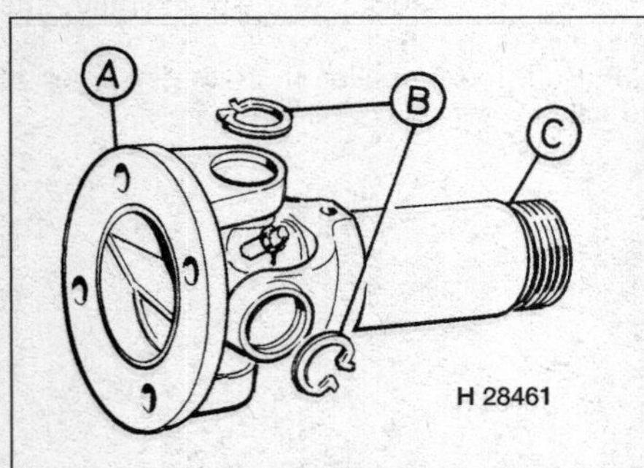
A
B
C
H 28461

3.15 Propeller shaft universal joint
A Coupling flange B Circlips C Shaft

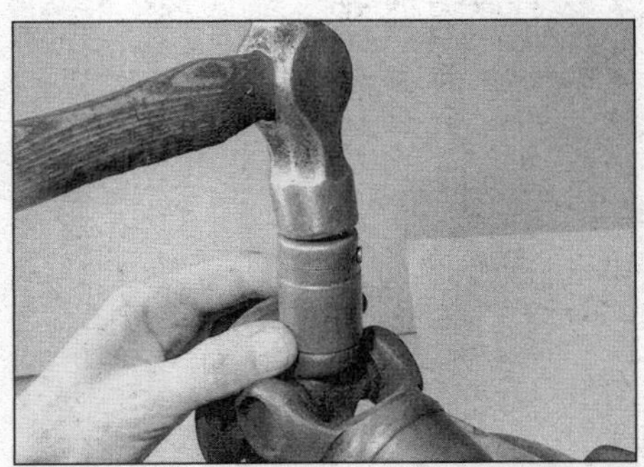

3.16 Tapping the uppermost bearing cup

3.21 Universal joint bearing components

all the needle rollers are present, and correctly positioned in the bearing cups.

26 Ensure that the bearing cups are one-third full of fresh grease (multi-purpose lithium-based grease - see *Lubricants and fluids* at the end of *Weekly checks*).

27 Fit the new spider, complete with seals, into the coupling flange yoke. Make sure that the grease nipple hole is aligned with the mark on the yoke made during dismantling, and note that the grease nipple hole must face away from the coupling flange.

28 Partially insert one of the bearing cups into the yoke, and enter the spider trunnion into the bearing cup, taking care not to dislodge the needle rollers **(see illustration)**.

29 Similarly, insert a bearing cup into the opposite yoke.

30 Using the vice, carefully press both bearing cups into place, ensuring that the spider trunnions do not dislodge any of the needle rollers.

31 Using a suitable tube or socket of a slightly smaller diameter than the bearing cups, press each cup into its respective yoke, until the top of the cup just reaches the lower land of the circlip groove. **Do not** press the cups below this point, as damage may be caused to the cups and seals.

32 Fit the new circlips to retain the bearing cups **(see illustration)**.

33 Engage the spider with the yokes on the relevant propeller shaft section, then partially fit both bearing cups to the yokes, taking care not to dislodge any of the needle rollers.

34 Press the bearing cups into position, and fit the new circlips, as described in paragraphs 30 to 32.

35 Screw the grease nipple into position in the joint spider.

36 Where applicable, repeat the operations described in paragraphs 25 to 35 to fit the remaining joint to the shaft.

37 Where applicable, screw the sliding joint grease nipple into position.

38 Smear the sliding joint splines on the end of the rear section of the shaft with grease, then slide the rear section of the shaft into the front section, ensuring that the marks made during dismantling are aligned. **Note:** *Do not pack grease into the open end of the shaft front section, as this may prevent the shaft from being pushed fully home.*

39 Screw the sliding joint dust cap into position.

40 If working on the front propeller shaft, slide the rubber gaiter over the sliding joint, and secure in position with the two clips. If screw-type clips are used, fit the clips with the screws 180°, apart to help maintain the balance of the shaft.

41 Refit the propeller shaft as described in Section 2, then lubricate the joints using a grease gun applied to the grease nipples (see the relevant part of Chapter 1).

3.28 Press the cups into place using a vice and socket

3.32 Fit new circlips to retain the bearing cups

4 Rear propeller shaft rubber coupling - inspection and renewal

Inspection

1 Later models use a flexible rubber coupling to connect the rear of the propeller shaft to the rear differential flange, instead of the universal joint used on earlier models.

2 Deterioration of the rubber coupling will be self-evident on inspection. Look particularly for cracks around the bolt holes.

Renewal

3 Remove the rear propeller shaft, as described in Section 2.

4 Counterhold the bolts, and unscrew the nuts securing the coupling to the rear differential flange, then withdraw the coupling. Recover the washers.

5 Thoroughly clean the differential flange and the spigot.

6 Fit the new coupling, and secure with the nuts and bolts, ensuring that the washers are in place under the nuts.

7 Counterhold the bolts, and tighten the nuts to the specified torque.

8 Refit the rear propeller shaft as described in Section 2.

5 Front propeller shaft rubber gaiter - renewal

1 Remove the propeller shaft as described in Section 2.

2 Loosen the two gaiter securing clips, and slide the gaiter towards the rear of the shaft.

3 Check that alignment marks are visible on the two halves of the shaft (normally two stamped arrows). If no marks can be found, scribe a line along the two halves of the shaft, to ensure that the two halves are reassembled in exactly the same position. This is vital, to ensure that the correct universal joint alignment and shaft balance is maintained.

4 Unscrew the dust cap, and withdraw the front section of the shaft from the splined end of the rear section.

5 Slide the gaiter and the clips from the shaft.

6 Clean the shaft splines, then slide the new gaiter onto the rear section of the shaft.

7 Smear the shaft splines with fresh grease, and slide the rear section of the shaft onto the front section, ensuring that the marks made during dismantling are aligned. **Note:** *Do not pack grease into the open end of the shaft front section, as this may prevent the shaft from being pushed fully home.*

8 Screw the sliding joint dust cap into position.

9 Slide the rubber gaiter over the sliding joint, and secure in position with the two clips. If screw-type clips are used, fit the clips with the screws 180° apart, to help maintain the balance of the shaft.

10 Refit the propeller shaft as described in Section 2.

Chapter 9
Front and rear axles

Contents

Degrees of difficulty

Easy, suitable for novice with little experience 

Fairly easy, suitable for beginner with some experience 

Fairly difficult, suitable for competent DIY mechanic

Difficult, suitable for experienced DIY mechanic

Very difficult, suitable for expert DIY or professional

Specifications

Type

Front	Spiral bevel with enclosed CV joints and fully-floating halfshafts
Rear	Spiral bevel with fully-floating halfshafts
Differential ratio (front and rear)	3.54:1

Adjustment data

Hub endfloat (front and rear):	
Early models	0.013 to 0.100 mm
Later models	0.010 mm
Front halfshaft endfloat (later models only)	0.08 to 0.25 mm
Front swivel pin housing bearing preload	See text

Torque wrench settings	Nm	lbf ft
Driving member retaining bolts (later models)*	65	48
Halfshaft flange retaining bolts	65	48
Hub adjusting nut:		
Early models	See text	
Later models:		
Stage 1	61	45
Fully slacken nut, then tighten to Stage 2	4	3
Hub locknut	100	74
Rear axle upper link balljoint nut	176	130
Roadwheel nuts	129	95
Stub axle bolts*	65	48
Swivel pin assembly-to-axle bolts*	73	54
Swivel pin housing oil seal retaining plate bolts	11	8
Swivel pin retaining bolts:		
Non-ABS models (upper and lower)*	78	58
ABS models:		
Upper pin bolts	65	48
Lower pin bolts*	25	18

**Use thread-locking fluid*

1 General information

Both the front and rear axles are of a similar design, comprising a one-piece steel casing, housing the differential assembly and two driveshafts (halfshafts). The rear shafts are of solid steel construction, the inner ends of which are splined into the differential assembly, while the outer ends are attached to the hubs **(see illustration)**.

To enable the front wheels to turn from lock-to-lock while being driven, the front halfshafts incorporate a CV joint on their outer ends. The CV joint runs inside an oil-filled swivel pin housing, the swivel pins being located in tapered roller bearings **(see illustration)**.

Refer to Chapter 11 for details of axle attachment and suspension details.

Throughout this Chapter, it is often necessary to identify models by their VIN number. Refer to *Vehicle identification numbers* at the end of this manual for information on VIN numbers.

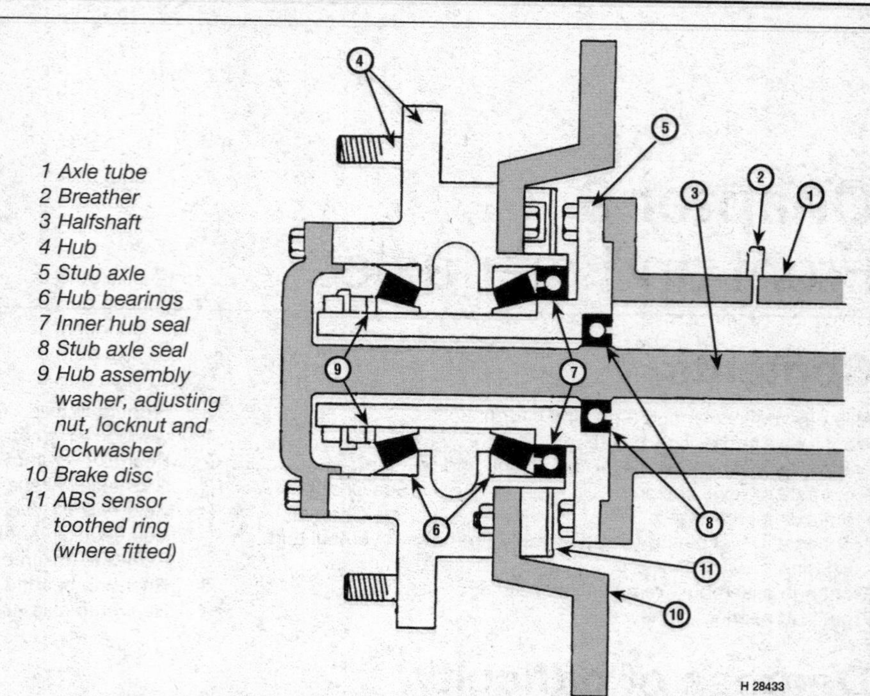
1 Axle tube
2 Breather
3 Halfshaft
4 Hub
5 Stub axle
6 Hub bearings
7 Inner hub seal
8 Stub axle seal
9 Hub assembly washer, adjusting nut, locknut and lockwasher
10 Brake disc
11 ABS sensor toothed ring (where fitted)
H 28433

1.1 Cross-sectional view of rear axle hub and associated components

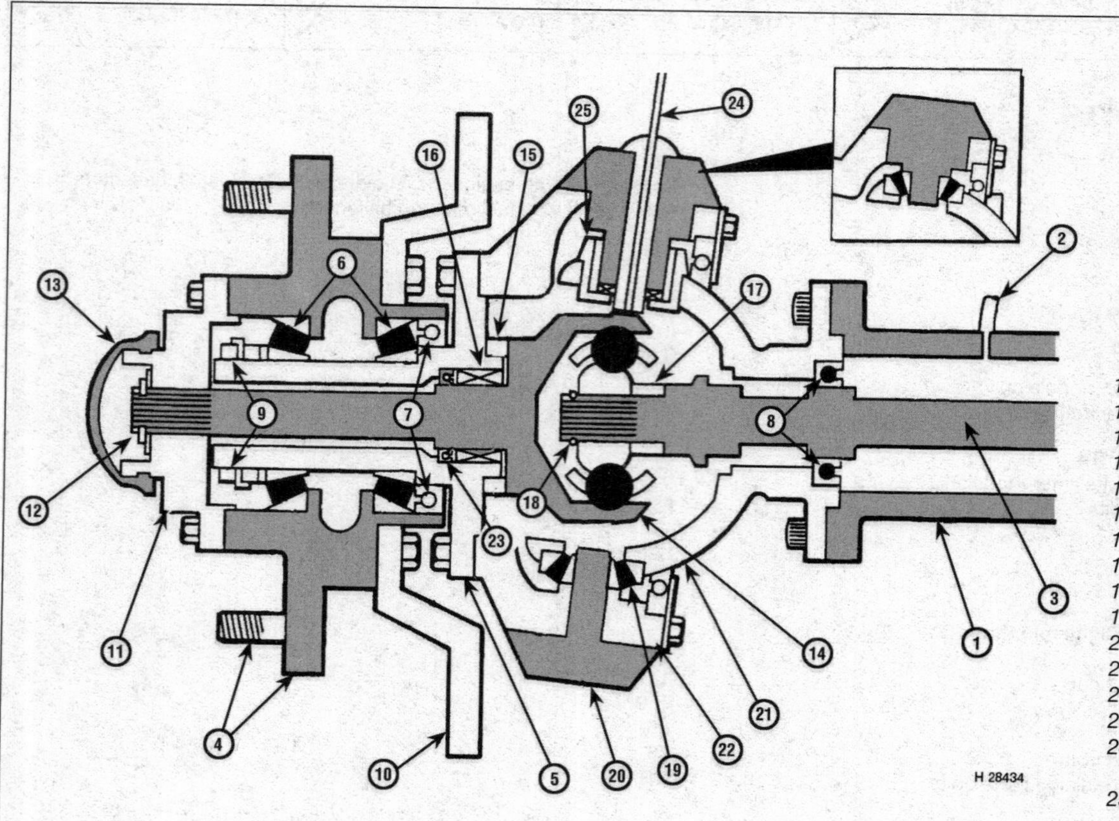
H 28434

1 Axle tube
2 Breather
3 Inner halfshaft section
4 Hub
5 Stub axle
6 Hub bearings
7 Inner hub seal
8 Circlip
9 Hub assembly washer, adjusting nut, locknut and lockwasher
10 Brake disc
11 Driving member
12 Shim and circlip
13 Hub cap
14 Outer halfshaft section
15 Bush
16 Needle-roller bearing
17 Spacer
18 Circlip
19 Swivel pin bearing
20 Swivel pin
21 Swivel ball
22 Swivel pin housing
23 Seal
24 ABS wheel sensor (where fitted)
25 Upper swivel pin bush

1.2 Cross-sectional view of front axle hub and associated components - later model with ABS (inset shows non-ABS upper swivel pin arrangement)

2 Front axle halfshaft - removal, inspection and refitting

Note: *Refer to Vehicle identification numbers at the end of this manual for information on VIN numbers.*

Removal - early models (up to VIN JA032850)

1 Apply the handbrake, and loosen the nuts on the relevant front roadwheel. Jack up the front of the vehicle and support it on axle stands positioned underneath the chassis (see *Jacking and vehicle support*). Remove the relevant front roadwheel. Proceed as described under the relevant sub-heading.

Halfshaft outer section

2 Drain the swivel pin housing oil as described in the relevant part of Chapter 1, or be prepared for some oil spillage as the shaft is removed.

3 Slacken and remove the five bolts and washers securing the halfshaft to the centre of the hub, and withdraw the outer shaft from the centre of the hub assembly. Recover the gasket from the halfshaft flange, and discard it.

Constant velocity joint and halfshaft inner section

4 Remove the stub axle as described in Section 5.

5 Remove the constant velocity joint and spacer from the end of the halfshaft inner section, then withdraw the halfshaft inner section from the axle, and slide the bush off the end of the shaft.

Removal - later models (from VIN JA032851)

6 Apply the handbrake, and loosen the nuts on the relevant front roadwheel. Jack up the front of the vehicle and support it on axle stands positioned underneath the chassis (see *Jacking and vehicle support*). Remove the relevant front roadwheel.

7 Remove the stub axle as described in Section 5. Pull the halfshaft assembly out from the axle **(see illustration)**.

8 Clamp the inner section of the shaft in a vice with soft jaws then, using a soft-faced mallet, tap the constant velocity joint off the end of the inner shaft.

2.7 Removing the halfshaft assembly - later models

9 Remove the circlip from the end of the inner shaft, and slide off the spacer. Discard the circlip; a new one must be used on refitting.

Inspection - early models (up to VIN JA032850)

Halfshaft outer section

10 Inspect the halfshaft splines and hub flange for signs of wear or damage, and renew if necessary.

Constant velocity joint and halfshaft inner section

11 Thoroughly clean all components using paraffin, or a suitable solvent, and dry thoroughly. Carry out a visual inspection as follows.

12 Inspect the halfshaft inner sections for signs of wear or damage, paying particular attention to its splines. Check the bush for signs of wear or damage, and renew worn components as necessary.

13 Move the constant velocity joint inner member from side to side, to expose each ball in turn at the top of its track. Examine the balls for cracks, flat spots or signs of surface pitting.

14 Inspect the ball tracks on the inner and outer members. If the tracks have widened, the balls will no longer be a tight fit. At the same time, check the ball cage windows for wear or cracking between the windows.

15 If the constant velocity joint assembly shows signs of wear or damage, it must be renewed.

Inspection - later models (from VIN JA032851)

16 Proceed as described above in paragraphs 11 to 15. Note that the constant velocity joint circlip must be renewed whenever it is disturbed.

Refitting - early models (up to VIN JA032850)

Halfshaft outer section

17 Ensure that the halfshaft and hub mating surfaces are clean and dry, and fit a new gasket.

3.3 Slide the brake caliper assembly off the disc, and tie it to the coil spring to prevent straining the brake hose

18 Slide the halfshaft outer section into position, then refit its retaining bolts and washers, tightening them to the specified torque setting.

19 Top-up/refill the swivel pin housing with oil as described in the relevant part of Chapter 1.

Constant velocity joint and halfshaft inner section

20 Lubricate the bush with a smear of oil, and slide it onto halfshaft inner section.

21 Insert the halfshaft inner section into the axle, aligning its splines with those of the differential sunwheel.

22 Check that the halfshaft inner section is correctly located, and fit the spacer to the shaft.

23 Fit the constant velocity joint to the halfshaft, making sure that it is fitted the correct way around.

24 Refit the stub axle as described in Section 5.

Refitting - later models (from VIN JA032851)

25 Slide the spacer onto the inner shaft, and fit a new circlip, making sure that it is correctly located in the shaft groove.

26 Locate the constant velocity joint on inner shaft splines, and tap it onto the driveshaft until the circlip engages in its groove. Make sure that the joint is securely retained by the circlip.

27 Insert the halfshaft inner section into the axle, aligning its splines with those of the differential sunwheel.

28 Check that the halfshaft inner section is correctly located, then refit the stub axle as described in Section 5.

3 Front hub assembly - removal and refitting

Note: *Refer to Vehicle identification numbers at the end of this manual for information on VIN numbers.*

Removal

1 Apply the handbrake, and loosen the nuts on the relevant front roadwheel. Jack up the front of the vehicle and support it on axle stands positioned underneath the chassis (see *Jacking and vehicle support*). Remove the relevant front roadwheel.

2 Undo the (upper swivel pin) bolts securing the brake hose retaining bracket to the swivel housing, position the bracket clear of the housing, then refit the bolts to prevent oil leakage.

3 Slacken and remove the two retaining bolts securing the brake caliper in position. Slide the caliper assembly off the disc and, using a piece of wire or string, tie the caliper to the front suspension coil spring, to avoid placing any strain on the hydraulic brake hose **(see illustration)**. Refit the upper swivel pin bolts,

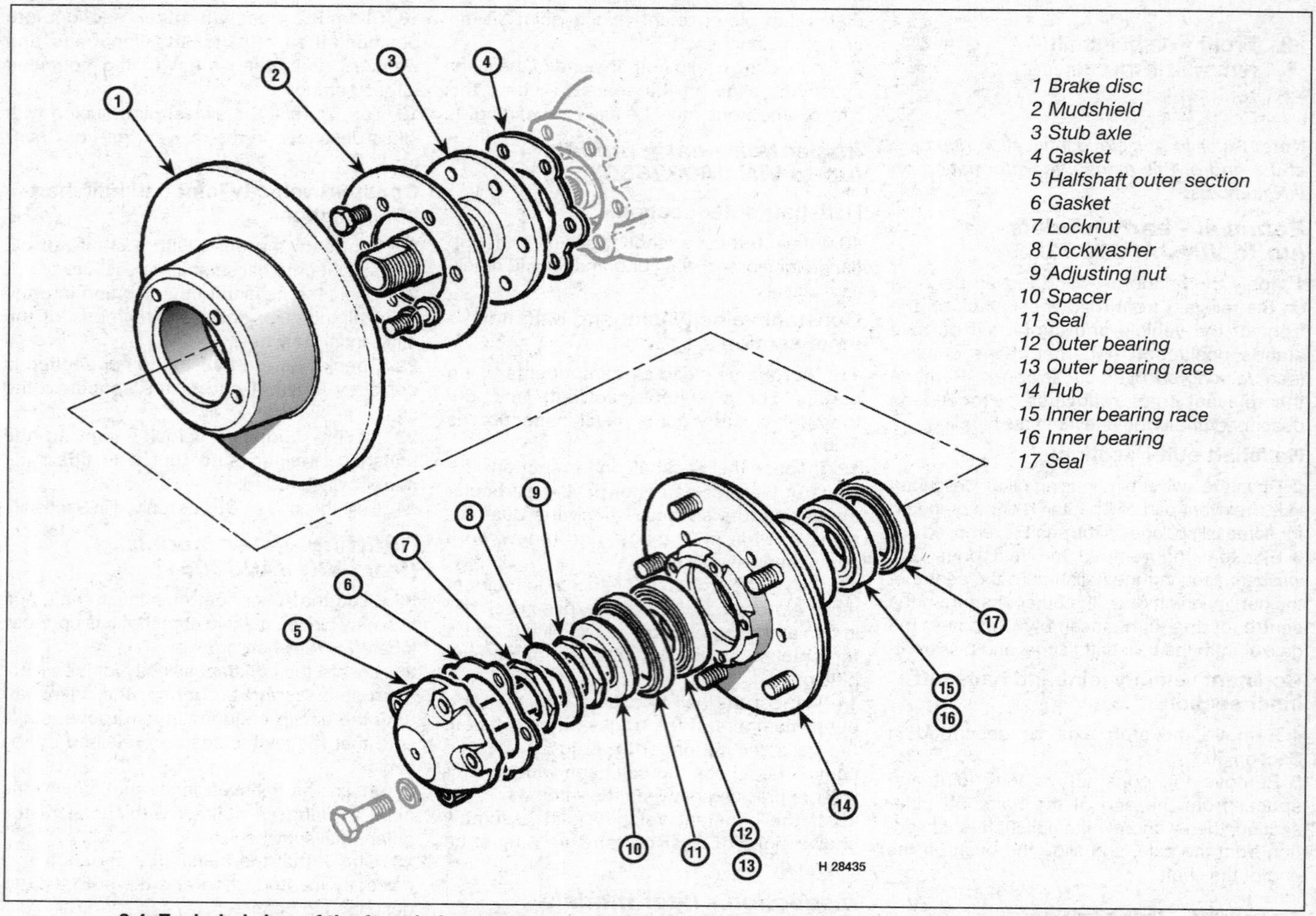

1 Brake disc
2 Mudshield
3 Stub axle
4 Gasket
5 Halfshaft outer section
6 Gasket
7 Locknut
8 Lockwasher
9 Adjusting nut
10 Spacer
11 Seal
12 Outer bearing
13 Outer bearing race
14 Hub
15 Inner bearing race
16 Inner bearing
17 Seal

H 28435

3.4 Exploded view of the front hub assembly and associated components - early models (up to VIN JA032850)

tighten them by hand only, then proceed as described under the relevant sub-heading.

Early models (up to VIN JA032850)

4 Remove the halfshaft outer section as described in Section 2 **(see illustration)**.

5 Using a hammer and suitable chisel, bend back the lockwasher tab from the hub locknut's flat **(see illustration)**.

6 Slacken and remove the hub locknut, and slide off the lockwasher. Discard the lockwasher - a new one must be used on refitting.

7 Unscrew the hub adjusting nut, then slide off the spacer, noting which way around it is fitted.

8 Slide the hub assembly off the stub axle **(see illustration)**.

3.5 Using a hammer and suitable chisel, bend back the lockwasher from the locknut's flat

3.8 Removing the front hub assembly

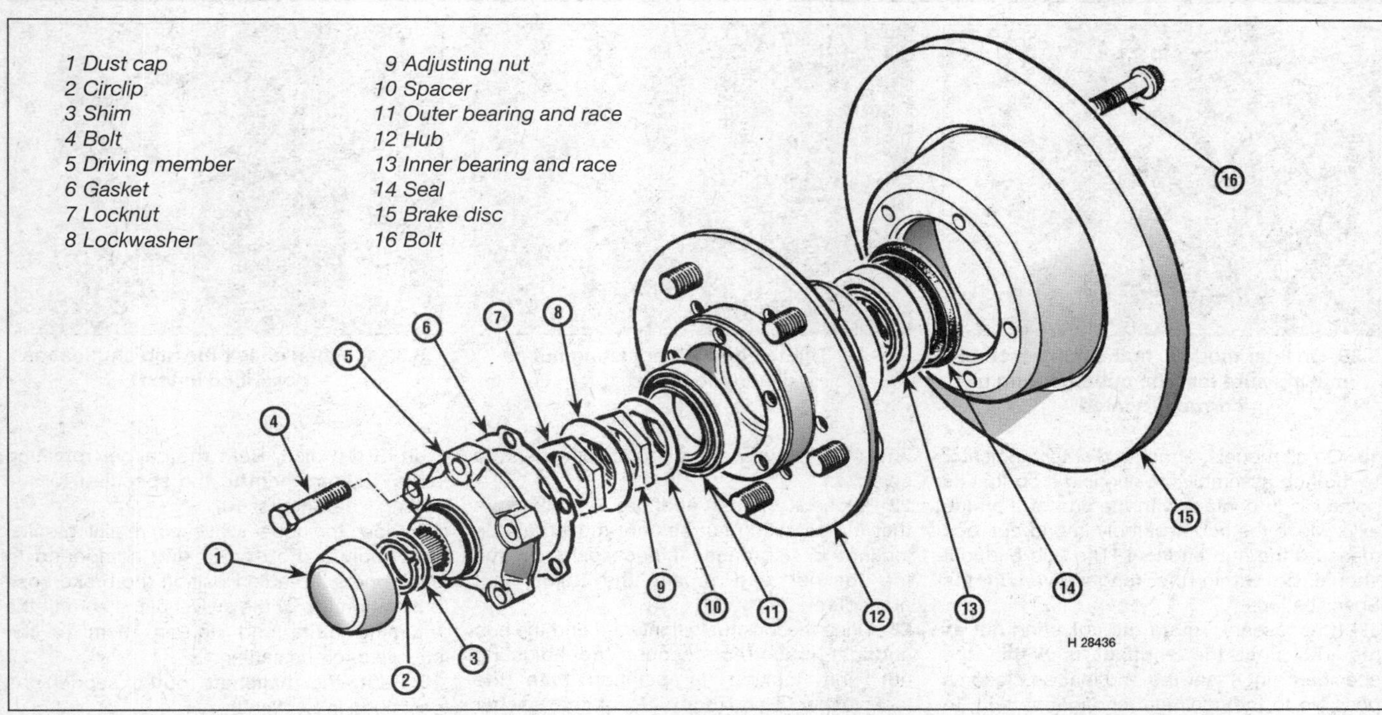
1 Dust cap
2 Circlip
3 Shim
4 Bolt
5 Driving member
6 Gasket
7 Locknut
8 Lockwasher
9 Adjusting nut
10 Spacer
11 Outer bearing and race
12 Hub
13 Inner bearing and race
14 Seal
15 Brake disc
16 Bolt
H 28436

3.9 Exploded view of the front hub assembly and associated components - later models (from VIN JA032851)

Later models (from VIN JA032851)

9 Lever off the dust cap from the centre of the hub assembly **(see illustration)**.

10 Using circlip pliers, remove the circlip from the end of the halfshaft, then slide off the thrustwasher(s) **(see illustrations)**.

11 Slacken and remove the five retaining bolts, then slide the driving member off the end of the halfshaft **(see illustration)**. Remove the member gasket and discard it - a new gasket must be used on refitting.

12 Remove the hub assembly as described above in paragraphs 5 to 8, taking care not to allow the outer bearing to fall out of the hub assembly.

Refitting

Early models (up to VIN JA032850)

13 Apply a smear of lithium-based grease to the lips of the hub oil seals.

14 Carefully slide the hub assembly onto the stub axle, taking care not to damage the oil seal lips.

15 Slide the spacer onto the stub axle, ensuring that it is fitted the correct way around **(see illustration)**.

16 Fit the hub adjusting nut, tightening it by hand only **(see illustration)**.

17 If a new hub/bearing has been installed, tighten the hub adjusting nut whilst rotating the hub to settle the bearings in position. Tighten the nut until all free play is removed from the bearings, then slacken it by a quarter of a turn; this will settle the bearings in position.

3.10a On later models, remove the circlip from the end of the halfshaft . . .

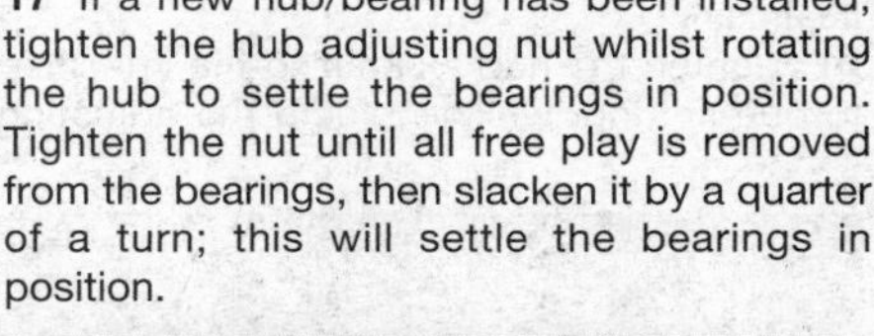

3.10b . . . and recover the thrustwasher(s)

3.11 Removing the hub driving member

3.15 Fit the spacer . . .

3.16 . . . then screw on the hub adjusting nut

3.28 On later models, fit the hub assembly, making sure that the outer bearing is correctly seated

3.29 Tighten the hub adjusting nut as described in text . . .

3.30 . . . then check the hub endfloat as described in text

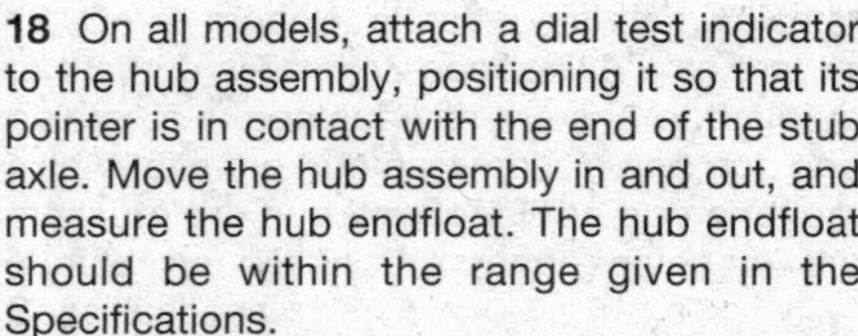

18 On all models, attach a dial test indicator to the hub assembly, positioning it so that its pointer is in contact with the end of the stub axle. Move the hub assembly in and out, and measure the hub endfloat. The hub endfloat should be within the range given in the Specifications.

19 If necessary, rotate the adjusting nut as required until the endfloat is within the specified range (set the endfloat as close as possible to the minimum endfloat setting, to allow for wear in use).

20 When the endfloat is correctly set, slide a new lockwasher onto the stub axle, then fit the locknut.

21 Tighten the hub locknut to the specified torque setting, whilst holding the adjusting nut stationary with a large open-ended spanner.

22 Recheck the hub endfloat, to make sure that the adjusting nut has not moved as the locknut is tightened. If necessary, loosen the locknut and repeat the adjustment procedure.

23 Once the locknut is tightened and the hub endfloat is correct, secure the adjusting nut and locknut in position with the lockwasher. Bend one side of the washer down so it contacts one of the adjusting nut flats, and bend the opposite side of the washer down so it contacts one of the locknut flats.

24 Slide the brake caliper assembly back into position, ensuring that its pads pass either side of the disc. Refit the caliper retaining bolts, tighten them to the specified torque setting (see Chapter 10).

25 Clean the upper swivel pin retaining bolts, and apply a drop of locking compound to each one's threads. Position the brake hose bracket on top of the swivel pin, then refit the retaining bolts and tighten them to the specified torque setting.

26 Refit the halfshaft outer section as described in Section 2.

3.31a Once the endfloat is correctly set, fit a new lockwasher . . .

3.31b . . . and screw on the locknut

3.33a Tighten the locknut to the specified torque, then bend one side of the lockwasher inwards so it contacts one of the adjusting nut flats . . .

3.33b . . . then bend the opposite side outwards so that it contacts one of the locknut flats

Later models (from VIN JA032851)

27 Prior to refitting, remove all traces of locking compound from the hub assembly threads, ideally by running a tap of the correct size and pitch down them.

28 Install the hub assembly as described in paragraphs 13 to 16, ensuring that the outer bearing is correctly fitted **(see illustration)**.

29 Tighten the hub adjusting nut to the Stage 1 torque setting, whilst rotating the hub to settle the bearings in position **(see illustration)**.

30 Fully slacken the adjusting nut, then tighten it to its Stage 2 torque setting. This should correctly set the hub endfloat (see *Specifications*). This can be checked using a dial test indicator as described in paragraph 18 **(see illustration)**.

31 Slide a new lockwasher onto the stub axle, then fit the locknut **(see illustrations)**. Tighten the hub locknut to the specified torque setting, whilst holding the adjusting nut stationary with a large open-ended spanner.

32 Recheck the hub endfloat (see paragraph 18), to make sure that the adjusting nut has not moved as the locknut is tightened. If necessary, loosen the locknut and repeat the adjustment procedure.

33 Once the locknut is tightened and the hub endfloat is correct, secure the adjusting nut and locknut in position with the lockwasher. Bend one side of the washer down so it contacts one of the adjusting nut flats, and bend the opposite side of the washer down so it contacts one of the lockwasher flats **(see illustrations)**.

34 Ensure that the hub and driving member

3.34 Ensure that the mating surfaces are clean and dry, and fit a new driving member gasket to the hub

3.36 Prior to installation, apply locking compound to the driving member retaining bolt threads

3.38 Checking halfshaft endfloat

mating surfaces are clean and dry, and fit a new gasket **(see illustration)**.

35 Slide the driving member into position.

36 Clean the threads of each driving member retaining bolt, and apply a drop of fresh locking compound to them. Install the bolts, and tighten them to the specified torque setting **(see illustration)**.

37 Slide the thrustwasher onto the halfshaft, and secure it in position with the circlip. Ensure that the circlip is correctly located in the halfshaft groove.

38 Screw a suitable bolt into the threaded end of the halfshaft, then attach a dial test indicator to the hub assembly, positioning it so that its pointer is in contact with the end of the bolt **(see illustration)**. Move the halfshaft in and out, using the bolt, and measure the endfloat. The halfshaft endfloat should be within the range given in the Specifications.

39 To adjust the endfloat, remove the circlip, and slide off the thrustwasher. Calculate the required thickness of shim needed, and obtain it from your Land Rover dealer. Fit the shim, and secure it in position with the circlip.

Set the endfloat as close as possible to the minimum endfloat setting, to allow for wear in use.

40 Once the halfshaft endfloat is correctly set, unscrew the bolt, and refit the dust cap to the hub assembly **(see illustration)**.

41 Slide the brake caliper assembly back into position, ensuring that its pads pass either side of the disc. Refit the caliper retaining bolts, tighten them to the specified torque setting (see Chapter 10).

42 Remove and clean the upper swivel pin retaining bolts, and apply a drop of locking compound to each one's threads. Position the brake hose bracket on top of the swivel pin, then refit the retaining bolts and tighten them to the specified torque setting **(see illustration)**.

43 Refit the roadwheel, then lower the vehicle to the ground and tighten the wheel nuts to the specified torque setting.

44 Top-up/refill the swivel pin housing as described in the relevant part of Chapter 1.

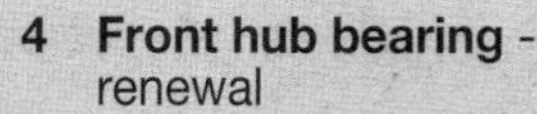

4 Front hub bearing - renewal

Note: *A press may be required to dismantle and rebuild the assembly if the bearing outer races are a tight fit in the hub. If such a tool is not available, a large bench vice and suitable spacers (such as large sockets) will serve as an adequate substitute.*

3.40 Once halfshaft endfloat is correctly set, refit the dust cap to the hub

1 Remove the hub assembly as described in Section 3.

2 Remove the brake disc as described in Chapter 10.

3 Using a large flat-bladed screwdriver, lever out the inner oil seal from the hub assembly **(see illustration)**. On early models, note the correct fitted depth of the outer seal in the hub, then lever it out of position.

4 Remove the outer and inner bearing inner races from the hub assembly.

5 Support the hub securely on blocks or in a vice, then using a hammer and suitable punch, carefully tap the inner and outer

3.42 With the caliper in position, apply locking compound to the threads of the upper swivel pin bolts, then tighten them to the specified torque setting

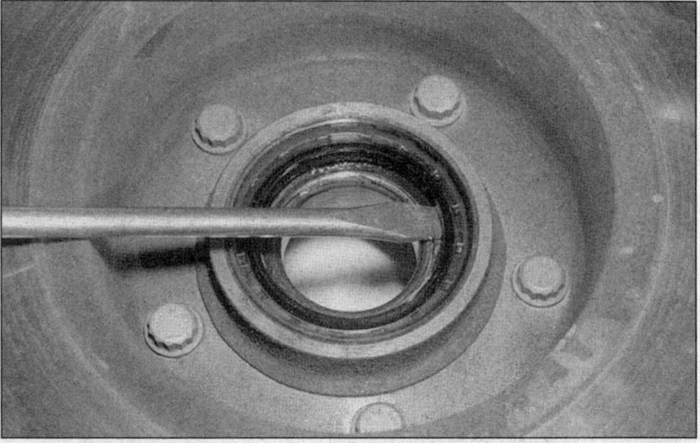

4.3 Lever the oil seal out from the hub using a large flat-bladed screwdriver

GREASE
LB 10
4.9 **Pack the hub bearings with a suitable multi-purpose lithium-based grease**

5.7 **On later models inspect the bearing, oil seal and thrust ring fitted to the rear of the stub axle for signs of wear or damage**

5.12 **Fit a new gasket (arrowed), then slide the stub axle into position**

bearing outer races out from the hub assembly.

6 Thoroughly clean the hub bore, removing all traces of dirt and grease. Polish away any burrs or raised edges which might hinder reassembly. Check both for cracks or any other signs of wear or damage, and renew them if necessary. Examine the stub axle for signs of wear or damage, and renew if necessary (see Section 5). Renew both bearings and oil seal(s) as a matter of course.

7 On reassembly, apply a light film of oil to the inner bearing outer race and hub bore, to aid installation.

8 Securely support the hub, and locate the inner bearing outer race in the hub. Press the race fully into position, ensuring that it enters the hub squarely, using a suitable tubular spacer which bears only on the bearing outer race.

9 Pack the bearing inner race with a multi-purpose lithium based grease. Work the grease well into the bearing race, apply a smear to the outer race surface, then fit the inner race to the hub assembly **(see illustration)**.

10 Install the new inner oil seal, making sure that its sealing lip is facing inwards. Press the seal into position, ensuring it enters the hub squarely, until it is flush with the hub surface.

11 Turn the hub over, and fit the outer bearing as described in paragraphs 7 to 9.

12 On early models, install the new outer oil seal, making sure that its sealing lip is facing inwards. Press the seal into position, ensuring that it enters the hub squarely, until it is positioned at the same depth as the original (noted prior to removal).

13 Refit the brake disc as described in Chapter 10.

14 Install the hub assembly as described in Section 3.

5 Front stub axle - removal and refitting

Removal

1 Remove the hub assembly as described in Section 3.

2 If not already done, drain the swivel pin housing oil as described in the relevant part of Chapter 1.

3 Make alignment marks between the stub axle and housing, then slacken and remove the six retaining bolts and washers.

4 Lift off the mudshield, then remove the stub axle from the swivel pin housing, and recover the gasket. Discard the gasket - a new one must be used on refitting.

5 Inspect the stub axle for signs of wear or damage, and renew if necessary.

6 On early models, check the bush fitted to the rear of the stub axle for signs of wear or damage. If renewal is necessary, it is recommended that the task is entrusted to a Land Rover dealer.

7 On later models, check the needle-roller bearing and oil seal arrangement fitted to the inside of the stub axle, and the thrust ring fitted to the rear of the axle flange, for signs of wear or damage **(see illustration)**. If renewal is necessary, the task should be entrusted to a Land Rover dealer.

Refitting

8 Prior to refitting, remove all traces of locking compound from the swivel housing threads, ideally by running a tap of the correct size and pitch down them.

9 Ensure that the halfshaft is correctly engaged with the differential splines.

10 Make sure that the stub axle and swivel pin housing mating surfaces are clean and dry, then fit a new gasket to the swivel housing.

11 Apply a smear of oil to the stub axle bush/bearing and seal (as applicable).

12 Slide the stub axle into position, aligning the marks made prior to removal **(see illustration)**. On early models, make sure that the constant velocity joint and halfshaft bush engage correctly as the stub axle is fitted.

13 Refit the mudshield to the stub axle **(see illustration)**.

14 Clean the threads of the retaining bolts, and apply a drop of fresh locking compound to them. Install the bolts and washers, and tighten them to the specified torque setting **(see illustrations)**.

15 Refit the hub assembly as described in Section 3.

5.13 **Refit the mudshield . . .**

5.14a **. . . then apply locking compound to the threads of the stub axle retaining bolts . . .**

5.14b **. . . and tighten them to the specified torque**

6 Front axle swivel pin housing assembly - removal, overhaul and refitting

Removal

1 Remove the complete halfshaft as described in Section 2.
2 Withdraw the split pin, then unscrew the nut securing the track rod to the swivel pin housing. Using a universal balljoint separator, free the track rod from the hub.
3 Where necessary, also free the drag link from the swivel pin housing, as described in paragraph 2.
4 On models with ABS, trace the wiring back from the sensor which is fitted to the top of the swivel pin housing. Disconnect the wiring connector, then work back along the wiring, freeing it from any relevant retaining clips.
5 On all models, slacken and remove the bolts and washers securing the swivel housing assembly to the axle, and remove it from the vehicle **(see illustrations)**. Recover the gasket and discard it - a new one must be used on refitting.

Overhaul

Models without ABS

6 Remove all traces of grease and dirt from the outside of the swivel housing assembly **(see illustration)**.
7 Undo the retaining bolts and washers, and remove the retaining plate and oil seal from the rear of the swivel housing, noting which way around the seal is fitted **(see illustration)**.
8 Undo the brake disc mudshield retaining bracket bolt and nut, and remove the shield **(see illustration)**.
9 Bend back the locking tabs (where necessary) then slacken and remove the two bolts securing the lower swivel pin to the housing. Remove the brake disc mudshield bracket **(see illustration)**.
10 Ease the lower swivel pin out of position, and recover the gasket.
11 Unscrew the upper swivel pin retaining bolts from the top of the swivel housing.
12 Ease the upper swivel pin from the housing, and recover the shim(s).

6.5a Slacken and remove the swivel pin housing retaining bolts . . .

6.5b . . . then lift off the housing assembly, and recover the gasket (arrowed)

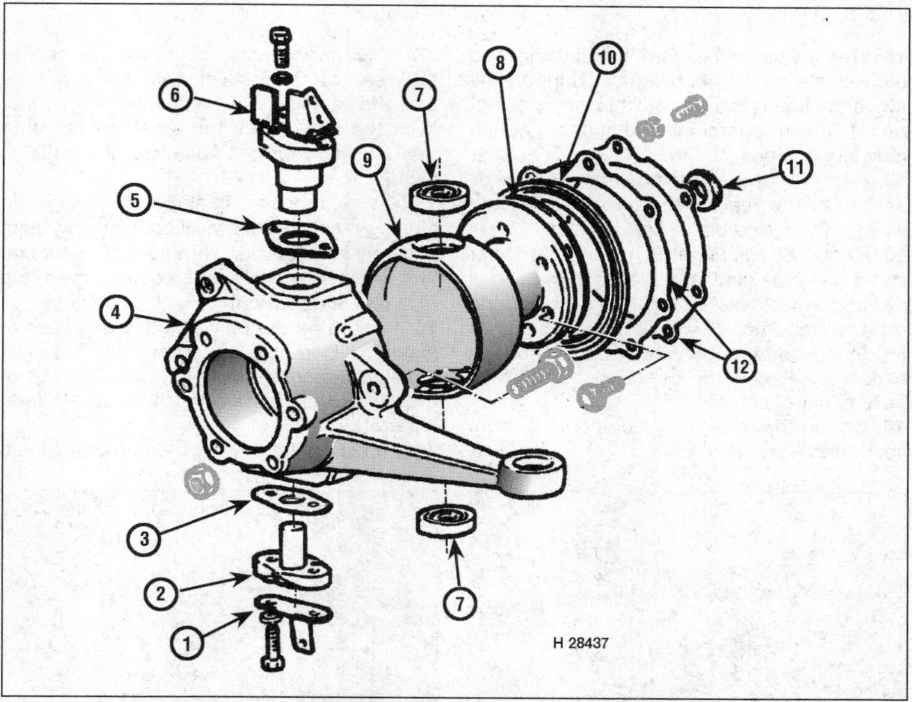
1
2
3
4
5
6
7
8
9
10
11
12
7
H 28437

6.6 Exploded view of the swivel pin housing components - non-ABS model (ABS model similar)

1 Mudshield bracket
2 Lower swivel pin
3 Gasket
4 Swivel pin housing
5 Shim
6 Upper swivel pin and brake hose bracket
7 Swivel pin bearing and race
8 Gasket
9 Swivel ball
10 Oil seal
11 Oil seal
12 Retaining plate and gasket

6.7 Remove the retaining plate from the rear of the swivel housing, and recover the oil seal

6.8 Removing the brake disc mudshield

6.9 Remove the lower swivel pin retaining bolts and recover the mudshield bracket, noting which way around it is fitted

6.13a Separate the swivel ball and housing, and recover the bearings

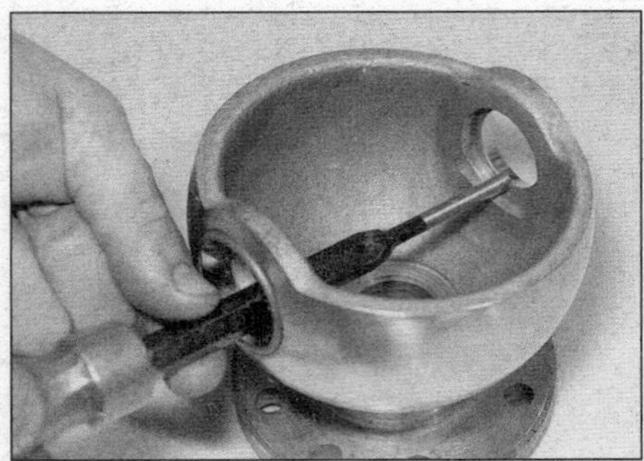

6.13b Tap the bearing outer races out of position using a hammer and suitable punch

6.18 Install the new bearing outer races using a suitable tubular drift which bears only on the hard outer edge of the race

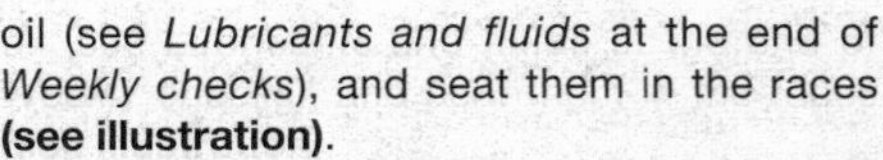

13 Free the swivel ball from the housing, and recover the swivel pin bearings. Support the swivel ball, and tap the bearing races out of position with a hammer and suitable punch **(see illustrations)**.

14 Where necessary, remove the smaller oil seal from the rear of the swivel ball. Note which way around the oil seal is fitted.

15 Check all components, paying particular attention to the contact surfaces of the swivel ball and swivel pins. Check that each bearing rotates smoothly, without any sign of roughness, and renew worn components as necessary. Renew the oil seal(s) and gaskets as a matter of course.

16 Obtain the necessary components from your Land Rover dealer.

17 Where necessary, fit the new oil seal to the rear of the swivel ball, making sure that its sealing lip is facing the away from the ball. Press the seal squarely into the housing until it is flush with the housing face.

18 On all models, fit the new swivel pin bearing races to the swivel ball, tapping them squarely into position with a suitable tubular drift which bears only on the outer edge of the race **(see illustration)**.

19 Prior to reassembly, remove all traces of locking compound from the swivel housing threads, ideally by running a tap of the correct size and pitch down them **(see illustration)**.

20 Lubricate the bearings with the specified oil (see *Lubricants and fluids* at the end of *Weekly checks*), and seat them in the races **(see illustration)**.

21 Reassemble the swivel ball with the housing, making sure that the bearings remain correctly seated.

22 Apply a smear of suitable sealant to either side of the lower swivel pin gasket, and fit the gasket to the pin.

23 Install the lower swivel pin with its lug outermost **(see illustration)**. Fit the mudshield bracket and refit the retaining bolts, tightening them loosely at this stage.

24 Fit the upper swivel pin and shim(s) to the top of the swivel housing, and install the retaining bolts, tightening them loosely at this stage **(see illustration)**.

25 With both pins in position, remove the lower pin retaining bolts, and clean their threads. Apply a drop of fresh locking compound to the bolt threads, then refit them and tighten them to the specified torque setting **(see illustration)**. Secure the bolts in position by bending down the locking tabs (where fitted).

26 Tighten the top swivel pin bolts to the specified torque setting.

27 It is now necessary to check the swivel pin bearing preload setting. Securely retain the swivel ball axle flange, and attach a spring balance to the swivel housing track rod balljoint hole. Use the spring balance to move the swivel housing back and forth,

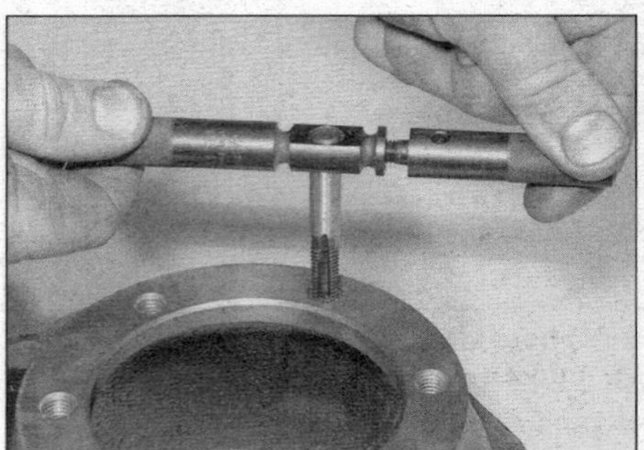

6.19 Prior to reassembly, remove all traces of old locking compound from the housing threads

6.20 Lubricate the bearings with the specified oil, and seat them in their races

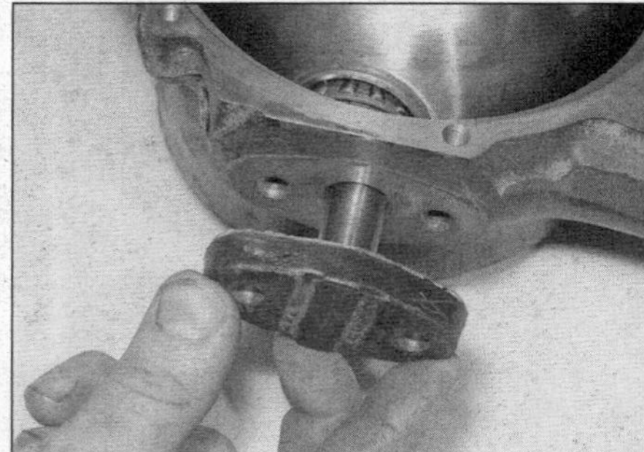

6.23 Insert the lower swivel pin and gasket . . .

6.24 . . . then fit the upper swivel pin and shim assembly

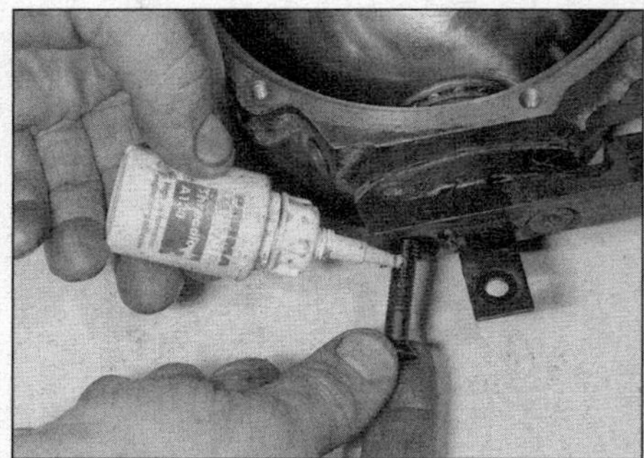

6.25 Apply locking compound to the lower swivel pin retaining bolts, and tighten them to the specified torque setting

noting the force necessary to do this **(see illustration)**.

28 If the bearing preload is correct, a weight (force) of approximately 1.16 to 1.46 kg (11 to 14 N) will be required to turn the housing.

29 The preload is adjusted by varying the thickness of the shim(s) fitted beneath the upper swivel pin. If the preload is too high (more force than specified required to turn housing), thicker shim(s) will be needed; if the preload is too low (less force than specified required to turn the housing), thinner shim(s) will be required.

30 Remove the upper swivel pin, measure that the thickness of the shims fitted, and obtain the relevant new shims from your Land Rover dealer. Refit the swivel pin and shim(s), and tighten the retaining bolts to the specified torque. Repeat the above procedure as necessary until the preload is correctly set.

31 Once the swivel housing bearing preload is correctly adjusted, apply a smear of lithium-based grease to the lip of the swivel housing oil seal. Apply a smear of oil to the outer edge seal to aid installation then, making sure that its sealing lip is facing inwards, fit the seal to the swivel housing, making sure that it enters the housing squarely **(see illustration)**.

32 Ensure that the housing and retaining plate mating surfaces are clean and dry, and refit the plate to the housing. Refit the plate retaining bolts, tightening them to the specified torque setting.

33 Refit the mudshield to the housing, and securely tighten its retaining nut and bolt.

Models with ABS

34 Carry out the operations described above in paragraphs 6 to 10.

35 Remove the wheel sensor from the housing, as described in Chapter 10, Section 21.

36 Undo the retaining bolts and washers, ease the upper swivel pin from the housing, and recover its shims.

37 Free the swivel ball from the housing. Recover the lower swivel pin bearing and the thrustwashers and bearing from the upper pin bush.

38 Support the swivel ball, and tap the bearing race and bush out of position with a hammer and suitable punch.

39 Check all components, paying particular attention to the contact surfaces of the swivel ball and swivel pins.

40 Check that each bearing rotates smoothly without any sign of roughness, and renew worn components as necessary. Renew the oil seals and gaskets as a matter of course.

41 Obtain the necessary components from your Land Rover dealer.

42 Lever out the oil seal from the rear of the swivel ball, noting which way around it is fitted. Fit the new oil seal to the rear of the swivel ball, making sure that its sealing lip is facing away from the ball. Press the seal squarely into the housing until it is flush with the housing face.

6.27 Checking swivel pin bearing preload (see text)

43 Fit the new lower swivel pin bearing race to the swivel ball, tapping it squarely into position with a suitable tubular drift which bears only on the outer edge of the race.

44 Fit the new upper swivel pin bush to the swivel ball, ensuring that the relieved lip of the bush is facing towards the rear of the ball **(see illustration)**.

45 Lubricate the bearings with the specified oil (see *Lubricants and fluids* at the end of *Weekly checks*) and insert the bearing and thrustwashers into the upper pin bush.

46 Reassemble the swivel ball with the housing, making sure that the bearings remain correctly seated.

47 Carry out the operations described above in paragraphs 22 to 33.

48 Refit the wheel sensor as described in Chapter 10, Section 21.

Refitting

49 Ensure that the swivel ball and axle mating surfaces are clean and dry. Remove all traces of locking compound from the axle threads, ideally by running a tap of the correct size and pitch down them.

50 Fit a new gasket, and locate the swivel pin housing assembly on the axle **(see illustration)**.

51 Apply a drop of locking compound to the thread of each retaining bolt. Refit the bolts and washers, and tighten them evenly and progressively to the specified torque setting.

52 On models with ABS, reconnect the wheel sensor wiring connector, ensuring that the wiring is correctly routed and retained by all the relevant clips.

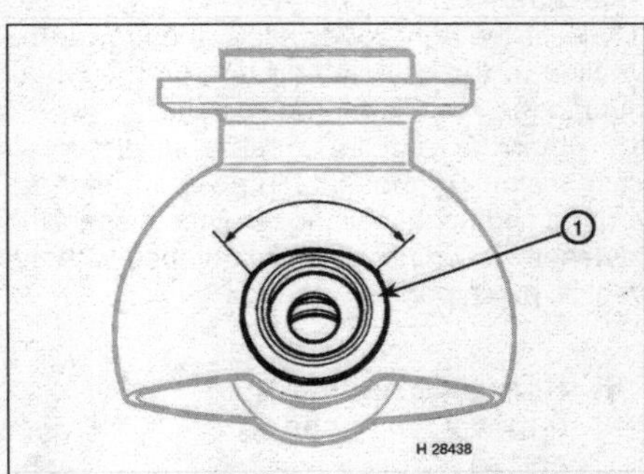
1
H 28438

6.44 On models with ABS, ensure that the relieved lip of the upper swivel pin bush is positioned as shown when fitting the bush (1) to the swivel ball

6.31 Fit a new oil seal to the rear of the swivel pin housing, making sure that it is fitted the correct way around

53 Engage the track rod balljoint with the swivel pin housing, and refit its retaining nut. Tighten the nut to the specified torque setting (see Chapter 11) and secure it in position with a new split pin.

54 Where necessary, reconnect the drag link to the swivel pin housing as described in paragraph 53.

55 Refit the halfshaft as described in Section 2.

56 On completion check and, if necessary, adjust the steering lock stops as described in Section 23 of Chapter 11.

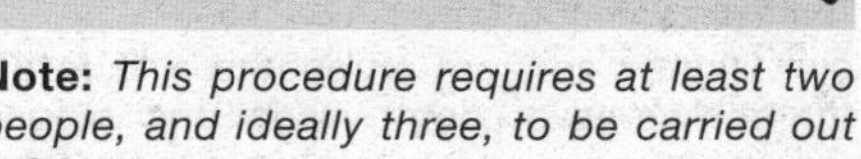

7 Front axle - removal and refitting

Note: *This procedure requires at least two people, and ideally three, to be carried out safely.*

Removal

1 Apply the handbrake, and loosen the front roadwheel nuts. Jack up the front of the vehicle and support it on axle stands positioned underneath the chassis (see *Jacking and vehicle support*). Remove both front roadwheels.

2 Undo the (upper swivel pin) bolts securing

6.50 Ensure that the axle mating surface is clean and dry, and fit a new swivel pin housing gasket

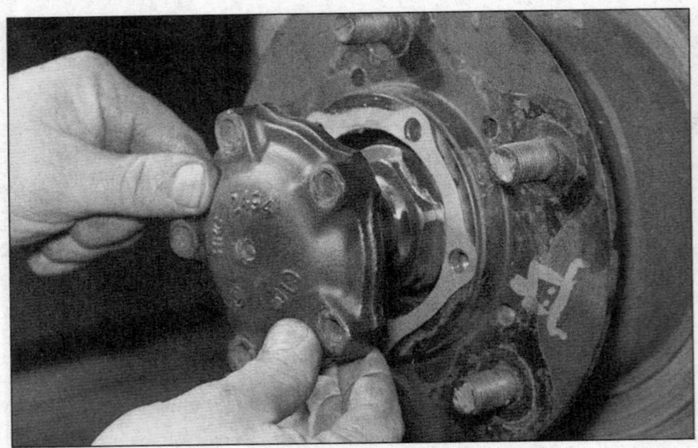
8.3 Removing a rear axle halfshaft

8.5 Fit a new gasket to the hub assembly . . .

the brake hose retaining bracket to the swivel housing. Position the bracket clear of the housing, then refit the bolts to prevent oil leakage. Repeat the procedure on the opposite side.

3 Slacken and remove the two retaining bolts securing the brake caliper in position. Slide the caliper assembly off the disc and, using a piece of wire or string, tie the caliper to the front suspension coil spring, to avoid placing any strain on the hydraulic brake hose. Repeat the procedure on the opposite side.

4 On models with ABS, trace the wiring back from each wheel sensor. Disconnect the wiring connectors, then work back along the wiring, freeing it from any relevant retaining clips so that both sensors are free to be removed with the axle.

5 Disconnect the propeller shaft from the front differential as described in Chapter 8.

6 Position a hydraulic jack beneath the front axle assembly, then raise the jack until it is supporting the axle weight.

7 Carry out the following procedures as described in Chapter 11:

a) Remove both radius arms.
b) Remove the Panhard rod.
c) Remove the track rod.
d) Disconnect the drag link from the swivel pin housing.
e) Disconnect the anti-roll bar connecting links from the axle.
f) Remove the nuts securing the shock absorbers to the axle.

8 With an assistant supporting either end of the axle, carefully lower the axle away from the vehicle, making sure that all the relevant components have been disconnected.

9 Remove the axle from underneath the vehicle, and recover the front coil springs.

Refitting

10 On refitting, position the axle assembly on the jack.

11 With the aid of two assistants, carefully raise the axle assembly into position, whilst aligning the front coil springs with their upper and lower spring seats.

12 With the axle raised and both coil springs correctly seated, carry out the following procedures as described in Chapter 11:

a) Refit the nuts securing the shock absorbers to the axle.
b) Connect the anti-roll bar connecting links from the axle.
c) Connect the drag link from the swivel pin housing.
d) Refit the track rod.
e) Refit the Panhard rod.
f) Refit both radius arms.

13 On models with ABS, reconnect the wheel sensor wiring connectors, ensuring that the wiring is correctly routed and retained by all the relevant clips.

14 Slide the brake caliper assembly back into position, ensuring that its pads pass either side of the disc. Refit the caliper retaining bolts, tighten them to the specified torque setting (see Chapter 10). Repeat the procedure on the opposite side.

15 Clean the upper swivel pin retaining bolts, and apply a drop of locking compound to each one's threads. Position the brake hose bracket on top of the swivel pin, then refit the retaining bolts and tighten them to the specified torque setting. Repeat the procedure on the opposite side.

16 Reconnect the propeller shaft to the axle as described in Chapter 8.

17 Refit the front roadwheels, then lower the vehicle to the ground and tighten the wheel nuts to the specified torque setting.

18 Rock the vehicle to settle all disturbed suspension components in position, then go around and tighten all the relevant suspension fasteners which need to be tightened with the vehicle resting on its wheels.

8 Rear axle halfshaft - removal, inspection and refitting

Removal

1 Loosen the rear roadwheel nuts, and chock the front wheels. Jack up the rear of the vehicle, and support it on axle stands positioned underneath the chassis (see *Jacking and vehicle support*). Remove the relevant rear roadwheel.

2 Drain the axle oil as described in the relevant part of Chapter 1, or be prepared for some oil spillage as the shaft is removed.

3 Slacken and remove the five bolts and washers securing the halfshaft to the centre of the hub, and withdraw the shaft from the centre of the hub assembly **(see illustration)**. Recover the gasket from the halfshaft flange, and discard it.

Inspection

4 Inspect the halfshaft splines and hub flange for signs of wear or damage, and renew if necessary.

Refitting

5 Ensure that the halfshaft and hub mating surfaces are clean and dry, and fit a new gasket **(see illustration)**.

6 Slide the halfshaft carefully into position. Refit its retaining bolts and washers, tightening them to the specified torque setting **(see illustration)**

7 Refit the roadwheel, then lower the vehicle to the ground and tighten the wheel nuts to the specified torque.

8 If necessary, top-up/refill the axle with oil as described in the relevant part of Chapter 1.

8.6 . . . then refit the halfshaft and tighten its retaining bolts to the specified torque

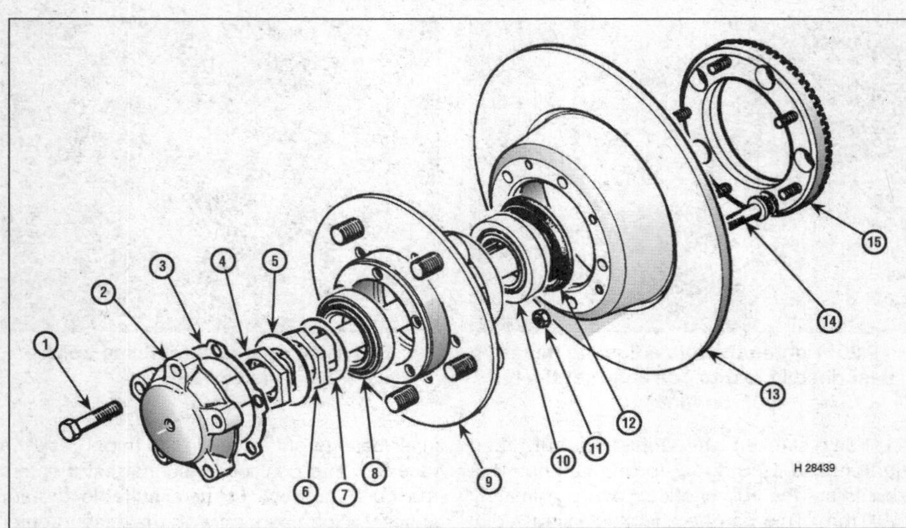
1
2
3
4
5
6
7
8
9
10
11
12
13
14
15
H 28439

9.1 Exploded view of the rear hub and associated components

1 Bolt
2 Halfshaft
3 Gasket
4 Locknut
5 Lockwasher
6 Adjusting nut
7 Spacer
8 Outer bearing and race
9 Hub
10 Inner bearing and race
11 Toothed wheel sensor nut (ABS models only)
12 Seal
13 Brake disc
14 Retaining bolt
15 Toothed wheel sensor (ABS models only)

9 Rear hub assembly - removal and refitting

Note: *Refer to Vehicle identification numbers at the end of this manual for information on VIN numbers.*

Removal

1 Remove the halfshaft as described in Section 8 **(see illustration)**.

2 Release the retaining clips securing the rear brake pipe to the axle. Slacken and remove the two retaining bolts securing the brake caliper in position. Slide the caliper assembly off the disc and, using a piece of wire or string, tie the caliper to the suspension coil spring, to avoid placing any strain on the hydraulic brake pipe **(see illustrations)**. **Note:** *Do not bend the pipe any more than is absolutely necessary.*

3 Using a hammer and suitable chisel, bend back the lockwasher tab from the hub locknut's flat **(see illustration)**.

4 Slacken and remove the hub locknut, and slide off the lockwasher. Discard the lockwasher - a new one must be used on refitting.

5 Unscrew the hub adjusting nut, then slide off the spacer, noting which way around it is fitted.

6 Slide the hub assembly off the stub axle, complete with bearings.

Refitting

Early models (up to VIN JA032850)

7 Apply a smear of lithium-based grease to the lips of the hub oil seal(s).

8 Carefully slide the hub assembly onto the stub axle, taking care not to damage the oil seal lips **(see illustration)**.

9 Slide the spacer onto the stub axle, ensuring that it is fitted the correct way around **(see illustration)**.

10 Fit the hub adjusting nut, tightening it by hand only **(see illustration)**.

11 If a new hub/bearing has been installed, tighten the hub adjusting nut whilst rotating the hub to settle the bearings in position. Tighten the nut until all freeplay is removed from the bearings, then slacken it by a quarter of a turn; this will settle the bearings in position.

9.2a Slide the brake caliper assembly off the disc . . .

9.2b . . . and tie it to the coil spring, to prevent the brake pipe being strained

9.3 Bend back the lockwasher from the locknut's flat using a suitable chisel

9.8 Slide the rear hub assembly into position . . .

9.9 . . . then refit the spacer . . .

9.10 . . . and screw on the hub adjusting nut

9.19 On later models, refit the rear hub assembly, making sure that the outer bearing is correctly seated

9.20 Tighten the hub adjusting nut as described in text to correctly set the hub endfloat

11.3 Rear stub axle retaining bolts (arrowed)

12 On all models, attach a dial test indicator to the hub assembly, positioning it so that its pointer is in contact with the end of the stub axle. Move the hub assembly in and out, and measure the hub endfloat. The hub endfloat should be within the range given in the Specifications. If necessary, rotate the adjusting nut as required until the endfloat is within the specified range.

Set the endfloat as close as possible to the minimum endfloat setting, to allow for wear in use.

13 When the endfloat is correctly set, slide a new lockwasher onto the stub axle, then fit the locknut.

14 Tighten the hub locknut to the specified torque setting, whilst holding the adjusting nut stationary with a large open-ended spanner.

15 Recheck the hub endfloat, to make sure that the adjusting nut has not moved as the locknut is tightened. If necessary, loosen the locknut and repeat the adjustment procedure.

16 Once the locknut is tightened and the hub endfloat is correct, secure the adjusting nut and locknut in position with the lockwasher. Bend one side of the washer down so it contacts one of the adjusting nut flats, and bend the opposite side of the washer down so it contacts one of the locknut flats.

17 Slide the brake caliper assembly back into position, ensuring that its pads pass either side of the disc. Refit the caliper retaining bolts, tighten them to the specified torque setting (see Chapter 10). Secure the brake pipe back in position with all the necessary retaining clips.

18 Refit the halfshaft as described in Section 8.

Later models (from VIN JA032851)

19 Install the hub assembly as described in paragraphs 7 to 10, ensuring that the outer bearing is correctly fitted **(see illustration)**. On models with ABS, take great care to ensure that the ABS wheel sensor is not damaged as the hub is installed.

20 Tighten the hub adjusting nut to the Stage 1 torque setting, whilst rotating the hub to settle the bearings in position **(see illustration)**.

21 Fully slacken the adjusting nut, then tighten it to its Stage 2 torque setting. This should set the hub endfloat to approximately 0.01 mm. This can be checked using a dial test indicator as described in paragraph 12.

22 Refit the remaining components as described above in paragraphs 13 to 18.

10 Rear hub bearing - renewal

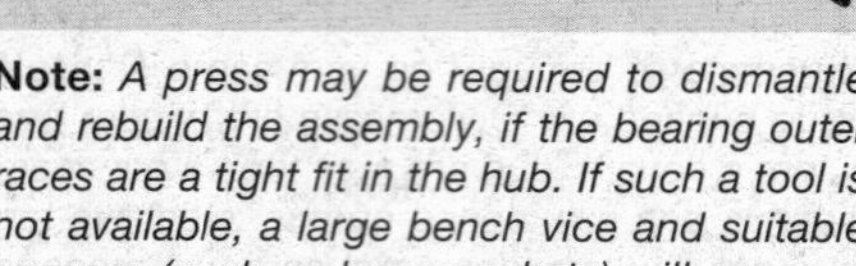

Note: *A press may be required to dismantle and rebuild the assembly, if the bearing outer races are a tight fit in the hub. If such a tool is not available, a large bench vice and suitable spacers (such as large sockets) will serve as an adequate substitute.*

Removal

1 Remove the hub assembly as described in Section 9.

2 Remove the brake disc as described in Chapter 10.

3 Using a large flat-bladed screwdriver, lever out the inner oil seal from the hub assembly and, where necessary, recover the shim(s) fitted behind the seal. On early models, note the correct fitted depth of the outer seal in the hub, then lever it out of position.

4 Remove the outer and inner bearing inner races from the hub assembly.

5 Support the hub securely on blocks or in a vice. Using a hammer and suitable punch, carefully tap the inner and outer bearing outer races out from the hub assembly.

6 Thoroughly clean the hub bore, removing all traces of dirt and grease. Polish away any burrs or raised edges which might hinder reassembly. Check both for cracks or any other signs of wear or damage, and renew them if necessary. Examine the stub axle for signs of wear or damage and renew, if necessary (see Section 11). Renew both bearings and oil seal(s) as a matter of course.

Refitting

7 On reassembly, apply a light film of oil to the inner bearing outer race and hub bore to aid installation.

8 Securely support the hub, and locate the inner bearing outer race in the hub. Press the race fully into position, ensuring that it enters the hub squarely, using a suitable tubular spacer which bears only on the bearing outer race.

9 Pack the bearing inner race with a multi-purpose lithium-based grease. Work the grease well into the bearing race, apply a smear to the outer race surface, then fit the inner race to the hub assembly.

10 Refit the shim(s) (where fitted), then install the new inner oil seal, making sure that its sealing lip is facing inwards. Press the seal into position, ensuring that it enters the hub squarely, until it is flush with the hub surface.

11 Turn the hub over, and fit the outer bearing as described in paragraphs 7 to 9.

12 On early models, install the new outer oil seal, making sure that its sealing lip is facing inwards. Press the seal into position, ensuring that it enters the hub squarely, until it is positioned at the same depth as the original (noted prior to removal).

13 Refit the brake disc as described in Chapter 10.

14 Install the hub assembly as described in Section 9.

11 Rear stub axle - removal and refitting

Removal

1 Remove the rear hub assembly as described in Section 9.

2 If not already done, drain the axle oil as described in the relevant part of Chapter 1.

3 Make alignment marks between the stub axle and axle, then slacken and remove the six retaining bolts and washers **(see illustration)**.

4 Lift off the mudshield, then remove the stub axle from the axle, and recover the gasket. Discard the gasket - a new one must be used on refitting.

5 Inspect the stub axle for signs of wear or damage, and renew if necessary.

6 On later models, check the oil seal fitted to the rear of the stub axle for signs of wear or damage. If renewal is necessary, lever out the old seal, noting which way around it is fitted. Apply a smear of grease to the new seal lip, to aid installation. Fit the new seal to the axle, making sure that its sealing lip is facing away from the stub axle. Press it into position using a suitable tubular spacer which bears only on the outer edge of the seal. Ensure that the seal squarely enters the stub axle, and is positioned flush with the axle end.

Refitting

7 Prior to refitting, remove all traces of locking compound from the axle housing threads, ideally by running a tap of the correct size and pitch down them.

8 Make sure that the stub axle and axle mating surfaces are clean and dry, then fit a new gasket to the axle.

9 Slide the stub axle into position, aligning the marks made prior to removal, and refit the mudshield to the stub axle.

10 Clean the threads of the retaining bolts, and apply a drop of fresh locking compound to them. Install the bolts and washers, and tighten them to the specified torque setting.

11 Refit the hub assembly as described in Section 9.

12 Rear axle - removal and refitting

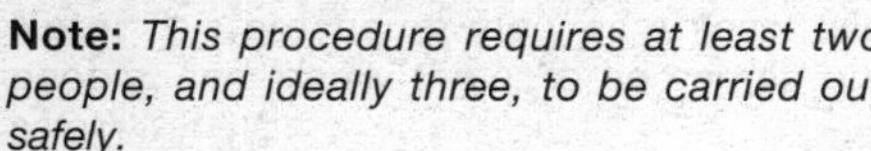

Note: *This procedure requires at least two people, and ideally three, to be carried out safely.*

Removal

1 Loosen the rear roadwheel nuts, and chock the front wheels. Jack up the rear of the vehicle and support it on axle stands positioned underneath the chassis (see *Jacking and vehicle support*). Remove both rear roadwheels.

2 Unscrew the master cylinder fluid reservoir cap, then tighten the cap down onto a piece of polythene, to minimise fluid loss. Trace the brake pipes back from the calipers to their union piece situated on top of the axle. Slacken the union nut(s), and disconnect the pipe(s). Remove the retaining clips, and release the pipes from the axle/vehicle body.

Plug the hydraulic pipe end(s), to minimise fluid loss and to prevent the entry of dirt into the hydraulic system.

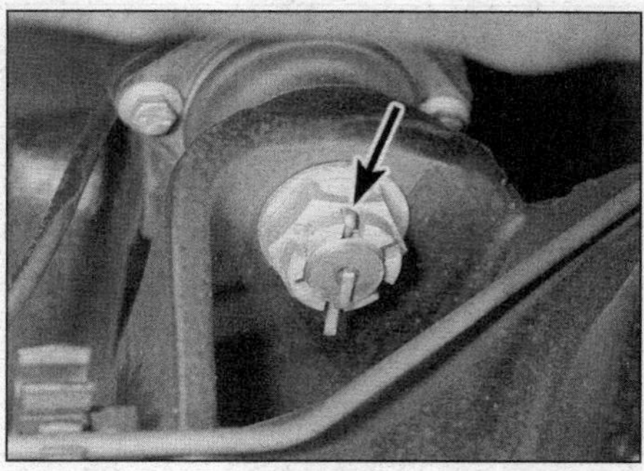

12.7 Withdraw the split pin (arrowed), then slacken and remove the nut securing the upper link balljoint to the rear axle

3 Trace the wiring back from each set of rear brake pads to its pad wear sensor wiring connector. Disconnect each connector, and free the wiring from any relevant retaining clips so that the calipers are free to be removed complete with the axle. On models with ABS, also free the rear wheel sensor wiring connectors.

4 Disconnect the propeller shaft from the rear differential as described in Chapter 8.

5 Position a hydraulic jack beneath the rear axle assembly, then raise the jack until it is supporting the axle weight.

6 Carry out the following procedures as described in Chapter 11:

a) Disconnect the lower links from the axle.
b) Disconnect the shock absorbers from the axle.
c) Disconnect the anti-roll bar connecting links from the axle.

7 Withdraw the split pin, then slacken and remove the nut securing the upper link balljoint to the top of the axle **(see illustration)**.

8 With an assistant supporting either end of the axle, carefully lower the axle away from the vehicle, making sure that all the relevant components have been disconnected.

9 Remove the axle from underneath the vehicle, and recover the spring seats from the tops of the front coil springs.

Refitting

10 On refitting, position the axle assembly on the jack, and refit the spring seats to the coil springs.

11 With the aid of two assistants, carefully raise the axle assembly into position, whilst aligning the front coil springs with their upper seats and the upper link balljoint with the axle.

12 With the axle raised and both coil springs correctly seated, refit the balljoint retaining nut, and tighten it to the specified torque setting (see Chapter 11). Secure the nut in position with a new split pin.

13 Carry out the following procedures as described in Chapter 11:

a) Connect the anti-roll bar connecting links from the axle.
b) Connect the shock absorbers to the axle.
c) Connect the lower links to the axle.

14 Reconnect the brake pad wear sensor wiring connectors, ensuring that the wiring is correctly routed and retained by all the relevant clips. On models with ABS, also reconnect the wheel sensor wiring connectors.

15 Reconnect the propeller shaft to the differential as described in Chapter 8.

16 Referring to Chapter 10, reconnect the brake pipe(s) to the axle, tightening them to the specified torque setting, then bleed the complete hydraulic braking system.

17 Refit the roadwheels, then lower the vehicle to the ground and tighten the wheel nuts to the specified torque setting.

18 Rock the vehicle to settle all disturbed suspension components in position, then tighten the lower link pivot bolts to the specified torque (See Chapter 11).

13 Axle differential overhaul - general information

Overhauling a differential unit is a difficult and involved job for the DIY home mechanic. In addition to dismantling and reassembling many small parts, clearances must be precisely measured and, if necessary, changed by selecting shims and spacers. Components are also often difficult to obtain and in many instances, extremely expensive. Because of this, if the differential develops a fault or becomes noisy, the best course of action is to have the unit overhauled by a specialist repairer, or to obtain an exchange reconditioned unit.

Nevertheless, it is not impossible for the more experienced mechanic to overhaul the differential, if the special tools are available and the job is done in a deliberate step-by-step manner so that nothing is overlooked.

The tools necessary for an overhaul include internal and external circlip pliers, bearing pullers, a slide hammer, a set of pin punches, a dial test indicator, and possibly a hydraulic press. In addition, a large, sturdy workbench and a vice will be required.

During dismantling, make careful notes of how each component is fitted, to make reassembly easier and more accurate.

Before dismantling, it will help if you have some idea what area is malfunctioning. Refer to *Fault finding* at the end of this manual for more information.

Notes

Chapter 10
Braking system

Contents

Degrees of difficulty

Easy, suitable for novice with little experience 	**Fairly easy,** suitable for beginner with some experience 	**Fairly difficult,** suitable for competent DIY mechanic	**Difficult,** suitable for experienced DIY mechanic	**Very difficult,** suitable for expert DIY or professional

Specifications

Front brakes

Type	Solid or ventilated disc, with opposed-piston caliper
Disc diameter	299 mm
Disc thickness	N/A
Maximum disc run-out	0.15 mm
Brake pad friction material minimum thickness	3.0 mm

Rear brakes

Type	Solid disc, with opposed-piston caliper
Disc diameter	290 mm
Disc thickness	N/A
Maximum disc run-out	0.15 mm
Brake pad friction material minimum thickness	3.0 mm

Torque wrench settings

Torque wrench settings	Nm	lbf ft
Brake caliper mounting bolts (front and rear)	82	61
Brake disc bolts (front and rear)*	73	54
Brake pipe unions	15	11
Handbrake backplate bolts	25	18
Handbrake linkage to transfer box	29	21
Master cylinder mounting nuts	26	19
Roadwheel nuts	129	95
Vacuum servo unit mounting nuts	26	19

**Use thread-locking fluid*

1 General information

The braking system is of the servo-assisted, dual-circuit hydraulic type, operating from a tandem master cylinder. On early models, the arrangement of the hydraulic system is such that the primary circuit operates one set of opposed-pistons of each front brake caliper, and the secondary circuit operates the other set of pistons and the rear brake calipers. On later models, the primary circuit operates the rear brake calipers, and the secondary circuit operates the front brake calipers. Under normal circumstances, both circuits operate in unison. However, in the event of hydraulic failure in one circuit, braking force will still be available at least at two wheels.

On diesel models, since there is insufficient vacuum in the inlet manifold to operate the braking system servo unit, a vacuum pump is fitted to the engine to provide the required vacuum.

All models have disc brakes all round as standard. An Anti-lock Braking System (ABS) was fitted to some high-specification models, and offered as an option on all later models (refer to Section 20 for further information on ABS operation).

Both the front and rear disc brakes are actuated by opposed-piston type calipers, which ensure that equal pressure is applied to each disc pad.

On all models, the handbrake is in the form of a drum brake assembly mounted onto the rear of the transfer box. When the handbrake is applied, it locks the rear axle by preventing propeller shaft rotation.

When servicing any part of the system, work carefully and methodically; also observe scrupulous cleanliness when overhauling any part of the hydraulic system. Always renew components (in axle sets, where applicable) if in doubt about their condition, and use only genuine Land Rover replacement parts, or at least those of known good quality. Note the warnings given in *Safety first!* and at relevant points in this Chapter concerning the dangers of asbestos dust and hydraulic fluid.

2 Hydraulic system - bleeding

Note: *Hydraulic fluid is poisonous; wash off immediately and thoroughly in the case of skin contact, and seek immediate medical advice if any fluid is swallowed or gets into the eyes. Certain types of hydraulic fluid are inflammable, and may ignite when allowed into contact with hot components. When servicing any hydraulic system, it is safest to assume that the fluid IS inflammable, and to take precautions against the risk of fire as though it is petrol that is being handled. Finally, it is hygroscopic (it absorbs moisture from the air) - old fluid may be contaminated and unfit for further use. When topping-up or renewing the fluid, always use the recommended type, and ensure that it comes from a freshly-opened sealed container.*

HAYNES
HiNT

Hydraulic fluid is an effective paint stripper, and will attack plastics; if any is spilt, it should be washed off immediately using copious quantities of fresh water.

General

1 The correct operation of any hydraulic system is only possible after removing all air from the components and circuit; this is achieved by bleeding the system.

2 During the bleeding procedure, add only clean, unused hydraulic fluid of the recommended type; never re-use fluid that has already been bled from the system. Ensure that sufficient fluid is available before starting work.

3 If there is any possibility of incorrect fluid being already in the system, the brake components and circuit must be flushed completely with uncontaminated, correct fluid, and new seals should be fitted to the various components.

4 If hydraulic fluid has been lost from the system (or air has entered) because of a leak, ensure that the fault is cured before proceeding further.

5 Park the vehicle on level ground, switch off the engine and select first or reverse gear, then chock the wheels and release the handbrake. On models with ABS, disconnect the battery negative lead.

6 Check that all pipes and hoses are secure, unions tight and bleed screws closed. Clean any dirt from around the bleed screws.

7 Unscrew the master cylinder reservoir cap, and top the master cylinder reservoir up to the MAX level line; refit the cap loosely. Remember to maintain the fluid level at least above the MIN level line throughout the procedure, or there is a risk of further air entering the system.

8 There are a number of one-man, do-it-yourself brake bleeding kits currently available from motor accessory shops. It is recommended that one of these kits is used whenever possible, as they greatly simplify the bleeding operation, and also reduce the risk of expelled air and fluid being drawn back into the system. If such a kit is not available, use the basic (two-man) method which is described in detail below.

9 If a kit is to be used, prepare the vehicle as described previously, and follow the kit manufacturer's instructions as the procedure may vary slightly according to the type being used; generally, they are as outlined below in the relevant sub-section.

10 Whichever method is used, the same sequence must be followed (paragraphs 11 and 12) to ensure the removal of all air from the system.

Bleeding sequence

11 If the system has been only partially disconnected, and suitable precautions were taken to minimise fluid loss, it should be necessary only to bleed that part of the system (ie. the primary or secondary circuit).

12 If the complete system is to be bled, then it should be done working in the following sequence:

a) Passenger's side rear brake.
b) Driver's side rear brake.
c) Passenger's side front brake.
d) Driver's side front brake.

Bleeding - basic (two-man) method

13 Collect a clean glass jar, a suitable length of plastic or rubber tubing which is a tight fit over the bleed screw, and a ring spanner to fit the screw. On early models with three front bleed screws, two pieces of tubing will be needed, as two of the three bleed screws must be bled simultaneously. The help of an assistant will also be required.

14 Remove the dust cap from the bleed screw on the passenger's side rear brake. Fit the spanner and tube to the screw, place the other end of the tube in the jar, and pour in sufficient fluid to cover the end of the tube.

15 Ensure that the master cylinder reservoir fluid level is maintained at least above the MIN level line throughout the procedure.

16 Have the assistant fully depress the brake pedal several times to build up pressure, then maintain it on the final stroke.

17 While pedal pressure is maintained, unscrew the bleed screw (approximately one turn) and allow the compressed fluid and air to flow into the jar. The assistant should maintain pedal pressure, following it down to the floor if necessary, and should not release it until instructed to do so. When the flow stops, tighten the bleed screw again, release the pedal slowly and recheck the reservoir fluid level.

18 Repeat the steps given in paragraphs 16 and 17 until the fluid emerging from the bleed screw is free from air bubbles. If the master cylinder has been drained and refilled, and air is being bled from the first screw in the sequence, allow approximately five seconds between cycles for the master cylinder passages to refill.

19 When no more air bubbles appear, tighten the bleed screw securely, remove the tube and spanner, and refit the dust cap. Do not overtighten the bleed screw.

20 Repeat the procedure on the remaining rear brake.

21 The procedure for bleeding the front brakes differs for early and later models. Early models were fitted with front calipers having three bleed screws each, while later models had a conventional caliper with just one bleed screw.

Early models

22 Bleeding the front brakes is similar to that described for the rears, but there are three bleed screws on each front caliper.

23 The two screws on the inner side of the caliper must be bled simultaneously, using the method described previously - ie a tube should be connected to both screws, both should be opened and bled, then both should be tightened before the pedal is released.

24 Once the two inner screws have been bled, the remaining outer screw should be bled on its own.

25 On completion of bleeding the passenger's side front caliper, the driver's side front caliper should be bled.

Later models

26 Later models have only one bleed screw per front caliper, and can be bled in exactly the same way as described previously for the rear calipers.

Bleeding - using a one-way valve kit

Note: *The inner side of the front caliper on early models has two bleed screws which must be bled simultaneously. Two one-way valves will be needed.*

27 As their name implies, these kits consist of a length of tubing with a one-way valve fitted, to prevent expelled air and fluid being drawn back into the system; some kits include a translucent container, which can be positioned so that the air bubbles can be more easily seen flowing from the end of the tube **(see illustration)**.

28 The kit is connected to the bleed screw, which is then opened. The user returns to the driver's seat and depresses the brake pedal with a smooth, steady stroke and slowly releases it; this is repeated until the expelled fluid is clear of air bubbles.

29 Note that these kits simplify work so much that it is easy to forget the master cylinder reservoir fluid level; ensure that this is maintained at least above the MIN level line at all times.

Bleeding - using a pressure-bleeding kit

Note: *Ensure that the pressure in the reservoir does not exceed 4.5 bars (60 psi approx).*

30 These kits are usually operated by the reservoir of pressurised air contained in the spare tyre, although note that it will probably be necessary to reduce the tyre pressure to a lower level than normal; refer to the instructions supplied with the kit.

31 By connecting a pressurised, fluid-filled container to the master cylinder reservoir, bleeding can be carried out simply by opening each screw in turn (in the specified sequence) and allowing the fluid to flow out until no more air bubbles can be seen in the expelled fluid.

32 This method has the advantage that the large reservoir of fluid provides an additional safeguard against air being drawn into the system during bleeding.

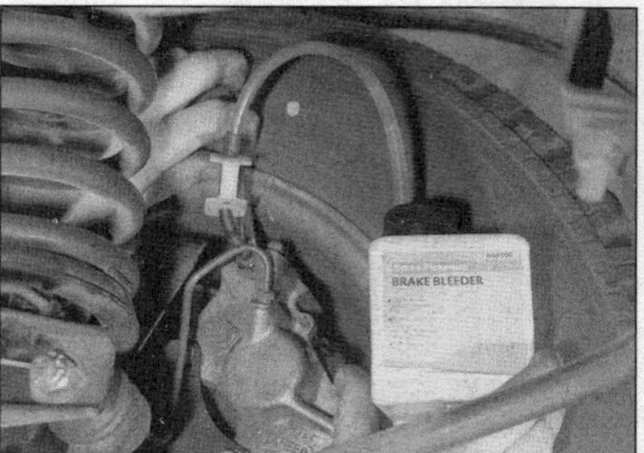
BRAKE BLEEDER

2.27 Bleeding a rear brake caliper using a one-way valve kit

33 Pressure bleeding is particularly effective when bleeding difficult systems, or when bleeding the complete system at the time of routine fluid renewal.

All methods

34 When bleeding is complete and firm pedal feel is restored, wash off any spilt fluid, tighten the bleed screws securely and refit their dust caps.

35 Check the hydraulic fluid level, and top-up if necessary (see *Weekly checks*).

36 Discard any hydraulic fluid that has been bled from the system; it will not be fit for re-use.

37 Check the feel of the brake pedal. If it feels at all spongy, air must still be present in the system, and further bleeding is required. Failure to bleed satisfactorily after a reasonable repetition of the bleeding procedure may be due to worn master cylinder seals.

3 Hydraulic pipes and hoses - renewal

Note: *Before starting work, refer to the note at the beginning of Section 2 concerning the dangers of hydraulic fluid.*

1 If any pipe or hose is to be renewed, minimise fluid loss as follows. Remove the master cylinder reservoir cap, then tighten it down onto a piece of polythene to obtain an airtight seal. Alternatively, flexible hoses can be sealed, if required, using a proprietary brake hose clamp, while metal brake pipe unions can be plugged (if care is taken not to allow dirt into the system) or capped immediately they are disconnected. Place a wad of rag under any union that is to be disconnected, to catch any spilt fluid.

2 If a flexible hose is to be disconnected, unscrew the brake pipe union nut before removing the spring clip which secures the hose to its mounting bracket (where fitted).

3 To unscrew the union nuts, it is preferable to obtain a brake pipe spanner of the correct size; these are available from most large motor accessory shops **(see illustration)**. Failing this, a close-fitting open-ended spanner will be required, though if the nuts are tight or corroded, their flats may be rounded-off if the spanner slips. In such a case, a self-locking wrench is often the only way to unscrew a stubborn union, but it follows that the pipe and the damaged nuts must be renewed on reassembly. Always clean a union and surrounding area before disconnecting it.

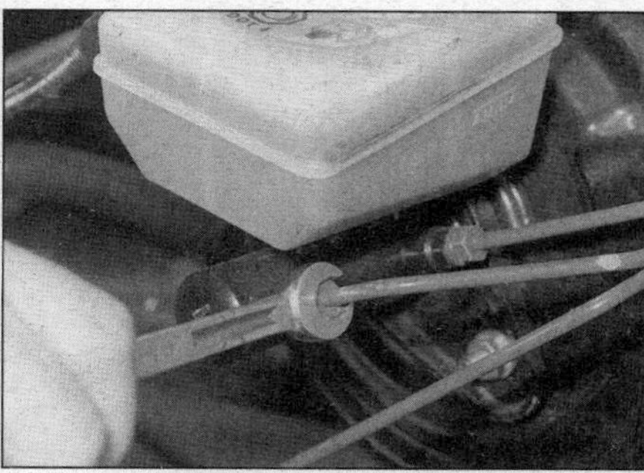

3.3 Using a brake pipe spanner to slacken and union nut

HAYNES
HiNT

If disconnecting a component with more than one union, make a careful note of the connections before disturbing any of them.

4 If a brake pipe is to be renewed, it can be obtained, cut to length and with the union nuts and end flares in place, from Land Rover dealers. All that is then necessary is to bend it to shape, following the line of the original, before fitting it to the car. Alternatively, most motor accessory shops can make up brake pipes from kits, but this requires very careful measurement of the original to ensure that the replacement is of the correct length. The safest answer is usually to take the original to the shop as a pattern.

5 On refitting, do not overtighten the union nuts. It is not necessary to exercise brute force to obtain a sound joint.

6 Ensure that the pipes and hoses are correctly routed with no kinks, and that they are secured in the clips or brackets provided. After fitting, remove the polythene from the reservoir, and bleed the hydraulic system as described in Section 2. Wash off any spilt fluid, and check carefully for fluid leaks.

4 Front brake pads - renewal

Warning: Renew BOTH sets of front brake pads at the same time - NEVER renew the pads on only one wheel, as uneven braking may result. Note that the dust created by wear of the pads may contain

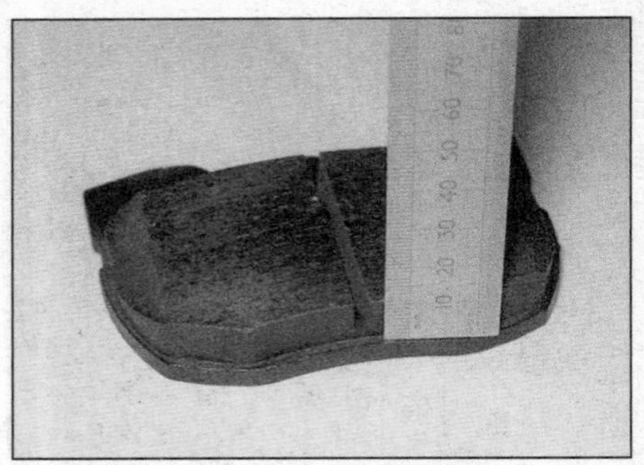

4.6 Measuring brake pad friction material thickness

asbestos, which is a health hazard. Never blow it out with compressed air, and don't inhale any of it. An approved filtering mask should be worn when working on the brakes. DO NOT use petroleum-based solvents to clean brake parts - use brake cleaner or methylated spirit only.

Note: *Models for certain markets may be fitted with ventilated front discs. These discs are fitted to compensate for the fitment of asbestos-free brake pads, which are required by law in some countries. To accommodate the thicker ventilated disc, the caliper is modified by the fitment in production of a wider spacer between the caliper halves (the caliper halves must NOT be separated). The procedures in this Chapter are unaffected by this, but it does mean that the front discs and calipers may not be interchangeable - bear this in mind when ordering new parts, or when obtaining second-hand items from vehicle breakers.*

1 Apply the handbrake, then loosen the front roadwheel nuts. Jack up the front of the vehicle and support it on axle stands. Remove both front roadwheels, and proceed as described under the relevant sub-heading.

Early models

2 Trace the pad wear sensor wiring (where fitted) back from the pad, and disconnect it at the wiring connector.

3 Noting the correct fitted locations of the pad anti-rattle springs, withdraw the pad retaining split-pins, and recover the springs from the top of the caliper.

4 Withdraw the pads from caliper.

5 Brush the dirt and dust from the caliper, but take care not to inhale it. Carefully remove any rust from the edge of the brake disc.

6 First measure the thickness of each brake pad's friction material **(see illustration)**. If either pad is worn at any point to the specified minimum thickness or less, all four pads must be renewed.

7 The pads should also be renewed if any are fouled with oil or grease; there is no satisfactory way of degreasing friction material, once contaminated. If any of the brake pads are worn unevenly, or are fouled with oil or grease, trace and rectify the cause before reassembly.

8 New pad retaining pins and anti-rattle springs should be fitted if the pads are to be renewed. New brake pads, pins and springs are available from Land Rover dealers.

9 If the brake pads are still serviceable, carefully clean them using a clean, fine wire brush or similar, paying particular attention to the sides and back of the metal backing. Clean out the grooves in the friction material, and pick out any large embedded particles of dirt or debris. Carefully clean the pad locations in the caliper body/mounting bracket.

10 Prior to fitting the pads, brush the dust and dirt from the caliper pistons, but **do not** inhale it, as it is a health hazard. Inspect the dust seal around the piston for damage, and the piston for evidence of fluid leaks, corrosion or damage. If attention to any of these components is necessary, refer to Section 8.

11 If new brake pads are to be fitted, the caliper pistons must be pushed back into the caliper, to make room for them. Either use a G-clamp or similar tool, or use suitable pieces of wood as levers. Provided that the master cylinder reservoir has not been overfilled with hydraulic fluid there should be no spillage, but keep a careful watch on the fluid level while retracting the piston. If the fluid level rises above the MAX level line at any time, the surplus should be syphoned off, or ejected via a plastic tube connected to the bleed screw (see Section 2). **Note:** *Do not syphon the fluid by mouth, as it is poisonous; use a syringe or an old poultry baster.*

12 Apply a thin smear of high-temperature brake grease or anti-seize compound to the sides and back of each pad's metal backing, and to those surfaces of the caliper body which bear on the pads. Do not allow the lubricant to foul the friction material.

13 Locate the pads in the caliper, ensuring that the friction material of each pad is against the brake disc. Where applicable, make sure that the pad with the wear sensor wiring is fitted on the inside.

14 Position the anti-rattle springs on top of the pads, ensuring that they are fitted the correct way around.

15 Insert the new retaining pins into the caliper, making sure that each pin is correctly engaged with its anti-rattle spring. Secure the pins in position by bending over their ends.

16 Depress the brake pedal repeatedly, until the pads are pressed into firm contact with the brake disc and normal (non-assisted) pedal pressure is restored.

17 Repeat the above procedure on the remaining front brake caliper.

18 Refit the roadwheels, then lower the vehicle to the ground and tighten the roadwheel nuts to the specified torque setting.

19 Check the hydraulic fluid level as described in *Weekly checks*.

Later models

20 Using a pair of pliers, remove the split-pin from the inner end of each pad retaining pin **(see illustration)**.

21 Carefully withdraw the pad retaining pins, recovering the anti-rattle springs as they are released **(see illustration)**.

22 Withdraw both pads from the caliper, and carry out the operations listed above in paragraphs 5 to 12 **(see illustration)**. Note that the retaining pin split-pins should also be renewed.

23 Locate the pads in the caliper, ensuring that the friction material of each pad is against the brake disc.

24 Fit the anti-rattle springs between the pads, then insert the pad retaining pins. Make sure that each pin passes through its anti-rattle spring.

25 Secure each retaining pin in position with a new split-pin.

4.20 On later models, remove the split pins (arrowed) . . .

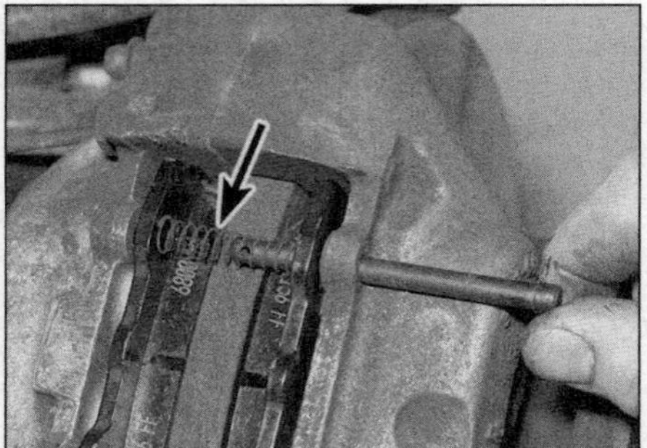

4.21 . . . then withdraw the pad retaining pins and recover the anti-rattle springs (arrowed)

4.22 Lift the brake pads out from the caliper

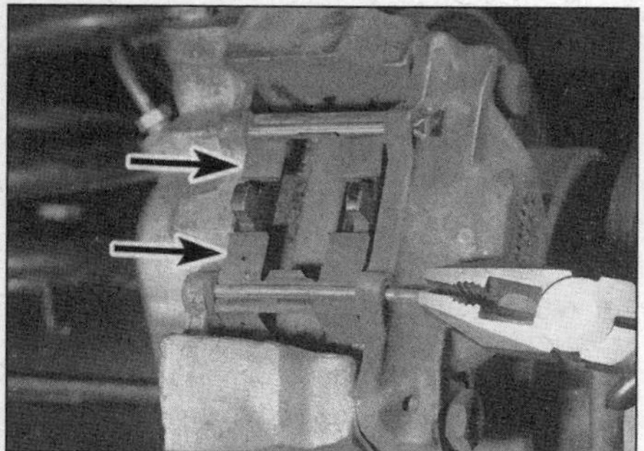

5.1a Withdraw the pad retaining split pins, then remove the anti-rattle springs (arrowed) . . .

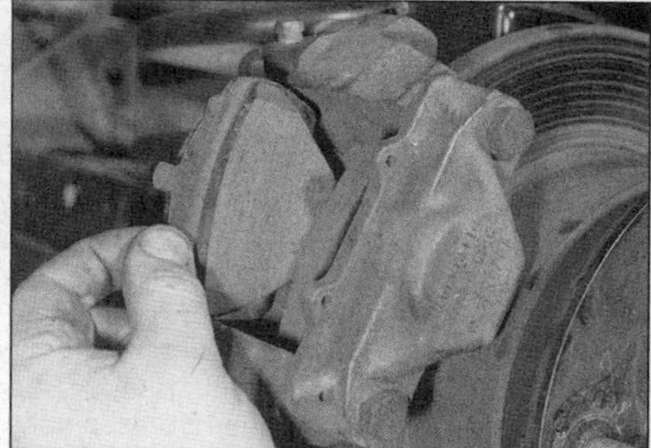

5.1b . . . and lift out the pads

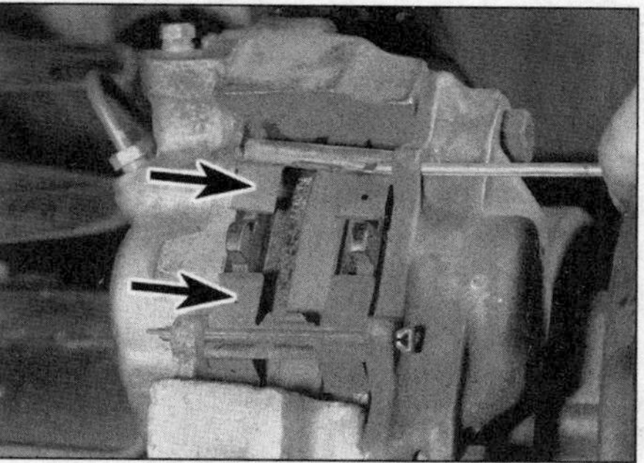

5.1c On refitting, ensure that the anti-rattle springs (arrowed) are correctly seated, and engage with the retaining split pins as they are inserted

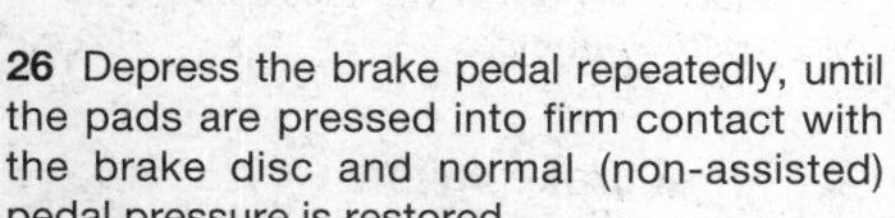

26 Depress the brake pedal repeatedly, until the pads are pressed into firm contact with the brake disc and normal (non-assisted) pedal pressure is restored.

27 Repeat the above procedure on the remaining front brake caliper.

28 Refit the roadwheels, then lower the vehicle to the ground and tighten the roadwheel nuts to the specified torque setting.

29 Check the hydraulic fluid level as described in *Weekly checks*.

5 Rear brake pads - renewal

Warning: Renew BOTH sets of rear brake pads at the same time - NEVER renew the pads on only one wheel, as uneven braking may result. Note that the dust created by wear of the pads may contain asbestos, which is a health hazard. Never blow it out with compressed air, and don't inhale any of it. An approved filtering mask should be worn when working on the brakes. DO NOT use petroleum-based solvents to clean brake parts - use brake cleaner or methylated spirit only.

The rear brake caliper is similar to the front brake caliper which is fitted to early models. Pad renewal can be carried out as described in paragraphs 1 to 19 of Section 4 **(see illustrations)**. Note that on some models, shims will be fitted to the rear of the brake pad(s). Where this is so, note their correct fitted locations on removal, and ensure that they are correctly positioned on refitting.

6 Front brake disc - inspection, removal and refitting

Note: *Before starting work, refer to the warning and note at the beginning of Section 4.*

Inspection

Note: *If either disc requires renewal, BOTH should be renewed at the same time, to ensure even and consistent braking.*

1 Firmly apply the handbrake, then loosen the front roadwheel nuts. Jack up the front of the car and support it on axle stands. Remove the appropriate front roadwheel.

2 Slowly rotate the brake disc, so that the full area of both sides can be checked; remove the brake pads if better access is required to the inner surface. Light scoring is normal in the area swept by the brake pads, but if heavy scoring is found, the disc must be renewed.

3 It is normal to find a lip of rust and brake dust around the disc's perimeter; this can be scraped off if required. If, however, a lip has formed due to excessive wear of the brake pad swept area, then the disc's thickness must be measured using a micrometer **(see illustration)**. Take measurements at several places around the disc, at the inside and outside of the pad swept area. Since the manufacturer does not quote a specified minimum thickness for the brake discs, it will be necessary to seek the advice of a Land Rover dealer. They will be able to advise you on the best course of action, ie whether it is permissible to have the disc refinished, or if disc renewal will be necessary.

4 If the disc is thought to be warped, it can be checked for run-out as follows. Either use a dial gauge mounted on any convenient fixed point, while the disc is slowly rotated, or use feeler blades to measure (at several points all around the disc) the clearance between the disc and a fixed point such as the brake caliper. If the measurements obtained are at the specified maximum or beyond, the disc is excessively warped and must be renewed; however, it is worth checking first that the axle hub bearing is in good condition (Chapter 9).

5 Check the disc for cracks, especially around the wheel studs, and any other wear or damage.

Removal

6 Remove the front hub assembly as described in Chapter 9.

7 Using chalk or paint, make alignment marks between the disc and hub.

8 Slacken and remove the bolts securing the brake disc to the hub assembly, and separate the two components **(see illustration)**.

Refitting

9 Refitting is the reverse of the removal procedure, noting the following points:

a) *Ensure that the mating surfaces of the disc and hub are clean and flat.*

b) *If a new disc has been fitted, use a suitable solvent to wipe any preservative coating from the disc before refitting the caliper.*

c) *Remove all traces of old locking compound from the brake disc holes in the hub assembly, ideally by running a tap of the correct size and pitch through them.*

d) *Fit the disc to the hub, aligning (if*

6.3 Measuring brake disc thickness using a micrometer

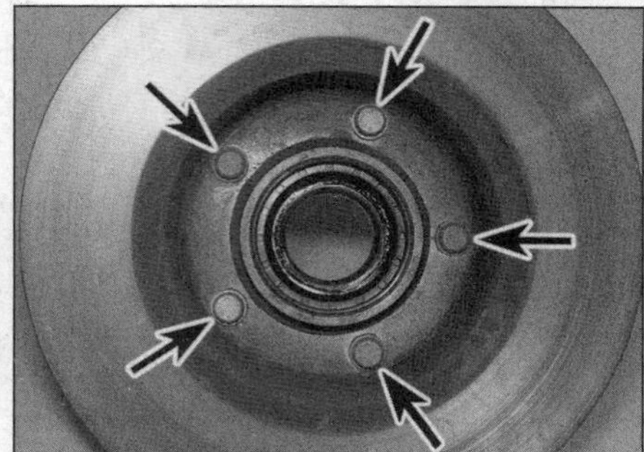

6.8 Front brake disc retaining bolts (arrowed)

applicable) the marks made prior to removal.

e) Apply a suitable locking compound to the threads of the disc retaining bolts, then fit the bolts and tighten them to the specified torque setting.

f) Refit the roadwheel, lower the vehicle to the ground, and tighten the roadwheel nuts to the specified torque. On completion, repeatedly depress the brake pedal, until normal (non-assisted) pedal pressure returns.

7 Rear brake disc - inspection, removal and refitting

Note: *Before starting work, refer to the warning at the beginning of Section 4 concerning the dangers of asbestos dust.*

Inspection

1 Refer to Section 6.

Removal

2 Remove the rear hub assembly as described in Chapter 9. Using chalk or paint, make alignment marks between the disc and hub.

3 On models fitted with ABS, undo the retaining nuts, and remove the sensor ring from the rear hub assembly. Discard the retaining nuts - they must be renewed whenever they are disturbed.

4 On all models, slacken and remove the bolts securing the disc to the hub assembly, and separate the two.

Refitting

5 Refitting is the reverse of the removal procedure, noting the following points:

a) Ensure that the mating surfaces of the disc and hub are clean and flat.

b) If a new disc has been fitted, use a suitable solvent to wipe any preservative coating from the disc before refitting the caliper.

c) Remove all traces of old locking compound from the brake disc holes in the hub assembly, ideally by running a tap of the correct size and pitch through them.

d) Fit the disc to the hub, aligning (if applicable) the marks made prior to removal.

e) Apply a suitable locking compound to the threads of the disc retaining bolts, then fit the bolts and tighten them to the specified torque setting.

f) Refit the roadwheel, lower the vehicle to the ground, and tighten the roadwheel nuts to the specified torque. On completion, repeatedly depress the brake pedal, until normal (non-assisted) pedal pressure returns.

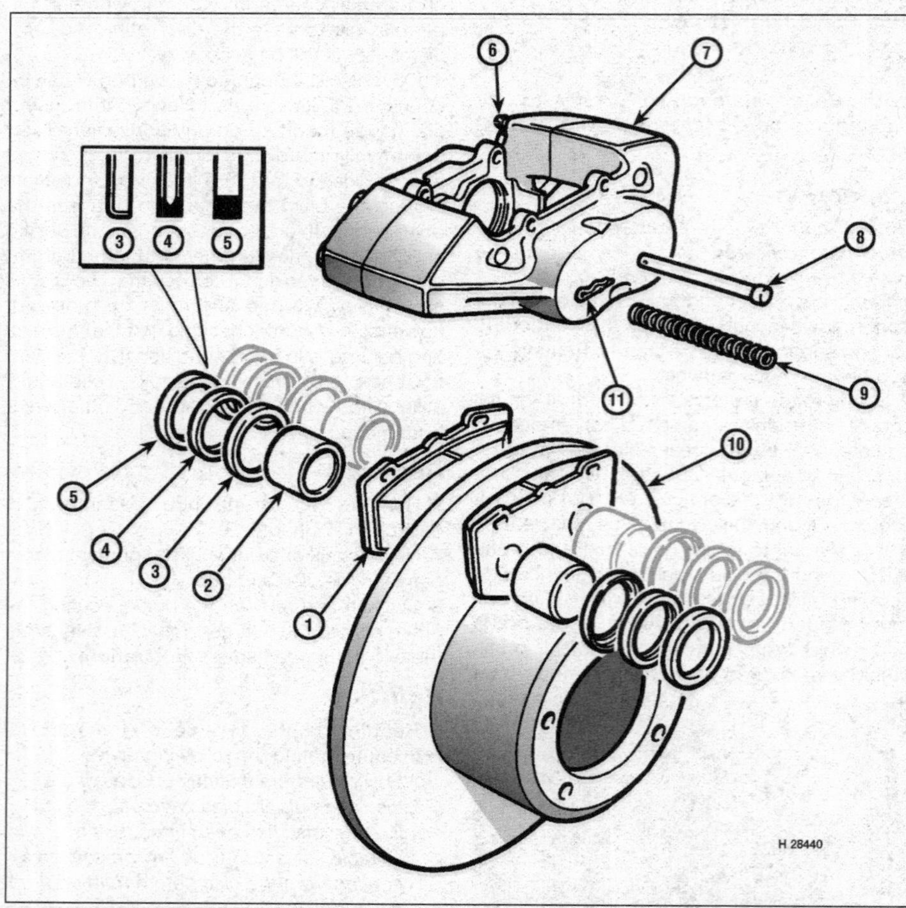
6
7
3
4
5
8
11
9
10
5
4
3
2
1
H 28440

8.6 Exploded view of the front brake caliper and associated components. Inset shows cross-section of each seal - later models shown (early models similar)

1 Brake pad
2 Piston
3 Wiper seal retainer
4 Wiper seal
5 Fluid seal
6 Bleed screw
7 Caliper
8 Pad retaining pin
9 Anti-rattle spring
10 Brake disc
11 R-clip

8 Front brake caliper - removal, overhaul and refitting

Note: *Before starting work, refer to the note at the beginning of Section 2 concerning the dangers of hydraulic fluid, and to the warning and note at the beginning of Section 4.*

Removal

1 Apply the handbrake, then loosen the relevant front roadwheel nuts. Jack up the front of the vehicle and support it on axle stands. Remove the appropriate roadwheel.

2 Remove the brake pads as described in Section 4.

3 To minimise fluid loss, remove the master cylinder reservoir cap, then tighten it down onto a piece of polythene to obtain an airtight seal. Alternatively, use a brake hose clamp, a G-clamp, or a similar tool to clamp the flexible hose at the nearest convenient point to the caliper.

4 Clean the area around the caliper brake hose union nut(s). Undo the union nut(s), and disconnect the brake pipe(s) from the caliper. Plug the hose end(s) and caliper hole(s), to minimise fluid loss and to prevent the ingress of dirt into the hydraulic system. **Note:** *On early models where there are two brake pipes, make identification marks between the pipes and caliper to use on refitting.*

5 Slacken and remove the two retaining bolts, and remove the caliper assembly from the vehicle.

Overhaul

Note: *Prior to dismantling the caliper, check the availability of spares from your Land Rover dealer; on some models, it may prove difficult to obtain caliper components.*

6 With the caliper on the bench, wipe away all traces of dust and dirt, but *avoid inhaling the dust, as it is a health hazard* **(see illustration).**

7 Push both the pistons on one side of the caliper fully into the caliper bore, and retain them in position with a suitable G-clamp.

8 Withdraw both the partially-ejected pistons

from the opposite side of the caliper body. The pistons can be withdrawn by hand, if loose. If one or both of the pistons are not loose enough to be withdrawn by hand, they can be pushed out by applying compressed air to the (relevant) brake hose union hole. Only low pressure should be required, such as is generated by a foot pump. **Note:** *On later models, ensure both pistons are expelled from the caliper at the same time.*

9 Extract both pistons from the caliper. Make identification marks between the caliper and bore to use on refitting, to ensure each piston is refitted to its original bore.

10 Using a small screwdriver, carefully remove the wiper seal retainer from the caliper, taking great care not to mark the bore. Repeat the procedure, and remove the wiper seal and piston (fluid) seal in the same way.

11 This is the limit of dismantling. The caliper halves must NOT be separated, as there is no guarantee that the fluid passages between the halves will be sealed effectively when reassembled, resulting in fluid leaks and/or air entry.

12 Thoroughly clean all components, using only methylated spirit, isopropyl alcohol or clean hydraulic fluid as a cleaning medium. Never use mineral-based solvents such as petrol or paraffin, which will attack the hydraulic system's rubber components. Dry the components immediately, using compressed air or a clean, lint-free cloth. Use compressed air to blow clear the fluid passages.

13 Check all components, and renew any that are worn or damaged. Check particularly the cylinder bores and pistons; these should be renewed if they are scratched, worn or corroded in any way.

14 If the assembly is fit for further use, obtain the necessary components from your Land Rover dealer. Renew the caliper seals and retainers as a matter of course; these should never be re-used.

15 On reassembly, ensure that all components are absolutely clean and dry.

16 Soak the pistons and the new piston (fluid) seals in clean hydraulic fluid. Smear clean fluid on the cylinder bore surface.

17 Fit the new piston (fluid) seals, using only your fingers to manipulate them into the cylinder bore grooves.

18 Ensure that the piston (fluid) seals are correctly located, then fit the new wiper seals in the same way.

19 Make sure that each wiper seal is correctly seated, then install the new wiper seal retainers in the caliper body, ensuring both are fitted the correct way around.

20 Fit each piston using a twisting motion, ensuring that they enter the caliper bore squarely. If the original pistons are being re-used, use the marks made on removal to ensure that they are refitted to the correct bores.

21 Remove the G-clamp from the caliper, and repeat the operations described in paragraphs 7 to 20 on the remaining two pistons in the caliper.

Refitting

22 Refit the caliper assembly to the vehicle, and tighten its retaining bolts to the specified torque setting.

23 Refit the brake pipe(s) to the caliper, tightening the union nut(s) to the specified torque setting. On early models, use the marks made on removal to ensure that the pipes are correctly reconnected.

24 Refit the brake pads as described in Section 4.

25 Remove the brake hose clamp or polythene, as applicable, and bleed the hydraulic system as described in Section 2. Note that, providing the precautions described were taken to minimise brake fluid loss, it should only be necessary to bleed the relevant front brake.

26 Refit the roadwheel, then lower the vehicle to the ground and tighten the roadwheel nuts to the specified torque.

9 Rear brake caliper - removal, overhaul and refitting

Note: *Before starting work, refer to the note at the beginning of Section 2 concerning the dangers of hydraulic fluid, and to the warning at the beginning of Section 5 concerning the dangers of asbestos dust.*

Removal

1 Chock the front wheels, then loosen the relevant rear roadwheel nuts. Jack up the rear of the vehicle and support on axle stands. Remove the relevant rear wheel.

2 Remove the brake pads as described in Section 5.

3 To minimise fluid loss, remove the master cylinder reservoir cap, then tighten it down onto a piece of polythene to obtain an airtight seal. Alternatively, use a brake hose clamp, a G-clamp, or a similar tool to clamp the flexible hose at the nearest convenient point to the caliper.

4 Wipe away all traces of dirt around the brake pipe union on the caliper, then undo the union nut and disconnect the brake pipe from the caliper. Plug the hose end and caliper hole, to minimise fluid loss and to prevent the ingress of dirt into the hydraulic system.

5 Slacken the two bolts securing the caliper assembly in position. Lift the caliper assembly away from the disc, and remove it from the vehicle.

Overhaul

Note: *Prior to dismantling the caliper, check the availability of spares from your Land Rover dealer; on some models, it may prove difficult to obtain caliper components.*

6 With the caliper on the bench, wipe away all traces of dust and dirt, but *avoid inhaling the dust, as it is a health hazard* **(see illustration)**.

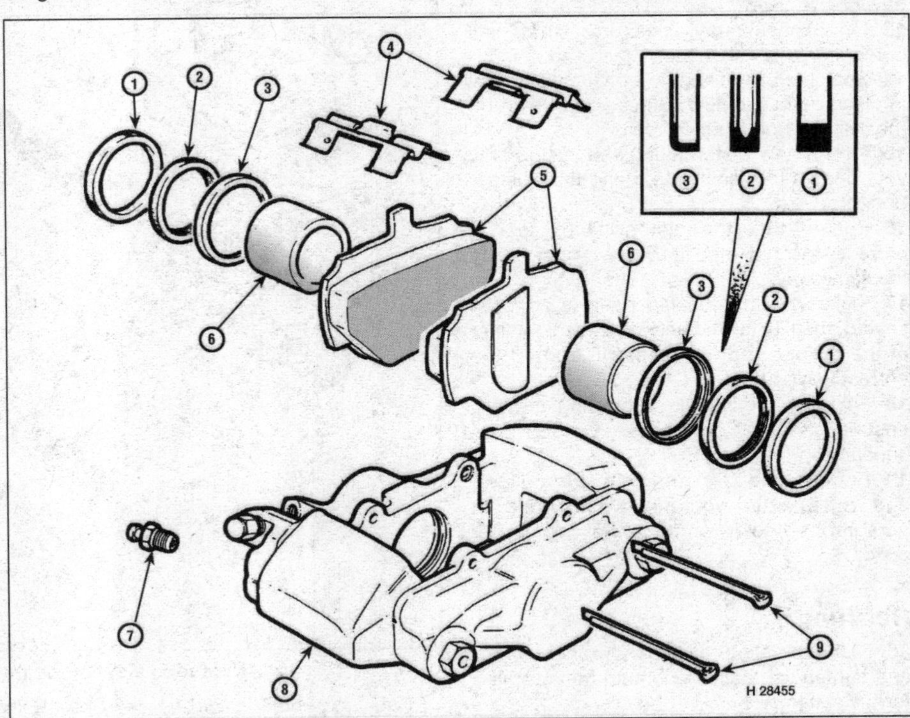
1
2
3
4
5
6
7
8
9
H 28455

9.6 Exploded view of the rear brake caliper and associated components. Inset shows cross-section of each seal

1 *Fluid seal*
2 *Wiper seal*
3 *Wiper seal retainer*
4 *Anti-rattle springs*
5 *Brake pads*
6 *Piston*
7 *Bleed screw*
8 *Caliper*
9 *Pad retaining pins*

7 Push the piston on one side of the caliper fully into the caliper bore, and retain it in position with a suitable G-clamp.
8 Withdraw the partially-ejected piston from the opposite side of the caliper body. The piston can be withdrawn by hand, if loose, or can be pushed out by applying compressed air to the brake hose union hole. Only low pressure should be required, such as is generated by a foot pump.
9 Using a small screwdriver, carefully remove the wiper seal retainer from the caliper, taking great care not to mark the bore. Repeat the procedure, and remove the wiper seal and piston (fluid) seal in the same way.
10 Thoroughly clean all components, using only methylated spirit, isopropyl alcohol or clean hydraulic fluid as a cleaning medium. Never use mineral-based solvents such as petrol or paraffin, which will attack the hydraulic system's rubber components. Dry the components immediately, using compressed air or a clean, lint-free cloth. Use compressed air to blow clear the fluid passages.
11 Check all components, and renew any that are worn or damaged. Check particularly the cylinder bore and piston; these should be renewed if they are scratched, worn or corroded in any way.
12 If the assembly is fit for further use, obtain the necessary components from your Land Rover dealer. Renew the caliper seals and retainers as a matter of course - these should never be re-used.
13 On reassembly, ensure that all components are absolutely clean and dry.
14 Soak the piston and new piston (fluid) seal in clean hydraulic fluid. Smear clean fluid on the cylinder bore surface.
15 Fit the new piston (fluid) seal, using only your fingers to manipulate it into the cylinder bore groove.
16 Ensure that the piston (fluid) seal is correctly located, then fit the new wiper seal in the same way.
17 Make sure that the wiper seal is correctly seated, then install the new wiper seal retainer in the caliper body, ensuring it is fitted the correct way around.
18 Fit the piston using a twisting motion, ensuring that it enters the caliper bore squarely.
19 Remove the G-clamp from the caliper, and repeat the operations described in paragraphs 7 to 18 on the remaining caliper piston.

Refitting

20 Refit the caliper assembly to the vehicle, and tighten its retaining bolts to the specified torque setting.
21 Refit the brake pipe to the caliper, and tighten its union nut to the specified torque setting.
22 Refit the brake pads as described in Section 5.
23 Remove the brake hose clamp or polythene, as applicable, and bleed the hydraulic system as described in Section 2. Note that, providing the precautions described were taken to minimise brake fluid loss, it should only be necessary to bleed the relevant rear brake.
24 Refit the roadwheel, then lower the vehicle to the ground and tighten the roadwheel nuts to the specified torque.

10 Master cylinder - removal, overhaul and refitting

Note: *Before starting work, refer to the warning at the beginning of Section 2 concerning the dangers of hydraulic fluid.*

Removal

1 Disconnect the wiring connector from the brake fluid level sender unit, then remove the master cylinder reservoir cap and syphon the hydraulic fluid from the reservoir. **Note:** *Do not syphon the fluid by mouth, as it is poisonous; use a syringe or an old poultry baster.* Alternatively, open any convenient bleed screw in the system, and gently pump the brake pedal to expel the fluid through a plastic tube connected to the screw (see Section 2).
2 Wipe clean the area around the brake pipe unions on the side of the master cylinder, and place absorbent rags beneath the pipe unions to catch any surplus fluid. Make a note of the correct fitted positions of the unions, then unscrew the union nuts and carefully withdraw the pipes. Wash off any spilt fluid immediately with cold water.

HAYNES HiNT ***Plug or tape over the pipe ends and master cylinder orifices to minimise the loss of brake fluid and to prevent the entry of dirt into the system.***

3 Slacken and remove the two nuts and washers securing the master cylinder to the vacuum servo unit. Withdraw the master

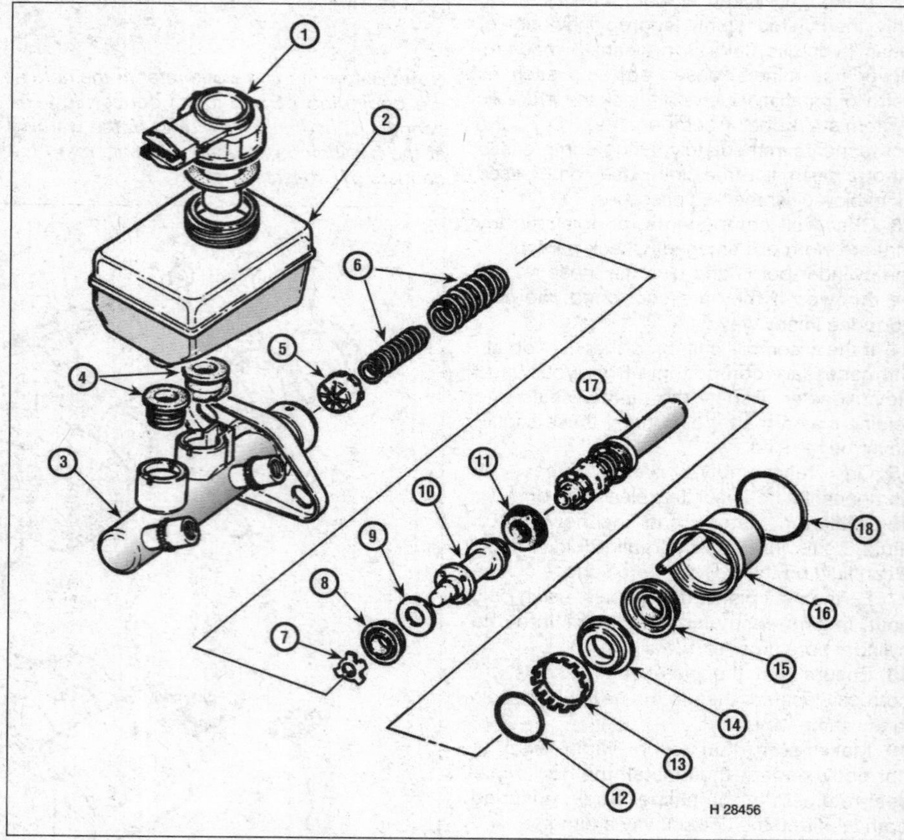
1
2
6
5
4
17
3
11
10
18
9
8
16
7
15
14
13
12
H 28456

10.6 Exploded view of the master cylinder - non-ABS models

1 Cap (incorporating fluid level sender unit)
2 Fluid reservoir
3 Master cylinder
4 Mounting seals
5 Swirl tube
6 Springs
7 Seal retainer
8 Seal
9 Washer
10 Secondary piston
11 Seal
12 O-ring seal
13 Retaining ring
14 Guide ring
15 Vacuum seal
16 Rear housing cover
17 Primary piston assembly
18 O-ring

cylinder assembly from the engine compartment. Recover the O-ring from the rear of the master cylinder.

Overhaul

Models with ABS

4 At the time of writing, master cylinder overhaul was not possible, since spares are not available. If the cylinder is thought to be faulty, it must be renewed.

5 The only parts available individually are the fluid reservoir and its mounting seals - these can be renewed as described below for the non-ABS models.

Models without ABS

Note: *Prior to dismantling the master cylinder, check the availability of spares from your Land Rover dealer.*

6 Carefully ease the reservoir out from the master cylinder body, and recover the two mounting seals from the master cylinder ports, noting each seal's correct fitted location **(see illustration opposite)**.

7 Carefully grip the master cylinder body in a vice fitted with soft jaws, then using a suitable pair of grips, ease the rear housing cover out from the cylinder. The housing should come away complete with the vacuum seal.

8 Carefully remove the retaining ring from the master cylinder, along with its O-ring.

9 Ease the guide ring out from the rear of the master cylinder. **Note:** *The guide is not supplied with the repair kit, and will have to be re-used, so take care not to damage it.*

10 Withdraw the primary piston assembly from the cylinder.

11 Noting the order of removal and the direction of fitting of each component, tap the body on a clean wooden surface, and withdraw the secondary piston assembly and springs, and the swirl tube, from the master cylinder. Note which way around the swirl tube is fitted.

12 Thoroughly clean all components, using only methylated spirit, isopropyl alcohol or clean hydraulic fluid as a cleaning medium. Never use mineral-based solvents such as petrol or paraffin, which will attack the hydraulic system's rubber components. Dry the components immediately, using compressed air or a clean, lint-free cloth.

13 Check all components, and renew any that are worn or damaged. Check particularly the cylinder bores and pistons; the complete assembly should be renewed if these are scratched, worn or corroded. If there is any doubt about the condition of the assembly or of any of its components, renew it. Check that the body's fluid passages are clear.

14 If the assembly is fit for further use, obtain a repair kit from your Land Rover dealer. The kit consists of the primary piston assembly, all seals and springs, as well as a rear housing. Renew all seals disturbed on dismantling and the rear housing as a matter of course; these should never be re-used.

15 Prior to reassembly, soak the piston assemblies and all new seals in clean hydraulic fluid. Smear clean fluid into the cylinder bore.

16 Using a small flat-bladed screwdriver, remove the seal retainer from the inner end of the secondary piston, and slide off the inner piston seal and washer. Remove the outer seal, taking great care not to mark the piston. Carefully manipulate the new outer seal into position on the piston, making sure that it is the correct way around. Fit the washer and inner seal, again making sure it is the correct way around, and secure it in position with the seal retainer **(see illustration)**.

17 Fit the new swirl tube to the master cylinder bore, ensuring that it is fitted the correct way around.

18 Locate both springs on the end of the secondary piston assembly, and insert the assembly into the master cylinder body. Insert the piston assembly using a twisting motion, ensuring that the piston seals do not become trapped as they enter the cylinder.

19 Fit the new primary piston assembly as described above.

20 With both piston assemblies in position, refit the guide ring to the end of the cylinder bore.

21 Fit the smaller O-ring to the groove on the master cylinder body.

22 Fit the new vacuum seal to the new rear housing, making sure its sealing lip is correctly positioned (facing the towards the primary piston).

23 Fit the new retaining ring to the rear of the master cylinder body, so that its teeth are in contact with the cylinder body.

24 Carefully ease the rear housing assembly into position on the master cylinder, and press it fully into the cylinder body. Fit the larger O-ring to the outside of the housing.

25 Press the new seals into the master cylinder ports, and refit the reservoir.

Refitting

26 Inspect the master cylinder O-ring for signs of damage or deterioration and, if necessary, renew it.

27 Remove all traces of dirt from the master cylinder and servo unit mating surfaces, then fit the master cylinder, ensuring that the servo unit pushrod enters the master cylinder bore centrally. Refit the master cylinder washers and mounting nuts, and tighten them to the specified torque.

28 Wipe clean the brake pipe unions, then refit them to the master cylinder ports and tighten them to the specified torque setting.

29 Refill the master cylinder reservoir with new fluid.

30 Slowly depress the brake pedal to the floor, and then slowly release it - repeat this five times. Wait for 10 seconds, then repeat this process. As this is done, air bubbles will rise into the reservoir, effectively bleeding the master cylinder.

31 Repeat the operations described in paragraph 30 until resistance is felt at the brake pedal, then bleed the complete hydraulic system as described in Section 2.

11 Brake pedal - removal and refitting

Removal

Early models

1 Release the two fasteners, and remove the driver's side lower facia panel (see Chapter 12).

2 Slide off the spring clip, and withdraw the clevis pin securing the pedal to the servo unit pushrod.

3 To relieve the tension of the pedal return spring, carefully unhook the spring from behind the pedal.

4 Where the pedal is retained by a pivot shaft, remove the circlip from one end of the pedal pivot shaft, then slide the pivot shaft out of position. Where the pedal is retained by a pivot bolt, unscrew the nut and washers from the end of the bolt, then slide the pivot bolt and washers out from its mounting bracket.

5 On all models, remove the pedal assembly from its mounting bracket, and recover the return spring and pivot bushes from the top end of the pedal.

6 Inspect the pedal pivot bushes and shaft/bolt (as applicable) for signs of wear, and renew if necessary.

Later models

7 Refer to the clutch pedal removal details given in Chapter 6.

Refitting

Early models

8 Press the pivot bushes into the pedal bore.

9 Apply a smear of multi-purpose grease to the bushes, and fit the return spring to the pedal.

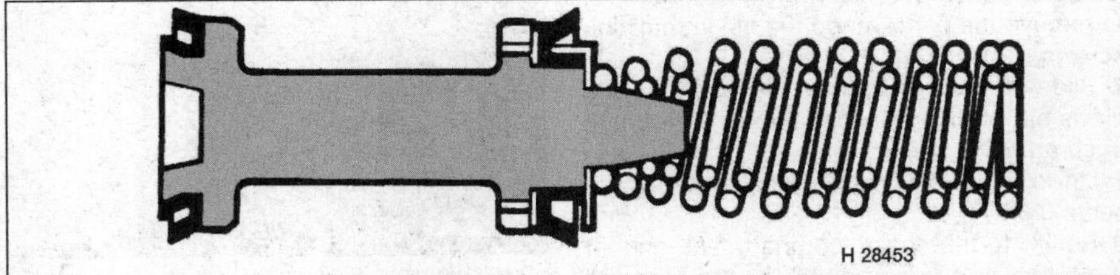
H 28453

10.16 Assemble the secondary piston and associated components as shown, noting that the inner and outer seals are different

10 Manoeuvre the pedal and spring into position, ensuring that it is correctly engaged with the servo pushrod, and insert the pivot shaft/bolt and washers (as applicable). On models with a pivot shaft, secure the shaft in position with the circlip, making sure it is correctly located in the shaft groove. On models with a pivot bolt, fit the washers and retaining nut, tightening it securely.

11 Align the pedal hole with the pushrod end, and insert the clevis pin. Secure the pin in position with the spring clip.

12 Hook the return spring over the pedal, and check the operation of the brake pedal.

13 On completion, refit the facia panel as described in Chapter 12.

Later models

14 Refer to the clutch pedal refitting details given in Chapter 6.

12 Vacuum servo unit - testing, removal and refitting

Testing

1 To test the operation of the servo unit, with the engine switched off, depress the footbrake several times to exhaust the vacuum. Keeping the pedal depressed, start the engine. As the engine starts, there should be a noticeable give in the brake pedal as the vacuum builds up. Allow the engine to run for at least two minutes, then switch it off. If the brake pedal is now depressed it should feel normal, but further applications should result in the pedal feeling firmer, with the pedal stroke decreasing with each application.

2 If the servo does not operate as described, first inspect the servo unit check valve as described in Section 13.

3 If the servo unit still fails to operate satisfactorily, the fault lies within the unit itself. Repairs to the unit are not possible, and if faulty, the servo unit must be renewed.

Removal

4 Remove the master cylinder as described in Section 10.

5 Release the retaining clip (where fitted), and disconnect the vacuum hose from the servo unit check valve.

6 From inside the vehicle, release the two fasteners and release the driver's side lower facia panel (see Chapter 12). On later models, to remove the panel, undo the hinge retaining screws.

7 Slide off the spring clip, and withdraw the clevis pin securing the pedal to the servo unit pushrod.

8 Undo the two retaining nuts securing the servo unit.

9 Return to the engine compartment, and lift the servo unit out of position. Recover the spacer which is fitted between the servo unit and bulkhead.

10 Whilst the servo unit is removed, peel back the rubber gaiter from the rear of the unit, and inspect the servo unit filter. If the filter is clogged or dirty, renew it. Carefully prise the old filter out of position, and ease the new one into place. Fit the rubber gaiter, making sure that it is correctly seated on the servo.

Refitting

11 Apply a smear of grease to the pushrod fork, then refit the spacer to the rear of the servo unit, and manoeuvre the assembly into position.

12 From inside the vehicle, ensure that the servo unit pushrod is correctly engaged with the brake pedal. Refit the mounting nuts, and tighten them to the specified torque setting.

13 Refit the servo unit pushrod-to-brake pedal clevis pin, and secure it in position with the spring clip.

14 Refit the facia panel as described in Chapter 12.

15 Return to the engine compartment, and reconnect the vacuum hose to the servo unit check valve.

16 Refit the master cylinder as described in Section 10.

13 Vacuum servo unit check valve - removal, testing and refitting

Removal

1 Slacken the retaining clip (where fitted), and disconnect the vacuum hose from the servo unit check valve.

2 Withdraw the valve from its rubber sealing grommet, using a pulling and twisting motion. Remove the grommet from the servo **(see illustration)**.

Testing

3 Examine the check valve for signs of damage, and renew if necessary. The valve may be tested by blowing through it in both directions, air should flow through the valve in one direction only - when blown through from the servo unit end of the valve. Renew the valve if this is not the case.

13.2 Withdraw the check valve from the servo unit, and recover the rubber grommet (arrowed)

4 Examine the rubber sealing grommet and flexible vacuum hose for signs of damage or deterioration, and renew as necessary.

Refitting

5 Fit the sealing grommet into position in the servo unit.

6 Carefully ease the check valve into position, taking great care not to displace or damage the grommet. Reconnect the vacuum hose to the valve and, where necessary, securely tighten its retaining clip.

7 On completion, start the engine, and check the check valve-to-servo unit connection for signs of air leaks.

14 Handbrake shoes - renewal

Note: *There are two types of handbrake assembly fitted. To distinguish which type is fitted, examine the rear of the handbrake assembly. On early models, the brake assembly is operated by a cable, with a rod operating linkage which is mounted onto the transfer box; on later models, the brake assembly is operated directly by cable.*

1 Chock the front wheels, then jack up the rear of the vehicle and support on axle stands.

2 Working as described in Chapter 8, disconnect the propeller shaft from the rear of the transfer box, and position the shaft clear of the handbrake assembly.

3 Apply the handbrake, then slacken and remove the handbrake drum retaining screw(s) **(see illustration)**.

4 Release the handbrake, and remove the brake drum from the rear of the transfer box. It may be difficult to remove the drum, due to the brake shoes binding on the inner circumference of the drum. If the brake shoes are binding, first check that the handbrake is fully released then, referring to the relevant part of Chapter 1 for further information, fully slacken the handbrake cable adjuster nut to obtain maximum freeplay in the cable, and rotate the adjuster bolt anti-clockwise so the shoes are retracted clear of the drum. The brake drum should then slide easily off the transfer box.

14.3 Removing the handbrake drum retaining screw

5 With the drum removed, inspect the shoes for signs of wear or damage. If the friction material of either shoe has worn down to, or close to, the rivets, the shoes must be renewed.

6 The shoes should also be renewed if any are fouled with oil; there is no satisfactory way of degreasing friction material, once contaminated. If there are traces of oil on the shoes, the transfer box output shaft seal should be renewed before new handbrake shoes are fitted by first draining the oil (see the relevant part of Chapter 1), then remove the rear propshaft and output flange. Lever out the old seal and fit a new one.

7 To remove the handbrake shoes, proceed as described under the relevant sub-heading.

Early models (with rod-actuated brake assembly)

8 To remove the shoes, note the correct fitted locations of the shoes and springs, then carefully unhook the shoes from the expander and adjuster assemblies **(see illustration)**. Remove the shoes and return spring assembly from the backplate, and separate the components.

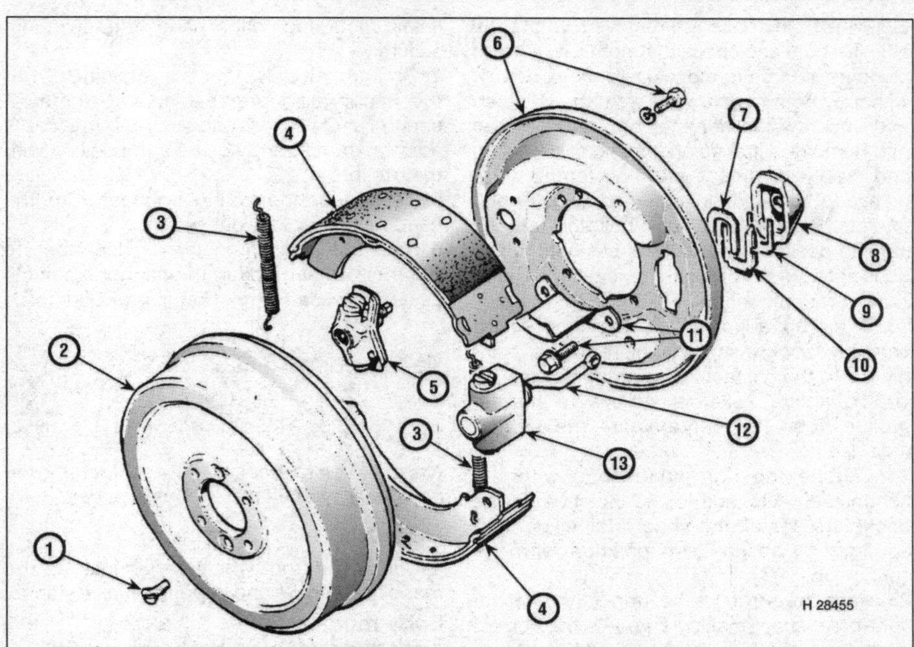
H 28455

14.8 Exploded view of the handbrake assembly components - early models (with rod-actuated brake assembly)

1 Retaining screw
2 Drum
3 Return springs
4 Shoe
5 Adjuster assembly
6 Backplate and retaining bolt
7 Spring plate
8 Rubber cover
9 Retaining clip
10 Packing plate
11 Oil catcher and retaining bolt (where fitted)
12 Drawlink
13 Expander assembly

9 Whilst the shoes are removed, take the opportunity to inspect the expander and adjuster assemblies as follows.

10 Operate the expander drawlink, and check that both plungers are free to move easily in the expander body. If necessary, withdraw both the plungers and their rollers from the expander body, and remove all traces of corrosion from them. Apply a smear of high-temperature grease to both rollers and the plungers, and refit them to the expander assembly. If this does not cure the problem, the expander assembly must be renewed as follows:

- *a) Withdraw the split-pin and clevis pin securing the drawlink to the actuating mechanism, then undo the four bolts and remove the backplate assembly and oil catcher (where fitted) from the rear of the transfer box.*
- *b) Peel back the rubber cover from the rear of the expander, slide out the horseshoe-type retaining clip, and recover the spring plate and packing plate, noting their correct fitted locations.*
- *c) Withdraw the expander assembly from the backplate.*
- *d) Install the new expander, securing it in position with the spring plate, packing plate and retaining clip, then fit the rubber cover to the rear of the assembly.*
- *e) Refit the oil catcher (where fitted) and backplate assembly to the transfer box, and tighten its retaining bolts.*
- *f) Apply a smear of grease to the clevis pin, then align the drawlink with the operating rod. Slide in the pin, securing it in position with a new split-pin.*

11 Rotate the adjuster bolt, and check that both the adjuster plungers are free to move easily. If necessary, withdraw both the plungers from the adjuster, and unscrew the adjuster bolt. Remove all traces of corrosion from them, and apply a smear of high-temperature grease to both the plungers and adjuster bolt threads. Screw the adjuster bolt into position, and refit the plungers. If this does not cure the problem, the adjuster assembly must be renewed. To renew the adjuster, undo the two retaining bolts and washers, and remove it from the backplate. Install the new adjuster assembly, and securely tighten the retaining bolts.

12 With both adjuster and expander assemblies operating correctly, apply a smear of high-melting point grease to the contact areas of the new shoes and backplate. Take care to ensure that the grease does not contaminate the friction material.

13 Position the handbrake shoes so that the fully-lined end of the lower shoe is next to the expander assembly, and the fully-lined end of the upper shoe is next to the adjuster assembly. Engage the new return springs with the shoes, then install the shoes and springs as an assembly.

14 Make sure that each shoe is correctly located on adjuster plunger slots, then refit the brake drum. Refit the brake drum retaining screws, and tighten them securely.

15 Adjust the cable as described in the relevant part of Chapter 1, then check the operation of the handbrake.

16 If all is well, reconnect the propeller shaft to the transfer box as described in Chapter 8.

Later models (with cable-actuated brake assembly)

17 Note the correct fitted locations of all components then, using a suitable pair of pliers, unhook the return springs and remove them from the brake shoes.

18 Using a pair of pliers, remove the left-hand shoe retainer spring cup by depressing and turning it through 90°. With the cup removed, lift off the spring, and withdraw the retainer pin from the rear of the backplate.

19 Remove the left-hand shoe, and recover the strut which is fitted between the shoe upper ends, noting which way around it is fitted.

20 Remove the right-hand shoe spring cup, spring and retainer pin as described in paragraph 18, then detach the shoe from the handbrake cable and remove it from the vehicle.

21 If the new handbrake shoes are supplied without the operating lever already fitted to the right-hand shoe, it will be necessary to transfer the old one over from the original shoe. Remove the spring clip, then withdraw the pivot pin and recover the spring washers, noting their correct fitted positions. Inspect the pivot pin and spring clip for signs of wear or damage, and renew if necessary. Apply a smear of high-melting-point grease to the pin, then fit the operating lever to the new shoe; insert the pin and spring washers, securing them in position with the spring clip.

22 Whilst the shoes are removed, rotate the adjuster bolt, and check that both the adjuster plungers are free to move easily. If necessary, withdraw both the plungers from the adjuster, and unscrew the adjuster bolt and tapered nut. Remove all traces of corrosion from them, and apply a smear of high-temperature grease to both the plungers and adjuster bolt threads. Screw the adjuster bolt and tapered nut into position, and refit the plungers. If this does not cure the problem, renew the adjuster assembly components.
23 With the adjuster assembly operating correctly, apply a smear of high-melting-point grease to the contact areas of the new shoes and backplate. Take care to ensure that the grease does not contaminate the friction material.
24 Engage the right-hand shoe with the handbrake cable, and locate the shoe on the backplate. Install the shoe retainer pin and spring, and secure it in position with the spring cup.
25 Refit the strut to the upper end of the right-hand shoe, making sure it is the correct way up.
26 Hook the lower return spring onto the right-hand shoe, then engage the left-hand shoe with the return spring. Locate the left-hand shoe on the backplate, engaging it with the adjuster plunger slot and strut, and secure it in position with its retainer pin, spring and spring cup.
27 Check that all components are correctly positioned, then refit the upper return spring.
28 Refit the brake drum to the transfer box, tightening its retaining screws securely.
29 Adjust the handbrake as described in the relevant part of Chapter 1 then, if all is well, reconnect the propeller shaft to the transfer box as described in Chapter 8.

15 Handbrake lever - removal and refitting

Removal

1 Remove the centre console as described in Chapter 12.
2 Disconnect the wiring connector from the handbrake warning light switch.
3 On early models, slacken the nut securing the handbrake outer cable to the base of the handbrake lever.
4 On later models, remove the circlip securing the cable to the lever assembly, and lift off the adjustment nut.
5 Undo the two mounting bolts and washers, then free the lever assembly from the outer cable, and lift it out of the vehicle **(see illustration)**.

Refitting

6 Refit the handbrake lever assembly, making sure that it is correctly engaged with the handbrake outer cable. Refit the handbrake lever mounting bolts, and tighten them securely.
7 On early models, refit the retaining nut to the handbrake outer cable, and tighten it securely. On later models, refit the cable adjustment nut, and secure it in position with the circlip.
8 Reconnect the wiring connector to the handbrake warning light switch.
9 Refit the centre console as described in Chapter 12, and adjust the handbrake cable as described in the relevant part of Chapter 1.

16 Handbrake cable - removal and refitting

Note: *Refer to Section 14 and identify the handbrake type fitted before proceeding.*

Removal

1 Chock the front wheels, then jack up the rear of the vehicle and support on axle stands.

Early models (with rod-actuated brake assembly)

2 Release the handbrake lever gaiter from the console, then carefully prise out the switch panel. Disconnect all the switch wiring connectors, and remove the panel from the console. If necessary, to improve access further, remove the centre console as described in Chapter 12.
3 If not already done, remove the split-pin/spring clip (as applicable) then withdraw the clevis pin securing the handbrake inner cable to the lever. Where a split-pin is used, discard it - a new one will be needed on refitting.
4 Slacken the nut securing the handbrake outer cable to the base of the handbrake lever.
5 From underneath the vehicle, work back along the cable, freeing it from any relevant retaining clips and ties whilst noting its correct routing.
6 Remove the split-pin, then withdraw the clevis pin securing the handbrake inner cable to the rod linkage on the rear of the handbrake assembly. Discard the split-pin - a new one will be needed on refitting.
7 Slacken the cable locknut and adjuster nut, then free the cable from its mounting bracket and withdraw the cable from underneath the vehicle.

Later models (with cable-actuated brake assembly)

8 Release the handbrake lever gaiter from the console, and remove the switch panel cover plate. Undo the retaining screws, then withdraw the switch panel and disconnect its wiring connectors. If necessary, to improve access further, remove the centre console as described in Chapter 12.
9 If not already done, remove the split-pin/spring clip (as applicable), then withdraw the clevis pin securing the handbrake inner cable to the lever. Where a split-pin is used, discard it - a new one will be needed on refitting.
10 Remove the circlip, and lift off the handbrake cable adjustment nut **(see illustration)**.
11 From underneath the vehicle, work back along the cable, freeing it from any relevant retaining clips and ties whilst noting its correct routing.
12 Referring to Section 14, remove the upper and lower return springs, then remove the spring cup, spring and retainer pin, and remove the right-hand handbrake shoe. Note that the left-hand shoe and strut can be left in position on the backplate.
13 Free the handbrake cable from the rear of the backplate, and withdraw it from underneath the vehicle.

Refitting

Early models (with rod-actuated brake assembly)

14 Engage the lower end of the cable with its mounting bracket, and tighten the adjuster nut and locknut by hand only.
15 Apply a smear of grease to the clevis pin. Align the inner cable with the rod linkage, then insert the clevis pin and secure it in position with a new split-pin.
16 Work along the cable, routing it correctly and securing it in position with all the relevant clips and ties, and feed it up through the base of the floorpan.

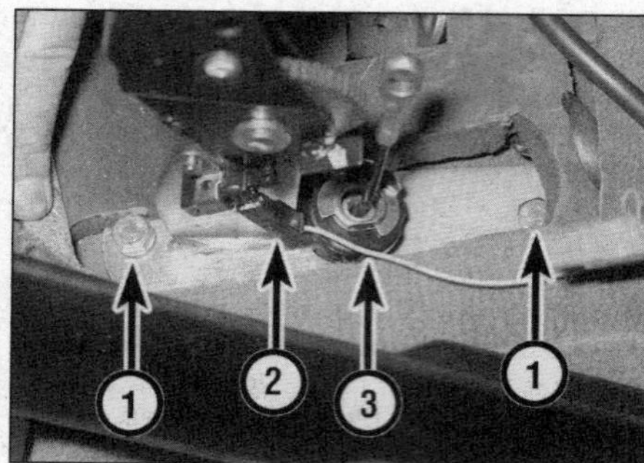
1
2
3
1

15.5 Handbrake lever retaining bolts (1), switch wiring connector (2) and cable adjusting nut (3) - later models

16.10 On later models, remove the circlip and lift off the handbrake cable adjusting nut (arrowed)

17 From inside the vehicle, refit the retaining nut to the outer cable, and tighten it securely.
18 Apply a smear of grease to the clevis pin, then align the inner cable with the lever, and insert the pin. Refit the washer, and secure the clevis pin in position with the spring clip/new split-pin (as applicable).
19 Refit the centre console (where removed) as described in Chapter 12, and adjust the handbrake as described in the relevant part of Chapter 1.

Later models (with cable-actuated brake assembly)

20 Apply a smear of high-melting-point grease to the cable lower end fitting, then insert the cable through the rear of the backplate.
21 Refit the right-hand brake shoe as described in Section 14, and refit the brake drum.
22 Work along the cable, routing it correctly and securing it in position with all the relevant clips and ties, and feed it up through the base of the floorpan.
23 From inside the vehicle, refit the adjustment nut to the cable, and secure it in position with the circlip.
24 Apply a smear of grease to the clevis pin, then align the inner cable with the lever, and insert the pin. Refit the washer, and secure the clevis pin in position with the spring clip/new new split-pin (as applicable).
25 Refit the centre console (where removed) as described in Chapter 12, and adjust the handbrake as described in the relevant part of Chapter 1.

17 Rear brake pressure-regulating valve - testing, removal and refitting

Testing

1 A pressure-regulating valve is incorporated in the hydraulic braking circuit, to regulate the pressure applied to the rear brakes, and thereby reduce the risk of the rear wheels locking under heavy braking. The valve is situated on either the left- or right-hand side of the engine compartment, mounted on the wing valance **(see illustration)**.
2 Specialist equipment is required to check the performance of the valve, and if the valve is thought to be faulty, the car should be taken to a suitably-equipped Land Rover dealer for testing. Repairs are not possible and, if faulty, the valve must be renewed.

Removal

Note: *Before starting work, refer to the note at the beginning of Section 2 concerning the dangers of hydraulic fluid.*
3 Disconnect the sender unit wiring connector, and unscrew the master cylinder reservoir filler cap. Place a piece of polythene over the filler neck, and securely refit the cap (taking care not to damage the sender unit). This will minimise brake fluid loss during subsequent operations. As an added precaution, place absorbent rags beneath the pressure-regulating valve brake pipe unions.
4 Wipe clean the area around the brake pipe unions on the side of the pressure-regulating valve, and place absorbent rags beneath the pipe unions to catch any surplus fluid. Make a note of the correct fitted positions of the unions, then unscrew the union nuts and carefully withdraw the pipes. Wash off any spilt fluid immediately with cold water.

HAYNES
HiNT

Plug or tape over the pipe ends and valve orifices to minimise the loss of brake fluid and to prevent the entry of dirt into the system.

5 Slacken the retaining bolt, and remove the valve from the engine compartment. Note that on some models, there is a spacer fitted behind the valve - take care not to lose this as the retaining bolt is withdrawn.

Refitting

6 Refit the pressure-regulating valve, positioning the spacer (where fitted) between the valve and body, and securely tighten its mounting bolt.
7 Wipe the brake pipe unions clean and refit them to the valve, using the notes made prior to removal to ensure that they are correctly positioned. Tighten the union nuts to the specified torque.
8 Remove the polythene from the master cylinder reservoir filler neck, and bleed the complete hydraulic system as described in Section 2.

18 Stop-light switch - removal, refitting and adjustment

Removal

1 The stop-light switch is located on the pedal bracket behind the facia. To remove the switch, first disconnect the battery negative lead, then release the fasteners and detach the driver's side lower facia panel from the facia (see Chapter 12).
2 Disconnect the wiring connector plug(s) from the stop-light switch **(see illustration)**. On models with cruise control, the stop-light switch is the higher-mounted of the two switches - the brake pedal vent valve switch is identified by its vacuum hose connection. If necessary, remove the brake pedal vent valve switch as described in Chapter 4B, Section 13.

Models without ABS

3 Depress the pedal, and remove the rubber from the front of the switch. Unscrew the switch retaining nut, and withdraw the switch from the rear of the pedal mounting bracket.

Models with ABS

4 Depress the pedal to gain access to the front of the switch. Pull the sleeve and plunger **fully** out of the front of the switch, then withdraw the switch from the rear of the mounting bracket **(see illustration)**.

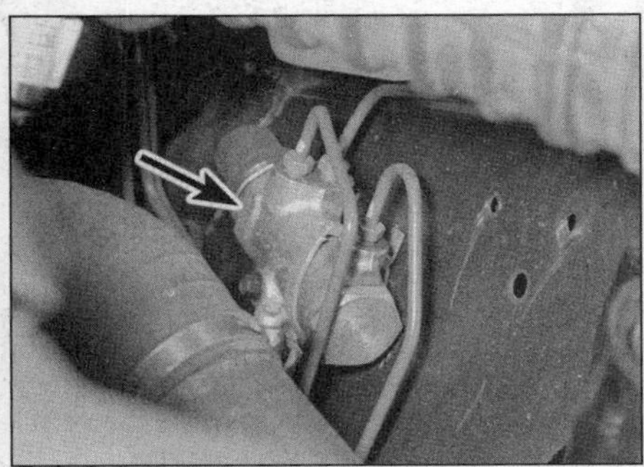

17.1 The rear brake pressure-regulating valve (arrowed) is mounted onto the wing valance

18.2 Stop-light switch (arrowed) is accessed from behind the driver's side lower facia panel

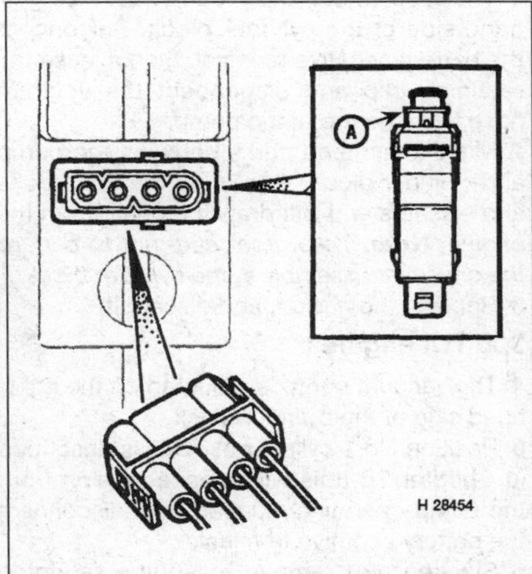
A
H 28454

18.4 On models with ABS, to release the stop-light switch, fully pull out the plunger (A), then slide the switch out from the mounting bracket

Refitting and adjustment

Models without ABS

5 Fit the switch to the mounting bracket, tightening its retaining nut securely, and refit its rubber.

6 Reconnect the switch wiring connectors and the battery negative terminal, then check the operation of the switch. Note that no adjustment of the switch is possible; if the switch does not function properly, it must be renewed.

7 On completion, refit the facia panel as described in Chapter 12.

Models with ABS

8 Make sure that the sleeve and plunger are pulled fully out of the front of the switch.

9 Depress the brake pedal, then push the switch fully into the mounting bracket so that its retaining clips are fully located. Hold the switch in this position, then pull the brake pedal back up towards the switch to lock the switch in position.

10 Reconnect the switch wiring connector and the battery negative terminal, then check the operation of the switch. If the switch does not function properly, first ensure that it is correctly located in the mounting bracket. If the switch is correctly located but fails to work, it must be renewed - no adjustment is possible.

11 On completion, refit the facia panel as described in Chapter 12.

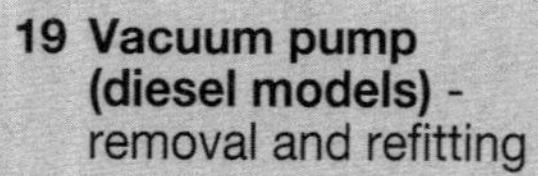

19 Vacuum pump (diesel models) - removal and refitting

Removal

200 TDi engine

1 The vacuum pump is mounted on the right-hand side of the cylinder block. Disconnect the battery negative terminal, then release the retaining clip and disconnect the vacuum hose from the top of the pump.

2 Make alignment marks between the pump and cylinder block, then undo the three bolts and washers and withdraw the pump from the engine. **Note:** *Take great care not to disturb the drivegear assembly in the cylinder block.*

3 Recover the gasket, and discard it.

300 TDi engine

4 The vacuum pump is mounted on the right-hand side of the cylinder block.

5 Position No 1 cylinder at TDC as described in Chapter 2B (this will release tension from the pump operating plunger) then disconnect the battery negative terminal.

6 Slacken and remove the pump retaining bolts and washers, noting the correct fitted location of the wiring bracket.

7 Remove the pump from the side of the block. Recover the gasket, and discard it.

19.13 On 300 TDi engines, ensure the mating surfaces are clean and dry, then fit a new gasket to the cylinder block and refit the braking system vacuum pump

Refitting

200 TDi engine

8 Ensure that the pump and drivegear mating surfaces are clean and dry, and position the new gasket on the driver gear.

9 Using the marks made prior to removal, refit the pump to the cylinder block, aligning its driveshaft correctly with the drivegear.

10 Refit the pump retaining bolts, and tighten them securely.

11 Reconnect the vacuum hose to the pump, and (where necessary) securely tighten its retaining clip.

300 TDi engine

12 Ensure that the pump and cylinder block mating surfaces are clean and dry.

13 Offer up a new gasket, and refit the pump to the cylinder block **(see illustration)**.

14 Refit the pump retaining bolts, not forgetting to fit the wiring bracket to the relevant bolt, and tighten them securely.

15 Reconnect the vacuum hose to the pump, and (where necessary) securely tighten its retaining clip.

20 Anti-lock braking system (ABS) - general information

ABS is fitted as standard to some high-specification models, and is available as an option on most other models in the range. The system comprises of the electronic control unit (ECU), a modulator block (which contains the hydraulic solenoid valves and accumulators, and the electrically-driven return pump), and four roadwheel sensors; one fitted to each hub. The brake pedal stop-light switch is used to indicate to the ECU that the brakes are applied. The purpose of the system is to prevent wheel(s) locking during heavy braking. This is achieved by automatic release of the brake on the relevant wheel, followed by reapplication of the brake.

The solenoid valves are controlled by the ECU, which itself receives signals from the four wheel sensors (one fitted on each hub), which monitor the speed of rotation of each wheel. By comparing these speed signals from the four wheels, the ECU can determine the speed at which the vehicle is travelling. It can then use this speed to determine when a wheel is decelerating at an abnormal rate compared to the speed of the vehicle, and therefore predicts when a wheel is about to lock. During normal operation, the system functions in the same way as a non-ABS braking system does.

During normal operation, the solenoid valves in the modulator assembly are closed, and the governor valves are in the at-rest position. The system then functions in the same way as a non-ABS braking system does.

If the ECU senses that a wheel is about to lock, the ABS operates the relevant solenoid valve in the modulator assembly, which then isolates the brake caliper on the wheel which is about to lock from the master cylinder, effectively sealing-in the hydraulic pressure.

If the speed of rotation of the wheel continues to decrease at an abnormal rate, the electrically-driven return pump operates, and pumps the hydraulic fluid back into the master cylinder, releasing pressure on the brake caliper so that the brake is released. Once the speed of rotation of the wheel returns to an acceptable rate, the pump stops and the solenoid valve opens, allowing the hydraulic master cylinder pressure to return to the caliper, which then reapplies the brake. This cycle can be carried out at many times a second.

The action of the solenoid valves and return pump creates pulses in the hydraulic circuit. When the ABS is functioning, these pulses can be felt through the brake pedal.

The operation of the ABS is entirely dependent on electrical signals. To prevent the system responding to any inaccurate signals, a built-in safety circuit monitors all signals received by the ECU. The first time the vehicle exceeds 5 mph (7 km/h) after the 'ignition' has been switched on, the ECU tests the readings from each wheel sensor, and the operation of the modulator solenoid valves. If a fault is present, the ABS is automatically shut down by the ECU, and the warning light on the instrument panel is illuminated to inform the driver that the ABS is not operational.

Every time the 'ignition' is switched on, the ECU performs a self-test and checks its memory for faults. This takes approximately 1 to 2 seconds, during which time the warning light in the instrument panel will illuminate. The warning light should then go out for approximately 0.5 seconds, indicating the end of the self-test, before illuminating again. The warning light will stay illuminated until the first time the vehicle speed exceeds 5 mph (7 km/h), at which point it should go out. If the warning light fails to go out, or illuminates whilst the vehicle is being driven, then a fault is present in the ABS.

If a fault does develop in the ABS, the vehicle must be taken to a Land Rover dealer for fault diagnosis and repair.

21 Anti lock braking system (ABS) components - removal and refitting

Modulator assembly

Note: *Before starting work, refer to the note at the beginning of Section 2 concerning the dangers of hydraulic fluid.*

Removal

1 Disconnect the battery negative terminal.

2 Disconnect the two wiring connectors from the ABS modulator assembly.

3 Unscrew the master cylinder reservoir filler cap, and top-up the reservoir to the MAX mark (see *Weekly checks*).

HAYNES
HiNT

Place a piece of polythene over the master cylinder filler neck, and securely refit the cap. This will minimise brake fluid loss during subsequent operations. As a precaution, place absorbent rags beneath the modulator brake pipe unions.

4 Wipe clean the area around the modulator brake pipe unions, then make a note of how the pipes are arranged, to use as a reference on refitting. Unscrew the union nuts, and carefully withdraw the pipes. Plug or tape over the pipe ends and modulator orifices, to minimise the loss of brake fluid and to prevent the entry of dirt into the system. Wash off any spilt fluid immediately with cold water.

5 Slacken and remove the mounting nuts, and release the modulator assembly from its mounting bracket. If necessary, unscrew the modulator rubber mounting bushes, and remove them. **Note:** *Do not attempt to dismantle the modulator block hydraulic assembly; overhaul of the unit is not possible.*

Refitting

6 Refitting is the reverse of the removal procedure, noting the following points:

a) Examine the rubber mounting bushes for signs of wear or damage, and renew if necessary.

b) Refit the brake pipes to their respective unions, and tighten the union nuts to the specified torque.

c) Ensure that the wiring is correctly routed, and that the connector is firmly pressed into position.

d) On completion, prior to refitting the battery, bleed the complete braking system as described in Section 2.

Electronic control unit (ECU)

Removal

7 The ABS electronic control unit (ECU) is mounted behind the glovebox. Prior to removing the ECU, disconnect the battery negative terminal.

8 Remove the central locking electronic control unit as described in Chapter 12.

9 Slacken and remove the two retaining screws, then lower the ABS ECU out of position.

10 Lift the wiring connector retaining clip, then twist the connector to release it and remove the ECU from the vehicle.

Refitting

11 Refitting is a reversal of the removal procedure, ensuring that the wiring connector is securely reconnected.

Front wheel sensor

Removal

Note: *A new sensor mounting bush and seal will be required on refitting.*

12 The front wheel sensors are mounted on top of the swivel housing. Prior to removal, disconnect the battery negative terminal.

13 Firmly apply the handbrake, then loosen the relevant front roadwheel nuts. Jack up the front of the vehicle and support on axle stands. Remove the appropriate front roadwheel.

14 Trace the wheel sensor wiring back to its wiring connector, and release it from its retaining clip. Disconnect the connector, and work back along the sensor wiring, freeing it from all the relevant retaining clips and ties.

15 Wipe clean the area around the top of the swivel housing, then carefully prise the sensor out from its mounting bush. Remove the sensor and lead assembly from the vehicle.

16 Undo the two retaining bolts securing the bracket to the top of the swivel housing, then withdraw the sensor mounting bush and seal.

Refitting

17 Remove all traces of locking compound from the threads of the bracket bolts and housing holes, ideally by running a tap of suitable size down them.

18 Carefully insert the new sensor mounting bush and seal into the switch housing.

19 Apply a drop of locking compound to the threads of the bracket bolts, then refit the bracket to the top of the swivel housing and securely tighten the retaining bolts.

20 Coat the outside of the sensor with a smear of EP90 gear oil to help aid installation, then carefully ease the sensor into position until it contacts the sensor ring. The sensor will then be pushed back by the ring, to set the correct air gap, the first time the vehicle is driven.

21 Ensure that the sensor wiring is correctly routed and retained by all the necessary clips. Reconnect it to its wiring connector, and clip the connector into the retaining clip.

22 Refit the roadwheel, then lower the vehicle to the ground and tighten the roadwheel nuts to the specified torque.

Rear wheel sensor

Note: *A new sensor mounting bush and seal will be required on refitting.*

Removal

23 The rear wheel sensors are mounted onto the rear of the hub assemblies. Prior to removal, disconnect the battery negative terminal.

24 Chock the front wheels, then jack up the rear of the vehicle and support it on axle stands.

25 Trace the wiring back from the sensor to its wiring connector. Free the connector from its retaining clip, disconnect it from the main wiring loom, then work back along the sensor wiring and free it from any relevant retaining clips.

26 Carefully prise the sensor out from its mounting bush, and remove it from underneath the vehicle.

27 Undo the retaining bolts, and remove the mudshield from the rear hub assembly.

28 Remove the sensor bush from the hub assembly.

Refitting

29 Carefully ease the new sensor bush into position in the hub.

30 Apply a thin coat of silicone grease to the sensor body to help aid installation, then carefully ease the sensor into position until it contacts the sensor ring. The sensor will then be pushed back by the ring, to set the correct air gap, the first time the vehicle is driven.

31 Ensure that the sensor wiring is correctly routed and retained by all the necessary clips. Reconnect it to its wiring connector, and clip the connector into the retaining clip.

32 Refit the roadwheel, then lower the vehicle to the ground and tighten the roadwheel nuts to the specified torque.

Front wheel sensor toothed rings

33 The front toothed rings are an integral part of the constant velocity (CV) joints, and cannot be renewed separately. If renewal is necessary, the complete constant velocity joint must be renewed as described in Chapter 9, Section 2.

Rear wheel sensor toothed rings

Note: *New retaining nuts will be required on refitting.*

Removal

34 Remove the rear hub assembly as described in Chapter 9.

35 Undo the retaining nuts, and remove the remove the sensor ring from the rear hub assembly. Discard the retaining nuts - they must be renewed whenever they are disturbed.

Refitting

36 Ensure that the disc and sensor mating surfaces are clean and dry, and fit the sensor to the disc.

37 Fit the new sensor retaining nuts, and tighten them securely.

38 Refit the rear hub assembly as described in Chapter 9.

Relays

39 See Chapter 13.

Chapter 11
Suspension and steering

Contents

Degrees of difficulty

Easy, suitable for novice with little experience

Fairly easy, suitable for beginner with some experience

Fairly difficult, suitable for competent DIY mechanic

Difficult, suitable for experienced DIY mechanic

Very difficult, suitable for expert DIY or professional

Specifications

Front suspension

Type	Axle with coil springs and shock absorbers. Axle movement controlled by radius arms and Panhard rod. Anti-roll bar fitted to all later models

Rear suspension

Type	Axle with coil springs and shock absorbers. Axle movement controlled by upper and lower links. Anti-roll bar fitted on most models

Steering

Type	Power-assisted steering box with drag link and track rod arrangement. Steering damper fitted to track rod
Power steering pump type:	
Petrol models	ZF Unicorn
Diesel models	Hobourn Eaton 500 series

Front wheel alignment and steering angles

Note: *All measurements should be taken with the vehicle unladen, with approximately five gallons of fuel in the tank.*

Camber angle	0°
Castor angle	3°
Swivel pin inclination	7°
Toe setting	0° 0' to 0° 16' toe-out (0 to 2.0 mm toe-out)

Roadwheels

Type	Pressed-steel or aluminium alloy (depending on model)

Tyres

Size	205 R 16 or 235/70 R 16 (depending on model)
Pressures	*See end of Weekly checks*

Torque wrench settings

	Nm	lbf ft
Front suspension		
Anti-roll bar:		
Connecting link balljoint nuts	40	30
Mounting clamp bolts	30	22
Pivot bolt nuts	68	50
Panhard rod:		
Mounting bracket bolts	88	65
Pivot bolts	88	65
Radius arm:		
Retaining nut	176	130
Pivot bolts	197	145
Upper spring seat retaining nuts	14	10
Rear suspension		
Anti-roll bar:		
Connecting link balljoint nuts	40	30
Mounting clamp bolts	30	22
Pivot bolt nuts	68	50
Lower link:		
Front nut	176	130
Pivot bolt	176	130
Shock absorber mounting nuts	37	27
Upper link:		
Balljoint bracket bolts	176	130
Mounting bracket bolts to crossmember	47	35
Pivot bolt	176	130
Upper link balljoint nut	176	130
Roadwheels		
Roadwheel nuts	129	95
Steering		
Drag link:		
Balljoint nuts	40	30
Clamp bolts	14	10
Drop arm retaining nut	176	130
Intermediate shaft/universal joint clamp bolt:		
Early models	35	26
Later models	25	18
Power steering pump:		
Feed pipe union nut	20	15
Front mounting plate bolts	9	7
Mounting bolts	35	26
Pulley retaining bolts*	10	7
Steering box:		
Mounting bolts	81	60
Tie-bar bolts/nuts	81	60
Steering column nuts/bolts:		
Early models	27	20
Later models	22	16
Steering pipe union nuts:		
14 mm thread	15	11
16 mm thread	20	15
Steering wheel nut:		
Early models	38	28
Later models	45	33
Track rod:		
Balljoint nuts	40	30
Clamp bolts	14	10

**Use thread-locking fluid*

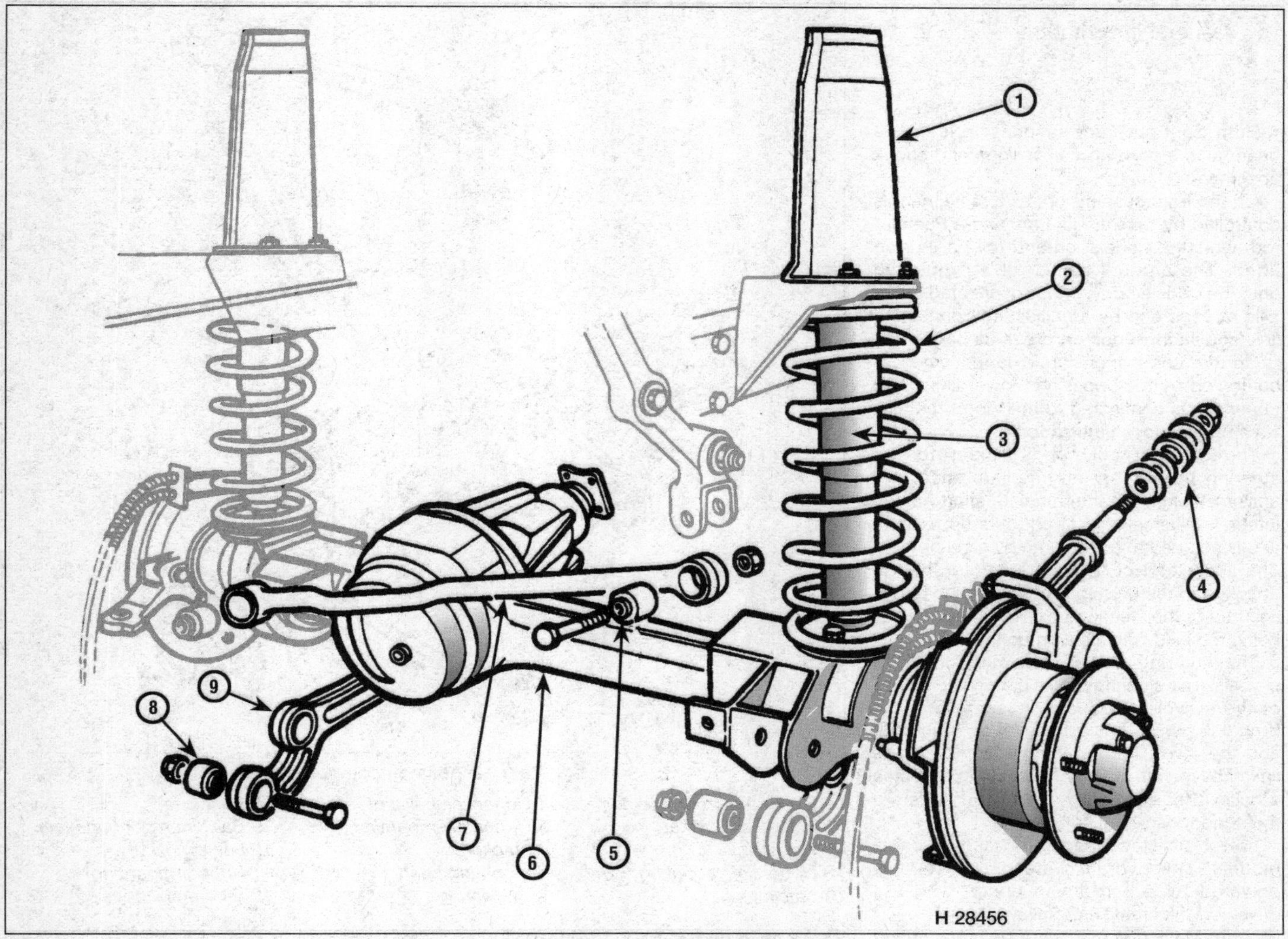

H 28456

1.2a Front suspension components

1 *Shock absorber mounting*
2 *Coil spring*
3 *Shock absorber*
4 *Mounting bush*
5 *Mounting bush*
6 *Front axle*
7 *Panhard rod*
8 *Mounting bush*
9 *Radius arm*

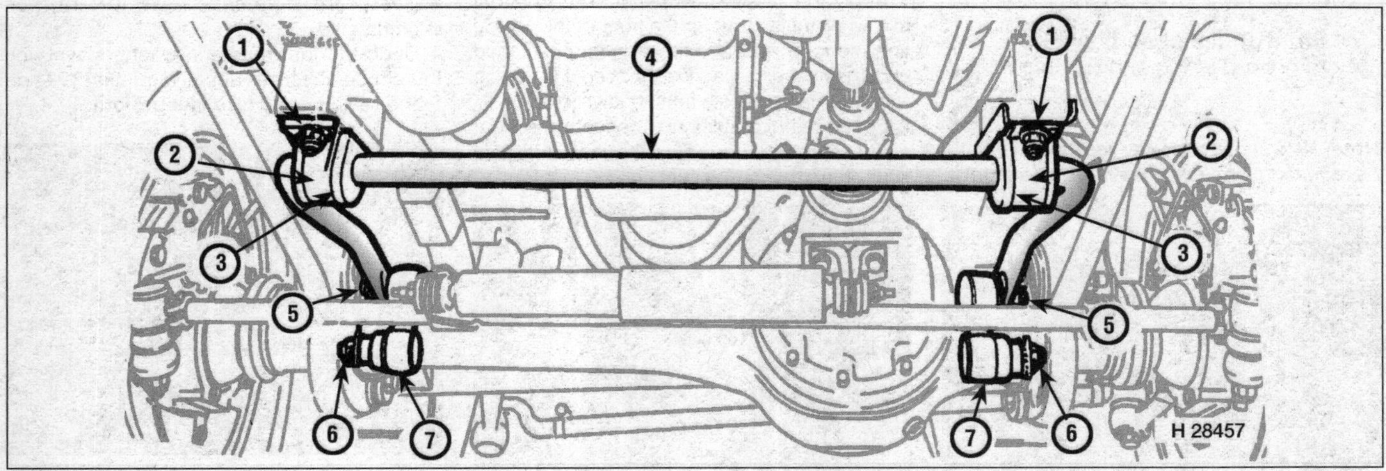
H 28457

1.2b Front suspension anti-roll bar components

1 *Clamp nut*
2 *Mounting clamp*
3 *Mounting rubber*
4 *Anti-roll bar*
5 *Retaining nut*
6 *Retaining nut*
7 *Connecting link*

1 General information

Both front and rear suspension is of live beam axle type, with coil springs and shock absorbers.

On the front suspension, axle movement is controlled by two radius arms and a Panhard rod. On later models, an anti-roll bar is also fitted. The anti-roll bar is rubber-mounted onto the vehicle body, and is connected to the axle at each end by a balljointed connecting link **(see illustrations on previous page)**.

On the rear suspension, axle movement is controlled by the upper and lower links. The upper link is connected to the top of the axle via a balljoint **(see illustration)**.

The steering column is linked to the steering box by an intermediate shaft and universal joint. The intermediate shaft has an integral universal joint fitted to its upper end, and is secured to the column by a clamp bolt. The lower end of the intermediate shaft is attached to the universal joint, which in turn is secured to the steering box pinion, both joints being retained with a clamp bolt.

The steering box is mounted onto the chassis. The steering box is connected to one of the swivel pin housing assemblies by a drag link, which has a balljoint at each end, and the swivel pin housing assemblies are linked by means of a track rod, which also has a balljoint at each end. All balljoint ends are threaded to facilitate adjustment.

Power-assisted steering is standard on all models. The hydraulic steering system is powered by a belt-driven pump, which is driven off the crankshaft pulley.

Note: *Many of the suspension and steering components are secured in position with self-locking nuts. Whenever a self-locking nut is disturbed, it must be discarded and a new nut fitted.*

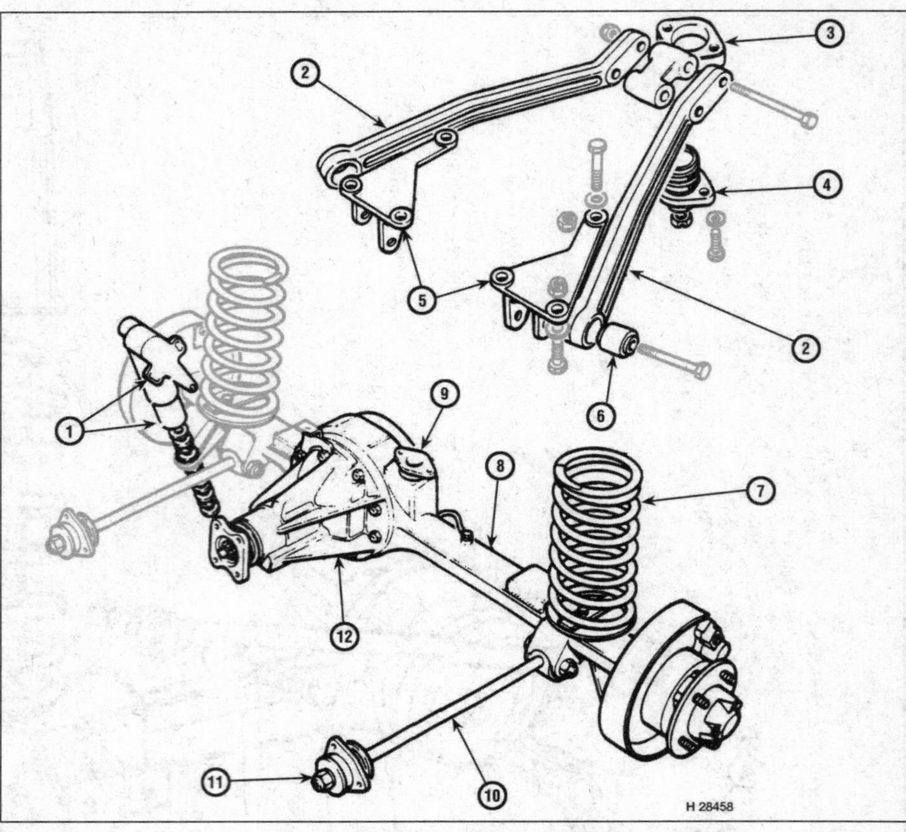
H 28458

1.3 Rear suspension components

1 Shock absorber and mounting bracket
2 Upper link
3 Upper link mounting bracket
4 Upper link balljoint
5 Upper link mounting bracket
6 Mounting bush
7 Coil spring
8 Rear axle
9 Balljoint mounting plate
10 Lower link
11 Rubber mounting
12 Differential housing

2 Front shock absorber - removal, testing and refitting

Note: *New shock absorber mounting nuts will be required on refitting (see note in Section 1). Shock absorbers must ALWAYS be renewed in pairs, even if only one appears to be defective, in order to preserve safe handling.*

Removal

1 Apply the handbrake, then loosen the front roadwheel nuts. Jack up the front of the vehicle and support it on axle stands positioned underneath the chassis (see *Jacking and vehicle support*). Remove both front roadwheels.

2 Position a hydraulic jack beneath the front axle assembly, then raise the jack until it is supporting the axle weight.

3 Slacken and remove the shock absorber lower mounting nut, and recover the outer washer and rubber mounting arrangement, noting each component's correct fitted position **(see illustrations)**. **Note:** *The washers are different, and must not be interchanged.*

4 Undo the four nuts and washers securing the shock absorber upper mounting bracket to the vehicle body **(see illustration)**.

2.3a Slacken and remove the shock absorber lower mounting nut (arrowed) . . .

2.3b . . . and slide off the washer and mounting rubber arrangement

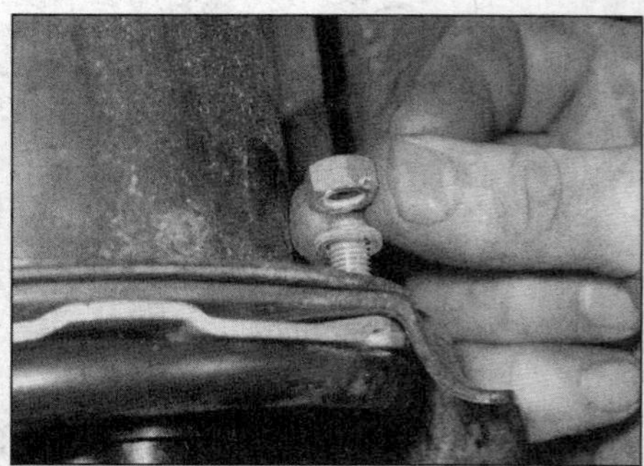

2.4 Unscrew the shock absorber upper mounting bracket retaining nuts and washers, then lift the shock absorber assembly out of position . . .

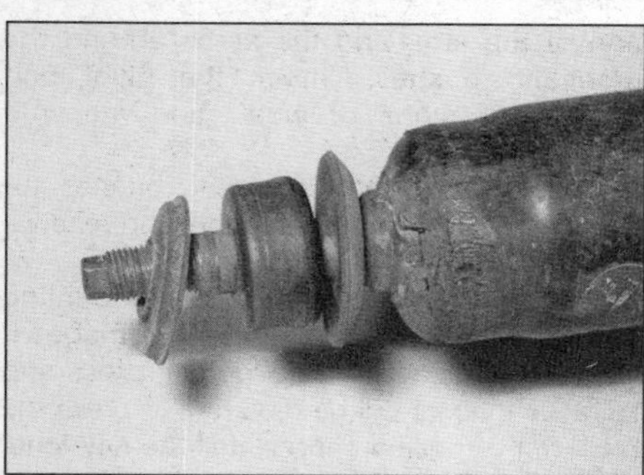

2.5 . . . and recover the second washer and mounting rubber arrangement from the shock absorber lower end

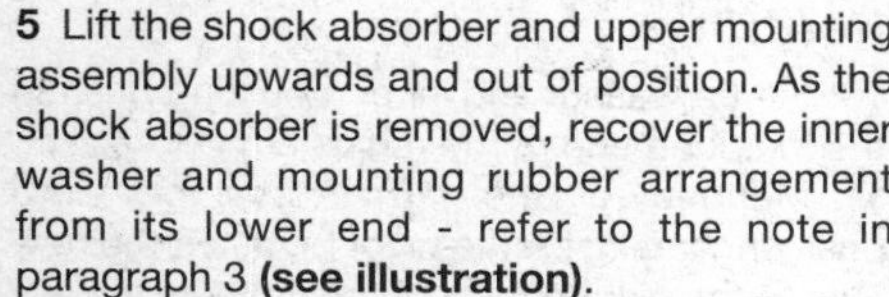

5 Lift the shock absorber and upper mounting assembly upwards and out of position. As the shock absorber is removed, recover the inner washer and mounting rubber arrangement from its lower end - refer to the note in paragraph 3 **(see illustration).**

6 With the assembly on a bench, unscrew the upper mounting nut, and lift off the outer washer and mounting rubber arrangement - refer to the note in paragraph 3 **(see illustration).**

7 Separate the shock absorber and mounting, and recover the inner washer and mounting rubber arrangement from the upper end of the shock absorber - refer to the note in paragraph 3.

Testing

8 Examine the shock absorber for signs of fluid leakage or damage.

9 Test the operation of the shock absorber, while holding it in an upright position, by moving the piston through a full stroke, and then through short strokes of 50 to 100 mm. In both cases, the resistance felt should be smooth and continuous. If the resistance is jerky, or uneven, or if there is any visible sign of wear or damage, renewal is necessary.

10 Renew the shock absorber complete if any damage or excessive wear is evident. Shock absorbers must always be renewed in axle sets, even if only one of the pair is damaged or leaking.

11 Inspect the mounting rubber for signs of damage or deterioration, and renew if necessary.

2.6 Shock absorber upper mounting nut

Refitting

12 Refitting is a reversal of the removal procedure, noting the following points:

a) Ensure that all washer and rubber mounting components are positioned correctly. The flat (seating) washer should be fitted so that its flat face abuts the upper mounting bracket/axle (as applicable), and the slightly cupped washer should be fitted with its concave side towards the rubber mounting **(see illustration).**

b) Fit new shock absorber mounting nuts, and tighten them securely.

3 Front coil spring - removal and refitting

Note: *A suitable tool to hold the coil spring in compression must be obtained. Adjustable coil spring compressors are readily available, and are recommended for this operation.*

Removal

1 Remove the relevant shock absorber assembly as described in Section 2. Note that it is not necessary to separate the shock absorber from the upper mounting bracket.

2 Fit the spring compressors to the coil spring, and compress the spring slightly to relieve the spring tension from its seats.

3 Carefully lower the axle until it is possible to withdraw the coil spring. Whilst lowering the axle, keep a careful watch on the brake pipes and hoses, to ensure that no excess strain is being placed on them.

4 Remove the coil spring, noting which way around it is fitted, and recover the upper spring seat **(see illustrations).**

5 Slacken and remove the retaining bolts and washers, and remove the lower spring seat from the axle **(see illustration).**

6 Inspect the spring closely for signs of damage, such as cracking, and check the spring seats for signs of wear or damage. Renew worn components as necessary.

Refitting

7 Refit the lower spring seat to the axle, and securely tighten its retaining bolt.

8 Fit the upper spring seat to the body, and secure it in position by temporarily fitting one of the strut nuts.

9 Install the coil spring, then carefully raise the axle into position whilst making sure that the upper spring seat studs remain correctly aligned with the body holes.

10 Refit the shock absorber as described in Section 2, then carefully remove the spring compressors.

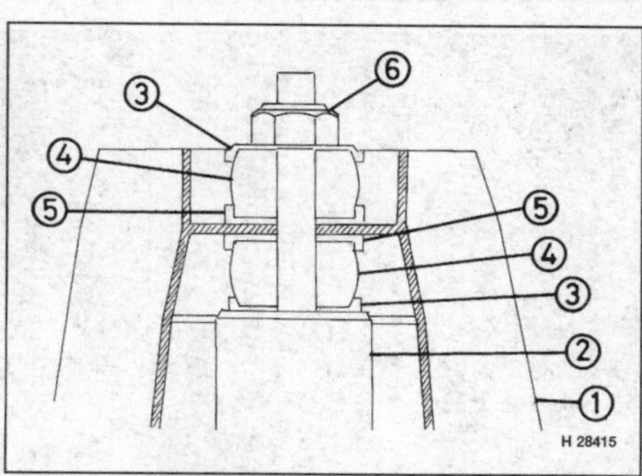

3
6
4
5
5
4
3
2
1
H 28415

2.12 On refitting, ensure that the shock absorber mounting rubbers and washers are correctly positioned as shown (upper mounting shown)

1 Shock absorber mounting
2 Shock absorber
3 Cupped washer
4 Mounting rubber
5 Flat (seating) washer
6 Mounting nut

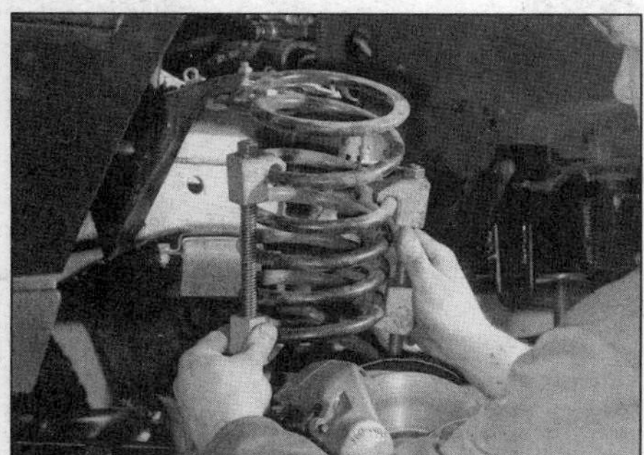

3.4a Remove the front coil spring . . .

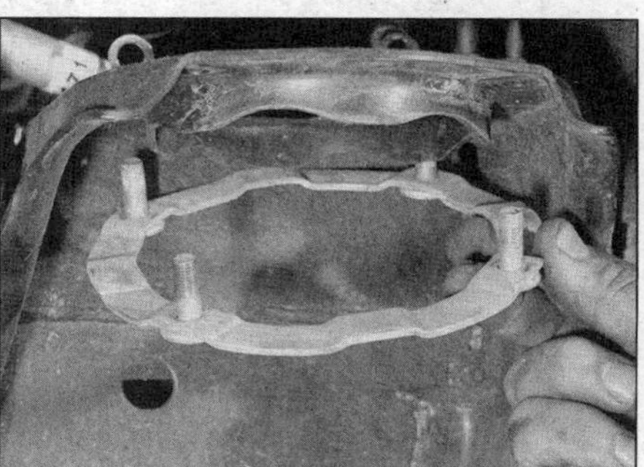

3.4b . . . and recover the upper spring seat

3.5 Lower spring seat is secured to the axle by two bolts (arrowed)

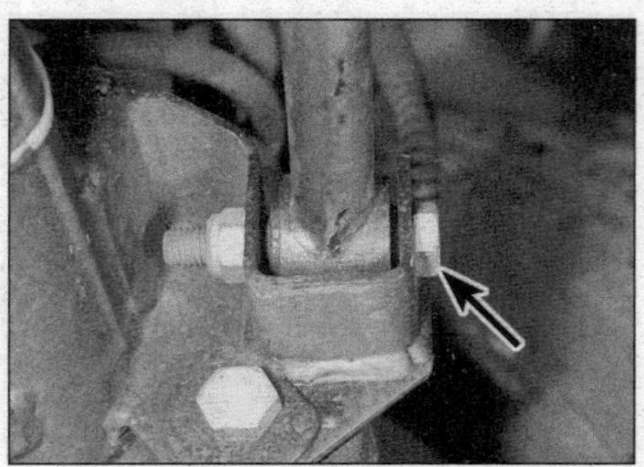

4.2 Panhard rod-to-axle pivot bolt (arrowed)

4 Front suspension Panhard rod - removal, inspection and refitting

Note: *New pivot bolt nuts will be required on refitting (see note in Section 1).*

Removal

1 To improve access, apply the handbrake, then jack up the front of the vehicle and support it on axle stands positioned underneath the chassis (see *Jacking and vehicle support*).

2 Slacken and remove the nuts and pivot bolts securing the Panhard rod to the chassis and axle, and remove the rod from underneath the vehicle **(see illustration)**.

3 If necessary, slacken and remove the retaining nuts and bolts, and remove the Panhard rod mounting bracket from the chassis.

Inspection

4 Inspect the rod and mounting bracket for signs of damage, paying particular attention to the areas around the mounting bushes. Check the pivot bolt shanks for signs of wear, and renew if necessary.

5 Examine the Panhard rod mounting bushes for signs of wear and damage. If renewal is necessary, a hydraulic press and suitable spacers will be required, to press the bush out of position and install the new one. Press the old bush out, and install the new bush using a suitable tubular spacer which bears only on the hard outer edge of the bush, not the bush rubber.

Refitting

6 Where removed, refit the mounting bracket to the chassis. Insert its retaining bolts and nuts, tightening them to the specified torque setting.

7 Offer up the Panhard rod, and insert both pivot bolts. Fit the new nuts to the pivot bolts, tightening them loosely only.

8 Lower the vehicle to the ground then, with it resting on its wheels, tighten both pivot bolt nuts to the specified torque setting.

5 Front suspension radius arm - removal, inspection and refitting

Note: *New radius arm upper and lower pivot bolt nuts will be required on refitting (see note in Section 1).*

Removal

1 Apply the handbrake, then loosen the relevant front roadwheel nuts. Jack up the front of the vehicle and support it on axle stands positioned underneath the chassis (see *Jacking and vehicle support*). Remove the relevant front roadwheel.

2 Position a hydraulic jack beneath the front axle assembly, then raise the jack until it is supporting the axle weight.

3 Unscrew the nut securing the radius arm to the chassis, and remove the washer and outer mounting bush **(see illustrations)**.

4 Remove the split-pin, then slacken and remove the nut and washer securing the steering gear track rod balljoint to the swivel pin housing. Release the balljoint tapered shank using a universal balljoint separator.

5 Slacken and remove the nuts and bolts securing the radius arm to the axle, and remove the arm from underneath the vehicle **(see illustration)**.

6 With the arm removed, slide off the inner mounting bush and washer from its upper end.

Inspection

7 Inspect the arm for signs of damage, paying particular attention to the threaded end of the arm, and the areas around the mounting bushes. Check the pivot bolt shanks for signs of wear, and renew if necessary.

8 Inspect the upper mounting bushes for signs of damage or deterioration, and renew if necessary.

9 Examine the radius arm lower mounting bushes for signs of wear and damage. If renewal is necessary, a hydraulic press and suitable spacers will be required, to press the bush out of position and install the new one. Press the old bush out, and install the new bush using a suitable tubular spacer which bears only on the hard outer edge of the bush, not the bush rubber.

Refitting

10 Fit the washer and inner mounting bush to the threaded end of the radius arm.

11 Manoeuvre the arm assembly into position, and insert the pivot bolts. Fit the new nuts to the pivot bolts, tightening them loosely only at this stage.

12 Reconnect the track rod balljoint to the swivel pin housing assembly, tightening its retaining nut to the specified torque setting. Secure the nut in position with a new split-pin.

13 Slide the outer mounting bush and washer onto the threaded end of the arm. Fit the new retaining nut, tightening it to the specified torque setting.

14 Refit the wheel, then lower the vehicle to the ground and tighten the wheel nuts to the specified torque.

15 With the vehicle resting on its wheels, tighten both radius arm pivot bolt nuts to the specified torque setting.

6 Front anti-roll bar - removal and refitting

Note: *New anti-roll bar mounting clamp and connecting link nuts will be required on refitting (see note in Section 1).*

Removal

1 Apply the handbrake, then jack up the front of the vehicle and support it on axle stands

5.3a Slacken and remove the nut and washer securing the radius arm to the chassis . . .

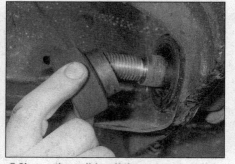

5.3b . . . then slide off the outer mounting bush

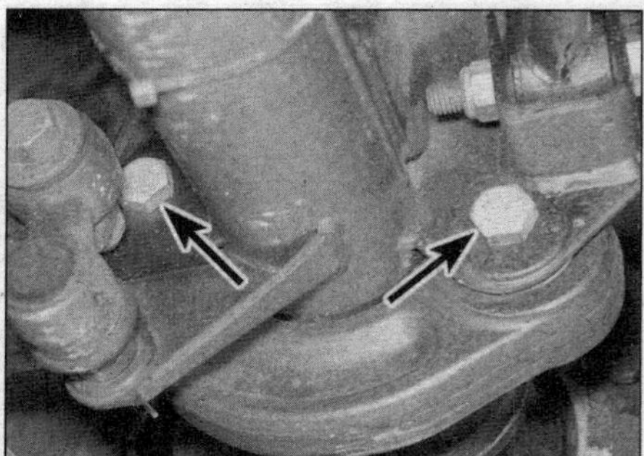

5.5 Unscrew the radius arm-to-axle bolts (arrowed), and remove the arm from underneath the vehicle

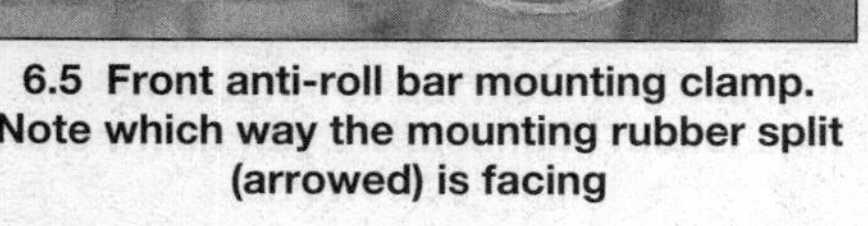

6.5 Front anti-roll bar mounting clamp. Note which way the mounting rubber split (arrowed) is facing

7.4a Release the balljoint shank with a balljoint separator . . .

7.4b . . . and remove the connecting link from underneath the vehicle

positioned underneath the chassis (see *Jacking and vehicle support*).

2 Position a hydraulic jack beneath the front axle assembly, then raise the jack until it is supporting the axle weight.

3 Prior to removal, mark the position of each mounting clamp rubber on the anti-roll bar.

4 Slacken and remove the nuts, and withdraw the bolts and washers securing each end of the anti-roll bar to the connecting links.

5 Unscrew the nuts and washers securing the mounting clamps to the vehicle body, then remove the bolts and mounting clamps, and lower the anti-roll bar out from underneath the vehicle **(see illustration)**.

6 Remove the mounting rubbers from the anti-roll bar, and inspect them for signs of damage. Renew both rubbers if they are damaged or show signs of deterioration.

Refitting

7 Fit the mounting rubbers to the anti-roll bar. Fit the right-hand rubber so that its split will be facing towards the axle, and the left-hand rubber so that its split will be facing away from the axle once the bar is installed.

8 Align both rubbers with the marks made prior to removal, and manoeuvre the anti-roll bar into position.

9 Ensure that the flat side of each rubber is against the vehicle body, then refit the mounting clamps. Insert the bolts, then fit the washers and new nuts, tightening them loosely only at this stage.

10 Align the anti-roll bar ends with the connecting links, and insert the pivot bolts and washers. Fit the new retaining nuts to the bolts, and tighten them loosely only.

11 Lower the vehicle to the ground and, with it resting on its wheels, tighten the mounting clamp and pivot bolt nuts to the specified torque.

7 Front anti-roll bar connecting link - removal, inspection and refitting

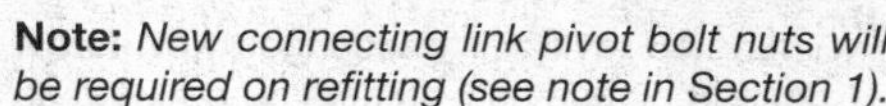

Note: *New connecting link pivot bolt nuts will be required on refitting (see note in Section 1).*

Removal

1 Apply the handbrake, then jack up the front of the vehicle and support it on axle stands positioned underneath the chassis (see *Jacking and vehicle support*). Remove the relevant front roadwheel.

2 Position a hydraulic jack beneath the front axle assembly, then raise the jack until it is supporting the axle weight.

3 Slacken and remove the nut, then withdraw the pivot bolt and washer securing the connecting link to the anti-roll bar.

4 Remove the split-pin, and undo the nut and washer securing the connecting link balljoint to the axle assembly. Release the balljoint tapered shank using a universal balljoint separator, and remove the connecting link from the vehicle **(see illustrations)**.

Inspection

5 Check that the link balljoint moves freely, without any sign of roughness. Check also that the balljoint gaiter shows no sign of deterioration, and is free from cracks and splits. If any sign of wear or damage is found, the complete link must be renewed.

6 Examine the upper mounting bushes for signs of wear and damage, and renew if necessary. A hydraulic press and suitable spacers may be required, to press the bushes out of position and install the new ones.

Refitting

7 Fit the connecting link assembly, and insert its pivot bolt and washer **(see illustration)**.

8 Locate the balljoint shank in the axle, and refit its washer and nut. Tighten the nut to the specified torque setting, and secure it in position with a new split-pin **(see illustrations)**.

9 Fit a new nut to the pivot bolt, tighten it to the specified torque setting, then refit the roadwheel and lower the vehicle to ground.

8 Front suspension bump stop - inspection, removal and refitting

Inspection

1 The bump stops are mounted onto the chassis, directly above the axle assembly

7.7 Offer up the connecting link, and insert its pivot bolt and washer

7.8a Locate the balljoint in the axle, and refit its retaining nut and washer

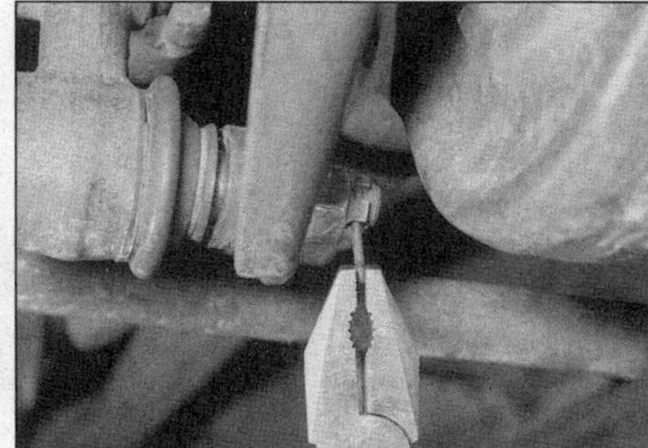

7.8b Tighten the nut to the specified torque, and secure it in position with a new split-pin

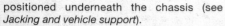

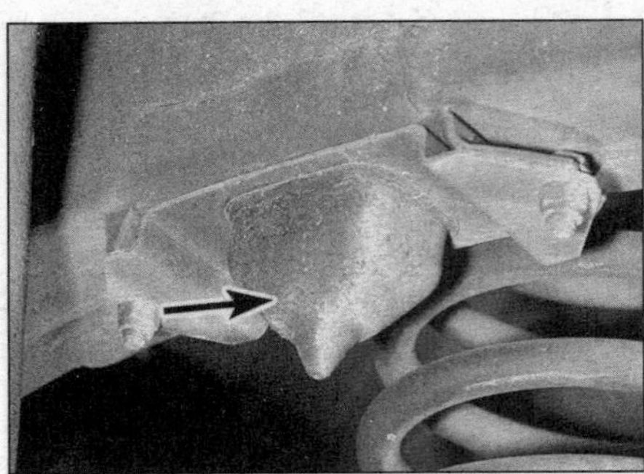

8.1 Bump stops are mounted onto the vehicle underbody, directly above each end of the axle

9.3 Slacken and remove the shock absorber upper mounting nut and washer . . .

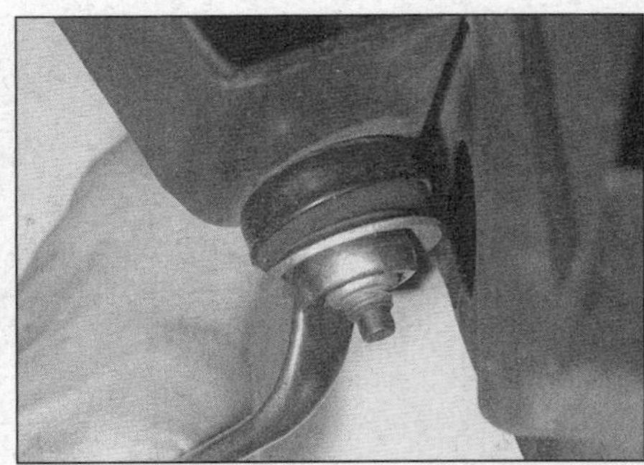

9.4 . . . then unscrew the lower mounting nut, and recover the washers and mounting rubber

(see illustration). Inspect each bump stop rubber for signs of damage or deterioration, and renew if necessary.

Removal

2 Slacken and remove the nuts, washers and bolts securing the bump stop in position, and remove it from the chassis.

Refitting

3 Fit the bolts to the slots in the chassis, then offer up the bump stop, ensuring that it is correctly located in the chassis slot. Refit the washers and nuts to the retaining bolts, and tighten them securely.

9 Rear shock absorber - removal, testing and refitting

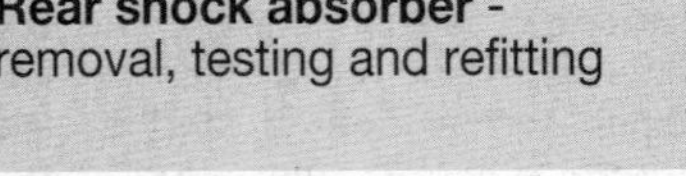

Note: *Shock absorbers must ALWAYS be renewed in pairs, even if only one appears to be defective, in order to preserve safe handling.*

Removal

1 Chock the front wheels, then loosen the relevant rear roadwheel nuts. Jack up the rear of the vehicle and support it on axle stands positioned underneath the chassis (see *Jacking and vehicle support*). Remove the relevant rear roadwheel.

2 Position a hydraulic jack beneath the rear axle assembly, then raise the jack until it is supporting the axle weight.

3 Slacken and remove the nut and outer washer from the shock absorber upper mounting **(see illustration)**.

4 Unscrew the nut from the lower mounting, and slide off the outer mounting rubber and its washers, noting their correct fitted positions **(see illustration)**. Free the shock absorber from the axle, and recover the second mounting rubber and washer arrangement from its lower end.

5 Remove the shock absorber from the vehicle, and recover the inner washer from its upper mounting.

6 If necessary, slacken and remove the retaining nuts and bolts, and remove the upper mounting bracket from the chassis.

Testing

7 Examine the shock absorber for signs of fluid leakage or damage.

8 Test the operation of the shock absorber, while holding it in an upright position, by moving the piston through a full stroke, and then through short strokes of 50 to 100 mm. In both cases, the resistance felt should be smooth and continuous. If the resistance is jerky, or uneven, or if there is any visible sign of wear or damage, renewal is necessary.

9 Renew the shock absorber complete if any damage or excessive wear is evident. Shock absorbers must always be renewed in axle sets, even if only one of the pair is damaged or leaking.

10 Inspect the upper mounting bush and the lower mounting rubbers for signs of damage or deterioration, and renew as necessary.

Refitting

11 Where removed, refit the upper mounting bracket to the chassis, and insert its retaining bolts and nuts, tightening them securely.

12 Fit the inner washer, then locate the shock absorber on the upper mounting bracket.

13 Fit the first mounting rubber and washer arrangement to the lower end of the shock absorber, positioning a washer on each side of the rubber. Engage the shock absorber with the axle, then fit the second rubber mounting and washer arrangement, followed by the retaining nut.

14 Refit the outer washer and upper retaining nut, then tighten both retaining nuts to the specified torque setting.

10 Rear coil spring - removal and refitting

Note: *A suitable tool to hold the coil spring in compression must be obtained. Adjustable coil spring compressors are readily available, and are recommended for this operation.*

Removal

1 Chock the front wheels, then loosen the relevant rear roadwheel nuts. Jack up the rear of the vehicle and support it on axle stands positioned underneath the chassis (see *Jacking and vehicle support*). Remove the relevant rear roadwheel.

2 Position a hydraulic jack beneath the rear axle assembly, then raise the jack until it is supporting the axle weight.

3 Slacken and remove the nut and outer washer from the shock absorber upper mounting, and disengage the shock absorber from its mounting bracket.

4 Fit the spring compressor, and compress the coil spring.

5 Carefully lower the axle until the upper end of the spring is released from its seat. Whilst lowering the axle, keep a careful watch on the brake pipes and hoses, to ensure that no excess strain is being placed on them.

6 Recover the upper spring seat, then slacken and remove the retaining bolts and washers and remove the retaining plate securing the spring to the axle. Withdraw the coil spring, and lift off the lower spring seat from the axle.

7 Inspect the spring closely for signs of damage, such as cracking, and check the spring seats for signs of wear or damage. Renew worn components as necessary.

Refitting

8 If a new spring is being installed, slowly release the old spring, then transfer the spring compressor from the old spring to the new one.

9 Refit the lower spring seat to the axle, then manoeuvre the coil spring into position.

10 Ensure that the spring is correctly seated, then refit the retaining plate to the axle and securely tighten its retaining bolts.

11 Fit the upper spring seat to the top of the coil spring.

12 Align the upper spring seat with the chassis, then carefully raise the axle assembly with the jack.

13 Locate the shock absorber on its upper mounting, then refit the outer washer and retaining nut, tightening it to the specified torque setting.

14 Carefully release the spring compressor whilst ensuring that the spring remains correctly seated.

15 Remove the jack from underneath the

11.2 Remove the pivot bolt securing the lower link to the axle . . .

11.3a . . . then unscrew the front retaining nut and washer . . .

11.3b . . . and manoeuvre the lower link out from underneath the vehicle

axle, refit the roadwheel and lower the vehicle to the ground.

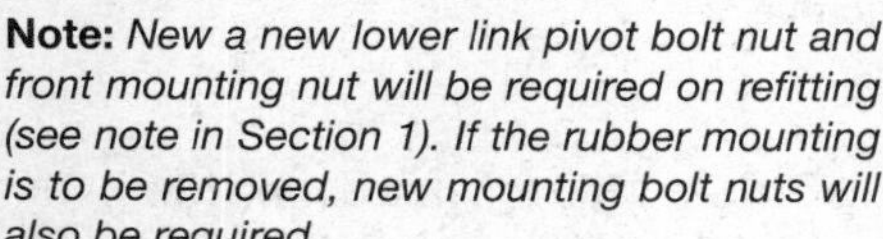

11 Rear suspension lower link - removal, inspection and refitting

Note: *New a new lower link pivot bolt nut and front mounting nut will be required on refitting (see note in Section 1). If the rubber mounting is to be removed, new mounting bolt nuts will also be required.*

Removal

1 Chock the front wheels, then jack up the rear of the vehicle and support it on axle stands positioned underneath the rear axle (see *Jacking and vehicle support*). Remove the relevant rear roadwheel.

2 Slacken and remove the nut, then withdraw the pivot bolt securing the lower link to the axle **(see illustration)**.

3 Slacken and remove the lower link front retaining nut and washer, then manoeuvre the link out from underneath the vehicle **(see illustrations)**.

4 If necessary, undo the three nuts and bolts securing the rubber mounting in position, and remove it from the chassis **(see illustration)**.

Inspection

5 Inspect the link for signs of damage, paying particular attention to its threaded end, and the area around its mounting bush. Check the pivot bolt shanks for signs of wear, and renew if necessary.

6 Examine the lower link mounting bush for signs of wear and damage. If renewal is necessary, a hydraulic press and suitable spacers will be required, to press the bush out of position and install the new one. Press the old bush out, and install the new bush using a suitable tubular spacer which bears only on the hard outer edge of the bush, not the bush rubber.

7 Inspect the rubber mounting for signs of damage or deterioration, and renew if necessary.

Refitting

8 Where necessary, fit the rubber mounting to the chassis, and insert its mounting bolts. Fit new nuts to the bolts, and tighten them securely.

9 Manoeuvre the link into position, and insert the pivot bolt.

10 Refit the washer to the threaded end of the link, then fit the new nuts to both the link and pivot bolt. Tighten each nut loosely only at this stage.

11 Refit the roadwheel, then lower the vehicle to the ground and tighten the wheel nuts to the specified torque.

12 With the vehicle resting on its wheels, tighten both the lower link front nut and pivot bolt nut to the specified torque setting **(see illustrations)**.

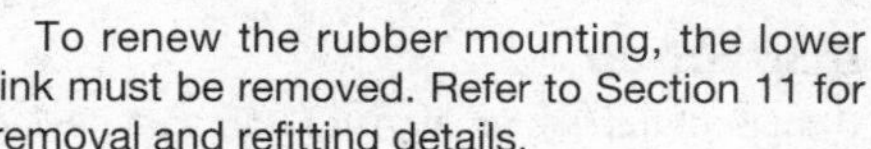

12 Rear suspension lower link mounting - renewal

To renew the rubber mounting, the lower link must be removed. Refer to Section 11 for removal and refitting details.

13 Rear suspension upper link - removal, inspection and refitting

Note: *New upper link pivot bolt and mounting bracket retaining bolt nuts will be required on refitting (see note in Section 1).*

Removal

1 Chock the front wheels, then jack up the rear of the vehicle and support it on axle stands positioned underneath the chassis (see Jacking and vehicle support).

2 Position a hydraulic jack beneath the rear axle assembly, then raise the jack until it is supporting the axle weight.

3 Slacken and remove the nuts and bolts securing the upper link mounting bracket to the chassis.

4 Slacken and remove the nuts securing the upper links to the balljoint bracket on the top

11.4 The lower link mounting is secured to the chassis by three bolts

11.12a With the vehicle standing on its wheels, tighten the lower link pivot bolt . . .

11.12b . . . and front retaining nut to the specified torque

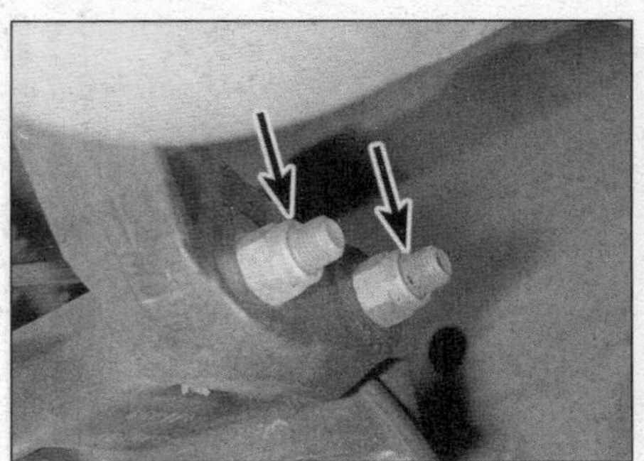

13.4 Upper link-to-balljoint bracket retaining bolts (arrowed)

of the axle **(see illustration)**. Withdraw both retaining bolts, and remove the relevant upper link and mounting bracket assembly from underneath the vehicle.

5 If necessary, undo the nut, withdraw the pivot bolt, and separate the link from its mounting bracket.

Inspection

6 Inspect the link for signs of damage, paying particular attention to the area around its mounting bush. Check the pivot bolt shanks for signs of wear, and renew if necessary.

7 Examine the upper link mounting bush for signs of wear and damage. If renewal is necessary, a hydraulic press and suitable spacers will be required, to press the bush out of position and install the new one. Press the old bush out, and install the new bush using a suitable tubular spacer which bears only on the hard outer edge of the bush, not the bush rubber.

8 Inspect the mounting bracket for signs of damage, and renew if necessary.

Refitting

9 Reassemble the upper link and mounting bracket, and insert the pivot bolts. Fit a new nut to the bolt, tightening it loosely only at this stage.

10 Manoeuvre the link and bracket assembly into position, and insert the bolts securing them to the balljoint bracket and second upper link. Fit new nuts to the bolts, and tighten them to the specified torque setting.

11 Insert the mounting bracket-to-chassis bolts, then fit the new nuts and tighten them to the specified torque setting.

12 Lower the vehicle to the ground and, with the vehicle resting on its wheels, tighten the upper pivot bolt nut to the specified torque setting.

14 Rear suspension upper link balljoint - removal and refitting

Removal

1 Remove both rear suspension upper links as described in Section 13.

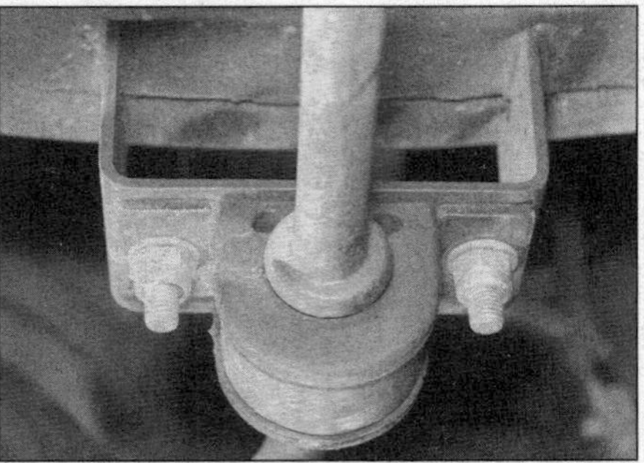

15.5 Rear anti-roll bar mounting clamp assembly

2 Withdraw the split-pin, then slacken and remove the nut securing the balljoint to the top of the rear axle.

3 Remove the balljoint and upper link bracket assembly from the top of the axle, then slacken and remove the two retaining bolts and washers, and separate the two components.

4 Check that the lower arm balljoint moves freely, without any sign of roughness. Check also that the balljoint gaiter shows no sign of deterioration, and is free from cracks and splits. If necessary, renew the balljoint.

Refitting

5 Refit the upper link bracket to the balljoint, and securely tighten its retaining bolts.

6 Locate the balljoint shank in its bracket on top of the axle, and refit its retaining nut. Tighten the balljoint nut to the specified torque setting, and secure it in position with a new split-pin.

7 Refit the rear suspension upper links as described in Section 13.

15 Rear anti-roll bar - removal and refitting

Note: *New anti-roll bar mounting clamp and connecting link nuts will be required on refitting (see note in Section 1).*

Removal

1 Chock the front wheels, then jack up the rear of the vehicle and support it on axle stands positioned underneath the chassis (see *Jacking and vehicle support*).

2 Position a hydraulic jack beneath the axle assembly, then raise the jack until it is supporting the axle weight.

3 Prior to removal, mark the position of each mounting clamp rubber on the anti-roll bar.

4 Slacken and remove the nuts, and withdraw the bolts and washers securing each end of the anti-roll bar to the connecting links. If they are loose, remove the mounting rubbers from the connecting link.

5 Unscrew the nuts and washers securing the mounting clamps to the vehicle body. Remove the bolts and mounting clamps, and lower the anti-roll bar out from underneath the vehicle **(see illustration)**.

6 Remove the mounting rubbers from the anti-roll bar, and inspect them for signs of damage. Renew both rubbers if they are damaged or show signs of deterioration.

Refitting

7 Fit the mounting rubbers to the anti-roll bar, aligning them with the marks made prior to removal.

8 Manoeuvre the anti-roll bar into position, ensuring that the flat side of each mounting rubber is against the vehicle body, then refit the mounting clamps. Insert the bolts and fit the washers and new nuts, tightening them loosely only at this stage.

9 Ensure that the mounting rubbers are in position, and align the anti-roll bar ends with the connecting links. Insert the pivot bolts and washers, then fit the new retaining nuts and tighten them loosely.

10 Lower the vehicle to the ground and, with it resting on its wheels, tighten the mounting clamp and pivot bolt nuts to the specified torque.

16 Rear anti-roll bar connecting link - removal, inspection and refitting

Note: *New connecting link pivot bolt nuts will be required on refitting (see note in Section 1).*

Removal

1 Chock the front wheels, then jack up the rear of the vehicle and support it on axle stands positioned underneath the chassis (see *Jacking and vehicle support).*

2 Position a hydraulic jack beneath the axle assembly, then raise the jack until it is supporting the axle weight.

3 Slacken and remove the nut, then withdraw the pivot bolt and washer securing the connecting link to the anti-roll bar. If they are loose, remove the mounting rubbers from the connecting link **(see illustrations)**.

4 Remove the split-pin, and undo the nut and washer securing the connecting link balljoint to the axle assembly. Release the balljoint tapered shank using a universal balljoint

16.3a Slacken and remove the nut . . .

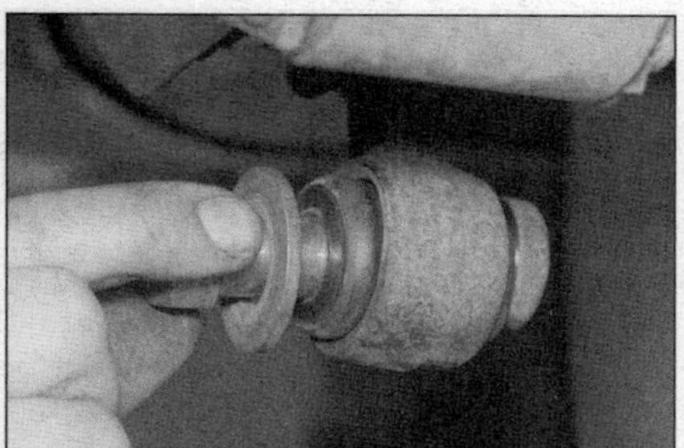
16.3b . . . then withdraw the pivot bolt and washer securing the anti-roll bar to the connecting link

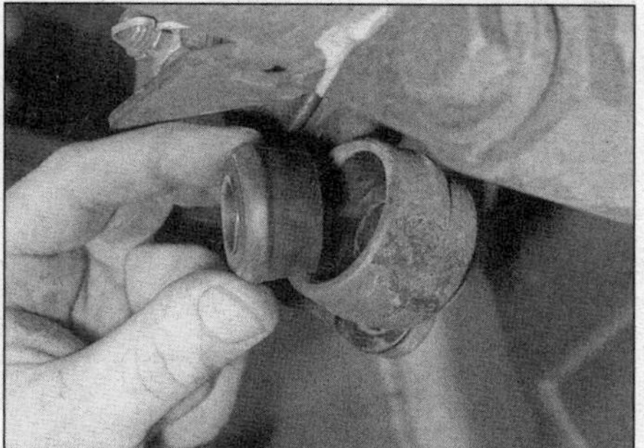
16.3c If they are loose, remove the mounting rubbers from the connecting link

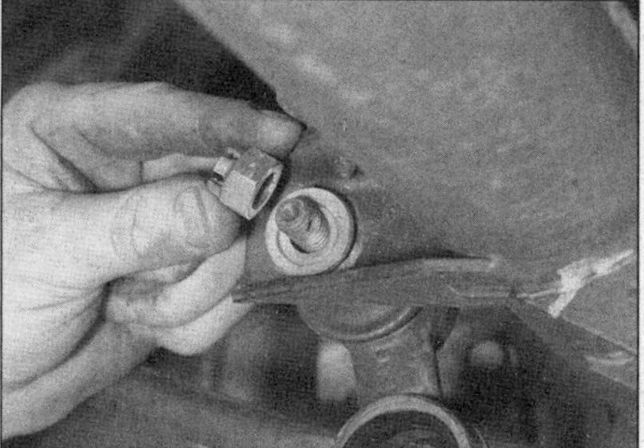
16.4a Slacken and remove the nut and washer . . .

16.4b . . . then use a universal balljoint separator . . .

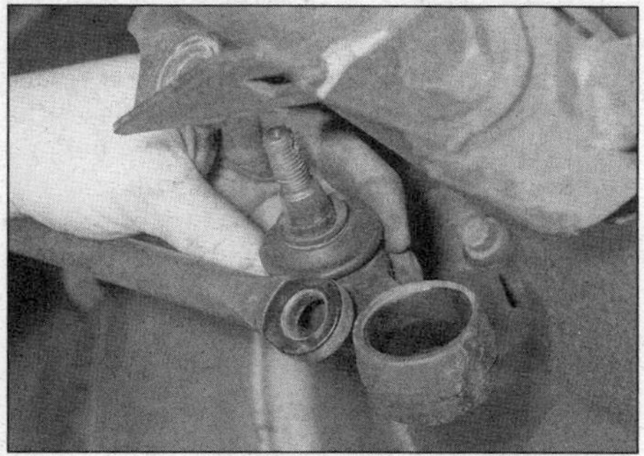
16.4c . . . to free the connecting link from the axle

16.7 Tighten the balljoint nut to the specified torque setting, and secure it in position with a new split-pin

separator, and remove the connecting link from the vehicle **(see illustrations)**.

Inspection

5 Check that the link balljoint moves freely, without any sign of roughness. Check also that the balljoint gaiter shows no sign of deterioration, and is free from cracks and splits. If any sign of wear or damage is found, the complete link must be renewed.

6 Examine the link mounting bushes for signs of wear or damage. If renewal is necessary, a hydraulic press and suitable spacers may be required, to press the bushes out of position and install the new ones.

Refitting

7 Locate the balljoint shank in the axle, and refit its washer and nut. Tighten the nut to the specified torque setting, and secure it in position with a new split-pin **(see illustration)**.

8 Ensure that the mounting rubbers are correctly fitted, and insert the pivot bolt and washer.

9 Fit a new nut to the pivot bolt, tighten it to the specified torque setting, then lower the vehicle to ground.

17 Rear suspension bump stop - inspection, removal and refitting

Refer to Section 8.

18 Steering wheel - removal and refitting

Removal

Models without an airbag

1 Disconnect the battery negative terminal.

2 Set the front wheels in the straight-ahead position, and release the steering lock by inserting the ignition key.

3 On early models, prise out the badge from the centre of the steering wheel, and remove the trim cap from the retaining nut.

4 On later models, prise out the horn button/trim pad from the centre of the steering wheel. This operation is harder than it first appears, as the steering wheel padding must be pulled considerably to free the edge of the horn pad. Take care to reduce the potential risk of damage to the wheel padding as this is done. Once the horn button has been removed, disconnect its wiring connectors. On models with cruise control, the horn and cruise control switch wiring is all fed through a single multi-plug - if this plug is separated, the individual wiring to each switch can be left connected **(see illustrations)**.

18.4a On later models, prise out the horn button from the centre of the steering wheel . . .

18.4b . . . and disconnect it from the wiring connectors

18.4c On models with cruise control, separate this plug if preferred

18.6 Unscrew the retaining nut, and withdraw the steering wheel from the end of the column

motorq 200

18.14 Ensure that the wheel is correctly located on the column splines, and tighten the retaining nut to the specified torque

5 Slacken the steering wheel retaining nut, but do not remove it at this stage.

6 Make alignment marks between the steering wheel and steering column shaft, then pull the wheel to release it from the splines **(see illustration)**. **Note:** *If the wheel is a tight fit on the column splines, a suitable legged puller will then be required to free the steering wheel.*

7 Remove the retaining nut and washer, then, checking that all wiring has been released from its retaining clips, remove the wheel from the steering column.

Models with an airbag

8 Set the front wheels in the straight-ahead position, and release the steering lock by inserting the ignition key.

9 Remove the airbag unit as described in Chapter 13, then return the steering wheel to the straight-ahead position.

10 Free the airbag unit wiring from its retaining clips on the wheel.

11 Remove the steering wheel as described above in paragraphs 6 and 7.

HAYNES
HiNT

Whilst the steering wheel is removed, wrap adhesive tape around the airbag (or cruise control) contact unit. This will prevent unnecessary rotation of the contact unit, and will ensure that it remains correctly positioned until the steering wheel is refitted.

Refitting

Models without an airbag

12 On models with cruise control, where applicable, remove the tape from the contact unit.

13 Locate the wheel on the column splines, aligning the marks made on removal. Take care to ensure that the wheel is correctly aligned with the indicator cancelling cam, and with the cruise control contact unit pegs (where applicable).

14 Refit the washer and retaining nut, and tighten the nut to the specified torque setting **(see illustration)**.

15 On later models, reconnect the wiring to the horn, then clip the horn button/trim pad back into position in the centre of the wheel. On models with cruise control, reconnect the multi-plug, then refit the steering wheel pad and secure with the two Torx screws.

16 On early models, refit the trim cap to the retaining nut, then fit the badge to the centre of the wheel.

17 On all models, reconnect the battery on completion.

Models with an airbag

18 Remove the tape from the contact unit, then feed the airbag unit wiring up through the wheel.

19 Locate the steering wheel on the column splines, aligning the marks made on removal, whilst making sure that the wheel is correctly engaged with the contact unit tabs.

20 Refit the washer and/or retaining nut (as applicable), and tighten it to the specified torque setting.

21 Clip the airbag unit wiring back into the steering wheel, then refit the airbag unit as described in Chapter 13.

19 Ignition switch/ steering column lock - removal and refitting

Note: *If the lock assembly is to be removed, new shear-bolts will be required on refitting.*

Removal

1 Disconnect the battery negative lead.

2 Release the fasteners and release the driver's side lower facia panel; on later models, undo the hinge retaining screws to remove the panel. Where necessary, undo the retaining screws and remove the support pad from the facia.

3 Undo the steering column shroud retaining screws, unclip the shroud halves, and remove both the upper and lower shrouds from the steering column. On early models, it may be necessary to pull off the hazard warning light switch button to allow the upper shroud to be removed. Proceed as described under the relevant sub-heading. If necessary, the steering wheel can be removed (see Section 18) to improve access.

Lock assembly

4 Trace the wiring back from the switch assembly, and disconnect its wiring connector(s). On later models, unclip the immobiliser reader coil from the lock assembly, and disconnect the wiring plug.

5 Release the bulbholder from the end of the lock assembly.

6 Using a hammer and suitable chisel, tap the head of each shear-bolt around anti-clockwise until each bolt is loose enough to be unscrewed by hand **(see illustration)**.

7 Unscrew both shear-bolts, then lift off the retaining clamp and remove the lock assembly from the steering column **(see illustration)**.

Ignition switch wiring block

8 Trace the wiring back from the switch assembly, and disconnect its wiring connector(s).

9 Slacken and remove the wiring block retaining screws, and withdraw the wiring block from the end of the switch assembly.

Refitting

Lock assembly

10 Refit the lock assembly retaining clamp, making sure its lug is correctly located in the steering column hole.

11 Manoeuvre the lock assembly into position and fit the new shear-bolts,

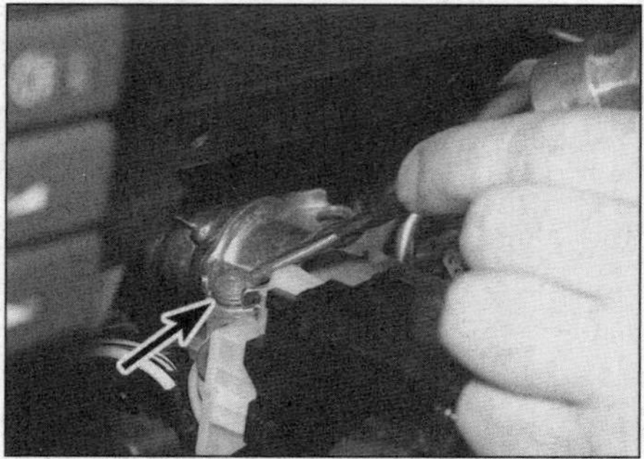

19.6 Remove the shear-bolts using a hammer and chisel . . .

19.7 . . . then remove the steering lock assembly from the column

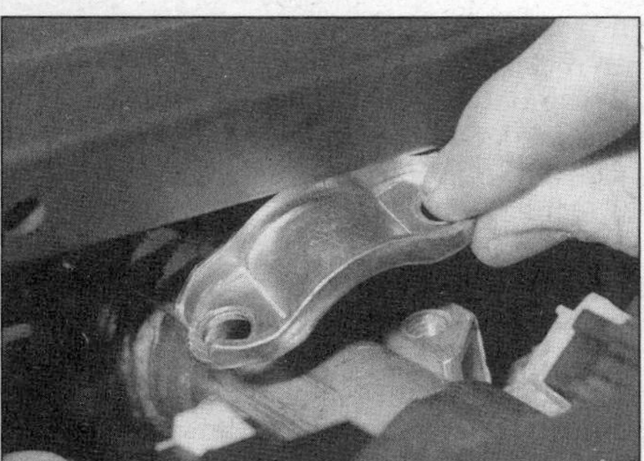

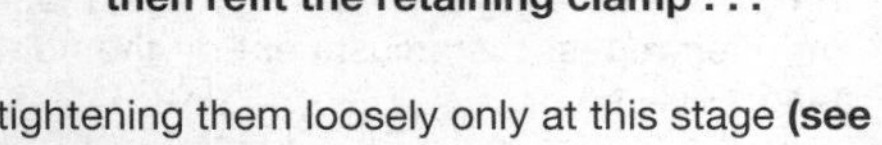

19.11a Engage the lock with the column, then refit the retaining clamp . . .

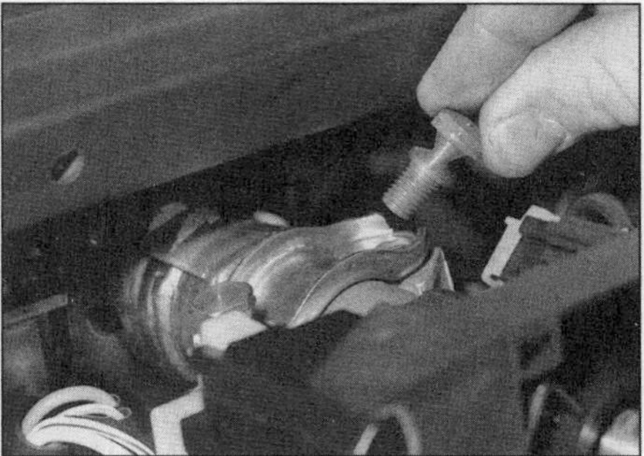

19.11b . . . and screw in the new shear-bolts

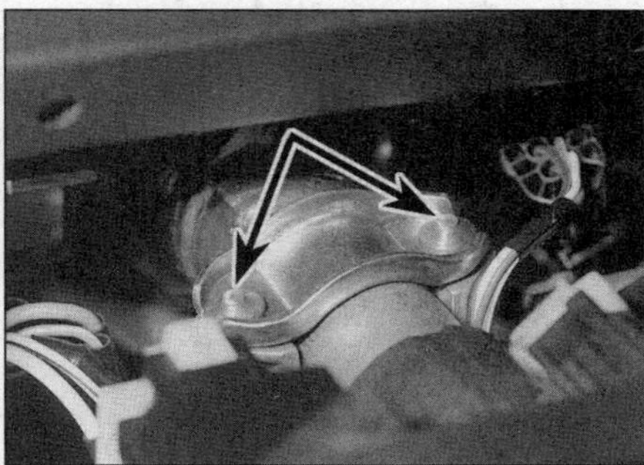

19.13 Check the operation of the lock, then fully tighten the shear-bolts until they break

tightening them loosely only at this stage **(see illustrations)**.

12 Reconnect the switch wiring, ensuring that it is correctly routed, and clip the bulbholder back into the lock.

13 Reconnect the battery, then check the operation of the ignition switch and steering column lock. If all is well, tighten each lock assembly bolt until its head shears off **(see illustration)**.

14 Manoeuvre the steering column shrouds into position, and clip them securely together. Refit the shroud retaining screws, and tighten them securely. Where necessary, refit the hazard warning switch button.

15 Refit the support pad (where removed), then install the lower facia panel and secure it in position.

Ignition switch wiring block

16 Fit the wiring block to the switch assembly, ensuring that its centre is correctly aligned with the lock cylinder rod flats.

17 Ensure that the wiring block is correctly seated, then securely tighten its retaining screw.

18 Reconnect the wiring connector(s) and the battery, and check the operation of the ignition switch.

19 Manoeuvre the steering column shrouds into position, and clip them securely together. Refit the shroud retaining screws, and tighten them securely. Where necessary, refit the hazard warning light switch button.

20 Refit the support pad (where removed), then install the lower facia panel and secure it in position.

20 Steering column - removal, inspection and refitting

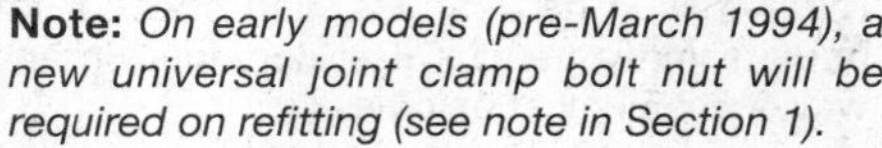

Note: *On early models (pre-March 1994), a new universal joint clamp bolt nut will be required on refitting (see note in Section 1).*

Removal

1 Remove the steering wheel as described in Section 18.

2 Release the two fasteners and release the driver's side lower facia panel; on later models, undo the hinge retaining screws to remove the panel. Where necessary, undo the retaining screws and remove the support pad from the facia.

3 Undo the steering column shroud retaining screws, unclip the shroud halves, and remove both the upper and lower shrouds from the steering column. On early models, it may be necessary to pull off the hazard warning light switch button to allow the upper shroud to be removed.

4 On models with an airbag, remove the airbag contact unit as described in Chapter 13.

5 Trace the wiring back from the column switch assembly and ignition switch, and disconnect the wiring connectors. Free the wiring from any relevant retaining clips.

6 Using paint or a marker pen, make alignment marks between the steering column and universal joint.

7 Slacken and remove the nut (early models only) and clamp bolt securing the intermediate shaft to the steering column.

8 On early models, slacken and remove the steering column upper and lower mounting nuts, washers and bolts, then remove the column assembly from the vehicle. Recover the gasket which is fitted to the lower end of the column.

9 On later models, slacken and remove the retaining nuts, and remove the support bracket from the lower end of the column. Unscrew the lower column mounting bolts and washers, and the upper mounting nuts and washers, and remove the steering column assembly from the vehicle **(see illustrations)**.

Inspection

10 Examine steering column and mountings for signs of damage and deformation, and check the steering shaft for signs of free play in the column bushes. If there are signs of damage or play, the column must be renewed. Overhaul of the column is not possible.

Refitting

11 Manoeuvre the steering column into position; engage it with the universal joint, aligning the marks made on removal.

12 On early models, fit a new gasket (where used) to the base of the column, then refit the column upper and lower mounting bolts, washers and nuts. Tighten all bolts by hand only at this stage.

13 On later models, refit the column upper mounting nuts and lower mounting bolts, tightening them by hand only. Refit the support bracket to the lower end of the column, and loosely tighten its retaining nuts.

14 On all models, check that the column is correctly positioned on its mountings, then go around and tighten all mounting nuts/bolts to the specified torque setting.

15 Insert the universal joint clamp bolt, fit a new nut (where necessary) and tighten it to the specified torque setting.

16 The remainder of refitting is a direct reversal of the removal procedure.

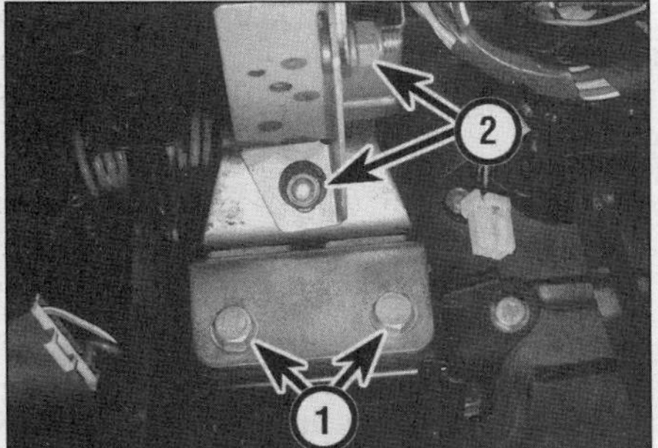
2
1

20.9a Lower steering column mounting bolts (1) and support bracket nuts (2) . . .

20.9b . . . and upper mounting nuts (arrowed)

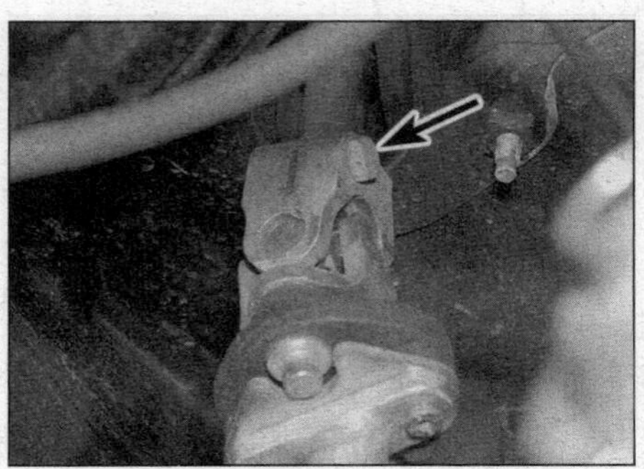

21.3 Intermediate shaft-to-steering column clamp bolt (arrowed)

21 Steering column intermediate shaft - removal, inspection and refitting

Note: *On early models (pre-March 1994), new clamp bolt nuts will be required on refitting (see note in Section 1).*

Removal

1 Set the front wheels in the straight-ahead position, then disconnect the battery negative terminal.

2 Using paint or a marker pen, make alignment marks between the intermediate shaft universal joint and steering column, and the shaft and lower universal joint.

3 Slacken and remove the nuts (early models only) and clamp bolts securing the intermediate shaft to the steering column and universal joint **(see illustration)**.

4 Disengage the shaft from the steering column and joint, and remove it from the vehicle.

Inspection

5 Inspect the intermediate shaft universal joints for signs of roughness in its bearings and ease of movement, and check the shaft coupling for signs of damage or deterioration. If either joint or the coupling is damaged in any way, the complete shaft assembly must be renewed.

6 On some models, the intermediate shaft incorporates a collapsible joint. In the event of a front-end crash, the joint collapses and prevents the steering wheel injuring the driver. On these models, inspect the shaft joint closely for signs of impact damage, and renew it if necessary.

Refitting

7 Aligning the marks made on removal, engage the shaft with the universal joint, then engage the upper end of the shaft with the steering column.

8 Make sure that the shaft is correctly seated, then insert both its clamp bolts. Fit a new nut to each clamp bolt (where necessary), then tighten them both to the specified torque setting.

22 Steering column universal joint - removal, inspection and refitting

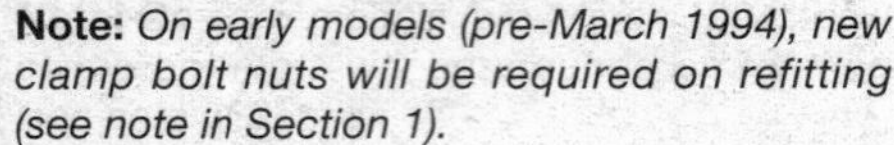

Note: *On early models (pre-March 1994), new clamp bolt nuts will be required on refitting (see note in Section 1).*

Removal

1 Set the front wheels in the straight-ahead position, then disconnect the battery negative terminal.

2 Using paint or a marker pen, make alignment marks between the universal joint and intermediate shaft, and the lower end of the joint and steering box pinion.

3 Slacken and remove the nuts (early models only) and clamp bolts securing the universal joint in position, then disengage it from the shaft and pinion, and remove it from the vehicle.

Inspection

4 Inspect the universal joint for signs of roughness in its bearings, and check it for ease of movement. If it is damaged in any way, the joint must be renewed.

Refitting

5 Aligning the marks made on removal, engage the universal joint with the steering box pinion and intermediate shaft splines.

6 Make sure that the joint is correctly seated, then insert both its clamp bolts. Fit a new nut to each clamp bolt (where necessary), then tighten them both to the specified torque setting.

23 Steering - adjustment

1 If at any time it is noted that the steering action has become stiff or sloppy, the vehicle should be taken to a Land Rover dealer for the steering components to be checked. Adjustments of the steering components and power steering box are possible, but specialist knowledge and equipment are needed. Therefore, this task must be entrusted to a Land Rover dealer.

2 The only adjustment which can easily be carried out by the home mechanic is steering lock stop adjustment.

3 Once the wheel alignment is known to be correct (see Section 33), turn the steering onto full left-hand lock, and measure the clearance between the left-hand front tyre wall and the radius arm. This should be 20 mm.

4 If adjustment is necessary, slacken the stop-bolt locknut, and rotate the bolt as required. Once the clearance is correctly set, securely tighten the locknut.

5 Turn the steering onto full right-hand lock, and then repeat the adjustment on the right-hand side.

24 Steering box - removal, inspection and refitting

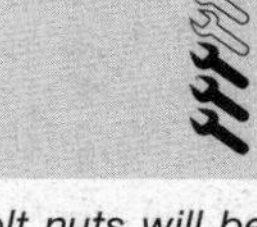

Note: *New tie-bar mounting bolt nuts will be required on refitting (see note in Section 1). On early models (pre-March 1994), a new clamp bolt nut will also be required.*

Removal

1 Apply the handbrake, then jack up the front of the vehicle and support it on axle stands positioned underneath the chassis (see *Jacking and vehicle support*).

2 Position the front wheels in the straight-ahead position, then disconnect the battery negative terminal.

3 Using brake hose clamps, clamp both the supply and return hoses near the power steering fluid reservoir. This will minimise fluid loss during subsequent operations.

4 Clean the area around the steering box hose unions, then make identification marks on each pipe to ensure that they are correctly positioned on reassembly. Unscrew the feed and return pipe union nuts from the steering box; be prepared for fluid spillage, and position a suitable container beneath the pipes whilst unscrewing the union nuts. Disconnect both pipes; plug the pipe ends and steering box orifices, to prevent excessive fluid leakage and the entry of dirt into the hydraulic system.

5 Withdraw the split-pin, then unscrew the nut securing the drag link to the steering box drop arm.

6 Using a universal balljoint separator, free the drag link from the drop arm **(see illustration)**.

24.6 Using a balljoint separator to release the drag link balljoint from the steering box drop arm

7 Using paint or a marker pen, make an alignment mark between the universal joint and steering box pinion.

8 Slacken and remove the nut (early models only) and clamp bolt securing the universal joint to the steering box pinion.

9 Loosen the nut securing the steering box tie-bar to its mounting. Slacken and remove the nuts, washers and bolts securing the tie-bar to the steering box, and position the tie-

24.9 Steering box tie-bar retaining nut locations (arrowed)

24.16a Refit the balljoint retaining nut . . .

24.16b . . . then tighten it to the specified torque and secure it in position with a new split-pin

bar clear of the box **(see illustration)**.

10 Unscrew the mounting bolts, and remove the steering box assembly from the vehicle.

Inspection

11 Inspect the steering box assembly for signs of wear or damage. If overhaul of the steering box assembly is necessary, the task must be entrusted to a Land Rover dealer.

Refitting

12 Manoeuvre the steering box into position, and engage it with the universal joint splines, aligning the marks made prior to removal.

13 Position the steering box assembly on the chassis, making sure its locating lug is correctly engaged, then fit the mounting bolts and tighten them to the specified torque setting.

14 Insert the clamp bolt securing the universal joint to the steering box. Fit a new nut to the clamp bolt (where necessary), and tighten the bolt to the specified torque.

15 Align the tie-bar with the box, and insert the retaining bolts and washers. Fit new nuts to the bolts, and tighten them to the specified torque setting. Tighten the tie-bar-to-mounting nut to the specified torque setting.

16 Connect the drag link to the drop arm, and refit its retaining nut. Tighten the nut to the specified torque setting, and secure it in position with a new split-pin **(see illustrations)**.

17 Wipe clean the feed and return pipe unions, and refit them to their respective unions on the steering box. Tighten the union nuts to the specified torque setting, and ensure that the pipes are securely retained by all the necessary retaining clips.

18 Remove the clamp from the steering hoses, then lower the vehicle to the ground. Bleed the hydraulic system as described in Section 27.

25 Steering box drop arm - removal and refitting

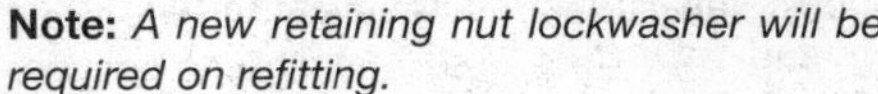

Note: *A new retaining nut lockwasher will be required on refitting.*

Removal

1 Apply the handbrake, then jack up the front of the vehicle and support it on axle stands positioned underneath the chassis (see *Jacking and vehicle support*).

2 Position the front wheels in the straight-ahead position, then disconnect the battery negative terminal.

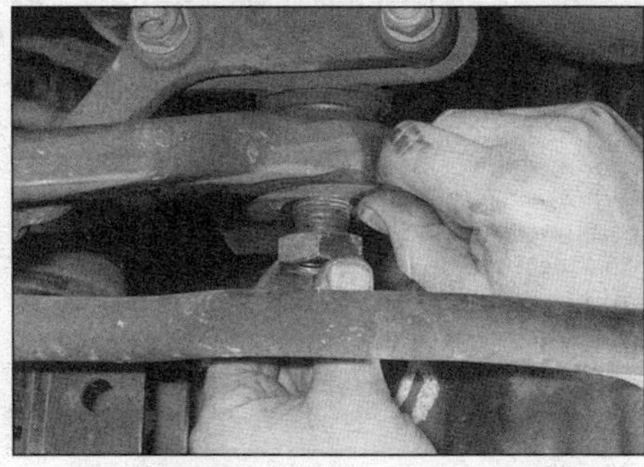
25.5a Unscrew the drop arm retaining nut . . .

3 Withdraw the split-pin, then unscrew the nut securing the drag link to the steering box drop arm.

4 Using a universal balljoint separator, free the drag link from the drop arm.

5 Bend down the lockwasher tab, then slacken and remove the drop arm retaining nut and lockwasher **(see illustrations)**.

6 Make alignment marks between the drop arm and steering box shaft.

7 A suitable legged puller will now be required to draw the arm off the box shaft. Locate the legs of the puller behind the arm, and carefully draw it off the steering box shaft **(see illustration)**.

25.5b . . . and recover the lockwasher

25.7 Using a legged puller to draw the drop arm off the steering box

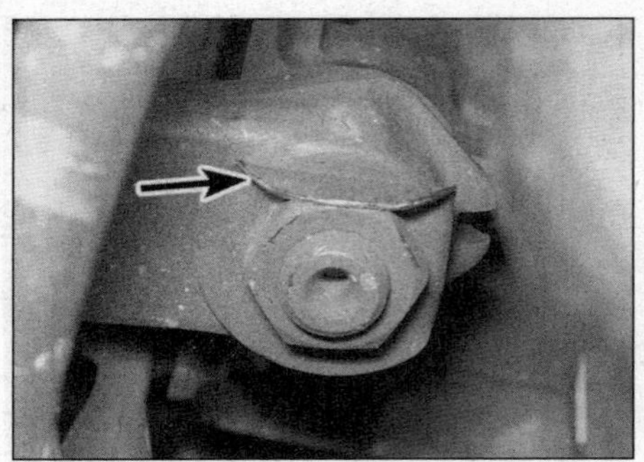

25.11 Tighten the drop arm retaining nut to the specified torque, and secure it in position by bending down the lockwasher against one of its flats

8 Once the arm is loose, remove the puller, then lower the drop arm away from the steering box.

9 On early models, check that the link balljoint moves freely, without any sign of roughness. Check also that the balljoint gaiter shows no sign of deterioration, and is free from cracks and splits. If any sign of wear or damage is found, the drop arm assembly should be renewed/overhauled. Overhaul of the balljoint components is possible, but the task requires the use of several special service tools, and should therefore be entrusted to a Land Rover dealer.

Refitting

10 Align the marks made prior to removal, and locate the drop arm on the steering box shaft splines.

11 Fit a new lockwasher to the shaft, and refit the retaining nut. Tighten the nut to the specified torque setting, then secure it in position by bending down the tab of the lockwasher so that it contacts one of the nut flats **(see illustration)**.

12 Connect the drag link to the drop arm, and refit its retaining nut. Tighten the nut to the specified torque setting, and secure it in position with a new split-pin.

13 Lower the vehicle to the ground, and reconnect the battery.

26 Power steering pump - removal and refitting

Removal

1 Apply the handbrake, then jack up the front of the vehicle and support it on axle stands positioned underneath the chassis (see *Jacking and vehicle support*).

2 On all except 200 TDi engines, remove the cooling fan and viscous coupling as described in Chapter 3.

3 On all engines, loosen the bolts securing the drivebelt pulley to the power steering pump. On petrol models, a 9 mm Allen key can be inserted into the centre of the pulley, to hold it against rotation.

4 Remove the auxiliary drivebelt as described in the relevant part of Chapter 1, then remove the retaining bolts and withdraw the power steering pump pulley, noting which way around it is fitted.

5 Using brake hose clamps, clamp both the supply and return hoses near the power steering fluid reservoir. This will minimise fluid loss during subsequent operations. **Note:** *If the reason for removing the pump is to replace it due to internal wear, then the fluid should be replaced as a matter of course.*

6 Release the fasteners, and remove the undershield from beneath the engine.

7 Slacken the retaining clip, and disconnect the fluid supply hose from the pump. Slacken the union nut, and disconnect the feed pipe from the pump. Be prepared for some fluid spillage as the pipe and hose are disconnected; plug the hose/pipe end and pump unions, to minimise fluid loss and to prevent the entry of dirt into the system.

8 On petrol models, release the HT lead from the clip above the pump, and move the lead to one side without disconnecting it.

9 Slacken and remove the power steering pump mounting bolts, and remove the pump from the engine.

10 Overhaul of the pump is not possible, if the pump is worn or damaged it must be renewed.

Refitting

11 Prior to refitting, remove all traces of locking compound from the pump pulley bolt holes, ideally by running a tap of the correct thread down them.

12 If a new pump is being fitted, unbolt the front mounting plate from the old pump (five bolts on petrol models, three on diesels) and transfer it to the new pump. Tighten the bolts to the specified torque.

13 Manoeuvre the pump into position, then refit its mounting bolts and tighten them to the specified torque setting.

14 On petrol models, clip the HT lead back into position above the pump.

15 Reconnect the feed pipe to the pump and tighten its union nut to the specified torque.

16 Reconnect the supply hose, and securely tighten its retaining clip.

17 Remove all traces of locking compound from the pulley bolts, and apply a drop of fresh locking compound to them.

18 Refit the pulley to the pump, making sure it is the correct way around, and install the mounting bolts.

19 Refit and tension the auxiliary drivebelt as described in the relevant part of Chapter 1, then tighten the pulley retaining bolts to the specified torque setting.

20 Where removed, refit the viscous coupling and cooling fan as described in Chapter 3.

21 Refit the undershield, then lower the vehicle to the ground.

22 Bleed the steering system as described in Section 27.

27 Power steering system - bleeding

1 With the engine stopped, top-up the fluid reservoir up to the maximum mark with the specified type of fluid.

2 Have an assistant start the engine, while you keep watch on the fluid level. Be prepared to add more fluid as the engine starts - the fluid level is likely to drop quickly.

3 Once the fluid level has stabilised, warm the engine up to normal operating temperature. Ensure that the front wheels are positioned in the straight-ahead position, then turn the engine off.

4 Check that the power steering fluid level is still up to the maximum mark, topping-up if necessary.

5 Start the engine and allow it idle. During the following procedure, the engine speed must not be raised above idle, and the steering must not be turned.

6 Slowly slacken the bleed screw which is situated on the top of the power steering box assembly. Ensuring that the fluid level in the reservoir remains at the maximum level, allow fluid to seep from the screw, until a steady flow of fluid which is free from air bubbles is seen to be emerging. Once this is so, securely tighten the bleed screw, and mop up all traces of fluid from the top of the steering box.

7 Turn the steering onto full left-hand lock, holding it there for a few seconds, and then onto full right-hand lock; check all steering hose/pipe unions for signs of leakage. **Note:** *Do not hold the steering at full lock for more than 30 seconds at a time, otherwise the hydraulic system may be damaged.*

8 Once all air is removed from the system, stop the engine, and check the fluid level as described in *Weekly checks*.

28 Steering damper - removal and refitting

Removal

1 Apply the handbrake, then jack up the front of the vehicle and support it on axle stands positioned underneath the chassis (see *Jacking and vehicle support*).

2 Slacken and unscrew the locknut and retaining nut securing the damper to the track rod. Slide off the outer washer, rubber mounting and mounting seat arrangement, noting each component's correct fitted location. Free the damper from the track rod, and recover the inner washer rubber mounting and mounting seat arrangement from the damper.

3 Repeat the operation described in paragraph 2, and detach the steering damper from the differential housing.

4 Remove the steering damper from underneath the vehicle.

5 Inspect the damper assembly for signs of wear or damage, and renew if necessary. Inspect

1
H 28420

28.6 On refitting, ensure that the steering damper (1) mounting rubber components are correctly arranged, as shown in the inset

the rubber mountings for signs of damage and deterioration, and renew if necessary.

Refitting

6 Refitting is the reverse of removal, ensuring that all mounting rubber arrangement components are correctly positioned **(see illustration)**. Securely tighten each retaining nut, then secure them in position by securely tighten the locknuts.

29 Drag link - removal, refitting and adjustment

Removal

1 Apply the handbrake, then jack up the front of the vehicle and support it on axle stands positioned underneath the chassis (see *Jacking and vehicle support*).

2 Position the front wheels in the straight-ahead position, then disconnect the battery negative terminal.

3 Withdraw the split-pin, then unscrew the nut securing the drag link to the steering box drop arm.

4 Using a universal balljoint separator, free the drag link from the drop arm.

5 Repeat paragraphs 3 and 4, and free the drag link from the swivel pin housing assembly. If necessary, remove the roadwheel to improve access to the balljoint nut. Remove the drag link from underneath the vehicle.

6 Check that the link balljoint(s) move freely, without any sign of roughness. Check also that the balljoint gaiter(s) show no sign of deterioration, and are free from cracks and splits. If any sign of wear or damage is found, the balljoint(s) must be renewed (see Section 30). If the drag link itself is damaged, it must be renewed - do not attempt to straighten it.

Refitting

7 Offer up the drag link, and engage it with the swivel pin housing and steering box drop arm. Refit the retaining nuts, and tighten them to the specified torque setting. Secure each nut in position with a new split-pin.

8 Refit the roadwheel (where removed), then lower the vehicle to the ground and reconnect the battery negative terminal. Where necessary, tighten the wheel nuts to the specified torque setting

9 Road test the vehicle, and check that the steering wheel is centralised when the vehicle is driven straight-ahead. If the steering wheel is more than 5° out of position, adjustment should be made by removing the wheel and repositioning it on the column splines. If the wheel is less than 5° out of alignment, adjustment can be made by altering the drag link length as follows.

Adjustment

10 Apply the handbrake, then raise the front of the vehicle and detach the outer balljoint from the swivel pin housing assembly, as described above in paragraphs 1 to 4.

11 Slacken the balljoint clamp bolt, and adjust the drag link length by screwing the balljoint in or out (as applicable):

a) *On right-hand drive models, if the steering wheel was found to be slightly right of centre, shorten the drag link length, and if it was found to be slightly left of centre, extend the drag link length.*

b) *On left-hand drive models, if the steering wheel was found to be slightly right of centre, extend the drag link length, and if it was found to be slightly left of centre, shorten the drag link length.*

12 Once the drag link length is correct, refit the balljoint to the swivel pin housing, and tighten its retaining nut to the specified torque setting.

13 Secure the nut in position with a new split-pin, then tighten the drag link clamp bolt to the specified torque.

14 Refit the roadwheel, then lower the vehicle to the ground and tighten the wheel nuts to the specified torque.

15 Road test the vehicle and, if necessary, repeat the adjustment procedure.

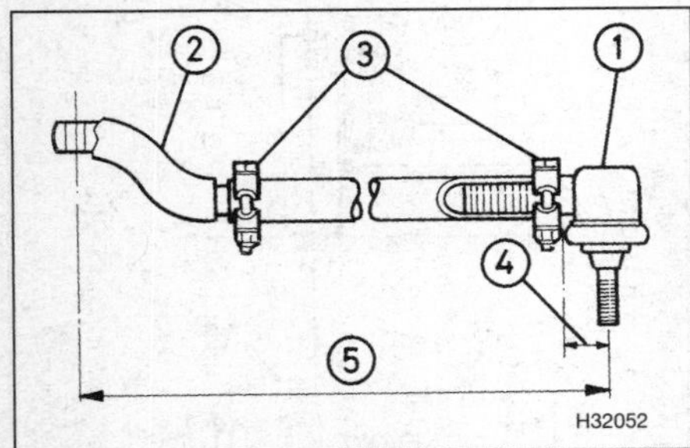
2
3
1
4
5
H32052

30.6 Drag link adjustment details - early models

1 *Balljoint*
2 *End fitting*
3 *Adjustment clamps*
4 *Balljoint centre-to-drag link end measurement = 28.5 mm*
5 *Balljoint centre-to-end fitting hole centre measurement = 919 mm*

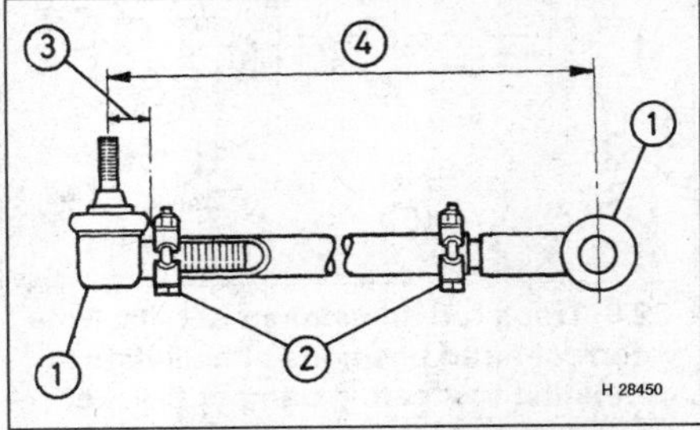
3
4
1
2
1
H 28450

30.7 Drag link adjustment details - later models

1 *Balljoint*
2 *Adjustment clamps*
3 *Balljoint centre-to-drag link end measurement = 28.5 mm*
4 *Balljoint centre to centre measurement = 924 mm*

30 Drag link balljoint/end fitting - removal and refitting

Removal

1 Remove the drag link as described in Section 29.

2 If the balljoint/end fitting is to be re-used, use a straight-edge and a scriber, or similar, to mark its relationship to the drag link.

3 Slacken the clamp bolt, then counting the **exact** number of turns necessary to do so, unscrew the balljoint/end fitting from the drag link end.

4 Carefully clean the balljoint/end fitting and the drag link threads. Renew the balljoint if its movement is sloppy or if it is too stiff, if it is excessively worn, or if it is damaged in any way; carefully check the stud taper and threads. If the balljoint gaiter is damaged, the complete balljoint assembly must be renewed; it is not possible to obtain the gaiter separately.

Refitting

5 If the original balljoint/end fitting is being refitted, screw it into the drag link by the number of turns noted on removal, and tighten the clamp bolt to the specified torque. This should line up the alignment marks that were made on removal.

6 On early models, if a new balljoint or end fitting are being installed, slacken both clamp bolts, and screw both the balljoint and end fitting into position. Referring to the accompanying illustration, position the balljoint so that the distance from its centre to the drag link end is as shown **(see illustration)**. Then position the drop arm end fitting so that the distance between the centre of the balljoint and the centre of the end fitting hole is as given. Make sure that the offset end fitting is correctly positioned in relation to the balljoint shank, and tighten both drag link clamp bolts to the specified torque setting.

7 On later models, if a new balljoint(s) is/are being fitted, slacken both clamp bolts, and screw both balljoints into the drag link. Position one of the balljoints so that the distance from its centre to the drag link end is as shown **(see illustration)**. Then position the second balljoint so that the distance between the balljoint centres is as given. Make sure that the balljoints are correctly positioned in relation to each other, and tighten both drag link clamp bolts to the specified torque setting.

8 Refit the drag link as described in Section 29, and check that the steering wheel is centralised.

31 Track rod - removal and refitting

Removal

1 Apply the handbrake, then jack up the front of the vehicle and support it on axle stands positioned underneath the chassis (see *Jacking and vehicle support*).

2 Position the front wheels in the straight-ahead position, then disconnect the battery negative terminal.

3 Free the steering damper from the track rod, as described in paragraph 2 of Section 28.

4 Withdraw the split-pin, then unscrew the nut securing the track rod to the left-hand swivel pin housing.

5 Using a universal balljoint separator, free the track rod from the swivel pin housing.

6 Repeat paragraphs 4 and 5, and free the track rod from the right-hand swivel pin housing assembly. Remove the track rod from underneath the vehicle.

7 Check that the track rod balljoints move freely, without any sign of roughness. Check also that the balljoint gaiters show no sign of deterioration, and are free from cracks and splits. If any sign of wear or damage is found, the balljoint(s) must be renewed (see Section 32). If the track rod itself is damaged, it must be renewed - do not attempt to straighten it.

Refitting

8 Offer up the track rod, and engage it with the swivel pin housings. Refit the retaining nuts, and tighten them to the specified torque setting. Secure each nut in position with a new split-pin.

9 Reconnect the steering damper to the track rod as described in Section 28.

10 Check the front wheel alignment as described in Section 33.

32 Track rod balljoint - removal and refitting

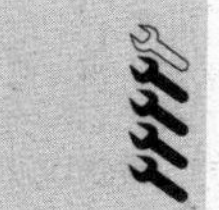

Removal

1 Remove the track rod as described in Section 31.

2 If the balljoint is to be re-used, use a straight-edge and a scriber, or similar, to mark its relationship to the track rod.

3 Slacken the clamp bolt, then counting the **exact** number of turns necessary to do so, unscrew the balljoint from the track rod end.

4 Carefully clean the balljoint and the track rod threads. Renew the balljoint if its movement is sloppy or if it is too stiff, if it is excessively worn, or if it is damaged in any way; carefully check the stud taper and threads. If the balljoint gaiter is damaged, the complete balljoint assembly must be renewed; it is not possible to obtain the gaiter separately.

Refitting

5 If the original balljoint is being refitted, screw it into the track rod by the number of turns noted on removal. This should line up the alignment marks that were made on removal.

6 If a new balljoint is being installed, slacken all the clamp bolts, and screw both balljoints fully into position. Position the track rod adjuster sleeve so that the distance between its end and the track rod is as shown **(see illustration)**. Position the adjuster sleeve balljoint so that the distance from its centre to the adjuster sleeve end is as given. Then position the track rod balljoint so that the distance between the balljoint centres is as shown. Make sure that both balljoints are correctly positioned in relation to the steering damper hole.

7 Refit the track rod as described in Section 31.

8 Prior to using the vehicle, check the front wheel alignment as described in Section 33. Tighten the track rod clamp bolts to the specified torque.

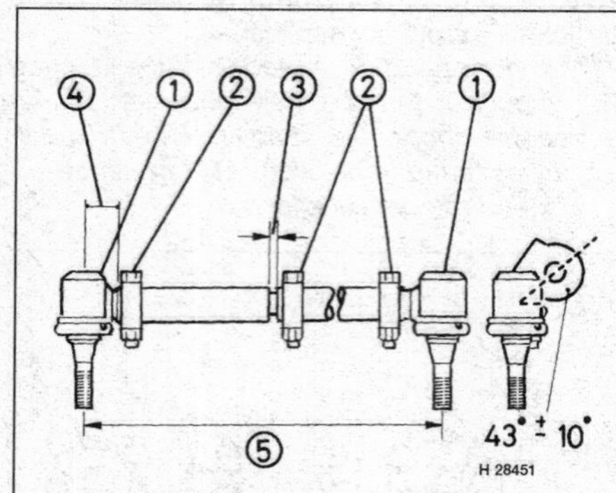
4
1
2
3
2
1
5
43° ± 10°
H 28451

32.6 Track rod adjustment details. Note correct fitted positions of balljoints in relation to steering damper bracket

1 *Balljoint*
2 *Adjustment clamps*
3 *Adjuster sleeve-to-track rod measurement = 9 mm*
4 *Balljoint centre-to-track rod end measurement = 28.5 mm*
5 *Balljoint centre-to-centre measurement = 1230 mm*

33 Wheel alignment and steering angles - general information

1 Accurate front wheel alignment is essential for precise steering and handling, and for even tyre wear. Before carrying out any checking or adjusting operations, make sure that the tyres are correctly inflated, that all steering and suspension joints and linkages are in sound condition, and that the wheels are not buckled or distorted, particularly around the rims. It will also be necessary to have the vehicle positioned on flat, level ground, with enough space to push the car backwards and forwards through about half its length.

2 Front wheel alignment consists of four factors **(see illustration)**:

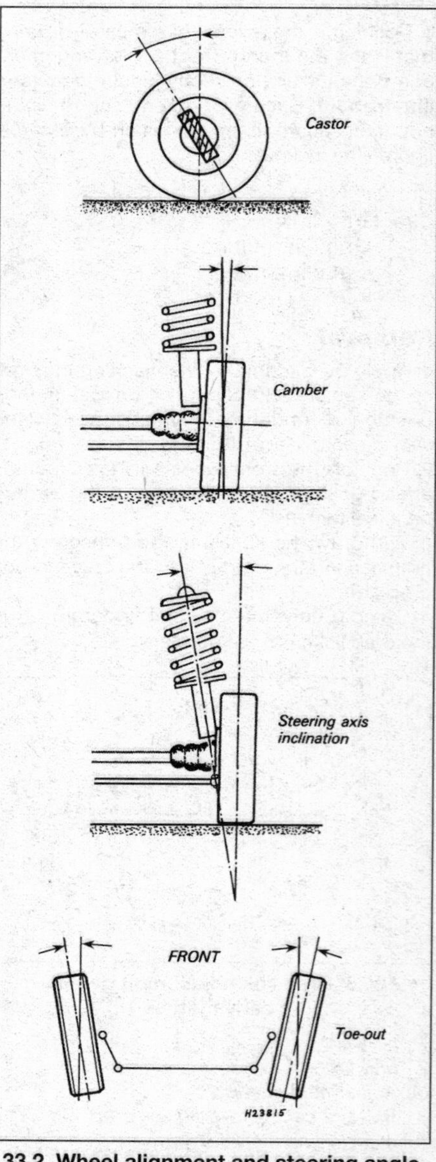
Castor
Camber
Steering axis inclination
FRONT
Toe-out
H23815

33.2 Wheel alignment and steering angle measurements

Camber is the angle at which the roadwheels are set from the vertical, when viewed from the front or rear of the vehicle. Positive camber is the angle (in degrees) that the wheels are tilted outwards at the top from the vertical.

Castor is the angle between the steering axis and a vertical line when viewed from each side of the vehicle. Positive castor is indicated when the steering axis is inclined towards the rear of the vehicle at its upper end.

Steering axis inclination is the angle, when viewed from the front or rear of the vehicle, between the vertical and an imaginary line drawn between the upper and lower front suspension strut mountings.

Toe setting is the amount by which the distance between the front inside edges of the roadwheels differs from that between the rear inside edges, when measured at hub height. If the distance between the front edges is less than at the rear, the wheels are said to toe-in. If it is greater than at the rear, the wheels are said to toe-out.

3 Camber, castor and steering axis inclination are set during manufacture, and are not adjustable. Unless the vehicle has suffered accident damage, or there is gross wear in the suspension mountings or joints, it can be assumed that these settings are correct. If for any reason it is believed that they are not correct, the task of checking them should be left to a Land Rover dealer, who will have the necessary special equipment needed to measure the small angles involved.

4 It is, however, within the scope of the home mechanic to check and adjust the front wheel toe setting. To do this, a tracking gauge must first be obtained. Two types of gauge are available, and can be obtained from motor accessory shops. The first type measures the distance between the front and rear inside edges of the roadwheels, as previously described, with the vehicle stationary. The second type, known as a scuff plate, measures the actual position of the contact surface of the tyre, in relation to the road surface, with the vehicle in motion. This is achieved by pushing or driving the front tyre over a plate, which then moves slightly according to the scuff of the tyre, and shows this movement on a scale. Both types have their advantages and disadvantages, but either can give satisfactory results if used correctly and carefully.

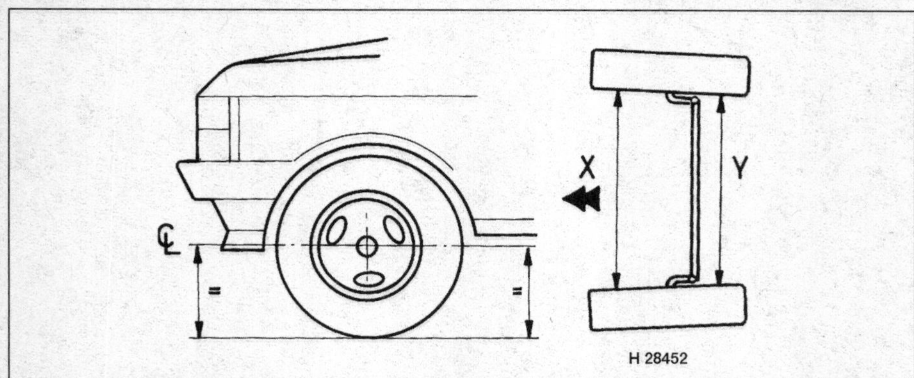
X
Y
=
=
H 28452

33.6 For the front wheel alignment check to be accurate, the vehicle must be at correct ride height, as shown. Take the measurements X and Y and calculate the toe setting

5 Many tyre specialists will also check toe settings free, or for a nominal charge.

6 Make sure that the steering is in the straight-ahead position when making measurements. The measurement will only be accurate if the vehicle ride height is as shown **(see illustration)**.

7 If adjustment is necessary, apply the handbrake, then jack up the front of the vehicle and support it securely on axle stands. Slacken the track rod adjuster sleeve clamp bolts, then rotate the adjuster sleeve to alter the length of the track rod (as necessary); shortening the track rod will reduce toe-in/increase toe-out.

8 When the setting is correct, tighten both the clamp bolts to the specified torque setting.

9 Recheck the toe setting and, if necessary, repeat the adjustment procedure.

Chapter 12
Bodywork and fittings

Contents

Degrees of difficulty

Easy, suitable for novice with little experience 

Fairly easy, suitable for beginner with some experience 

Fairly difficult, suitable for competent DIY mechanic 

Difficult, suitable for experienced DIY mechanic 

Very difficult, suitable for expert DIY or professional 

Specifications

Torque wrench settings

Torque wrench settings	Nm	lbf ft
Seat belt mounting nuts and bolts:		
Up to 1996	20	15
1996 onwards	32	24

1 General information

The bodyshell and panels are a mix of steel and aluminium panels; the aluminium being used to increase corrosion resistance properties. Both three- and 5-door versions are available. Most components are welded together, but some use is made of structural adhesives; the front wings are bolted on.

Extensive use is made of plastic materials, mainly on the interior but also in exterior components. The front and rear bumpers are injection-moulded from a synthetic material, which is very strong and yet light. Plastic components such as wheelarch liners are fitted to the underside of the vehicle, to improve the body's resistance to corrosion.

2 Maintenance - bodywork and underframe

The general condition of a vehicle's bodywork is the one thing that significantly affects its value. Maintenance is easy, but needs to be regular. Neglect, particularly after minor damage, can lead quickly to further deterioration and costly repair bills. It is important also to keep watch on those parts of the vehicle not immediately visible, for instance the underside, inside all the wheel arches, and the lower part of the engine compartment.

The basic maintenance routine for the bodywork is washing - preferably with a lot of water, from a hose. This will remove all the loose solids which may have stuck to the vehicle. It is important to flush these off in such a way as to prevent grit from scratching the finish. The wheel arches and underframe need washing in the same way, to remove any accumulated mud, which will retain moisture and tend to encourage rust. Paradoxically enough, the best time to clean the underframe and wheel arches is in wet weather, when the mud is thoroughly wet and soft. In very wet weather, the underframe is usually cleaned of large accumulations automatically, and this is a good time for inspection.

Periodically, except on vehicles with a wax-based underbody protective coating, it is a good idea to have the whole of the underframe of the vehicle steam-cleaned, engine compartment included, so that a thorough inspection can be carried out to see what minor repairs and renovations are necessary. Steam-cleaning is available at many garages, and is necessary for the removal of the accumulation of oily grime, which sometimes is allowed to become thick in certain areas. If steam-cleaning facilities are not available, there are some excellent grease solvents available which can be brush-applied; the dirt can then be simply hosed off. Note that these methods should not be used on vehicles with wax-based underbody protective coating, or the coating will be removed. Such vehicles should be inspected annually, preferably just prior to Winter, when the underbody should be washed down, and any damage to the wax coating repaired. Ideally, a completely fresh coat should be applied. It would also be worth considering the use of such wax-based protection for injection into door panels, sills, box sections, etc, as an additional safeguard against rust damage, where such protection is not provided by the vehicle manufacturer.

After washing paintwork, wipe off with a chamois leather to give an unspotted clear finish. A coat of clear protective wax polish will give added protection against chemical pollutants in the air. If the paintwork sheen has dulled or oxidised, use a cleaner/polisher combination to restore the brilliance of the shine. This requires a little effort, but such dulling is usually caused because regular washing has been neglected. Care needs to be taken with metallic paintwork, as special non-abrasive cleaner/polisher is required to avoid damage to the finish. Always check that the door and ventilator opening drain holes and pipes are completely clear, so that water can be drained out. Brightwork should be treated in the same way as paintwork. Windscreens and windows can be kept clear of the smeary film which often appears, by the use of proprietary glass cleaner. Never use any form of wax or other body or chromium polish on glass.

3 Maintenance - upholstery and carpets

Mats and carpets should be brushed or vacuum-cleaned regularly, to keep them free of grit. If they are badly stained, remove them from the vehicle for scrubbing or sponging, and make quite sure they are dry before refitting. Seats and interior trim panels can be kept clean by wiping with a damp cloth. If they do become stained (which can be more apparent on light-coloured upholstery), use a little liquid detergent and a soft nail brush to scour the grime out of the grain of the material. Do not forget to keep the headlining clean in the same way as the upholstery. When using liquid cleaners inside the vehicle, do not over-wet the surfaces being cleaned. Excessive damp could get into the seams and padded interior, causing stains, offensive odours or even rot.

HAYNES
HiNT

If the inside of the vehicle gets wet accidentally, it is worthwhile taking some trouble to dry it out properly, particularly where carpets are involved. Do not leave oil or electric heaters inside the vehicle for this purpose.

4 Minor body damage - repair

Repair of minor scratches in the vehicle's bodywork

If the scratch is very superficial, and does not penetrate to the metal of the bodywork, repair is very simple. Lightly rub the area of the scratch with a paintwork renovator, or a very fine cutting paste, to remove loose paint from the scratch and to clear the surrounding bodywork of wax polish. Rinse the area with clean water.

In the case of metallic paint, the most commonly-found 'scratches' are not in the paint, but in the lacquer top coat, and appear white. If care is taken , these can sometimes be rendered less obvious by very careful use of paintwork renovator (which would otherwise not be used on metallic paintwork); otherwise, repair of these scratches can be achieved by applying lacquer with a fine brush.

Apply touch-up paint to the scratch using a thin paintbrush; continue to apply thin layers of paint until the surface of the paint in the scratch is level with the surrounding paintwork. Allow the new paint at least two weeks to harden, then blend it into the surrounding paintwork by rubbing the paintwork in the scratch area with a paintwork renovator or a very fine cutting paste. Finally, apply wax polish.

Where the scratch has penetrated right through to the metal of the bodywork, a different repair technique is required. Remove any loose paint, etc from the bottom of the scratch with a penknife. Using a rubber or nylon applicator, fill the scratch with bodystopper paste. If required, this paste can be mixed with cellulose thinners to provide a very thin paste which is ideal for filling narrow scratches. Before the stopper-paste in the scratch hardens, wrap a piece of smooth cotton rag around the top of a finger. Dip the finger in cellulose thinners, and then quickly sweep it across the surface of the stopper-paste in the scratch; this will ensure that the surface of the stopper-paste is lightly hollowed. The scratch can now be painted over as described earlier in this Section.

Repair of dents in the vehicle's bodywork

The alloy body panels on the Land Rover are easier to work on than steel, and minor dents or creases can be beaten out fairly easily. However, if the damaged area is quite large, prolonged hammering will cause the metal to harden; to avoid the possibility of cracking, it must be softened or 'annealed'. This can be done easily with a gas blowlamp, but great care is required to avoid actually melting the metal. The blowlamp must always be kept moving in a circular pattern, whilst being held a respectable distance from the metal.

One method of checking when the alloy is hot enough is to rub down the surface to be annealed, and then apply a thin film of oil over it. The blowlamp should be played over the rear side of the oiled surface, until the oil evaporates and the surface is dry. Turn off the blowlamp, and allow the metal to cool naturally; the treated areas will now be softened, and it will be possible to work it with a hammer or mallet. After panel-beating, the damaged section should be rubbed down and painted as described later in this Section.

When deep denting of the vehicle's bodywork has taken place, the first task is to pull the dent out until the affected bodywork almost attains its original shape. There is little point in trying to restore the original shape completely, as the metal in the damaged area will have stretched on impact, and cannot be reshaped to its original contour. It is better to bring the level of the dent up to a point which is about 3 mm below the level of the surrounding bodywork. In cases where the dent is very shallow anyway, it is not worth trying to pull it out at all.

If the underside of the dent is accessible, it can be hammered out gently from behind using the method described earlier.

Should the dent be in a section of the bodywork which has a double skin, or some other factor making it inaccessible from behind, a different technique is called for. Drill several small holes through the metal inside the dent area, particularly in the deeper sections. Then screw long self-tapping screws into the holes just sufficiently for them to gain a good purchase in the metal. Now the dent can be pulled out by pulling on the protruding heads of the screws with a pair of pliers.

The next stage of the repair is the removal of the paint from the damaged area, and from an inch or so of the surrounding 'sound' bodywork.

Note: *On no account should coarse abrasives be used on aluminium panels in order to remove paint. The use of a wire brush or abrasive on a power drill for example, will cause deep scoring of the metal and in extreme cases, penetrate the thickness of the relatively soft aluminium alloy.*

Removal of paint is best achieved by applying paint remover to the area, allowing it to act on the paintwork for the specified time, and then removing the softened paint with a wood or nylon scraper. This method may have to be repeated in order to remove all traces of paint. A good method of removing small stubborn traces of paint is to rub the area with a nylon scouring pad soaked in thinners or paint remover. **Note:** *If it is necessary to use this method, always wear rubber gloves to protect the hands from burns from the paint remover. It is also advisable to wear eye protection, as any paint remover that gets into the eyes will cause severe inflammation, or worse.*

Finally, remove all traces of paint and remover by washing the area with plenty of clean fresh water.

To complete the preparations for filling, score the surface of the bare metal with a screwdriver or the tang of a file, or alternatively, drill small holes in the affected area. This will provide a really good 'key' for the filler paste.

To complete the repair, see the Section on filling and respraying.

Repair of holes or gashes in the vehicle's bodywork

Remove all the paint from the affected area, and from an inch or so of the surrounding 'sound' bodywork, using the method described in the previous Section. With the paint removed, you will be able to gauge the severity of the damage, and therefore decide whether to replace the whole panel (if this is possible) or to repair the affected area. It is often quicker and more satisfactory to fit a new panel than to attempt to repair large areas of damage.

Remove all fittings from the affected area, except those which will act as a guide to the original shape of the damaged bodywork (eg. headlight shells, etc). Then, using tin snips or a hacksaw blade, remove all loose metal and other metal badly affected by damage. Hammer the edges of the hole inwards, in order to create a slight depression for the filler paste.

Before filling can take place, it will be necessary to block the hole in some way. This can be achieved by the use of zinc gauze or aluminium tape.

Zinc gauze is probably the best material to use for a large hole. Cut a piece to the approximate size and shape of the hole to be filled, then position it in the hole so that its edges are below the level of the surrounding bodywork. It can be retained in position by several blobs of filler paste around its periphery.

Aluminium tape should be used for small or very narrow holes. Pull a piece off the roll and trim it to the approximate size and shape required, then pull off the backing paper (if used) and stick the tape over the hole; it can be overlapped if the thickness of one piece is insufficient. Burnish down the edges of the tape with the handle of a screwdriver or similar, to ensure that the tape is securely attached to the metal underneath.

Bodywork repairs - filling and respraying

Before using this Section, see the Section on dent, deep scratch, hole and gash repairs.

Many types of bodyfiller are available, but generally speaking, those proprietary kits which contain a tin of filler paste and a tube of resin hardener are best for this type of repair. A wide, flexible plastic or nylon applicator will be found invaluable for imparting a smooth and well-contoured finish to the surface of the filler.

Mix up a little filler on a clean piece of card or board. Use the hardener sparingly (follow the maker's instructions on the packet) otherwise the filler will set rapidly.

Using the applicator, apply the filler paste to the prepared area; draw the applicator across the surface of the filler to achieve the correct contour, and to level the filler surfaces. As soon as a contour that approximates the correct one is achieved, stop working the paste; if you carry on too long, the paste will become sticky and begin to 'pick-up' on the applicator. Continue to add thin layers of filler paste at twenty-minute intervals until the level of the filler is just 'proud' of the surrounding bodywork.

Once the filler has hardened, excess can be removed using a metal plane or file. From then on, progressively finer grades of abrasive paper should be used, starting with a 40-grade production paper, and finishing with a 400-grade wet-or-dry paper. Always wrap the abrasive paper around a flat rubber, cork, or wooden block, otherwise the surface of the filler will not be completely flat. During the smoothing of the filler surface, the wet-or-dry paper should be periodically rinsed in water. This will ensure that a very fine smooth finish is imparted to the filler at the final stage.

At this stage, the 'dent' should be surrounded by a ring of bare metal, which in turn should be encircled by the finely 'feathered' edge of the good paintwork. Rinse the repair with clean water, until all the dust produced by the rubbing-down operation is gone.

Spray the whole area with a light coat of grey primer, this will show up any imperfections in the surface of the filler. If at all possible, it is recommended that an etch-primer is used on untreated alloy surfaces, otherwise the primer may not be keyed sufficiently, and may subsequently flake off. Repair imperfections with fresh filler paste or bodystopper and once more, smooth the surface with abrasive paper. Repeat the spray-and-repair procedures until you are satisfied that the surface of the filler, and the feathered edge of the paintwork, is perfect. Clean the repair area with clean water, and allow it to dry fully.

HAYNES
HiNT

If bodystopper is used, it can be mixed with cellulose thinners, to form a really thin paste which is ideal for filling small holes.

The repair area is now ready for spraying. Paint spraying must be carried out in a warm, dry, windless and dust-free atmosphere. This condition can be created artificially if you have access to a large indoor working area, but if you are forced to work in the open, you will have to pick your day very carefully. If you are working indoors, dousing the floor in the work area with water will 'lay' the dust which would otherwise be in the atmosphere. If the repair is confined to one body panel, mask off the surrounding panels; this will help to minimise the effects of a slight mis-match in paint colours. Bodywork fittings will also need to be masked off. Use genuine masking tape and several thickness of newspaper for the masking operation.

Before commencing to spray, agitate the aerosol can thoroughly, then spray a test area (an old tin, or similar) until the technique is mastered. Cover the repair area with a thick coat of primer; the thickness should be built up using several thin layers of paint, rather than one thick one. Using 400-grade wet-or-dry paper, rub down the surface of the primer until it is really smooth. Whilst doing this, the work area should be thoroughly doused with water, and the wet-or-dry paper periodically rinsed in water. Allow to dry before spraying on more paint.

Spray on the top coat, again building up the thickness by using several thin layers of paint. Start spraying at the top of the repair area and then, using a side-to-side motion, work downwards until the whole repair area and about 50 mm of the surrounding original paintwork is covered. Remove all masking material 10 to 15 minutes after spraying on the final coat of paint.

Allow the new paint at least two weeks to harden, then, using a paintwork renovator or a very fine cutting paste, blend the edges of the paint into the existing paintwork. Finally, apply wax polish.

Plastic components

With the use of more and more plastic body components by the vehicle manufacturers (eg bumpers. spoilers, and in some cases major body panels), rectification of more serious damage to such items has become a matter of either entrusting repair work to a specialist in this field, or renewing complete components. Repair of such damage by the DIY owner is not really feasible, owing to the cost of the equipment and materials required for effecting such repairs. The basic technique involves making a groove along the line of the crack in the plastic, using a rotary burr in a power drill. The damaged part is then welded back together, using a hot-air gun to heat up and fuse a plastic filler rod into the groove. Any excess plastic is then removed, and the area rubbed down to a smooth finish. It is important that a filler rod of the correct plastic is used, as body components can be made of a variety of different types (eg polycarbonate, ABS, polypropylene).

Damage of a less serious nature (abrasions, minor cracks etc) can be repaired by the DIY owner using a two-part epoxy filler repair material. Once mixed in equal proportions, or applied directly from the tube, this is used in

6.2 Slacken the retaining clip, and disconnect the washer hose (arrowed) from the T-piece

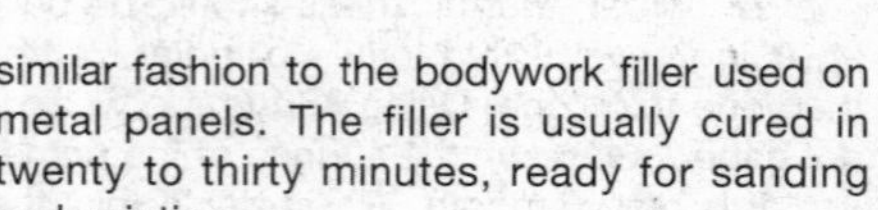

6.3 Undo the bumper end retaining nut (arrowed) . . .

6.4 . . . and the bumper-to-mounting bracket nuts and bolts (arrowed)

similar fashion to the bodywork filler used on metal panels. The filler is usually cured in twenty to thirty minutes, ready for sanding and painting.

If the owner is renewing a complete component himself, or if he has repaired it with epoxy filler, he will be left with the problem of finding a suitable paint for finishing which is compatible with the type of plastic used. At one time, the use of a universal paint was not possible, owing to the complex range of plastics encountered in body component applications. Standard paints, generally speaking, will not bond to plastic or rubber satisfactorily. However, it is now possible to obtain a plastic body parts finishing kit which consists of a pre-primer treatment, a primer and coloured top coat. Full instructions are normally supplied with a kit, but basically, the method of use is to first apply the pre-primer to the component concerned, and allow it to dry for up to 30 minutes. Then the primer is applied, and left to dry for about an hour before finally applying the special-coloured top coat. The result is a correctly-coloured component, where the paint will flex with the plastic or rubber, a property that standard paint does not normally possess.

5 Major body damage - repair

Where serious damage has occurred, or large areas need renewal due to neglect, it means that complete new panels will need welding in, and this is best left to professionals. If the damage is due to impact, it will also be necessary to check completely the alignment of the bodyshell, and this can only be carried out accurately by a Land Rover dealer using special jigs. If the body is left misaligned, it is primarily dangerous, as the car will not handle properly. Secondly, uneven stresses will be imposed on the steering, suspension and possibly transmission, causing abnormal wear, or complete failure, particularly to such items as the tyres.

6 Front bumper - removal and refitting

Removal

1 If necessary to improve access, firmly apply the handbrake, then jack up the front of the vehicle and support it on axle stands.

2 Where necessary, trace the headlight washer hose back to its T-piece, and disconnect the main supply hose **(see illustration)**.

3 Slacken and remove the nut and washer securing each end of the bumper in position **(see illustration)**.

4 With the aid of an assistant, support the bumper, then slacken and remove the four nuts and bolts securing bumper to its chassis mounting brackets **(see illustration)**.

5 Manoeuvre the bumper away from the vehicle, and recover the front towing eye

6 If necessary, with the bumper removed, undo the retaining screws and bolts, and separate the various sections of bumper.

Refitting

7 Reassemble the bumper sections (where necessary), and securely tighten its retaining screws and bolts.

8 Manoeuvre the bumper into position, not forgetting the towing eye, and insert its four mounting bolts and nuts.

9 Refit the washers and nuts securing the bumper ends in position, then go around and securely tighten all the bumper mounting bolts and nuts.

10 Reconnect the headlight washer hose (where necessary), and lower the vehicle to the ground.

7 Rear bumper - removal and refitting

Removal

1 If necessary to improve access, chock the front wheels, then jack up the rear of the vehicle and support it on axle stands.

2 With the aid of an assistant, support the bumper, then slacken and remove the nuts and bolts securing bumper to its chassis mounting brackets. Manoeuvre the bumper assembly away from the vehicle.

3 If necessary, with the bumper removed, undo the retaining nuts and bolts, and separate the various sections of bumper.

Refitting

4 Refitting is the reverse of removal.

8 Bonnet - removal, refitting and adjustment

Removal

1 Open the bonnet, and have an assistant support it. Using a pencil or felt tip pen, mark the outline position of each bonnet hinge relative to the bonnet, to use as a guide on refitting.

2 Undo the bonnet retaining bolts and, with the help of an assistant, carefully lift the bonnet clear. Recover any shims which are fitted between the bonnet and hinges.

3 Inspect the bonnet hinges for signs of wear or damage; the hinges are bolted in position, and can easily be renewed.

Refitting and adjustment

4 With the aid of an assistant, offer up the bonnet, not forgetting any shims which were fitted between the hinge and bonnet, and loosely fit the retaining bolts. Align the hinges with the marks made on removal, then tighten the retaining bolts securely.

5 Close the bonnet, and check for alignment with the adjacent panels. If necessary, slacken the bonnet bolts and realign the bonnet to suit. The bonnet height is adjusted by adding/removing the shims fitted between it and the hinge. Once the bonnet is correctly aligned, securely tighten the bolts.

6 Once the bonnet is correctly aligned, check that the bonnet fastens and releases in a satisfactory manner, and if necessary adjust the lock striker as described in Section 10.

1.4Z

10.5a Bonnet lock assembly retaining bolts (arrowed)

10.5b Undo the bolt, and remove the bonnet adjusting plates

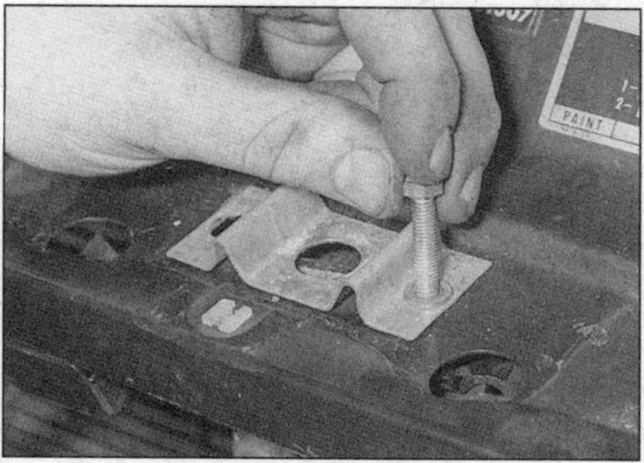

10.6 Undo the two bolts and remove the bonnet lock top plate

9 Bonnet release cable - removal and refitting

Removal

1 Remove the bonnet lock assembly as described in Section 10.

2 Work back along the cable, releasing it from all the relevant retaining clips and ties, whilst noting its correct routing. Release the rubber sealing grommets from the body, and slide them off the end of the cable. Tie a piece of string to the cable end - this can then be used to draw the cable back into position.

3 From inside the vehicle, unscrew the retaining nut securing the bonnet release handle to its mounting bracket.

4 Withdraw the lever and cable assembly from inside the vehicle. Once the cable end appears, untie the string and leave it in position in the vehicle; the string can then be used to draw the new cable back into position.

Refitting

5 Tie the string to the end of the cable, and use the string to draw the bonnet release cable through from inside the vehicle into the engine compartment. Once the cable is through, untie the string and slide on both the rubber sealing grommets. Seat the handle in its mounting bracket, and securely tighten the retaining nut.

6 Ensure that the cable is correctly routed, and retained by all the relevant clips and ties, then seat the cable grommets in the vehicle body.

7 Refit the bonnet lock assembly as described in Section 10.

10 Bonnet lock - removal and refitting

Removal

1 Disconnect the battery negative terminal.

2 On later models (March 1994 onwards), remove the left-hand direction indicator light as described in Chapter 13, Section 7. Undo the retaining screw and nut, and remove the trim panel from underneath the headlight unit, freeing it from the radiator grille.

3 On all models, undo the retaining screws situated along the top edge of the grille, then free the grille lower locating pegs and remove it from the vehicle. On later models, also free the grille from the right-hand headlight trim panel as it is removed.

4 Using a suitable marker pen, draw around the outline of the bonnet lock top plate and adjusting plates. These marks can then be used as a guide on refitting.

5 Undo the single bolt and remove both the bonnet adjusting plates, noting their correct fitted locations **(see illustrations)**.

6 Undo the two retaining bolts, and lift the top plate away from the bonnet crossmember **(see illustration)**.

7 Free the lock assembly and mounting plate from the underside of the bonnet crossmember, and detach the lock assembly from its return spring **(see illustration)**.

8 Slacken the release cable clamp, then detach the cable and remove the lock and mounting plate from the vehicle **(see illustration)**.

Refitting

9 Refitting is the reverse of the removal procedure, using the alignment marks made prior to removal. Prior to refitting the radiator grille, check the operation of the release mechanism. Adjustment of the cable can be made by either slackening the clamp and adjusting the inner cable or, alternately, by releasing the outer cable retaining clip and repositioning the clip on the cable (as applicable).

11 Door - removal, refitting and adjustment

Removal

Front door

1 Disconnect the battery negative lead.

2 Release the rubber seal from the lower edge of the door pillar, then release the two fasteners securing the footwell side trim panel in position, and remove the panel from the vehicle.

3 Disconnect the wiring connectors, then release the rubber wiring harness grommet from the door pillar. Withdraw the wiring from the pillar, so that it is free to be removed with the door assembly **(see illustration)**.

ROVER GROUP

10.7 Free the lock assembly . . .

10.8 . . . then slacken the clamp (arrowed) and detach the operating cable

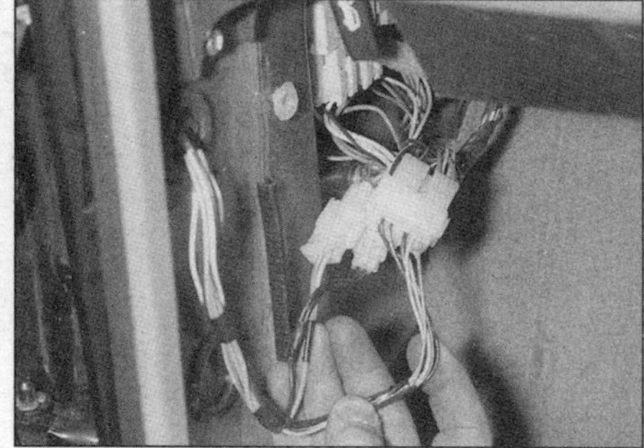

11.3 The front door wiring connectors are located behind the footwell side trim panel

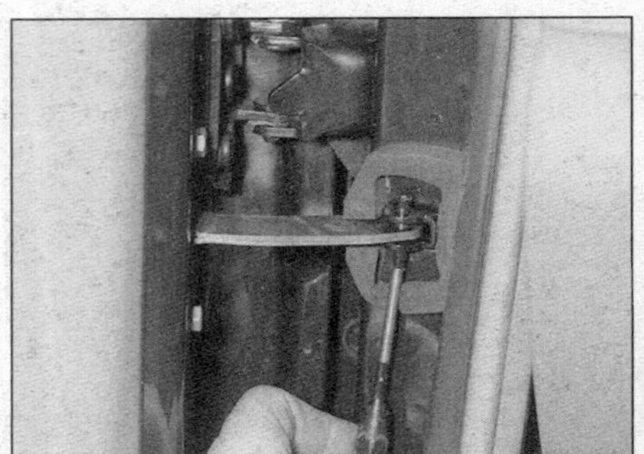

11.4 Using a hammer and punch to tap out the check link roll pin

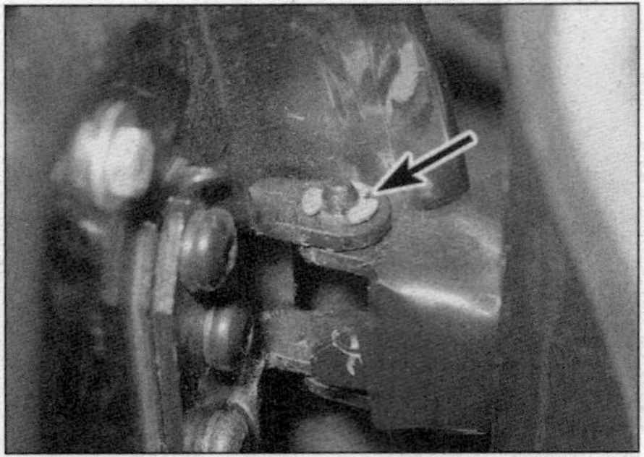

11.5 Remove the C-clip (arrowed) from each hinge, and lift the door upwards and away from the vehicle

11.8a Release the rubber grommet from the door pillar . . .

4 Using a hammer and suitable punch, carefully tap out the roll pin securing the check link to the door pillar **(see illustration)**. Discard the roll pin - a new one should be used on refitting.

5 Prise off the C-clips from each of the hinge pins then, with the aid of an assistant, carefully lift the door upwards and away from the vehicle **(see illustration)**. If the C-clips show signs of distortion, renew them.

6 Examine the hinges for signs of wear or damage. If renewal is necessary, mark the outline of the original hinge on the door/pillar, then slacken and remove the retaining bolts and remove the hinge brackets. Note the correct fitted location of the shim(s) and spacer plates which are positioned behind them. Fit the new brackets, making sure that the shim(s) and spacer plates are correctly arranged, and refit the retaining bolts. Align the brackets with the marks made prior to removal, and securely tighten the retaining bolts.

Rear door

7 Disconnect the battery negative lead.

8 Release the wiring harness rubber grommet from the door pillar, then withdraw the wiring and disconnect its connectors **(see illustrations)**.

9 Slacken and remove the bolts and washers securing the check link to the door pillar.

10 Prise off the C-clips from each of the hinge pins then, with the aid of an assistant, carefully lift the door upwards and away from the vehicle. If the C-clips show signs of distortion, renew them.

11 Inspect the hinges as described above in paragraph 6.

Refitting

Front door

12 Apply a smear of multi-purpose grease to the hinge pivots then, with the aid of an assistant, manoeuvre the door back into position. Secure the door in position by fitting a C-clip to each of the hinge pins.

13 Align the check link with its mounting bracket, and secure it in position with a new roll pin.

14 Feed the wiring back through the pillar, reconnect the wiring connectors, and seat the rubber grommet back in the door pillar.

15 Refit the footwell side panel, and secure it in position.

16 Reconnect the battery and, if necessary, adjust the door position as described below.

Rear door

17 Apply a smear of multi-purpose grease to the hinge pivots then, with the aid of an assistant, manoeuvre the door back into position. Secure the door in position by fitting a C-clip to each of the hinge pins.

18 Reconnect the wiring connectors, feed the wiring back into the door pillar, and seat the wiring grommet in position.

19 Reconnect the battery and, if necessary, adjust the door position as described below.

Adjustment

20 Some vertical adjustment of the doors can be achieved by slackening the hinge retaining bolts and repositioning the hinge/door.

21 Some front-to-rear adjustment of the door position can be achieved by adding/removing shims between the door and hinge bracket. To do this, loosen (do not remove) the hinge retaining bolts, then add/remove the relevant number of shims; the shims are slotted to allow the thickness to be adjusted without removing the door. Once the door is correctly positioned, securely tighten the hinge retaining bolts.

22 Door closure may be adjusted by altering the position of the door lock striker on the body. Slacken the striker, reposition it as required, then securely retighten it. The striker can also be adjusted by adding/removing shims from behind it.

12 Door inner trim panel - removal and refitting

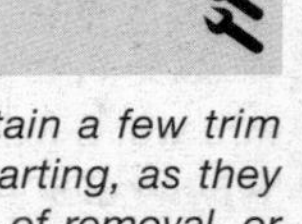

Note: *It is a good idea to obtain a few trim panel retaining clips before starting, as they are often broken in the course of removal, or will be found to have broken during previous removal attempts.*

Removal

Front door

1 Disconnect the battery negative terminal.

2 Undo the retaining screws, and remove the armrest handle from the door **(see illustrations)**.

3 Lift the inner door lock handle, and carefully

11.8b . . . and withdraw the rear door wiring connectors from the pillar

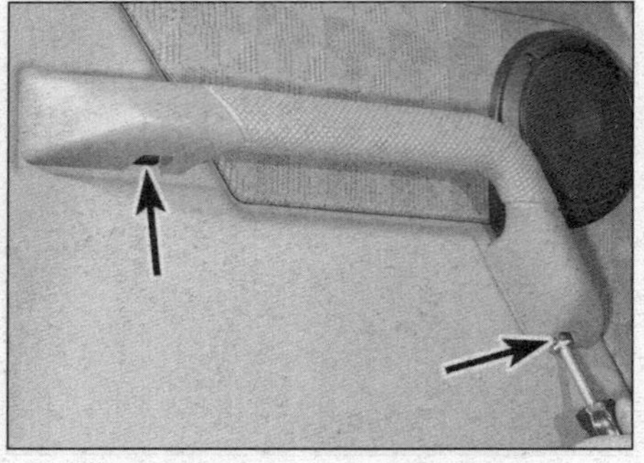

12.2a Undo the two retaining screws (arrowed) . . .

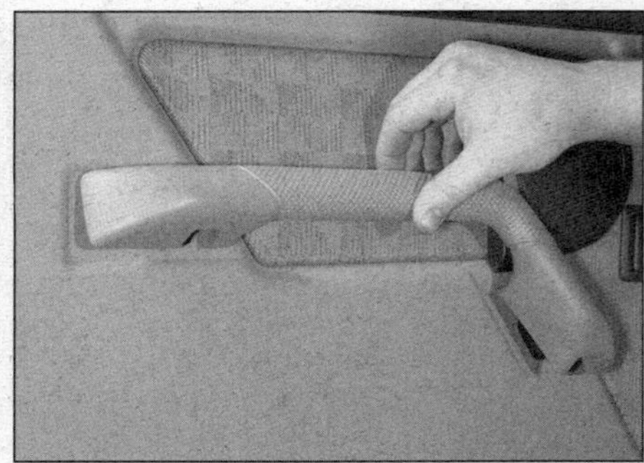

12.2b . . . and remove the armrest handle from the door

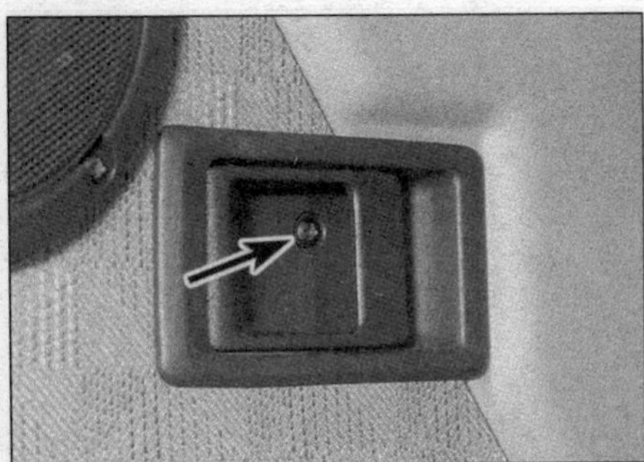

12.3a Undo the retaining screw (arrowed) . . .

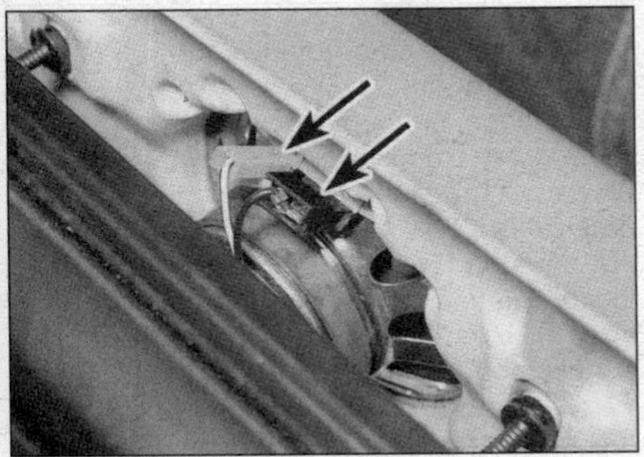

12.5b . . . disconnecting the speaker wiring as it becomes accessible

prise the trim cap out from the handle surround. Undo the retaining screw, and remove the handle surround from the door panel **(see illustrations)**.

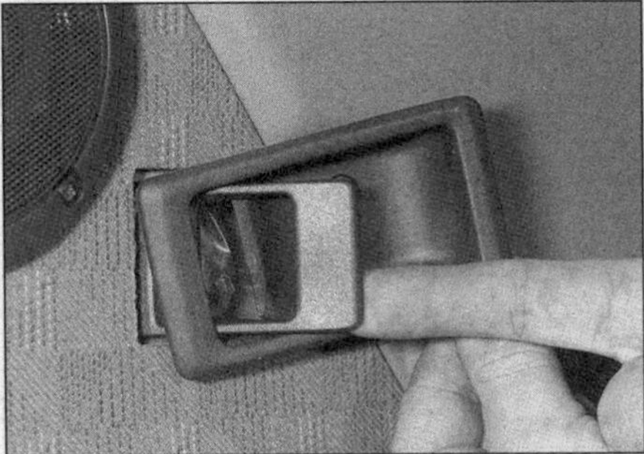

12.3b . . . and unclip the handle surround from the trim panel

4 On models with manual windows, carefully prise the trim cap out from the centre of the regulator handle, then slacken and remove the retaining screw and washer. Remove the handle from the regulator, and recover the handle escutcheon.

5 Release the door trim panel studs, working around the outside of the panel, carefully levering between the panel and door with a suitable flat-bladed screwdriver. When all the studs are released, slide the panel upwards and away from the door, disconnecting the speaker wiring connectors as they become accessible **(see illustrations)**.

Rear door

6 Remove the panel as described above in paragraphs 1 to 6, noting that there is no speaker in the rear door. On models with electric windows, it will be necessary to disconnect the window switch wiring as the panel is removed **(see illustration)**.

12.5a Unclip the trim panel from the door . . .

Refitting

7 Refitting is a reverse of the removal procedure. Prior to refitting, examine the panel retaining clips for signs of damage - renew any broken clips. On refitting, do not forget to align the inner lock button with its guide in the top of the trim panel.

13 Door handle and lock components - removal, refitting and adjustment

Removal

Front door interior handle

1 Remove the door inner trim panel as described in Section 12. Peel the polythene weathershield away from the door to gain access to the door lock components **(see illustration)**.

2 Slacken and remove the screws securing the door handle to the door **(see illustration)**.

3 Working through the cut-out in the door, prise off the metal retaining clip and release the handle link rod from the plastic connector **(see illustration)**.

4 Withdraw the handle and link rod assembly from the door **(see illustration)**.

Front door exterior handle

5 On models with central locking, remove the servo unit as described in Section 17.

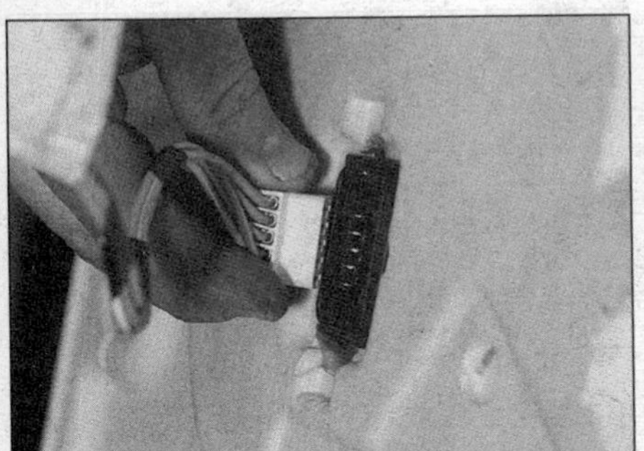

12.6 Disconnecting the rear door window switch wiring connector

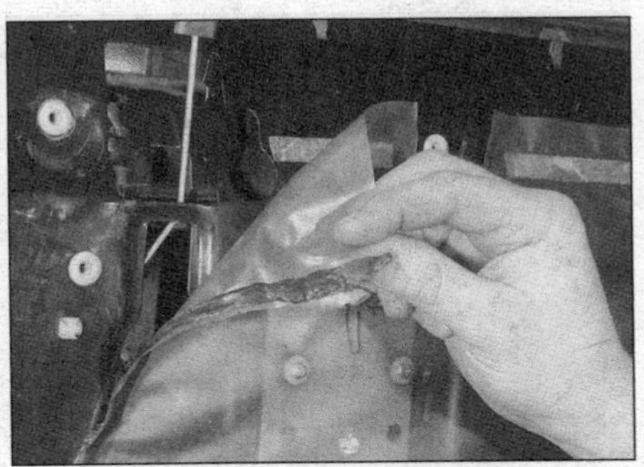

13.1 Peel the polythene weathershield away from the door to gain access to the lock components

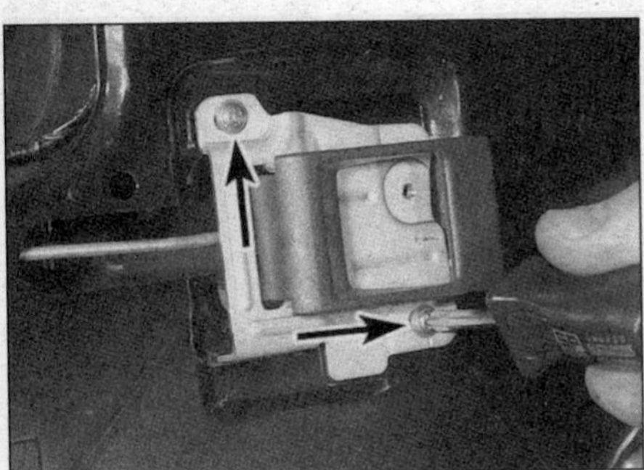

13.2 Undo the retaining screws . . .

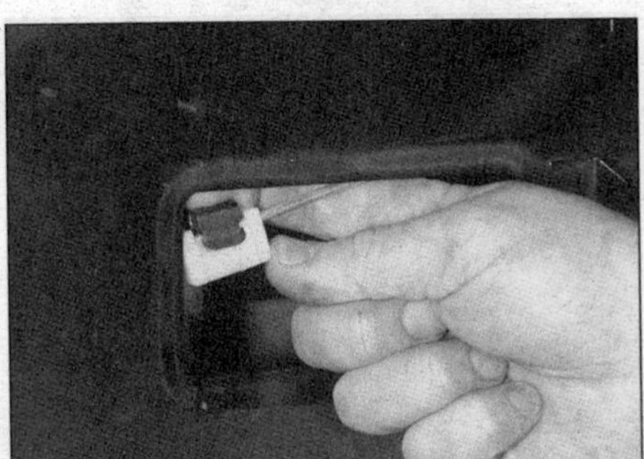

13.3 . . . then detach the link rod from its plastic connector . . .

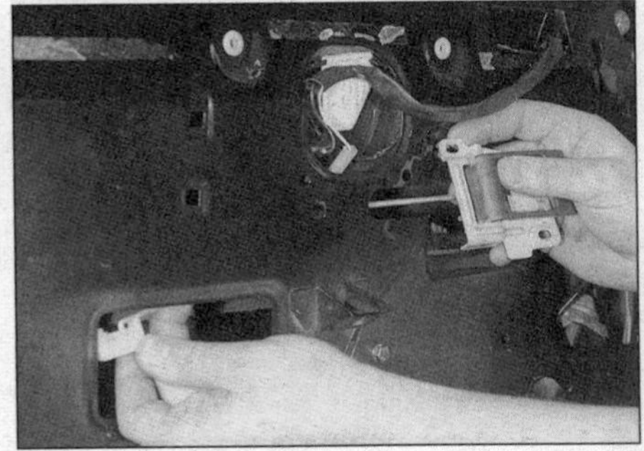

13.4 . . . and remove the interior handle from the door

13.8a Undo the two retaining nuts (arrowed) . . .

13.8b . . . and remove the handle bracket from inside the door

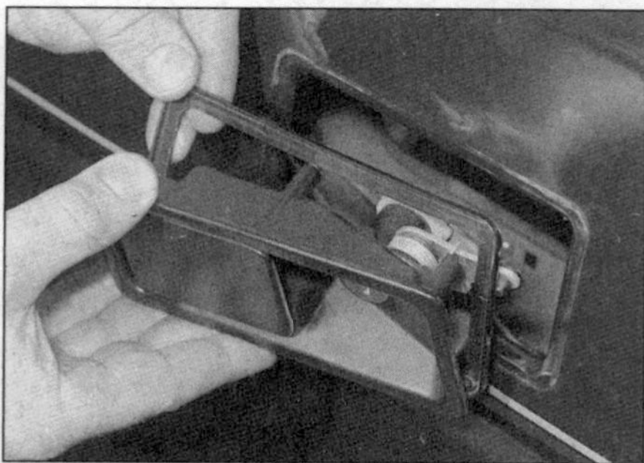
13.8c Remove the exterior handle from the door, and recover the handle seal

6 Release the retaining clips by pivoting them away from the link rods, and free the link rods from the handle.

7 Where necessary, trace the wiring back from the central locking/alarm microswitch, and disconnect it at the wiring connector.

8 Unscrew and remove the two handle retaining nuts and washers, and remove the assembly from the outside of the door. Recover the bracket from inside of the door. Examine the handle seal for signs of damage or deterioration, and renew if necessary **(see illustrations)**.

Front lock cylinder

9 Remove the exterior door handle as described above.

10 Insert the key into the lock cylinder, then prise off the C-clip and washer from the rear of the mounting plate **(see illustration)**. Lift off the link rod bracket and spring, noting their correct fitted locations, and withdraw the lock cylinder.

Front door lock

11 Remove the door inner trim panel as described in Section 12.

12 Remove the door window regulator and glass as described in Section 14.

13 On models with central locking, remove the servo unit as described in Section 17. Push out the pin and free the servo unit pivot, which is situated directly above the lock assembly, from the door **(see illustration)**.

14 Release the retaining clip securing the interior lock button rod to the lock, and withdraw the button from the top of the door **(see illustration)**.

15 Release the retaining clips by pivoting them away from the rods, and detach both exterior handle link rods from the lock **(see illustration)**.

16 Working through the cut-out in the door, lift the metal retaining clip, and release the interior handle link rod from the plastic connector.

17 Undo the three retaining screws, and manoeuvre the lock assembly out of the door **(see illustrations)**.

Rear interior door handle

18 Remove the door inner trim panel as described in Section 12.

19 Peel the polythene weathershield away

13.10 Lock cylinder is retained by a C-clip

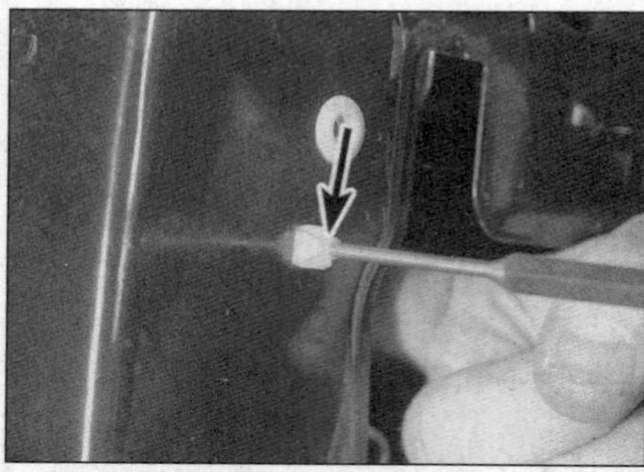
13.13 Push out the pivot pin, and free the servo unit pivot from the door

13.14 Release the retaining clip, and detach the lock button from the lock

13.15 Release the retaining clip (arrowed) and detach the exterior handle link rod from the lock

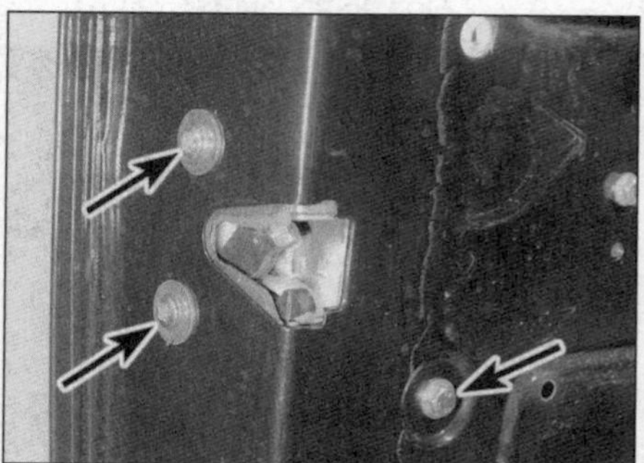
13.17a Undo the three retaining screws (arrowed) . . .

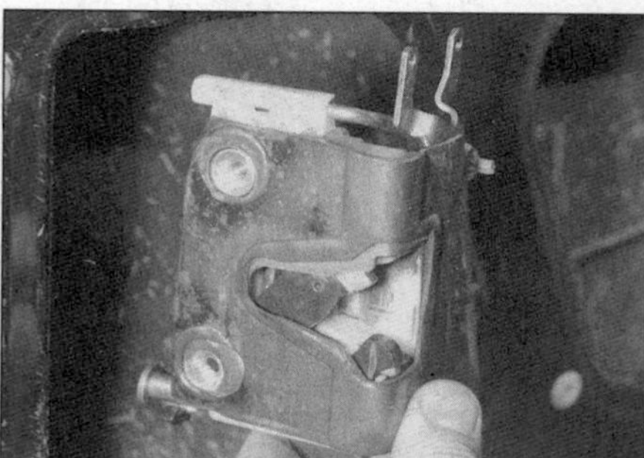
13.17b . . . and withdraw the lock assembly from the door

13.19 Peel the polythene weathershield away from the door, to gain access to the lock components

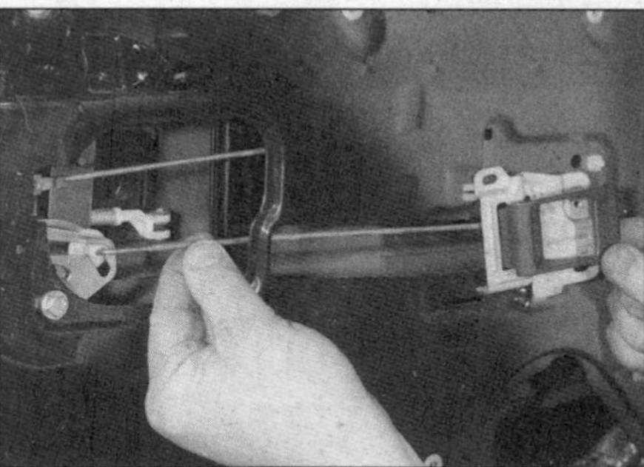
13.20 Detach the link rod from the lock, and remove the interior handle from the rear door

13.24a Undo the two retaining nuts (arrowed) and recover the bracket . . .

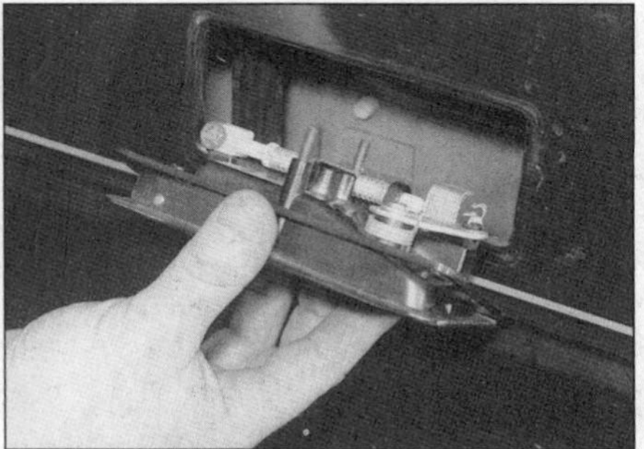
13.24b . . . then remove the exterior handle from the door

from the door, to gain access to the door lock components **(see illustration)**.

20 Detach the link rod from the lock assembly, then undo the retaining screws and withdraw the handle and rod from the door **(see illustration)**.

Rear exterior door handle

21 Remove the door inner trim panel as described in Section 12.

22 Peel the polythene weathershield away from the door to gain access to the door lock components.

23 Release the retaining clip by pivoting it away from the link rod, and detach the rod from the rear of the handle.

24 Unscrew the two handle retaining nuts and washers, and remove the assembly from the outside of the door. Recover the bracket from inside of the door. Examine the handle seal for signs of damage or deterioration, and renew if necessary **(see illustrations)**.

Rear door lock

25 Remove the door inner trim panel as described in Section 12.

26 Peel the polythene weathershield away from the door to gain access to the door lock components.

27 Release the retaining clip by pivoting it away from the link rod, and detach the rod from the rear of the exterior handle.

28 Release the retaining clip, and detach the interior button rod from the lock **(see illustration)**.

29 Release the interior handle link rod from the lock, then undo the three retaining screws and remove the lock assembly from the door **(see illustration)**.

Refitting

30 Refitting is the reverse of the removal sequence, noting the following points:

a) *If a lock cylinder has been removed, on refitting, ensure that the spring and link rod bracket are correctly positioned, and are securely held by the C-clip. Check the operation of the lock cylinder before refitting the handle to the door.*
b) *Ensure that all link rods are securely held in position by their retaining clips.*
c) *Apply grease to all lock and link rod pivot points.*
d) *Before installing the relevant trim panel, thoroughly check the operation of all the door lock handles and, where necessary, the central locking system. If necessary, adjust as described below.*

Adjustment

Front door lock

31 The length of the exterior handle-to-lock link rod can be adjusted by screwing/unscrewing it from the lock assembly. The length of the lock assembly interior handle link rod can be altered by rotating the spring-tensioned nyloc nut which is situated at the lock end of the rod.

Rear door lock

32 The length of the exterior handle-to-lock link rod can be adjusted by screwing/unscrewing it from the lock assembly.

13.28 Detach the link rods . . .

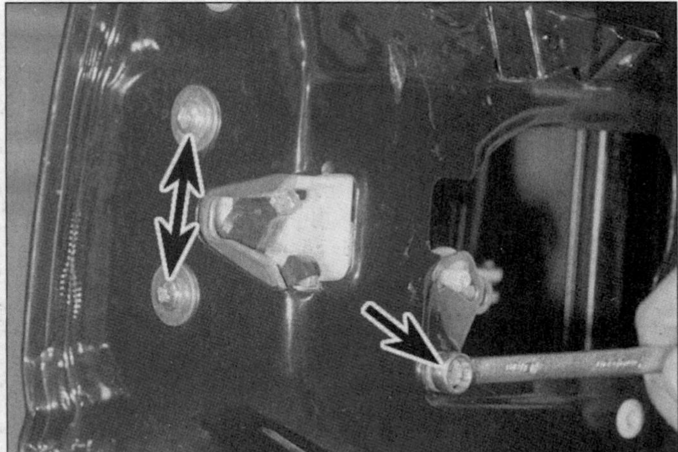
13.29 . . . then undo the three retaining bolts and remove the lock assembly from the door

14.5 Remove the inner and outer sealing strips from the top edge of the door

14.6 Undo the two front retaining bolts (arrowed) . . .

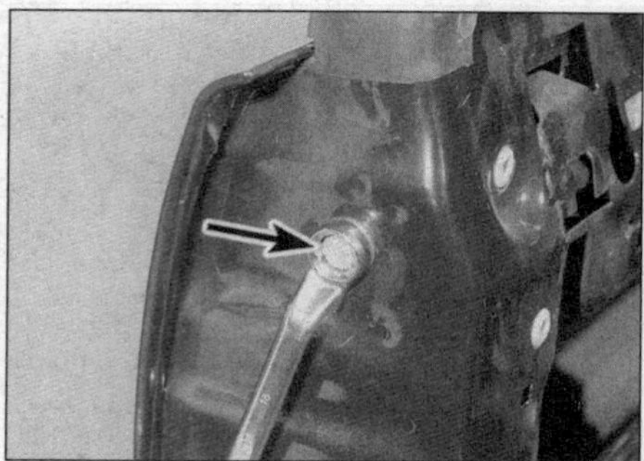
14.7 . . . and the rear upper frame retaining bolt

14 Door window glass and regulator - removal and refitting

Removal

1 Remove the door inner trim panel as described in Section 12.

2 Peel the polythene weathershield away from the door, to gain access to the door lock components. Proceed as described under the relevant sub-heading.

Front door window glass

3 Remove the exterior mirror as described in Section 19.

4 Remove the regulator assembly as described below. On models with central locking, also remove the servo unit as described in Section 17.

5 Remove the inner and outer sealing strips from the top of the door **(see illustration)**.

6 Slacken and remove the window frame front retaining bolts from the front and inner edges of the door **(see illustration)**.

7 Unscrew the window frame rear retaining bolt and washer from the rear edge of the door **(see illustration)**.

8 Slacken and remove two window frame lower retaining screws and washers (one at the front, and one at the back edge of frame) **(see illustration)**.

9 Carefully lift the window frame and glass assembly upwards and away from the door **(see illustration)**.

10 With the assembly on a bench, remove the tape, and separate the glass and frame.

Rear door window glass

11 Remove the regulator assembly as described below.

12 Remove the inner and outer sealing strips from the top of the door **(see illustrations)**.

13 Slacken and remove the bolt and washers securing the shorter side of the window guide to the door, and the two bolts and washers securing the frame to the front edge of the door **(see illustration)**.

14 Undo the two bolts and washers securing the rear of the frame in position **(see illustration)**.

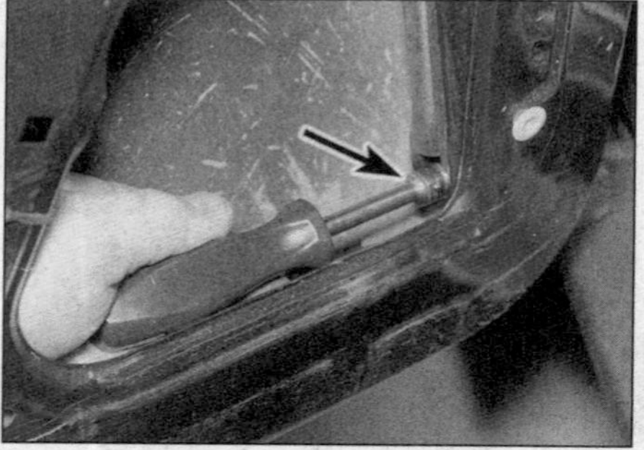
14.8 Undo the window frame lower retaining bolts . . .

14.9 . . . then lift the frame and window glass assembly out from the door

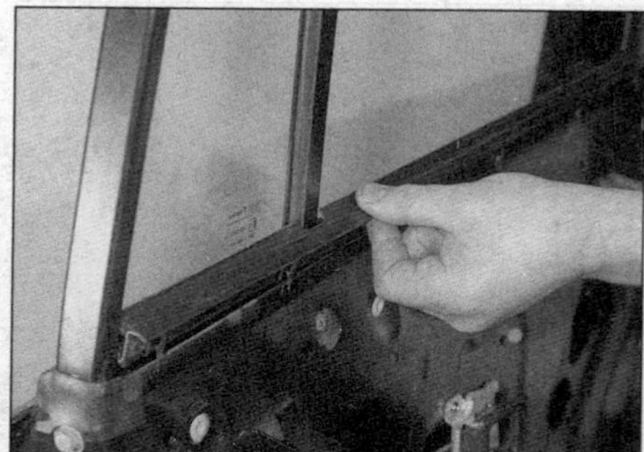
14.12a Remove the inner . . .

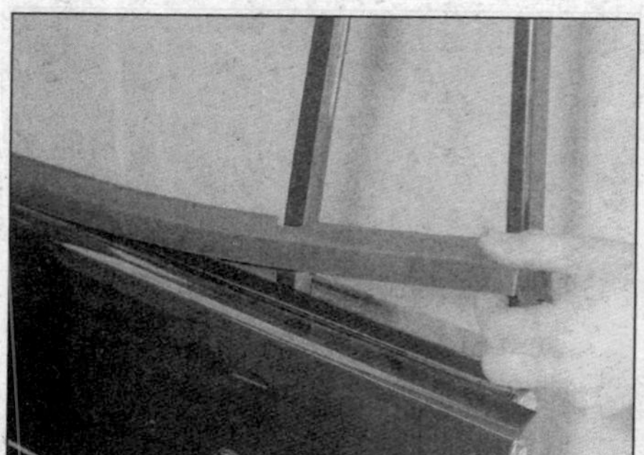
14.12b . . . and outer sealing strips from the top edge of the rear door

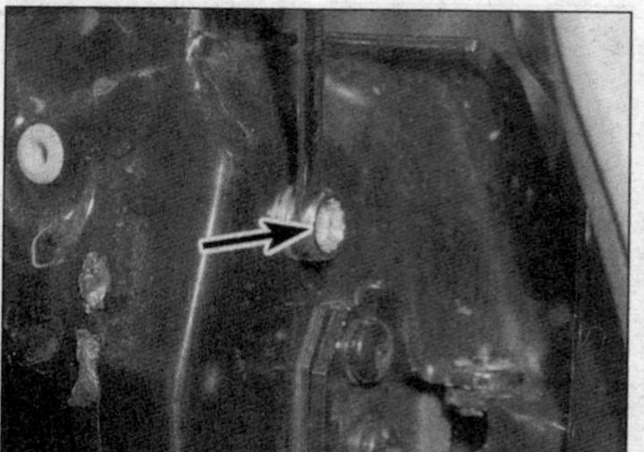
14.13 Undo the front retaining bolt . . .

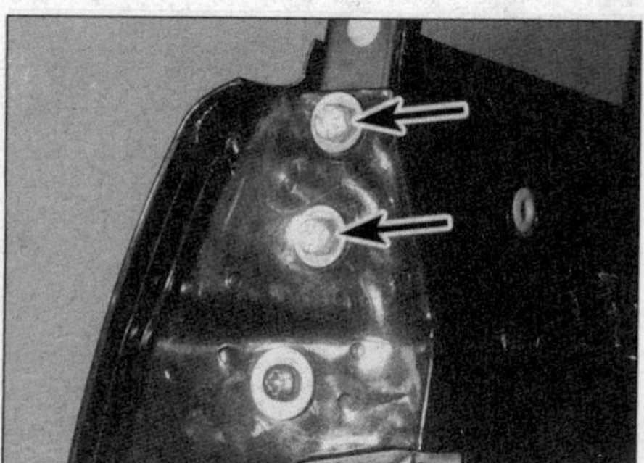
14.14 . . . and the two rear window frame retaining bolts (arrowed) . . .

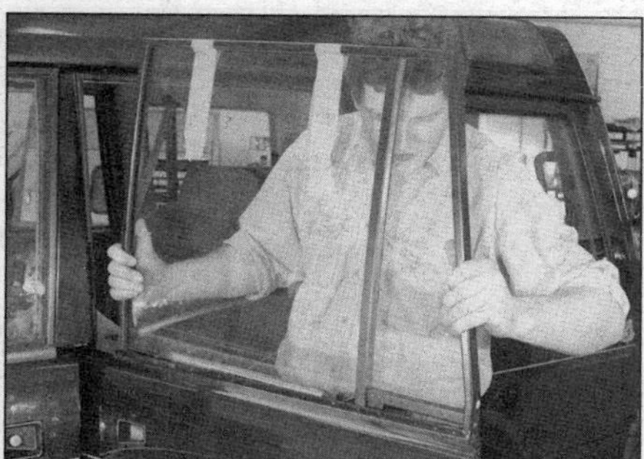
14.15 . . . then lift the window glass and frame out from the rear door

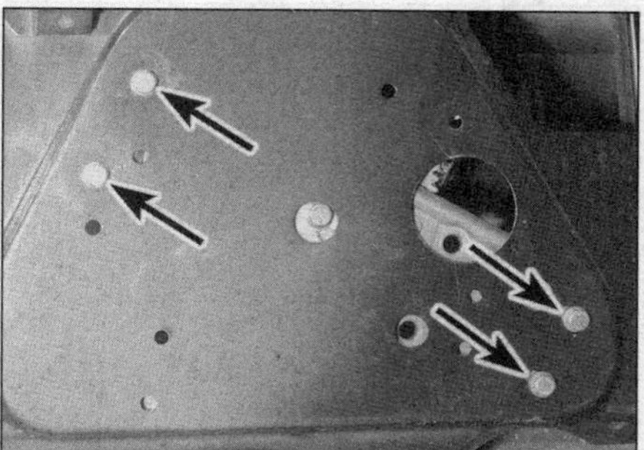
14.19 Undo the four retaining bolts (arrowed) . . .

14.20 . . . and remove the regulator from the front door

15 Carefully lift the window frame and glass assembly upwards and away from the door **(see illustration)**.

16 With the assembly on a bench, remove the tape, and separate the glass and frame.

Front door window regulator

17 Ensure that the window is fully raised, then securely tape the window glass to its frame, to prevent the window dropping when the regulator is removed.

18 On models with electric windows, remove the window lift motor as described in Section 18.

19 Slacken and remove the four screws and washers securing the regulator assembly to the door panel **(see illustration)**.

20 Disengage the regulator arms from the window glass guides, then manoeuvre the regulator out through the door aperture **(see illustration)**.

Rear door window regulator

21 Ensure that the window is fully raised, then securely tape the window glass to its frame, to prevent the window dropping when the regulator is removed.

22 On models with electric windows, remove the window lift motor as described in Section 18.

23 Slacken and remove the four screws and washers securing the regulator assembly to the door panel **(see illustration)**.

24 Disengage the regulator arm from the window glass guides.

25 Manoeuvre the regulator out through the door aperture **(see illustration)**.

Refitting

26 Refitting is the reverse of the removal procedure, noting the following points:

a) *Prior to tightening the window frame retaining bolts and screws, close the door, and check that the frame is correctly aligned with the surrounding body panels. Adjust as necessary, then securely tighten all bolts.*

b) *Refit the weathershield, making sure it is securely stuck to the door, then install the trim panel as described in Section 12.*

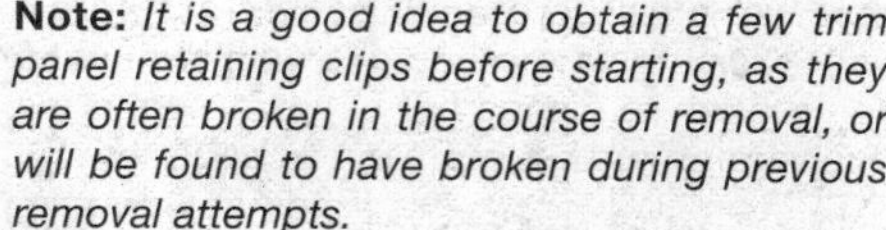

15 Tailgate - removal and refitting

Note: *It is a good idea to obtain a few trim panel retaining clips before starting, as they are often broken in the course of removal, or will be found to have broken during previous removal attempts.*

Removal

1 Disconnect the battery negative terminal, then remove the spare wheel from the tailgate.

2 Undo the two retaining screws, and remove the handle from the inside of the tailgate.

3 Lift the tailgate lock interior handle, and carefully prise the trim cap out from the handle surround. Undo the retaining screw, and remove the handle surround from the trim panel.

4 On later models, remove the tailgate speaker assembly as described in Chapter 13.

5 Release the trim panel studs, working around the outside of the panel, carefully levering between the panel and tailgate with a suitable flat-bladed screwdriver. When all the studs are released, pull the panel away from the tailgate **(see illustration)**.

6 Release the tailgate wiring harness rubber grommet from the pillar, then withdraw the wiring and disconnect its connectors.

7 Remove the circlip and washer securing the check link to the body, and free it from its bracket.

8 Using a suitable marker pen, make alignment marks between the tailgate and hinges.

9 Have an assistant support the tailgate. Undo the four bolts and washers securing the tailgate to its hinges, and remove the tailgate assembly from the vehicle.

10 Examine the tailgate hinges for signs of wear or damage. If renewal is necessary, first mark the outline of the hinge on the pillar. Undo the retaining bolts and remove the hinge, along with any relevant shims which are fitted behind it. Fit the new hinges, along with all the necessary shims, then align them with the marks made prior to removal before securely tighten their retaining bolts.

Refitting

11 Refitting is the reverse of removal, noting the following points:

a) *Locate the tailgate on its hinges, and refit the retaining bolts and washers, tightening them by hand only. Align the marks made prior to removal, then securely tighten the hinge retaining bolts. Reconnect the check link, then close the*

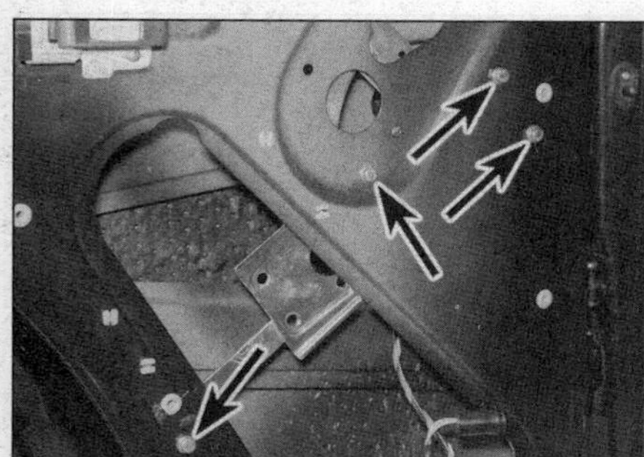
14.23 Undo the four retaining bolts . . .

14.25 . . . and remove the regulator from the rear door

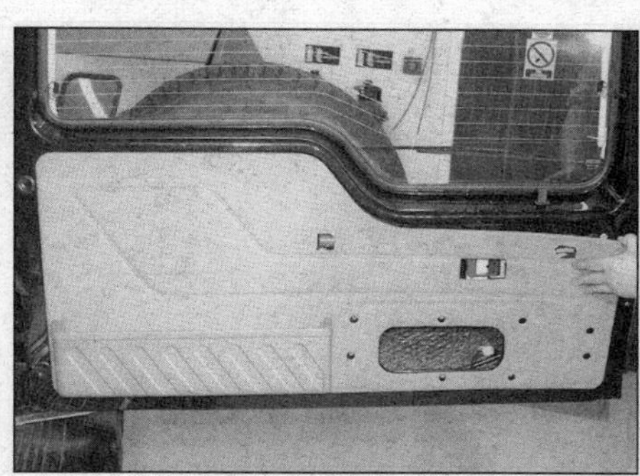
15.5 Removing the tailgate trim panel

16.5 Remove the tailgate interior lock handle

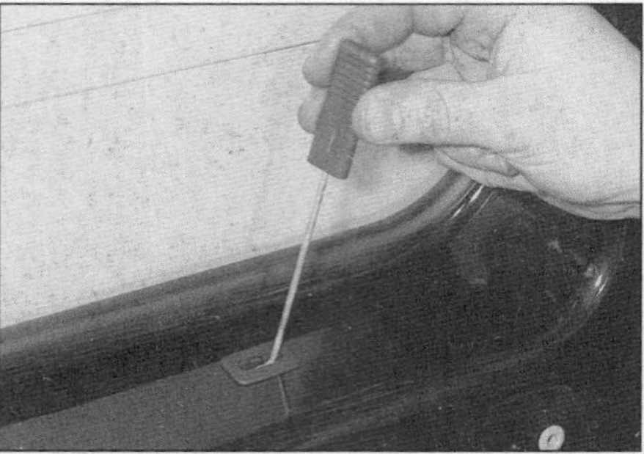
16.7 Detach the retaining clip, and remove the interior lock button from the tailgate

16.8 Release the retaining clips and detach the link rods . . .

tailgate and check for alignment with the surrounding body panels. Slight adjustments can be made by loosening the hinge bolts and repositioning the tailgate.

b) *Check the trim panel retaining clips for signs of damage - renew any broken ones before installing the panel.*

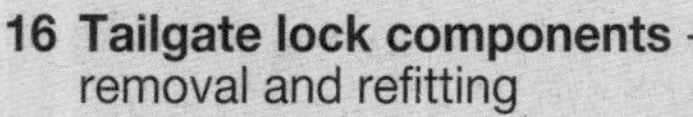

16 Tailgate lock components - removal and refitting

Removal

1 Disconnect the battery negative terminal.
2 Remove the tailgate trim panel as described in paragraphs 2 to 5 of Section 15.
3 Peel the polythene weathershield (where fitted) away from the tailgate, to gain access to the lock components. Proceed as described under the relevant sub-heading.

Interior lock handle

4 Release the retaining clip, and free the handle link rod from the lock assembly.
5 Slacken and remove the retaining screws, and remove the handle and link rod assembly from the door **(see illustration)**.

Lock assembly

Note: *The tailgate lock assembly is complicated. Make a note of how all the link rods and pivots are arranged before disturbing them.*
6 Remove the interior handle as described above.
7 Release the retaining clip by pivoting it away from the link rod, then detach the interior lock button from the lock and remove it from the tailgate **(see illustration)**.
8 Release the retaining clips, and detach the central locking servo unit (where fitted), the exterior handle, and the lock link rods from the inner Y-shaped lock mechanism pivot lever **(see illustration)**.
9 Slacken and remove the screws securing the inner Y-shaped pivot lever mounting bracket in position, then manoeuvre the assembly out from the tailgate. Recover the armrest bracket, noting its correct fitted location **(see illustrations)**.
10 Undo the two retaining screws, and remove the childproof lock actuator from the tailgate **(see illustration)**.
11 Release the retaining clip, and detach the exterior handle lock link rod from the outer Y-shaped pivot lever **(see illustration)**.
12 Withdraw the pivot pin and bush from the outer Y-shaped pivot lever, undo the three retaining screws, then manoeuvre the lock and pivot lever assembly out from the tailgate **(see illustrations)**.

16.9a . . . then undo the retaining screws . . .

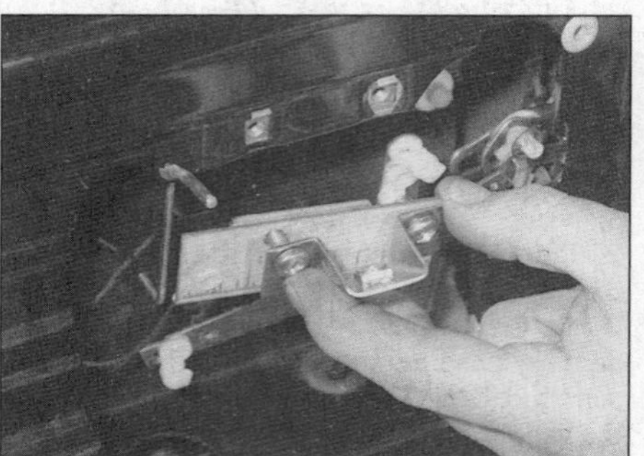
16.9b . . . and remove the inner Y-shaped pivot assembly from the door, complete with the armrest handle bracket

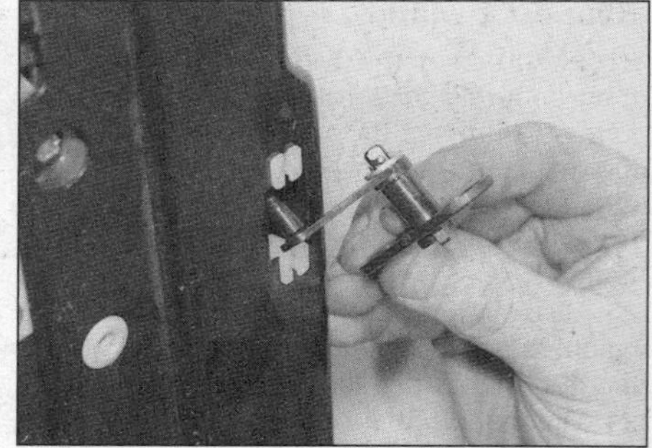
16.10 Undo the two screws, and remove the childproof lock actuator from the tailgate

16.11 Release the retaining clip (arrowed) and detach the link rod . . .

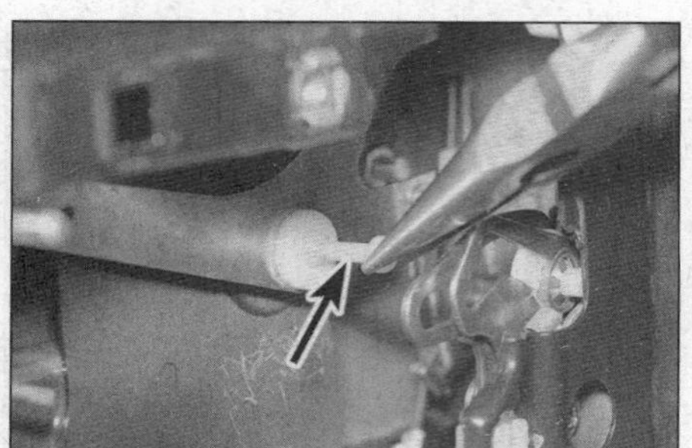
16.12a . . . then pull out the pivot pin securing the outer Y-shaped pivot assembly to the tailgate

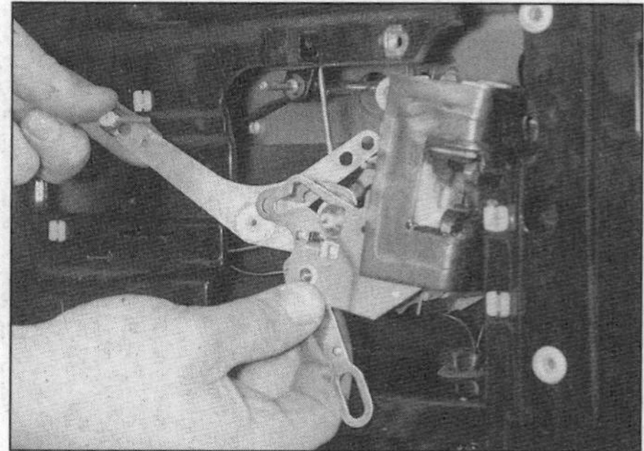
16.12b Undo the retaining bolts, and remove the lock and pivot as an assembly

16.14 Disconnecting the tailgate number plate wiring

16.15a Remove the circlip . . .

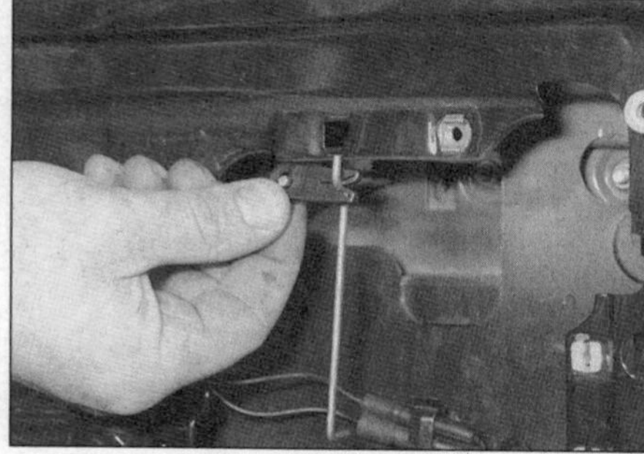
16.15b . . . and detach the link rod and bracket from the lock cylinder

Exterior lock handle

13 Remove the lock assembly as described above.

14 Disconnect the number plate light wiring from the tailgate harness **(see illustration)**.

15 Carefully remove the circlip securing the link rod bracket to the rear of the lock cylinder, and remove the bracket and rod assembly **(see illustrations)**.

16 From inside the tailgate, slacken and remove the nuts and washers securing the lock and number plate light housing in position.

17 From outside the tailgate, carefully prise the badge out from the centre of the number plate light housing, to gain access to the retaining bolt **(see illustrations)**.

18 Remove the number plate light housing from the tailgate, freeing its wiring and sealing grommet from any retaining clips as necessary **(see illustration)**. Inspect the housing seal for signs of wear or damage and renew if necessary.

19 Working inside the tailgate, disconnect the link rod from the exterior lock handle, then slacken and remove its two retaining nuts and washers **(see illustrations)**.

20 Remove the handle from the outside of the tailgate, and recover its seal. Inspect the seal for signs of wear or damage, and renew if necessary.

Lock cylinder

21 Remove the number plate light housing from the tailgate as described above in paragraphs 13 to 18.

22 With the housing on the bench, undo the retaining bolt, and withdraw the cylinder and mounting bracket from the rear of the housing **(see illustrations)**. Recover the O-ring seal.

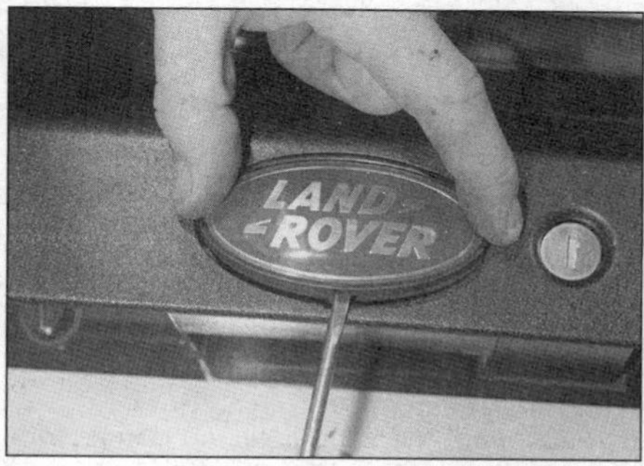
LAND
ROVER
16.17a Prise out the badge from the housing . . .

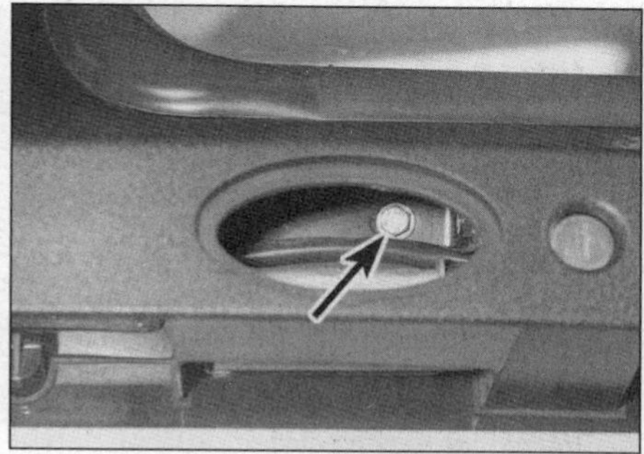
16.17b . . . to gain access to the housing retaining bolt (arrowed)

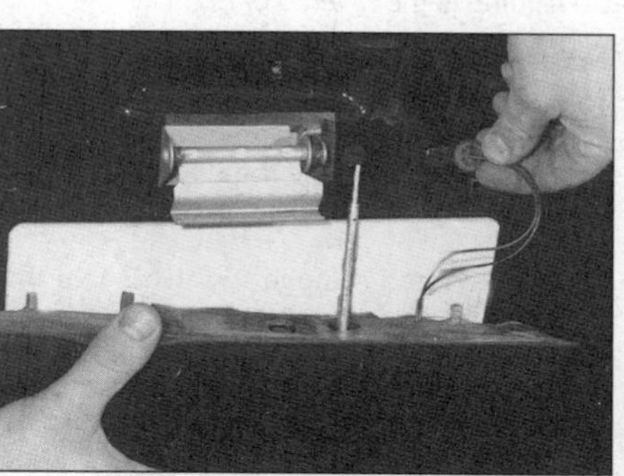
16.18 Removing the number plate light housing from the tailgate

16.19a Undo the two retaining nuts . . .

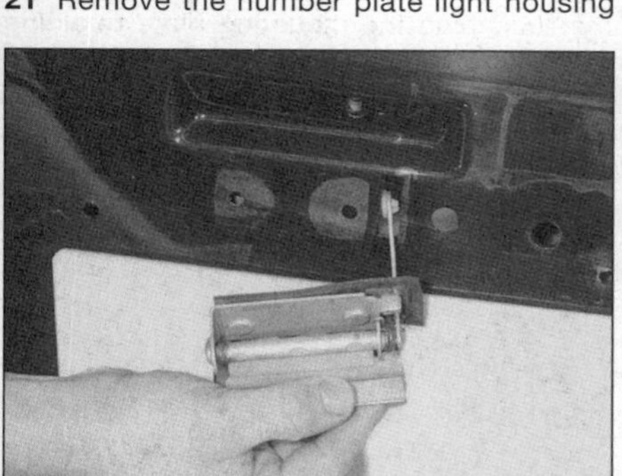
16.19b . . . and remove the handle from the outside of the tailgate

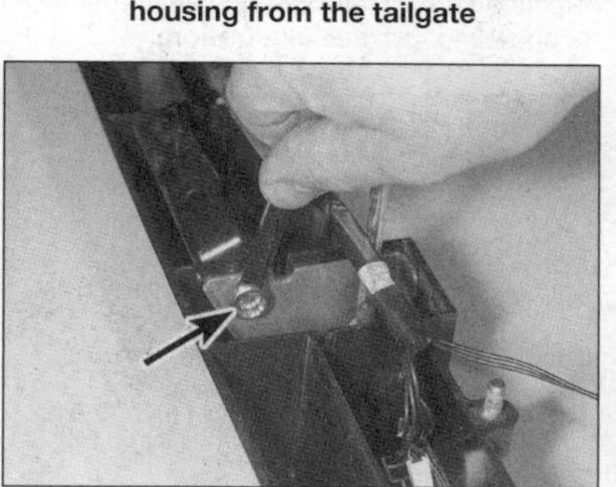
16.22a Undo the retaining bolt, then remove the lock cylinder mounting bracket . . .

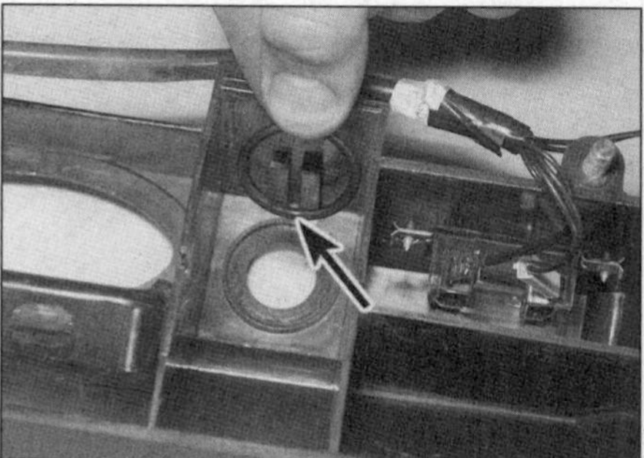
16.22b . . . and recover its O-ring from the number plate housing

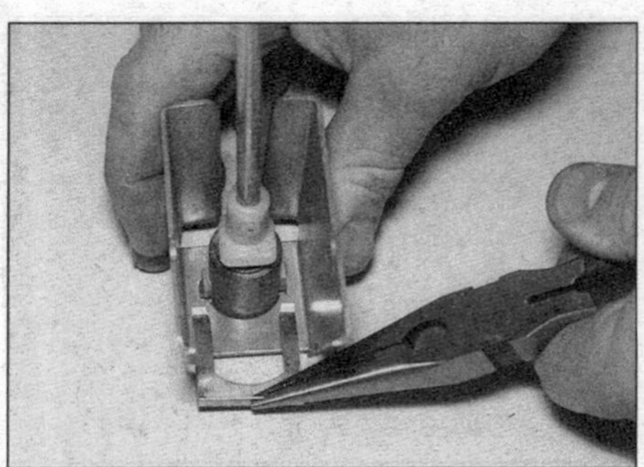
16.23 Slide out the spring clip, and separate the cylinder from its mounting bracket

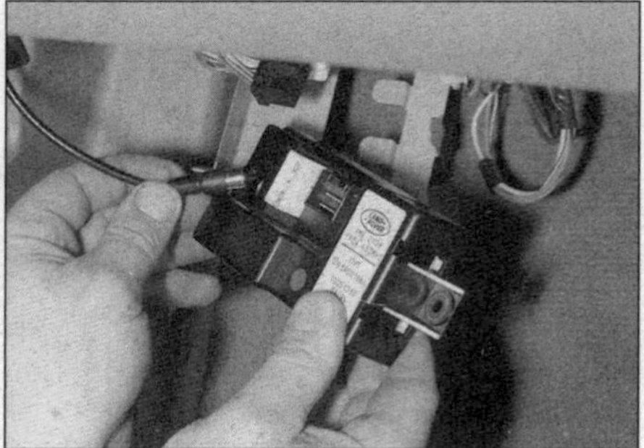
17.8 Removing the central locking control unit - later models

17.12 Undo the upper retaining screws, and remove the armrest handle bracket and retaining plate from the door

23 Slide out the spring clip, separate the lock cylinder from its mounting bracket, and recover the seal **(see illustration)**.

24 Remove the spring clip, and separate the lock cylinder and its operating rod.

Refitting

25 Refitting is the reverse of the relevant removal procedure, noting the following:

a) *Ensure that all link rods are securely held in position by their retaining clips.*

b) *Apply grease to all lock and link rod pivot points.*

c) *Before installing the relevant trim panel, thoroughly check the operation of all the door lock handles and, where necessary, the central locking system.*

17 Central locking components - removal and refitting

Electronic control unit

Note: *On models with a factory-fitted alarm, the electronic control unit also controls the alarm system.*

Early models (pre-March 1994)

1 The control unit is situated behind the driver's footwell side trim panel. Prior to removal, disconnect the battery negative terminal.

2 To gain access to the unit, release the rubber seal from the lower edge of the door pillar, then release the two fasteners securing the footwell side trim panel in position, and remove the panel from the vehicle.

3 Disconnect the wiring connectors from the control unit, then undo the retaining nut and remove the unit from the vehicle.

4 Refitting is the reverse of removal.

Later models (March 1994 onwards)

5 The control unit is located beneath the passenger side of the facia. Prior to removal, disconnect the battery negative terminal.

6 Release the fasteners and remove the lower cover from the passenger side of the facia.

7 Undo the nut securing the relay bracket to the facia, and lower the bracket down into the footwell.

8 Disconnect the various wiring connectors, then undo the retaining nuts and remove the control unit **(see illustration)**.

9 Refitting is the reverse of removal.

Front door servo unit

10 Remove the door trim panel as described in Section 12.

11 Peel the polythene weathershield away from the door, to gain access to the servo unit.

12 Slacken and remove the two servo unit mounting bracket upper retaining screws, and recover the door handle mounting bracket from the outside of the door **(see illustration)**. Also recover the caged nut retaining plate from inside the door.

13 Slacken and remove the two lower retaining screws, and free the servo unit from its operating rod **(see illustration)**.

14 Withdraw the servo unit and mounting plate from the door, disconnecting its wiring connector as it becomes accessible **(see illustration)**.

15 If necessary, undo the retaining screws, and separate the servo unit from its mounting bracket.

16 Refitting is the reverse of removal. Prior to refitting the door trim panel, reconnect the battery and check the operation of the servo unit. If necessary, adjustments can be made by slackening the mounting plate retaining screws and repositioning the plate as required.

Rear door servo unit

17 Remove the door trim panel as described in Section 12.

18 Peel the polythene weathershield away from the door, to gain access to the servo unit.

19 Slacken and remove the four servo unit mounting bracket retaining screws **(see illustration)**.

20 Free the servo unit from its link rod, then withdraw it from the door, disconnecting its wiring connector as it becomes accessible.

21 If necessary, undo the retaining screws and separate the servo unit from its mounting bracket.

22 Refitting is the reverse of removal. Prior to refitting the door trim panel, reconnect the battery and check the operation of the servo unit. If necessary, adjustments can be made by slackening the mounting plate retaining

17.13 Detach the servo unit from its link rod . . .

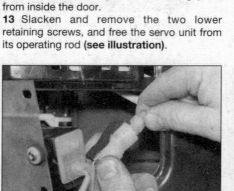

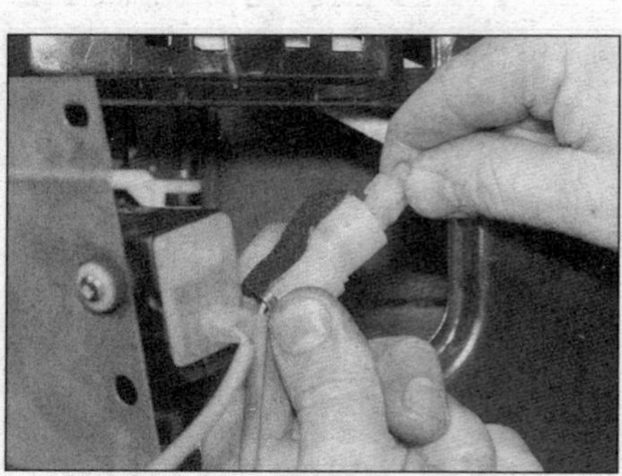
17.14 . . . and disconnect its wiring connector

17.19 Removing a rear door servo unit

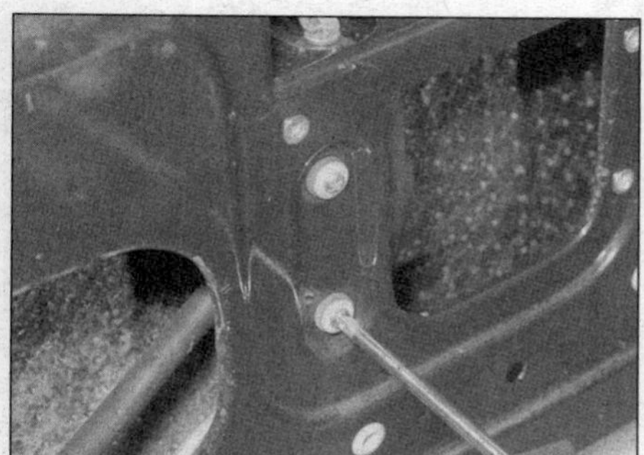

17.26a Undo the two retaining screws . . .

screws and repositioning the plate as required.

Tailgate servo unit

23 Remove the tailgate inner trim panel as described in paragraphs 2 to 5 of Section 15.

24 Peel the polythene weathershield away from the door, to gain access to the servo unit.

25 Trace the wiring back from the servo unit, and disconnect it at the connector.

26 Undo the two retaining screws, then free the servo unit from its link rod and remove it from the door **(see illustrations)**.

27 Refitting is the reverse of removal. Prior to refitting the door trim panel, reconnect the battery and check the operation of the servo unit.

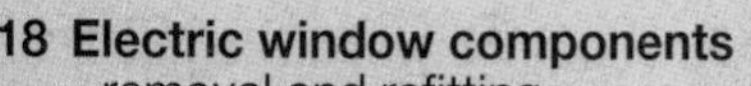

18 Electric window components - removal and refitting

Window switches

1 Refer to Chapter 13.

Window lift motor

2 Remove the door inner trim panel as described in Section 12.

3 Peel the polythene weathershield away from the door, to gain access to the motor. On the rear door, where necessary, remove the central locking servo unit as described in Section 17.

4 Ensure that the window glass is fully raised, and secure it in position by taping it to the window frame.

5 Trace the wiring back from the motor, and disconnect it at the wiring connectors **(see illustration)**.

6 Support the motor, then slacken and remove its three retaining bolts and manoeuvre the motor assembly out from the door panel **(see illustrations)**.

7 Refitting is the reverse of removal, ensuring that the motor gear is correctly engaged with the regulator mechanism. Check the operation of the motor before refitting the trim panel to the door.

17.26b . . . then free the servo unit from its link rod, and withdraw it from the tailgate

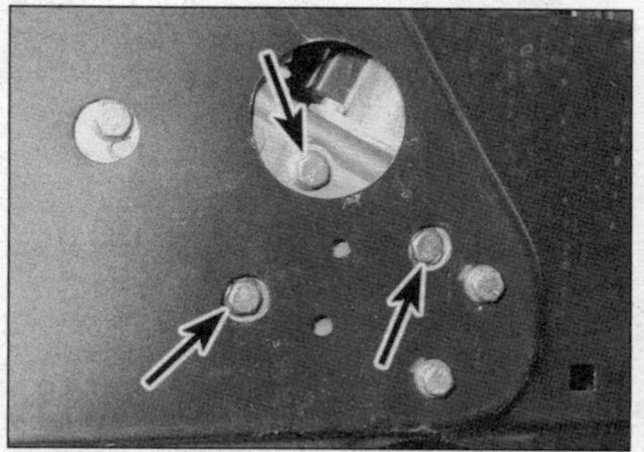

18.6a . . . then undo the three retaining bolts (arrowed) . . .

Electronic control unit - later models (March 1994 onwards) only

8 The control unit is located behind the glovebox. Prior to removal, disconnect the battery negative terminal.

9 Open up the glovebox, and release its hinge springs to allow the box to be fully opened. To improve access, release the clips and remove the lower cover from the facia.

10 Disconnect the wiring connectors and undo the two nuts securing the control unit mounting bracket to the bulkhead **(see illustration)**.

11 Manoeuvre the bracket assembly out of position, then undo the three retaining nuts and separate the control unit from the bracket **(see illustration)**.

12 Refitting is the reverse of removal.

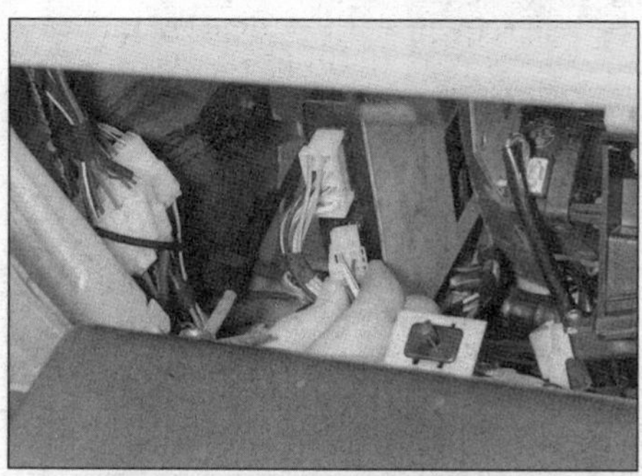

18.10 Disconnect the wiring connectors, then undo the retaining bolts and remove the window lift control unit from underneath the facia

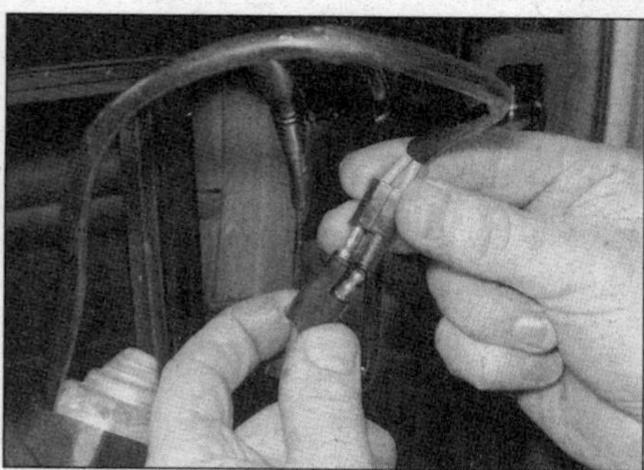

18.5 Disconnect the window lift motor wiring connector . . .

18.6b . . . and remove the motor from the door (front door shown)

19 Exterior mirrors and associated components - removal and refitting

Manually-operated mirror

1 Pull off the knob from the mirror adjusting lever.

2 Carefully unclip the mirror inner trim panel from the door.

3 Support the mirror assembly, then undo the three retaining screws and washers. Remove

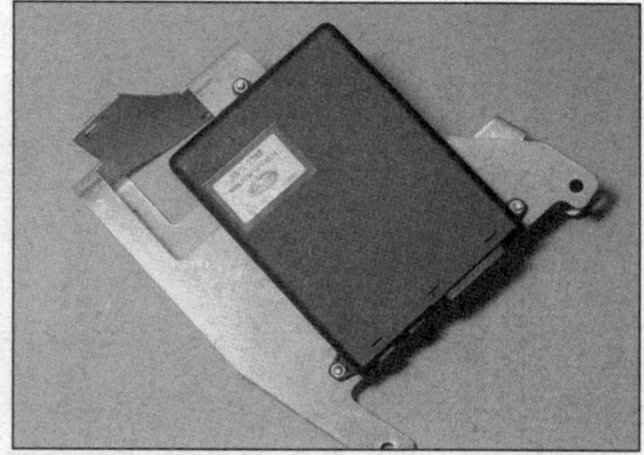

18.11 Window lift control unit is secured to its bracket by three nuts

19.6 Unclip the inner trim panel . . .

19.7 . . . and disconnect the mirror wiring connector

19.8 Undo the retaining bolts, and recover the mounting plate (arrowed) . . .

the mounting plate from the inner edge of the door, and recover its retaining clips.

4 Remove the mirror assembly from the door, along with its sealing rubber.

5 Refitting is the reverse of removal. If the mirror seal shows signs of damage or deterioration, renew it.

Electrically-operated mirror

6 Carefully unclip the mirror inner trim panel from the door **(see illustration)**.

7 Disconnect the mirror wiring connector(s) **(see illustration)**.

8 Support the mirror assembly, then undo the three retaining screws and washers **(see illustration)**. Remove the mounting plate from the inner edge of the door, and recover its retaining clips.

9 Remove the mirror assembly from the door, along with its sealing rubber **(see illustration)**.

10 Refitting is the reverse of removal, using a new mirror seal if the original shows signs of damage or deterioration. Take care to ensure that the wiring is not trapped as the interior trim panel is refitted.

19.9 . . . then remove the mirror from the door

Mirror glass

Caution: If the glass is broken, wear sturdy gloves. Even if the glass is not broken, wearing gloves is a sensible precaution, should the glass break as it is being removed or refitted.

11 Position the glass so its inner edge is fully in, then carefully ease your fingers in behind the outer edge of the glass, and gently pull the glass outwards until it is released from its retaining clips **(see illustration)**. Take great care when removing the glass; do not use excessive force, as the glass is easily broken.

12 Remove the glass from the mirror. On models with electric mirrors, disconnect the wiring connectors from the mirror heating element as they become accessible **(see illustration)**.

13 On refitting, reconnect the wiring connectors (where necessary). Carefully clip the glass back into position, ensuring that it is securely retained by each of the clips.

Mirror motor - electrically-operated mirror

14 Remove the mirror glass as described above.

15 Undo the retaining screws and remove the motor assembly, disconnecting its wiring connectors as they become accessible **(see illustration)**.

16 Refitting is the reverse of removal.

Mirror switch - electrically-operated mirror

17 Refer to Chapter 13.

20 Windscreen, tailgate and fixed windows - general information

These areas of glass are secured by the tight fit of the weatherstrip in the body aperture, and are bonded in position with a special adhesive. The removal and refitting of these areas of fixed glass is difficult, messy and time-consuming task, which is considered beyond the scope of the home mechanic. It is difficult, unless one has plenty of practice, to obtain a secure, waterproof fit. Furthermore, the task carries a high risk of breakage; this applies especially to the laminated glass windscreen. In view of this, owners are strongly advised to have this sort of work carried out by one of the many specialist windscreen fitters.

21 Opening rear passenger windows (3-door models) - removal and refitting

Removal

Window glass

1 Slacken and remove the screws securing the window catch to the body, and detach the catch.

19.11 Remove the mirror glass as described in text . . .

19.12 . . . disconnecting its wiring connectors as they become accessible

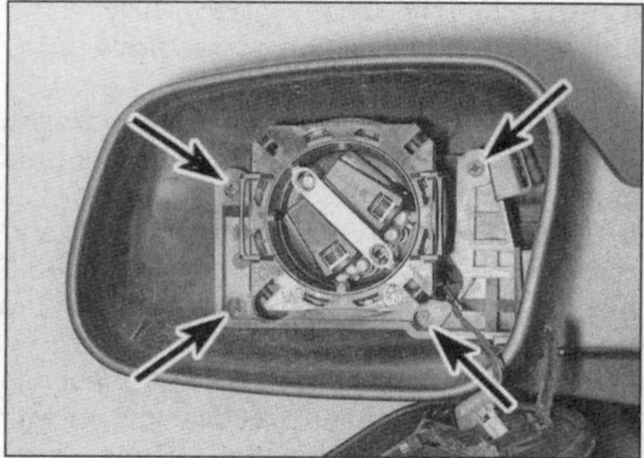
19.15 Electric mirror retaining screws (arrowed)

2 Remove the trim caps from the hinges, then have an assistant support the window.

3 Slacken and remove the window retaining screws and washers, noting each washer's correct fitted location, and remove the window glass from the vehicle.

Window hinge

4 Remove the window glass as described above.

5 Undo the two retaining screws, and remove the passenger grab handle from the door pillar.

6 Unclip the trim cover from the seat belt upper mounting point, then unscrew the retaining nut/bolt (as applicable) and free the belt from its mounting. Recover the flanged spacer and washers which are fitted to the rear of the belt anchorage, noting their correct fitted locations.

7 Ease the trim panel away from the pillar, then undo the hinge retaining screw, and withdraw the hinge and its washers.

Refitting

Window glass

8 Refitting is the reverse of removal, making sure that the washers are correctly positioned on either side of the window glass. Do not overtighten the glass retaining screws, as there is a risk of cracking the glass.

Window hinge

9 Refitting is the reverse of removal, tightening the seat belt retaining nut to the specified torque setting.

22 Sunroof - general information

On early models (pre-March 1994), a simple tilt-only sunroof was offered as an optional extra on most models, and fitted as standard equipment to some models.

On later models (March 1994 onwards), twin tilt/sliding sunroofs were fitted as standard to some models, and offered as an optional extra on others. The sunroof(s) is/are either manually or electrically-operated.

Due to the complexity of the tilt/slide sunroof mechanism, considerable expertise is needed to repair, replace or adjust the sunroof components successfully. Removal of the sunroof first requires the headlining to be removed, which is a complex and tedious operation in itself, and not a task to be undertaken lightly (see Section 26). Therefore, any problems with the sunroof should be referred to a Land Rover dealer.

On models with an electric sunroof, if the sunroof motor fails to operate, first check the relevant fuse. The motor incorporates an automatic cut-out facility, which cuts the motor if the sunroof encounters an obstruction - the motor may therefore cut-out if the mechanism is partially seized (see the relevant part of Chapter 1). If the fault cannot be traced and rectified, the sunroof can be opened and closed manually using a suitable Allen key to turn the motor spindle. To gain access to the motor spindle, carefully prise out the trim cover situated at the rear of the sunroof. Insert the Allen key in the motor spindle, and rotate the key to move the sunroof to the required position. A suitable key was supplied with the vehicle, and should be found in the glovebox.

23 Body exterior fittings - removal and refitting

Wheel arch liners and body under-panels

1 The various plastic covers fitted to the underside of the vehicle are secured in position by a mixture of screws, nuts and retaining clips. Removal will be fairly obvious on inspection. Work methodically around the panel, removing its retaining screws and releasing its retaining clips until the panel is free and can be removed from the underside of the vehicle. Most clips used on the vehicle, with the exception of the fasteners which are used to secure the sill finishers in position, are simply prised out of position. The sill finisher clips are release by pressing out their centre pins and then removing the outer section of the clip; new clips will be required on refitting if the centre pins are not recovered.

2 On refitting, renew any retaining clips that may have been broken on removal, and ensure that the panel is securely retained by all the relevant clips, nuts and screws.

Body trim strips and badges

3 Most of the various body trim strips and badges are held in position with a special adhesive tape. Removal requires the trim/badge to be heated, to soften the adhesive, and then cut away from the surface. Due to the high risk of damage to the vehicle's paintwork during this operation, it is recommended that this task should be entrusted to a Land Rover dealer.

24 Seats - removal and refitting

Removal

Front seat - 3-door models

1 Slide the seat fully rearwards, then slacken and remove the rear bolts securing the seat to its base.

2 Slide the seat fully forwards, then undo the front bolts securing the seat to its base, and remove the seat from the vehicle.

Warning: Whilst the seat is removed, take great care not to operate the seat tilting mechanism, as this could cause personal injury.

3 To remove the seat base assembly, release the tilt mechanism, and carefully relieve the spring pressure. Undo the rear retaining bolts, then return the tilt mechanism to the upright position. Slacken and remove the front retaining bolts, and remove the seat base assembly from the vehicle, bearing in mind the warning above.

Front seat - 5-door models

4 Prise out the three retaining clips, then carefully unclip the trim panel from the side of the seat; remove the panel from the vehicle.

5 Slide the seat fully rearwards, then slacken and remove the bolts securing the front of the seat base to the floor. Where necessary, recover the nut(s) from underneath the vehicle.

6 Slide the seat fully forwards, then undo the nut and bolts (or the two Torx bolts) securing the rear of the seat base to the floor.

7 On models with heated or electrically-operated seats, disconnect the battery negative lead. Locate and disconnect the wiring plugs from under the rear of the seat, noting their locations for refitting.

8 On models from 1996 onwards, unscrew and remove the large Torx bolt securing the seat belt lower mounting to the seat.

9 Lift the seat assembly out of the vehicle. Where necessary, recover the nut(s) from underneath the vehicle.

Rear seat

10 Release the seat belt(s) from the seat, then slacken and remove the front retaining bolts securing the seat to the floor.

11 Fold the seat forwards, then slacken and remove the seat rear retaining bolts and manoeuvre the rear seat out from the vehicle.

12 If necessary, unscrew the retaining bolts securing the seat back to the cushion, and separate the two.

Luggage compartment seats

13 Open the seat up, and release the seat belt from the seat. Slacken and remove the two seat upper retaining screws **(see illustration)**.

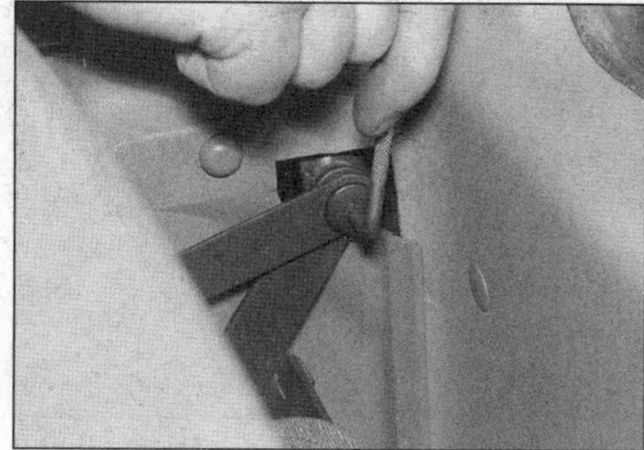

24.13 Undo the upper retaining screws . . .

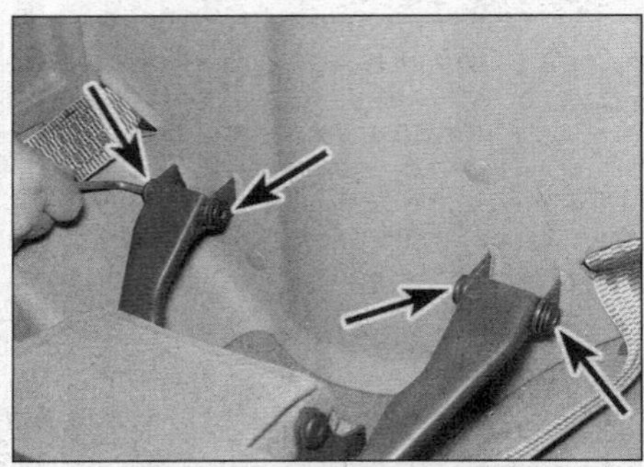

24.14 . . . then undo the four lower retaining screws and remove the seat from the luggage compartment

14 Fold the seat down, then unscrew the four lower retaining bolts and remove the seat assembly from the vehicle **(see illustration)**.

Refitting

15 Refitting is a reversal of the relevant removal procedure. Make sure that all seat mountings are securely tightened.

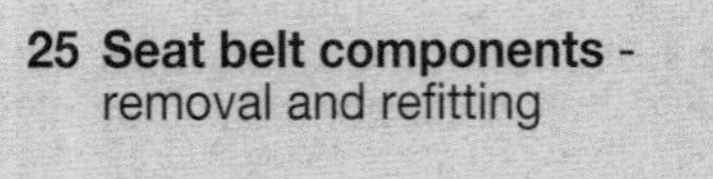

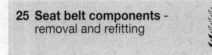

25 Seat belt components - removal and refitting

Removal

Front seat belt

1 Unclip the trim cover from the seat belt upper mounting point, then unscrew the retaining nut/bolt (as applicable) and free the belt from its mounting. Recover the flanged spacer and washers which are fitted to the rear of the belt anchorage, noting their correct fitted locations **(see illustrations)**.

2 On models up to 1996, prise off the trim cap from the seat belt lower mounting, then slacken and remove the lower mounting bolt. Recover the washers and spacer fitted between the seat belt anchorage and floor, noting their correct fitted locations **(see illustration)**.

3 On models with electric front seats, prise out the three plastic retaining studs and remove the side trim panel from the seat.

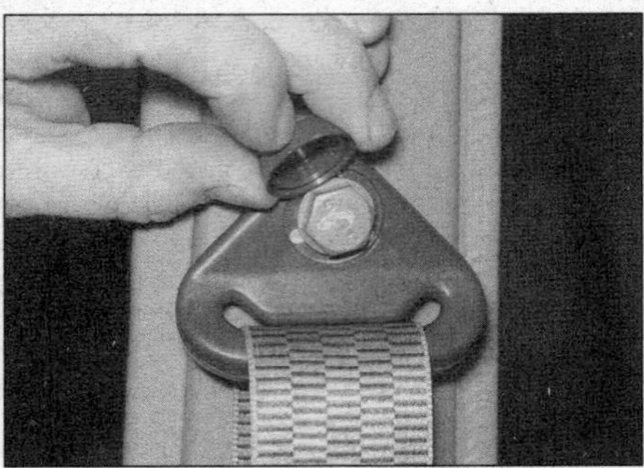

25.1a Remove the trim cover from the upper mounting . . .

25.1b . . . then undo the retaining bolt, and recover the spacer which is fitted between the seat belt and pillar

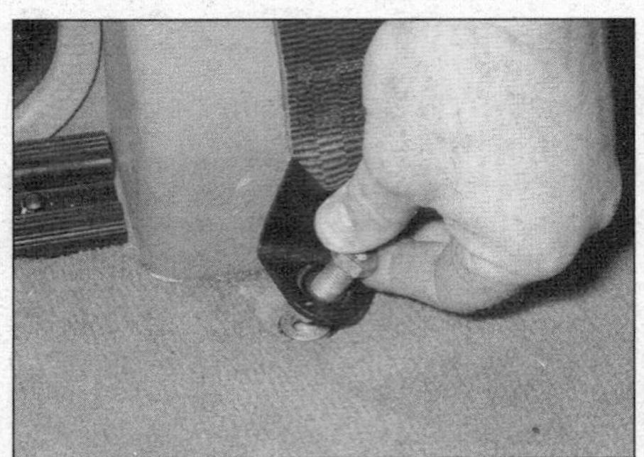

25.2 Slacken and remove the lower mounting bolt, and recover the spacer fitted between the belt and floor

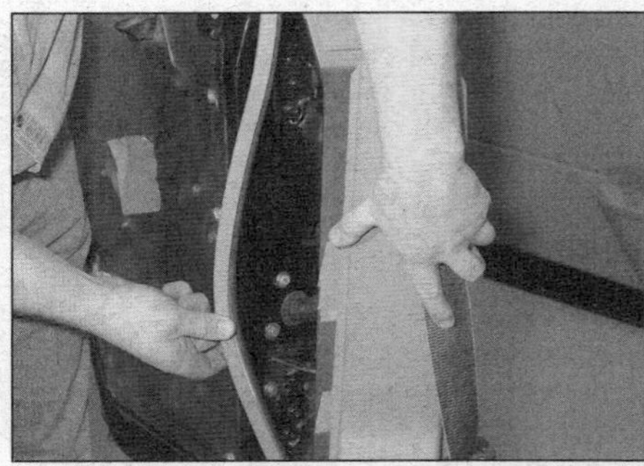

25.5 Release the sealing strips from either side of the door pillar, then unclip the lower trim panel

4 On models from 1996 onwards, remove the large Torx bolt securing the seat belt lower mounting to the seat.

5 Release the sealing strips from each side of the door pillar lower trim panel. Carefully unclip the panel, release it from the seat belt, and remove it from the vehicle **(see illustration)**.

6 Unscrew the bolt securing the inertia reel to the door pillar, and remove the seat belt from the vehicle **(see illustration)**.

Front seat belt stalk

7 Prise off the trim cap, then slacken and remove the stalk mounting bolt. Remove the stalk and recover the washers and spacer, noting their correct fitted location.

Rear seat side belt

8 Remove the rear side seat (where fitted) as described in Section 24.

9 Undo the retaining screws, remove the speaker/speaker grille from the trim panel, then remove panel itself **(see illustration)**.

10 Unclip the load space cover, then undo the two screws and remove the cover pivot from the top of the trim panel. Remove the rear light access cover, then prise out the relevant trim clips, undo the relevant screws, and remove the luggage compartment side trim cover from the vehicle **(see illustrations)**.

11 Unclip the trim cover from the seat belt upper mounting point, then unscrew the

25.6 Undo the inertia reel retaining bolt, and remove the front seat belt from the vehicle

25.9 Removing the speaker trim panel

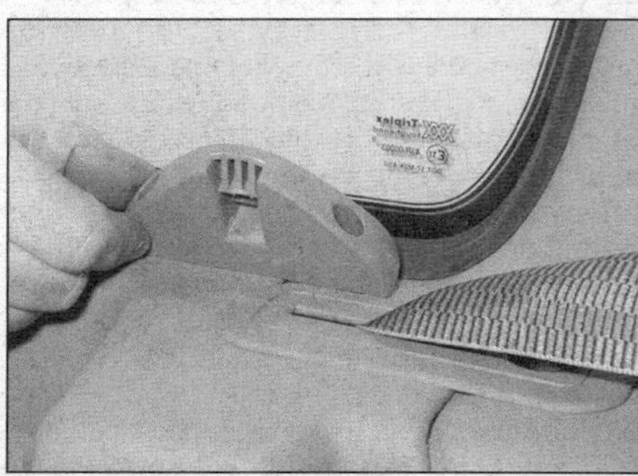

25.10a Remove the load space cover pivot from the top of the trim panel . . .

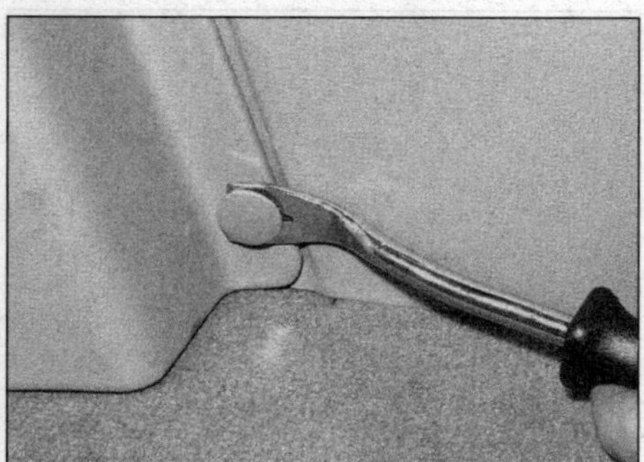

25.10b . . . then prise out the retaining clips . . .

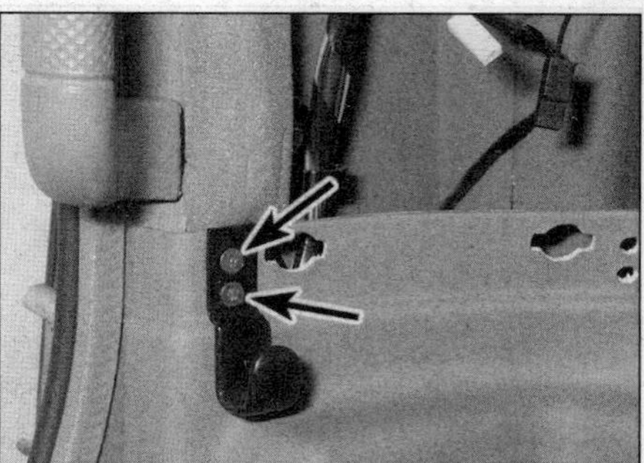

25.10c . . . and undo the relevant screws (arrowed) . . .

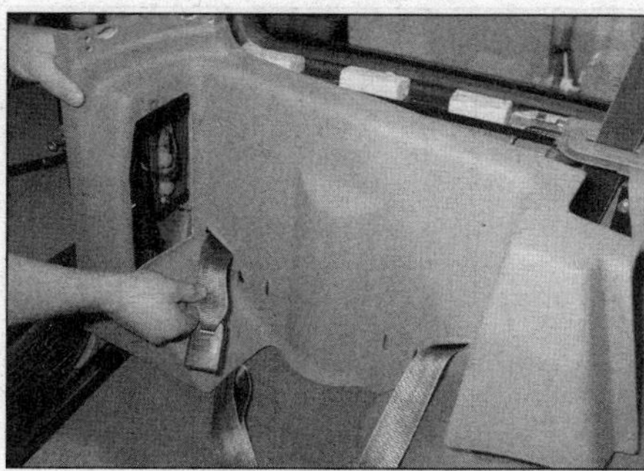

25.10d . . . and remove the trim panel from the luggage compartment

mounting bolt and free the belt from its mounting. Recover the washers and spacer fitted between the seat belt anchorage and body, noting their correct fitted locations.

12 Prise off the trim cap from the seat belt lower mounting, then slacken and remove the lower mounting bolt. Recover the washers and spacer fitted between the seat belt anchorage and floor, noting their correct fitted locations.

13 Unscrew the bolt securing the inertia reel to the body, and remove the seat belt from the vehicle **(see illustration)**.

Rear seat belt centre belt and buckles

14 Free the seat belt/buckle (as applicable) from the rear seat, and unbolt it from its mounting point.

25.13 Rear seat side belt inertia reel retaining bolt

Luggage compartment seat belt and buckle

15 Remove the rear side seat (where fitted) as described in Section 24.

16 Remove the trim panels as described above in paragraphs 9 and 10.

17 Slacken and remove the retaining bolt, then remove the belt/buckle and recover the washers which are fitted to either side of the belt anchorage.

Refitting

18 Refitting is a reversal of the removal procedure, ensuring that all the mounting bolts are tightened to the specified torque (where given) and all disturbed trim panels are securely retained by all the relevant retaining clips.

26 Interior trim - removal and refitting

Interior trim panels

1 The interior trim panels are secured using either screws or various types of trim fasteners, usually studs or clips.

2 Check that there are no other panels overlapping the one to be removed; usually there is a sequence to be followed that will become obvious on close inspection.

3 Remove all obvious fasteners, such as screws. If the panel will not come free, it is held by hidden clips or fasteners. These are usually situated around the edge of the panel, and can be prised up to release them. Note, however, that they can break quite easily, so replacements should be available. The best way of releasing such clips in the absence of the correct type of tool, is to use a large flat-bladed screwdriver. Note in many cases that an adjacent sealing strip (such as the rubber door seal) must be prised back to release a panel.

4 When removing a panel, **never** use excessive force, or the panel may be damaged. Always check carefully that all fasteners have been removed or released before attempting to withdraw a panel.

5 Refitting is the reverse of the removal procedure; secure the fasteners by pressing them firmly into place, and ensure that all disturbed components are correctly secured, to prevent rattles.

Glovebox

6 Open up the glovebox, and release its hinge springs **(see illustration)**.

7 Slacken and remove the hinge retaining screws, and remove the glovebox from the facia.

8 Refitting is the reverse of removal.

Cup holder (later models)

9 Remove the central facia ashtray, and the switch panel from the left-and right-hand sides of the facia centre section **(see illustrations)**.

10 Working inside the apertures at each side,

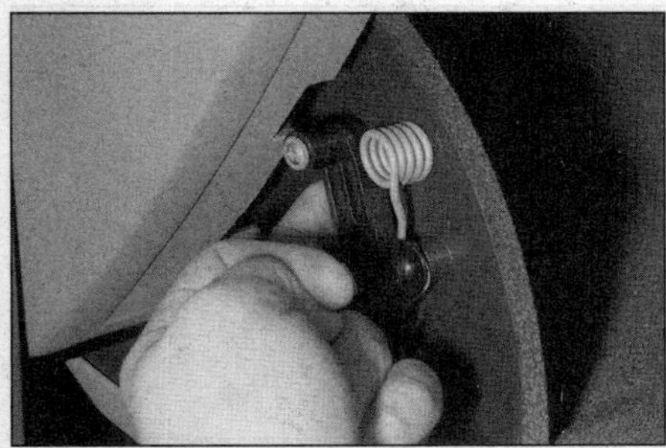

26.6 Lift the hinge springs, and release them from the facia to allow the glovebox to the fully opened

26.9a Remove the central ashtray . . .

26.9b . . . and the switch panel

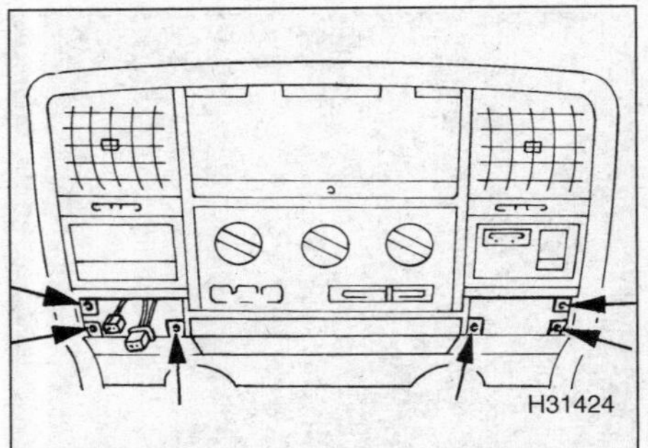
H31424
26.10a Remove six screws (arrowed) . . .

26.10b . . . and withdraw the cup holder from the facia

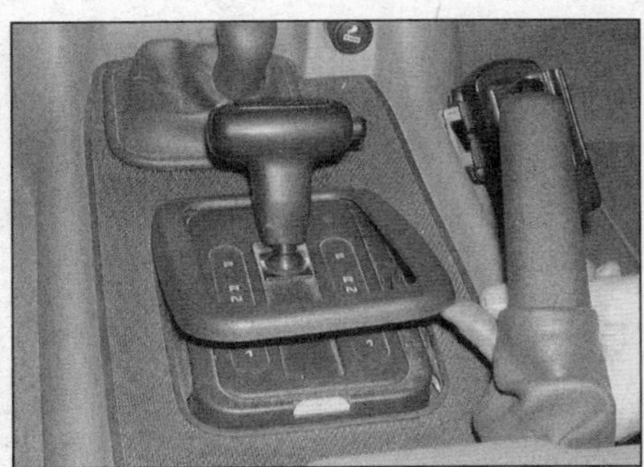
27.6 Unclip and remove the selector panel surround

remove a total of six screws (three each side) securing the cup holder. Carefully slide the holder out from its location **(see illustrations)**.

11 Further dismantling the cup holder is not advisable. Refitting is a reversal of removal.

Carpets

12 The passenger compartment floor carpet is in one piece, and is secured at its edges by screws or clips, usually the same fasteners used to secure the various adjoining trim panels.

13 Carpet removal and refitting is reasonably straightforward, but very time-consuming, due to the fact that all adjoining trim panels must be removed first, as must components such as the seats, the centre console and seat belt lower anchorages.

Headlining

14 The headlining is clipped to the roof, and can only be withdrawn once all fittings such as the grab handles, sunvisors, windscreen and rear quarter windows, and related trim panels have been removed, and the door, tailgate and sunroof aperture sealing strips have been prised clear.

27.8a Remove the spring clip (arrowed) . . .

15 Note that headlining removal requires considerable skill and experience if it is to be carried out without damage, and is therefore best entrusted to an expert.

27 Centre console - removal and refitting

Removal

Early models (pre-March 1994)

1 Disconnect the battery negative terminal.

2 Remove the radio/cassette player as described in Chapter 13.

3 Release the handbrake lever gaiter from the console, then carefully prise out the switch panel. Disconnect all the switch wiring connectors, and remove the panel from the console.

4 Unclip the transfer lever gaiter from the console, then unscrew the knob from the manual gearchange lever.

5 On manual transmission models, unclip the gearchange lever gaiter from the console. Slacken and remove the gearchange lever clamp screw, and remove the lever and gaiter assembly.

6 On automatic transmission models, either remove the selector lever trim panel retaining screws, or carefully unclip the surround from the selector panel, starting at the rear edge **(see illustration)**.

7 Chock the wheels to prevent the vehicle moving, then release the handbrake.

8 Remove the split-pin/spring clip (as applicable), then withdraw the clevis pin securing the handbrake inner cable to the lever **(see illustrations)**. Fully raise the handbrake lever. Where a split-pin is used, discard it - a new one will be needed on refitting.

9 Lift the front of the rubber mat which is fitted to the front of the console, and unscrew the console front retaining screws. Also remove the retaining screw which is accessed through the handbrake lever aperture.

10 Remove the mat from the shelf at the rear of the console, then slacken and remove the four rear retaining screws.

11 Lift the console upwards and out of the vehicle.

Later models (March 1994 onwards)

12 Disconnect the battery negative lead.

13 Release the handbrake lever gaiter from the console, and remove the switch panel cover plate. Undo the retaining screws, then withdraw the switch panel and disconnect its wiring connectors **(see illustrations)**. On models with electric seats, disconnect the wiring from the seat switches in the console.

14 Carry out the operations described above in paragraphs 4 to 9.

15 Open the console storage box, then slacken and remove all the console retaining screws.

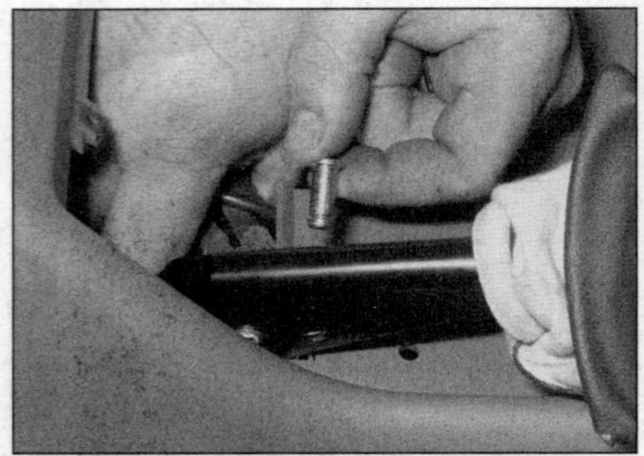
27.8b . . . and withdraw the clevis pin securing the cable to the handbrake lever

27.13a Lift off the cover plate . . .

27.13b . . . then undo the retaining screws . . .

16 Release the retaining clips securing the front of the console to its retaining bracket, then lift the console out of position, disconnecting the wiring connectors from the cigarette lighter as they become accessible **(see illustration)**.

Refitting

17 Refitting is a reversal of the removal procedure, noting the following:

a) *Ensure that all the wiring is correctly routed, and does not become trapped as the console is refitted.*
b) *Apply a smear of grease to the handbrake cable mechanism, and secure the cable in position with a new split-pin. Adjust the cable as described in the relevant part of Chapter 1.*
c) *On completion, reconnect the battery, and check the operation of all the switches.*

27.13c . . . and withdraw the switch panel from the console, disconnecting its wiring connectors

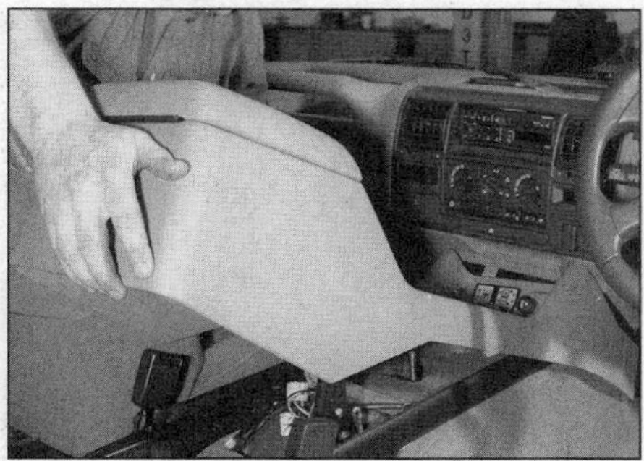

27.16 Removing the centre console

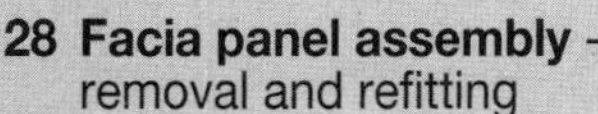

28 Facia panel assembly - removal and refitting

HAYNES
HiNT

Label each wiring connector as it is disconnected from its relevant component. The labels will prove useful on refitting when routing the wiring and feeding the wiring through the facia apertures.

Removal

Early models (pre-March 1994)

1 Disconnect the battery negative terminal.
2 Remove the steering wheel as described in Chapter 11.
3 Remove the instrument panel and steering column combination switches as described in Chapter 13.
4 Remove the centre console as described in Section 27.
5 Pull the control knobs off the heater levers, then slacken and remove the retaining screws securing the centre panel to the facia. Ease the panel away from the facia, then disconnect each of the panel wiring connectors, noting their correct fitted locations, and remove the panel.
6 Unclip the instrument panel housing and remove it from the facia panel.
7 Release the fasteners and remove driver's side lower panel from the facia.
8 Lift up the rubber mat, then unscrew the passenger grab handle retaining screws. Remove the handle and mat from the facia, and recover the spacers from the facia mounting bracket.
9 Slacken and remove the two retaining bolts and washers securing the facia central mounting bracket to the floor.
10 Release the retaining clips, and remove the driver's side footwell side trim panel, to gain access to the side facia retaining bolts. Slacken and remove both the right-hand lower retaining bolts, and the screw securing the end of the facia in position.
11 Repeat the operation described in paragraph 10 on the passenger side of the facia, and remove the facia left-hand lower retaining bolts and end screw.
12 Slacken and remove the two facia retaining bolts and washers which are situated where the instrument panel is mounted.
13 The facia panel is now free to be removed. Pull the panel away from the bulkhead, and manoeuvre it out from inside the vehicle.

Later models (March 1994 onwards)

14 Disconnect the battery negative terminal.
15 Remove the steering wheel as described in Chapter 11.
16 Prise out the clips, and remove both the driver's and passenger side facia lower covers **(see illustrations)**. Remove the following components as described in Chapter 13.

a) *Instrument panel.*
b) *Radio/cassette player.*
c) *Steering column combination switches.*
d) *Clock.*
e) *Passenger airbag unit (where fitted).*

17 Remove the centre console as described in Section 27.
18 Release the two fasteners and release the driver's side lower facia panel; on later models, also undo the hinge retaining screws to remove the panel. Where necessary, undo the retaining screws and remove the support pad from the facia
19 Using a suitable flat-bladed screwdriver, carefully prise the exterior mirror switch panel out from the facia, taking care not to mark

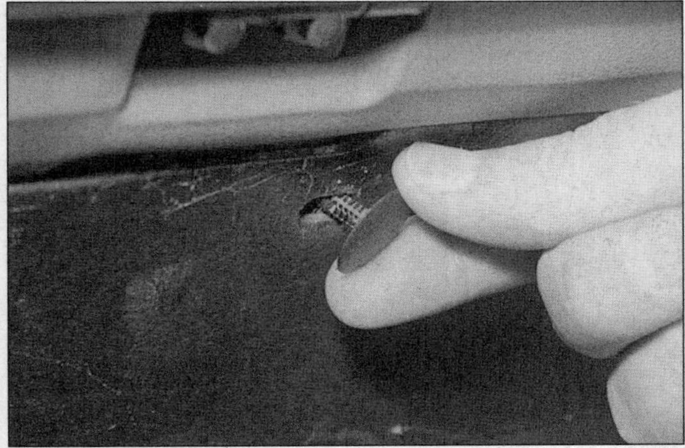

28.16a Prise out the retaining clips . . .

28.16b . . . and remove the lower covers from the facia

28.19 Remove the mirror switch panel from the facia, and disconnect its wiring connectors

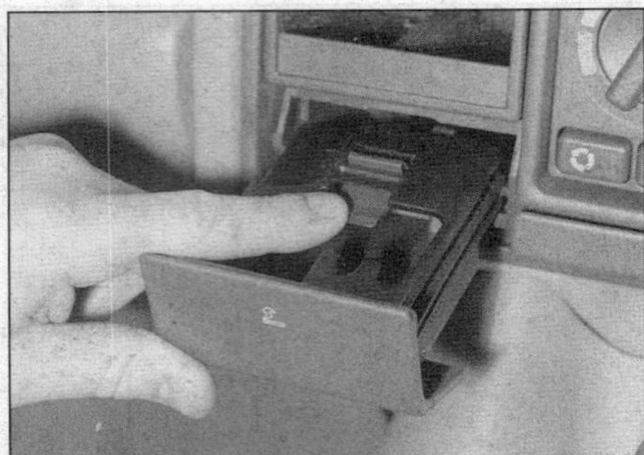
28.20a Remove the ashtray . . .

28.20b . . . then push out the coin box from the facia centre panel

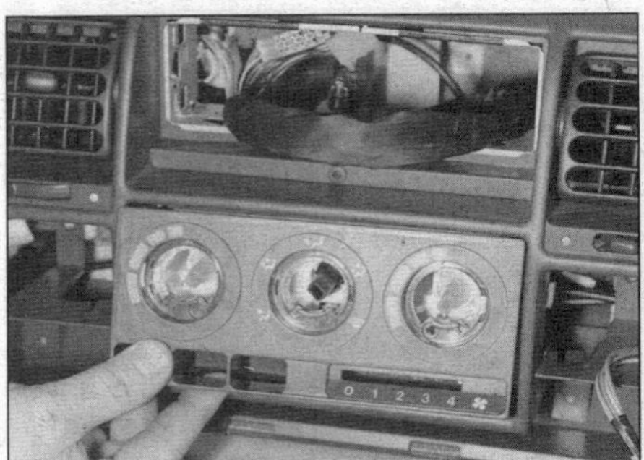
0 1 2 3 4
28.23 Pull the control knobs off the blower motor switch and heater controls, then undo the retaining screws and remove the front plate

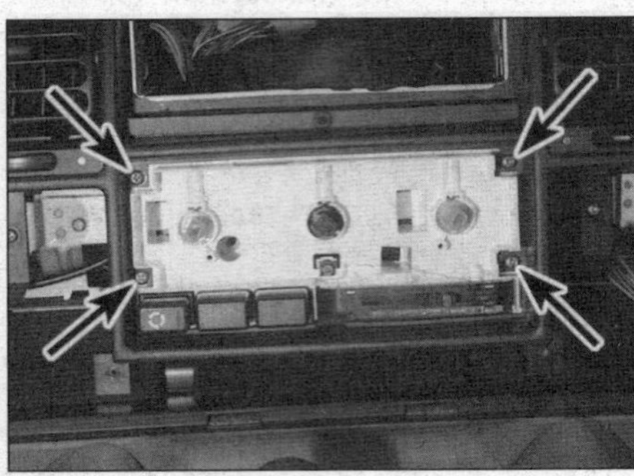
28.24 Heater control panel retaining screws (arrowed)

either. Disconnect the wiring connectors and remove the panel **(see illustration)**.

20 Remove the ashtray, then release the retaining clips and carefully ease the coin box out from the centre vent panel **(see illustrations)**.

21 Referring to Section 26, undo the retaining screws, and withdraw the cup holder assembly from the base of the facia centre panel.

22 Pull off the control knobs from the three heater controls, and the knob from the blower motor switch.

23 Undo the two retaining screws, and remove the front plate from the heater control panel **(see illustration)**.

24 Undo the four retaining screws securing the heater control unit to the facia, and free the unit from the centre panel **(see illustration)**.

25 Bend back the retaining tangs, and withdraw the radio/cassette player mounting cage from the centre vent panel **(see illustrations)**.

26 Carefully prise the alarm system LED panel out from the centre vent panel, taking great care not to mark either component. Free the bulbholder, and remove the panel **(see illustrations)**.

27 Slacken and remove the retaining screws, then unclip the centre vent panel and remove it from the facia **(see illustrations)**.

28 Open up the glovebox, and release its

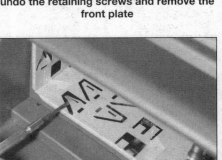

28.25a Bend up the retaining tangs . . .

28.25b . . . and remove the radio/cassette player mounting cage

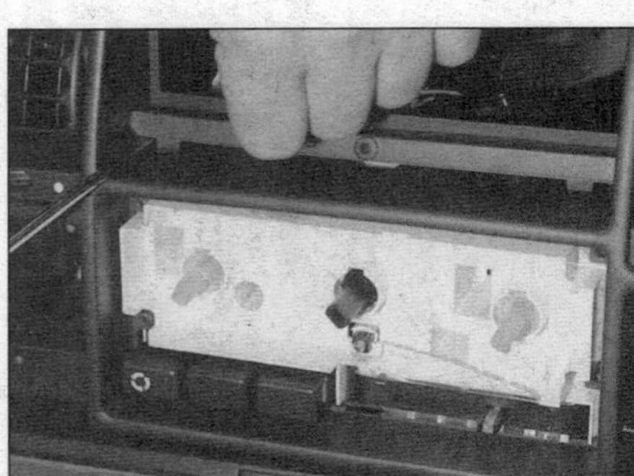
28.26a Prise out the alarm system LED panel . . .

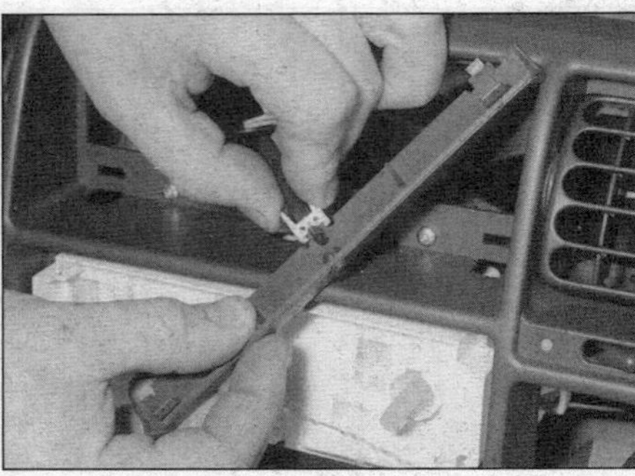
28.26b . . . and free it from its bulbholder

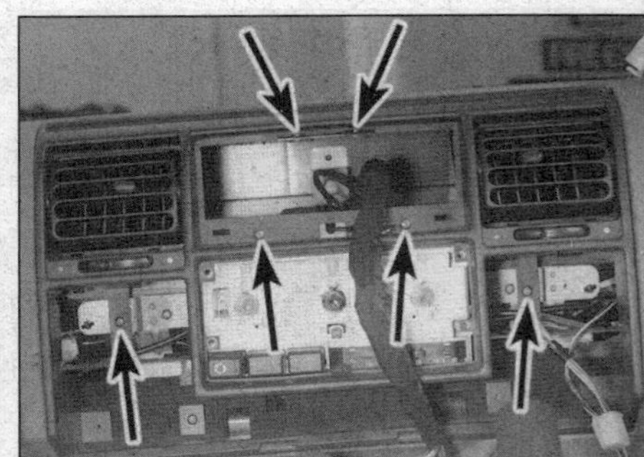
28.27a Undo the retaining screws (arrowed) . . .

28.27b . . . and remove the centre vent panel from the facia

28.29 Undo the retaining nut (arrowed) and release the relay mounting bracket from the facia frame

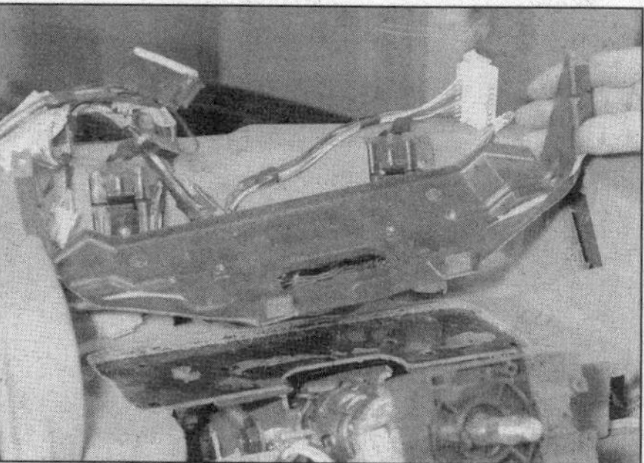
28.30 Removing the instrument panel mounting bracket

hinge springs. Slacken and remove the hinge retaining screws, and remove the glovebox from the facia.

29 Slacken and remove the nut securing the passenger side relay mounting bracket to the base of the facia, and free the bracket assembly from the facia frame **(see illustration)**.

30 Slacken and remove the retaining nuts and bolts, and remove the instrument panel mounting bracket from the facia aperture **(see illustration)**.

31 Detach the operating cables and wiring connectors from the heater control unit, and remove the unit from the facia (see Chapter 3).

32 Slacken and remove the four bolts (two each side of the transmission tunnel) securing the centre mounting brackets to the base of the facia **(see illustration)**.

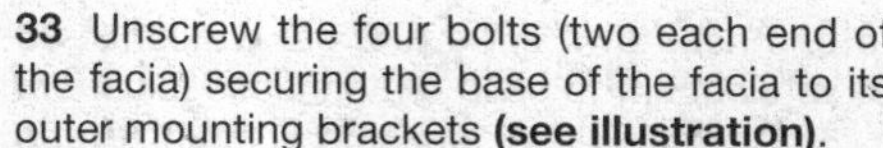

33 Unscrew the four bolts (two each end of the facia) securing the base of the facia to its outer mounting brackets **(see illustration)**.

34 Working through the glovebox aperture, slacken and remove the two bolts securing the facia to the bulkhead.

35 With the aid of an assistant, carefully ease the facia assembly partially away from the bulkhead. As they become accessible, disconnect the wiring connectors connecting the facia wiring harness to the main harness (situated on both the right- and left-hand side of the air distribution housing) and those connecting the harness to the fusebox assembly **(see illustration)**.

36 The facia panel is now free to be removed. With the aid of an assistant, pull the panel away from the bulkhead, and manoeuvre it out from inside the vehicle.

Refitting

37 Refitting is a reversal of the removal procedure, noting the following points:

a) *Manoeuvre the facia into position and, using the labels stuck on during removal, ensure that the wiring is correctly routed and fed through the relevant facia apertures. Take great care not to trap the wiring as the facia is installed.*
b) *Clip the facia back into position, then refit all the facia fasteners and tighten them securely.*
c) *On completion, reconnect the battery and check that all the electrical components and switches function correctly.*

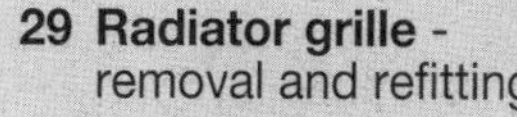

29 Radiator grille - removal and refitting

Removal

Models up to March 1994

1 Open the bonnet, then undo the retaining screws situated along the top edge of the grille.

2 Free the grille lower locating pegs and remove the grille from the car.

Models from March 1994 onwards

3 Disconnect the battery negative terminal.

4 Remove the left-hand direction indicator light as described in Chapter 13, Section 7.

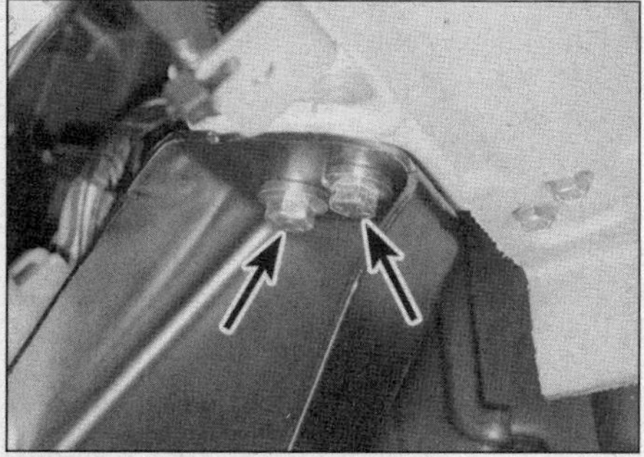
28.32 Slacken and remove the facia centre mounting bracket bolts (arrowed) . . .

28.33 . . . and the side mounting bracket bolts (arrowed)

28.35 Remove the facia from the vehicle

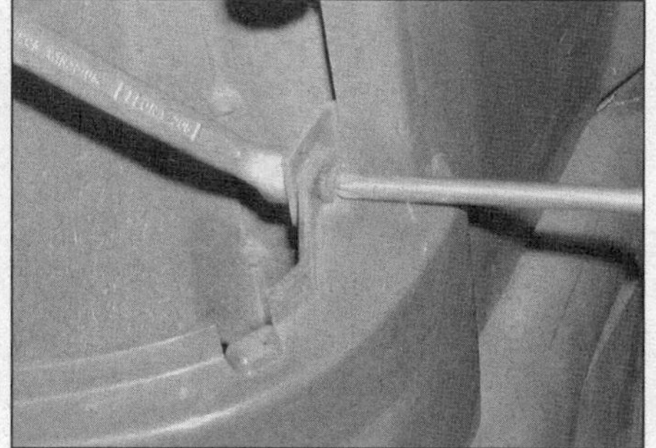
29.4a With the indicator removed, undo the screw and nut . . .

29.4b . . . then release the locating pegs at either end . . .

29.4c . . . and remove the headlight trim panel

29.6 Remove the grille retaining screws (arrowed)

29.7 Engage the grille locating pegs correctly when refitting

Undo the retaining screw and nut, then remove the trim panel from underneath the headlight unit, bending it carefully to free the locating pegs at either end. This operation carries a high risk of damaging the trim panel - work slowly and carefully **(see illustrations)**.

5 Repeat the operations in paragraph 4 to remove the right-hand headlight trim panel.

6 Undo the retaining screws situated along the top edge of the grille **(see illustration)**, then free the grille lower locating pegs and remove it from the car.

Refitting

7 Refitting is the reverse of removal, ensuring that the grille locating pegs engage correctly with their mounting rubbers **(see illustration)**.

Chapter 13
Body electrical systems

Contents

Degrees of difficulty

Easy, suitable for novice with little experience 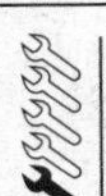	**Fairly easy,** suitable for beginner with some experience 	**Fairly difficult,** suitable for competent DIY mechanic	**Difficult,** suitable for experienced DIY mechanic 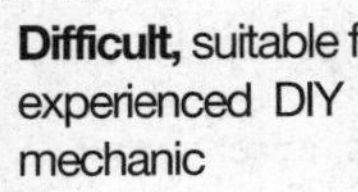	**Very difficult,** suitable for expert DIY or professional 

Specifications

System type .... 12-volt negative-earth

Fuses - early models (pre-March 1994)

No	Circuit(s) protected*	Rating (amps)
A1	Headlight dipped beam and headlight washers	10
A2	Headlight dipped beam	10
A3	Right-hand headlight main beam	10
A4	Left-hand headlight main beam	10
A5	Right-hand front and rear sidelights, facia switches and instrument panel illumination	5
A6	Left-hand front and rear sidelights, number plate lights, radio, cigar lighter, clock and heater control panel illumination	5
A7	Windscreen washer/wiper	20
A8	Air conditioning/heater relay and fan	20
A9	Heated rear window	30
B1	Radio memory, interior lights and clock	5
B2	Rear foglights	10
B3	Direction indicators, stop-lights, reversing lights, headlight levelling system, air conditioning/heater relay and warning lights	15
B4	Trailer socket	15
B5	Horns	15
B6	Tailgate washer/wiper and clock	10
B7	Cigarette lighter	10
B8	Fuel pump relay	10
B9	Radio	10
C1	Electric window relay	30
C2	Electric window relay	30
C3	Central locking system	15
C4	Exterior mirrors	3
C5	Air conditioning fans	20
C6	Air conditioning fans	20
C7	Air conditioning compressor clutch	5
C8	Hazard warning lights	15
C9	- Not used	

**Not all items fitted to all models*

Passenger compartment fuses - later models (March 1994 onwards)

Main fuse panel

No	Circuit(s) protected*	Rating (amps)
1	Stop-lights and direction indicators	15
2	Left-hand sidelight	10
3	Radio/cassette, CD player	10
4	Right-hand headlight main beam	10
5	Left-hand headlight main beam	10
6	Cigarette lighter, vanity mirror light, heated seats	20
7	Airbag system	10
8	Right-hand sidelight	10
9	Rear foglights	10
10	Right-hand headlight dipped beam	10
11	Left-hand headlight dipped beam	10
12	Multi-function unit	10
13	Ignition feed for multi-function unit	10
14	Instruments, clock, speed sensor and reversing lights	10
15	Air conditioning and electric windows	10
16	Windscreen washers/wipers	20
17	Starter and pre-heating system	10
18	Tailgate wash/wipe, electric mirrors, cruise control	10

**Not all items fitted to all models*

Upper auxiliary fuse panel

No	Circuit(s) protected*	Rating (amps)
1	Front electric windows	30
2	Rear electric windows	30
3	Anti-lock braking system	10
4	Central locking system	15
5	Electric sunroof	30
6	Radio, clock, alarm, interior lights, trailer socket	20

**Not all items fitted to all models*

Lower auxiliary fuse panel

No	Circuit(s) protected*	Rating (amps)
1	Anti-theft alarm	15
2	Headlight washers	20
3	Engine management system	10
4	Anti-lock braking system	5
5	Anti-theft alarm	10
6	Rear air conditioning and blower motor	25

**Not all items fitted to all models*

Engine compartment fuses and fusible links - later models (March 1994 onwards)

No	Circuit(s) protected*
1	Heated rear window
2	Sidelights
3	Air conditioning
4	Hazard warning lights and horn
5	Anti-lock braking system
6	Fuel pump
7	Fuel injection system
8	Anti-lock braking system pump
9	Ignition system
10	Lighting
11	Electric windows, central locking and rear blower motor
12	Air conditioning/heater
13	Alternator

**Not all items fitted to all models*

Relay locations - early models (pre-March 1994)

Component*	Location
Air conditioning compressor clutch relay	Behind passenger compartment fusebox (red wiring connector)
Air conditioning (low-speed) relay	Behind driver's footwell side panel (below the main relay bank)
Air conditioning (medium-speed) relay	Behind driver's footwell side panel (below the main relay bank)
Air conditioning fresh air solenoid relay	Behind passenger footwell side panel (inner red wiring connector)
Air conditioning heater relay	Behind passenger footwell side panel (outer red wiring connector)
Air conditioning/blower motor relay	Behind driver's footwell side panel (below the main relay bank)
Blower motor relay (non-air conditioning models)	Behind driver's footwell side panel (below the main relay bank)
Cooling fan relay	Behind passenger compartment fusebox (red wiring connector)
Direction indicator relay	Behind passenger compartment fusebox (blue wiring connector)
Front electric window relay	Behind driver's footwell side panel (white wiring connector)
Fuel pump relay	Behind passenger footwell side panel (yellow wiring connector)
Headlight levelling relay	Behind driver's footwell side panel (outer black wiring connector)
Headlight washer relay	Behind passenger footwell side panel (blue wiring connector)
Heated rear window relay	Behind driver's footwell side panel (inner black wiring connector)
Pre-heating system relay	On engine compartment bulkhead
Rear electric window relay	Behind driver's footwell side panel (yellow wiring connector)
Starter relay	Behind passenger footwell side panel (black wiring connector)
Tailgate wiper relay	Behind passenger footwell side panel (red wiring connector)
Voltage switch relay	Behind passenger compartment fusebox (yellow wiring connector)
Windscreen wiper relay	Behind driver's footwell side panel (red wiring connector)

**Not all items fitted to all models*

Relay locations - later models (March 1994 onwards)

Component*	Location
Accessory relay	Behind passenger footwell side panel
Air conditioning compressor clutch relay	Behind driver's side footwell side panel
Air conditioning logic relay	Behind driver's footwell side panel
Anti-lock braking system load relay	Behind passenger side of facia, on bracket
Anti-lock braking system pump relay	Behind passenger side of facia, on bracket
Anti-lock braking system warning relay	Behind passenger side of facia, on bracket
Anti-theft alarm relay	Behind passenger footwell side panel
Condenser fan relay	Behind passenger side of facia, on bracket
Cooling fan relay	Behind driver's side footwell side panel
Dim/dip relay	Behind passenger side of facia, on bracket
Direction indicator relay	Passenger compartment fusebox
Engine control load relay	Behind driver's side footwell side panel
Front blower motor relay	Behind passenger side of facia

Relay locations - later models (March 1994 onwards) (continued)

Component*	Location
Fuel pump relay	Behind driver's footwell side panel
Headlight washer relay	Behind passenger side of facia, on bracket
Heated rear window relay	Passenger compartment fusebox
Horn relay	Behind passenger footwell side panel
Interlock relay 1	Behind passenger side of facia
Interlock relay 2	Behind passenger side of facia
Multi-function unit	Behind driver's footwell side panel
Power amplifier relay	Behind passenger side of facia
Rear air conditioning control relay	Left-hand side of luggage compartment on rear evaporator
Rear air conditioning fan speed relay	Left-hand side of luggage compartment on rear evaporator
Rear air conditioning illumination relay	Left-hand side of luggage compartment on rear evaporator
Rear blower motor relay	Left-hand side of luggage compartment on rear evaporator
Sounder relay	Behind passenger footwell side panel
Starter relay	Behind driver's footwell side panel
Tailgate wiper relay	Behind passenger footwell side panel
Windscreen wiper relay	Behind driver's footwell side panel

**Not all items fitted to all models*

Bulbs

	Wattage
Automatic transmission selector illumination light	5
Direction indicator	21
Direction indicator side repeater	5
Front foglight	55
Front sidelight	5
Headlight	60/55
Instrument panel lights:	
Ignition warning light	2
All other warning/illumination lights	1.2
Interior lights	10
Number plate light	5
Rear foglight	21
Reversing light	21
Stop/tail light	21/5

Torque wrench settings

	Nm	lbf ft
Airbag components:		
Airbag unit screws	8	6
Control unit screws	10	7
Impact sensor screws	10	7

1 General information and precautions

Warning: Before carrying out any work on the electrical system, read through the precautions given in Safety first! at the beginning of this manual, and in Chapter 5A.

The electrical system is of the 12-volt negative-earth type. Power for the lights and all electrical accessories is supplied by a lead-acid type battery which is charged by the alternator.

This Chapter covers repair and service procedures for the various electrical components not associated with engine. Information on the battery, alternator and starter motor can be found in Chapter 5A.

Prior to working on any component in the electrical system, the battery negative terminal should first be disconnected, to prevent the possibility of electrical short-circuits and/or fires.

Disconnecting the battery - precautions

If the radio/cassette player fitted to the vehicle is with an anti-theft security code, as the unit fitted as standard is, refer to the information given in *Radio/cassette unit anti-theft system - precaution* at the end of this manual before disconnecting the battery.

On models from 1996 onwards, the standard anti-theft alarm system has a battery back-up facility, meaning that the alarm will still sound even if the battery is disconnected. To avoid accidentally setting off the alarm, switch the ignition on, then off, and disconnect the battery terminals **within 15 seconds**. If the alarm sounds, disarm the system with the handset, then reconnect the battery, switch on the ignition, and try again.

2 Electrical fault-finding - general information

Note: *Refer to the precautions given in Safety first! and in Section 1 of this Chapter before starting work. The following tests relate to testing of the main electrical circuits, and should not be used to test delicate electronic circuits (such as anti-lock braking systems), particularly where an electronic control module is used.*

General

1 A typical electrical circuit consists of an electrical component, any switches, relays, motors, fuses, fusible links or circuit breakers related to that component, and the wiring and connectors which link the component to both the battery and the chassis. To help to pinpoint a problem in an electrical circuit, wiring diagrams are included at the end of this Chapter.

2 Before attempting to diagnose an electrical fault, first study the appropriate wiring diagram to obtain a complete understanding of the components included in the particular circuit concerned. The possible sources of a fault can be narrowed down by noting if other components related to the circuit are operating properly. If several components or circuits fail at one time, the problem is likely to be related to a shared fuse or earth connection.

3 Electrical problems usually stem from simple causes, such as loose or corroded connections, a faulty earth connection, a blown fuse, a melted fusible link, or a faulty relay (refer to Section 3 for details of testing relays). Visually inspect the condition of all fuses, wires and connections in a problem circuit before testing the components. Use the wiring diagrams to determine which terminal connections will need to be checked in order to pinpoint the trouble-spot.

4 The basic tools required for electrical fault finding include a circuit tester or voltmeter (a 12-volt bulb with a set of test leads can also be used for certain tests); a self-powered test light (sometimes known as a continuity tester); an ohmmeter (to measure resistance); a battery and set of test leads; and a jumper wire, preferably with a circuit breaker or fuse incorporated, which can be used to bypass suspect wires or electrical components. Before attempting to locate a problem with test instruments, use the wiring diagram to determine where to make the connections.

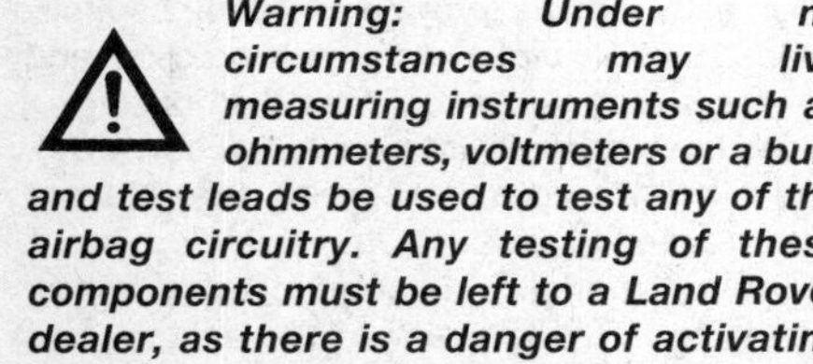

Warning: Under no circumstances may live measuring instruments such as ohmmeters, voltmeters or a bulb and test leads be used to test any of the airbag circuitry. Any testing of these components must be left to a Land Rover dealer, as there is a danger of activating the system if the correct procedures are not followed.

5 To find the source of an intermittent wiring fault (usually due to a poor or dirty connection, or damaged wiring insulation), a 'wiggle' test can be performed on the wiring. This involves wiggling the wiring by hand to see if the fault occurs as the wiring is moved. It should be possible to narrow down the source of the fault to a particular section of wiring. This method of testing can be used in conjunction with any of the tests described in the following sub-Sections.

6 Apart from problems due to poor connections, two basic types of fault can occur in an electrical circuit - open-circuit, or short-circuit.

7 Open-circuit faults are caused by a break somewhere in the circuit, which prevents current from flowing. An open-circuit fault will prevent a component from working, but will not cause the relevant circuit fuse to blow.

8 Short-circuit faults are caused by a short somewhere in the circuit, which allows the current flowing in the circuit to escape along an alternative route, usually to earth. Short-circuit faults are normally caused by a breakdown in wiring insulation, which allows a feed wire to touch either another wire, or an earthed component such as the bodyshell. A short-circuit fault will normally cause the relevant circuit fuse to blow.

Finding an open-circuit

9 To check for an open-circuit, connect one lead of a circuit tester or voltmeter to either the negative battery terminal or a known good earth.

10 Connect the other lead to a connector in the circuit being tested, preferably nearest to the battery or fuse.

11 Switch on the circuit, bearing in mind that some circuits are live only when the ignition switch is moved to a particular position.

12 If voltage is present (indicated either by the tester bulb lighting or a voltmeter reading, as applicable), this means that the section of the circuit between the relevant connector and the battery is problem-free.

13 Continue to check the remainder of the circuit in the same fashion.

14 When a point is reached at which no voltage is present, the problem must lie between that point and the previous test point with voltage. Most problems can be traced to a broken, corroded or loose connection.

Finding a short-circuit

15 To check for a short-circuit, first disconnect the load(s) from the circuit (loads are the components which draw current from a circuit, such as bulbs, motors, heating elements, etc).

16 Remove the relevant fuse from the circuit, and connect a circuit tester or voltmeter to the fuse connections.

17 Switch on the circuit, bearing in mind that some circuits are live only when the ignition switch is moved to a particular position.

18 If voltage is present (indicated either by the tester bulb lighting or a voltmeter reading, as applicable), this means that there is a short-circuit.

19 If no voltage is present, but the fuse still blows with the load(s) connected, this indicates an internal fault in the load(s).

Finding an earth fault

20 The battery negative terminal is connected to earth - the metal of the engine/transmission and the car body - and most systems are wired so that they only receive a positive feed, the current returning via the metal of the car body.

21 This means that the component mounting and the body form part of that circuit. Loose or corroded mountings can therefore cause a range of electrical faults, ranging from total failure of a circuit, to a puzzling partial fault. In particular, lights may shine dimly (especially when another circuit sharing the same earth point is in operation), motors (eg. wiper motors or the radiator cooling fan motor) may run slowly, and the operation of one circuit may have an apparently-unrelated effect on another.

22 Note that on many vehicles, earth straps are used between certain components, such as the engine/transmission and the body, usually where there is no metal-to-metal contact between components due to flexible rubber mountings, etc.

23 To check whether a component is properly earthed, disconnect the battery and connect one lead of an ohmmeter to a known good earth point. Connect the other lead to the wire or earth connection being tested. The resistance reading should be zero; if not, check the connection as follows.

24 If an earth connection is thought to be faulty, dismantle the connection and clean back to bare metal both the bodyshell and the wire terminal or the component earth connection mating surface. Be careful to remove all traces of dirt and corrosion, then use a knife to trim away any paint, so that a clean metal-to-metal joint is made.

25 On reassembly, tighten the joint fasteners securely; if a wire terminal is being refitted, use serrated washers between the terminal and the bodyshell to ensure a clean and secure connection. When the connection is remade, prevent the onset of corrosion in the future by applying a coat of petroleum jelly or silicone-based grease. Alternatively, spray on (at regular intervals) a proprietary ignition sealer, or a water-dispersant lubricant.

3 Fuses and relays - general information

Fuses

1 On early models (pre-March 1994), the fuses are located behind the driver's side lower facia panel. On later models (March 1994 onwards), most of the fuses are located in the fusebox behind the driver's side lower facia panel, with a few fuses and the main fusible links being located in the engine compartment fusebox **(see illustrations)**.

3.1a Passenger compartment fusebox is located behind the driver's side lower facia panel

3.1b On later models, unclip the engine compartment fusebox cover . . .

3.1c . . . to gain access to the fuses (arrowed) . . .

3.1d . . . then remove the inner cover to gain access to the fusible links

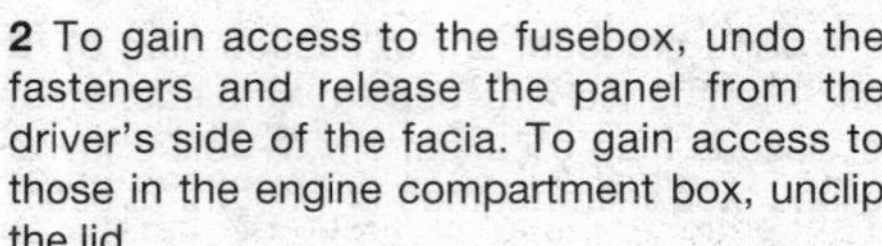

2 To gain access to the fusebox, undo the fasteners and release the panel from the driver's side of the facia. To gain access to those in the engine compartment box, unclip the lid.

3 A label identifying each fuse should be attached to the cover/lid, and a list of the circuits each fuse protects is given in the Specifications at the start of this Chapter.

4 To remove a fuse, first switch off the circuit concerned (or the ignition), then pull the fuse out of its terminals. The wire within the fuse is clearly visible; if the fuse is blown, it will be broken or melted.

5 To renew a fusible link (later models only), prise off its plastic cover, then undo its two retaining screws. The wire within the fuse will be broken if the fusible link has gone.

6 Always renew a fuse/fusible link with one of an identical rating; never use one with a different rating from the original, nor substitute anything else. Never renew a fuse/fusible link more than once without tracing the source of the trouble. The rating is stamped on top of the fuse/fusible link; note that are also colour-coded for easy recognition.

7 If a new fuse/fusible link blows immediately, find the cause before renewing it again - a short to earth as a result of faulty insulation is most likely. Where more than one circuit is protected, try to isolate the defect by switching on each circuit in turn (if possible) until it blows again. Always carry a supply of spare fuses/fusible links of each relevant rating on the vehicle; a spare of each fuse rating should be clipped into the base of the fusebox.

Relays

8 The relay locations are given in the Specifications at the start of this Chapter.

9 If a circuit or system controlled by a relay develops a fault and the relay is suspect, operate the system; if the relay is functioning, it should be possible to hear it click as it is energised. If it clicks, the fault lies with the components or wiring of the system. If the relay is not being energised, then either the relay is not receiving a main supply or a switching voltage, or the relay itself is faulty. Testing is by the substitution of a known good unit, but be careful; while some relays are identical in appearance and in operation, others look similar but perform different functions.

10 To renew a relay, first ensure that the ignition switch is off. The relay can then simply be pulled out from the socket, and the new relay pressed in **(see illustration)**.

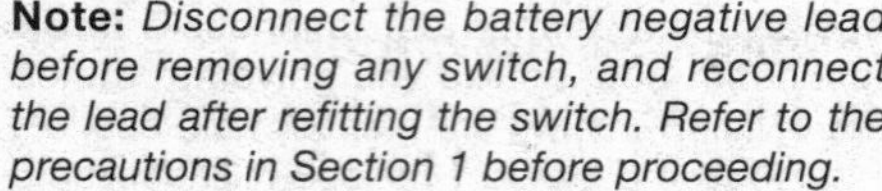

4 Switches - removal and refitting

Note: *Disconnect the battery negative lead before removing any switch, and reconnect the lead after refitting the switch. Refer to the precautions in Section 1 before proceeding.*

Ignition switch/ steering column lock

1 Refer to Chapter 11.

Steering column combination switches

2 Remove the steering wheel as described in Chapter 11.

3 Undo the steering column shroud retaining screws, unclip the shroud halves, and remove both the upper and lower shrouds from the steering column. On early models, it may be necessary to pull off the hazard warning light switch to allow the upper shroud to be removed.

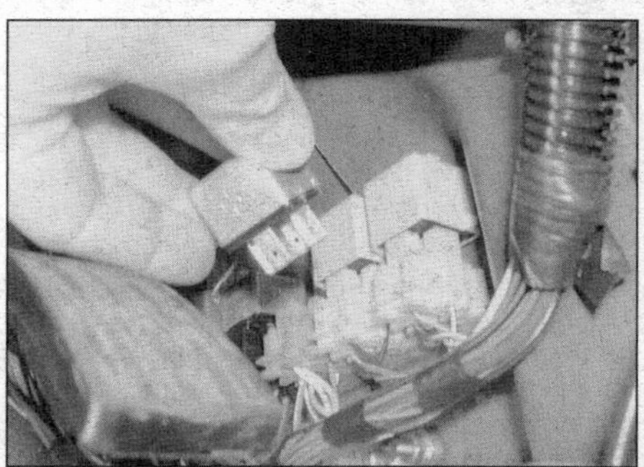

3.10 Removing the fuel injection pump relay

4 On early models (pre-March 1994), carefully release the relevant switch retaining clips, and pull the switch guides out from the housing.

5 On later models (March 1994 onwards), undo the two screws securing the relevant switch assembly in position.

6 On all models, disconnect the wiring connector from the rear of the switch, and remove the switch assembly. On models without an airbag, when removing the left-hand switch assembly, it will also be necessary to remove the horn contact wire **(see illustrations)**.

7 Refitting is a reversal of the removal procedure.

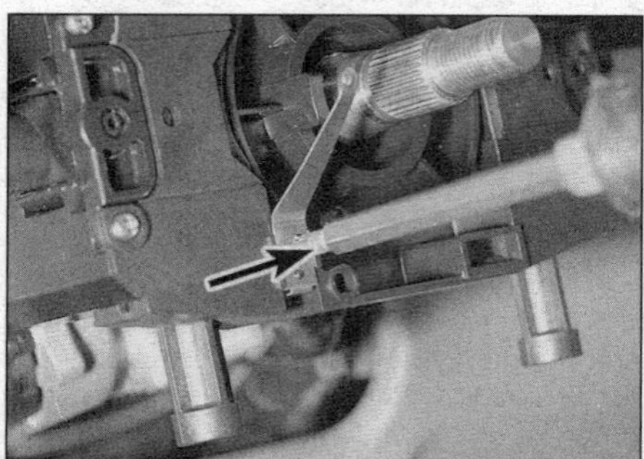

4.6a Where necessary, undo the retaining screw (arrowed) and remove the horn contact from the steering column switch assembly

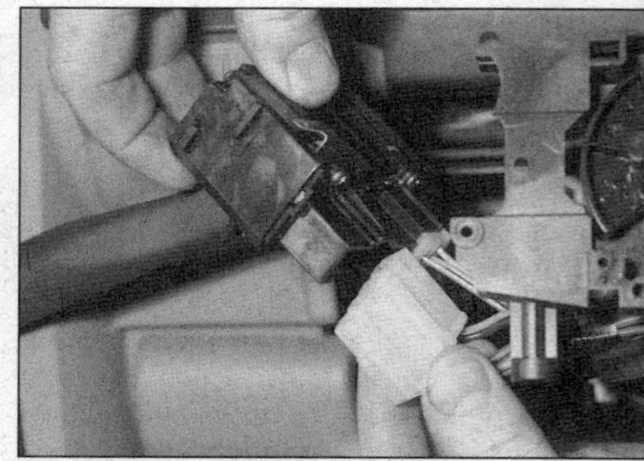

4.6b Release the switch from the steering column, and disconnect its wiring connector

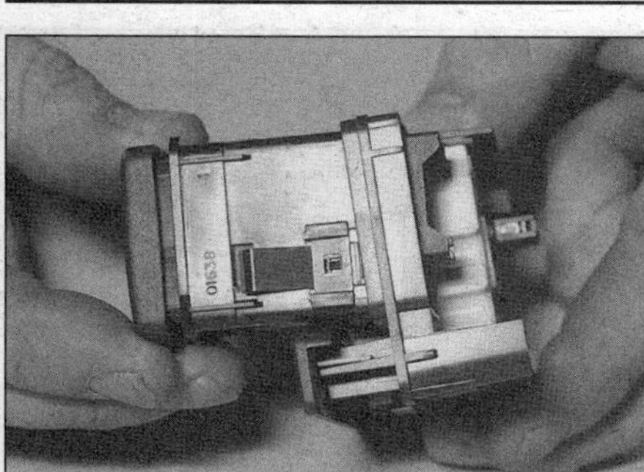
4.18 Removing the hazard warning light switch from the clock - later models

4.22 Handbrake warning light switch is mounted onto the side of the handbrake lever (arrowed)

4.26 On later models, undo the four retaining screws and remove the switch panel from the centre console

Instrument panel surround switches

Early models (pre-March 1994)

8 Slacken and remove the four retaining screws securing the instrument panel surround in position. Move the panel forwards until access can be gained to the panel switch wiring connectors. Disconnect each switch wiring connector, noting its correct fitted location, then remove the panel from the vehicle. Note that the wiring connectors are colour-coded to aid identification.

9 Depress the retaining clips, and slide the relevant switch out from the panel.

10 On refitting, slide the switch in until it clips into position then refit the panel surround, making sure that all wiring connectors are securely reconnected to the correct switches.

Later models (March 1994 onwards)

11 Slacken and remove the retaining screws securing the instrument panel surround in position. Ease the panel out of position, disconnect the wiring connectors from the rear of the switches, and remove the shroud.

12 Release the retaining clips, and push the relevant switch out from the shroud.

13 Refitting is the reverse of removal, ensuring that the wiring connectors are securely reconnected.

Hazard warning light switch

Early models (pre-March 1994)

14 Remove the steering column combination switches as described earlier in this Section.

15 Disconnect the wiring connector from the base of the hazard warning light switch, and remove it from the top of the steering column.

16 On refitting, ensure that the switch is correctly located on the steering column, then reconnect its wiring connector.

17 Refit the steering wheel as described in Chapter 11.

Later models (March 1994 onwards)

18 Remove the clock as described in Section 11, and slide the switch out of the clock **(see illustration)**.

19 Refitting is the reverse of removal.

Stop-light switch

20 Refer to Chapter 10.

Handbrake warning light switch

21 Remove the centre console as described in Chapter 12.

22 Disconnect the wiring connector from the switch, then undo the two retaining screws and remove the switch from the lever **(see illustration)**.

23 Refitting is the reverse of removal.

Electric window switches

Centre console switches

24 Release the handbrake lever gaiter from the switch panel on the centre console.

25 On early models (pre-March 1994), carefully unclip the switch panel from the console.

26 On later models (March 1994 onwards), remove the switch panel trim plate, then undo the retaining screws and remove the switch panel from the console **(see illustration)**.

27 Disconnect the wiring connector from the relevant switch, then depress the retaining clips and push the switch out of position **(see illustration)**.

28 Refitting is the reverse of removal.

Rear door switches

29 Remove the door trim panel as described in Chapter 12.

30 Release the retaining clip, and slide the switch out from the trim panel **(see illustrations)**.

31 On refitting, clip the switch into the trim panel then fit the panel as described in Chapter 12.

Electric mirror switch

Early models (pre-March 1994)

32 Refer to paragraphs 24 to 28.

Later models (March 1994 onwards)

33 Undo the fasteners and release the driver's lower facia panel.

34 Reach in behind the switch, then push it

4.27 Depress the retaining clips, and slide the relevant switch out from the panel

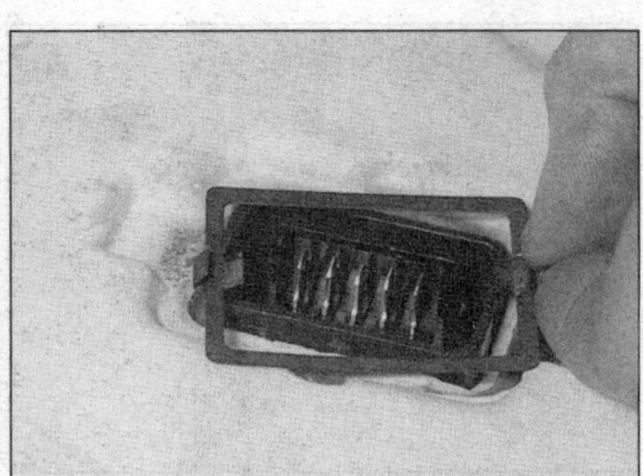
4.30a Release the retaining clip . . .

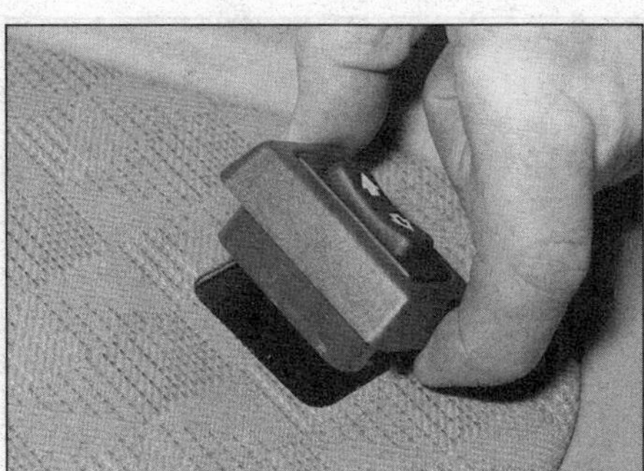
4.30b . . . and remove the window switch from the rear door trim panel

4.34 Removing the exterior mirror switch - later models

out of position and disconnect its wiring connector **(see illustration)**.

35 On refitting, reconnect the wiring connector, clip the switch back into the panel, and secure the facia panel in position with its fasteners.

Headlight levelling system switch

Early models (pre-March 1994)

36 Release the handbrake lever gaiter from the switch panel on the centre console.

37 Undo the retaining screws (later models only), and unclip the switch panel from the console.

38 Disconnect the wiring connector from the switch.

39 Pull off the levelling switch knob, then unscrew the retaining nut and free the switch from the panel.

40 On refitting, locate the switch in the panel, making sure that it is fitted the correct way around. Securely tighten the switch retaining nut, then refit its control knob.

41 Reconnect the wiring connectors, then clip the switch panel back into position, followed by the handbrake lever gaiter.

Later models (March 1994 onwards)

42 Undo the fasteners, and lower the driver's side lower facia panel. Using a suitable flat-bladed screwdriver, carefully prise the switch panel out from the facia, taking care not to mark either.

43 Disconnect the wiring connectors from both the mirror and levelling switches, and remove the panel assembly.

44 Pull off the levelling switch knob, then

4.44a On later models, pull off the headlight adjustment switch knob, then unscrew the retaining nut (arrowed) . . .

unscrew the retaining nut and free the switch from the panel **(see illustrations)**.

45 On refitting, locate the switch in the panel, tightening its retaining nut securely, and refit its control knob.

46 Reconnect the wiring connectors, then clip the switch panel back into position on the facia.

Electric sunroof switch

Front switches

47 Using a suitable flat-bladed screwdriver, carefully prise the switch panel out from the overhead console, taking care not to mark either.

48 Disconnect the wiring connector from the relevant switch, then depress the retaining clips and push the switch out from the panel.

49 On refitting, clip the switch back into the panel, reconnect the wiring connector, then clip the switch panel back into the overhead console.

Rear switch

50 Using a suitable flat-bladed screwdriver, carefully prise the switch from the overhead console, taking care not to mark either.

51 Disconnect the wiring connector and remove the switch.

52 On refitting, reconnect the wiring connector, then clip the switch back into the overhead console.

Courtesy light switches

53 Open the door, then undo the retaining screw from the door pillar. Withdraw the switch from the pillar, disconnecting its wiring connector as it becomes accessible **(see illustrations)**. Tape the wiring to the door pillar, to prevent it falling back into the hole.

4.44b . . . and remove the switch from the panel

54 Refitting is a reverse of the removal procedure.

Heater blower motor, air recirculation and front air conditioning system switches

Early models (pre-March 1994)

55 Remove the centre console as described in Chapter 12.

56 Pull the control knobs off the heater levers.

57 Slacken and remove the retaining screws securing the centre panel to the facia, then ease the panel away from the facia. Disconnect each of the panel wiring connectors, noting their correct fitted locations, and remove the panel.

58 Undo the relevant switch retaining screws and remove the switch, disconnecting its wiring connector as it becomes accessible.

59 Refitting is the reverse of removal, ensuring that all wiring connectors are reconnected to their original positions.

Later models (March 1994 onwards)

60 Remove the heater control unit as described in Chapter 3.

61 Release the retaining tangs, and slide the relevant switch out of position.

62 Refitting is the reverse of removal.

Centre facia panel switches - later models (March 1994 onwards)

63 Carefully pull the switch panel assembly out from the bottom of the facia centre panel **(see illustration)**.

4.53a Slacken and remove the retaining screw . . .

4.53b . . . then withdraw the courtesy light switch and disconnect its wiring connector

4.63 Pull out the switch panel assembly

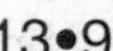

4.64a Disconnect the wiring plug from the relevant switch . . .

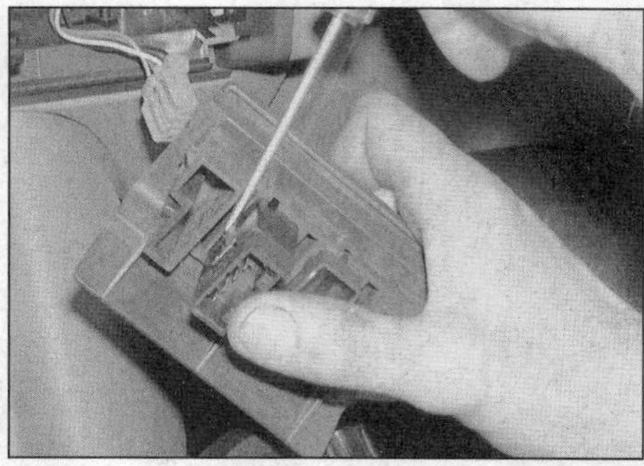

4.64b . . . then use a small screwdriver to release the switch retaining clips . . .

4.64c . . . and slide the switch from the panel

64 Disconnect the wiring connectors from the relevant switch, then depress the retaining clips and slide the switch out from the panel **(see illustrations)**.

65 Refitting is a reversal of the removal procedure.

Glovebox illumination switch - later models (March 1994 onwards)

66 Release the clips and remove the passenger side lower facia panel.

67 Open up the glovebox, and release its hinge springs. This will allow the glovebox to be fully opened.

68 Release the clip, withdraw the switch from the facia, and disconnect its wiring connectors **(see illustration)**.

69 Refitting is the reverse of removal.

Heated seat switches

70 Release the handbrake lever gaiter from the switch panel on the centre console.

71 Remove the switch panel trim plate, then undo the retaining screws and remove the switch panel from the console.

72 Disconnect the wiring connector from the relevant switch, then depress the retaining clips and push the switch out of position.

73 Refitting is the reverse of removal.

Electric seat switches

74 Using a small screwdriver, carefully release the two upper and lower retaining clips securing the switch panel to the side of the centre console.

75 Withdraw the switch panel, disconnect the two wiring plugs, and remove it **(see illustration)**.

76 Refitting is a reversal of removal.

Cruise control switches

77 Refer to Chapter 4B or 4C.

Oil pressure warning light switch

78 Refer to Chapter 2A or 2B.

5 Bulbs (exterior lights) - renewal

General

1 Whenever a bulb is renewed, note the following points:

a) Disconnect the battery negative lead before starting work. Refer to the precautions in Section 1 before proceeding.

b) Remember that if the light has just been in use, the bulb may be extremely hot.

c) Always check the bulb contacts and holder, ensuring that there is clean metal-to-metal contact between the bulb and its live(s) and earth. Clean off any corrosion or dirt before fitting a new bulb.

d) Wherever bayonet-type bulbs are fitted ensure that the live contact(s) bear firmly against the bulb contact.

e) Always ensure that the new bulb is of the correct rating, and that it is completely clean before fitting it; this applies particularly to headlight bulbs (see below).

Headlight

Early models (pre-March 1994)

2 Working in the engine compartment, disconnect the wiring connector from the rear of the headlight, then remove the rubber dust cover.

3 Unhook and release the ends of the bulb retaining clip, and release it from the rear of the light unit.

4 Withdraw the bulb.

5 When handling the new bulb, use a tissue or clean cloth to avoid touching the glass with the fingers; moisture and grease from the skin can cause blackening and rapid failure of this type of bulb.

HAYNES
HiNT

If the headlight bulb glass is accidentally touched, wipe it clean using methylated spirit.

6 Install the new bulb, ensuring that its locating tabs are correctly located in the light cut-outs, and secure it in position with the retaining clip.

7 Refit the dust cover to the rear of the light unit, and reconnect the wiring connector.

Later models (March 1994 onwards)

8 Remove the headlight unit as described in Section 7.

9 Remove the rubber dust cover, and renew the bulb as described above in paragraphs 3 to 6 **(see illustrations)**.

4.68 Release the glovebox illumination light switch from the facia, and disconnect its wiring connectors (arrowed)

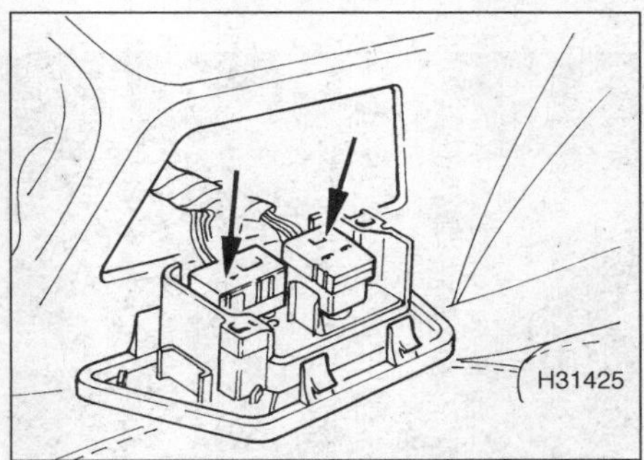
H31425

4.75 Unclip the electric seat switch panel, then disconnect the wiring plugs (arrowed)

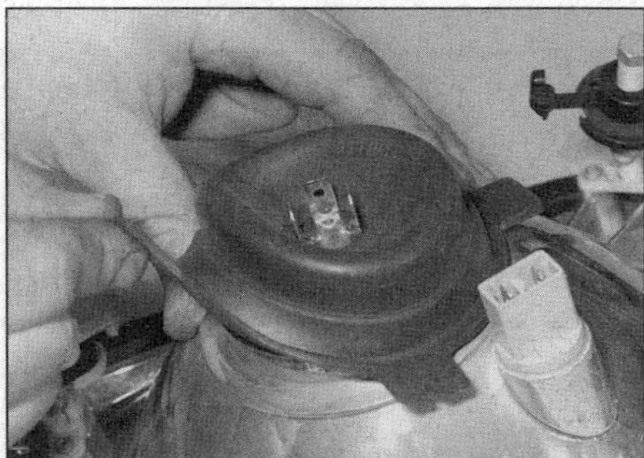

5.9a On later models, with the headlight on the bench, remove the rubber dust cover . . .

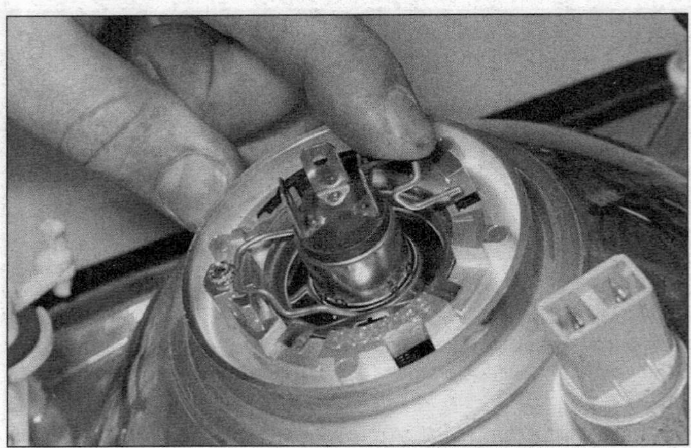

5.9b . . . then release the retaining clip . . .

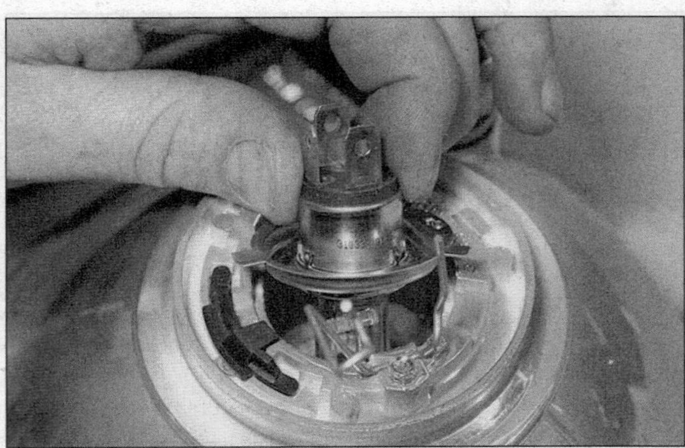

5.9c . . . and withdraw the bulb from the light unit

10 Refit the rubber dust cover to the bulb, making sure that it is correctly seated, and fit the headlight unit as described in Section 7.

Front sidelight

Early models (pre-March 1994)

11 Working in the engine compartment, disconnect the wiring connector from the rear of the headlight bulb, then remove the rubber dust cover.

12 Free the sidelight bulbholder, and remove the bulb. The bulb is of the capless (push-fit) type, and can be removed by simply pulling it out of the bulbholder.

13 Refitting is the reverse of the removal procedure, ensuring that the rubber dust cover is correctly fitted.

Later models (March 1994 onwards)

14 Remove the headlight unit as described in Section 7.

15 Twist the bulbholder anti-clockwise, and remove it from the rear of the headlight unit **(see illustration)**.

16 The bulb is of the capless (push-fit) type, and can be removed by simply pulling it out of the bulbholder **(see illustration)**.

17 Refitting is the reverse of removal.

Front direction indicator

Early models (pre-March 1994)

18 Slacken and remove the two screws securing the headlight surround in position, and pull the surround forwards.

19 Twist the bulbholder anti-clockwise, and remove it from the rear of the surround.

20 The bulb is a bayonet fit in the holder, and can be removed by pressing it and twisting in an anti-clockwise direction.

21 Refitting is the reverse of removal.

Later models (March 1994 onwards)

22 From within the engine compartment, unhook the direction indicator light retaining spring, and release the light unit from the vehicle **(see illustrations)**.

23 Twist the bulbholder anti-clockwise, and remove it from the rear of the light unit **(see illustration)**.

24 The bulb is a bayonet fit in the holder, and can be removed by pressing it and twisting in an anti-clockwise direction.

25 Refitting is the reverse of removal, making sure the two locating pegs at the base if the unit engage with the slots on the car body.

Front direction indicator side repeater

26 Carefully push the light unit to the right, to

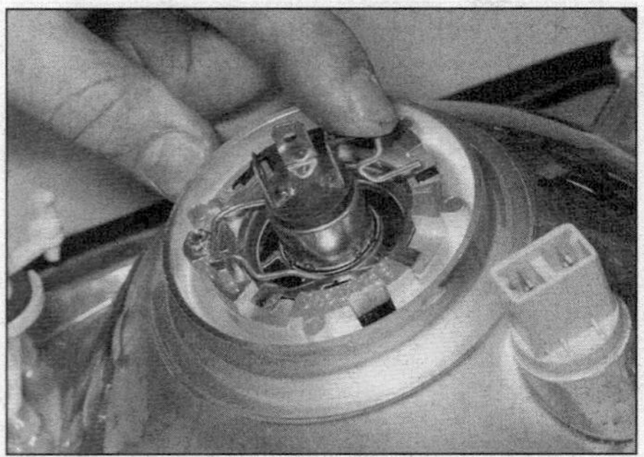

5.15 Twist the sidelight bulbholder anti-clockwise and remove it . . .

5.16 . . . then pull the bulb out from its holder

5.22a On later models, release the retaining spring (arrowed) . . .

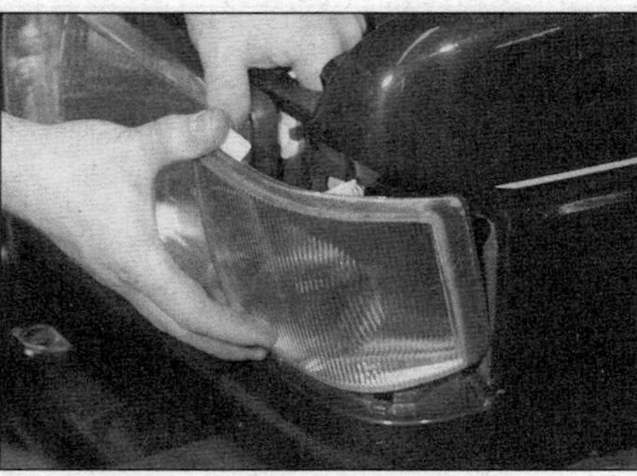

5.22b . . . then remove the direction indicator light unit from the wing . . .

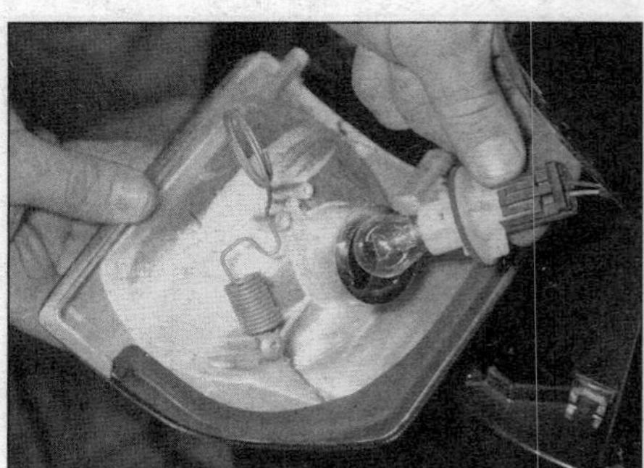

5.23 . . . and free the bulbholder from the rear of the light unit

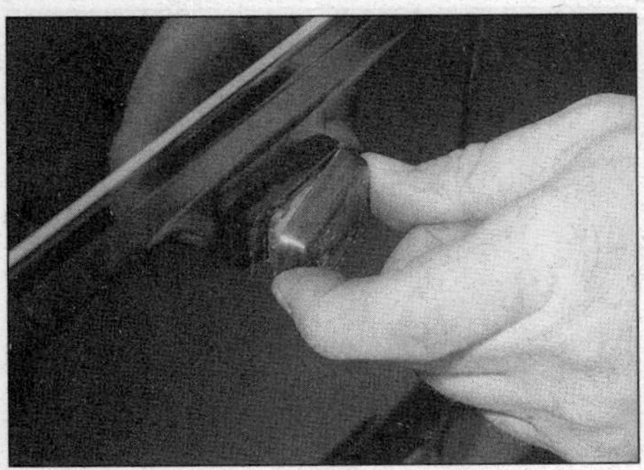

5.26 **Push the side repeater light to the right to release its retaining clip . . .**

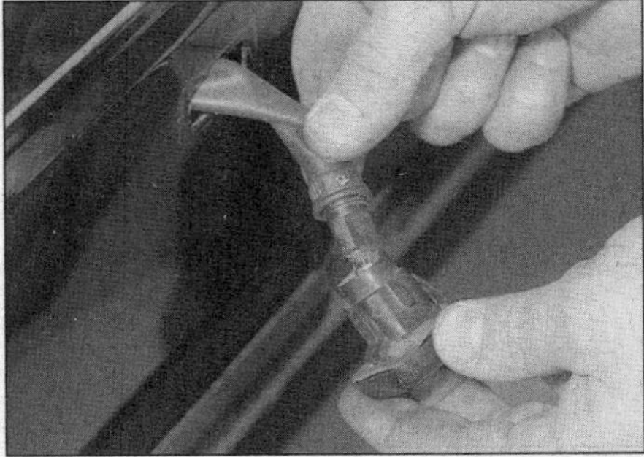

5.27 **. . . then free the bulbholder from the rear of the light unit . . .**

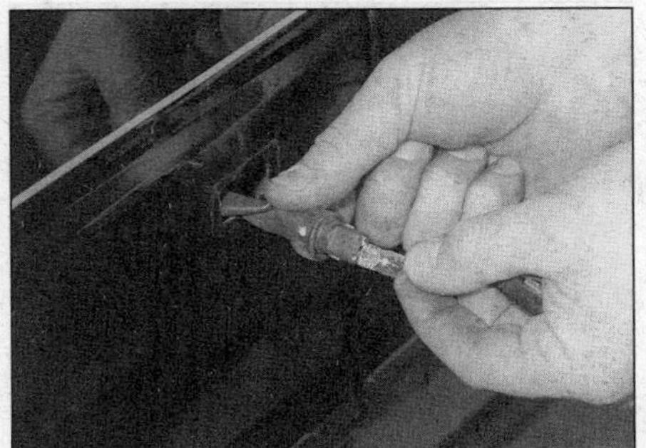

5.28 **. . . and pull out the bulb**

release its retaining clip, then withdraw the unit from the wing **(see illustration)**.

27 Turn the lens unit anti-clockwise to release it, then remove it from the bulbholder **(see illustration)**.

28 The bulb is of the capless (push-fit) type, and can be removed by simply pulling it out of the bulbholder **(see illustration)**.

29 Refitting is a reverse of the removal procedure.

Rear light cluster

30 Pull out the side-facing seat/pocket cover (as applicable), then undo the fastener and remove the access panel to reveal the rear of the light cluster assembly **(see illustration)**. To improve access, the seat can be removed (see Chapter 12).

31 Twist the relevant bulbholder anti-clockwise, and withdraw it from the rear of the light unit **(see illustration)**. The bulb is a bayonet fit in the holder, and can be removed by pressing it and twisting in an anti-clockwise direction.

32 Refitting is a reverse of the removal procedure.

Bumper-mounted rear lights - later models (March 1994 onwards)

33 Reach up behind the bumper, then twist the relevant bulbholder anti-clockwise and withdraw it from the rear of the light unit. The bulb is a bayonet fit in the holder, and can be removed by pressing it and twisting in an anti-clockwise direction.

34 Refitting is a reverse of the removal procedure.

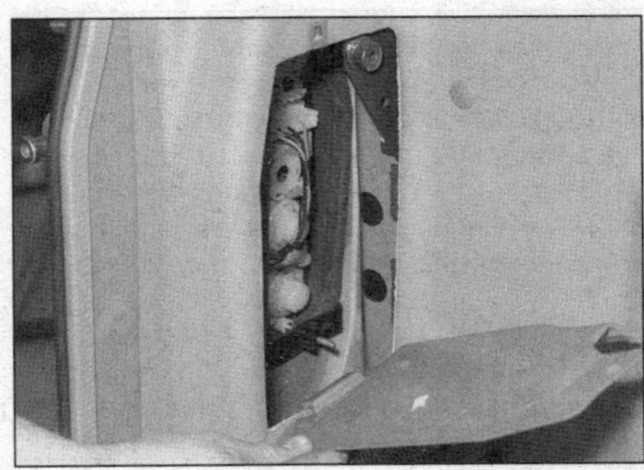

5.30 **Remove the access cover . . .**

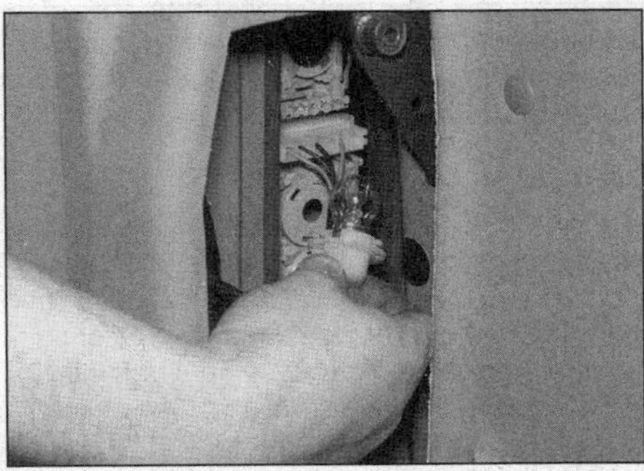

5.31 **. . . and twist the relevant bulbholder anti-clockwise to release it from the rear of the rear light unit**

High-level stop-light - later models (March 1994 onwards)

35 Undo the two retaining screws, and detach the rear of the light unit.

36 Twist the bulbholder anti-clockwise, and withdraw it from the rear of the light unit.

37 The bulb is a bayonet fit in the holder, and can be removed by pressing it and twisting in an anti-clockwise direction.

38 Refitting is a reverse of the removal procedure.

Bumper-mounted sidelights - later models (March 1994 onwards)

39 Reach up behind the bumper, then twist the bulbholder anti-clockwise and withdraw it from the rear of the light unit. The bulb is of the capless (push-fit) type, and can be removed by simply pulling it out of the bulbholder.

40 Refitting is a reverse of the removal procedure.

Door edge light

41 Using a small screwdriver, carefully prise the lens out from the door to reveal the bulb.

42 The bulb is a bayonet fit in the holder, and can be removed by pressing it and twisting in an anti-clockwise direction.

43 Refitting is the reverse of removal.

Number plate light

44 Slacken and remove the two retaining screws, then lift out the light unit and release the bulb from its contacts.

45 On refitting, ensure that the contacts securely grip the bulb ends (bend them carefully if necessary), then refit the light unit and tighten its retaining screws.

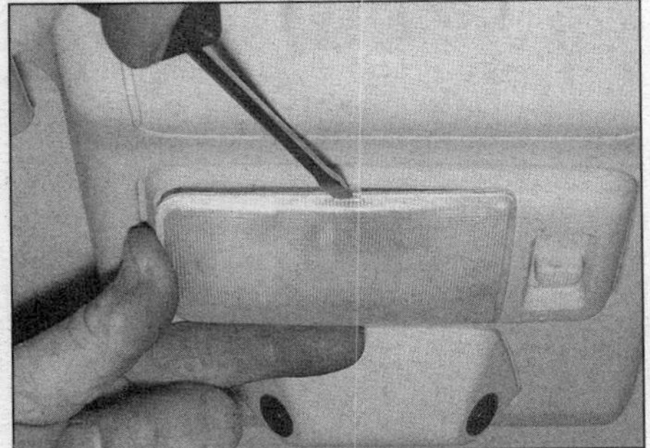

6.2a **Carefully prise out the light lens . . .**

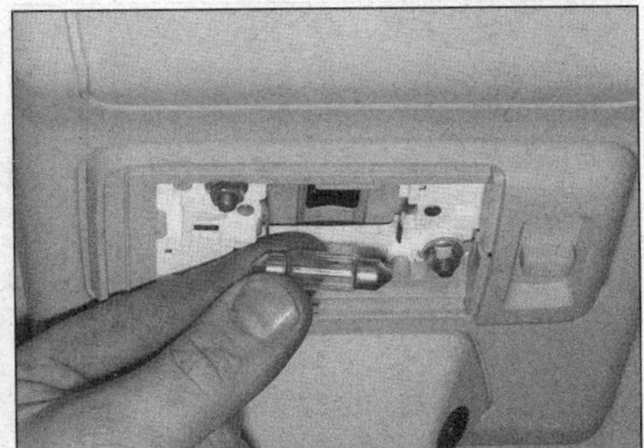

6.2b **. . . then remove the bulb from the courtesy light unit**

6 Bulbs (interior lights) - renewal

General

1 Refer to Section 5, paragraph 1.

Courtesy light

2 Using a suitable screwdriver, carefully prise the light unit lens out of position, and release the bulb from the light unit contacts **(see illustrations)**.

6.4 Carefully prise the luggage compartment light unit out from the trim panel . . .

6.5 . . . then twist the bulb and remove it from the light unit

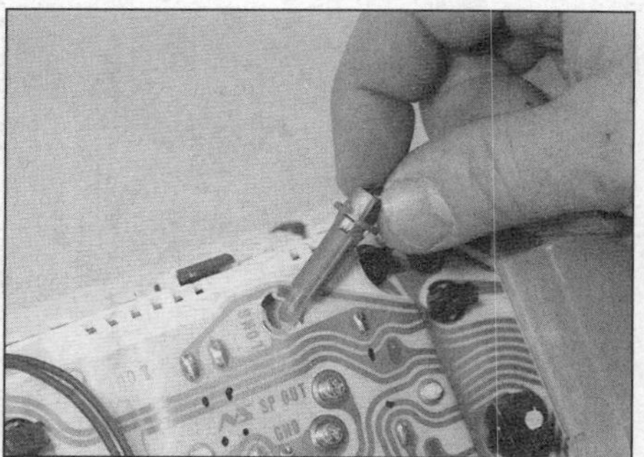

6.8 Removing an instrument panel bulb

3 Install the new bulb, ensuring that it is securely held in position by the contacts (bend them carefully if necessary), then clip the lens back into position.

Luggage compartment light

4 Using a suitable screwdriver, carefully prise the light unit out of position **(see illustration)**.
5 Disconnect the wiring connector, then remove the bulb by pressing it and twisting in an anti-clockwise direction **(see illustration)**.
6 Refitting is the reverse of removal.

Instrument panel illumination/warning lights

Note: *On models with an airbag, refer to Section 25 for information on airbag system warning light bulb renewal.*
7 Remove the instrument panel as described in Section 9.
8 Twist the relevant bulbholder anti-clockwise, and withdraw it from the rear of the panel **(see illustration)**.
9 Most bulbs are integral with their holders, although a few are of the capless (push-fit) type. Be very careful to ensure that the new bulbs are of the correct rating, the same as those removed; this is especially important in the case of the ignition/no-charge warning light.
10 Refit the bulbholder to the rear of the instrument panel, then refit the instrument panel as described in Section 9.

Glovebox illumination light bulb

11 Open the glovebox. Using a small flat-bladed screwdriver, carefully prise the light unit out of position, then release the bulb from its contacts **(see illustrations)**.
12 Install the new bulb, ensuring that it is securely held in position by the contacts, and clip the light unit back into position.

Cigarette lighter, heater control panel and clock illumination bulbs - early models (pre-March 1994)

13 Remove the centre console as described in Chapter 12.
14 Pull the control knobs off the heater levers, then slacken and remove the retaining screws securing the centre panel to the facia. Ease the panel away from the facia.
15 To renew the cigarette lighter bulb, pull the bulbholder out from the cigarette lighter. The bulb is of the capless (push-fit) type, and can be removed by pulling it out of the bulbholder.
16 To renew the heater control panel bulb(s), pull the bulbholder from the rear of the panel. The bulbs are of the capless (push-fit) type, and can be removed by simply pulling out of the bulbholder.
17 To renew the clock illumination bulb, twist the bulbholder anti-clockwise and withdraw it from the rear of the clock. The bulb is integral with the holder.
18 Refitting is the reverse of removal.

Heater control panel illumination bulb - later models (March 1994 onwards)

19 Pull off the control knobs from the three heater controls, and the knob from the blower motor switch **(see illustration)**.
20 Undo the two retaining screws, then carefully ease the front plate away from the heater control panel to reveal the illumination bulb **(see illustration)**.
21 The bulb is of the capless (push-fit) type, and can be removed by simply pulling it out of the bulbholder **(see illustration)**.

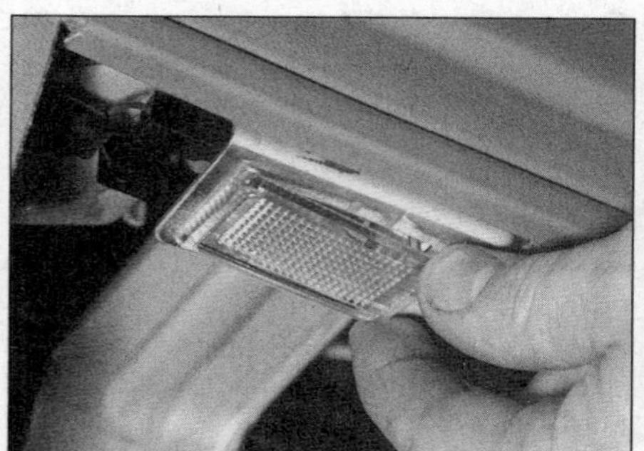

6.11a Release the glovebox illumination light from the facia frame . . .

6.11b . . . then remove the bulb from the light contacts

6.19 On later models, pull the control knobs off from the heater controls and the blower motor switch . . .

6.20 . . . then undo the retaining screws and remove the front plate from the heater control unit

6.21 The illumination bulb is a push-fit in the panel

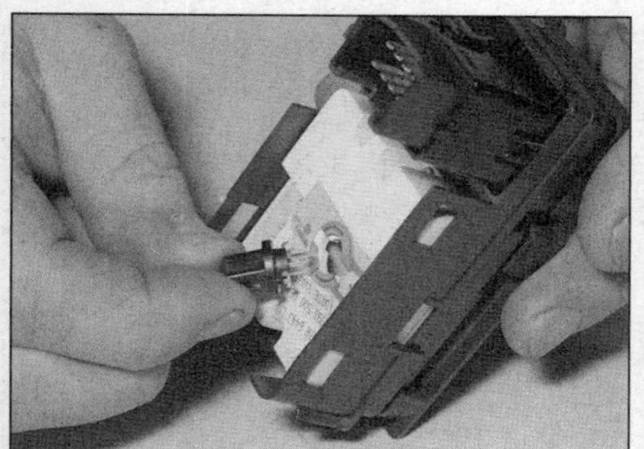

6.28 Removing the clock illumination bulb - later models

22 Carefully push the new bulb into position, then refit the front plate to the control panel

23 Securely tighten the panel retaining screws, then refit the control knobs.

Cigarette lighter illumination bulb - later models (March 1994 onwards)

24 Remove the centre console as described in Chapter 12.

25 Pull the bulbholder out from the rear of the lighter. The bulb is of the capless (push-fit) type, and can be removed by simply pulling it out of the bulbholder.

26 Refitting is the reverse of removal.

Clock illumination bulb - later models (March 1994 onwards)

27 Remove the clock as described in Section 11.

28 Twist the bulbholder anti-clockwise, and withdraw it from the rear of the clock. The bulb is integral with the holder **(see illustration)**.

29 Fit the new bulb to the rear of the clock, and refit the clock as described in Section 11.

Switch illumination bulbs

Hazard warning light switch bulb - early models (pre-March 1994)

30 Pull the knob off the hazard warning light switch.

31 Remove the bulb by carefully pulling it upwards and out of position.

32 Carefully push the new bulb into place, and refit the knob.

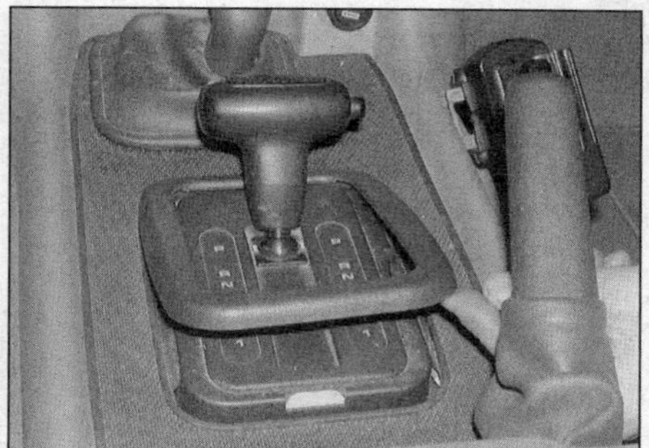

6.45 Unclip the selector panel surround

Steering column switch illumination bulb - early models (pre-March 1994)

33 Undo the steering column shroud retaining screws, unclip the shroud halves, and remove both the upper and lower shrouds from the steering column. It may be necessary to pull off the hazard warning light switch button to allow the upper shroud to be removed.

34 Twist the bulbholder anti-clockwise, and withdraw it from the rear of the switch housing.

35 The bulb is of the capless (push-fit) type, and can be removed by simply pulling it out of the bulbholder.

36 Refitting is the reverse of removal.

Instrument panel surround switch illumination bulbs - early models (pre-March 1994)

37 Slacken and remove the four retaining screws securing the instrument panel surround in position. Move the panel forwards until access can be gained to the panel switch wiring connectors. Disconnect each switch wiring connector, noting its correct fitted location, then remove the panel from the vehicle. Note that the wiring connectors are colour-coded to aid identification.

38 Each bulb is of the capless (push-fit) type, and can be removed by simply pulling it out of the bulbholder.

39 Carefully push the new bulb into position then refit the surround panel, making sure that each wiring connector is securely connected to the correct switch.

Electric window/heated seat switch illumination bulbs

40 Using the information in Section 4, withdraw the switch from the switch panel - the wiring plug does not have to be removed.

41 The bulbholder is fitted to the side of the switch - using a small screwdriver, turn the bulbholder through 90° and remove it from the switch.

42 The bulb and holder are one unit - the bulb cannot be replaced separately. Fit a new bulb and holder, then refit the switch as described in Section 4.

All other switches

43 All of the switches are fitted with illuminating bulbs; some are also fitted with a bulb to show when the circuit concerned is operating. These bulbs are an integral part of the switch assembly, and cannot be obtained separately. Bulb replacement will therefore require the renewal of the complete switch assembly.

Automatic transmission selector panel bulb

44 On early models, slacken and remove the selector lever trim panel retaining screws; carefully unclip the panel.

45 On later models, carefully unclip the panel at the rear, using a piece of card to protect the trim; release the panel from the front clips once the rear edge is free **(see illustration)**. Fold back the console rubber mat to improve access.

46 There is a bulbholder on either side of the selector panel. Remove the relevant bulbholder from the selector lever surround, using a small screwdriver to prise it out from behind. The bulb is of the capless (push-fit) type, and can be removed by simply pulling it out of the bulbholder **(see illustrations)**.

47 Refitting is the reverse of removal.

7 Exterior light units - removal and refitting

Note: *Disconnect the battery negative lead before removing any light unit, and reconnect the lead after refitting the light. Refer to the precautions in Section 1 before proceeding.*

6.46a Using a small screwdriver . . .

6.46b . . . prise out the bulbholders . . .

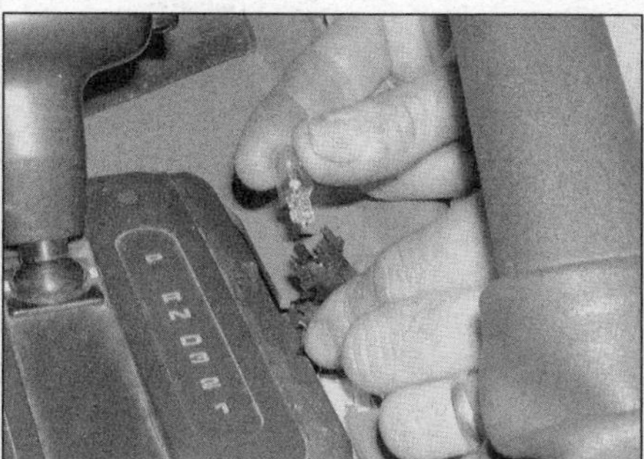

6.46c . . . then pull out the wedge-base bulb

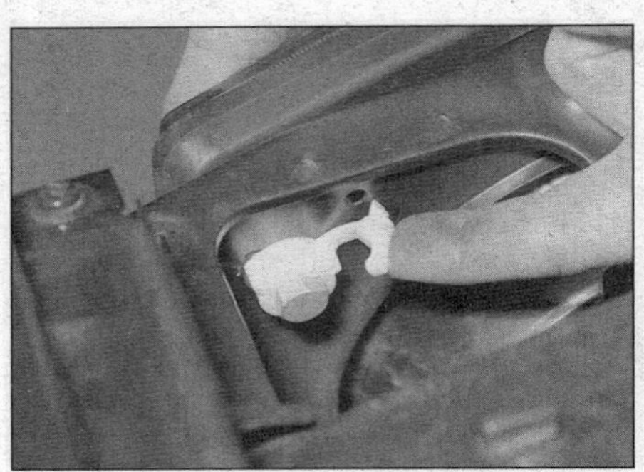
7.6 On later models, release the light unit retaining clips . . .

7.7 . . . then pull the headlight unit off from its adjustment motor balljoint (shown with indicator light removed)

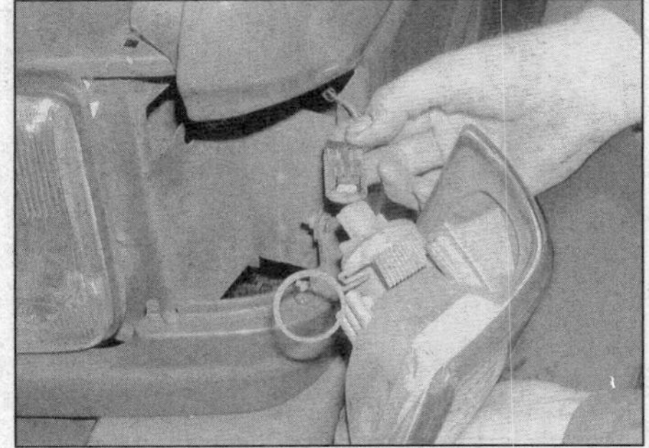
7.13 Disconnect the wiring plug from the bulbholder, and remove the front direction indicator

Headlight

Early models (pre-March 1994)

1 Slacken and remove the two screws securing the headlight surround in position, and pull the surround forwards. Disconnect the direction indicator light wiring connector, and remove the surround from the vehicle.

2 Disconnect the wiring connector from the rear of the headlight unit, and remove the rubber dust cover.

3 Free the sidelight bulbholder from the rear of the headlight unit.

4 Remove the knobs from the headlight alignment adjustment screws, then release the plastic retainers and withdraw the headlight unit from the vehicle.

5 Refitting is a direct reversal of the removal procedure. On completion, check the headlight beam alignment using the information given in Section 8.

Later models (March 1994 onwards)

6 Rotate the retaining clips through approximately 10° to align with the slots in the headlight mounting plate **(see illustration)**.

7 Withdraw the headlight unit from its aperture, and disconnect the headlight and sidelight wiring connectors. Note that on models equipped with an electric headlight levelling system, it will be necessary to disconnect the levelling motor link rod balljoint as the headlight is removed **(see illustration)**. To improve access, remove the direction indicator light (see below).

8 Refitting is a direct reversal of the removal procedure. On completion, check the headlight beam alignment using the information given in Section 8. Where necessary, check the operation of the headlight levelling system.

Front direction indicator light

Early models (pre-March 1994)

9 Slacken and remove the two screws securing the headlight surround in position, and pull the surround forwards. Disconnect the direction indicator light wiring connector, and remove the surround from the vehicle.

10 Undo the two retaining screws, and separate the indicator light from the surround.

11 Refitting is the reverse of removal.

Later models (March 1994 onwards)

12 From within the engine compartment, unhook the direction indicator light retaining spring, and release the light unit from the vehicle.

13 Twist the bulbholder anti-clockwise to free it from the rear of the light unit (or alternatively, disconnect the wiring plug from the rear of the bulbholder), and remove the light unit from the vehicle **(see illustration)**.

14 Refitting is the reverse of removal.

Front direction side repeater light

15 Carefully push the light unit to the right, to release its retaining clip, then withdraw the unit from the wing.

16 Turn the lens unit anti-clockwise to release it, then remove the light unit from the vehicle.

17 Refitting is a reverse of the removal procedure.

Rear light cluster

18 Pull out the side-facing seat/pocket cover (as applicable), then undo the fastener and remove the access panel to reveal the rear of the light cluster assembly. To improve access, remove the seat (see Chapter 12).

19 Disconnect the wiring connector, then undo the two retaining nuts and washers and remove the rear light cluster assembly from the vehicle. Recover the rubber seal which is fitted between the light unit and body **(see illustrations)**.

20 Refitting is the reverse of removal. If the rubber seal shows signs of damage or deterioration, renew it.

Bumper-mounted rear lights - later models (March 1994 onwards)

21 Reach up behind the bumper, trace the wiring back from each of the bulbholders to their wiring connectors, then disconnect each wiring connector.

22 Unscrew the two retaining nuts, and remove the light unit from the bumper.

23 Refitting is a reverse of the removal procedure.

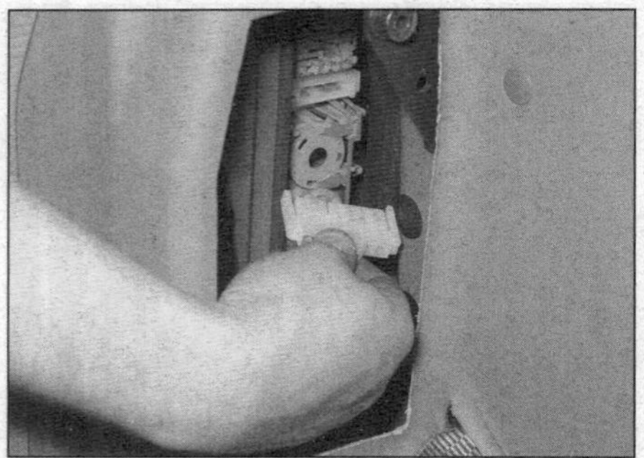
7.19a Disconnect the wiring connector, then undo the retaining nuts . . .

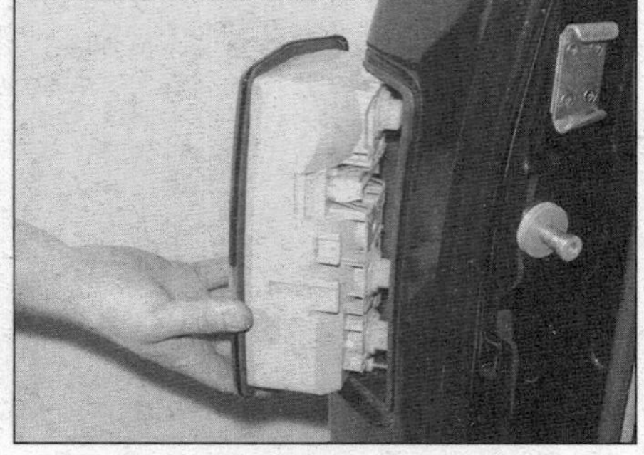
7.19b . . . withdraw the rear light cluster from the vehicle . . .

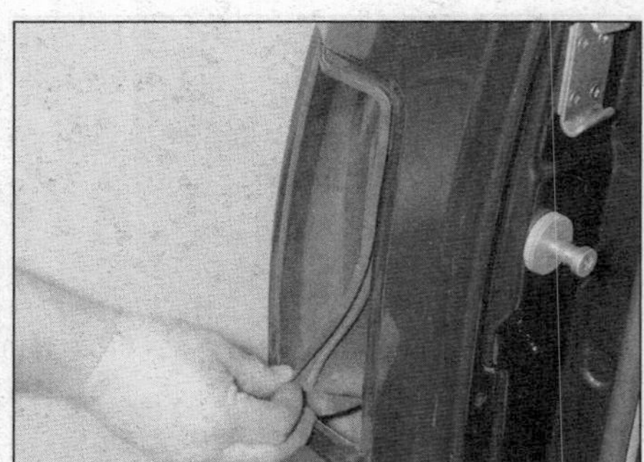
7.19c . . . and recover the rubber seal

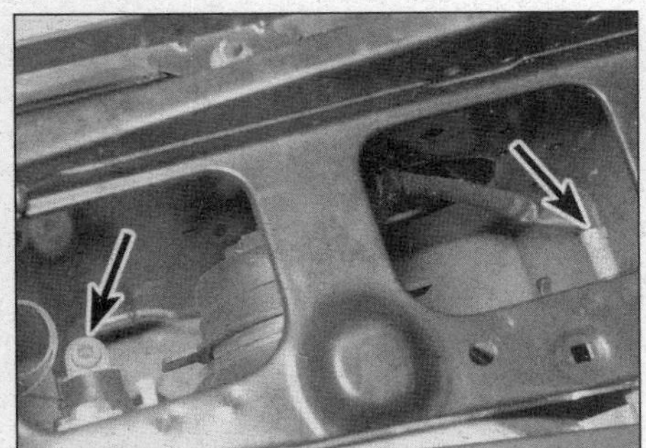

8.2 Headlight unit adjustment screws (arrowed) - model with electric headlight adjustment shown

High-level stop-light - later models (March 1994 onwards)

24 Undo the two retaining screws, and detach the rear of the light unit.

25 Undo the retaining nut, and remove the light unit from the window glass.

26 Refitting is a reverse of the removal procedure.

Number plate light

27 Slacken and remove the two retaining screws, then lift out the light unit of position.

28 Disconnect the wiring connectors from the terminals, and remove the light unit from the vehicle.

29 Refitting is the reverse of removal.

8 Headlight beam alignment - general information

Accurate adjustment of the headlight beam is only possible using optical beam-setting equipment, and this work should therefore be carried out by a Land Rover dealer or suitably-equipped workshop.

For reference, the headlights can be adjusted using the adjuster assemblies fitted to the rear of each light unit. On models equipped with electrically-operated headlight beam levelling, one of the adjusters is built into the top of the motor assembly **(see illustration)**.

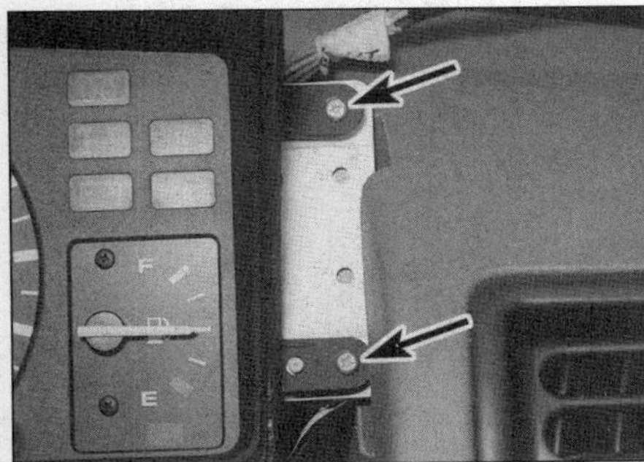

9.7 Undo the panel retaining screws (right-hand screws shown) . . .

9.6a On later models, undo the retaining screws (arrowed) . . .

Some models are equipped with an electrically-operated headlight beam adjustment system - the recommended settings are as follows:

0 *Front seat(s) occupied*
1 *All seats occupied*
2 *All seats occupied and load in luggage compartment*
3 *Driver's seat occupied and load in the luggage compartment*

When adjusting the headlight aim, ensure that the switch is set in position 0.

9 Instrument panel - removal and refitting

Removal

Early models (pre-March 1994)

1 Disconnect the battery negative terminal.

2 Slacken and remove the four retaining screws securing the instrument panel surround in position.

3 Move the surround forwards until access can be gained to the switch wiring connectors. Disconnect each switch wiring connector, noting its correct fitted location, then remove the surround; the wiring connectors are colour-coded to aid identification.

4 Reach behind the panel, and detach the speedometer cable from the instrument panel by depressing its retaining clip.

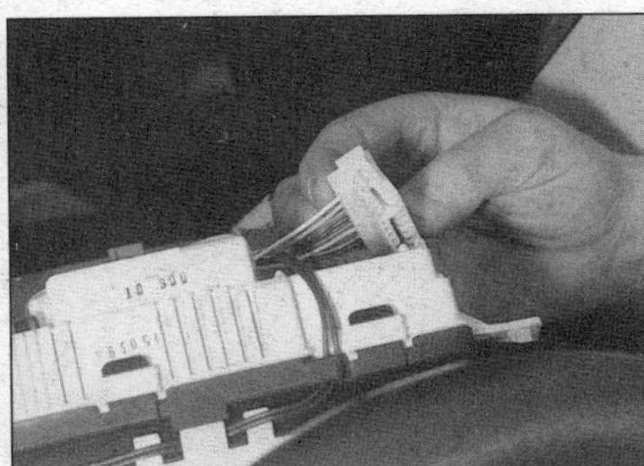

9.8 . . . then remove the panel, disconnecting its wiring connectors as they become accessible

9.6b . . . then remove the instrument panel surround, disconnecting the wiring connectors from its switches

5 Slacken and remove the four retaining nuts and washers and the two retaining screws, then carefully manoeuvre the instrument panel out of position.

Later models (March 1994 onwards)

6 Disconnect the battery negative terminal. Slacken and remove the retaining screws securing the instrument panel surround in position. Ease the panel out of position, disconnecting the wiring connectors from the switches as they become accessible **(see illustrations)**.

7 Undo the four panel retaining screws, then carefully manoeuvre the panel assembly out of position until access can be gained to the wiring connectors **(see illustration)**.

8 Disconnect each wiring connector, noting their correct fitted positions, and remove the instrument panel from the vehicle **(see illustration)**.

Refitting

Early models (pre-March 1994)

9 Ease the instrument panel into position, and reconnect the speedometer cable.

10 Refit the panel retaining nuts and screws, and tighten them securely.

11 Manoeuvre the surround panel into position and reconnect each switch wiring connector, making sure that they are all connected to the correct switches.

12 Seat the panel in position, and securely tighten its retaining screws.

13 Reconnect the battery negative terminal. Check the operation of all the panel surround switches and the warning lights.

Later models (March 1994 onwards)

14 Ease the instrument panel into position, and securely reconnect all the wiring connectors.

15 Refit the panel retaining screws, and tighten them securely.

16 Refit the instrument panel surround, not forgetting to reconnect the dimmer switch wiring connector, and securely tighten its retaining screws.

17 Reconnect the battery, and check the operation of the instrument panel warning lights.

10.17 Release the illumination bulbholder . . .

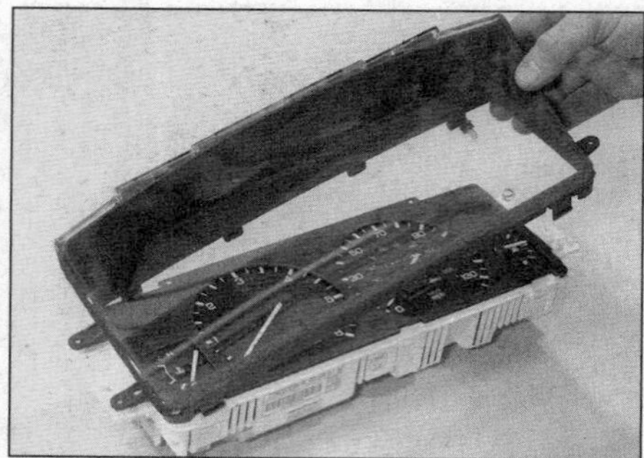

10.18 . . . then release the retaining clips and remove the lens unit

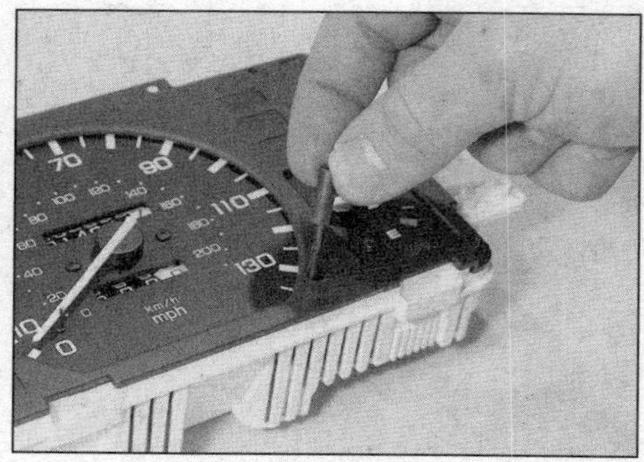

10.19 Pull out the trip odometer reset pin, and remove the instrument cover plate

10 Instrument panel components - removal and refitting

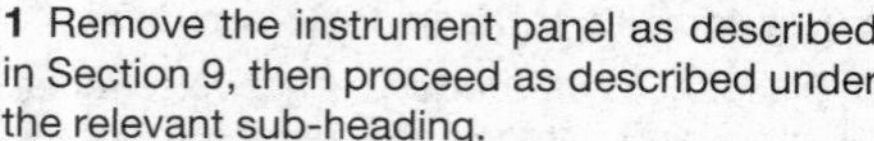

1 Remove the instrument panel as described in Section 9, then proceed as described under the relevant sub-heading.

Early models (pre-March 1994)

Speedometer

2 Release the panel illumination bulbs and the speedometer bulb from the panel, then remove the bulbholder and wiring assembly from the panel.

3 Remove the button from the trip odometer reset pin.

4 Undo the retaining screws, then release the retaining clips and remove the lens from the front of the instrument panel.

5 Undo the retaining screws and remove the speedometer from the rear of the instrument panel.

6 Refitting is a reverse of the removal procedure. Do not overtighten the instrument panel fasteners, as the plastic is easily cracked.

Tachometer (incorporating fuel and temperature gauges)

7 Remove the lens from the panel as described in paragraphs 2 to 4.

8 Slacken and remove the seven retaining screws securing the tachometer assembly in position. Note each screw's correct fitted location as it is removed, since three different sizes of screw are used.

9 Lift the tachometer out of position.

10 Refitting is the reverse of removal, making sure that each retaining screw is fitted in its correct location. Do not overtighten the screws, as the plastic is easily cracked.

Warning light panel

11 Remove the speedometer and tachometer as described above, and lift the panel out of position.

12 On refitting, ensure that the panel is correctly seated and fitted the correct way around, then refit the tachometer and speedometer.

Printed circuit

13 Remove all bulbholders from the rear of the panel, noting each one's correct fitted position.

14 Slacken and remove the five tachometer retaining screws which secure the printed circuit in position, noting each screw's correct fitted position.

15 Release the resistor from its retaining clips, and carefully withdraw the printed circuit assembly from the instrument panel.

16 Refitting is a reversal of the removal procedure, ensuring that the printed circuit is correctly located on all the necessary retaining pins, and that its retaining screws are refitted in their correct positions.

Later models (March 1994 onwards)

Speedometer

17 Release the illumination bulbholder from the rear of the instrument panel so that it is free to be removed with the lens unit **(see illustration)**.

18 Release the retaining clips, and remove the lens assembly from the front of the panel **(see illustration)**.

19 Remove the button from the trip odometer reset pin, then lift off the instrument cover plate **(see illustration)**.

20 Undo the retaining screws and remove the speedometer from the instrument panel **(see illustration)**.

21 Refitting is a reverse of the removal procedure. Do not overtighten the instrument panel fasteners, as the plastic is easily cracked.

Tachometer

22 Remove the instrument panel lens and cover plate as described in paragraphs 17 to 19.

23 Remove the circuit board as described in paragraph 33.

24 Undo the retaining screws and remove the tachometer from the housing **(see illustration)**.

25 Refitting is the reverse of removal. Do not overtighten the screws, as the plastic is easily cracked.

Coolant temperature gauge

26 Remove the instrument panel lens and cover plate as described in paragraphs 17 to 19.

27 Remove the circuit board as described in paragraph 33.

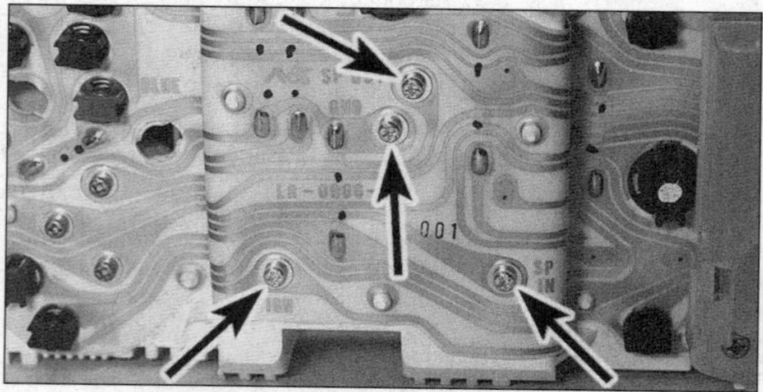

10.20 Speedometer retaining screws (arrowed)

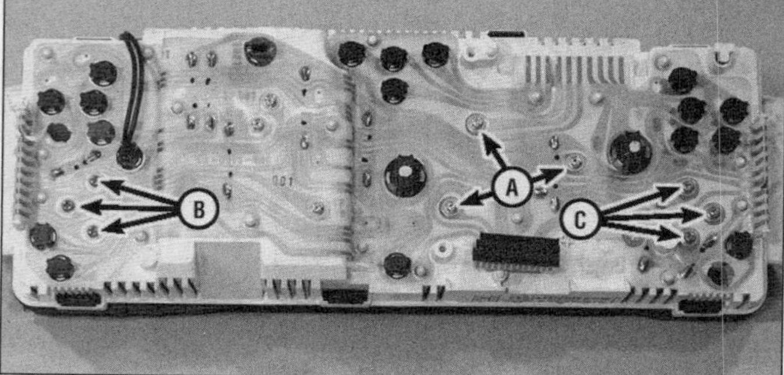
B
A
C

10.24 Tachometer retaining screws (A), coolant temperature gauge retaining screws (B) and fuel gauge retaining screws (C)

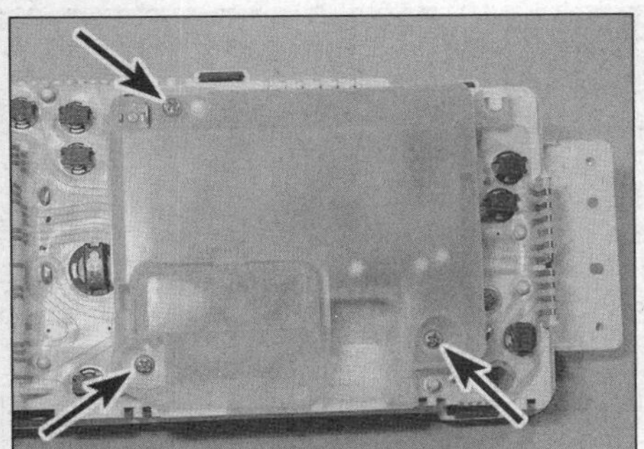

10.33a Undo the retaining screws (arrowed) . . .

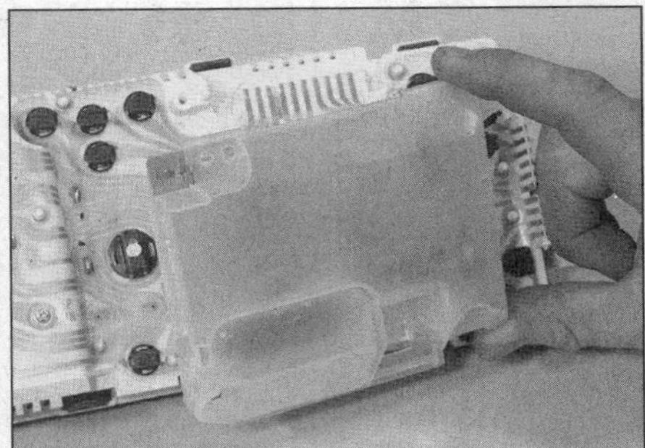

10.33b . . . then lift off the plastic cover . . .

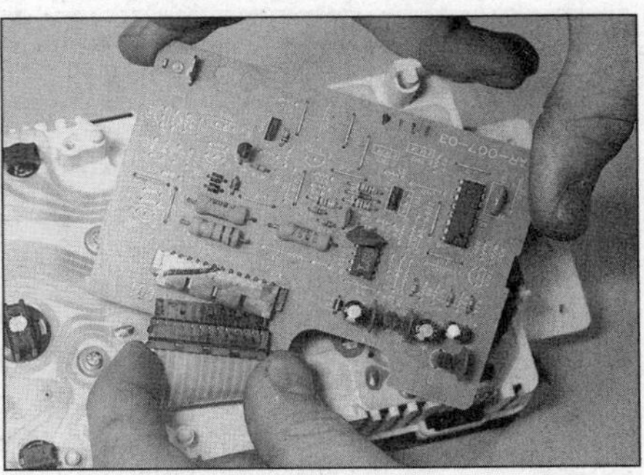

10.33c . . . and disconnect the wiring connector from the circuit board

28 Undo the gauge retaining screws, and lift it out from the housing **(refer to illustration 10.24)**.

29 Refitting is the reverse of removal. Do not overtighten the screws, as the plastic is easily cracked.

Fuel gauge

30 Remove the instrument panel lens and cover plate as described in paragraphs 17 to 19.

31 Undo the gauge retaining screws, and lift it out from the housing **(refer to illustration 10.24)**.

32 Refitting is the reverse of removal. Do not overtighten the screws, as the plastic is easily cracked.

Circuit board

33 Undo the three retaining screws securing the circuit board to the rear of the panel. Unclip the plastic cover, then disconnect the wiring connector and remove the board **(see illustrations)**.

34 On refitting, ensure that the wiring connector is securely reconnected. Take care not to overtighten the retaining screws.

Printed circuit

35 Remove the instrument panel lens and cover plate as described in paragraphs 17 to 19.

36 Remove the circuit board as described in paragraph 33.

37 Remove all bulbholders from the rear of the panel, noting each one's correct fitted position.

38 Slacken and remove the printed circuit retaining screws, then carefully withdraw the printed circuit assembly from the instrument panel.

39 Refitting is a reversal of the removal procedure, ensuring that the printed circuit is correctly located on all the necessary retaining pins. Do not overtighten any screws, as the plastic is easily cracked.

11 Clock - removal and refitting

Removal

Early models (pre-March 1994)

1 Remove the centre console as described in Chapter 12.

2 Pull the control knobs off the heater levers.

3 Slacken and remove the retaining screws securing the centre panel to the facia, then ease the panel away from the facia.

4 Disconnect the wiring connector from the rear of the clock, then depress the retaining tang and push the clock out from the centre panel.

Later models (March 1994 onwards)

5 Using a suitable screwdriver, carefully prise the facia (dummy) switch panel assembly out from the centre panel, taking great care not to mark either **(see illustration)**. Disconnect the wiring connectors (where necessary) and remove the panel.

6 Reach in behind the clock, release its lower retaining clips, then push the clock assembly out from the facia **(see illustration)**.

7 Disconnect the wiring connectors, and remove the clock from the vehicle **(see illustration)**.

Refitting

Early models (pre-March 1994)

8 Slide the clock back into position in the panel, and reconnect its wiring connector.

9 Refit the centre panel to the facia, and securely tighten its retaining screws.

10 Refit the knobs to the heater controls, then install the centre console as described in Chapter 12.

Later models (March 1994 onwards)

11 Reconnect the wiring connector, then slide the clock back into position in the facia.

12 Reconnect the wiring connectors (where applicable), then the (dummy) switch panel back into place.

12 'Lights-on' warning system - general information

Most vehicles covered in this manual have a 'lights-on' warning system. The purpose of the system is to inform the driver that the lights have been left on - if the ignition switch

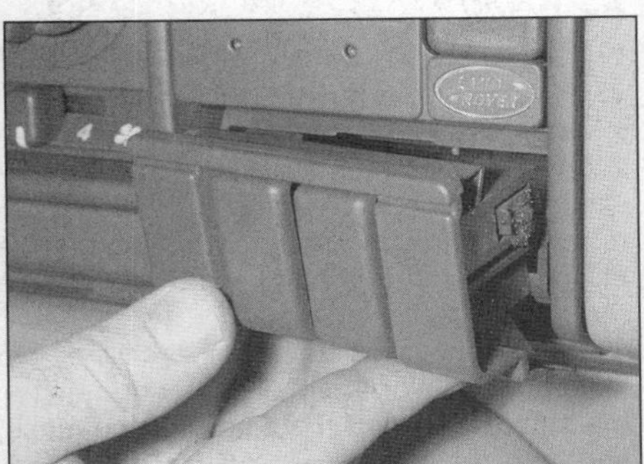

11.5 On later models, unclip the (dummy) switch panel . . .

11.6 . . . then remove the clock unit from the facia . . .

11.7 . . . and disconnect its wiring connectors

14.3 Horn unit seen with radiator grille removed

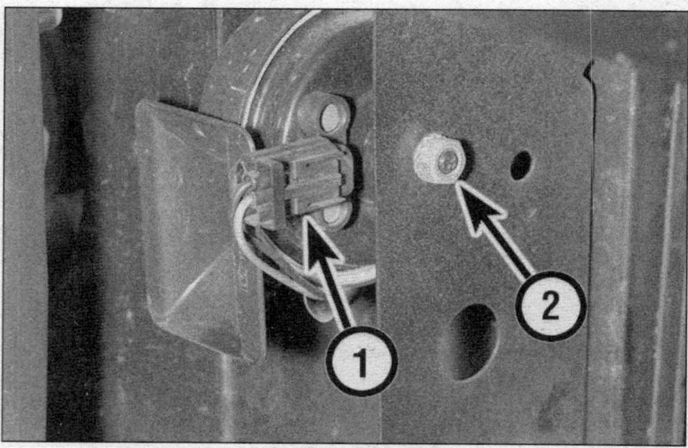
1
2
14.4 Horn wiring connectors (1) and retaining nut (2)

is turned off with the lights still switched on; the buzzer will sound when a door is opened. The system consists of a buzzer relay unit which is linked to the driver's door courtesy light switch.

13 Cigarette lighter - removal and refitting

Removal

Early models (pre-March 1994)

1 Remove the centre console as described in Chapter 12.
2 Pull the control knobs off the heater levers.
3 Slacken and remove the retaining screws securing the centre panel to the facia, then ease the panel away from the facia.
4 Disconnect the wiring connectors from the rear of the lighter, then depress the retaining tangs and push the lighter out from the centre panel.

Later models (March 1994 onwards)

5 Remove the centre console as described in Chapter 12.
6 Depress the retaining tangs, then push the lighter out from the centre console.

Refitting

Early models (pre-March 1994)

7 Clip the lighter back into position in the centre panel, and reconnect its wiring connectors.
8 Refit the centre panel to the facia, and securely tighten its retaining screws.
9 Refit the knobs to the heater controls, then install the centre console as described in Chapter 12.

Later models (March 1994 onwards)

10 Clip the lighter back into position, then refit the centre console as described in Chapter 12.

14 Horn - removal and refitting

Removal

1 Disconnect the battery negative terminal.
2 Remove the radiator grille as described in Chapter 12.
3 Disconnect the wiring connector from the relevant horn **(see illustration)**.
4 Slacken and remove the retaining nut and washer, then remove the horn from the vehicle **(see illustration)**.

Refitting

5 Refitting is the reverse of removal.

15 Speedometer drive cable - removal and refitting

Early models (pre-March 1994)

Removal

1 Firmly apply the handbrake, then jack up the front of the vehicle and support it on axle stands.
2 Detach the lower end of the speedometer cable from its drive on the transfer box.
3 Remove the instrument panel as described in Section 9. Tie a piece string to the upper end of the cable - this can then be used to draw the cable back into position.
4 From within the engine compartment, free the speedometer cable from any relevant retaining clips and ties, noting its correct routing.
5 Release the cable grommet from the engine compartment bulkhead, and withdraw the cable forwards and out through the bulkhead. Once the cable is free, untie the string and leave it in position in the vehicle; the string can then be used to draw the new cable back into position.

Refitting

6 Tie the end of the string to the end of the cable, then use the string to draw the speedometer cable through from the engine compartment and into position. Once the cable is through, untie the string.
7 Ensure that the cable is correctly routed and retained by all the relevant clips and ties, then seat the outer cable grommet in the engine compartment bulkhead.
8 Reconnect the lower end of the cable to its drive, ensuring it is securely reconnected, then lower the vehicle to the ground.
9 Refit the instrument panel as described in Section 9.

Later models (March 1994 onwards)

10 On later models, the speedometer is of the electronic type, and has no drive cable. If the speed-ometer fails, the fault must be due either to a faulty vehicle speed sensor (see Chapter 4B, Section 6, or Chapter 4C, Section 21) or speedometer unit, or in the wiring connecting the two components.

16 Wiper arm - removal and refitting

Removal

1 Operate the wiper motor, then switch it off so that the wiper arm returns to the at rest (parked) position.
2 Stick a piece of masking tape to the windscreen along the edge of the wiper blade, to use as an alignment aid on refitting. If the tailgate wiper arm is being removed, remove the spare wheel.
3 Lift up/remove (as applicable) the wiper arm spindle nut cover, then slacken and remove the spindle nut. Lift the blade off the glass, and pull the wiper arm off its spindle. If necessary, the arm can be levered off the spindle using a suitable flat-bladed

17.3a Unscrew the large nut from each wiper spindle . . .

17.3b . . . and remove the washers, noting their correct fitted locations

17.4 Remove the bonnet seal from the bulkhead . . .

screwdriver. Where necessary, remove the rubber seal which is fitted to the spindle.

Refitting

4 Ensure that the wiper arm and spindle splines are clean and dry and, where necessary, refit the rubber seal.

5 Locate the wiper arm on the spindle, aligning the wiper blade with the tape fitted on removal.

6 Refit the spindle nut, tightening it securely, and clip the nut cover back in position.

17 Windscreen wiper motor and linkage - removal and refitting

Removal

1 Disconnect the battery negative terminal.

2 Remove both windscreen wiper arms as described in Section 16.

3 Undo the large nut from each wiper spindle, and remove the washers, noting each one's correct fitted position **(see illustrations)**.

4 Open the bonnet, and remove the bonnet seal from the engine compartment bulkhead **(see illustration)**.

5 Disconnect the washer hoses from the windscreen washer jets **(see illustration)**.

6 Slacken and remove the bolt securing the centre of the windscreen motor cowl in position. Release the fasteners securing the centre cowl section to the outer sections, and remove it from the vehicle **(see illustrations)**.

7 Slacken and remove the nut securing the wiper motor earth lead to the vehicle body **(see illustration)**.

8 Undo the wiper motor mounting plate retaining bolts, then remove the assembly from the vehicle, disconnecting its wiring connector as it becomes accessible. Recover the motor rubber gasket. Inspect the gasket for signs of damage or deterioration, and renew if necessary **(see illustrations)**.

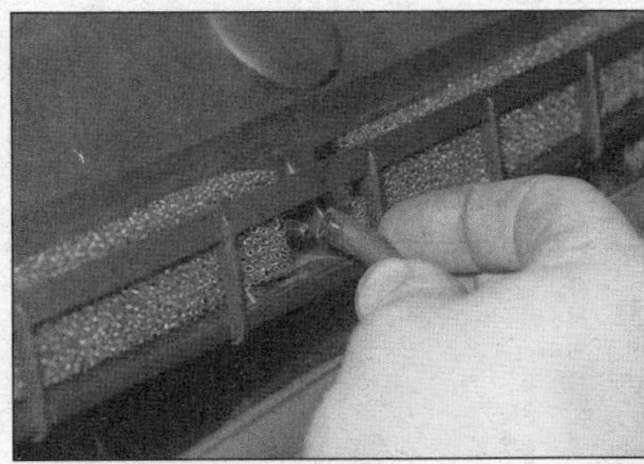
17.5 . . . and disconnect the hoses from the washer jets

17.6a Undo the centre retaining bolt . . .

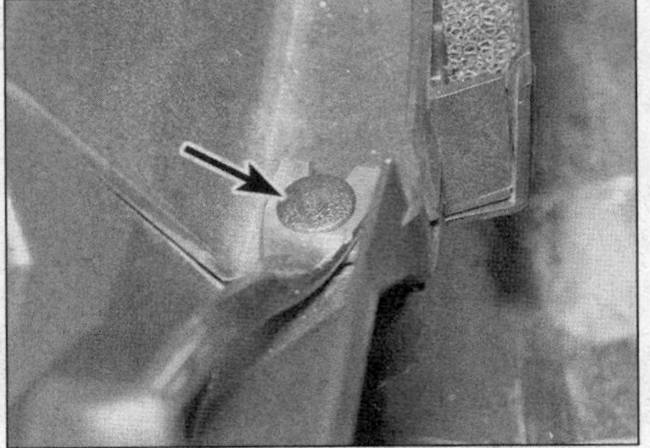
17.6b . . . then prise out the retaining clips . . .

17.6c . . . and remove the windscreen motor cowl from the vehicle

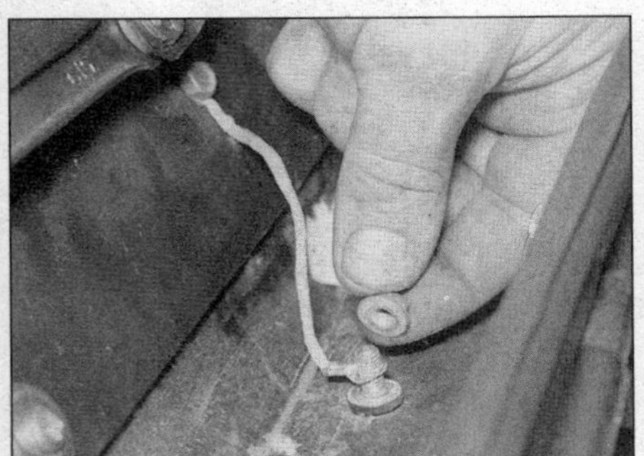
17.7 Release the earth lead from the body . . .

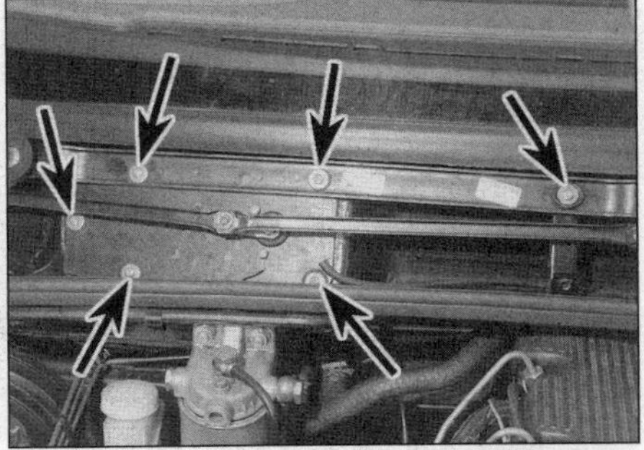
17.8a . . . then undo the retaining bolts (arrowed) . . .

17.8b . . . and remove the wiper motor . . .

9 If necessary, mark the relative positions of the motor shaft and linkage arm, then unscrew the retaining nut from the motor spindle. Free the wiper linkage from the spindle, then remove the motor retaining bolts and separate the motor and linkage. Recover the motor earth lead, noting its correct fitted position.

Refitting

10 Where necessary, assemble the motor and linkage, not forgetting the motor earth lead, and securely tighten the motor retaining bolts. Locate the linkage arm on the motor spindle, aligning the marks made prior to removal, and securely tighten its retaining nut.
11 Position the rubber gasket on the bulkhead, then manoeuvre the motor assembly back into position in the vehicle and reconnect the wiring connector **(see illustration)**. Refit the three retaining bolts and tighten them securely.
12 Refit the earth lead retaining bolt, and tighten it securely.
13 Refit the centre cowl section, securing it in position with the retaining bolt and fasteners, and reconnect the washer hoses.
14 Fit the washers to the wiper spindles, and secure them in position with the large nuts.
15 Refit the wiper arms as described in Section 16, and reconnect the battery.

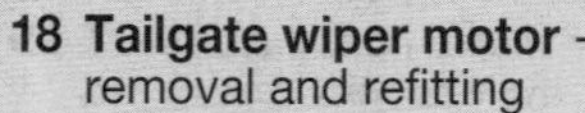

18 Tailgate wiper motor - removal and refitting

Removal

1 Disconnect the battery negative terminal, and remove the spare wheel.
2 Remove the wiper arm as described in Section 16. On most models, it will be necessary to remove the spare wheel for access.
3 Unscrew the large nut from the wiper spindle, and recover the washer and rubber seal **(see illustrations)**.
4 Remove the tailgate inner trim panel as described in Section 15 of Chapter 12.
5 Disconnect the motor wiring connector, then slacken and remove the wiper motor mounting bolts, noting the correct fitted position of the earth lead **(see illustrations)**.
6 Manoeuvre the motor assembly out from the tailgate, and recover the spindle spacer and washer **(see illustration)**.
7 If necessary, undo the retaining nuts and bolts, and separate the motor and its mounting bracket.

Refitting

8 Where necessary, reassemble the motor and its mounting bracket, and securely tighten the retaining nuts and bolts.
9 Ensure that the spindle spacer and washer are correctly fitted, and manoeuvre the assembly into position in the tailgate.
10 Refit the motor mounting bolts, not forgetting the earth lead, and tighten them securely.
11 Reconnect the wiring connector, then refit the inner trim panel as described in Chapter 12.
12 Slide the rubber seal and washer onto the outside of the spindle, and securely tighten the spindle nut.
13 Refit the wiper arm as described in Section 16, then refit the spare wheel and reconnect the battery.

19 Windscreen/tailgate washer system components - removal and refitting

Washer system reservoir

1 Disconnect the battery negative lead, then proceed as described under the relevant sub-heading.

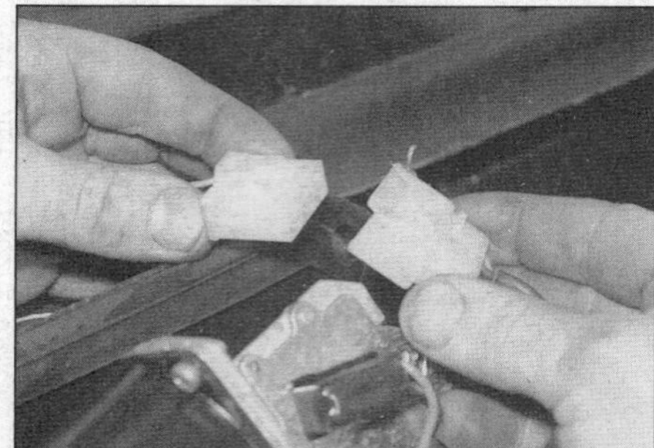

17.8c . . . disconnecting its wiring connector as it becomes accessible

17.11 On refitting, ensure that the motor seal is in good condition

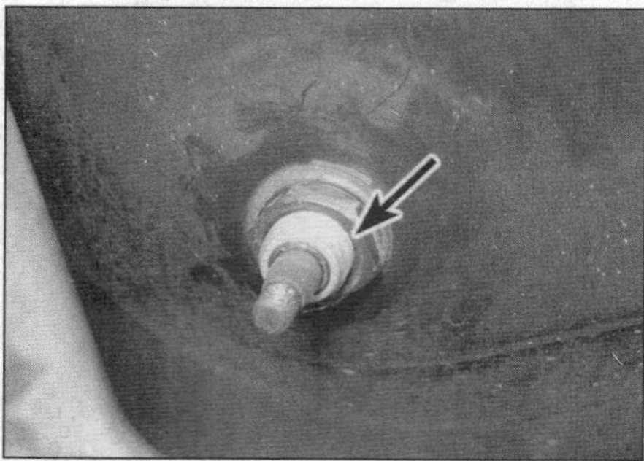

18.3a Unscrew the nut (arrowed) from the wiper spindle . . .

18.3b . . . and remove the rubber seal

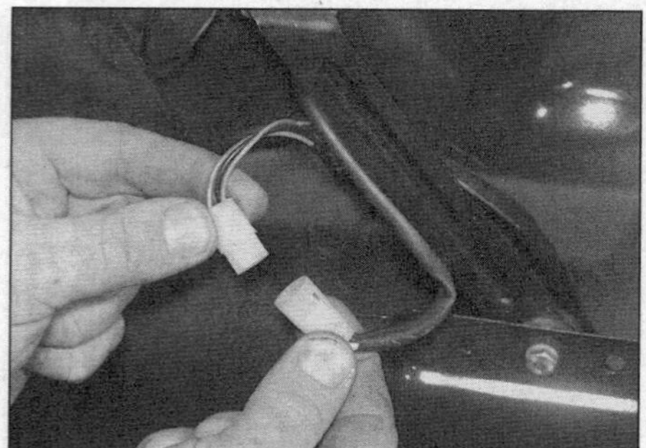

18.5a Disconnect the wiring connector . . .

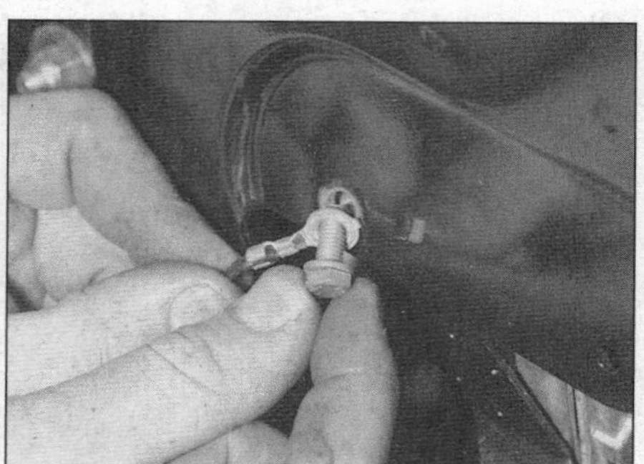

18.5b . . . then undo the retaining bolts, noting the correct fitted position of the earth lead

18.6 Remove the wiper motor from the tailgate, and recover the washer and spacer from its spindle

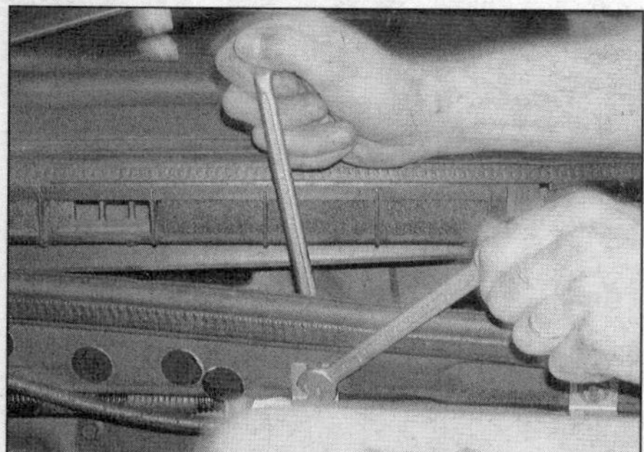
19.5 Unscrew and remove the upper mounting bolts

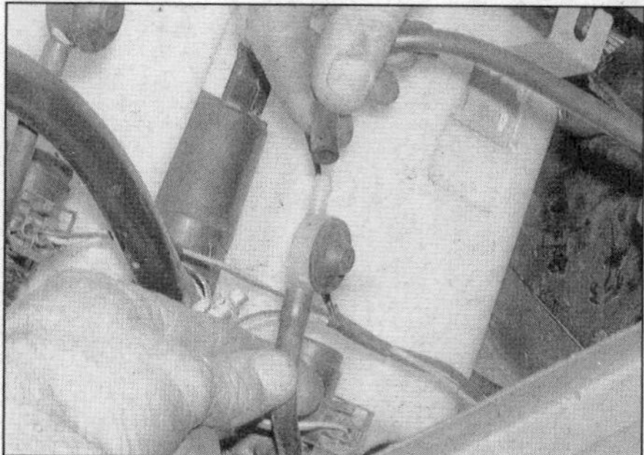
19.7 Disconnect the washer hoses, noting their positions

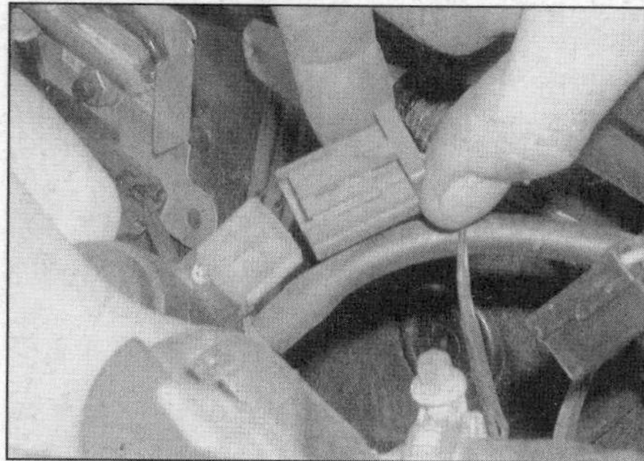
19.8 Disconnect the washer pump wiring plugs

Early models (pre-March 1994)

2 Slacken the retaining clips (where fitted), and disconnect the hoses from the washer pumps. Mark each hose for identification purposes, to avoid the possibility of incorrectly reconnecting the hoses on refitting.

3 Disconnect the wiring connector from each washer pump.

4 From underneath the wheelarch, slacken and remove the two retaining bolts, then remove the washer reservoir from the engine compartment.

Later models (March 1994 onwards)

5 Slacken and remove the two bolts securing the top of the reservoir to the bulkhead **(see illustration)**.

6 From underneath the wheelarch, slacken and remove the two retaining nuts securing the reservoir to the body.

We had some difficulty with this on our project car, as the nuts in the wheelarch would not loosen, and the bolts turned (these are screwed into the plastic of the reservoir, and had stripped their threads). In the end, the nuts had to be drilled and split off, and new conventional nuts and bolts fitted on reassembly.

7 Withdraw the reservoir, and disconnect the hoses from the washer pumps **(see illustration)**. Mark each hose for identification purposes, to avoid the possibility of incorrectly reconnecting the hoses on refitting.

8 Disconnect the wiring connector from each washer pump **(see illustration)**, and remove the reservoir from the engine compartment.

Washer pump

9 Remove the washer reservoir as described above.

10 Tip out the contents of the reservoir, then carefully ease the pump out from the reservoir, and recover its sealing grommet **(see illustration)**.

11 Refitting is the reverse of removal, using a new sealing grommet if the original one shows signs of damage or deterioration.

Non-return valves

12 A non-return valve is fitted to both the windscreen and tailgate washer hoses.

13 To remove the valve, trace the hose back from the relevant pump to the valve, then disconnect the hoses and remove the valve from the vehicle.

14 On refitting, ensure that the valve is fitted the correct way around.

Windscreen washer jets

15 Disconnect the washer hose from the base of the jet, then unscrew the retaining nut and washer and remove the jet from the cowl panel **(see illustration)**.

16 On refitting, refit the washer and retaining nut, tightening it securely. Reconnect the washer hose, then check the operation of the jet. If necessary adjust the nozzle using a pin, aiming the spray to a point slightly above the centre of the wiper blade swept area.

Tailgate washer jet

17 Rotate the washer jet to release it from the body **(see illustration)**.

18 Withdraw the washer jet and disconnect it from the washer hose, taking great care not to allow the hose to fall back into the body. While the jet is removed, tie a piece of string to the supply pipe (or tape it to the vehicle body) to ensure that it does not disappear. If the hose does fall back into the hole, the interior trim panel will have to be removed (see Chapter 12, Section 26) to allow it to be reconnected.

19 On refitting, reconnect the washer hose, then clip the jet back into position. Check the operation of the jet and, If necessary, adjust the nozzle using a pin, aiming the spray to a point slightly above the centre of the swept area.

20 Headlight washer system components - removal and refitting

Washer system reservoir

1 Refer to Section 19.

Washer pump

Early models (pre-March 1994)

2 Slacken the retaining clip (where fitted), and disconnect the hose from the washer pump.

19.10 Ease the pump out of the reservoir body

19.15 The windscreen washer jets (arrowed) are located in the windscreen cowl panel

19.17 Twist the tailgate washer jet to release it from the vehicle

21.3 Prise out the cover plates . . .

21.4a . . . then insert the removal tools and slide out the radio/cassette unit . . .

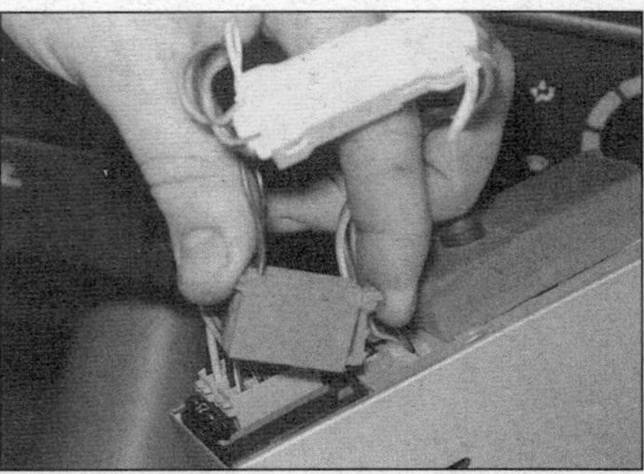

21.4b . . . disconnecting its wiring connectors and aerial lead as they become accessible

3 Disconnect the wiring connector from the pump.
4 Undo the screws and remove the pump retaining bracket.
5 Carefully ease the pump out from the reservoir, and recover its sealing grommet.
6 Refitting is the reverse of removal, using a new sealing grommet if the old one shows signs of damage or deterioration.

Later models (March 1994 onwards)

7 Refer to Section 19.

Washer jet

8 If necessary to improve access, chock the rear wheels, then jack up the front of the vehicle and support it on axle stands.
9 Slacken the retaining clip, and detach the washer hose from the rear of the relevant washer jet.
10 Unscrew the retaining nut, and remove the washer jet from the bumper.
11 Refitting is the reverse of removal.

21 Radio/cassette and CD player - removal and refitting

Note: *The following removal and refitting procedure is for the range of radio/cassette units which Land Rover fit as standard equipment. Removal and refitting procedures of non-standard units may differ slightly. Before removing the unit, refer to Radio/cassette unit anti-theft system - precaution at the end of this manual.*

Removal

Radio/cassette player

1 All the radio/cassette players fitted by Land Rover have DIN standard fixings. Two special tools, obtainable from most car accessory shops, are required for removal. Alternatively, suitable tools can be fabricated from 3 mm diameter wire, such as welding rod.
2 Disconnect the battery negative lead.
3 Unclip the small access covers (where fitted) from either side of the radio/cassette unit, to reveal the fixing holes **(see illustration)**.
4 Insert the tools into the holes, and push them until they snap into place. The radio/cassette player can then be slid out of the facia, and the aerial lead and wiring connectors disconnected **(see illustrations)**.

CD autochanger

5 Disconnect the battery negative lead.
6 The autochanger unit is located under the right-hand front seat. To gain access to the unit, release the top catches and drop down the seat outer side panel, which is further located by a velcro pad **(see illustrations)**.
7 The unit is mounted in a cradle bracket, and is secured by four bolts (two at the front, two at the rear). Check that the unit is free to move, then slide it out from the front of the seat **(see illustrations)**.

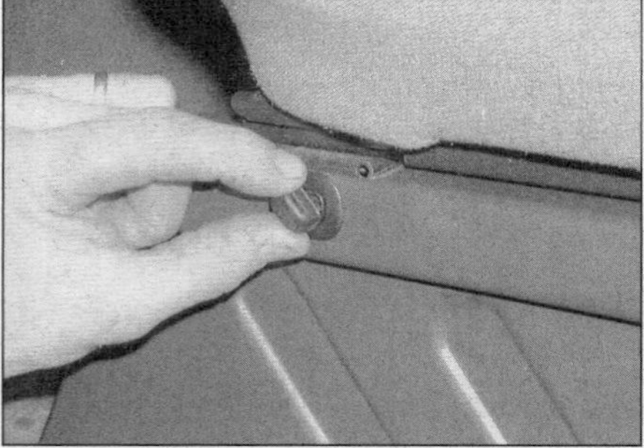

21.6a Twist the top catches to release . . .

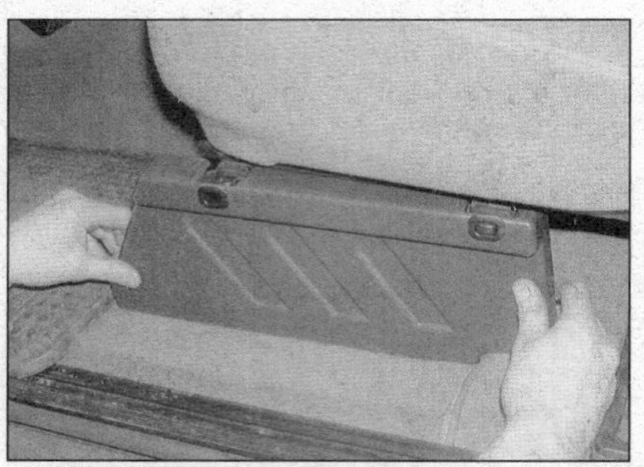

21.6b . . . then lower the seat side panel, and detach the velcro pad

21.7a The autochanger is secured by two bolts at the front . . .

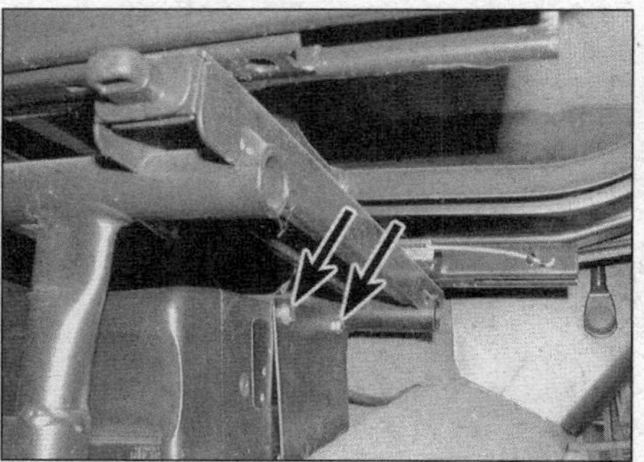

21.7b . . . and two more at the rear

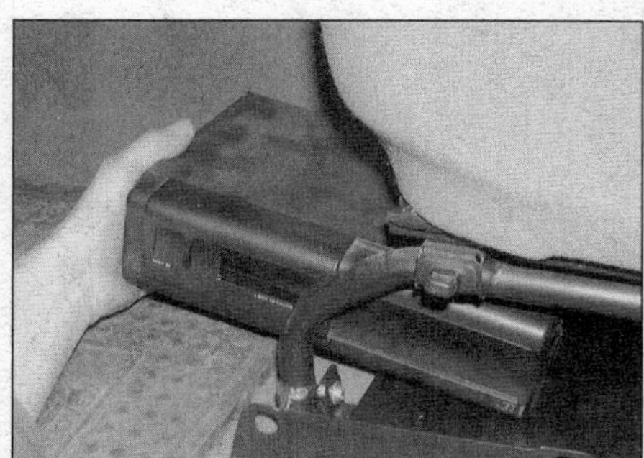

21.7c Slide the autochanger out from the front

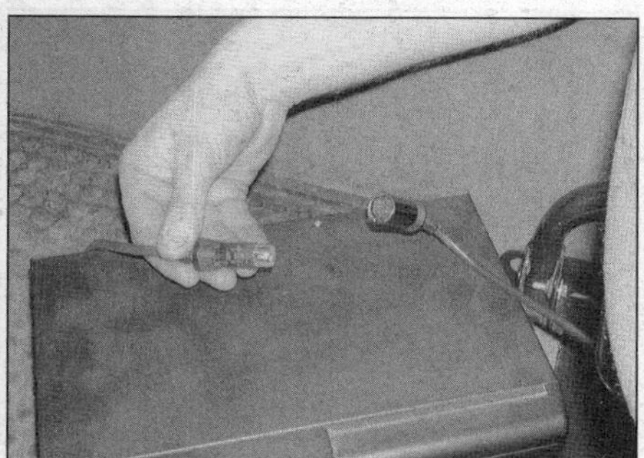
21.8 Disconnect the main data lead

22.1a Undo the retaining screws . . .

22.1b . . . then withdraw the speaker from the door panel, and disconnect its wiring connectors

8 Unplug the main data lead from the autochanger unit **(see illustration)**.
9 At this stage, the mounting bracket retaining nuts and bolts can also be removed, and the bracket taken out if required.

Refitting

Radio/cassette player

10 To refit the radio/cassette player, reconnect the aerial lead and wiring connectors, then push the unit into the facia until the retaining lugs snap into place.
11 Refit the access covers and reconnect the battery.
12 Enter the radio security code using the information supplied in the owner's handbook supplied with the vehicle. For security reasons, the procedure is not given here - refer to a Land Rover dealer in case of difficulty.

CD autochanger

13 Refitting is a reversal of removal. Make sure the data lead connection is securely made.

22 Speakers - removal and refitting

Door speakers

1 Undo the retaining screws, then withdraw the speaker from the door panel, disconnecting its wiring connectors as they become accessible **(see illustrations)**.
2 Refitting is the reverse of removal.

Rear speakers

3 On early models, prise out the retaining clips, undo the relevant retaining screw, and remove the trim panel to gain access to the speaker. Disconnect the speaker wiring connectors, then drill out the pop-rivets and remove the speaker assembly from the vehicle.
4 On later models, slacken and remove the retaining screws, then withdraw the speaker assembly from the rear trim panel, disconnecting its wiring connectors as they become accessible **(see illustrations)**.
5 Refitting is the reverse of removal. On early models, secure the speaker in position with new pop-rivets.

Tailgate speakers - later models (March 1994 onwards)

6 Undo the retaining screws, and remove the speaker grille from the tailgate **(see illustration)**.
7 Slacken and remove the retaining screws, and withdraw the trim panel from around the speakers **(see illustration)**.
8 Undo the retaining screws, then withdraw the speakers from the tailgate, disconnecting the wiring connectors as they become accessible **(see illustrations)**.
9 If necessary, undo the retaining screws and

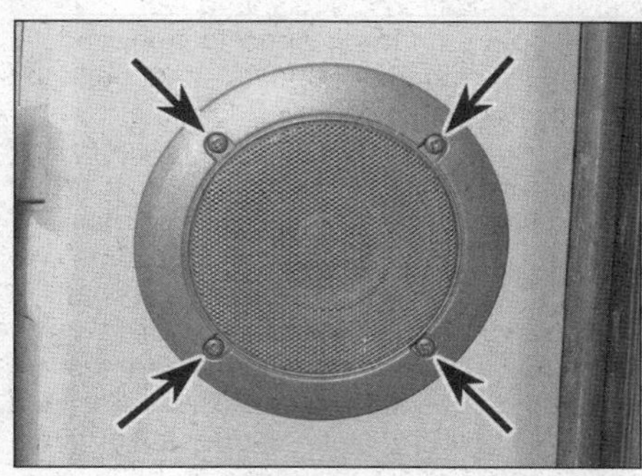
22.4a On later models, undo the retaining screws (arrowed) . . .

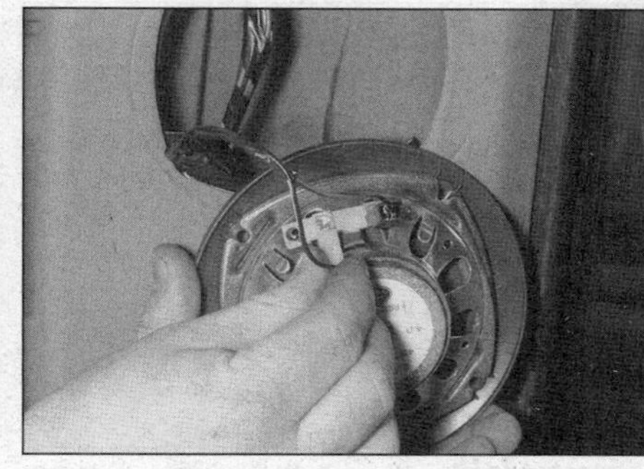
22.4b . . . then withdraw the speaker from the rear pillar, and disconnect its wiring connectors

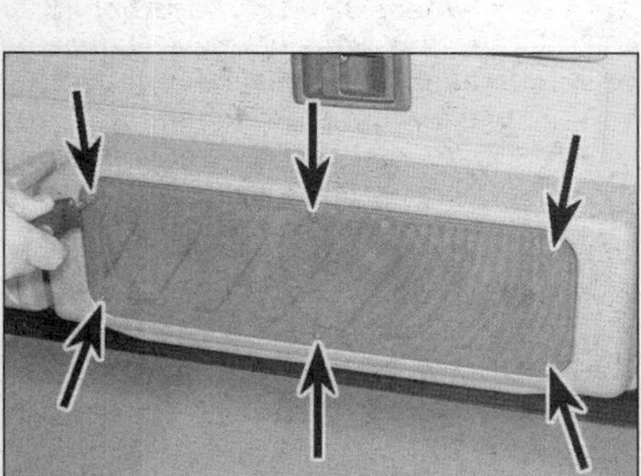
22.6 Undo the retaining screws (arrowed) and remove the speaker grille from the tailgate

22.7 Remove the trim panel . . .

22.8a . . . then undo the retaining screws (arrowed) . . .

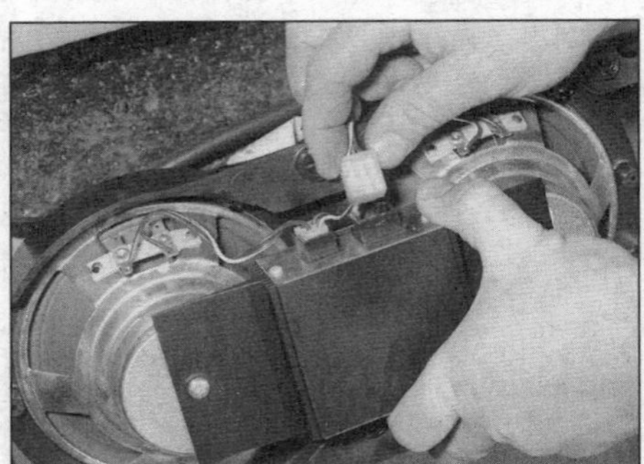

22.8b . . . and withdraw the speakers, disconnecting the wiring connectors as they become accessible

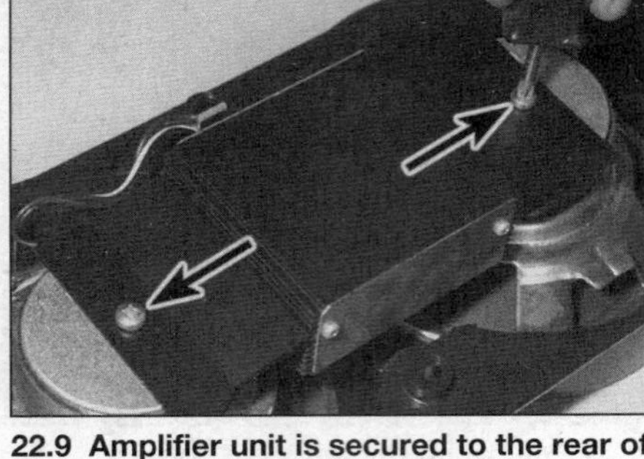

22.9 Amplifier unit is secured to the rear of the tailgate speakers by two screws

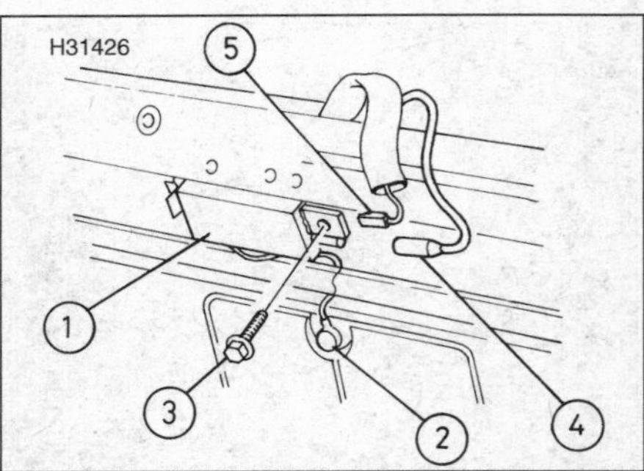
H31426
1
2
3
4
5

23.9 Aerial amplifier unit details

1 Amplifier
2 Element wiring plug
3 Amplifier bolt
4 Co-axial cable
5 Lucar connector

remove the amplifier module **(see illustration)**.

10 Refitting is the reverse of the removal procedure.

23 Radio aerial and amplifier - removal and refitting

Aerial

Removal

1 Disconnect the battery negative terminal.

2 Prise out the retaining clips, and drill out the pop-rivets securing the wheelarch liner in position. Unclip the liner, and remove it from the wing.

3 From underneath the wing, release the grommet, then withdraw the aerial lead and disconnect it at its connector.

4 Unscrew the aerial nut, remove the washer and rubber, then release the aerial from its lower retaining clip. Remove the aerial and lead from underneath the wing.

Refitting

5 Refitting is the reverse of removal.

Amplifier (1997 models onwards)

Removal

6 The aerial amplifier, fitted as standard to models from 1997, is located behind the trim panel surrounding the right-hand rear 'alpine light' glass.

7 To remove the alpine light trim panel, first unbolt the rear seat belt upper mounting, using the information in Chapter 12, Section 25. Remove the screw which secures the E-pillar trim panel to the alpine light surround. Prise out the two upper trim panel securing studs, then carefully prise the surround to release the two clips next to the seat belt mounting.

8 Carefully disconnect the wiring plug from the aerial element in the side glass, and feed the wiring though the seal.

9 Remove the amplifier retaining bolt, and release the amplifier from the roof location **(see illustration)**.

10 Disconnect the co-axial cable and the Lucar connector from the amplifier, and remove it from the car.

Refitting

11 Refitting is a reversal of removal. Tighten the seat belt upper mounting bolt to the torque specified in Chapter 12.

24 Airbag system - general information and precautions

Driver's and passenger's airbags are fitted as standard to later (March 1994 onwards) high-specification models, and were offered as an option on lower-specification models. Lower-specification models may have an airbag fitted to the driver's side alone.

The driver's airbag unit is fitted to the steering wheel, and the passenger's airbag unit is fitted to the top of the facia panel. In addition to the airbag unit(s), there are two impact sensors, the control unit, and a warning light in the instrument panel.

The airbag system is triggered in the event of a frontal impact. The airbag(s) is/are inflated (by a built-in gas generator) within milliseconds, and forms a safety cushion between the driver and steering wheel/passenger and facia. This prevents contact between the driver's/passenger's upper body and wheel/facia, and therefore greatly reduces the risk of injury. The airbag then deflates almost immediately.

Every time the ignition is switched on, the airbag control unit performs a self-test. The self-test takes between 5 and 8 seconds, and during this time, the airbag warning light in the instrument panel is illuminated. After the self-test has been completed, the warning light should go out. If the warning light fails to come on, remains illuminated after the initial period, or comes on at any time when the vehicle is being driven, there is a fault in the airbag system. The vehicle should be taken to a Land Rover dealer for examination at the earliest possible opportunity.

Warning: Before carrying out any operations on the airbag system, disconnect the battery positive and negative terminals, and wait AT LEAST 20 minutes, to ensure that the system capacitor has been discharged.

Warning: Note that the airbag must not be subjected to temperatures in excess of 90°C (194°F). When the airbag is removed, ensure that it is stored the correct way up, to prevent possible inflation.

Warning: Do not use electrical test equipment on the airbag system components or wiring connectors, as this could lead to the system being accidentally triggered. Testing of the airbag system can only be carried out by a Land Rover dealer with access to the special electronic test equipment.

Warning: Do not allow any water, solvents or cleaning agents to contact the airbag unit(s). They must only be cleaned using a damp cloth.

Warning: The airbag(s) and control unit are both sensitive to impact. If either is dropped or shows signs of physical damage or deterioration, they must be renewed.

Warning: Disconnect the airbag(s) and control unit wiring plugs prior to using arc-welding equipment on the vehicle.

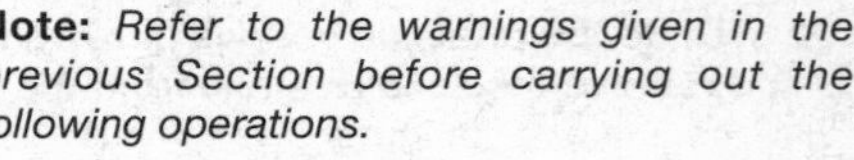

25 Airbag system components - removal and refitting

Note: *Refer to the warnings given in the previous Section before carrying out the following operations.*

Note: *A special Torx socket will be required to remove the retaining screws used to secure each of the airbag system components in position. Refer to your Land Rover dealer for further details. New airbag retaining screws will be required on refitting.*

1 Disconnect the battery negative then positive leads, and wait at least 20 minutes before proceeding as described under the relevant sub-heading.

Driver's airbag unit

Note: *New airbag retaining screws will be required on refitting.*

2 Release the two fasteners and release the driver's side lower facia panel.

3 Disconnect the airbag unit wiring connector from the steering column harness.

4 Position the steering at 90° from the straight-ahead position, then slacken and remove the two special retaining screws.

5 Lift off the airbag unit, disconnecting its wiring connector as it becomes accessible.

6 On refitting, reconnect the wiring connector, then fit the airbag unit to the centre of the steering wheel.

7 Install the new airbag unit retaining screws, and tighten them to the specified torque setting.

8 Reconnect the airbag unit wiring connector to the steering column harness, then refit the lower facia panel. **Note:** *The vehicle should be taken to a Land Rover dealer at the earliest possible opportunity, to have the airbag system checked using the special electronic test equipment. This will ensure that the airbag system is fully operational.*

Passenger's airbag unit

9 Open the glovebox, to gain access to the airbag unit retaining screws.

10 Using the special socket, slacken and remove the four airbag unit retaining screws.

11 Lift the airbag unit away from the facia, disconnecting its wiring connector as it becomes accessible.

12 Refitting is the reverse of removal, tightening the airbag retaining screws to the specified torque setting. **Note:** *The vehicle should be taken to a Land Rover dealer at the earliest possible opportunity, to have the airbag system checked using the special electronic test equipment. This will ensure that the airbag system is fully operational.*

Airbag control unit

13 Remove the centre console as described in Chapter 12.

Up to 1997 model year

14 Undo the retaining screws, and release both rear passenger air ducts.

15 Using a flat-bladed screwdriver, prise out the retaining clip (the clip should be coloured yellow) and extend it fully. The wiring connector can then be disconnected from the control unit.

16 Using the special socket, undo the retaining bolts and remove the control unit.

1997 model year onwards

17 Disconnect the control unit wiring plug.

18 Unscrew and remove the two Torx retaining bolts, then remove the unit from the car.

All models

19 Refitting is the reverse of removal, tightening the retaining screws to the specified torque setting. Ensure that the wiring connector is securely reconnected and its retaining clip is correctly seated. **Note:** *The vehicle should be taken to a Land Rover dealer at the earliest possible opportunity, to have the airbag system checked using the special electronic test equipment. This will ensure that the airbag system is fully operational.*

Driver's airbag wiring contact unit

20 Remove the driver's airbag unit as described above.

21 Remove the steering wheel as described in Chapter 11.

22 Undo the steering column shroud retaining screws, unclip the shroud halves, and remove both the upper and lower shrouds from the steering column.

23 Trace the wiring back from the contact unit, and disconnect it at the wiring connector.

24 Release the two retaining clips, then free the contact unit from the top of the combination switch assembly. If the contact unit is to be re-used, wrap adhesive tape around the unit as shown **(see illustration).** This will prevent unnecessary rotation of the wiring unit, and ensure that it remains correctly positioned until it is refitted.

25 If a new contact unit is being installed, ensure that the tape on the unit is unbroken. Do not install the unit if the tape has been broken.

26 Ensure that the front wheels are positioned in the straight-ahead position, then remove the tape from the contact unit.

27 Clip the contact into position on the steering column combination switch assembly, and connect its wiring connector.

28 Refit the steering column shrouds, and securely tighten the retaining screws.

29 Refit the steering wheel as described in Chapter 11, making sure that it engages correctly with the contact unit.

30 Refit the driver's airbag unit as described above.

Impact sensors (up to 1997 model year)

Note: *The impact sensors are incorporated into the control unit from 1997 model year onwards.*

31 There are two impact sensors - one is fitted behind each headlight assembly. To gain access to the left-hand sensor, it will first be necessary to remove the jack, and the jack mounting bracket.

32 Disconnect the sensor wiring connector then, using the special socket, slacken and remove the two retaining screws and remove the impact sensor from the vehicle.

33 Refitting is the reverse of removal, tightening the retaining screws to the specified torque setting. **Note:** *The vehicle should be taken to a Land Rover dealer at the earliest possible opportunity, to have the airbag system checked using the special electronic test equipment. This will ensure that the airbag system is fully operational.*

Airbag system warning light bulb renewal

34 Remove the tachometer from the instrument panel as described in Section 10.

35 Carefully undo the two retaining screws securing the tachometer face plate in position then, taking great care not to damage the tachometer needle, unclip the airbag warning light bulbholder from the rear of the tachometer.

36 Remove both warning light bulbs from the holder.

37 On refitting, ensure that the bulbs are correctly fitted, then carefully clip the bulbholder back into position. Refit the face plate retaining screws, but do not overtighten them. Refit the tachometer as described in Section 10.

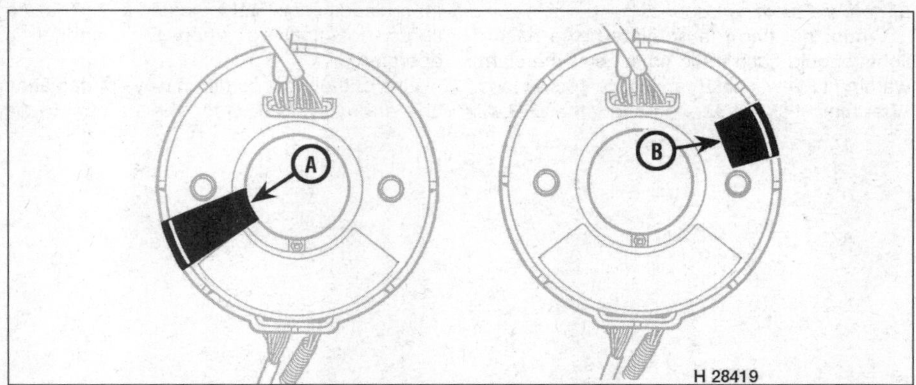
A
B
H 28419

25.24 On removal, wrap adhesive tape (A) around the contact unit as shown in the left-hand illustration, to prevent rotation. If a new unit is being installed, make sure that the tape (B) is in position and unbroken, as shown in the right-hand illustration

27.2 Removing the electric headlight levelling system motor

28.1 Headlight dim-dip resistor on engine compartment bulkhead

26 Anti-theft alarm system - general information

Note: *This information is applicable only to the anti-theft alarm system fitted by Land Rover as standard equipment.*

Most later models in the range are fitted with an anti-theft alarm system as standard equipment. The alarm system has ultrasonic (movement) sensing, as well as switches on all the doors (including the tailgate) and the bonnet. If movement is detected inside the vehicle, or if the tailgate, bonnet or any of the doors are opened whilst the alarm is set, the alarm siren will sound and the hazard warning lights will flash. The alarm also has an immobiliser function, which makes the ignition and starter circuits inoperable whilst the alarm is triggered.

Models up to 1996

The alarm can be activated in either of two ways. The first is by using the remote control unit, this turns on the ultrasonic (movement) sensing facility, as well as all the door switches. The second way is to lock the doors using the key in the driver's door lock, this will only turn on the door switches, leaving the ultrasonic (movement) sensing facility disabled. **Note:** *If the key is left in the door lock for more than 5 seconds without being turned, the alarm will sound.*

When the alarm is activated, the hazard lights should flash three times, and the alarm warning LED will flash rapidly for 10 seconds. After the initial 10-second period, the LED will flash at a slower rate, to indicate that the alarm is active. On disarming the alarm, the hazard warning lights will flash once, and the LED will go out.

Models from 1996 onwards

The system fitted to later models is a development of the earlier system, and features a number of key upgrades.

If the alarm handset is not pressed, or the doors are not locked, the immobiliser function still cuts in automatically on leaving the car. This occurs either after 30 seconds (when the engine is switched off and the driver's door is opened), or after 5 minutes following the engine being switched off or the alarm being deactivated. This passive arming feature means that the car cannot be left for long periods without at least being immobilised.

The passive immobiliser disables the starter circuit, and the ignition circuit (petrol models) or fuel supply using the injection pump stop solenoid (diesel models). The system is disarmed as follows. The alarm handset contains a transponder micro-chip, and the ignition switch contains a reader coil. When the handset is close to the ignition switch, the reader coil recognises the signal from the micro-chip, and de-activates the immobiliser. For this reason, it is essential that the handset is kept on the same key ring as the rest of the car keys. It is also essential that the handset battery is replaced when necessary - the need for replacement is first indicated by the hazard lights not flashing when the handset is operated.

One of the most common ways of defeating any alarm system is for the battery to be disconnected. The alarm siren on later models has a battery back-up feature, and will sound the alarm if the vehicle battery is tampered with. If the vehicle battery is disconnected for repair work, there is a procedure to be followed, to avoid setting off the alarm - see Chapter 5A, Section 4.

All models

Should the alarm system develop a fault, the vehicle should be taken to a Land Rover dealer for examination.

27 Electric headlight levelling system components - removal and refitting

Electric motor

1 Remove the headlight as described in Section 7.

2 The motor is a bayonet fit in the body; twist the motor to free it, and disconnect its wiring connector **(see illustration)**.

3 Refitting is the reverse of removal.

Switch

4 Refer to Section 4.

28 Dim-dip lighting system (UK models only) - general information

To comply with UK regulations, a dim-dip lighting system is fitted to most UK models. On early models (pre-March 1994), the system comprises a control unit which is mounted onto the rear of the steering column support bracket. Later models use a relay (see Specifications for location) and a resistor unit situated at the rear left-hand corner of engine compartment, mounted onto the bulkhead **(see illustration)**.

The system is supplied with current from the sidelight circuit, and energised by a feed from the ignition switch. When energised, the unit allows battery voltage to pass through the resistor to the headlight dipped-beam circuits; this lights the headlights with approximately one-sixth of their normal power, so that the car cannot be driven using sidelights alone.

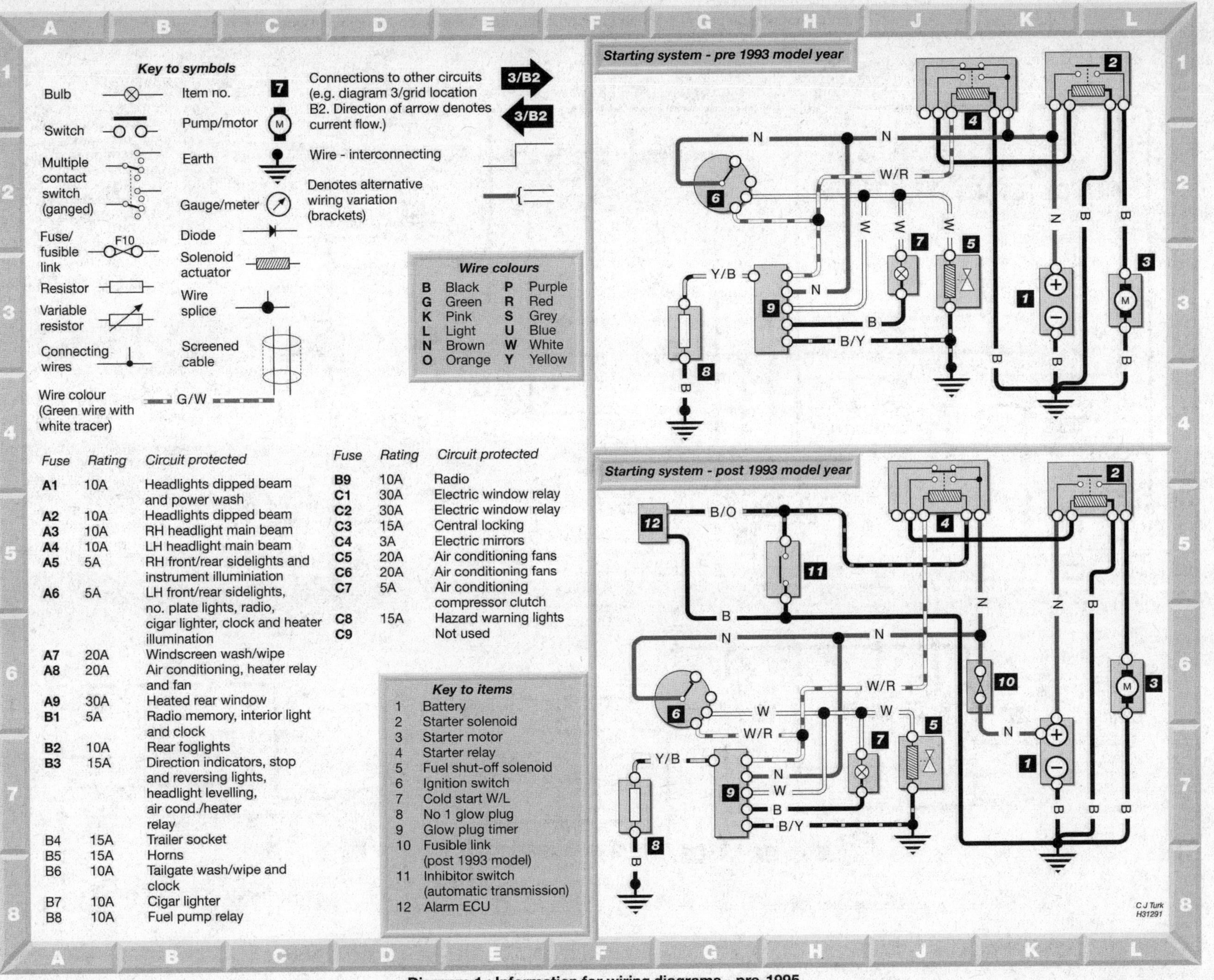
Key to symbols
Bulb
Switch
Multiple contact switch (ganged)
Fuse/ fusible link
F10
Resistor
Variable resistor
Connecting wires
Wire colour (Green wire with white tracer)
G/W
Item no.
7
Pump/motor
M
Earth
Gauge/meter
Diode
Solenoid actuator
Wire splice
Screened cable
Connections to other circuits (e.g. diagram 3/grid location B2. Direction of arrow denotes current flow.)
3/B2
3/B2
Wire - interconnecting
Denotes alternative wiring variation (brackets)
Wire colours
B Black
G Green
K Pink
L Light
N Brown
O Orange
P Purple
R Red
S Grey
U Blue
W White
Y Yellow
Starting system - pre 1993 model year
Starting system - post 1993 model year
N
W/R
W
B
B/Y
Y/B
B/O
Key to items
1 Battery
2 Starter solenoid
3 Starter motor
4 Starter relay
5 Fuel shut-off solenoid
6 Ignition switch
7 Cold start W/L
8 No 1 glow plug
9 Glow plug timer
10 Fusible link (post 1993 model)
11 Inhibitor switch (automatic transmission)
12 Alarm ECU
C J Turk
H31291

Fuse	Rating	Circuit protected
A1	10A	Headlights dipped beam and power wash
A2	10A	Headlights dipped beam
A3	10A	RH headlight main beam
A4	10A	LH headlight main beam
A5	5A	RH front/rear sidelights and instrument illuminiation
A6	5A	LH front/rear sidelights, no. plate lights, radio, cigar lighter, clock and heater illumination
A7	20A	Windscreen wash/wipe
A8	20A	Air conditioning, heater relay and fan
A9	30A	Heated rear window
B1	5A	Radio memory, interior light and clock
B2	10A	Rear foglights
B3	15A	Direction indicators, stop and reversing lights, headlight levelling, air cond./heater relay
B4	15A	Trailer socket
B5	15A	Horns
B6	10A	Tailgate wash/wipe and clock
B7	10A	Cigar lighter
B8	10A	Fuel pump relay
B9	10A	Radio
C1	30A	Electric window relay
C2	30A	Electric window relay
C3	15A	Central locking
C4	3A	Electric mirrors
C5	20A	Air conditioning fans
C6	20A	Air conditioning fans
C7	5A	Air conditioning compressor clutch
C8	15A	Hazard warning lights
C9		Not used

Diagram 1 : Information for wiring diagrams - pre-1995

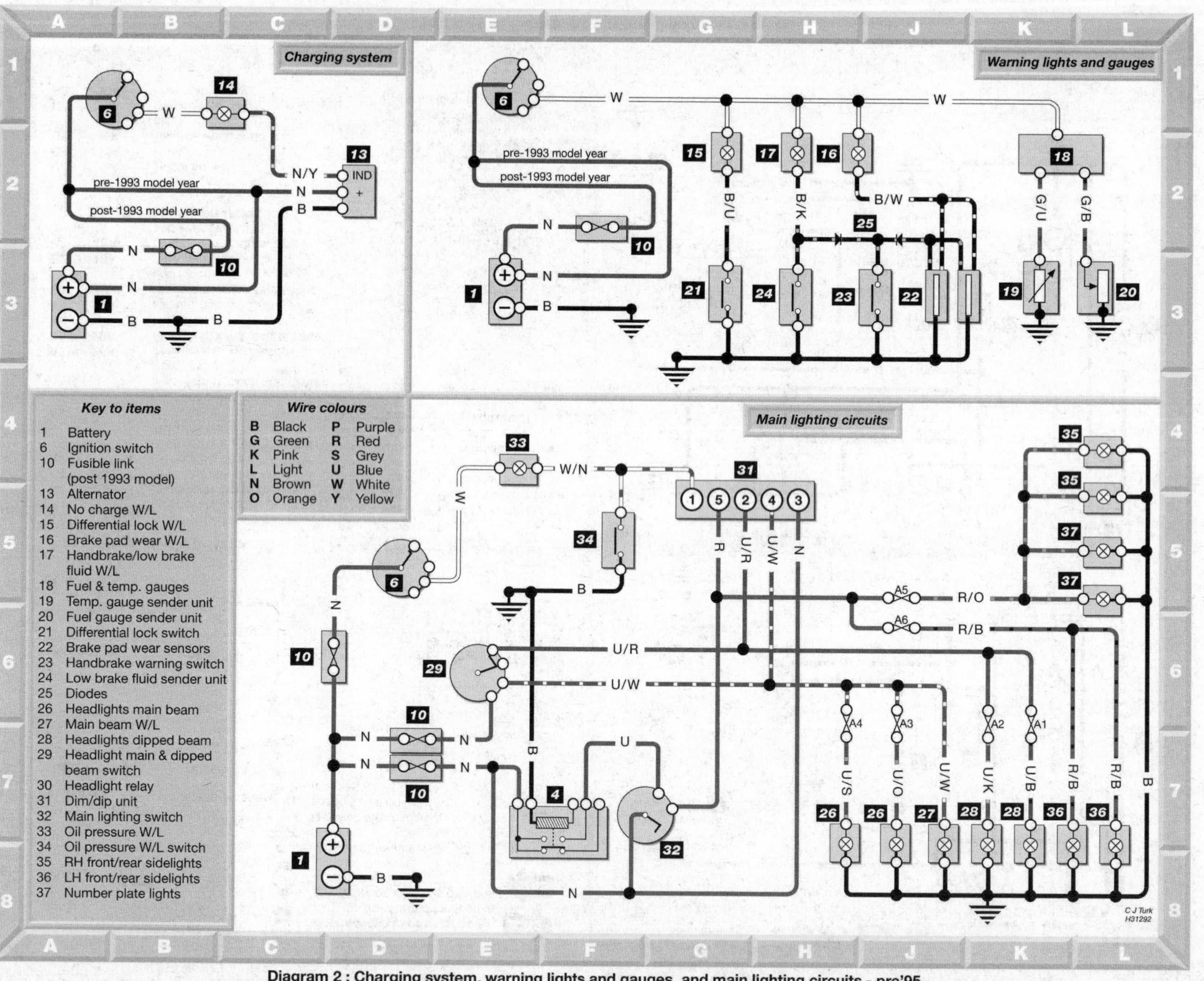

Charging system
Warning lights and gauges
Main lighting circuits
pre-1993 model year
post-1993 model year
Key to items
1 Battery
6 Ignition switch
10 Fusible link (post 1993 model)
13 Alternator
14 No charge W/L
15 Differential lock W/L
16 Brake pad wear W/L
17 Handbrake/low brake fluid W/L
18 Fuel & temp. gauges
19 Temp. gauge sender unit
20 Fuel gauge sender unit
21 Differential lock switch
22 Brake pad wear sensors
23 Handbrake warning switch
24 Low brake fluid sender unit
25 Diodes
26 Headlights main beam
27 Main beam W/L
28 Headlights dipped beam
29 Headlight main & dipped beam switch
30 Headlight relay
31 Dim/dip unit
32 Main lighting switch
33 Oil pressure W/L
34 Oil pressure W/L switch
35 RH front/rear sidelights
36 LH front/rear sidelights
37 Number plate lights
Wire colours
B Black
G Green
K Pink
L Light
N Brown
O Orange
P Purple
R Red
S Grey
U Blue
W White
Y Yellow
C J Turk
H31292

Diagram 2 : Charging system, warning lights and gauges, and main lighting circuits - pre'95

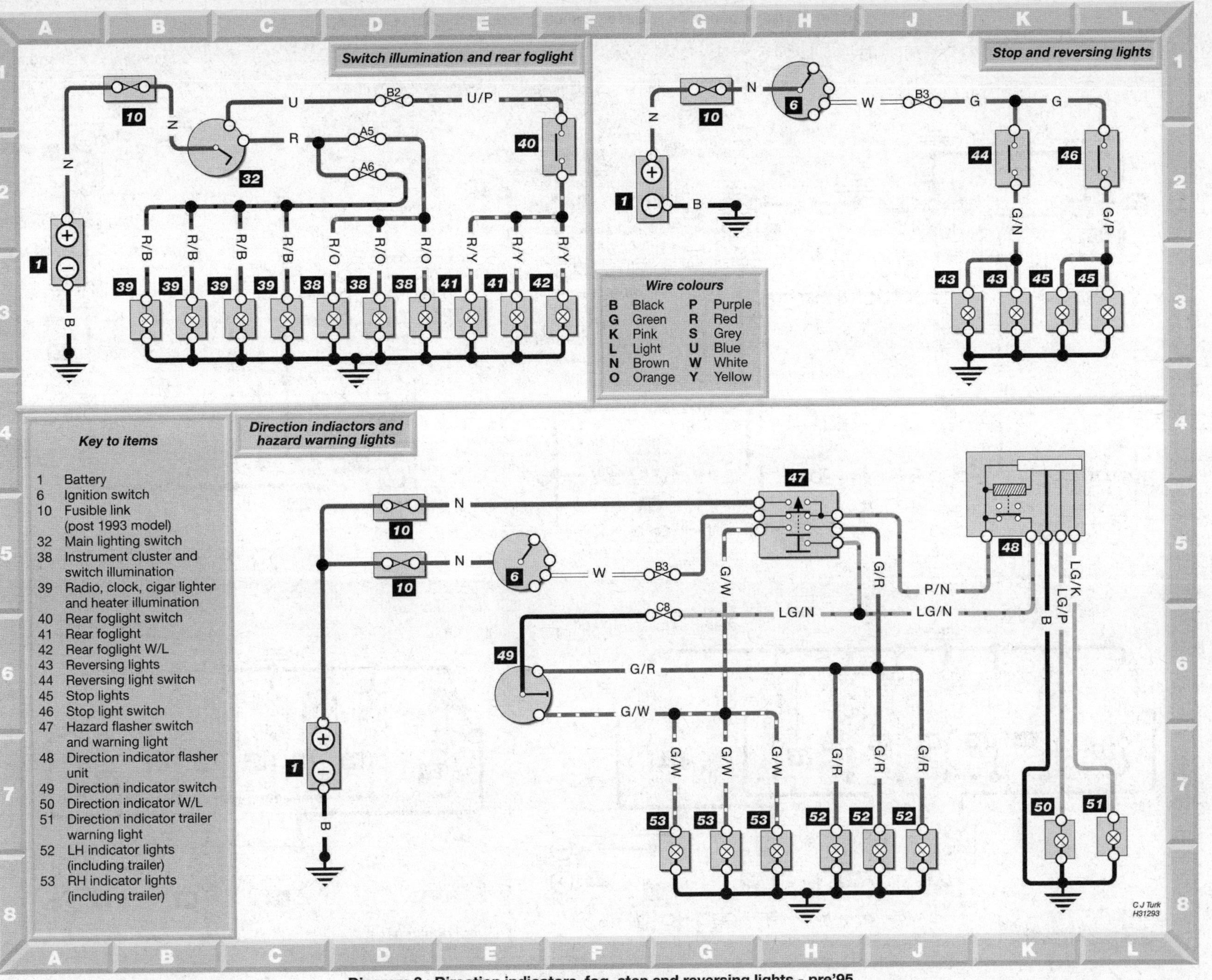
Switch illumination and rear foglight
Stop and reversing lights
Direction indiactors and hazard warning lights
Wire colours
B Black
G Green
K Pink
L Light
N Brown
O Orange
P Purple
R Red
S Grey
U Blue
W White
Y Yellow
Key to items
1 Battery
6 Ignition switch
10 Fusible link (post 1993 model)
32 Main lighting switch
38 Instrument cluster and switch illumination
39 Radio, clock, cigar lighter and heater illumination
40 Rear foglight switch
41 Rear foglight
42 Rear foglight W/L
43 Reversing lights
44 Reversing light switch
45 Stop lights
46 Stop light switch
47 Hazard flasher switch and warning light
48 Direction indicator flasher unit
49 Direction indicator switch
50 Direction indicator W/L
51 Direction indicator trailer warning light
52 LH indicator lights (including trailer)
53 RH indicator lights (including trailer)
C J Turk
H31293

Diagram 3 : Direction indicators, fog, stop and reversing lights - pre'95

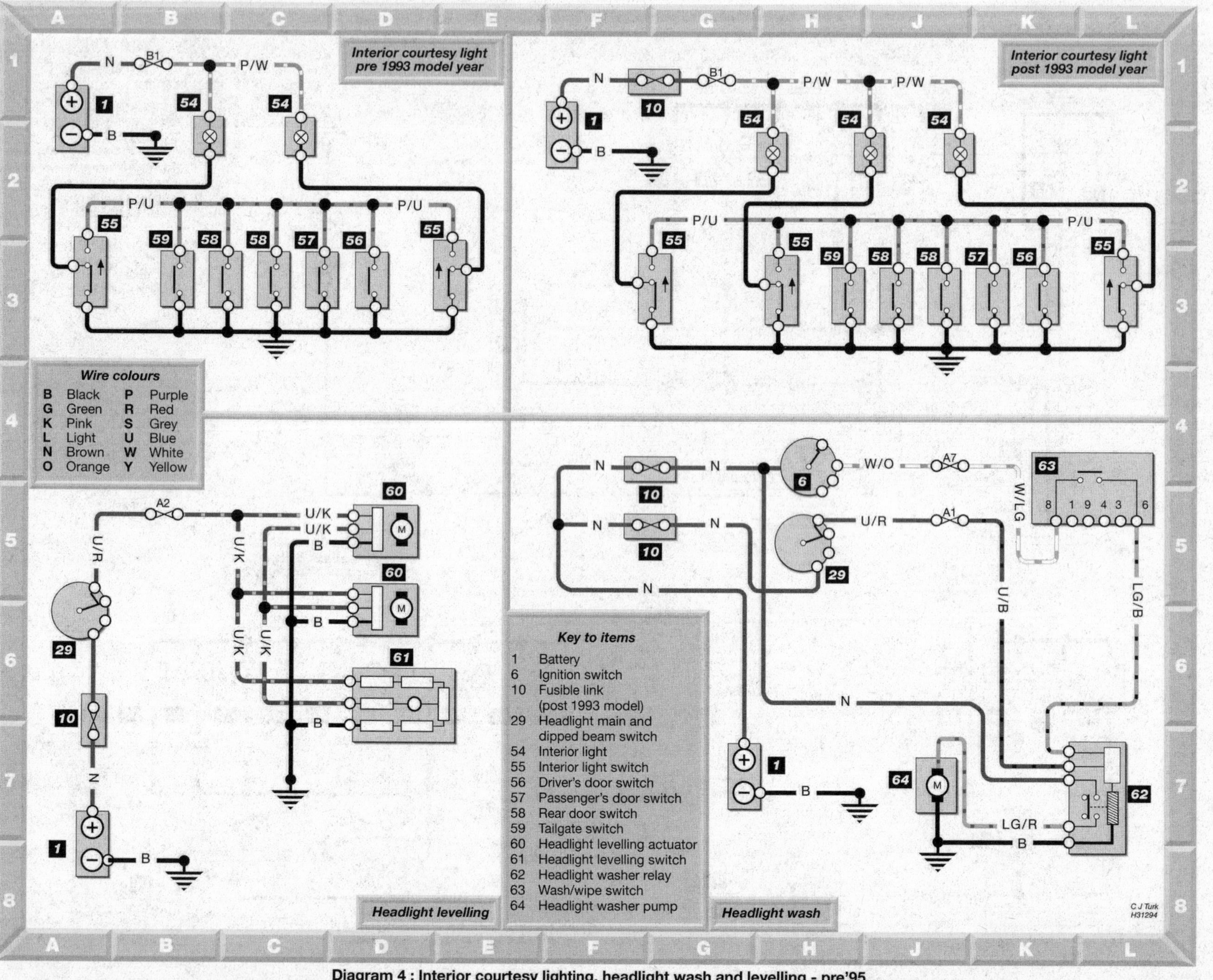
Interior courtesy light pre 1993 model year
Interior courtesy light post 1993 model year
Headlight levelling
Headlight wash
Wire colours
B Black
G Green
K Pink
L Light
N Brown
O Orange
P Purple
R Red
S Grey
U Blue
W White
Y Yellow
Key to items
1 Battery
6 Ignition switch
10 Fusible link (post 1993 model)
29 Headlight main and dipped beam switch
54 Interior light
55 Interior light switch
56 Driver's door switch
57 Passenger's door switch
58 Rear door switch
59 Tailgate switch
60 Headlight levelling actuator
61 Headlight levelling switch
62 Headlight washer relay
63 Wash/wipe switch
64 Headlight washer pump
N
B1
P/W
P/U
B
A2
U/K
U/R
W/O
A7
W/LG
A1
U/B
LG/B
LG/R
8 1 9 4 3 6
M
C J Turk
H31294

Diagram 4 : Interior courtesy lighting, headlight wash and levelling - pre'95

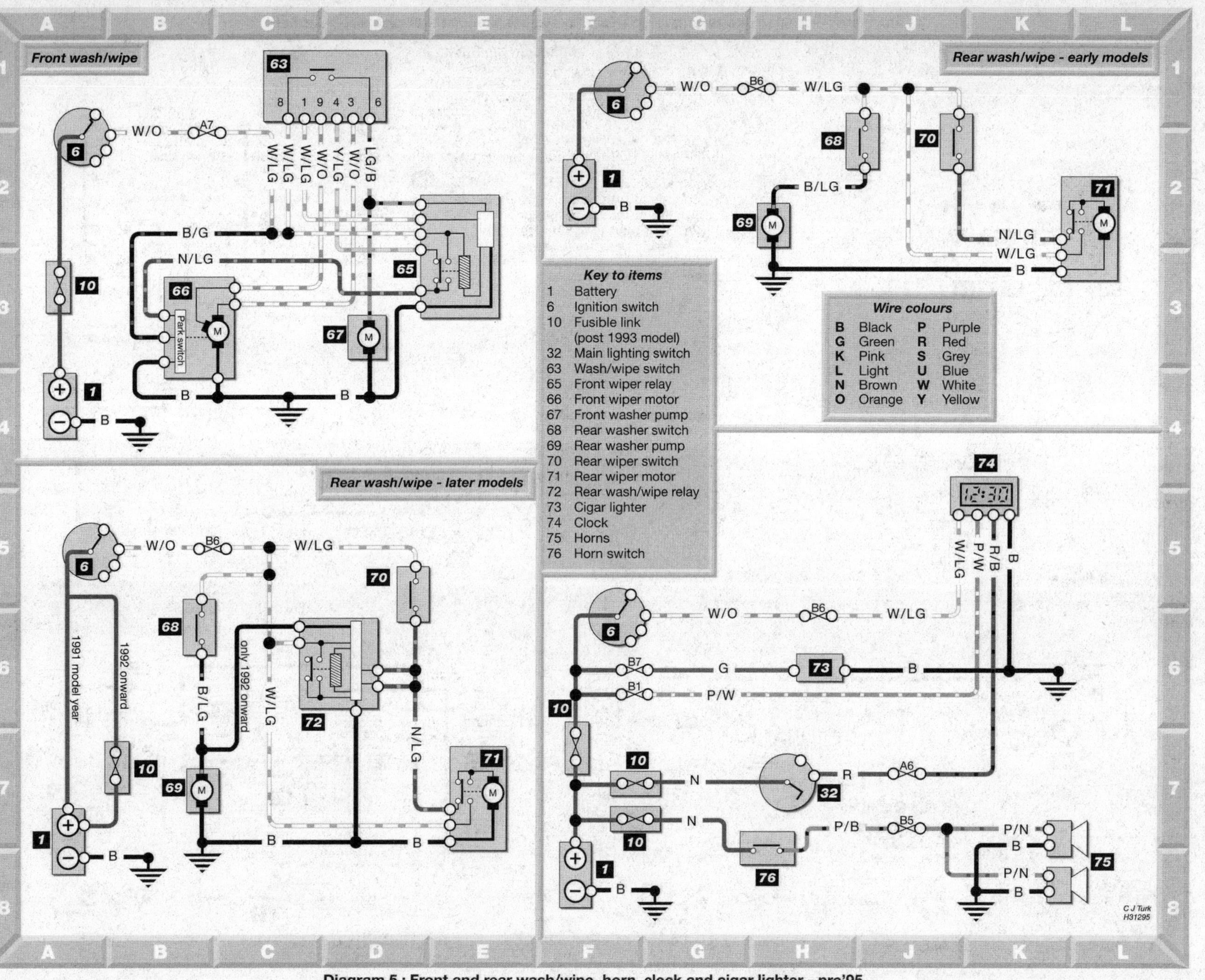
Front wash/wipe
Rear wash/wipe - early models
Rear wash/wipe - later models
Key to items
1 Battery
6 Ignition switch
10 Fusible link (post 1993 model)
32 Main lighting switch
63 Wash/wipe switch
65 Front wiper relay
66 Front wiper motor
67 Front washer pump
68 Rear washer switch
69 Rear washer pump
70 Rear wiper switch
71 Rear wiper motor
72 Rear wash/wipe relay
73 Cigar lighter
74 Clock
75 Horns
76 Horn switch
Wire colours
B Black
G Green
K Pink
L Light
N Brown
O Orange
P Purple
R Red
S Grey
U Blue
W White
Y Yellow
Park switch
only 1992 onward
1992 onward
1991 model year
LG/B
W/O
Y/LG
W/LG
N/LG
B/G
B/LG
R/B
P/W
P/N
P/B
C J Turk
H31295
Diagram 5 : Front and rear wash/wipe, horn, clock and cigar lighter - pre'95

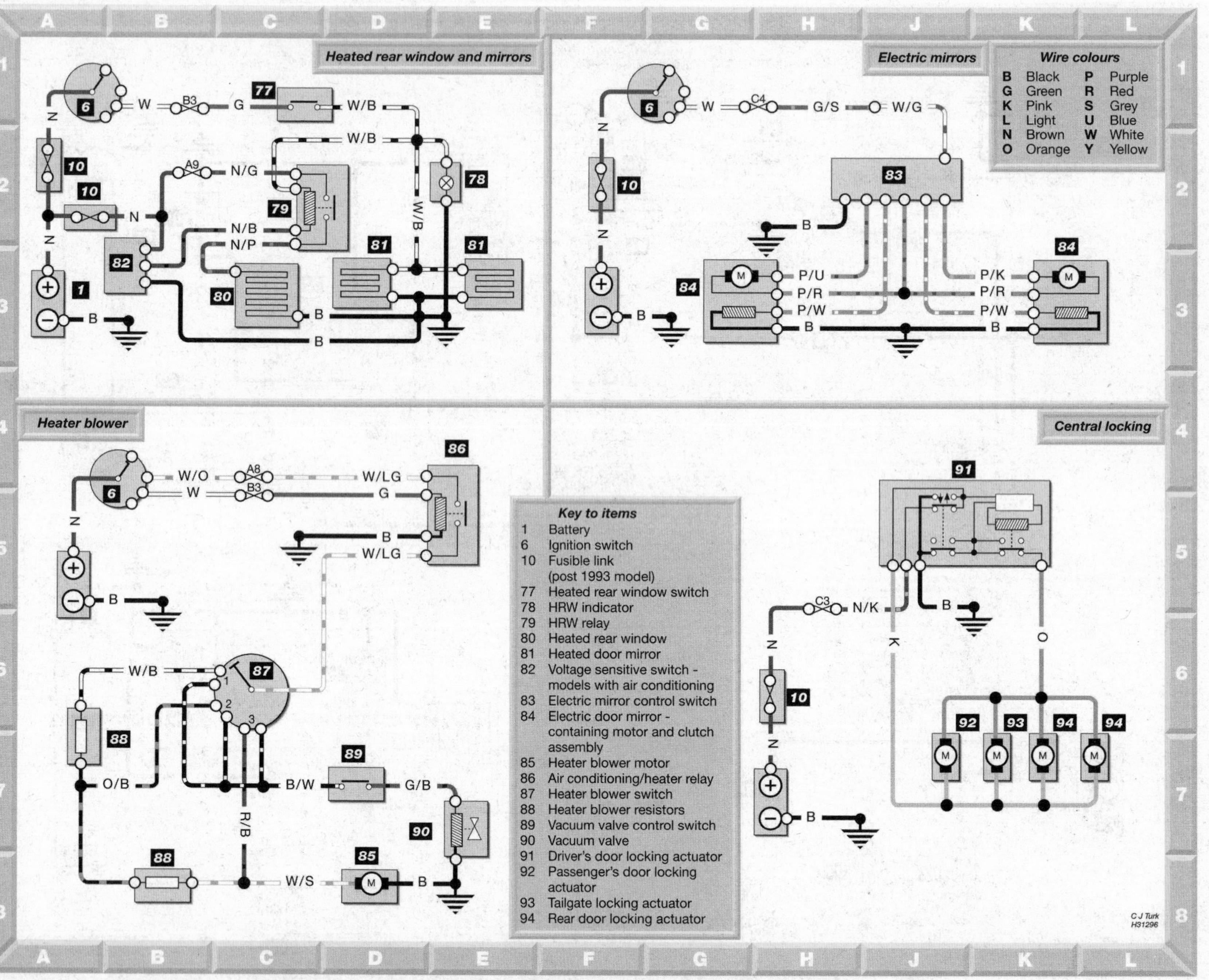
Heated rear window and mirrors
Electric mirrors
Wire colours
B Black
G Green
K Pink
L Light
N Brown
O Orange
P Purple
R Red
S Grey
U Blue
W White
Y Yellow
Heater blower
Central locking
Key to items
1 Battery
6 Ignition switch
10 Fusible link (post 1993 model)
77 Heated rear window switch
78 HRW indicator
79 HRW relay
80 Heated rear window
81 Heated door mirror
82 Voltage sensitive switch - models with air conditioning
83 Electric mirror control switch
84 Electric door mirror - containing motor and clutch assembly
85 Heater blower motor
86 Air conditioning/heater relay
87 Heater blower switch
88 Heater blower resistors
89 Vacuum valve control switch
90 Vacuum valve
91 Driver's door locking actuator
92 Passenger's door locking actuator
93 Tailgate locking actuator
94 Rear door locking actuator
C J Turk
H31296

Diagram 6 : Heated rear window, electric mirrors, heater blower and central locking - pre'95

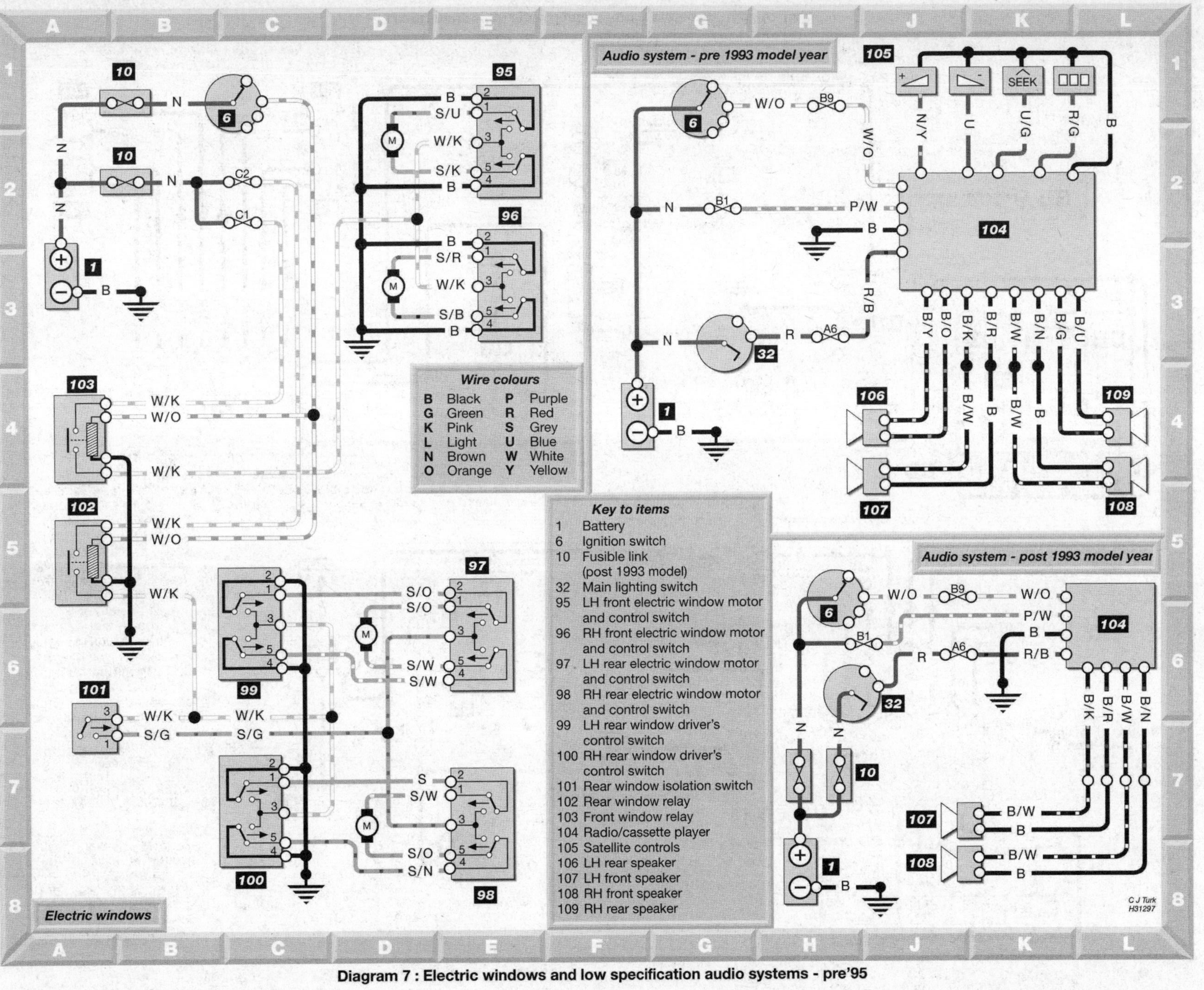
Electric windows
Audio system - pre 1993 model year
Audio system - post 1993 model year
Wire colours
B Black
G Green
K Pink
L Light
N Brown
O Orange
P Purple
R Red
S Grey
U Blue
W White
Y Yellow
Key to items
1 Battery
6 Ignition switch
10 Fusible link (post 1993 model)
32 Main lighting switch
95 LH front electric window motor and control switch
96 RH front electric window motor and control switch
97 LH rear electric window motor and control switch
98 RH rear electric window motor and control switch
99 LH rear window driver's control switch
100 RH rear window driver's control switch
101 Rear window isolation switch
102 Rear window relay
103 Front window relay
104 Radio/cassette player
105 Satellite controls
106 LH rear speaker
107 LH front speaker
108 RH front speaker
109 RH rear speaker
C J Turk
H31297

Diagram 7 : Electric windows and low specification audio systems - pre'95

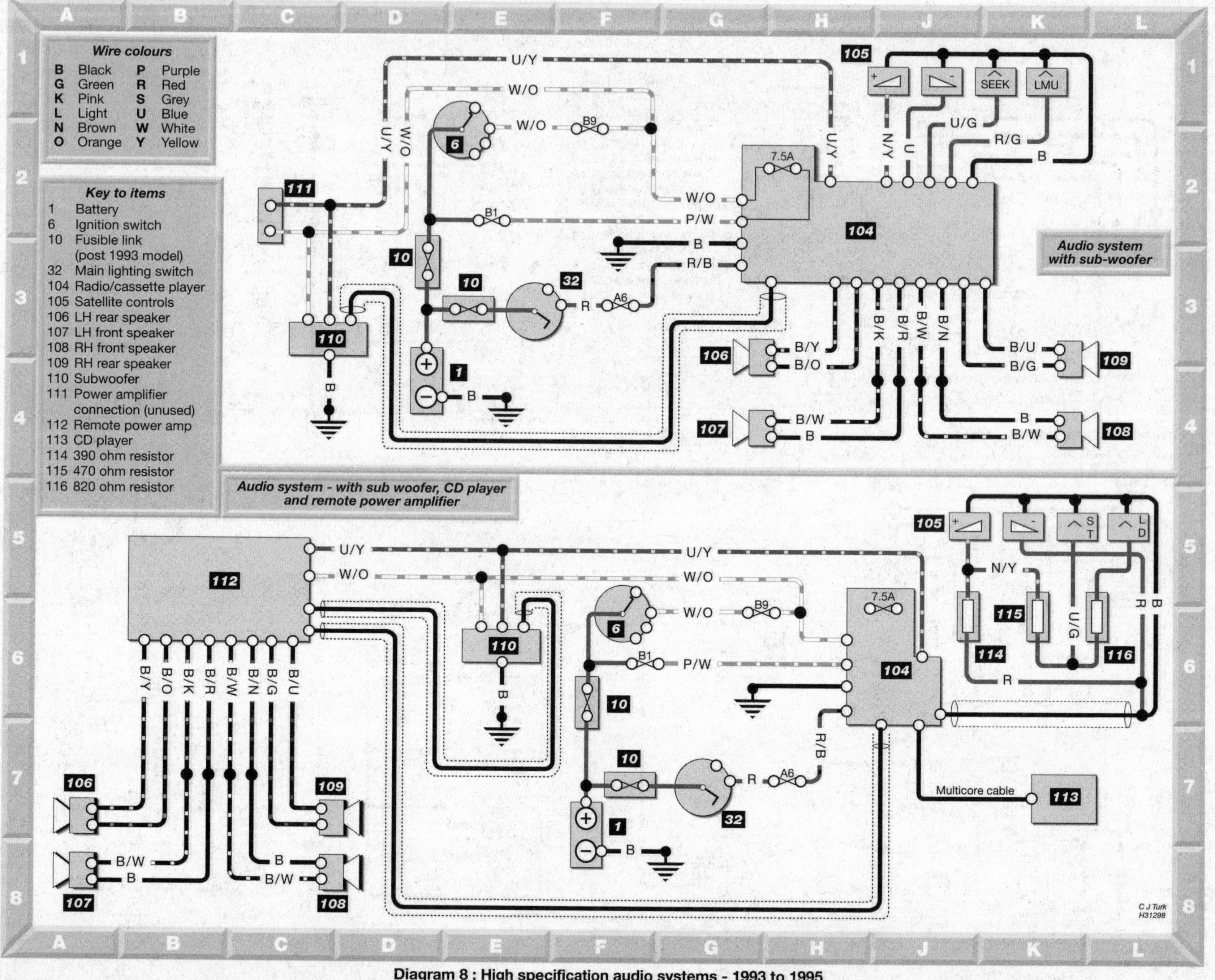
Wire colours
B Black
G Green
K Pink
L Light Blue
N Brown
O Orange
P Purple
R Red
S Grey
U Blue
W White
Y Yellow
Key to items
1 Battery
6 Ignition switch
10 Fusible link (post 1993 model)
32 Main lighting switch
104 Radio/cassette player
105 Satellite controls
106 LH rear speaker
107 LH front speaker
108 RH front speaker
109 RH rear speaker
110 Subwoofer
111 Power amplifier connection (unused)
112 Remote power amp
113 CD player
114 390 ohm resistor
115 470 ohm resistor
116 820 ohm resistor
Audio system with sub-woofer
Audio system - with sub woofer, CD player and remote power amplifier
Multicore cable
C J Turk
H31298

Diagram 8 : High specification audio systems - 1993 to 1995

Key to symbols

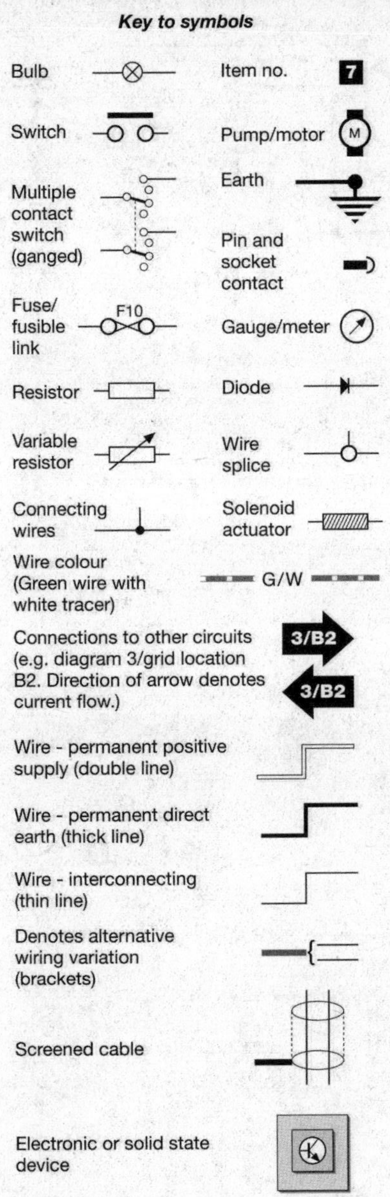

Bulb
Item no. 7
Switch
Pump/motor
Multiple contact switch (ganged)
Earth
Pin and socket contact
Fuse/fusible link (F10)
Gauge/meter
Resistor
Diode
Variable resistor
Wire splice
Connecting wires
Solenoid actuator
Wire colour (Green wire with white tracer) G/W
Connections to other circuits (e.g. diagram 3/grid location B2. Direction of arrow denotes current flow.) 3/B2 3/B2
Wire - permanent positive supply (double line)
Wire - permanent direct earth (thick line)
Wire - interconnecting (thin line)
Denotes alternative wiring variation (brackets)
Screened cable
Electronic or solid state device

Engine fusebox

Fuse	Rating	Circuit protected
F1	30A	Heated rear window
F2	20A	Sidelights, headlights
F3	30A	Cooling fan relay (petrol), air con. compressor clutch and condenser fan relays
F4	20A	Horn relay, hazard warning switch
F5	30A	ABS load relay
F6	15A	Fuel pump relay (petrol), multifunction relay unit (petrol)
F7	20A	Engine load control relay

Satellite fusebox 1 (on passenger fusebox)

Fuse	Rating	Circuit protected
F1	15A	Alarm
F2	20A	Alarm, power wash relay
F3	10A	Engine management and air cond. (petrol), glow plugs and EGR valve control module (Diesel)
F4	5A	Stop light switch, ABS
F5	10A	Alarm
F6	25A	Ignition load relay and air cond.

Satellite fusebox 2 (on passenger fusebox)

Fuse	Rating	Circuit protected
F1	30A	Electric window control unit
F2	30A	Electric window control unit
F3	10A	ABS diagnostic connector
F4	15A	Right front door lock actuator
F5	30A	Sunroof control unit
F6	20A	Clock, radio, interior lighting, alarm, trailer socket

Standard terminal identification (typical)

15	Ignition switch 'ignition' position
30	Battery +ve
31	Earth
50	Ignition switch 'start' position
85	Relay winding input
86	Relay winding earth
87	Relay output
R	ignition switch 'accessory' position

Denotes white 7 way connector, terminal no 3. Dashed outline denotes part of a larger item (W/7/3)

Denotes standard terminal identification i.e. battery +ve (30)

Passenger fusebox

Fuse	Rating	Circuit protected
F1	15A	Stop light switch, hazard warning switch, multifunction unit
F2	10A	Multifunction unit, headlight levelling, LH side/tail light, number plate light, rear air cond. switch illumination
F3	10A	Radio
F4	10A	Instrument cluster, RH headlight
F5	10A	LH headlight
F6	20A	Cigar lighter
F7	10A	Airbag control module, instrument cluster
F8	10A	RH side/tail light, multifunction unit, glovebox light switch, headlight levelling, interior illumination
F9	10A	Rear foglight switch
F10	10A	LH headlight
F11	10A	RH headlight, multifunction switch
F12	10A	Multifunction unit, key in switch, shiftlock illumination, CD changer
F13	10A	Multifunction unit, interlock relay 2
F14	10A	Multifunction unit, park/neutral switch (auto.), reversing light switch (manual), instrument cluster, airbag, clock
F15	10A	Ignition load relay, electric window control unit
F16	20A	Front wash/wipe
F17	10A	Starter relay
F18	10A	Rear wash/wipe, gear selelector illumination, cruise control switch, mirror control switch

Earth locations

E1	RH front of engine compartment, behind battery
E2	LH front of engine compartment inner wing
E3	RH front of engine compartment, behind battery
E4	Lower RH rear engine compartment
E5	Lower LH front of engine compartment
E6	Lower RH rear engine compartment
E7	Mounted on bonnet
E8	Near starter
E9	LH rear corner of engine
E10	RH side of bulkhead
E11	Behind RH footwell trim panel
E12	Behind LH footwell trim panel
E13	Behind LH side of facia
E14	Behind LH footwell trim panel
E15	Beneath centre console
E16	LH side of luggage compartment
E17	RH side of luggage compartment
E18	RH side of tailgate

H31299

Diagram 9 : Information for wiring diagrams - 1995 on

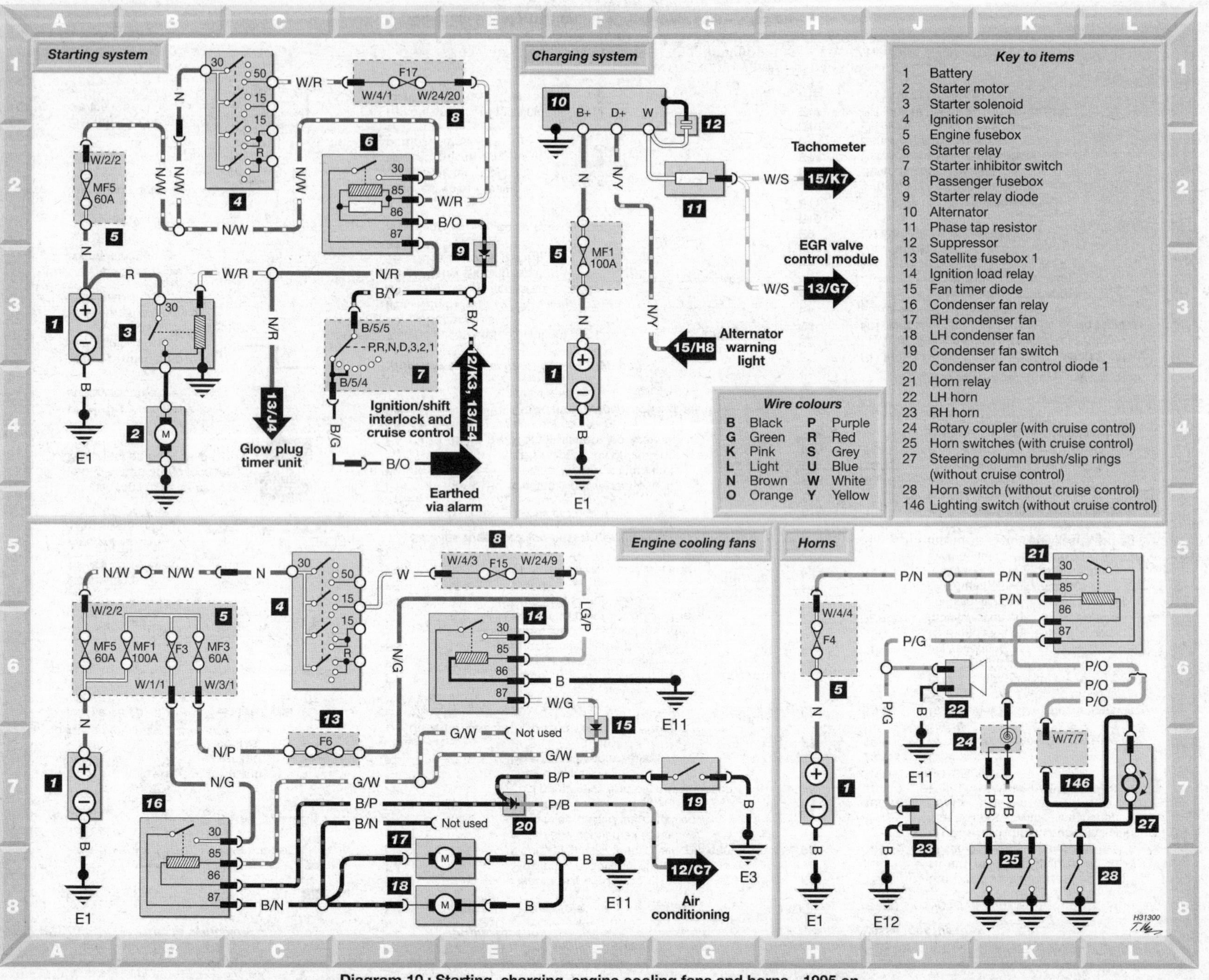
Starting system
Charging system
Tachometer
15/K7
EGR valve control module
13/G7
Alternator warning light
15/H8
Glow plug timer unit
13/J4
Ignition/shift interlock and cruise control
12/K3, 13/E4
Earthed via alarm
Key to items
1 Battery
2 Starter motor
3 Starter solenoid
4 Ignition switch
5 Engine fusebox
6 Starter relay
7 Starter inhibitor switch
8 Passenger fusebox
9 Starter relay diode
10 Alternator
11 Phase tap resistor
12 Suppressor
13 Satellite fusebox 1
14 Ignition load relay
15 Fan timer diode
16 Condenser fan relay
17 RH condenser fan
18 LH condenser fan
19 Condenser fan switch
20 Condenser fan control diode 1
21 Horn relay
22 LH horn
23 RH horn
24 Rotary coupler (with cruise control)
25 Horn switches (with cruise control)
27 Steering column brush/slip rings (without cruise control)
28 Horn switch (without cruise control)
146 Lighting switch (without cruise control)
Wire colours
B Black
G Green
K Pink
L Light
N Brown
O Orange
P Purple
R Red
S Grey
U Blue
W White
Y Yellow
Engine cooling fans
Horns
Not used
12/C7
Air conditioning
MF5 60A
MF1 100A
F3
MF3 60A
F17
F15
F6
F4
E1
E3
E11
E12
H31300
Diagram 10 : Starting, charging, engine cooling fans and horns - 1995 on

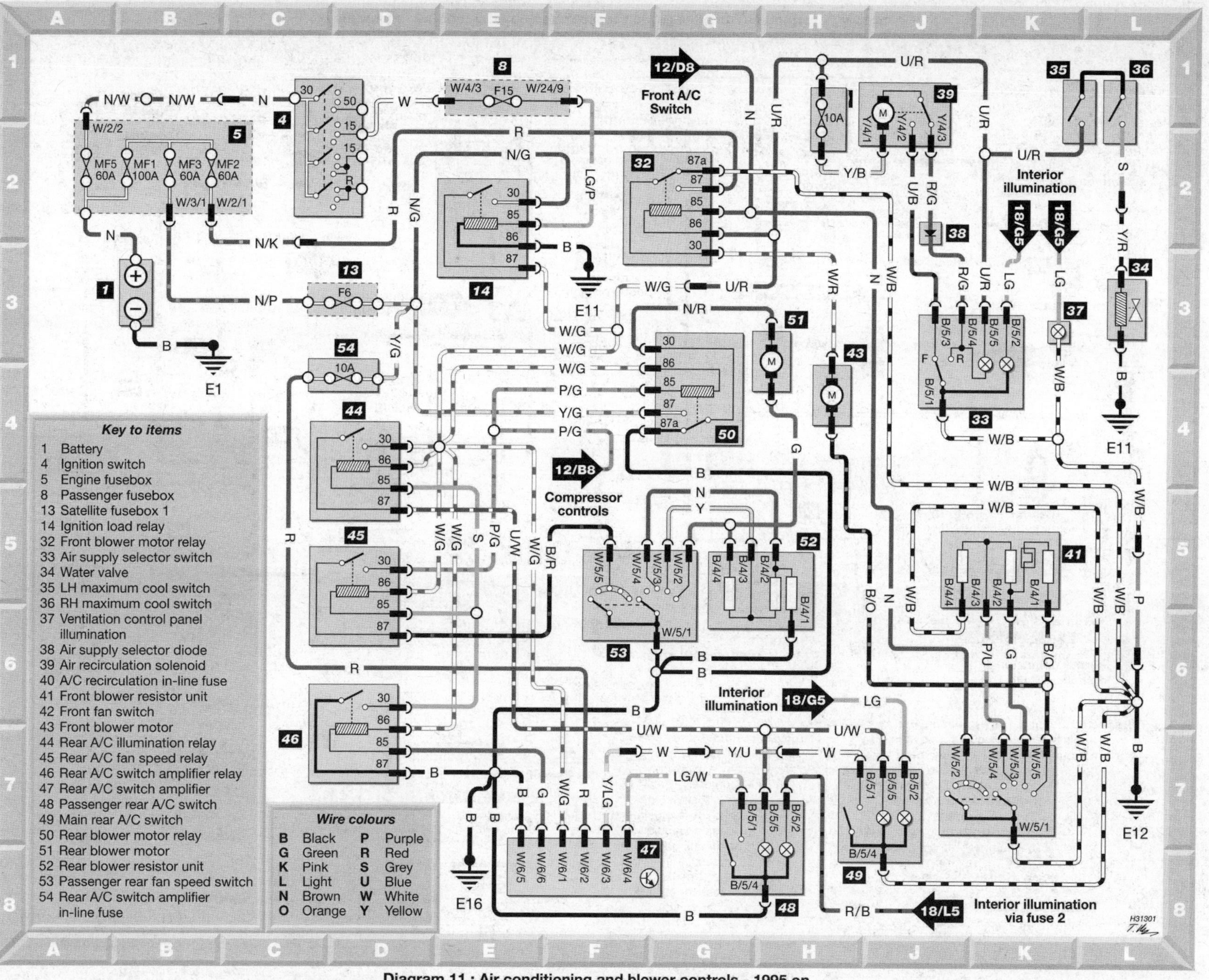
Key to items
1 Battery
4 Ignition switch
5 Engine fusebox
8 Passenger fusebox
13 Satellite fusebox 1
14 Ignition load relay
32 Front blower motor relay
33 Air supply selector switch
34 Water valve
35 LH maximum cool switch
36 RH maximum cool switch
37 Ventilation control panel illumination
38 Air supply selector diode
39 Air recirculation solenoid
40 A/C recirculation in-line fuse
41 Front blower resistor unit
42 Front fan switch
43 Front blower motor
44 Rear A/C illumination relay
45 Rear A/C fan speed relay
46 Rear A/C switch amplifier relay
47 Rear A/C switch amplifier
48 Passenger rear A/C switch
49 Main rear A/C switch
50 Rear blower motor relay
51 Rear blower motor
52 Rear blower resistor unit
53 Passenger rear fan speed switch
54 Rear A/C switch amplifier in-line fuse
Wire colours
B Black
G Green
K Pink
L Light
N Brown
O Orange
P Purple
R Red
S Grey
U Blue
W White
Y Yellow
Front A/C Switch
Compressor controls
Interior illumination
Interior illumination via fuse 2
H31301

Diagram 11 : Air conditioning and blower controls - 1995 on

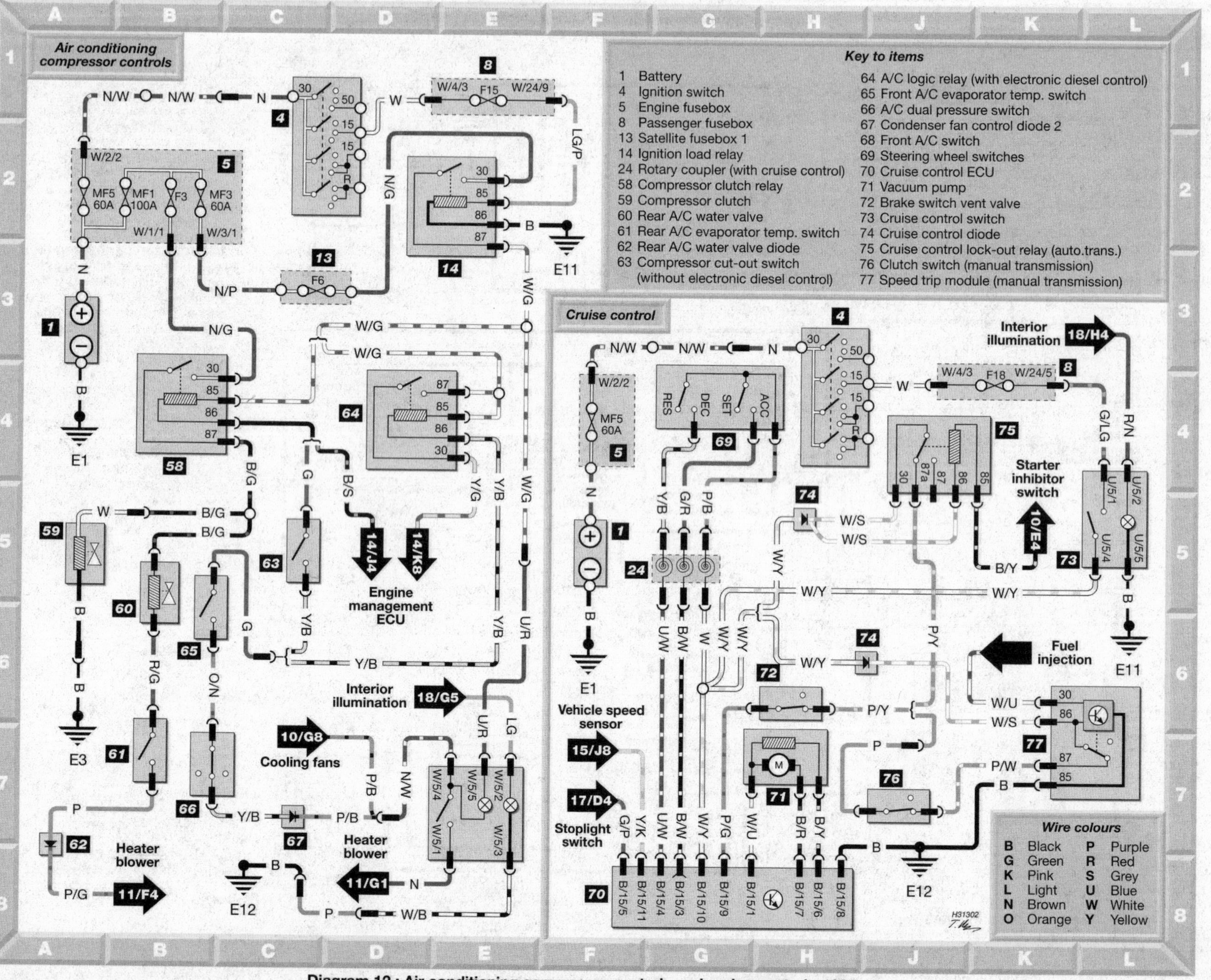
Air conditioning compressor controls
Cruise control
Key to items
1 Battery
4 Ignition switch
5 Engine fusebox
8 Passenger fusebox
13 Satellite fusebox 1
14 Ignition load relay
24 Rotary coupler (with cruise control)
58 Compressor clutch relay
59 Compressor clutch
60 Rear A/C water valve
61 Rear A/C evaporator temp. switch
62 Rear A/C water valve diode
63 Compressor cut-out switch (without electronic diesel control)
64 A/C logic relay (with electronic diesel control)
65 Front A/C evaporator temp. switch
66 A/C dual pressure switch
67 Condenser fan control diode 2
68 Front A/C switch
69 Steering wheel switches
70 Cruise control ECU
71 Vacuum pump
72 Brake switch vent valve
73 Cruise control switch
74 Cruise control diode
75 Cruise control lock-out relay (auto.trans.)
76 Clutch switch (manual transmission)
77 Speed trip module (manual transmission)
Wire colours
B Black
G Green
K Pink
L Light
N Brown
O Orange
P Purple
R Red
S Grey
U Blue
W White
Y Yellow
Engine management ECU
Interior illumination
Cooling fans
Heater blower
Vehicle speed sensor
Stoplight switch
Starter inhibitor switch
Fuel injection
H31302
Diagram 12 : Air conditioning compressor controls and cruise control - 1995 on

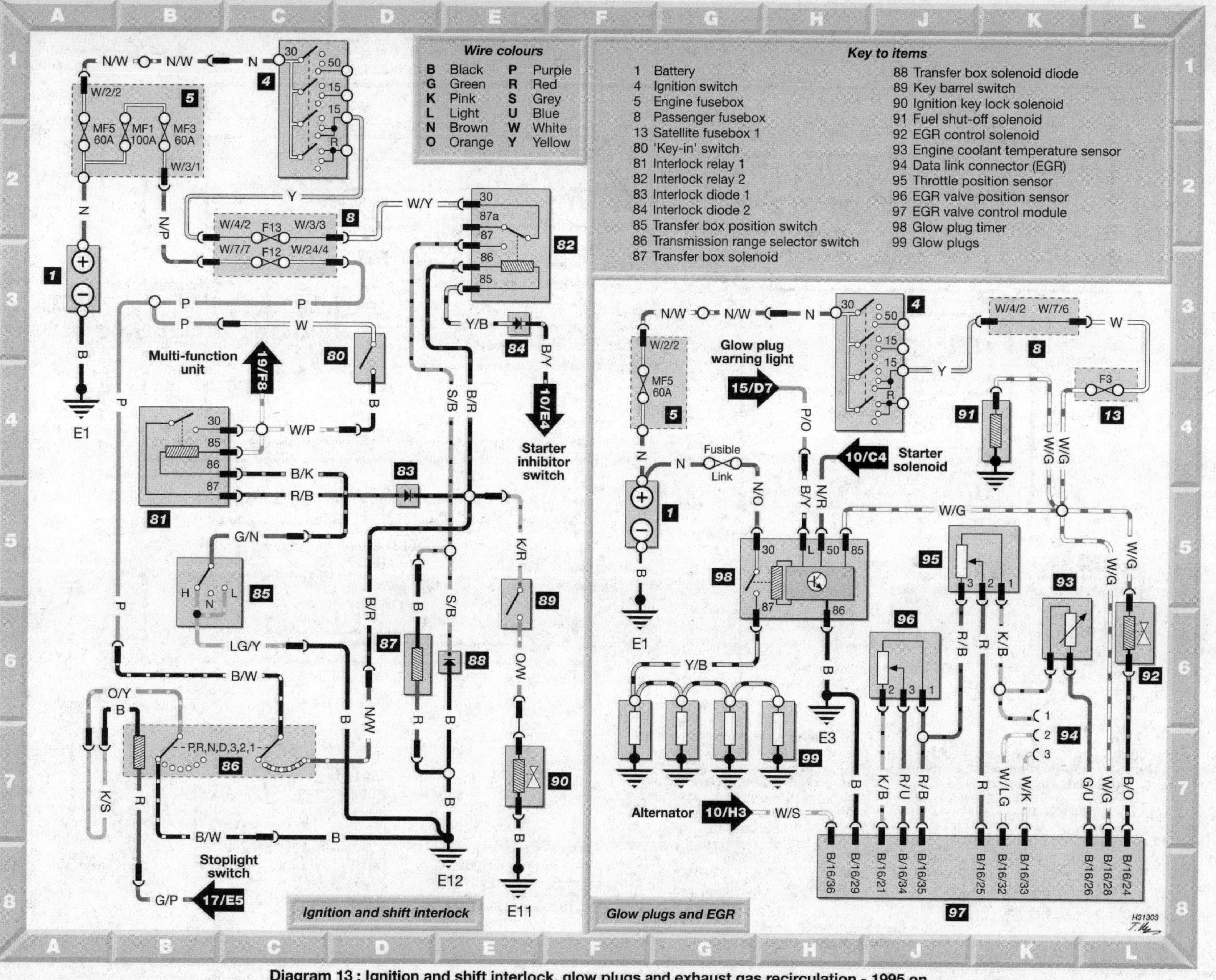
Wire colours
B Black
G Green
K Pink
L Light
N Brown
O Orange
P Purple
R Red
S Grey
U Blue
W White
Y Yellow
Key to items
1 Battery
4 Ignition switch
5 Engine fusebox
8 Passenger fusebox
13 Satellite fusebox 1
80 'Key-in' switch
81 Interlock relay 1
82 Interlock relay 2
83 Interlock diode 1
84 Interlock diode 2
85 Transfer box position switch
86 Transmission range selector switch
87 Transfer box solenoid
88 Transfer box solenoid diode
89 Key barrel switch
90 Ignition key lock solenoid
91 Fuel shut-off solenoid
92 EGR control solenoid
93 Engine coolant temperature sensor
94 Data link connector (EGR)
95 Throttle position sensor
96 EGR valve position sensor
97 EGR valve control module
98 Glow plug timer
99 Glow plugs
Multi-function unit
Starter inhibitor switch
Stoplight switch
Glow plug warning light
Starter solenoid
Alternator
Ignition and shift interlock
Glow plugs and EGR
H31303
Diagram 13 : Ignition and shift interlock, glow plugs and exhaust gas recirculation - 1995 on

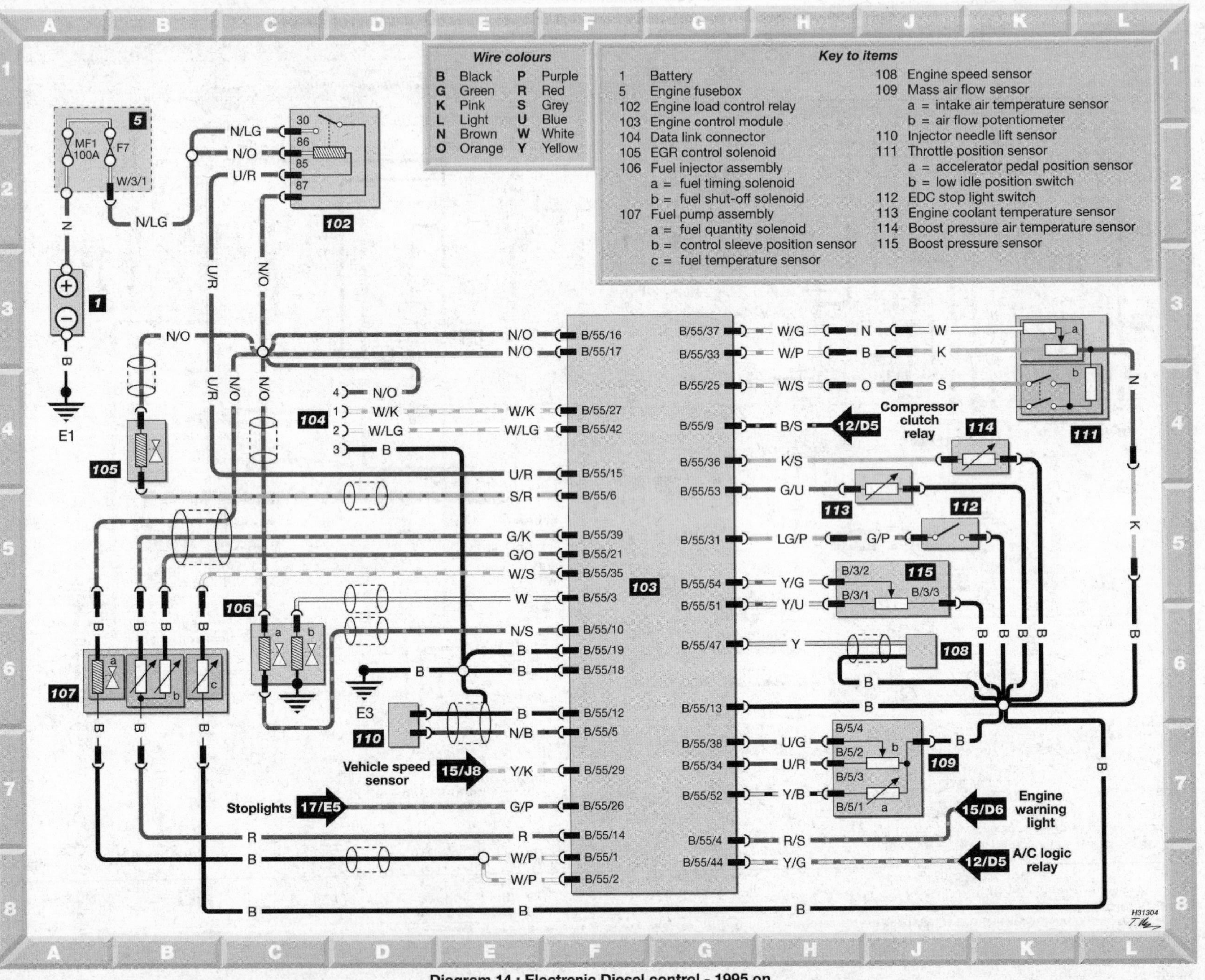
Wire colours
B Black
G Green
K Pink
L Light
N Brown
O Orange
P Purple
R Red
S Grey
U Blue
W White
Y Yellow
Key to items
1 Battery
5 Engine fusebox
102 Engine load control relay
103 Engine control module
104 Data link connector
105 EGR control solenoid
106 Fuel injector assembly
a = fuel timing solenoid
b = fuel shut-off solenoid
107 Fuel pump assembly
a = fuel quantity solenoid
b = control sleeve position sensor
c = fuel temperature sensor
108 Engine speed sensor
109 Mass air flow sensor
a = intake air temperature sensor
b = air flow potentiometer
110 Injector needle lift sensor
111 Throttle position sensor
a = accelerator pedal position sensor
b = low idle position switch
112 EDC stop light switch
113 Engine coolant temperature sensor
114 Boost pressure air temperature sensor
115 Boost pressure sensor
Compressor clutch relay
Vehicle speed sensor
Stoplights
Engine warning light
A/C logic relay
12/D5
15/J8
17/E5
15/D6
E1
E3
MF1 100A
F7
W/3/1
H31304
Diagram 14 : Electronic Diesel control - 1995 on

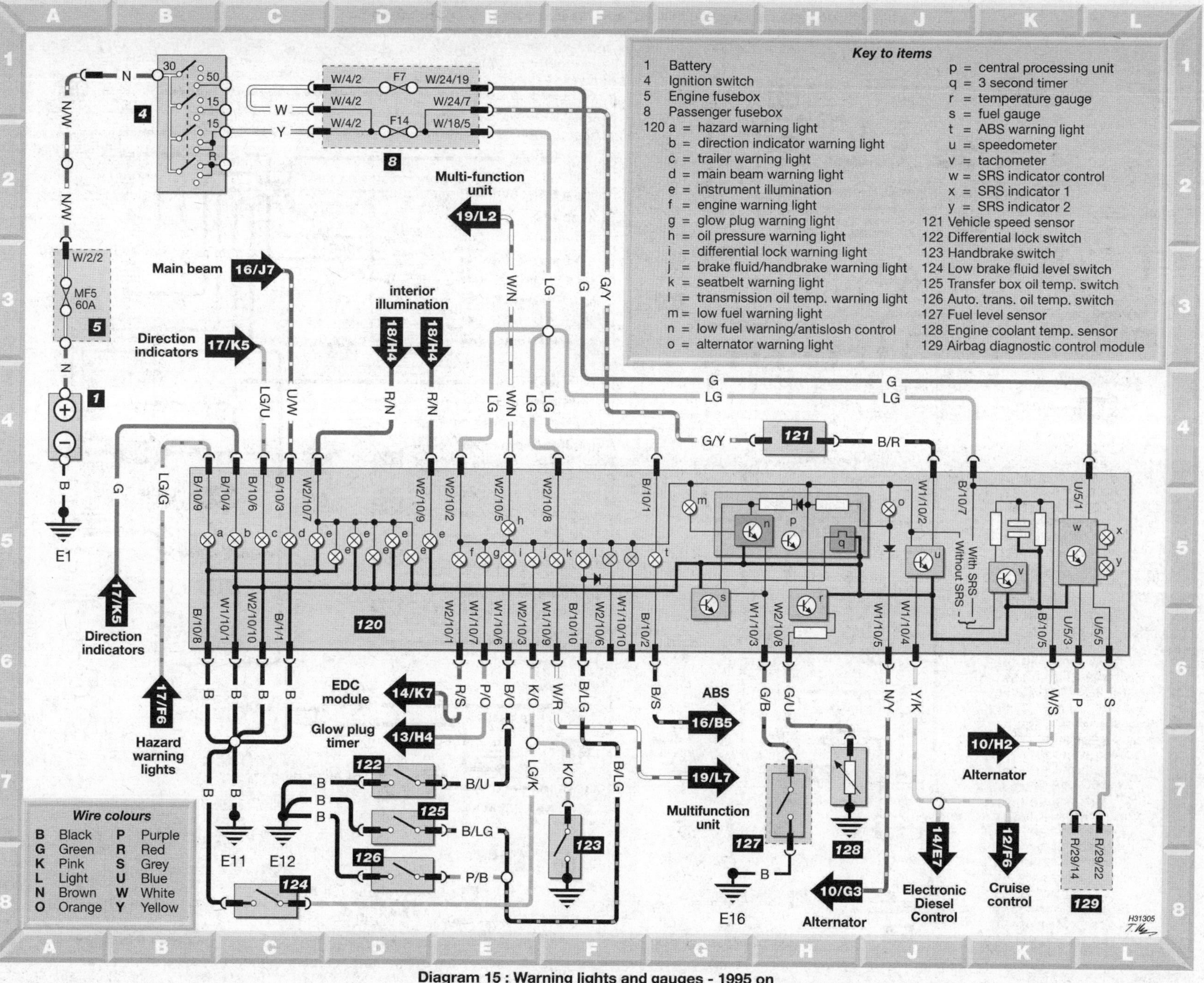
Key to items
1 Battery
4 Ignition switch
5 Engine fusebox
8 Passenger fusebox
120 a = hazard warning light
b = direction indicator warning light
c = trailer warning light
d = main beam warning light
e = instrument illumination
f = engine warning light
g = glow plug warning light
h = oil pressure warning light
i = differential lock warning light
j = brake fluid/handbrake warning light
k = seatbelt warning light
l = transmission oil temp. warning light
m = low fuel warning light
n = low fuel warning/antislosh control
o = alternator warning light
p = central processing unit
q = 3 second timer
r = temperature gauge
s = fuel gauge
t = ABS warning light
u = speedometer
v = tachometer
w = SRS indicator control
x = SRS indicator 1
y = SRS indicator 2
121 Vehicle speed sensor
122 Differential lock switch
123 Handbrake switch
124 Low brake fluid level switch
125 Transfer box oil temp. switch
126 Auto. trans. oil temp. switch
127 Fuel level sensor
128 Engine coolant temp. sensor
129 Airbag diagnostic control module
Wire colours
B Black
G Green
K Pink
L Light
N Brown
O Orange
P Purple
R Red
S Grey
U Blue
W White
Y Yellow
Main beam
Direction indicators
interior illumination
Multi-function unit
Hazard warning lights
EDC module
Glow plug timer
ABS
Multifunction unit
Alternator
Electronic Diesel Control
Cruise control
With SRS
Without SRS
E1
E11
E12
E16
H31305

Diagram 15 : Warning lights and gauges - 1995 on

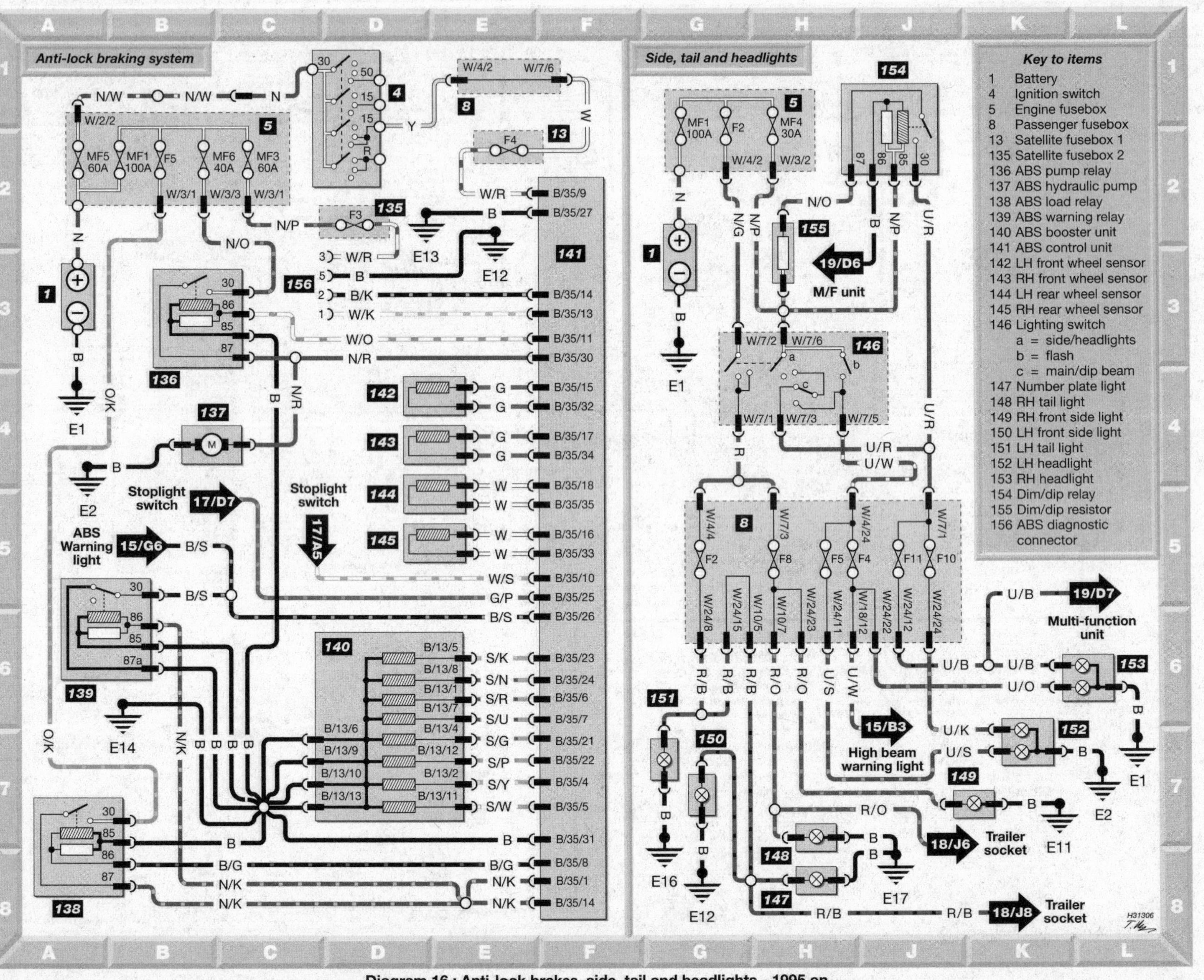
Anti-lock braking system
Side, tail and headlights
Key to items
1 Battery
4 Ignition switch
5 Engine fusebox
8 Passenger fusebox
13 Satellite fusebox 1
135 Satellite fusebox 2
136 ABS pump relay
137 ABS hydraulic pump
138 ABS load relay
139 ABS warning relay
140 ABS booster unit
141 ABS control unit
142 LH front wheel sensor
143 RH front wheel sensor
144 LH rear wheel sensor
145 RH rear wheel sensor
146 Lighting switch
a = side/headlights
b = flash
c = main/dip beam
147 Number plate light
148 RH tail light
149 RH front side light
150 LH front side light
151 LH tail light
152 LH headlight
153 RH headlight
154 Dim/dip relay
155 Dim/dip resistor
156 ABS diagnostic connector
Stoplight switch
ABS Warning light
M/F unit
Multi-function unit
High beam warning light
Trailer socket
H31306

Diagram 16 : Anti-lock brakes, side, tail and headlights - 1995 on

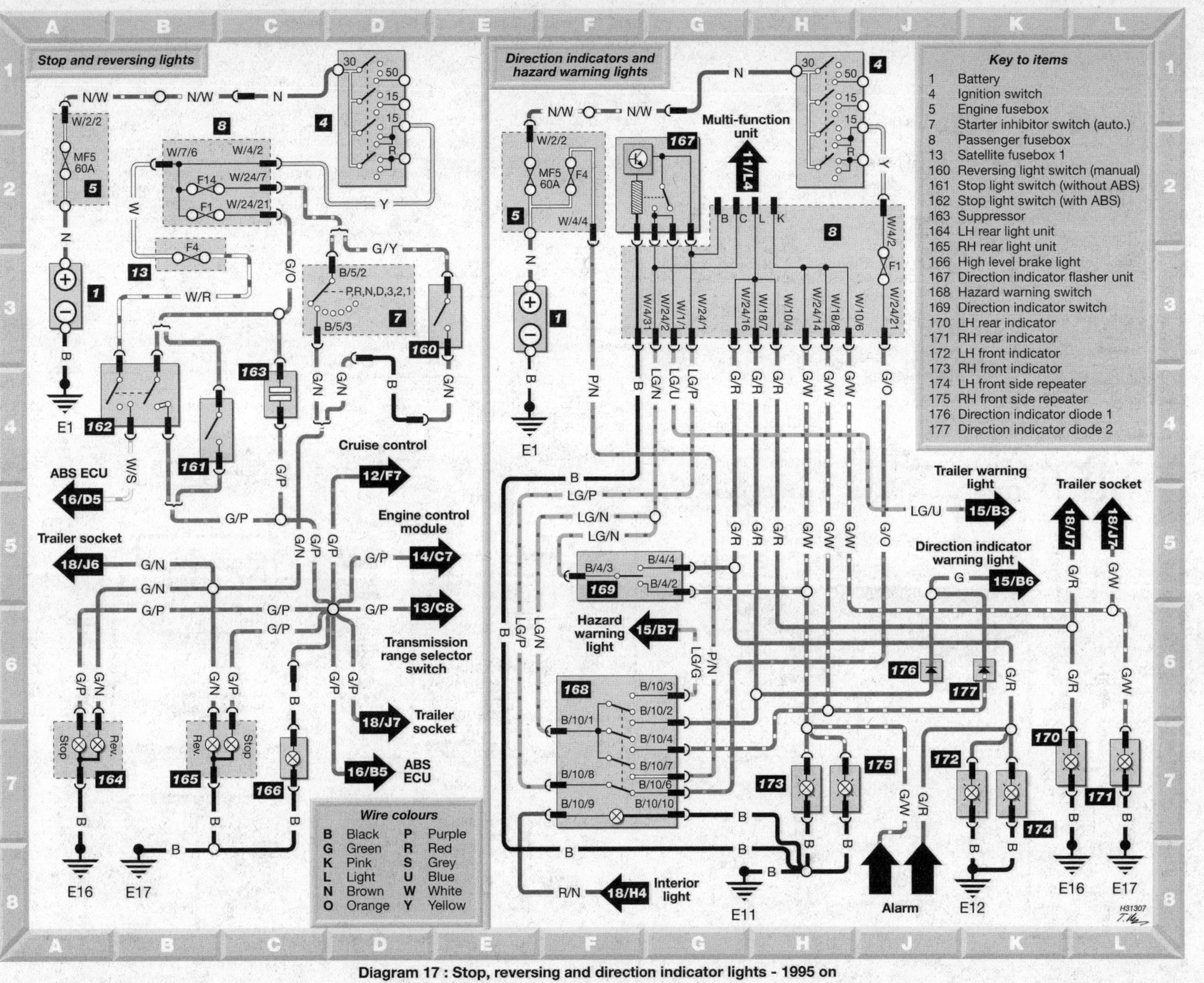

Stop and reversing lights
Direction indicators and hazard warning lights
Key to items
1 Battery
4 Ignition switch
5 Engine fusebox
7 Starter inhibitor switch (auto.)
8 Passenger fusebox
13 Satellite fusebox 1
160 Reversing light switch (manual)
161 Stop light switch (without ABS)
162 Stop light switch (with ABS)
163 Suppressor
164 LH rear light unit
165 RH rear light unit
166 High level brake light
167 Direction indicator flasher unit
168 Hazard warning switch
169 Direction indicator switch
170 LH rear indicator
171 RH rear indicator
172 LH front indicator
173 RH front indicator
174 LH front side repeater
175 RH front side repeater
176 Direction indicator diode 1
177 Direction indicator diode 2
ABS ECU 16/D5
Trailer socket 18/J6
Cruise control 12/F7
Engine control module 14/C7
Transmission range selector switch 13/C8
Trailer socket 18/J7
ABS ECU 16/B5
Multi-function unit 11/L4
Trailer warning light 15/B3
Trailer socket 18/J7
Direction indicator warning light 15/B6
Hazard warning light 15/B7
Interior light 18/H4
Alarm
Wire colours
B Black
G Green
K Pink
L Light
N Brown
O Orange
P Purple
R Red
S Grey
U Blue
W White
Y Yellow
H31307

Diagram 17 : Stop, reversing and direction indicator lights - 1995 on

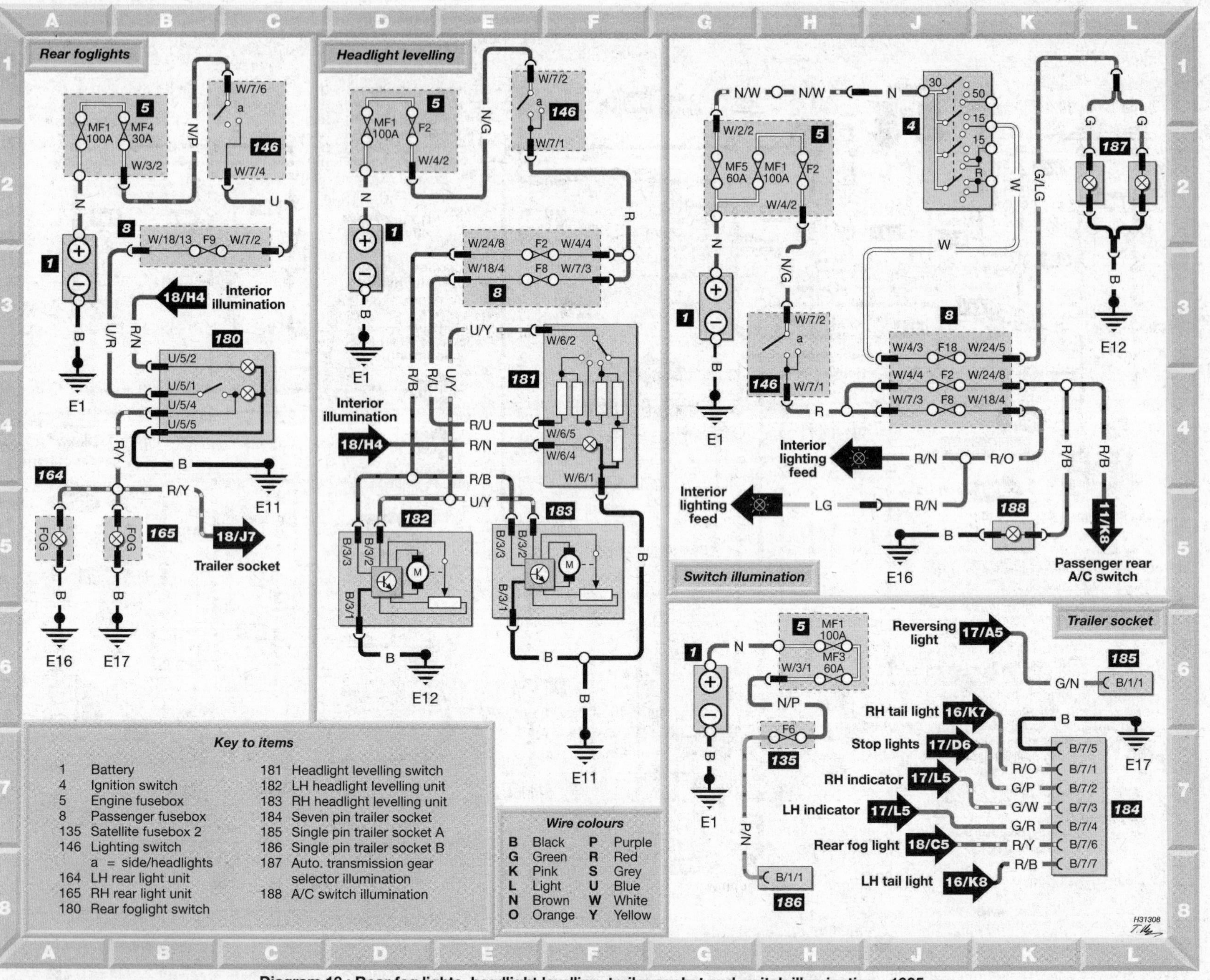
Rear foglights
Headlight levelling
Switch illumination
Trailer socket
Interior illumination
Interior lighting feed
Passenger rear A/C switch
Trailer socket
Reversing light
RH tail light
Stop lights
RH indicator
LH indicator
Rear fog light
LH tail light
18/H4
18/J7
11/K8
17/A5
16/K7
17/D6
17/L5
18/C5
16/K8
FOG
H31308

Key to items
1 Battery
4 Ignition switch
5 Engine fusebox
8 Passenger fusebox
135 Satellite fusebox 2
146 Lighting switch
a = side/headlights
164 LH rear light unit
165 RH rear light unit
180 Rear foglight switch
181 Headlight levelling switch
182 LH headlight levelling unit
183 RH headlight levelling unit
184 Seven pin trailer socket
185 Single pin trailer socket A
186 Single pin trailer socket B
187 Auto. transmission gear selector illumination
188 A/C switch illumination

Wire colours
B Black
G Green
K Pink
L Light
N Brown
O Orange
P Purple
R Red
S Grey
U Blue
W White
Y Yellow

Diagram 18 : Rear fog lights, headlight levelling, trailer socket and switch illumination - 1995 on

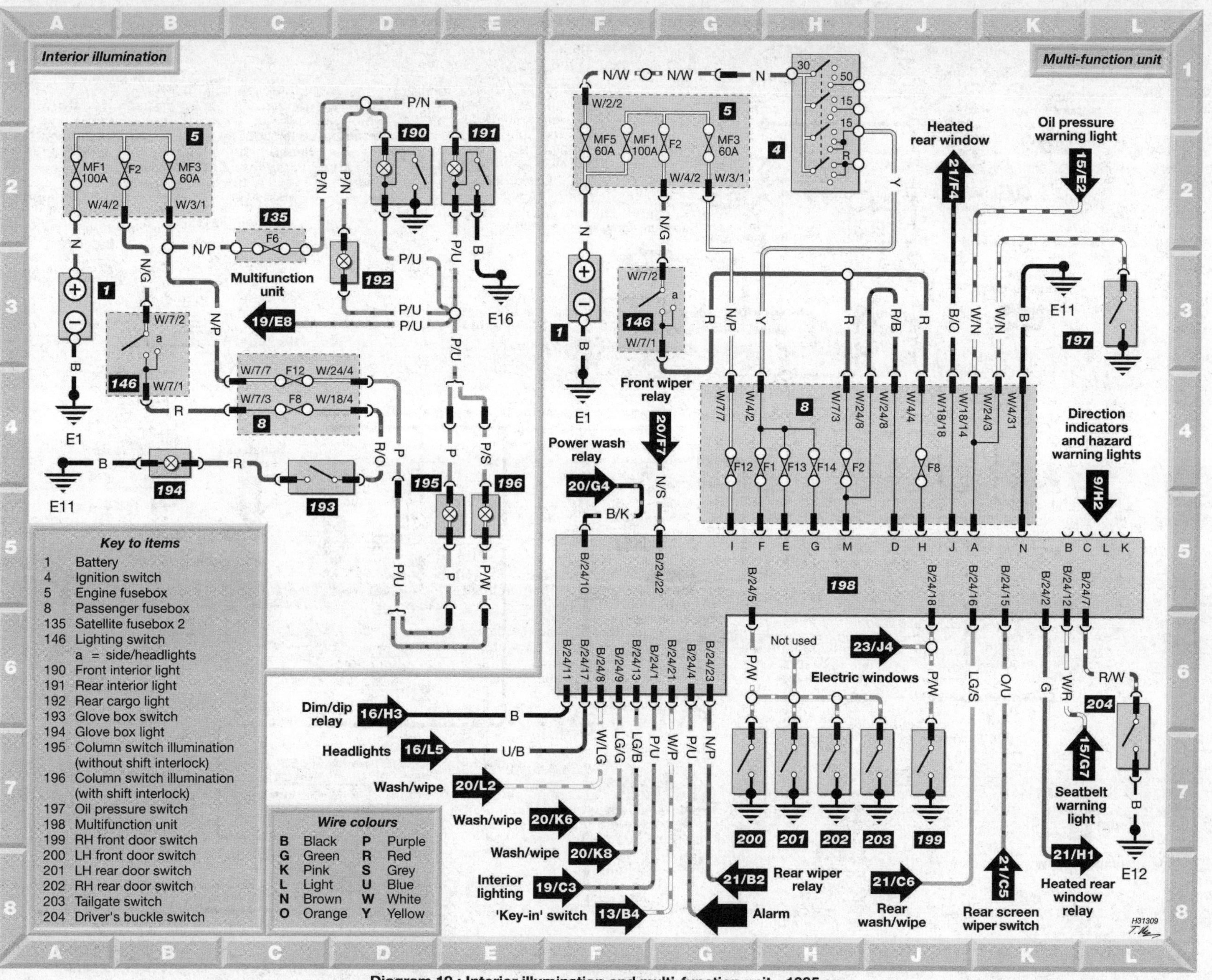
Interior illumination
Multi-function unit
Key to items
1 Battery
4 Ignition switch
5 Engine fusebox
8 Passenger fusebox
135 Satellite fusebox 2
146 Lighting switch
a = side/headlights
190 Front interior light
191 Rear interior light
192 Rear cargo light
193 Glove box switch
194 Glove box light
195 Column switch illumination (without shift interlock)
196 Column switch illumination (with shift interlock)
197 Oil pressure switch
198 Multifunction unit
199 RH front door switch
200 LH front door switch
201 LH rear door switch
202 RH rear door switch
203 Tailgate switch
204 Driver's buckle switch
Wire colours
B Black
G Green
K Pink
L Light
N Brown
O Orange
P Purple
R Red
S Grey
U Blue
W White
Y Yellow
Multifunction unit
Heated rear window
Oil pressure warning light
Front wiper relay
Power wash relay
Direction indicators and hazard warning lights
Not used
Electric windows
Dim/dip relay
Headlights
Wash/wipe
Interior lighting
'Key-in' switch
Alarm
Rear wiper relay
Rear wash/wipe
Rear screen wiper switch
Seatbelt warning light
Heated rear window relay

Diagram 19 : Interior illumination and multi-function unit - 1995 on

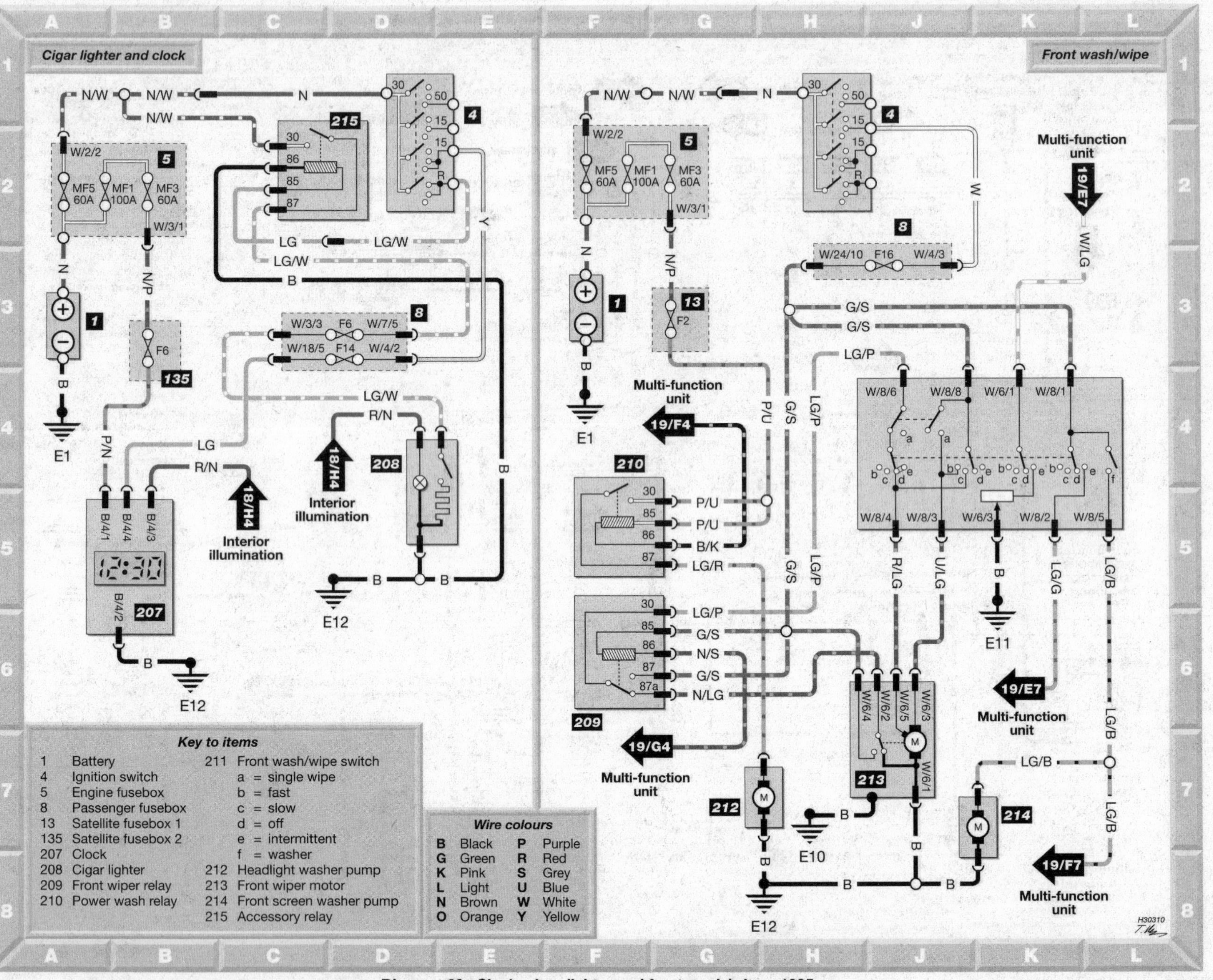
Cigar lighter and clock
Front wash/wipe
Multi-function unit
19/E7
19/F4
19/G4
19/F7
18/H4
Interior illumination
Key to items
1 Battery
4 Ignition switch
5 Engine fusebox
8 Passenger fusebox
13 Satellite fusebox 1
135 Satellite fusebox 2
207 Clock
208 Cigar lighter
209 Front wiper relay
210 Power wash relay
211 Front wash/wipe switch
a = single wipe
b = fast
c = slow
d = off
e = intermittent
f = washer
212 Headlight washer pump
213 Front wiper motor
214 Front screen washer pump
215 Accessory relay
Wire colours
B Black
G Green
K Pink
L Light
N Brown
O Orange
P Purple
R Red
S Grey
U Blue
W White
Y Yellow
H30310
Diagram 20 : Clock, cigar lighter and front wash/wipe - 1995 on

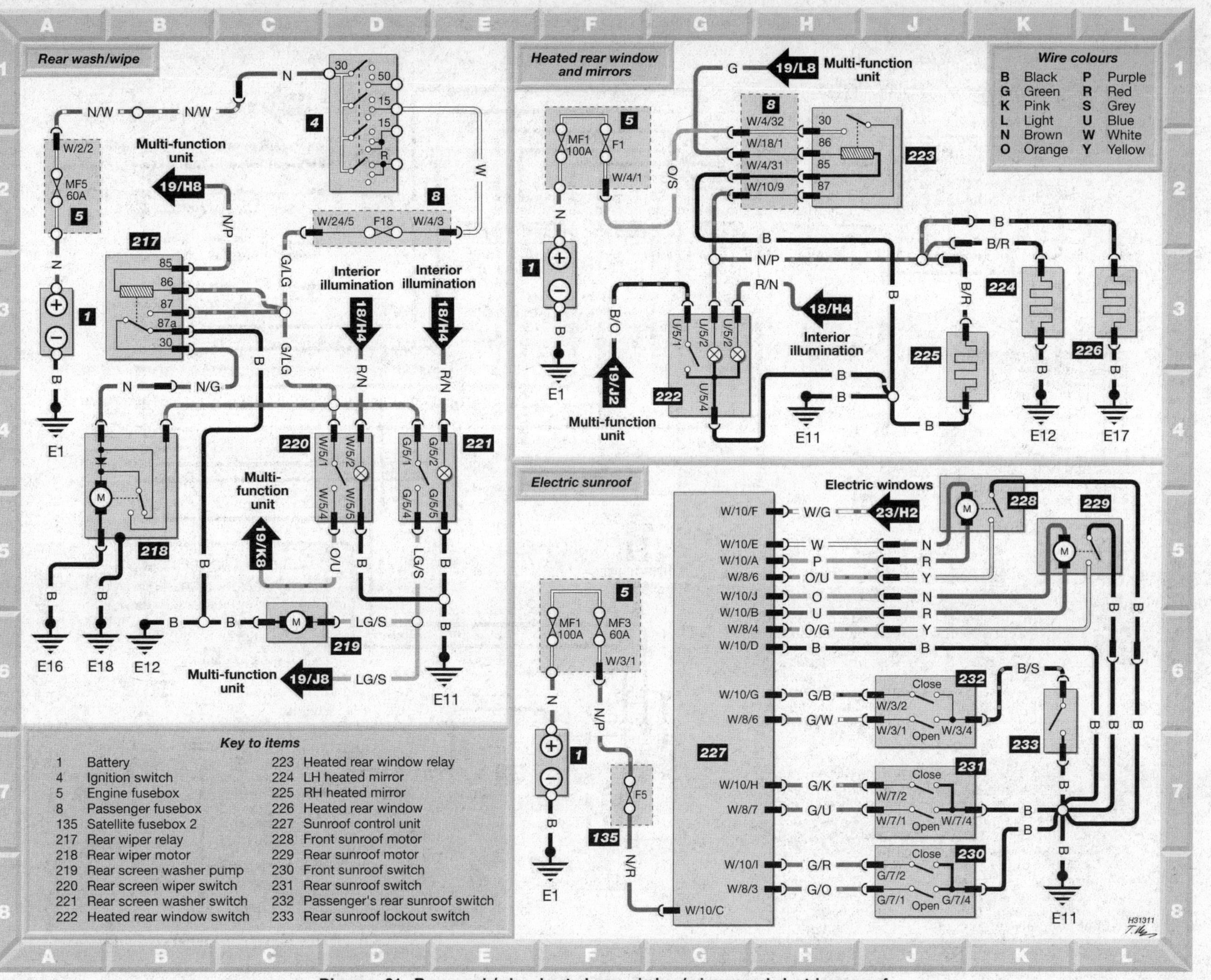
Rear wash/wipe
Heated rear window and mirrors
Electric sunroof
Electric windows
Multi-function unit
Interior illumination
Wire colours
B Black
G Green
K Pink
L Light
N Brown
O Orange
P Purple
R Red
S Grey
U Blue
W White
Y Yellow
Key to items
1 Battery
4 Ignition switch
5 Engine fusebox
8 Passenger fusebox
135 Satellite fusebox 2
217 Rear wiper relay
218 Rear wiper motor
219 Rear screen washer pump
220 Rear screen wiper switch
221 Rear screen washer switch
222 Heated rear window switch
223 Heated rear window relay
224 LH heated mirror
225 RH heated mirror
226 Heated rear window
227 Sunroof control unit
228 Front sunroof motor
229 Rear sunroof motor
230 Front sunroof switch
231 Rear sunroof switch
232 Passenger's rear sunroof switch
233 Rear sunroof lockout switch
H31311
Diagram 21 : Rear wash/wipe, heated rear window/mirrors and electric sunroof

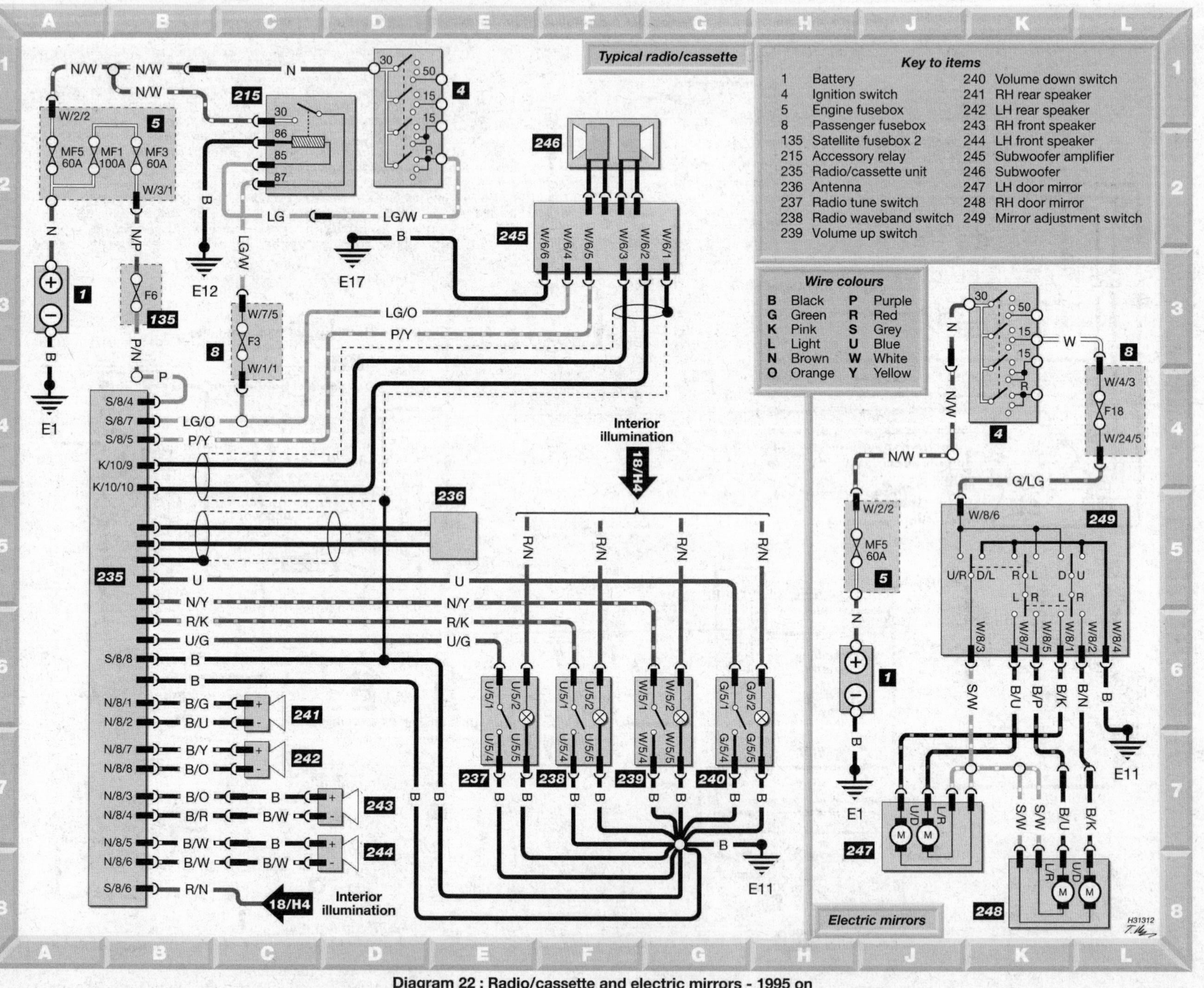
Typical radio/cassette
Key to items
1 Battery
4 Ignition switch
5 Engine fusebox
8 Passenger fusebox
135 Satellite fusebox 2
215 Accessory relay
235 Radio/cassette unit
236 Antenna
237 Radio tune switch
238 Radio waveband switch
239 Volume up switch
240 Volume down switch
241 RH rear speaker
242 LH rear speaker
243 RH front speaker
244 LH front speaker
245 Subwoofer amplifier
246 Subwoofer
247 LH door mirror
248 RH door mirror
249 Mirror adjustment switch
Wire colours
B Black
G Green
K Pink
L Light
N Brown
O Orange
P Purple
R Red
S Grey
U Blue
W White
Y Yellow
Interior illumination
18/H4
Electric mirrors
H31312

Diagram 22 : Radio/cassette and electric mirrors - 1995 on

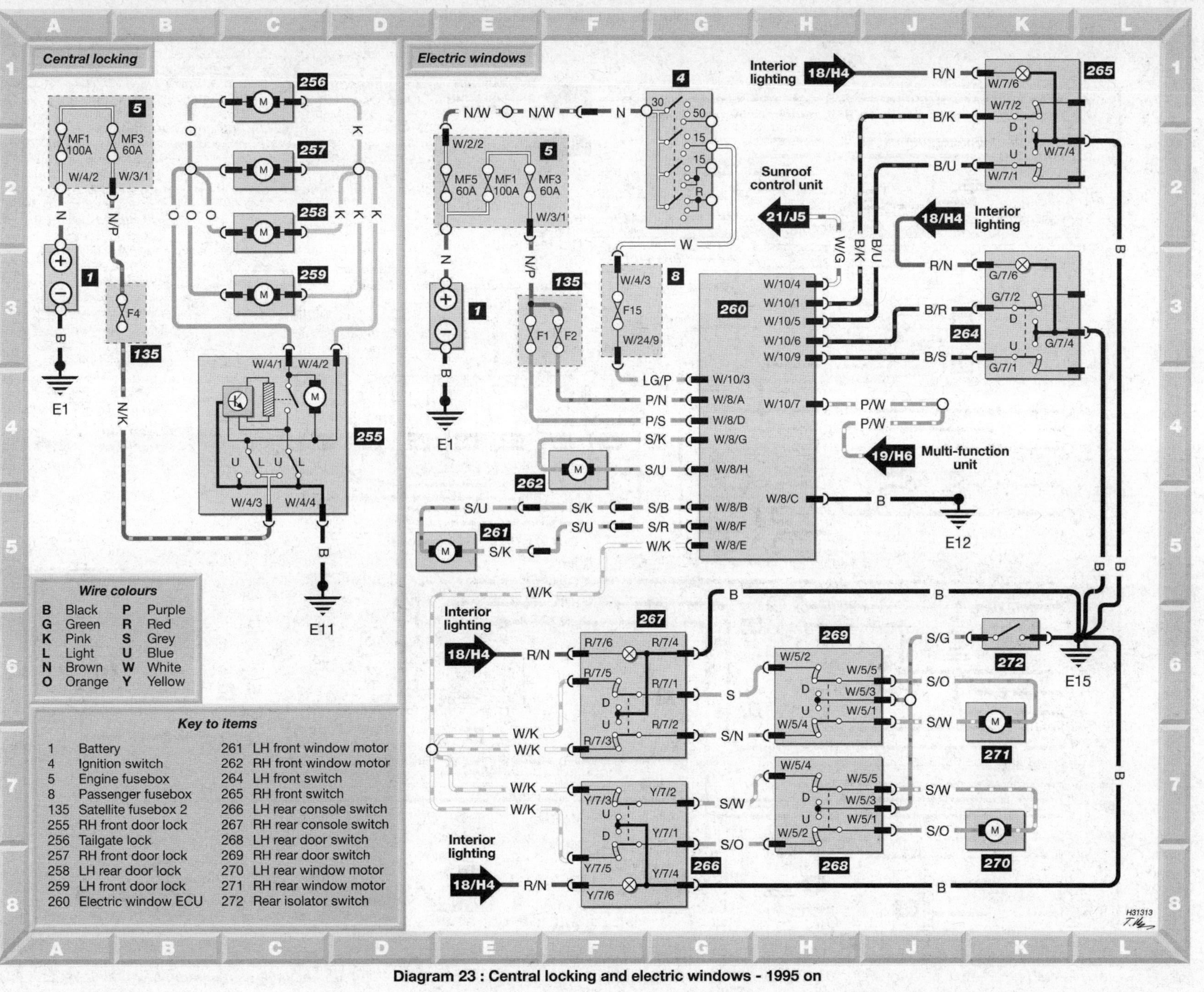
Central locking
Electric windows
Interior lighting
Sunroof control unit
Multi-function unit
Wire colours
B Black
G Green
K Pink
L Light
N Brown
O Orange
P Purple
R Red
S Grey
U Blue
W White
Y Yellow
Key to items
1 Battery
4 Ignition switch
5 Engine fusebox
8 Passenger fusebox
135 Satellite fusebox 2
255 RH front door lock
256 Tailgate lock
257 RH front door lock
258 LH rear door lock
259 LH front door lock
260 Electric window ECU
261 LH front window motor
262 RH front window motor
264 LH front switch
265 RH front switch
266 LH rear console switch
267 RH rear console switch
268 LH rear door switch
269 RH rear door switch
270 LH rear window motor
271 RH rear window motor
272 Rear isolator switch
H31313
Diagram 23 : Central locking and electric windows - 1995 on

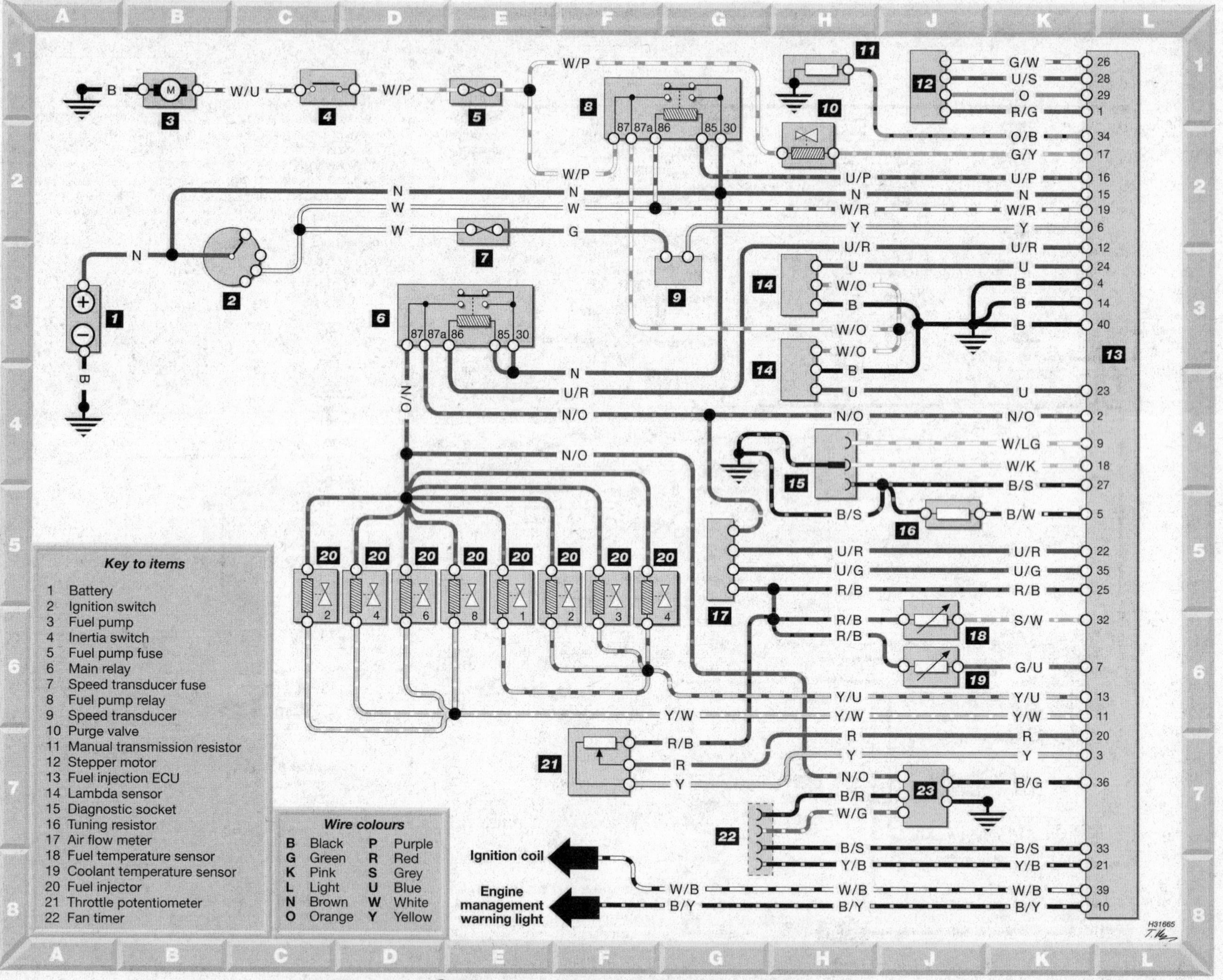
H31665
Key to items
1 Battery
2 Ignition switch
3 Fuel pump
4 Inertia switch
5 Fuel pump fuse
6 Main relay
7 Speed transducer fuse
8 Fuel pump relay
9 Speed transducer
10 Purge valve
11 Manual transmission resistor
12 Stepper motor
13 Fuel injection ECU
14 Lambda sensor
15 Diagnostic socket
16 Tuning resistor
17 Air flow meter
18 Fuel temperature sensor
19 Coolant temperature sensor
20 Fuel injector
21 Throttle potentiometer
22 Fan timer
Wire colours
B Black
G Green
K Pink
L Light
N Brown
O Orange
P Purple
R Red
S Grey
U Blue
W White
Y Yellow
Ignition coil
Engine management warning light

Supplementary diagram for fuel injection - pre '95

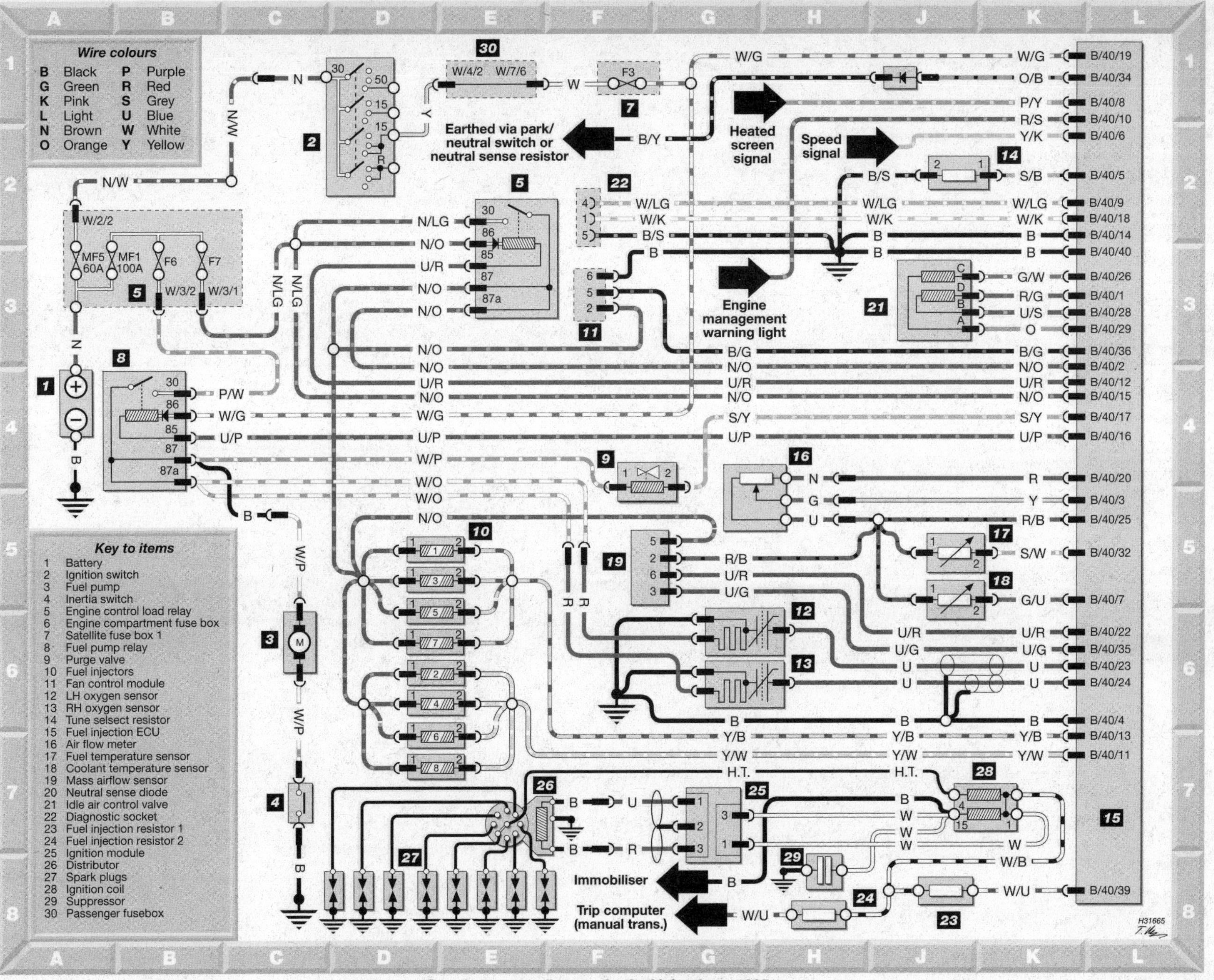
Wire colours
B Black
G Green
K Pink
L Light
N Brown
O Orange
P Purple
R Red
S Grey
U Blue
W White
Y Yellow
Key to items
1 Battery
2 Ignition switch
3 Fuel pump
4 Inertia switch
5 Engine control load relay
6 Engine compartment fuse box
7 Satellite fuse box 1
8 Fuel pump relay
9 Purge valve
10 Fuel injectors
11 Fan control module
12 LH oxygen sensor
13 RH oxygen sensor
14 Tune selsect resistor
15 Fuel injection ECU
16 Air flow meter
17 Fuel temperature sensor
18 Coolant temperature sensor
19 Mass airflow sensor
20 Neutral sense diode
21 Idle air control valve
22 Diagnostic socket
23 Fuel injection resistor 1
24 Fuel injection resistor 2
25 Ignition module
26 Distributor
27 Spark plugs
28 Ignition coil
29 Suppressor
30 Passenger fusebox
Earthed via park/neutral switch or neutral sense resistor
Heated screen signal
Speed signal
Engine management warning light
Immobiliser
Trip computer (manual trans.)
H31665
Supplementary diagram for fuel injection - 1995 on

LAND ROVER
HAYNES

Dimensions and weights

Note: *All figures are approximate, and may vary according to model. Refer to manufacturer's data for exact figures.*

Dimensions

Overall length:	
Including spare wheel	4538 mm
Including tow hitch	4581 mm
Overall width	2189 mm
Overall height (unladen)	1914 mm

Weights

Kerb weight:	**3-door**	**5-door**
Petrol engine models:		
Carburettor engine	1979 kg	-
Fuel injection engine	2089 kg	2128 kg
200 TDi engine models	2008 kg	2053 kg
300 TDi engine models	2040 kg	2065 kg
Maximum gross vehicle weight (all models)	2720 kg	
Maximum roof rack load:		
On-road	50 kg	
Off-road	30 kg	
Maximum trailer nose weight	75 kg	
Maximum towing weight:		
Unbraked trailer:		
On-road	750 kg	
Off-road	500 kg	
Trailer with overrun brakes:		
On-road	3500 kg	
Off-road	1000 kg	

Conversion factors

Length (distance)

Inches (in)	x 25.4	= Millimetres (mm)	x 0.0394	= Inches (in)
Feet (ft)	x 0.305	= Metres (m)	x 3.281	= Feet (ft)
Miles	x 1.609	= Kilometres (km)	x 0.621	= Miles

Volume (capacity)

Cubic inches (cu in; in^3)	x 16.387	= Cubic centimetres (cc; cm^3)	x 0.061	= Cubic inches (cu in; in^3)
Imperial pints (Imp pt)	x 0.568	= Litres (l)	x 1.76	= Imperial pints (Imp pt)
Imperial quarts (Imp qt)	x 1.137	= Litres (l)	x 0.88	= Imperial quarts (Imp qt)
Imperial quarts (Imp qt)	x 1.201	= US quarts (US qt)	x 0.833	= Imperial quarts (Imp qt)
US quarts (US qt)	x 0.946	= Litres (l)	x 1.057	= US quarts (US qt)
Imperial gallons (Imp gal)	x 4.546	= Litres (l)	x 0.22	= Imperial gallons (Imp gal)
Imperial gallons (Imp gal)	x 1.201	= US gallons (US gal)	x 0.833	= Imperial gallons (Imp gal)
US gallons (US gal)	x 3.785	= Litres (l)	x 0.264	= US gallons (US gal)

Mass (weight)

Ounces (oz)	x 28.35	= Grams (g)	x 0.035	= Ounces (oz)
Pounds (lb)	x 0.454	= Kilograms (kg)	x 2.205	= Pounds (lb)

Force

Ounces-force (ozf; oz)	x 0.278	= Newtons (N)	x 3.6	= Ounces-force (ozf; oz)
Pounds-force (lbf; lb)	x 4.448	= Newtons (N)	x 0.225	= Pounds-force (lbf; lb)
Newtons (N)	x 0.1	= Kilograms-force (kgf; kg)	x 9.81	= Newtons (N)

Pressure

Pounds-force per square inch (psi; lbf/in^2; lb/in^2)	x 0.070	= Kilograms-force per square centimetre (kgf/cm^2; kg/cm^2)	x 14.223	= Pounds-force per square inch (psi; lbf/in^2; lb/in^2)
Pounds-force per square inch (psi; lbf/in^2; lb/in^2)	x 0.068	= Atmospheres (atm)	x 14.696	= Pounds-force per square inch (psi; lbf/in^2; lb/in^2)
Pounds-force per square inch (psi; lbf/in^2; lb/in^2)	x 0.069	= Bars	x 14.5	= Pounds-force per square inch (psi; lbf/in^2; lb/in^2)
Pounds-force per square inch (psi; lbf/in^2; lb/in^2)	x 6.895	= Kilopascals (kPa)	x 0.145	= Pounds-force per square inch (psi; lbf/in^2; lb/in^2)
Kilopascals (kPa)	x 0.01	= Kilograms-force per square centimetre (kgf/cm^2; kg/cm^2)	x 98.1	= Kilopascals (kPa)
Millibar (mbar)	x 100	= Pascals (Pa)	x 0.01	= Millibar (mbar)
Millibar (mbar)	x 0.0145	= Pounds-force per square inch (psi; lbf/in^2; lb/in^2)	x 68.947	= Millibar (mbar)
Millibar (mbar)	x 0.75	= Millimetres of mercury (mmHg)	x 1.333	= Millibar (mbar)
Millibar (mbar)	x 0.401	= Inches of water (inH_2O)	x 2.491	= Millibar (mbar)
Millimetres of mercury (mmHg)	x 0.535	= Inches of water (inH_2O)	x 1.868	= Millimetres of mercury (mmHg)
Inches of water (inH_2O)	x 0.036	= Pounds-force per square inch (psi; lbf/in^2; lb/in^2)	x 27.68	= Inches of water (inH_2O)

Torque (moment of force)

Pounds-force inches (lbf in; lb in)	x 1.152	= Kilograms-force centimetre (kgf cm; kg cm)	x 0.868	= Pounds-force inches (lbf in; lb in)
Pounds-force inches (lbf in; lb in)	x 0.113	= Newton metres (Nm)	x 8.85	= Pounds-force inches (lbf in; lb in)
Pounds-force inches (lbf in; lb in)	x 0.083	= Pounds-force feet (lbf ft; lb ft)	x 12	= Pounds-force inches (lbf in; lb in)
Pounds-force feet (lbf ft; lb ft)	x 0.138	= Kilograms-force metres (kgf m; kg m)	x 7.233	= Pounds-force feet (lbf ft; lb ft)
Pounds-force feet (lbf ft; lb ft)	x 1.356	= Newton metres (Nm)	x 0.738	= Pounds-force feet (lbf ft; lb ft)
Newton metres (Nm)	x 0.102	= Kilograms-force metres (kgf m; kg m)	x 9.804	= Newton metres (Nm)

Power

Horsepower (hp)	x 745.7	= Watts (W)	x 0.0013	= Horsepower (hp)

Velocity (speed)

Miles per hour (miles/hr; mph)	x 1.609	= Kilometres per hour (km/hr; kph)	x 0.621	= Miles per hour (miles/hr; mph)

Fuel consumption*

Miles per gallon, Imperial (mpg)	x 0.354	= Kilometres per litre (km/l)	x 2.825	= Miles per gallon, Imperial (mpg)
Miles per gallon, US (mpg)	x 0.425	= Kilometres per litre (km/l)	x 2.352	= Miles per gallon, US (mpg)

Temperature

Degrees Fahrenheit = (°C x 1.8) + 32

Degrees Celsius (Degrees Centigrade; °C) = (°F - 32) x 0.56

** It is common practice to convert from miles per gallon (mpg) to litres/100 kilometres (l/100km), where mpg x l/100 km = 282*

Spare parts are available from many sources, including maker's appointed garages, accessory shops, and motor factors. To be sure of obtaining the correct parts, it may sometimes be necessary to quote the vehicle identification number. If possible, it can also be useful to take the old parts along for positive identification. Items such as starter motors and alternators may be available under a service exchange scheme - any parts returned should always be clean.

Our advice regarding spare part sources is as follows.

Officially-appointed garages

This is the best source of parts which are peculiar to your vehicle, and are not otherwise generally available (eg badges, interior trim, certain body panels, etc). It is also the only place at which you should buy parts if the vehicle is still under warranty.

Accessory shops

These are very good places to buy materials and components needed for the maintenance of your vehicle (oil, air and fuel filters, spark plugs, light bulbs, drivebelts, oils and greases, brake pads, touch-up paint, etc). Parts like this sold by a reputable shop are of the same standard as those used by the vehicle manufacturer.

Motor factors

Good factors will stock all the more important components which wear out comparatively quickly and can sometimes supply individual components needed for the overhaul of a larger assembly. They may also handle work such as cylinder block reboring, crankshaft regrinding and balancing, etc.

Tyre and exhaust specialists

These outlets may be independent or members of a local or national chain. They frequently offer competitive prices when compared with a main dealer or local garage, but it will pay to obtain several quotes before making a decision. Also ask what 'extras' may be added to the quote - for instance, fitting a new valve and balancing the wheel are both often charged on top of the price of a new tyre.

Other sources

Beware of parts or materials obtained from market stalls, car boot sales or similar outlets. Such items are not invariably sub-standard, but there is little chance of compensation if they do prove unsatisfactory. In the case of safety-critical components such as brake pads, there is the risk not only of financial loss, but also of an accident causing injury or death.

Second-hand components or assemblies obtained from a car breaker can be a good buy in some circumstances, but this sort of purchase is best made by the experienced DIY mechanic.

Whenever servicing, repair or overhaul work is carried out on the car or its components, observe the following procedures and instructions. This will assist in carrying out the operation efficiently and to a professional standard of workmanship.

Joint mating faces and gaskets

When separating components at their mating faces, never insert screwdrivers or similar implements into the joint between the faces in order to prise them apart. This can cause severe damage which results in oil leaks, coolant leaks, etc upon reassembly. Separation is usually achieved by tapping along the joint with a soft-faced hammer in order to break the seal. However, note that this method may not be suitable where dowels are used for component location.

Where a gasket is used between the mating faces of two components, a new one must be fitted on reassembly; fit it dry unless otherwise stated in the repair procedure. Make sure that the mating faces are clean and dry, with all traces of old gasket removed. When cleaning a joint face, use a tool which is unlikely to score or damage the face, and remove any burrs or nicks with an oilstone or fine file.

Make sure that tapped holes are cleaned with a pipe cleaner, and keep them free of jointing compound, if this is being used, unless specifically instructed otherwise.

Ensure that all orifices, channels or pipes are clear, and blow through them, preferably using compressed air.

Oil seals

Oil seals can be removed by levering them out with a wide flat-bladed screwdriver or similar implement. Alternatively, a number of self-tapping screws may be screwed into the seal, and these used as a purchase for pliers or some similar device in order to pull the seal free.

Whenever an oil seal is removed from its working location, either individually or as part of an assembly, it should be renewed.

The very fine sealing lip of the seal is easily damaged, and will not seal if the surface it contacts is not completely clean and free from scratches, nicks or grooves. If the original sealing surface of the component cannot be restored, and the manufacturer has not made provision for slight relocation of the seal relative to the sealing surface, the component should be renewed.

Protect the lips of the seal from any surface which may damage them in the course of fitting. Use tape or a conical sleeve where possible. Lubricate the seal lips with oil before fitting and, on dual-lipped seals, fill the space between the lips with grease.

Unless otherwise stated, oil seals must be fitted with their sealing lips toward the lubricant to be sealed.

Use a tubular drift or block of wood of the appropriate size to install the seal and, if the seal housing is shouldered, drive the seal down to the shoulder. If the seal housing is unshouldered, the seal should be fitted with its face flush with the housing top face (unless otherwise instructed).

Screw threads and fastenings

Seized nuts, bolts and screws are quite a common occurrence where corrosion has set in, and the use of penetrating oil or releasing fluid will often overcome this problem if the offending item is soaked for a while before attempting to release it. The use of an impact driver may also provide a means of releasing such stubborn fastening devices, when used in conjunction with the appropriate screwdriver bit or socket. If none of these methods works, it may be necessary to resort to the careful application of heat, or the use of a hacksaw or nut splitter device.

Studs are usually removed by locking two nuts together on the threaded part, and then using a spanner on the lower nut to unscrew the stud. Studs or bolts which have broken off below the surface of the component in which they are mounted can sometimes be removed using a stud extractor. Always ensure that a blind tapped hole is completely free from oil, grease, water or other fluid before installing the bolt or stud. Failure to do this could cause the housing to crack due to the hydraulic action of the bolt or stud as it is screwed in.

When tightening a castellated nut to accept a split pin, tighten the nut to the specified torque, where applicable, and then tighten further to the next split pin hole. Never slacken the nut to align the split pin hole, unless stated in the repair procedure.

When checking or retightening a nut or bolt to a specified torque setting, slacken the nut or bolt by a quarter of a turn, and then retighten to the specified setting. However, this should not be attempted where angular tightening has been used.

For some screw fastenings, notably cylinder head bolts or nuts, torque wrench settings are no longer specified for the latter stages of tightening, “angle-tightening” being called up instead. Typically, a fairly low torque wrench setting will be applied to the bolts/nuts in the correct sequence, followed by one or more stages of tightening through specified angles.

Locknuts, locktabs and washers

Any fastening which will rotate against a component or housing during tightening should always have a washer between it and the relevant component or housing.

Spring or split washers should always be renewed when they are used to lock a critical component such as a big-end bearing retaining bolt or nut. Locktabs which are folded over to retain a nut or bolt should always be renewed.

Self-locking nuts can be re-used in non-critical areas, providing resistance can be felt when the locking portion passes over the bolt or stud thread. However, it should be noted that self-locking stiffnuts tend to lose their effectiveness after long periods of use, and should then be renewed as a matter of course.

Split pins must always be replaced with new ones of the correct size for the hole.

When thread-locking compound is found on the threads of a fastener which is to be re-used, it should be cleaned off with a wire brush and solvent, and fresh compound applied on reassembly.

Special tools

Some repair procedures in this manual entail the use of special tools such as a press, two or three-legged pullers, spring compressors, etc. Wherever possible, suitable readily-available alternatives to the manufacturer’s special tools are described, and are shown in use. In some instances, where no alternative is possible, it has been necessary to resort to the use of a manufacturer’s tool, and this has been done for reasons of safety as well as the efficient completion of the repair operation. Unless you are highly-skilled and have a thorough understanding of the procedures described, never attempt to bypass the use of any special tool when the procedure described specifies its use. Not only is there a very great risk of personal injury, but expensive damage could be caused to the components involved.

Environmental considerations

When disposing of used engine oil, brake fluid, antifreeze, etc, give due consideration to any detrimental environmental effects. Do not, for instance, pour any of the above liquids down drains into the general sewage system, or onto the ground to soak away. Many local council refuse tips provide a facility for waste oil disposal, as do some garages. If none of these facilities are available, consult your local Environmental Health Department, or the National Rivers Authority, for further advice.

With the universal tightening-up of legislation regarding the emission of environmentally-harmful substances from motor vehicles, most vehicles have tamperproof devices fitted to the main adjustment points of the fuel system. These devices are primarily designed to prevent unqualified persons from adjusting the fuel/air mixture, with the chance of a consequent increase in toxic emissions. If such devices are found during servicing or overhaul, they should, wherever possible, be renewed or refitted in accordance with the manufacturer’s requirements or current legislation.

OIL CARE
FOLLOW THE CODE
OIL BANK LINE
0800 66 33 66
www.oilbankline.org.uk

Note: It is antisocial and illegal to dump oil down the drain. To find the location of your local oil recycling bank, call this number free.

Modifications are a continuing and unpublicised process in vehicle manufacture, quite apart from major model changes. Spare parts manuals and lists are compiled upon a numerical basis, the individual vehicle identification numbers being essential to correct identification of the component concerned.

When ordering spare parts, always give as much information as possible. Quote the vehicle model, year of manufacture, body and engine numbers as appropriate.

The *Vehicle Identification Number (VIN) plate* is riveted to the top of the body front panel, and can be viewed once the bonnet is open **(see illustrations)**. The plate carries the VIN number, vehicle weight information and paint and trim colour codes.

The *Vehicle Identification Number (VIN)* is given on the VIN plate, and is also stamped into front right-hand side of the chassis, forward of the coil spring mounting **(see illustration)**.

The petrol *engine number* is stamped onto the left-hand bank of the cylinder block (left as seen from the driver's seat), between the centre branches of the exhaust manifold. The engine compression ratio also appears above the engine number **(see illustration)**.

The diesel *engine number* is stamped into the cylinder block, on the right-hand side of the engine, above the camshaft front cover plate.

The *manual transmission identification number* is stamped into a flat on the bottom right-hand side of the transmission casing **(see illustration)**.

The *automatic transmission identification number* is stamped on a plate riveted to the bottom left-hand side of the transmission casing **(see illustration)**.

The *transfer gearbox identification number* is stamped into the lower left-hand side of the gearbox casing **(see illustration)**.

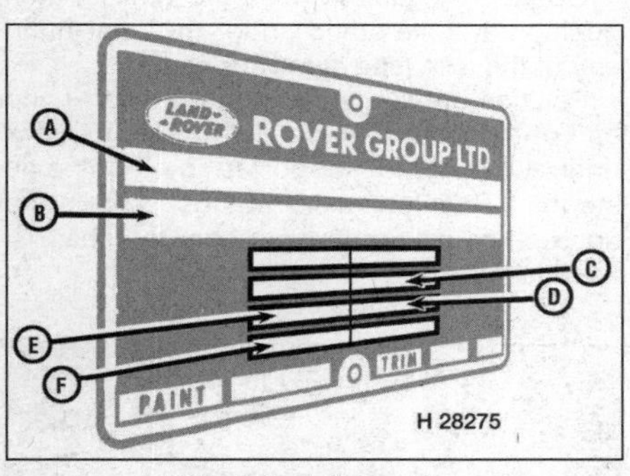
ROVER GROUP LTD

VIN plate (arrowed)

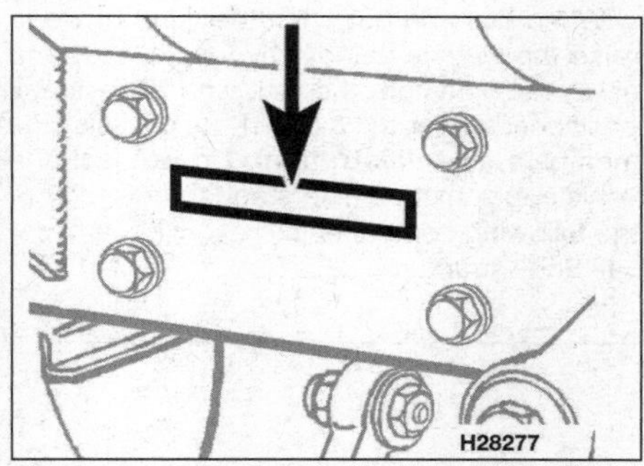
LAND-ROVER
ROVER GROUP LTD
A
B
C
D
E
F
PAINT
TRIM
H 28275

VIN plate information

A Type approval number
B VIN (minimum 17 digits)
C Maximum permitted laden weight for vehicle
D Maximum vehicle and trailer weight
E Maximum road weight - front axle
F Maximum road weight - rear axle

VIN stamped on right-hand side of chassis

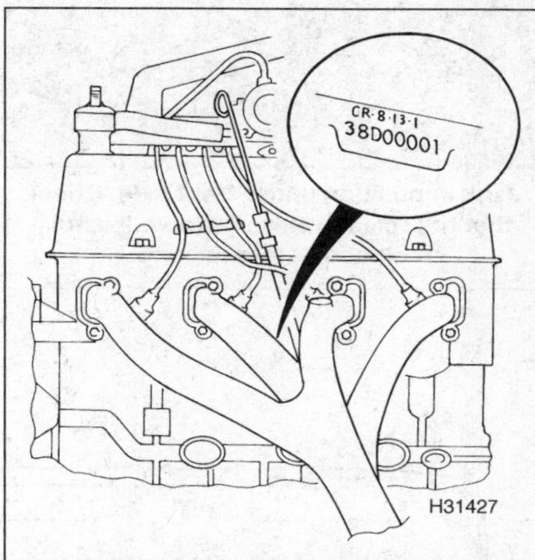
H28277
CR-8·13·1
38D00001
H31427

Petrol engine number location - note compression ratio (CR) details which appear above

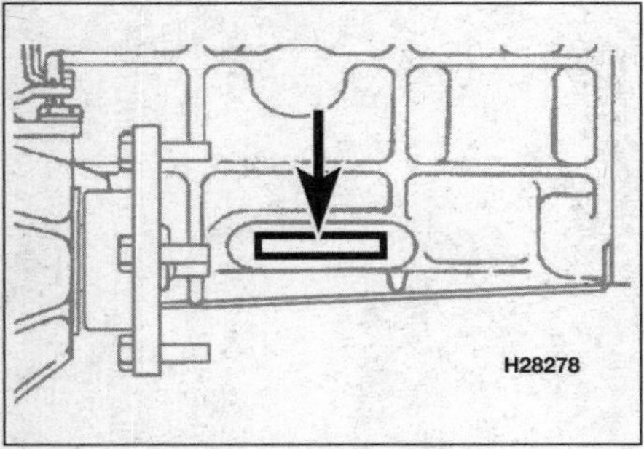
H28278

Manual gearbox identification number location

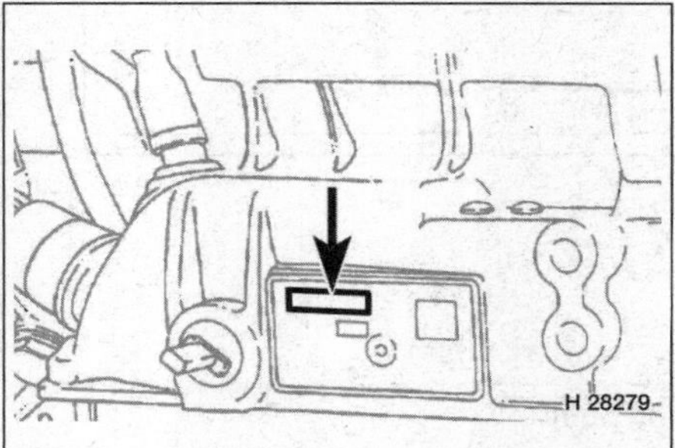
H 28279

Automatic transmission identification number location

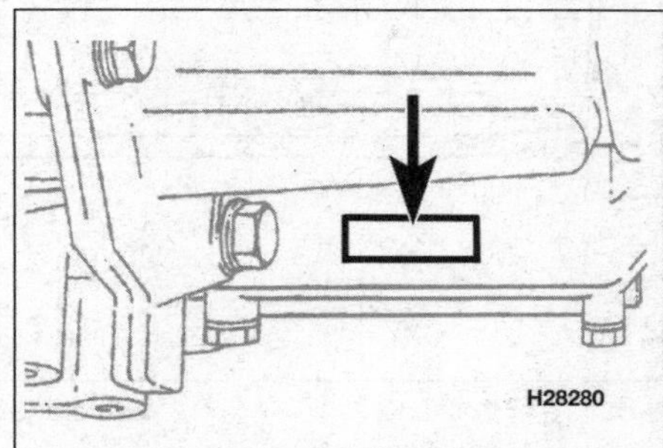
H28280

Transfer gearbox identification number location

Warning: The handbrake acts on the transmission, not the rear wheels, and may not hold the vehicle stationary when jacking. If one front wheel and one rear wheel are raised, no vehicle holding or braking effect is possible using the handbrake, therefore the wheels must always be chocked (using the chock supplied in the tool kit). If the vehicle is coupled to a trailer, disconnect the trailer from the vehicle before commencing jacking. This is to prevent the trailer pulling the vehicle off the jack and causing personal injury.

Using the vehicle jack

The jack supplied with the vehicle tool kit should only be used for changing the roadwheels, as described in *Wheel changing* at the front of this Manual.

If jacking up a front wheel, slide the jack into position from the front of the vehicle (not from the side). Position the jack head so that when raised, it will engage with the front axle casing immediately below the coil spring. The jack head must locate between the flange at the end of the axle casing and large bracket to which the front suspension components are secured (see illustration).

Jack in position under front axle. Check that the release valve (arrowed) is fully closed before jacking

If raising a rear wheel, push the rear mudflap up behind the tyre to allow a clear view of the jacking point. Slide the jack into position from the rear of the vehicle. Position the jack head so that when raised, it will engage with the rear axle casing immediately below the coil spring, and as close as possible to the shock absorber mounting bracket.

Using a hydraulic (trolley) jack and axle stands

Note: *To raise the vehicle, a hydraulic jack with a minimum load capacity of 1500 kg must be used.* ***Never*** *work under a vehicle supported solely by a hydraulic jack, as even a hydraulic jack could fail under load - always supplement the jack with axle stands. Do not use piles of bricks or wooden blocks for supporting - the Discovery is a heavy vehicle, and makeshift methods should not be used.*

When carrying out any other kind of work, raise the vehicle using a hydraulic jack, and always supplement the jack with axle stands positioned under the axles or the chassis side members **(see illustration)**. **Do not** jack the vehicle, or position axle stands under any of the following components:

a) Body structure.
b) Bumpers.
c) Underbody pipes and hoses.
d) Suspension components.
e) Gearbox/transmission/transfer gearbox housings.
f) Engine sump.
g) Fuel tank.

Only ever jack the vehicle up on a solid, level surface. If there is even a slight slope, take great care that the vehicle cannot move as the wheels are lifted off the ground. Jacking up on an uneven or gravelled surface is not recommended, as the weight of the vehicle will not be evenly distributed, and the jack may slip as the vehicle is raised.

As far as possible, do not leave the vehicle unattended once it has been raised, particularly if children are playing nearby.

To raise the front or the rear of the vehicle, chock the appropriate roadwheels, then position the jack head under the front or rear differential casing, as appropriate **(see illustration)**. **Note:** *The differential casing is not in the centre of the axle, and the vehicle will tilt when jacked under the differential casing. This is particularly noticeable when jacking up the front of the vehicle.*

Operate the jack to raise the vehicle, then position an axle stand under the right-hand end of the axle **(see illustration)**.

Position an axle stand under the left-hand end of the axle, then carefully lower the jack until the axle is supported by both axle stands. Position axle stands under the appropriate axle tubes, or under the chassis, as required.

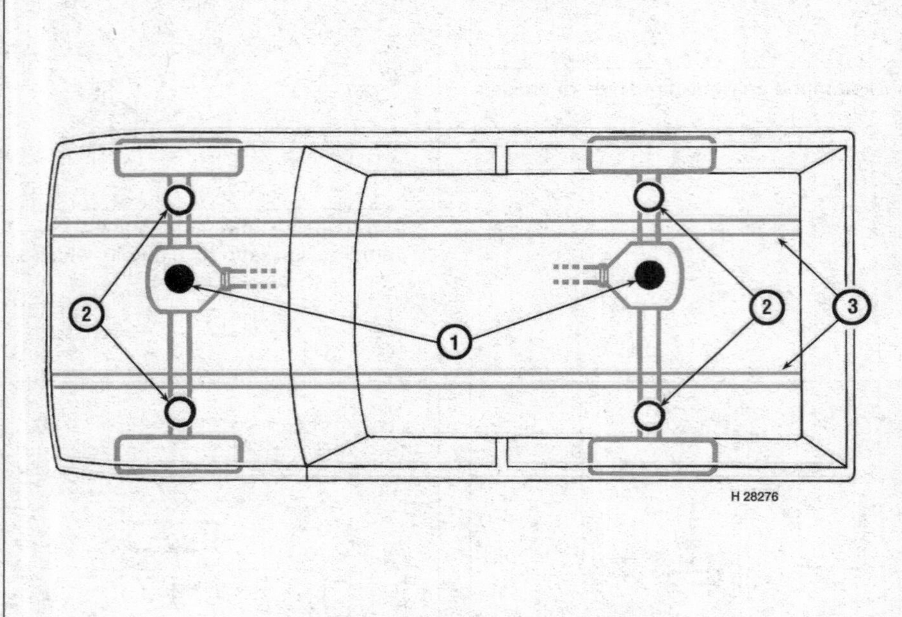
1
2
2
3
H 28276

Vehicle jacking points

1 *Jacking points for use with hydraulic jack (under differential housing)*
2 *Support points for use with axle stands (under axle tubes)*
3 *Chassis side members*

Jack positioned under front differential casing

Axle stand positioned under right-hand end of front axle

Radio/cassette unit anti-theft system - precaution

The radio/cassette unit fitted as standard equipment by Land Rover may be equipped with a built-in security code, to deter thieves. If the power source to the unit is cut, the anti-theft system will activate. Even if the power source is immediately reconnected, the radio/cassette unit will not function until the correct security code has been entered. Therefore, if you do not know the correct security code for the radio/cassette unit, **do not** disconnect the battery negative terminal of the battery, or remove the radio/cassette unit from the vehicle.

To enter the correct security code, follow the instructions provided with the radio/cassette player handbook.

If an incorrect code is entered, the unit will become locked, and cannot be operated.

If this happens or if the security code is lost or forgotten, seek the advice of your Land Rover dealer. On presentation of proof of ownership, a Land Rover dealer will be able to unlock the unit and provide you with a new security code.

Introduction

A selection of good tools is a fundamental requirement for anyone contemplating the maintenance and repair of a motor vehicle. For the owner who does not possess any, their purchase will prove a considerable expense, offsetting some of the savings made by doing-it-yourself. However, provided that the tools purchased meet the relevant national safety standards and are of good quality, they will last for many years and prove an extremely worthwhile investment.

To help the average owner to decide which tools are needed to carry out the various tasks detailed in this manual, we have compiled three lists of tools under the following headings: *Maintenance and minor repair*, *Repair and overhaul*, and *Special*. Newcomers to practical mechanics should start off with the *Maintenance and minor repair* tool kit, and confine themselves to the simpler jobs around the vehicle. Then, as confidence and experience grow, more difficult tasks can be undertaken, with extra tools being purchased as, and when, they are needed. In this way, a *Maintenance and minor repair* tool kit can be built up into a *Repair and overhaul* tool kit over a considerable period of time, without any major cash outlays. The experienced do-it-yourselfer will have a tool kit good enough for most repair and overhaul procedures, and will add tools from the *Special* category when it is felt that the expense is justified by the amount of use to which these tools will be put.

Maintenance and minor repair tool kit

The tools given in this list should be considered as a minimum requirement if routine maintenance, servicing and minor repair operations are to be undertaken. We recommend the purchase of combination spanners (ring one end, open-ended the other); although more expensive than open-ended ones, they do give the advantages of both types of spanner.

- ☐ *Combination spanners:*
  Metric - 8 to 19 mm inclusive
- ☐ *Adjustable spanner - 35 mm jaw (approx.)*
- ☐ *Spark plug spanner (with rubber insert) - petrol models*
- ☐ *Spark plug gap adjustment tool - petrol models*
- ☐ *Set of feeler gauges*
- ☐ *Brake bleed nipple spanner*
- ☐ *Screwdrivers:*
  Flat blade - 100 mm long x 6 mm dia
  Cross blade - 100 mm long x 6 mm dia
  Torx - various sizes (not all vehicles)
- ☐ *Combination pliers*
- ☐ *Hacksaw (junior)*
- ☐ *Tyre pump*
- ☐ *Tyre pressure gauge*
- ☐ *Oil can*
- ☐ *Oil filter removal tool*
- ☐ *Fine emery cloth*
- ☐ *Wire brush (small)*
- ☐ *Funnel (medium size)*
- ☐ *Sump drain plug key (not all vehicles)*

Repair and overhaul tool kit

These tools are virtually essential for anyone undertaking any major repairs to a motor vehicle, and are additional to those given in the *Maintenance and minor repair* list. Included in this list is a comprehensive set of sockets. Although these are expensive, they will be found invaluable as they are so versatile - particularly if various drives are included in the set. We recommend the half-inch square-drive type, as this can be used with most proprietary torque wrenches.

The tools in this list will sometimes need to be supplemented by tools from the *Special* list:

- ☐ *Sockets (or box spanners) to cover range in previous list (including Torx sockets)*
- ☐ *Reversible ratchet drive (for use with sockets)*
- ☐ *Extension piece, 250 mm (for use with sockets)*
- ☐ *Universal joint (for use with sockets)*
- ☐ *Flexible handle or sliding T "breaker bar" (for use with sockets)*
- ☐ *Torque wrench (for use with sockets)*
- ☐ *Self-locking grips*
- ☐ *Ball pein hammer*
- ☐ *Soft-faced mallet (plastic or rubber)*
- ☐ *Screwdrivers:*
  Flat blade - long & sturdy, short (chubby), and narrow (electrician's) types
  Cross blade – long & sturdy, and short (chubby) types
- ☐ *Pliers:*
  Long-nosed
  Side cutters (electrician's)
  Circlip (internal and external)
- ☐ *Cold chisel - 25 mm*
- ☐ *Scriber*
- ☐ *Scraper*
- ☐ *Centre-punch*
- ☐ *Pin punch*
- ☐ *Hacksaw*
- ☐ *Brake hose clamp*
- ☐ *Brake/clutch bleeding kit*
- ☐ *Selection of twist drills*
- ☐ *Steel rule/straight-edge*
- ☐ *Allen keys (inc. splined/Torx type)*
- ☐ *Selection of files*
- ☐ *Wire brush*
- ☐ *Axle stands*
- ☐ *Jack (strong trolley or hydraulic type)*
- ☐ *Light with extension lead*
- ☐ *Universal electrical multi-meter*

Sockets and reversible ratchet drive

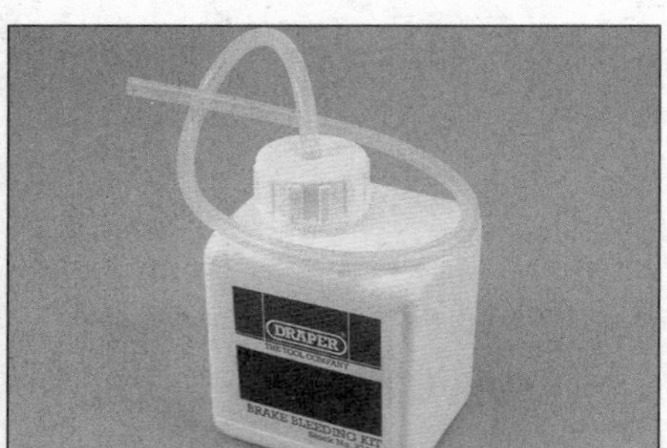
DRAPER
BRAKE BLEEDING KIT
Brake bleeding kit

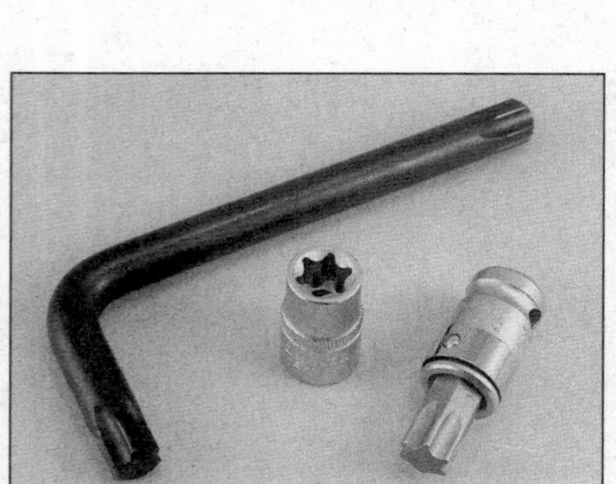
Torx key, socket and bit

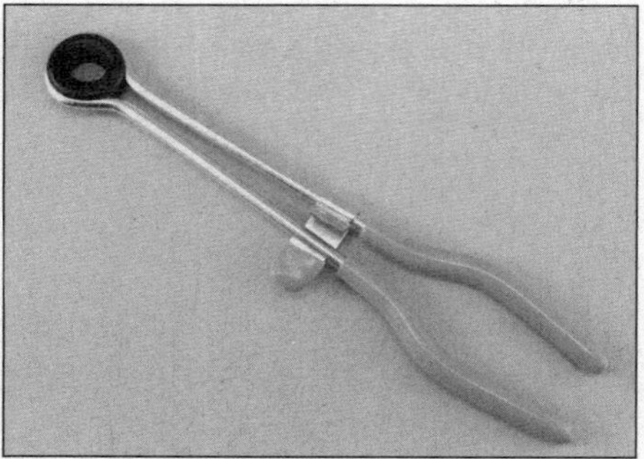
Hose clamp

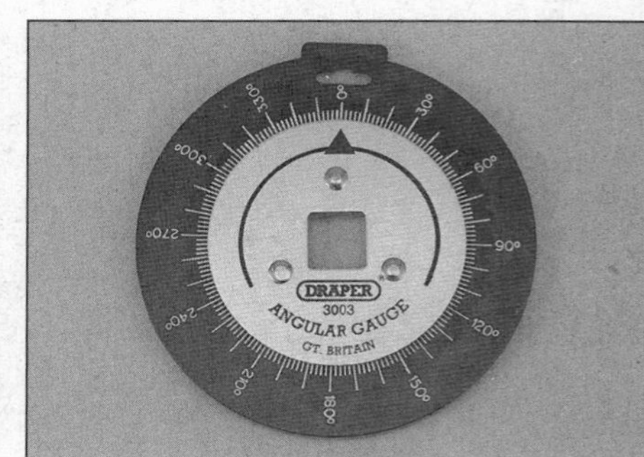
DRAPER
3003
ANGULAR GAUGE
GT. BRITAIN
Angular-tightening gauge

Special tools

The tools in this list are those which are not used regularly, are expensive to buy, or which need to be used in accordance with their manufacturers' instructions. Unless relatively difficult mechanical jobs are undertaken frequently, it will not be economic to buy many of these tools. Where this is the case, you could consider clubbing together with friends (or joining a motorists' club) to make a joint purchase, or borrowing the tools against a deposit from a local garage or tool hire specialist. It is worth noting that many of the larger DIY superstores now carry a large range of special tools for hire at modest rates.

The following list contains only those tools and instruments freely available to the public, and not those special tools produced by the vehicle manufacturer specifically for its dealer network. You will find occasional references to these manufacturers' special tools in the text of this manual. Generally, an alternative method of doing the job without the vehicle manufacturers' special tool is given. However, sometimes there is no alternative to using them. Where this is the case and the relevant tool cannot be bought or borrowed, you will have to entrust the work to a dealer.

- ☐ *Angular-tightening gauge*
- ☐ *Valve spring compressor*
- ☐ *Valve grinding tool*
- ☐ *Piston ring compressor*
- ☐ *Piston ring removal/installation tool*
- ☐ *Cylinder bore hone*
- ☐ *Balljoint separator*
- ☐ *Coil spring compressors (where applicable)*
- ☐ *Two/three-legged hub and bearing puller*
- ☐ *Impact screwdriver*
- ☐ *Micrometer and/or vernier calipers*
- ☐ *Dial gauge*
- ☐ *Stroboscopic timing light*
- ☐ *Dwell angle meter/tachometer*
- ☐ *Fault code reader*
- ☐ *Cylinder compression gauge*
- ☐ *Hand-operated vacuum pump and gauge*
- ☐ *Clutch plate alignment set*
- ☐ *Brake shoe steady spring cup removal tool*
- ☐ *Bush and bearing removal/installation set*
- ☐ *Stud extractors*
- ☐ *Tap and die set*
- ☐ *Lifting tackle*
- ☐ *Trolley jack*

Buying tools

Reputable motor accessory shops and superstores often offer excellent quality tools at discount prices, so it pays to shop around.

Remember, you don't have to buy the most expensive items on the shelf, but it is always advisable to steer clear of the very cheap tools. Beware of 'bargains' offered on market stalls or at car boot sales. There are plenty of good tools around at reasonable prices, but always aim to purchase items which meet the relevant national safety standards. If in doubt, ask the proprietor or manager of the shop for advice before making a purchase.

Care and maintenance of tools

Having purchased a reasonable tool kit, it is necessary to keep the tools in a clean and serviceable condition. After use, always wipe off any dirt, grease and metal particles using a clean, dry cloth, before putting the tools away. Never leave them lying around after they have been used. A simple tool rack on the garage or workshop wall for items such as screwdrivers and pliers is a good idea. Store all normal spanners and sockets in a metal box. Any measuring instruments, gauges, meters, etc, must be carefully stored where they cannot be damaged or become rusty.

Take a little care when tools are used. Hammer heads inevitably become marked, and screwdrivers lose the keen edge on their blades from time to time. A little timely attention with emery cloth or a file will soon restore items like this to a good finish.

Working facilities

Not to be forgotten when discussing tools is the workshop itself. If anything more than routine maintenance is to be carried out, a suitable working area becomes essential.

It is appreciated that many an owner-mechanic is forced by circumstances to remove an engine or similar item without the benefit of a garage or workshop. Having done this, any repairs should always be done under the cover of a roof.

Wherever possible, any dismantling should be done on a clean, flat workbench or table at a suitable working height.

Any workbench needs a vice; one with a jaw opening of 100 mm is suitable for most jobs. As mentioned previously, some clean dry storage space is also required for tools, as well as for any lubricants, cleaning fluids, touch-up paints etc, which become necessary.

Another item which may be required, and which has a much more general usage, is an electric drill with a chuck capacity of at least 8 mm. This, together with a good range of twist drills, is virtually essential for fitting accessories.

Last, but not least, always keep a supply of old newspapers and clean, lint-free rags available, and try to keep any working area as clean as possible.

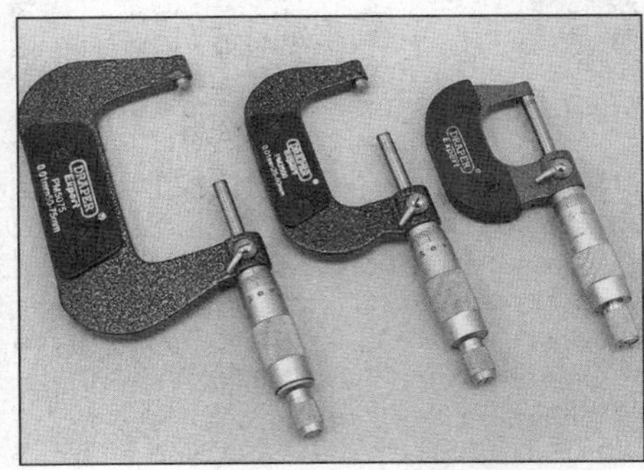
DRAPER

Micrometers

Dial test indicator ("dial gauge")

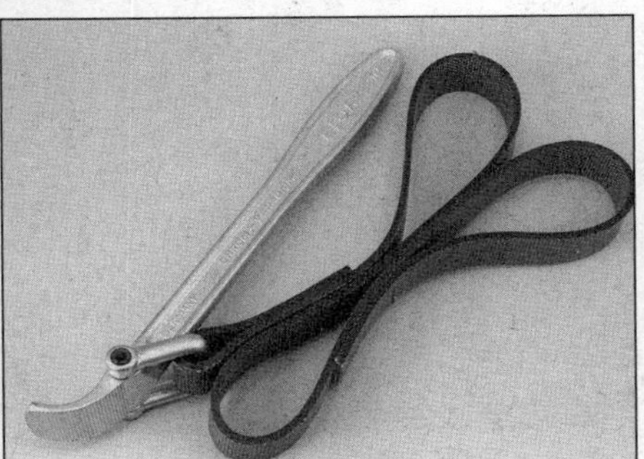

Strap wrench

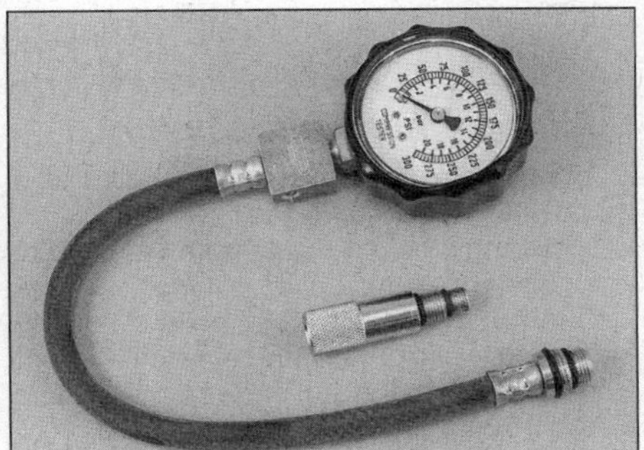

Compression tester

PFCR

Fault code reader

MOT test checks

This is a guide to getting your vehicle through the MOT test. Obviously it will not be possible to examine the vehicle to the same standard as the professional MOT tester. However, working through the following checks will enable you to identify any problem areas before submitting the vehicle for the test.

Where a testable component is in borderline condition, the tester has discretion in deciding whether to pass or fail it. The basis of such discretion is whether the tester would be happy for a close relative or friend to use the vehicle with the component in that condition. If the vehicle presented is clean and evidently well cared for, the tester may be more inclined to pass a borderline component than if the vehicle is scruffy and apparently neglected.

It has only been possible to summarise the test requirements here, based on the regulations in force at the time of printing. Test standards are becoming increasingly stringent, although there are some exemptions for older vehicles.

An assistant will be needed to help carry out some of these checks.

The checks have been sub-divided into four categories, as follows:

1 Checks carried out **FROM THE DRIVER'S SEAT**

2 Checks carried out **WITH THE VEHICLE ON THE GROUND**

3 Checks carried out **WITH THE VEHICLE RAISED AND THE WHEELS FREE TO TURN**

4 Checks carried out on **YOUR VEHICLE'S EXHAUST EMISSION SYSTEM**

1 Checks carried out FROM THE DRIVER'S SEAT

Handbrake

☐ Test the operation of the handbrake. Excessive travel (too many clicks) indicates incorrect brake or cable adjustment.

☐ Check that the handbrake cannot be released by tapping the lever sideways. Check the security of the lever mountings.

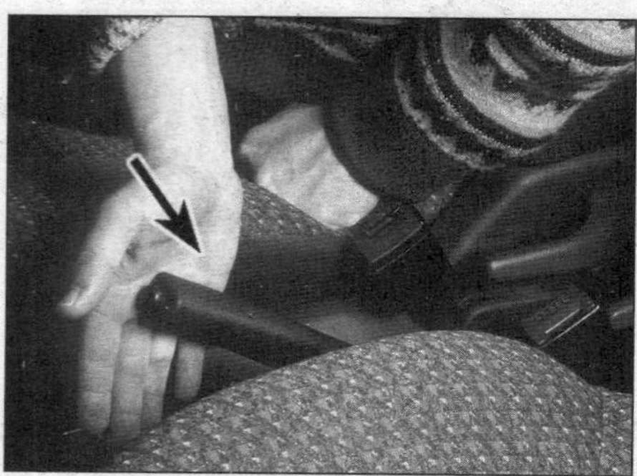

Footbrake

☐ Depress the brake pedal and check that it does not creep down to the floor, indicating a master cylinder fault. Release the pedal, wait a few seconds, then depress it again. If the pedal travels nearly to the floor before firm resistance is felt, brake adjustment or repair is necessary. If the pedal feels spongy, there is air in the hydraulic system which must be removed by bleeding.

☐ Check that the brake pedal is secure and in good condition. Check also for signs of fluid leaks on the pedal, floor or carpets, which would indicate failed seals in the brake master cylinder.

☐ Check the servo unit (when applicable) by operating the brake pedal several times, then keeping the pedal depressed and starting the engine. As the engine starts, the pedal will move down slightly. If not, the vacuum hose or the servo itself may be faulty.

Steering wheel and column

☐ Examine the steering wheel for fractures or looseness of the hub, spokes or rim.

☐ Move the steering wheel from side to side and then up and down. Check that the steering wheel is not loose on the column, indicating wear or a loose retaining nut. Continue moving the steering wheel as before, but also turn it slightly from left to right.

☐ Check that the steering wheel is not loose on the column, and that there is no abnormal

movement of the steering wheel, indicating wear in the column support bearings or couplings.

Windscreen, mirrors and sunvisor

☐ The windscreen must be free of cracks or other significant damage within the driver's field of view. (Small stone chips are acceptable.) Rear view mirrors must be secure, intact, and capable of being adjusted.

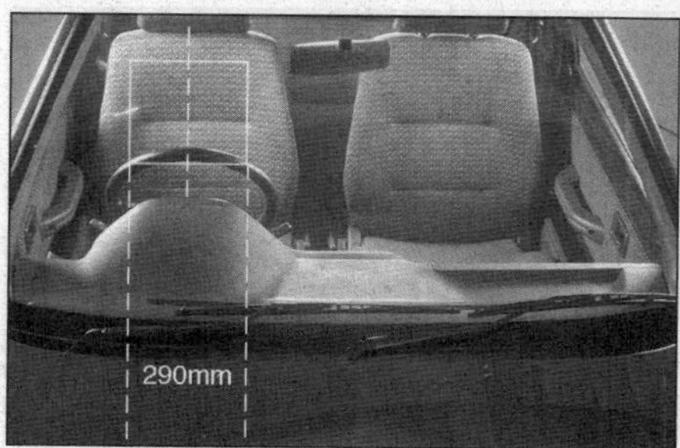
290mm

☐ The driver's sunvisor must be capable of being stored in the "up" position.

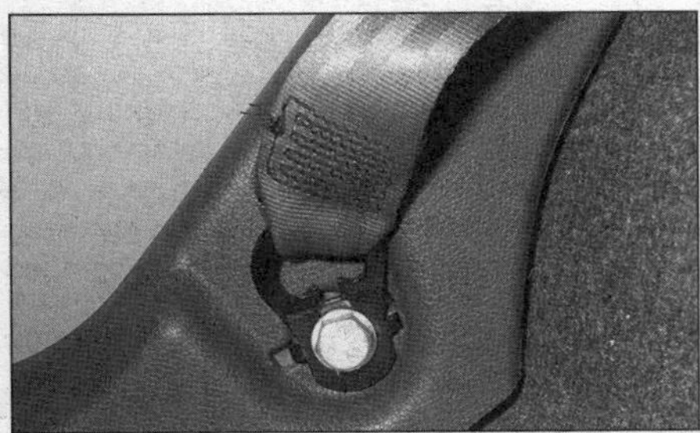

Seat belts and seats

Note: *The following checks are applicable to all seat belts, front and rear.*

☐ Examine the webbing of all the belts (including rear belts if fitted) for cuts, serious fraying or deterioration. Fasten and unfasten each belt to check the buckles. If applicable, check the retracting mechanism. Check the security of all seat belt mountings accessible from inside the vehicle.

☐ Seat belts with pre-tensioners, once activated, have a "flag" or similar showing on the seat belt stalk. This, in itself, is not a reason for test failure.

☐ The front seats themselves must be securely attached and the backrests must lock in the upright position.

Doors

☐ Both front doors must be able to be opened and closed from outside and inside, and must latch securely when closed.

2 Checks carried out WITH THE VEHICLE ON THE GROUND

Vehicle identification

☐ Number plates must be in good condition, secure and legible, with letters and numbers correctly spaced – spacing at (A) should be at least twice that at (B).

B
A

☐ The VIN plate and/or homologation plate must be legible.

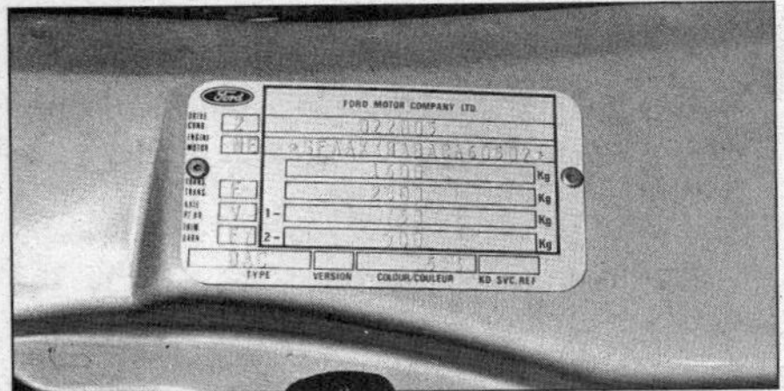

Electrical equipment

☐ Switch on the ignition and check the operation of the horn.

☐ Check the windscreen washers and wipers, examining the wiper blades; renew damaged or perished blades. Also check the operation of the stop-lights.

☐ Check the operation of the sidelights and number plate lights. The lenses and reflectors must be secure, clean and undamaged.

☐ Check the operation and alignment of the headlights. The headlight reflectors must not be tarnished and the lenses must be undamaged.

☐ Switch on the ignition and check the operation of the direction indicators (including the instrument panel tell-tale) and the hazard warning lights. Operation of the sidelights and stop-lights must not affect the indicators - if it does, the cause is usually a bad earth at the rear light cluster.

☐ Check the operation of the rear foglight(s), including the warning light on the instrument panel or in the switch.

☐ The ABS warning light must illuminate in accordance with the manufacturers' design. For most vehicles, the ABS warning light should illuminate when the ignition is switched on, and (if the system is operating properly) extinguish after a few seconds. Refer to the owner's handbook.

Footbrake

☐ Examine the master cylinder, brake pipes and servo unit for leaks, loose mountings, corrosion or other damage.

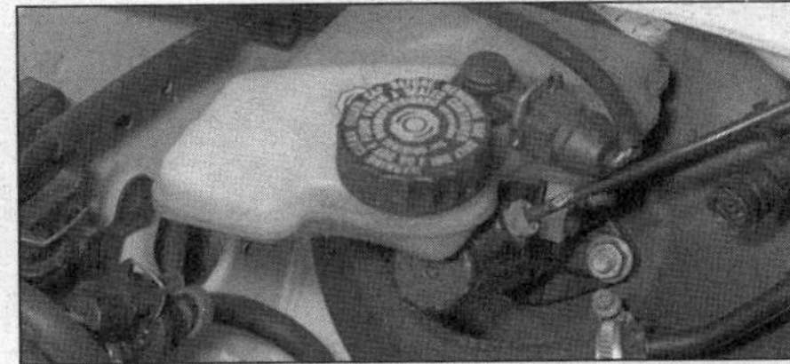

☐ The fluid reservoir must be secure and the fluid level must be between the upper (**A**) and lower (**B**) markings.

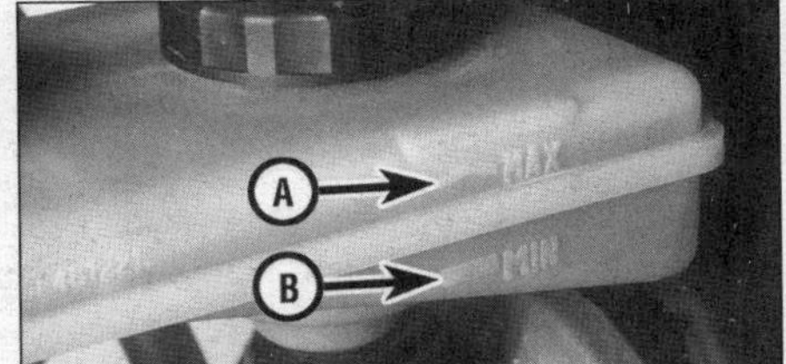
A
MAX
B
MIN

☐ Inspect both front brake flexible hoses for cracks or deterioration of the rubber. Turn the steering from lock to lock, and ensure that the hoses do not contact the wheel, tyre, or any part of the steering or suspension mechanism. With the brake pedal firmly depressed, check the hoses for bulges or leaks under pressure.

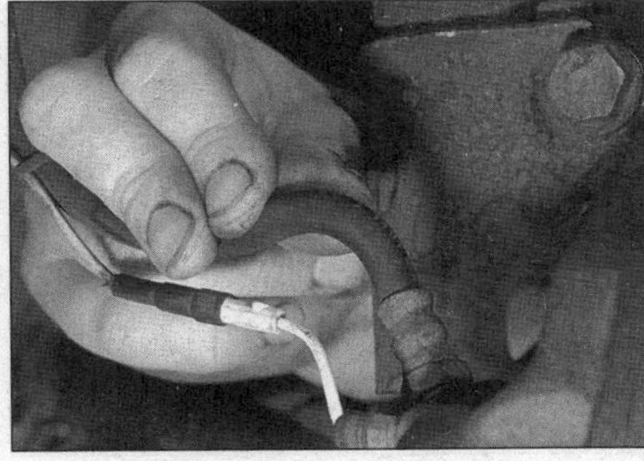

Steering and suspension

☐ Have your assistant turn the steering wheel from side to side slightly, up to the point where the steering gear just begins to transmit this movement to the roadwheels. Check for excessive free play between the steering wheel and the steering gear, indicating wear or insecurity of the steering column joints, the column-to-steering gear coupling, or the steering gear itself.

☐ Have your assistant turn the steering wheel more vigorously in each direction, so that the roadwheels just begin to turn. As this is done, examine all the steering joints, linkages, fittings and attachments. Renew any component that shows signs of wear or damage. On vehicles with power steering, check the security and condition of the steering pump, drivebelt and hoses.

☐ Check that the vehicle is standing level, and at approximately the correct ride height.

Shock absorbers

☐ Depress each corner of the vehicle in turn, then release it. The vehicle should rise and then settle in its normal position. If the vehicle continues to rise and fall, the shock absorber is defective. A shock absorber which has seized will also cause the vehicle to fail.

Exhaust system

☐ Start the engine. With your assistant holding a rag over the tailpipe, check the entire system for leaks. Repair or renew leaking sections.

3 Checks carried out WITH THE VEHICLE RAISED AND THE WHEELS FREE TO TURN

Jack up the front and rear of the vehicle, and securely support it on axle stands. Position the stands clear of the suspension assemblies. Ensure that the wheels are clear of the ground and that the steering can be turned from lock to lock.

Steering mechanism

☐ Have your assistant turn the steering from lock to lock. Check that the steering turns smoothly, and that no part of the steering mechanism, including a wheel or tyre, fouls any brake hose or pipe or any part of the body structure.

☐ Examine the steering rack rubber gaiters for damage or insecurity of the retaining clips. If power steering is fitted, check for signs of damage or leakage of the fluid hoses, pipes or connections. Also check for excessive stiffness or binding of the steering, a missing split pin or locking device, or severe corrosion of the body structure within 30 cm of any steering component attachment point.

Front and rear suspension and wheel bearings

☐ Starting at the front right-hand side, grasp the roadwheel at the 3 o'clock and 9 o'clock positions and rock gently but firmly. Check for free play or insecurity at the wheel bearings, suspension balljoints, or suspension mountings, pivots and attachments.

☐ Now grasp the wheel at the 12 o'clock and 6 o'clock positions and repeat the previous inspection. Spin the wheel, and check for roughness or tightness of the front wheel bearing.

☐ If excess free play is suspected at a component pivot point, this can be confirmed by using a large screwdriver or similar tool and levering between the mounting and the component attachment. This will confirm whether the wear is in the pivot bush, its retaining bolt, or in the mounting itself (the bolt holes can often become elongated).

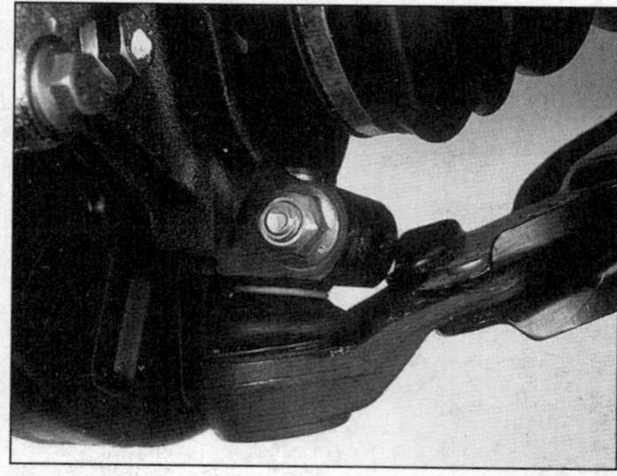

☐ Carry out all the above checks at the other front wheel, and then at both rear wheels.

Springs and shock absorbers

☐ Examine the suspension struts (when applicable) for serious fluid leakage, corrosion, or damage to the casing. Also check the security of the mounting points.

☐ If coil springs are fitted, check that the spring ends locate in their seats, and that the spring is not corroded, cracked or broken.

☐ If leaf springs are fitted, check that all leaves are intact, that the axle is securely attached to each spring, and that there is no deterioration of the spring eye mountings, bushes, and shackles.

☐ The same general checks apply to vehicles fitted with other suspension types, such as torsion bars, hydraulic displacer units, etc. Ensure that all mountings and attachments are secure, that there are no signs of excessive wear, corrosion or damage, and (on hydraulic types) that there are no fluid leaks or damaged pipes.

☐ Inspect the shock absorbers for signs of serious fluid leakage. Check for wear of the mounting bushes or attachments, or damage to the body of the unit.

Driveshafts (fwd vehicles only)

☐ Rotate each front wheel in turn and inspect the constant velocity joint gaiters for splits or damage. Also check that each driveshaft is straight and undamaged.

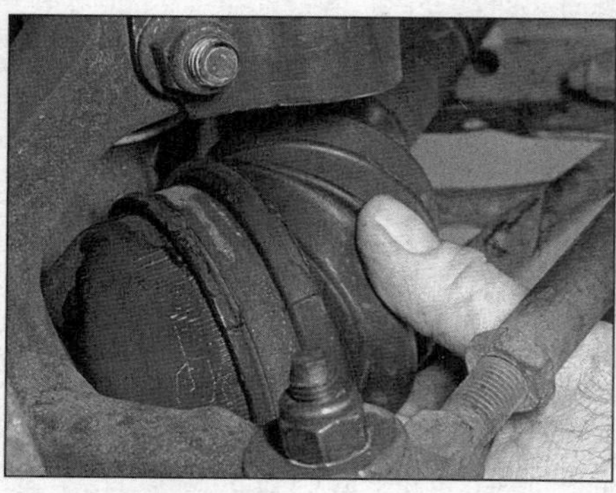

Braking system

☐ If possible without dismantling, check brake pad wear and disc condition. Ensure that the friction lining material has not worn excessively, (A) and that the discs are not fractured, pitted, scored or badly worn (B).

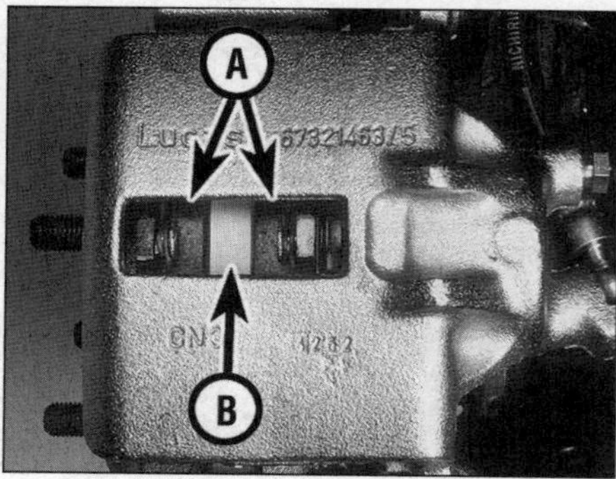
A
B

☐ Examine all the rigid brake pipes underneath the vehicle, and the flexible hose(s) at the rear. Look for corrosion, chafing or insecurity of the pipes, and for signs of bulging under pressure, chafing, splits or deterioration of the flexible hoses.

☐ Look for signs of fluid leaks at the brake calipers or on the brake backplates. Repair or renew leaking components.

☐ Slowly spin each wheel, while your assistant depresses and releases the footbrake. Ensure that each brake is operating and does not bind when the pedal is released.

☐ Examine the handbrake mechanism, checking for frayed or broken cables, excessive corrosion, or wear or insecurity of the linkage. Check that the mechanism works on each relevant wheel, and releases fully, without binding.

☐ It is not possible to test brake efficiency without special equipment, but a road test can be carried out later to check that the vehicle pulls up in a straight line.

Fuel and exhaust systems

☐ Inspect the fuel tank (including the filler cap), fuel pipes, hoses and unions. All components must be secure and free from leaks.

☐ Examine the exhaust system over its entire length, checking for any damaged, broken or missing mountings, security of the retaining clamps and rust or corrosion.

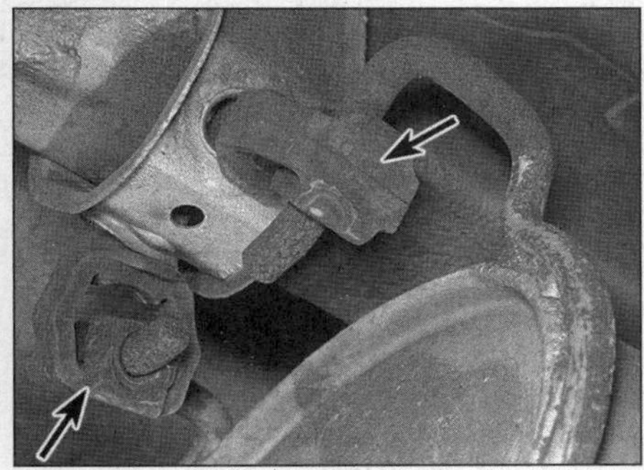

Wheels and tyres

☐ Examine the sidewalls and tread area of each tyre in turn. Check for cuts, tears, lumps, bulges, separation of the tread, and exposure of the ply or cord due to wear or damage. Check that the tyre bead is correctly seated on the wheel rim, that the valve is sound and properly seated, and that the wheel is not distorted or damaged.

☐ Check that the tyres are of the correct size for the vehicle, that they are of the same size and type on each axle, and that the pressures are correct.

☐ Check the tyre tread depth. The legal minimum at the time of writing is 1.6 mm over at least three-quarters of the tread width. Abnormal tread wear may indicate incorrect front wheel alignment.

Body corrosion

☐ Check the condition of the entire vehicle structure for signs of corrosion in load-bearing areas. (These include chassis box sections, side sills, cross-members, pillars, and all suspension, steering, braking system and seat belt mountings and anchorages.) Any corrosion which has seriously reduced the thickness of a load-bearing area is likely to cause the vehicle to fail. In this case professional repairs are likely to be needed.

☐ Damage or corrosion which causes sharp or otherwise dangerous edges to be exposed will also cause the vehicle to fail.

4 Checks carried out on YOUR VEHICLE'S EXHAUST EMISSION SYSTEM

Petrol models

☐ Have the engine at normal operating temperature, and make sure that it is in good tune (ignition system in good order, air filter element clean, etc).

☐ Before any measurements are carried out, raise the engine speed to around 2500 rpm, and hold it at this speed for 20 seconds. Allow the engine speed to return to idle, and watch for smoke emissions from the exhaust tailpipe. If the idle speed is obviously much too high, or if dense blue or clearly-visible black smoke comes from the tailpipe for more than 5 seconds, the vehicle will fail. As a rule of thumb, blue smoke signifies oil being burnt (engine wear) while black smoke signifies unburnt fuel (dirty air cleaner element, or other carburettor or fuel system fault).

☐ An exhaust gas analyser capable of measuring carbon monoxide (CO) and hydrocarbons (HC) is now needed. If such an instrument cannot be hired or borrowed, a local garage may agree to perform the check for a small fee.

CO emissions (mixture)

☐ At the time of writing, for vehicles first used between 1st August 1975 and 31st July 1986 (P to C registration), the CO level must not exceed 4.5% by volume. For vehicles first used between 1st August 1986 and 31st July 1992 (D to J registration), the CO level must not exceed 3.5% by volume. Vehicles first used after 1st August 1992 (K registration) must conform to the manufacturer's specification. The MOT tester has access to a DOT database or emissions handbook, which lists the CO and HC limits for each make and model of vehicle. The CO level is measured with the engine at idle speed, and at "fast idle". The following limits are given as a general guide:

At idle speed -
CO level no more than 0.5%
At "fast idle" (2500 to 3000 rpm) -
CO level no more than 0.3%
(Minimum oil temperature 60°C)

☐ If the CO level cannot be reduced far enough to pass the test (and the fuel and ignition systems are otherwise in good condition) then the carburettor is badly worn, or there is some problem in the fuel injection system or catalytic converter (as applicable).

HC emissions

☐ With the CO within limits, HC emissions for vehicles first used between 1st August 1975 and 31st July 1992 (P to J registration) must not exceed 1200 ppm. Vehicles first used after 1st August 1992 (K registration) must conform to the manufacturer's specification. The MOT tester has access to a DOT database or emissions handbook, which lists the CO and HC limits for each make and model of vehicle. The HC level is measured with the engine at "fast idle". The following is given as a general guide:

At "fast idle" (2500 to 3000 rpm) -
HC level no more than 200 ppm
(Minimum oil temperature 60°C)

☐ Excessive HC emissions are caused by incomplete combustion, the causes of which can include oil being burnt, mechanical wear and ignition/fuel system malfunction.

Diesel models

☐ The only emission test applicable to Diesel engines is the measuring of exhaust smoke density. The test involves accelerating the engine several times to its maximum unloaded speed.

Note: *It is of the utmost importance that the engine timing belt is in good condition before the test is carried out.*

☐ The limits for Diesel engine exhaust smoke, introduced in September 1995 are:

Vehicles first used before 1st August 1979:
Exempt from metered smoke testing, but must not emit "dense blue or clearly visible black smoke for a period of more than 5 seconds at idle" or "dense blue or clearly visible black smoke during acceleration which would obscure the view of other road users".
Non-turbocharged vehicles first used after 1st August 1979: 2.5m^{-1}
Turbocharged vehicles first used after 1st August 1979: 3.0m^{-1}

☐ Excessive smoke can be caused by a dirty air cleaner element. Otherwise, professional advice may be needed to find the cause.

Engine

- ☐ Engine fails to rotate when attempting to start
- ☐ Starter motor turns engine slowly
- ☐ Starter motor spins without turning engine
- ☐ Starter motor noisy or excessively-rough in engagement
- ☐ Engine rotates but will not start
- ☐ Engine fires but will not run
- ☐ Engine difficult to start when cold
- ☐ Engine difficult to start when hot
- ☐ Engine idles erratically
- ☐ Engine misfires at idle speed
- ☐ Engine misfires throughout the driving speed range
- ☐ Engine stalls
- ☐ Engine lacks power
- ☐ Oil pressure warning light illuminated with engine running
- ☐ Engine runs-on after switching off
- ☐ Engine noises

Cooling system

- ☐ Overheating
- ☐ Overcooling
- ☐ External coolant leakage
- ☐ Internal coolant leakage
- ☐ Corrosion

Fuel and exhaust systems

- ☐ Excessive fuel consumption
- ☐ Fuel leakage and/or fuel odour
- ☐ Excessive noise or fumes from exhaust system

Clutch

- ☐ Pedal travels to floor - no pressure or very little resistance
- ☐ Clutch fails to disengage (unable to select gears)
- ☐ Clutch slips (engine speed increases, with no increase in vehicle speed)
- ☐ Judder as clutch is engaged
- ☐ Noise when depressing or releasing clutch pedal

Manual gearbox

- ☐ Noisy in neutral with engine running
- ☐ Noisy in one particular gear
- ☐ Difficulty engaging gears
- ☐ Jumps out of gear
- ☐ Vibration
- ☐ Lubricant leaks

Automatic transmission

- ☐ Fluid leakage
- ☐ Transmission fluid brown, or has burned smell
- ☐ General gear selection problems
- ☐ Transmission will not downshift (kickdown) with accelerator fully depressed
- ☐ Engine will not start in any gear, or starts in gears other than Park or Neutral
- ☐ Transmission slips, shifts roughly, is noisy, or has no drive in forward or reverse gears

Transfer gearbox

- ☐ Noisy in neutral with engine running
- ☐ Noisy in Low or High positions
- ☐ Difficulty engaging ranges
- ☐ Jumps out of gear
- ☐ Vibration
- ☐ Lubricant leaks

Propeller shafts

- ☐ Knock or clunk when taking up drive
- ☐ Oil leak where propeller shaft enters transfer gearbox
- ☐ Oil leak where propeller shaft enters axle
- ☐ Metallic grating sound consistent with vehicle speed
- ☐ Scraping noise
- ☐ Vibration

Front and rear axles

- ☐ Vibration
- ☐ Noise on drive and overrun
- ☐ Noise consistent with roadspeed
- ☐ Knock or clunk when taking up drive
- ☐ Oil leakage

Braking system

- ☐ Vehicle pulls to one side under braking
- ☐ Noise (grinding or high-pitched squeal) when brakes applied
- ☐ Excessive brake pedal travel
- ☐ Brake pedal feels spongy when depressed
- ☐ Excessive brake pedal effort required to stop vehicle
- ☐ Judder felt through brake pedal or steering wheel when braking
- ☐ Brakes binding
- ☐ Rear wheels locking under normal braking

Suspension and steering

- ☐ Vehicle pulls to one side
- ☐ Wheel wobble and vibration
- ☐ Excessive pitching and/or rolling around corners, or during braking
- ☐ Wandering or general instability
- ☐ Excessively-stiff steering
- ☐ Excessive play in steering
- ☐ Lack of power assistance
- ☐ Tyre wear excessive

Electrical system

- ☐ Battery will not hold a charge for more than a few days
- ☐ Ignition/no-charge warning light remains illuminated with engine running
- ☐ Ignition/no-charge warning light fails to come on
- ☐ Lights inoperative
- ☐ Instrument readings inaccurate or erratic
- ☐ Horn inoperative, or unsatisfactory in operation
- ☐ Windscreen/tailgate wipers inoperative, or unsatisfactory in operation
- ☐ Windscreen/tailgate washers inoperative, or unsatisfactory in operation
- ☐ Electric windows inoperative, or unsatisfactory in operation
- ☐ Central locking system inoperative, or unsatisfactory in operation

Introduction

The vehicle owner who does his or her own maintenance according to the recommended service schedules should not have to use this section of the manual very often. Modern component reliability is such that, provided those items subject to wear or deterioration are inspected or renewed at the specified intervals, sudden failure is comparatively rare. Faults do not usually just happen as a result of sudden failure, but develop over a period of time. Major mechanical failures in particular are usually preceded by characteristic symptoms over hundreds or even thousands of miles. Those components which do occasionally fail without warning are often small and easily carried in the vehicle.

With any fault-finding, the first step is to decide where to begin investigations. Sometimes this is obvious, but on other occasions, a little detective work will be necessary. The owner who makes half a dozen haphazard adjustments or replacements may be successful in curing a fault (or its symptoms), but will be none the wiser if the fault recurs, and ultimately may have spent more time and money than was necessary. A calm and logical approach will be found to be more satisfactory in the long run. Always take into account any warning signs or abnormalities that may have been noticed in the period preceding the fault - power loss, high or low gauge readings, unusual smells, etc - and remember that failure of components such as fuses or relays may only be pointers to some underlying fault.

The pages which follow provide an easy reference guide to the more common problems which may occur during the operation of the vehicle. These problems and their possible causes are grouped under headings denoting various components or systems, such as Engine, Cooling system, etc. The Chapter and/or Section which deals with the problem is also shown in brackets. Whatever the fault, certain basic principles apply. These are as follows:

Verify the fault. This is simply a matter of being sure that you know what the symptoms are before starting work. This is particularly important if you are investigating a fault for someone else, who may not have described it very accurately.

Don't overlook the obvious. For example, if the vehicle won't start, is there fuel in the tank? (Don't take anyone else's word on this particular point, and don't trust the fuel gauge either!) If an electrical fault is indicated, look for loose or broken wires before digging out the test gear.

Cure the disease, not the symptom. Substituting a flat battery with a fully-charged one will get you off the hard shoulder, but if the underlying cause is not attended to, the new battery will go the same way.

Don't take anything for granted. Particularly, don't forget that a 'new' component may itself be defective (especially if it's been rattling around in the boot for months), and don't leave components out of a fault diagnosis sequence just because they are new or recently fitted. When you do finally diagnose a difficult fault, you'll probably realise that all the evidence was there from the start.

Engine

Engine fails to rotate when attempting to start

- ☐ Battery terminal connections loose or corroded (*Weekly checks*).
- ☐ Battery discharged or faulty (Chapter 5A).
- ☐ Broken, loose or disconnected wiring in the starting circuit (Chapter 5A).
- ☐ Automatic transmission not in P or N (Chapter 7B)
- ☐ Defective starter solenoid or switch (Chapter 5A).
- ☐ Defective starter motor (Chapter 5A).
- ☐ Starter pinion or flywheel ring gear teeth loose or broken (Chapters 2A, 2B, 2C and 5A).
- ☐ Engine earth strap broken or disconnected (Chapter 5A).

Engine rotates, but will not start

- ☐ Fuel tank empty.
- ☐ Battery discharged (engine rotates slowly) (Chapter 5A).
- ☐ Battery terminal connections loose or corroded (*Weekly checks*).
- ☐ Immobiliser fault (Chapter 13).
- ☐ Ignition components damp or damaged - petrol models (Chapters 1 and 5B).
- ☐ Ignition timing incorrect (Chapter 5B)
- ☐ Broken, loose or disconnected wiring in the ignition circuit - petrol models (Chapter 5B).
- ☐ Worn, faulty or incorrectly-gapped spark plugs - petrol models (Chapter 1A).
- ☐ Preheating system faulty - diesel models (Chapter 5C).
- ☐ Fuel injection system fault - petrol models (Chapter 4A or 4B).
- ☐ Fuel cut-off (stop) solenoid faulty - diesel models (Chapter 4C).
- ☐ Air in fuel system - diesel models (Chapter 4C).
- ☐ Major mechanical failure (eg camshaft drive) (Chapter 2A, 2B or 2C).

Engine difficult to start when cold

- ☐ Battery discharged (Chapter 5A).
- ☐ Ignition timing incorrect (Chapter 5B)
- ☐ Battery terminal connections loose or corroded (*Weekly checks*).
- ☐ Worn, faulty or incorrectly-gapped spark plugs - petrol models (Chapter 1A).
- ☐ Preheating system faulty - diesel models (Chapter 5C).
- ☐ Wax formed in fuel - diesel models (in very cold weather).
- ☐ Fuel injection system fault - petrol models (Chapter 4A or 4B).
- ☐ Other ignition system fault - petrol models (Chapter 5B).
- ☐ Low cylinder compressions (Chapter 2A or 2B).

Engine difficult to start when hot

- ☐ Air filter element dirty or clogged (Chapter 1).
- ☐ Carburettor or fuel injection system fault - petrol models (Chapter 4A or 4B).
- ☐ Low cylinder compressions (Chapter 2A or 2B).
- ☐ Ignition timing incorrect (Chapter 5B)

Starter motor noisy or excessively-rough in engagement

- ☐ Starter pinion or flywheel ring gear teeth loose or broken (Chapters 2A, 2B and 5A).
- ☐ Starter motor mounting bolts loose or missing (Chapter 5A).
- ☐ Starter motor internal components worn or damaged (Chapter 5A).

Engine starts, but stops immediately

- ☐ Loose or faulty electrical connections in the ignition circuit - petrol models (Chapter 5B).
- ☐ Vacuum leak at the carburettor/plenum chamber, inlet manifold or associated hoses - petrol models (Chapter 4A or 4B).
- ☐ Carburettor/fuel injection system fault - petrol models (Chapter 4A or 4B).
- ☐ Fuel pump fault - petrol models (Chapter 4A or 4B).
- ☐ Fuel lines restricted (Chapter 4).
- ☐ Wax formed in fuel - diesel models (in very cold weather).

Engine idles erratically

- ☐ Air filter element clogged (Chapter 1).
- ☐ Vacuum leak at the carburettor/plenum chamber, inlet manifold or associated hoses - petrol models (Chapter 4A or 4B).
- ☐ Worn, faulty or incorrectly-gapped spark plugs - petrol models (Chapter 1A).
- ☐ Uneven or low cylinder compressions (Chapter 2A or 2B).
- ☐ Camshaft lobes worn (Chapter 2A or 2B).
- ☐ Valve clearances incorrect - diesel models (Chapter 1B).
- ☐ Timing belt incorrectly tensioned - diesel models (Chapter 2B).
- ☐ Carburettor/fuel injection system fault - petrol models (Chapter 4A or 4B).
- ☐ Faulty injector(s) - diesel models (Chapter 4C).
- ☐ Wax formed in fuel - diesel models (in very cold weather).

Engine misfires at idle speed

- ☐ Worn, faulty or incorrectly-gapped spark plugs - petrol models (Chapter 1A).
- ☐ Faulty spark plug HT leads - petrol models (Chapter 5B).
- ☐ Vacuum leak at the carburettor/plenum chamber, inlet manifold or associated hoses - petrol models (Chapter 4A or 4B).
- ☐ Carburettor/fuel injection system fault - petrol models (Chapter 4A or 4B).
- ☐ Faulty injector(s) - diesel models (Chapter 4C).
- ☐ Valve clearances incorrect - diesel models (Chapter 1B).
- ☐ Distributor cap cracked or tracking internally - petrol models (Chapter 5B).
- ☐ Uneven or low cylinder compressions (Chapter 2A or 2B).
- ☐ Disconnected, leaking, or perished crankcase ventilation hoses (Chapter 4D).

Engine (continued)

Engine misfires throughout the driving speed range

- ☐ Fuel filter choked (Chapter 1).
- ☐ Fuel pump faulty, or delivery pressure low - petrol models (Chapter 4A or 4B).
- ☐ Fuel tank vent blocked, or fuel pipes restricted (Chapter 4A, 4B or 4C).
- ☐ Vacuum leak at the carburettor/plenum chamber, inlet manifold or associated hoses - petrol models (Chapter 4A or 4B).
- ☐ Worn, faulty or incorrectly-gapped spark plugs - petrol models (Chapter 1A).
- ☐ Faulty spark plug HT leads - petrol models (Chapter 5B).
- ☐ Faulty injector(s) - diesel models (Chapter 4C).
- ☐ Valve clearances incorrect - diesel models (Chapter 1B).
- ☐ Distributor cap cracked or tracking internally - petrol models (Chapter 5B).
- ☐ Faulty ignition coil - petrol models (Chapter 5B).
- ☐ Uneven or low cylinder compressions (Chapter 2A or 2B).
- ☐ Carburettor/fuel injection system fault - petrol models (Chapter 4A or 4B).

Engine hesitates on acceleration

- ☐ Worn, faulty or incorrectly-gapped spark plugs - petrol models (Chapter 1A).
- ☐ Vacuum leak at the carburettor/plenum chamber, inlet manifold or associated hoses - petrol models (Chapter 4A or 4B).
- ☐ Carburettor/fuel injection system fault - petrol models (Chapter 4A or 4B).
- ☐ Faulty injector(s) - diesel models (Chapter 4C).
- ☐ Valve clearances incorrect - diesel models (Chapter 1B).

Engine stalls

- ☐ Vacuum leak at the carburettor/plenum chamber, inlet manifold or associated hoses - petrol models (Chapter 4A or 4B).
- ☐ Fuel filter choked (Chapter 1).
- ☐ Fuel pump faulty, or delivery pressure low - petrol models (Chapter 4A or 4B).
- ☐ Fuel tank vent blocked, or fuel pipes restricted (Chapter 4A, 4B or 4C).
- ☐ Carburettor/fuel injection system fault - petrol models (Chapter 4A or 4B).
- ☐ Faulty injector(s) - diesel models (Chapter 4C).
- ☐ Wax formed in fuel - diesel models (in very cold weather).

Engine lacks power

- ☐ Timing chain or belt incorrectly fitted or tensioned (Chapter 2A or 2B).
- ☐ Fuel filter choked (Chapter 1).
- ☐ Ignition timing incorrect - petrol models (Chapter 5B)
- ☐ Fuel pump faulty, or delivery pressure low - petrol models (Chapter 4A or 4B).
- ☐ Fuel lines leaking or restricted (Chapter 4A, 4B, or 4C).
- ☐ Uneven or low cylinder compressions (Chapter 2A or 2B).
- ☐ Worn, faulty or incorrectly-gapped spark plugs - petrol models (Chapter 1A).
- ☐ Vacuum leak at the carburettor/plenum chamber, inlet manifold or associated hoses - petrol models (Chapter 4A or 4B).
- ☐ Carburettor/fuel injection system fault - petrol models (Chapter 4A or 4B).
- ☐ Faulty injector(s) - diesel models (Chapter 4C).
- ☐ Injection pump timing incorrect - diesel models (Chapter 4C).
- ☐ Wax formed in fuel - diesel models (in very cold weather).
- ☐ Brakes binding (Chapters 1 and 10).
- ☐ Clutch slipping (Chapter 6).

Engine backfires

- ☐ Timing chain or belt incorrectly fitted or tensioned (Chapter 2A or 2B).
- ☐ Vacuum leak at the carburettor/plenum chamber, inlet manifold or associated hoses - petrol models (Chapter 4A or 4B).
- ☐ Carburettor/fuel injection system fault - petrol models (Chapter 4A or 4B).
- ☐ Ignition timing incorrect - petrol models (Chapter 5B)

Oil pressure warning light illuminated with engine running

- ☐ Low oil level, or incorrect oil grade (*Weekly checks*).
- ☐ Worn engine bearings and/or oil pump (Chapter 2C).
- ☐ High engine operating temperature (Chapter 3).
- ☐ Oil pressure relief valve defective (Chapter 2A or 2B).
- ☐ Oil pick-up strainer clogged (Chapter 2A or 2B).

Engine runs-on after switching off

- ☐ Excessive carbon build-up in engine (Chapter 2C).
- ☐ High engine operating temperature (Chapter 3).
- ☐ Carburettor/fuel injection system fault - petrol models (Chapter 4A or 4B).
- ☐ Faulty fuel cut-off (stop) solenoid - diesel models (Chapter 4C).

Engine noises

Note: *To inexperienced ears, a diesel engine can sound alarming even when there is nothing wrong with it, so it may be prudent to have an unusual noise expertly diagnosed before making renewals or repairs.*

Pre-ignition (pinking) or knocking during acceleration or under load

- ☐ Ignition timing incorrect/ignition system fault - petrol models (Chapter 5B).
- ☐ Incorrect grade of spark plug - petrol models (Chapter 1A).
- ☐ Incorrect grade of fuel.
- ☐ Vacuum leak at the carburettor/plenum chamber, inlet manifold or associated hoses - petrol models (Chapter 4A or 4B).
- ☐ Excessive carbon build-up in engine (Chapter 2C).
- ☐ Carburettor/fuel injection system fault - petrol models (Chapter 4A or 4B).
- ☐ Overheating (Refer to *Cooling system* of Fault finding).

Whistling or wheezing noises

- ☐ Leaking carburettor/plenum chamber or inlet manifold gasket - petrol models (Chapter 4A or 4B).
- ☐ Leaking exhaust manifold gasket or pipe-to-manifold joint (Chapter 4A, 4B or 4C).
- ☐ Leaking vacuum hose (Chapters 4, 5B and 10).
- ☐ Blowing cylinder head gasket (Chapter 2A or 2B).

Tapping or rattling noises

- ☐ Insufficient oil reaching hydraulic tappets (petrol models) - check oil level, or change oil (*Weekly checks* or Chapter 1A).
- ☐ Valve clearances incorrect - diesel models (Chapter 1B).
- ☐ Worn hydraulic tappet or camshaft - petrol models (Chapter 2A).
- ☐ Worn timing chain - petrol models (Chapter 2A).
- ☐ Worn camshaft - diesel models (Chapter 2B).
- ☐ Ancillary component fault (water pump, alternator, etc) (Chapters 3, 5A, etc).

Knocking or thumping noises

- ☐ Worn big-end bearings (regular heavy knocking, perhaps less under load) (Chapter 2C).
- ☐ Worn main bearings (rumbling and knocking, perhaps worsening under load) (Chapter 2C).
- ☐ Piston slap (indicating piston and/or bore wear - most noticeable when cold) (Chapter 2C).
- ☐ Ancillary component fault (water pump, alternator, etc) (Chapters 3, 5A, etc).

Cooling system

Overheating

- ☐ Insufficient coolant in system (*Weekly checks*).
- ☐ Auxiliary drivebelt broken or drivebelt tensioner faulty (Chapter 1)
- ☐ Thermostat faulty (Chapter 3).
- ☐ Radiator core blocked, or grille restricted (Chapter 3).
- ☐ Electric cooling fan or thermoswitch faulty (Chapter 3 or 13).
- ☐ Pressure cap faulty (Chapter 3).
- ☐ Ignition timing incorrect/ignition system fault - petrol models (Chapter 5B).
- ☐ Inaccurate temperature gauge sender unit (Chapter 3).
- ☐ Airlock in cooling system (Chapter 1).

Overcooling

- ☐ Thermostat faulty (Chapter 3).
- ☐ Inaccurate temperature gauge sender unit (Chapter 3).

External coolant leakage

- ☐ Deteriorated or damaged hoses or hose clips (Chapter 1).
- ☐ Radiator core or heater matrix leaking (Chapter 3).
- ☐ Pressure cap faulty (Chapter 3).
- ☐ Water pump seal leaking (Chapter 3).
- ☐ Boiling due to overheating (Chapter 3).
- ☐ Core plug leaking (Chapter 2C).

Internal coolant leakage

- ☐ Leaking cylinder head gasket (Chapter 2A or 2B).
- ☐ Cracked cylinder head or cylinder bore (Chapter 2A or 2B).

Corrosion

- ☐ Infrequent draining and flushing (Chapter 1).
- ☐ Incorrect coolant mixture or inappropriate coolant type (Chapter 1).

Fuel and exhaust systems

Excessive fuel consumption

- ☐ Air filter element dirty or clogged (Chapter 1).
- ☐ Carburettor float level too high - petrol models (Chapter 4A).
- ☐ Fuel injectors partially blocked - petrol models (Chapter 4B).
- ☐ Other carburettor or fuel injection system fault - petrol models (Chapter 4A or 4B).
- ☐ Faulty injector(s) - diesel models (Chapter 4C).
- ☐ Fuel tank/lines damaged or leaking, or fuel return line restricted (Chapter 4).
- ☐ Ignition timing incorrect/ignition system fault - petrol models (Chapter 5B).
- ☐ Tyres under-inflated (*Weekly checks*).
- ☐ Brakes binding (Chapter 10).

Fuel leakage and/or fuel odour

- ☐ Damaged or corroded fuel tank, pipes or connections (Chapter 4).

Excessive noise or fumes from exhaust system

- ☐ Leaking exhaust system or manifold joints (Chapters 1 and 4).
- ☐ Leaking, corroded or damaged silencers or pipe (Chapters 1 and 4).
- ☐ Broken mountings causing body or suspension contact (Chapter 1).

Clutch

Judder as clutch is engaged

- ☐ Clutch disc linings contaminated with oil or grease (Chapter 6).
- ☐ Clutch disc linings excessively worn (Chapter 6).
- ☐ Clutch cable sticking or frayed (Chapter 6).
- ☐ Faulty or distorted pressure plate or diaphragm spring (Chapter 6).
- ☐ Worn or loose engine/transmission mountings (Chapter 2).
- ☐ Clutch disc hub or gearbox input shaft splines worn (Chapter 6).

Clutch fails to disengage (unable to select gears)

- ☐ Leak in clutch hydraulic system (Chapter 6).
- ☐ Faulty hydraulic master or slave cylinder (Chapter 6).
- ☐ Clutch disc sticking on gearbox input shaft splines (Chapter 6).
- ☐ Clutch disc sticking to flywheel or pressure plate (Chapter 6).
- ☐ Faulty pressure plate assembly (Chapter 6).
- ☐ Clutch release mechanism worn or incorrectly assembled (Chapter 6).

Clutch slips (engine speed increases, with no increase in vehicle speed)

- ☐ Clutch disc linings excessively worn (Chapter 6).
- ☐ Clutch disc linings contaminated with oil or grease (Chapter 6).
- ☐ Faulty pressure plate or weak diaphragm spring (Chapter 6).

Pedal travels to floor - no pressure or very little resistance

- ☐ Leak in clutch hydraulic system (Chapter 6).
- ☐ Faulty hydraulic master or slave cylinder (Chapter 6).
- ☐ Broken clutch release bearing or fork (Chapter 6).
- ☐ Broken diaphragm spring in clutch pressure plate (Chapter 6).

Noise when depressing or releasing clutch pedal

- ☐ Worn clutch release bearing (Chapter 6).
- ☐ Worn or dry clutch pedal bushes (Chapter 6).
- ☐ Faulty pressure plate assembly (Chapter 6).
- ☐ Pressure plate diaphragm spring broken (Chapter 6).
- ☐ Broken clutch disc cushioning springs (Chapter 6).

Manual transmission

Difficulty engaging gears

- ☐ Clutch fault (Chapter 6).
- ☐ Worn or damaged gear linkage (Chapter 7A).
- ☐ Worn synchroniser units (Chapter 7A).*

Jumps out of gear

- ☐ Worn or damaged gear linkage (Chapter 7A).
- ☐ Incorrectly-adjusted gear linkage (Chapter 7A).
- ☐ Worn synchroniser units (Chapter 7A).*
- ☐ Worn selector forks (Chapter 7A).*

Vibration

- ☐ Lack of oil (Chapter 1).
- ☐ Worn bearings (Chapter 7A).*

Noisy in one particular gear

- ☐ Worn, damaged or chipped gear teeth (Chapter 7A).*

Noisy in neutral with engine running

- ☐ Input shaft and/or mainshaft bearings worn (noise apparent with clutch pedal released, but not when depressed) (Chapter 7A).*
- ☐ Clutch release bearing worn (noise apparent with clutch pedal depressed, possibly less when released) (Chapter 6).

Lubricant leaks

- ☐ Leaking oil seal (Chapter 7A).
- ☐ Leaking housing joint (Chapter 7A).*

**Although the corrective action necessary to remedy the symptoms described is beyond the scope of the home mechanic, the above information should be helpful in isolating the cause of the condition, so that the owner can communicate clearly with a professional mechanic.*

Automatic transmission

Note: *Due to the complexity of the automatic transmission, it is difficult for the home mechanic to properly diagnose and service this unit. For problems other than the following, the vehicle should be taken to a dealer service department or automatic transmission specialist.*

Fluid leakage

- ☐ Automatic transmission fluid is usually deep red in colour. Fluid leaks should not be confused with engine oil, which can easily be blown onto the transmission by air flow.
- ☐ To determine the source of a leak, first remove all built-up dirt and grime from the transmission housing and surrounding areas, using a degreasing agent or by steam-cleaning. Drive the vehicle at low speed, so that air flow will not blow the leak far from its source. Raise and support the vehicle, and determine where the leak is coming from. The following are common areas of leakage.
  - *a) Fluid pan (transmission sump).*
  - *b) Dipstick tube (Chapter 1).*
  - *c) Transmission-to-fluid cooler fluid pipes/unions (Chapter 7B).*

Transmission fluid brown, or has burned smell

- ☐ Transmission fluid level low, or fluid in need of renewal (Chapter 1).

Transmission will not downshift (kickdown) with accelerator pedal fully depressed

- ☐ Low transmission fluid level (Chapter 1).
- ☐ Incorrect selector cable adjustment (Chapter 7B).

General gear selection problems

- ☐ The most likely cause of gear selection problems is a faulty or poorly-adjusted gear selector mechanism. The following are common problems associated with a faulty selector mechanism:
  - *a) Engine starting in gears other than Park or Neutral.*
  - *b) Indicator on gear selector lever pointing to a gear other than the one actually being used.*
  - *c) Vehicle moves when in Park or Neutral.*
  - *d) Poor gear shift quality, or erratic gear changes.*
- ☐ Refer any problems to a Land Rover dealer, or an automatic transmission specialist.

Engine will not start in any gear, or starts in gears other than Park or Neutral

- ☐ Incorrect starter inhibitor switch adjustment (Chapter 7B).
- ☐ Incorrect selector cable adjustment (Chapter 7B).

Transmission slips, shifts roughly, is noisy, or has no drive in forward or reverse gears

- ☐ There are many probable causes for the above problems, but the home mechanic should be concerned with only one possibility - fluid level. Before taking the vehicle to a dealer or transmission specialist, check the fluid level and condition of the fluid as described in Chapter 1. Correct the fluid level as necessary, or change the fluid and filter if needed. If the problem persists, professional help will be necessary.

Transfer gearbox

Noisy in neutral with engine running

☐ Worn mainshaft or output shaft bearings (Chapter 7C).*

Noisy in Low or High positions

☐ Worn, damaged or chipped gear teeth (Chapter 7C).*

Jumps out of gear

☐ Worn or damaged gear linkage (Chapter 7C).*
☐ Worn selector fork (Chapter 7C).*

Vibration

☐ Lack of oil (Chapter 1).
☐ Worn bearings (Chapter 7C).*

Difficulty engaging ranges

☐ Clutch fault (Chapter 6).
☐ ☐ain transmission fault (Chapter 7A or 7B).
☐ Worn selector fork (Chapter 7C).*

Lubricant leaks

☐ Leaking oil seal (Chapter 7C).*
☐ Leaking housing joint (Chapter 7C).*

**Although the corrective action necessary to remedy the symptoms described is beyond the scope of the home mechanic, the above information should be helpful in isolating the cause of the condition, so that the owner can communicate clearly with a professional mechanic.*

Propeller shafts

Knock or clunk when taking up drive

☐ Worn universal joint bearings (Chapter 8).
☐ Worn axle drive pinion splines (Chapter 9).
☐ Loose drive flange bolts (Chapter 8).
☐ Excessive backlash in axle gears (Chapter 9).

Metallic grating sound, consistent with vehicle speed

☐ Severe wear in universal joint bearings (Chapter 8).

Vibration

☐ Wear in sliding sleeve splines (Chapter 8).
☐ Worn universal joint bearings (Chapter 8).
☐ Propeller shaft out of balance (Chapter 8).

Front and rear axles

Vibration

☐ Propeller shaft out of balance (Chapter 8).
☐ Worn hub bearings (Chapter 9).
☐ Wheels out of balance.
☐ Propeller shaft or halfshaft joints worn (Chapters 8 and 9).
☐ Suspension or steering fault (Chapter 11).

Noise on drive and overrun

☐ Worn crownwheel and pinion gears (Chapter 9).
☐ Worn differential bearings (Chapter 9).
☐ Lack of lubrication in axle or swivel pin housings (Chapters 9 and 11).
☐ ☐ain transmission or transfer gearbox fault (Chapter 7).

Noise consistent with road speed

☐ Worn hub bearings (Chapter 9).
☐ Worn differential bearings (Chapter 9).
☐ Lack of lubrication in axle or swivel pin housings (Chapters 9 and 11).
☐ ☐ain transmission or transfer gearbox fault (Chapter 7).

Knock or clunk when taking up drive

☐ Excessive crownwheel and pinion backlash (Chapter 9).
☐ Worn propeller shaft or halfshaft joints (Chapters 8 and 9).
☐ Worn halfshaft splines (Chapter 9).
☐ Halfshaft bolts or roadwheel nuts loose (Chapter 9).
☐ Broken, damaged, or worn suspension components or axle mountings (Chapters 11 and 9).
☐ Main transmission or transfer gearbox fault (Chapter 7).

Oil leakage

☐ Faulty differential pinion or halfshaft oil seals (Chapter 9).
☐ Blocked axle breather valve (Chapter 9).
☐ Damaged swivel pin housing or oil seal (Chapter 11).

Braking system

Note: *Before assuming that a brake problem exists, make sure that the tyres are in good condition and correctly inflated, the front wheel alignment is correct, and the vehicle is not loaded with weight in an unequal manner. Apart from checking the condition of all pipe and hose connections, any faults occurring on the anti-lock braking system should be referred to a Land Rover dealer for diagnosis.*

Vehicle pulls to one side under braking

☐ Worn, defective, damaged or contaminated front or rear brake pads on one side (Chapter 10).
☐ Seized or partially-seized front or rear brake caliper piston (Chapter 10).
☐ A mixture of brake pad lining materials fitted between sides (Chapter 10).
☐ Brake caliper mounting bolts loose (Chapter 10).
☐ Worn or damaged steering or suspension components (Chapter 11).

Noise (grinding or high-pitched squeal) when brakes applied

☐ Brake pad friction lining material worn down to metal backing (Chapter 10).
☐ Brake pads incorrectly fitted, or pad backing plates dry (Chapter 10).
☐ Excessive corrosion of brake disc - may be apparent after the vehicle has been standing for some time (Chapter 10).

Excessive brake pedal travel

☐ Faulty master cylinder (Chapter 10).
☐ Air in hydraulic system (Chapter 10).
☐ Faulty vacuum servo unit (Chapter 10).
☐ Faulty brake vacuum pump - diesel models (Chapter 10).

Brake pedal feels spongy when depressed

☐ Air in hydraulic system (Chapter 10).
☐ Deteriorated flexible rubber brake hoses (Chapter 10).
☐ Master cylinder mountings loose (Chapter 10).
☐ Faulty master cylinder (Chapter 10).

Excessive brake pedal effort required to stop vehicle

☐ Faulty vacuum servo unit (Chapter 10).
☐ Disconnected, damaged or insecure brake servo vacuum hose (Chapters 1 and 10).
☐ Faulty brake vacuum pump (Chapter 10).
☐ Primary or secondary hydraulic circuit failure (Chapter 10).
☐ Seized brake caliper piston(s) (Chapter 10).
☐ Brake pads incorrectly fitted (Chapter 10).
☐ Incorrect grade of brake pads fitted (Chapter 10).
☐ Brake pads contaminated (Chapter 10).

Judder felt through brake pedal or steering wheel when braking

Note: *Under heavy braking, models equipped with ABS may exhibit a 'pulsing' sensation felt through the brake pedal. This is a normal feature of ABS operation, and does not necessarily indicate a fault.*

☐ Excessive run-out or distortion of brake disc(s) (Chapter 10).
☐ Brake pad linings worn (Chapter 10).
☐ Brake caliper mounting bolts loose (Chapter 10).
☐ Wear in suspension or steering components or mountings (Chapter 11).

Brakes binding

☐ Seized brake caliper piston(s) (Chapter 10).
☐ Faulty master cylinder (Chapter 10).

Rear wheels locking under normal braking

☐ Faulty brake pressure regulator (Chapter 10).

Suspension and steering

Note: *Before diagnosing suspension or steering faults, be sure that the trouble is not due to incorrect tyre pressures, mixtures of tyre types or binding brakes.*

Vehicle pulls to one side

- ☐ Defective tyre (*Weekly checks*).
- ☐ Excessive wear in suspension or steering components (Chapter 11).
- ☐ Incorrect front wheel alignment (Chapter 11).
- ☐ Accident damage to steering or suspension components (Chapter 11).

Wheel wobble and vibration

- ☐ Front roadwheels out of balance - vibration felt mainly through the steering wheel (Chapter 11).
- ☐ Rear roadwheels out of balance - vibration felt throughout the vehicle (Chapter 11).
- ☐ Roadwheels damaged or distorted (*Weekly checks*).
- ☐ Faulty or damaged tyre (*Weekly checks*).
- ☐ Worn steering or suspension joints, bushes or components (Chapter 11).
- ☐ Wheel nuts loose (*Wheel changing*).

Excessive pitching and/or rolling around corners or during braking

- ☐ Defective shock absorbers (Chapter 11).
- ☐ Broken or weak coil spring and/or suspension component (Chapter 11).
- ☐ Worn or damaged anti-roll bar or mountings (Chapter 11).

Wandering or general instability

- ☐ Incorrect front wheel alignment (Chapter 11).
- ☐ Worn steering or suspension joints, bushes or components (Chapter 11).
- ☐ Roadwheels out of balance (*Weekly checks*).
- ☐ Faulty or damaged tyre (*Weekly checks*).
- ☐ Wheel nuts loose (*Wheel changing*).
- ☐ Defective shock absorbers (Chapter 11).

Excessively-stiff steering

- ☐ Lack of steering gear lubricant (Chapter 11).
- ☐ Seized track-rod end balljoint (Chapter 11).
- ☐ Broken or incorrectly-adjusted power steering pump drivebelt (Chapter 1).
- ☐ Incorrect front wheel alignment (Chapter 11).
- ☐ Steering box or column damaged (Chapter 11).

Excessive play in steering

- ☐ Worn steering column universal joint(s) or intermediate coupling (Chapter 11).
- ☐ Worn steering track-rod end balljoints (Chapter 11).
- ☐ Worn steering box (Chapter 11).
- ☐ Worn steering or suspension joints, bushes or components (Chapter 11).

Lack of power assistance

- ☐ Broken or incorrectly-adjusted power steering pump drivebelt (Chapter 1).
- ☐ Incorrect power steering fluid level (*Weekly checks*).
- ☐ Restriction in power steering fluid hoses (Chapter 1).
- ☐ Faulty power steering pump (Chapter 11).
- ☐ Faulty steering box (Chapter 11).

Tyre wear excessive

Tyres worn on inside or outside edges

- ☐ Tyres under-inflated (wear on both edges) (*Weekly checks*).
- ☐ Incorrect camber or castor angles (wear on one edge only) (Chapter 11).
- ☐ Worn steering or suspension joints, bushes or components (Chapter 11).
- ☐ Excessively hard cornering.
- ☐ Accident damage.

Tyre treads exhibit feathered edges

- ☐ Incorrect toe setting (Chapter 11).

Tyres worn in centre of tread

- ☐ Tyres over-inflated (*Weekly checks*).

Tyres worn on inside and outside edges

- ☐ Tyres under-inflated (*Weekly checks*).

Tyres worn unevenly

- ☐ Tyres out of balance (*Weekly checks*).
- ☐ Faulty tyre (*Weekly checks*).
- ☐ Excessive wheel or tyre run-out (*Weekly checks*).
- ☐ Worn shock absorbers (Chapter 11).

Electrical system

Note: *For problems associated with the starting system, refer to the faults listed under Engine earlier in this Section.*

Battery will not hold a charge for more than a few days

- ☐ Battery defective internally (Chapter 5A).
- ☐ Battery electrolyte level low - where applicable (Chapter 1).
- ☐ Battery terminal connections loose or corroded (*Weekly checks*).
- ☐ Alternator drivebelt worn or incorrectly adjusted (Chapter 1).
- ☐ Alternator not charging at correct output (Chapter 5A).
- ☐ Alternator or voltage regulator faulty (Chapter 5A).
- ☐ Short-circuit causing continual battery drain (Chapter 5A or 13).

Ignition/no-charge warning light remains illuminated with engine running

- ☐ Alternator drivebelt broken, worn, or incorrectly adjusted (Chapter 1).
- ☐ Alternator brushes worn, sticking, or dirty (Chapter 5A).
- ☐ Alternator brush springs weak or broken (Chapter 5A).
- ☐ Internal fault in alternator or voltage regulator (Chapter 5A).
- ☐ Broken, disconnected, or loose wiring in charging circuit (Chapter 5A).

Ignition/no-charge warning light fails to come on

- ☐ Warning light bulb blown (Chapter 13).
- ☐ Broken, disconnected, or loose wiring in warning light circuit (Chapter 13).
- ☐ Alternator faulty (Chapter 5A).

Lights inoperative

- ☐ Bulb blown (*Weekly checks* or Chapter 13).
- ☐ Corrosion of bulb or bulbholder contacts (Chapter 13).
- ☐ Blown fuse (*Weekly checks* or Chapter 13).
- ☐ Faulty relay (Chapter 13).
- ☐ Broken, loose, or disconnected wiring (Chapter 13).
- ☐ Faulty switch (Chapter 13).

Instrument readings inaccurate or erratic

Instrument readings increase with engine speed

- ☐ Faulty voltage regulator (Chapter 13).

Fuel or temperature gauge give no reading

- ☐ Faulty gauge sender unit (Chapters 3 or 4).
- ☐ Wiring open-circuit (Chapter 13).
- ☐ Faulty gauge (Chapter 13).

Fuel or temperature gauges give continuous maximum reading

- ☐ Faulty gauge sender unit (Chapters 3 or 4).
- ☐ Wiring short-circuit (Chapter 13).
- ☐ Faulty gauge (Chapter 13).

Horn inoperative, or unsatisfactory in operation

Horn operates all the time

- ☐ Horn push either earthed or stuck down (Chapter 13).
- ☐ Horn cable to horn push earthed (Chapter 13).

Horn fails to operate

- ☐ Blown fuse (*Weekly checks* or Chapter 13).
- ☐ Cable or cable connections loose, broken or disconnected (Chapter 13).
- ☐ Faulty horn (Chapter 13).

Horn emits intermittent or unsatisfactory sound

- ☐ Cable connections loose (Chapter 13).
- ☐ Horn mountings loose (Chapter 13).
- ☐ Faulty horn (Chapter 13).

Windscreen/tailgate wipers inoperative, or unsatisfactory in operation

Wipers fail to operate, or operate very slowly

- ☐ Wiper blades stuck to screen, or linkage seized or binding (Chapters 1 and 13).
- ☐ Blown fuse (*Weekly checks* or Chapter 13).
- ☐ Cable or cable connections loose, broken or disconnected (Chapter 13).
- ☐ Faulty relay (Chapter 13).
- ☐ Faulty wiper motor (Chapter 13).

Wiper blades sweep over too large or too small an area of the glass

- ☐ Wiper arms incorrectly positioned on spindles (Chapter 13).
- ☐ Excessive wear of wiper linkage (Chapter 13).
- ☐ Wiper motor or linkage mountings loose or insecure (Chapter 13).

Wiper blades fail to clean the glass effectively

- ☐ Wiper blade rubbers worn or perished (*Weekly checks*).
- ☐ Wiper arm tension springs broken, or arm pivots seized (Chapter 13).
- ☐ Insufficient windscreen washer additive to adequately remove road film (*Weekly checks*).

Windscreen/tailgate washers inoperative, or unsatisfactory in operation

One or more washer jets inoperative

- ☐ Blocked washer jet (Chapter 13).
- ☐ Disconnected, kinked or restricted fluid hose (Chapter 13).
- ☐ Insufficient fluid in washer reservoir (*Weekly checks*).

Washer pump fails to operate

- ☐ Broken or disconnected wiring or connections (Chapter 13).
- ☐ Blown fuse (*Weekly checks* or Chapter 13).
- ☐ Faulty washer switch (Chapter 13).
- ☐ Faulty washer pump (Chapter 13).

Washer pump runs for some time before fluid is emitted from jets

- ☐ Faulty one-way valve in fluid supply hose (Chapter 13).

Electric windows inoperative, or unsatisfactory in operation

Window glass will only move in one direction

- ☐ Faulty switch (Chapter 12).

Window glass slow to move

- ☐ Regulator seized or damaged, or in need of lubrication (Chapter 12).
- ☐ Door internal components or trim fouling regulator (Chapter 12).
- ☐ Faulty motor (Chapter 12).

Window glass fails to move

- ☐ Blown fuse (*Weekly checks* or Chapter 13).
- ☐ Faulty relay (Chapter 13).
- ☐ Broken or disconnected wiring or connections (Chapter 13).
- ☐ Faulty motor (Chapter 12).

Electrical system (continued)

Central locking system inoperative, or unsatisfactory in operation

Complete system failure

- ☐ Blown fuse (*Weekly checks* or Chapter 13).
- ☐ Faulty relay (Chapter 13).
- ☐ Broken or disconnected wiring or connections (Chapter 13).

Latch locks but will not unlock, or unlocks but will not lock

- ☐ Faulty switch (Chapter 13).
- ☐ Broken or disconnected latch operating rods or levers (Chapter 12).
- ☐ Faulty relay (Chapter 13).

One solenoid/motor fails to operate

- ☐ Broken or disconnected wiring or connections (Chapter 13).
- ☐ Faulty solenoid/motor (Chapter 12).
- ☐ Broken, binding or disconnected latch operating rods or levers (Chapter 12).
- ☐ Fault in door latch (Chapter 12).

A

ABS (Anti-lock brake system) A system, usually electronically controlled, that senses incipient wheel lockup during braking and relieves hydraulic pressure at wheels that are about to skid.

Air bag An inflatable bag hidden in the steering wheel (driver's side) or the dash or glovebox (passenger side). In a head-on collision, the bags inflate, preventing the driver and front passenger from being thrown forward into the steering wheel or windscreen.

Air cleaner A metal or plastic housing, containing a filter element, which removes dust and dirt from the air being drawn into the engine.

Air filter element The actual filter in an air cleaner system, usually manufactured from pleated paper and requiring renewal at regular intervals.

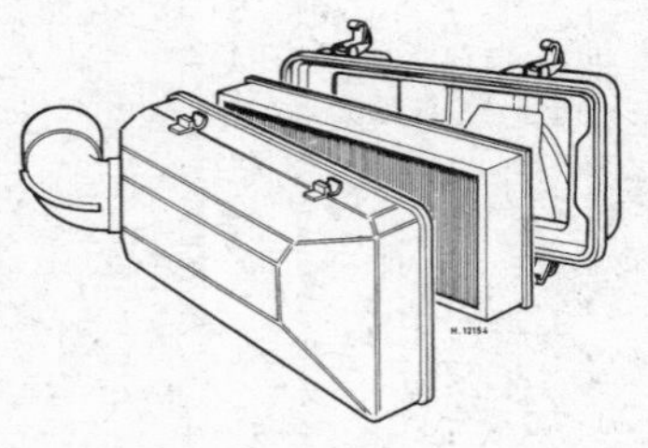

Air filter

Allen key A hexagonal wrench which fits into a recessed hexagonal hole.

Alligator clip A long-nosed spring-loaded metal clip with meshing teeth. Used to make temporary electrical connections.

Alternator A component in the electrical system which converts mechanical energy from a drivebelt into electrical energy to charge the battery and to operate the starting system, ignition system and electrical accessories.

Alternator (exploded view)

Ampere (amp) A unit of measurement for the flow of electric current. One amp is the amount of current produced by one volt acting through a resistance of one ohm.

Anaerobic sealer A substance used to prevent bolts and screws from loosening. Anaerobic means that it does not require oxygen for activation. The Loctite brand is widely used.

Antifreeze A substance (usually ethylene glycol) mixed with water, and added to a vehicle's cooling system, to prevent freezing of the coolant in winter. Antifreeze also contains chemicals to inhibit corrosion and the formation of rust and other deposits that would tend to clog the radiator and coolant passages and reduce cooling efficiency.

Anti-seize compound A coating that reduces the risk of seizing on fasteners that are subjected to high temperatures, such as exhaust manifold bolts and nuts.

Anti-seize compound

Asbestos A natural fibrous mineral with great heat resistance, commonly used in the composition of brake friction materials. Asbestos is a health hazard and the dust created by brake systems should never be inhaled or ingested.

Axle A shaft on which a wheel revolves, or which revolves with a wheel. Also, a solid beam that connects the two wheels at one end of the vehicle. An axle which also transmits power to the wheels is known as a live axle.

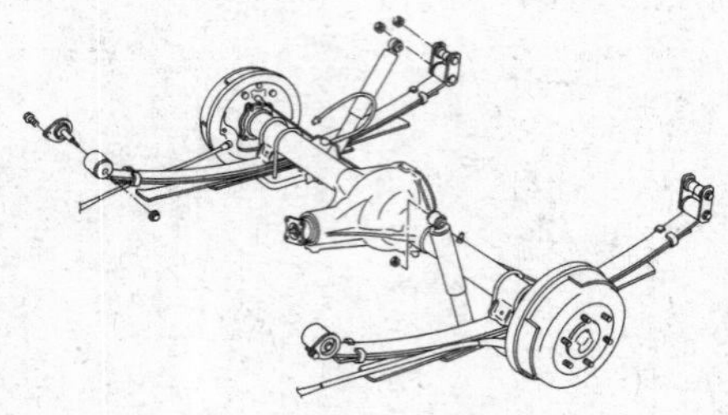

Axle assembly

Axleshaft A single rotating shaft, on either side of the differential, which delivers power from the final drive assembly to the drive wheels. Also called a driveshaft or a halfshaft.

B

Ball bearing An anti-friction bearing consisting of a hardened inner and outer race with hardened steel balls between two races.

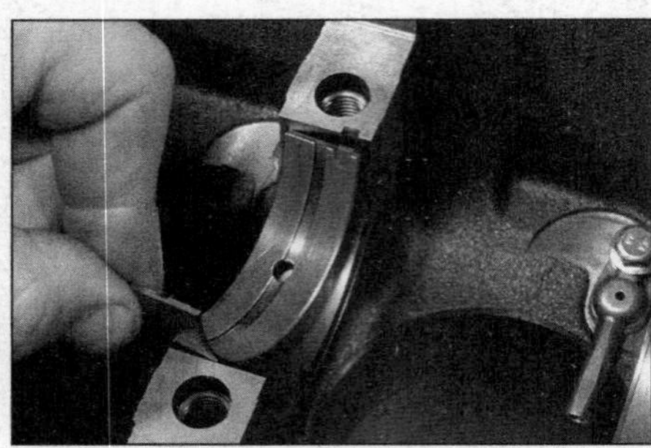

Bearing

Bearing The curved surface on a shaft or in a bore, or the part assembled into either, that permits relative motion between them with minimum wear and friction.

Big-end bearing The bearing in the end of the connecting rod that's attached to the crankshaft.

Bleed nipple A valve on a brake wheel cylinder, caliper or other hydraulic component that is opened to purge the hydraulic system of air. Also called a bleed screw.

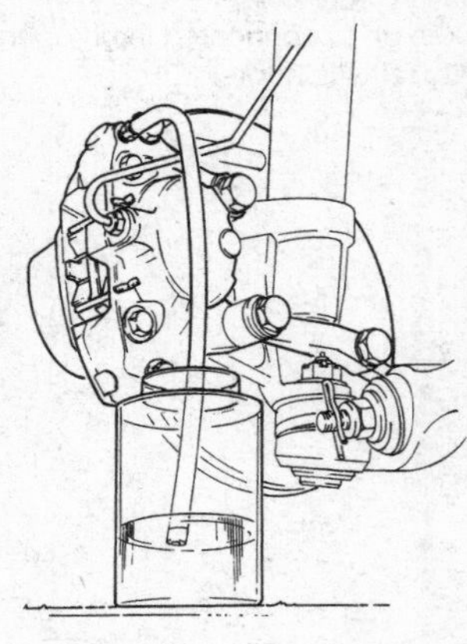

Brake bleeding

Brake bleeding Procedure for removing air from lines of a hydraulic brake system.

Brake disc The component of a disc brake that rotates with the wheels.

Brake drum The component of a drum brake that rotates with the wheels.

Brake linings The friction material which contacts the brake disc or drum to retard the vehicle's speed. The linings are bonded or riveted to the brake pads or shoes.

Brake pads The replaceable friction pads that pinch the brake disc when the brakes are applied. Brake pads consist of a friction material bonded or riveted to a rigid backing plate.

Brake shoe The crescent-shaped carrier to which the brake linings are mounted and which forces the lining against the rotating drum during braking.

Braking systems For more information on braking systems, consult the *Haynes Automotive Brake Manual*.

Breaker bar A long socket wrench handle providing greater leverage.

Bulkhead The insulated partition between the engine and the passenger compartment.

C

Caliper The non-rotating part of a disc-brake assembly that straddles the disc and carries the brake pads. The caliper also contains the hydraulic components that cause the pads to pinch the disc when the brakes are applied. A caliper is also a measuring tool that can be set to measure inside or outside dimensions of an object.

Camshaft A rotating shaft on which a series of cam lobes operate the valve mechanisms. The camshaft may be driven by gears, by sprockets and chain or by sprockets and a belt.

Canister A container in an evaporative emission control system; contains activated charcoal granules to trap vapours from the fuel system.

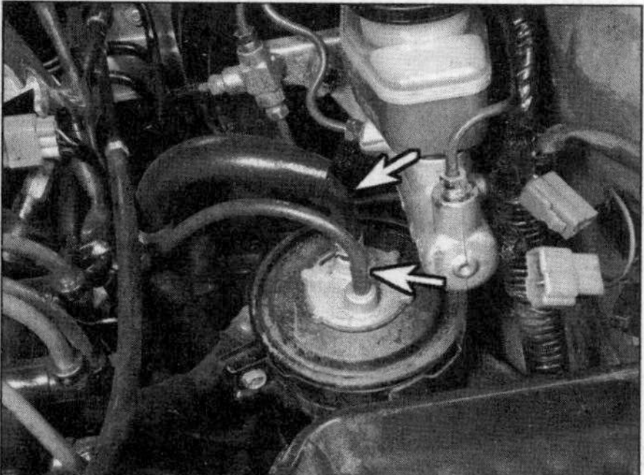

Canister

Carburettor A device which mixes fuel with air in the proper proportions to provide a desired power output from a spark ignition internal combustion engine.

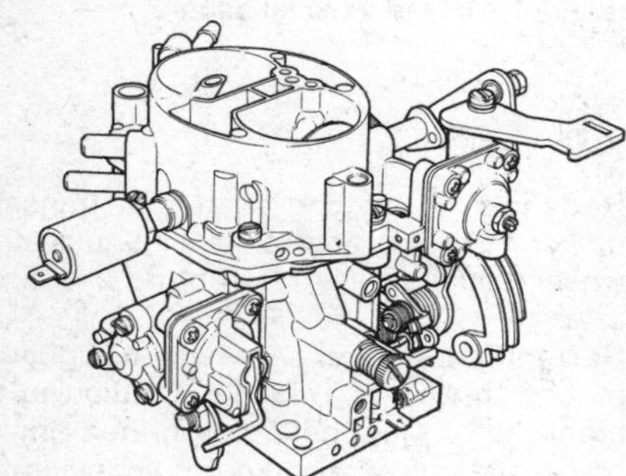

Carburettor

Castellated Resembling the parapets along the top of a castle wall. For example, a castellated balljoint stud nut.

Castellated nut

Castor In wheel alignment, the backward or forward tilt of the steering axis. Castor is positive when the steering axis is inclined rearward at the top.

Catalytic converter A silencer-like device in the exhaust system which converts certain pollutants in the exhaust gases into less harmful substances.

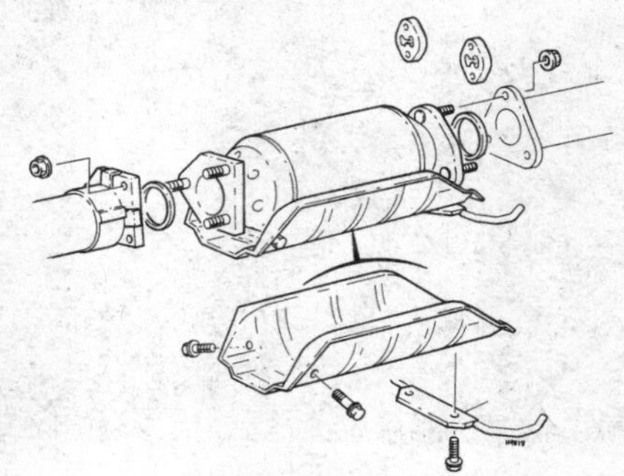

Catalytic converter

Circlip A ring-shaped clip used to prevent endwise movement of cylindrical parts and shafts. An internal circlip is installed in a groove in a housing; an external circlip fits into a groove on the outside of a cylindrical piece such as a shaft.

Clearance The amount of space between two parts. For example, between a piston and a cylinder, between a bearing and a journal, etc.

Coil spring A spiral of elastic steel found in various sizes throughout a vehicle, for example as a springing medium in the suspension and in the valve train.

Compression Reduction in volume, and increase in pressure and temperature, of a gas, caused by squeezing it into a smaller space.

Compression ratio The relationship between cylinder volume when the piston is at top dead centre and cylinder volume when the piston is at bottom dead centre.

Constant velocity (CV) joint A type of universal joint that cancels out vibrations caused by driving power being transmitted through an angle.

Core plug A disc or cup-shaped metal device inserted in a hole in a casting through which core was removed when the casting was formed. Also known as a freeze plug or expansion plug.

Crankcase The lower part of the engine block in which the crankshaft rotates.

Crankshaft The main rotating member, or shaft, running the length of the crankcase, with offset "throws" to which the connecting rods are attached.

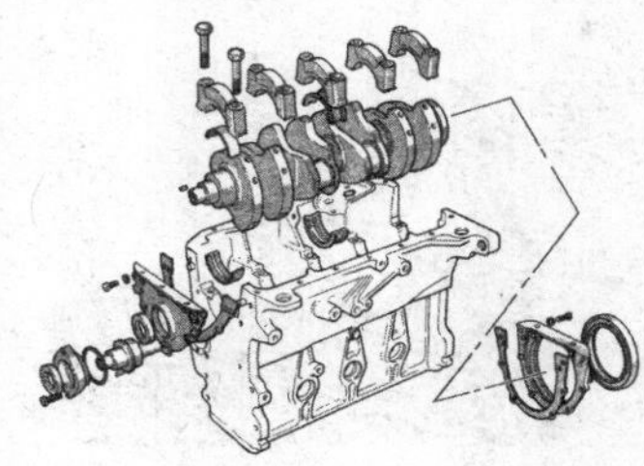

Crankshaft assembly

Crocodile clip See Alligator clip

D

Diagnostic code Code numbers obtained by accessing the diagnostic mode of an engine management computer. This code can be used to determine the area in the system where a malfunction may be located.

Disc brake A brake design incorporating a rotating disc onto which brake pads are squeezed. The resulting friction converts the energy of a moving vehicle into heat.

Double-overhead cam (DOHC) An engine that uses two overhead camshafts, usually one for the intake valves and one for the exhaust valves.

Drivebelt(s) The belt(s) used to drive accessories such as the alternator, water pump, power steering pump, air conditioning compressor, etc. off the crankshaft pulley.

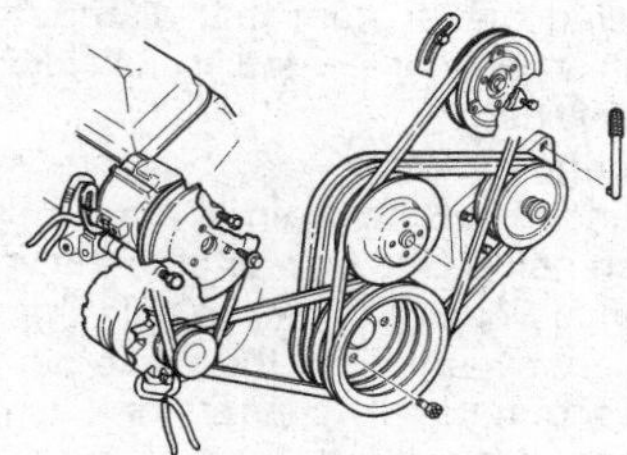

Accessory drivebelts

Driveshaft Any shaft used to transmit motion. Commonly used when referring to the axleshafts on a front wheel drive vehicle.

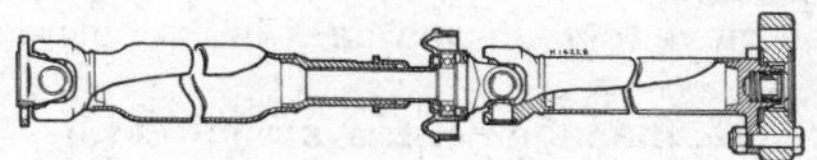

Driveshaft

Drum brake A type of brake using a drum-shaped metal cylinder attached to the inner surface of the wheel. When the brake pedal is pressed, curved brake shoes with friction linings press against the inside of the drum to slow or stop the vehicle.

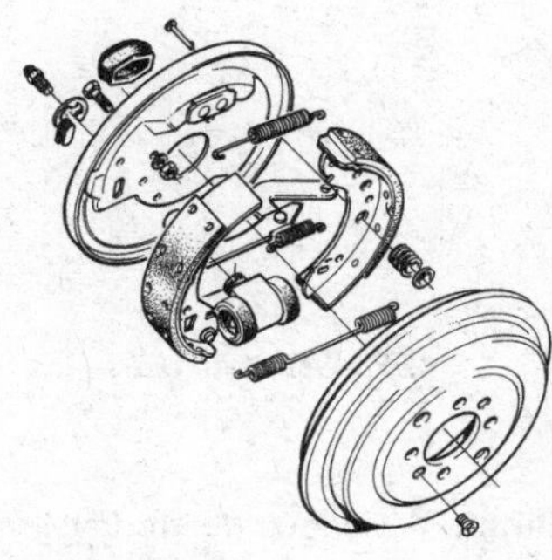

Drum brake assembly

E

EGR valve A valve used to introduce exhaust gases into the intake air stream.

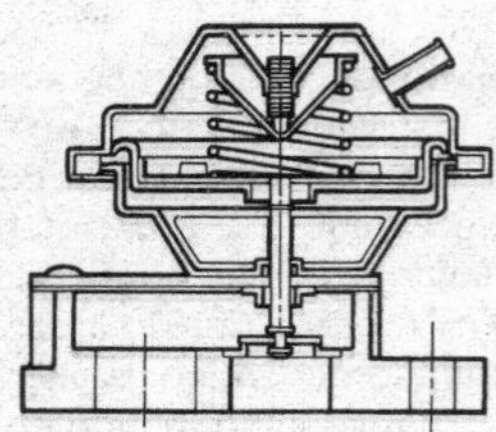

EGR valve

Electronic control unit (ECU) A computer which controls (for instance) ignition and fuel injection systems, or an anti-lock braking system. For more information refer to the *Haynes Automotive Electrical and Electronic Systems Manual.*

Electronic Fuel Injection (EFI) A computer controlled fuel system that distributes fuel through an injector located in each intake port of the engine.

Emergency brake A braking system, independent of the main hydraulic system, that can be used to slow or stop the vehicle if the primary brakes fail, or to hold the vehicle stationary even though the brake pedal isn't depressed. It usually consists of a hand lever that actuates either front or rear brakes mechanically through a series of cables and linkages. Also known as a handbrake or parking brake.

Endfloat The amount of lengthwise movement between two parts. As applied to a crankshaft, the distance that the crankshaft can move forward and back in the cylinder block.

Engine management system (EMS) A computer controlled system which manages the fuel injection and the ignition systems in an integrated fashion.

Exhaust manifold A part with several passages through which exhaust gases leave the engine combustion chambers and enter the exhaust pipe.

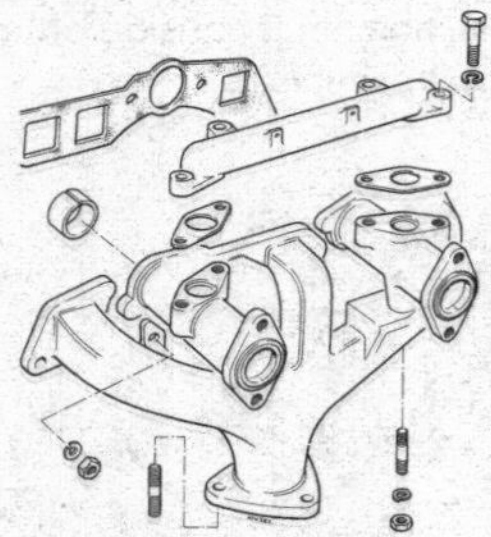

Exhaust manifold

F

Fan clutch A viscous (fluid) drive coupling device which permits variable engine fan speeds in relation to engine speeds.

Feeler blade A thin strip or blade of hardened steel, ground to an exact thickness, used to check or measure clearances between parts.

Feeler blade

Firing order The order in which the engine cylinders fire, or deliver their power strokes, beginning with the number one cylinder.

Flywheel A heavy spinning wheel in which energy is absorbed and stored by means of momentum. On cars, the flywheel is attached to the crankshaft to smooth out firing impulses.

Free play The amount of travel before any action takes place. The "looseness" in a linkage, or an assembly of parts, between the initial application of force and actual movement. For example, the distance the brake pedal moves before the pistons in the master cylinder are actuated.

Fuse An electrical device which protects a circuit against accidental overload. The typical fuse contains a soft piece of metal which is calibrated to melt at a predetermined current flow (expressed as amps) and break the circuit.

Fusible link A circuit protection device consisting of a conductor surrounded by heat-resistant insulation. The conductor is smaller than the wire it protects, so it acts as the weakest link in the circuit. Unlike a blown fuse, a failed fusible link must frequently be cut from the wire for replacement.

G

Gap The distance the spark must travel in jumping from the centre electrode to the side electrode in a spark plug. Also refers to the spacing between the points in a contact breaker assembly in a conventional points-type ignition, or to the distance between the reluctor or rotor and the pickup coil in an electronic ignition.

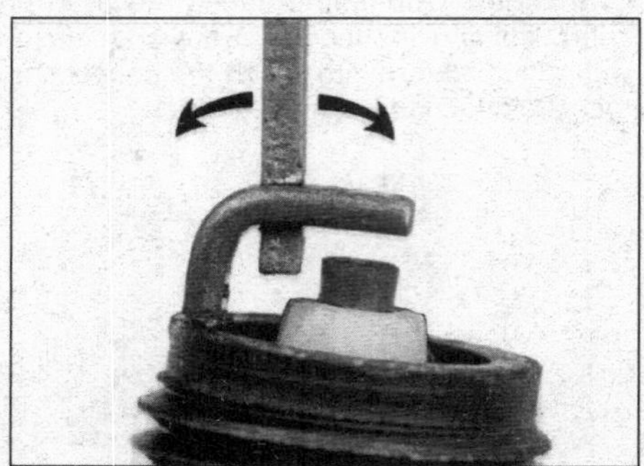

Adjusting spark plug gap

Gasket Any thin, soft material - usually cork, cardboard, asbestos or soft metal - installed between two metal surfaces to ensure a good seal. For instance, the cylinder head gasket seals the joint between the block and the cylinder head.

Gasket

Gauge An instrument panel display used to monitor engine conditions. A gauge with a movable pointer on a dial or a fixed scale is an analogue gauge. A gauge with a numerical readout is called a digital gauge.

H

Halfshaft A rotating shaft that transmits power from the final drive unit to a drive wheel, usually when referring to a live rear axle.

Harmonic balancer A device designed to reduce torsion or twisting vibration in the crankshaft. May be incorporated in the crankshaft pulley. Also known as a vibration damper.

Hone An abrasive tool for correcting small irregularities or differences in diameter in an engine cylinder, brake cylinder, etc.

Hydraulic tappet A tappet that utilises hydraulic pressure from the engine's lubrication system to maintain zero clearance (constant contact with both camshaft and valve stem). Automatically adjusts to variation in valve stem length. Hydraulic tappets also reduce valve noise.

I

Ignition timing The moment at which the spark plug fires, usually expressed in the number of crankshaft degrees before the piston reaches the top of its stroke.

Inlet manifold A tube or housing with passages through which flows the air-fuel mixture (carburettor vehicles and vehicles with throttle body injection) or air only (port fuel-injected vehicles) to the port openings in the cylinder head.

J

Jump start Starting the engine of a vehicle with a discharged or weak battery by attaching jump leads from the weak battery to a charged or helper battery.

L

Load Sensing Proportioning Valve (LSPV) A brake hydraulic system control valve that works like a proportioning valve, but also takes into consideration the amount of weight carried by the rear axle.
Locknut A nut used to lock an adjustment nut, or other threaded component, in place. For example, a locknut is employed to keep the adjusting nut on the rocker arm in position.
Lockwasher A form of washer designed to prevent an attaching nut from working loose.

M

MacPherson strut A type of front suspension system devised by Earle MacPherson at Ford of England. In its original form, a simple lateral link with the anti-roll bar creates the lower control arm. A long strut - an integral coil spring and shock absorber - is mounted between the body and the steering knuckle. Many modern so-called MacPherson strut systems use a conventional lower A-arm and don't rely on the anti-roll bar for location.
Multimeter An electrical test instrument with the capability to measure voltage, current and resistance.

N

NOx Oxides of Nitrogen. A common toxic pollutant emitted by petrol and diesel engines at higher temperatures.

O

Ohm The unit of electrical resistance. One volt applied to a resistance of one ohm will produce a current of one amp.
Ohmmeter An instrument for measuring electrical resistance.
O-ring A type of sealing ring made of a special rubber-like material; in use, the O-ring is compressed into a groove to provide the sealing action.

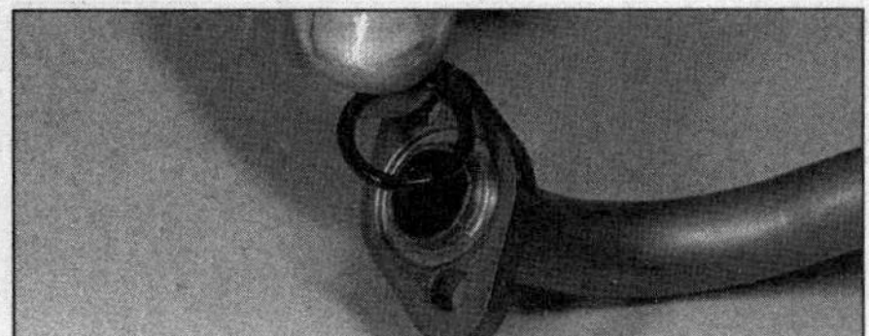

O-ring

Overhead cam (ohc) engine An engine with the camshaft(s) located on top of the cylinder head(s).
Overhead valve (ohv) engine An engine with the valves located in the cylinder head, but with the camshaft located in the engine block.
Oxygen sensor A device installed in the engine exhaust manifold, which senses the oxygen content in the exhaust and converts this information into an electric current. Also called a Lambda sensor.

P

Phillips screw A type of screw head having a cross instead of a slot for a corresponding type of screwdriver.
Plastigage A thin strip of plastic thread, available in different sizes, used for measuring clearances. For example, a strip of Plastigage is laid across a bearing journal. The parts are assembled and dismantled; the width of the crushed strip indicates the clearance between journal and bearing.

Plastigage

Propeller shaft The long hollow tube with universal joints at both ends that carries power from the transmission to the differential on front-engined rear wheel drive vehicles.
Proportioning valve A hydraulic control valve which limits the amount of pressure to the rear brakes during panic stops to prevent wheel lock-up.

R

Rack-and-pinion steering A steering system with a pinion gear on the end of the steering shaft that mates with a rack (think of a geared wheel opened up and laid flat). When the steering wheel is turned, the pinion turns, moving the rack to the left or right. This movement is transmitted through the track rods to the steering arms at the wheels.
Radiator A liquid-to-air heat transfer device designed to reduce the temperature of the coolant in an internal combustion engine cooling system.
Refrigerant Any substance used as a heat transfer agent in an air-conditioning system. R-12 has been the principle refrigerant for many years; recently, however, manufacturers have begun using R-134a, a non-CFC substance that is considered less harmful to the ozone in the upper atmosphere.
Rocker arm A lever arm that rocks on a shaft or pivots on a stud. In an overhead valve engine, the rocker arm converts the upward movement of the pushrod into a downward movement to open a valve.
Rotor In a distributor, the rotating device inside the cap that connects the centre electrode and the outer terminals as it turns, distributing the high voltage from the coil secondary winding to the proper spark plug. Also, that part of an alternator which rotates inside the stator. Also, the rotating assembly of a turbocharger, including the compressor wheel, shaft and turbine wheel.
Runout The amount of wobble (in-and-out movement) of a gear or wheel as it's rotated. The amount a shaft rotates "out-of-true." The out-of-round condition of a rotating part.

S

Sealant A liquid or paste used to prevent leakage at a joint. Sometimes used in conjunction with a gasket.
Sealed beam lamp An older headlight design which integrates the reflector, lens and filaments into a hermetically-sealed one-piece unit. When a filament burns out or the lens cracks, the entire unit is simply replaced.
Serpentine drivebelt A single, long, wide accessory drivebelt that's used on some newer vehicles to drive all the accessories, instead of a series of smaller, shorter belts. Serpentine drivebelts are usually tensioned by an automatic tensioner.

Serpentine drivebelt

Shim Thin spacer, commonly used to adjust the clearance or relative positions between two parts. For example, shims inserted into or under bucket tappets control valve clearances. Clearance is adjusted by changing the thickness of the shim.
Slide hammer A special puller that screws into or hooks onto a component such as a shaft or bearing; a heavy sliding handle on the shaft bottoms against the end of the shaft to knock the component free.
Sprocket A tooth or projection on the periphery of a wheel, shaped to engage with a chain or drivebelt. Commonly used to refer to the sprocket wheel itself.

Starter inhibitor switch On vehicles with an automatic transmission, a switch that prevents starting if the vehicle is not in Neutral or Park.
Strut See MacPherson strut.

T

Tappet A cylindrical component which transmits motion from the cam to the valve stem, either directly or via a pushrod and rocker arm. Also called a cam follower.
Thermostat A heat-controlled valve that regulates the flow of coolant between the cylinder block and the radiator, so maintaining optimum engine operating temperature. A thermostat is also used in some air cleaners in which the temperature is regulated.
Thrust bearing The bearing in the clutch assembly that is moved in to the release levers by clutch pedal action to disengage the clutch. Also referred to as a release bearing.
Timing belt A toothed belt which drives the camshaft. Serious engine damage may result if it breaks in service.
Timing chain A chain which drives the camshaft.
Toe-in The amount the front wheels are closer together at the front than at the rear. On rear wheel drive vehicles, a slight amount of toe-in is usually specified to keep the front wheels running parallel on the road by offsetting other forces that tend to spread the wheels apart.
Toe-out The amount the front wheels are closer together at the rear than at the front. On front wheel drive vehicles, a slight amount of toe-out is usually specified.
Tools For full information on choosing and using tools, refer to the *Haynes Automotive Tools Manual.*
Tracer A stripe of a second colour applied to a wire insulator to distinguish that wire from another one with the same colour insulator.
Tune-up A process of accurate and careful adjustments and parts replacement to obtain the best possible engine performance.
Turbocharger A centrifugal device, driven by exhaust gases, that pressurises the intake air. Normally used to increase the power output from a given engine displacement, but can also be used primarily to reduce exhaust emissions (as on VW's "Umwelt" Diesel engine).

U

Universal joint or U-joint A double-pivoted connection for transmitting power from a driving to a driven shaft through an angle. A U-joint consists of two Y-shaped yokes and a cross-shaped member called the spider.

V

Valve A device through which the flow of liquid, gas, vacuum, or loose material in bulk may be started, stopped, or regulated by a movable part that opens, shuts, or partially obstructs one or more ports or passageways. A valve is also the movable part of such a device.
Valve clearance The clearance between the valve tip (the end of the valve stem) and the rocker arm or tappet. The valve clearance is measured when the valve is closed.
Vernier caliper A precision measuring instrument that measures inside and outside dimensions. Not quite as accurate as a micrometer, but more convenient.
Viscosity The thickness of a liquid or its resistance to flow.
Volt A unit for expressing electrical "pressure" in a circuit. One volt that will produce a current of one ampere through a resistance of one ohm.

W

Welding Various processes used to join metal items by heating the areas to be joined to a molten state and fusing them together. For more information refer to the *Haynes Automotive Welding Manual.*
Wiring diagram A drawing portraying the components and wires in a vehicle's electrical system, using standardised symbols. For more information refer to the *Haynes Automotive Electrical and Electronic Systems Manual.*

Note: *References through-out this index are in the form - "Chapter number" • "Page number"*

D

E

F

G

H

I

J

T

U

V

W

Y

Notes

Notes

Notes

Notes

Preserving Our Motoring Heritage

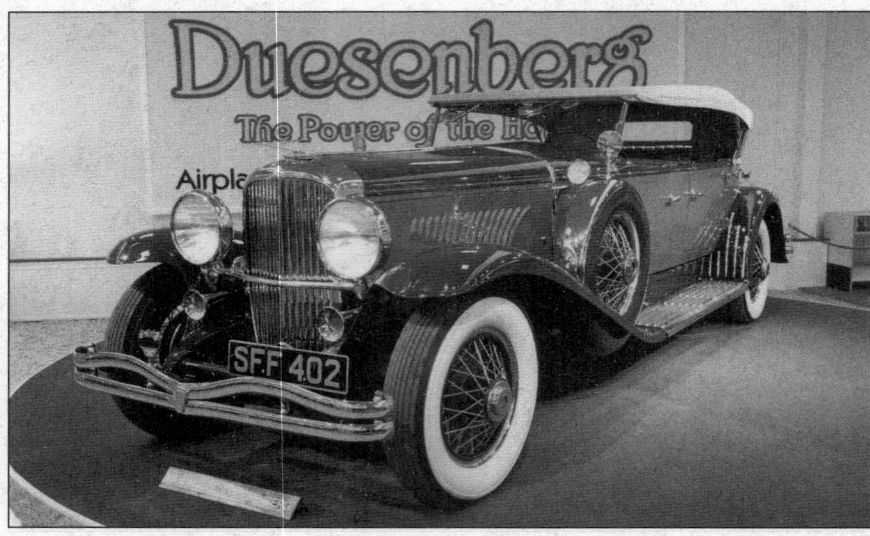
Duesenberg
SFF 402

<
The Model J Duesenberg Derham Tourster. Only eight of these magnificent cars were ever built – this is the only example to be found outside the United States of America

Almost every car you've ever loved, loathed or desired is gathered under one roof at the Haynes Motor Museum. Over 300 immaculately presented cars and motorbikes represent every aspect of our motoring heritage, from elegant reminders of bygone days, such as the superb Model J Duesenberg to curiosities like the bug-eyed BMW Isetta. There are also many old friends and flames. Perhaps you remember the 1959 Ford Popular that you did your courting in? The magnificent 'Red Collection' is a spectacle of classic sports cars including AC, Alfa Romeo, Austin Healey, Ferrari, Lamborghini, Maserati, MG, Riley, Porsche and Triumph.

A Perfect Day Out

Each and every vehicle at the Haynes Motor Museum has played its part in the history and culture of Motoring. Today, they make a wonderful spectacle and a great day out for all the family. Bring the kids, bring Mum and Dad, but above all bring your camera to capture those golden memories for ever. You will also find an impressive array of motoring memorabilia, a comfortable 70 seat video cinema and one of the most extensive transport book shops in Britain. The Pit Stop Cafe serves everything from a cup of tea to wholesome, home-made meals or, if you prefer, you can enjoy the large picnic area nestled in the beautiful rural surroundings of Somerset.

23
MOTOR MUSEUM
A303 ANDOVER
A359 CASTLE CARY
SPARKFORD
A303 EXETER TO M5 J 25 TAUNTON
A359 YEOVIL
HAYNES PUBLISHING
OLD A303
NOT TO SCALE

>
John Haynes O.B.E., Founder and Chairman of the museum at the wheel of a Haynes Light 12.

<
Graham Hill's Lola Cosworth Formula 1 car next to a 1934 Riley Sports.

The Museum is situated on the A359 Yeovil to Frome road at Sparkford, just off the A303 in Somerset. It is about 40 miles south of Bristol, and 25 minutes drive from the M5 intersection at Taunton.

Open 9.30am - 5.30pm (10.00am - 4.00pm Winter) 7 days a week, *except Christmas Day, Boxing Day and New Years Day*

Special rates available for schools, coach parties and outings Charitable Trust No. 292048